third edition

The THEORY of BUSINESS FINANCE

A Book of Readings

Macmillan Publishing Co., Inc.
NEW YORK

Collier Macmillan Publishers
LONDON

Copyright © 1983, Macmillan Publishing Co., Inc.

Printed in the United States of America

Earlier edition copyright © 1967, 1976
by Macmillan Publishing Co., Inc.

Macmillan Publishing Co., Inc.
866 Third Avenue, New York, New York 10022

Collier Macmillan Canada, Inc.

Library of Congress Cataloging in Publication Data
Main entry under title:

The Theory of business finance.

   Includes bibliographies.
   1. Corporations—Finance—Addresses, essays,
lectures.   2. Business enterprises—Finance—Addresses, essays, lectures.   3. Capital—Addresses,
essays, lectures.   I. Archer, Stephen Hunt.
II. D'Ambrosio, Charles A.
HG4011.T48   1983   658.1'5   82-9911
ISBN 0-02-304150-1   AACR2

Printing: 1 2 3 4 5 6 7 8   Year: 3 4 5 6 7 8 9 0

ISBN   0-02-304150-1

Preface

Sixteen years ago, when we wrote the preface to the first edition, we felt that finance literature was leading the field into new areas and that a collection of readings capturing the essence of that development was the order of the day. The marketplace agreement is attested to by the initial and sustained reception of both the first and second editions. This, the third edition of *The Theory of Business Finance: A Book of Readings,* continues to be a body of substantive articles for microfinance, although many of them serve as a foundations for all fields of finance.

Our goal in this edition is the same as that of the prior two, namely, to collate those readings that clearly stand out as landmarks in the study of finance, that constitute the minimal set of literature for every serious student, and that will hold readers in good stead for some years to come.

The selection process for the first edition was relatively easy, but it became much more difficult in the second edition, and was almost forbidding in this third edition, so rapidly has the generation of new and substantive material been. Consequently, not everyone will agree with our selections. That an optimal set is attainable is doubtful, given the tastes of each possible user. In some areas a reasonable consensus exists regarding the important articles to be studied, and we restrict our collection to that set. In other areas, however, little consensus exists; in those instances we exercised our judgment regarding the reasonably acceptable set. For reasons readily explicable by imperfect knowledge and other human frailties, the emergent set is necessarily preferred, *in toto,* perhaps only by us. Our hope is that it will be preferred by others as well, at least within the theory of second best.

The foregoing implies, among other things, that many fine articles have been excluded. As in prior editions, such exclusions are not intended to slight these significant contributions. The budget constraint of a collection of readings had to be acknowledged.

As anyone who has followed the literature of the past twenty years knows, the overlap in content and coverage among published works is considerable.

Perforce, much of each selection, when incorporated into a collection such as this, is duplicative. Paradoxically, to have shorn the various selections of paragraphs or sections redundant of materials in other selections would have been to detract from their overall quality and intent. As a result, each reading is presented intact.

Moreover, segmentation of a collected set of readings according to various section headings is a hazardous task inasmuch as some selections could easily be included in more than one section. The current topical arrangement is our preferred choice. Obviously, as the articles are unedited, each user can freely create his own variation. In general, the papers within each section are presented chronologically. Some articles are comments, criticisms, or replies of other works, and therefore some care should be exercised in random selection.

The nature of the readings, it will quickly be observed, is challenging. However, many can be handled by the beginning student, requiring in most instances acquaintance with simple mathematical expressions. Prior editions found use in many types of classes: as a supplementary text for a beginning class in finance, as the main body of material for advanced classes, and in graduate seminars. The choice depended on the selection of the articles and the preparation of the students.

The third edition consists of the following five sections:

   I. Theory of Choice
  II. Portfolio Theory and Capital Asset Pricing
 III. Contingent Claims
  IV. Investment Decisions, Financing Decisions, and the Cost of Capital
   V. Dividends

We have added four important contributions to Part II—articles by Fama (2), Roll, and Roll and Ross. Part III, "Contingent Claims," contains articles by Black and Scholes, and MacBeth and Merville. To Part IV we have added the important Miller article, the pioneering Jensen and Mekling article, the incisive and innovative articles by Fama, Ross, and Fama, and the perspicuity-adding article of Barnea, Haugen, and Senbet. To Part V we have added Miller-Scholes and Litzenberger and Ramaswamy. We wish we could have included more. Similarly, deleting certain articles to make room for the new caused considerable anguish.

Because so many of the readings are usable with texts and theory books, a list of selected texts is included. These texts may be used in combination with our volume, to the advantage of readers and authors alike.

In this and prior editions we obtained the evaluations of colleagues and hereby acknowledge our considerable debt to them: Richard A. Brealey, London Business School; Harry DeAngelo, University of Rochester; Robert S. Hamada, The University of Chicago; Alan Kraus, University of British Columbia; Cheng-Few Lee, University of Illinois at Urbana-Champaign; John

J. McConnell, Purdue University; Larry J. Merville, The University of Texas at Dallas; Richard Roll, University of California, Los Angeles; Harold Stevenson, Arizona State University; Seha M. Tinic, The University of Alberta; Richard C. West, Dartmouth College.

Because the final selections were ours, we assume full culpability both for them and for the order in which they are presented. We acknowledge the generosity of each of the authors for his permission to reproduce his paper. Our gratitude is also extended to the various editors and copyright holders who are acknowledged herein.

S. H. ARCHER

C. A. D'AMBROSIO

Selected Companion Texts

Listed below are several textbooks which can be used easily in conjunction with *The Theory of Price: A Book of Readings*. Of course, not all such texts could be listed here and there are many other excellent choices on the market.

Archer, Stephen H., G. Marc Choate, and George Racette. *Financial Management*. 2d ed. New York: John Wiley & Sons, 1983.

Brealey, Richard and Stewart Myers. *Principles of Corporate Finance*. New York: McGraw-Hill Book Company, 1981.

Brigham, Eugene F. *Financial Management*. Hinsdale, Illinois: The Dryden Press, 1977.

Copeland, Thomas E. and J. Fred Weston. *Financial Theory and Corporate Policy*. Reading, Massachusetts: Addison-Wesley Publishing Company, Inc., 1979.

Elton, Edwin J. and Martin J. Gruber. *Modern Portfolio Theory and Investment Analysis*. New York: John Wiley & Sons, 1981.

Fama, Eugene F. *Foundations of Finance*. New York: Basic Books, Inc., 1976.

Fama, Eugene F. and Merton H. Miller. *The Theory of Finance*. New York: Holt, Rinehart and Winston, 1972.

Francis, Jack Clark. *Investments Analysis and Management*. 3d ed. New York: McGraw-Hill Book Company, 1980.

Haley, Charles W. and Lawrence D. Schall. *The Theory of Financial Decisions*. 2d ed. New York: McGraw-Hill Book Company, 1979.

Hirshleifer, J. *Investment, Interest and Capital*. Englewood Cliffs, New Jersey: Prentice-Hall, Inc., 1970.

Levy, Haim and Marshall Sarnat. *Capital Investment and Financial Decisions*. Englewood Cliffs, New Jersey: Prentice-Hall International, 1982.

Mossin, Jan. *Theory of Financial Markets*. Englewood Cliffs, New Jersey: Prentice-Hall, Inc., 1973.

Reilly, Frank K. *Investment Analysis & Portfolio Management*. Hinsdale, Illinois: The Dryden Press, 1979.

Sharpe, William F. *Investments*. 2d ed. Englewood Cliffs, New Jersey: Prentice-Hall, Inc., 1981.

Van Horne, James C. *Financial Management and Policy*. 4th ed. Englewood Cliffs, New Jersey: Prentice-Hall, Inc., 1977.

Contents

PART V.   DIVIDENDS   621

PART **I**

THE THEORY OF CHOICE

* *

1. EXPOSITION OF A NEW THEORY ON THE MEASUREMENT OF RISK[1]

DANIEL BERNOULLI

Reprinted from *Econometrica*, Vol. 22, No. 1 (January 1954), pp. 23–36, by permission of the publisher.

§1. Ever since mathematicians first began to study the measurement of risk there has been general agreement on the following proposition: *Expected values are computed by multiplying each possible gain by the number of ways in which it can occur, and then dividing the sum of these products by the total*

[1] Translated from Latin into English by Dr. Louise Sommer, The American University, Washington, D.C., from " Specimen Theoriae Novae de Mensura Sortis," *Commentarii Academiae Scientiarum Imperialis Petropolitanae*, Tomus V [*Papers of the Imperial Academy of Sciences in Petersburg*, Vol. V], 1738, pp. 175–192. Professor Karl Menger, Illinois Institute of Technology has written footnotes 4, 9, 10, and 15.

Editor's Note: In view of the frequency with which Bernoulli's famous paper has been referred to in recent economic discussion, it has been thought appropriate to make it more generally available by publishing this English version. In her translation Professor Sommer has sought, in so far as possible, to retain the eighteenth century spirit of the original. The mathematical notation and much of the punctuation are reproduced without change. References to some of the recent literature concerned with Bernoulli's theory are given at the end of the article.

Translator's Note: I highly appreciate the help of Karl Menger, Professor of Mathematics, Illinois Institute of Technology, a distinguished authority on the Bernoulli problem, who has read this translation and given me expert advice. I am also grateful to Mr. William J. Baumol, Professor of Economics, Princeton University, for his valuable assistance in interpreting Bernoulli's paper in the light of modern econometrics. I wish to thank also Mr. John H. Lingenfeld, Economist, U.S. Department of Labor, for his cooperation in the English rendition of this paper. The translation is based solely upon the original Latin text.

Biographical Note: Daniel Bernoulli, a member of the famous Swiss family of distinguished mathematicians, was born in Groningen, January 29, 1700, and died in Basle, March 17, 1782. He studied mathematics and medical sciences at the University of Basle. In 1725 he accepted an invitation to the newly established academy in Petersburg, but returned to Basle in 1733 where he was appointed professor of physics and philosophy. Bernoulli was a member of the academies of Paris, Berlin, and Petersburg and the Royal Academy in London. He was the first to apply mathematical analysis to the problem of the movement of liquid bodies.

number of possible cases where, in this theory, the consideration of cases which are all of the same probability is insisted upon. If this rule be accepted, what remains to be done within the framework of this theory amounts to the enumeration of all alternatives, their breakdown into equi-probable cases and, finally, their insertion into corresponding classifications.

§2. Proper examination of the numerous demonstrations of this proposition that have come forth indicates that they all rest upon one hypothesis: *since there is no reason to assume that of two persons encountering identical risks,*[2] *either should expect to have his desires more closely fulfilled, the risks anticipated by each must be deemed equal in value.* No characteristic of the persons themselves ought to be taken into consideration; only those matters should be weighed carefully that pertain to the terms of the risk. The relevant finding might then be made by the highest judges established by public authority. But really there is here no need for judgment but of deliberation, i.e., rules would be set up whereby anyone could estimate his prospects from any risky undertaking in light of one's specific financial circumstances.

§3. To make this clear it is perhaps advisable to consider the following example: Somehow a very poor fellow obtains a lottery ticket that will yield with equal probability either nothing or twenty thousand ducats. Will this man evaluate his chance of winning at ten thousand ducats? Would he not be ill-advised to sell this lottery ticket for nine thousand ducats? To me it seems that the answer is in the negative. On the other hand I am inclined to believe that a rich man would be ill-advised to refuse to buy the lottery ticket for nine thousand ducats. If I am not wrong then it seems clear that all men cannot use the same rule to evaluate the gamble. The rule established in §1 must, therefore, be discarded. But anyone who considers the problem with perspicacity and interest will ascertain that the concept of *value* which we have used in this rule may be defined in a way which renders the entire procedure universally acceptable without reservation. To do this the determination of the *value* of an item must not be based on its *price*, but rather on the *utility* it yields. The price of the item is dependent only on the thing itself and is equal for everyone; the utility, however, is dependent on the particular circumstances of the person making the estimate. Thus there is no doubt that a gain of one thousand ducats is more significant to a pauper than to a rich man though both gain the same amount.

§4. The discussion has now been developed to a point where anyone may proceed with the investigation by the mere paraphrasing of one and the same principle. However, since the hypothesis is entirely new, it may nevertheless

---

(On Bernoulli see: *Handwörterbuch der Naturwissenschaften*, second edition, 1931, pp. 800–801; "Die Basler Mathematiker Daniel Bernoulli und Leonhard Euler. Hundert Jahre nach ihrem Tode gefeiert von der Naturforschenden Gesellschaft," Basle, 1884. (Annex to part VII of the proceedings of this Society); and *Correspondance mathematique* ... , edited by Paul Heinrich Fuss, 1843 containing letters written by Daniel Bernoulli to Leonhard Euler, Nicolaus Fuss, and C. Goldbach.)

[2] i.e., risky propositions (gambles). [Translator].

require some elucidation. I have, therefore, decided to explain by example what I have explored. Meanwhile, let us use this as a fundamental rule: *If the utility of each possible profit expectation is multiplied by the number of ways in which it can occur, and we then divide the sum of these products by the total number of possible cases, a mean utility*[3] *[moral expectation] will be obtained, and the profit which corresponds to this utility will equal the value of the risk in question.*

§5. Thus it becomes evident that no valid measurement of the value of a risk can be obtained without consideration being given to its *utility*, that is to say, the utility of whatever gain accrues to the individual or, conversely, how much profit is required to yield a given utility. However it hardly seems plausible to make any precise generalizations since the utility of an item may change with circumstances. Thus, though a poor man generally obtains more utility than does a rich man from an equal gain, it is nevertheless conceivable, for example, that a rich prisoner who possesses two thousand ducats but needs two thousand ducats more to repurchase his freedom, will place a higher value on a gain of two thousand ducats than does another man who has less money than he. Though innumerable examples of this kind may be constructed, they represent exceedingly rare exceptions. We shall, therefore, do better to consider what usually happens, and in order to perceive the problem more correctly we shall assume that there is an imperceptibly small growth in the individual's wealth which proceeds continuously by infinitesimal increments. Now it is highly probable that *any increase in wealth, no matter how insignificant, will always result in an increase in utility which is inversely proportionate to the quantity of goods already possessed.* To explain this hypothesis it is necessary to define what is meant by the *quantity of goods.* By this expression I mean to connote food, clothing, all things which add to the conveniences of life, and even to luxury—anything that can contribute to the adequate satisfaction of any sort of want. There is then nobody who can be said to possess nothing at all in this sense unless he starves to death. For the great majority the most valuable portion of their possessions so defined will consist in their productive capacity, this term being taken to include even the beggar's talent: a man who is able to acquire ten ducats yearly by begging will scarcely be willing to accept a sum of fifty ducats on condition that he henceforth refrain from begging or otherwise trying to earn money. For he would have to live on this amount, and after he had spent it his existence must also come to an end. I doubt whether even those who do not possess a farthing and are burdened with financial obligations would be willing to free themselves of their debts or even to accept a still greater gift on such a condition. But if the beggar were to refuse such a contract unless immediately paid no less than one hundred ducats and the man pressed by creditors similarly demanded one thousand ducats, we might say that the former is possessed of wealth

---

[3] Free translation of Bernoulli's "emolumentum medium," literally: "mean utility." [Translator].

worth one hundred, and the latter of one thousand ducats, though in common parlance the former owns nothing and the latter less than nothing.

§6. Having stated this definition, I return to the statement made in the previous paragraph which maintained that, in the absence of the unusual, the *utility resulting from any small increase in wealth will be inversely proportionate to the quantity of goods previously possessed*. Considering the nature of man, it seems to me that the foregoing hypothesis is apt to be valid for many people to whom this sort of comparison can be applied. Only a few do not spend their entire yearly incomes. But, if among these, one has a fortune worth a hundred thousand ducats and another a fortune worth the same number of semi-ducats and if the former receives from it a yearly income of five thousand ducats while the latter obtains the same number of semi-ducats it is quite clear that to the former a ducat has exactly the same significance as a semi-ducat to the latter, and that, therefore, the gain of one ducat will have to the former no higher value than the gain of a semi-ducat to the latter. Accordingly, if each makes a gain of one ducat the latter receives twice as much utility from it, having been enriched by two semi-ducats. This argument applies to many other cases which, therefore, need not be discussed separately. The proposition is all the more valid for the majority of men who possess no fortune apart from their working capacity which is their only source of livelihood. True, there are men to whom one ducat means more than many ducats do to others who are less rich but more generous than they. But since we shall now concern ourselves only with one individual (in different states of affluence) distinctions of this sort do not concern us. The man who is emotionally less affected by a gain will support a loss with greater patience. Since, however, in special cases things can conceivably occur otherwise, I shall first deal with the most general case and then develop our special hypothesis in order thereby to satisfy everyone.

§7. Therefore, let *AB* represent the quantity of goods initially possessed. Then after extending *AB*, a curve *BGLS* must be constructed, whose ordinates *CG*, *DH*, *EL*, *FM*, etc., designate *utilities* corresponding to the abscissas *BC*, *BD*, *BE*, *BF*, etc., designating gains in wealth. Further, let *m*, *n*, *p*, *q*, etc., be the numbers which indicate the number of ways in which gains in wealth *BC*, *BD*, *BE*, *BF* [misprinted in the original as *CF*], etc., can occur. Then (in accord with §4) the *moral* expectation of the risky proposition referred to is given by:

$$PO = \frac{m \cdot CG + n \cdot DH + p \cdot EL + q \cdot FM + \cdots}{m + n + p + q + \cdots}$$

Now, if we erect *AQ* perpendicular to *AR*, and on it measure off *AN = PO*, the straight line *NO − AB* represents the gain which may properly be expected, or the value of the risky proposition in question. If we wish, further, to know how large a stake the individual should be willing to venture on this risky proposition, our curve must be extended in the opposite direction in such a way that the abscissa *Bp* now represents a loss and the ordinate *po* represents

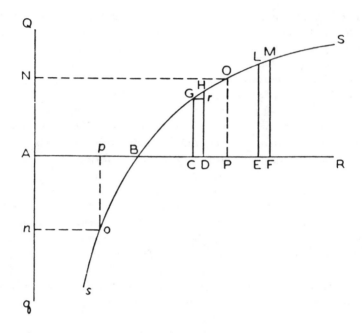

the corresponding decline in utility. Since in a fair game the disutility to be suffered by losing must be equal to the utility to be derived by winning, we must assume that $An = AN$, or $po = PO$. Thus Bp will indicate the stake more than which persons who consider their own pecuniary status should not venture.

COROLLARY I

§8. Until now scientists have usually rested their hypothesis on the assumption that all gains must be evaluated exclusively in terms of themselves, i.e., on the basis of their intrinsic qualities, and that these gains will always produce a *utility* directly proportionate to the gain. On this hypothesis the curve BS becomes a straight line. Now if we again have:

$$PO = \frac{m \cdot CG + n \cdot DH + p \cdot EL + q \cdot FM + \cdots}{m + n + p + q + \cdots},$$

and if, on both sides, the respective factors are introduced it follows that:

$$BP = \frac{m \cdot BC + n \cdot BD + p \cdot BE + q \cdot BF + \cdots}{m + n + p + q + \cdots},$$

which is in conformity with the usually accepted rule.

COROLLARY II

§9. If AB were infinitely great, even in proportion to BF, the greatest possible gain, the arc BM may be considered very like an infinitesimally small straight line. Again in this case the usual rule [for the evaluation of risky propositions] is applicable, and may continue to be considered approximately valid in games of insignificant moment.

§10. Having dealt with the problem in the most general way we turn now to the aforementioned particular hypothesis, which, indeed, deserves prior attention to all others. First of all the nature of curve sBS must be investigated under the conditions postulated in §7. Since on our hypothesis we must consider infinitesimally small gains, we shall take gains BC and BD to be nearly equal, so that their difference CD becomes infinitesimally small. If we draw Gr parallel to BR, then rH will represent the infinitesimally small gain in *utility* to a man whose fortune is AC and who obtains the small gain, CD. This *utility*, however, should be related not only to the tiny gain CD, to which it is, other things being equal, proportionate, but also to AC, the fortune previously owned to which it is inversely proportionate. We therefore set: $AC = x$, $CD = dx$, $CG = y$, $rH = dy$ and $AB = \alpha$; and if b designates some constant we obtain $dy = \dfrac{b\,dx}{x}$ or $y = b \log \dfrac{x}{\alpha}$. The curve sBS is therefore a logarithmic curve, the subtangent[4] of which is everywhere b and whose asymptote is Qq.

§11. If we now compare this result with what has been said in paragraph 7, it will appear that: $PO = b \log AP/AB$, $CG = b \log AC/AB$, $DH = b \log AD/AB$ and so on; but since we have

$$PO = \frac{m \cdot CG + n \cdot DH + p \cdot EL + q \cdot FM + \cdots}{m + n + p + q + \cdots}$$

it follows that

$$b \log \frac{AP}{AB} = \left(mb \log \frac{AC}{AB} + nb \log \frac{AD}{AB} + pb \log \frac{AE}{AB} + qb \log \frac{AF}{AB} + \cdots \right) :$$

$$(m + n + p + q + \cdots)$$

and therefore

[4] The tangent to the curve $y = b \log \dfrac{x}{\alpha}$ at the point $\left(x_o, \log \dfrac{x_o}{\alpha} \right)$ is the line $y - b \log \dfrac{x_o}{\alpha} = \dfrac{b}{x_o}(x - x_o)$. This tangent intersects the Y-axis $(x = 0)$ at the point with the ordinate $b \log \dfrac{x_o}{\alpha} - b$. The point of contact of the tangent with the curve has the ordinate $b \log \dfrac{x_o}{\alpha}$. So also does the projection of this point on the Y-axis. The segment between the two points on the Y-axis that have been mentioned has the length b. That segment is the projection of the segment on the tangent between its intersection with the Y-axis and the point of contact. The length of this projection (which is b) is what Bernoulli here calls the "sub-tangent." Today, by the subtangent of the curve $y = f(x)$ at the point $(x_o, f(x_o))$ is meant the length of the segment on the X-axis (and not the Y-axis) between its intersection with the tangent and the projection of the point of contact. This length is $f(x_o)/f'(x_o)$. In the case of the logarithmic curve it equals $x_o \log \dfrac{x_o}{\alpha}$.—Karl Menger.

$$AP = (AC^m . AD^n . AE^p . AF^q ....)^{1/m+n+p+q+ \cdots}$$

and if we subtract AB from this, the remaining magnitude, BP, will represent the value of the risky proposition in question.

§12. Thus the preceding paragraph suggests the following rule: *Any gain must be added to the fortune previously possessed, then this sum must be raised to the power given by the number of possible ways in which the gain may be obtained; these terms should then be multiplied together. Then of this product a root must be extracted the degree of which is given by the number of all possible cases, and finally the value of the initial possessions must be subtracted therefrom; what then remains indicates the value of the risky proposition in question.* This principle is essential for the mesurement of the value of risky propositions in various cases. I would elaborate it into a complete theory as has been done with the traditional analysis, were it not that, despite its usefulness and originality, previous obligations do not permit me to undertake this task. I shall therefore, at this time, mention only the more significant points among those which have at first glance occurred to me.

§13. First, it appears that in many games, even those that are absolutely fair, both of the players may expect to suffer a loss; indeed this is Nature's admonition to avoid the dice altogether. . . . This follows from the concavity of curve sBS to BR. For in making the stake, Bp, equal to the expected gain, BP, it is clear that the disutility po which results from a loss will always exceed the expected gain in utility, PO. Although this result will be quite clear to the mathematician, I shall nevertheless explain it by example, so that it will be clear to everyone. Let us assume that of two players, both possessing one hundred ducats, each puts up half this sum as a stake in a game that offers the same probabilities to both players. Under this assumption each will then have fifty ducats plus the expectation of winning yet one hundred ducats more. However, the sum of the values of these two items amounts, by the rule of §12, to only $(50^1 . 150^1)^{1/2}$ or $\sqrt{50 . 150}$, i.e., less than eighty-seven ducats, so that, though the game be played under perfectly equal conditions for both, either will suffer an expected loss of more than thirteen ducats. We must strongly emphasize this truth, although it be self evident: the imprudence of a gambler will be the greater the larger the part of his fortune which he exposes to a game of chance. For this purpose we shall modify the previous example by assuming that one of the gamblers, before putting up his fifty ducat stake possessed two hundred ducats. This gambler suffers an expected loss of $200 - \sqrt{150 . 250}$, which is not much greater than six ducats.

§14. Since, therefore, everyone who bets any part of his fortune, however small, on a mathematically fair game of chance acts irrationally, it may be of interest to inquire how great an advantage the gambler must enjoy over his opponent in order to avoid any expected loss. Let us again consider a game which is as simple as possible, defined by two equiprobable outcomes one of which is favorable and the other unfavorable. Let us take a to be the gain to be won in case of a favorable outcome, and x to be the stake which is lost in the unfavorable case. If the initial quantity of goods possessed is α we have $AB = \alpha$; $BP = a$; $PO = b \log \dfrac{\alpha + a}{\alpha}$ (see §10), and since (by §7) $po = PO$ it follows by the nature of a logarithmic curve that $Bp = \dfrac{\alpha a}{\alpha + a}$. Since however Bp represents the stake x, we have $x = \dfrac{\alpha a}{\alpha + a}$ a magnitude which is always smaller than a, the expected gain. It also follows from this that a man who risks his entire fortune acts like a simpleton, however great may be the possible gain. No one will have difficulty in being persuaded of this if he has carefully examined our definitions given above. Moreover, this result sheds light on a statement which is universally accepted in practice: it may be reasonable for some individuals to invest in a doubtful enterprise and yet be unreasonable for others to do so.

§15. The procedure customarily employed by merchants in the insurance of commodities transported by sea seems to merit special attention. This may again be explained by an example. Suppose Caius,[5] a Petersburg merchant, has purchased commodities in Amsterdam which he could sell for ten thousand rubles if he had them in Petersburg. He therefore orders them to be shipped there by sea, but is in doubt whether or not to insure them. He is well aware of the fact that at this time of year of one hundred ships which sail from Amsterdam to Petersburg, five are usually lost. However, there is no insurance available below the price of eight hundred rubles a cargo, an amount which he considers outrageously high. The question is, therefore, how much wealth must Caius possess apart from the goods under consideration in order that it be sensible for him to abstain from insuring them? If x represents his fortune, then this together with the value of the expectation of the safe arrival of his goods is given by

$$\sqrt[100]{(x + 10000)^{95} x^5} = \sqrt[20]{(x + 10000)^{19} x}$$

in case he abstains. With insurance he will have a certain fortune of $x + 9200$. Equating these two magnitudes we get: $(x + 10000)^{19} x = (x + 9200)^{20}$ or, approximately, $x = 5043$. If, therefore, Caius, apart from the expectation of receiving his commodities, possesses an amount greater than 5043 rubles he will be right in not buying insurance. If, on the contrary, his wealth is less than this amount he should insure his cargo. And if the question be asked "What minimum fortune should be possessed by the man who offers to provide this insurance in order for him to be rational in doing so?" We must answer thus: let y be his fortune, then

$$\sqrt[20]{(y + 800)^{19} \cdot (y - 9200)} = y$$

or approximately, $y = 14243$, a figure which is obtained from the foregoing without additional calculation. A man less wealthy than this would be foolish to provide the surety, but it makes sense for a wealthier man to do so.

---

[5] Caius is a Roman name, used here in the sense of our " Mr. Jones." Caius is the older form; in the later Roman period it was spelled "Gaius." [Translator].

Fom this it is clear that the introduction of this sort of insurance has been so useful since it offers advantages to all persons concerned. Similarly, had Caius been able to obtain the insurance for six hundred rubles he would have been unwise to refuse it if he possessed less than 20478 rubles, but he would have acted much too cautiously had he insured his commodities at this rate when his fortune was greater than this amount. On the other hand a man would act unadvisedly if he were to offer to sponsor this insurance for six hundred rubles when he himself possesses less than 29878 rubles. However, he would be well advised to do so if he possessed more than that amount. But no one, however rich, would be managing his affairs properly if he individually undertook the insurance for less than five hundred rubles.

§16. Another rule which may prove useful can be derived from our theory. This is the rule that it is advisable to divide goods which are exposed to some danger into several portions rather than to risk them all together. Again I shall explain this more precisely by an example. Sempronius owns goods at home worth a total of 4000 ducats and in addition possesses 8000 ducats worth of commodities in foreign countries from where they can only be transported by sea. However, our daily experience teaches us that of ten ships one perishes. Under these conditions I maintain that if Sempronius trusted all his 8000 ducats of goods to one ship his expectation of the commodities is worth 6751 ducats. That is

$$\sqrt[10]{12000^9 \cdot 4000^1} - 4000.$$

If, however, he were to trust equal portions of these commodities to two ships the value of his expectation would be

$$\sqrt[100]{12000^{81} \cdot 8000^{18} \cdot 4000} - 4000, \quad \text{i.e., } 7033 \text{ ducats.}$$

In this way the value of Sempronius' prospects of success will grow more favorable the smaller the proportion committed to each ship. However, his expectation will never rise in value above 7200 ducats. This counsel will be equally serviceable for those who invest their fortunes in foreign bills of exchange and other hazardous enterprises.

§17. I am forced to omit many novel remarks though these would clearly not be unserviceable. And, though a person who is fairly judicious by natural instinct might have realized and spontaneously applied much of what I have here explained, hardly anyone believed it possible to define these problems with the precision we have employed in our examples. Since all our propositions harmonize perfectly with experience it would be wrong to neglect them as abstractions resting upon precarious hypotheses. This is further confirmed by the following example which inspired these thoughts, and whose history is as follows: My most honorable cousin the celebrated *Nicolas Bernoulli*, Professor utriusque iuris[6] at the University of Basle, once submitted five

---

[6] Faculties of law of continental European universities bestow up to the present time the title of a Doctor utriusque juris, which means Doctor of both systems of laws, the Roman and the canon law. [Translator].

problems to the highly distinguished[7] mathematician *Montmort*.[8] These problems are reproduced in the work *L'analyse sur les jeux de hazard de M. de Montmort*, p. 402. The last of these problems runs as follows: *Peter tosses a coin and continues to do so until it should land "heads" when it comes to the ground. He agrees to give Paul one ducat if he gets "heads" on the very first throw, two ducats if he gets it on the second, four if on the third, eight if on the fourth, and so on, so that with each additional throw the number of ducats he must pay is doubled. Suppose we seek to determine the value of Paul's expectation.* My aforementioned cousin discussed this problem in a letter to me asking for my opinion. Although the standard calculation shows[9] that the value of Paul's expectation is infinitely great, it has, he said, to be admitted that any fairly reasonable man would sell his chance, with great pleasure, for twenty ducats. The accepted method of calculation does, indeed, value Paul's prospects at infinity though no one would be willing to purchase it at a moderately high price. If, however, we apply our new rule to this problem we may see the solution and thus unravel the knot. The solution of the problem by our principles is as follows.

§18. The number of cases to be considered here is infinite: in one half of the cases the game will end at the first throw, in one quarter of the cases it will conclude at the second, in an eighth part of the cases with the third, in a sixteenth part with the fourth, and so on.[10] If we designate the number of

---

[7] Cl., i.e., Vir Clarissimus, a title of respect. [Translator].

[8] Montmort, Pierre Remond, de (1678–1719). The work referred to here is the then famous "Essai d'analyse sur les jeux de hazard," Paris, 1708. Appended to the second edition, published in 1713, is Montmort's correspondence with Jean and Nicolas Bernoulli referring to the problems of chance and probabilities. [Translator].

[9] The probability of heads turning up on the 1st throw is $1/2$. Since in this case Paul receives one ducat, this probability contributes $1/2 . 1 = 1/2$ ducats to his expectation. The probability of heads turning up on the 2nd throw is $1/4$. Since in this case Paul receives 2 ducats, this possibility contributes $1/4 . 2 = 1/2$ to his expectation. Similarly, for every integer n, the possibility of heads turning up on the n-th throw contributes $1/2^n . 2^{n-1} = 1/2$ ducats to his expectation. Paul's total expectation is therefore $1/2 + 1/2 + \cdots + 1/2 + \cdots$, and that is infinite.—Karl Menger.

[10] Since the number of cases is infinite, it is impossible to speak about one half of the cases, one quarter of the cases, etc., and the letter N in Bernoulli's argument is meaningless. However, Paul's expectation on the basis of Bernoulli's hypothesis concerning evaluation can be found by the same method by which, in footnote 9, Paul's classical expectation was determined. If Paul's fortune is ducats, then, according to Bernoulli, he attributes to a gain of 2^{n-1} ducats the value $b \log \dfrac{\alpha + 2^{n-1}}{\alpha}$. If the probability of this gain is $1/2^n$, his expectation is $b/2^n \log \dfrac{\alpha + 2^{n-1}}{\alpha}$. Paul's expectation resulting from the game is therefore $\dfrac{b}{2} \log \dfrac{\alpha + 1}{\alpha} + \dfrac{b}{4} \log \dfrac{\alpha + 2}{\alpha} + \cdots + \dfrac{b}{2^n} \log \dfrac{\alpha + 2^{n-1}}{\alpha} + \cdots = b \log [(\alpha + 1)^{1/2}(\alpha + 2)^{1/4} . \cdots . (\alpha + 2^{n-1})^{1/2^n} . \cdots] - b \log \alpha$. What addition D to Paul's fortune has the same value for him? Clearly, $b \log \dfrac{\alpha + D}{\alpha}$ must equal the above sum. Therefore $D = (\alpha + 1)^{1/2}(\alpha + 2)^{1/4} . \cdots . (\alpha + 2^{n-1})^{1/2^n} . \cdots - \alpha$.—Karl Menger.

cases through infinity by N it is clear that there are $\frac{1}{2}N$ cases in which Paul gains one ducat, $\frac{1}{4}N$ cases in which he gains two ducats, $\frac{1}{8}N$ in which he gains four, $\frac{1}{16}N$ in which he gains eight, and so on, ad infinitum. Let us represent Paul's fortune by α; the proposition in question will then be worth

$$\sqrt[N]{(\alpha+1)^{N/2}.(\alpha+2)^{N/4}.(\alpha+4)^{N/8}.(\alpha+8)^{N/16}\cdots}-\alpha$$
$$=\sqrt{(\alpha+1)}.\sqrt[4]{(\alpha+2)}.\sqrt[8]{(\alpha+4)}.\sqrt[16]{(\alpha+8)}\cdots-\alpha.$$

§19. From this formula which evaluates Paul's prospective gain it follows that this value will increase with the size of Paul's fortune and will never attain an infinite value unless Paul's wealth simultaneously becomes infinite. In addition we obtain the following corollaries. If Paul owned nothing at all the value of his expectation would be

$$\sqrt[2]{1}.\sqrt[4]{2}.\sqrt[8]{4}.\sqrt[16]{8}\cdots$$

which amounts to two ducats, precisely. If he owned ten ducats his opportunity would be worth approximately three ducats; it would be worth approximately four if his wealth were one hundred, and six if he possessed one thousand. From this we can easily see what a tremendous fortune a man must own for it to make sense for him to purchase Paul's opportunity for twenty ducats. The amount which the buyer ought to pay for this proposition differs somewhat from the amount it would be worth to him were it already in his possession. Since, however, this difference is exceedingly small if α (Paul's fortune) is great, we can take them to be equal. If we designate the purchase price by x its value can be determined by means of the equation

$$\sqrt[2]{(\alpha+1-x)}.\sqrt[4]{(\alpha+2-x)}.\sqrt[8]{(\alpha+4-x)}.\sqrt[16]{(\alpha+8-x)}\cdots=\alpha$$

and if α is a large number this equation will be approximately satisfied by

$$x=\sqrt[2]{\alpha+1}.\sqrt[4]{\alpha+2}.\sqrt[8]{\alpha+4}.\sqrt[16]{\alpha+8}\cdots-\alpha.$$

After having read this paper to the Society[11] I sent a copy to the aforementioned Mr. Nicolas Bernoulli, to obtain his opinion of my proposed solution to the difficulty he had indicated. In a letter to me written in 1732 he declared that he was in no way dissatisfied with my proposition on the evaluation of risky propositions when applied to the case of a man who is to evaluate his own prospects. However, he thinks that the case is different if a third person, somewhat in the position of a judge, is to evaluate the prospects of any participant in a game in accord with equity and justice. I myself have discussed this problem in §2. Then this distinguished scholar informed me that the celebrated mathematician, Cramer,[12] had developed a theory on the same subject several years

[11] Bernoulli's paper had been submitted to the Imperial Academy of Sciences in Petersburg. [Translator].

[12] Cramer, Gabriel, famous mathematician, born in Geneva, Switzerland (1704–1752). [Translator].

before I produced my paper. Indeed I have found his theory so similar to mine that it seems miraculous that we independently reached such close agreement on this sort of subject. Therefore it seems worth quoting the words with which the celebrated Cramer himself first described his theory in his letter of 1728 to my cousin. His words are as follows: [13]

" Perhaps I am mistaken, but I believe that I have solved the extraordinary problem which you submitted to M. *de Montmort*, in your letter of September 9, 1713 (problem 5, page 402). For the sake of simplicity I shall assume that A tosses a coin into the air and B commits himself to give A 1 ducat if, at the first throw, the coin falls with its cross upward; 2 if it falls thus only at the second throw, 4 if at the third throw, 8 if at the fourth throw, etc. The paradox consists in the infinite sum which calculation yields as the equivalent which A must pay to B. This seems absurd since no reasonable man would be willing to pay 20 ducats as equivalent. You ask for an explanation of the discrepancy between the mathematical calculation and the vulgar evaluation. I believe that it results from the fact that, *in their theory*, mathematicians evaluate money in proportion to its quantity while, *in practice*, people with common sense evaluate money in proportion to the utility they can obtain from it. The mathematical expectation is rendered infinite by the enormous amount which I can win if the coin does not fall with its cross upward until rather late, perhaps at the hundredth or thousandth throw. Now, as a matter of fact, if I reason as a sensible man, this sum is worth no more to me, causes me no more pleasure and influences me no more to accept the game than does a sum amounting only to ten or twenty million ducats. Let us suppose, therefore, that any amount above 10 millions, or (for the sake of simplicity) above $2^{24} = 166777216$ ducats be deemed by him equal in value to 2^{24} ducats or, better yet, that I can never win more than that amount, no matter how long it takes before the coin falls with its cross upward. In this case, my expectation is $\frac{1}{2}.1 + \frac{1}{4}.2 + \frac{1}{8}.4 \cdots + \frac{1}{2^{25}}.2^{24} + \frac{1}{2^{26}}.2^{24} + \frac{1}{2^{27}}.2^{24} + \cdots = \frac{1}{2} + \frac{1}{2} + \frac{1}{2} + \cdots$ (24 times) $\cdots + \frac{1}{2} + \frac{1}{4} + \frac{1}{8} + \cdots = 12 + 1 = 13$. Thus, my moral expectation is reduced in value to 13 ducats and the equivalent to be paid for it is similarly reduced—a result which seems much more reasonable than does rendering it infinite."

Thus far [14] *the exposition is somewhat vague and subject to counter argument. If it, indeed, be true that the amount 2^{25} appears to us to be no greater than 2^{24}, no attention whatsoever should be paid to the amount that may be won after the twenty-fourth throw, since just before making the twenty-fifth throw I am certain to end up with no less than $2^{24} - 1$,* [15] *an amount that, according to this theory, may be considered equivalent to 2^{24}. Therefore it may be said correctly that my expectation is only worth twelve ducats, not thirteen. However, in*

---

[13] The following passage of the original text is in French. [Translator].

[14] From here on the text is again translated from Latin. [Translator].

[15] This remark of Bernoulli's is obscure. Under the conditions of the game a gain of $2^{24} - 1$ ducats is impossible.—Karl Menger.

view of the coincidence between the basic principle developed by the afore-
mentioned author and my own, the foregoing is clearly not intended to be taken
to invalidate that principle. I refer to the proposition that reasonable men should
evaluate money in accord with the utility they derive therefrom. I state this to
avoid leading anyone to judge that entire theory adversely. And this is exactly
what Cl. C.[16] *Cramer states, expressing in the following manner precisely what*
we would ourselves conclude. He continues thus.[17]

" The equivalent can turn out to be smaller yet if we adopt some alternative
hypothesis on the moral value of wealth. For that which I have just assumed is
not entirely valid since, while it is true that 100 millions yield more satisfaction than do 10 millions, they do not give ten times as much. If, for example,
we suppose the moral value of goods to be directly proportionate to the
square root of their mathematical quantities, e.g., that the satisfaction
provided by 40000000 is double that provided by 10000000, my psychic
expectation becomes

$$\tfrac{1}{2}\sqrt{1} + \tfrac{1}{4}\sqrt{2} + \tfrac{1}{8}\sqrt{4} + \tfrac{1}{16}\sqrt{8} + \cdots = \frac{1}{2 - \sqrt{2}}.$$

However this magnitude is not the equivalent we seek, for this equivalent
need not be equal to my moral expectation but should rather be of such a
magnitude that the pain caused by its loss is equal to the moral expectation
of the pleasure I hope to derive from my gain. Therefore, the equivalent
must, on our hypothesis, amount to $\left(\dfrac{1}{2 - \sqrt{2}}\right)^2 = \left(\dfrac{1}{6 - 4\sqrt{2}}\right) = 2.9 \ldots,$
which is consequently less than 3, truly a trifling amount, but nevertheless, I
believe, closer than is 13 to the vulgar evaluation."

REFERENCES

There exists only one other translation of Bernoulli's paper:
Pringsheim, Alfred, *Die Grundlage der modernen Wertlehre: Daniel Bernoulli,*
Versucheiner neuen Theorie der Wertbestimmung von Glücksfällen (Specimen
Theoriae novae de Mensura Sortis). Aus dem Lateinischen übersetzt und mit
Eläuterungen versehen von Alfred Pringsheim, Leipzig, Duncker und Humblot,
1896, Sammlung älterer und neuerer staats-wissenschaftlicher Schriften des Inund
Auslandes hrsg. von L. Brentano und E. Leser, No. 9.

For an early discussion of the Bernoulli problem, reference is made to
Malfatti, Gianfrancesco, " Esame critico di un problema di probabilita del Signor
Daniele Bernoulli, e soluzione d'un altro problema analogo al Bernoulliano" in
" *Memorie di Matematica e Fisica della Societa italiana,*" Vol. I, Verona, 1782, pp.
768–824.

For more on the " St. Petersburg Paradox," including material on later discussions, see
Menger, Karl, " Das Unsicherheitsmoment in der Wertlehre. Betrachtungen im

[16] To be translated as " the distinguished Gabriel." [Translator].
[17] Text continues in French. [Translator].

Anschluss an das sogenannte Petersburger Spiel," *Zeitschrift für Nationalökonomie*, Vol. 5, 1934.

This paper by Professor Menger is the most extensive study on the literature of the problem, and the problem itself.

Recent interest in the Bernoulli hypothesis was aroused by its appearance in von Neumann, John, and Oskar Morgenstern, *The Theory of Games and Economic Behavior*, second edition, Princeton: Princeton University Press, 1947, Ch. III and Appendix: "The Axiomatic Treatment of Utility."

Many contemporary references and a discussion of the utility maximization hypothesis are to be found in

Arrow, Kenneth J., "Alternative Approaches to the Theory of Choice in Risk-Taking Situations," *Econometrica*, Vol. 19, October, 1951.

More recent writings in the field include

Alchian, A. A., "The Meaning of Utility Measurement," *American Economic Review*, Vol. XLIII, March, 1953.

Friedman, M., and Savage, L. J., "The Expected Utility-Hypothesis and the Measurability of Utility," *Journal of Political Economy*, Vol. LX, December, 1952.

Herstein, I. N., and John Milnor, "An Axiomatic Approach to Measurable Utility," *Econometrica*, Vol. 21, April, 1953.

Marschak, J., "Why 'Should' Statisticians and Businessmen Maximize 'Moral Expectation'?," *Second Berkeley Symposium on Mathematical Statistics and Probability*, 1953.

Mosteller, Frederick, and Philip Nogee, "An Experimental Measurement of Utility," *Journal of Political Economy*, lix, 5, Oct., 1951.

Samuelson, Paul A., "Probability, Utility, and the Independence Axiom," *Econometrica*, Vol. 20, Oct., 1952.

Strotz, Robert H., "Cardinal Utility," *Papers and Proceedings of the Sixty-Fifth Annual Meeting of the American Economic Association, American Economic Review*, Vol. 43, May, 1953, and the comment by W. J. Baumol.

For dissenting views, see:

Allais, M., "Les Theories de la Psychologie du Risque de l'Ecole Americaine," *Revue d'Economie Politique*, Vol. 63, 1953.

———. "Le Comportement de l'Homme Rationnel devant le Risque: Critique des postulats et Axiomes de l'Ecole Americaine," *Econometrica*, Oct., 1953, and

Edwards, Ward, "Probability-Preferences in Gambling," *The American Journal of Psychology*, Vol. 66, July, 1953.

Textbooks dealing with Bernoulli:

Anderson, Oskar, *Einführung in die mathematische Statistik*, Wien: J. Springer, 1935.

Davis, Harold, *The Theory of Econometrics*, Bloomington, Ind.: Principia Press, 1941.

Loria, Gino, *Storia delle Matematiche, dall'albadella civiltá al secolo XIX*, Second revised ed., Milan: U. Hopli, 1950.

2. THE UTILITY ANALYSIS OF CHOICES INVOLVING RISK[1]

MILTON FRIEDMAN*
and
LEONARD J. SAVAGE†

Reprinted from *The Journal of Political Economy*, Vol. LVI, No. 4 (August 1948), pp. 279–304, by permission of the authors.

I. THE PROBLEM AND ITS BACKGROUND

The purpose of this paper is to suggest that an important class of reactions of individuals to risk can be rationalized by a rather simple extension of orthodox utility analysis.

Individuals frequently must, or can, choose among alternatives that differ, among other things, in the degree of risk to which the individual will be subject. The clearest examples are provided by insurance and gambling. An individual who buys fire insurance on a house he owns is accepting the certain loss of a small sum (the insurance premium) in preference to the combination of a small chance of a much larger loss (the value of the house) and a large chance of no loss. That is, he is choosing certainty in preference to uncertainty. An individual who buys a lottery ticket is subjecting himself to a large chance of losing a small amount (the price of the lottery ticket) plus a small chance of winning a large amount (a prize) in preference to avoiding both risks. He is choosing uncertainty in preference to certainty.

This choice among different degrees of risk, so prominent in insurance and gambling, is clearly present and important in a much broader range of economic choices. Occupations differ greatly in the variability of the income they promise: in some, for example, civil service employment, the prospective income is rather clearly defined and is almost certain to be within rather narrow limits; in others, for example, salaried employment as an accountant, there is somewhat more variability yet almost no chance of either an extremely high or an extremely low income; in still others, for example, motion-picture acting, there is extreme variability, with a small chance of an extremely high income and a larger chance of an extremely low income. Securities vary similarly, from government bonds and industrial "blue chips" to "blue-sky" common stocks; and so do business enterprises or lines of business activity. Whether or not they realize it and whether or not they take explicit

* Professor of Economics, University of Chicago.
† Professor of Statistics, Yale University.
[1] The fundamental ideas of this paper were worked out jointly by the two authors. The paper was written primarily by the senior author.

account of the varying degree of risk involved, individuals choosing among occupations, securities, or lines of business activity are making choices analogous to those that they make when they decide whether to buy insurance or to gamble. Is there any consistency among the choices of this kind that individuals make? Do they neglect the element of risk? Or does it play a central role? If so, what is that role?

These problems have, of course, been considered by economic theorists, particularly in their discussions of earnings in different occupations and of profits in different lines of business.[2] Their treatment of these problems has, however, never been integrated with their explanation of choices among riskless alternatives. Choices among riskless alternatives are explained in terms of maximization of utility: individuals are supposed to choose as they would if they attributed some common quantitative characteristic—designated utility—to various goods and then selected the combination of goods that yielded the largest total amount of this common characteristic. Choices among alternatives involving different degrees of risk, for example, among different occupations, are explained in utterly different terms—by ignorance of the odds or by the fact that "young men of an adventurous disposition are more attracted by the prospects of a great success than they are deterred by the fear of failure," by "the overweening conceit which the greater part of men have of their own abilities," by "their absurd presumption in their own good fortune," or by some similar *deus ex machina*.[3]

The rejection of utility maximization as an explanation of choices among different degrees of risk was a direct consequence of the belief in diminishing marginal utility. If the marginal utility of money diminishes, an individual seeking to maximize utility will never participate in a "fair" game of chance, for example, a game in which he has an equal chance of winning or losing a dollar. The gain in utility from winning a dollar will be less than the loss in utility from losing a dollar, so that the expected utility from participation in the game is negative. Diminishing marginal utility plus maximization of expected utility would thus imply that individuals would always have to be paid to induce them to bear risk.[4] But this implication is clearly contradicted

---

[2] E.g., see Adam Smith, *The Wealth of Nations*, Book I, Ch. x (Modern Library reprint of Cannan ed.), pp. 106–11; Alfred Marshall, *Principles of Economics* (8th ed.; London: Macmillan & Co., Ltd., 1920), pp. 398–400, 554–55, 613.

[3] Marshall, *op. cit.*, p. 554 (first quotation); Smith, *op. cit.*, p. 107 (last two quotations).

[4] See Marshall, *op. cit.*, p. 135 n.; Mathematical Appendix, n. ix (p. 843). "Gambling involves an economic loss, even when conducted on perfectly fair and even terms. . . . A theoretically fair insurance against risks is always an economic gain" (p. 135). "The argument that fair gambling is an economic blunder . . . requires no further assumption than that, firstly the pleasures of gambling may be neglected; and, secondly $\phi''(x)$ is negative for all values of x, where $\phi(x)$ is the pleasure derived from wealth equal to x. . . . It is true that this loss of probable happiness need not be greater than the pleasure derived from the excitement of gambling, and we are then thrown back upon the induction that pleasures of gambling are in Bentham's phrase 'impure'; since experience shows that they are likely to engender a restless, feverish character, unsuited for steady work as well as for the higher and more solid pleasures of life" (p. 843).

by actual behavior. People not only engage in fair games of chance, they engage freely and often eagerly in such unfair games as lotteries. Not only do risky occupations and risky investments not always yield a higher average return than relatively safe occupations or investments, they frequently yield a much lower average return.

Marshall resolved this contradiction by rejecting utility maximization as an explanation of choices involving risk. He need not have done so, since he did not need diminishing marginal utility—or, indeed, any quantitative concept of utility—for the analysis of riskless choices. The shift from the kind of utility analysis employed by Marshall to the indifference-curve analysis of F. Y. Edgeworth, Irving Fisher, and Vilfredo Pareto revealed that to rationalize riskless choices, it is sufficient to suppose that individuals can rank baskets of goods by total utility. It is unnecessary to suppose that they can compare differences between utilities. But diminishing, or increasing, marginal utility implies a comparison of differences between utilities and hence is an entirely gratuitous assumption in interpreting riskless choices.

The idea that choices among alternatives involving risk can be explained by the maximization of expected utility is ancient, dating back at least to D. Bernoulli's celebrated analysis of the St. Petersburg paradox.[5] It has been repeatedly referred to since then but almost invariably rejected as the correct explanation—commonly because the prevailing belief in diminishing marginal utility made it appear that the existence of gambling could not be so explained. Even since the widespread recognition that the assumption of diminishing marginal utility is unnecessary to explain riskless choices, writers have continued to reject maximization of expected utility as "unrealistic."[6] This rejection of maximization of expected utility has been challenged by John von

---

[5] See Daniel Bernoulli, *Versuch einer neuen Theorie der Wertbestimmung von Glücksfällen* (Leipzig, 1896), translated by A. Pringsheim from "Specimen theoriae novae de mensura sortis," *Commentarii academiae scientiarum imperialis Petropolitanae*, Vol. V, for the years 1730 and 1731, published in 1738.

In an interesting note appended to his paper Bernoulli points out that Cramer [presumably Gabriel Cramer (1704–52)], a famous mathematician of the time, had anticipated some of his own views by a few years. The passages that he quotes from a letter in French by Cramer contain what, to us, is the truly essential point in Bernoulli's paper, namely, the idea of using the mathematical expectation of utility (the "moral expectation") instead of the mathematical expectation of income to compare alternatives involving risk. Cramer has not in general been attributed this much credit, apparently because the essential point in Bernoulli's paper has been taken to be the suggestion that the logarithm of income is an appropriate utility function.

[6] "It has been the assumption in the classical literature on this subject that the individual in question will always try to maximize the mathematical expectation of his gain or utility. . . . This may appear plausible, but it is certainly not an assumption which must hold true in all cases. It has been pointed out that the individual may also be interested in, and influenced by, the range or the standard deviation of the different possible utilities derived or some other measure of dispersion. It appears pretty evident from the behavior of people in lotteries or football pools that they are not a little influenced by the skewness of the probability distribution" [Gerhard Tintner, "A Contribution to the Non-Static Theory of Choice," *Quarterly Journal of Economics*, Vol. LVI (February, 1942), p. 278].

Neumann and Oskar Morgenstern in their recent book, *Theory of Games and Economic Behavior*.[7] They argue that " under the conditions on which the indifference curve analysis is based very little extra effort is needed to reach a numerical utility," the expected value of which is maximized in choosing among alternatives involving risk.[8] The present paper is based on their treatment but has been made self-contained by the paraphrasing of esssential parts of their argument.

If an individual shows by his market behavior that he prefers A to B and B to C, it is traditional to rationalize this behavior by supposing that he attaches more utility to A than to B and more utility to B than to C. All utility functions that give the same ranking to possible alternatives will provide equally good rationalizations of such choices, and it will make no difference which particular one is used. If, in addition, the individual should show by his market behavior that he prefers a 50-50 chance of A or C to the certainty of B, it seems natural to rationalize this behavior by supposing that the *difference* between the utilities he attaches to A and B is greater than the *difference* between the utilities he attaches to B and C, so that the *expected* utility of the preferred combination is greater than the utility of B. The class of utility functions, if there be any, that can provide the same ranking of alternatives that involve risk is much more restricted than the class that can provide the same ranking of alternatives that are certain. It consists of utility functions that differ only in origin and unit of measure (i.e., the utility functions in the class are linear functions of one another).[9] Thus, in effect, the ordinal properties of utility functions can be used to rationalize riskless choices, the numerical properties to rationalize choices involving risk.

It does not, of course, follow that there will exist a utility function that will rationalize in this way the reactions of individuals to risk. It may be that individuals behave inconsistently—sometimes choosing a 50-50 chance of A or C instead of B and sometimes the reverse; or sometimes choosing A instead of B, B instead of C, and C instead of A—or that in some other way their behavior is different from what it would be if they were seeking rationally to maximize expected utility in accordance with a given utility function. Or it may be that some types of reactions to risk can be rationalized in this way

---

" It would be definitely unrealistic . . . to confine ourselves to the mathematical expectation only, which is the usual but not justifiable practice of the traditional calculus of 'moral probabilities'" [J. Marschak, " Money and the Theory of Assets," *Econometrica*, Vol. VI (1938), p. 320].

Tintner's inference, apparently also shared by Marschak, that the facts he cites are necessarily inconsistent with maximization of expected utility is erroneous (see Secs. III and IV below). He is led to consider a formerly more general solution because of his failure to appreciate the real generality of the kinds of behavior explicable by the maximization of expected utility.

[7] Princeton University Press, 1st ed., 1944; 2d ed., 1947; pp. 15–31 (both eds.), pp. 617–32 (2d ed. only); succeeding references are to 2d ed.

[8] *Ibid.*, p. 17.

[9] *Ibid.*, pp. 15–31, esp. p. 25.

while others cannot. Whether a numerical utility function will in fact serve to rationalize any particular class of reactions to risk is an empirical question to be tested; there is no obvious contradiction such as was once thought to exist.

This paper attempts to provide a crude empirical test by bringing together a few broad observations about the behavior of individuals in choosing among alternatives involving risk (Sec. II) and investigating whether these observations are consistent with the hypothesis revived by von Neumann and Morgenstern (Secs. III and IV). It turns out that these empirical observations are entirely consistent with the hypothesis if a rather special shape is given to the total utility curve of money (Sec. IV). This special shape, which can be given a tolerably satisfactory interpretation (Sec. V), not only brings under the aegis of rational utility maximization much behavior that is ordinarily explained in other terms but also has implications about observable behavior not used in deriving it (Sec. VI). Further empirical work should make it possible to determine whether or not these implications conform to reality.

It is a testimony to the strength of the belief in diminishing marginal utility that it has taken so long for the possibility of interpreting gambling and similar phenomena as a contradiction of universal diminishing marginal utility, rather than of utility maximization, to be recognized. The initial mistake must have been at least partly a product of a strong introspective belief in diminishing marginal utility: a dollar must mean less to a rich man than to a poor man; see how much more a man will spend when he is rich than when he is poor to avoid any given amount of pain or discomfort.[10] Some of the comments that have been published by competent economists on the utility analysis of von Neumann and Morgenstern are even more remarkable testimony to the hold that diminishing marginal utility has on economists. Vickrey remarks: " There is abundant evidence that individual decisions in situations involving risk are not always made in ways that are compatible with the assumption that the decisions are made rationally with a view to maximizing the mathematical expectation of a utility function. The purchase of tickets in lotteries, sweepstakes, and 'numbers' pools would imply, on such a basis, that the marginal utility of money is an increasing rather than a decreasing function of income. Such a conclusion is obviously unacceptable as a guide to social policy."[11] Kaysen remarks, " Unfortunately, these postulates (underlying

---

[10] This elemental argument seems so clearly to justify diminishing marginal utility that it may be desirable even now to state explicitly how this phenomenon can be rationalized equally well on the assumption of increasing marginal utility of money. It is only necessary to suppose that the avoidance of pain and the other goods that can be bought with money are related goods and that, while the marginal utility of money increases as the amount of money increases, the marginal utility of avoiding pain increases even faster.

[11] William Vickrey, " Measuring Marginal Utility by Reactions to Risk," *Econometrica*, Vol. XIII (1945), pp. 319–33. The quotation is from pp. 327 and 328. "The purchase of tickets in lotteries, sweepstakes, and 'numbers' pools does not imply that marginal utility of money increases with income everywhere (see Sec. IV below). Moreover, it is entirely unnecessary to identify the quantity that individuals are to be interpreted as maximizing with a quantity that should be given special importance in public policy."

the von Neumann and Morgenstern discussion of utility measurement) involve an assumption about economic behavior which is contrary to experience.... That this assumption is contradicted by experience can easily be shown by hundreds of examples (including) the participation of individuals in lotteries in which their mathematical expectation of gain (utility) is negative."[12]

II. OBSERVABLE BEHAVIOR TO BE RATIONALIZED

The economic phenomena to which the hypothesis revived by von Neumann and Morgenstern is relevant can be divided into, first, the phenomena ordinarily regarded as gambling and insurance; second, other economic phenomena involving risk. The latter are clearly the more important, and the ultimate significance of the hypothesis will depend primarily on the contribution it makes to an understanding of them. At the same time, the influence of risk is revealed most markedly in gambling and insurance, so that these phenomena have a significance for testing and elaborating the hypothesis out of proportion to their importance in actual economic behavior.

At the outset it should be confessed that we have conducted no extensive empirical investigation of either class of phenomena. For the present, we are content to use what is already available in the literature, or obvious from casual observation, to provide a first test of the hypothesis and to impose significant substantive restrictions on it.

The major economic decisions of an individual in which risk plays an important role concern the employment of the resources he controls: what occupation to follow, what entrepreneurial activity to engage in, how to invest (nonhuman) capital. Alternative possible uses of resources can be classified into three broad groups according to the degree of risk involved: (a) those involving little or no risk about the money return to be received—occupations like schoolteaching, other civil service employment, clerical work; business undertakings of a standard predictable type like many public utilities; securities like government bonds, high-grade industrial bonds; some real property, particularly owner-occupied housing; (b) those involving a moderate degree of risk but unlikely to lead to either extreme gains or extreme losses—occupations like dentistry, accountancy, some kinds of managerial work; business undertakings of fairly standard kinds in which, however, there is sufficient competition to make the outcome fairly uncertain; securities like lower-grade bonds, preferred stocks, higher-grade common stocks; (c) those involving much risk, with some possibility of extremely large gains and some of extremely large losses—occupations involving physical risks, like piloting aircraft, automobile racing, or professions like medicine and law; business undertakings in untried fields; securities like highly speculative stocks; some types of real property.

[12] C. Kaysen, "A Revolution in Economic Theory?" *Review of Economic Studies*, Vol. XIV, No. 35 (1946–47), pp. 1–15; quotation is from p. 13.

The most significant generalization in the literature about choices among these three uses of resources is that, other things the same, uses *a* or *c* tend in general to be preferred to use *b*; that is, people must in general be paid a premium to induce them to undertake moderate risks instead of subjecting themselves to either small or large risks. Thus Marshall says:

There are many people of a sober steady-going temper, who like to know what is before them, and who would far rather have an appointment which offered a certain income of say £400 a year than one which was not unlikely to yield £600, but had an equal chance of affording only £200. Uncertainty, therefore, which does not appeal to great ambitions and lofty aspirations, has special attractions for very few; while it acts as a deterrent to many of those who are making their choice of a career. And as a rule the certainty of moderate success attracts more than an expectation of an uncertain success that has an equal actuarial value.

But on the other hand, if an occupation offers a few extremely high prizes, its attractiveness is increased out of all proportion to their aggregate value.[13]

Adam Smith comments similarly about occupational choices and, in addition, says of entrepreneurial undertakings:

The ordinary rate of profits always rises more or less with the risk. It does not, however, seem to rise in proportion to it, or so as to compensate it completely. . . . The presumptuous hope of success seems to act here as upon all other occasions, and to entice so many adventurers into those hazardous trades, that their competition reduces the profit below what is sufficient to compensate the risk.[14]

Edwin Cannan, in discussing the rate of return on investments, concludes that "the probability is that the classes of investments which on the average return most to the investor are neither the very safest of all nor the very riskiest, but the intermediate classes which do not appeal either to timidity or to the gambling instinct."[15]

This asserted preference for extremely safe or extremely risky investments over investments with an intermediate degree of risk has its direct counterpart in the willingness of persons to buy insurance and also to buy lottery tickets or engage in other forms of gambling involving a small chance of a large gain. The extensive market for highly speculative stocks—the kind of stocks that "blue-sky" laws are intended to control—is a border-line case that could equally well be designated as investment or gambling.

The empirical evidence for the willingness of persons of all income classes to buy insurance is extensive.[16] Since insurance companies have costs of

---

[13] *Op. cit.*, pp. 554–55.

[14] *Op. cit.*, p. 111.

[15] Article on "Profit," in *Dictionary of Political Economy*, ed. R. H. Inglis Palgrave (new edition, ed. Henry Higgs; London, 1926); see also the summary of the views of different writers on risk-taking in F. H. Knight, *Risk, Uncertainty, and Profit* (New York, 1921; reprint London School of Economics and Political Science, 1933), pp. 362–67.

[16] E.g., see U.S. Bureau of Labor Statistics, *Bulletin 648: Family Expenditures in Selected Cities, 1935–36*; Vol. I: *Family Expenditures for Housing, 1935–36*; Vol. VI: *Family Expenditures for Transportation, 1935–36*; and Vol. VIII: *Changes in Assets and Liabilities, 1935–36*.

operation that are covered by their premium receipts, the purchaser is obviously paying a larger premium than the average compensation he can expect to receive for the losses against which he carries insurance. That is, he is paying something to escape risk.

The empirical evidence for the willingness of individuals to purchase lottery tickets, or engage in similar forms of gambling, is also extensive. Many governments find, and more governments have found, lotteries an effective

---

Table 6 of the Tabular Summary of Vol. I gives the percentage of home-owning families reporting the payment of premiums for insurance on the house. These percentages are given separately for each income class in each of a number of cities or groups of cities. Since premiums are often paid less frequently than once a year, the percentages given definitely understate the percentage of families carrying insurance. Yet the bulk of the percentages are well over 40.

Table 5 of the Tabular Summary of Vol. VI gives the percentage of families (again by income classes and cities or groups of cities) reporting expenditures for automobile insurance. These figures show a very rapid increase in the percentage of automobile operators that had insurance (this figure is derived by dividing the percentage of families reporting automobile insurance by the percentage of families operating cars) as income increases. In the bottom income classes, where operation of a car is infrequent, only a minority of those who operate cars carry insurance. In the upper income classes, where most families operate cars, the majority of operators carry insurance. A convenient summary of these percentages for selected income classes in six large cities, given in text Table 10 (p. 26), has 42 entries. These vary from 4% to 98%, and 23 are over 50%.

Table 3 of the Tabular Summary of Vol. VIII gives the percentage of families in each income class in various cities or groups of cities reporting the payment of life, endowment, or annuity insurance premiums. The percentages are uniformly high. For example, for New York City the percentage of white families reporting the payment of insurance premiums is 75% or higher for every income class listed and varies from 75% in the income class $500–$749 to over 95% in the upper-income classes; the percentage of Negro families purchasing insurance was 38% for the $1,000–$1,249 class but 60% or higher for every other class. This story is repeated for city after city, the bulk of the entries in the table for the percentage of families purchasing insurance being above 80%.

These figures cannot be regarded as direct estimates of the percentage of families willing to pay something—that is, to accept a smaller actuarial value—in order to escape risk, the technical meaning of the purchase of insurance that is relevant for our purpose. (1) The purchase of automobile and housing insurance may not be a matter of choice. Most owned homes have mortgages (see Vol. I, p. 361, Table L) and the mortgage may require that insurance be carried. The relevant figure for mortgaged homes would be the fraction of owners carrying a larger amount of insurance than is required by the mortgage. Similarly, finance companies generally require that insurance be carried on automobiles purchased on the instalment plan and not fully paid for, and the purchase of automobile insurance is compulsory in some states. (2) For automobile property damage and liability insurance (but not collision insurance) the risks to the operator and to the insurance company may not be the same, particularly to persons in the lower-income classes. The loss to the uninsured operator is limited by his wealth and borrowing power, and the maximum amount that he can lose may be well below the face value of the policy that he would purchase. The excess of the premium over the expected loss is thus greater for him than for a person with more wealth or borrowing power. The rise in the percentage of persons carrying automobile insurance as income rises may therefore reflect not an increased willingness to carry insurance but a reduction in the effective price that must be paid for insurance. (3) This tendency may be reversed for the relatively high-income classes for both automobile and housing insurance

means of raising revenue.[17] Though illegal, the " numbers " game and similar forms of gambling are reported to flourish in the United States,[18] particularly among the lower-income classes.

It seems highly unlikely that there is a sharp dichotomy between the individuals who purchase insurance and those who gamble. It seems much more likely that many do both or, at any rate, would be willing to. We can cite no direct evidence for this asserted fact, though indirect evidence and casual observation give us considerable confidence that it is correct. Its validity is suggested by the extensiveness of both gambling and the purchase of insurance. It is also suggested by some of the available evidence on how people invest their funds. The widespread legislation against " bucket shops " suggests that relatively poor people must have been willing to buy extremely speculative stocks of a " blue-sky " variety. Yet the bulk of the property income of the lower-income classes consists of interest and rents and relatively little of dividends, whereas the reverse is true for the upper-income classes.[19] Rents

---

by the operation of the income tax. Uninsured losses are in many instances deductible from income before computation of income tax under the United States federal income tax, while insurance premiums are not. This tends to make the net expected loss less for the individual than for the insurance company. This effect is almost certainly negligible for the figures cited above, both because they do not effectively cover very high incomes and because the federal income tax was relatively low in 1935–36. (4) Life insurance at times comes closer to gambling (the choice of an uncertain alternative in preference to a certain alternative with a higher expected value) than to the payment of a premium to escape risk. For example, special life insurance policies purchased to cover a single railroad or airplane trip are probably more nearly comparable to a lottery ticket than a means of achieving certainty. (5) Even aside from these qualifications, actual purchase of insurance would give at best a lower limit to the number willing to buy insurance, since there will always be some who will regard the price asked as too high.

These qualifications offset one another to some extent. It seems highly unlikely that their net effect could be sufficient to reverse the conclusion suggested by the evidence cited that a large fraction of people in all income classes are willing to buy insurance.

[17] France, Spain, and Mexico, to name but three examples, currently conduct lotteries for revenue. Russia attaches a lottery feature to bonds sold to the public. Great Britain conducted lotteries from 1694 to 1826. In the United States lotteries were used extensively before the Revolution and for some time thereafter, both directly by state governments and under state charters granted to further specific projects deemed to have a state interest. For the history of lotteries in Great Britain see C. L'Estrange Ewen, *Lotteries and Sweepstakes* (London, 1932); in New York State, A. F. Ross, " History of Lotteries in New York," *Magazine of History*, Vol. V (New York, 1907). There seem to be no direct estimates of the fraction of the people who purchase tickets in state or other legal lotteries, and it is clear that such figures would be difficult to get from data obtained in connection with running the lotteries. The receipts from legal lotteries, and casual impressions of observers, suggest that a substantial fraction of the relevant units (families or, alternatively, individual income recipients) purchase tickets.

[18] Evidence from wagering on horse races, where this has been legalized, is too ambiguous to be of much value. Since most legal wagering is at the track, gambling is available only to those who go to watch the races and is combined with participation in the mechanics of the game of chance.

[19] *Delaware Income Statistics*, Vol. I (Bureau of Economic and Business Research,

and interest are types of receipts that tend to be derived from investments with relatively little risk, and so correspond to the purchase of insurance, whereas investment in speculative stocks corresponds to the purchase of lottery tickets.

Offhand it appears inconsistent for the same person both to buy insurance and to gamble: he is willing to pay a premium, in the one case, to avoid risk, in the other, to bear risk. And indeed it would be inconsistent for a person to be willing to pay something (no matter how little) in excess of actuarial value to avoid every possible risk and also something in excess of actuarial value to assume every possible risk. One must distinguish among different kinds of insurance and different kinds of gambling, since a willingness to pay something for only some kinds of insurance would not necessarily be inconsistent with a willingness to engage in only some kinds of gambling. Unfortunately, very little empirical evidence is readily available on the kinds of insurance that people are willing to buy and the kinds of gambling that they are willing to engage in. About the only clear indication is that people are willing to enter into gambles that offer a small chance of a large gain—as in lotteries and " blue-sky " securities.

Lotteries seem to be an extremely fruitful, and much neglected, source of information about reactions of individuals to risk. They present risk in relatively pure form, with little admixture of other factors; they have been conducted in many countries and for many centuries, so that a great deal of evidence is available about them; there has been extensive experimentation with the terms and conditions that would make them attractive, and much competition in conducting them, so that any regularities they may show would have to be interpreted as reflecting corresponding regularities in human behavior.[20] It is, of course, not certain that inferences from lotteries would carry over to other choices involving risk. There would, however, seem to be some presumption that they would do so, though of course the validity of this presumption would have to be tested.[21]

The one general feature of lotteries that is worth noting in this preliminary survey, in addition to the general willingness of people to participate in them, is the structure of prizes that seems to have developed. Lotteries rarely have just a single prize equal to the total sum to be paid out as prizes. Instead, they tend to have several or many prizes. The largest prize is ordinarily not very

---

University of Delaware, 1941), Table 1; *Minnesota Incomes*, 1938–39, Vol. II (Minnesota Resources Commission, 1942), Table 27; F. A. Hanna, J. A. Pechman, S. M. Lerner, *Analysis of Wisconsin Income* [" Studies in Income and Wealth," Vol. IX (National Bureau of Economic Research, 1948)], Part II, Table 1.

[20] Aside from their value in providing information about reactions to risk, data from lotteries may be of broader interest in providing evidence about the stability of tastes and preferences over time and their similarity in different parts of the world. Here is a " commodity " which has remained unchanged over centuries, which is the same all over the globe, and which has been dealt in widely for the entire period and over much of the globe. It is hard to conceive of any other commodity for which this is true.

[21] See Smith, *op. cit.*, p. 108, for a precedent.

much larger than the next largest, and often there is not one largest prize but several of the same size.[22] This tendency is so general that one would expect it to reflect some consistent feature of individual reactions, and any hypothesis designed to explain reactions to uncertainty should explain it.

III. THE FORMAL HYPOTHESIS

The hypothesis that is proposed for rationalizing the behavior just summarized can be stated compactly as follows: In choosing among alternatives open to it, whether or not these alternatives involve risk, a consumer unit (generally a family, sometimes an individual) behaves as if (a) it had a consistent set of preferences; (b) these preferences could be completely described by a function attaching a numerical value—to be designated "utility"—to alternatives each of which is regarded as certain; (c) its objective were to make its expected utility as large as possible. It is the contribution of von Neumann and Morgenstern to have shown that an alternative statement of the same hypothesis is: An individual chooses in accordance with a system of preferences which has the following properties:

1. The system is complete and consistent; that is, an individual can tell which of two objects he prefers or whether he is indifferent between them, and if he does not prefer C to B and does not prefer B to A, then he does not prefer C to A.[23] (In this context, the word "object" includes combinations of objects with stated probabilities; for example, if A and B are objects, a 40-60 chance of A or B is also an object.)

2. Any object which is a combination of other objects with stated probabilities is never preferred to every one of these other objects, nor is every one of them ever preferred to the combination.

3. If the object A is preferred to the object B and B to the object C, there will be some probability combination of A and C such that the individual is indifferent between it and B.[24]

---

[22] See Ewen, *op. cit.*, *passim*, but esp. descriptions of state lotteries in Ch. VII, pp. 199–244; see also the large numbers of bills advertising lotteries in John Ashton, *A History of English Lotteries* (London: Leadenhall Press, 1893).

[23] The transitivity of the relation of indifference assumed in this postulate is, of course, an idealization. It is clearly possible that the difference between successive pairs of alternatives in a series might be imperceptible to an individual, yet the first of the series definitely preferable to the last. This idealization, which is but a special case of the idealization involved in the geometric concept of a dimensionless point, seems to us unobjectionable. However, the use of this idealization in indifference-curve analysis is the major criticism offered by W. E. Armstrong in an attack on indifference-curve analysis in his article "The Determinateness of the Utility Function," *Economic Journal*, Vol. XLIX (September, 1939), pp. 453–67. In a more recent article ["Uncertainty and the Utility Function," *Economic Journal*, Vol. LVIII (March, 1948), pp. 1–10] Armstrong repeats this criticism and adds to it the criticism that choices involving risk cannot be rationalized by the ordinal properties of utility functions.

[24] For a rigorous presentation of the second statement and a rigorous proof that the statements are equivalent see von Neumann and Morgenstern, *op. cit.*, pp. 26–27, 617–32.

This form of statement is designed to show that there is little difference between the plausibility of this hypothesis and the usual indifference-curve explanation of riskless choices.

These statements of the hypothesis conceal by their very compactness most of its implications. It will pay us, therefore, to elaborate them. It simplifies matters, and involves no loss in generality, to regard the alternatives open to the consumer unit as capable of being expressed entirely in terms of money or money income. Actual alternatives are not, of course, capable of being so expressed: the same money income may be valued very differently according to the terms under which it is to be received, the nonpecuniary advantages or disadvantages associated with it, and so on. We can abstract from these factors, which play no role in the present problem, by supposing either that they are the same for different incomes compared or that they can be converted into equivalent sums of money income.[25] This permits us to consider total utility a function of money income alone.

Let I represent the income of a consumer unit per unit time, and $U(I)$ the utility attached to that income if it is regarded as certain. Measure I along the horizontal axis of a graph and U along the vertical. In general, $U(I)$ will not be defined for all values of I, since there will be a lower limit to the income a consumer unit can receive, namely, a negative income equal (in absolute value to) the maximum amount that the consumer unit can lose per unit time for the period to which the utility curve refers.

Alternatives open to the consumer unit that involve no risk consist of possible incomes, say I', I'', ... The hypothesis then implies simply that the consumer unit will choose the income to which it attaches the most utility. Other things the same, we know from even casual observation that the consumer unit will in general choose the largest income: put differently, we consider it pathological for an individual literally to throw money away, yet this means of choosing a smaller income is always available. It follows that the hypothesis can rationalize riskless choices of the limited kind considered here if, and only if, the utility of money income is larger, the higher the income. Consideration of riskless choices imposes no further requirements on the utility function.

Alternatives involving risk consist of probability distributions of possible incomes. Fortunately, it will suffice for our purpose to consider only a particularly simple kind of alternative involving risk, namely (A) a chance $a(0 < a < 1)$ of an income I_1, and a chance $(1 - a)$ of an income I_2, where for

---

[25] The other factors abstracted from must not, of course, include any that cannot in fact be held constant while money income varies. For example, a higher income is desired because it enables a consumer unit to purchase a wider variety of commodities. The consumption pattern of the consumer unit must not therefore be supposed to be the same at different incomes. As another example, a higher income may mean that a consumer unit must pay a higher price for a particular commodity (e.g., medical service). Such variation in price should not be impounded in *ceteris paribus*, though price changes not necessarily associated with changes in the consumer unit's income should be.

simplicity I_2 is supposed always greater than I_1. This simplification is possible because, as we shall see later, the original hypothesis implies that choices of consumer units among more complicated alternatives can be predicted from complete knowledge of their preferences among alternatives like A and a riskless alternative (B) consisting of a certain income I_0.

Since "other things" are supposed the same for alternatives A and B, the utility of the two alternatives may be taken to be functions solely of the incomes and probabilities involved and not also of attendant circumstances. The utility of alternative B is $U(I_0)$. The expected utility of A is given by

$$\overline{U}(A) = aU(I_1) + (1 - a)U(I_2)$$

According to the hypothesis, a consumer unit will choose A if $\overline{U} > U(I_0)$, will choose B if $\overline{U} < U(I_0)$, and will be indifferent between A and B if $\overline{U} = U(I_0)$.

Let $\bar{I}(A)$ be the actuarial value of A, i.e., $\bar{I}(A) = aI_1 + (1 - a)I_2$. If I_0 is equal to $\bar{I}$, the "gamble" or "insurance" is said to be "fair" since the consumer unit gets the same actuarial value whichever alternative it chooses. If, under these circumstances, the consumer unit chooses A, it shows a preference for this risk. This is to be interpreted as meaning that $\overline{U} > U(\bar{I})$ and indeed $\overline{U} - U(\bar{I})$ may be taken to measure the utility it attaches to this particular risk.[26] If the consumer unit chooses B, it shows a preference for certainty. This is to be interpreted as meaning that $\overline{U} < U(\bar{I})$. Indifference between A and B is to be interpreted as meaning that $\overline{U} = U(\bar{I})$.

Let I^* be the certain income that has the same utility as A, that is, $U(I^*) = \overline{U}$.[27] Call I^* the income equivalent to A. The requirement, derived from consideration of riskless choices, that utility increase with income means that

$$\overline{U} \gtreqless U(\bar{I})$$

implies

$$I^* \gtreqless \bar{I}$$

If I^* is greater than $\bar{I}$, the consumer unit prefers this particular risk to a certain income of the same actuarial value and would be willing to pay a

[26] This interpretation of $\overline{U} - U(I)$ as the utility attached to a particular risk is directly relevant to a point to which von Neumann and Morgenstern and commentators on their work have given a good deal of attention, namely, whether there may "not exist in an individual a (positive or negative) utility of the mere act of 'taking a chance,' of gambling, which the use of the mathematical expectation obliterates" (von Neumann and Morgenstern, op. cit., p. 28). In our view the hypothesis is better interpreted as a rather special explanation why gambling has utility or disutility to a consumer unit, and as providing a particular measure of the utility or disutility, than as a denial that gambling has utility (see ibid., pp. 28, 629–32).

[27] Since U has been assumed strictly monotonic to rationalize riskless choices, there will be only one income, if any, that has the same utility as A. There will be one if U is continuous which, for simplicity, we assume to be the case throughout this paper.

Illustration of Utility Analysis of Choices Involving Risk
a, Preference for Certainty; b, Preference for Risk

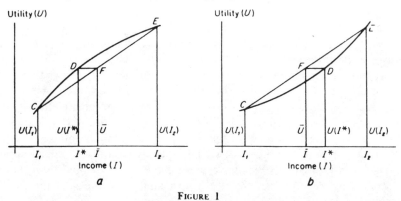

FIGURE 1

maximum of $I^* - \bar{I}$ for the privilege of "gambling." If I^* is less than $\bar{I}$, the consumer unit prefers certainty and is willing to pay a maximum of $\bar{I} - I^*$ for "insurance" against this risk.

These concepts are illustrated for a consumer unit who is willing to pay for insurance ($\bar{I} > I^*$) in Figure 1a, and for a consumer unit who is willing to pay for the privilege of gambling ($\bar{I} < I^*$) in Figure 1b. In both figures, money income is measured along the horizontal axis, and utility along the vertical. On the horizontal axis, designate I_1 and I_2. $\bar{I}$, the actuarial value of I_1 and I_2, is then represented by a point that divides the interval I_1 to I_2 in the proportion

$$\frac{1-a}{a} \left(\text{i.e., } \frac{\bar{I} - I_1}{I_2 - \bar{I}} = \frac{1-a}{a} \right)$$

Draw the utility curve (CDE in both figures). Connect the points $[I_1, U(I_1)]$, $[I_2, U(I_2)]$ by a straight line (CFE). The vertical distance of this line from the horizontal axis at $\bar{I}$ is then equal to $\bar{U}$. [Since $\bar{I}$ divides the distance between I_1 and I_2 in the proportion $(1 - a)/a$, F divides the vertical distance between C and E in the same proportion, so the vertical distance from F to the horizontal axis is the expected value of $U(I_1)$ and $U(I_2)$.] Draw a horizontal line through F and find the income corresponding to its intersection with the utility curve (point D). This is the income the utility of which is the same as the expected utility of A, hence by definition is I^*.

In Figure 1a, the utility curve is so drawn as to make I^* less than $\bar{I}$. If the consumer unit is offered a choice between A and a certain income I_0 greater than I^*, it will choose the certain income. If this certain income I_0 were less than $\bar{I}$, the consumer unit would be paying $\bar{I} - I_0$ for certainty—in ordinary parlance it would be "buying insurance"; if the certain income were greater than $\bar{I}$, it would be being paid $I_0 - \bar{I}$ for accepting certainty, even though it is willing to pay for certainty—we might say that it is "selling a gamble" rather than "buying insurance." If the consumer unit were offered a choice between A and a certain income I_0 less than I^*, it would choose A because, while it is willing to pay a price for certainty, it is being asked to pay more than the maximum amount $(\bar{I} - I^*)$ that it is willing to pay. The price of insurance has become so high that it has, as it were, been converted into a seller rather than a buyer of insurance.

In Figure 1b, the utility curve is so drawn as to make I^* greater than $\bar{I}$. If the consumer unit is offered a choice between A and a certain income I_0 less than I^*, it will choose A. If this certain income I_0 were greater than $\bar{I}$, the consumer unit would be paying $I_0 - \bar{I}$ for this risk—in ordinary parlance, it would be choosing to gamble or, one might say, " to buy a gamble "; if the certain income were less than $\bar{I}$, it would be being paid $\bar{I} - I_0$ for accepting this risk even though it is willing to pay for the risk—we might say that it is " selling insurance " rather than " buying a gamble." If the consumer unit is offered a choice between A and a certain income I_0 greater than I^*, it will choose the certain income because, while it is willing to pay something for a gamble, it is not willing to pay more than $I^* - \bar{I}$. The price of the gamble has become so high that it is converted into a seller, rather than a buyer, of gambles.

It is clear that the graphical condition for a consumer unit to be willing to pay something for certainty is that the utility function be above its chord at $\bar{I}$. This is simply a direct translation of the condition that $U(\bar{I}) > \bar{U}$. Similarly, a consumer unit will be willing to pay something for a risk if the utility function is below its chord at $\bar{I}$. The relationship between these formalized " insurance " and " gambling " situations and what are ordinarily called insurance and gambling is fairly straight-forward. A consumer unit contemplating buying insurance is to be regarded as having a current income of I_2 and as being subject to a chance of losing a sum equal to $I_2 - I_1$, so that if this loss should occur its income would be reduced to I_1. It can insure against this loss by paying a premium equal to $I_2 - I_0$. The premium, in general, will be larger than $I_2 - \bar{I}$, the "loading" being equal to $\bar{I} - I_0$. Purchase of insurance therefore means accepting the certainty of an income equal to I_0 instead of a pair of alternative incomes having a higher expected value. Similarly, a consumer unit deciding whether to gamble (e.g., to purchase a lottery ticket) can be interpreted as having a current income equal to I_0. It can have a chance $(1 - a)$ of a gain equal to $I_2 - I_0$ by subjecting itself to a chance a of losing a sum equal to $I_0 - I_1$. If it gambles, the actuarial value of its income is $\bar{I}$, which in general is less than I_0. $I_0 - \bar{I}$ is the premium it is paying for the chance to gamble (the " take " of the house, or the " banker's cut ").

It should be emphasized that this analysis is all an elaboration of a particular hypothesis about the way consumer units choose among alternatives involving risk. This hypothesis describes the reactions of consumer units in terms of a utility function, unique except for origin and unit of measure, which gives the utility assigned to certain incomes and which has so far been taken for granted. Yet for choices among certain incomes only a trivial characteristic of this function is relevant, namely, that it rises with income. The remaining characteristics of the function are relevant only to choices among alternatives involving risk and can therefore be inferred only from observation of such choices. The precise manner in which these characteristics are implicit in the consumer unit's preferences among alternatives involving risk can be indicated most easily by describing a conceptual experiment for determining the utility function.

Select any two incomes, say $500 and $1,000. Assign any arbitrary utilities to these incomes, say 0 utiles and 1 utile, respectively. This corresponds to an arbitrary choice of origin and unit of measure. Select any intermediate income, say $600. Offer the consumer unit the choice between (A) a chance a of $500 and $(1 - a)$ of $1,000 or ($B$) a certainty of $600, varying a until the consumer unit is indifferent between the two (i.e., until $I^* = \$600$). Suppose this indifference value of a is 2/5. If the hypothesis is correct, it follows that

$$U(600) = 2/5 U(500) + 3/5 U(1000) = 2/5 \cdot 0 + 3/5 \cdot 1 = 3/5 = .60$$

In this way the utility attached to every income between $500 and $1,000 can be determined. To get the utility attached to any income outside the interval $500 to $1,000, say $10,000, offer the consumer unit a choice between (A) a chance a of $500 and $(1 - a)$ of $10,000 or ($B$) a certainty of $1,000, varying a until the consumer unit is indifferent between the two (i.e., until $I^* = \$1,000$). Suppose this indifference value of a is 4/5. If the hypothesis is correct, it follows that

$$4/5 U(500) + 1/5 U(10,000) = U(1000)$$

or

$$4/5 \cdot 0 + 1/5 U(10,000) = 1$$

or

$$U(10,000) = 5$$

In principle, the possibility of carrying out this experiment, and the reproducibility of the results, would provide a test of the hypothesis. For example, the consistency of behavior assumed by the hypothesis would be contradicted if a repetition of the experiment using two initial incomes other than $500 and $1,000 yielded a utility function differing in more than origin and unit of measure from the one initially obtained.

Given a utility function obtained in this way, it is possible, if the hypothesis is correct, to compute the utility attached to (that is, the expected utility of) any set or sets of possible incomes and associated probabilities and thereby to predict which of a number of such sets will be chosen. This is the precise meaning of the statement made toward the beginning of this section that, if the hypothesis were correct, complete knowledge of the preferences of consumer units among alternatives like A and B would make it possible to predict their reactions to any other choices involving risk.

The choices a consumer unit makes that involve risk are typically far more complicated than the simple choice between A and B that we have used to elaborate the hypothesis. There are two chief sources of complication: Any particular alternative typically offers an indefinitely large number of possible incomes, and "other things" are generally not the same.

The multiplicity of possible incomes is very general: losses insured against ordinarily have more than one possible value; lotteries ordinarily have more than one prize; the possible income from a particular occupation, investment, or business enterprise may be equal to any of an indefinitely large number of values. A hypothesis that the essence of choices among the degrees of risk involved in such complex alternatives is contained in such simple choices as the choice between A and B is by no means tautological.

The hypothesis does not, of course, pretend to say anything about how consumer choices will be affected by differences in things other than degree of risk. The significance for our purposes of such differences is rather that they greatly increase the difficulty of getting evidence about reactions to differences in risk alone. Much casual experience, particularly experience bearing on what is ordinarily regarded as gambling, is likely to be misinterpreted, and erroneously regarded as contradictory to the hypothesis, if this difficulty is not explicitly recognized. In much so-called gambling the individual chooses not only to bear risk but also to participate in the mechanics of a game of chance; he buys, that is, a gamble, in our technical sense, and entertainment. We can conceive of separating these two commodities: he could buy entertainment alone by paying admission to participate in a game using valueless chips; he could buy the gamble alone by having an agent play the game of chance for him according to detailed instructions.[28] Further, insurance and gambles are often purchased in almost pure form. This is notably true of insurance. It is true also of gambling by the purchase of lottery tickets when the purchaser is not a spectator to the drawing of the winners (e.g., Irish sweepstakes tickets bought in this country or the "numbers" game), and of much stockmarket speculation.

An example of behavior that would definitely contradict the assertion, contained in the hypothesis, that the same utility function can be used to explain choices that do and do not involve risk would be willingness by an individual to pay more for a gamble than the maximum amount he could win. In order to explain riskless choices it is necessary to suppose that utility increases with income. It follows that the average utility of two incomes can never exceed the utility of the larger income and hence that an individual will never be willing to pay, for example, a dollar for a chance of winning, at most, 99 cents.

More subtle observation would be required to contradict the assertion that

---

[28] It does not, of course, follow that the price an individual is willing to pay for the joint commodity is simply the sum of the prices he is willing to pay for them separately. Indeed, it may well be the possible existence of such a difference that people have in mind when they speak of a "specific utility of gambling."

the reactions of persons to complicated gambles can be inferred from their reactions to simple gambles. For example, suppose an individual refuses an opportunity to toss a coin for a dollar and also to toss a coin for two dollars but then accepts an opportunity to toss two coins in succession, the first to determine whether the second toss is to be for one dollar or for two dollars. This behavior would definitely contradict the hypothesis. On the hypothesis, the utility of the third gamble is an average of the utility of the first two. His refusal of the first two indicates that each of them has a lower utility than the alternative of not gambling; hence, if the hypothesis were correct, the third should have a lower utility than the same alternative, and he should refuse it.

IV. RESTRICTIONS ON UTILITY FUNCTION REQUIRED TO RATIONALIZE OBSERVABLE BEHAVIOR

The one restriction imposed on the utility function in the preceding section is that total utility increase with the size of money income. This restriction was imposed to rationalize the first of the facts listed below. We are now ready to see whether the behavior described in Section II can be rationalized by the hypothesis, and, if so, what additional restrictions this behavior imposes on the utility function. To simplify the task, we shall take as a summary of the essential features of the behavior described in Section II the following five statements, alleged to be facts: (1) consumer units prefer larger to smaller certain incomes; (2) low-income consumer units buy, or are willing to buy, insurance; (3) low-income consumer units buy, or are willing to buy, lottery tickets; (4) many low-income consumer units buy, or are willing to buy, both insurance and lottery tickets; (5) lotteries typically have more than one prize.

These particular statements are selected not because they are the most important in and of themselves but because they are convenient to handle and the restrictions imposed to rationalize them turn out to be sufficient to rationalize all the behavior described in Section II.

It is obvious from Figure 1 and our discussion of it that if the utility function were everywhere convex from above (for utility functions with a continuous derivative, if the marginal utility of money does not increase for any income), the consumer unit, on our hypothesis, would be willing to enter into any fair insurance plan but would be unwilling to pay anything in excess of the actuarial value for any gamble. If the utility function were everywhere concave from above (for functions with a continuous derivative, if the marginal utility of money does not diminish for any income), the consumer unit would be willing to enter into any fair gamble but would be unwilling to pay anything in excess of the actuarial value for insurance against any risk.

It follows that our hypothesis can rationalize statement 2, the purchase of insurance by low-income consumer units, only if the utility functions of the corresponding units are not everywhere concave from above; that it can rationalize statement 3, the purchase of lottery tickets by low-income consumer units, only if the utility functions of the corresponding units are not everywhere convex from above; and that it can rationalize statement 4, the

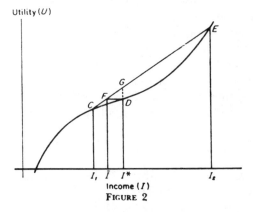

Illustration of Utility Function Consistent with Willingness of a Low-Income Consumer Unit Both to Purchase Insurance and to Gamble

FIGURE 2

purchase of both insurance and lottery tickets by low-income consumer units, only if the utility functions of the corresponding units are neither everywhere concave from above nor everywhere convex from above.

The simplest utility function (with a continuous derivative) that can rationalize all three statements simultaneously is one that has a segment convex from above followed by a segment concave from above and no other segments.[29] The convex segment must precede the concave segment because of the kind of insurance and of gambling the low-income consumer units are said to engage in: a chord from the existing income to a lower income must be below the utility function to rationalize the purchase of insurance against the risk of loss; a chord from the immediate neighborhood of the existing income to a higher income must be above the utility function at the existing income to rationalize the purchase for a small sum of a small chance of a large gain.[30]

Figure 2 illustrates a utility function satisfying these requirements. Let this utility function be for a low-income consumer unit whose current income is in the initial convex segment, say at the point designated I^*. If some risk should arise of incurring a loss, the consumer unit would clearly (on our hypothesis) be willing to insure against the loss (if it did not have to pay too much "loading") since a chord from the utility curve at I^* to the utility curve at the lower income that would be the consequence of the actual occurrence of the loss would everywhere be below the utility function. The consumer unit would not be willing to engage in small gambling. But suppose it is offered a fair gamble of the kind represented by a lottery involving a small chance of

---

[29] A kink or a jump in the utility function could rationalize either the gambling or the insurance. For example, the utility function could be composed of two convex or two concave segments joined in a kink. There is no essential loss in generality in neglecting such cases, as we shall do from here on, since one can always think of rounding the kink ever so slightly.

[30] If there are more than two segments and a continuous derivative, a convex segment necessarily precedes a concave segment.

winning a relatively large sum equal to $I_2 - I^*$ and a large chance of losing a relatively small sum equal to $I^* - I_1$. The consumer unit would clearly prefer the gamble, since the expected utility (I^*G) is greater than the utility of I^*. Indeed it would be willing to pay any premium up to $I^* - \bar{I}$ for the privilege of gambling; that is, even if the expected value of the gamble were almost as low as $\bar{I}$, it would accept the gamble in preference to a certainty of receiving I^*. The utility curve in Figure 2 is therefore clearly consistent with statements 2, 3, and 4.

These statements refer solely to the behavior of relatively low-income consumer units. It is tempting to seek to restrict further the shape of the utility function, and to test the restrictions so far imposed, by appealing to casual observation of the behavior of relatively high-income consumer units.[31] It does not seem desirable to do so, however, for two major reasons: (1) it is far more difficult to accumulate reliable information about the behavior of relatively high-income consumer units than about the behavior of the more numerous low-income units: (2) perhaps even more important, the progressive income tax so affects the terms under which the relatively high-income consumer units purchase insurance or gamble as to make evidence on their behavior hard to interpret for our purposes.[32] Therefore, instead of using

[31] For example, a high-income consumer unit that had a utility function like that in Fig. 2 and a current income of I_2 would be willing to participate in a wide variety of gambling, including the purchase of lottery tickets; it would be unwilling to insure against losses that had a small expected value (i.e., involved payment of a small premium) though it might be willing to insure against losses that had a large expected value. Consequently, unwillingness of relatively high-income consumer units to purchase lottery tickets, or willingness to purchase low-premium insurance, would contradict the utility function of Fig. 2 and require the imposition of further restrictions.

[32] The effect of the income tax, already referred to in footnote 16 above, depends greatly on the specific provisions of the tax law and of the insurance or gambling plan. For example, if an uninsured loss is deductible in computing taxable income (as is loss of an owned home by fire under the federal income tax) while the premium for insuring against the loss is not (as a fire insurance premium on an owned home is not), the expected value of the loss is less to the consumer unit than to the firm selling insurance. A premium equal to the actuarial value of the loss to the insurance company then exceeds the actuarial value of the loss to the consumer unit. That is, the government in effect pays part of the loss but none of the premium. On the other hand, if the premium is deductible (as a health insurance premium may be), while an uninsured loss is not (as the excess of medical bills over $2,500 for a family is not), the net premium to the consumer unit is less than the premium received by the insurance company. Similarly, gambling gains in excess of gambling losses are taxable under the federal income tax, while gambling losses in excess of gambling gains are not deductible. The special treatment of capital gains and losses under the existing United States federal income tax adds still further complications.

Even if both the premium and the uninsured loss are deductible, or a gain taxable and the corresponding loss deductible, the income tax may change the terms because of the progressive rates. The tax saving from a large loss may be a smaller fraction of the loss than the tax payable on the gain is of the gain.

These comments clearly apply not only to insurance and gambling proper but also to other economic decisions involving risk—the purchase of securities, choice of occupation or business, etc. The neglect of these considerations has frequently led to the erroneous belief

observations about the behavior of relatively high-income consumer units, we shall seek to learn more about the upper end of the curve by using statement 5, the tendency for lotteries to have more than one prize.

In order to determine the implications of this statement for the utility function, we must investigate briefly the economics of lotteries. Consider an entrepreneur conducting a lottery and seeking to maximize his income from it. For simplicity, suppose that he conducts the lottery by deciding in advance the number of tickets to offer and then auctioning them off at the highest price he can get.[33] Aside from advertising and the like, the variables at his disposal are the terms of the lottery: the number of tickets to sell, the total amount to offer as prizes (which together, of course, determine the actuarial value of a ticket), and the structure of prizes to offer. For any given values of the first two, the optimum structure of prizes is clearly that which maximizes the price he can get per ticket or, what is the same thing, the excess of the price of a ticket over its actuarial value—the "loading" per ticket.

In the discussion of Figure 2, it was noted that $I^* - \bar{I}$ was the maximum amount in excess of the actuarial value that the corresponding consumer unit would pay for a gamble involving a chance $(1 - a)$ of winning $I_2 - I^*$ and a chance a of losing $I^* - I_1$. This gamble is equivalent to a lottery offering a chance $(1 - a)$ of a prize $I_2 - I_1$ in return for the purchase of a ticket at a price of $I^* - I_1$, the chance of winning the prize being such that $\bar{I} - I_1$ is the actuarial worth of a ticket [i.e., is equal to $(1 - a) \times (I_2 - I_1)$]. If the consumer unit won the prize, its net winnings would be $I_2 - I^*$, since it would have to subtract the cost of the ticket from the gross prize. The problem of the entrepreneur, then, is to choose the structure of prizes that will maximize $I^* - \bar{I}$ for a given actuarial value of a ticket, that is, for a given value of $\bar{I} - I_1$. Changes in the structure of prizes involve changes in $I_2 - I_1$. If there is a single prize, $I_2 - I_1$ is equal to the total amount to be distributed [$(1 - a)$ is equal to the reciprocal of the number of tickets]. If there are two equal prizes, $I_2 - I_1$ is cut in half [$(1 - a)$ is then equal to twice the reciprocal of the number of tickets]. Suppose Figure 2 referred to this latter situation in which there were two equal prizes, I^* on the diagram designating both the current income of the consumer unit and the income equivalent to the lottery. If the price and actuarial worth of the ticket were kept unchanged, but a single prize was substituted for the two prizes [and $(1 - a)$ correspondingly reduced], the gamble would clearly become more attractive to the consumer unit. I_2 would move to the right, the chord connecting $U(I_1)$ and $U(I_2)$ would rotate upward, $\bar{U}$ would increase, and the consumer unit would be paying less

---

that a progressive income tax does not affect the allocation of resources and is in this way fundamentally different from excise taxes.

[33] This was, in fact, the way in which the British government conducted many of its official lotteries. It frequently auctioned off the tickets to lottery dealers, who served as the means of distributing the tickets to the public (see Ewen, *op. cit.*, pp. 234–40).

Illustration of Typical Shape of Utility Curve

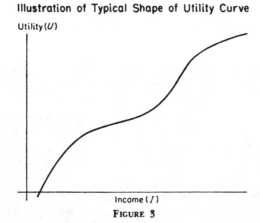

FIGURE 3

than the maximum amount it was willing to pay. The price of the ticket could accordingly be increased; that is, I_2, $\bar{I}$, and I_1 could be moved to the left until the I^* for the new gamble were equal to the consumer unit's current income (the I^* for the old gamble). The optimum structure of prizes clearly consists therefore of a single prize, since this makes $I_2 - I_1$ as large as possible.

Statement 5, that lotteries typically have more than one prize, is therefore inconsistent with the utility function of Figure 2. This additional fact can be rationalized by terminating the utility curve with a suitable convex segment. This yields a utility curve like that drawn in Figure 3. With such a utility curve, $I^* - \bar{I}$ would be a maximum at the point at which a chord from $U(I_1)$ was tangent to the utility curve, and a larger prize would yield a smaller value of $I^* - \bar{I}$.[34]

A utility curve like that drawn in Figure 3 is the simplest one consistent with the five statements listed at the outset of this section.

V. A DIGRESSION

It seems well to digress at this point to consider two questions that, while not strictly relevant to our main theme, are likely to occur to many readers:

[34] An additional convex segment guarantees that there will always exist current incomes of the consumer unit for which (a) attractive gambles exist and (b) the optimum prize for attractive gambles has a maximum. It does not guarantee that b will be true for every income for which attractive gambles exist. The condition on the current income that attractive gambles exist is that the tangent to the utility curve at the current income be below the utility curve for some income (this argument, like many in later technical footnotes, holds not only for the utility function of Fig. 3 but for any differentiable utility function). A single prize will be the optimum, no matter what the amount distributed in prizes or the fixed actuarial worth of the prize if, and only if, every chord from the utility curve at the current income to the utility of a higher income is everywhere above the utility curve. A particular, and somewhat interesting, class of utility functions for which b will be true for every income for which a is true is the class for which utility approaches a finite limit as income increases.

first, is not the hypothesis patently unrealistic; second, can any plausible interpretation be given to the rather peculiar utility function of Figure 3?

THE DESCRIPTIVE " REALISM " OF THE HYPOTHESIS

An objection to the hypothesis just presented that is likely to be raised by many, if not most, readers is that it conflicts with the way human beings actually behave and choose. Is it not patently unrealistic to suppose that individuals consult a wiggly utility curve before gambling or buying insurance, that they know the odds involved in the gambles or insurance plans open to them, that they can compute the expected utility of a gamble or insurance plan, and that they base their decision on the size of the expected utility?

While entirely natural and understandable, this objection is not strictly relevant. The hypothesis does not assert that individuals explicitly or consciously calculate and compare expected utilities. Indeed, it is not at all clear what such an assertion would mean or how it could be tested. The hypothesis asserts rather that, in making a particular class of decisions, individuals behave *as if* they calculated and compared expected utility and *as if* they knew the odds. The validity of this assertion does not depend on whether individuals know the precise odds, much less on whether they say that they calculate and compare expected utilities or think that they do, or whether it appears to others that they do, or whether psychologists can uncover any evidence that they do, but solely on whether it yields sufficiently accurate predictions about the class of decisions with which the hypothesis deals. Stated differently, the test by results is the only possible method of determining whether the *as if* statement is or is not a sufficiently good approximation to reality for the purpose at hand.

A simple example may help to clarify the point at issue. Consider the problem of predicting, before each shot, the direction of travel of a billiard ball hit by an expert billiard player. It would be possible to construct one or more mathematical formulas that would give the directions of travel that would score points and, among these, would indicate the one (or more) that would leave the balls in the best positions. The formulas might, of course, be extremely complicated, since they would necessarily take account of the location of the balls in relation to one another and to the cushions and of the complicated phenomena introduced by "english." Nonetheless, it seems not at all unreasonable that excellent predictions would be yielded by the hypothesis that the billiard player made his shots *as if* he knew the formulas, could estimate accurately by eye the angles, etc., describing the location of the balls, could make lightning calculations from the formulas, and could then make the ball travel in the direction indicated by the formulas. It would in no way disprove or contradict the hypothesis, or weaken our confidence in it, if it should turn out that the billiard player had never studied any branch of mathematics and was utterly incapable of making the necessary calculations: unless he was capable in some way of reaching approximately the same result as that obtained from the formulas, he would not in fact be likely to be an expert billiard player.

The same considerations are relevant to our utility hypothesis. Whatever the psychological mechanism whereby individuals make choices, these choices appear to display some consistency, which can apparently be described by our utility hypothesis. This hypothesis enables predictions to be made about phenomena on which there is not yet reliable evidence. The hypothesis cannot be declared invalid for a particular class of behavior until a prediction about that class proves false. No other test of its validity is decisive.

A POSSIBLE INTERPRETATION OF THE UTILITY FUNCTION

A possible interpretation of the utility function of Figure 3 is to regard the two convex segments as corresponding to qualitatively different socioeconomic levels, and the concave segment to the transition between the two levels. On this interpretation, increases in income that raise the relative position of the consumer unit in its own class but do not shift the unit out of its class yield diminishing marginal utility, while increases that shift it into a new class, that give it a new social and economic status, yield increasing marginal utility. An unskilled worker may prefer the certainty of an income about the same as that of the majority of unskilled workers to an actuarially fair gamble that at best would make him one of the most prosperous unskilled workers and at worst one of the least prosperous. Yet he may jump at an actuarially fair gamble that offers a small chance of lifting him out of the class of unskilled workers and into the " middle " or " upper " class, even though it is far more likely than the preceding gamble to make him one of the least prosperous unskilled workers. Men will and do take great risks to distinguish themselves, even when they know what the risks are. May not the concave segment of the utility curve of Figure 3 translate the economic counterpart of this phenomenon appropriately?

A number of additions to the hypothesis are suggested by this interpretation. In the first place, may there not be more than two qualitatively distinguishable socioeconomic classes? If so, might not each be reflected by a convex segment in the utility function? At the moment, there seems to be no observed behavior that requires the introduction of additional convex segments, so it seems undesirable and unnecessary to complicate the hypothesis further. It may well be, however, that it will be necessary to add such segments to account for behavior revealed by further empirical evidence. In the second place, if different segments of the curve correspond to different socioeconomic classes, should not the dividing points between the segments occur at roughly the same income for different consumer units in the same community? If they did, the fruitfulness of the hypothesis would be greatly extended. Not only could the general shape of the utility function be supposed typical; so also could the actual income separating the various segments. The initial convex segment could be described as applicable to "relatively low-income consumer units " and the terminal convex segment as applicable to

" relatively high-income consumer units "; and the groups so designated could be identified by the actual income or wealth of different consumer units.

Interpreting the different segments of the curve as corresponding to different socioeconomic classes would, of course, still permit wide variation among consumer units in the exact shape and height of the curve. In addition, it would not be necessary to suppose anything more than rough similarity in the location of the incomes separating the various segments. Different socioeconomic classes are not sharply demarcated from one another; each merges into the next by imperceptible gradations (which, of course, accounts for the income range encompassed by the concave segment); and the generally accepted dividing line between classes will vary from time to time, place to place, and consumer unit to consumer unit. Finally, it is not necessary that every consumer unit have a utility curve like that in Figure 3. Some may be inveterate gamblers; others, inveterately cautious. It is enough that many consumer units have such a utility curve.

VI. FURTHER IMPLICATIONS OF THE HYPOTHESIS

To return to our main theme, we have two tasks yet to perform: first, to show that the utility function of Figure 3 is consistent with those features of the behavior described in Section II not used in deriving it; second, to suggest additional implications of the hypothesis capable of providing a test of it.

The chief generalization of Section II not so far used is that people must in general be paid a premium to induce them to bear moderate risks instead of either small or large risks. Is this generalization consistent with the utility function of Figure 3?

It clearly is for a consumer unit whose income places it in the initial convex segment. Such a relatively low-income consumer unit will be willing to pay something more than the actuarial value for insurance against any kind of risk that may arise; it will be averse to small fair gambles; it may be averse to all fair gambles; if not, it will be attracted by fair gambles that offer a small chance of a large gain; the attractiveness of such gambles, with a given possible loss and actuarial value, will initially increase as the size of the possible gain increases and will eventually decrease.[35] Such consumer units therefore

---

[35] The willingness of a consumer unit in the initial convex segment to pay something more than the actuarial value for insurance against any kind of risk follows from the fact that a chord connecting the utility of its current income with the utility of any lower income to which it might be reduced by the risk in question will everywhere be below the utility curve. The expected utility is therefore less than the utility of the expected income.

To analyze the reaction of such a consumer unit to different gambles, consider the limiting case in which the gamble is fair, i.e., $I = I_0$. I then is both the expected income of the consumer unit if it takes the gamble and its actual income if it does not (i.e., its current income). The possible gains (and associated probabilities) that will be attractive to the unit for a given value of I_1 (i.e., a given possible loss) can be determined by drawing a straight line through $U(I_1)$ and $U(I)$. All values of $I_2 > I$ for which $U(I_2)$ is greater than the ordinate of the extended straight line will be attractive; no others will be.

Since I is assumed to be in the first convex segment, there will always exist some values of

prefer either certainty or a risk that offers a small chance of a large gain to a risk that offers the possibility of moderate gains or losses. They will therefore have to be paid a premium to induce them to undertake such moderate risks.

The generalization is clearly false for a consumer unit whose income places it in the concave segment. Such an "intermediate-income" consumer unit will be attracted by every small fair gamble; it may be attracted by every fair gamble; it may be averse to all fair insurance; if not, it will be attracted by insurance against relatively large losses.[36] Such consumer units will therefore be willing to pay a premium in order to assume moderate risks.

The generalization is partly true, partly false, for a consumer unit whose income places it in the terminal convex segment. Such a relatively high-income consumer unit will be willing to insure against any small possible loss and may be attracted to every fair insurance plan; the only insurance plans it may be averse to are plans involving rather large losses; it may be averse to all fair gambles; if not, it will be attracted by gambles that involve a reasonably sure, though fairly small, gain, with a small possibility of a sizable loss; it will be averse to gambles of the lottery variety.[37] These consumer units therefore prefer certainty to moderate risks; in this respect they conform to the generalization. However, they may prefer moderate risks to extreme risks, though these adjectives hardly suffice to characterize the rather complex pattern of risk preferences implied for high-income consumer units by a utility curve like

---

$I_2 > I$ for which $U(I_2)$ is less than the ordinate of the extended straight line. This is the basis for the statement that the consumer unit will be averse to small gambles.

Consider the line that touches the curve at only two points and is nowhere below the utility curve. Call the income at the first of the points at which it touches the curve, which may be the lowest possible income, I', and the income at the second point, I''. The consumer unit will be averse to all gambles if its income ($I_0 = I$) is equal to or less than I'. This follows from the fact that a tangent to the curve at I will then be steeper than the "double tangent" and will intersect the latter prior to I'; a chord from I to a lower income will be even steeper. This is the basis for the statement that the consumer unit may be averse to all gambles.

If the income is above I', there will always be some attractive gambles. These will offer a small chance of a large gain. The statement about the changing attractiveness of the gamble as the size of the possible gain changes follows from the analysis in Sec. IV of the conditions under which it would be advantageous to have a single prize in a lottery.

[36] Consider the tangent to the utility curve at the income the consumer unit would have if it did not take the gamble ($I - I_0$). If this income is in the concave section, the tangent will be below the utility curve at least for an interval of incomes surrounding I. A chord connecting any two points of the utility curve on opposite sides of I and within this interval will always be above the utility curve at I (i.e., the expected utility will be above the utility of the expected income), so these gambles will be attractive. The tangent may lie below the utility curve for all incomes. In this case, every fair gamble will be attractive. The unit will be averse to insuring against a loss, whatever the chance of its occurring, if a chord from the current income to the lower income to which it would be reduced by the loss is everywhere above the utility curve. This will surely be true for small losses and may be true for all possible losses.

[37] These statements follow directly from considerations like those in the two preceding footnotes.

that of Figure 3. Nonetheless, in this respect the implied behavior of the high-income consumer units is either neutral or contrary to the generalization.

Our hypothesis does not therefore lead inevitably to a rate of return higher to uses of resources involving moderate risk than to uses involving little or much risk. It leads to a rate of return higher for uses involving moderate risk than for uses involving little risk only if consumer units in the two convex segments outweigh in importance, for the resource use in question, consumer units in the concave segment.[38] Similarly, it leads to a rate of return higher for uses involving moderate risk than for uses involving much risk only if consumer units in the initial convex segment outweigh in importance consumer units in both the concave and the terminal convex segments—though this may be a more stringent condition than is necessary in view of the uncertainty about the exact role of consumer units in the terminal convex segment.

This relative distribution of consumer units among the various segments could be considered an additional restriction that would have to be imposed to rationalize the alleged higher rate of return to moderately risky uses of resources. It is not clear, however, that it need be so considered, since there are two independent lines of reasoning that, taken together, establish something of a presumption that relatively few consumer units are in the concave segment.

One line of reasoning is based on the interpretation of the utility function suggested in Section V above. If the concave segment is a border line between two qualitatively different social classes, one would expect relatively few consumer units to be between the two classes.

The other line of reasoning is based on the implications of the hypothesis for the relative stability of the economic status of consumer units in the different segments. Units in the intermediate segment are tempted by every small gamble and at least some large ones. If opportunities are available, they will be continually subjecting themselves to risk. In consequence, they are likely to move out of the segment; upwards, if they are lucky; downwards, if they are not. Consumer units in the two convex segments, on the other hand, are less likely to move into the intermediate segment. The gambles that units in the initial segment accept will rarely pay off and, when they do, are likely to shift them all the way into the terminal convex segment. The gambles that units in the terminal segment accept will rarely involve losses and, when they do, may shift them all the way into the lower segment. Under these conditions, maintenance of a stable distribution of the population among the three segments would require that the two convex segments contain many more individuals than the concave segment. These considerations, while persuasive, are not, of course, conclusive. Opportunities to assume risks may

---

[38] This statement is deliberately vague. The actual relative rates of return will depend not only on the conditions of demand for risks of different kinds but also on the conditions of supply, and both would have to be taken into account in a comprehensive statement.

not exist. More important, the status of consumer units is determined not alone by the outcome of risks deliberately assumed but also by random events over which they cannot choose and have no control; and it is conceivable that these random events might be distributed in such a way that their main effect was to multiply the number in the concave segment.

The absolute number of persons in the various segments will count most for choices among the uses of human resources; wealth will count most for choices among uses of nonhuman resources.[39] In consequence, one might expect that the premium for bearing moderate risks instead of large risks would be greater for occupations than for investments. Indeed, for investments, the differential might in some cases be reversed, since the relatively high-income consumer units (those in the terminal segment) count for more in wealth than in numbers and they may prefer moderate to extreme risks.

In judging the implications of our hypothesis for the market as a whole, we have found it necessary to consider separately its implications for different income groups. These offer additional possibilities of empirical test. Perhaps the most fruitful source of data would be the investment policies of different income groups.

It was noted in Section II that, although many persons with low incomes are apparently willing to buy extremely speculative stocks, the low-income group receives the bulk of its property income in the form of interest and rents. These observations are clearly consistent with our hypothesis. Relatively high-income groups might be expected, on our hypothesis, to prefer bonds and relatively safe stocks. They might be expected to avoid the more speculative common stocks but to be attracted to higher-grade preferred stocks, which pay a higher nominal rate of return than high-grade bonds to compensate for a small risk of capital loss. Intermediate income groups might be expected to hold relatively large shares of their assets in moderately speculative common stocks and to furnish a disproportionate fraction of entrepreneurs.

Of course, any empirical study along these lines will have to take into account, as noted above, the effect of the progressive income tax in modifying the terms of investment. The current United States federal income tax has conflicting effects: the progressive rates discourage risky investments; the favored treatment of capital gains encourages them. In addition, such a study will have to consider the risk of investments as a group, rather than of individual investments, since the rich may be in a position to "average" risks.

Another implication referred to above that may be susceptible of empirical test, and the last one we shall cite, is the implied difference in the stability of the relative income status of various economic groups. The unattractiveness of small risks to both high- and low-income consumer units would tend to

[39] This distinction requires qualification because of the need for capital to enter some types of occupations and the consequent existence of "noncompeting groups"; see Milton Friedman and Simon Kuznets, *Income from Independent Professional Practice* (New York: National Bureau of Economic Research, 1945), Ch. III, Sec. 3; Ch. IV, Sec. 2.

give them a relatively stable status. By contrast, suppose the utility curve had no terminal convex segment but was like the curve of Figure 2. Low-income consumer units would still have a relatively stable status: their willingness to take gambles at long odds would pay off too seldom to shift many from one class to another. High-income consumer units would not. They would then take almost any gamble, and those who had high incomes today almost certainly would not have high incomes tomorrow. The average period from "shirt sleeves to shirt sleeves" would be far shorter than "three generations."[40] Unlike the other two groups, the middle-income class might be expected to display considerable instability of relative income status.[41]

VII. CONCLUSION

A plausible generalization of the available empirical evidence on the behavior of consumer units in choosing among alternatives open to them is provided by the hypothesis that a consumer unit (generally a family, sometimes an individual) behaves as if

1. It had a consistent set of preferences;
2. These preferences could be completely described by attaching a numerical value—to be designated "utility"—to alternatives each of which is regarded as certain;
3. The consumer unit chose among alternatives not involving risk that one which has the largest utility;
4. It chose among alternatives involving risk that one for which the expected utility (as contrasted with the utility of the expected income) is largest;
5. The function describing the utility of money income had in general the following properties:
   a. Utility rises with income, i.e., marginal utility of money income everywhere positive;
   b. It is convex from above below some income, concave between that income and some larger income, and convex for all higher incomes, i.e., diminishing marginal utility of money income for incomes below some income, increasing marginal utility of money income for incomes between that income and some larger income, and diminishing marginal utility of money income for all higher incomes;

---

[40] We did not use the absence of such instability to derive the upper convex segment because of the difficulty of allowing for the effect of the income tax.

[41] The existing data on stability of relative income status are too meager to contradict or to confirm this implication. In their study of professional incomes Friedman and Kuznets found that relative income status was about equally stable at all income levels. However, this study is hardly relevant, since it was for homogeneous occupational groups that would tend to fall in a single one of the classes considered here. Mendershausen's analysis along similar lines for family incomes in 1929 and 1933 is inconclusive. See Friedman and Kuznets, *op. cit.*, chap. VII; Horst Mendershausen, *Changes in Income Distribution during the Great Depression* (New York: National Bureau of Economic Research, 1946), chap. III.

6. Most consumer units tend to have incomes that place them in the segments of the utility function for which marginal utility of money income diminishes.

Points 1, 2, 3, and 5a of this hypothesis are implicit in the orthodox theory of choice; point 4 is an ancient idea recently revived and given new content by von Neumann and Morgenstern; and points 5b and 6 are the consequence of the attempt in this paper to use this idea to rationalize existing knowledge about the choices people make among alternatives involving risk.

Point 5b is inferred from the following phenomena: (a) low-income consumer units buy, or are willing to buy, insurance; (b) low-income consumer units buy, or are willing to buy, lottery tickets; (c) many consumer units buy, or are willing to buy, both insurance and lottery tickets; (d) lotteries typically have more than one prize. These statements are taken as a summary of the essential features of observed behavior not because they are the most important features in and of themselves but because they are convenient to handle and the restrictions imposed to rationalize them turn out to be sufficient to rationalize all the behavior described in Section II of this paper.

A possible interpretation of the various segments of the utility curve specified in 5b is that the segments of diminishing marginal utility correspond to socioeconomic classes, the segment of increasing marginal utility to a transitional stage between a lower and a higher socioeconomic class. On this interpretation the boundaries of the segments should be roughly similar for different people in the same community; and this is one of several independent lines of reasoning leading to point 6.

This hypothesis has implications for behavior, in addition to those used in deriving it, that are capable of being contradicted by observable data. In particular, the fundamental supposition that a single utility curve can generalize both riskless choices and choices involving risk would be contradicted if (a) individuals were observed to choose the larger of two certain incomes offered to them but (b) individuals were willing to pay more than the largest possible gain for the privilege of bearing risk. The supposition that individuals seek to maximize expected utility would be contradicted if individuals' reactions to complicated gambles could not be inferred from their reactions to simple ones. The particular shape of the utility curve specified in 5b would be contradicted by any of a large number of observations, for example, (a) general willingness of individuals, whatever their income, who buy insurance against small risks to enter into small fair gambles under circumstances under which they are not also buying "entertainment," (b) the converse of (a), namely an unwillingness to engage in small fair gambles by individuals who are not willing to buy fair insurance against small risks, (c) a higher average rate of return to uses of resources involving little risk than to uses involving a moderate amount of risk when other things are the same, (d) a concentration of investment portfolios of relatively low-income groups on speculative (but not highly speculative) investments or of relatively high-income groups on either moderately or highly speculative investments, (e) great instability in the relative income status of high-income groups or of low-income groups as a consequence of a propensity to engage in speculative activities.

3. RISK AVERSION IN THE SMALL AND IN THE LARGE[1]

JOHN W. PRATT*

Reprinted by permission of the author and publisher from *Econometrica*, Vol. 32, 1–2 (January–April 1964), pp. 122–136.

This paper concerns utility functions for money. A measure of risk aversion in the small, the risk premium or insurance premium for an arbitrary risk, and a natural concept of decreasing risk aversion are discussed and related to one another. Risks are also considered as a proportion of total assets.

1. SUMMARY AND INTRODUCTION

Let $u(x)$ be a utility function for money. The function $r(x) = -u''(x)/u'(x)$ will be interpreted in various ways as a measure of local risk aversion (risk aversion in the small); neither $u''(x)$ nor the curvature of the graph of u is an appropriate measure. No simple measure of risk aversion in the large will be introduced. Global risks will, however, be considered, and it will be shown that one decision maker has greater local risk aversion $r(x)$ than another at all x if and only if he is globally more risk-averse in the sense that, for every risk, his cash equivalent (the amount for which he would exchange the risk) is smaller than for the other decision maker. Equivalently, his risk premium (expected monetary value minus cash equivalent) is always larger, and he would be willing to pay more for insurance in any situation. From this it will be shown that a decision maker's local risk aversion $r(x)$ is a decreasing function of x if and only if, for every risk, his cash equivalent is larger the larger his assets, and his risk premium and what he would be willing to pay for insurance are smaller. This condition, which many decision makers would subscribe to, involves the third derivative of u, as $r' \leqq 0$ is equivalent to $u'''u' \geqq u''^2$. It is not satisfied by quadratic utilities in any region. All this means that some natural ways of thinking casually about utility functions may be misleading. Except for one family, convenient utility functions for which $r(x)$ is decreasing are not so very easy to find. Help in this regard is given by some theorems showing that certain combinations of utility functions, in particular linear combinations with positive weights, have decreasing $r(x)$ if all the functions in the combination have decreasing $r(x)$.

[1] This research was supported by the National Science Foundation (grant NSF-G24035). Reproduction in whole or in part is permitted for any purpose of the United States Government.

* Harvard University.

The related function $r^*(x) = xr(x)$ will be interpreted as a local measure of aversion to risks measured as a proportion of assets, and monotonicity of $r^*(x)$ will be proved to be equivalent to monotonicity of every risk's cash equivalent measured as a proportion of assets, and similarly for the risk premium and insurance.

These results have both descriptive and normative implications. Utility functions for which $r(x)$ is decreasing are logical candidates to use when trying to describe the behavior of people who, one feels, might generally pay less for insurance against a given risk the greater their assets. And consideration of the yield and riskiness per investment dollar of investors' portfolios may suggest, at least in some contexts, description by utility functions for which $r^*(x)$ is first decreasing and then increasing.

Normatively, it seems likely that many decision makers would feel they ought to pay less for insurance against a given risk the greater their assets. Such a decision maker will want to choose a utility function for which $r(x)$ is decreasing, adding this condition to the others he must already consider (consistency and probably concavity) in forging a satisfactory utility from more or less malleable preliminary preferences. He may wish to add a further condition on $r^*(x)$.

We do not assume or assert that utility may not change with time. Strictly speaking, we are concerned with utility at a specified time (when a decision must be made) for money at a (possibly later) specified time. Of course, our results pertain also to behavior at different times if utility does not change with time. For instance, a decision maker whose utility for total assets is unchanging and whose assets are increasing would be willing to pay less and less for insurance against a given risk as time progresses if his $r(x)$ is a decreasing function of x. Notice that his actual expenditure for insurance might nevertheless increase if his risks are increasing along with his assets.

The risk premium, cash equivalent, and insurance premium are defined and related to one another in Section 2. The local risk aversion function $r(x)$ is introduced and interpreted in Sections 3 and 4. In Section 5, inequalities concerning global risks are obtained from inequalities between local risk aversion functions. Section 6 deals with constant risk aversion, and Section 7 demonstrates the equivalence of local and global definitions of decreasing (and increasing) risk aversion. Section 8 shows that certain operations preserve the property of decreasing risk aversion. Some examples are given in Section 9. Aversion to proportional risk is discussed in Sections 10 to 12. Section 13 concerns some related work of Kenneth J. Arrow.[2]

Throughout this paper, the utility $u(x)$ is regarded as a function of total

[2] The importance of the function $r(x)$ was discovered independently by Kenneth J. Arrow and by Robert Schlaifer, in different contexts. The work presented here was, unfortunately, essentially completed before I learned of Arrow's related work. It is, however, a pleasure to acknowledge Schlaifer's stimulation and participation throughout, as well as that of John Bishop at certain points.

assets rather than of changes which may result from a certain decision, so that $x = 0$ is equivalent to ruin, or perhaps to loss of all readily disposable assets. (This is essential only in connection with proportional risk aversion.) The symbol $\sim$ indicates that two functions are equivalent as utilities, that is, $u_1(x) \sim u_2(x)$ means there exist constants a and b (with $b > 0$) such that $u_1(x) = a + bu_2(x)$ for all x. The utility functions discussed may, but need not, be bounded. It is assumed, however, that they are sufficiently regular to justify the proofs; generally it is enough that they be twice continuously differentiable with positive first derivative, which is already required for $r(x)$ to be defined and continuous. A variable with a tilde over it, such as $\tilde{z}$, is a random variable. The risks $\tilde{z}$ considered may, but need not, have "objective" probability distributions. In formal statements, $\tilde{z}$ refers only to risks which are not degenerate, that is, not constant with probability one, and interval refers only to an interval with more than one point. Also, increasing and decreasing mean nondecreasing and nonincreasing respectively; if we mean strictly increasing or decreasing we will say so.

2. THE RISK PREMIUM

Consider a decision maker with assets x and utility function u. We shall be interested in the *risk premium* π such that he would be indifferent between receiving a risk $\tilde{z}$ and receiving the non-random amount $E(\tilde{z}) - \pi$, that is, π less than the actuarial value $E(\tilde{z})$. If u is concave, then $\pi \geqq 0$, but we don't require this. The risk premium depends on x and on the distribution of $\tilde{z}$, and will be denoted $\pi(x, \tilde{z})$. (It is not, as this notation might suggest, a function $\pi(x, z)$ evaluated at a randomly selected value of z, which would be random.) By the properties of utility,

$$(1) \qquad u(x + E(\tilde{z}) - \pi(x, \tilde{z})) = E\{u(x + \tilde{z})\}.$$

We shall consider only situations where $E\{u(x + \tilde{z})\}$ exists and is finite. Then $\pi(x, \tilde{z})$ exists and is uniquely defined by (1), since $u(x + E(\tilde{z}) - \pi)$ is a strictly decreasing, continuous function of π ranging over all possible values of u. It follows immediately from (1) that, for any constant μ,

$$(2) \qquad \pi(x, \tilde{z}) = \pi(x + \mu, \tilde{z} - \mu).$$

By choosing $\mu = E(\tilde{z})$ (assuming it exists and is finite), we may thus reduce consideration to a risk $\tilde{z} - \mu$ which is actuarially neutral, that is, $E(\tilde{z} - \mu) = 0$.

Since the decision maker is indifferent between receiving the risk $\tilde{z}$ and receiving for sure the amount $\pi_a(x, \tilde{z}) = E(\tilde{z}) - \pi(x, \tilde{z})$, this amount is sometimes called the cash equivalent or value of $\tilde{z}$. It is also the asking price for $\tilde{z}$, the smallest amount for which the decision maker would willingly sell $\tilde{z}$ if he had it. It is given by

$$(3a) \qquad u(x + \pi_a(x, \tilde{z})) = E\{u(x + \tilde{z})\}.$$

It is to be distinguished from the bid price $\pi_b(x, \tilde{z})$, the largest amount the decision maker would willingly pay to obtain $\tilde{z}$, which is given by

(3b) $$u(x) = E\{u(x + \tilde{z} - \pi_b(x, \tilde{z}))\}.$$

For an unfavorable risk $\tilde{z}$, it is natural to consider the insurance premium $\pi_I(x, \tilde{z})$ such that the decision maker is indifferent between facing the risk $\tilde{z}$ and paying the non-random amount $\pi_I(x, \tilde{z})$. Since paying π_I is equivalent to receiving $-\pi_I$, we have

(3c) $$\pi_I(x, \tilde{z}) = -\pi_a(x, \tilde{z}) = \pi(x, \tilde{z}) - E(\tilde{z}).$$

If $\tilde{z}$ is actuarially neutral, the risk premium and insurance premium coincide.

The results of this paper will be stated in terms of the risk premium π, but could equally easily and meaningfully be stated in terms of the cash equivalent or insurance premium.

3. LOCAL RISK AVERSION

To measure a decision maker's local aversion to risk, it is natural to consider his risk premium for a small, actuarially neutral risk $\tilde{z}$. We therefore consider $\pi(x, \tilde{z})$ for a risk $\tilde{z}$ with $E(\tilde{z}) = 0$ and small variance σ_z^2; that is, we consider the behavior of $\pi(x, \tilde{z})$ as $\sigma_z^2 \to 0$. We assume the third absolute central moment of $\tilde{z}$ is of smaller order than σ_z^2. (Ordinarily it is of order σ_z^3.) Expanding u around x on both sides of (1), we obtain under suitable regularity conditions[3]

(4a) $$u(x - \pi) = u(x) - \pi u'(x) + O(\pi^2),$$

(4b) $$E\{u(x + \tilde{z})\} = E\{u(x) + \tilde{z}u'(x) + \tfrac{1}{2}\tilde{z}^2 u''(x) + O(\tilde{z}^3)\}$$
$$= u(x) + \tfrac{1}{2}\sigma_z^2 u''(x) + o(\sigma_z^2).$$

Setting these expressions equal, as required by (1), then gives

(5) $$\pi(x, \tilde{z}) = \tfrac{1}{2}\sigma_z^2 r(x) + o(\sigma_z^2),$$

where

(6) $$r(x) = -\frac{u''(x)}{u'(x)} = -\frac{d}{dx} \log u'(x).$$

Thus the decision maker's risk premium for a small, actuarially neutral risk $\tilde{z}$ is approximately $r(x)$ times half the variance of $\tilde{z}$; that is, $r(x)$ is twice the risk premium per unit of variance for infinitesimal risks. A sufficient regularity condition for (5) is that u have a third derivative which is continuous and bounded over the range of all $\tilde{z}$ under discussion. The theorems to follow will not actually depend on (5), however.

If $\tilde{z}$ is not actuarially neutral, we have by (2), with $\mu = E(\tilde{z})$, and (5):

(7) $$\pi(x, \tilde{z}) = \tfrac{1}{2}\sigma_z^2 r(x + E(\tilde{z})) + o(\sigma_z^2).$$

[3] In expansions, $O(\ )$ means "terms of order at most" and $o(\ )$ means "terms of smaller order than."

Thus the risk premium for a risk $\tilde{z}$ with arbitrary mean $E(\tilde{z})$ but small variance is approximately $r(x + E(\tilde{z}))$ times half the variance of $\tilde{z}$. It follows also that the risk premium will just equal and hence offset the actuarial value $E(\tilde{z})$ of a small risk $(\tilde{z})$; that is, the decision maker will be indifferent between having $\tilde{z}$ and not having it when the actuarial value is approximately $r(x)$ times half the variance of $\tilde{z}$. Thus $r(x)$ may also be interpreted as twice the actuarial value the decision maker requires per unit of variance for infinitesimal risks.

Notice that it is the variance, not the standard deviation, that enters these formulas. To first order any (differentiable) utility is linear in small gambles. In this sense, these are second order formulas.

Still another interpretation of $r(x)$ arises in the special case $\tilde{z} = \pm h$, that is, where the risk is to gain or lose a fixed amount $h > 0$. Such a risk is actuarially neutral if $+h$ and $-h$ are equally probable, so $P(\tilde{z} = h) - P(\tilde{z} = -h)$ measures the *probability premium* of $\tilde{z}$. Let $p(x, h)$ be the probability premium such that the decision maker is indifferent between the status quo and a risk $\tilde{z} = \pm h$ with

(8) $$P(\tilde{z} = h) - P(\tilde{z} = -h) = p(x, h).$$

Then $P(\tilde{z} = h) = \frac{1}{2}[1 + p(x, h)]$, $P(\tilde{z} = -h) = \frac{1}{2}[1 - p(x, h)]$, and $p(x, h)$ is defined by

(9) $$u(x) = E\{u(x + \tilde{z})\} = \frac{1}{2}[1 + p(x, h)]\, u(x + h) + \frac{1}{2}[1 - p(x, h)]u(x - h).$$

When u is expanded around x as before, (9) becomes

(10) $$u(x) = u(x) + hp(x, h)\, u'(x) + \frac{1}{2}h^2 u''(x) + O(h^3).$$

Solving for $p(x, h)$, we find

(11) $$p(x, h) = \frac{1}{2}hr(x) + O(h^2).$$

Thus for small h the decision maker is indifferent between the status quo and a risk of $\pm h$ with a probability premium of $r(x)$ times $\frac{1}{2}h$; that is, $r(x)$ is twice the probability premium he requires for unit risked for small risks.

In these ways we may interpret $r(x)$ as a measure of the *local risk aversion* or *local propensity to insure* at the point x under the utility function u; $-r(x)$ would measure locally liking for risk or propensity to gamble. Notice that we have not introduced any measure of risk aversion in the large. Aversion to ordinary (as opposed to infinitesimal) risks might be considered measured by $\pi(x, \tilde{z})$, but π is a much more complicated function than r. Despite the absence of any simple measure of risk aversion in the large, we shall see that comparisons of aversion to risk can be made simply in the large as well as in the small.

By (6), integrating $-r(x)$ gives $\log u'(x) + c$; exponentiating and integrating again then gives $e^c u(x) + d$. The constants of integration are immaterial because $e^c u(x) + d \sim u(x)$. (Note $e^c > 0$). Thus we may write

(12)
$$u \sim \int e^{-\int r},$$

and we observe that the local risk aversion function r associated with any utility function u contains all essential information about u while eliminating everything arbitrary about u. However, decisions about ordinary (as opposed to "small") risks are determined by r only through u as given by (12), so it is not convenient entirely to eliminate u from consideration in favor of r.

4. CONCAVITY

The aversion to risk implied by a utility function u seems to be a form of concavity, and one might set out to measure concavity as representing aversion to risk. It is clear from the foregoing that for this purpose $r(x) = -u''(x)/u'(x)$ can be considered a measure of the concavity of u at the point x. A case might perhaps be made for using instead some one-to-one function of $r(x)$, but it should be noted that $u''(x)$ or $-u''(x)$ is not in itself a meaningful measure of concavity in utility theory, nor is the curvature (reciprocal of the signed radius of the tangent circle) $u''(x) (1 + [u'(x)]^2)^{-3/2}$. Multiplying u by a positive constant, for example, does not alter behavior but does alter u'' and the curvature.

A more striking and instructive example is provided by the function $u(x) = -e^{-x}$. As x increases, this function approaches the asymptote $u = 0$ and looks graphically less and less concave and more and more like a horizontal straight line, in accordance with the fact that $u'(x) = e^{-x}$ and $u''(x) = -e^{-x}$ both approach 0. As a utility function, however, it does not change at all with the level of assets x, that is, the behavior implied by $u(x)$ is the same for all x, since $u(k + x) = -e^{-k-x} \sim u(x)$. In particular, the risk premium $\pi(x, \tilde{z})$ for any risk $\tilde{z}$ and the probability premium $p(x, h)$ for any h remain absolutely constant as x varies, Thus, regardless of the appearance of its graph, $u(x) = -e^{-x}$ is just as far from implying linear behavior at $x = \infty$ as at $x = 0$ or $x = -\infty$. All this is duly reflected in $r(x)$, which is constant: $r(x) = -u''(x)/u'(x) = 1$ for all x.

One feature of $u''(x)$ does have a meaning, namely its sign, which equals that of $-r(x)$. A negative (positive) sign at x implies unwillingness (willingness) to accept small, actuarially neutral risks with assets x. Furthermore, a negative (positive) sign for all x implies strict concavity (convexity) and hence unwillingness (willingness) to accept any actuarially neutral risk with any assets. The absolute magnitude of $u''(x)$ does not in itself have any meaning in utility theory, however.

5. COMPARATIVE RISK AVERSION

Let u_1 and u_2 be utility functions with local risk aversion functions r_1 and r_2, respectively. If, at a point x, $r_1(x) > r_2(x)$, then u_1 is locally more risk-averse than u_2 at the point x; that is, the corresponding risk premiums satisfy

$\pi_1(x, \tilde{z}) > \pi_2(x, \tilde{z})$ for sufficiently small risks $\tilde{z}$, and the corresponding probability premiums satisfy $p_1(x, h) > p_2(x, h)$ for sufficiently small $h > 0$. The main point of the theorem we are about to prove is that the corresponding global properties also hold. For instance, if $r_1(x) > r_2(x)$ for all x, that is, u_1, has greater local risk aversion than u_2 everywhere, then $\pi_1(x, \tilde{z}) > \pi_2(x, \tilde{z})$ for every risk $\tilde{z}$, so that u_1 is also globally more risk-averse in a natural sense.

It is to be understood in this section that the probability distribution of $\tilde{z}$, which determines $\pi_1(x, \tilde{z})$ and $\pi_2(x, \tilde{z})$, is the same in each. We are comparing the risk premiums for the same probability distribution of risk but for two different utilities. This does not mean that when Theorem 1 is applied to two decision makers, they must have the same personal probability distributions, but only that the notation is imprecise. The theorem could be stated in terms of $\pi_1(x, \tilde{z}_1)$ and $\pi_2(x, \tilde{z}_2)$ where the distribution assigned to $\tilde{z}_1$ by the first decision maker is the same as that assigned to $\tilde{z}_2$ by the second decision maker. This would be less misleading, but also less convenient and less suggestive, especially for later use. More precise notation would be, for instance, $\pi_1(x, F)$ and $\pi_2(x, F)$, where F is a cumulative distribution function.

Theorem 1. *Let $r_i(x)$, $\pi_i(x, \tilde{z})$, and $p_i(x)$ be the local risk aversion, risk premium, and probability premium corresponding to the utility function u_i, $i = 1, 2$. Then the following conditions are equivalent, in either the strong form (indicated in brackets), or the weak form (with the bracketed material omitted).*

(a) $r_1(x) \geqq r_2(x)$ *for all x [and $>$ for at least one x in every interval].*
(b) $\pi_1(x, \tilde{z}) \geqq [>] \pi_2(x, \tilde{z})$ *for all x and $\tilde{z}$.*
(c) $p_1(x, h) \geqq [>] p_2(x, h)$ *for all x and all $h > 0$.*
(d) $u_1(u_2^{-1}(t))$ *is a [strictly] concave function of t.*
(e) $\dfrac{u_1(y) - u_1(x)}{u_1(w) - u_1(v)} \leqq [<] \dfrac{u_2(y) - u_2(x)}{u_2(w) - u_2(v)}$ *for all v, w, x, y with $v < w \leqq x < y$.*

The same equivalences hold if attention is restricted throughout to an interval, that is, if the requirement is added that x, $x + \tilde{z}$, $x + h$, $x - h$, $u_2^{-1}(t)$, v, w, and y, all lie in a specified interval.

Proof. We shall prove things in an order indicating somewhat how one might discover that (a) implies (b) and (c).

To show that (b) follows from (d), solve (1) to obtain

(13) $\pi_i(x, \tilde{z}) = x + E(\tilde{z}) - u_i^{-1}(E\{u_i(x + \tilde{z})\})$.

Then

(14) $\pi_1(x, \tilde{z}) - \pi_2(x, \tilde{z}) = u_2^{-1}(E\{u_2(x + \tilde{z})\}) - u_1^{-1}(E\{u_1(x + \tilde{z})\})$
$= u_2^{-1}(E\{\tilde{t}\}) - u_1^{-1}(E\{u_1(u_2^{-1}(\tilde{t}))\})$,

where $\tilde{t} = u_2(x + \tilde{z})$. If $u_1(u_2^{-1}(t))$ is [strictly] concave, then (by Jensen's inequality)

(15) $E\{u_1(u_2^{-1}(\tilde{t}))\} \leqq [<] u_1(u_2^{-1}(E\{\tilde{t}\}))$.

Substituting (15) in (14), we obtain (b).

To show that (a) implies (d), note that

$$\text{(16)} \qquad \frac{d}{dt} u_1(u_2^{-1}(t)) = \frac{u_1'(u_2^{-1}(t))}{u_2'(u_2^{-1}(t))},$$

which is [strictly] decreasing if (and only if) $\log u_1'(x)/u_2'(x)$ is. The latter follows from (a) and

$$\text{(17)} \qquad \frac{d}{dx} \log \frac{u_1'(x)}{u_2'(x)} = r_2(x) - r_1(x).$$

That (c) is implied by (e) follows immediately upon writing (9) in the form

$$\text{(18)} \qquad \frac{1 - p_i(x, h)}{1 + p_i(x, h)} = \frac{u_i(x + h) - u_i(x)}{u_i(x) - u_i(x - h)}.$$

To show that (a) implies (e), integrate (a) from w to x, obtaining

$$\text{(19)} \qquad - \log \frac{u_1'(x)}{u_1'(w)} \geq [>] - \log \frac{u_2'(x)}{u_2'(w)} \quad \text{for } w < x,$$

which is equivalent to

$$\text{(20)} \qquad \frac{u_1'(x)}{u_1'(w)} \leq [<] \frac{u_2'(w)}{u_2'(w)} \quad \text{for } w < x.$$

This implies

$$\text{(21)} \qquad \frac{u_1(y) - u_1(x)}{u_1'(w)} \leq [<] \frac{u_2(y) - u_2(x)}{u_2'(w)} \quad \text{for } w \leq x < y,$$

as may be seen by applying the Mean Value Theorem of differential calculus to the difference of the two sides of (21) regarded as a function of y. Condition (e) follows from (21) upon application of the Mean Value Theorem to the difference of the reciprocals of the two sides of (e) regarded as a function of w.

We have now proved that (a) implies (d) implies (b), and (a) implies (e) implies (c). The equivalence of (a)–(e) will follow if we can prove that (b) implies (a), and (c) implies (a), or equivalently that not (a) implies not (b) and not (c). But this follows from what has already been proved, for if the weak [strong] form of (a) does not hold, then the strong [weak] form of (a) holds on some interval with u_1 and u_2 interchanged. Then the strong [weak] forms of (b) and (c) also hold on this interval with u_1 and u_2 interchanged, so the weak [strong] forms of (b) and (c) do not hold. This completes the proof.

We observe that (e) is equivalent to (20), (21), and

$$\text{(22)} \qquad \frac{u_1(w) - u_1(v)}{u_1'(x)} \geq [>] \frac{u_2(w) - u_2(v)}{u_2'(x)} \quad \text{for } v < w \leq x.$$

6. CONSTANT RISK AVERSION

If the local risk aversion function is constant, say $r(x) = c$, then by (12):

(23) $\qquad\qquad u(x) \sim x \qquad\quad$ if $r(x) = 0$;

(24) $\qquad\qquad u(x) \sim -e^{-cx} \quad$ if $r(x) = c > 0$;

(25) $\qquad\qquad u(x) \sim e^{-cx} \quad$ if $r(x) = c < 0$.

These utilities are, respectively, linear, strictly concave and strictly convex.

If the risk aversion is constant locally, then it is also constant globally, that is, a change in assets makes no change in preference among risks. In fact, for any k, $u(k + x) \sim u(x)$ in each of the cases above, as is easily verified. Therefore it makes sense to speak of "constant risk aversion" without the qualification "local" or "global."

Similar remarks apply to constant risk aversion on an interval, except that global consideration must be restricted to assets x and risks $\tilde{z}$ such that $x + \tilde{z}$ is certain to stay within the interval.

7. INCREASING AND DECREASING RISK AVERSION

Consider a decision maker who (i) attaches a positive risk premium to any risk, but (ii) attaches a smaller risk premium to any given risk the greater his assets x. Formally this means

(i) $\pi(x, \tilde{z}) > 0$ for all x and $\tilde{z}$;
(ii) $\pi(x, \tilde{z})$ is a strictly decreasing function of x for all $\tilde{z}$.

Restricting $\tilde{z}$ to be actuarially neutral would not affect (i) or (ii), by (2) with $\mu = E(\tilde{z})$.

We shall call a utility function (or a decision maker possessing it) *risk-averse* if the weak form of (i) holds, that is, if $\pi(x, \tilde{z}) \geq 0$ for all x and $\tilde{z}$; it is well known that this is equivalent to concavity of u, and hence to $u'' \leq 0$ and to $r \geq 0$. A utility function is *strictly risk-averse* if (i) holds as stated; this is equivalent to strict concavity of u and hence to the existence in every interval of at least one point where $u'' < 0$, $r > 0$.

We turn now to (ii). Notice that it amounts to a definition of strictly decreasing risk aversion in a global (as opposed to local) sense. One would hope that decreasing global risk aversion would be equivalent to decreasing local risk aversion $r(x)$. The following theorem asserts that this is indeed so. Therefore it makes sense to speak of "decreasing risk aversion" without the qualification "local" or "global." What is nontrivial is that $r(x)$ decreasing implies $\pi(x, \tilde{z})$ decreasing, inasmuch as $r(x)$ pertains directly only to infinitesimal gambles. Similar considerations apply to the probability premium $p(x, h)$.

> *Theorem 2. The following conditions are equivalent.*
> (a) *The local risk aversion function $r(x)$ is [strictly] decreasing.*
> (b') *The risk premium $\pi(x, \tilde{z})$ is a [strictly] decreasing function of x for all $\tilde{z}$.*

(c′)   *The probability premium $p(x, h)$ is a [strictly] decreasing function of x for all $h > 0$.*

The same equivalences hold if "increasing" is substituted for "decreasing" throughout and/or attention is restricted throughout to an interval, that is, the requirement is added that x, $x + \tilde{z}$, $x + h$, and $x - h$ all lie in a specified interval.

Proof. This theorem follows upon application of Theorem 1 to $u_1(x) = u(x)$ and $u_2(x) = u(x + k)$ for arbitrary x and k.

It is easily verified that (a′) and hence also (b′) and (c′) are equivalent to

(d′) $u'(u^{-1}(t))$ is a [strictly] convex function of t.

This corresponds to (d) of Theorem 1. Corresponding to (e) of Theorem 1 and (20)–(22) is

(e′) $u'(x)u'''(x) \geqq (u''(x))^2$ [and $>$ for at least one x in every interval].

The equivalence of this to (a′)–(c′) follows from the fact that the sign of $r'(x)$ is the same as that of $(u''(x))^2 - u'(x)u'''(x)$. Theorem 2 can be and originally was proved by way of (d′) and (e′), essentially as Theorem 1 is proved in the present paper.

8. OPERATIONS WHICH PRESERVE DECREASING RISK AVERSION

We have just seen that a utility function evinces decreasing risk aversion in a global sense if and only if its local risk aversion function $r(x)$ is decreasing. Such a utility function seems of interest mainly if it is also risk-averse (concave, $r \geqq 0$). Accordingly, we shall now formally define a utility function to be [strictly] decreasingly risk-averse if its local risk aversion function r is [strictly] decreasing and nonnegative. Then by Theorem 2, conditions (i) and (ii) of Section 7 are equivalent to the utility's being strictly decreasingly risk-averse.

In this section we shall show that certain operations yield decreasingly risk-averse utility functions if applied to such functions. This facilitates proving that functions are decreasingly risk-averse and finding functions which have this property and also have reasonably simple formulas. In the proofs, $r(x)$, $r_1(x)$, etc., are the local risk aversion functions belonging to $u(x)$, $u_1(x)$, etc.

Theorem 3.   *Suppose $a > 0$: $u_1(x) = u(ax + b)$ is [strictly] decreasingly risk-averse for $x_0 \leqq x \leqq x_1$ if and only if $u(x)$ is [strictly] decreasingly risk-averse for $ax_0 + b \leqq x \leqq ax_1 + b$.*

Proof. This follows directly from the easily verified formula:

(26) $r_1(x) = ar(ax + b).$

Theorem 4.   *If $u_1(x)$ is decreasingly risk-averse for $x_0 \leqq x \leqq x_1$, and $u_2(x)$ is decreasingly risk-averse for $u_1(x_0) \leqq x \leqq u_1(x_1)$, then $u(x) = u_2(u_1(x))$ is decreasingly risk-averse for $x_0 \leqq x \leqq x_1$, and strictly so unless one of u_1 and*

u_2 is linear from some x on and the other has constant risk aversion in some interval.

Proof. We have $\log u'(x) = \log u_2'(u_1'(x)) + \log u_1'(x)$, and therefore

$$(27) \qquad r(x) = r_2(u_1(x))u_1'(x) + r_1(x).$$

The functions $r_2(u_1(x))$, $u_1'(x)$, and $r_1(x)$ are ≥ 0 and decreasing, and therefore so is $r(x)$. Furthermore, $u_1'(x)$ is strictly decreasing as long as $r_1(x) > 0$, so $r(x)$ is strictly decreasing as long as $r_1(x)$ and $r_2(u_1(x))$ are both > 0. If one of them is 0 for some x, then it is 0 for all larger x, but if the other is strictly decreasing, then so is r.

Theorem 5. If $u, \ldots, u_n$ are decreasingly risk-averse on an interval $[x_0, x_1]$, and $c, \ldots, c_n$ are positive constants, then $u = \sum_1^n c_i u_i$ is decreasingly risk-averse on $[x_0, x_1]$, and strictly so except on subintervals (if any) where all u_i have equal and constant risk aversion.

Proof. The general statement follows from the case $u = u_1 + u_2$. For this case

$$(28) \qquad r = -\frac{u_1'' + u_2''}{u_1' + u_2'} = \frac{u_1'}{u_1' + u_2'} r_1 + \frac{u_2'}{u_1' + u_2'} r_2;$$

$$(29) \qquad r' = \frac{u_1'}{u_1' + u_2'} r_1' + \frac{u_2'}{u_1' + u_2'} r_2' + \frac{u_1'' u_2' - u_1' u_2''}{(u_1' + u_2')^2} (r_1 - r_2)$$

$$= \frac{u_1' r_1' + u_2' r_2'}{u_1' + u_2'} - \frac{u_1' u_2'}{(u_1' + u_2')^2} (r_1 - r_2)^2.$$

We have $u_1' > 0$, $u_2' > 0$, $r_1' \leq 0$, and $r_2' \leq 0$. Therefore $r \leq 0$, and $r' < 0$ unless $r_1 = r_2$ and $r_1' = r_2' = 0$. The conclusion follows.

9. EXAMPLES

9.1 *Example 1.* The utility $u(x) = -(b - x)^c$ for $x \leq b$ and $c > 1$ is strictly increasing and strictly concave, but it also has strictly *increasing* risk aversion: $r(x) = (c - 1)/(b - x)$. Notice that the most general concave quadratic utility $u(x) = \alpha + \beta x - \gamma x^2$, $\beta > 0$, $\gamma > 0$, is equivalent as a utility to $-(b - x)^c$ with $c = 2$ and $b = \frac{1}{2}\beta/\gamma$. Therefore a quadratic utility cannot be decreasingly risk-averse on any interval whatever. This severely limits the usefulness of quadratic utility, however nice it would be to have expected utility depend only on the mean and variance of the probability distribution. Arguing "in the small" is no help: decreasing risk aversion is a local property as well as a global one.

9.2 *Example 2.* If

$$(30) \qquad u'(x) = (x^a + b)^{-c} \quad \text{with} \quad a > 0, c > 0,$$

then $u(x)$ is strictly decreasingly risk-averse in the region

$$(31) \qquad x > [\max\{0, -b, b(a - 1)\}]^{1/a}.$$

To prove this, note

$$(32) \qquad r(x) = -\frac{d}{dx} \log u'(x) = \frac{ac}{x + bx^{1-a}},$$

which is ≥ 0 and strictly decreasing in the region where the denominator $x + bx^{1-a}$ is ≥ 0 and strictly increasing, which is the region (30). (The condition $x \geq 0$ is included to insure that x^a is defined; for $a \geq 1$ it follows from the other conditions.)

By Theorem 3, one can obtain a utility function that is strictly decreasingly risk-averse for $x > 0$ by substituting $x + d$ for x above, where d is at least the right-hand side of (31). Multiplying x by a positive factor, as in Theorem 3, is equivalent to multiplying b by a positive factor.

Given below are all the strictly decreasingly risk-averse utility functions $u(x)$ on $x > 0$ which can be obtained by applying Theorem 3 to (30) with the indicated choices of the parameters a and c:

(33) $a = 1, 0 < c < 1$: $u(x) \sim (x + d)^q$ with $d \geq 0, 0 < q < 1$;

(34) $a = 1, c = 1$: $u(x) \sim \log(x + d)$ with $d \geq 0$;

(35) $a = 1, c > 1$: $u(x) \sim -(x + d)^{-q}$ with $d \geq 0, q > 0$;

(36) $a = 2, c = 5$: $u(x) \sim \log (x + d + [(x + d)^2 + b])$ with $d \geq |b|^{\frac{1}{2}}$;

(37) $a = 2, c = 1$: $u(x) \sim \arctan(\alpha x + \beta)$ or $\log (1 - (\alpha x + \beta)^{-1})$ with $a > 0, \beta \geq 1$;

(38) $a = 2, c = 1.5$: $u(x) \sim [1 + (\alpha x + \beta)^{-2}]^{-\frac{1}{2}}$ or $-[1 - (\alpha x + \beta)^{-2}]^{-\frac{1}{2}}$ with $\alpha > 0, \beta \geq 1$.

9.3 *Example 3.*   Applying Theorems 4 and 5 to the utilities of Example 2 and Section 6 gives a very wide class of utilities which are strictly decreasingly risk-averse for $x > 0$, such as

(39) $u(x) \sim -c_1 e^{-cx} - c_2 e^{-dx}$ with $c_1 > 0, c_2 > 0, c > 0, d > 0$.

(40) $u(x) \sim \log (d_1 + \log (x + d_2))$ with $d_1 \geq 0, d_2 \geq 0, d_1 + \log d_2 \geq 0$.

10. PROPORTIONAL RISK AVERSION

So far we have been concerned with risks that remained fixed while assets varied. Let us now view everything as a proportion of assets. Specifically, let $\pi^*(x, \tilde{z})$ be the *proportional risk premium* corresponding to a proportional risk $\tilde{z}$; that is, a decision maker with assets x and utility function u would be indifferent between receiving a risk $x\tilde{z}$ and receiving the non-random amount $E(x\tilde{z}) - x\pi^*(x, \tilde{z})$. Then $x\pi^*(x, \tilde{z})$ equals the risk premium $\pi(x, x\tilde{z})$, so

$$(41) \qquad \pi^*(x, \tilde{z}) = \frac{1}{x}\, \pi(x, x\tilde{z}).$$

For a small, actuarially neutral, proportional risk $\tilde{z}$ we have, by (5),

$$(42) \qquad \pi^*(x, \tilde{z}) = \tfrac{1}{2}\sigma_z^2\, r^*(x) + o(\sigma_z^2),$$

where

$$(43) \qquad r^*(x) = xr(x).$$

If $\tilde{z}$ is not actuarially neutral, we have, by (7),

$$(44) \qquad \pi^*(x, \tilde{z}) = \tfrac{1}{2}\sigma_z^2 r^*(x + E(\tilde{z})) + o(\sigma_z^2).$$

We will call r^* the *local proportional risk aversion* at the point x under the utility function u. Its interpretation by (42) and (44) is like that of r by (5) and (7).

Similarly, we may define the *proportional probability premium* $p^*(x, h)$, corresponding to a risk of gaining or losing a proportional amount h, namely

$$(45) \qquad p^*(x, h) = p(x, xh).$$

Then another interpretation of $r^*(x)$ is provided by

$$(46) \qquad p^*(x, h) = \tfrac{1}{2}hr^*(x) + O(h^2),$$

which follows from (45) and (11).

11. CONSTANT PROPORTIONAL RISK AVERSION

If the local proportional risk aversion function is constant, say $r^*(x) = c$, then $r(x) = c/x$, so the utility is strictly decreasingly risk-averse for $c > 0$ and has negative, strictly increasing risk aversion for $c < 0$. By (12), the possibilities are:

$$(47) \qquad u(x) \sim x^{1-c} \qquad \text{if}\quad r^*(x) = c < 1,$$

$$(48) \qquad u(x) \sim \log x \qquad \text{if}\quad r^*(x) = 1,$$

$$(49) \qquad u(x) \sim -x^{-(c-1)} \quad \text{if}\quad r^*(x) = c > 1.$$

If the proportional risk aversion is constant locally, then it is constant globally, that is, a change in assets makes no change in preferences among proportional risks. This follows immediately from the fact that $u(kx) \sim u(x)$ in each of the cases above. Therefore it makes sense to speak of "constant proportional risk aversion" without the qualification "local" or "global." Similar remarks apply to constant proportional risk aversion on an interval.

12. INCREASING AND DECREASING PROPORTIONAL RISK AVERSION

We will call a utility function [strictly] increasingly or decreasingly proportionally risk-averse if it has a [strictly] increasing or decreasing local proportional risk aversion function. Again the corresponding local and global properties are equivalent, as the next theorem states.

Theorem 6.   The following conditions are equivalent.

(a″)   *The local proportional risk aversion function $r^*(x)$ is [strictly] decreasing.*

(b″)   *The proportional risk premium $\pi^*(x, \tilde{z})$ is a [strictly] decreasing function of x for all $\tilde{z}$.*

(c″)   *The proportional probability premium $p^*(x, h)$ is a [strictly] decreasing function of x for all $h > 0$.*

The same equivalences hold if "increasing" is substituted for "decreasing" throughout and/or attention is restricted throughout to an interval, that is, if the requirement is added that x, $x + x\tilde{z}$, $x + xh$, and $x - xh$ all lie in a specified interval.

Proof.   This theorem follows upon application of Theorem 1 to $u_1(x) = u(x)$ and $u_2(x) = u(kx)$ for arbitrary x and k.

A decreasingly risk-averse utility function may be increasingly or decreasingly proportionally risk-averse or neither. For instance, $u(x) \sim -\exp[-q^{-1}(x + b)^q]$, with $b \geq 0$, $q < 1, q \neq 0$, is strictly decreasingly risk-averse for $x > 0$ while its local proportional risk aversion function $r^*(x) = x(x + b)^{-1}[(x + b)^q + 1 - q]$ is strictly increasing if $0 < q < 1$, strictly decreasing if $q < 0$ and $b = 0$, and neither if $q < 0$ and $b > 0$.

13. RELATED WORK OF ARROW

Arrow[4] has discussed the optimum amount to invest when part of the assets x are to be held as cash and the rest invested in a specified, actuarially favorable risk. If $\tilde{i}$ is the return per unit invested, then investing the amount a will result in assets $x + a\tilde{i}$. Suppose $a(x, \tilde{i})$ is the optimum amount to invest, that is, $a(x, \tilde{i})$ maximizes $E\{u(x + a\tilde{i})\}$. Arrow proves that if $r(x)$ is [strictly] decreasing, increasing, or constant for all x, then $a(x, \tilde{i})$ is [strictly] increasing, decreasing, or constant, respectively, except that $a(x, \tilde{i}) = x$ for all x below a certain value (depending on $\tilde{i}$). He also proves a theorem about the asset elasticity of the demand for cash which is equivalent to the statement that if $r^*(x)$ is [strictly] decreasing, increasing, or constant for all x, then the optimum proportional investment $a^*(x, \tilde{i}) = a(x, \tilde{i})/x$ is [strictly] increasing, decreasing, or constant, respectively, except that $a^*(x, \tilde{i}) = 1$ for all x below a certain value. In the present framework it is natural to deduce these results from the following theorem, whose proof bears essentially the same relation to Arrow's proofs as the proof of Theorem 1 to direct proofs of Theorems 2 and 6. For convenience we assume that $a_1(x, \tilde{i})$ and $a_2(x, \tilde{i})$ are unique.

Theorem 7.   Condition (a) of Theorem 1 is equivalent to

---

[4] Kenneth J. Arrow, "Liquidity Preference," Lecture VI in "Lecture Notes for Economics 285, The Economics of Uncertainty," pp. 33–53, undated, Stanford University.

(f) $a_1(x, \bar{\imath}) \leq a_2(x, \bar{\imath})$ *for all* x *and* $\bar{\imath}$ [*and* $<$ *if* $0 < a_1(x, \bar{\imath}) < x$].
The same equivalence holds if attention is restricted throughout to an interval,
that is, if the requirement is added that x *and* $x + \bar{\imath}x$ *lie in a specified interval.*

Proof. To show that (a) implies (f), note that $a_j(x, \bar{\imath})$ maximizes

$$(50) \qquad v_j(a) = \frac{1}{u'_j(x)} E\{u_j(x + a\bar{\imath})\}, \qquad j = 1, 2.$$

Therefore (f) follows from

$$(51) \qquad \frac{d}{da}\{v_1(a) - v_2(a)\} = E\left\{\bar{\imath}\left(\frac{u'_1(x + a\bar{\imath})}{u'_1(x)} - \frac{u'_2(x + a\bar{\imath})}{u'_2(x)}\right)\right\} \leq [<] 0,$$

which follows from (a) by (20).

If, conversely, the weak [strong] form of (a) does not hold, then its strong [weak] form holds on some interval with u_1 and u_2 interchanged, in which case the weak [strong] form of (f) cannot hold, so (f) implies (a). (The fact must be used that the strong form of (f) is actually stronger than the weak form, even when x and $x + \bar{\imath}x$ are restricted to a specified interval. This is easily shown.)

Assuming u is bounded, Arrow proves that (i) it is impossible that $r^*(x) \leq 1$ for all $x > x_0$, and he implies that (ii) $r^*(0) \leq 1$. It follows, as he points out, that if u is bounded and r^* is monotonic, then r^* is increasing. (i) and (ii) can be deduced naturally from the following theorem, which is an immediate consequence of Theorem 1 (a) and (e).

Theorem 8. If $r_1(x) \geq r_2(x)$ *for all* $x > x_0$ *and* $u_1(\infty) = \infty$, *then* $u_2(\infty) = \infty$. *If* $r_1(x) \geq r_2(x)$ *for all* $x < \varepsilon$, $\varepsilon > 0$, *and* $u_2(0) = -\infty$, *then* $u_1(0) = -\infty$.
This gives (i) when $r_1(x) = 1/x$, $r_2(x) = r(x)$, $u_1(x) = \log x$, $u_2(x) = u(x)$. It gives (ii) when $r_1(x) = r(x)$, $r_2(x) = c/x$, $c > 1$, $u_1(x) = u(x)$, $u_2(x) = -x^{1-c}$.

This section is not intended to summarize Arrow's work,[4] but only to indicate its relation to the present paper. The main points of overlap are that Arrow introduces essentially the functions r and r^* (actually their negatives) and uses them in significant ways, in particular those mentioned already, and that he introduces essentially $p^*(x, h)$, proves an equation like (46) in order to interpret decreasing r^*, and mentions the possibility of a similar analysis for r.

4. INVESTMENT DECISION UNDER UNCERTAINTY: CHOICE— THEORETIC APPROACHES*

J. HIRSHLEIFER

Reprinted by permission of the author and publishers from *The Quarterly Journal of Economics,* Vol. LXXIX, No. 4 (November 1965), pp. 509–536 (Cambridge, Mass.: Harvard University Press, Copyright 1965 by the President and Fellows of Harvard College).

Investment is, in essence, *present* sacrifice for *future* benefit. But the present is relatively well known, whereas the future is always an enigma. Investment is also, therefore, *certain* sacrifice for *uncertain* benefit. The theory of investment decision has been satisfactorily developed, in the great work of Irving Fisher,[1] only under the artificial assumption of certainty.[2] Despite the restrictiveness of this assumption, Fisher's theory does succeed in explaining substantial portions of observed investment behavior.[3] But other portions cannot apparently be explained without bringing in attitudes toward risk and differences of opinion, sources of behavior that only come into existence under uncertainty. Among the phenomena left unexplained under the certainty assumption are: the value attached to "liquidity," the willingness to buy insurance, the existence of debt and equity financing, and the bewildering variety of returns or yields on various forms of investment simultaneously ruling in the market.

---

* The editors have numbered all footnotes of this article consecutively although they are not presented that way in the original article. To aid in identification with the original article, at the end of each footnote, beginning with number 10, the editors have indicated in parenthesis the original footnote designation and the page on which it appears in the original article.

[1] Irving Fisher, *The Theory of Interest* (New York: Macmillan, 1930; reprinted, Augustus M. Kelley, 1961). Fisher's earlier work, *The Rate of Interest* (New York: Macmillan, 1907), is also important.

[2] Fisher takes account of uncertainty in his "third approximation" to the theory of interest. Significantly, Chap. 14 of *The Theory of Interest* is entitled: "The Third Approximation Unadapted to Mathematical Formulation."

[3] *Theory of Interest, op. cit.,* Chaps. 18–19.

The object of this paper is to develop, and show some of the implications of, a treatment of risky or uncertain choice that is a generalization of Fischer's theory of riskless choice over time (itself a generalization of the standard theory of timeless choice). In the section immediately following I provide an interpretation of Fisher's theory designed (a) to examine its character as a model of *choice-theoretic structure*, and (b) to introduce the *firm* as a decision-making unit, where Fisher treated only of atomic individuals. The next sections review alternative lines of approach to the theory of riskv choice, showing how they diverge in specification of the *choice-objects* of individuals. The major analytical sections then follow, developing a theory of uncertain choice over time in terms of comparisons between consumption possibilities in different possible dated contingencies or "states of the world." A successor article[4] will apply this "time-state-preference" approach to several normative and positive issues: (1) risk aversion and the coexistence of gambling and insurance; (2) the Modigliani-Miller problem concerning the existence or nonexistence of an optimum corporate financial structure (debt-equity mix); and (3) the discount rate to be employed in evaluating public investment projects not subject to the market test.

I. FISHER'S THEORY OF INVESTMENT DECISION: INTERPRETATION AND REFORMULATION

Only a brief exposition of Fisher's theory will be provided here, as a prelude to the introduction of the firm as an economic agent into Fisher's system. The concepts and terms of Fisher's presentation will be somewhat modified to suit my purposes. To avoid needless complications, the explicit presentation will be limited to two-period comparisons between the present (time "0") and the future (time "1").

In Fisher's system the primitive concept, in terms of which all others are defined, is *consumption*. The objects of choice are present consumption (c_0) and future consumption (c_1). The *time-preference* function for the j-th individual may be denoted $U^j = g^j(c_0^j, c_1^j), = 1, 2, \ldots, J$. Each individual attempts to maximize utility within his *opportunity set*. It is useful to distinguish three different categories within the opportunity set: endowment, financial opportunities, and productive opportunities. The endowment $Y^j = (y_0^j, y_1^j)$ is the individual's initial position (see Figure I); it provides a base point for the analysis of investment as a redistribution of consumption opportunities over time. The endowment element y_0 may be interpreted as *current income* and y_1 correspondingly as *future income*. The justification for this interpretation (which departs from Fisher's terminology, but is consistent with the spirit of his analysis) is that y_0 is the amount that can be consumed

[4] "Investment Decision Under Uncertainty: Applications of the State-Preference Approach," forthcoming in this *Journal*.

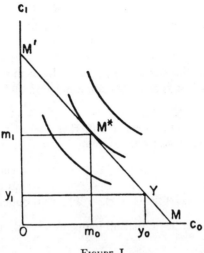

FIGURE I

without trenching on future consumptive possibilities.[5] We then define investment $i_0 = y_0 - c_0$, negative values of investment being possible.[6]

Financial opportunities for investment permit transormation of the endowment into alternative (c_0, c_1) combinations, but only by trading with other individuals. In such trading, motivated by disparities between endowed or attained income-sequences and desired time-patterns of consumption, a rate of exchange between units of present consumption (present dollars) and of future consumption (future dollars) would be established in the market. This rate of exchange can be expressed as $(dc_1)/(dc_0) = -(1 + r)$, where r is the *rate of interest*, or premium on current dollars. In Figure I the financial opportunities facing the investor are shown by the "market line" MM'

---

[5] "Income" is a troublesome concept. Fisher attempted to dispose of it by defining income as identical with consumption; this is unsatisfactory, since one cannot avoid distinguishing *actual* and *potential* consumption. Income is a potential-consumption concept: in principle, it is what can be consumed in the current period without impairing future income or consumption. But this statement of principle leaves open a number of possible interpretations. For accounting or tax purposes, a *net* concept of income is ordinarily adopted: the gross yield of any income source in the current period is reduced by allowance for "depreciation of capital." Depreciation represents the amount which, if reinvested, would replenish the income source so as to permit maintenance of the net income to the time-horizon envisaged—under the ordinary assumption of an infinite horizon, this is equivalent to maintaining capital value intact. The analytical inconvenience of this concept, for our purposes, is that depreciation (and therefore net income) cannot in general be calculated independently of the rate of interest—which is what we seek to explain. For this reason the income concept used here is *gross* income: for any time-period, this is the corresponding element of the gross yield sequence (the endowment) itself, without any accounting adjustments. This interpretation qualifies as a potential-consumption concept; it is what can be consumed without borrowing, or (equivalently) without trenching on the future-consumption elements of the endowment itself.

[6] This is a *gross* rather than a *net* investment concept (see footnote above).

through Y. Along this market line *wealth* $W = c_0 + c_1/(1 = r)$ equals $y_0 + y_1/(1 + r)$, a constant, so that the market line is a budget or wealth constraint. The time-preference optimum for the individual under pure exchange (financial opportunities only) is M^*, and at the interest rate r he seeks to invest (lend) the amount $(y_0 - m_0)$. Under pure exchange the social totals of present and of future consumption, $\sum_j y_0^j$ and $\sum_j y_1^j$ are conserved, while the social total of investment is zero (for each borrower there is a lender). This condition determines the market interest rate r.

The basic equations under pure exchange may be represented as follows:

(1) $U^j = g^j(c_0^j, c_1^j)$

Time-preference function

wealth constraint, or

(2) $c_0^j + c_1^j/(1 + r) = y_0^j + y_1^j/(1 + r)$ financial opportunities.

These equations also indicate that all loans are repaid.

(3) $\dfrac{dc_1^j}{dc_0^j}\bigg|_{U^j} = -(1 + r)$ Time-preference optimum

The symbol on the left represents the marginal rate of substitution of c_1 for c_0 that leaves utility constant—the marginal rate of time preference. Note that this is equated for all individuals (if we rule out corner solutions).

$$
\left.\begin{aligned}
\sum_{j=1}^{J} c_0^j &= \sum_{j=1}^{J} y_0^j \\
\sum_{j=1}^{J} c_1^j &= \sum_{j=1}^{J} y_1^j
\end{aligned}\right\}
$$

(4)   Conservation equations[7]

These market-clearing equations also indicate that the social total of investment, $\sum(y_0 - c_0)$ is zero, as required for the case of pure exchange.

If the opportunity set also contains *productive opportunities*, then it is possible to engage in transactions with nature (e.g., planting a seed), as well as with other individuals. Under such circumstances, in Fisher's system the individual investor attains his utility optimum at X^* (in Figure II) by a two-step procedure. First, he moves from his endowment Y along his productive opportunity locus PP' (note that his opportunities are ordered according to diminishing marginal productivity of investment) to his productive optimum P^*. The productive optimum is characterized by attainment of the highest possible market line—that is, highest wealth level. The productive investor can then "finance" by borrowing, if need be, to attain his utility optimum X^*. In Figure II, his productive investment is $(y_0 - p_0)$, and he borrows $(x_0 - p_0)$ to replenish current consumption. It is the transaction with nature that creates wealth; the associated financial transfers leave wealth unchanged.

---

[7] One of the conservation equations can be shown to follow from the remainder of the system.

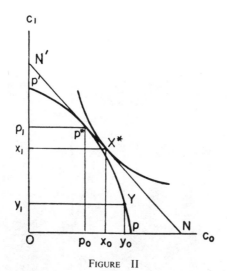

FIGURE II

In the equations allowing productive opportunities, the elements (p_0, p_1) of the "productive solution" P^* appear as variables:

(1')	$U^j = g^j(c_0^j, c_1^j)$	Time-preference function
		wealth constraint, or
(2')	$c_0^j + c_1^j/(1 + r) = p_0^j + p_1^j/(1 + r)$	financial opportunities.

The wealth level attained by productive transformations, rather than the endowment wealth level, becomes the financial constraint.

(3')	$\left.\dfrac{dc_1^j}{dc_0^j}\right|_{U^j} = -(1 + r)$	Time-preference optimum
(4')	$p^j(p_0^j, p_1^j; y_0^j, y_1^j) = 0$	Productive opportunity set
(5')	$\dfrac{dp_1^j}{dp_0^j} = -(1 + r)$	Productive optimum

This condition also represents attainment of maximum wealth or "present value."[8]

$$
(6') \quad \left.
\begin{array}{l}
\sum\limits_{j=1}^{J} c_0^j = \sum\limits_{j=1}^{J} p_0^j \\[2mm]
\sum\limits_{j=1}^{J} c_1^j = \sum\limits_{j=1}^{J} p_1^j
\end{array}
\right\} \qquad \text{Conservation equations}
$$

[8] In more general cases, where the productive opportunity locus need not have the simple concavity properties of Figure II (because of lumpiness or interdependence among investments), the tangency condition of equation (5') is insufficient to determine the optimum. The more general maximum-wealth condition permits selection among multiple local maxima, whether tangencies or corner solutions. See J. Hirshleifer, "On the Theory of Optimal Investment Decision," *Journal of Political Economy*, *LXVI* (Aug. 1958), reprinted in E. Solomon (ed.), *The Management of Corporate Capital* (Glencoe, Ill.: Free Press, 1959).

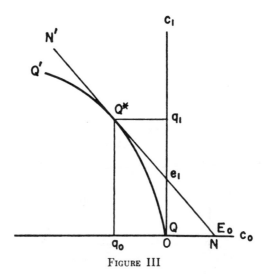

FIGURE III

These market-clearing equations make the interest rate depend upon the productive as well as the consumptive supply and demand for funds. The social total of current investment

$$\sum_{j=1}^{J} i_0^j = \sum_{j=1}^{J} (y_0^j - p_0^j).$$

We may now introduce firms as the specialized agencies of individuals in their time-productive capacities. We specify: (a) firms do not consume; (b) firms have null endowments; and (c) all productive opportunities appertain to firms. Let there be F firms, and let o_f^j be the fraction of the f-th firm owned by the j-th individual. The o_f^j here are constants, such that $\sum_{j=1}^{J} o_f^j = 1$; for $f = 1; 2; \ldots, F$. The equilibrium of the firm (see Figure III) is the productive solution Q^* where the highest market line NN' is attained; this represents maximum wealth for the firm, and so for the owners. The firm, having null endowment, must borrow q_0, an amount equal to the productive investment. It repays lenders $-q_0(1 + r) = q_1 - e_1$ (see Figure III). The firm income e_1^f is distributed to the owners as an increment to their endowments y_1^j.[9]

With the introduction of firms, the equation system may be represented:

(1″) $U^j = g^j(c_0^j, c_1^j)$ Time-preference function

(2″) $c_0^j + c_1^j/(1 + r) =$

$y_0^j + \left(y_1^j + \sum_{f=1}^{F} o_f^j e_1^f\right)/(1 + r)$ Wealth constraint.

[9] Alternatively, in a world of certainty the firm's payout could be in current funds c_0. That is, the firm could immediately distribute to owners the amount E_0, the present value of the future net income e_1.

On this interpretation, the firms use no "equity" funds. In a world of certainty, full-debt financing is possible. However, the effect of profitable investment is an increment e_1^f to equity (wealth of owners) in time "1".

(3″) $\left.\dfrac{dc_1^j}{dc_0^j}\right|_{U^j} = -(1 + r)$ Time-preference optimum

(4″) $q^f(q_0^f, q_1^f) = 0$ Productive opportunity set

(5″) $\dfrac{dq_1^f}{dq_0^f} = -(1 + r)$ Productive optimum

The productive decisions are all made by the firms.

(6″) $q_1^f = -q_0^f(1 + r) + e_1^f$ Firm's Financial Distributions

Since the firm does not consume, it must distribute its productive gross earnings, q_1. This amount is divided between repayment of debt and equity income to owners.

(7″) $\left.\begin{aligned}\sum_{j=1}^{J} y_0^j + \sum_{f=1}^{F} q_0^f = \sum_{j=1}^{J} c_0^j \\[2mm] \sum_{j=1}^{J} y_1^j + \sum_{f=1}^{F} q_1^f = \sum_{j=1}^{J} c_1^j\end{aligned}\right\}$ Conservation equations

Note that $\sum_{j=1}^{J} p_0^j$ in (6′) of the previous formulation becomes $\sum_{j=1}^{J} y_0^j + \sum_{f=1}^{F} q_0^f$ here, and similarly $\sum p_1^j$ becomes $\sum y_1^j + \sum q_1^f$.

An alternative form of the wealth or financial constraints is also useful. Let P_0 be the price of c_0, and P_1 the price of c_1. If c_0 is taken as numeraire we have $P_0 = 1$ and $P_1 = 1/(1 + r)$. Then:

Equation (2) becomes: $P_0 c_0 + P_1 c_1 = P_0 y_0 + P_1 y_1$.

Equation (2′) becomes: $P_0 c_0 + P_1 c_1 = P_0 p_0 + P_1 p_1$.

Equation (2″) becomes: $P_0 c_0 + P_1 c_1 = P_0 y_0 + P_1 y_1 + P_1 \left[\sum_{f=1}^{F} (o_f e_1^f) \right]$.

And, after dividing through by $(1 + r)$, equation (6″) becomes:

(6‴) $P_1 q_1 = -P_0 q_0 + P_1 e_1$.

This can be given the interpretation: the "wealth of the firm" (i.e., the present worth of the firm's gross or productive income q_1) is the sum of the values of the debt and equity—the sum of the borrowings and the increment to wealth of the owners.[10]

---

[10] This looks very much like the famous "Proposition I" in F. Modigliani and M. H. Miller, "The Cost of Capital, Corporation Finance and the Theory of Investment," *American Economic Review*, XLVIII (June, 1958), 268. Of course, that the Modigliani-Miller theorem holds under conditions of certainty is not surprising; in the successor to this article it will be proved that the theorem continues to hold even under some forms of uncertainty. (1, p. 516).

II. CHOICE-THEORETIC APPROACHES TO INVESTMENT DECISION UNDER UNCERTAINTY

While Fisher's model is a special application to the problem of investment decision under certainty, it can also be regarded as an archetype of choice-theoretic system for any decision problem. By "choice-theoretic system" I will mean a model containing the following features: (1) objects of choice (commodities), and decision-making units (economic agents); (2) a preference function ordering such objects, for each economic agent; (3) an opportunity set, again for each agent, which is equivalent to specifying the constraints upon the agent's range of choice; and (4) balancing or conservation equations, which specify the social interactions among the individual decisions. The competing approaches to investment decision considered in this section diverge in their specification of the basic objects of choice.

Investment decision under uncertainty involves purchase of *assets*—more or less complex claims or titles to present and future incomes. The most direct theoretical formulation of this decision is the *Asset-preference Approach*; this postulates that assets themselves are the desired objects of choice. On the theoretical level, comparisons usually run in terms of exchanges between a riskless asset and one or more risky assets (or lotteries) with arbitrary but specified probability distributions.[11] The main appeal of this approach is the attractiveness of the direct analogy between assets in investment theory and the commodities of ordinary price theory. The central disadvantage of the approach is that assets are clearly not the elemental desired objects; what we would like to do analytically would be to show how the prices of assets are determined by the valuations placed by individuals upon the underlying income opportunities to which the assets represent claims. In other words, what we really are seeking is a means of resolving assets into more fundamental choice-objects. A second difficulty, which will reappear below in connection with each of the alternative formulations for the objects of choice, is that the total of the various types of assets cannot be assumed fixed, even under pure exchange. Thus, an individual owning a real asset can issue claims against the security of his original asset—i.e., he can "finance" his holdings of assets, and in doing so has a wide variety of options ("debt-equity mix"). But each such action generates a more or less complex pattern of new "financial" assets which can substitute for productive assets in the portfolios of investors. It is clear, therefore, that conservation relations do not hold in any simple way when the objects of choice are taken to be assets.

The approach currently most popular in the analysis of investment decision under uncertainty postulates that the fundamental objects of choice, standing behind the particularities of individual assets, are the *mean* and the *variability* of future return—where variability refers to probabilistic rather

[11] An asset-preference approach is adopted in my paper, "Risk, the Discount Rate, and Investment Decisions," *American Economic Review*, LI (May 1961). A much more complete working out of this approach was independently developed by Gordon B. Pye in his 1963 M.I.T. Ph.D. thesis, "Investment Rules for Corporations." (2, p. 517)

than chronological fluctuation. This *Mean, Variability Approach*, to be critically analyzed in the next section, reduces assets (or portfolios of assets) to underlying mean and variability measures which, it is postulated, enter into investors' preference functions. An alternative reduction will be developed next, under the heading of *State-preference Approach*. Here the underlying objects of choice are postulated to be contingent consumption opportunities or claims defined over a complete listing of all possible " states of the world." It will be shown that this latter approach can easily be developed into a choice-theoretic system that represents a natural extension of Fisher's into the domain of uncertainty.

III. THE MEAN, VARIABILITY APPROACH

The mean, variability approach to investment decision under uncertainty selects as the objects of choice *expected returns* and *variability of returns* from investments.[12] In accordance with the common beliefs of observers of

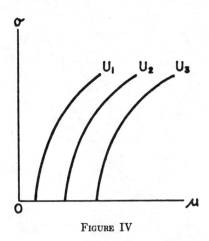

FIGURE IV

financial markets, the assumption is made that investors desire high values of the former and low values of the latter—as usually measured by the mean (μ) and standard deviation (σ), respectively, of the probability distri-

[12] The most complete development of this viewpoint is in H. M. Markowitz, *Portfolio Selection* (New York: Wiley, 1959). The earliest conception is apparently that of Fisher in *The Nature of Capital and Income* (New York: Macmillan, 1912). Other important contributions are J. R. Hicks, "A Suggestion for Simplifying the Theory of Money," *Economica*, N.S., II (Feb. 1935); J. Marschak, "Money and the Theory of Assets," *Econometrica*, VI (Oct. 1938); and James Tobin, "Liquidity Preference as Behavior Towards Risk," *Review of Economic Studies*, XXV (Feb. 1958). A convenient condensed formulation will be found in D. E. Farrar, *The Investment Decision Under Uncertainty* (Englewood Cliffs, N.J.: Prentice-Hall, 1962). An important recent contribution, breaking into entirely new ground, is William F. Sharpe, "Capital Asset Prices: A Theory of Market Equilibrium under Conditions of Risk," *Journal of Finance*, XIX (Sept. 1964). (3, p. 518)

bution of returns—and show increasing aversion to σ as risk increases. Under these assumptions a preference function can be shown as in Figure IV ordering all possible (μ, σ) combinations.

Theorists following the mean, variability approach have concentrated upon the problem of portfolios, i.e., holdings of financial assets (securities). Little or no attention has been paid to productive assets or investments. Also, the usual portfolio analysis keeps constant the amount of current investment and concerns itself only with the distribution of that amount over the available securities. Neither restriction is, however, essential. The same approach could be extended, on the level of the individual investor, to include real productive investments in addition to a financial portfolio,[13] and a simultaneous solution could be provided for the amount of investment together with the choice of securities to be held.

For our purposes, it will suffice to present only the broad outlines of the mean, variability formulation. Turning first to the opportunity set, and letting X be the random variable of prospective gross portfolio value[14] consequent

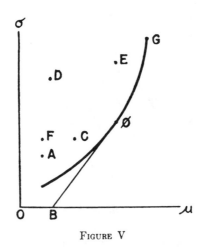

FIGURE V

upon given current investment, the possible combinations of $\mu(X)$ and $\sigma(X)$ attainable by holding individual securities (i.e., combinations attainable in one-security portfolios) are suggested by the typical points B, C, D, etc., in Figure V. The point B is on the horizontal axis; it is intended to represent investment in riskless bonds. The solid curve shows the efficient frontier (minimum σ attainable for each possible value of μ) when the investor does

[13] Although, as indicated above, such an extension would involve some difficulties in specifying conservation relations when both productive and financial assets are considered. (4, p. 519)

[14] Since a portfolio is a collection of assets, the gross value X cannot be negative. (5, p. 519)

not have the riskless opportunity B available. In general, one-security port-folios are not on the efficient frontier, because of the advantage of diversi-fication: the over-all μ for any mixed portfolio will be the weighted average of the component μ_i values for the individual securities, but the over-all σ will in general be lower than the corresponding average of the σ_i.[15] However, the security G, whose expected future value is greater than any other security's, is an efficient one-security portfolio. This suggests why the efficient frontier is convex to the right: as we move to higher and higher portfolio μ, we are forced to concentrate increasingly on the small number of high-μ_i securities, thus progressively reducing the power of diversification. The introduction of the riskless security B, with mean future value μ_B, changes the opportunity set to incorporate the area bounded by the line through B and tangent at ϕ to the efficient frontier constructed from the risky securities.[16]

The preference function has been the focus of attention in controversial discussion of the mean, variability approach. There have been attempts to derive indifference maps like that portrayed in Figure IV from the Neumann-Morgenstern axioms of rational choice—together with a specification of a concave-downward utility-of-income $v(X)$ function like that shown in Figure VI. The latter shape is necessary in order to obtain risk aversion (positive-sloping U-curves in Figure IV).[17] (Whether observed behavior can be re-garded as reflecting risk aversion rather than risk preference, or some mixture of the two, is a subject of disagreement that will be considered in the succes-sor article alluded to earlier.) Here v is the Neumann-Morgenstern utility indicator that permits use of the expected-utility theorem in rationalizing

[15] Let X be the future value of the over-all portfolio, x_i the future value of the i-th security, a_i the fraction of the fixed original investment held in the i-th security, and n the number of securities. Then:

(a) $\quad X = \sum_{i=1}^{n} a_i x_i$

(b) $\quad \mu = E(X) = \sum_{i=1}^{n} a_i \mu_i$

(c) $\quad \sigma = \left[\sum_{i=1}^{n} a_i^2 \sigma_i^2 + 2 \sum_{i=1}^{n} \sum_{j=1}^{i=1} a_i \sigma_i \sigma_j \right]^{1/2}$

Here σ_{ij} is the covariance of the i-th and the j-th security.

There are two important exceptions to the statement that σ will be lower than the average of the σ_i: (1) if all the securities are perfectly correlated (each $\sigma_{ij} = \sigma_i \sigma_j$), or (2) if one secu-rity of a two-security portfolio has zero σ_i, from which it follows that covariance also equals zero. In either of these cases, $\sigma = \sum_{i=1}^{n} a_i \sigma_i$. (6, p. 520)

[16] The portfolio μ and σ represented by combinations of B and the "security" ϕ (itself generally a combination of securities) plot along a straight line because σ_B and therefore $\sigma_{B\phi}$ equal zero (see footnote above). (7, p. 520)

[17] See M. Friedman and L. J. Savage, "The Utility Analysis of Choices Involving Risk," *Journal of Political Economy*, LVI (Aug. 1948). Reprinted in American Economic Associa-tion, *Readings in Price Theory* (Homewood, Ill.: Irwin, 1952). Page references to the latter volume. (8, p. 520)

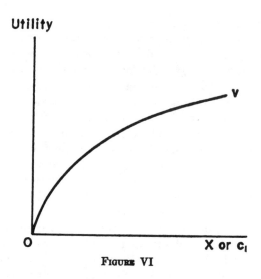

Utility

V

O   X or c_i

FIGURE VI

choice under uncertainty, and the argument X is really consumption income in the future period. It has been shown that a μ, σ indifference map can be derived (i.e., that each indifference curve represents a locus of constant expected utility-of-income) only if one of the following conditions obtains: (a) the utility-of-income function v is quadratic, or (b) in considering alternative portfolios, the investor's probability distributions for X under the various portfolios considered are all members of a two-parameter family.[18]

It is clear that a quadratic utility-of-income function is unacceptable. To make $v(X)$ concave downward with such a function, the coefficient of the squared term must be negative—but in this case a point must be reached where additional income decreases utility! Furthermore, we cannot accept the quadratic even as an approximation, however well it may fit in the neighborhood of the mean return $\mu(X)$, because we are dealing with risky portfolios that require us to evaluate the utility of values for the random variable X diverging considerably from the mean.

One's first impression is that the second condition should be much more widely applicable. In particular, if (on the efficient frontier, at least) all portfolios consist of relatively large numbers of securities, the Central Limit Theorem indicates that the probability distributions for the returns X under any such "well-diversified" portfolio will approach normality—and, of course, the normal distribution is two-parameter. Nevertheless, this does not really help us, though to explain why will require an illustration anticipating the main ideas of the next section. Let us suppose that an investor contemplates the uncertain future as the set of three equally probable "states of the world" A, B, and C—one and only one of which will actually obtain. A "state" here is a complete world-environment for the individual. For two

[18] Tobin, *loc. cit.*, pp. 74–77. (9, p. 521)

different portfolios, the distribution of future values over these states (X_A, X_B, X_C), might be (3, 2, 1) and (1, 2, 3) respectively. Since these two distributions or "prospects" have the same μ and σ, they would have to be identical in preference ordering in order for it to be possible to construct a preference map on μ, σ axes. But we have no right to assume that an investor would be indifferent between the two prospects. The nature of the world-environments A, B, and C might be such that he prefers the distribution biased toward wealth in state A over that biased toward wealth in state C. Here the *ordering* on A, B, and C of the elements of the distribution cannot be neglected; a distribution that is two-parameter disregarding ordering turns out to be insufficiently specified, for preference ranking purposes, by the mean and standard deviation.

One element of the choice-theoretic structure under the mean, variability approach has not received the attention it deserves: the role of conservation relations. Waiving the difficulties turning upon the existence and shape of μ, σ preference functions, and accepting the efficient frontier as defining the useful limits of the opportunity set, the individual will presumably attain a tangency solution. Note in Figure V that there are two main classes of solutions: mixtures of riskless bonds and risky assets in the range $B\phi$, and portfolios excluding riskless bonds in the range ϕG.[19] But this is only an individual solution, not a market solution. The analytical system requires a specification of the social interactions that determine a set of asset prices P_i, which in turn modify the μ_i, σ_i, and σ_{ij} of the various securities until finally an equilibrium is reached.

In equations (4) describing Fisher's system, the social interaction takes the form of conservation equations fixing the social totals of the various objects of choice. Sharpe, apparently the first to realize the need for completion of the mean, variability theoretic structure, employed a formulation fixing the social totals of the various *securities* available. He has succeeded in deriving a number of theorems, based essentially upon the consideration that in equilibrium security prices P_i must be such as to permit the existing totals of securities to be exactly held in terms of the summation of the individuals' tangency solutions. These results are important, but they cannot be regarded as a final completion of the choice-theoretic system.[20] The reason is that securities are artificial commodities or objects of choice. Without changing the underlying real investment yields, alternative patterns of securities can be

---

[19] Sharpe (*loc. cit.*) extends the line $B\phi$ beyond the point ϕ, arguing that the extension represents negative amounts of the asset B, or "selling B short" to hold more of the μ, σ combination represented by ϕ. But this amounts to the investor issuing a new bond to "finance" his asset-holdings—which is inconsistent with the spirit of Sharpe's analysis that postulates fixed social totals of each class of risky and riskless assets. (If the analysis were to permit the investor to issue new bonds, it should also permit him to issue new risky securities as well.) (1, p. 522)

[20] They are analogous to the results derived in ordinary price theory in the so-called "very short run" where, with fixed supplies, demand alone governs price. (2, p. 523)

generated as claims to these real yields. On the individual or firm level, the question of the optimal pattern of securities to issue against one's assets— which latter may be real assets, or may themselves be securities one step or more removed from the ultimate real assets—is known in capital-budgeting literature as the "financing" problem, or in the simplest case as the problem of the "debt-equity mix." To complete the system fully under pure exchange, analysis must go beyond the principles on which individuals decide both to hold assets and to finance asset-holdings, to the social interactions that determine the equilibrium set of financial securities issued by all individuals together as the set of claims to the underlying real assets of the community. Presumably, these interactions will be governed by the μ and σ represented by the given real assets. And, when production is introduced, the real assets themselves can no longer be held constant, and analysis must go back to the forces determining the balance between μ and σ in the real investments undertaken. We are thus still a considerable distance from a market theory of the risk premium under the mean, variability approach.

IV. THE STATE-PREFERENCE APPROACH

The approach to investment decision under uncertainty that begins by postulating the objects of choice to be contingent consumption opportunities, in alternative possible states of the world, is comparatively unfamiliar.[21] But it has great advantages. There is a close formal analogy with Fisher's model for riskless choice over time; in fact, the state-and-time-preference choice-theoretic model is a natural generalization of Fisher's system. The approach leads, we shall see, to important theorems concerning investment and financing decisions.

In the interest of minimizing complications, it will be assumed that there is only one present state; i.e., there is certainty as to the present (time "0"). The future is represented by a point in time (time "1"), in which there are two alternative "states of the world" (state a or state b must obtain). The two states might be thought of as war versus peace, or prosperity versus depression. Two-state uncertainty is, of course, a very radical oversimplification, adopted here for purposes of presentation only. In the two-period *certainty* case we needed to consider only the single type of exchange between present and future consumption, c_0 and c_1. But now there are three objects of choice: c_0, c_{1a}, and c_{1b}. We may think of two dimensions of choice: the contemporaneous balance of risky claims between c_{1a} and c_{1b} (Figure VII), and the time-plus-risk exchange between a present certain c_0 and a future uncertain c_{1b} or

[21] The pioneering work here is Kenneth J. Arrow, "Le Rôle des Valeurs Boursières pour la Répartition la Meilleure des Risques," *International Colloquium on Econometrics*, 1952, Centre National de la Recherche Scientifique (Paris, 1953). An English version appeared under the title "The Role of Securities in the Optimal Allocation of Risk-bearing," *Review of Economic Studies*, XXXI (April 1964). See also G. Debreu, *Theory of Value* (New York: Wiley, 1959), Chap. 7, and J. Hirshleifer, "Efficient Allocation of Capital in an Uncertain World," *American Economic Review*, LIV (May 1964), 77–85. (3, p. 523)

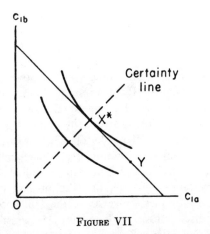

FIGURE VII

c_{1a} (Figure VIII portrays the choice between c_0 and c_{1b}). We will consider here situations of pure exchange, deferring the problems introduced by the existence of productive opportunities.

Under the conditions of Figure VII, the amount of c_0 is implicitly fixed so that we can deal with simple exchange between contemporaneous risky claims. The 45° line through the origin represents points along which $c_{1a} = c_{1b}$, so that the amount c_1 is sure to be received—this is the "certainty line." The figure portrays the preference function for an individual attaching subjective probabilities $\pi_a = \pi_b = 1/2$ to the two possible states.

The convex indifference curves shown in Figure VII can be justified on several levels. General observation of behavior probably suffices to convince us that almost no one is so reckless to prefer, if $\pi_a = \pi_b = 1/2$, the prospect $(c_{1a}, c_{1b}) = (1000, 0)$ to a prospect like (500, 500). (It must be understood that the statement $c_{1b} = 0$ does not mean merely a possibly tolerable loss of a

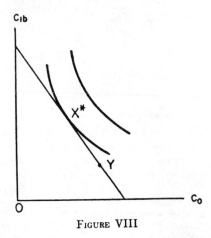

FIGURE VIII

gamble, but an actual zero consumption level—starvation—if state b should occur.) Thus, even the very mild degree of conservatism, implicit in observed "nonspecialization" among claims to consumption in alternative states of the world, requires convex utility isoquants.[22]

Interesting questions arise concerning the interpretation of the convex preference function in Figure VII in terms of subjective probabilities and Neumann-Morgenstern utilities. Let a Neumann-Morgenstern function $v(c_1)$ be postulated, concave downward as in Figure VI, and assume that this function can be applied to the risky choice between c_{1a} and c_{1b}. This special assumption says that the function $v(c_1)$ is independent of the state—the world-environment—that obtains; it will be called the "uniqueness" assumption. Then concavity of $v(c_1)$, or "diminishing marginal utility of (consumption) income," implies convexity of the utility isoquants in Figure VII. The converse also holds, so Neumann-Morgenstern risk aversion is implied by nonspecialization of risky choice. (Convexity is more general than diminishing marginal utility, in that convexity at a particular (c_{1a}, c_{1b}) point does not necessarily imply diminishing marginal utility at c_{1a} and c_{1b}— but convexity *everywhere* requires diminishing marginal utility.)[23] In the

---

[22] The statement above is correct provided that the choice is between simple convex and simple concave curvature. Other, more complex, shapes would also be consistent with the observation. (4, p. 525)

[23] Convexity requires $(d^2c_{1b})/(dc_{1a}^2) > 0$. Under the Neumann-Morgenstern postulates, it is possible to attribute a utility function $v(c_1)$ to "income" (here, to consumption) such that the utility of a risky prospect equals the expectation of the v's attached to the elements of the prospect. Then $U(c_{1a}, c_{1b}; \pi_a, \pi_b) = \pi_a v(c_{1a}) + \pi_b v(c_{1b})$, or, simplifying notation:

$$= \pi_a v_{1a} + \pi_b v_{1b}$$

$$\frac{dc_{1b}}{dc_{1a}}\bigg|_U = -\frac{\partial U/\partial c_{1a}}{\partial U/\partial c_{1b}} = -\frac{\pi_a v'_{1a}}{\pi_b v'_{1b}}$$

$$\frac{d^2 c_{1b}}{dc^2_{1a}} = \frac{d}{dc_{1a}}\left(\frac{dc_{1b}}{dc_{1a}}\right) = \frac{\partial}{\partial c_{1a}}\left(\frac{dc_{1b}}{dc_{1a}}\right) + \frac{\partial}{\partial c_{1b}}\left(\frac{dc_{1b}}{dc_{1a}}\right) \cdot \frac{dc_{1b}}{dc_{1a}}$$

$$= -\frac{\pi_a v''_{1a}}{\pi_b v'_{1b}} + \frac{\pi_a v'_{1a} v''_{1b}}{\pi_b (v'_{1b})^2}\left(-\frac{\pi_a v'_{1a}}{\pi_b v'_{1b}}\right)$$

$$= -\frac{\pi_a v''_{1a}}{\pi_b v'_{1b}} - \frac{\pi_a^2 (v'_{1a})^2 v''_{1b}}{\pi_b^2 (v'_{1b})^2}$$

It should be noted that $\dfrac{\partial v'_{1b}}{\partial c_{1a}} = \dfrac{\partial v'_{1a}}{\partial c_{1b}} = 0$.

That is, the slope of the "utility-of-income" curve for state b is independent of the amount scheduled for consumption in state a, and vice versa. This follows from the Neumann-Morgenstern "independence" or "substitutability" postulate (R. D. Luce and H. Raiffa, *Games and Decisions* (New York: Wiley, 1957), p. 27). Since $\pi_a, \pi_b, v'_{1a}, v'_{1b} > 0$, diminishing marginal utility ($v''_{1a} < 0$ and $v''_{1b} < 0$) is sufficient for convexity but is not a necessary condition for convexity at (c_{1a}, c_{1b}); a sufficiently negative v''_{1a} may outweigh a positive v''_{1b}, or vice versa. But in this latter case it will be possible to find risky prospects for which v''_{1a} and v''_{1b} are both positive, so that convexity would not hold everywhere. (5, p. 526)

special case where $\pi_a = \pi_b = 1/2$, and holding to the uniqueness assumption so that the single function $v(c_1)$ is applicable to consumption in state a or state b, concavity of $v(c_1)$ implies not merely convex indifference curves in Figure VII but indifference curves symmetrical about the 45° certainty line. For, with a single $v(c_1)$ function, utility of any prospect $(y, x; 1/2, 1/2)$ would then be the same as that of the prospect $(x, y; 1/2, 1/2)$.

Under the simplified model investigated here, any commodity basket consists of time-state consumption elements c_0, c_{1a}, and c_{1b}. In particular, the endowment Y may be denoted (y_0, y_{1a}, y_{1b}). Since we are considering a pure-exchange situation, there are no productive opportunities. But financial opportunities exist for individuals to trade elements of their endowed combinations. In such trading each is constrained by his endowed wealth: $W = P_0 c_0 + P_{1a} c_{1a} + P_{1b} c_{1b}$. Here P_0, P_{1a}, and P_{1b} are the prices of the correspondingly subscribed time-state claims—the commodities of this model. The constant W is determined by $P_0 y_0 + P_{1a} y_{1a} + P_{1b} y_{1b}$, the present value of the endowment. Let c_0 be the numeraire, so that $P_0 = 1$. At this point we may generalize the concept of discount rate by defining the *time-and-state discount rates* r_{1a} and r_{1b} in terms of the prices of the corresponding time-state claims: $P_{1a} = 1/(1 + r_{1a})$ and $P_{1b} = 1/(1 + r_{1b})$. Note that these rates discount for both futurity and probability (or, rather, improbability). In the degenerate case of only one future state, the riskless rate, discounting for time only, is defined in $P_1 = 1/(1 + r_1)$.

In the special case where $\pi_a = \pi_b = 1/2$, and if the price of claims to c_{1a} happens to equal that of claims to c_{1b}, under the uniqueness assumption the wealth constraint and preference function for contemporaneous exchanges (i.e., given the amount of c_0) are as portrayed in Figure VII—the former is a 135° line, and the latter is symmetrical about the 45° certainty line. Then, the state-preference tangency optimum must be along the certainty line. More generally, given uniqueness of $v(c_1)$, if the price ratio P_{1b}/P_{1a} is equal to the probability ratio π_b/π_a, the optimum is along the certainty line.[24] This result corresponds to the well-known theorem that, if $v(c_1)$ is concave, a fair gamble will not be accepted.[25] (N.B., assuming the individual is already on the certainty line!)[26]

---

[24] The utility function is: $U = \pi_a v(c_{1a}) + \pi_b v(c_{1b})$. It is to be maximized subject to the constraint: $P_{1a} c_{1a} + P_{1b} c_{1b} = K$, a parameter equal to $W - c_0$. The condition resulting is:

$$\frac{P_{1b}}{P_{1a}} = \frac{\pi_b v'(c_{1b})}{\pi_a v'(c_{1a})}$$

The equality of price and probability ratios must hold along the certainty line, since there $c_{1b} = c_{1a}$. Convexity of the indifference curves assures that the condition cannot be met elsewhere. (6, p. 527)

[25] Friedman and Savage, *loc. cit.*, pp. 73 *ff*. (7, p. 527)

[26] If the individual is not on the certainty line, there may exist "gambles" that can move him toward that line. We call such gambles "insurance." Under the present assumptions fair insurance will be purchased. It is important to note that, depending on the endowed or attained position, the same contractual arrangement could be a risk-increasing gamble for

The final elements in the choice system are the conservation equations. These take on almost trivially simple forms: in each separate time-state, the total social endowment must be conserved (under pure exchange).

The entire time-and-state choice-theoretic system, for the special case of pure exchange with a single present state and two future states, and excluding generation of "financial" assets, may be summarized in the equations below:

(8) $U^j = g(c_0^j, c_{1a}^j, c_{1b}^j; \pi_a^j, \pi_b^j)$ Time-and-state Preference Function

This formulation emphasizes that utility depends upon the subjective probability estimates, π_a^j and π_b^j.[27]

(9) $c_0^j + \dfrac{c_{1a}^j}{1 + r_{1a}} + \dfrac{c_{1b}^j}{1 + r_{1b}} = y_0^j + \dfrac{y_{1a}^j}{1 + r_{1a}} + \dfrac{y_{1b}^j}{1 + r_{1b}}$ Wealth constraint

(10)
$$\left.\begin{array}{l} \dfrac{\partial c_{1a}^j}{\partial c_0^j}\Big|_{U^j} = -(1 + r_{1a}) \\[2ex] \dfrac{\partial c_{1b}^j}{\partial c_0^j}\Big|_{U^j} = -(1 + r_{1b}) \\[2ex] \dfrac{\partial c_{1b}^j}{\partial c_{1a}^j}\Big|_{U^j} = -\dfrac{1 + r_{1b}}{1 + r_{1a}} \end{array}\right\}$$
Optimum conditions

(11)
$$\left.\begin{array}{l} \sum c_0^j = \sum y_0^j \\[1ex] \sum c_{1a}^j = \sum y_{1a}^j \\[1ex] \sum c_{1b}^j = \sum y_{1b}^j \end{array}\right\}$$
Conservation equations

A numerical illustration may help provide an intuitive grasp of the above relationships. Imagine a simple economy consisting of 100 identically situated individuals with one consumption commodity ("corn"). Each individual has an endowment distributed as follows: 100 bushels of present corn (y_0),

---

one person and a risk-decreasing insurance for another. A very clear case exists in the futures market, where the same contract can be either a hedge or a speculation, depending upon the risk status of the purchaser. (8, p. 527)

[27] But note that the subjective probability estimates nowhere appear in the equations directly, so that up to this point the formulation does not require the existence of subjective probabilities. Actually, it is not necessary to go behind the preference function in this way. After specifying the time-state consumption claims as the basic objects of choice, we could assert convexity of indifference curves as a generalization of ordinary consumption theory. This is indeed the line pursued by Arrow and Debreu, and has the advantage of parsimony of assumptions. On the other hand, explicit introduction of probabilities does enable us to derive results (e.g., about fair gambles) not otherwise attainable. For discussions of the conditions permitting the simultaneous identification of subjective probabilities and numerical utilities, see L. J. Savage, *The Foundations of Statistics* (New York: Wiley, 1954) and Jacques Drèze, "Fondements Logiques de la Probabilité Subjective et de L'Utilité," *La Décision* (Centre National de la Recherche Scientifique, Paris, 1961). (9, p. 528)

and contingent claims to the future crop $y_{1a} = 150$ and $y_{1b} = 50$. Thus, the individual is entitled to 150 bushels if state a obtains, but only 50 bushels if state b obtains—only these two states, regarded as equally probable, being considered possible for the future crop. In a pure-exchange situation, it is impossible to change these endowments by planting seed, carry-over of crop, or "consumption of capital"; individuals can only modify their positions by trading. If, however, all individuals have identical preferences in addition to identical endowments and identical (null) productive opportunities, the markets must establish a set of prices such that each individual is satisfied to hold his original endowment. Let the numeraire $P_0 = 1$, and assume that with this time-state distribution there is on the margin for each individual zero time preference with respect to certainties. Thus, denoting the price of a certainty as P_1, where necessarily $P_1 = P_{1a} + P_{1b}$, we have $P_1 = 1$. To deal with the contemporaneous choices in time "1", it will be convenient to define a cardinal utility U_1 which assigns a numerical value to probabilistic combinations by the use of the expected-utility theorem and an underlying Neumann-Morgenstern utility-of-income function $v(c_1)$. Then $U_1 = 1/2v(c_{1a}) + 1/2v(c_{1b})$. For concreteness, we may use a logarithmic formulation: $v(c_1) = \ln c_1$. It may then be verified that the indifference curves are rectangular hyperbolas on axes as in Figure VII with slope $-c_{1b}/c_{1a}$, or at the endowment point $-1/3$. It follows that $P_{1a} = 1/4$, and $P_{1b} = 3/4$, at which prices everyone prefers to hold his endowment rather than exchange it for any alternative combination. Our numerical assumptions have implied discount rates $r_{1a} = 300$ per cent and $r_{1b} = 33\frac{1}{3}$ per cent.

It is often illuminating to introduce the concept of the riskless ("pure") interest rate, which we have denoted r_1. This would represent the marginal *time* preference alone. The relation defining the riskless discount rate in terms of the more basic time-and-risk exchanges is:

$$\frac{1}{1 + r_1} = \frac{1}{1 + r_{1a}} + \frac{1}{1 + r_{1b}}.$$

This follows immediately from $P_1 = P_{1a} + P_{1b}$—that is, the price of a riskless holding is simply the sum of the prices of a corresponding holding for each possible contingency. It would then be possible to reformulate the choice situation in terms of future risky and future riskless assets. The set of objects of choice, instead of (c_0, c_{1a}, c_{1b}) would be (c_0, c_1, c_{1x}), where c_1 is the lesser of c_{1a} and c_{1b}, and c_{1x} is the excess of the greater over the lesser of these two. This route leads toward the asset-preference approach alluded to earlier; its disadvantage lies in obscuring the state in which the risky asset pays off (that is, it will in general make a difference to an individual if a unit of c_{1x} represents a claim to time-state $1a$ or $1b$).

Waiving explicit introduction of productive opportunities, and generalizations to T times and S states, it is possible in a few sentences to sum up the main nature of the results yielded by the time-and-state-preference approach. The discount rates are determined by the interaction of individual attempts to move to preferred time-and-state consumption combinations by productive and financial transformations. The equilibrium rates will depend upon the composition of endowments among individuals, states, and times; the natures of the productive and financial opportunities; and the time-and-state preferences of individuals, these in turn being connected with their subjective probability estimates for the states. In the case of certainty the interest rate was determined by the interaction of endowments, time preferences, and time productivity. The additional elements entering under certainty are state endowments, state productivity, and state preferences. Probability opinions will enter into state preferences.

Corresponding to the theorem under certainty that all investors (barring corner solutions) adapt their subjective marginal rates of time preference to the market rate of interest is the following: each investor will adapt his marginal rate of time-and-state preference to the market discount rate for claims of the corresponding state and time. This conclusion indicates that it is not necessary to allow an additional degree of freedom in the form of the interposition of a "personal discount rate" to reach an optimum under certainty.[28] The error here is analogous to that sometimes committed of imposing a personal *time-preference* discount rate on future certain returns—whereas attainment of an optimum requires adjusting the marginal personal rate of time preference to the objective market rate.

V. RISK AVERSION AND THE UNIQUENESS ASSUMPTION

In the section preceding, the observation of "nonspecialization" among time-state contingencies was employed to justify convex indifference curves between state incomes. The further assumption of uniqueness of the underlying Neumann-Morgenstern utility-of-income $v(c_1)$ function, for uncertain future consumption, led to a kind of symmetry of state preferences such that if the price ratio for state incomes P_{1b}/P_{1a} is equal to the probability ratio π_b/π_a, the preferred combination will be along the certainty line. This last condition is the ordinary definition of risk aversion: given an initial combination along the certainty line, a fair gamble would not be accepted.[29]

But, it may be asked, if reasonable assumptions under the state-preference approach lead to risk aversion in the ordinary sense, what is the advantage of the approach over the mean, variability formulation that directly postulates aversion to variability risk? The crucial advantage, developed at length in the previous sections, is that time-state claims are commodities capable of being exchanged in markets—so that a complete choice-theoretic structure, including

---

[28] Lacking a formal solution to investment decision under uncertainty, Fisher recommended discounting anticipated future receipts by a personal "caution coefficient" (*Rate of Interest, op. cit.*, p. 215). The analysis here indicates that the interaction of personal time-and-risk preferences will establish a *market* time-and-risk discount rate, to which individuals will adjust on the margin. (1, p. 530)

[29] As mentioned above, the proviso about the initial situation being one of certainty should not be omitted. (2, p. 531)

conservation equations, can be constructed as in equations (8) through (11) above. Mean return and variability of return are not commodities in this sense, or at least there are as yet unresolved difficulties in regarding them as such. Furthermore, even in terms of the preference function alone, there is a gain in depth of understanding in deriving risk aversion from more fundamental considerations as compared with merely postulating it.[30] But the consideration to be examined further in this section is whether some types of behavior that seem to violate risk aversion can be rationalized in terms of the state-preference approach.

If one asked a responsible family man why he carries life insurance, presumably he would give a reply consistent with our risk-avoiding picture in Figure VII. Letting the state a represent the contingency "Breadwinner dies" and b the contingency "Breadwinner lives," our family man purchases life insurance to move his heirs in the direction of the certainty line. But a similarly thoughtful man, who happened to be a bachelor without family, would be unlikely to purchase insurance. Are we to say that he prefers risk? In a sense, perhaps, but it is more natural to explain his behavior by saying that a consumption opportunity contingent upon his death does not have the same appeal to the bachelor as it does to the family man.

This extreme case suggests the more general consideration that the utility-of-income function for any individual may not be invariant with respect to the state that obtains. It will be useful here to distinguish between true *gambles* (artificially generated risks, as at roulette) and natural *hazards*. There seems no reason to believe that anyone would rationally value consumption opportunities differently depending upon which end of a winning gamble he held. Money won on Black at roulette means exactly the same as an equivalent sum won on Red.[31] Therefore, within our model and ruling out pleasure-oriented gambling,[32] it continues to follow that fair *gambles* would never be accepted. A natural *hazard*, in contrast, will in general affect the external or internal context for choice by modifying the significance of the "same" consumption opportunity or sum of money.[33] We might say, somewhat

[30] In suppressing the information about the state-distributed composition of a particular combination being analyzed, essential information may be lost. One example would be the comparison of two-state prospects like (3, 1) and (6, 2)—where, for each combination, the first number gives the income for state a and the second for state b, the two states being equally probable. Evidently, the combination (6, 2) is dominant. But in terms of mean and variability measures this would not be evident, since (6, 2) has both a larger mean and a larger standard deviation. A somewhat related point is discussed in W. J. Baumol, "An Expected Gain-Confidence Limit Criterion for Portfolio Selection," *Management Science*, X (Oct. 1963). (3, p. 531)

[31] Though one of the appeals of long-shot betting may be that it provides more thrill and conversation value than an equivalent sum won on favorites. (4, p. 532)

[32] The successor to this article will consider the question of how observed gambling can be rationalized. (5, p. 532)

[33] A rather similar conception has been put forward and analyzed by Jacques Drèze, *loc. cit.* (6, p. 532)

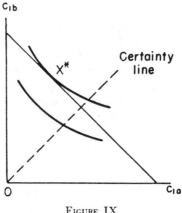

FIGURE IX

loosely, that states may vary in respect to "nonpecuniary income." As a result, state preferences for income become asymmetrical. For the bachelor in the above example, occurrence of the state " Death "eliminates practically any significance he might otherwise place upon titles to consumption. Again, a particular individual might weight his present choices in such a way as to have *more* income in depression· or famine than in prosperity, because he would then be able to assist his neighbors in their day of need. More typically, perhaps, we do not mind being poor so much if our neighbors (the Joneses) are also poor, since keeping up with them would then require less effort. The example cited in Section III, that an investor would not in general find the state-distributed portfolios (3, 2, 1) and (1, 2, 3) indifferent even if all three states were equally probable, would also be an instance of asymmetrical state preferences.

In all these cases we would observe risk-taking at fair odds in the sense that the preferred state distributions would not be along the certainty line (see Figure IX). But the reason is not nonconcavity of the $v(c_1)$ function—Neumann-Morgenstern risk preference—but rather nonuniqueness. That is, we would have to admit that, in general, we would have differing *conditional* utility-of-income functions $v_{1a}(c_{1a})$ and $v_{1b}(c_{1b})$. These separate functions can, however, be given a common scaling[34] so that we can find the utility of any prospect $(c_{1a}, c_{1b}; \pi_a, \pi_b)$ via the expected-utility theorem:

$$U(c_{1a}, c_{1b}; \pi_a, \pi_b) = \pi_a v_{1a}(c_{1a}) + \pi_b v_{1b}(c_{1b}).$$

Convexity of the state-distributed indifference curve follows, by the same reasoning employed in Section IV, making use again of the "independence" postulate which asserts that the marginal utilities of income in state *a* are unaffected by the level of consumption available for state *b*, and vice versa.

---

[34] See Appendix. (7, p. 533)

The equilibrium condition is

$$\frac{P_{1b}}{P_{1a}} = \frac{\pi_b v'_{1b}(c_{1b})}{\pi_a v'_{1a}(c_{1b})}.$$

However, since in general $v'_{1a}(c_{1a}) \neq v'_{1b}(c_{1b})$ when $c_{1a} = c_{1b}$, the tangencies will not occur on the certainty line, as was the case with a single utility-of-income function and consequent symmetrical state preferences.

The situation portrayed in Figure IX can be interpreted as indicating that in hazard situations people will be inclined to take risks. This is true in an actuarial sense (the decision-maker prefers at fair odds to move away from the certainty line), and yet the behavior remains essentially conservative. The "risk" is undertaken because quantitative equality of incomes in the two states does not properly balance the marginal utilities. We have shown, therefore, that the state-preference approach leads to a generalized concept which might be called "conservative behavior"—of which ordinary risk aversion in the sense of minimizing variability of outcome is only a special case.

VI. CONCLUDING REMARK

One surprising aspect of the time-and-state preference model is that it leads to a theory of decision under uncertainty while entirely excluding the "vagueness" we usually associate with uncertainty.[35] Uncertainty in this model takes the form not of vagueness but rather of completely precise beliefs as to endowments, productive opportunities, etc., just as in the case of certainty—the only difference being that the beliefs span alternative possible states of the world as well as successive time periods. Again, precise beliefs as to the probabilities of these alternative states are assumed. The assumption that uncertainty takes the form of precise beliefs about alternative possible states of the world certainly lacks psychological verisimilitude to the mental state of confusion and doubt commonly experienced in this connection. It is generally recognized, however, that descriptive reality of assumptions is no essential criterion for a useful theory. So far as vagueness is concerned, we have already in our simplest timeless and riskless models assumed a precision in preference (as when we draw maps of indifference between shoes and apples) that can scarcely be regarded as closely descriptive of mental states. A similarly "unrealistic" or "depsychologized" portraying of uncertainty may really be what is required for comparably fruitful results in our analysis of risky choice.

APPENDIX: SCALING OF UTILITY-OF-INCOME FUNCTIONS CONDITIONAL UPON STATE

We seek to show informally here that conditional utility-of-income functions, each defined for a particular state of the world, can nevertheless be

---

[35] Compare Fisher's declaration: "The third approximation cannot avoid some degree of vagueness" (*Theory of Interest, op. cit.*, p. 227). (8, p. 534)

given a common utility scaling consistent with the Neumann-Morgenstern postulates. In the case of a single (independent of state) utility-of-income function $v(c)$,[36] unique up to a linear transformation, a convenient scaling sets $v(0) = 0$, and $v(\overline{M}) = 1$, where $\overline{M}$ is the maximum income (consumption) level contemplated. The scaling used here will preserve analogues of these properties, for a hazard situation consisting of two alternative states of the world a and b $(\pi_a + \pi_b = 1)$, and where $v_a(c_a)$ is not identical with $v_b(c_b)$. As before, the elemental object of choice is a *conditional* claim to consumption in a specified state of the world. The "independence axiom" continues to apply: that is, $v_a(c_a)$ is independent of c_b, and *vice versa*.

To fix our desired scaling, it will suffice to assign utility values to two incomes on each conditional function: specifically to fix $v_a(0)$, $v_b(0)$, $v_a(\overline{M})$, and $v_b(\overline{M})$. We wish to continue assigning the utility value 1 to the certain receipt of $\overline{M}$, and the value 0 to the certain receipt of 0. Writing this in prospect notation, and using the expected-utility theorem:

$$U(\overline{M}, \overline{M}; \pi_a, \pi_b) = 1 = \pi_a v_a(\overline{M}) + \pi_b v_b(\overline{M})$$

$$U(0, 0; \pi_a, \pi_b) = 0 = \pi_a v_a(0) + \pi_b v_b(0).$$

We may now denote by the symbols X_a and X_b the prospects $(X, 0; \pi_a, \pi_b)$ and $(0, X; \pi_a, \pi_b)$, respectively. We can then adopt the scaling rule $v_a(X) = U(X_a)/\pi_a$, and similarly for $v_b(X)$. It follows immediately that $v_a(0) = v_b(0) = 0$, since 0_a and 0_b are identical and both have utility value zero; we may call this principle the Equivalence of Nulls. The interpretation is that, since we cannot do worse than zero in either state, a title or claim to zero in a particular state is worthless. Note that this does not deny that we might be happier with zero in state a (should state a obtain) than with zero in state b (should state b obtain) —but we cannot in fact ever be offered a choice among states, but only among claims to income conditional upon states occurring.

By the ordering postulate,[37] the individual can compare $\overline{M}_a$ with $\overline{M}_b$, and they need not be indifferent. Suppose he prefers the former. Then, by the continuity postulate[38] there is some probability π (in a pure gamble) such that $\overline{M}_b$ is indifferent to a lottery ticket offering $\overline{M}_a$ or zero.[39] Thus:

$$U(0, \overline{M}; \pi_a, \pi_b) = U[(\overline{M}, 0; \pi_a, \pi_b), 0; \pi, 1 - \pi]$$

$$\pi_b v_b(\overline{M}) = \pi \pi_a v_a(\overline{M}).$$

Using the property that the certain receipt of $\overline{M}$ has utility 1, we get the results $v_a(\overline{M}) = 1/(\pi_a + \pi_a \pi)$ and $v_b(\overline{M}) = \pi/(\pi_b + \pi_b \pi)$. The import of this

[36] The time subscript will be dropped in this Appendix, which deals only with utility functions for synchronous decisions. (9, p. 534)

[37] Luce and Raiffa, *op. cit.*, p. 25. (1, p. 535)

[38] *Ibid.*, p. 27. (1, p. 535)

[39] This π is a variable in an artificial gamble constructed to test preferences, whereas π_a and π_b are to be regarded as constants by nature (or at least by belief) in a real hazard situation. (1, p. 535)

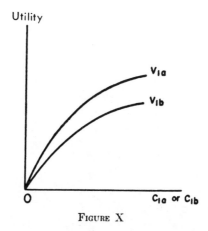

FIGURE X

is that we are now able, in principle, to use the two points thus provided for each state so as to construct in Figure X two separate curves, $v_{1a}(c_{1a})$ and $v_{1b}(c_{1b})$, to serve as *conditional* utility-of-income scales. The expected-utility theorem can then be used with these scales to calculate the over-all preference ordering of any income distribution over these states.

PART **II**

PORTFOLIO THEORY AND CAPITAL ASSET PRICING

* *

5. PORTFOLIO SELECTION*

HARRY MARKOWITZ†

Reprinted from *The Journal of Finance,* Vol. VII, No. 1
(March 1952), pp. 77–91, by permission of the author and
the publisher.

The process of selecting a portfolio may be divided into two stages. The first stage starts with observation and experience and ends with beliefs about the future performances of available securities. The second stage starts with the relevant beliefs about future performances and ends with the choice of portfolios. This paper is concerned with the second stage. We first consider the rule that the investor does (or should) maximize discounted expected, or anticipated, returns. This rule is rejected both as a hypothesis to explain, and as a maximum to guide investment behavior. We next consider the rule that the investor does (or should) consider expected return a desirable thing *and* variance of return an undesirable thing. This rule has many sound points, both as a maxim for, and hypothesis about, investment behavior. We illustrate geometrically relations between beliefs and choice of portfolio according to the " expected returns—variance of returns " rule.

One type of rule concerning choice of portfolio is that the investor does (or should) maximize the discounted (or capitalized) value of future returns.[1] Since the future is not known with certainty, it must be " expected " or " anticipated " returns which we discount. Variations of this type of rule can be suggested. Following Hicks, we could let " anticipated " returns include an

* This paper is based on work done by the author while at the Cowles Commission for Research in Economics and with the financial assistance of the Social Science Research Council. It will be reprinted as Cowles Commission Paper, New Series, No. 60.

† The Rand Corporation.

[1] See, for example, J. B. Williams, *The Theory of Investment Value* (Cambridge, Mass.: Harvard University Press, 1938), pp. 55–75.

allowance for risk.[2] Or, we could let the rate at which we capitalize the returns from particular securities vary with risk.

The hypothesis (or maxim) that the investor does (or should) maximize discounted return must be rejected. If we ignore market imperfections the foregoing rule never implies that there is a diversified portfolio which is preferable to all nondiversified portfolios. Diversification is both observed and sensible; a rule of behavior which does not imply the superiority of diversification must be rejected both as a hypothesis and as a maxim.

The foregoing rule fails to imply diversification no matter how the anticipated returns are formed; whether the same or different discount rates are used for different securities; no matter how these discount rates are decided upon or how they vary over time.[3] The hypothesis implies that the investor places all his funds in the security with the greatest discounted value. If two or more securities have the same value, then any of these or any combination of these is as good as any other.

We can see this analytically: suppose there are N securities; let r_{it} be the anticipated return (however decided upon) at time t per dollar invested in security i; let d_{it} be the rate at which the return on the ith security at time t is discounted back to the present; let X_i be the relative amount invested in security i. We exclude short sales, thus $X_i \geq 0$ for all i. Then the discounted anticipated return of the portfolio is

$$R = \sum_{t=1}^{\infty} \sum_{i=1}^{N} d_{it} r_{it} X$$

$$= \sum_{i=1}^{N} X_i \left(\sum_{t=1}^{\infty} d_{it} r_{it} \right)$$

$R_i = \sum_{t=1}^{\infty} d_{it} r_{it}$ is the discounted return of the ith security, therefore $R = \Sigma X_i R_i$ where R_i is independent of X_i. Since $X_i \geq 0$ for all i and $\Sigma X_i = 1$, R is a weighted average of R_i with the X_i as non-negative weights. To maximize R, we let $X_i = 1$ for i with maximum R_i. If several Ra_a, $a = 1, \ldots, K$ are maximum then any allocation with

$$\sum_{a=1}^{K} Xa_a = 1$$

maximizes R. In no case is a diversified portfolio preferred to all non-diversified portfolios.[4]

It will be convenient at this point to consider a static model. Instead of

---

[2] J. R. Hicks, *Value and Capital* (New York: Oxford University Press, 1939), p. 126. Hicks applies the rule to a firm rather than a portfolio.

[3] The results depend on the assumption that the anticipated returns and discount rates are independent of the particular investor's portfolio.

[4] If short sales were allowed, an infinite amount of money would be placed in the security with highest r.

speaking of the time series of returns from the ith security $(r_{i1}, r_{i2}, \ldots, r_{it}, \ldots)$ we will speak of "the flow of returns" (r_i) from the ith security. The flow of returns from the portfolio as a whole is $R = \Sigma X_i r_i$. As in the dynamic case if the investor wished to maximize "anticipated" return from the portfolio he would place all his funds in that security with maximum anticipated returns.

There is a rule which implies both that the investor should diversify and that he should maximize expected return. The rule states that the investor does (or should) diversify his funds among all those securities which give maximum expected return. The law of large numbers will insure that the actual yield of the portfolio will be almost the same as the expected yield.[5] This rule is a special case of the expected returns—variance of returns rule (to be presented below). It assumes that there is a portfolio which gives both maximum expected return and minimum variance, and it commends this portfolio to the investor.

This presumption, that the law of large numbers applies to a portfolio of securities, cannot be accepted. The returns from securities are too intercorrelated. Diversification cannot eliminate all variance.

The portfolio with maximum expected return is not necessarily the one with minimum variance. There is a rate at which the investor can gain expected return by taking on variance, or reduce variance by giving up expected return.

We saw that the expected returns or anticipated returns rule is inadequate. Let us now consider the expected returns-variance of returns $(E-V)$ rule. It will be necessary to first present a few elementary concepts and results of mathematical statistics. We will then show some implications of the $E-V$ rule. After this we will discuss its plausibility.

In our presentation we try to avoid complicated mathematical statements and proofs. As a consequence a price is paid in terms of rigor and generality. The chief limitations from this source are 1) we do not derive our results analytically for the n-security case; instead, we present them geometrically for the 3 and 4 security cases; 2) we assume static probability beliefs. In a general presentation we must recognize that the probability distribution of yields of the various securities is a function of time. The writer intends to present, in the future, the general, mathematical treatment which removes this limitation.

We will need the following elementary concepts and results of mathematical statistics:

Let Y be a random variable, i.e., a variable whose value is decided by chance. Suppose, for simplicity of exposition, that Y can take on a finite number of values $y_1, y_2, \ldots, y_N$. Let the probability that $Y = y_1$, be p_1; that $Y = y_2$ be p_2; etc. The expected value (or mean) of Y is defined to be

$$E = p_1 y_1 + p_2 y_2 + \cdots + p_N y_N$$

The variance of Y is defined to be

[5] Williams, *op. cit.*, pp. 68, 69.

$$V = p_1(y_1 - E)^2 + p_2(y_2 - E)^2 + \cdots + p_N(y_N - E)^2$$

V is the average squared deviation of Y from its expected value. V is a commonly used measure of dispersion. Other measures of dispersion, closely related to V are the standard deviation, $\sigma = \sqrt{V}$, and the coefficient of variation, σ/E.

Suppose we have a number of random variables: $R_1, \ldots, R_n$. If R is a weighted sum (linear combination) of the R_i

$$R = a_1 R_1 + a_2 R_2 + \cdots + a_n R_n$$

then R is also a random variable. (For example, R_1 may be the number which turns up on one die; R_2, that of another die; and R the sum of these numbers. In this case $n = 2$, $a_1 = a_2 = 1$.)

It will be important for us to know how the expected value and variance of the weighted sum (R) are related to the probability distribution of the R_1, $\ldots, R_n$. We state these relations below; we refer the reader to any standard text for proof.[6]

The expected value of a weighted sum is the weighted sum of the expected values. I.e. $E(R) = a_1 E(R_1) + a_2 E(R_2) + \ldots + a_n E(R_n)$. The variance of a weighted sum is not as simple. To express it we must define "covariance." The covariance of R_1 and R_2 is

$$\sigma_{12} = E\{[R_1 = E(R_1)][R_2 - E(R_2)]\}$$

i.e., the expected value of [(the deviation of R_1 from its mean) times (the deviation of R_2 from its mean)]. In general we define the covariance between R_i and R_j as

$$\sigma_{ij} = E\{[R_i - E(R_i)][R_j - E(R_j)]\}.$$

σ_{ij} may be expressed in terms of the familiar correlation coefficient (ρ_{ij}). The covariance between R_i and R_j is equal to [(their correlation) times (the standard deviation of R_i) times (the standard deviation of R_j)]:

$$\sigma_{ij} = \rho_{ij}\sigma_i\sigma_j.$$

The variance of a weighted sum is

$$V(R) = \sum_{i=1}^{N} a_i^2 \, V(X_i) + 2\sum_{i=1}^{N} \sum_{i>1}^{N} a_i a_j \sigma_{ij}.$$

If we use the fact that the variance of R_i is σ_{ii} then

$$V(R) = \sum_{i=1}^{N} \sum_{j=1}^{N} a_i a_j \sigma_{ij}.$$

Let R_i be the return on the ith security. Let μ_i be the expected value of R_i; σ_{ij}, be the covariance between R_i and R_j (thus σ_{ii} is the variance of R_i). Let

[6] For example, J. V. Uspensky, *Introduction to Mathematical Probability* (New York: McGraw-Hill, 1937), Ch. 9, pp. 161–81.

X_i be the percentage of the investor's assets which are allocated to the ith security. The yield (R) on the portfolio as a whole is

$$R = \sum R_i X_i.$$

The R_i (and consequently R) are considered to be random variables.[7] The X_i are not random variables, but are fixed by the investor. Since the X_i are percentages we have $\Sigma X_i = 1$. In our analysis we will exclude negative values of the X_i (i.e., short sales); therefore $X_i \geq 0$ for all i.

The return (R) on the portfolio as a whole is a weighted sum of random variables (where the investor can choose the weights). From our discussion of such weighted sums we see that the expected return E from the portfolio as a whole is

$$E = \sum_{i=1}^{N} X_i \mu_i$$

and the variance is

$$V = \sum_{i=1}^{N} \sum_{j=1}^{N} \sigma_{ij} X_i X.$$

For fixed probability beliefs (μ_i, σ_{ij}) the investor has a choice of various combinations of E and V depending on his choice of portfolio $X_1, \ldots, X_N$. Suppose that the set of all obtainable (E, V) combinations were as in Figure 1. The E-V rule states that the investor would (or should) want to select one of those portfolios which give rise to the (E, V) combinations indicated as efficient in the figure; i.e., those with minimum V for given E or more and maximum E for given V or less.

There are techniques by which we can compute the set of efficient portfolios and efficient (E, V) combinations associated with given μ_i and σ_{ij}. We will not present these techniques here. We will, however, illustrate geometrically the nature of the efficient surfaces for cases in which N (the number of available securities) is small.

The calculation of efficient surfaces might possibly be of practical use. Perhaps there are ways, by combining statistical techniques and the judgment of experts, to form reasonable probability beliefs (μ_i, σ_{ij}). We could use these beliefs to compute the attainable efficient combinations of (E, V).

---

[7] That is, we assume that the investor does (and should) act as if he had probability beliefs concerning these variables. In general we would expect that the investor could tell us, for any two events (A and B), whether he personally considered A more likely than B, B more likely than A, or both equally likely. If the investor were consistent in his opinions on such matters, he would possess a system of probability beliefs. We cannot expect the investor to be consistent in every detail. We can, however, expect his probability beliefs to be roughly consistent on important matters that have been carefully considered. We should also expect that he will base his actions upon these probability beliefs—even though they be in part subjective.

This paper does not consider the difficult question of how investors do (or should) form their probability beliefs.

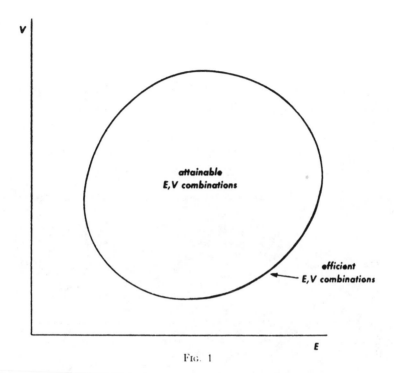

FIG. 1

The investor, being informed of what (E, V) combinations were attainable, could state which he desired. We could then find the portfolio which gave this desired combination.

Two conditions—at least—must be satisfied before it would be practical to use efficient surfaces in the manner described above. First, the investor must desire to act according to the E-V maxim. Second, we must be able to arrive at reasonable μ_i and σ_{ij}. We will return to these matters later.

Let us consider the case of three securities. In the three security case our model reduces to

(1) $$E = \sum_{i=1}^{3} X_i \mu_i$$

(2) $$V = \sum_{i=1}^{3} \sum_{j=1}^{3} X_i X_j \sigma_{ij}$$

(3) $$\sum_{i=1}^{3} X_i = 1$$

(4) $$X_i \geq 0 \quad \text{for } i = 1, 2, 3.$$

From (3) we get

(3') $$X_3 = 1 - X_1 - X_2.$$

If we substitute (3') in (1) and (2), we get E and V as functions of X_1 and X_2. For example we find

(1') $$E = \mu_3 + X_1(\mu_1 - \mu_3) + X_2(\mu_2 - \mu_3).$$

The exact formulas are not too important here (that of V is given below).[8] We can simply write

(a) $$E = E(X_1, X_2)$$

(b) $$V = V(X_1, X_2)$$

(c) $$X_1 \geq 0, X_2 \geq 0, 1 - X_1 - X_2 \geq 0.$$

By using relations (a), (b), (c), we can work with two dimensional geometry.

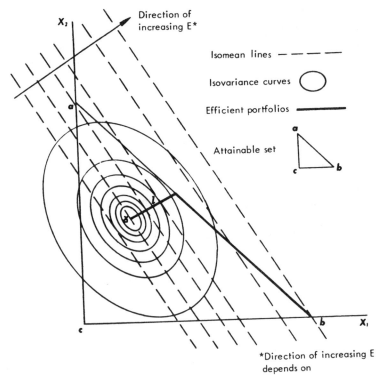

FIGURE 2.

The attainable set of portfolios consists of all portfolios which satisfy constraints (c) and (3') (or equivalently (3) and (4)). The attainable combinations of X_1, X_2 are represented by the triangle abc in Figure 2. Any point to the left of the X_2 axis is not attainable because it violates the condition that

[8] $V = X_1^2(\sigma_{11} - 2\sigma_{13} + \sigma_{33}) + X_2^2(\sigma_{22} - 2\sigma_{23} + \sigma_{33}) + 2 X_1 X_2(\sigma_{12} - \sigma_{13} - \sigma_{23} + \sigma_{33})$
$+ 2X_1(\sigma_{13} - \sigma_{33}) + 2X_2(\sigma_{23} - \sigma_{33}) + \sigma_{33}.$

$X_1 \geq 0$. Any point below the X_1 axis is not attainable because it violates the condition that $X_2 \geq 0$. Any point above the line $(1 - X_1 - X_2 = 0)$ is not attainable because it violates the condition that $X_3 = 1 - X_1 - X_2 \geq 0$.

We define an *isomean* curve to be the set of all points (portfolios) with a given expected return. Similarly an *isovariance* line is defined to be the set of all points (portfolios) with a given variance of return.

An examination of the formulae for E and V tells us the shapes of the isomean and isovariance curves. Specificallly, they tell us that typically[9] the isomean curves are a system of parallel straight lines; the isovariance curves are a system of concentric ellipses (see Fig 2). For example, if $\mu_2 \neq \mu_3$ equation (1') can be written in the familiar form $X_2 = a + bX_1$; specifically

$$X_2 = \frac{E - \mu_3}{\mu_2 - \mu_3} - \frac{\mu_1 - \mu_3}{\mu_2 - \mu_3} X_1.$$

Thus the slope of the isomean line associated with $E = E_o$ is $-(\mu_1 - \mu_3)/(\mu_2 - \mu_3)$; its intercept is $(E_o - \mu_3)/(\mu_2 - \mu_3)$. If we change E we change the intercept but not the slope of the isomean line. This confirms the contention that the isomean lines form a system of parallel lines.

Similarly, by a somewhat less simple application of analytic geometry, we can confirm the contention that the isovariance lines form a family of concentric ellipses. The "center" of the system is the point which minimizes V. We will label this point X. Its expected return and variance we will label E and V. Variance increases as you move away from X. More precisely, if one isovariance curve, C_1, lies closer to X than another, C_2, then C_1 is associated with a smaller variance than C_2.

With the aid of the foregoing geometric apparatus let us seek the efficient sets.

X, the center of the system of isovariance ellipses, may fall either inside or outside the attainable set. Figure 4 illustrates a case in which X falls inside the attainable set. In this case: X is efficient. For no other portfolio has a V as low as X; therefore no portfolio can have either smaller V (with the same or greater E) or greater E with the same or smaller V. No point (portfolio) with expected return E less than E is efficient. For we have $E > E$ and $V < V$.

Consider all points with a given expected return E; i.e., all points on the isomean line associated with E. The point of the isomean line at which V takes on its least value is the point at which the isomean line is tangent to an isovariance curve. We call this point $\hat{X}(E)$. If we let E vary, $\hat{X}(E)$ traces out a curve.

Algebraic considerations (which we omit here) show us that this curve is a straight line. We will call it the critical line l. The critical line passes through X for this point minimizes V for all points with $E(X_1, X_2) = E$. As we go along

---

[9] The isomean "curves" are as described above except when $\mu_1 = \mu_2 = \mu_3$. In the latter case all portfolios have the same expected return and the investor chooses the one with minimum variance.

As to the assumptions implicit in our description of the isovariance curves, see footnote 12.

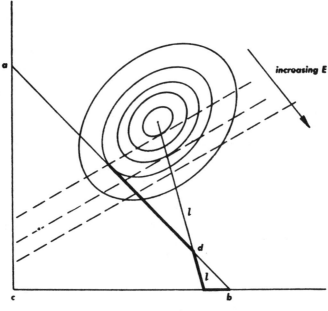

FIG. 3

l in either direction from *X*, *V* increases. The segment of the critical line from *X* to the point where the critical line crosses the boundary of the attainable set is part of the efficient set. The rest of the efficient set is (in the case illustrated) the segment of the $\overline{ab}$ line from *d* to *b*. *b* is the point of maximum attainable *E*. In Figure 3, *X* lies outside the admissible area but the critical line cuts the

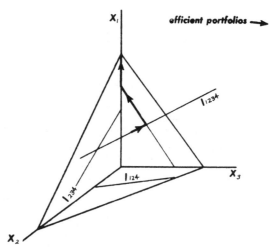

FIG. 4

admissible area. The efficient line begins at the attainable point with minimum variance (in this case on the $\overline{ab}$ line). It moves toward b until it intersects the critical line, moves along the critical line until it intersects a boundary and finally moves along the boundary to b. The reader may wish to construct and examine the following other cases: (1) X lies outside the attainable set and the critical line does not cut the attainable set. In this case there is a security which does not enter into any efficient portfolio. (2) Two securities have the same μ_i. In this case the isomean lines are parallel to a boundary line. It may happen that the efficient portfolio with maximum E is a diversified portfolio. (3) A case wherein only one portfolio is efficient.

The efficient set in the 4 security case is, as in the 3 security and also the N security case, a series of connected line segments. At one end of the efficient set is the point of minimum variance; at the other end is a point of maximum expected return[10] (see Fig. 4).

Now that we have seen the nature of the set of efficient portfolios, it is not difficult to see the nature of the set of efficient (E, V) combinations. In the three security case $E = a_o + a_1 X_1 + a_2 X_2$ is a plane; $V = b_o + b_1 X_1 + b_2 X_2 + b_{12} X_1 X_2 + b_{11} X_1^2 + b_{22} X_2^2$ is a paraboloid.[11] As shown in Figure 5, the section of the E-plane over the efficient portfolio set is a series of connected line segments. The section of the V-paraboloid over the efficient portfolio set is a series of connected parabola segments. If we plotted V against E for efficient portfolios we would again get a series of connected parabola segments (see Fig. 6). This result obtains for any number of securities.

Various reasons recommend the use of the expected return-variance of return rule, both as a hypothesis to explain well-established investment behavior and as a maxim to guide one's own action. The rule serves better, we

---

[10] Just as we used the equation $\sum_{i=1}^{4} X_i = 1$ to reduce the dimensionality in the three security case, we can use it to represent the four security case in 3 dimensional space. Eliminating X_4 we get $E = E(X_1, X_2, X_3)$, $V = V(X_1, X_2, X_3)$. The attainable set is represented, in three space, by the tetrahedron with vertices $(0, 0, 0)$, $(0, 0, 1)$, $(0, 1, 0)$, $(1, 0, 0)$, representing portfolios with, respectively, $X_4 = 1$, $X_3 = 1$, $X_2 = 1$, $X_1 = 1$.

Let s_{123} be the subspace consisting of all points with $X_4 = 0$. Similarly we can define $s_{a1}, \ldots, a_a$ to be the subspace consisting of all points with $X_i = 0$, $i \neq a_1, \ldots, a_a$. For each subspace $s_{a1}, \ldots, a_a$ we can define a *critical line $1a_1, \ldots a_a$*. This line is the locus of points P where P minimizes V for all points in $s_{a1}, \ldots, a_a$ with the same E as P. If a point is in $s_{a1}, \ldots, a_a$ and is efficient it must be on $la_1, \ldots, a_a$. The efficient set may be traced out by starting at the point of minimum available variance, moving continuously along various $la_1, \ldots, a_a$ according to definite rules, ending in a point which gives maximum E. As in the two dimensional case the point with minimum available variance may be in the interior of the available set or on one of its boundaries. Typically we proceed along a given critical line until either this line intersects one of a larger subspace or meets a boundary (and simultaneously the critical line of a lower dimensional subspace). In either of these cases the efficient line turns and continues along the new line. The efficient line terminates when a point with maximum E is reached.

[11] See footnote 8.

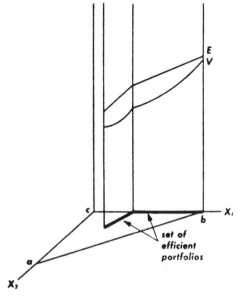

Fig. 5

will see, as an explanation of, and guide to, "investment" as distinguished from "speculative" behavior.

Earlier we rejected the expected returns rule on the grounds that it never implied the superiority of diversification. The expected return-variance of return rule, on the other hand, implies diversification for a wide range of μ_i, σ_{ij}. This does not mean that the E-V rule never implies the superiority of an undiversified portfolio. It is conceivable that one security might have an

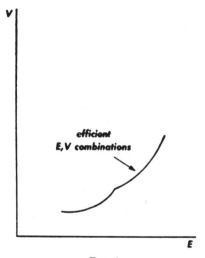

Fig. 6

extremely higher yield and lower variance than all other securities; so much so that one particular undiversified portfolio would give maximum E and minimum V. But for a large, presumably representative range of μ_i, σ_{ij} the E-V rule leads to efficient portfolios almost all of which are diversified.

Not only does the E-V hypothesis imply diversification, it implies the "right kind" of diversification for the "right reason." The adequacy of diversification is not thought by investors to depend on the number of different securities held. A portfolio with sixty different railway securities for example, would not be as well diversified as the same size portfolio with some railroad, some public utility, mining, various sort of manufacturing, etc. The reason is that it is generally more likely for firms within the same industry to do poorly at the same time than for firms in dissimilar industries.

Similarly in trying to make variance small it is not enough to invest in many securities. It is necessary to avoid investing in securities with high covariances among themselves. We should diversify across industries because firms in different industries, especially industries with different economic characteristics, have lower covariances than firms within an industry.

The concepts "yield" and "risk" appear frequently in financial writings. Usually if the term "yield" were replaced by "expected yield" or "expected return," and "risk" by "variance of return," little change of apparent meaning would result.

Variance is a well-known measure of dispersion about the expected. If instead of variance the investor was concerned with standard error, $\sigma = \sqrt{V}$, or with the coefficient of dispersion, σ/E, his choice would still lie in the set of efficient portfolios.

Suppose an investor diversifies between two portfolios (i.e., if he puts some of his money in one portfolio, the rest of his money in the other. An example of diversifying among portfolios is the buying of the shares of two different investment companies). If the two original portfolios have *equal* variance then typically [12] the variance of the resulting (compound) portfolio will be less than the variance of either original portfolio. This is illustrated by Figure 7. To interpret Figure 7 we note that a portfolio P which is built out of two portfolios $P' = (X'_1, X'_2)$ and $P'' = (X''_1, X''_2)$ is of the form $P = \lambda P' + (1 - \lambda)P'' = [\lambda X'_1 + (1 - \lambda)X''_1, \lambda X'_2 + (1 - \lambda)X''_2]$. P is on the straight line connecting P' and P''.

The E-V principle is more plausible as a rule for investment behavior as distinguished from speculative behavior. The third moment [13] M_3 of the probability distribution of returns from the portfolio may be connected with a

---

[12] In no case will variance be increased. The only case in which variance will not be decreased is if the return from both portfolios are perfectly correlated. To draw the isovariance curves as ellipses it is both necessary and sufficient to assume that no two distinct portfolios have perfectly correlated returns.

[13] If R is a random variable that takes on a finite number of values $r_1, \ldots, r_n$ with probabilities $p_1, \ldots, p_n$ respectively, and expected value E, then $M_3 = \sum_{i=1}^{n} p_i(r_i - E)^3$.

propensity to gamble. For example if the investor maximizes utility U which depends on E and V $[U = U(E, V), \partial U/\partial E > 0, \partial U/\partial E < 0]$, he will never accept an actuarially fair[14] bet. But if $U = U(E, V, M_3)$ and if $\partial U/\partial M_3 \neq 0$ then there are some fair bets which would be accepted.

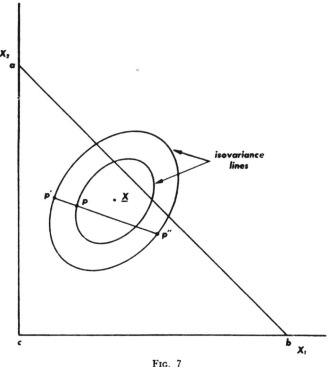

Fig. 7

Perhaps—for a great variety of investing institutions which consider yield to be a good thing; risk, a bad thing; gambling, to be avoided—E, V efficiency is reasonable as a working hypothesis and a working maxim.

Two uses of the E-V principle suggest themselves. We might use it in theoretical analyses, or we might use it in the actual selection of portfolios.

In theoretical analyses we might inquire, for example, about the various effects of a change in the beliefs generally held about a firm, or a general change in preference as to expected return versus variance of return, or a change in the supply of a security. In our analyses the X_i might represent individual securities or they might represent aggregates such as, say, bonds, stocks, and real estate.[15]

To use the E-V rule in the selection of securities we must have procedures

[14] One in which the amount gained by winning the bet times the probability of winning is equal to the amount lost by losing the bet, times the probability of losing.

[15] Care must be used in using and interpreting relations among aggregates. We cannot deal here with the problems and pitfalls of aggregation.

for finding reasonable μ_i and σ_{ij}. These procedures, I believe, should combine statistical techniques and the judgment of practical men. My feeling is that the statistical computations should be used to arrive at a tentative set of μ_i and σ_{ij}. Judgment should then be used in increasing or decreasing some of these μ_i and σ_{ij} on the basis of factors or nuances not taken into account by the formal computations. Using this revised set of μ_i and σ_{ij}, the set of efficient E, V combinations could be computed, the investor could select the combination he preferred, and the portfolio which gave rise to this E, V combination could be found.

One suggestion as to tentative μ_i, σ_{ij} is to use the observed μ_i, σ_{ij} for some period of the past. I believe that better methods, which take into account more information, can be found. I believe that what is needed is essentially a "probabilistic" reformulation of security analysis. I will not pursue this subject here, for this is "another story." It is a story of which I have read only the first page of the first chapter.

In this paper we have considered the second stage in the process of selecting a portfolio. This stage starts with the relevant beliefs about the securities involved and ends with the selection of a portfolio. We have not considered the first stage: the information of the relevant beliefs on the basis of observation.

6. LIQUIDITY PREFERENCE AS BEHAVIOUR TOWARDS RISK*

J. TOBIN†

Reprinted from *The Review of Economic Studies,* Vol. XXVI, No. 1 (February 1958), pp. 65–86, by permission of the author and the publisher.[1]

One of the basic functional relationships in the Keynesian model of the economy is the liquidity preference schedule, an inverse relationship between the demand for cash balances and the rate of interest. This aggregative function must be derived from some assumptions regarding the behavior of the decision-making units of the economy, and those assumptions are the concern

* I am grateful to Challis Hall, Arthur Okun, Walter Salant, and Leroy Wehrle for helpful comments on earlier drafts of this paper.

† New Haven, Conn., U.S.A.

[1] The footnotes below are numbered consecutively throughout, although in the original article they are numbered consecutively only on each page. To ease the reader's transference between this reprint and the original, at the end of each footnote, in parentheses, is the footnote citation and the page number of the original article.

of this paper. Nearly two decades of drawing downward-sloping liquidity preference curves in textbooks and on classroom blackboards should not blind us to the basic implausibility of the behavior they describe. Why should anyone hold the non-interest bearing obligations of the government instead of its interest bearing obligations? The apparent irrationality of holding cash is the same, moreover, whether the interest rate is 6%, 3% or $\frac{1}{2}$ of 1%. What needs to be explained is not only the existence of a demand for each when its yield is less than the yield on alternative assets but an inverse relationship between the aggregate demand for cash and the size of this differential in yields.[2]

1. TRANSACTIONS BALANCES AND INVESTMENT BALANCES.

Two kinds of reasons for holding cash are usually distinguished: transactions reasons and investment reasons.

1.1 *Transactions balances: size and composition.*   No economic unit—firm or household or government—enjoys perfect synchronization between the seasonal patterns of its flow of receipts and its flow of expenditures. The discrepancies give rise to balances which accumulate temporarily, and are used up later in the year when expenditures catch up. Or, to put the same phenomenon the other way, the discrepancies give rise to the need for balances to meet seasonal excesses of expenditures over receipts. These balances are *transactions balances.* The aggregate requirement of the economy for such balances depends on the institutional arrangements that determine the degree of synchronization between individual receipts and expenditures. Given these institutions, the need for transactions balances is roughly proportionate to the aggregate volume of transactions.

The obvious importance of these institutional determinants of the demand for transactions balances has led to the general opinion that other possible determinants, including interest rates, are negligible.[3] This may be true of the

---

[2] " . . . in a world involving no transaction friction and no uncertainty, there would be no reason for a spread between the yield on any two assets, and hence there would be no difference in the yield on money and on securities . . . in such a world securities themselves would circulate as money and be acceptable in transactions; demand bank deposits would bear interest, just as they often did in this country in the period of the twenties." Paul A. Samuelson, *Foundations of Economic Analysis* (Cambridge: Harvard University Press, 1947), p. 123. The section pp. 122–124, from which the passage is quoted makes it clear that liquidity preference must be regarded as an explanation of the existence and level not of the interest rate but of the differential between the yield on money and the yields on other assets.

[3] The traditional theory of the velocity of money has, however, probably exaggerated the invariance of the institutions determining the extent of lack of synchronization between individual receipts and expenditures. It is no doubt true that such institutions as the degree of vertical integration of production and the periodicity of wage, salary, dividend, and tax payments are slow to change. But other relevant arrangements can be adjusted in response to money rates. For example, there is a good deal of flexibility in the promptness and regularity with which bills are rendered and settled. (1, p. 66)

size of transactions balances, but the composition of transactions balances is another matter. Cash is by no means the only asset in which transactions balances may be held. Many transactors have large enough balances so that holding part of them in earning assets, rather than in cash, is a relevant possibility. Even though these holdings are always for short periods, the interest earnings may be worth the cost and inconvenience of the financial transactions involved. Elsewhere[4] I have shown that, for such transactors, the proportion of cash in transactions balances varies inversely with the rate of interest; consequently this source of interest-elasticity in the demand for cash will not be further discussed here.

1.2 *Investment balances and portfolio decisions.*   In contrast to transactions balances, the investment balances of an economic unit are those that will survive all the expected seasonal excesses of cumulative expenditures over cumulative receipts during the year ahead. They are balances which will not have to be turned into cash within the year. Consequently the cost of financial transactions—converting other assets into cash and vice versa—does not operate to encourage the holding of investment balances in cash.[5] If cash is to have any part in the composition of investment balances, it must be because of expectations or fears of loss on other assets. It is here, in what Keynes called the speculative motives of investors, that the explanation of liquidity preference and of the interest-elasticity of the demand for cash has been sought.

The alternatives to cash considered, both in this paper and in prior discussions of the subject, in examining the speculative motive for holding cash are assets that differ from cash only in having a variable market yield. They are obligations to pay stated cash amounts at future dates, with no risk of default. They are, like cash, subject to changes in real value due to fluctuations in the price level. In a broader perspective, all these assets, including cash, are merely minor variants of the same species, a species we may call monetary assets—marketable, fixed in money value, free of default risk. The differences of members of this species from each other are negligible compared to their differences from the vast variety of other assets in which wealth may be invested: corporate stocks, real estate, unincorporated business and professional practice, etc. The theory of liquidity preference does not concern the choices investors make between the whole species of monetary assets, on the one hand, and other broad classes of assets, on the other.[6] Those choices are

---

[4] "The Interest Elasticity of the Transactions Demand for Cash," *Review of Economics and Statistics*, Volume 38 (August, 1956), pp. 241–247. (2, p. 66)

[5] Costs of financial transactions have the effect of deterring changes from the existing portfolio, whatever its composition; they may thus operate against the holding of cash as easily as for it. Because of these costs, the *status quo* may be optimal even when a different composition of assets would be preferred if the investor were starting over again. (3, p. 66)

[6] For an attempt by the author to apply to this wider choice some of the same theoretical tools that are here used to analyze choices among the narrow class of monetary assets, see "A Dynamic Aggregative Model," *Journal of Political Economy*, Vol. 63 (April, 1955), pp. 103–115. (4, p. 66)

the concern of other branches of economic theory, in particular theories of investment and of consumption. Liquidity preference theory takes as given the choices determining how much wealth is to be invested in monetary assets and concerns itself with the allocation of these amounts among cash and alternative monetary assets.

Why should any investment balances be held in cash, in preference to other monetary assets? We shall distinguish two possible sources of liquidity preference, while recognizing that they are not mutually exclusive. The first is inelasticity of expectations of future interest rates. The second is uncertainty about the future of interest rates. These two sources of liquidity preference will be examined in turn.

2. INELASTICITY OF INTEREST RATE EXPECTATIONS.

2.1 *Some simplifying assumptions.* To simplify the problem, assume that there is only one monetary asset other than cash, namely, consols. The current yield of consols is r per "year." \$1 invested in consols today will purchase an income of \$$r$ per "year" in perpetuity. The yield of cash is assumed to be zero; however, this is not essential, as it is the current and expected differentials of consols over cash that matter. An investor with a given total balance must decide what proportion of this balance to hold in cash, A_1, and what proportion in consols, A_2. This decision is assumed to fix the portfolio for a full "year."[7]

2.2 *Fixed expectations of future rate.* At the end of the year, the investor expects the rate on consols to be r_e. This expectation is assumed, for the present, to be held with certainty and to be independent of the current rate r. The investor may therefore expect with certainty that every dollar invested in consols today will earn over the year ahead not only the interest \$$r$, but also a capital gain or loss g:

$$g = \frac{r}{r_e} - 1. \tag{2.1}$$

[7] As noted above, it is the costs of financial transactions that impart inertia to portfolio composition. Every reconsideration of the portfolio involves the investor in expenditure of time and effort as well as of money. The frequency with which it is worth while to review the portfolio will obviously vary with the investor and will depend on the size of his portfolio and on his situation with respect to costs of obtaining information and engaging in financial transactions. Thus the relevant "year" ahead for which portfolio decisions are made is not the same for all investors. Moreover, even if a decision is made with a view to fixing a portfolio for a given period of time, a portfolio is never so irrevocably frozen that there are no conceivable events during the period which would induce the investor to reconsider. The fact that this possibility is always open must influence the investor's decision. The fiction of a fixed investment period used in this paper is, therefore, not a wholly satisfactory way of taking account of the inertia in portfolio composition due to the costs of transactions and of decision making. (1, p. 67)

For this, investor, the division of his balance into proportions A_1 of cash and A_2 of consols is a simple all-or-nothing choice. If the current rate is such that $r + g$ is greater than zero, then he will put everything in consols. But if $r + g$ is less than zero, he will put everything in cash. These conditions can be expressed in terms of a critical level of the current rate r_c, where:

$$r_c = \frac{r_e}{1 + r_e}. \tag{2.2}$$

At current rates above r_c, everything goes into consols; but for r less than r_c, everything goes into cash.

2.3 *Sticky and certain interest rate expectations.* So far the investor's expected interest rate r_e has been assumed to be completely independent of the current rate r. This assumption can be modified so long as some independence of the expected rate from the current rate is maintained. In Figure2.1,

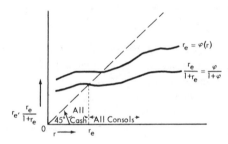

Fig. 2. 1 — Stickiness in the relation between expected and current interest rate.

for example, r_e is shown as a function of r, namely $\phi(r)$. Correspondingly $\frac{r_e}{1 + r_e}$ is a function of r. As shown in the figure, this function $\frac{\phi}{1 + \phi}$ has only one intersection with the 45° line, and at this intersection its slope $\frac{\phi'}{(1 + \phi)^2}$ is less than one. If these conditions are met, the intersection determines a critical rate r_c such that if r exceeds r_c the investor holds no cash, while if r is less than r_c he holds no consols.

2.4 *Differences of opinion and the aggregate demand for cash.* According to this model, the relationship of the individual's investment demand for cash to the current rate of interest would be the discontinuous step function shown by the heavy vertical lines $LMNW$ in Figure 2.2. How then do we get the familiar Keynesian liquidity preference function, a smooth, continuous inverse relationship between the demand for cash and the rate of interest? For the economy as a whole, such a relationship can be derived from individual behavior of the sort depicted in Figure 2.2 by assuming that individual investors differ in their critical rates r_c. Such an aggregate relationship is shown in Figure 2.3.

At actual rates above the maximum of individual critical rates the aggregate demand for cash is zero, while at rates below the minimum critical rate it is

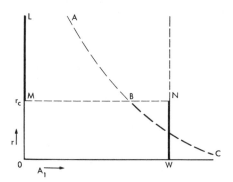

Fig. 2.2 — Individual demand for cash assuming certain
but inelastic interest rate expectations.

equal to the total investment balances for the whole economy. Between these two extremes the demand for cash varies inversely with the rate of interest r. Such a relationship is shown as $LMN\Sigma W$ in Figure 2.3. The demand for cash at r is the total of investment balances controlled by investors whose critical rates r_c exceed r. Strictly speaking, the curve is a step function; but, if the number of investors is large, it can be approximated by a smooth curve. Its

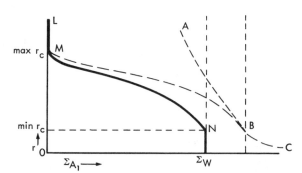

Fig. 2.3 — Aggregate demand for cash assuming differences
among individuals in interest rate expectations.

shape depends on the distribution of dollars of investment balances by the critical rate of the investor controlling them; the shape of the curve in Figure 2.3 follows from a unimodal distribution.

2.5 Capital gains or losses and open market operations. In the foregoing analysis the size of investment balances has been taken as independent of the current rate on consols r. This is not the case if there are already consols outstanding. Their value will depend inversely on the current rate of interest. Depending on the relation of the current rate to the previously fixed coupon on consols, owners of consols will receive capital gains or losses. Thus the investment balances of an individual owner of consols would not be constant at W but would depend on r in a manner illustrated by the curve ABC in Figure 2.2.[8] Similarly, the investment balances for the whole economy would follow a curve like ABC in Figure 2.3, instead of being constant at ΣW. The demand for cash would then be described by $LMBC$ in both figures. Correspondingly the demand for consols at any interest rate would be described by the horizontal distance between $LMBC$ and ABC. The value of consols goes to infinity as the rate of interest approaches zero; for this reason, the curve BC may never reach the horizontal axis. The size of investment balances would be bounded if the monetary assets other than cash consisted of bonds with definite maturities rather than consols.

According to this theory, a curve like $LMBC$ depicts the terms on which a central bank can engage in open-market operations, given the claims for future payments outstanding in the form of bonds or consols. The curve tells what the quantity of cash must be in order for the central bank to establish a particular interest rate. However, the curve will be shifted by open market operations themselves, since they will change the volume of outstanding bonds or consols. For example, to establish the rate at or below min r_c, the central bank would have to buy all outstanding bonds or consols. The size of the community's investment balances would then be independent of the rate of interest; it would be represented by a vertical line through, or to the right of, B, rather than the curve ABC. Thus the new relation between cash and interest would be a curve lying above LMB, of the same general contour as $LMN\Sigma W$.

2.6 *Keynesian theory and its critics.*   I believe the theory of liquidity preference I have just presented is essentially the original Keynesian explanation. The *General Theory* suggests a number of possible theoretical explanations, supported and enriched by the experience and insight of the author. But the explanation to which Keynes gave the greatest emphasis is the notion of a "normal" long-term rate, to which investors expect the rate of interest to return. When he refers to uncertainty in the market, he appears to mean disagreement among investors concerning the future of the rate rather than subjective doubt in the mind of an individual investor.[9] Thus Kaldor's correction of Keynes is more verbal than substantive when he says, "It is . . . not

---

[8] The size of their investment balances, held in cash and consols may not vary by the full amount of these changes in wealth; some part of the changes may be reflected in holdings of assets other than monetary assets. But presumably the size of investment balances will reflect at least in part these capital gains and losses. (1, p. 69)

[9] J. M. Keynes, *The General Theory of Employment, Interest, and Money* (New York: Harcourt Brace, 1936), Chapters 13 and 15, especially pp. 168–172 and 201–203. One quotation from p. 172 will illustrate the point: "It is interesting that the stability of the system and its sensitiveness to changes in the quantity of money should be so dependent on the existence

so much the *uncertainty* concerning future interest rates as the *inelasticity* of interest expectations which is responsible for Mr. Keynes' 'liquidity preference function,' ... "[10]

Keynes' use of this explanation of liquidity preference as a part of his theory of underemployment equilibrium was the target of important criticism by Leontief and Fellner. Leontief argued that liquidity preference must necessarily be zero *in equilibrium*, regardless of the rate of interest. Divergence between the current and expected interest rate is bound to vanish as investors learn from experience; no matter how low an interest rate may be, it can be accepted as "normal" if it persists long enough. This criticism was a part of Leontief's general methodological criticism of Keynes, that unemployment was not a feature of equilibrium, subject to analysis by tools of static theory, but a phenomenon of disequilibrium requiring analysis by dynamic theory.[11] Fellner makes a similar criticism of the logical appropriateness of Keynes' explanation of liquidity preference for the purposes of his theory of underemployment equilibrium. Why, he asks, are interest rates the only variables to which inelastic expectations attach? Why don't wealth owners and others regard pre-depression price levels as "normal" levels to which prices will return? If they did, consumption and investment demand would respond to reductions in money wages and prices, no matter how strong and how elastic the liquidity preference of investors.[12]

These criticisms raise the question whether it is possible to dispense with the assumption of stickiness in interest rate expectations without losing the implication that Keynesian theory drew from it. Can the inverse relationship of demand for cash to the rate of interest be based on a different set of assumptions about the behavior of individual investors? This question is the subject of the next part of the paper.

3. UNCERTAINTY, RISK AVERSION, AND LIQUIDITY PREFERENCE.

3.1 *The locus of opportunity for risk and expected return.* Suppose that an investor is not certain of the future rate of interest on consols; investment in consols then involves a risk of capital gain or loss. The higher the proportion of his investment balance that he holds in consols, the more risk the investor assumes. At the same time, increasing the proportion in consols also increases

---

of a variety of opinion about what is uncertain. Best of all that we should know the future. But if not, then, if we are to control the activity of the economic system by changing the quantity of money, it is important that opinions should differ." (1, p. 70)

[10] N. Kaldor, "Speculation and Economic Stability," *Review of Economic Studies*, Vol. 7 (1939), p. 15. (2, p. 70)

[11] W. Leontief, "Postulates: Keynes' General Theory and the Classicists," Chapter XIX in S. Harris, editor, *The New Economics* (New York: Knopf, 1947), pp. 232–242. Section 6, pp. 238–239, contains the specific criticism of Keynes' liquidity preference theory. (3, p. 70)

[12] W. Fellner, *Monetary Policies and Full Employment* (Berkeley: University of California Press, 1946), p. 149. (4, p. 70)

his expected return. In the upper half of Figure 3.1, the vertical axis represents expected return and the horizontal axis risk. A line such as OC_1 pictures the fact that the investor can expect more return if he assumes more risk. In the lower half of Figure 3.1, the left-hand vertical axis measures the proportion

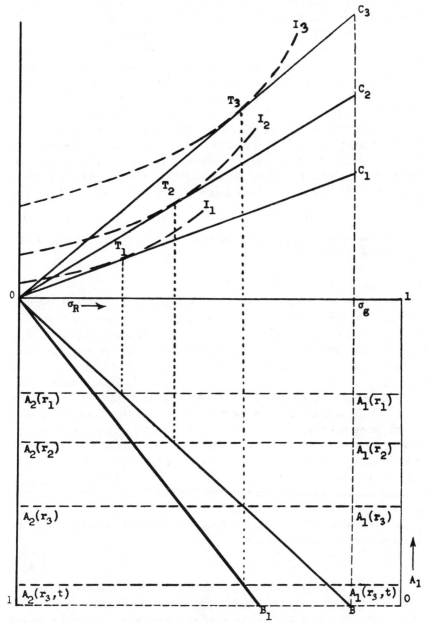

FIGURE 3.1
Portfolio Selection at Various Interest Rates and Before and After Taxation.

invested in consols. A line like OB shows risk as proportional to the share of the total balance held in consols.

The concepts of expected return and risk must be given more precision.

The individual investor of the previous section was assumed to have, for any current rate of interest, a definite expectation of the capital gain or loss g (defined in expression (2.1) above) he would obtain by investing one dollar in consols. Now he will be assumed instead to be uncertain about g but to base his actions on his estimate of its probability distribution. This probability distribution, it will be assumed, has an expected value of zero and is independent of the level of r, the current rate on consols. Thus the investor considers a doubling of the rate just as likely when rate is 5% as when it is 2%, and a halving of the rate just as likely when it is 1% as when it is 6%.

A portfolio consists of a proportion A_1 of cash and A_2 of consols, where A_1 and A_2 add up to 1. We shall assume that A_1 and A_2 do not depend on the absolute size of the initial investment balance in dollars. Negative values of A_1 and A_2 are excluded by definition; only the government and the banking system can issue cash and government consols. The return on a portfolio R is:

$$R = A_2(r + g) \qquad 0 \leq A_2 \leq 1. \tag{3.1}$$

Since g is a random variable with expected value zero, the expected return on the portfolio is:

$$E(R) = \mu_R = A_2 r. \tag{3.2}$$

The risk attached to a portfolio is to be measured by the standard deviation of R, σ_R. The standard deviation is a measure of the dispersion of possible returns around the mean value μ_R. A high standard deviation means, speaking roughly, high probability of large deviations from μ_R, both positive and negative. A low standard deviation means low probability of large deviations from μ_R; in the extreme case, a zero standard deviation would indicate certainty of receiving the return μ_R. Thus a high-σ_R portfolio offers the investor the chance of large capital gains at the price of equivalent chances of large capital losses. A low-σ_R portfolio protects the investor from capital loss, and likewise gives him little prospect of unusual gains. Although it is intuitively clear that the risk of a portfolio is to be identified with the dispersion of possible returns, the standard deviation is neither the sole measure of dispersion nor the obviously most relevant measure. The case for the standard deviation will be further discussed in section 3.3 below.

The standard deviation of R depends on the standard deviation of g, σ_g, and on the amount invested in consols:

$$\sigma_R = A_2 \sigma_g \qquad 0 \leq A_2 \leq 1. \tag{3.3}$$

Thus the proportion the investor holds in consols A_2 determines both his expected return μ_R and his risk σ_R. The terms on which the investor can obtain greater expected return at the expense of assuming more risk can be derived from (3.2) and (3.3):

$$\mu_R = \frac{r}{\sigma_g} \sigma_R \qquad 0 \leq \sigma_R \leq \sigma_g. \qquad (3.4)$$

Such an *opportunity locus* is shown as line OC_1 (for $r = r_1$) in Figure 3.1. The slope of the line is $\frac{r_1}{\sigma_g}$. For a higher interest rate r_2, the opportunity locus would be OC_2; and for r_3, a still higher rate, it would be OC_3. The relationship (3.3) between risk and investment in consols is shown as line OB in the lower half of the Figure. Cash holding $A_1(= 1 - A_2)$ can also be read off the diagram on the right-hand vertical axis.

3.2 *Loci of indifference between combinations of risk and expected return.* The investor is assumed to have preferences between expected return μ_R and risk σ_R that can be represented by a field of indifference curves. The investor is indifferent between all pairs (μ_R, σ_R) that lie on a curve such as I_1 in Figure 3.1. Points on I_2 are preferred to those on I_1; for given risk, an investor always prefers a greater to a smaller expectation of return. Conceivably, for some investors, *risk-lovers*, these indifference curves have negative slopes. Such individuals are willing to accept lower expected return in order to have the chance of unusually high capital gains afforded by high values of σ_R. Risk-averters, on the other hand, will not be satisfied to accept more risk unless they can also expect greater expected return. Their indifference curves will be positively sloped. Two kinds of risk-averters need to be distinguished. The first type, who may be called *diversifiers* for reasons that will become clear below, have indifference curves that are concave upward, like those in Figure 3.1. The second type, who may be called *plungers*, have indifference curves that are upward sloping, but either linear or convex upward.

3.3 *Indifference curves as loci of constant expected utility of wealth.* The reader who is willing to accept the indifference fields that have just been introduced into the analysis may skip to section 3.4 without losing the main thread of the argument. But these indifference curves need some explanation and defence. Indifference curves between μ_R and σ_R do not necessarily exist. It is a simplification to assume that the investor chooses among the alternative probability distributions of R available to him on the basis of only two parameters of those distributions. Even if this simplification is accepted, the mean and standard deviation may not be the pair of parameters that concern the investor.

3.3.1 One justification for the use of indifference curves between μ_R and σ_R would be that the investor evaluates the future of consols only in terms of some two-parameter family of probability distributions of g. For example, the investor might think in terms of a range of equally likely gains or losses, centered on zero. Or he might think in terms that can be approximated by a normal distribution. Whatever two-parameter family is assumed—uniform, normal, or some other—the whole probability distribution is determined as soon as the mean and standard deviation are specified. Hence the investor's choice among probability distributions can be analyzed by μ_R-σ_R indifference curves; any other pair of independent parameters could serve equally well.

If the investor's probability distributions are assumed to belong to some two-parameter family, the shape of his indifference curves can be inferred from the general characteristics of his utility-of-return function. This function will be assumed to relate utility to R, the percentage growth in the investment balance by the end of the period. This way of formulating the utility function makes the investor's indifference map, and therefore his choices of proportions of cash and consols, independent of the absolute amount of his initial balance.

On certain postulates, it can be shown that an individual's choice among probability distributions can be described as the maximization of the expected value of a utility function.[13] The ranking of probability distributions with respect to the expected value of utility will not be changed if the scale on which utility is measured is altered either by the addition of a constant or by multiplication by a positive constant. Consequently we are free to choose arbitrarily the zero and unit of measurement of the utility function $U(R)$ as follows: $U(0) = 0$; $U(-1) = -1$.

Suppose that the probability distribution of R can be described by a two-parameter density function $f(R; \mu_R, \sigma_R)$. Then the expected value of utility is:

$$E[U(R)] = \int_{-\infty}^{\infty} U(R)f(R; \mu_R, \sigma_R)dR. \qquad (3.5)$$

$$\text{Let } z = \frac{R - \mu_R}{\sigma_R}.$$

$$E[U(R)] = E(\mu_R, \sigma_R) = \int_{-\infty}^{\infty} U(\mu_R + \sigma_R z)f(z; 0, 1)dz. \qquad (3.6)$$

An indifference curve is a locus of points (μ_R, σ_R) along which expected utility is constant. We may find the slope of such a locus by differentiating (3.6) with

---

[13] See Von Neumann, J. and Morgenstern, O., *Theory of Games and Economic Behavior*, 3rd Edition (Princeton: Princeton University Press, 1953), pp. 15-30, pp. 617-632; Herstein, I. N. and Milnor, J., "An Axiomatic Approach to Measurable Utility," *Econometrica*, Vol. 23 (April, 1953), pp. 291-297; Marschak, J., "Rational Behavior, Uncertain Prospects, and Measurable Utility," *Econometrica*, Vol. 18 (April, 1950), pp. 111-141; Friedman, M. and Savage, L. J., "The Utility Analysis of Choices Involving Risk," *Journal of Political Economy*, Vol. 56 (August, 1948), pp. 279-304, and "The Expected Utility Hypothesis and the Measurability of Utility," *Journal of Political Economy*, Vol. 60 (December, 1952), pp. 463-474. For a treatment which also provides an axiomatic basis for the subjective probability estimates here assumed, see Savage, L. J., *The Foundations of Statistics* (New York: Wiley, 1954). (1, p. 74)

respect to σ_R:

$$0 = \int_{-\infty}^{\infty} U'(\mu_R + \sigma_R z)\left[\frac{d\mu_R}{d\sigma_R} + z\right] f(z; 0, 1)dz.$$

$$\frac{d\mu_R}{d\sigma_R} = -\frac{\displaystyle\int_{-\infty}^{\infty} z U'(R) f(z; 0, 1)dz}{\displaystyle\int_{-\infty}^{\infty} U'(R) f(z; 0, 1)dz}. \tag{3.7}$$

$U'(R)$, the marginal utility of return, is assumed to be everywhere non-negative. If it is also a decreasing function of R, then the slope of the indifference locus must be positive; an investor with such a utility function is a risk-averter. If it is an increasing function of R, the slope will be negative; this kind of utility function characterizes a risk-lover.

Similarly, the curvature of the indifference loci is related to the shape of the utility function. Suppose, that (μ_R, σ_R) and (μ_R', σ_R') are on the same indifference locus, so that $E(\mu_R, \sigma_R) = E(\mu_R', \sigma_R')$. Is $\left(\dfrac{\mu_R + \mu_R'}{2}, \dfrac{\sigma_R + \sigma_R'}{2}\right)$ on the same locus, or on a higher or a lower one? In the case of declining marginal utility we know that for every z:

$$\tfrac{1}{2}U(\mu_R + \sigma_R z) + \tfrac{1}{2}U(\mu_R' + \sigma_R' z) < U\left(\frac{\mu_R + \mu_R'}{2} + \frac{\sigma_R + \sigma_R'}{2} z\right)$$

Consequently $E\left(\dfrac{\mu_R + \mu_R'}{2}, \dfrac{\sigma_R + \sigma_R'}{2}\right)$ is greater than $E(\mu_R, \sigma_R)$ or $E(\mu_R', \sigma_R')$, and

$$\left(\frac{\mu_R + \mu_R'}{2}, \frac{\sigma_R + \sigma_R'}{2}\right),$$

which lies on a line between (μ_R, σ_R) and (μ_R', σ_R'), is on a higher locus than those points. Thus it is shown that a risk-averter's indifference curve is necessarily concave upwards, provided it is derived in this manner from a two parameter family of probability distributions and declining marginal utility of return. All risk-averters are diversifiers; plungers do not exist. The same kind of argument shows that a risk-lover's indifference curve is concave downwards.

3.3.2 In the absence of restrictions on the subjective probability distribution of the investor, the parameters of the distribution relevant to his choice can be sought in parametric restrictions on his utility-of-return function. Two parameters of the utility function are determined by the choice of the utility scale. If specification of the utility function requires no additional parameters, one parameter of the probability distribution summarizes all the information relevant for the investor's choice. For example, if the utility function is linear

$[U(R) = R]$, then the expected value of utility is simply the expected value of R, and maximizing expected utility leads to the same behavior as maximizing return in a world of certainty. If, however, one additional parameter is needed to specify the utility function, then two parameters of the probability distribution will be relevant to the choice; and so on. Which parameters of the distribution are relevant depends on the form of the utility function.

Focus on the mean and standard deviation of return can be justified on the assumption that the utility function is quadratic. Following our conventions as to utility scale, the quadratic function would be:

$$U(R) = (1 + b)R + bR^2. \tag{3.8}$$

Here $0 < b < 1$ for a risk-lover, and $-1 < b < 0$ for a risk-averter. However (3.8) cannot describe the utility function for the whole range of R, because marginal utility cannot be negative. The function given in (3.8) can apply only for:

$$(1 + b) + 2bR \geq 0;$$

that is, for:

$$R \geq -\left(\frac{1 + b}{2b}\right)(b > 0) \quad \text{(Risk lover)} \tag{3.9}$$

$$R \leq -\left(\frac{1 + b}{2b}\right)(b < 0) \quad \text{(Risk averter)}.$$

In order to use (3.8), therefore, we must exclude from the range of possibility values of R outside the limits (3.9). At the maximum investment in consols $(A_2 = 1)$, $R = r + g$. A risk-averter must be assumed therefore, to restrict the range of capital gains g to which he attaches non-zero probability so that, for the highest rate of interest r to be considered:

$$r + g \leq -\left(\frac{1 + b}{2b}\right). \tag{3.10}$$

The corresponding limitation for a risk-lover is that, for the lowest interest rate r to be considered:

$$r + g \geq -\left(\frac{1 + b}{2b}\right). \tag{3.11}$$

Given the utility function (3.8) , we can investigate the slope and curvature of the indifference curves it implies. The probability density function for R, $f(R)$, is restricted by the limit (3.10) or (3.11); but otherwise no restriction on its shape is assumed.

$$E[U(R)] = \int_{-\infty}^{\infty} U(R)f(R)dR = (1 + b)\mu_R + b(\sigma_R^2 + \mu_R^2). \tag{3.12}$$

Holding $E[U(R)]$ constant and differentiating with respect to σ_R to obtain the slope of an indifference curve, we have:

$$\frac{d\mu_R}{d\sigma_R} = \frac{\sigma_R}{-\dfrac{1+b}{2b} - \mu_R}. \tag{3.13}$$

For a risk-averter, $-\dfrac{1+b}{2b}$ is positive and is the upper limit for R, according to (3.9); $-\dfrac{1+b}{2b}$ is necessarily larger than μ_R. Therefore the slope of an indifference locus is positive. For a risk-lover, on the other hand, the corresponding argument shows that the slope is negative.

Differentiating (3.13) leads to the same conclusions regarding curvature as the alternative approach of section 3.3.1, namely that a risk-averter is necessarily a diversifier.

$$\frac{d^2\mu_R}{d\sigma_R} = \frac{1 + \left(\dfrac{d\mu_R^2}{d\sigma_R}\right)}{\left(-\dfrac{1+b}{2b} - \mu_R\right)^2}. \tag{3.14}$$

For a risk-averter, the second derivative is positive and the indifference locus is concave upwards; for a risk-lover, it is concave downwards.

3.4 *Effects of changes in the rate of interest.*   In section 3.3 two alternative rationalizations of the indifference curves introduced in section 3.2 have been presented. Both rationalizations assume that the investor (1) estimates subjective probability distributions of capital gain or loss in holding consols, (2) evaluates his prospective increase in wealth in terms of a cardinal utility function, (3) ranks alternative prospects according to the expected value of utility. The rationalization of section 3.3.1 derives the indifference curves by restricting the subjective probability distributions to a two-parameter family. The rationalization of section 3.3.2 derives the indifference curves by assuming the utility function to be quadratic within the relevant range. On either rationalization, a risk-averter's indifference curves must be concave upwards, characteristic of the diversifiers of section 3.2, and those of a risk-lover concave downwards. If the category defined as *plungers* in 3.2 exists at all, their indifference curves must be determined by some process other than those described in 3.3.

The opportunity locus for the investor is described in 3.1 and summarized in equation (3.4). The investor decides the amount to invest in consols so as to reach the highest indifference curve permitted by his opportunity-locus. This maximization may be one of three kinds:

I. Tangency between an indifference curve and the opportunity locus, as

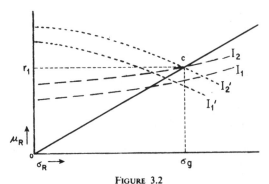

FIGURE 3.2
" Risk-lovers " and " Diversifiers " : Optimum Portfolio at Maximum Risk and Expected Return.

illustrated by points T_1, T_2, and T_3 in Figure 3.1. A regular maximum of this kind can occur only for a risk-averter, and will lead to diversification. Both A_1, cash holding, and A_2, consol holding, will be positive. They too are shown in Figure 3.1, in the bottom half of the diagram, where, for example, $A_1(r_1)$ and $A_2(r_1)$ depict the cash and consol holdings corresponding to point T_1.

II. A corner maximum at the point $\mu_R = r$, $\sigma_R = \sigma_g$, as illustrated in Figure 3.2. In Figure 3.2 the opportunity locus is the ray OC, and point C represents the highest expected return and risk obtainable by the investor i.e. the expected return and risk from holding his entire balance in consols. A utility maximum at C can occur either for a risk-averter or for a risk-lover. I_1 and I_2 represent indifference curves of a diversifier; I_2 passes through C and has a lower slope, both at C and everywhere to the left of C, than the opportunity locus. I_1' and I_2' represent the indifference curves of a risk-lover, for whom it is clear that C is always the optimum position. Similarly, a plunger may, if his indifference curves stand with respect to his opportunity locus as in Figure 3.3 (OC_2) plunge his entire balance in consols.

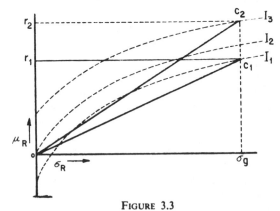

FIGURE 3.3
" Plungers "—Optimum Portfolio at Minimum or Maximum Risk and Expected Return.

III. A corner maximum at the origin, where the entire balance is held in cash. For a plunger, this case is illustrated in Figure 3.3, (OC_1). Conceivably it could also occur for a diversifier, if the slope of his indifference curve at the origin exceeded the slope of the opportunity locus. However, case III is entirely excluded for investors whose indifference curves represent the constant-expected-utility loci of section 3.3. Such investors, we have already noted, cannot be plungers. Furthermore, the slope of all constant-expected-utility loci at $\sigma_R = 0$ must be zero, as can be seen from (3.7) and (3.13).

We can now examine the consequences of a change in the interest rate r, holding constant the investor's estimate of the risk of capital gain or loss. An increase in the interest rate will rotate the opportunity locus OC to the left. How will this affect the investor's holdings of cash and consols? We must consider separately the three cases.

I. In Figure 3.1, OC_1, OC_2, and OC_3 represent opportunity loci for successively higher rates of interest. The indifference curves I_1, I_2, and I_3 are drawn so that the points of tangency T_1, T_2, and T_3, correspond to successively higher holdings of consols A_2. In this diagram, the investor's demand for cash depends inversely on the interest rate.

This relationship is, of course, in the direction liquidity preference theory has taught us to expect, but it is not the only possible direction of relationship. It is quite possible to draw indifference curves so that the point of tangency moves left as the opportunity locus is rotated counter-clockwise. The ambiguity is a familiar one in the theory of choice, and reflects the ubiquitous conflict between income and substitution effects. An increase in the rate of interest is an incentive to take more risk; so far as the substitution effect is concerned, it means a shift from security to yield. But an increase in the rate of interest also has an income effect, for it gives the opportunity to enjoy more security along with more yield. The ambiguity is analogous to the doubt concerning the effect of a change in the interest rate on saving; the substitution effect argues for a positive relationship, the income effect for an inverse relationship.

However, if the indifference curves are regarded as loci of constant expected utility, as derived in section 3.3, part of this ambiguity can be resolved. We have already observed that these loci all have zero slopes at $\sigma_R = 0$. As the interest rate r rises from zero, so also will consul holding A_2. At higher interest rates, however, the inverse relationship may occur.

This reversal of direction can, however, virtually be excluded in the case of the quadratic utility function (section 3.3.2). The condition for a maximum is that the slope of an indifference locus as given by (3.13) equal the slope of the opportunity locus (3.4).

$$\frac{r}{\sigma_g} = \frac{A_2\sigma_g}{-\dfrac{1+b}{2b} - A_2 r} \; ; \; A_2 = \frac{r}{r^2 + \sigma_g^2}\left(-\frac{1+b}{2b}\right). \tag{3.15}$$

Equation (3.15) expresses A_2 as a function of r, and differentiating gives:

$$\frac{dA_2}{dr} = \frac{\sigma_g^2 - r^2}{(\sigma_g^2 + r^2)^2}\left(-\frac{1+b}{2b}\right); \frac{r}{A_2}\frac{dA_2}{dr} = \frac{\sigma_g^2 - r^2}{\sigma_g^2 + r^2}. \tag{3.16}$$

Thus the share of consols in the portfolio increases with the interest rate for r less than σ_g. Moreover, if r exceeds σ_g, a tangency maximum cannot occur unless r also exceeds g_{max}, the largest capital gain the investor conceives possible (see 3.10).[14] The demand for consols is less elastic at high interest rates than at low, but the elasticity is not likely to become negative.

II and III. A change in the interest rate cannot cause a risk-lover to alter his position, which is already the point of maximum risk and expected yield. Conceivably a "diversifier" might move from a corner maximum to a regular interior maximum in response either to a rise in the interest rate or to a fall. A "plunger" might find his position altered by an increase in the interest rate, as from r_1 to r_2 in Figure 3.3; this would lead him to shift his entire balance from cash to consols.

3.5 *Effects of changes in risk.*   Investor's estimates σ_g of the risk of holding monetary assets other than cash, "consols," are subjective. But they are undoubtedly affected by market experience, and they are also subject to influence by measures of monetary and fiscal policy. By actions and words, the central bank can influence investors' estimates of the variability of interest rates; its influence on these estimates of risk may be as important in accomplishing or preventing changes in the rate as open-market operations and other direct interventions in the market. Tax rates, and differences in tax treatment of capital gains, losses, and interest earnings, affect in calculable ways the investor's risks and expected returns. For these reasons it is worth while to examine the effects of a change in an investor's estimate of risk on his allocation between cash and consols.

In Figure 3.4, T_1 and A_2 (r_1, σ_g) represent the initial position of an investor, at interest rate r_1 and risk σ_g. OC_1 is the opportunity locus (3.4), and OB_1 is the risk-consols relationship (3.3). If the investor now cuts his estimate of risk in half, to $\frac{\sigma_g}{2}$, the opportunity locus will double in slope, from OC_1 to OC_2,

---

[14] For this statement and its proof, I am greatly indebted to my colleague Arthur Okun. The proof is as follows:

If $r^2 \geq \sigma_g^2$, then by (3.15) and (3.10):

$$1 \geq A_2 \geq \frac{r}{2r^2}\left(-\frac{1+b}{2b}\right) \geq \frac{1}{2r}(r + g_{max}).$$

From the two extremes of this series of inequalities it follows that $2r \geq r + g_{max}$ or $r \geq g_{max}$. Professor Okun also points out that this condition is incompatible with a tangency maximum if the distribution of g is symmetrical. For then $r \geq g_{max}$ would imply $r + g_{min} \geq 0$. There would be no possibility of net loss on consols and thus no reason to hold any cash. (1, p. 79)

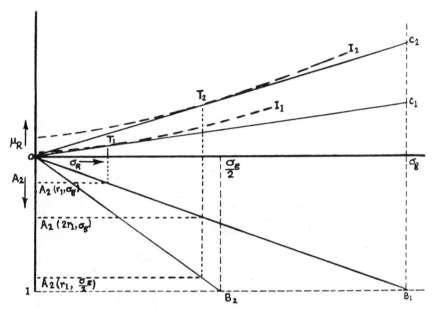

FIGURE 3.4
Comparison of effects of changes in interest rate (r) and in " risk " (σ_g) on holding of consols.

and the investor will shift to point T_2. The risk-consols relationship will have also doubled in slope, from OB_1 to OB_2. Consequently points T_2 corresponds to an investment in consols of $A_2 \left(r_1, \dfrac{\sigma_g}{2} \right)$. This same point T_2 would have been reached if the interest rate had doubled while the investor's risk estimate σ_g remained unchanged. But in that case, since the risk-consols relationship would remain at OB_1, the corresponding investment in consols would have been only half as large, i.e., $A_2 (2r_1, \sigma_g)$. In general, the following relationship exists between the elasticity of the demand for consols with respect to risk and its elasticity with respect to the interest rate:

$$\frac{\sigma_g}{A_2} \frac{dA_2}{d\sigma_g} = -\frac{r}{A_2} \frac{dA_2}{dr} - 1. \tag{3.17}$$

The implications of this relationship for analysis of effects of taxation may be noted in passing, with the help of Figure 3.4. Suppose that the initial position of the investor is T_2 and $A_2 (2r_1, \sigma_g)$. A tax of 50% is now levied on interest income and capital gains alike, with complete loss offset provisions. The result of the tax is to reduce the expected net return per dollar of consols from $2r_1$ to r_1 and to reduce the risk to the investor per dollar of consols from σ_g to $\sigma_g/2$. The opportunity locus will remain at OC_2, and the investor will still wish to obtain the combination of risk and expected return depicted by T_2. To obtain this combination, however, he must now double his holding of consols, to $A_2 (r_1, \sigma_g/2)$; the tax shifts the risk-consols line from OB_1 to OB_2.

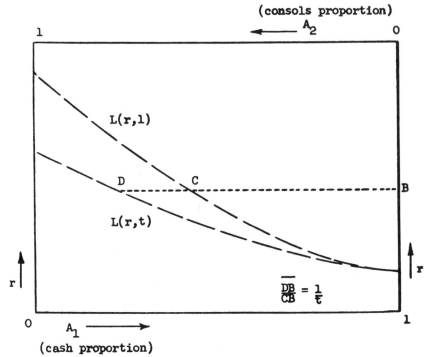

FIGURE 3.5
Effect of Tax (at Rate 1—*t*) on Liquidity Preference Function.

A tax of this kind, therefore, would reduce the demand for cash at any market rate of interest, shifting the investor's liquidity preference schedule in the manner shown in Figure 3.5. A tax on interest income only, with no tax on capital gains and no offset privileges for capital losses, would have quite different effects. If the Treasury began to split the interest income of the investor in Figure 3.4 but not to share the risk, the investor would move from his initial position, T_2 and $A_2\,(2r_1\,,\sigma_g)$; to T_1 and $A_2\,(r_1\,,\sigma_g)$. His demand for cash at a given market rate of interest would be increased and his liquidity preference curve shifted to the right.

3.6 *Multiple alternatives to cash.*   So far it has been assumed that there is only one alternative to cash, and A_2 has represented the share of the investor's balance held in that asset, "consols." The argument is not essentially changed, however, if A_2 is taken to be the aggregate share invested in a variety of non-cash assets, e.g. bonds and other debt instruments differing in maturity, debtor, and other features. The return R and the risk σ_g on "consols" will then represent the average return and risk on a composite of these assets.

Suppose that there are m assets other than cash, and let $x_i(i = 1, 2, \ldots m)$ be the amount invested in the i-th of these assets. All x_i are non-negative, and $\sum_{i=1}^{m} x_i = A_2 \leq 1$. Let r_i be the expected yield, and let g_i be the capital gain or loss, per dollar invested in the i-th asset. We assume $E(g_i) = 0$ for all i. Let v_{ij} be the variance or covariance of g_i and g_j as estimated by the investor.

$$v_{ij} = E(g_i g_j) \quad (i, j, = 1, 2, \ldots m). \tag{3.18}$$

The over-all expected return is:

$$\mu_R = A_2 r = \sum_{i=1}^{m} x_i r_i. \tag{3.19}$$

The over-all variance of return is:

$$\sigma_R^2 = A_2^2 \sigma_g^2 = \sum_{i=1}^{m} \sum_{j=1}^{m} x_i x_j v_{ij}. \tag{3.20}$$

A set of points x_i for which $\sum_{i=1}^{m} x_i r_i$ is constant may be defined as a *constant-return locus*. A constant-return locus is linear in the x_i. For two assets x_1 and x_2, two loci are illustrated in Figure 3.6. One locus of combinations of x_1 and x_2 that give the same expected return μ_R is the line from $\dfrac{\mu_R}{r_2}$ to $\dfrac{\mu_R}{r_1}$, through

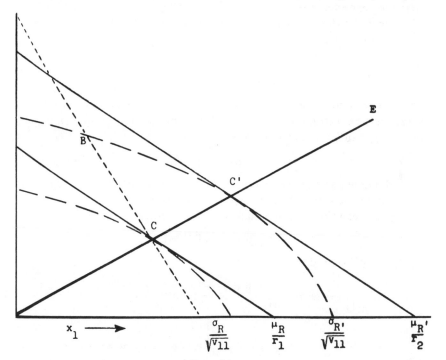

FIGURE 3.6
Dominant Combinations of Two Assets.

C; another locus, for a higher constant, μ'_R, is the parallel line from $\dfrac{\mu'_R}{r_2}$ to $\dfrac{\mu'_R}{r_1}$, through C'.

A set of points x_i for which σ^2_R is constant may be defined as a *constant-risk locus*. These loci are ellipsoidal. For two assets x_1 and x_2, such a locus is illustrated by the quarter-ellipse from $\dfrac{\sigma_R}{\sqrt{v_{22}}}$ to $\dfrac{\sigma_R}{\sqrt{v_{11}}}$, through point C. The equation of such an ellipse is:

$$x_1^2 v_{11} + 2x_1 x_2 v_{12} + x_2^2 v_{22} = \sigma^2_R = \text{constant.}$$

Another such locus, for a higher risk level, σ'_R, is the quarter-ellipse from

$\dfrac{\sigma'_R}{\sqrt{v_{22}}}$ to $\dfrac{\sigma'_R}{\sqrt{v_{11}}}$ through point C'.

From Figure 3.6, it is clear that C and C' exemplify *dominant* combinations of x_1 and x_2. If the investor is incurring a risk of σa, somewhere on the ellipse through C, he will have the highest possible expectation of return available to him at that level of risk. The highest available expected return is represented by the constant-expected-return line tangent to the ellipse at C. Similarly C' is a dominant point: it would not be possible to obtain a higher expected return than at C' without incurring additional risk, or to diminish risk without sacrificing expected return.

In general, a dominant combination of assets is defined as a set x_i which minimizes σ^2_R for μ_R constant:

$$\sum_i \left(\sum_j v_{ij} x_j \right) x_i - \lambda \left(\sum_i r_i x_i - \mu_R \right) = \min \tag{3.21}$$

where λ is a Lagrange multiplier. The conditions for the minimum are that the x_i satisfy the constraint (3.19) and the following set of m simultaneous linear equations, written in matrix notation:

$$[v_{ij}][x_i] = [\lambda r_i]. \tag{3.22}$$

All dominant sets lie on a ray from the origin. That is, if $[x_i^{(0)}]$ and $[x_i^{(1)}]$ are dominant sets, then there is some non-negative scalar κ such that $[x_i^{(1)}] = [\kappa x_i^{(0)}]$. By definition of a dominant set, there is some $\lambda^{(0)}$ such that:

$$[v_{ij}][x_i^{(0)}] = [\lambda^{(0)} r_i],$$

and some $\lambda^{(1)}$ such that:

$$[v_{ij}][x_i^{(1)}] = [\lambda^{(1)} r_i].$$

Take $\kappa = \dfrac{\lambda(1)}{\lambda(0)}$. Then:

$$[v_{ij}][\kappa x_i^{(0)}] = [\kappa \lambda^{(0)} r_i] = [\lambda^{(1)} r_i] = [v_{ij}][x_i^{(1)}].$$

At the same time, $\Sigma r_i \, x_i^{(0)} = \mu_R^{(0)}$ and $\Sigma r_i \, x_i^{(1)} = \mu_R^{(1)}$.

Hence, $\mu_R^{(1)} = [\kappa\mu_R^{(0)}]$. Conversely, every set on this ray is a dominant set. If $[x_i^{(0)}]$ is a dominant set, then so is $[\kappa x_i^{(0)}]$ for any non-negative constant κ. This is easily proved. If $[x_i^{(0)}]$ satisfies (3.19) and (3.22) for $\mu_R^{(0)}$ and $\lambda^{(0)}$, then $[\kappa x_i^{(0)}]$ satisfies (3.19) and (3.22) for $\lambda^{(K)} = \kappa\lambda^{(0)}$ and $\mu_R^{(K)} = \kappa\mu_R^{(0)}$. In the two dimensional case pictured in Figure 3.6, the dominant pairs lie along the ray $OCC'E$.

There will be some point on the ray (say E in Figure 3.6) at which the investor's holdings of non-cash assets will exhaust his investment balance ($\sum_i x_i = 1$) and leave nothing for cash holding. Short of that point the balance will be divided among cash and non-cash assets in proportion to the distances along the ray; in Figure 3.6 at point C for example, $\dfrac{OC}{OE}$ of the balance would be non-cash, and $\dfrac{CE}{OE}$ cash. But the convenient fact that has just been proved is that the proportionate composition of the non-cash assets is independent of their aggregate share of the investment balance. This fact makes it possible to describe the investor's decisions as if there were a single non-cash asset, a composite formed by combining the multitude of actual non-cash assets in fixed proportions.

Corresponding to every point on the ray of dominant sets is an expected return μ_R and risk σ_R; these pairs (μ_R, σ_R) are the opportunity locus of sections 3.1 and 3.4. By means of (3.22), the opportunity locus can be expressed in terms of the expected return and variances and covariances of the non-cash assets: Let:

$$[V_{ij}] = [V_{ij}]^{-1}.$$

Then:

$$\mu_R = \lambda \sum_i \sum_j r_i r_j V_{ij} \qquad (3.23)$$

$$\sigma_R^2 = \lambda^2 \sum_i \sum_j r_i r_j V_{ij}. \qquad (3.24)$$

Thus the opportunity locus is the line:

$$\mu_R = \sigma_R \sqrt{\sum_i \sum_j r_i r_j V_{ij}} = \sigma_R \frac{r}{\sigma_g} \qquad (3.25)$$

This analysis is applicable only so long as cash is assumed to be a riskless asset. In the absence of a residual riskless asset, the investor has no reason to confine his choices to the ray of dominant sets. This may be easily verified in the two-asset case. Using Figure 3.6 for a different purpose now, suppose that the entire investment balance must be divided between x_1 and x_2. The point (x_1, x_2) must fall on the line $x_1 + x_2 = 1$, represented by the line through BC in the diagram. The investor will not necessarily choose point C. At point B, for example, he would obtain a higher expected yield as well as a higher risk;

he may prefer B to C. His opportunity locus represents the pairs (μ_R, σ_R) along the line through $BC(x_1 + x_2 = 1)$ rather than along the ray OC, and is a hyperbola rather than a line. It is still possible to analyze portfolio choices by the apparatus of (μ_R, σ_R) indifference and opportunity loci, but such analysis is beyond the scope of the present paper.[15]

It is for this reason that the present analysis has been deliberately limited, as stated in section 1.2, to choices among monetary assets. Among these assets cash is relatively riskless, even though in the wider context of portfolio selection, the risk of changes in purchasing power, which all monetary assets share, may be relevant to many investors. Breaking down the portfolio selection problem into stages at different levels of aggregation—allocation first among, and then within, asset categories—seems to be a permissible and perhaps even indispensable simplification both for the theorist and for the investor himself.

4. IMPLICATIONS OF THE ANALYSIS FOR LIQUIDITY PREFERENCE THEORY

The theory of risk-avoiding behavior has been shown to provide a basis for liquidity preference and for an inverse relationship between the demand for cash and the rate of interest. This theory does not depend on inelasticity of expectations of future interest rates, but can proceed from the assumption that the expected value of capital gain or loss from holding interest-bearing assets is always zero. In this respect, it is a logically more satisfactory foundation for liquidity preference than the Keynesian theory described in section 2. Moreover, it has the empirical advantage of explaining diversification—the same individual holds both cash and "consols"—while Keynesian theory implies that each investor will hold only one asset.

The risk aversion theory of liquidity preference mitigates the major logical objection to which, according to the argument of section 2.6, the Keynesian theory is vulnerable. But it cannot completely meet Leontief's position that in a strict stationary equilibrium liquidity preference must be zero unless cash and consols bear equal rates. By their very nature consols and, to a lesser degree, all time obligations contain a potential for capital gain or loss that cash and other demand obligations lack. Presumably, however, there is some length of experience of constancy in the interest rate that would teach the most stubbornly timid investor to ignore that potential. In a pure stationary state, it could be argued, the interest rate on consols would have been the same for so long that investors would unanimously estimate σ_g to be zero. So stationary a state is of very little interest. Fortunately the usefulness of comparative

[15] A forthcoming book by Harry Markowitz, *Techniques of Portfolio Selection*, will treat the general problem of finding dominant sets and computing the corresponding opportunity locus, for sets of securities all of which involve risk. Markowitz's main interest is prescription of rules of rational behavior for investors; the main concern of this paper is the implications for economic theory, mainly comparative statics, that can be derived from assuming that investors do in fact follow such rules. For the general nature of Markowitz's approach, see his article, "Portfolio Selection," *Journal of Finance*, Volume VII, No. 1 (March, 1952), pp. 77–91. (1, p. 85)

statics does not appear to be confined to comparisons of states each of which would take a generation or more to achieve. As compared to the Keynesian theory of liquidity preference, the risk aversion theory widens the applicability of comparative statics in aggregate analysis; this is all that need be claimed for it.

The theory, however, is somewhat ambiguous concerning the direction of relationship between the rate of interest and the demand for cash. For low interest rates, the theory implies a negative elasticity of demand for cash with respect to the interest rate, an elasticity that becomes larger and larger in absolute value as the rate approaches zero. This implication, of course, is in accord with the usual assumptions about liquidity preference. But for high interest rates, and especially for individuals whose estimates σ_g of the risk of capital gain or loss on "consols" are low, the demand for cash may be an increasing, rather than a decreasing, function of the interest rate. However, the force of this reversal of direction is diluted by recognition, as in section 2.5, that the size of investment balances is not independent of the current rate of interest r. In section 3.4 we have considered the proportionate allocation between cash and "consols" on the assumption that it is independent of the size of the balance. An increase in the rate of interest may lead an investor to desire to shift towards cash. But to the extent that the increase in interest also reduces the value of the investor's consol holdings, it automatically gratifies this desire, at least in part.

The assumption that investors expect on balance no change in the rate of interest has been adopted for the theoretical reasons explained in section 2.6 rather than for reasons of realism. Clearly investors do form expectations of changes in interest rates and differ from each other in their expectations. For the purposes of dynamic theory and of analysis of specific market situations, the theories of sections 2 and 3 are complementary rather than competitive. The formal apparatus of section 3 will serve just as well for a non-zero expected capital gain or loss as for a zero expected value of g. Stickiness of interest rate expectations would mean that the expected value of g is a function of the rate of interest r, going down when r goes down and rising when r goes up. In addition to the rotation of the opportunity locus due to a change in r itself, there would be a further rotation in the same direction due to the accompanying change in the expected capital gain or loss. At low interest rates expectation of capital loss may push the opportunity locus into the negative quadrant, so that the optimal position is clearly no consols, all cash. At the other extreme, expectation of capital gain at high interest rates would increase sharply the slope of the opportunity locus and the frequency of no cash, all consols positions, like that of Figure 3.3. The stickier the investor's expectations, the more sensitive his demand for cash will be to changes in the rate of interest.

7. CAPITAL ASSET PRICES: A THEORY OF MARKET EQUILIBRIUM UNDER CONDITIONS OF RISK*

WILLIAM F. SHARPE†

Reprinted from *The Journal of Finance,* Vol. XIX, No. 3 (September 1964), pp. 425–42, by permission of the author and the publisher.

I. INTRODUCTION

One of the problems which has plagued those attempting to predict the behavior of capital markets is the absence of a body of positive micro-economic theory dealing with conditions of risk. Although many useful insights can be obtained from the traditional models of investment under conditions of certainty, the pervasive influence of risk in financial transactions has forced those working in this area to adopt models of price behavior which are little more than assertions. A typical classroom explanation of the determination of capital asset prices, for example, usually begins with a careful and relatively rigorous description of the process through which individual preferences and physical relationships interact to determine an equilibrium pure interest rate. This is generally followed by the assertion that somehow a market risk-premium is also determined, with the prices of assets adjusting accordingly to account for differences in their risk.

A useful representation of the view of the capital market implied in such discussions is illustrated in Figure 1. In equilibrium, capital asset prices have adjusted so that the investor, if he follows rational procedures (primarily diversification), is able to attain any desired point along a *capital market line.*[1] He may obtain a higher expected rate of return on his holdings only by incurring additional risk. In effect, the market presents him with two prices: the *price of time,* or the pure interest rate (shown by the intersection of the line with the horizontal axis) and the *price of risk,* the additional expected return per unit of risk borne (the reciprocal of the slope of the line).

At present there is no theory describing the manner in which the price of

---

* A great many people provided comments on early versions of this paper which led to major improvements in the exposition. In addition to the referees, who were most helpful, the author wishes to express his appreciation to Dr. Harry Markowitz of the Rand Corporation, Professor Jack Hirshleifer of the University of California at Los Angeles, and to Professors Yoram Barzel, George Brabb, Bruce Johnson, Walter Oi and R. Haney Scott of the University of Washington.

† Associate Professor of Operations Research, University of Washington.

[1] Although some discussions are also consistent with a non-linear (but monotonic) curve.

risk results from the basic influences of investor preferences, the physical attributes of capital assets, etc. Moreover, lacking such a theory, it is difficult to give any real meaning to the relationship between the price of a single asset and its risk. Through diversification, some of the risk inherent in an asset can be avoided so that its total risk is obviously not the relevant influence on its price; unfortunately little has been said concerning the particular risk component which is relevant.

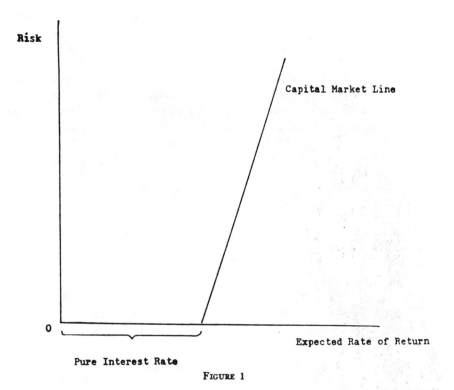

FIGURE 1

In the last ten years a number of economists have developed *normative* models dealing with asset choice under conditions of risk. Markowitz,[2] following Von Neumann and Morgenstern, developed an analysis based on the expected utility maxim and proposed a general solution for the portfolio selection problem. Tobin[3] showed that under certain conditions Markowitz's model implies that the process of investment choice can be broken down into two phases: first, the choice of a unique optimum combination of risky assets;

[2] Harry M. Markowitz, *Portfolio Selection, Efficient Diversification of Investments* (New York: John Wiley and Sons, Inc., 1959). The major elements of the theory first appeared in his article " Portfolio Selection," *The Journal of Finance*, XII (March 1952), 77–91.

[3] James Tobin, " Liquidity Preference as Behavior Towards Risk," *The Review of Economic Studies*, XXV (February 1958), 65–86.

and second, a separate choice concerning the allocation of funds between such a combination and a single riskless asset. Recently, Hicks[4] has used a model similar to that proposed by Tobin to derive corresponding conclusions about individual investor behavior, dealing somewhat more explicitly with the nature of the conditions under which the process of investment choice can be dichotomized. An even more detailed discussion of this process, including a rigorous proof in the context of a choice among lotteries has been presented by Gordon and Gangolli.[5]

Although all the authors cited use virtually the same model of investor behavior,[6] none has yet attempted to extend it to construct a *market* equilibrium theory of asset prices under conditions of risk.[7] We will show that such an extension provides a theory with implications consistent with the assertions of traditional financial theory described above. Moreover, it sheds considerable light on the relationship between the price of an asset and the various components of its overall risk. For these reasons it warrants consideration as a model of the determination of capital asset prices.

Part II provides the model of individual investor behavior under conditions of risk. In Part III the equilibrium conditions for the capital market are considered and the capital market line derived. The implications for the relationship between the prices of individual capital assets and the various components of risk are described in Part IV.

II. OPTIMAL INVESTMENT POLICY FOR THE INDIVIDUAL

THE INVESTOR'S PREFERENCE FUNCTION

Assume that an individual views the outcome of any investment in probabilistic terms; that is, he thinks of the possible results in terms of some probability distribution. In assessing the desirability of a particular investment, however, he is willing to act on the basis of only two parameters of this

---

[4] John R. Hicks, "Liquidity," *The Economic Journal*, LXXII (December 1962), 787–802.

[5] M. J. Gordon and Ramesh Gangolli, "Choice Among and Scale of Play on Lottery Type Alternatives," College of Business Administration, University of Rochester, 1962. For another discussion of this relationship see W. F. Sharpe, "A Simplified Model for Portfolio Analysis," *Management Science*, Vol. 9, No. 2 (January 1963), 277–293. A related discussion can be found in F. Modigliani and M. H. Miller, "The Cost of Capital, Corporation Finance, and the Theory of Investment," *The American Economic Review*, XLVIII (June 1958), 261–297.

[6] Recently Hirshleifer has suggested that the mean-variance approach used in the articles cited is best regarded as a special case of a more general formulation due to Arrow. See Hirshleifer's "Investment Decision Under Uncertainty," *Papers and Proceedings of the Seventy-Sixth Annual Meeting of the American Economic Association*, December 1963, or Arrow's "Le Role des Valeurs Boursieres pour la Repartition la Meilleure des Risques," *International Colloquium on Econometrics*, 1952.

[7] After preparing this paper the author learned that Mr. Jack L. Treynor, of Arthur D. Little, Inc., had independently developed a model similar in many respects to the one described here. Unfortunately Mr. Treynor's excellent work on this subject is, at present, unpublished.

distribution—its expected value and standard deviation.[8] This can be represented by a total utility function of the form:

$$U = f(E_W, \sigma_W)$$

where E_W indicates expected future wealth and σ_W the predicted standard deviation of the possible divergence of actual future wealth from E_W.

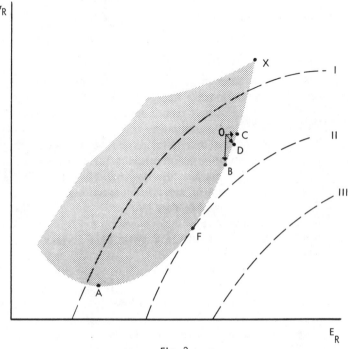

Fig. 2

Investors are assumed to prefer a higher expected future wealth to a lower value, *ceteris paribus* $(dU/dE_W > 0)$. Moreover, they exhibit risk-aversion, choosing an investment offering a lower value of σ_W to one with a greater level, given the level of E_W $(dU/d\sigma_W < 0)$. These assumptions imply that indifference curves relating E_W and σ_W will be upward-sloping.[9]

To simplify the analysis, we assume that an investor has decided to commit a given amount (W_i) of his present wealth to investment. Letting W_t be his

---

[8] Under certain conditions the mean-variance approach can be shown to lead to unsatisfactory predictions of behavior. Markowitz suggests that a model based on the semi-variance (the average of the squared deviations below the mean) would be preferable; in light of the formidable computational problems, however, he bases his analysis on the variance and standard deviation.

[9] While only these characteristics are required for the analysis, it is generally assumed that the curves have the property of diminishing marginal rates of substitution between E_W and σ_W, as do those in our diagrams.

terminal wealth and R the rate of return on his investment:

$$R \equiv \frac{W_t - W_i}{W_i},$$

we have

$$W_t = RW_i + W_i.$$

This relationship makes it possible to express the investor's utility in terms of R, since terminal wealth is directly related to the rate of return:

$$U = g(E_R, \sigma_R).$$

Figure 2 summarizes the model of investor preferences in a family of indifference curves; successive curves indicate higher levels of utility as one moves down and/or to the right.[10]

THE INVESTMENT OPPORTUNITY CURVE

The model of investor behavior considers the investor as choosing from a set of investment opportunities that one which maximizes his utility. Every investment plan available to him may be represented by a point in the E_R, σ_R plane. If all such plans involve some risk, the area composed of such points will have an appearance similar to that shown in Figure 2. The investor will choose from among all possible plans the one placing him on the indifference curve representing the highest level of utility (point F). The decision can be made in two stages: first, find the set of efficient investment plans and, second, choose one from among this set. A plan is said to be efficient if (and only if) there is no alternative with either (1) the same E_R and a lower σ_R, (2) the same σ_R and a higher E_R or (3) a higher E_R and a lower σ_R. Thus investment O is inefficient since investments B, C, and D (among others) dominate it. The only plans which would be chosen must lie along the lower right-hand boundary ($AFBDCX$)—*the investment opportunity curve.*

---

[10] Such indifference curves can also be derived by assuming that the investor wishes to maximize expected utility and that his total utility can be represented by a quadratic function of R with decreasing marginal utility. Both Markowitz and Tobin present such a derivation. A similar approach is used by Donald E. Farrar in *The Investment Decision Under Uncertainty* (Prentice-Hall, 1962). Unfortunately Farrar makes an error in his derivation; he appeals to the Von-Neumann-Morgenstern cardinal utility axioms to transform a function of the form:

$$E(U) = a + bE_R - cE_R^2 - c\sigma_R^2$$

into one of the form:

$$E(U) = k_1 E_R - k_2 \sigma_R^2.$$

That such a transformation is not consistent with the axioms can readily be seen in this form, since the first equation implies non-linear indifference curves in the E_R, σ_R^2 plane while the second implies a linear relationship. Obviously no three (different) points can lie on both a line and a non-linear curve (with a monotonic derivative). Thus the two functions must imply different orderings among alternative choices in at least some instance.

To understand the nature of this curve, consider two investment plans—A and B, each including one or more assets. Their predicted expected values and standard deviations of rate of return are shown in Figure 3. If the proportion

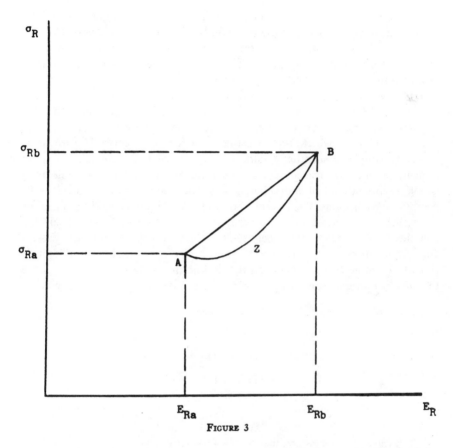

FIGURE 3

α of the individual's wealth is placed in plan A and the remainder $(1-\alpha)$ in B, the expected rate of return of the combination will lie between the expected returns of the two plans:

$$E_{Rc} = \alpha E_{Ra} + (1 - \alpha)E_{Rb}$$

The predicted standard deviation of return of the combination is:

$$\sigma_{Rc} = \sqrt{\alpha^2\sigma_{Ra}^2 + (1 - \alpha)^2\sigma_{Rb}^2 + 2r_{ab}\alpha(1 - \alpha)\sigma_{Ra}\sigma_{Rb}}$$

Note that this relationship includes r_{ab}, the correlation coefficient between the predicted rates of return of the two investment plans. A value of $+1$ would indicate an investor's belief that there is a precise positive relationship between the outcomes of the two investments. A zero value would indicate a belief that the outcomes of the two investments are completely independent and -1 that the investor feels that there is a precise inverse relationship between them. In the usual case r_{ab} will have a value between 0 and $+1$.

Figure 3 shows the possible values of E_{Rc} and σ_{Rc} obtainable with different combinations of A and B under two different assumptions about the value of r_{ab}. If the two investments are perfectly correlated, the combinations will lie along a straight line between the two points, since in this case both E_{Rc} and σ_{Rc} will be linearly related to the proportions invested in the two plans.[11] If they are less than perfectly positively correlated, the standard deviation of any combination must be less than that obtained with perfect correlation (since r_{ab} will be less); thus the combinations must lie along a curve below the line AB.[12] AZB shows such a curve for the case of complete independence ($r_{ab} = 0$); with negative correlation the locus is even more U-shaped.[13]

The manner in which the investment opportunity curve is formed is relatively simple conceptually, although exact solutions are usually quite difficult.[14] One first traces curves indicating E_R, σ_R values available with simple combinations of individual assets, then considers combinations of combinations of assets. The lower right-hand boundary must be either linear or increasing at an increasing rate ($d^2\sigma_R/dE_R^2 > 0$). As suggested earlier, the complexity of the relationship between the characteristics of individual assets and the location of the investment opportunity curve makes it difficult to provide a simple rule for assessing the desirability of individual assets, since the effect of an asset on an investor's over-all investment opportunity curve

---

[11] $E_{Rc} = \alpha E_{Ra} + (1 - \alpha)E_{Rb} = E_{Rb} + (E_{Ra} - E_{Rb})\alpha$

$$\sigma_{Rc} = \sqrt{\alpha^2\sigma_{Ra}^2 + (1 - \alpha)^2\sigma_{Rb}^2 + 2r_{ab}\alpha(1 - \alpha)\sigma_{Ra}\sigma_{Rb}}$$

but $r_{ab} = 1$, therefore the expression under the square root sign can be factored:

$$\sigma_{Rc} = \sqrt{[\alpha\sigma_{Ra} + (1 - \alpha)\sigma_{Rb}]^2}$$
$$= \alpha\sigma_{Ra} + (1 - \alpha)\sigma_{Rb}$$
$$= \sigma_{Rb} + (\sigma_{Ra} - \sigma_{Rb})\alpha$$

[12] This curvature is, in essence, the rationale for diversification.

[13] When $r_{ab} = 0$, the slope of the curve at point A is

$$-\frac{\sigma_{Ra}}{E_{Rb} - E_{Ra}},$$

at point B it is

$$\frac{\sigma_{Rb}}{E_{Rb} - E_{Ra}}.$$

When $r_{ab} = -1$, the curve degenerates to two straight lines to a point on the horizontal axis.

[14] Markowitz has shown that this is a problem in parametric quadratic programming. An efficient solution technique is described in his article, "The Optimization of a Quadratic Function Subject to Linear Constraints," *Naval Research Logistics Quarterly*, Vol. 3 (March and June, 1956), 111–133. A solution method for a special case is given in the author's "A Simplified Model for Portfolio Analysis," *op. cit.*

depends not only on its expected rate of return (E_{Ri}) and risk (σ_{Ri}), but also on its correlations with the other available opportunities $(r_{i1}, r_{i2}, \ldots, r_{in})$. However, such a rule is implied by the equilibrium conditions for the model, as we will show in part IV.

THE PURE RATE OF INTEREST

We have not yet dealt with riskless assets. Let P be such an asset; its risk is zero $(\sigma_{Rp} = 0)$ and its expected rate of return, E_{Rp}, is equal (by definition) to the pure interest rate. If an investor places α of his wealth in P and the remainder in some risky asset A, he would obtain an expected rate of return:

$$E_{Rc} = \alpha E_{Rp} + (1 - \alpha)E_{Ra}$$

The standard deviation of such a combination would be:

$$\sigma_{Rc} = \sqrt{\alpha^2\sigma_{Rp}^2 + (1 - \alpha)^2\sigma_{Ra}^2 + 2r_{pa}\alpha(1 - \alpha)\sigma_{Rp}\sigma_{Ra}}$$

but since $\sigma_{Rp} = 0$, this reduces to:

$$\sigma_{Rc} = (1 - \alpha)\sigma_{Ra}.$$

This implies that all combinations involving any risky asset or combination of assets plus the riskless asset must have values of E_{Rc} and σ_{Rc} which lie along a straight line between the points representing the two components. Thus in Figure 4 all combinations of E_R and σ_R lying along the line PA are attainable

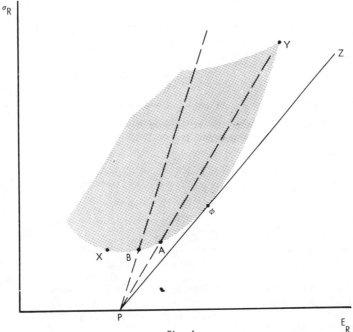

Fig. 4

if some money is loaned at the pure rate and some placed in A. Similarly, by lending at the pure rate and investing in B, combinations along PB can be attained. Of all such possibilities, however, one will dominate: that investment plan lying at the point of the original investment opportunity curve where a ray from point P is tangent to the curve. In Figure 4 all investments lying along the original curve from X to ϕ are dominated by some combination of investment in ϕ and lending at the pure interest rate.

Consider next the possibility of borrowing. If the investor can borrow at the pure rate of interest, this is equivalent to disinvesting in P. The effect of borrowing to purchase more of any given investment than is possible with the given amount of wealth can be found simply by letting α take on negative values in the equations derived for the case of lending. This will obviously give points lying along the extension of line PA if borrowing is used to purchase more of A; points lying along the extension of PB if the funds are used to purchase B, etc.

As in the case of lending, however, one investment plan will dominate all others when borrowing is possible. When the rate at which funds can be borrowed equals the lending rate, this plan will be the same one which is dominant if lending is to take place. Under these conditions, the investment opportunity curve becomes a line ($P\phi Z$ in Figure 4). Moreover, if the original investment opportunity curve is not linear at point ϕ, the process of investment choice can be dichotomized as follows: first select the (unique) optimum combination of risky assets (point ϕ), and second borrow or lend to obtain the particular point on PZ at which an indifference curve is tangent to the line.[15]

Before proceeding with the analysis, it may be useful to consider alternative assumptions under which only a combination of assets lying at the point of tangency between the original investment opportunity curve and a ray from P can be efficient. Even if borrowing is impossible, the investor will choose ϕ (and lending) if his risk-aversion leads him to a point below ϕ on the line $P\phi$. Since a large number of investors choose to place some of their funds in relatively risk-free investments, this is not an unlikely possibility. Alternatively, if borrowing is possible but only up to some limit, the choice of ϕ would be made by all those investors willing to undertake considerable risk. These alternative paths lead to the main conclusion, thus making the assumption of borrowing or lending at the pure interest rate less onerous than it might initially appear to be.

---

[15] This proof was first presented by Tobin for the case in which the pure rate of interest is zero (cash). Hicks considers the lending situation under comparable conditions but does not allow borrowing. Both authors present their analysis using maximization subject to constraints expressed as equalities. Hicks' analysis assumes independence and thus insures that the solution will include no negative holdings of risky assets; Tobin's covers the general case, thus his solution would generally include negative holdings of some assets. The discussion in this paper is based on Markowitz' formulation, which includes non-negativity constraints on the holdings of all assets.

III. EQUILIBRIUM IN THE CAPITAL MARKET

In order to derive conditions for equilibrium in the capital market we invoke two assumptions. First, we assume a common pure rate of interest, with all investors able to borrow or lend funds on equal terms. Second, we assume homogeneity of investor expectations:[16] investors are assumed to agree on the prospects of various investments—the expected values, standard deviations and correlation coefficients described in Part II. Needless to say, these are highly restrictive and undoubtedly unrealistic assumptions. However, since the proper test of a theory is not the realism of its assumptions but the acceptability of its implications, and since these assumptions imply equilibrium conditions which form a major part of classical financial doctrine, it is far from clear that this formulation should be rejected—especially in view of the dearth of alternative models leading to similar results.

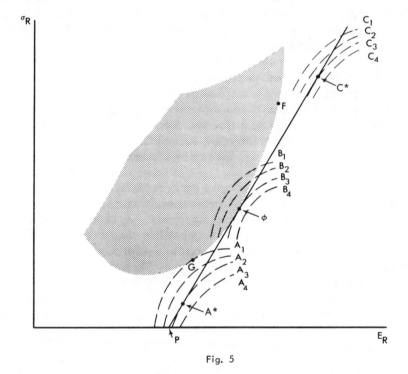

Fig. 5

Under these assumptions, given some set of capital asset prices, each investor will view his alternatives in the same manner. For one set of prices the alternatives might appear as shown in Figure 5. In this situation, an investor with the preferences indicated by indifference curves A_1 through A_4 would seek to lend some of his funds at the pure interest rate and to invest the remainder in the combination of assets shown by point ϕ, since this would

[16] A term suggested by one of the referees.

give him the preferred over-all position A^*. An investor with the preferences indicated by curves B_1 through B_4 would seek to invest all his funds in combination ϕ, while an investor with indifference curves C_1 through C_4 would invest all his funds plus additional (borrowed) funds in combination ϕ in order to reach his preferred position (C^*). In any event, all would attempt to purchase only those risky assets which enter combination ϕ.

The attempts by investors to purchase the assets in combination ϕ and their lack of interest in holding assets not in combination ϕ would, of course, lead to a revision of prices. The prices of assets in ϕ will rise and, since an asset's expected return relates future income to present price, their expected returns will fall. This will reduce the attractiveness of combinations which include such assets; thus point ϕ (among others) will move to the left of its initial position.[17] On the other hand, the prices of assets not in ϕ will fall, causing an increase in their expected returns and a rightward movement of points representing combinations which include them. Such price changes will lead to a revision of investors' actions; some new combination or combinations will become attractive, leading to different demands and thus to further revisions in prices. As the process continues, the investment opportunity curve will tend to become more linear, with points such as ϕ moving to the left and formerly inefficient points (such as F and G) moving to the right.

Capital asset prices must, of course, continue to change until a set of prices is attained for which every asset enters at least one combination lying on the capital market line. Figure 6 illustrates such an equilibrium condition.[18] All possibilities in the shaded area can be attained with combinations of risky assets, while points lying along the line PZ can be attained by borrowing or lending at the pure rate plus an investment in some combination of risky assets. Certain possibilities (those lying along PZ from point A to point B) can be obtained in either manner. For example, the E_R, σ_R values shown by point A can be obtained solely by some combination of risky assets; alternatively, the point can be reached by a combination of lending and investing in combination C of risky assets.

It is important to recognize that in the situation shown in Figure 6 many alternative combinations of risky assets are efficient (i.e., lie along line PZ), and thus the theory does not imply that all investors will hold the same combination.[19] On the other hand, all such combinations must be perfectly

---

[17] If investors consider the variability of future dollar returns unrelated to present price, both E_R and σ_R will fall; under these conditions the point representing an asset would move along a ray through the origin as its price changes.

[18] The area in Figure 6 representing E_R, σ_R values attained with only risky assets has been drawn at some distance from the horizontal axis for emphasis. It is likely that a more accurate representation would place it very close to the axis.

[19] This statement contradicts Tobin's conclusion that there will be a unique optimal combination of risky assets. Tobin's proof of a unique optimum can be shown to be incorrect for the case of perfect correlation of efficient risky investment plans if the line connecting their E_R, σ_R points would pass through point P. In the graph on page 83 of this article (*op. cit.*)

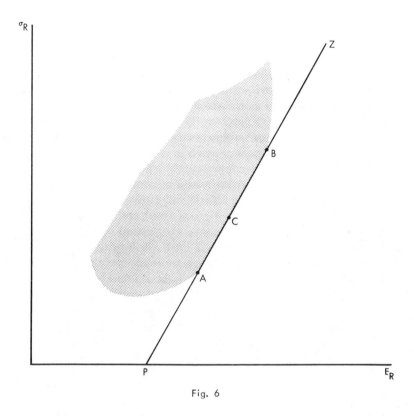

Fig. 6

(positively) correlated, since they lie along a linear border of the E_R, σ_R region.[20] This provides a key to the relationship between the prices of capital assets and different types of risk.

IV. THE PRICES OF CAPITAL ASSETS

We have argued that in equilibrium there will be a simple linear relationship between the expected return and standard deviation of return for efficient combinations of risky assets. Thus far nothing has been said about such a relationship for individual assets. Typically the E_R, σ_R values associated with single assets will lie above the capital market line, reflecting the inefficiency of undiversified holdings. Moreover, such points may be scattered throughout the feasible region, with no consistent relationship between their expected

the constant-risk locus would, in this case, degenerate from a family of ellipses into one of straight lines parallel to the constant-return loci, thus giving multiple optima.

[20] E_R, σ_R values given by combinations of any two combinations must lie within the region and cannot plot above a straight line joining the points. In this case they cannot plot below such a line. But since only in the case of perfect correlation will they plot along a straight line, the two combinations must be perfectly correlated. As shown in Part IV, this does not necessarily imply that the individual securities they contain are perfectly correlated.

return and total risk (σ_R). However, there will be a consistent relationship between their expected returns and what might best be called systematic risk, as we will now show.

Figure 7 illustrates the typical relationship between a single capital asset (point i) and an efficient combination of assets (point g) of which it is a part. The curve igg' indicates all E_R, σ_R values which can be obtained with feasible combinations of asset i and combination g. As before, we denote such a combination in terms of a proportion α of asset i and $(1 - \alpha)$ of combination g.

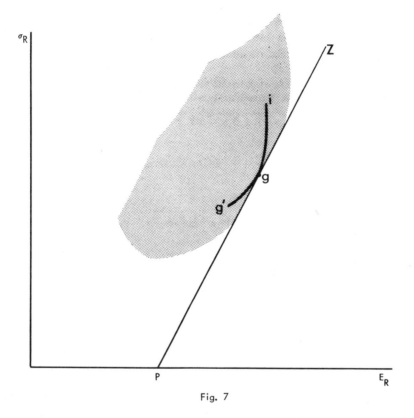

Fig. 7

A value of $\alpha = 1$ would indicate pure investment in asset i while $\alpha = 0$ would imply investment in combination g. Note, however, that $\alpha = .5$ implies a total investment of more than half the funds in asset i, since half would be invested in i itself and the other half used to purchase combination g, which also includes some of asset i. This means that a combination in which asset i does not appear at all must be represented by some negative value of α. Point g' indicates such a combination.

In Figure 7 the curve igg' has been drawn tangent to the capital market line (PZ) at point g. This is no accident. All such curves must be tangent to the capital market line in equilibrium, since (1) they must touch it at the point representing the efficient combination and (2) they are continuous at the point.[21] Under these conditions a lack of tangency would imply that the curve intersects PZ. But then some feasible combination of assets would lie to the right of the capital market line, an obvious impossibility since the capital market line represents the efficient boundary of feasible values of E_R and σ_R.

The requirement that curves such as igg' be tangent to the capital market line can be shown to lead to a relatively simple formula which relates the expected rate of return to various elements of risk for all assets which are included in combination g.[22] Its economic meaning can best be seen if the relationship between the return of asset i and that of combination g is viewed in a manner similar to that used in regression analysis.[23] Imagine that we were

[21] Only if $r_{ig} = -1$ will the curve be discontinuous over the range in question.

[22] The standard deviation of a combination of g and i will be:

$$\sigma = \sqrt{\alpha^2 \sigma_{Ri}^2 + (1-\alpha)^2 \sigma_{Rg}^2 + 2r_{ig}\alpha(1-\alpha)\sigma_{Ri}\sigma_{Rg}}$$

at $\alpha = 0$:

$$\frac{d\sigma}{d\alpha} = -\frac{1}{\sigma}[\sigma_{Rg}^2 - r_{ig}\sigma_{Ri}\sigma_{Rg}]$$

but $\sigma = \sigma_{Rg}$ at $\alpha = 0$. Thus:

$$\frac{d\sigma}{d\alpha} = -[\sigma_{Rg} - r_{ig}\sigma_{Ri}]$$

The expected return of a combination will be:

$$E = \alpha E_{Ri} + (1-\alpha)E_{Rg}$$

Thus, at all values of α:

$$\frac{dE}{d\alpha} = -[E_{Rg} - E_{Ri}]$$

and, at $\alpha = 0$:

$$\frac{d\sigma}{dE} = \frac{\sigma R_g - r_{ig}\sigma_{Ri}}{E_{Rg} - E_{Ri}}.$$

Let the equation of the capital market line be:

$$\sigma_R = s(E_R - P)$$

where P is the pure interest rate. Since igg' is tangent to the line when $\alpha = 0$, and since (E_{Rg}, σ_{Rg}) lies on the line:

$$\frac{\sigma_{Rg} - r_{ig}\sigma_{Ri}}{E_{Rg} - E_{Ri}} = \frac{\sigma_{Rg}}{E_{Rg} - P}$$

or:

$$\beta \simeq \frac{r_{ig}\sigma_{Ri}}{\sigma_{Rg}} = -\left[\frac{P}{E_{Rg} - P}\right] + \left[\frac{1}{E_{Rg} - P}\right]E_{Ri}.$$

[23] This model has been called the diagonal model since its portfolio analysis solution can be facilitated by re-arranging the data so that the variance-covariance matrix becomes diagonal. The method is described in the author's article, cited earlier.

given a number of (ex post) observations of the return of the two investments. The points might plot as shown in Figure 8. The scatter of the R_i observation around their mean (which will approximate E_{Ri}) is, of course, evidence of the total risk of the asset—σ_{Ri}. But part of the scatter is due to an underlying relationship with the return on combination g, shown by B_{ig}, the slope of the

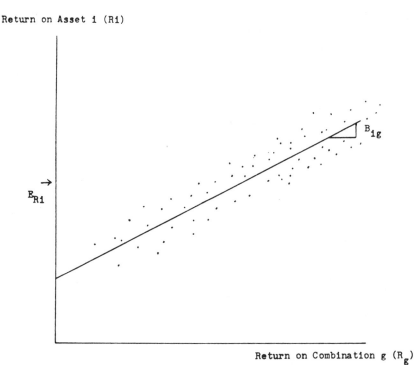

Return on Asset 1 (R1)

E_{R1}

B_{1g}

Return on Combination g (R_g)

FIGURE 8

regression line. The response of R_i to changes in R_g (and variations in R_g itself) account for much of the variation in R_i. It is this component of the asset's total risk which we term the *systematic* risk. The remainder,[24] being uncorrelated with R_g, is the unsystematic component. This formulation of the relationship between R_i and R_g can be employed *ex ante* as a predictive model. B_{ig} becomes the *predicted* response of R_i to changes in R_g. Then, given σR_g (the predicted risk of R_g), the systematic portion of the predicted risk of each asset can be determined.

This interpretation allows us to state the relationship derived from the tangency of curves such as *igg'* with the capital market line in the form shown in Figure 9. All assets entering efficient combination g must have (predicted)

---

[24] ex post, the standard error.

B_{ig} and E_{Ri} values lying on the line PQ.[25] Prices will adjust so that assets which are more responsive to changes in R_g will have higher expected returns than those which are less responsive. This accords with common sense.

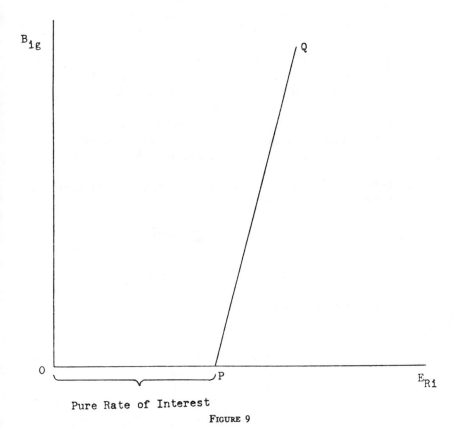

Pure Rate of Interest

FIGURE 9

Obviously the part of an asset's risk which is due to its correlation with the return on a combination cannot be diversified away when the asset is added to the combination. Since B_{ig} indicates the magnitudes of this type of risk it should be directly related to expected return.

25

$$r_{ig} = \sqrt{\frac{B_{ig}^2 \sigma_{Rg}^2}{\sigma_{Ri}^2}} = \frac{B_{ig}\sigma_{Rg}}{\sigma_{Ri}}$$

$$B_{ig} = \frac{r_{ig}\sigma_{Ri}}{\sigma_{Rg}}.$$

The expression on the right is the expression on the left-hand side of the last equation in footnote 22. Thus:

$$B_{ig} = -\left[\frac{P}{E_{Rg} - P}\right] + \left[\frac{1}{E_{Rg} - P}\right] E_{Ri}.$$

The relationship illustrated in Figure 9 provides a partial answer to the question posed earlier concerning the relationship between an asset's risk and its expected return. But thus far we have argued only that the relationship holds for the assets which enter some particular efficient combination (g). Had another combination been selected, a different linear relationship would have been derived. Fortunately this limitation is easily overcome. As shown in the footnote,[26] we may arbitrarily select *any* one of the efficient combinations, then measure the predicted responsiveness of *every* asset's rate of return to that of the combination selected; and these coefficients will be related to the expected rates of return of the assets in exactly the manner pictured in Figure 9.

The fact that rates of return from all efficient combinations will be perfectly correlated provides the justification for arbitrarily selecting any one of them. Alternatively we may choose instead any variable perfectly correlated with the

---

[26] Consider the two assets i and i^*, the former included in efficient combination g and the latter in combination g^*. As shown above:

and:

$$B_{ig} = -\left[\frac{P}{E_{Rg} - P}\right] + \left[\frac{1}{E_{Rg} - P}\right] E_{Rl}$$

and:

$$B_{i^*g^*} = -\left[\frac{P}{E_{Rg^*} - P}\right] + \left[\frac{1}{E_{Rg^*} - P}\right] E_{Ri^*}.$$

Since R_g and R_{g^*} are perfectly correlated:

$$r_{i^*g^*} = r_{i^*g}$$

Thus:

$$\frac{B_{i^*g^*}\sigma_{Rg^*}}{\sigma_{Ri^*}} = \frac{B_{i^*g}\sigma_{Rg}}{\sigma_{Ri^*}}$$

and:

$$B_{i^*g^*} = B_{i^*g}\left[\frac{\sigma_{Rg}}{\sigma_{Rg^*}}\right].$$

Since both g and g^* lie on a line which intercepts the E-axis at P:

$$\frac{\sigma_{Rg}}{\sigma_{Rg^*}} = \frac{E_{Rg} - P}{E_{Rg^*} - P}$$

and:

$$B_{i^*g^*} = B_{i^*g}\left[\frac{E_{Rg} - P}{E_{Rg^*} - P}\right].$$

Thus:

$$-\left[\frac{P}{E_{Rg^*} - P}\right] + \left[\frac{1}{E_{Rg^*} - P}\right] E_{Ri^*} = B_{i^*g}\left[\frac{E_{Rg} - P}{E_{Rg^*} - P}\right]$$

from which we have the desired relationship between R_{i^*} and g:

$$B_{i^*g} = -\left[\frac{P}{E_{Rg} - P}\right] + \left[\frac{1}{E_{Rg} - P}\right] E_{Ri^*}.$$

B_{i^*g} must therefore plot on the same line as does B_{ig}.

rate of return of such combinations. The vertical axis in Figure 9 would then indicate alternative levels of a coefficient measuring the sensitivity of the rate of return of a capital asset to changes in the variable chosen.

This possibility suggests both a plausible explanation for the implication that all efficient combinations will be perfectly correlated and a useful interpretation of the relationship between an individual asset's expected return and its risk. Although the theory itself implies only that rates of return from efficient combinations will be perfectly correlated, we might expect that this would be due to their common dependence on the over-all level of economic activity. If so, diversification enables the investor to escape all but the risk resulting from swings in economic activity—this type of risk remains even in efficient combinations. And, since all other types can be avoided by diversification, only the responsiveness of an asset's rate of return to the level of economic activity is relevant in assessing its risk. Prices will adjust until there is a linear relationship between the magnitude of such responsiveness and expected return. Assets which are unaffected by changes in economic activity will return the pure interest rate; those which move with economic activity will promise appropriately higher expected rates of return.

This discussion provides an answer to the second of the two questions posed in this paper. In Part III it was shown that with respect to equilibrium conditions in the capital market as a whole, the theory leads to results consistent with classical doctrine (i.e., the capital market line). We have now shown that with regard to capital assets considered individually, it also yields implications consistent with traditional concepts: it is common practice for investment counselors to accept a lower expected return from defensive securities (those which respond little to changes in the economy) than they require from aggressive securities (which exhibit significant response). As suggested earlier, the familiarity of the implications need not be considered a drawback. The provision of a logical framework for producing some of the major elements of traditional financial theory should be a useful contribution in its own right.

8. EQUILIBRIUM IN A CAPITAL ASSET MARKET[1]

JAN MOSSIN[2]*

Reprinted by permission of the author and publisher from
Econometrica, Vol. 34, No. 4 (October 1966), pp. 768–83.

This paper investigates the properties of a market for risky assets on the basis of a simple model of general equilibrium of exchange, where individual investors seek to maximize preference functions over expected yield and variance of yield on their portfolios. A theory of market risk premiums is outlined, and it is shown that general equilibrium implies the existence of a so-called "market line," relating per dollar expected yield and standard deviation of yield. The concept of price of risk is discussed in terms of the slope of this line.

1. INTRODUCTION

In recent years several studies have been made of the problem of selecting optimal portfolios of risky assets ([6, 8], and others). In these models the investor is assumed to possess a preference ordering over all possible portfolios and to maximize the value of this preference ordering subject to a budget restraint, taking the prices and probability distributions of yield for the various available assets as given data.

From the point of view of positive economics, such decision rules can, of course, be postulated as implicitly describing the individual's demand schedules for the different assets at varying prices. It would then be a natural next step to enquire into the characteristics of the whole market for such assets when the individual demands are interacting to determine the prices and the allocation of the existing supply of assets among individuals.

These problems have been discussed, among others, by Allais [1], Arrow [2], Borch [3], Sharpe [7], and also to some extent by Brownlee and Scott [5].

Allais' model represents in certain respects a generalization relative to the model to be discussed here. In particular, Allais does not assume general risk aversion. This generalization requires, on the other hand, certain other assumptions that we shall not need in order to lead to definite results.

Arrow's brief but important paper is also on a very general and even ab-

[1] Revised manuscript received December, 1965.

[2] The author is indebted to Karl Borch, Jacques Drèze, and Sten Thore for their valuable comments and suggestions.

* The Norwegian School of Economics and Business Administration.

stract level. He uses a much more general preference structure than we do here and also allows differences in individual perceptions of probability distributions. He then proves that under certain assumptions there exists a competitive equilibrium which is also Pareto optimal.

Borch has investigated the problem with special reference to a reinsurance market. He suggests, however, that his analysis can be reversed and extended to a more general market for risky assets. The present paper may be seen as an attempt in that direction. The general approach is different in important respects, however, particularly as concerns the price concept used. Borch's price implies in our terms that the price of a security should depend only on the stochastic nature of the yield, not on the number of securities outstanding. This may be accounted for by the particular characteristics of a reinsurance market, where such a price concept seems more reasonable than is the case for a security market. A rational person will not buy securities on their own merits without considering alternative investments. The failure of Borch's model to possess a Pareto optimal solution appears to be due to this price concept.

Generality has its virtues, but it also means that there will be many questions to which definite answers cannot be given. To obtain definite answers, we must be willing to impose certain restrictive assumptions. This is precisely what our paper attempts to do, and it is believed that this makes it possible to come a long way towards providing a theory of the market risk premium and filling the gap between demand functions and equilibrium properties.

Brownlee and Scott specify equilibrium conditions for a security market very similar to those given here, but are otherwise concerned with entirely different problems. The paper by Sharpe gives a verbal-diagrammatical discussion of the determination of asset prices in quasi-dynamic terms. His general description of the character of the market is similar to the one presented here, however, and his main conclusions are certainly consistent with ours. But his lack of precision in the specification of equilibrium conditions leaves parts of his arguments somewhat indefinite. The present paper may be seen as an attempt to clarify and make precise some of these points.

2. THE EQUILIBRIUM MODEL

Our general approach is one of determining conditions for *equilibrium of exchange* of the assets. Each individual brings to the market his present holdings of the various assets, and an exchange takes place. We want to know what the prices must be in order to satisfy demand schedules and also fulfill the condition that supply and demand be equal for all assets. To answer this question we must first derive relations describing individual demand. Second, we must incorporate these relations in a system describing general equilibrium. Finally, we want to discuss properties of this equilibrium.

We shall assume that there is a large number m of individuals labeled i, $(i = 1, 2, \ldots, m)$. Let us consider the behavior of one individual. He has to select a portfolio of assets, and there are n different assets to choose from, labeled j, $(j = 1, 2, \ldots, n)$. The yield on any asset is assumed to be a random variable whose distribution is known to the individual. Moreover, all individuals are assumed to have identical perceptions of these probability distributions.[3] The yield on a whole portfolio is, of course, also a random variable. The portfolio analyses mentioned earlier assume that, in his choice among all the possible portfolios, the individual is satisfied to be guided by its expected yield and its variance only. This assumption will also be made in the present paper.[4]

It is important to make precise the description of a portfolio in these terms. It is obvious (although the point is rarely made explicit) that the holdings of the various assets must be measured in some kind of units. The Markowitz analysis, for example, starts by picturing the investment alternatives open to the individual as a point set in a mean-variance plane, each point representing a specific investment opportunity. The question is: to what do this expected yield and variance of yield refer? For such a diagram to make sense, they must necessarily refer to some unit common to all assets. An example of such a unit would be one dollar's worth of investment in each asset. Such a choice of units would evidently be of little use for our purposes, since we shall consider the prices of assets as variables to be determined in the market. Consequently, we must select some arbitrary "physical" unit of measurement and define expected yield and variance of yield relative to this unit. If, for example, we select one share as our unit for measuring holdings of Standard Oil stock and say that the expected yield is μ and the variance σ^2, this means expected yield and variance of yield per share; if instead we had chosen a hundred shares as our unit, the relevant expected yield and variance of yield would have been 100μ, and $10,000 \sigma^2$, respectively.

We shall find it convenient to give an interpretation of the concept of "yield" by assuming discrete market dates with intervals of one time unit. The yield to be considered on any asset on a given market date may then be thought of as the value per unit that the asset will have at the next market date (including possible accrued dividends, interest or other emoluments). The terms "yield" and "future value" may then be used more or less interchangeably.

We shall, in general, admit stochastic dependence among yields of different

---

[3] This assumption is not crucial for the analysis, but simplifies it a good deal. It also seems doubtful whether the introduction of subjective probabilities would really be useful for deriving propositions about market behavior. In any case, it may be argued, as Borch [3, p. 439] does: "Whether two rational persons on the basis of the same information can arrive at different evaluations of the probability of a specific event, is a question of semantics. That they may act differently on the same information is well known, but this can usually be explained assuming that the two persons attach different utilities to the event."

[4] Acceptance of the von Neumann—Morgenstern axioms (leading to their theorem on measurable utility), together with this assumption, implies a quadratic utility function for yield (see [4]). But such a specification is not strictly necessary for the analysis to follow, and so, by the principle of Occam's razor, has not been introduced.

assets. But the specification of the stochastic properties poses the problem of identification of "different" assets. It will be necessary to make the convention that two units of assets are of the same kind only if their yields will be identical. The reason for this convention can be clarified by an example. In many lotteries (in particular national lotteries), several tickets wear the same number. When a number is drawn, all tickets with that number receive identical prizes. Suppose all tickets have mean μ and variance σ^2 of prizes. Then the expected yield on *two* tickets is clearly 2μ, regardless of their numbers. But while the variance on two tickets is $2\sigma^2$ when they have different numbers, it is $4\sigma^2$ when they have identical numbers. If such lottery tickets are part of the available assets, we must therefore identify as many "different" assets as there are different numbers (regardless of the fact that they have identical means and variances). For ordinary assets such as corporate stock, it is of course known that although the yield is random it will be the same on all units of each stock.

We shall denote the expected yield per unit of asset j by μ_j and the covariance between unit yield of assets j and k by σ_{jk}. We shall also need the rather trivial assumption that the covariance matrix for the yield of the risky assets is nonsingular.

An individual's portfolio can now be described as an n-dimensional vector with elements equal to his holdings of each of the n assets. We shall use x_j^i to denote individual i's holdings of assets j (after the exchange), and so his portfolio may be written $(x_1^i, x_2^i, \ldots, x_n^i)$.

One of the purposes of the analysis is to compare the relations between the prices and yields of different assets. To facilitate such comparisons, it will prove useful to have a *riskless asset* as a yardstick. We shall take the riskless asset to be the nth. That it is riskless of course means that $\sigma_{nk} = 0$ for all k. But it may also be suggestive to identify this asset with *money*, and with this in mind we shall write specifically $u_n = 1$, i.e., a dollar will (with certainty) be worth a dollar a year from now.

We denote the price per unit of asset j by p_j. Now, general equilibrium conditions are capable of determining relative prices only: we can arbitrarily fix one of the prices and express all others in terms of it. We may therefore proceed by fixing the price of the nth asset as q, i.e., $p_n = q$. This means that we select the nth asset as *numéraire*. We shall return to the implications of this seemingly innocent convention below.

With the above assumptions and conventions, the expected yield on individual i's portfolio can be written:

(1)
$$y_1^i = \sum_{j=1}^{n-1} \mu_j x_j^i + x_n^i,$$

and the variance:

(2)
$$y_2^i = \sum_{j=1}^{n-1} \sum_{\alpha=1}^{n-1} \sigma_{j\alpha} x_i^i x_\alpha^j.$$

As mentioned earlier, we postulate for each individual a *preference ordering* (utility function) of the form:

(3) $$U^i = f^i(y_1^i, y_2^i)$$

over all possible portfolios, i.e., we postulate that an individual will behave as if he were attempting to maximize U^i. With respect to the form of U^i, we shall assume that it is concave, with the first derivative positive and the second negative. This latter assumption of general risk aversion seems to be generally accepted in the literature on portfolio selection. The investor is constrained, however, to the points that satisfy his *budget equation*:

(4) $$\sum_{j=1}^{n-1} p_j(x_j^i - \bar{x}_j^i) + q(x_n^i - \bar{x}_n^i) = 0,$$

where $\bar{x}_j^i$ are the quantities of asset j that he brings to the market; these are given data. The budget equation simply states that his total receipts from the sale of the "old" portfolio should equal total outlays on the "new" portfolio.

Formally, then, we postulate that each individual i behaves as if attempting to maximize (3), subject to (4), (1), and (2). Forming the Lagrangean:

$$V^i = f^i(y_1^i, y_2^i) + \theta^i \left[\sum_{j=1}^{n-1} p_j(x_j^i - \bar{x}_j^i) + g(x_n^i - \bar{x}_n^i) \right],$$

we can then write the first-order conditions for the maxima for all i as:

$$\frac{\partial V^i}{\partial x_j^i} = f_1^i \mu_j + 2f_2^i \sum_{\alpha=1}^{n-1} \sigma_{j\alpha} x_\alpha^i + \theta^i p_j = 0 \qquad (j = 1, \ldots, n-1),$$

$$\frac{\partial V^i}{\partial x_n^i} = f_1^i + \theta^i q = 0,$$

$$\frac{\partial V^i}{\partial \theta^i} = \sum_{j=1}^{n-1} p_j(x_j^i - \bar{x}_j^i) + q(x_n^i - \bar{x}_n^i) = 0,$$

where f_1^i and f_2^i denote partial derivatives with respect to y_1^i and y_2^i, respectively. Eliminating θ^i, this can be written as:

(5) $$-\frac{f_1^i}{f_2^i} = \frac{2 \sum_\alpha \sigma_{j\alpha} x_\alpha^i}{u_j - p_j/q} \qquad (j = 1, \ldots, n-1),$$

(6) $$\sum_{j=1}^{n-1} p_j(x_j^i - \bar{x}_j^i) + q(x_n^i - \bar{x}_n^i) = 0.$$

In (5), the $-f_1^i/f_2^i$ is the marginal rate of substitution dy_2^i/dy_1^i between the variance and mean of yield. Equations (5) and (6) constitute, for each individual, n equations describing his demand for the n assets.

To determine general equilibrium, we must also specify equality between demand and supply for each asset. These market clearing conditions can be written:

(7')
$$\sum_{i=1}^{m} (x_j^i - \bar{x}_j^i) = 0 \qquad (j = 1, \ldots, n).$$

As we would suspect, one of these conditions is superfluous. This can be seen by first summing the budget equations over all individuals:

$$\sum_{i=1}^{m} \sum_{j=1}^{n-1} p_j(x_j^i - \bar{x}_j^i) + q \sum_{i=1}^{m} (x_n^i - \bar{x}_n^i) = 0,$$

or

(8)
$$\sum_{j=1}^{n-1} p_j \sum_{i=1}^{m} (x_j^i - \bar{x}_j^i) + q \sum_{i=1}^{m} (x_n^i - \bar{x}_n^i) = 0.$$

Suppose that (7') were satisfied for all j except n. This would mean that the first term on the left of (8) vanishes, so that

$$q \sum_{i=1}^{m} (x_n^i - \bar{x}_n^i) = 0.$$

Hence also the nth equation of (7') must hold. We may therefore instead write:

(7)
$$\sum_{i=1}^{m} x_j^i = \bar{x}_j \qquad (j = 1, \ldots, n - 1),$$

where $\bar{x}_j$ denotes the given total supply of asset j: $\bar{x}_j = \sum_{i=1}^{m} \bar{x}_j^i$.

This essentially completes the equations describing general equilibrium. The system consists of the m equations (4), the $m(n - 1)$ equations (5) and (6), and the $(n - 1)$ equations (7); altogether $(mn + n - 1)$ equations. The unknowns are the mn quantities x_j^i and the $(n - 1)$ prices p_j.

We have counted our equations and our unknowns and found them to be equal in number. But we cannot rest with this; our main task has hardly begun. We shall bypass such problems as the existence and uniqueness of a solution to the system and rather concentrate on investigating properties of the equilibrium values of the variables, assuming that they exist.

We may observe, first of all, that the equilibrium allocation of assets represents a Pareto optimum, i.e., it will be impossible by some reallocation to increase one individual's utility without at the same time reducing the utility of one or more other individuals. This should not need any explicit proof, since it is a well known general property of a competitive equilibrium where preferences are concave. We should also mention the problem of nonnegativity of the solution to which we shall return at a later stage.

3. RISK MARGINS

The expected *rate of return* r_j on a unit of a risky asset can be defined by $\mu_j/(1 + r_j) = p_j$, i.e., $r_j = (\mu_j/p_j) - 1$, $(j = 1, \ldots, n - 1)$. Similarly, the rate of return of a unit of the riskless asset r_n is defined by $1/(1 + r_n) = q$, i.e., $r_n = 1/q - 1$. With our earlier interpretation of the riskless asset in mind, r_n may be regarded as the *pure rate of interest*.

The natural definition of the pure rate of interest is the rate of return on a riskless asset. In general, we may think of the rate of return of any asset as separated into two parts: the pure rate of interest representing the "price for waiting," and a remainder, a risk margin, representing the "price of risk." When we set the future yield of the riskless asset at 1 and decided to fix its current price at q, we thereby implicitly fixed the pure rate of interest. And to say that the market determines only relative asset prices is seen to be equivalent to saying that the pure rate of interest is not determined in the market for risky assets. Alternatively, we may say that the asset market determines only the risk margins.

The risk margin on asset j, m_j, is defined by

$$m_j = r_j - r_n = \frac{u_j - p_j/q}{p_j}.$$

To compare the risk margins of two assets j and k, we write:

$$\frac{m_j}{m_k} = \frac{\mu_j - p_j/q}{\mu_k - p_k/q} \frac{p_k}{p_j}.$$

We now make use of the equilibrium conditions. From (5) we have:

(9)
$$\frac{\sum\limits_{\alpha} \sigma_{j\alpha} x_\alpha^i}{u_j - p_j/q} = \frac{\sum\limits_{\alpha} \sigma_{k\alpha} x_\alpha^i}{\mu_k - p_k/q} \qquad (j, k = 1, \ldots, n - 1).$$

Summing over i and using (7), we then get:

(10)
$$\frac{\sum\limits_{\alpha} \sigma_{j\alpha} \bar{x}_\alpha}{\mu_j - p_j/q} = \frac{\sum\limits_{\alpha} \sigma_{k\alpha} \bar{x}_\alpha}{\mu_k - p_k/q}.$$

These equations define relationships between the prices of the risky assets in terms of given parameters only. We can then write:

$$\frac{m_j}{m_k} = \frac{\bar{x}_j \sum\limits_{\alpha} \sigma_{j\alpha} \bar{x}_\alpha}{\bar{x}_k \sum\limits_{\alpha} \sigma_{k\alpha} \bar{x}_\alpha} \cdot \frac{p_k \bar{x}_k}{p_j \bar{x}_j}.$$

Now, $\bar{x}_j \sum_{\alpha} \sigma_{j\alpha} \bar{x}_\alpha$ is the variance of yield on the total outstanding stock of asset j; $p_j \bar{x}_j$ is similarly the total value, at market prices, of all of asset j. Let us denote these magnitudes by V_j and R_j, respectively. In equilibrium, therefore, the risk margins satisfy:

(11)
$$\frac{m_j R_j}{V_j} = \frac{m_k R_k}{V_k} \qquad (j, k = 1, \ldots, n - 1),$$

i.e., the risk margins are such that *the ratio between the total risk compensation paid for an asset and the variance of the total stock of the asset is the same for all assets.*

4. COMPOSITION OF EQUILIBRIUM PORTFOLIOS

We can now derive an important property of an individual's equilibrium portfolio.

When (10) is substituted back in (9), the result is:

(12)
$$\frac{\sum_\alpha \sigma_{j\alpha} x_\alpha^i}{\sum_\alpha \sigma_{j\alpha} \bar{x}_\alpha} = \frac{\sum_\alpha \sigma_{k\alpha} x_\alpha^i}{\sum_\alpha \sigma_{k\alpha} \bar{x}_\alpha}.$$

Now define for each individual $z_j^i = x_j^i/\bar{x}_j$ $(j = 1,\dots, n-1)$, i.e., z_j^i is the proportion of the outstanding stock of asset h held by individual i. Further, let

$$b_{j\alpha} = \frac{\sigma_{j\alpha}\bar{x}_\alpha}{\sum_\alpha \sigma_{j\alpha}\bar{x}_\alpha},$$

so that $\sum_\alpha j\alpha = 1$. Then (12) can be written

(13)
$$\sum_\alpha b_{j\alpha} z_\alpha^i = \sum_\alpha b_{k\alpha} z_\alpha^i \qquad (j, k = 1,\dots, n-1).$$

It is easily proved[5] that these equations imply that the z_j^i are the same for all j (equal to, say, z^i), i.e.,

(14)
$$z_j^i = z_k^i = z^i \qquad (j, k = 1,\dots, n-1).$$

What this means is that in equilibrium, prices must be such that *each individual will hold the same percentage of the total outstanding stock of all risky assets*. This percentage will of course be different for different individuals, but it means that if an individual holds, say, 2 per cent of all the units outstanding of one risky asset, he also holds 2 per cent of the units outstanding of all the other risky assets. Note that we cannot conclude that he also holds the same percentage of the riskless asset; this proportion will depend upon his attitude towards risk, as expressed by his utility function. But the relation nevertheless permits us to summarize the description of an individual's portfolio by stating (a) his holding of the riskless asset, and (b) the percentage z^i held of the outstanding stock of the risky assets. We also observe that if an individual holds any risky assets at all (i.e., if he is not so averse to risk as to place everything in the riskless asset), then he holds some of *every* asset. (The analysis assumes, of course, that all assets are perfectly divisible.)

Looked at from another angle, (13) states that for any two individuals r and s, and any two risky assets j and k, we have $x_j^r/x_k^r = x_j^s/x_k^s$, i.e., the ratio between the holdings of two risky assets is the same for all individuals.

With these properties of equilibrium portfolios, we can return to the prob-

---

[5] Let the common value of the $n-1$ terms $\sum_{\alpha=1}^{n-1} b_{j\alpha} z_\alpha^i$ be a^i, and let $c_{j\alpha}$ be the elements of the inverse of the matrix of the $b_{j\alpha}$ (assuming nonsingularity). It is well known that when $\sum_\alpha b_{j\alpha} = 1$, then also $\sum_\alpha c_{j\alpha} = 1$. The solutions for the z_j^i are then: $z_j^i = \sum_\alpha c_{j\alpha} a^i = a^i \sum_\alpha c_{j\alpha} = a^i$, which proves our proposition.

lem of nonnegativity of the solution. With risk aversion it follows from (5) that

$$\sum_\alpha \sigma_{j\alpha} x_\alpha^i / \left(\mu_j - \frac{p_j}{q} \right) > 0.$$

The sum of such positive terms must also be positive, i.e.,

$$\sum_\alpha \sigma_{j\alpha} \bar{x}_\alpha / \left(\mu_j - \frac{p_j}{q} \right) > 0.$$

But then also, $\sum_\alpha \sigma_{j\alpha} x_\alpha^i / \sum_\alpha \sigma_{j\alpha} \bar{x}_\alpha > 0$, so that the a^i of footnote 4 is positive, which then implies $z^i > 0$. Hence, negative asset holdings are ruled out.

Our results are not at all unreasonable. At *any* set of prices, it will be rational for investors to diversify. Suppose that before the exchange takes place investors generally come to the conclusion that the holdings they would prefer to have of some asset are small relative to the supply of that asset. This must mean that the price of this asset has been too high in the past. It is then only natural to expect the exchange to result in a fall in this price, and hence in an increase in desired holdings. What the relations of (14) do is simply to give a precise characterization of the ultimate outcome of the equilibrating effects of the market process.

5. THE MARKET LINE

The somewhat diffuse concept of a "price of risk" can be made more precise and meaningful through an analysis of the rate of substitution between expected yield and risk (in equilibrium). Specification of such a rate of substitution would imply the existence of a so-called "market curve." Sharpe illustrates a market curve as a line in a mean-standard deviation plane and characterizes it by saying: "In equilibrium, capital asset prices have adjusted so that the investor, if he follows rational procedures (primarily diversification), is able to attain any desired point along a *capital market line*" (p. 425). He adds that ". . . some discussions are also consistent with a nonlinear (but monotonic) curve" (p. 425, footnote).

We shall attempt to formulate these ideas in terms of our general equilibrium system.

As we have said earlier, a relation among points in a mean-variance diagram makes sense only when the means and variances refer to some unit common to all assets, for example, a dollar's worth of investment. We therefore had to reject such representations as a starting point for the derivation of general equilibrium conditions. When we study properties of this equilibrium, however, the situation is somewhat different. After equilibrium has been attained, each individual has specific portfolios with specific expected yields and variances of yield. Also, the individual's total wealth, i.e., the value at market prices of his portfolio, has been determined. This wealth, w^i, can be expressed as

$$w^i = \sum_{j=1}^{n-1} p_j x_j^i + q x_n^i = \sum_{j=1}^{n-1} p_j \bar{x}_j^i + q \bar{x}_n^i.$$

(The latter equality follows from (6).) We can now meaningfully define, for each individual, the per dollar expected yield of his equilibrium portfolio, u_1^i, and the per dollar standard deviation of yield of his equilibrium portfolio, u_2^i. These magnitudes are defined in terms of y_1^i and y_2^i by the relations: $u_1^i = y_1^i/w^i$, and $u_2^i = \sqrt{y_2^i}/w^i$. More concretely, we may think of individual i's portfolio as divided into w^i equal "piles," with each asset in equal proportion in all "piles." Each such "pile" has a market value of one dollar; its expected yield is u_1^i, and its standard deviation of yield is u_2^i. We are interested in the relationship between u_1^i and u_2^i.

From (5) we have:

$$\frac{dy_2^i}{dy_1^i} = \frac{2x_j^i \sum_\alpha \sigma_{j\alpha} x_\alpha^i}{(u_j - p_j/q)x_j^i} \qquad (j = 1,\ldots, n-1).$$

But by "corresponding addition,"[6] we also have

$$\frac{dy_2^i}{dy_1^i} = \frac{2 \sum_j \sum_\alpha \sigma_{j\alpha} x_j^i x_\alpha^i}{\sum_j (\mu_j - p_j/q)x_j^i} = \frac{2y_2^i}{(y_1^i - x_n^i) - (w^i - qx_n^i)/q} = \frac{2y_2^i}{y_1^i - w^i q}.$$

We thus have a differential equation in y_1^i and y_2^i, the general solution form of which is given by

$$\lambda^i \sqrt{y_2^i} = y_1^i - w^i/q,$$

where λ^i is a constant of integration. With this solution, we have

$$\frac{dy_2^i}{dy_1^i} = \frac{2}{\lambda^i} \sqrt{y_2^i},$$

and so λ^i can be determined by the condition

$$\frac{2}{\lambda^i} \sqrt{y_2^i} = \frac{2 \sum_a \sigma_{j\alpha} x_\alpha^i}{\mu_j - p_j/q},$$

which gives

$$\lambda^i = \frac{\mu_j - p_j/q}{\sum_\alpha \sigma_{j\alpha} x_\alpha^i} \sqrt{\sum_j \sum_\alpha \rho_{j\alpha} x_j^i x_\alpha^i}.$$

But substituting from (14) $x_j^i = z^i \bar{x}_j$, we end up with

$$\lambda^i = \frac{\mu_j - p_j/q}{\sum_\alpha \sigma_{j\alpha} \bar{x}_\alpha} \sqrt{\sum_j \sum_\alpha \sigma_{j\alpha} \bar{x}_j \bar{x}_\alpha}.$$

[6] If $u = a/b = c/d$, then also $u = (a + c)/(b + d)$.

The important thing to note here is that the righthand side is independent of i, so that we conclude that the λ^i are the same for all i—equal to, say, λ. This means that all points (u_1^i, u_2^i) lie on a straight line, $u_1 = \lambda u_2 + 1/q$, with

$$(15) \qquad \lambda = \frac{\mu_j - p_j/q}{\sum_\alpha p_{j\alpha}\bar{x}_\alpha} \sqrt{\sum_j \sum_\alpha \sigma_{j\alpha}\bar{x}_j\bar{x}_\alpha}.$$

We note also that according to (10) the factor $(\mu_j - p_j/q)/\sum_\alpha \sigma_{j\alpha}\bar{x}_\alpha$ is the same for all assets, so that the choice of the jth asset as "reference point" is perfectly arbitrary.

We shall analyse λ in detail in the next section, but it may be worth while to give a general appreciation of the results so far, as they are of some interest in themselves.

We have shown, first of all, that a "market line" in the sense discussed above can be derived from the conditions for general equilibrium (if it exists). Second, the fact that the market line is a straight line means that the rate of substitution between per dollar expected yield and per dollar standard deviation of yield is constant, i.e., for any two individuals r and s:

$$\frac{u_1^r - u_1^s}{u_2^r - u_2^s} = \lambda.$$

Third, these results are independent of any individual characteristics, not only with respect to initial holdings, but also with respect to the individuals' utility functions (except, possibly, that they depend upon the first two moments only of the probability distribution for yield). This is not to say that the *value* of λ is independent of the utility functions, which is clearly not the case, depending as it does upon the prices which in turn cannot be determined without knowledge of the utility functions. But the demonstration of this general property of equilibrium is nevertheless valuable.

The intercept with the u_1-axis, i.e., the point $u_2 = 0$, $u_1 = 1/q$, corresponds to a portfolio consisting entirely of the riskless asset and would be the location for an individual showing an extreme degree of risk aversion. And the further upward along the line an individual is located, the more willing he is to assume risk in order to gain in expected yield.

This concept of the market line as a locus of a finite number of points (u_1^i, u_2^i) describing individual portfolios should be contrasted with the characterization given by Sharpe and cited earlier. At least with the interpretation we have been able to give to the market line, it is not something along which an individual may or may not choose to place himself. It would be misleading to give the impression that if an individual does not behave rationally he is somehow "off" this line. For the market line is not a construct that can be maintained independently of investor behavior, and it has no meaning as a criterion for testing whether an individual behaves rationally or not. Rather, it is a way of summarizing the result of rational behavior, and nothing more. It describes in a concise fashion the market conditions in general equilibrium, and this equilibrium is defined in terms of conditions implied by the attempts of individuals to maximize their utility functions, i.e., to behave rationally (and this is the only meaning that the term "rational behavior" can have in this context). If one or more individuals do not behave rationally, the whole foundation of the analysis is destroyed, and the concept of equilibrium, and hence also of the market line, becomes meaningless. The only statements that (15) does permit are those involving comparisons of different individuals' equilibrium portfolios with respect to their per dollar yield characteristics.

There is one more property of the market equilibrium that should be made explicit, namely, that it is independent of the definition of assets. More precisely: given society's real investments and their stochastic nature, the existence and slope of the market line is (under assumptions to be specified) independent of the distribution of ownership of these investments among companies.

So far, we have not been very precise about the nature of the various risky assets, although company shares were mentioned as examples of assets. Consider now the possibility of a merger of two companies into a new company. How will such a merger affect market equilibrium?

A detailed analysis of this kind of reorganization would evidently require specification of details of the merger agreements. But the most important results can be derived without this knowledge. We shall, as a matter of fact, consider any reorganization of the original $n - 1$ companies into any number $\hat{n}$ of new companies. In the remainder of this section, we shall label the original companies j or k—$j, k = 1, \ldots, n - 1$—and retain our earlier notation for the parameters and variables in the original situation. The new companies will be labeled α or β; $\alpha, \beta = 1, \ldots, \hat{n}$, and the corresponding parameters and variables will be distinguished by hats ($\hat{\mu}_\alpha$, $\hat{x}_\alpha^i$, $\hat{w}^i$, etc.). The riskless asset is labeled n in both cases.

We shall make two basic assumptions. The first is that the yield on the securities of a company can be identified with the yield of the real investments that it owns. The second is that the yield on real investments are independent of ownership conditions.

It should be clear that these assumptions imply that we neglect those factors that may account for most real-world mergers, namely, the possibility of reorganization of productive activities so as to improve their yield prospects. Further, it is implicitly taken for granted that the ownership reallocation does not affect investors' perceptions of probability distributions of yield. We are really attempting to compare two entirely different worlds—one with and one without merged companies. There is then no logical reason why there should exist any connections between probability distributions in the two worlds: the μ's and σ's are given data summarizing investors' perceptions when things are organized in a particular way, and would conceivably be different if things were organized differently.

Be that as it may, the immediate results of the assumptions are, first, that the expected yield on total outstanding stock of all companies is the same in both situations, i.e.,

(16)
$$\sum_{j=1}^{n-1} \mu_j \bar{x}_j = \sum_{\alpha=1}^{\hat{n}} \hat{\mu}_\alpha \hat{\bar{x}}_\alpha,$$

and, second, that a similar condition holds for the total variance:

(17)
$$\sum_{j=1}^{n-1} \sum_{k=1}^{n-1} \sigma_{jk} \bar{x}_j \bar{x}_k = \sum_{\alpha=1}^{\hat{n}} \sum_{\beta=1}^{\hat{n}} \hat{\sigma}_{\alpha\beta} \hat{\bar{x}}_\alpha \hat{\bar{x}}_\beta.$$

From (5) we must have, for each i and any j or α,

$$\frac{\sum_\beta \hat{\sigma}_{\alpha\beta} \hat{x}_\beta^i}{\hat{\mu}_\alpha - \dfrac{\hat{p}_\alpha}{q}} = \frac{\sum_k \sigma_{jk} x_k^i}{\mu_j - \dfrac{p_j}{q}},$$

so that (by summing over i):

(18)
$$\frac{\sum_\beta \hat{\sigma}_{\alpha\beta} \hat{\bar{x}}_\beta}{\hat{\mu}_\alpha - \dfrac{\hat{p}_\alpha}{q}} = \frac{\sum_k \sigma_{jk} \bar{x}_k}{\mu_j - \dfrac{p_j}{q}}.$$

This equation corresponds to (10), and it therefore follows that

$$\frac{\hat{x}_\alpha^i}{\hat{\bar{x}}_\alpha} = \frac{x_j^i}{\bar{x}_j} = z^i,$$

i.e., the proportion held of the outstanding stock of the various risky assets is the same in both situations. Looking now at the expression (15) for λ, we observe that by (18) the first factor is the same in both situations, and that by (17) this also holds for the second factor. Hence we conclude that the market line remains the same.

By corresponding addition on both sides of (18), we also get

$$\frac{\sum_\alpha \sum_\beta \hat{\sigma}_{\alpha\beta} \hat{\bar{x}}_\alpha \hat{\bar{x}}_\beta}{\sum_\alpha \hat{\mu}_\alpha \hat{\bar{x}}_\alpha - \dfrac{1}{q}\sum_\alpha \hat{p}_\alpha \hat{\bar{x}}_\alpha} = \frac{\sum_j \sum_k \sigma_{jk} \bar{x}_j \bar{x}_k}{\sum_j \mu_j \bar{x}_j - \dfrac{1}{q}\sum_j p_j \bar{x}_j}$$

Therefore,

$$\sum_\alpha \hat{p}_\alpha \hat{\bar{x}}_\alpha = \sum_j p_j \bar{x}_j.$$

Next we can show that each individual will be located at the same point on the market line in both situations, so that his utility remains the same. This is seen by directly observing the means and variances of yield of portfolios in the two cases:

$$\hat{y}_1^i = \sum_\alpha \hat{\mu}_\alpha \hat{x}_\alpha^i + \hat{x}_n^i = z^i \sum_\alpha \hat{\mu}_\alpha \hat{\bar{x}}_\alpha + \hat{x}_n^i = z^i \sum_j \mu_j \bar{x}_j + \hat{x}_n^i$$

$$= \sum_j \mu_j x_j^i + \hat{x}_n^i = y_1^i - x_n^i + \hat{x}_n^i.$$

But since the budget equations must also hold, we have

$$\sum_{\alpha} \hat{p}_{\alpha} \hat{x}_{\alpha}^i + q\hat{x}_n^i = \sum_j p_j x_j^i + qx_n^i,$$

$$z^i \sum_{\alpha} p_{\alpha} \hat{\bar{x}}_{\alpha} + q\hat{x}_n^i = z^i \sum_j p_j \bar{x}_j + qx_n^i,$$

Therefore, $\hat{x}_n^i = x_n^i$, and so $\hat{y}_1^i = y_1^i$. Similarly, we find $\hat{y}_2^i = y_2^i$.

In short, then, everything remains essentially the same as before. Investors will just accept the exchange of securities caused by the reorganization of companies, but will not undertake any further adjustment.

The meaning of these results are, then, that when probability distributions are assumed to apply to the real side of the economy, the organization of productive activities is immaterial from the standpoint of valuation. Accordingly, companies may be formed in the way which is the most efficient for carrying out the productive activities (given such phenomena as economies of scale and the like), and that organization will also prove adequate from a "financial markets" point of view.

6. THE PRICE OF RISK

The concept of the "price of risk" can now be explored somewhat more fully in terms of λ, the slope of the market line. The "price of risk" is not a very fortunate choice of terms: "price of risk reduction" might be more satisfactory, since it is the relief of risk for which we must assume individuals are willing to pay. (We would, to make an analogy, certainly hesitate to use the term "price of garbage" for a city sanitation fee.) The price of risk reduction, however, is not only related to the rate of substitution between expected yield and risk, but must indeed be directly identified with it. That is to say, the only sensible meaning we can impute to the "price of risk reduction" is the amount of expected yield that must be sacrificed in order to reduce risk.

We note that when risk is measured, as we have done above, by the value (in dollars, say) of the standard deviation of yield, then the dimension of the price of risk reduction is that of an interest rate. This observation would lead us to try to establish a relation between λ and the risk margins m_j, discussed earlier. These risk margins may, of course, also be looked upon as representing prices of risk reduction, each one, however, referring to the risk aspects of that particular asset. We might then suspect that the equilibrating mechanisms of the market are such that all these risk margins are somehow "averaged" out into an overall market price of risk reduction. And it would certainly be reasonable to conjecture that the larger an asset looms in the market, the larger the weight carried by that asset in the total. Such an interpretation of λ can indeed be given an exact formulation.

Recalling our earlier definitions of m_j, R_j, and V_j, we can write (15) as:

$$\lambda = \frac{p_j \bar{x}_j m_j}{\bar{x}_j \sum_{\alpha} \sigma_{j\alpha} \bar{x}_{\alpha}} \sqrt{\sum_j V_j} = \frac{R_j m_j}{V_j} \sqrt{\sum_j V_j}.$$

Since this holds for any $j, j = 1, \ldots, n - 1$, we must also have

(19)
$$\lambda = \frac{\sum_j R_j m_j}{\sum_j V_j} \sqrt{\sum_j V_j} = \frac{\sum_j R_j m_j}{\sqrt{\sum_j V_j}}.$$

This means that λ is proportional to an arithmetical average of the m_j, the weights for each asset being the outstanding stock of that asset. The factor of proportionality is $\sum_j R_j / \sqrt{\sum_j V_j}$, the mean-standard deviation ratio for the market as a whole.

Another substitution allows us to write λ in still another fashion, which also throws some light on its composition. We may write (15) as

$$\lambda = \frac{m_k p_k}{\sum_\alpha \sigma_{k\alpha} \bar{x}_\alpha} \sqrt{\sum_j x_j \sum_\alpha \sigma_{j\alpha} \bar{x}_\alpha}$$

$$= \frac{m_k p_k}{\sum_\alpha \sigma_{k\alpha} \bar{x}_\alpha} \sqrt{\sum_j x_j \frac{(\sum_\alpha \sigma_{j\alpha} \bar{x}_\alpha)^2}{\sum_\alpha \sigma_{j\alpha} \bar{x}_\alpha}}.$$

From (10), however, we get

$$(\sum \sigma_{j\alpha} \bar{x}_\alpha)^2 = (m_j p_j)^2 \left(\frac{\sum_\alpha \sigma_{k\alpha} \bar{x}_\alpha}{m_k p_k} \right)^2.$$

When this is substituted above, the factor $m_k p_k / \sum_\alpha \sigma_{k\alpha} \bar{x}_\alpha$ drops out, and we are left with

$$\lambda = \sqrt{\sum_j \frac{(m_j p_j)^2}{\frac{1}{x_j} \sum_\alpha \sigma_{j\alpha} \bar{x}_\alpha}}.$$

Now define $s_j^2 = \frac{1}{\bar{x}_j} \sum_\alpha \sigma_{j\alpha} \bar{x}_\alpha$; this gives

(20)
$$\lambda = \sqrt{\sum_j \left(\frac{m_j p_j}{s_j} \right)^2}.$$

This expression is not only simple, but affords an interesting interpretation. Since $s_j^2 = V_j / \bar{x}_j^2$, s_j can be interpreted as the standard deviation of yield per unit of asset j (with the given quantities $\bar{x}_j$); i.e., it measures the risk per unit of asset j. Hence, $m_j p_j$ is clearly the risk of compensation per unit of asset j; $p_j m_j / s_j$ is then the risk compensation per unit of risk on a unit of asset j, or, to put it differently, the gain in expected yield per unit's increase in the risk on a unit of asset j. The characterization given to λ as a description of equilibrium for the market as a whole was completely analogous. Then (20) specifies λ as the square root of the sum of squares of the individual components $p_j m_j / s_j$;

this is a natural result of the properties of the standard deviation as a measure of risk.

REFERENCES

1. Allais, M.: "L'extension des théories de l'équilibre économique général et du rendement social au cas du risque," *Econometrica*, April, 1953.
2. Arrow, K. J.: "The Role of Securities in the Optimal Allocation of Risk-Bearing," *Review of Economic Studies*, 86, 1964.
3. Borch, Karl: "Equilibrium in a Reinsurance Market," *Econometrica*, July, 1962.
4. ———: "A Note on Utility and Attitudes to Risk," *Management Science*, 1963.
5. Brownlee, O. H., and I. O. Scott: "Utility, Liquidity, and Debt Management," *Econometrica*, July, 1963.
6. Markowitz, H.: *Portfolio Selection*, New York, John Wiley and Sons, 1959.
7. Sharpe, W. F.: "Capital Asset Prices: A Theory of Market Equilibrium under Conditions of Risk," *The Journal of Finance*, September, 1964.
8. Tobin, J.: "Liquidity Preference as Behavior Towards Risk," *Review of Economic Studies*, 67, 1959.

9. A TIME-STATE-PREFERENCE MODEL OF SECURITY VALUATION**

STEWART C. MYERS*

Reprinted by permission of the author and the publisher from *Journal of Financial and Quantitative Analysis,* Vol. III, No. 1 (March 1968), pp. 1–33.

I. INTRODUCTION AND SUMMARY

Determining the market values of streams of future returns is a task common to many sorts of economic analysis. The literature on this subject is extensive at all levels of abstraction. However, most work has not taken uncertainty into account in a meaningful way.

This paper presents a model of security valuation in which uncertainty takes the central role. The model is based on the requirements for equilibrium in a world in which uncertainty is described by a set of possible event-sequences, or states of nature. This "time-state-preference" framework is a generalized version of that used in articles by Arrow, Debreu, and Hirshleifer, as well as in several more recent studies.[1]

The valuation formulas presented here are, of course, imperfect. They cannot be represented as handy empirical tools. On the theoretical front, moreover, new results and new problems seem always to arrive hand in hand. Although the problems are duly noted, the time-state-preference model will be defended as a plausible approximation and a useful analytical tool.

* Assistant Professor of Finance, Sloan School of Management, Massachusetts Institute of Technology.

** This paper is a further development of my doctoral dissertation [20], which was submitted to the Graduate School of Business, Stanford University, in 1967. I am indebted for good advice and apt suggestions to my dissertation committee, Professors Alexander Robichek, Gert von der Linde, and Ezra Solomon. Also, Professor Kenneth Arrow was kind enough to read and comment on the entire dissertation. I wish also to thank Professors Jack Hirshleifer, Avraham Beja, Paul Cootner, and Peter Diamond, as well as this paper's referees, for helpful comments.

My research was supported by a Ford Foundation Doctoral Fellowship and a Ford Foundation Grant to the Sloan School for research in business finance. Neither the Ford Foundation nor the persons cited above are responsible for my opinions or mistakes.

[1] The framework is due to Arrow [2] and has been extended and expounded by Debreu [5], Ch. VII, and Hirshleifer [9], [10], [11]. See also Radner [24], Drèze [7], Pye [23], Diamond [4], and Beja [3] for examples of related work. Lancaster [14] has used a similar analytical framework in recent discussions of theory of consumer choice.

The paper is organized as follows. The basic time-state-preference model is derived in Section II. This requires careful statement of the assumed market characteristics and the constraints on investors' strategies: although the general characteristics of the formulas obtained are intuitively appealing, their precise form is sensitive to the range of trading opportunities open to investors. The Kuhn-Tucker conditions are used to obtain the necessary conditions for equilibrium. In Section III, the special case discussed by other authors is related to my more general model. Some implications are considered in Section IV.

Finally, I consider the possible effects of "the interdependence of investors' strategies," which arise whenever the value of a security to an investor depends on other investors' beliefs and market strategies. This interdependence leads to price uncertainty, which greatly complicates the necessary conditions for equilibrium. Thus, it is difficult to evaluate its systematic effect, if any, on the structure of security prices. It is possible, however, to make qualitative comments on the nature of the problem and its possible effects.

The main contributions of this paper are as follows:

1. It is a general description of how markets for risky assets would work under a variety of conditions. Although it is more exploratory than definitive, this should not be surprising: work in the area has a relatively short history, and has concentrated mostly on issues that are even broader than those considered here. This paper is one of the first detailed investigations of a particular market under uncertainty.
2. It is widely agreed that the time-state-preference framework as developed by Arrow, Debreu, and Hirshleifer[2] is an important addition to the economist's theoretical tool-kit. This paper shows that the framework is amenable to considerable generalization, and that it allows explicit statement of the effects of certain "imperfections"—e.g., restrictions on short selling or borrowing.
3. The model was originally developed as a contribution to the theory of corporate financial management. Although details are not included here, it has already proved useful in this context.[3] Thus it should be worthwhile to set out the logic of the model in detail as a basis for further work.

II. THE BASIC TIME-STATE-PREFERENCE MODEL

One way of describing uncertainty about conditions in a future period[4] is to say that one of a set of possible states of nature will occur at that time.

---

[2] In the articles already cited.

[3] See Myers [20] [21], Robichek and Myers [25], and Hirshleifer [10], esp. pp. 264–68.

[4] The most common alternative is to specify the mean, variance and possibly other statistical measures of risk and return. See Sharpe [26] and Lintner [16] [17], for formal models using a mean-variance framework, and Hirshleifer [11] for a detailed comparison of the two approaches.

Definition of a set of states, in turn, provides a means of describing risk characteristics of securities, since any security can be regarded as a contract to pay an amount which depends on the state which actually occurs.

For instance, we might regard a share of stock as a contract to pay an x dollar dividend if state 1 occurs at $t = 1$, a y dollar dividend if state 2 occurs at $t = 1$, etc. Let the dividend paid be $R(s, t)$ and suppose 100 states of nature are being considered for $t = 1$. Then the set $\{R(s, 1)\} = \{R(1, 1), R(2, 1), \ldots, R(100, 1)\}$ specifies the particular bundle of *contingent payments* which the investor obtains for $t = 1$ by purchasing one share. In this case, $R(1, 1) = x$, $R(2, 1) = y$, and so on.

The following model relates the present value of a security to the present value of the contingent returns the security must pay to its owner. This relationship will be derived from the *necessary* conditions of security market equilibrium. First, however, the assumed characteristics of the market must be carefully specified.

ASSUMPTIONS

1. *States of Nature.* A state of nature which may occur at time τ is defined as a particular *sequence of events* during the time span from $t = 1$ to $t = \tau$. Constructing a set of possible states is simply a means of identifying the possible event-sequences relevant to present decisions.

   The concept of an event-sequence is ambiguous, however, if "event" is left undefined, since a possibility that is relevant in one context may not be in another. A benchmark can be established by imagining a set of states defined in such great detail that the knowledge of the state that will occur at any time t would allow specification of every characteristic of the future world from the present to time t. Let this set be S. The sets of states which would be considered relevant to actual decisions may be regarded as *partitions* of S. Thus, if an investor finds it useful to identify a state by "GM's dividend is increased at $t = 1$," the state refers to that subset of S for which this "event" takes place.

   In the model presented here, it is assumed that investors agree on a particular partition,[5] which defines a set of states $\{(s, t)\}$. The set is assumed to apply to the time span from $t = 1$ to $t = T$.[6] Conditions at

---

[5] The choice of a particular partition is arbitrary. An even coarser partition than that used here would undoubtedly be more "realistic," since investors would in practice regard computational efforts as a scarce resource. The intuitive meaning of a still finer partition is difficult to pin down, if only because no one person is likely to be *interested* in more than a small subset of the additional event-sequences which could be defined.

The interpretation of time-state-preference models given coarser partitions than $\{(s, t)\}$ is discussed in Section IV.

[6] The horizon $t = T$ is introduced for analytical convenience; it is not a "planning horizon" in the usual sense of the phrase. There is some error because of the lack of explicit analysis of events subsequent to the horizon, but the effect of any such errors on the market's valuation of securities at $t = 0$ may be considered negligible if the horizon is far enough distant in time.

$t = 0$ are known with certainty. The set $\{(s, t)\}$ is sufficiently detailed that, if state s occurs at time t, then returns on every security are uniquely specified for period t and all previous periods. Also, the set of states is finite and exhaustive with respect to possible sequences of security returns.[7]

Given these conditions, a security's contingent returns $\{R(s, t)\}$ are not random variables; the return $R(s, t)$ is *certain* to be paid in period t *if* state s occurs. However, it is important to remember that the set $\{(s, t)\}$ does not catalogue all possible future events. Even if it could be known that a particular state (s, t) is to occur, an investor would still face a residual uncertainty about his health, tastes, family status, employment, etc.

2. *The Economy.* We will imagine an economy split into real and financial sectors. For present purposes, "financial sector" and "security markets" are synonymous.

It is clearly meaningless to speak of the equilibrium of security markets except in relation to a particular set of conditions in the real sector. Accordingly, the following items are taken as given:

a. The set of states $\{(s, t)\}$.
b. Investors' assessments of the probabilities that the various states will occur.
c. The (sequences of) security returns contingent on each state (s, t).

Also, it is assumed that investors have given endowments of wealth available for allocation among securities and other uses, which will be referred to collectively as "consumption."

3. *Available Securities.* Taking conditions in the economy's real sector as given necessitates a restriction on the types of securities that may be issued (or retired) in response to security prices at $t = 0$. There is no need to hold supplies of all securities constant; however, it is not consistent to admit changes in the supply of securities that are part and parcel of changes in the allocation of resources within the real sector.

To illustrate, suppose that interest rates fall at $t = 0$. In response, a firm issues bonds to finance purchases of additional plant and equipment. Because the additional real assets enable the firm to pay higher returns in some or all future contingencies, a link is created between current interest rates and the bundle of contingent returns which the firm offers to present investors. This is unacceptable if the analysis is to be limited to conditions for equilibrium in the financial sectors.

If, on the other hand, the firm uses the bond issue to retire a portion of its outstanding common stock, conditions in the real sector may be con-

---

[7] The assumption is that security returns may take specific, discrete values. Continuous variables could just as well be used—e.g., $R_k(s, t)$ could be regarded as a continuous function of s and t. Diamond's argument [4] is cast in this form.

sidered unchanged. The substitution of debt for equity in a firm's capital structure is a financing decision, and changes in the firm's real assets or investment strategy are not a necessary consequence.[8]

To generalize, changes in the supply of securities, or the issue of new types of securities, are not ruled out in what follows. It is assumed, however, that such adjustments are not of the sort that imply changed conditions in the real sector. It has already been noted that the concept "equilibrium of security markets" is meaningful only if conditions in the real sector are given.

4. *Market Characteristics.* Markets are assumed to be perfect.

5. *Reinvestment of Contingent Returns.* Investment in securities amounts to the purchase of contingent returns, which may, in general, be either consumed or reinvested when and if they are realized. For this model, however, we will effectively rule out reinvestment by assuming that investors hold their original portfolios unchanged at least until $t = T$. (This assumption is reconsidered in Section V below.) Accordingly, a security's return in (s, t) will be interpreted as the *cash* payment (i.e., dividend, interest, or principal payment) which its owner receives in (s, t). Capital gains or losses will not be considered, except that the price of the security in the most distant future time period under consideration will be treated as if it were a liquidating dividend.[9]

For stocks, this assures that market value is determined solely by the present value of future dividends.

6. *Utility Functions.* Investors choose portfolios which we assume maximize the expected utility of future returns on the portfolio. In addition, the total expected utility associated with any portfolio is a linear function of utility functions defined for each state. Specifically, if $\pi(s, t)$ is an investor's judgment of the probability of occurrence of contingency (s, t) and $U(s, t)$ is the utility of returns to be received in (s, t), then the overall utility of a portfolio's contingent returns will be given by

$$(1) \qquad \psi = \sum_{s,t} \pi(s, t)U(s, t).$$

---

[8] It is true that the contingent returns received by stock- and bond-holders are affected if the firm replaces equity with debt. However, the bundles of contingent returns offered by the firm's securities can still be clearly specified within the set of states $\{(s, t)\}$, provided that (a) there is no change in the total contingent returns paid by the firm on all its outstanding securities and (b) investors are certain about how the firm's total payout is to be divided among stock- and bond-holders in every possible contingency. Although these conditions may not always hold in practice (see Robichek and Myers [25], esp. pp. 15–19), they are a reasonable approximation for present purposes.

[9] However, there is no requirement that all securities offer contingent returns in all time periods from $t = 1$ to $t = T$. Bonds, in particular, will often mature before the horizon period.

The notation $\sum\limits_{s,t}$ denotes summation over all states in the set $\{(s, t)\}$, $t = 1, 2, \ldots, T.$

Further, we assume that each utility function $U(s, t)$ is defined only in terms of returns to be received in (s, t). That is, if an investor holds a portfolio yielding y in (s, t), then the utility of y is independent of the utility of returns in all other contingencies, and vice versa.

This assumption would not be reasonable without our proviso that contingent returns on securities are consumed, rather than reinvested. If, say, the amount y were invested in real assets, the investor's income in subsequent contingencies would be increased. As a consequence, the marginal utility of income in these contingencies would not be the same, in general, as it would be if y were consumed.

In this framework $U'(s, t)$, the marginal utility of income in a given contingency, may be high for either or both of two reasons:[10]

a. Assuming that the investor is risk-averse, $U'(s, t)$ will be relatively high to the extent that the total income to be received in (s, t) is low.
b. The utility of a given amount of money income may differ from state to state, since the utility *functions* $U(s, t)$ are not necessarily the same for each contingency.

One class of reasons why the functions $U(s, t)$ may depend on (s, t) is fairly obvious: differences can arise, for instance, if commodity prices differ from state to state and over time, or if the investor's need for income depends on, say, his age at (s, t).

Another kind of reason follows from the way we have set up the problem. The set $\{(s, t)\}$ assumed for purposes of analysis is exhaustive in the sense that it offers a complete catalogue of possible future returns on *securities*, but it does not catalogue *all* future events exhaustively. The risks inherent in these "uncatalogued" contingencies will not, in general, be independent of the state being considered. An investor will perhaps be less certain of the amount of income he will receive from sources other than securities in wartime, but the occurrence of a war will also affect returns on securities. The functions $U(s, t)$ will reflect such inter-relationships.

Formally, then, the phrase "utility of a contingent return A in (s, t)" must be taken to mean "the *expected* utility to the investor of the (certain) amount A at time t given that state s occurs." We thus consider only a part of the investor's overall decision problem: the possible incremental effects on his future income of his portfolio choice at $t = 0$.

---

[10] As noted by Hirshleifer [11], pp. 523–34.

THE BASIC MODEL

We begin by considering N different securities which investors can purchase at $t = 0$. These securities may have been issued at $t = 0$, or they may be "left over" from previous periods. The word "share" will be used to refer to a single unit of investment in a given security.

For the kth security, the set $\{R_k(s, t)\}$ of contingent returns per share will be written in vector form, and referred to as R_k, where

$$R_k = [R_k(0), \ldots, R_k(s, t), \ldots]$$

for $s = 1, 2, \ldots, m(t)$, and for each period $t = 1, 2, \ldots, T$. The "state" $s = 0$ refers to the present—i.e., to $t = 0$—and for each security $R_k(0) = -P_k$, where P_k is the ex-dividend market price per share of the kth security at $t = 0$.

We define a dummy security $k = 0$ to be "consumption" at $t = 0$, with

$$R_0 = [1, 0, \ldots, 0].$$

That is, purchasing one share of security zero is interpreted as the consumption of one dollar at $t = 0$. P_0, the "price" of consumption, is likewise one dollar.

Consider the portfolio selection problem of a particular investor. Let h_k be the number of shares of the kth security which he purchases. His decision problem at $t = 0$ is to choose $[h_0, h_1, \ldots, h_N]$ to maximize expected utility ψ, where

(2) $$\psi = \sum_{s,t} \pi(s, t)U(s, t) + U(0),$$

with $U(s, t) = f[\sum_{k=1}^{N} h_k R_k(s, t)]$ and $U(0) = f[h_0]$. The variables $\pi(s, t)$ represent the investor's assessments of the probabilities that the states (s, t) actually will occur. (Note that we have made no assumption ruling out disagreement among investors on the probabilities $\pi(s, t)$.)

In addition, the investor is constrained in that he has only a given amount of wealth, W, available for allocation among consumption and investment. The constraint is

(3) $$\phi = \sum_{k=0}^{N} h_k P_k - W = 0.$$

Since consumption and investment in securities are the only available uses for this wealth, Equation (3) is necessarily an equality.

If no short selling or borrowing is permitted, then $h_k \geq 0$ for all k. In this case, maximizing Equation (2) subject to the stated constraint is a problem in non-linear programming. The necessary conditions for the maximum may be inferred from the Kuhn-Tucker conditions.[11] If a maximum exists, we know from these conditions that we can assign a positive number $\lambda(\phi)$ to the constraint Equation (3).[12] Maximizing utility implies that

$$(4) \qquad \frac{\delta\psi}{\delta h_k} - \lambda(\phi)\frac{\delta\phi}{\delta h_k} \leq 0,$$

for $k = 0, 1, \ldots, N$. The left hand side of Equation (4) is zero if $h_k > 0$.

Note that $\delta\phi/\delta h_k = P_k$ for $k > 0$, and $\delta\phi/\delta h_0 = 1$. Substituting in Equation (4) for security $k = 0$ (i.e. consumption at $t = 0$), we obtain

$$(5) \qquad \lambda(\phi) = U'(0),$$

where $U'(0)$ is the marginal utility of income used for present consumption.

Using these results, we can rewrite Equation (4) as

$$\delta\psi/\delta h_k - U'(0)P_k \leq 0,$$

or

$$P_k \geq 1/U'(0)[\delta\psi/\delta h_k].$$

Since, for $k \neq 0$, $\delta\psi/\delta h_k = \sum_{s,t} \pi(s,t)U'(s,t)R_k(s,t)$, we have the fundamental result

$$(6) \qquad P_k \geq \sum_{s,t} q(s,t)R_k(s,t),$$

where

$$(7) \qquad q(s,t) = \pi(s,t)\frac{U'(s,t)}{U'(0)}.$$

Equation (6) is the basic valuation formula for the time-state-preference framework. In words, it tells us that when an investor maximizes the expected utility of his portfolio, the price of each security is at least equal to the expectation of the marginal utility associated with a small increment in his holdings of that security, when the utility of money in future contingencies is

---

[11] Kuhn and Tucker [13]. Also, see Dorfman, Samuelson, and Solow [6], Ch. VII, for the exposition which prompted my use of the conditions. Remember that the conditions to be presented are not sufficient for equilibrium. For instance, one necessary condition not mentioned is that the utility functions $U(s,t)$ be convex—i.e., risk-averse. See Arrow [2], p. 95. Also, in the absence of any direct or indirect restraints on the ability of investors to *sell* single contingent payments, we must require that $\pi_i(s,t) > 0$ for all investors (indexed by i) and all (s,t). If an investor really believes that the contingency (s,t) is impossible, he will be willing to sell contingent payments in (s,t) in unlimited amounts. This latter point was mentioned to me by Avraham Beja. For a detailed treatment of the existence of equilibrium, see Debreu [5].

[12] Since, from the nature of the problem, the constraint Equation (3) must be satisfied exactly, $\lambda(\phi)$ cannot be zero.

measured in terms of the utility of money used for present consumption. If the investor actually holds that security in his portfolio, then its price is exactly equal to the expectation of the marginal utility associated with the security. The terms $q(s, t)$ thus indicate the present value to this investor of an incremental dollar of portfolio return to be received at time t if state (s, t) occurs.

A necessary condition for equilibrium is that Equation (6) holds for all securities from the point of view of each investor. In effect, it establishes a lower bound on the price of each security, expressed in terms of investors' marginal valuations of contingent returns. For if P_k were less than the right hand side of Equation (6) from the point of view of any investor, then that investor could increase the total expected utility of returns to his portfolio by purchasing security k in at least marginal amounts. Equilibrium cannot exist until all such opportunities are exhausted.

BORROWING

The introduction of investors' borrowing opportunities does not change the necessary conditions for equilibrium given by Equation (6). Borrowing is simply the purchase of a particular type of security. If the jth security is a borrowing contract open to an investor, then its contingent cash "returns" can be written in the same format used above:

$$R_j = [R_j(0), \ldots, R_j(s, t), \ldots].$$

The vector R_j is unusual only in that $R_j(0) > Q$ and $R_j(s, t) \leq 0$.

SELLING SHORT

Selling short can be most conveniently analyzed within the present framework by regarding the short sale of security k as the purchase of a dummy security k^* with a vector of contingent returns R_k^* derived from R_k. The vector R_k^* will be roughly a mirror image of R_k. If there are no margin requirements, then $R_k^* = R_k$, in which case selling security k short is algebraically equivalent to purchasing negative amounts of security k, assuming k^* is held to time $t = T$.[13]

It is entirely feasible to incorporate dummy securities such as k^* in the investor's portfolio problem wherever short sales make sense. The necessary conditions for the maximum imply a result comparable to Equation (6) for each dummy security—that is,

---

[13] Given the distant horizon T, the short sale becomes a promise to pay security k's dividends from period $t = 1$ to $t = T$ to the lender of the security. The payments include the security's price at $t = T$, which we have interpreted as a liquidating dividend. Thus selling short is the sale of future contingent returns. That we do not actually find short sales undertaken as long-term commitments is apparently due to uncertainty about whether any particular investor could fulfill such a contract. Margin requirements are a reaction to this uncertainty.

$$(8) \qquad P_k^* \geq \sum_{s,t} q(s, t) R_k^*(s, t).$$

This holds with an equality if $h_k^* > 0$.

For the case in which there are no margin requirements, comparison of Equations (6) and (8) leads to an interesting result. As we have observed, for this case $R_k^* = -R_k$, implying that $P_k^* = -P_k$ and that $R_k^*(s, t) = -R_k(s, t)$ for all (s, t). Substituting in Equation (8),

$$(9) \qquad P_k^* \leq \sum_{s,t} q(s, t) R_k(s, t).$$

Equations (6) and (9) taken together require[14]

$$(10) \qquad P_k = \sum_{s,t} q(s, t) R_k(s, t).$$

Note that Equation (10) implies that all investors agree, at the margin, on the equilibrium values of all securities, although not necessarily on the value of any particular contingent return. Because each investor is willing to "take a position" in each security, there can be no such thing as a "clientele effect." That is, investors holding a particular security will *not* value it more highly that other investors do.

On the other hand, Equation (6) *is* in itself consistent with a clientele effect. Any such effect must therefore be ascribed to restricted trading opportunities, not to the existence of uncertainty or differences in investors' expectations.

OTHER CONSTRAINTS

The frictions and imperfections which exist in actual markets, have for the most part, been left out of the above analysis. However, those which impose constraints on investors' portfolio choices can be analyzed with relative ease if portfolio choice is viewed as a problem of non-linear programming.

For example, suppose the investor must invest at least 100 percent of his funds in securities from the set K. Now the objective function must be maximized subject to two constraints:

$$\phi_1 = \sum_{k=0}^{N} h_k P_k - W = 0,$$

(11)

$$\phi_2 = bW - \sum_{k \in K} h_k P_k \leq 0.$$

[14] In words, the argument is this. If the investor's total expected utility is reduced by selling a marginal amount of security k short, he will necessarily be better off by purchasing a marginal amount of k long. Conversely, if the investor's total expected utility is reduced by purchasing a marginal amount of security k, then it will pay him to sell security k short. Therefore, each investor at equilibrium will be willing to hold at least marginal amounts of each security either long or short in his portfolio. Only if this condition is satisfied will Equations (6) and (9) be consistent.

For securities not included in the set K, $\delta\phi_2/\delta h_k = 0$. Here the constraint $\phi_2 = 0$ is irrelevant, and Equation (6) holds. For $k \in K$, however, the Kuhn-Tucker conditions are:

$$(12) \qquad \frac{\delta\psi}{\delta h_k} - \lambda(\phi_1)\frac{\delta\phi_1}{\delta h_k} - \lambda(\phi_2)\frac{\delta\phi_2}{\delta h_k} \leq 0.$$

Computing $\lambda(\phi_1)$ and the partial derivatives, and solving for P_k, we have:

$$(13) \qquad P_k = \frac{1}{U'(\phi) - \lambda(\phi_2)} \sum_{s,t} \pi(s, t)U'(s, t)R_k(s, t),$$

assuming that k is actually included in the investor's optimal portfolio. The variable $\lambda(\phi_2)$ is the expected utility lost (at the margin) by investing one dollar in a security $k \in K$ instead of consuming the dollar.[15]

III. A SPECIAL CASE

We now return to the main thread of the argument. A necessary condition for equilibrium if short sales are permitted, and if there are no margin requirements or other imperfections, is that Equation (10) holds for each investor and each security. For the ith investor, then,

$$(10) \qquad P_k = \sum_{s,t} q_i(s, t)R_k(s, t),$$

$k = 1, 2, \ldots, N$. In other words, if there are N securities, equilibrium requires that N equations of this form hold for each investor. The "unknowns" are the variables $q_i(s, t)$, since security prices and contingent returns are taken as given by investors in a perfect market. The set $\{q_i(s, t)\}$ represents the present values of contingent returns to the ith investor, given by Equation (7).

In general, there is no requirement that investors agree on the present value of contingent returns. However, consider the special case in which $N \geq M$, where M is the number of future states, and M of the vectors R_k is linearly independent. Here the equations may be solved to yield a unique set of *prices* $\{q_1(1, 1), \ldots, q_i(s, t), \ldots\}$. Moreover, since P_k and R_k are the same for all investors, *the set must be identical for all investors*. Given the structure of security prices at equilibrium, we can thus infer an entirely objective set of prices $\{q(s, t)\}$, where $q(s, t)$ is the price at $t = 0$ of one dollar to be paid contingent on the occurrence of (s, t). We have, therefore:

$$(14) \qquad P_k = \sum_{s,t} q(s, t)R_k(s, t),$$

with $q(s, t) = q_i(s, t)$ for all i and all (s, t).[16]

[15] It is given by $\lambda(\phi_2) = U'(0) - \sum\limits_{s,t} \pi(s, t) U'(s, t) [R_k(s, t)/P_k]$.

[16] This result *may* hold even if short sales are restricted. But this requires that (a) the vectors of returns of available securities—including borrowing and any "dummy securities" used to describe types of trading different from simple purchases—span a cone equivalent to the M-dimensional space created by the set $\{(s, t)\}$, and (b) that Equation (16) holds with an equality for all securities and all investors. In this case the number of securities would have to be substantially *more* than the number of states.

In reality, of course, the number of securities is likely to be much less than the number of states. Nevertheless, this simplest possible case is important in several respects.

1. It is customarily argued that, since investors will disagree in their subjective evaluations of the size and risk of streams of future returns, their estimates of the value of these streams will also differ. This may well be true in fact, but Equation (14) establishes that any such disagreement is not a necessary consequence of either (a) the existence of uncertainty or (b) differences in investors' expectations. In fact, Equation (14) implies that all investors would agree on the value of any conceivable bundle of contingent returns, no matter how bizarre, which could be specified in terms of the catalogue of contingencies $\{(s, t)\}$.

2. Equation (14) is closely related to (and, in fact, depends on) the ability of any investor to achieve any desired *pattern* of contingent returns from his portfolio. To be specific, let the vector X_p represent the desired pattern:

$$(15) \qquad X_p = [X_p(1, 1), \ldots, X_p(s, t), \ldots] = \frac{1}{\sum\limits_{s,t} R_p(s, t)} R_p.$$

Here $R_p(s, t)$ is the return of the portfolio in (s, t) and R_p is the vector of these returns. The numbers $X_p(s, t)$ represent the pattern of the contingent returns $R_p(s, t)$. Because $1/\sum\limits_{s,t} R_p(s, t)$ adjusts for the *scale* of the portfolio's returns, $\sum\limits_{s,t} X_p(s, t) = 1$. The pattern of returns for a security can be described similarly:

$$(16) \qquad X_k = [X_k(1, 1), \ldots, X_k(s, t), \ldots] = \frac{1}{\sum\limits_{s,t} R_k(s, t)} R_k.$$

Since, in this special case, there are M securities with linearly independent vectors X_k, and there are no margin requirements for short sales, the vectors span the M-dimensional space defined by the catalogue of M states. The portfolio vector X_p lies in this same space. It follows that any vector X_p can be obtained by a linear combination of the vectors X_k.

To put this another way, we have established that an investor can adjust his portfolio to change a particular contingent return $R_p(s, t)$, while leaving returns in all other contingencies unchanged. In effect, he can buy or sell returns for any contingency. It is as if there were a separate forward market for dollars to be delivered in each future state. Viewed in this light, it is not surprising that a unique set of prices $\{q(s, t)\}$ is a necessary condition for equilibrium.

3. Previous time-state-preference models have, without significant exception, confined their analysis to this special case. In fact, it is usually assumed that trading of contingent returns takes place in explicit markets, rather than implicitly, via portfolio adjustments. Arrow and Hirshliefer, for

instance, have assumed markets for "primitive securities":[17] the primitive security for (s, t) pays one dollar contingent on (s, t), but nothing in any other state. Thus the equilibrium price of such a security would be simply $q(s, t)$.[18]

Without denying the theoretical productivity of this special case,[19] it is important to recognize that the time-state-preference framework can be generalized and adapted to particular market characteristics.

IV. SOME IMPLICATIONS

This section notes some implications of the time-state-preference model of security valuation. First, the conventional valuation formulas are briefly re-examined. Observations follow on the implications of individual risk aversion for market prices, the interpretation of time-state-preference models if the catalogue of states is not exhaustively defined, and the concept of a risk-equivalent class of securities.

CONVENTIONAL FORMULAS

Consider the ith investor, who holds at least one share of the kth stock. Then Equation (12) holds at equilibrium:

$$(10) \qquad P_k = \sum_{s,t} q_i(s, t)R_k(s, t).$$

This investor may or may not agree with others on the present value of contingent returns. For simplicity's sake, however, we will drop the subscript i in what follows.

The formulas normally used are:

$$(17) \qquad P_k = \sum_{t=1}^{T} \frac{\bar{R}_k(t)}{(1 + r)^t} = \sum_{t=1}^{T} \frac{C_k(t)}{(1 + i)^t},$$

where $\bar{R}_k(t)$ is the investor's expected return in t; r is his required rate of return; $C_k(t)$ is the certainty equivalent of $\bar{R}_k(t)$, and i is the riskless rate of interest. These formulas may be regarded as simplifications of Equation (10). Thus the size of r or $C_k(t)$ depends on (1) the pattern across states of stock k's contingent dividends, (2) the investor's valuations of contingent returns, and (3) his probability assessments. Specifically,[20]

---

[17] See Arrow [2]. Hirshleifer calls these primitive securities "time-state claims." [11], p. 527, and passim.

[18] The set of primitive securities and the M normal securities considered above are simply alternative bases for the vector space defined in terms of $\{(s, t)\}$.

[19] For instance, the special case has generated considerable insight into the problem of determining optimal capital structure for corporations. See Robichek and Myers [25] and Hirshleifer [10], pp. 264–8.

[20] This is purely algebraic juggling. Note that $Z_k(t)D_k(t)$ is equivalent to the vector $[R_k(1, t) \cdots R_k(m(t), t)]$. Also, $Q(t) = [1/\sum_s q(s, t)] [q(1, t) \cdots q(m(t), t)] = (1 + i)^t[q(1, t) \cdots q(m(t), t)]$. That is, $\sum_s q(s, t)$ is the value to the investor of one dollar to be delivered with certainty in period t.

(18) $$C_k(t) = Z_k(t)Q'(t)D_k(t),$$

where $D_k(t) = \sum\limits_{s=1}^{m(t)} R_k(s, t)$, a measure of the *scale* of the bundle of contingent returns for period t, and $Z_k(t)$ and $Q(t)$ are $1 \times m(t)$ row vectors:

$$Z_k(t) = \frac{1}{D_k(t)} [R_k(1, t) \cdots R_k(m(t), t)]$$

$$Q(t) = \frac{1}{\sum\limits_{s=1}^{m(t)} q(s, t)} [q(1, t) \cdots q(m(t), t)].$$

The variables $\bar{R}_k(t)$ and $C_k(t)$ are related as follows:[21]

(19) $$C_k(t) = \alpha(t)\bar{R}_k(t) = \frac{Z_k(t)Q'(t)}{Z_k(t)\pi'(t)} \bar{R}_k(t).$$

Here $\pi(t)$ is a row vector of the investor's probability assessments $\pi(s, t)$ for period t.

There is, of course, no guarantee that investors will agree on the appropriate size for $C_k(t)$, $\bar{R}_k(t)$, $\alpha(t)$ or r.

Equation (17) is one among many ways of simplifying the more basic valuation formula, Equation (10). Alternative forms based on continuous compounding and exponential growth are often seen, as are rules of thumb using price-earnings ratios or "multipliers." Given a little algebraic ingenuity, the possible formats are endless.

Consequently, it is pointless to say that any particular simplification is *the* correct way to represent present value.

RISK AVERSION

The next few paragraphs investigate the implications of investors' risk aversion for the structure of security prices. The conclusions are generally consistent with those obtained elsewhere.[22] I repeat them because they serve as a basis for discussing implications of coarse partitions of states, and because of the persistence of the notion that security prices are adequately explained by simply considering the characteristics of individual investors' utility functions.

It is generally accepted that most investors are risk averse. From this, it is

[21] This is obtained by multiplying $C_k(t)$ as given by Equation (18) by

$$\frac{\bar{R}_k(t)}{\bar{R}_k(t)} = \frac{\bar{R}_k(t)}{Z_k(t)\pi'(t)D_k(t)} = 1.$$

Confidence in the theoretical appropriateness of certainty equivalents may be somewhat increased by finding that they can be conveniently expressed in a time-state-preference framework. Unfortunately, the required rate r cannot be conveniently expressed—a fact which corroborates Lintner's view that r is not a "primary" variable for theoretical uses. See Lintner [19], pp. 27–8.

[22] See, for instance, Drèze [7], pp. 36–8; Lintner [17], pp. 22–3.

often inferred that "the market" should be risk averse, in the sense that the certainty equivalent of an uncertain return should always be no more than the expectation of the return. In other words, the prediction would be that $\alpha(t) \le 1$, or that $r \ge i$, where i is the pure rate of interest.

Actually, it is always possible to construct patterns of contingent returns for which $\alpha(t) > 1$ for all t,—i.e., such that $r < i$. Note that the numerator and denominator of Equation (18) are weighted averages of relative prices and probabilities, respectively. In general, the relative price for (s, t) may be more or less than $\pi(s, t)$. By changing the weights $Z_k(t)$, therefore, we can always[23] assure that $Z_k(t)Q(t)' > Z_k(t)\pi(t)'$, or that $\alpha(t) > 1$. The economic meaning of this manipulation is that a bundle of contingent returns will be relatively more valuable if it pays higher returns in states in which contingent returns have a high value.

On the other hand, suppose the weights $Z_k(t)$ are chosen randomly, subject to the condition that the elements of $Z_k(t)$ sum to one. The expected result of this experiment is that[24]

(20) $$E[C_k(t)] = E[Z_k(t)Q'(t)D_k(t)] = \frac{D_k(t)}{m(t)}.$$

That is, period t's bundle of contingent returns is, on the average, exactly as valuable as a *certain* return $D_k(t)/m(t)$. Securities constructed in this manner would tend to be no more or less valuable than riskless securities with the same scale of returns.[25]

These mental experiments indicate that rewards for risk bearing are not explained by uncertainty per se, but by some systematic relationship between the relative sizes of the returns $R_k(s, t)$ and the "prices" $q(s, t)$. In actual markets, the relationship seems to be that returns on most available securities are positively correlated, so that securities tend to pay high returns precisely when most portfolio returns are high and low returns in times of scarcity. The normal risk premium is thus explained, given the inverse relationship between supplies of contingent returns and their present values.

INTERPRETATION OF THE MODEL GIVEN COARSE PARTITIONS OF STATES

The application of the time-state-preference model within a relatively coarse partition of the set S of possible event-sequences is entirely feasible, given attention to several complicating factors. One of these is that investors will not, in general, adopt identical partitions, so that agreement among

[23] If $\pi(t) = Q(t)$, $\alpha(t) = 1$ for any pattern of contingent returns. This is improbable.
[24] That is, the expected value of each of the elements of $Z_k(t)$ is $1/m(t)$; $m(t)$ is the number of states defined for period t.
[25] Unfortunately it would not be correct to predict that, on the average, such securities would be priced so that investors would anticipate an *expected* rate of return equal to the riskless rate of interest. Although $E[Z_k(t) Q'(t)] = E[Z_k(t) \pi'(t)]$, it is not true that

$$E[\alpha_t] = E\left[\frac{Z_k(t) Q'(t)}{Z_k(t) \pi'(t)}\right] = 1.$$

investors on the risk characteristics of securities cannot be taken for granted. Nevertheless, postulating agreement will often prove to be appropriate.

Another problem is that our previous definition of contingent returns will no longer serve. Given a partition $\{(\sigma, t)\}$ which is coarser than $\{(s, t)\}$, the returns contingent on (σ, t) are the *random* variables $R_k(\sigma, t)$. They cannot be used in the same sense as the variables $R_k(s, t)$—which are *certain* returns, given (s, t)—without further explanation.

Adopting the partition $\{(\sigma, t)\}$, the investor's decision problem is to maximize

$$(21) \qquad \psi = \sum_{\sigma, t} \pi(\sigma, t) E[U(\sigma, t)] + U(0),$$

subject to a wealth constraint, where

$$(22) \qquad E[U(\sigma, t)] = E\left[U\left(\sum_{k=1}^{N} h_k \tilde{R}_k(\sigma, t) \right) \right].$$

The value of $E[U(\sigma, t)]$ could be computed readily if the investor had specified the returns $R_k(s, t)$, the probabilities $\pi(s, t)$, given (σ, t), and the functions $U(s, t)$; but he does not have this information. A reasonable heuristic tool is to rewrite his decision problem as:

$$(21a) \qquad \psi = \sum_{\sigma, t} \pi(\sigma, t) U^*(\sigma, t) + U(0),$$

$$(22a) \qquad U^*(\sigma, t) = U\left(\sum_{k=1}^{N} h_k C_k(\sigma, t) \right).$$

Here $C_k(\sigma, t)$ is the certainty equivalent of $\tilde{R}_k(\sigma, t)$—that is, if state (σ, t) occurs, the investor is indifferent to receiving $\tilde{R}_k(\sigma, t)$ or a certain amount $C_k(\sigma, t)$. The investor is assumed to act as if he is certain to receive a portfolio return of $\sum_{k=1}^{N} h_k C_k(\sigma, t)$ if (σ, t) occurs.

The decision problem shown as Equations (21a) and (22a) may be solved by exactly the same procedure used in Section II to derive the basic time-state-preference model. However, this provides an easy way out only if the certainty equivalent can itself be explained without undue complication. Various simple relationships might be assumed if the partition represented by the set (σ, t) is not too coarse.[26]

---

[26] If, for instance, the partition is fine enough to describe all systematic interrelationships among returns, then the returns $\tilde{R}_k(\sigma, t)$ of the N securities are independent random variables. So long as the states (s, t) are not explicitly considered, the securities' returns can be distinguished only by summary measures of the residual uncertainty—e.g., by $\text{Var}[\tilde{R}_k(\sigma, t)]$. Consequently, a relation such as $C_k(\sigma, t) = E[\tilde{R}_k(\sigma, t)] - A \text{Var}[\tilde{R}_k(\sigma, t)]$ could be assumed. The result would be a hybrid model, in which a security's price is related to (a) the pattern of its returns across the states $\{(\sigma, t)\}$ and (b) the mean and variability of its contingent returns. It might even be fruitful to set $A = 0$, on the grounds that most of the uncertainty about security returns is resolved by the occurrence of a state (σ, t), and that diversification can eliminate most of the residual variance. Note that the covariance of $\tilde{R}_j(\sigma, t)$ and $\tilde{R}_k(\sigma, t)$ would be zero for all $j \neq k$.

One interesting thing is that the special case discussed in Section III is less unlikely when a coarse partition of states is used. The coarser $\{(\sigma, t)\}$, the smaller the number of states, and the more likely it is that the available vectors of security returns will span the vector space associated with $\{(\sigma, t)\}$. It would not be entirely unreasonable, therefore, to attempt to measure the price of one dollar to be delivered (with certainty) at $t = 1$ contingent on, say, an increase in GNP of more than five percent.[27]

"RISK CLASSES" AS A CONSEQUENCE OF COARSE PARTITIONS

In a time-state-preference framework, the risk characteristics of the kth security are determined by its pattern of returns across the possible states of nature. The vector X_k, defined by Equation (16), is one way to describe this pattern.

Unfortunately, it is not very helpful to say that securities j and k are in the same risk class if $X_j = X_k$, for this requires the return $R_k(s, t)$ to be the same proportion of $R_j(s, t)$ in every contingency. If this is true, there is little point in calling j and k different securities. The use of such a definition would thus require creating a risk class for every security, and it implies that no two securities can be considered perfect substitutes.

This is not surprising, considering that individuals are assumed to have made the computational investment necessary to evaluate securities within the set of states $\{(s, t)\}$. A smaller computational effort yields a coarser partition, and a corresponding reduction in the investor's ability to distinguish among the risk characteristics of securities. If computation is costly, it is perfectly conceivable that an investor will consider the jth and kth securities to be perfect substitutes, knowing that $X_j \neq X_k$, but not being able to specify the differences between the two (because of a coarse partition of future states) in any way which would allow a choice between them.[28] Thus the concept of a class of securities with homogeneous risk characteristics—found useful by Modigliani and Miller, for instance[29]—is not unreasonable if computational effort is a scarce resource.

V. THE INTERDEPENDENCE OF INVESTORS' STRATEGIES

The model of security valuation presented in this paper is not descriptive in any strict sense. On the other hand, the assumptions used are mostly familiar ones; few readers will be surprised to encounter such abstractions as the Perfect Market or the Rational Investor.

[27] This would also establish the market price of the certainty equivalent of a random return to be delivered contingent on this event.

[28] However, because of the general benefits of diversification, the investor may hold both securities in his portfolio.

[29] See Modigliani and Miller [18]. These comments are not meant to imply that the concept of a risk class is necessary to the proof of Modigliani and Miller's Proposition I—that the market value of the firm is independent of financial leverage in the absence of taxes on corporate income. The proposition can be readily proved given the detailed partition defined by $\{(s, t)\}$, in which no two securities can be said to belong to the same risk class. See Hirschleifer [10], pp. 264–68, and Robichek and Myers [25].

One novel assumption is that all investors purchase portfolios at $t = 0$ with the certain intention of holding them unchanged at least until period $t = T$. This proviso insures that investors' portfolio choices are *independent*, in the sense that the expected utility of any investor's portfolio depends only on the cash returns of the securities included, and in no way on possible future actions of other investors.

It takes only cursory observation of actual security markets to see that this assumption of a "one-shot" portfolio choice is inaccurate. Investors' strategies are clearly interdependent, for instance, if securities are purchased partly for anticipated capital gains. Here, the return realized by any particular investor depends not only on the state (s, t) occurring, but also on what other investors will think the security is worth.

The interdependence of investors' strategies is a matter of considerable theoretical interest and uncertain practical importance. It is discussed briefly and qualitatively in this section.

WHY INVESTORS REVISE THEIR PORTFOLIOS

There are two sorts of reasons why an investor may sell securities from his original portfolio.

1. *To provide funds for consumption.* An investor may sell securities if the cash returns on his portfolio do not sustain his "desired" consumption expenditures. Some of these consumption needs, such as retirement income, are fairly predictable, but others are not: security investment serves in part as a cushion or reserve source of funds which may be needed unexpectedly for other uses.

   It is important, however, to look one step behind this proximate cause of the sale of securities. Our previous assumption of a one-shot investment decision is *not necessarily* inconsistent with an investor's providing exactly for a large contingent cash payment, since there may be some portfolio with a pattern of returns across the set of states which is appropriate. If this pattern lies within the cone spanned by the vectors X_k of available securities, then the investor can purchase a portfolio now to meet these contingent needs precisely.

   However, such opportunities do not generally exist for all types of consumption needs, since the actual number of securities is too small to span more than a small portion of the different patterns of portfolio returns which may be desired. Moreover, the problem is only partially solved by postulating the "special case" in which an investor can obtain any conceivable pattern in the vector space defined by the set of states $\{(s, t)\}$. Suppose, for instance, that an investor perceives the possibility of a personal emergency at $t = 1$. He will not be able to provide for the emergency situation by his portfolio choice unless securities exist which give different returns *contingent on the occurrence of the emergency*. Unless this event is related in some way to economic conditions on a broader scale, this will not be the case. One would not expect to find securities offering different returns contingent on the occurrence of an event of purely personal interest.[30] Even in this special case, therefore, an investor's need for a large amount of money income contingent on a personal event cannot always be met without portfolio adjustments when the event occurs.

2. *Portfolio choice is a sequential decision problem.*[31] Whereas the contingent needs just discussed are needs for funds to be consumed, investors may also wish to *reinvest* these funds in other securities. In this case, formal analysis requires explicit treatment of portfolio choice as a *sequential* decision problem. The nature of the problem may be indicated by noting that, in our model, the marginal utility to an investor of money in (s, t) is dependent only on his portfolio choice at $t = 0$, since the returns yielded by the portfolio are determined solely by this choice. In general, however, the return received in (s, t) also depends on (a) the opportunities which develop before time t and (b) the investor's strategy in pursuing these opportunities. In this more general case, the marginal utility of income in (s, t) cannot be deduced solely from consideration of the initial portfolio choice. The result is that this variable cannot be derived and used to evaluate contingent returns in (s, t) without further analysis.

TREATMENT OF THESE PROBLEMS IN THE LITERATURE OF FINANCE

The problems raised by the interdependence of investors' strategies have been recognized, but not emphasized, in the literature. In essence, what has been done is to assume that these problems have no systematic effect on the valuation process.

Suppose we begin by comparing (a) an investor's valuation of an incre-

---

[30] It may be possible for an investor to issue securities which are differentiated in this regard. We see this in practice as insurance. But many risks are not insurable, so that we can count on some emergencies remaining.

The reasons why investors usually cannot issue securities to cover all contingent needs have been discussed by Radner [27] and Arrow [1], pp. 45–56. Transaction costs are an obvious reason. Another is the difficulty of writing a contract in which the duties of the parties depend on which state of nature actually occurs, when the catalogue of states is not exhaustively defined and agreed upon. A third reason is that the very existence of a contract may change the subsequent actions of the parties to it, in turn affecting the probabilities of occurrence of the states on which the contract is contingent. As Arrow [1] notes (p. 55) this problem arises in practice when insurance policies may make the issuing company vulnerable to a "moral hazard."

[31] One of the referees remarked: "The discussion of portfolio choice over time is very weak. The introduction of opportunities developing between t and T means that (s, t) can never be completely specified, which is a good part of what uncertainty is about. Furthermore, information processing is central to what goes on in portfolio management (the sequential problem). In fact, information is of the essence."

The referee is absolutely right. The only defense available is that my model is no weaker in this regard than other formal security valuation models. The tools available are clearly less powerful than we would like; we must do what we can with what we have.

mental share of a security on the assumption that he will hold the share until time T to (b) his valuation of this share, assuming that it is to be sold in some period $t < T$. The bundle of contingent returns he receives in case (b) differs from (a) in the substitution of the security's price at t for the contingent dividends paid by the firm between t and T. Since the level and risk characteristics of the security's price at time t are closely associated with those of the security's bundle of contingent returns subsequent to that time, it is a reasonable first approximation to assume that the present value of the price at t and the bundle of subsequent returns is the same. Given this assumption, the value of any security can be expressed solely as a function of its contingent cash returns.

This argument, which has been widely used in the literature,[32] *also justifies any of the results which can be obtained by use of the basic time-state-preference model presented above.*

The difficulty is that the risk characteristics of a security price at some future date t are also dependent on all investors' demands for this security at that time. Therefore, the investor who may sell a security at time t is exposed to uncertainty about other investors' future demands *in addition to* the uncertainty inherent in its bundle of subsequent contingent returns. This *price uncertainty* is precisely why the interdependence of investors' strategies is potentially important to any theory of security valuation. Its actual importance cannot be determined here, but the next subsection considers a situation in which it is likely to be relevant.

COMMITMENTS TO FUTURE SALE OR PURCHASE OF SECURITIES

· Interesting theoretical problems are not always empirically relevant. Could we improve a prediction of the structure of security prices by taking the interdependence of investors' strategies into account? Such an improvement could take place only if (a) securities differ in ways not reflected in their sets of contingent cash returns and (b) these differences are relevant to the investor because of the interdependence of investors' strategies.

The *commitment* to buy or sell a security at a future date (or in a particular state of nature) clearly increases an investor's exposure to price uncertainty; the extent of the increase depends on the extent of the commitment. Therefore, security prices should be affected by the interdependence of investors' strategies where strong commitments are common. It should suffice here to cite two examples.

The many studies of the term structure of interest rates have investigated the effects, if any, of price uncertainty. The liquidity premium found by most such studies is interpreted as an extra payment made by holders of short-term bonds for protection from price uncertainty. It may not be clear, however, how a commitment to buy or sell bonds is involved.

If an investor "needs" a certain amount of funds in ten years, we might

---

[32] For example, see Gordon [8], pp. 131–32, Porterfield [22], p. 19, Lintner [17], p. 27. Lintner uses a slight variant of this assumption in another paper. See [15], p. 69.

refer to $t = 10$ as his "preferred habitat,"[33] since a bond maturing at that time would be ideal for him. Higher anticipated yields on bonds of different maturities may lure him from his habitat, but if he does so, he is exposed to price uncertainty. If the "need" is in fact given, purchasing a five-year bond now commits him to buy another bond at $t = 5$, and bond yields at that time are uncertain. On the other hand, buying a fifteen-year bond effectively commits him to selling, at an uncertain price, at $t = 10$. Thus an investor can be said to commit himself to future sales or purchases when he forsakes his habitat. These commitments are one consideration which may explain the liquidity premiums just noted.[34]

A second type of implied commitment is found in much corporate borrowing, evidenced by the frequent refinancing of corporate issues. Most firms borrow for relatively short periods, compared with the *de facto* maturities of their assets. When this is done, the firm commits itself to refinancing when the borrowed funds are due.[35] If new borrowing is to be undertaken, the firm's shareholders are indirectly exposed to the price uncertainty reflected in uncertainty about the level and term structure of interest rates.

To be sure, the commitment to borrow is not absolute, since the shareholders always have the option of providing additional future financing themselves. This may be done by retention of earnings or by issue of new securities. Unfortunately, the effects of price uncertainty are not avoided in either case. If refinancing by shareholders is anticipated, ownership of the firm's shares implies a commitment to make an additional investment in some future period or contingencies. In general, there is no guarantee that such an investment is consistent with portfolios which would otherwise be optimal at that time.[36] If it is not consistent, we would expect an adverse effect on the present price of the firm's shares. The magnitude of the effect would depend on the firm's debt-equity ratio and the disparity between the maturity structures of its assets and liabilities.

VII. CONCLUDING NOTE

Hirshleifer has remarked that "one surprising aspect of the time-and-state preference model is that it leads to a theory of decision under uncertainty while entirely excluding the 'vagueness' we usually associate with uncertainty."[37] It should now be clear that such precision is not a necessary characteristic of all time-state-preference models, but only of the special case

[33] The term is Modigliani and Sutch's [19].

[34] They are not sufficient explanations. For instance, see Modigliani and Sutch [19], pp. 183–84.

[35] Robichek and Myers [25] discuss how the necessity to refinance may affect the optimal degree of leverage for highly leveraged firms.

[36] In the "special case" discussed in Section IV above, however, the investor could always offset the effect of the additional investment by short sales and/or sale of other securities in his portfolio. Thus the commitment to invest additional amounts does not constrain his portfolio choice. In less idealized worlds, the commitment may be binding.

[37] Hirshleifer [11], p. 534.

Hirshleifer was concerned with. Given a limited number of securities, restrictions on short sales, the possible effects of the interdependence of investors' strategies, etc., a certain amount of vagueness—i.e. indetermination—seems unavoidable. It should not be surprising that Equation (5), the most basic valuation formula, is an inequality. I do not find this particularly discouraging. Such properties seem to be characteristic of actual problems, not of the models we invent to solve them.

To be sure, it will often be sufficient to assume that prices are determined as if the world were perfectly precise. But we have shown that the usefulness of time-state-preference models does not rest on this assumption.

REFERENCES

1. Arrow, Kenneth J., *Aspects of the Theory of Risk-Bearing* (Helsinki: Yrjö Jahansson Lectures, 1965).
2. ———, "The Role of Securities in the Optimal Allocation of Risk-Bearing," *Review of Economic Studies*, XXXI (1963-64), pp. 91-96.
3. Beja, Avraham, "A General Framework for the Analysis of Capital Markets and Some Results for Equilibrium," (Unpublished manuscript, Stanford University, 1966).
4. Diamond, Peter A., "The Role of a Stock Market in a General Equilibrium Model with Technological Uncertainty," *American Economic Review*, LVII (September 1967), pp. 759-78.
5. Debreu, Gerard, *The Theory of Value* (New York: John Wiley & Sons, Inc., 1959).
6. Dorfman, Robert, Paul A. Samuelson, and Robert M. Solow, *Linear Programming and Economic Analysis* (New York: McGraw-Hill Book Co., Inc., 1958).
7. Drèze, Jacques H., "Market Allocation Under Uncertainty" (Preliminary draft of paper presented at the First World Congress of the Econometric Society, Rome, September 9-14, 1965).
8. Gordon, Myron J., *The Investment, Financing and Valuation of the Corporation* (Homewood, Ill.: Richard D. Irwin, Inc., 1962).
9. Hirshleifer, J., "Efficient Allocation of Capital in an Uncertain World," *American Economic Review*, LIV (May 1964), pp. 77-85.
10. ———, "Investment Decision Under Uncertainty: Application of the State-Preference Approach," *Quarterly Journal of Economics*, LXXX (May 1966), pp. 252-77.
11. ———, "Investment Decision Under Uncertainty: Choice-Theoretic Approaches," *Quarterly Journal of Economics*, LXXIX (November 1965), pp. 509-36.
12. ———, "On the Theory of Optimal Investment Decision," *Journal of Political Economy*, LXVI (August 1958), pp. 329-52.
13. Kuhn, H. W., and A. W. Tucker, "Nonlinear Programming," in U. Neyman (ed.), *Proceedings of the Second Berkeley Symposium on Mathematical Statistics and Probability* (Berkeley: University of California Press, 1951).
14. Lancaster, Kevin, "Change and Innovation in the Technology of Consumption," *American Economic Review*, LVI (May 1966), pp. 14-23.
15. Lintner, John, "Optimal Dividends and Corporate Growth Under Un-

certainty," *Quarterly Journal of Economics*, LXXVII (February 1964), pp. 49–95.

16. ———, "Security Prices, Risk and Maximal Gains from Diversification," *Journal of Finance*, XX (December 1965), pp. 587–616.

17. ———, "The Valuation of Risk Assets and the Selection of Risky Investments," *Review of Economics and Statistics*, XLVII (February 1967), pp. 13–37.

18. Modigliani, Franco, and M. H. Miller, "The Cost of Capital, Corporation Finance and the Theory of Investment," *American Economic Review*, XLVIII (June 1958), pp. 261–97.

19. ———, and Richard Sutch, "Innovations in Interest Rate Policy," *American Economic Review*, LVI (May 1966), pp. 178–97.

20. Myers, Stewart C., *Effects of Uncertainty on the Valuation of Securities and the Financial Decisions of the Firm* (Unpublished Doctoral Dissertation, Stanford University, 1967).

21. ———, "Procedures for Capital Budgeting Under Uncertainty," Massachusetts Institute of Technology, Sloan School of Management Working Paper 257–67 (mimeo).

22. Porterfield, James T. S., *Investment Decisions and Capital Costs* (Englewood Cliffs, N.J.: Prentice-Hall, Inc., 1965).

23. Pye, Gordon, "Portfolio Selection and Security Prices," *Review of Economics and Statistics*, XLIX (February 1967), pp. 111–15.

24. Radner, Roy, "Competitive Equilibrium Under Uncertainty," Technical Report No. 20, Prepared under Contract Nonr-222(77) for the Office of Naval Research, Center for Research in Management Science (Berkeley, California: University of California, 1967) (mimeo).

25. Robichek, Alexander A., and Stewart C. Myers, "Problems in the Theory of Optimal Capital Structure," *Journal of Financial and Quantitative Analysis*, I (June 1966), pp. 1–35.

26. Sharpe, William F., "Capital Asset Prices: A Theory of Market Equilibrium Under Conditions of Risk," *Journal of Finance*, XIX (September 1964), pp. 425–42.

10. EFFICIENT CAPITAL MARKETS: A REVIEW OF THEORY AND EMPIRICAL WORK*

EUGENE F. FAMA†

Reprinted from *The Journal of Finance*, Vol. XXV, No. 2 (May 1970), pp. 383–417, by permission of the author and the publisher.

I. INTRODUCTION

The primary role of the capital market is allocation of ownership of the economy's capital stock. In general terms, the ideal is a market in which prices provide accurate signals for resource allocation: that is, a market in which firms can make production-investment decisions, and investors can choose among the securities that represent ownership of firms' activities under the assumption that security prices at any time "fully reflect" all available information. A market in which prices always "fully reflect" available information is called "efficient."

This paper reviews the theoretical and empirical literature on the efficient markets model. After a discussion of the theory, empirical work concerned with the adjustment of security prices to three relevant information subsets is considered. First, *weak form* tests, in which the information set is just historical prices, are discussed. Then *semi-strong form* tests, in which the concern is whether prices efficiently adjust to other information that is obviously publicly available (e.g., announcements of annual earnings, stock splits, etc.) are considered. Finally, *strong form* tests concerned with whether given investors or groups have monopolistic access to any information relevant for price formation are reviewed.[1] We shall conclude that, with but a few exceptions, the efficient markets model stands up well.

Though we proceed from theory to empirical work, to keep the proper historical perspective we should note to a large extent the empirical work in this

---

* Research on this project was supported by a grant from the National Science Foundation. I am indebted to Arthur Laffer, Robert Aliber, Ray Ball, Michael Jensen, James Lorie, Merton Miller, Charles Nelson, Richard Roll, William Taylor, and Ross Watts for their helpful comments.

† University of Chicago—Joint Session with the Econometric Society.

[1] The distinction between weak and strong form tests was first suggested by Harry Roberts.

area preceded the development of the theory. The theory is presented first here in order to more easily judge which of the empirical results are most relevant from the viewpoint of the theory. The empirical work itself, however, will then be reviewed in more or less historical sequence.

Finally, the perceptive reader will surely·recognize instances in this paper where relevant studies are not specifically discussed. In such cases my apologies should be taken for granted. The area is so bountiful that some such injustices are unavoidable. But the primary goal here will have been accomplished if a coherent picture of the main lines of the work on efficient markets is presented, along with an accurate picture of the current state of the arts.

II. THE THEORY OF EFFICIENT MARKETS

A. EXPECTED RETURN OR "FAIR GAME" MODELS

The definitional statement that in an efficient market prices "fully reflect" available information is so general that it has no empirically testable implications. To make the model testable, the process of price information must be specified in more detail. In essence we must define somewhat more exactly what is meant by the term "fully reflect."

One possibility would be to posit that equilibrium prices (or expected returns) on securities are generated as in the "two parameter" Sharpe [40]-Lintner [24, 25] world. In general, however, the theoretical models and especially the empirical tests of capital market efficiency have not been this specific. Most of the available work is based only on the assumption that the conditions of market equilibrium can (somehow) be stated in terms of expected returns. In general terms, like the two parameter model such theories would posit that conditional on some relevant information set, the equilibrium expected return on a security is a function of its "risk." And different theories would differ primarily in how "risk" is defined.

All members of the class of such "expected return theories" can, however, be described notationally as follows:

$$E(\tilde{p}_{j,t+1}|\Phi_t) = [1 + E(\tilde{r}_{j,t+1}|\Phi_t)]p_{jt}, \tag{1}$$

where E is the expected value operator; p_{jt} is the price of security j at time t; $p_{j,t+1}$ is its price at $t + 1$ (with reinvestment of any intermediate cash income from the security); $r_{j,t+1}$ is the one-period percentage return $(p_{j,t+1} - p_{jt})/p_{jt}$; Φ_t is a general symbol for whatever set of information is assumed to be "fully reflected" in the price at t; and the tildes indicate that $p_{j,t+1}$ and $r_{j,t+1}$ are random variables at t.

The value of the equilibrium expected return $E(\tilde{r}_{j,t+1}|\Phi_t)$ projected on the basis of the information Φ_t would be determined from the particular expected return theory at hand. The conditional expectation notation of (1) is meant to imply, however, that whatever expected return model is assumed to apply, the information in Φ_t is fully utilized in determining equilibrium expected returns. And this is the sense in which Φ_t is "fully reflected" in the formation of the price p_{jt}.

But we should note right off that, simple as it is, the assumption that the conditions of market equilibrium can be stated in terms of expected returns elevates the purely mathematical concept of expected value to a status not necessarily implied by the general notion of market efficiency. The expected value is just one of many possible summary measures of a distribution of returns, and market efficiency per se (i.e., the general notion that prices "fully reflect" available information) does not imbue it with any special importance. Thus, the results of tests based on this assumption depend to some extent on its validity as well as on the efficiency of the market. But some such assumption is the unavoidable price one must pay to give the theory of efficient markets empirical content.

The assumptions that the conditions of market equilibrium can be stated in terms of expected returns and that equilibrium expected returns are formed on the basis of (and thus "fully reflect") the information set Φ_t have a major empirical implication—they rule out the possibility of trading systems based only on information in Φ_t that have expected profits or returns in excess of equilibrium expected profits or returns. Thus let

$$x_{j,t+1} = p_{j,t+1} - E(p_{j,t+1}|\Phi_t). \tag{2}$$

Then

$$E(\tilde{x}_{j,t+1}|\Phi_t) = 0 \tag{3}$$

which, *by definition*, says that the sequence $\{x_{jt}\}$ is a "fair game" with respect to the information sequence $\{\Phi_t\}$. Or, equivalently, let

$$z_{j,t+1} = r_{j,t+1} - E(\tilde{r}_{j,t+1}|\Phi_t), \tag{4}$$

then

$$E(\tilde{z}_{j,t+1}|\Phi_t) = 0, \tag{5}$$

so that the sequence $\{z_{jt}\}$ is also a "fair game" with respect to the information sequence $\{\Phi\}$.

In economic terms, $x_{j,t+1}$ is the excess market value of security j at time $t +$ 1: it is the difference between the observed price and the expected value of the price that was projected at t on the basis of the information Φ_t. And similarly, $z_{j,t+1}$ is the return at $t + 1$ in excess of the equilibrium expected return projected at t. Let

$$\alpha(\Phi_t) = [\alpha_1(\Phi_t), \alpha_2(\Phi_t), \ldots, \alpha_n(\Phi_t)]$$

be any trading system based on Φ_t which tells the investor the amounts $\alpha_j(\Phi_t)$ of funds available at t that are to be invested in each of the n available securities. The total excess market value at $t + 1$ that will be generated by such a system is

$$V_{t+1} = \sum_{j=1}^{n} \alpha_j(\Phi_t)[r_{j,t+1} - E(\tilde{r}_{j,t+1}|\Phi_t)],$$

which, from the "fair game" property of (5) has expectation,

$$E(\tilde{V}_{t+1}|\Phi_t) = \sum_{j=1}^{n} \alpha_j(\Phi_t)E(\tilde{z}_{j,t+1}|\Phi_t) = 0.$$

The expected return or "fair game" efficient markets model[2] has other important testable implications, but these are better saved for the later discussion of the empirical work. Now we turn to two special cases of the model, the submartingale and the random walk, that (as we shall see later) play an important role in the empirical literature.

B. THE SUBMARTINGALE MODEL

Suppose we assume in (1) that for all t and Φ_t

$$E(\tilde{p}_{j,t+1}|\Phi_t) \geq p_{jt}, \quad \text{or equivalently,} \quad E(\tilde{r}_{j,t+1}|\Phi_t) \geq 0. \quad (6)$$

This is a statement that the price sequence $\{p_{jt}\}$ for security j follows a submartingale with respect to the information sequence $\{\Phi_t\}$, which is to say nothing more than that the expected value of next period's price, as projected on the basis of the information Φ_t, is equal to or greater than the current price. If (6) holds as an equality (so that expected returns and price changes are zero), then the price sequence follows a martingale.

A submartingale in prices has one important empirical implication. Consider the set of "one security and cash" mechanical trading rules by which we mean systems that concentrate on individual securities and that define the conditions under which the investor would hold a given security, sell it short, or simply hold cash at any time t. Then the assumption of (6) that expected returns conditional on Φ_t are non-negative directly implies that such trading rules based

---

[2] Though we shall sometimes refer to the model summarized by (1) as the "fair game" model, keep in mind that the "fair game" properties of the model are *implications* of the assumptions that (i) the conditions of market equilibrium can be stated in terms of expected returns, and (ii) the information Φ_t is fully utilized by the market in forming equilibrium expected returns and thus current prices.

The role of "fair game" models in the theory of efficient markets was first recognized and studied rigorously by Mandelbrot [27] and Samuelson [38]. Their work will be discussed in more detail later.

only on the information in Φ_t cannot have greater expected profits than a policy of always buying-and-holding the security during the future period in question. Tests of such rules will be an important part of the empirical evidence on the efficient markets model.[3]

C. THE RANDOM WALK MODEL

In the early treatments of the efficient markets model, the statement that the current price of a security "fully reflects" available information was assumed to imply that successive price changes (or more usually, successive one-period returns) are independent. In addition, it was usually assumed that successive changes (or returns) are identically distributed. Together the two hypotheses constitute the random walk model. Formally, the model says

$$f(r_{j,t+1} \mid \Phi_t) = f(r_{j,t+1}), \tag{7}$$

which is the usual statement that the conditional and marginal probability distributions of an independent random variable are identical. In addition, the density function f must be the same for all t.[4]

Expression (7) of course says much more than the general expected return model summarized by (1). For example, if we restrict (1) by assuming that the expected return on security j is constant over time, then we have

$$E(\tilde{r}_{j,t+1} \mid \Phi_t) = E(\tilde{r}_{j,t+1}). \tag{8}$$

[3] Note that the expected profitability of "one security and cash" trading systems vis-à-vis buy-and-hold is not ruled out by the general expected return or "fair game" efficient markets model. The latter rules out systems with expected profits in excess of equilibrium expected returns, but since in principle it allows equilibrium expected returns to be negative, holding cash (which always has zero actual and thus expected return) may have higher expected return than holding some security.

And negative equilibrium expected returns for some securities are quite possible. For example, in the Sharpe [40]-Lintner [24, 25] model (which is in turn a natural extension of the portfolio models of Markowitz [30] and Tobin [43]) the equilibrium expected return on a security depends on the extent to which the dispersion in the security's return distribution is related to dispersion in the returns on all other securities. A security whose returns on average move opposite to the general market is particularly valuable in reducing dispersion of portfolio returns, and so its equilibrium expected return may well be negative.

[4] The terminology is loose. Prices will only follow a random walk if price changes are independent, identically distributed; and even then we should say "random walk with drift" since expected price changes can be non-zero. If one-period returns are independent, identically distributed, prices will not follow a random walk since the distribution of price changes will depend on the price level. But though rigorous terminology is usually desirable, our loose use of terms should not cause confusion; and our usage follows that of the efficient markets literature.

Note also that in the random walk literature, the information set Φ_t in (7) is usually assumed to include only the past return history, $r_{j,t}, r_{j,t-1}, \ldots$

This says that the mean of the distribution of $r_{j,t+1}$ is independent of the information available at t, Φ_t, whereas the random walk model of (7) in addition says that the entire distribution is independent of Φ_t.[5]

We argue later that it is best to regard the random walk model as an extension of the general expected return or "fair game" efficient markets model in the sense of making a more detailed statement about the economic environment. The "fair game" model just says that the conditions of market equilibrium can be stated in terms of expected returns, and thus it says little about the details of the stochastic process generating returns. A random walk arises within the context of such a model when the environment is (fortuitously) such that the evolution of investor tastes and the process generating new information combine to produce equilibria in which return distributions repeat themselves through time.

Thus it is not surprising that empirical tests of the "random walk" model that are in fact tests of "fair game" properties are more strongly in support of the model than tests of the additional (and, from the viewpoint of expected return market efficiency, superfluous) pure independence assumption. (But it is perhaps equally surprising that, as we shall soon see, the evidence against the independence of returns over time is as weak as it is.)

D. MARKET CONDITIONS CONSISTENT WITH EFFICIENCY

Before turning to the empirical work, however, a few words about the market conditions that might help or hinder efficient adjustment of prices to information are in order. First, it is easy to determine *sufficient* conditions for capital market efficiency. For example, consider a market in which (i) there are no transactions costs in trading securities, (ii) all available information is costlessly available to all market participants, and (iii) all agree on the implications of current information for the current price and distributions of future prices of each security. In such a market, the current price of a security obviously "fully reflects" all available information.

But a frictionless market in which all information is freely available and investors agree on its implications is, of course, not descriptive of markets met in practice. Fortunately, these conditions are sufficient for market efficiency, but not necessary. For example, as long as transactors take account of all available information, even large transactions costs that inhibit the flow of transactions do not in themselves imply that when transactions do take place, prices will not "fully reflect" available information. Similarly (and speaking, as

---

[5] The random walk model does not say, however, that past information is of no value in *assessing* distributions of future returns. Indeed since return distributions are assumed to be stationary through time, past returns are the best source of such information. The random walk model does say, however, that the *sequence* (or the order) of the past returns is of no consequence in assessing distributions of future returns.

above, somewhat loosely), the market may be efficient if "sufficient numbers" of investors have ready access to available information. And disagreement among investors about the implications of given information does not in itself imply market inefficiency unless there are investors who can consistently make better evaluations of available information than are implicit in market prices.

But though transactions costs, information that is not freely available to all investors, and disagreement among investors about the implications of given information are not necessarily sources of market inefficiency, they are potential sources. And all three exist to some extent in real world markets. Measuring their effects on the process of price formation is, of course, the major goal of empirical work in this area.

III. THE EVIDENCE

All the empirical research on the theory of efficient markets has been concerned with whether prices "fully reflect" particular subsets of available information. Historically, the empirical work evolved more or less as follows. The initial studies were concerned with what we call *weak form* tests in which the information subset of interest is just past price (or return) histories. Most of the results here come from the random walk literature. When extensive tests seemed to support the efficiency hypothesis at this level, attention was turned to *semi-strong form* tests in which the concern is the speed of price adjustment to other obviously publicly available information (e.g., announcements of stock splits, annual reports, new security issues, etc.). Finally, *strong form* tests in which the concern is whether any investor or groups (e.g., managements of mutual funds) have monopolistic access to any information relevant for the formation of prices have recently appeared. We review the empirical research in more or less this historical sequence.

First, however, we should note that what we have called *the* efficient markets model in the discussions of earlier sections is the hypothesis that security prices at any point in time "fully reflect" *all* available information. Though we shall argue that the model stands up rather well to the data, it is obviously an extreme null hypothesis. And, like any other extreme null hypothesis, we do not expect it to be literally true. The categorization of the tests into weak, semi-strong, and strong form will serve the useful purpose of allowing us to pinpoint the level of information at which the hypothesis breaks down. And we shall contend that there is no important evidence against the hypothesis in the weak and semi-strong form tests (i.e., prices seem to efficiently adjust to obviously publicly available information), and only limited evidence against the hypothesis in the strong form tests (i.e., monopolistic access to information about prices does not seem to be a prevalent phenomenon in the investment community).

1. *Random Walks and Fair Games: A Little Historical Background.* As noted earlier, all of the empirical work on efficient markets can be considered within the context of the general expected return or "fair game" model, and much of the evidence bears directly on the special submartingale expected return model of (6). Indeed, in the early literature, discussions of the efficient markets model were phrased in terms of the even more special random walk model, though we shall argue that most of the early authors were in fact concerned with more general versions of the "fair game" model.

Some of the confusion in the early random walk writings is understandable. Research on security prices did not begin with the development of a theory of price formation which was then subjected to empirical tests. Rather, the impetus for the development of a theory came from the accumulation of evidence in the middle 1950's and early 1960's that the behavior of common stock and other speculative prices could be well approximated by a random walk. Faced with the evidence, economists felt compelled to offer some rationalization. What resulted was a theory of efficient markets stated in terms of random walk, but usually implying some more general "fair game" model.

It was not until the work of Samuelson [38] and Mandelbrot [27] in 1965 and 1966 that the role of "fair game" expected return models in the theory of efficient markets and the relationships between these models and the theory of random walks were rigorously studied.[6] And these papers came somewhat after the major empirical work on random walks. In the earlier work, "theoretical" discussions, though usually intuitively appealing, were always lacking in rigor and often either vague or *ad hoc*. In short, until the Mandelbrot-Samuelson models appeared, there existed a large body of empirical results in search of a rigorous theory.

Thus, though his contributions were ignored for sixty years, the first statement and test of the random walk model was that of Bachelier [3] in 1900. But his "fundamental principle" for the behavior of prices was that speculation should be a "fair game"; in particular, the expected profits to the speculator

---

[6] Basing their analyses on futures contracts in commodity markets, Mandelbrot and Samuelson show that if the price of such a contract at time t is the expected value at t (given information Φ_t) of the spot price at the termination of the contract, then the futures price will follow a martingale with respect to the information sequence $\{\Phi_t\}$; that is, the expected price change from period to period will be zero, and the price changes will be a "fair game." If the equilibrium expected return is not assumed to be zero, our more general "fair game" model, summarized by (1), is obtained.

But though the Mandelbrot-Samuelson approach certainly illuminates the process of price formation in commodity markets, we have seen that "fair game" expected return models can be derived in much simpler fashion. In particular, (1) is just a formalization of the assumptions that the conditions of market equilibrium can be stated in terms of expected returns and that the information Φ_t is used in forming market prices at t.

should be zero. With the benefit of the modern theory of stochastic processes, we know now that the process implied by this fundamental principle is a martingale.

After Bachelier, research on the behavior of security prices lagged until the coming of the computer. In 1953 Kendall [21] examined the behavior of weekly changes in nineteen indices of British industrial share prices and in spot prices for cotton (New York) and wheat (Chicago). After extensive analysis of serial correlations, he suggests, in quite graphic terms:

The series looks like a wandering one, almost as if once a week the Demon of Chance drew a random number from a symetrical population of fixed dispersion and added it to the current price to determine the next week's price [21, p. 13].

Kendall's conclusion had in fact been suggested earlier by Working [47], though his suggestion lacked the force provided by Kendall's empirical results. And the implications of the conclusion for stock market research and financial analysis were later underlined by Roberts [36].

But the suggestion by Kendall, Working, and Roberts that series of speculative prices may be well described by random walks was based on observation. None of these authors attempted to provide much economic rationale for the hypothesis, and, indeed, Kendall felt that economists would generally reject it. Osborne [33] suggested market conditions, similar to those assumed by Bachelier, that would lead to a random walk. But in his model, independence of successive price changes derives from the assumption that the decisions of investors in an individual security are independent from transaction to transaction—which is little in the way of an economic model.

Whenever economists (prior to Mandelbrot and Samuelson) tried to provide economic justification for the random walk, their arguments usually implied a "fair game." For example, Alexander [8, p. 200] states:

If one were to start out with the assumption that a stock or commodity speculation is a "fair game" with equal expectation of gain or loss or, more accurately, with an expectation of zero gain, one would be well on the way to picturing the behavior of speculative prices as a random walk.

There is an awareness here that the "fair game" assumption is not sufficient to lead to a random walk, but Alexander never expands on the comment. Similarly, Cootner [8, p. 232] states:

If any substantial group of buyers thought prices were too low, their buying would force up the prices. The reverse would be true for sellers. Except for appreciation due to earnings retention, the conditional expectation of tomorrow's price, given today's price, is today's price.

In such a world, the only price changes that would occur are those that result from new information. Since there is no reason to expect that information to be non-random in appearance, the period-to-period price changes of a stock should be random movements, statistically independent of one another.

Though somewhat imprecise, the last sentence of the first paragraph seems to point to a "fair game" model rather than a random walk.[7] In this light, the second paragraph can be viewed as an attempt to describe environmental conditions that would reduce a "fair game" to a random walk. But the specification imposed on the information generating process is insufficient for this purpose; one would, for example, also have to say something about investor tastes. Finally, lest I be accused of criticizing others too severely for ambiguity, lack of rigor and incorrect conclusions,

> By contrast, the stock market trader has a much more practical criterion for judging what constitutes important dependence in successive price changes. For his purposes the random walk model is valid as long as knowledge of the past behavior of the series of price changes cannot be used to increase expected gains. Most specifically, the independence assumption is an adequate description of reality as long as the actual degree of dependence in the series of price changes is not sufficient to allow the past history of the series to be used to predict the future in a way which makes expected profits greater than they would be under a naive buy-and-hold model [10, p. 35].

We know now, of course, that this last condition hardly requires a random walk. It will in fact be met by the submartingale model of (6).

But one should not be too hard on the theoretical efforts of the early empirical random walk literature. The arguments were usually appealing; where they fell short was in awareness of developments in the theory of stochastic processes. Moreover, we shall now see that most of the empirical evidence in the random walk literature can easily be interpreted as tests of more general expected return or "fair game" models.[8]

2. *Tests of Market Efficiency in the Random Walk Literature.* As discussed earlier, "fair game" models imply the "impossibility" of various sorts of trading systems. Some of the random walk literature has been concerned with testing the profitability of such systems. More of the literature has, however, been concerned with tests of serial covariances of returns. We shall now show that, like a random walk, the serial covariances of a "fair game" are zero, so that these tests are also relevant for the expected return models.

If x_t is a "fair game," its unconditional expectation is zero and its serial covariance can be written in general form as:

---

[7] The appropriate conditioning statement would be "Given the sequence of historical prices."

[8] Our brief historical review is meant only to provide perspective, and it is, of course, somewhat incomplete. For example, we have ignored the important contributions to the early random walk literature in studies of warrants and other options by Sprenkle, Kruizenga, Boness, and others. Much of this early work on options is summarized in [8].

$$E(\tilde{x}_{t+\tau}\tilde{x}_t) = \int_{x_t} x_t E(\tilde{x}_{t+\tau}|x_t)f(x_t)dx_t,$$

where f indicates a density function. But if x_t is a "fair game,"

$$E(\tilde{x}_{t+\tau}|x_t) = 0.^9$$

From this it follows that for all lags, the serial covariances between lagged values of a "fair game" variable are zero. Thus, observations of a "fair game" variable are linearly independent.[10]

But the "fair game" model does not necessarily imply that the serial covariances of *one-period returns* are zero. In the weak form tests of this model the "fair game" variable is

$$z_{j,t} = r_{j,t} - E(\tilde{r}_{j,t}|r_{j,t-1}, r_{j,t-2}, \ldots). \text{ (Cf. fn. 9)} \qquad (9)$$

But the covariance between, for example, r_{jt} and $r_{j,t+1}$ is

$$E([\tilde{r}_{j,t+1} - E(\tilde{r}_{j,t+1})][\tilde{r}_{jt} - E(\tilde{r}_{jt})])$$

$$= \int_{r_{jt}} [r_{jt} - E(\tilde{r}_{jt})][E(\tilde{r}_{j,t+1}|r_{jt}) - E(\tilde{r}_{j,t+1})]f(r_{jt})dr_{jt},$$

[9] More generally, if the sequence $\{x_t\}$ is a fair game with respect to the information sequence $\{\Phi_t\}$, (i.e., $E(\tilde{x}_{t+1}|\Phi_t) = 0$ for all Φ_t); then x_t is a fair game with respect to any Φ'_t that is a subset of Φ_t (i.e., $E(\tilde{x}_{t+1}|\Phi'_t) = 0$ for all Φ'_t). To show this, let $\Phi_t = (\Phi'_t, \Phi''_t)$. Then, using Stieltjes integrals and the symbol F to denote cumulative distinction functions, the conditional expectation

$$E(\tilde{X}_{j+1}|\Phi'_t) = \int_{\Phi_t}\int_{x_{t+1}} x_{t+1}dF(x_{t+1}, \Phi''_t|\Phi'_t) = \int_{\Phi_t}\left[\int_{x_{t+1}} x_{t+1}dF(x_{t+1}|\Phi'_t, \Phi''_t)\right]dF(\Phi'_t|\Phi'_t).$$

But the integral in brackets is just $E(\tilde{x}_{t+1}|\Phi_t)$ which by the "fair game" assumption is 0, so that

$$E(x_{t+1}|\Phi'_t) = 0 \text{ for all } \Phi'_t \subset \Phi_t.$$

[10] But though zero serial covariances are consistent with a "fair game," they do not imply such a process. A "fair game" also rules out many types of nonlinear dependence. Thus using arguments similar to those above, it can be shown that if x is a "fair game," $E(\tilde{x}_t\tilde{x}_{t+1} \ldots \tilde{x}_{t+\tau}) = 0$ for all τ, which is not implied by $E(\tilde{x}_t\tilde{x}_{t+\tau}) = 0$ for all τ. For example, consider a three-period case where x must be either ± 1. Suppose the process is $x_{t+2} = \text{sign}(x_tx_{t+1})$, i.e.,

x_t	x_{t+1}	$\rightarrow$	x_{t+2}
+	+	$\rightarrow$	+
+	−	$\rightarrow$	−
−	+	$\rightarrow$	−
−	−	$\rightarrow$	+.

If probabilities are uniformly distributed across events,

$$E(\tilde{x}_{t+2}|x_{t+1}) = E(\tilde{x}_{t+2}|x_t) = E(\tilde{x}_{t+1}|x_t) = E(\tilde{x}_{t+2}) = E(\tilde{x}_{t+1}) = E(\tilde{x}_t) = 0,$$

so that all pairwise serial covariances are zero. But the process is not a "fair game," since $E(\tilde{x}_{t+2}|x_{t+1}, x_t) \neq 0$, and knowledge of (x_{t+1}, x_t) can be used as the basis of a simple "system" with positive expected profit.

and (9) does not imply that $E(\tilde{r}_{j,t+1}|r_{jt}) = E(\tilde{r}_{j,t+1})$: In the "fair game" efficient markets model, the deviation of the return for $t + 1$ from its conditional expectation is a "fair game" variable, but the conditional expectation itself can depend on the return observed for t.[11]

In the random walk literature, this problem is not recognized, since it is assumed that the expected return (and indeed the entire distribution of returns) is stationary through time. In practice, this implies estimating serial covariances by taking cross products of deviations of observed returns from the overall sample mean return. It is somewhat fortuitous, then, that this procedure, which represents a rather gross approximation from the viewpoint of the general expected return efficient markets model, does not seem to greatly affect the results of the covariance tests, at least for common stocks.[12]

For example, Table 1 (taken from [10]) shows the serial correlations between successive changes in the natural log of price for each of the thirty stocks of the Dow Jones Industrial Average, for time periods that vary slightly from stock to stock, but usually run from about the end of 1957 to September 26, 1962. The serial correlations of successive changes in $\log_e$ price are shown for differencing intervals of one, four, nine, and sixteen days.[13]

The results in Table 1 are typical of those reported by others for tests based on serial covariances. (Cf. Kendall [21], Moore [31], Alexander [1], and the results of Granger and Morgenstern [17] and Godfrey, Granger and Morgenstern [16] obtained by means of spectral analysis.) Specifically, there is no evidence of substantial linear dependence between lagged price changes or returns. In absolute terms the measured serial correlations are always close to zero.

Looking hard, though, one can probably find evidence of statistically "significant" linear dependence in Table 1 (and again this is true of results reported by others). For the daily returns eleven of the serial correlations are more than twice their computed standard errors, and twenty-two out of thirty are positive. On the other hand, twenty-one and twenty-four of the coefficients for the four and nine day differences are negative. But with samples of the size underlying

---

[11] For example, suppose the level of one-period returns follows a martingale so that

$$E(\tilde{r}_{j,t+1}|r_{jt}, r_{j,t-1} \ldots) = r_{jt}.$$

Then covariances between successive returns will be nonzero (though in this special case first differences of returns will be uncorrelated).

[12] The reason is probably that for stocks, changes in equilibrium expected returns for the common differencing intervals of a day, a week, or a month, are trivial relative to other sources of variation in returns. Later, when we consider Roll's work [37], we shall see that this it not true for one week returns on U.S. Government Treasury Bills.

[13] The use of changes in $\log_e$ price as the measure of return is common in the random walk literature. It can be justified in several ways. But for current purposes, it is sufficient to note that for price changes less than fifteen per cent, the change in $\log_e$ price is approximately the percentage price change or one-period return. And for differencing intervals shorter than one month, returns in excess of fifteen per cent are unusual. Thus [10] reports that for the data of Table 1, tests carried out on percentage or one-period returns yielded results essentially identical to the tests based on changes in $\log_e$ price.

TABLE 1
FIRST-ORDER SERIAL CORRELATION COEFFICIENTS FOR ONE-, FOUR-, NINE-,
AND SIXTEEN-DAY CHANGES IN LOG$_e$ PRICE

STOCK	DIFFERENCING INTERVAL (DAYS)			
	ONE	FOUR	NINE	SIXTEEN
Allied Chemical	.017	.029	−.091	−.118
Alcoa	.118*	.095	−.112	−.044
American Can	−.087*	−.124*	−.060	.031
A. T. & T.	−.039	−.010	−.009	−.003
American Tobacco	.111*	−.175*	.033	.007
Anaconda	.067*	−.068	−.125	.202
Bethlehem Steel	.013	−.122	−.148	.112
Chrysler	.012	.060	−.026	.040
Du Pont	.013	.069	−.043	−.055
Eastman Kodak	.025	−.006	−.053	−.023
General Electric	.011	.020	−.004	.000
General Foods	.061*	−.005	−.140	−.098
General Motors	−.004	−.128*	.009	−.028
Goodyear	−.123*	.001	−.037	.033
International Harvester	−.017	−.068	−.244*	.116
International Nickel	.096*	.038	.124	.041
International Paper	.046	.060	−.004	−.010
Johns Manville	.006	−.068	−.002	.002
Owens Illinois	−.021	−.006	.003	−.022
Procter & Gamble	.099*	−.006	.098	.076
Sears	.097*	−.070	−.113	.041
Standard Oil (Calif.)	.025	−.143*	−.046	.040
Standard Oil (N.J.)	.008	−.109	−.082	−.121
Swift & Co.	−.004	−.072	.118	−.197
Texaco	.094*	−.053	−.047	−.178
Union Carbide	.107*	.049	−.101	.124
United Aircraft	.014	−.190*	−.192*	−.040
U.S. Steel	.040	−.006	−.056	.236*
Westinghouse	−.027	−.097	−.137	.067
Woolworth	.028	−.033	−.112	.040

* Coefficient is twice its computed standard error.
Reprinted from Fama [10].

Table 1 (N = 1200–1700 observations per stock on a daily basis) statistically "significant" deviations from zero covariance are not necessarily a basis for rejecting the efficient markets model. For the results in Table 1, the standard errors of the serial correlations were approximated as $(1/(N - 1))^{1/2}$, which for the daily data implies that a correlation as small as .06 is more than twice its standard error. But a coefficient this size implies that a linear relationship with the lagged price change can be used to explain about .36% of the variation in the current price change, which is probably insignificant from an economic viewpoint. In particular, it is unlikely that the small absolute levels of serial correlation that are always observed can be used as the basis of substantially profitable trading systems.[14]

It is, of course, difficult to judge what degree of serial correlation would imply the existence of trading rules with substantial expected profits. (And indeed we shall soon have to be a little more precise about what is implied by "substantial" profits.) Moreover, zero serial covariances are consistent with a "fair game" model, but as noted earlier (fn. 10), there are types of nonlinear dependence that imply the existence of profitable trading systems, and yet do not imply nonzero serial covariances. Thus, for many reasons it is desirable to directly test the profitability of various trading rules.

The first major evidence on trading rules was Alexander's [1, 2]. He tests a variety of systems, but the most thoroughly examined can be described as follows: If the price of a security moves up at least y% , buy and hold the security until its price moves down at least y% from a subsequent high, at which time simultaneously sell and go short. The short position is maintained until the price rises at least y% above a subsequent low, at which time one covers the short position and buys. Moves less than y% in either direction are ignored. Such a system is called a y% filter. It is obviously a "one security and cash" trading rule, so that the results it produces are relevant for the submartingale expected return model of (6).

After extensive tests using daily data on price indices from 1897 to 1959 and filters from one to fifty per cent, and after correcting some incorrect presumptions in the initial results of [1] (see fn. 25), in his final paper on the subject, Alexander concludes:

In fact, at this point I should advise any reader who is interested only in practical results, and who is not a floor trader and so must pay commissions, to turn to other sources on how to beat buy and hold. The rest of this article is devoted principally to a theoretical consideration of whether the observed results are consistent with a random walk hypothesis [8], p. 351).

---

[14] Given the evidence of Kendall [21], Mandelbrot [28], Fama [10] and others that large price changes occur much more frequently than would be expected if the generating process were Gaussian, the expression $(1/(N - 1))^{1/2}$ understates the sampling dispersion of the serial correlation coefficient, and thus leads to an overstatement of significance levels. In addition, the fact that sample serial correlations are predominantly of one sign or the other is not in itself evidence of linear dependence. If, as the work of King [23] and Blume [7] indicates, there is a market factor whose behavior affects the returns on all securities, the sample behavior of this market factor may lead to a predominance of signs of one type in the serial correlations for individual securities, even though the population serial correlations for both the market factor and the returns on individual securities are zero. For a more extensive analysis of these issues see [10].

Later in the paper Alexander concludes that there is some evidence in his results against the independence assumption of the random walk model. But market efficiency does not require a random walk, and from the viewpoint of the submartingale model of (6), the conclusion that the filters cannot beat buy-and-hold is support for the efficient markets hypothesis. Further support is provided by Fama and Blume [13] who compare the profitability of various filters to buy-and-hold for the individual stocks of the Dow-Jones Industrial Average. (The data are those underlying Table 1.)

But again, looking hard one can find evidence in the filter tests of both Alexander and Fama-Blume that is inconsistent with the submartingale efficient markets model, if that model is interpreted in a strict sense. In particular, the results for very small filters (1 per cent in Alexander's tests and .5, 1.0, and 1.5 per cent in the tests of Fama-Blume) indicate that it is possible to devise trading schemes based on very short-term (preferably intra-day but at most daily) price swings that will on average outperform buy-and-hold. The average profits on individual transactions from such schemes are miniscule, but they generate transactions so frequently that over longer periods and ignoring commissions they outperform buy-and-hold by a substantial margin. These results are evidence of persistence or positive dependence in very short-term price movements. And, interestingly, this is consistent with the evidence for slight positive linear dependence in successive daily price changes produced by the serial correlations.[15]

But when one takes account of even the minimum trading costs that would be generated by small filters, their advantage over buy-and-hold disappears. For example, even a floor trader (i.e., a person who owns a seat) on the New York Stock Exchange must pay clearinghouse fees on his trades that amount to about .1 per cent per turnaround transaction (i.e., sales plus purchase). Fama-Blume show that because small filters produce such frequent trades,

---

[15] Though strictly speaking, such tests of pure independence are not directly relevant for expected return models, it is interesting that the conclusion that very short-term swings in prices persist slightly longer than would be expected under the martingale hypothesis is also supported by the results of non-parametric runs tests applied to the daily data of Table 1. (See [10], Tables 12–15.) For the daily price changes, the actual number of runs of price changes of the same sign is less than the expected number for 26 out of 30 stocks. Moreover, of the eight stocks for which the actual number of runs is more than two standard errors less than the expected number, five of the same stocks have positive daily, first order serial correlations in Table 1 that are more than twice their standard errors. But in both cases the statistical "significance" of the results is largely a reflection of the large sample sizes. Just as the serial correlations are small in absolute terms (the average is .026), the differences between the expected and actual number of runs on average are only three per cent of the total expected number.

On the other hand, it is also interesting that the runs tests do not support the suggestion of slight negative dependence in four and nine day changes that appeared in the serial correlations. In the runs tests such negative dependence would appear as a tendency for the actual number of runs to exceed the expected number. In fact, for the four and nine day price changes, for 17 and 18 of the 30 stocks in Table 1 the actual number of runs is less than the expected number. Indeed, runs tests in general show no consistent evidence of dependence for any differencing interval longer than a day, which seems especially pertinent in light of the comments in footnote 14.

these minimum trading costs are sufficient to wipe out their advantage over buy-and-hold.

 Thus the filter tests, like the serial correlations, produce empirically noticeable departures from the strict implications of the efficient markets model. But, in spite of any statistical significance they might have, from an economic viewpoint the departures are so small that it seems hardly justified to use them to declare the market inefficient.

3. *Other Tests of Independence in the Random Walk Literature.* It is probably best to regard the random walk model as a special case of the more general expected return model in the sense of making a more detailed specification of the economic environment. That is, the basic model of market equilibrium is the "fair game" expected return model, with a random walk arising when additional environmental conditions are such that distributions of one-period returns repeat themselves through time. From this viewpoint violations of the pure independence assumption of the random walk model are to be expected. But when judged relative to the benchmark provided by the random walk model, these violations can provide insights into the nature of the market environment.

For example, one departure from the pure independence assumption of the random walk model has been noted by Osborne [34], Fama ([10], Table 17 and Figure 8), and others. In particular, large daily price changes tend to be followed by large daily changes. The signs of the successor changes are apparently random, however, which indicates that the phenomenon represents a denial of the random walk model but not of the market efficiency hypothesis. Nevertheless, it is interesting to speculate why the phenomenon might arise. It may be that when important new information comes into the market it cannot always be immediately evaluated precisely. Thus, sometimes the initial price will overadjust to the information, and other times it will underadjust. But since the evidence indicates that the price changes on days following the initial large change are random in sign, the initial large change at least represents an unbiased adjustment to the ultimate price effects of the information, and this is sufficient for the expected return efficient markets model.

Niederhoffer and Osborne [32] document two departures from complete randomness in common stock price changes from transaction to transaction. First, their data indicate that reversals (pairs of consecutive price changes of opposite sign) are from two or three times as likely as continuations (pairs of consecutive price changes of the same sign). Second, a continuation is slightly more frequent after a preceding continuation than after a reversal. That is, let $(+|++)$ indicate the occurrence of a positive price change, given two preceding positive changes. Then the events $(+|++)$ and $(-|--)$ are slightly more frequent than $(+|+-)$ or $(-|-+)$.[16]

---

[16] On a transaction to transaction basis, positive and negative price changes are about equally likely. Thus, under the assumption that price changes are random, any pair of non-zero changes should be as likely as any other, and likewise for triplets of consecutive non-zero changes.

Niederhoffer and Osborne offer explanations for these phenomena based on the market structure of the New York Stock Exchange (N.Y.S.E.). In particular, there are three major types of orders that an investor might place in a given stock: (a) buy limit (buy at a specified price or lower), (b) sell limit (sell at a specified price or higher), and (c) buy or sell at market (at the lowest selling or highest buying price of another investor). A book of unexecuted limit orders in a given stock is kept by the specialist in that stock on the floor of the exchange. Unexecuted sell limit orders are, of course, at higher prices than unexecuted buy limit orders. On both exchanges, the smallest non-zero price change allowed is ⅛ point.

Suppose now that there is more than one unexecuted sell limit order at the lowest price of any such order. A transaction at this price (initiated by an order to buy at market[17]) can only be followed either by a transaction at the same price (if the next market order is to buy) or by a transaction at a lower price (if the next market order is to sell). Consecutive price increases can usually only occur when consecutive market orders to buy exhaust the sell limit orders at a given price.[18] In short, the excessive tendency toward reversal for consecutive non-zero price changes could result from bunching of unexecuted buy and sell limit orders.

The tendency for the events $(+\,|\,+\,+)$ and $(-\,|\,-\,-)$ to occur slightly more frequently than $(+\,|\,+\,-)$ and $(-\,|\,-\,+)$ requires a more involved explanation which we shall not attempt to reproduce in full here. In brief, Niederhoffer and Osborne contend that the higher frequency of $(+\,|\,+\,+)$ relative to $(+\,|\,+\,-)$ arises from a tendency for limit orders "to be concentrated at integers (26, 43), halves (26½, 43½), quarters and odd eighths in descending order of preference."[19] The frequency of the event $(+\,|\,+\,+)$, which usually requires that sell limit orders be exhausted at at least two consecutively higher prices (the last of which is relatively more frequently at an odd eighth), more heavily reflects the absence of sell limit orders at odd eighths than the event $(+\,|\,+\,-)$, which usually implies that sell limit orders at only one price have been exhausted and so more or less reflects the average bunching of limit orders at all eighths.

But though Niederhoffer and Osborne present convincing evidence of statistically significant departures from independence in price changes from transaction to transaction, and though their analysis of their findings presents interesting insights into the process of market making on the major exchanges, the types of dependence uncovered do not imply market inefficiency. The best doc-

---

[17] A buy limit order for a price equal to or greater than the lowest available sell limit price is effectively an order to buy at market, and is treated as such by the broker.

[18] The exception is when there is a gap of more than ⅛ between the highest unexecuted buy limit and the lowest unexecuted sell limit order, so that market orders (and new limit orders) can be crossed at intermediate prices.

[19] Their empirical documentation for this claim is a few samples of specialists' books for selected days, plus the observation [34] that actual trading prices, at least for volatile high period stocks, seem to be concentrated at integers, halves, quarters and odd eighths in descending order.

umented source of dependence, the tendency toward excessive reversals in pairs of non-zero price changes, seems to be a direct result of the ability of investors to place limit orders as well as orders at market, and this negative dependence in itself does not imply the existence of profitable trading rules. Similarly, the apparent tendency for observed transactions (and, by implication, limit orders) to be concentrated at integers, halves, even eighths and odd eighths in descending order is an interesting fact about investor behavior, but in itself is not a basis on which to conclude that the market is inefficient.[20]

The Niederhoffer-Osborne analysis of market making does, however, point clearly to the existence of market inefficiency, but with respect to strong form tests of the efficient markets model. In particular, the list of unexecuted buy and sell limit orders in the specialist's book is important information about the likely future behavior of prices, and this information is only available to the specialist. When the specialist is asked for a quote, he gives the prices and can give the quantities of the highest buy limit and lowest sell limit orders on his book, but he is prevented by law from divulging the book's full contents. The interested reader can easily imagine situations where the structure of limit orders in the book could be used as the basis of a profitable trading rule.[21] But the record seems to speak for itself:

It should not be assumed that these transactions undertaken by the specialist, and in which he is involved as buyer or seller in 24 per cent of all market volume, are necessarily a burden to him. Typically, the specialist sells above his last purchase on 83 per cent of all his sales, and buys below his last sale on 81 per cent of all his purchases ([32], p. 908).

Thus it seems that the specialist has monopoly power over an important block of information, and, not unexpectedly, uses his monopoly to turn a profit. And

---

[20] Niederhoffer and Osborne offer little to refute this conclusion. For example ([32], p. 914):

Although the specific properties reported in this study have a significance from a statistical point of view, the reader may well ask whether or not they are helpful in a practical sense. Certain trading rules emerge as a result of our analysis. One is that limit and stop orders should be placed at odd eights, preferably at ⅞ for sell orders and at ⅛ for buy orders. Another is to buy when a stock advances through a barrier and to sell when it sinks through a barrier.

The first "trading rule" tells the investor to resist his innate inclination to place orders at integers, but rather to place sell orders ⅛ below an integer and buy orders ⅛ above. Successful execution of the orders is then more likely, since the congestion of orders that occur at integers is avoided. But the cost of this success is apparent. The second "trading rule" seems no more promising, if indeed it can even be translated into a concrete prescription for action.

[21] See, for example, ([32], p. 908). But it is unlikely that anyone but the specialist could earn substantial profits from knowledge of the structure of unexecuted limit orders on the book. The specialist makes trading profits by engaging in many transactions, each of which has a small average profit; but for any other trader, including those with seats on the exchange, these profits would be eaten up by commissions to the specialist.

this, of course, is evidence of market inefficiency in the strong form sense. The important economic question, of course, is whether the market making function of the specialist could be fulfilled more economically by some nonmonopolistic mechanism.[22]

4. *Distributional Evidence.* At this date the weight of the empirical evidence is such that economists would generally agree that whatever dependence exists in series of historical returns cannot be used to make profitable predictions of the future. Indeed, for returns that cover periods of a day or longer, there is little in the evidence that would cause rejection of the stronger random walk model, at least as a good first approximation.

Rather, the last burning issue of the random walk literature has centered on the nature of the distribution of price changes (which, we should note immediately, is an important issue for the efficient markets hypothesis since the nature of the distribution affects both the types of statistical tools relevant for testing the hypothesis and the interpretation of any results obtained). A model implying normally distributed price changes was first proposed by Bachelier [3], who assumed that price changes from transaction to transaction are independent, identically distributed random variables with finite variances. If transactions are fairly uniformly spread across time, and if the number of transactions per day, week, or month is very large, then the Central Limit Theorem leads us to expect that these price changes will have normal or Gaussian distributions.

Osborne [33], Moore [31], and Kendall [21] all thought their empirical evidence supported the normality hypothesis, but all observed high tails (i.e., higher proportions of large observations) in their data distributions vis-à-vis what would be expected if the distributions were normal. Drawing on these findings and some empirical work of his own, Mandelbrot [28] then suggested that these departures from normality could be explained by a more general form of the Bachelier model. In particular, if one does not assume that distributions of price changes from transaction to transaction necessarily have finite variances, then the limiting distributions for price changes over longer differencing intervals could be any member of the stable class, which includes the normal as a special case. Non-normal stable distributions have higher tails than the normal, and so can account for this empirically observed feature of distributions of price changes. After extensive testing (involving the data from the stocks in Table 1), Fama [10] concludes that non-normal stable distributions

---

[22] With modern computers, it is hard to believe that a more competitive and economical system would not be feasible. It does not seem technologically impossible to replace the entire floor of the N.Y.S.E. with a computer, fed by many remote consoles, that kept all the books now kept by the specialists, that could easily make the entire book on any stock available to anybody (so that interested individuals could then compete to "make a market" in a stock) and that carried out transactions automatically.

are a better description of distributions of daily returns on common stocks than the normal. This conclusion is also supported by the empirical work of Blume [7] on common stocks, and it has been extended to U.S. Government Treasury Bills by Roll [37].

Economists have, however, been reluctant to accept these results,[23] primarily because of the wealth of statistical techniques available for dealing with normal variables and the relative paucity of such techniques for non-normal stable variables. But perhaps the biggest contribution of Mandelbrot's work has been to stimulate research on stable distributions and estimation procedures to be applied to stable variables. (See, for example, Wise [46], Fama and Roll [15], and Blattberg and Sargent [6], among others.) The advance of statistical sophistication (and the importance of examining distributional assumptions in testing the efficient markets model) is well illustrated in Roll [37], as compared, for example, with the early empirical work of Mandelbrot [28] and Fama [10].

5. *"Fair Game" Models in the Treasury Bill Market.* Roll's work is novel in other respects as well. Coming after the efficient markets models of Mandelbrot [27] and Samuelson [38], it is the first weak form empirical work that is consciously in the "fair game" rather than the random walk tradition.

More important, as we saw earlier, the "fair game" properties of the general expected return models apply to

$$z_{jt} = r_{jt} - E(\tilde{r}_{jt} | \Phi_{t-1}).$$ (10)

For data on common stocks, tests of "fair game" (and random walk) properties seem to go well when the conditional expected return is estimated as the average return for the sample of data at hand. Apparently the variation in common stock returns about their expected values is so large relative to any changes in the expected values that the latter can safely be ignored. But, as Roll demon-

---

[23] Some have suggested that the long-tailed empirical distributions might result from processes that are mixtures of normal distributions with different variances. Press [35], for example, suggests a Poisson mixture of normals in which the resulting distributions of price changes have long tails but finite variances. On the other hand, Mandelbrot and Taylor [29] show that other mixtures of normals can still lead to non-normal stable distributions of price changes for finite differencing intervals.

If, as Press' model would imply, distributions of price changes are long-tailed but have finite variances, then distributions of price changes over longer and longer differencing intervals should be progressively closer to the normal. No such convergence to normality was observed in [10] (though admittedly the techniques used were somewhat rough). Rather, except for origin and scale, the distributions for longer differencing intervals seem to have the same "high-tailed" characteristics as distributions for shorter differencing intervals, which is as would be expected if the distributions are non-normal stable.

strates, this result does not hold for Treasury Bills. Thus, to test the "fair game" model on Treasury Bills requires explicit economic theory for the evolution of expected returns through time.

Roll uses three existing theories of the term structure (the pure expectations hypothesis of Lutz [26] and two market segmentation hypotheses, one of which is the familiar "liquidity preference" hypothesis of Hicks [18] and Kessel [22]) for this purpose.[24] In his models r_{jt} is the rate observed from the term structure at period t for one week loans to commence at $t + j - 1$, and can be thought of as a "futures" rate. Thus $r_{j+1,t-1}$ is likewise the rate on one week loans to commence at $t + j - 1$, but observed in this case at $t - 1$. Similarly, L_{jt} is the so-called "liquidity premium" in r_{jt}; that is

$$r_{jt} = E(\tilde{r}_{0,t+j-1}|\Phi_t) + L_{jt}.$$

In words, the one week "futures" rate for period $t + j - 1$ observed from the term structure at t is the expectation at t of the "spot" rate for $t + j - 1$ plus a "liquidity premium" (which could, however, be positive or negative).

In all three theories of the term structure considered by Roll, the conditional expectation required in (10) is of the form

$$E(\tilde{r}_{j,t}|\Phi_{t-1}) = r_{j+1,t-1} + E(\tilde{L}_{jt}|\Phi_{t-1}) - L_{j+1,t-1}.$$

The three theories differ only in the values assigned to the "liquidity premiums." For example, in the "liquidity preference" hypothesis, investors must always be paid a positive premium for bearing interest rate uncertainty, so that the L_{jt} are always positive. By contrast, in the "pure expectations" hypothesis, all liquidity premiums are assumed to be zero, so that

$$E(\tilde{r}_{jt}|\Phi_{t-1}) = r_{j+1,t-1}.$$

After extensive testing, Roll concludes (i) that the two market segmentation hypothesis fit the data better than the pure expectations hypothesis, with perhaps a slight advantage for the "liquidity preference" hypothesis, and (ii) that as far as his tests are concerned, the market for Treasury Bills is efficient. Indeed, it is interesting that when the best fitting term structure model is used to estimate the conditional expected "futures" rate in (10), the resulting variable z_{jt} seems to be serially independent! It is also interesting that if he simply assumed that his data distributions were normal, Roll's results would not be so strongly in support of the efficient markets model. In this case taking account

---

[24] As noted early in our discussions, all available tests of market efficiency are implicitly also tests of expected return models of market equilibrium. But Roll formulates explicitly the economic models underlying his estimates of expected returns, and emphasizes that he is simultaneously testing economic models of the term structure as well as market efficiency.

of the observed high tails of the data distributions substantially affected the interpretation of the results.[25]

6. *Tests of a Multiple Security Expected Return Model.* Though the weak form tests support the "fair game" efficient markets model, all of the evidence examined so far consists of what we might call "single security tests." That is, the price or return histories of individual securities are examined for evidence of dependence that might be used as the basis of a trading system for *that* security. We have not discussed tests of whether securities are "appropriately priced" vis-à-vis one another.

But to judge whether differences between average returns are "appropriate" an economic theory of equilibrium expected returns is required. At the moment, the only fully developed theory is that of Sharpe [40] and Lintner [24, 25] referred to earlier. In this model (which is a direct outgrowth of the mean-standard deviation portfolio models of investor equilibrium of Markowitz [30] and Tobin [43]), the expected return on security j from time t to t + 1 is

$$
E(\tilde{r}_{j,t+1} | \Phi_t) = r_{f,t+1} + \left[\frac{E(\tilde{r}_{m,t+1} | \Phi_t) - r_{f,t+1}}{\sigma(\tilde{r}_{m,t+1} | \Phi_t)} \right] \frac{\text{cov}(\tilde{r}_{j,t+1}, \tilde{r}_{m,t+1} | \Phi_t)}{\sigma(\tilde{r}_{m,t+1} | \Phi_t)}, \quad (11)
$$

where $r_{f,t+1}$ is the return from t to t + 1 on an asset that is riskless in money terms; $r_{m,t+1}$ is the return on the "market portfolio" m (a portfolio of all investment assets with each weighted in proportion to the total market value of all its outstanding units); $\sigma^2(\tilde{r}_{m,t+1} | \Phi_t)$ is the variance of the return on m; cov $(\tilde{r}_{j,t+1}, \tilde{r}_{m,t+1} | \Phi_t)$ is the covariance between the returns on j and m; and the appearance of Φ_t indicates that the various expected returns, variance and covariance, could in principle depend on Φ_t. Though Sharpe and Lintner derive (11) as a one-period model, the result is given a multiperiod justification and interpretation in [11]. The model has also been extended in (12) to the case where the one-period returns could have stable distributions with infinite variances.

In words, (11) says that the expected one-period return on a security is the one-period riskless rate of interest $r_{f,t+1}$ plus a "risk premium" that is proportional to cov $(\tilde{r}_{j,t+1}, \tilde{r}_{m,t+1} | \Phi_t)/\sigma(\tilde{r}_{m,t+1} | \Phi_t)$. In the Sharpe-Lintner model each investor holds some combination of the riskless asset and the market portfolio,

---

[25] The importance of distributional assumptions is also illustrated in Alexander's work on trading rules. In his initial tests of filter systems [1], Alexander assumed that purchases could always be executed exactly (rather than at least) y% above lows and sales exactly y% below highs. Mandelbrot [28] pointed out, however, that though this assumption would do little harm with normally distributed price changes (since price series are then essentially continuous), with non-normal stable distributions it would introduce substantial positive bias into the filter profits (since with such distributions price series will show many discontinuities). In his later tests [2], Alexander does indeed find that taking account of the discontinuities (i.e., the presence of large price changes) in his data substantially lowers the profitability of the filters.

so that, given a mean-standard deviation framework, the risk of an individual asset can be measured by its contribution to the standard deviation of the return on the market portfolio. This contribution is in fact cov $(\tilde{r}_{j,t+1}, \tilde{r}_{m,t+1}|\Phi_t)/\sigma(\tilde{r}_{m,t+1}|\Phi_t)$.[26] The factor

$$[E(\tilde{r}_{m,t+1}|\Phi_t) - r_{f,t+1}]/\sigma(\tilde{r}_{m,t+1}|\Phi_t),$$

which is the same for all securities, is then regarded as the market price of risk.

Published empirical tests of the Sharpe-Lintner model are not yet available, though much work is in progress. There is some published work, however, which, though not directed at the Sharpe-Lintner model, is at least consistent with some of its implications. The stated goal of this work has been to determine the extent to which the returns on a given security are related to the returns on other securities. It started (again) with Kendall's [21] finding that though common stock price changes do not seem to be serially correlated, there is a high degree of cross-correlation between the *simultaneous* returns of different securities. This line of attack was continued by King [23] who (using factor analysis of a sample of monthly returns on sixty N.Y.S.E. stocks for the period 1926–60) found that on average about 50% of the variance of an individual stock's returns could be accounted for by a "market factor" which affects the returns on all stocks, with "industry factors" accounting for at most an additional 10% of the variance.

For our purposes, however, the work of Fama, Fisher, Jensen, and Roll [14] (henceforth FFJR) and the more extensive work of Blume [7] on monthly return data is more relevant. They test the following "market model," originally suggested by Markowitz [30]:

$$\tilde{r}_{j,t+1} = \alpha_j + \beta_j \tilde{r}_{M,t+1} + \tilde{u}_{j,t+1} \tag{12}$$

where $r_{j,t+1}$ is the rate of return on security j for month t, $r_{M,t+1}$ is the corresponding return on a market index M, α_j and β_j are parameters that can vary from security to security, and $u_{j,t+1}$ is a random disturbance. The tests of FFJR and subsequently those of Blume indicate that (12) is well specified as a linear regression model in that (i) the estimated parameters $\hat{\alpha}_j$ and $\hat{\beta}_j$ remain fairly constant over long periods of time (e.g., the entire post-World War II period in the case of Blume), (ii) $r_{M,t+1}$ and the estimated $\hat{u}_{j,t+1}$, are close to serially independent, and (iii) the $\hat{u}_{j,t+1}$ seem to be independent of $r_{M,t+1}$.

Thus the observed properties of the "market model" are consistent with the expected return efficient markets model, and, in addition, the "market model" tells us something about the process generating expected returns from security to security. In particular,

$$E(\tilde{r}_{j,t+1}) = \alpha_j + \beta_j E(\tilde{r}_{M,t+1}). \tag{13}$$

[26] That is,

$$\sum_j \text{cov}(\tilde{r}_{j,t+1}, \tilde{r}_{m,t+1}|\Phi_t)/\sigma(\tilde{r}_{m,t+1}|\Phi_t) = \sigma(\tilde{r}_{m,t+1}|\Phi_t).$$

The question now is to what extent (13) is consistent with the Sharpe-Lintner expected return model summarized by (11). Rearranging (11) we obtain

$$E(\tilde{r}_{j,t+1}|\Phi_t) = \alpha_j(\Phi_t) + \beta_j(\Phi_t)E(\tilde{r}_{m,t+1}|\Phi_t), \tag{14}$$

where, noting that the riskless rate $r_{f,t+1}$ is itself part of the information set Φ_t, we have

$$\alpha_j(\Phi_t) = r_{f,t+1}[1 - \beta_j(\Phi_t)], \tag{15}$$

and

$$\beta_j(\Phi_t) = \frac{\text{cov}\,(\tilde{r}_{j,t+1}, \tilde{r}_{m,t+1}|\Phi_t)}{\sigma^2(\tilde{r}_{m,t+1}|\Phi_t)}. \tag{16}$$

With some simplifying assumptions, (14) can be reduced to (13). In particular, if the covariance and variance that determine $\beta_j(\Phi_t)$ in (16) are the same for all t and Φ_t, then $\beta_j(\Phi_t)$ in (16) corresponds to β_j in (12) and (13), and the least squares *estimate* of β_j in (12) is in fact just the ratio of the sample values of the covariance and variance in (16). If we also assume that $r_{f,t+1}$ is the same for all t, and that the behavior of the returns on the market portfolio m are closely approximated by the returns on some representative index M, we will have come a long way toward equating (13) and (11). Indeed, the only missing link is whether in the estimated parameters of (12)

$$\hat{\alpha}_j \cong r_f(1 - \hat{\beta}_j). \tag{17}$$

Neither FFJR nor Blume attack this question directly, though some of Blume's evidence is at least promising. In particular, the magnitudes of the estimated $\hat{\alpha}_j$ are roughly consistent with (17) in the sense that the estimates are always close to zero (as they should be with monthly return data).[27]

In a sense, though, in establishing the apparent empirical validity of the "market model" of (12), both too much and too little have been shown *vis-à-vis* the Sharpe-Lintner expected return model of (11). We know that during the post-World War II period one-month interest rates on riskless assets (e.g., government bills with one month to maturity) have not been constant. Thus, if expected security returns were generated by a version of the "market model"

---

[27] With least squares applied to monthly return data, the estimate of α_j in (12) is

$$\hat{\alpha}_j = \bar{r}_{j,t} - \hat{\beta}_j\bar{r}_{M,t},$$

where the bars indicate sample mean returns. But, in fact, Blume applies the market model to the wealth relatives $R_{jt} = 1 + r_{jt}$ and $R_{Mt} = 1 + r_{Mt}$. This yields precisely the same estimate of β_j as least squares applied to (12), but the intercept is now

$$\hat{\alpha}'_j = \bar{R}_{jt} - \hat{\beta}_j\bar{R}_{Mt} = 1 + \bar{r}_{jt} - \hat{\beta}_j(1 + \bar{r}_{Mt}) = 1 - \hat{\beta}_j + \hat{\alpha}_j.$$

Thus what Blume in fact finds is that for almost all securities, $\hat{\alpha}'_j + \hat{\beta}_j \cong 1$, which implies that $\hat{\alpha}_j$ is close to 0.

that is fully consistent with the Sharpe-Lintner model, we would, according to (15), expect to observe some non-stationarity in the estimates of α_j. On a monthly basis, however, variation through time in one-period riskless interest rates is probably trivial relative to variation in other factors affecting monthly common stock returns, so that more powerful statistical methods would be necessary to study the effects of changes in the riskless rate.

In any case, since the work of FFJR and Blume on the "market model" was not concerned with relating this model to the Sharpe-Lintner model, we can only say that the results for the former are somewhat consistent with the implications of the latter. But the results for the "market model" are, after all, just a statistical description of the return generating process, and they are probably somewhat consistent with other models of equilibrium expected returns. Thus the only way to generate strong empirical conclusions about the Sharpe-Lintner model is to test it directly. On the other hand, any alternative model of equilibrium expected returns must be somewhat consistent with the "market model," given the evidence in its support.

B. TESTS OF MARTINGALE MODELS OF THE SEMI-STRONG FORM

In general, semi-strong form tests of efficient markets models are concerned with whether current prices "fully reflect" all obviously publicly available information. Each individual test, however, is concerned with the adjustment of security prices to one kind of information generating event (e.g., stock splits, announcements of financial reports by firms, new security issues, etc.). Thus each test only brings supporting evidence for the model, with the idea that by accumulating such evidence the validity of the model will be "established."

In fact, however, though the available evidence is in support of the efficient markets model, it is limited to a few major types of information generating events. The initial major work is apparently the study of stock splits by Fama, Fisher, Jensen, and Roll (FFJR) [14], and all the subsequent studies summarized here are adaptations and extensions of the techniques developed in FFJR. Thus, this paper will first be reviewed in some detail, and then the other studies will be considered.

1. *Splits and the Adjustment of Stock Prices to New Information.* Since the only apparent result of a stock split is to multiply the number of shares per shareholder without increasing claims to real assets, splits in themselves are not necessarily sources of new information. The presumption of FFJR is that splits may often be associated with the appearance of more fundamentally important information. The idea is to examine security returns around split dates to see first if there is any "unusual" behavior, and, if so, to what extent it can be accounted for by relationships between splits and other more fundamental variables.

The approach of FFJR to the problem relies heavily on the "market model"

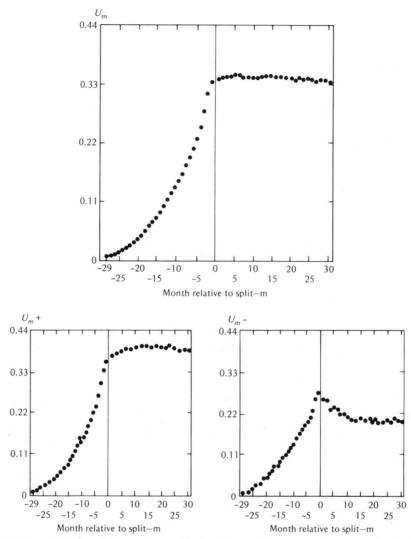

FIGURE 1. (top) Cumulative average residuals—all splits; (left) cumulative average residuals for dividend "increases;" (right) cumulative average residuals for dividend "decreases."

of (12). In this model if a stock split is associated with abnormal behavior, this would be reflected in the estimated regression residuals for the months surrounding the split. For a given split, define month O as the month in which the effective date of a split occurs, month 1 as the month immediately following the split month, month -1 as the month preceding, etc. Now define the average residual over all split securities for month m (where for each security m is measured relative to the split month) as

$$u_m = \sum_{j=1}^{N} \frac{\hat{u}_{jm}}{N},$$

where $\hat{u}_{jm}$ is the sample regression residual for security j in month m and N is the number of splits. Next, define the cumulative average residual U_m as

$$U_m = \sum_{k=-29}^{m} u_k.$$

The average residual u_m can be interpreted as the average deviation (in month m relative to split months) of the returns of split stocks from their normal relationships with the market. Similarly, U_m can be interpreted as the cumulative deviation (from month -29 to month m). Finally, define u_m^+, u_m^-, U_m^+, and U_m^- as the average and cumulative average residuals for splits followed by "increased" $(+)$ and "decreased" $(-)$ dividends. An "increase" is a case where the percentage change in dividends on the split share in the year after the split is greater than the percentage change for the N.Y.S.E. as a whole, while a "decrease" is a case of relative dividend decline.

The essence of the results of FFJR are then summarized in Figure 1, which shows the cumulative average residuals U_m, U_m^+, and U_m^- for $-29 \leq m \leq 30$. The sample includes all 940 stock splits on the N.Y.S.E. from 1927–59, where the exchange was at least five new shares for four old, and where the security was listed for at least twelve months before and after the split.

For all three dividend categories the cumulative average residuals rise in the 29 months prior to the split, and in fact the average residuals (not shown here) are uniformly positive. This cannot be attributed to the splitting process, since in only about ten per cent of the cases is the time between the announcement and effective dates of a split greater than four months. Rather, it seems that firms tend to split their shares during "abnormally" good times—that is, during periods when the prices of their shares have increased more than would be implied by their normal relationships with general market prices, which itself probably reflects a sharp improvement, relative to the market, in the earnings prospects of these firms sometime during the years immediately preceding a split.[28]

After the split month there is almost no further movement in U_m, the cumulative average residual for all splits. This is striking, since 71.5 per cent (672

---

[28] It is important to note, however, that as FFJR indicate, the persistent upward drift of the cumulative average residuals in the months preceding the split is not a phenomenon that could be used to increase expected trading profits. The reason is that the behavior of the average residuals is not representative of the behavior of the residuals for individual securities. In months prior to the split, successive sample residuals for individual securities seem to be independent. But in most cases, there are a few months in which the residuals are abnormally large and positive. The months of large residuals differ from security to security, however, and these differences in timing explain why the signs of the average residuals are uniformly positive for many months preceding the split.

out of 940) of all splits experienced greater percentage dividend increases in the year after the split than the average for all securities on the N.Y.S.E. In light of this, FFJR suggest that when a split is announced the market interprets this (and correctly so) as a signal that the company's directors are probably confident that future earnings will be sufficient to maintain dividend payments at a higher level. Thus the large price increases in the months immediately preceding a split may be due to an alteration in expectations concerning the future earning potential of the firm, rather than to any intrinsic effects of the split itself.

If this hypothesis is correct, return behavior subsequent to splits should be substantially different for the cases where the dividend increase materializes than for the cases where it does not. FFJR argue that in fact the differences are in the directions that would be predicted. The fact that the cumulative average residuals for the "increased" dividends (Figure 1, left) drift upward but only slightly in the year *after* the split is consistent with the hypothesis that when the split is *declared,* there is a price adjustment in anticipation of future dividend increases. But the behavior of the residuals for stock splits associated with "decreased" dividends offers even stronger evidence for the split hypothesis. The cumulative average residuals for these stocks (Figure 1, right) rise in the few months before the split, but then fall dramatically in the few months after the split when the anticipated dividend increase is not forthcoming. When a year has passed after the split, the cumulative average residual has fallen to about where it was five months prior to the split, which is about the earliest time reliable information about a split is likely to reach the market. Thus by the time it becomes clear that the anticipated dividend increase is not forthcoming, the apparent effects of the split seem to have been wiped away, and the stock's returns have reverted to their normal relationship with market returns.

Finally, and most important, although the behavior of post-split returns will be very different depending on whether or not dividend "increases" occur, and in spite of the fact that a large majority of split securities do experience dividend "increases," when all splits are examined together (Figure 1, top) subsequent to the split there is no net movement up or down in the cumulative average residuals. Thus, apparently the market makes unbiased forecasts of the implications of a split for future dividends, and these forecasts are fully reflected in the prices of the security by the end of the split month. After considerably more data analysis than can be summarized here, FFJR conclude that their results lend considerable support to the conclusion that the stock market is efficient, at least with respect to its ability to adjust to the information implicit in a split.

2. *Other Studies of Public Announcements.* Variants of the method of residual analysis developed in [14] have been used by others to study the effects of

different kinds of public announcements, and all of these also support the efficient markets hypothesis.

Thus using data on 261 major firms for the period 1946–66, Ball and Brown [4] apply the method to study the effects of annual earnings announcements. They use the residuals from a time series regression of the annual earnings of a firm on the average earnings of all their firms to classify the firm's earnings for a given year as having "increased" or "decreased" relative to the market. Residuals from regressions of monthly common stock returns on an index of returns (i.e., the market model of (12)) are then used to compute cumulative average return residuals separately for the earnings that "increased," and those that "decreased." The cumulative average return residuals rise throughout the year in advance of the announcement for the earnings "increased" category, and fall for the earnings "decreased" category.[29] Ball and Brown [4, p. 175] conclude that in fact no more than about ten to fifteen percent of the information in the annual earnings announcement has not been anticipated by the month of the announcement.

On the macro level, Waud [45] has used the method of residual analysis to examine the effects of announcements of discount rate changes by Federal Reserve Banks. In this case the residuals are essentially just the deviations of the daily returns on the Standard and Poor's 500 Index from the average daily return. He finds evidence of a statistically significant "announcement effect" on stock returns for the first trading day following an announcement, but the magnitude of the adjustment is small, never exceeding .5%. More interesting from the viewpoint of the efficient markets hypothesis is his conclusion that, if anything, the market anticipates the announcements (or information is somehow leaked in advance). This conclusion is based on the non-random patterns of the signs of average return residuals on the days immediately preceding the announcement.

Further evidence in support of the efficient markets hypothesis is provided in the work of Scholes [39] on large secondary offerings of common stock (i.e., large underwritten sales of existing common stocks by individuals and institutions) and on new issues of stock. He finds that on average secondary issues are associated with a decline of between one and two per cent in the cumulative average residual returns for the corresponding common stocks. Since the magnitude of the price adjustment is unrelated to the size of the issue, Scholes concludes that the adjustment is not due to "selling pressure" (as is commonly believed), but rather results from negative information implicit in the fact that somebody is trying to sell a large block of a firm's stock. Moreover, he presents evidence that the value of the information is a secondary depends to some extent on the vendor; somewhat as would be expected, by far the largest negative cumulative average residuals occur where the vendor is the corporation

---

[29] But the comment of footnote 28 is again relevant here.

itself or one of its officers, with investment companies a distant second. But the identity of the vendor is not generally known at the time of the secondary, and corporate insiders need only report their transactions in their own company's stock to the S.E.C. within six days after a sale. By this time the market on average has fully adjusted to the information in the secondary, as indicated by the fact that the average residuals behave randomly thereafter.

Note, however, that though this is evidence that prices adjust efficiently to public information, it is also evidence that corporate insiders at least sometimes have important information about their firm that is not yet publicly known. Thus Scholes' evidence for secondary distributions provides support for the efficient markets model in the semi-strong sense, but also some strong-form evidence against the model.

Though his results here are only preliminary, Scholes also reports on an application of the method of residual analysis to a sample of 696 new issues of common stock during the period 1926–66. As in the FFJR study of splits, the cumulative average residuals rise in the months preceding the new security offering (suggesting that new issues tend to come after favorable recent events)[30] but behave randomly in the months following the offering (indicating that whatever information is contained in the new issue is on average fully reflected in the price of the month of the offering).

In short, the available semi-strong form evidence on the effect of various sorts of public announcements on common stock returns is all consistent with the efficient markets model. The strong point of the evidence, however, is its consistency rather than its quantity; in fact, few different types of public information have been examined, though those treated are among the obviously most important. Moreover, as we shall now see, the amount of semi-strong form evidence is voluminous compared to the strong form tests that are available.

C. STRONG FORM TESTS OF THE EFFICIENT MARKETS MODELS

The strong form tests of the efficient markets model are concerned with whether all available information is fully reflected in prices in the sense that no individual has higher expected trading profits than others because he has monopolistic access to some information. We would not, of course, expect this model to be an exact description of reality, and indeed, the preceding discussions have already indicated the existence of contradictory evidence. In particular, Niederhoffer and Osborne [32] have pointed out that specialists on the N.Y.S.E. apparently use their monopolistic access to information concerning unfilled limit orders to generate monopoly profits, and Scholes' evidence [39] indicates that offers of corporations sometimes have monopolistic access to information about their firms.

---

[30] Footnote 28 is again relevant here.

Since we already have enough evidence to determine that the model is not strictly valid, we can now turn to other interesting questions. Specifically, how far down through the investment community do deviations from the model permeate? Does it pay for the average investor (or the average economist) to expend resources searching out little known information? Are such activities even generally profitable for various groups of market "professionals"? More generally, who are the people in the investment community that have access to "special information"?

Though this is a fascinating problem, only one group has been studied in any depth—the managements of open end mutual funds. Several studies are available (e.g., Sharpe [41, 42] and Treynor [44]), but the most thorough are Jensen's [19, 20], and our comments will be limited to his work. We shall first present the theoretical model underlying his tests, and then go on to his empirical results.

1. *Theoretical Framework.* In studying the performance of mutual funds the major goals are to determine (a) whether in general fund managers seem to have access to special information which allows them to generate "abnormal" expected returns, and (b) whether some funds are better at uncovering such special information than others. Since the criterion will simply be the ability of funds to produce higher returns than some norm with no attempt to determine what is responsible for the high returns, the "special information" that leads to high performance could be either keener insight into the implications of publicly available information than is implicit in market prices or monopolistic access to specific information. Thus the tests of the performance of the mutual fund industry are not strictly strong form tests of the efficient markets model.

The major theoretical (and practical) problem in using the mutual fund industry to test the efficient markets model is developing a "norm" against which performance can be judged. The norm must represent the results of an investment policy based on the assumption that prices fully reflect all available information. And if one believes that investors are generally risk averse and so on average must be compensated for any risks undertaken, then one has the problem of finding appropriate definitions of risk and evaluating each fund relative to a norm with its chosen level of risk.

Jensen uses the Sharpe [40]-Lintner [24, 25] model of equilibrium expected returns discussed above to derive a norm consistent with these goals. From (14)–(16), in this model the expected return on an asset or portfolio j from t to t + 1 is

$$E(\tilde{r}_{j,t+1}|\Phi_t) = r_{f,t+1}[1 - \beta_j(\Phi_t)] + E(\tilde{r}_{m,t+1}|\Phi_t)\beta_j(\Phi_t), \qquad (18)$$

where the various symbols are as defined in Section III. A. 6. But (18) is an *ex ante* relationship, and to evaluate performance an *ex post* norm is needed.

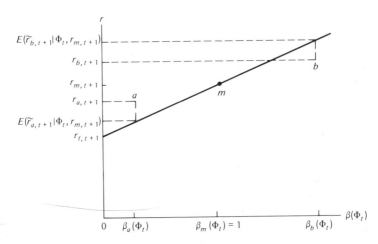

FIGURE 2. Performance evaluation graph.

·One way the latter can be obtained is to substitute the realized return on the market portfolio for the expected return in (18) with the result[31]

$$E(\tilde{r}_{j,t+1}\,|\,\Phi_t, r_{m,t+1}) = r_{f,t+1}[1 - \beta_j(\Phi_t)] + r_{m,t+1}\beta_j(\Phi_t). \qquad (19)$$

Geometrically, (19) says that within the context of the Sharpe-Lintner model, the expected return on j (given information Φ_t and the return $r_{m,t+1}$ on the market portfolio) is a linear function of its risk

$$\beta_j(\Phi_t) = \text{cov}\,(\tilde{r}_{j,t+1}, \tilde{r}_{m,t+1}\,|\,\Phi_t)/\sigma^2(\tilde{r}_{m,t+1}\,|\,\Phi_t),$$

as indicated in Figure 2. Assuming that the value of $\beta_j(\Phi_t)$ is somehow known, or can be reliably estimated, if j is a mutual fund, its *ex post* performance from t to t + 1 might now be evaluated by plotting its combination of realized return $r_{j,t+1}$ and risk in Figure 2. If (as for the point a) the combination falls above the expected return line (or, as it is more commonly called, the "market line"), it has done better than would be expected given its level of risk, while if (as for the point b) it falls below the line it has done worse.

Alternatively, the market line shows the combinations of return and risk provided by portfolios that are simple mixtures of the riskless asset and the market portfolio m. The returns and risks for such portfolios (call them c) are

$$r_{c,t+1} = \alpha r_{f,t+1} + (1 - \alpha)r_{m,t+1}$$

$$\beta_c(\Phi_t) = \frac{\text{cov}\,(\tilde{r}_{c,t+1}, \tilde{r}_{m,t+1}\,|\,\Phi_t)}{\sigma^2(\tilde{r}_{m,t+1}\,|\,\Phi_t)} = \frac{\text{cov}\,((1 - \alpha)\tilde{r}_{m,t+1}, \tilde{r}_{m,t+1}\,|\,\Phi_t)}{\sigma^2(\tilde{r}_{m,t+1}\,|\,\Phi_t)} = 1 - \alpha,$$

[31] The assumption here is that the return $\tilde{r}_{j,t+1}$ is generated according to

$$\tilde{r}_{j,t+1} = r_{f,t+1}[1 - \beta_j(\Phi_t)] + r_{m,t+1}\beta_j(\Phi_t) + \tilde{u}_{j,t+1},$$

and

$$E(\tilde{u}_{j,t+1}\,|\,r_{m,t+1}) = 0 \text{ for all } r_{m,t+1}.$$

where α is the proportion of portfolio funds invested in the riskless asset. Thus, when $1 \geq \alpha \geq 0$ we obtain the combinations of return and risk along the market line from $r_{f,t+1}$ to m in Figure 2, while when $\alpha < 0$ (and under the assumption that investors can borrow at the same rate that they lend) we obtain the combinations of return and risk along the extension of the line through m. In this interpretation, the market line represents the results of a naive investment strategy, which the investor who thinks prices reflect all available information might follow. The performance of a mutual fund is then measured relative to this naive strategy.

2. *Empirical Results.* Jensen uses this risk-return framework to evaluate the performance of 115 mutual funds over the ten year period 1955–64. He argues at length for measuring return as the nominal ten-year rate with continuous compounding (i.e., the natural log of the ratio of terminal wealth after ten years to initial wealth) and for using historical data on nominal one-year rates with continuous compounding to estimate risk. The Standard and Poor Index of 500 major common stocks is used as the proxy for the market portfolio.

The general question to be answered is whether mutual fund managements have any special insights or information which allows them to earn returns above the norm. But Jensen attacks the question on several levels. First, can the funds in general do well enough to compensate investors for loading charges, management fees, and other costs that might be avoided by simply choosing the combination of the riskless asset f and the market portfolio m with risk level comparable to that of the fund's actual portfolio? The answer seems to be an emphatic no. As far as net returns to investors are concerned, in 89 out of 115 cases, the fund's risk-return combination for the ten-year period is below the market line for the period, and the average over all funds of the deviations of ten year returns from the market time is −14.6%. That is, on average the consumer's wealth after ten years of holding mutual funds is about fifteen per cent less than if he held the corresponding portfolios along the market line.

But the loading charge that an investor pays in buying into a fund is usually a pure salesman's commission that the fund itself never gets to invest. Thus one might ask whether, ignoring loading charges (i.e., assuming no such charges were paid by the investor), in general fund managements can earn returns sufficiently above the norm to cover all other expenses that are presumably more directly related to the management of the fund portfolios. Again, the answer seems to be no. Even when loading charges are ignored in computing returns, the risk-return combinations for 72 out of 115 funds are below the market line, and the average deviation of ten-year returns from the market line is −8.9%.

Finally, as a somewhat stronger test of the efficient markets model, one would like to know if, ignoring all expenses, fund managements in general showed any ability to pick securities that outperformed the norm. Unfortunately, this question cannot be answered with precision for individual funds since, curiously, data on brokerage commissions are not published regularly. But Jensen suggests the available evidence indicates that the answer to the question is again probably negative. Specifically, adding back all other published expenses of funds to their returns, the risk-return combinations for 58 out of 115 funds were below the market line, and the average deviation of ten-year return from the line was −2.5%. But part of this result is due to the absence of a correction for brokerage commissions. Estimating these commissions from average portfolio turnover rates for all funds for the period 1953–58, and adding them back to returns for all funds increases the average deviation from the market line from −2.5% to .09%, which still is not indicative of the existence of special information among mutual fund managers.

But though mutual fund managers in general do not seem to have access to information not already fully reflected in prices, perhaps there are individual funds that consistently do better than the norm, and so provide at least some strong form evidence against the efficient markets model. If there are such funds, however, they escape Jensen's search. For example, for individual funds. returns above the norm in one subperiod do not seem to be associated with performance above the norm in other subperiods. And regardless of how returns are measured (i.e., net or gross of loading charges and other expenses), the number of funds with large positive deviations of returns from the market line of Figure 2 is less than the number that would be expected by chance with 115 funds under the assumption that fund managements have no special talents in predicting returns.[32]

Jensen argues that though his results apply to only one segment of the investment community, they are nevertheless striking evidence in favor of the efficient markets model:

Although these results certainly do not imply that the strong form of the martingale hypothesis holds for all investors and for all time, they provide strong evidence in support of that hypothesis. One must realize that these analysts are extremely well endowed. Moreover, they operate in the securities markets every day and have wide-ranging contacts and associations in both the business and financial communities. Thus, the fact that they are apparently unable to forecast returns accurately enough to recover their research and transactions costs is a striking piece of evidence in favor of the strong form of the martingale hypothesis—at least as far as the extensive subset of information available to these analysts is concerned [20, p. 170].

---

[32] On the other hand, there is some suggestion in Scholes' [39] work on secondary issues that mutual funds may occassionally have access to "special information." After corporate insiders, the next largest negative price changes occur when the secondary seller is an investment company (including mutual funds), though on average the price changes are much smaller (i.e., closer to 0) than when the seller is a corporate insider.

Moreover, Jensen's evidence itself, though not indicative of the existence of special information among mutual fund managers, is not sufficiently precise to conclude that such information never exists. This stronger conclusion would require exact data on unavoidable expenses (including brokerage commissions) of portfolio management incurred by funds.

IV. SUMMARY AND CONCLUSIONS

The preceding (rather lengthy) analysis can be summarized as follows. In general terms, the theory of efficient markets is concerned with whether prices at any point in time "fully reflect" available information. The theory only has empirical content, however, within the context of a more specific model of market equilibrium, that is, a model that specifies the nature of market equilibrium when prices "fully reflect" available information. We have seen that all of the available empirical literature is implicitly or explicitly based on the assumption that the conditions of market equilibrium can be stated in terms of expected returns. This assumption is the basis of the expected return or "fair game" efficient markets models.

The empirical work itself can be divided into three categories depending on the nature of the information subset of interest. *Strong-form* tests are concerned with whether individual investors or groups have monopolistic access to any information relevant for price information. One would not expect such an extreme model to be an exact description of the world, and it is probably best viewed as a benchmark against which the importance of deviations from market efficiency can be judged. In the less restrictive *semi-strong-form* tests the information subset of interest includes all obviously publicly available information, while in the *weak form* tests the information subset is just historical price or return sequences.

Weak form tests of the efficient market model are the most voluminous, and it seems fair to say that the results are strongly in support. Though statistically significant evidence for dependence in successive price changes or returns has been found, some of this is consistent with the "fair game" model and the rest does not appear to be sufficient to declare the market inefficient. Indeed, at lease for price changes or returns covering a day or longer, there isn't much evidence against the "fair game" model's more ambitious offspring, the random walk.

Thus, there is consistent evidence of positive dependence in day-to-day price changes and returns on common stocks, and the dependence is of a form that can be used as the basis of marginally profitable trading rules. In Fama's data [10] the dependence shows up as serial correlations that are consistently positive but also consistently close to zero, and as a slight tendency for observed numbers of runs of positive and negative price changes to be less than the numbers that would be expected from a purely random process. More important, the dependence also shows up in the filter tests of Alexander [1, 2] and those of Fama and Blume [13] as a tendency for very small filters to produce profits in excess of buy-and-hold. But any systems (like the filters) that attempt to turn short-term dependence into trading profits of necessity generate so many transactions that their expected profits would be absorbed by even the minimum commissions (security handling fees) that floor traders on major exchanges must pay. Thus, using a less than completely strict interpretation of market efficiency, this positive dependence does not seem of sufficient importance to warrant rejection of the efficient markets model.

Evidence in contradiction of the "fair game" efficient markets model for price changes or returns covering periods longer than a single day is more difficult to find. Cootner [9], and Moore [31] report preponderantly negative (but again small) serial correlations in weekly common stock returns, and this result appears also in the four day returns analyzed by Fama [10]. But it does not appear in runs tests of [10], where, if anything, there is some slight indication of positive dependence, but actually not much evidence of any dependence at all. In any case, there is no indication that whatever dependence exists in weekly returns can be used as the basis of profitable trading rules.

Other existing evidence of dependence in returns provides interesting insights into the process of price formation in the stock market, but it is not relevant for testing the efficient markets model. For example, Fama [10] shows that large daily price changes tend to be followed by large changes, but of unpredictable sign. This suggests that important information cannot be completely evaluated immediately, but that the initial first day's adjustment of prices to the information is unbiased, which is sufficient for the martingale model. More interesting and important, however, is the Niderhoffer-Osborne [32] finding of a tendency toward excessive reversals in common stock price changes from transaction to transaction. They explain this as a logical result of the mechanism whereby orders to buy and sell at market are matched against existing limit orders on the books of the specialist. Given the way this tendency toward excessive reversals arises, however, there seems to be no way it can be used as the basis of a profitable trading rule. As they rightly claim, their results are a strong refutation of the theory of random walks, at least as applied to price changes from transaction to transaction, but they do not constitute refutation of the economically more relevant "fair game" efficient markets model.

Semi-strong form tests, in which prices are assumed to fully reflect all obviously publicly available information, have also supported the efficient markets hypothesis. Thus Fama, Fisher, Jensen, and Roll [14] find that the information in stock splits concerning the firm's future dividend payments is on average fully reflected in the price of a split share at the time of the split. Ball and Brown [4] and Scholes [39] come to similar conclusions with respect to the information contained in (i) annual earning announcements by firms and (ii) new issues and large block secondary issues of common stock. Though only a few different types of information generating events are represented here, they are among the more important, and the results are probably indicative of what can be expected in future studies.

As noted earlier, the strong-form efficient markets model, in which prices are assumed to fully reflect all available information, is probably best viewed as a benchmark against which deviations from market efficiency (interpreted in its strictest sense) can be judged. Two such deviations have in fact been observed. First, Niederhoffer and Osborne [32] point out that specialists on major security exchanges have monopolistic access to information on unexecuted limit orders and they use this information to generate trading profits. This raises the question of whether the "market making" function of the specialist (if indeed this is a meaningful economic function) could not as effectively be carried out by some other mechanism that did not imply monopolistic access to information. Second, Scholes [39] finds that, not unexpectedly, corporate insiders often have monopolistic access to information about their firms.

At the moment, however, corporate insiders and specialists are the only two groups whose monopolistic access to information has been documented. There is no evidence that deviations from the strong form of the efficient markets model permeate down any further through the investment community. For the purposes of most investors the efficient markets model seems a good first (and second) approximation to reality.

In short, the evidence in support of the efficient markets model is extensive, and (somewhat uniquely in economics) contradictory evidence is sparse. Nevertheless, we certainly do not want to leave the impression that all issues are closed. The old saw, "much remains to be done," is relevant here as elsewhere. Indeed, as is often the case in successful scientific research, now that we know we've been in the past, we are able to pose and (hopefully) to answer an even more interesting set of questions for the future. In this case the most pressing field of future endeavor is the development and testing of models of market equilibrium under uncertainty. When the process generating equilibrium expected returns is better understood (and assuming that some expected return model turns out to be relevant), we will have a more substantial framework for more sophisticated intersecurity tests of market efficiency.

REFERENCES

1. Sidney S. Alexander. "Price Movements in Speculative Markets: Trends or Random Walks." *Industrial Management Review,* 2 (May 1961), 7–26. Also reprinted in [8], 199–218.
2. ———. "Price Movements in Speculative Markets: Trends or Random Walks. No. 2," in [8], 338–72.
3. Louis Bachelier. *Théorie de la Speculation* (Paris: Gauthier-Villars, 1900), and reprinted in English in [8], 17–78.
4. Ray Ball and Phillip Brown. "An Empirical Evaluation of Accounting Income Numbers." *Journal of Accounting Research,* 6 (Autumn, 1968), 159–78.
5. William Beaver. "The Information Content of Annual Earnings Announcements." *Empirical Research in Accounting: Selected Studies, 1968,* supplement to Vol. 7 of the *Journal of Accounting Research,* 67–92.

6. Robert Blattberg and Thomas Sargent. "Regression with Non-Gaussian Disturbances: Some Sampling Results," forthcoming in *Econometrica*.
7. Marshall Blume. "The Assessment of Portfolio Performance." Unpublished Ph.D. thesis, University of Chicago, 1968. A paper summarizing much of this work will appear in the April, 1970, Journal of Business.
8. Paul Cootner (ed.). *The Random Character of Stock Market Prices*. Cambridge: M.I.T., 1964.
9. ———. "Stock Prices: Random vs. Systematic Changes." *Industrial Management Review,* 3 (Spring 1962), 24–45. Also reprinted in [8], 231–52.
10. Eugene F. Fama. "The Behavior of Stock Market Prices." *Journal of Business,* 38 (January, 1965), 34–105.
11. ———. "Multiperiod Consumption-Investment Decisions." *American Economic Review,* (March, 1970).
12. ———. "Risk, Return and Equilibrium." Report No. 6831, University of Chicago, Center for Math. Studies in Business and Economics, June, 1968.
13. ——— and Marshall Blume. "Filter Rules and Stock Market Trading Profits." *Journal of Business,* 39 (Special Supplement, January, 1966), 226–41.
14. ———, Lawrence Fisher, Michael Jensen and Richard Roll. "The Adjustment of Stock Prices to New Information." *International Economic Review,* X (February, 1969), 1–21.
15. ——— and Richard Roll. "Some Properties of Symmetric Stable Distributions." *Journal of the American Statistical Association,* 63 (September, 1968), 817–36.
16. Michael D. Godfrey, C. W. J. Granger and O. Morgenstern. "The Random Walk Hypothesis of Stock Market Behavior." *Kyklos,* 17 (1964), 1–30.
17. C. W. J. Granger and O. Morgenstern. "Spectral Analysis of New York Stock Market Prices," *Kyklos,* 16 (1963), 1–27. Also reprinted in [8], 162–88.
18. John R. Hicks. *Value and Capital.* Oxford: The Clarendon Press, 1946.
19. Michael Jensen. "The Performance of Mutual Funds in the Period 1945–64," *Journal of Finance,* 23 (May, 1968), 389–416.
20. ———. "Risk, the Pricing of Capital Assets, and the Evaluation of Investment Portfolios," *Journal of Business,* 42 (April, 1969), 167–247.
21. Maurice G. Kendall. "The Analysis of Economic Time-Series, Part I: Prices," *Journal of the Royal Statistical Society,* 96 (Part I, 1953), 11–25.
22. Ruben A. Kessel. "The Cyclical Behavior of the Term Structure of Interest Rates," National Bureau of Economic Research Occasional Paper No. 91. New York: Columbia University Press, 1965.
23. Benjamin F. King. "Market and Industry Factors in Stock Price Behav-

ior," *Journal of Business,* 39 (Special Supplement January, 1966), 139–90.

24. John Lintner. "Security Prices, Risk, and Maximal Gains from Diversification," *Journal of Finance,* 20 (December, 1965), 587–615.

25. ———. "The Valuation of Risk Assets and the Selection of Risky Investments in Stock Portfolios and Capital Budgets," *Review of Economics and Statistics,* 47 (February, 1965), 13–37.

26. Fredrich A. Lutz. "The Structure of Interest Rates," *Quarterly Journal of Economics,* 40 (1940–41).

27. Benoit Mandelbrot. "Forecasts of Future Prices, Unbiased Markets, and Martingale Models," *Journal of Business,* 39 (Special Supplement, January, 1966), 242–55.

28. ———. "The Variation of Certain Speculative Prices." *Journal of Business,* 36 (October, 1963), 394–419.

29. ——— and Howard M. Taylor. "On the Distribution of Stock Price Differences." *Operations Research,* 15 (November–December, 1967), 1057–62.

30. Harry Markowitz. *Portfolio Selection: Efficient Diversification of Investment.* New York: John Wiley & Sons, 1959.

31. Arnold Moore. "A Statistical Analysis of Common Stock Prices. Unpublished Ph.D. thesis, Graduate School of Business, University of Chicago, 1962.

32. Victor Niederhoffer and M. F. M. Osborne. "Market Making and Reversal on the Stock Exchange." *Journal of the American Statistical Association,* 61 (December, 1966), 897–916.

33. M. F. M. Osborne. "Brownian Motion in the Stock Market," *Operations Research,* 7 (March–April, 1959), 145–73. Also reprinted in [8], 100–28.

34. ———. "Periodic Structure in the Brownian Motion of Stock Prices." *Operations Research,* 10 (May–June, 1962), 345–79. Also reprinted in [8], 262–96.

35. S. James Press. "A Compound Events Model for Security Prices." *Journal of Business,* 40 (July, 1968), 317–35.

36. Harry V. Roberts. "Stock Market 'Patterns' and Financial Analysis: Methodological Suggestions." *Journal of Finance,* 14 (March, 1959), 1–10.

37. Richard Roll. "The Efficient Market Model Applied to U.S. Treasury Bill Rates." Unpublished Ph.D. thesis, Graduate School of Business, University of Chicago, 1968.

38. Paul A. Samuelson. "Proof That Properly Anticipated Prices Fluctuate Randomly." *Industrial Management Review,* 6 (Spring, 1965), 41–9.

39. Myron Scholes. "A Test of the Competitive Hypothesis: The Market for New Issues and Secondary Offerings." Unpublished Ph.D. thesis, Graduate School of Business, University of Chicago, 1969.

40. William F. Sharpe. "Capital Asset Prices: A Theory of Market Equilib-

rium under Conditions of Risk." *Journal of Finance,* 19 (September, 1964), 425–42.

41. ——. "Mutual Fund Performance." *Journal of Business,* 39 (Special Supplement, January, 1966), 119–38.

42. ——. "Risk Aversion in the Stock Market." *Journal of Finance,* 20 (September, 1965), 416–22.

43. James Tobin. "Liquidity Preference as Behavior Towards Risk," *Review of Economic Studies,* 25 (February, 1958), 65–85.

44. Jack L. Treynor. "How to Rate Management of Investment Funds." *Harvard Business Review,* 43 (January–February, 1965), 63–75.

45. Roger N. Waud. "Public Interpretation of Discount Rate Changes: Evidence on the 'Announcement Effect,'" forthcoming in *Econometrica.*

46. John Wise. "Linear Estimators for Linear Regression Systems Having Infinite Variances." Unpublished paper presented at the Berkeley-Stanford Mathematical Economics Seminar, October, 1963.

47. Holbrook Working. "A Random Difference Series for Use in the Analysis of Time Series." *Journal of the American Statistical Association,* 29 (March, 1934), 11–24.

11. AMBIGUITY WHEN PERFORMANCE IS MEASURED BY THE SECURITIES MARKET LINE

RICHARD ROLL*

Reprinted from *The Journal of Finance,* Vol. XXXIII, No. 4 (September 1978), pp. 1051–1069, by permission of the author and publisher.

I. INTRODUCTION

Imagine an idealized analog to the activities of professional money managers, a contest whose rules are as follows:

a. Each contestant selects a portfolio from a specified set of individual assets.
b. Returns are observed on the assets.

* Graduate School of Management U.C.L.A. Comments and suggestions by Alan Kraus, David Mayers, Stephen Ross and Eduardo Schwartz are gratefully acknowledged.

c. After each period of return observation, the portfolios are re-balanced to the initial selections.

d. After an interval consisting of several periods, "winners" and "losers" are declared for that interval.

e. Contestants choose a new portfolio, or keep the old one, and the process (b) through (d) is repeated.

f. After several intervals, consistent winners are declared to be superior portfolio managers and consistent losers are declared inferior. In the absence of any consistency, everyone is declared non-superior.

The sponsors of the contest face only a single problem of intellectual interest. They must develop criteria to partition contestants at step (d) into winners and losers. Of course, the criteria must be acceptable to participants and to disinterested observers. There should be a correspondence between "consistency in winning" and an intuitive notion of ability in portfolio selection.

We might think of many desirable qualities to be possessed by such criteria. For example, they should be robust to stochastic changes in the return sequence; true ability should be detectable over many intervals regardless of the sequence. If the criteria are employed by different sponsors, the same judgements about ability should be obtained. It should not be possible to reverse judgements by making changes in the computation of the criteria, if such changes are deemed insignificant by all observers. In other words, the criteria must provide decisions about ability that are *unambiguous* to rational judges.

A criterion that is widely employed in the financial community for assessing portfolio performance is the "securities market line," the (linear) relation between mean returns on assets or portfolios and the betas[1] of these assets or portfolios calculated against a market index. Judging from the academic literature, this criterion is even more widely-accepted by scholars as a tool for assessing the ex ante or ex post qualities of securities, portfolios and investment projects. There seems little doubt that it is currently the most widely-accepted criterion for inferences about the quality of risky assets.

It is quite simple to employ, particularly in a situation such as the contest mentioned above. There are only two steps to accomplish. First, an index must be chosen by the judges; second, the betas must be computed against this index for each asset (and portfolio). The second step can be accomplished in many ways, including purely subjective, but the most common method is to employ historical data over the same interval as the contest itself.

Given the computed betas and the returns on assets or portfolios, the crite-

---

[1] The "beta" is the covariance of the asset and the market index returns divided by the variance of the market index' return.

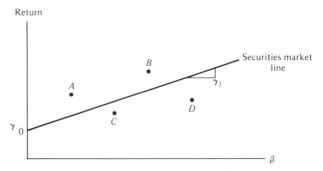

FIGURE 1.   The securities market line employed as a criterion for assessing asset quality.

rion can be illustrated as in Figure 1. A line, $R = \gamma_0 + \gamma_1\beta$ is fit[2] to the observations and assets are declared "winners" if they are above the line (such as A and B) or losers if they are below (C or D).

My purpose here is to expose the ambiguity in this criterion. It is not robust, is likely to yield different judgements when employed by different judges, and can completely reverse its judgements after seemingly innocuous changes in its computation. Reasons for these deficiencies will be explained in detail. By implication, the concept of the beta as an unambiguous measure of risk will be disputed.

A NUMERICAL EXAMPLE

To illustrate the ambiguity of the securities market line criterion, let us consider a specific numerical example—the idealized contest conducted with 15 hypothetical contestants and a hypothetical four asset universe.

Table 1 begins the example with portfolios selected by the fifteen contestants. Nothing is unusual about the selections. The first four contestants plunged into the individual assets and contestants 14 and 15 sold short some securities, but there seems little reason to exclude such possibilities. The idealization of the contest is evident only because trading costs and restrictions on short sales have not even been mentioned.

After the portfolios were selected, a sample period was observed with the results for individual assets reported in Table 2. Again, there is nothing abnor-

---

[2] The method of fit is not crucial for this discussion. It is often done by regression, sometimes with sophisticated econometric corrections of the betas. It could also be done by choosing γ_0 and γ_1 based on theories of market equilibrium. For example, the Sharpe [1964], Lintner [1965] theory requires that $\gamma_0 = R_F$, the riskless rate of interest, and that $\gamma_1 = E(R_m) - R_F$, the difference between the expected return on the market index and the riskless rate of interest. Thus, *estimates* of $E(R_m)$ and of R_F can be used to fix the line. Alternatively, the Black [1972] theory would require $\gamma_1 = E(R_m - R_z)$ and $\gamma_0 = E(R_z)$ where z is a portfolio with minimal variance uncorrelated with m.

TABLE 1
PORTFOLIOS SELECTED BY FIFTEEN CONTESTANTS

	ASSET			
	1	2	3	4
CONTESTANT	PERCENTAGE INVESTED IN INDIVIDUAL ASSET			
1	100.	0.	0.	0.
2	0.	100.	0.	0.
3	0.	0.	100.	0.
4	0.	0.	0.	100.
5	50.	50.	0.	0.
6	33⅓	33⅓	33⅓	0.
7	40.	30.	20.	10.
8	25.	25.	25.	25.
9	10.	20.	30.	40.
10	0.	33⅓	33⅓	33⅓
11	0.	0.	50.	50.
12	59.6	27.6	7.69	5.08
13	40.7	31.9	14.0	13.4
14	−4.4	42.2	29.0	33.3
15	−49.6	52.4	44.1	53.1

Note: The last four portfolios' weights may not sum to 100% because of rounding. The exact weights were used in all calculations.

TABLE 2
SAMPLE STATISTICS FOR INDIVIDUAL ASSETS WHICH CONSTITUTED THE UNIVERSE OF SECURITIES FOR THE PORTFOLIO SELECTION CONTEST

		ASSET			
	SAMPLE MEAN RETURN	1	2	3	4
ASSET	(%/PERIOD)	SAMPLE VARIANCE/COVARIANCE MATRIX			
1	6.	10.			
2	7.	2.	20.		
3	8.	4.	4.	40.	
4	9.	5.	1.	10.	60.

TABLE 3

INDICES AND SECURITIES MARKET LINES USED BY THE THREE JUDGES IN THE
PORTFOLIO SELECTION CONTEST

JUDGE	1	2	3	4	MEAN RETURN	VARIANCE OF RETURN	SLOPE	INTERCEPT
	COMPOSITION OF INDEX (PERCENTAGE OF INDEX IN SECURITY)						SECURITIES MARKET LINE[a]	
						INDEX		
1	25	25	25	25	7.5	11.4	2.31 (.119)	5.22 (.127)
2	10	40	40	10	7.5	13.0	2.40 (.486)	5.46 (.444)
3[b]	18.2	37	21.5	23.3	7.5	11.0	2.57 (0.)	4.93 (0.)

[a] Standard errors are in parentheses. These lines were fitted cross-sectionally by ordinary least squares applied to mean returns and betas of the fifteen portfolios in the contest.

[b] Judge three actually specified more precise weights. The weights reported here have been rounded. (For example, the proportion of his index in asset 4 was actually 23.3214%.) The exact weights were used in all calculations.

Coefficients of Correlation Between Indices

	2	3
1	.897	.982
2		.920

mal nor pathological about these numbers. The mean returns were different on different assets and the covariance matrix was non-singular, certainly the most usual and desirable feature of real asset return samples. Indeed, all of the qualitative results to be reported hereafter could be obtained from any other numbers with these same general characteristics. For the purposes of illustration, there is not even any need to be concerned with the statistical properties of the sample. The ambiguities are not related in any way to the sampling error in the estimates. The same problems are present when the true population means, variances and covariances are known and used in computing the criterion.

The observed means and variances of the 15 portfolios are easy to compute by applying the compositions of Table 1 to the observed individual asset returns, variances and covariances of Table 2.

Because of its wide acceptance, the securities market line criterion will be used by the three hypothetical sponsors of the contest in order to distinguish winners from losers. Let us suppose, however, that a dispute arises about the best index to use in calculating the "betas." Sponsor/judge no. 1 admits total ignorance about this question. He concludes that an index composed of equal weights in the individual assets would be the most sensible portrayal of this ignorance and the fairest to all contestants. Sponsor/judge no. 2, however, has studied asset pricing theory and argues that the appropriate index should have weights proportional to the aggregate market values of individual assets. He finds that the aggregate values of assets 2 and 3 are roughly four times larger than those of assets 1 and 4, so he suggests the index (10%, 40%, 40%, 10%). Sponsor/judge no. 3, also a theorist, thinks that a good index should be mean-variance efficient in the sense of Markowitz (1959)[3], so he makes some calculations and obtains an index with the same mean return as the indices of the other judges but with a different composition. His index turns out to be (18.2%, 37.0%, 21.5%, 23.3%), the proportions being rounded to three significant digits.

The compositions of the indices, their observed mean returns and variances, and the securities market lines computed against them are reported in Table 3. Notice that the three indices have equal means, similar variances and closely adjacent securities market lines. (The securities market lines would have been identical if they had been fit using an asset pricing theory rather than by regression. See Note 2.)

What about their assessments of "winners" and "losers"? Judge no. 1 ranks the 15 contestants from best (largest positive deviation from his securities market line) to worst as follows:

Rankings of Contestants by Judge no. 1

Winners (Best)→   2 15 14 5 10 /
(above the line)

Losers   6 13 9 8 7 12 4 11 3 1 ←(Worst)
(below the line)

A graph of the contestants' positions relative to the judge's criterion is given by Figure 2(a).

The second judge has a different set of assessments, as shown in the following list and depicted in Figure 2(b):

Rankings of Contestants by Judge no. 2

Winners (Best)→   4 15 11 9 14 10 8 /

Losers   13 1 12 7 5 2 6 3 ←(Worst)

---

[3] That is, a portfolio which has the smallest sample variance of return for a given level of sample mean return.

Although some contestants were similarly rated by both judges (e.g., contestant 15 was ranked second by both and contestant 3 was ranked 14th by judge no. 1 and 15th by judge no. 2), other contestants were rated quite differently (e.g., the number one winner according to judge no. 1 was a loser and ranked 13th out of 15 by judge no. 2.) The rank correlation between the deci-

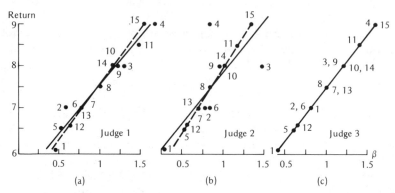

FIGURE 2. Securities market lines and positions of selected portfolios as perceived by the three judges of the contest. The solid lines are ordinary least squares estimated securities market lines fitted through the fifteen contestants' portfolios. The dotted lines pass through portfolios 12–15, which were exactly mean/variance efficient ex post.

sions of these two judges is only .0036 and the lack of agreement is clearly evident in the figure.

As for judge no. 3, after calculating his securities market line and plotting the selected portfolios, he observes Figure 2(c). Every single contestant is exactly on the line. Of course, this judge is unable to construct a ranking and can draw no inference about the relative abilities of contestants.

This example was not constructed to generate bizarre results. The same results can be obtained from every sample of asset returns. They were not caused by any of the example's parameters, by the numbers of assets and contestants, nor by the pattern of returns.

The results in the example and the ambiguity in the securities market line criterion can be attributed to the following fact: corresponding to every index, there is a beta for every individual asset (and thus for every portfolio); but these betas can be different for different indices and will be different for most. To consider the beta as an attribute of the individual asset alone is a significant mistake. For every asset, an index can be found to produce a beta of any desired magnitude, however large or small. Thus, for every asset (or portfolio) judicious choice of the index can produce any desired measured "performance" (positive or negative), against the securities market line.

II. MATHEMATICS OF THE SECURITIES MARKET LINE CRITERION

In this section, the mathematical causes of the preceding numerical results will be made more precise. Since there are general principles involved that would bring similar results to every ex post sample and ex ante application of the criterion, it seems worthwhile to have a unified list of the principles in one place.

Let us presuppose the existence of a mean return vector, R, and a non-singular covariance matrix, V, of N *individual* assets. There is no need to require that these be of any particular dimension nor that they be ex ante (nor ex post sample statistics). The following statements are true for any R and V, however obtained. These statements constitute the mathematics that explains the behavior of the criterion:

S1: Let X_p be the $N \times 1$ column vector of investment proportions (or "weights") that defines a portfolio p. Let X_I define the index I used by a judge. Then the "beta" for portfolio P with respect to the index is given by

$$\beta_{p,I} = X_p'VX_I/\sigma_I^2 \tag{1}$$

where $\sigma_I^2 = X_I'VX_I$.
Proof: obvious.

S2: If the portfolio q is mean/variance efficient (in the Markowitz sense) with respect to R and V, then its weights are given by

$$X_q = V^{-1}(R\iota)A^{-1}(r_q 1) \tag{2}$$

where ι is the $N \times 1$ unit vector, A is the efficient set information matrix[4] and $r_q \equiv X_q'R$ is the return of portfolio q.
Proof: Merton [1972] or Roll [1977].

S3: If the selected index is mean/variance efficient, then the betas of all assets are related to their mean returns by the same linear function.
Proof: Set $q = I$ in (2) and use the results in (1). Then simplify to

$$\beta_{p,I} = (r_p 1)A^{-1}(r_I 1)/\sigma_I^2 \tag{3}$$

A, r_I, and σ_I^2 are cross-sectional constants.[5] *Q.E.D.*

S4: If, for some selected index, the betas of all assets are related to their

---

[4] That is,

$$A = \begin{bmatrix} R'V^{-1}R & \iota'V^{-1}R \\ \iota'V^{-1}R & \iota'V^{-1}\iota \end{bmatrix}$$

[5] It can be shown easily that $r_p = \gamma_0 + \gamma_1\beta_{p,I}$ where γ_0 is the return on a portfolio orthogonal to I and $\gamma_1 = r_I - \gamma_0$.

mean returns by the same linear function, then that index is mean/variance efficient.

Proof: Roll [1977, p. 185.]

S5: The betas of all mean/variance efficient portfolios are related to their mean returns by the same linear function, even if the index used to compute the betas is not itself mean/variance efficient.

S6: For every ranking of performance obtained with a mean/variance non-efficient index, there exists another non-efficient index which reverses the ranking.

Proof: Let Z be the $(K \times N)$ matrix of selected portfolios (each row containing the weights for N individual assets in the portfolio selected by one of the K contestants). Let $_A$ be a subscript which denotes the first ranking, (based on index "$_A$"). The scatter of selected portfolios in the return/beta space can be denoted

$$ZR = \alpha_A + \gamma_{0A}\iota_k + \gamma_{1A}(ZVX_A/\sigma_A^2) \tag{4}$$

where γ_{0A} and γ_{1A} are, respectively, the (estimated) intercept and slope of the securities market line and α_A is the $(K \times 1)$ vector of deviations. The jth element of α_A is the "performance measure" for contestant j. (ι_k is the K-element unit vector).

A reversal of rankings can be achieved by finding a second index, denoted B, such that $\alpha_B = d\alpha_A$ where d is a positive scalar constant. Choose $d/\sigma_A^2/\sigma_B^2$. Then (4) can be written twice, once for $_A$ and once for $_B$, and the equations can be added to obtain

$$\sigma_A^2\alpha_A + \sigma_B^2\alpha_B \equiv 0 = ZR(\sigma_A^2 + \sigma_B^2) - (\sigma_A^2\gamma_{0A} + \sigma_B^2\gamma_{0B})\iota_k \tag{5}$$
$$- ZV(\gamma_{1A}X_A + \gamma_{1B}X_B)$$

We suppose that there are more contestants (K) than individual assets (N) and that all selected portfolios are different. Under these circumstances $Z'Z$ is non-singular. Furthermore, since each row of Z sums to unity, we must have $Z\iota_N = \iota_k$ and thus $\iota_N = (Z'Z)^{-1}Z'\iota_k$. Multiplying both sides of (5) by Z' and simplifying, we find

$$R(\sigma_A^2 + \sigma_B^2) - (\sigma_A^2\gamma_{0A} + \sigma_B^2\gamma_{0B})\iota_N = V(\gamma_{1A}X_A + \gamma_{1B}X_B) \tag{6}$$

In the equation system (6), there are $N + 3$ unknowns: the N elements of X_B plus γ_{0B}, γ_{1B}, and σ_B^2. (Recall that X_A, σ_A^2, γ_{0A}, and γ_{1A}, were already known.) There are only N equations in (6) but we must also add the portfolio additivity condition, $X_B'\iota_N = 1$, the definition of the variance,

$$\sigma_B^2 = X_B'VX_B \tag{7}$$

and the usual requirement,

$$\gamma_{1B} = X'_B R - \gamma_{0B},\tag{8}$$

which guarantees that the securities market line passes through the mean return of the index ($X'_B R$) at a beta of unity. Thus, there obtains an identified system of three non-linear equations in three unknowns and at least one solution is guaranteed.

When there are fewer contestants than assets, the system (5) is underidentified and there is an infinity of solutions. *Q.E.D.*[6]

Statements S1 through S6 explain all the facts of the numerical example. For example, Judge no. 3's inability to discriminate among the contestants was caused by his choice of a mean/variance efficient index. As S3 indicates, any such index will cause the scatter of returns and betas to fall exactly along a line.

The portfolios selected by contestants 12 through 15 fall exactly along another line (shown dashed in all three panels of Figure 2). These selections turned out to be mean/variance efficient portfolios which, as S5 indicates, always fall exactly along a line regardless of the index. Note that this line is not necessarily the securities market line. The latter is usually a line of best fit to selected portfolios and this can deviate from the line through efficient portfolios when the index itself is not efficient.[7]

Finally, the deviations of portfolios from the securities market lines used by Judge no. 1 and Judge no. 2 are a consequence of S4. These judges did not use efficient portfolios as their indices so the *individual* asset returns could not be exactly linear in the individual betas. Of course, contestants could have made choices such that their portfolio's betas and returns were linear; but this was not the case for the example nor is it likely in general. S6 shows that these judges might even have selected indices which reversed the rankings of contestants.

It is quite easy to show how the beta of an arbitrary portfolio varies with the index. Suppose we simplify matters by assuming that all the indices being considered have the same return but different compositions (as in the example).

---

[6] A computational problem is present in solving (6) because the system of equations is non-linear. An *approximate* reversal of rankings can be obtained by ignoring the difference in the securities market lines, setting $\gamma_{0A} = \gamma_{0B}$ and $\gamma_{1A} = \gamma_{1B}$. This provides an X_B which approximately reverses the rankings based on X_A. For example, the X_B obtained in this manner corresponding to the index selected by the first judge (which was equally-weighted), is the portfolio $X' = (-.0422, .526, .232, .285)$. It provides the ranking of the 15 selected portfolios from "best" to "worst", of 3, 1, 11, 4, 9, 8, 12, 7/13, 6, 10, 14, 5, 15, 2. Compare judge no. 1's rankings above. The rank correlation between them is $-.961$.

[7] Portfolio 12 was selected to be the global minimum variance portfolio and its return was 6.58 percent. Since portfolios 13, 14, and 15 all had returns of at least 7 percent and since they were mean-variance efficient, they were all located on the positively-sloped segment of the ex-post efficient frontier.

Of course, only one will be mean/variance efficient. If I^* is the index that is mean/variance efficient and I is another index with the same return, the difference in the beta of p from using I^* rather than I is

$$\Delta\beta_p = X_p V[(\sigma_I^2/\sigma_{I^*}^2)X_{I^*} - X_I]/\sigma_I^2 \qquad (9)$$

The sum of elements in the bracketed vector of (9) is equal to $\sigma_I^2/\sigma_{I^*}^2 - 1$, which is positive (because $\sigma_{I^*}^2 < \sigma_I^2$). Thus, the numerator of (9) is proportional to the covariance between p and a hybrid portfolio whose investment proportions vector is $[(\sigma_I^2/\sigma_{I^*}^2)X_{I^*} - X_I]/(\sigma_I^2/\sigma_{I^*}^2 - 1)$. The closer the pattern of p's weights to the pattern of weights in this hybrid portfolio, the larger is beta. Roughly speaking, if the weights of p match the difference in weights between an efficient index and the index actually employed, the observed beta will be "small" relative to the magnitude of beta had the efficient index been employed. Since the return of p is invariant to the index employed, a relatively smaller beta corresponds to better measured performance and vice versa.

As an example, consider contestant no. 2, who was ranked first by Judge no. 1 and 13th by Judge no. 2. His portfolio and the vectors $[(\sigma_I^2/\sigma_{I^*}^2)X_{I^*} - X_I]/(\sigma_I^2/\sigma_{I^*}^2 - 1)$ for the two judges are given in Table 4. Clearly, contestant no. 2 selected a portfolio that was "different" from the first judge's index.[8] The beta perceived by this judge was correspondingly lower and the performance was highly rated. The opposite was the case for this contestant as perceived by Judge no. 2.[9] Similar situations for the other selected portfolios are evident in the example. Roughly speaking, contestants' hybrid portfolios are ranked low when their weight patterns are "close" to the judge's hybrid portfolio weight patterns, and vice versa.

Another measure of the alteration in beta caused by using an inefficient index is the displacement of portfolio p's beta from the line connecting all efficient portfolios (the dashed line of Figure 2). Note that all assets and portfolios would be situated on such a line if an efficient portfolio had been employed as an index. Formally,

S7: the displacement, from the line connecting efficient portfolios, induced in p's beta by using an inefficient index is $X_p V(X_I - X_{I^*})/\sigma_I^2$, where I^* is the efficient portfolio whose return is the same as the return of I, the index.

Proof: Let p^* be the efficient portfolio whose return is the same as p. Then the displacement of p's beta from the dashed line of efficient portfolios is $\beta_{p,I} - \beta_{p^*,I} = (X_p' - X_{p^*}')VX_I/\sigma_I^2$. Since the information

---

[8] Different in the sense that the largest weight of contestant no. 2's portfolio corresponded to the (algebraically) smallest value of $X_I - X_{I^*}(\sigma_I^2/\sigma_{I^*}^2)$ for judge no. 1; and thus the largest weight of the hybrid portfolio for judge no. 1 matched the largest weight for contestant no. 2.

[9] Correlations between this contestant's weights and the judges' hybrid portfolio weights are .73 for judge no. 1 and $-.11$ for judge no. 2.

TABLE 4

AN EXAMPLE OF THE RELATIONSHIP BETWEEN A SELECTED PORTFOLIO AND
THE INDEX' DEVIATION FROM MEAN/VARIANCE EFFICIENCY

| | WEIGHTS | | |
| | | HYBRID PORTFOLIOS WHICH REPRESENT DEVIATIONS OF INDEX FROM EFFICIENCY | |
ASSET	SELECTED PORTFOLIO NO. 2	JUDGE NO. 1	JUDGE NO. 2
1	0.	-1.77	.622
2	1.00	3.82	.209
3	0.	$-.79$	$-.778$
4	0.	$-.26$	.947

matrix A in (3) is symmetric, the covariance between any efficient portfolio and any arbitrary asset or portfolio depends only on their returns. Thus $X'_{p*}VX_I = X'_p VX_{I*}$ and $\beta_{p,I} - \beta_{p*,I} = X'_p V(X_I - X_{I*})/\sigma_I^2$. Q.E.D.

Still a third way to measure alteration in beta with alteration of the index is provided in the appendix.

III. MEASUREMENT OF ABILITY, MARKET EFFICIENCY, AND INDEX FUNDS

Individual *differences* in portfolio selection ability cannot be measured by the securities market line criterion. This was the general thrust of the preceding argument. If the index is ex ante mean/variance efficient, the criterion will be unable to discriminate between winners and losers. If the index is not ex ante efficient, the criterion will designate winners and losers; but another index could cause the criterion to designate different winners and losers and there is no objective way to ascertain which index is correct.

Although the securities market line cannot distinguish between superior and inferior selected portfolios, it does contain information about the quality of one portfolio, the index itself. In fact, a repeated running of a contest such as the one described on pages 222 and 223 will, in principle, provide the necessary information to infer whether the *index* is ex ante mean/variance efficient. It will provide no information about any other portfolio.

We must be very careful to delineate the difference between running the contest, (or conducting an experiment with actual returns), in order to measure relative abilities of different individuals and in order to test the ex ante efficiency of the particular portfolio employed as an index. These two purposes are not the same.

To clarify the difference in measuring ability and in testing for ex ante efficiency of the index, it will be convenient to make the concept of ability more precise. Begin with an *objective* ex ante expected return vector and covariance matrix, the "state of nature," perhaps unknown to anyone. Perfect ability should be defined as selecting a portfolio located on the ex ante mean/variance efficient set computed with these objective parameters.[10] Less than perfect ability would be revealed by the selection of an ex ante non-efficient portfolio. Such a lapse might be caused by incorrect estimates of the true objective means, variances, and covariances, by an inability to compute the efficient set, given correct estimates, by transaction's costs, etc. Now consider the task of separating individuals with perfect and imperfect abilities. If we employ the securities market line criterion and choose *any* index that is itself ex ante mean/variance efficient, and such indices will always be present, we would be unable to ascertain which individuals have imperfect ability. All portfolios would be *on* the securities market line. This would be exactly true ex ante, using the true objective expected returns and betas, and it would be true on average ex post. (There would be no observed ex post consistency in winning.)

On the other hand, if we choose an inefficient index, we would judge some of the individuals with perfect ability to be inferior and some individuals with less than perfect ability to be superior. In the numerical example, for instance, both judges no. 1 and no. 2, who used non-mean/variance efficient indices, concluded that contestants 12 and 13 were losers. Actually, 12 and 13 selected portfolios that turned out to be exactly efficient, thus indicating perfect ability (ex post).

Considering the second purpose, suppose we wish to infer whether a particular portfolio is ex ante mean/variance efficient. This is a statistical problem since we could make the inference directly if the ex ante probability parameters were known. Given uncertainty about means, variances, and covariances, however, it becomes necessary to employ the portfolio in question as the index in a selection contest (or experiment). From mathematical principles S3 and S4, we see that repeated calculations of the securities market line over many intervals will discover *no* consistent winners *or* losers if and only if the index is ex ante efficient. In other and more precise words, if no measured deviation from the line is statistically significant, the hypothesis of the index' ex ante efficiency cannot be rejected. Some contestants will be adjudged winners and some losers at every intermediate stage, step (d) of the contest, but if these judgements can be attributed to chance alone, the index is efficient.

Suppose that such contests or experiments are conducted and the hypothesis

---

[10] Note that there is no use discussing this topic at all if individuals do not have utility functions that depend on the expected return and variance of return of their portfolios.

of ex ante efficiency for the index is not rejected. The particular collection of individual assets, the index, would then be certified as a non-dominated portfolio in the ex ante mean/variance space. No portfolio manager, regardless of his skill, could possibly pick a superior portfolio. Notice, however, that many observed, managed portfolios might also be ex ante efficient and thus be just as good as the index (gross of fees). This fact could not be determined by using the securities market line criterion with the original index, of course, but it could be determined by employing each managed portfolio as the index in another contest.

If managers charge fees, and if the original index were found to be ex ante efficient, investors could select one point on the ex ante efficient frontier very cheaply. This seems to be the rationale for index funds. To the extent that the empirical articles on performance measurement (Jensen [1968, 1969]) present evidence that the indices employed were ex ante mean/variance efficient, a free management consulting service was provided to all investors.[11]

In order to know whether index funds make sense for a particular investor, two questions must be answered affirmatively:

a. Was the empirical judgement correct about the index' ex ante efficiency?
b. Was the index positioned at an efficient frontier tangency point with respect to a line drawn from the measured riskless asset?

The answer to both questions is no.

Question b's answer can be obtained by noting the wide-spread Friend/ Blume [1970] phenomenon—that securities market lines, computed with value-weighted market indices consisting of equities only, produce positive performance measures for low-beta portfolios and negative measures for high-beta portfolios. This is equivalent to the index having a larger return than the tangency position of a line drawn from the riskless asset.[12]

Question (a) requires a critical evaluation of evidence offered in the literature, which consists of tests on the deviations of selected portfolios about measured securities market lines. All of these tests presume that such deviations are cross-sectionally independent. *This presumption is false and the tests are therefore inconclusive.*

---

[11] There was another important product of these empirical papers, a test of the generalized (by Black [1972]) capital asset pricing theory originally due to Sharpe [1964] and Lintner [1965]. The principal implication of this theory is that the market value-weighted portfolio of all assets is ex ante mean/variance efficient. A proxy for the market portfolio is employed as an index in the empirical performance measurement literature. To the extent that deviations about the securities market line computed with such an index are non-systematic, and to the extent that the index is an accurate measure of the true value-weighted market portfolio, a test of the theory is conducted—and the theory is not rejected. Interestingly, the original and best empirical papers (Jensen [1968, 1969]) were finished *before* the Black version of the theory was developed. A more detailed examination of the theory's testability is given in Roll [1977].

[12] See Roll [1977, pp. 140–144].

The cross-sectional statistical dependence of performance measures (deviations about the securities market line) is easily recognized by noting their complete functional dependence on the index. If the index happened to be *exactly* on the ex post efficient frontier during a given sample period, all deviations would be identically zero. If, as usual, the index does not turn out to be exactly ex post efficient, each observed deviation is determined analytically by the distance of the index' position from the ex post efficient frontier. This is obvious from equation (4). If betas are recomputed each period, the deviations (α's in 4) are linear functions of the observed return vector (R) and observed covariance matrix (V). Even if the betas are not recomputed, the α's are still functions of these two sampling statistics (R and V) because the index' position, the sample efficient set, and the sample securities market line depend only on R and V.[13] Thus, the sampling variation of the deviations is much more complex than might at first be imagined. A proper test of the index' efficiency must regard the entire set of deviations as a single sample statistic. Thus, a multinomial type test based on their presumed independence will produce incorrect significance levels and incorrect inferences.[14]

Even the best empirical literature does not take this problem into account. For example, in Jensen [1968], a scatter diagram of t-ratios of the deviations is presented and an inference is drawn about the average t-ratios. Of course, t-ratio tests rely on independence among observations.

More sophisticated tests are presented in Jensen [1969, Fig. 19] which depicts a highly significant positive relation between deviations, net of management expenses, in two successive periods. If truly significant, this result would be inconsistent with the index' ex ante efficiency. However, Jensen argued that the observed relation was caused by the high fees charged by some managers in both periods and he provided a still more sophisticated test in Table 9, p. 239. In this test, a run of k years of positive deviations from the securities market line, *gross* of expenses, is used as a predictor for the deviation in the subsequent year. For $1 \leq k \leq 4$, where sample sizes are large, the predictor does better than average but, it was claimed, not significantly better. The computed significance level was based on the supposition of cross-sectional independence. Some doubt remains about the actual level of statistical significance.

Based on these facts, might it still be rational for investors to incur positive management costs to achieve a portfolio on or close to the objective ex ante efficient frontier? No direct evidence has appeared to indicate that some portfolio selectors do indeed have ability; but there seems to be plenty of indirect

---

[13] Note that the observed return vector is cross-sectionally dependent unless the population covariance matrix is diagonal. Furthermore, portfolios would be cross-sectionally dependent even if individual assets were not.

[14] In Roll [1977b] the econometric problems of testing a given portfolio's efficiency are discussed in more detail.

evidence: the continued existence of professional money managers. The existence of managers who collect fees would itself be a violation of the theory of efficient markets if publicly-available information implied that no fees need be expended to select an optimal portfolio. If index funds were optimal, the aggregate market value for the portfolio advisory industry would be zero. Clearly, the market wage per advisor does not contain all relevant information (or does it?)

IV. CHANGING-COMPOSITION PORTFOLIOS

As the portfolio contest is repeated, players are allowed to select different portfolios during each trial or series of trials. This mimics real-world portfolio managers, who seem inclined to alter their portfolios' compositions rather frequently. Does the very fact that selected portfolios change composition over time have any implications for the conclusions drawn so far?

In looking into this question, it will be convenient to distinguish two cases. First, the case of stationarity in which the true objective (and perhaps unknown) ex ante mean return vector and covariance matrix are constant. If we denote these parameters by R_t^* and V_t^*, then we require $R_t^* = R_\tau^*$, $V_t^* = V_\tau$ for all t and τ. In this case, none of the conclusions can possibly be altered.

For example, suppose that an index is employed which is mean/variance efficient with respect to R_t^* and V_t^*. (It is on the ex ante objective efficient frontier.) Then the deviations of every individual asset about the securities market line will be zero ex ante and zero on average ex post. The manager can change compositions as often as he likes, but since every asset is neither a consistent winner nor loser, *no* portfolio of assets that he selects can *significantly* win or lose in any trial. It follows that changing compositions cannot matter for assessing ability.[15]

Similarly, if the index is inefficient (with respect to R_t^* and V_t^*), the manager can consistently "win." As we have seen, he can do so even with a constant composition portfolio. But since "winning" with respect to the securities market line does not imply selection ability (or vice versa) again the fact of changing composition does not alter the basic conclusion that the criterion cannot distinguish good managers from bad ones.

The second case of non-stationarity is probably the situation most people have in mind when they think of the manager possibly "outperforming" the index by altering his portfolio's composition over time. The intuitive notion seems to be that a manager might not do well if he is required to pick a port-

---

[15] Changing compositions will matter, however, for the appropriate statistical test to use in determining whether the index is significantly nonefficient ex post. The statistical sampling portfolios change compositions within the sample period.

folio and stick with it but that he might be able to predict when general market conditions are going to turn out more or less favorably than normal. Alternatively he might have privileged information about certain assets during some periods.

The intuition is certainly correct in the sense that clairvoyance of one kind or another will yield "superior" performance. The question here, however, is whether that superiority can be *detected* by the securities market line. Imagine that the objective ex ante mean return vector and covariance matrix R_t^* and V_t^* are not constant, but depend on t. In addition, suppose that the manager knows their time paths perfectly. Each period, he selects an ex ante mean/variance efficient portfolio with respect to the R_t^* and V_t^* prevailing at that time. Suppose also that the index used to assess his performance has a constant composition. It may have been ex ante mean/variance efficient for some period, say against R_t^* and V_t^*, but it need not be ex ante efficient at every period. In fact, there may be no constant composition portfolio which is efficient for all t.

The sample observed covariance matrix and mean return vector, $\hat{V}$ and $\hat{R}$, are convolutions of the sequences $\{V_1^*, \ldots, V_T^*\}$ and $\{R_1^*, \ldots, R_T^*\}$ actually followed by the objective parameters during the sample, (which covers, say, periods 1 to T). Thus, with respect to the sample, the manager's portfolio may turn out to be either above or below the securities market line since the index is mean/variance inefficient, and statistically significantly inefficient. Needless to say, another manager who does not know the sequences $\{V^*\}$ and $\{R^*\}$, and thus may have selected an inefficient portfolio, can find his "performance" rated highly by the securities market line, and higher than the manager with perfect information.

Finally, an index could conceivably be ex ante mean/variance efficient with respect to every V_t^* and R_t^* even though it has constant composition. The index might also remain efficient because it changes composition along a simple path which happens to match the paths $\{V^*\}$ and $\{R^*\}$. For example a buy-and-hold index, (not rebalanced), would be a feasible choice for many investors because it is even easier to monitor than a constant composition index. In either case, investors would not need to pay for the services of professional portfolio managers if the index were always efficient. If a simple index possesses mean/variance efficiency, no portfolio manager could be found who consistently placed a portfolio above or below the securities market line in repeated samples. This lack of consistency would constitute evidence that the index itself is efficient with respect to the sequences $\{V^*\}$ and $\{R^*\}$. However, it would constitute no information about the efficiency of the selected portfolios. Selected portfolios which were also mean/variance efficient with respect to $\{V^*\}$ and $\{R^*\}$ *and* selected portfolios which were not efficient would both show no consistency in their positions with respect to the securities market line.

Of course, if the scenario above described the state of nature, investors would be advised to select the simple index and pocket the management fees. We have not yet determined empirically, however, whether the scenario contains even the slightest element of realism.

V. THE SECURITIES MARKET LINE AND THE RETURN GENERATING PROCESS: RESOLUTION OF A PARADOX[16]

This paper has presented some negative aspects of the securities market line as a performance measuring device. Yet the theory of portfolio diversification and the concept of "beta" ($\beta_{jp} = \sigma_{jp}/\sigma_p^2$) as a systematic risk measure constitute a pervasive paradigm among financial economists. Is the paradigm without merit? I hope to argue persuasively in this section that the paradigm has some merit but that the usual implementation of the paradigm leads to the problems discussed in the preceding sections.

The argument is: when discussing the securities market line and beta, most people are actually thinking intuitively about a one-factor linear return generating process of the form

$$R_{jt} = \alpha_j + \rho + \beta_j(R_{Gt} - \rho) + \zeta_{jt}; j = 1, \dots N \qquad (10)$$

The t subscript indicates time period; ζ_{jt} is a stochastic error with zero mean and is unrelated to R_G or to $\zeta_{i\tau}$ for $i \neq j$ or $t \neq \tau$; R_{Gt} is a common generating factor and ρ is a constant across assets.

Process (10) looks similar to a securities market line. Indeed, by taking expectations of both sides of (10), a system of equations is obtained which is indistinguishable from (4) with $\gamma_0 = \rho$ and $\gamma_1 = E(R_{Gt} - \rho)$. However, it is a mistake to interpret the expection of (10) as a securities market line because G is not a portfolio. Instead, G is the *unique* source of common variation in the ensemble of asset returns. This seemingly innocuous distinction is actually critical.

The interpretation usually given to deviations about the securities market line is validly applicable to the deviations, (α_j's), about the return generating process (10).[17] As Ross [1976] showed in the development of his theory of asset pricing, a riskless profit can be obtained when there is at least one asset j for which α_j is not zero, provided that (10) describes the return generating process and that there exists a "sufficiently" large number of individual assets. Furthermore, the hedge portfolio formed to obtain this profit should contain long positions in securities with positive α_j's. Clearly α_j in (10) could be interpreted as an ex ante measure of an asset's desirability and ex post as a measure of performance.

But a problem arises because G is not necessarily observable and because

---

[16] I am greatly indebted to Stephen A. Ross for many conversations about the material in this section.
[17] This argument is presented in a somewhat different form by Mayers and Rice [1977].

replacing G by some portfolio index can result in the problems described earlier in this paper. For example, suppose that there are truly some non-zero α_j's in (10). In this case, a riskless profit is possible. But the portfolio used to replace G might be mean/variance efficient. As S3 shows, the "betas" computed against this index would be exactly linear in the mean returns. Of course, these computed betas would not be equal in value to the slope coefficients in the generating process (10).

Alternatively, the selected index might not be mean/variance efficient. However, the $\hat{\alpha}_j$'s it produces would be equal in value to the α_j's of (10) if and only if the index is perfectly positively correlated with G. One would be fortunate indeed to happen upon such a perfect index. As we have seen, imperfect correlation could cause the computed performance measures to be of different magnitudes and even of opposite sign from the α_j's of (10). Incorrect inferences about performance would thereby be obtained.

The same problems arise when there are no available arbitrage profits. In this case, all the true α_j's in (10) are zero. Furthermore, G *does* have the same mean and variance as some mean/variance efficient portfolio. But if the index employed is not efficient, non-zero $\hat{\alpha}_j$'s will be found and non-neutral performance will be falsely indicated.

The analytic components of the problem can be examined by selecting an index, say with investment proportions vector X_I, and then using it as a replacement for G. From (10), the index' return is

$$R_{It} = X_I'R_t = X_I'[\alpha + \rho + \beta(R_{Gt} - \rho) + \zeta_t]$$

where the absence of j subscript indicates an $N \times 1$ column vector. Thus,

$$R_{It} = \alpha_I + \rho + \beta_I(R_{Gt} - \rho) + \zeta_{It} \tag{11}$$

Solving (11) for $R_{Gt} - \rho$ and substituting back into (10), we have

$$R_{jt} = \alpha_j - \frac{\beta_j}{\beta_I}\alpha_I + \rho + \frac{\beta_j}{\beta_I}(R_{It} - \rho) + \zeta_{jt} - \frac{\beta_j}{\beta_I}\zeta_{It} \quad j = 1, \ldots N \tag{12}$$

Equation (12) is now in a form similar to the true generating process, but with the common factor, R_G, replaced by the return on the operational index, R_I. We can observe that there are basically two differences between (12) and (10) and these must be responsible for the problems encountered previously.

First, the index may be imperfectly diversified; i.e., ζ_{It} may not be identically zero in every period. This is basically an econometric problem which will cause mis-estimation of the slope and intercept of (12). Conceivably, it alone could result in incorrect measures of performance. Second, the index may have its own non-zero deviation α_I about the true generating process. If there are arbitrage opportunities, there would be no a priori reason that $\alpha_I = X_I'\alpha$ should be zero. Unfortunately, if α_I is non-zero, the performance measure for asset or portfolio j becomes $\alpha_j - \alpha_I(\beta_j/\beta_I)$. Since it depends now also on β_j, assets with large slope coefficients in the true process (10) will have positively (negatively) biased performance as the true but unknowable performance of the index is itself negative (positive).

If and only if the index has no residual variation (is perfectly correlated with the common factor), *and has exactly neutral performance* ex post will the observed securities market line generate the same performance measures as the true generating process. In this unlikely circumstance, $\zeta_{It} \equiv 0$ and $\alpha_I = 0$ and thus

$$R_{jt} = \alpha_j + \rho + (\beta_j/\beta_I)(R_{It} - \rho) + \zeta_{jt}, \quad j = 1, \ldots N \qquad (13)$$

Of course, we have no way to ascertain, either ex ante or for a given sample, whether such conditions are satisfied.

Finally, there remains the possibility that (10) is false and that more than a single common factor affects asset returns. Using a single index securities market line when the true process contains several factors will give incorrect measures of performance. For example, riskless and profitable hedge portfolios may be completely unavailable. Yet a single index that is perfectly diversified in the sense of exact linear dependence on the factors will not be mean/variance efficient. It will, therefore, indicate the presence of non-zero deviations about a computed securities market line.

APPENDIX

ALTERATION IN MEASURED BETA WITH CHANGES IN THE INDEX

As an illustration of some possible beta pitfalls, consider changing the index against which beta is computed while retaining the index' position *on* the mean/variance efficient frontier. There is a functional relation between β_{jp} for individual asset j and the mean return r_p on a mean/variance efficient portfolio p.[18] As illustrated in Figure 3, the relation is nonmonotonic and has a unique maximum and minimum. It follows that a β_{ip} for asset i can be increasing with respect to a movement along the efficient set (a change in the efficient index) while $\beta_{jp}(j \neq i)$ is at the same time decreasing. In particular, if we begin at the global minimum variance portfolio, all β's are equal to 1.0. Then moving upward toward higher efficient mean returns, some β's will decrease and some will increase, and for those that move in the same direction, the rates of change will generally differ.

The individual asset's *weight* in the efficient portfolio changes monotonically along the efficient frontier.[19] If the weight decreases (increases) at any point, it decreases (increases) at all points. Suppose it increases with the return. Then

[18] The function is derived in Roll [1977, pp. 169–171].
[19] For a proof of this assertion, see Roll [1977, pp. 168–169].

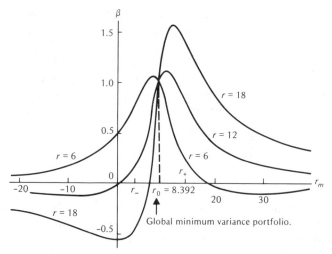

FIGURE 3.   The variation of individual betas according to the efficient portfolio used in their calculation. The numbers used to construct this figure were obtained from Black, Jensen, and Scholes [1972]. Using a method described in Roll [1977], the equation of the ex post efficient set was estimated as $\sigma_p^2 = 7993 - 1398r_p + 83.3r_p^2$, where returns are measured in percent per annum. Movements along this equation were then linked to changes in the betas of three illustrative securities, with mean returns of 6., 12., and 18. percent per annum. Points $r+$ and $r-$ indicate the returns of efficient portfolios which maximized the cross-sectional variance of all individual betas. See Roll [1977, p. 170].

it represents an ever larger proportion of efficient portfolios as we move upward in return. And yet, its beta will decrease after a certain point, which should mean, given the usual interpretation, that its "contribution" toward the portfolio's total risk declines. The variance of the efficient index grows without limit as its return increases, yet the betas of *all* individual assets converge to zero. See Figure 3.

There is only one point of intersection for the betas of all assets—at the global minimum variance portfolio, r_0 as shown in Figure 3. This implies that betas give an unambiguous ranking of assets which is the same for all efficient portfolios with return larger than r_0. (It is reversed for portfolios below r_0.) Thus, β has a desirable property which admits the following interpretation: "If for any mean/variance efficient index I with $r_I > r_0$ a given pair of individual securities has $\beta_{iI} > \beta_{jI}$ then $\beta_{ip} > \beta_{jp}$ for all p with $r_p > r_0$. Unfortunately, no similar statement is true for non-efficient indices.

REFERENCES

1. Fischer Black. "Capital Market Equilibrium with Restricted Borrowing," *Journal of Business,* 45 (July 1972), pp. 444–454.

2. ———, Michael C. Jensen, and Myron Scholes. "The Capital Asset Pricing Model: Some Empirical Tests," in M. C. Jensen, ed., *Studies in the Theory of Capital Markets.* (New York: Praeger, 1972).

3. Irwin Friend and Marshall Blume. "Measurement of Portfolio Performance under Uncertainty," *American Economic Review,* 60 (September 1970), pp. 561–575.

4. Michael C. Jensen. "The Performance of Mutual Funds in the Period 1945–1964," *Journal of Finance,* 23 (May 1968), pp. 389–416.

5. ———. "Risk, the Pricing of Capital Assets, and the Evaluation of Investment Portfolios," *Journal of Business,* 62 (April 1969), pp. 167–247.

6. John Lintner. "The Valuation of Risk Assets and the Selection of Risky Investments in Stock Portfolios and Capital Budgets," *Review of Economics and Statistics,* 47 (February 1965), pp. 13–37.

7. Harry M. Markowitz. *Portfolio Selection: Efficient Diversification of Investments,* New York: John Wiley and Sons, Inc., 1959.

8. David Mayers and Edward M. Rice. "The Securities Market Line as a Benchmark for Portfolio Performance," UCLA Working Paper, August, 1977.

9. Robert C. Merton. "An Analytic Derivation of the Efficient Portfolio Frontier," *Journal of Financial and Quantitative Analysis,* 7, (September 1972), pp. 1850–1872.

10. Richard Roll. "A Critique of the Asset Pricing Theory's Tests," *Journal of Financial Economics,* 4 (March 1977), pp. 129–176.

11. ———. "Testing a Portfolio for Ex Ante Mean/Variance Efficiency," Working Paper, UCLA, March, 1977.

12. Stephen A. Ross. "Portfolios and Capital Market Theory with Arbitrary Preferences and Distributions—the General Validity of the Mean-Variance Approach in Large Markets," Working Paper 12-72, Rodney L. White Center for Financial Research, University of Pennsylvania, 1972.

13. ———. "The Arbitrage Theory of Asset Pricing," *Journal of Economic Theory,* 13, (Dec. 1976), pp. 341–360.

14. William F. Sharpe. "Capital Asset Prices: A Theory of Market Equilibrium Under Conditions of Risk," *Journal of Finance,* 19 (September 1964), pp. 425–442.

15. ———. *Portfolio Theory and Capital Markets* (New York: McGraw-Hill, 1970).

12. AN EMPIRICAL INVESTIGATION OF THE ARBITRAGE PRICING THEORY

RICHARD ROLL and STEPHEN A. ROSS

Reprinted from *The Journal of Finance,* Vol. XXXV, No. 5 (December 1980), pp. 1073–1103, by permission of the authors and the publisher.

Empirical tests are reported for Ross' [48] arbitrage theory of asset pricing. Using data for individual equities during the 1962–72 period, at least three and probably four "priced" factors are found in the generating process of returns. The theory is supported in that estimated expected returns depend on estimated factor loadings, and variables such as the "own" standard deviation, though highly correlated (simply) with estimated expected returns, do not add any further explanatory power to that of the factor loadings.

THE ARBITRAGE PRICING THEORY (APT) formulated by Ross [48] offers a testable alternative to the well-known capital asset pricing model (CAPM) introduced by Sharpe [51], Lintner [30] and Mossin [38]. Although the CAPM has been predominant in empirical work over the past fifteen years and is the basis of modern portfolio theory, accumulating research has increasingly cast doubt on its ability to explain the empirical constellation of asset returns.

More than a modest level of disenchantment with the CAPM is evidenced by the number of related but different theories, e.g., Hakansson [18], Mayers [34], Merton [35], Kraus and Litzenberger [23]; by anomalous empirical evidence, e.g., Ball [2], Basu [4], Reinganum [40]; and by questioning of the CAPM's viability as a scientific theory, e.g., Roll [41]. Nonetheless, the CAPM retains a central place in the thoughts of academic scholars and of finance practitioners such as portfolio managers, investment advisors, and security analysts.

There is good reason for its durability: it is compatible with the single most widely-acknowledged empirical regularity in asset returns, their common variability. Apparently, intuition readily ascribes such common variation to a single factor which, with a random disturbance, generates returns for each individual asset via some (linear) functional relationship. Oddly, though, this intuition is wholly divorced from the formal CAPM theory. To the contrary, elegant deriva-

Graduate School of Management, University of California, Los Angeles, and School of Organization and Management, Yale University, respectively.

tions of the CAPM equation have been concocted beginning from the first principles of utility theory; but the model's popularity is not due to such analyses, for they make all too obvious the assumptions required for the CAPM's validity and make no use of the common variability of returns. A review of recent finance texts (e.g., Van Horne, [54, pp. 57–63]) reveals that rationalizations of the CAPM are based instead on the dichotomy between diversifiable and non-diversifiable risk, a distinction which refers to a linear generating process, not to the CAPM derived from utility theory.

The APT is a particularly appropriate alternative because it agrees perfectly with what appears to be the intuition behind the CAPM. Indeed, the APT is based on a linear return generating process *as a first principle*, and requires no utility assumptions beyond monotonicity and concavity. Nor is it restricted to a single period; it will hold in both the multiperiod and single period cases. Though consistent with every conceivable prescription for portfolio diversification, no particular portfolio plays a role in the APT. Unlike the CAPM, there is no requirement that the market portfolio be mean variance efficient.

There are two major differences between the APT and the original Sharpe [50] "diagonal" model, a single factor generating model which we believe is the intuitive grey eminence behind the CAPM. First, and most simply, the APT allows more than just one generating factor. Second, the APT demonstrates that since any market equilibrium must be consistent with no arbitrage profits, every equilibrium will be characterized by a linear relationship between each asset's expected return and its return's response amplitudes, or loadings, on the common factors. With minor caveats, given the factor generating model, the absence of riskless arbitrage profits—an easy enough condition to accept a priori—leads immediately to the APT. Its modest assumptions and its pleasing implications surely render the APT worthy of being the object of empirical testing.

To our knowledge, though, there has so far been just one published empirical study of the APT, by Gehr [17]. He began with a procedure similar to the one reported here. We can claim to have extended Gehr's analysis with a more comprehensive set of data (he used 24 industry indices and 41 individual stocks) and to have carried the analysis farther—to a stage actually required if the tests are to be definitive. Nonetheless, Gehr's paper is well worth reading and it must be given precedence as the first empirical work directly on this subject.

Another empirical study related to the APT is an early paper by Brennan [6], which is unfortunately still unpublished. Brennan's approach was to decompose the residuals from a market model regression. He found two factors present in the residuals and concluded that "the true return generating process must be represented by at least a two factor model rather than by the single factor diagonal model" (p. 30). Writing before the APT, Brennan saw clearly that "it is not possible to devise cross-sectional tests of the Capital Asset Pricing Model, since only in the case of a single factor model is it possible to relate *ex ante* and *ex post* returns" (p. 34). Of course, the APT's empirical usefulness rests precisely in its ability to permit such cross-sectional tests whether there is one factor or many.

The possibility of multiple generating factors was recognized long ago. Farrar

[15] and King [22], for example, employed factor analytic methods. Their work focused on industry influences and was pure (and very worthwhile) empiricism. Since the APT was not available to predict the cross-sectional effects of industry factors on expected returns, no tests were conducted for the presence of such effects.

More recently, Rosenberg and Marathe [44] have analyzed what they term "extra-market" components of return. They find unequivocal empirical support for the presence of such components. Rosenberg and Marathe's work employs extraneous "descriptor variables" to predict intertemporal changes in the CAPM's parameters. They state that "the appropriateness of the multiple-factor model of security returns, with loadings equal to predetermined descriptors, as opposed to a single-factor or market model, is conclusively demonstrated" (p. 100). But, they do not ascertain the *separate* influences of these multiple factors on individual expected returns, and focus instead on a combined influence working through the market portfolio. In other words, they assume the CAPM and decompose the single market beta into its constitutent parts.

Regarding the market portfolio as a construct which captures the influences of many factors follows the theoretical ideas in Rosenberg [45] and Sharpe [52]. Thus, Rosenberg and Marathe's work does not provide a definitive test of the APT.

There are a number of other recent papers which are more or less related to this one. In particular, Langetieg [25], Lee and Vinso [28], and Meyers [36] contain evidence of more than just a single market factor influencing returns. In contrast, Kryzanowski and To [24] give a formal test for the presence of additional factors but find "that only the first factor is non-trivial" (p. 23).

Nevertheless, there seems to be enough evidence in past empirical work to conclude that there may exist multiple factors in the returns generating processes of assets. The APT provides a solid theoretical framework for ascertaining whether those factors, if they exist, are "priced," i.e., are associated with risk premia. The purpose of our paper is to use the APT framework to investigate both the existence and the pricing questions.

In the following section, (I), a more complete discussion of the unique testable features of the APT is provided. Then section II gives our basic tests. It concludes that three factors are definitely present in the "prices" (actually in the expected returns) of equities traded on the New York and American Exchanges. A fourth factor may be present also but the evidence there is less conclusive.

Sections III and IV present two additional tests of the APT. The most important and powerful is in section III, where the APT is compared against a specific alternative hypothesis that "own" variance influences expected returns. If the APT is true, the "own" variance should not be important, even though its sample value is known to be highly correlated cross-sectionally with sample mean returns. We find that the "own" variance's sample influence arises spuriously from skewness in the returns distribution.

In section IV, we present a test of the consistency of the APT across groups of assets. Although the power of this test is probably weak, it gives no indication whatsoever of differences among groups.

Our conclusion is that the APT performs well under empirical scrutiny and that it should be considered a reasonable model for explaining the cross-sectional variation in average asset returns.

I. The APT and its Testability

A. The APT

This section outlines the APT in a fashion that makes it suitable for empirical work. A detailed development of theory is presented in Ross [47, 48] and the intent here is to highlight those conclusions of the theory which are tested in subsequent sections.

The theory begins with the traditional neoclassical assumptions of perfectly competitive and frictionless asset markets. Just as the CAPM is derived from the assumption that random asset returns follow a multivariate normal distribution, the APT also begins with an assumption on the return generating process. Individuals are assumed to believe (homogeneously) that the random returns on the set of assets being considered are governed by a k-factor generating model of the form:

$$\tilde{r}_i = E_i + b_{i1}\tilde{\delta}_1 + \cdots + b_{ik}\tilde{\delta}_k + \tilde{\epsilon}_i,$$

$$i = 1, \cdots, n. \tag{1}$$

The first term in (1), E_i, is the expected return on the ith asset. The next k terms are of the form $b_{ij}\tilde{\delta}_j$ where $\tilde{\delta}_j$ denotes the mean zero j^{th} factor common to the returns of all assets under consideration. The coefficient b_{ij} quantifies the sensitivity of asset i's returns to the movements in the common factor $\tilde{\delta}_j$. The common factors capture the systematic components of risk in the model. The final term, $\tilde{\epsilon}_i$, is a noise term, i.e., an unsystematic risk component, idiosyncratic to the ith asset. It is assumed to reflect the random influence of information that is unrelated to other assets. In keeping with this assumption, we also have that

$$E\{\tilde{\epsilon}_i \,|\, \tilde{\delta}_j\} = 0,$$

and that $\tilde{\epsilon}_i$ is (quite) independent of $\tilde{\epsilon}_j$ for all i and j. Too strong a dependence in the $\tilde{\epsilon}_i$'s would be like saying that there are more than simply the k hypothesized common factors. Finally, we assume for the set of n assets under consideration, that n is much greater than the number of factors, k.

Before developing the theory, it is worth pausing to examine (1) in a bit more detail. The assumption of a k-factor generating model is very similar in spirit to a restriction on the Arrow-Debreu tableau that displays the returns on the assets in different states of nature. If the $\tilde{\epsilon}_i$ terms were omitted, then (1) would say that each asset i has returns r_i that are an exact linear combination of the returns on a riskless asset (with identical return in each state) and the returns on k other factors or assets or column vectors, $\delta_1, \cdots, \delta_k$. In such a setting, the riskless return and each of the k factors can be expressed as a linear combination of $k + 1$ other returns, say r_1 through r_{k+1}. Any other asset's return, since it is a linear combination of the factors, must also be a linear combination of the first $k + 1$

assets' returns. And thus, portfolios of the first $k + 1$ assets are perfect substitutes for all other assets in the market. Since perfect substitutes must be priced equally, there must be restrictions on the individual returns generated by the model. This is the core of the APT: there are only a few systematic components of risk existing in nature. As a consequence, many portfolios are close substitutes and as such, they must have the same value.

What are the common or systematic factors? This question is equivalent to asking what causes the particular values of covariance terms in the CAPM. If there are only a few systematic components of risk, one would expect these to be related to fundamental economic aggregates, such as GNP, or to interest rates or weather (although no causality is implied by such relations). The factor model formalism suggests that a whole theoretical and empirical structure must be explored to better understand what economic forces actually affect returns systematically. But in testing the APT, it is no more appropriate for us to examine this issue than it would be for tests of the CAPM to examine what, if anything, causes returns to be multivariate normal. In both instances, the return generating process is taken as one of the primitive assumptions of the theory. We do consider the basic underlying causes of the generating process of returns to be a potentially important area of research, but we think it is an area that can be investigated separately from testing asset pricing theories.

Now let us develop the APT itself from the return generating process (1). Consider an individual who is currently holding a portfolio and is contemplating an alteration of his portfolio. Any new portfolio will differ from the old portfolio by investment proportions x_i $(i = 1, \cdots, m)$, which is the dollar amount purchased or sold of asset i as a fraction of total invested wealth. The sum of the x_i proportions,

$$\sum_i x_i = 0,$$

since the new portfolio and the old portfolio put the same wealth into the n assets. In other words, additional purchases of assets must be financed by sales of others. Portfolios that use no wealth such as $\underline{x} \equiv (x_1, \cdots x_n)^1$ are called arbitrage portfolios.

In deciding whether or not to alter his current holdings, an individual will examine all the available arbitrage portfolios. The additional return obtainable from altering the current portfolio by n is given by

$$\underline{x\bar{r}} \equiv \sum_i x_i\bar{r}_i$$

$$= (\sum_i x_iE_i) + (\sum_i x_ib_{i1})\delta_1 + \cdots + (\sum_i x_ib_{ik})\delta_k + \sum_i x_i\bar{\epsilon}_i$$

$$\equiv \underline{xE} + (\underline{xb_1})\delta_1 + \cdots + (\underline{xb_k})\delta_k + \underline{x\bar{\epsilon}}.$$

Consider the arbitrage portfolio chosen in the following fashion. First, we will keep each element, x_i, of order $1/n$ in size; i.e., we will choose the arbitrage portfolio $\underline{x}$ to be well diversified. Second, we will choose $\underline{x}$ in such a way that it

---

[1] An underscored symbol indicates a vector or matrix.

has no systematic risk; i.e., for each j

$$\underline{x}b_j \equiv \sum_i x_i b_{ij} = 0.$$

Any such arbitrage portfolio, $\underline{x}$, will have returns of

$$
\begin{aligned}
\underline{x}\tilde{r} &= (\underline{x}E) + (\underline{x}\underline{b_1})\tilde{\delta}_1 + \cdots + (\underline{x}\underline{b_k})\tilde{\delta}_k + (\underline{x}\tilde{\epsilon}\,) \\
&\approx \underline{x}E + (\underline{x}\underline{b_1})\tilde{\delta}_1 + \cdots + (\underline{x}\underline{b_k})\tilde{\delta}_k \\
&= \underline{x}E.
\end{aligned}
$$

The term $(\underline{x}\tilde{\epsilon})$ is (approximately) eliminated by applying the law of large numbers. For example, if σ^2 denotes the average variance of the $\tilde{\epsilon}_i$ terms, and if, for simplicity, each x_i exactly equals $\pm 1/n$, then

$$
\begin{aligned}
\mathrm{Var}(\underline{x}\tilde{\epsilon}) &= \mathrm{Var}(1/n \sum_i \tilde{\epsilon}_i) \\
&= [\mathrm{Var}(\tilde{\epsilon}_i)]/n^2 \\
&= \sigma^2/n,
\end{aligned}
$$

where we have assumed that the ϵ_i are mutually independent. It follows that for large numbers of assets, the variance of $\underline{x}\tilde{\epsilon}$ will be negligible, and we can diversify away the unsystematic risk.

Recapitulating, we have shown that it is possible to choose arbitrage portfolios with neither systematic *nor* unsystematic risk terms! If the individual is in equilibrium and is content with his current portfolio, we must also have $\overline{\underline{x}E} = 0$. No portfolio is an equilibrium (held) portfolio if it can be improved upon without incurring additional risk or committing additional resources.

To put the matter somewhat differently, in equilibrium all portfolios of these n assets which satisfy the conditions of using no wealth and having no risk must also earn no return on average.

The above conditions are really statements in linear algebra. Any vector, $\underline{x}$, which is orthogonal to the constant vector and to each of the coefficient vectors, $\underline{b_j}(j = 1, \cdots, k)$, must also be orthogonal to the vector of expected returns. An algebraic consequence of this statement is that the expected return vector, $\underline{E}$, must be a linear combination of the constant vector and the $\underline{b_j}$ vectors. In algebraic terms, there exist $k + 1$ weights, $\lambda_0, \lambda_1, \cdots, \lambda_k$ such that

$$E_i = \lambda_0 + \lambda_1 b_{i1} + \cdots + \lambda_k b_{ik}, \qquad \text{for all } i. \tag{2}$$

If there is a riskless asset with return, E_0, then $b_{0j} = 0$ and

$$E_0 = \lambda_0,$$

hence we will write

$$E_i - E_0 = \lambda_1 b_{i1} + \cdots + \lambda_k b_{ik},$$

with the understanding that E_0 is the riskless rate of return if such an asset exists, and is the common return on all "zero-beta" assets, i.e., assets with $b_{ij} = 0$, for all j, whether or not a riskless asset exists.

If there is a single factor, then the APT pricing relationship is a line in expected return, E_i, systematic risk, b_i, space:

$$E_i - E_0 = \lambda b_i.$$

Figure 1 can be used to illustrate our argument geometrically. Suppose, for example, that assets 1, 2, and 3 are presently held in positive amounts in some portfolio and that asset 2 is above the line connecting assets 1 and 3. Then a portfolio of 1 and 3 could be constructed with the same systematic risk as asset 2, but with a lower expected return. By selling assets 1 and 3 in the proportions they represent of the initial portfolio and buying more of asset 2 with the proceeds, a new position would be created with the same overall risk and a greater return. Such arbitrage opportunities will be unavailable *only* when assets lie along a line. Notice that the intercept on the expected return axis would be E_0 when no arbitrage opportunities are present.

The pricing relationship (2) is the central conclusion of the APT and it will be the cornerstone of our empirical testing, but it is natural to ask what interpretation can be given to the λ_j factor risk premia. By forming portfolios with unit systematic risk on each factor and no risk on other factors, each λ_j can be interpreted as

$$\lambda_j = E^j - E_0,$$

the excess return or market risk premium on portfolios with only systematic factor j risk. Then (2) can be rewritten as,

$$E_i - E_0 = (E^1 - E_0)b_{i1} + \cdots + (E^k - E_0)b_{ik}. \tag{3}$$

Is the "market portfolio" one such systematic risk factor? As a well diversified portfolio, indeed a convex combination of diversified portfolios, the market

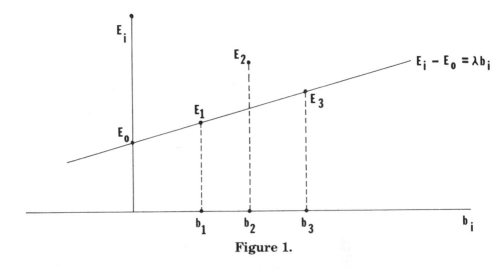

Figure 1.

portfolio probably should not possess much idiosyncratic risk. Thus, it might serve as a substitute for one of the factors. Furthermore, individual asset b's calculated against the market portfolio would enter the pricing relationship and the excess return on the market would be the weight on these b's. But, it is important to understand that *any* well-diversified portfolio could serve the same function and that, in general, k well-diversified portfolios could be found that approximate the k factors *better* than any single market index. In general, the market portfolio plays no special role whatsoever in the APT, unlike its pivotal role in the CAPM, (Cf. Roll [41, 42] and Ross [49]).

The lack of a special role in the APT for the market portfolios is particularly important. As we have seen, the APT pricing relationship was derived by considering any set of n assets which followed the generating process (1). In the CAPM, it is crucial to both the theory and the testing that all of the universe of available assets be included in the measured market portfolio. By contrast, the APT yields a statement of relative pricing on subsets of the universe of assets. As a consequence, the APT can, in principle, be tested by examining only subsets of the set of all returns. We think that in many discussions of the CAPM, scholars were actually thinking intuitively of the APT and of process (1) with just a single factor. Problems of identifying that factor and testing for others were not considered important.

To obtain a more precise understanding of the factor risk premia, $E^j - E_0$, in (3), it is useful to specialize the APT theory to an explicit stochastic environment within which individual equilibrium is achieved. Since the APT is valid in intertemporal as well as static settings and in discrete as well as in continuous time, the choice of stochastic models is one of convenience alone. The only critical assumption is the returns be generated by (1) over the shortest trading period.

A particularly convenient specialization is to a rational anticipations intertemporal diffusion model. (See Cox, Ingersoll and Ross [8] for a more elaborate version of such a model and for the relevant literature references.) Suppose there are k exogenous, independent (without loss of generality) factors, s^j, which follow a multivariate diffusion process and whose current values are sufficient statistics to determine the current state of the economy. As a consequence, the current price, p_i, of each asset i will be a function only of $\underline{s} = (s^1, \cdots, s^k)$ and the particular fixed contractual conditions which define that asset in the next differential time unit. Similarly the random return, dr_i, on asset i will depend on the random movements of the factors. By the diffusion assumption we can write

$$d\tilde{r}_i = E_i \, dt + b_{i1} \, d\tilde{s}^1 + \cdots + b_{ik} \, d\tilde{s}^k. \tag{4}$$

It follows immediately that the conditions of the APT are satisfied exactly—with $d\tilde{\epsilon}_i = 0$ and the APT pricing relationship (3) must hold exactly to prevent arbitrage. In this setting, however, we can go further and examine the premia, $E^j - E_0$, themselves.

If individuals in this economy are solving consumption withdrawal problems, then the current utility of future consumption, e.g., the discounted expected value of the utility of future consumption, V, will be a function only of the individual's current wealth, w, and the current state of nature, $\underline{s}$. The individual will optimize by choosing a consumption withdrawal plan, c, and an optimal portfolio choice, $\underset{\sim}{x}$, so as to maximize the expected increment in V; i.e.,

$$\max_{\underset{\sim}{x}, c} E\{dV\}.$$

At an optimum, consumption will be withdrawn to the point where its marginal utility equals the marginal utility of wealth,

$$u'(c) = V_w.$$

The individual portfolio choice will result from the optimization of a locally quadratic form exactly as in the static CAPM theory with the additional feature that covariances of the change in wealth, $d\bar{w}$, with the changes in state variables, ds^i, will now be influenced by portfolio choice and will, in general, alter the optimal portfolio. By solving this optimization problem and using the marginal utility condition, $u'(c) = V_w$, the individual equilibrium sets factor risk premia equal to

$$E^j - E_0 = (R/c)(\partial c/\partial s^j)\sigma_j^2;$$

where $R = -(wV_{ww})/V_w$, the individual coefficient of relative risk aversion and σ_j^2 is the local variance of (independent) factor s_j. (The interested reader is referred to Cox, Ingersoll and Ross [8] for details.) Notice that the premia $E^j - E_0$ can be negative if consumption moves counter to the state variable. In this case portfolios which bear positive factor s^j risk hedge against adverse movements in consumption, but too much can be made of this, since by simply redefining s^j to be $-s^j$ the sign can be reversed. The sign, therefore, is somewhat arbitrary and we will assume it is normalized to be positive. Aggregating over individuals yields (3).

One special case of particular interest occurs when state dependencies can be ignored. In the log case, $R = 1$, for example, or any case with a relative wealth criteria (see Ross [48]) the risk premia take the special form

$$E^j - E_0 = R\left(\sum_i x_i b_{ij}\right)\sigma_j^2$$

where $\underset{\sim}{x}$ is the individual optimal portfolio. This form emphasizes the general relationship between b_j and σ_j^2. Normalizing $\sum_i x_i b_{ij}$ to unity by scaling s^j, we have

$$E^j - E_0 = R\sigma_j^2.$$

The risk premium of factor j is proportional to its variance and the constant of proportionality is a measure of relative risk aversion.

For other utility functions, individual consumption vectors can be expressed in terms of portfolios of returns and similar expressions can be obtained. In effect, since the weighted state consumption elasticities for all individuals satisfy the APT pricing relationships, they must all be proportional.[2]

---

[2] Breeden [5] has developed the observation that homogenous beliefs about E's and b's imply perfect correlation between individual random consumption changes. His results depend on the assumption, made also by APT, that $k < N$.

The risk premium can be written in general as

$$E^j - E_0 = \left[\sum_l w_l R_l \left(\frac{1}{c_l}\right) \frac{\partial c_l}{\partial s_j} \right] \sigma_j^2$$

where l indexes individual agents, w_l is the proportion of total wealth held by agent l, R_l is his coefficient of relative risk aversion, $-\dfrac{1}{c_l} \dfrac{\partial c_l}{\partial s_j}$ is the partial elasticity of his consumption with respect to changes in the jth factor, and σ_j^2 is the variance of the jth factor. Not very much is known about the term in parentheses and, all other things being equal, about all we can conclude is that risk premia should be larger, the larger the own variance of the factor. We would not expect this result to be specialized to the diffusion model and, in general, we would expect, with beta weights appropriately normalized, that factors with larger own variances would have larger associated risk premia.[3]

Let us return now to the general APT model and aggregate it to a testable market relationship. The key point in aggregation is to make strong enough assumptions on the homogeneity of individual anticipations to produce a testable theory. To do so with the APT we need to assume that individuals agree on both the factor coefficients, b_{ij}, and the expected returns, E_i. It now follows that the pricing relationship (2) which holds for each individual holds at the market level as well. Notice that individual, and aggregate risk premia must coincide when there are homogenous beliefs on the expected returns and the factor coefficients.

As with the CAPM, the purpose of assuming homogenous anticipations is not to facilitate the algebra of aggregation. Rather, it is to take the final step to a testable theory. We can now make the rational anticipations assumption that (1) not only describes the *ex ante* individual perceptions of the returns process but also that *ex post* returns are described by the same equation. This fundamental intertemporal rationality assumption permits the *ex ante* theory to be tested by examining *ex post* data. In the next section we will discuss the possibilities for empirical testing which derive from this assumption.

B. Testing the APT

Our empirical tests of the APT will follow a two step procedure. In the first step, the expected returns and the factor coefficients are estimated from time series data on individual asset returns. The second step uses these estimates to test the basic cross-sectional pricing conclusion, (2), of the APT. This procedure is analogous to familiar CAPM empirical work in which time series analysis is used to obtain market betas, and cross-sectional regressions are then run of expected returns, estimated for various time periods, on the estimated betas. While flawed in some respects, the two step procedure is free of some major conceptual difficulties in CAPM tests. In particular, the APT applies to subsets

---

[3] We have not, of course, developed a complete rational anticipations model in diffusion setting, but it should be clear from this outline that the APT is compatible with the more specific results of Merton [35], Lucas [31], Cox, Ingersoll, and Ross [8], and Ross [48].

of the universe of assets; this eliminates the need to justify a particular choice of a surrogate for the market portfolio.

If we assume that returns are generated by (1), then the basic hypothesis we wish to test is the pricing relationship,

H_0: There exist non-zero constants, $(E_0, \lambda_1, \cdots, \lambda_k)$

such that

$$E_i - E_0 = \lambda_1 b_{i1} + \cdots + \lambda_k b_{ik}, \quad \text{for all } i.$$

The theory should be tested by its conclusions, not by its assumptions. One should not reject the APT hypothesis that assets were priced as if (2) held by merely observing that returns do not exactly fit a k-factor linear process. The theory says nothing about how close the assumptions must fit. Rejection is justified only if the conclusions are inconsistent with the observed data.[4]

To estimate the b coefficients, we appeal to the statistical technique of factor analysis. In factor analysis, these coefficients are called factor loadings and they are inferred from the sample covariance matrix, $\hat{V}$. From (1), the population variance, $\underline{V}$, is decomposed into

$$\underline{V} = \underline{B}\Lambda\underline{B}' + \underline{D}, \tag{5}$$

where $\underline{B} = [b_{ij}]$ is the matrix of factor loadings, Λ is the matrix of factor covariances, and D is the diagonal matrix of own asset variances, $\sigma_i^2 = E\{\bar{\epsilon}_i^2\}$.

From (5), $\underline{V}$ will be unaltered by any transformation which leaves $\underline{B}\Lambda\underline{B}'$ unaltered. In particular, if $\underline{G}$ is an orthogonal transformation matrix, $\underline{GG}' = I$, then

$$\underline{V} = \underline{B}\Lambda\underline{B}' + \underline{D}$$
$$= \underline{BGG'\Lambda GG'B'} + \underline{D}$$
$$= (\underline{BG})(\underline{G'\Lambda G})(\underline{BG})' + \underline{D}$$

If $\underline{B}$ is to be estimated from $\hat{V}$, then all transforms $\underline{BG}$ will be equivalent. For example, it clearly makes no difference in (1) if the first two factors switch places. More importantly, we could obviously scale up factor j's loadings and scale down factor j by the same constant g and since $bz_{ij}\delta_j = gb_{ij}\left(\dfrac{1}{g}\delta_j\right)$ the distributions of returns would be unaltered. To some extent we can eliminate ambiguity by restricting the factors to be orthonormal so they are independent and have unit variance. Alternatively, we could maintain the independence of the factors and construct the loadings for each factor to have a particular norm value, e.g., to

---

[4] This is a strongly positive view. Testing the APT involves testing H_0 and *not* testing the k-factor model. The latter tests may be of interest in their own right just as any examination of the distribution of returns is of interest, but it is irrelevant for the APT. As Friedman [16, pp. 19–20] points out: one would not be inclined to reject the hypothesis that the leaves on a tree arranged themselves so as to maximize the amount of sunlight they received by observing that trees did not have free will. Similarly, one should not reject the conclusions derived from firm profit maximization on the basis of sample surveys in which managers claim that they trade off profit for social good.

sum to 1 (or −1) and let the factor variances vary. From a theoretical viewpoint these are all equivalent constraints. While they alter the form of the APT null hypotheses, H_0, the statistical rejection region is unaffected.

To see this note that if

$$E_i - E_0 = \underline{b}_i \cdot \lambda,$$

or, in matrix form,

$$\underline{E} - E_0 = \underline{B}\lambda,$$

then

$$\underline{E} - E_0 = (\underline{B}G)(\underline{G'\lambda})$$

and the linear hypothesis remains true with the exact weights altered by the orthogonal transform.[5] This is a very sensible result. The APT concludes that excess expected returns lie in the space spanned by the factor loadings. Orthogonal transforms leave that space unchanged, altering only the directions of the defining basis vectors, the column vectors of the loadings. As a consequence, we will adopt a statistically convenient restriction to estimate B, keeping the arbitrariness of the procedure in mind. Notice that this is quite different from the ordinary uses of factor analysis. We are not "rotating" the factors in an arbitrary fashion to try to "interpret" them. Rather, our results are independent of the rotation chosen.

Once the expected returns, E_i, and the loadings, B, have been estimated, we can then move to the test of H_0. The general procedure is to examine cross-sectional regressions of the form

$$E_i = E_0 + \lambda_1 \hat{b}_{i1} + \cdots + \lambda_k \hat{b}_{ik},$$

where E_0 and $\lambda_1, \cdots, \lambda_k$ are to be estimated. The theory will not be rejected if the joint hypothesis that $\lambda_1 = \cdots = \lambda_k = 0$, is rejected. This is the usual state of statistical testing; we cannot "prove" that a theory is true against an unspecified alternative. We can only fail to reject it.

In Section III a specific alternative will be proposed, namely that the "own" variances, $\sigma^2_{\epsilon_i}$, affect excess returns, and the APT will be tested against this alternative. (This is probably the standard structure which most tests of the APT will take. A specific alternative will be proposed in which some idiosyncratic feature of the assets not reflected in their loadings is hypothesized to explain returns.)

We deal with the specifics of the above tests below, but for the present point out some of the major deficiencies of the procedure. The estimates of b_{ij} found in

---

[5] Notice, that if we knew the λ_i weights, we could obviously use them to aggregate the factors into a single factor which "explains" excess returns. In this trivial sense the number of factors does not matter. Without further assumptions, though, this begs the question since the λ_i weights must first be estimated to find the proper combination of the factors. For example, if we chose G such that its first column is proportional to λ, then $G'\lambda$ will be a vector with only the first entry non-zero. Under this rotation only a single factor is used to explain excess returns, but as noted above, the result has no empirical content.

the first step are, of course, just estimates and, as such, are subject to sampling error. Let $\tilde{e}_i$ and $\tilde{\beta}_{ij}$ denote the respective sample errors,

$$\hat{E}_i = E_i + \tilde{e}_i$$

and

$$\hat{b}_{ij} = b_{ij} + \tilde{\beta}_{ij}.$$

Under the null hypothesis, then, the cross-sectional regression for any period will be of the form

$$\hat{E}_i = E_i + \tilde{e}_i$$

$$= E_0 + \lambda_1 b_{i1} + \cdots + \lambda_k b_{ik} + \tilde{e}_i$$

$$= E_0 + \lambda_1 \hat{b}_{i1} + \cdots + \lambda_k \hat{b}_{ik} + \xi_i,$$

where the regression error

$$\xi_i \equiv \tilde{e}_i - \lambda_1 \tilde{\beta}_{il} - \cdots - \lambda_k \tilde{\beta}_{ik}.$$

Since the factor analytic estimation procedure to be employed is a maximum likelihood procedure, in a multivariate normal world the estimates will be asymptotically consistent; but very little is known about their small sample properties. In general, we expect ξ_i to be correlated with $\hat{b}_i$ and the cross-sectional regression to suffer from the usual errors-in-variables problems. Clearly, there is a considerable amount of statistical analysis to be carried out before one can feel comfortable with this approach. As a consequence, we stress the tentative and "first try" nature of the empirical work which follows.

II. Empirical Results

A. Data

The data are described in Table I. In selecting them, several more or less arbitrary choices were necessary. For instance, although daily data were available through 1977, the calculations reported in this paper used data only through 1972. The motivation was to secure a calibration or "holdout" sample without sacrificing the advantages of a large estimation sample, large enough for some statistical reliability even after aggregating the basic daily returns into monthly returns. The calibration sample is thereby reserved for later replication and for investigation of problems such as non-stationarity. The cutoff data of 31 December 1972 was selected also to correspond with other published studies of asset pricing, most of which used a pre-1973 period. This should facilitate a comparison of the results.

In our empirical analysis, estimated covariance matrices of returns were computed for groups of individual assets. Calculation of covariances necessitates simultaneous observations—so the beginning and ending dates were specified in order to exclude exceedingly short-lived securities. Although this assured a reasonably large time series sample for every group, there remained some variation across groups in number of observations. This was due evidently to suspen-

Table I

Data Description

Source:	Center for Research in Security Prices Graduate School of Business University of Chicago Daily Returns File
Selection Criterion:	By alphabetical order into groups of 30 individual securities from those listed on the New York or American Exchanges on *both* 3 July 1962 and 31 December 1972. The (alphabetically) last 24 such securities were not used since complete groups of 30 were required.
Basic Data Unit:	Return adjusted for all capital changes and including dividends, if any, between adjacent trading days; i.e., $[(p_{j,t} + d_{j,t})/p_{j,t-1}] - 1$, where p = price, d = dividend, j = security index, t = trading day index.
Maximum Sample Size per Security:	2619 daily returns
Number of Selected Securities	1260, (42 groups of 30 each)

sion of trading, temporary delisting, or simply to missing data for individual securities. None of the 42 groups contained data for all 2619 trading days. The minimum sample size was still 1445 days, however, and only three groups had less than 2000 days. Thirty-six groups (86%) had at least 2400 observations.

The group size of 30 individual securities was a compromise. For some purposes, such as estimating the number of return generating factors present in the economy, the best group size would have included *all* individual assets; but this would have dictated a covariance matrix larger than the processing capacity of the computer. For other purposes, such as comparing covariance structures across groups, statistical power increases with the number of groups, *cet. par.* Unfortunately, the *ceteris* are not *paribus*; for the number of securities *per* group also improves power and the reliability of estimates. We guessed that 30 securities per group would confer reasonable precision for all of the tests envisaged initially and we stuck with 30 as the work proceeded.

B. Estimating the Factor Model

The analysis proceeds in the following stages:
1) For a group of individual assets, (in this case, a group of 30 selected alphabetically), a sample product-moment covariance matrix is computed from a time series of returns, (of New York and American Exchange listed stocks from July 1962 through December 1972).
2) A maximum-likelihood factor analysis is performed on the covariance matrix. This estimates the number of factors and the matrix of loadings.
3) The individual-asset factor loading estimates from the previous step are used to explain the cross-sectional variation of individual estimated expected returns. The procedure here is similar to a cross-sectional generalized least squares regression.
4) Estimates from the cross-sectional model are used to measure the size and statistical significance of risk premia associated with the estimated factors.

This procedure is similar to estimating the size and significance of factor "scores."

5) Steps (1) through (4) are repeated for all groups and the results are tabulated.

The first stage is straightforward and should require no further explanation. There was only one curiosity: every element in the covariance matrix was divided by one-half the largest of the 30 individual variances. This was done to prevent rounding error in the factor analysis and it has no effect whatever on the results since factor analysis is scale free.

In the second stage, an optimization technique suggested by Jöreskog [20] was employed in the form of a program described by Jöreskog and Sörbom [21]. There are several available choices of types of factor analysis. In addition to the maximum likelihood method, there are generalized least squares, unweighted least squares, and approximate methods, among others. The maximum-likelihood method is usually preferable since more is known about its statistical properties, (Cf. Lawley and Maxwell [26]). As we shall see later, however, there may be some problems attendant to the M.L.E. method because the likelihood function involved is that of a multivariate gaussian distribution. To the extent that the data have been generated by a non-gaussian probability law, unknown biases and inconsistencies may be introduced.

Assuming away these problems for the moment, the M.L.E. method provides the capability of estimating the number of factors. This can be accomplished by specifying an arbitrary number of factors, say k, then solving for the maximum likelihood conditional on a covariance matrix generated by exactly k factors. Of course k is set less than the number of securities in the group of 30. A second value of the likelihood function is also found; this one being conditional on the observed sample covariance matrix without any restriction as to number of factors. Then a likelihood ratio, (first likelihood value divided by second), is computed. Under the null hypothesis of exactly k factors, twice the natural logarithm of the likelihood ratio is distributed asymptotically as chi-square with $\frac{1}{2}[(n - k)^2 - (n + k)]$ degrees of freedom. Thus, if the computed chi-square statistic is large (small), then more (fewer) than k factors are required to explain the structure of the generating process. So $k + 1$ $(k - 1)$ factors are specified and another chi-square statistic is computed. The process terminates when the chi-square statistic indicates a pre-selected level, (usually 50%), that an additional factor is required.

We used the alphabetically first group of 30 securities to estimate the number of factors in the way just described, but with the added intention of retaining more factors than a 50% probability level would dictate. We could afford these extra, perhaps superfluous, factors since the third stage of our procedure provides a direct check on the true number of factors in the underlying generating process. An estimated factor introduced spuriously at the factor analysis stage would not be "priced" in the cross-sectional regression; its estimated coefficient should not differ significantly from zero. We wanted to allow the possibility of spurious factors because the same number of true (priced) factors should be present in every group *and* the first group might have been unrepresentative. Fewer than the true number of common factors could have been estimated for group one because of sampling variation. The third stage protects against too many factors estimated at stage two but it does not protect against too few.

For five factors using daily returns over the entire sample period, the chi-square statistic computed from the first group was 246.1. The number of degrees of freedom was 295 and the probability level (.980) implied only two chances in 100 that at least six factors were present in the data. Thus, we specified five factors, retaining this same number in the factor analysis computation for all 42 groups. Table II presents frequencies of the chi-square statistic for the 42 groups of daily returns. The monthly returns used later display a similar pattern.

As the table shows, in 38.1% of the groups, (16 of 42), the likelihood ratio test implied more than a 90% chance that five factors were sufficient. Over three-quarters of the groups had at least an even chance that five were enough. Some sampling variation in the estimated number of factors is inevitable; but the results indicate clearly that five is conservative in the sense of including, with high probability, at least as many estimated factors as there are true factors. Note, however, that a formal goodness-of-fit test using the results in Table II would not quite be legitimate. Since the original covariance matrices were computed over the same time period for all groups, there is probably some statistical dependence across the groups. Thus, the cross-group sample of any statistic is not likely to be a random sample. Since there is positive cross-sectional dependence among the returns, there is also likely to be positive cross group dependence in any statistic calculated from their returns.

With five factors, the model envisaged for each security can be written

$$\tilde{r}_{jt} \equiv \tilde{R}_{jt} - E_j = b_{1j}\tilde{\delta}_{1t} + \cdots + b_{5j}\tilde{\delta}_{5t} + \tilde{\epsilon}_{jt} \tag{6}$$

where R_{jt} is the daily return for day t and security j, E_j is the expected return for j, the b_j's are factor coefficients, the $\tilde{\delta}$'s are the true common factors, and $\tilde{\epsilon}_{jt}$ is a random disturbance completely unrelated to anything else including its own values in other periods. In matrix notation, a group of n individual securities whose returns conform to (6) can be expressed as

$$\tilde{r}_t = \underline{B}\tilde{\delta}_t + \epsilon_t$$

where $\tilde{r}_t$ and $\tilde{\epsilon}_t$ are $(n \times 1)$ column vectors, $\underline{B}$ is an $(n \times 5)$ matrix and $\underline{\delta}_t$ is a (5×1) vector. Without loss of generality, the factors can be assumed orthogonal and scaled to have unit variance. Then the null hypothesis represented by equation (6) implies that the covariance matrix of returns takes the form

$$\underline{V} = \underline{B}\underline{B}' + \underline{D}$$

Table II

Probability that no more than five factors are needed to explain returns	.9	.8	.7	.6	.5	.4	.3	.2	.1	0
Frequency (%)	38.1	16.7	7.14	2.38	11.9	2.38	4.76	4.76	9.52	2.38

Cross-sectional distribution of the Chi-square statistic from a likelihood ratio test that no more than five factors are necessary to explain daily returns, 42 covariance matrices of 30 securities each, NYSE and AMEX listed securities, 1962–72.

where $\underline{D}$ is a (diagonal) matrix whose j^{th} diagonal element is the variance of $\tilde{\epsilon}_{jt}$.

As noted in Section I, although maximum likelihood factor analysis provides a unique estimate of $\underline{V}$, this estimate is compatible with an infinity of estimates for $\underline{B}$, "all equally good from a statistical point of view. In this situation, all the statistician can do is to select a particular solution, one which is convenient to find, and leave the experimenter to apply whatever rotation he thinks desirable" (Lawley and Maxwell [26, p. 11]).

Our program chooses an estimate $\hat{\underline{B}}$ of $\underline{B}$ such that the matrix $\hat{B}'\hat{D}^{-1}\hat{B}$ is diagonal and arranged with its diagonal elements in descending order of magnitude. This constitutes a restriction that guarantees uniqueness, except that $-\hat{\underline{B}}$ is statistically equivalent and, in fact, any column of $\hat{B}$ can be reversed in sign. The problem of sign reversal is solved quite easily for the restricted estimates, (see below), but the general non-uniqueness of factor loadings is very troublesome. Essentially, one cannot ascertain with certainty that the first factor in one group of securities is the same as the first factor in another group. For instance, factor number one in group A could conceivably correspond to factor number three in group $K(K \neq A)$. Thus, when the cross-sectional distributions of the loading coefficients are tabulated, there could be a mixing of estimates which apply to different "true" factors.

C. A First Test of the APT

The factor model can be written as

$$\tilde{\underline{R}}_t = \underline{E} + B\tilde{\underline{\delta}}_t + \tilde{\underline{\epsilon}}_t$$

and the arbitrage pricing theory requires

$$\underline{E} = \lambda_0 + \underline{B}\lambda.$$

Combining the two gives the basic factor process under the null hypothesis that the APT is true,

$$\tilde{r}_t = \tilde{\underline{R}}_t - \lambda_0 = \underline{B}\lambda + (\underline{B}\tilde{\underline{\delta}}_t + \tilde{\underline{\epsilon}}_t), \tag{7}$$

or, more compactly,

$$\tilde{r}_t = \underline{B}\lambda + \underline{\xi}_t, \tag{8}$$

where $\underline{\xi}_t$ is the mean zero disturbance at date t caused by intertemporal variation in the factors $\tilde{\underline{\delta}}_t$ and in the diversifiable component $\tilde{\underline{\epsilon}}_t$.

It might seem natural to test the APT via (8) by first estimating the factor loadings, $\underline{B}$, and the mean return vector $\bar{r} = \Sigma r_t / T$ from time series, and then running a simple OLS cross-sectional regression analogous to (8),

$$\bar{r} = \hat{B}\hat{\lambda} + \hat{\xi} \tag{9}$$

where $\hat{\lambda}$ the OLS regression coefficients, would be the estimated risk premia. A closer examination of (7), however, reveals that this procedure would be biased toward finding risk premia for "priced" factors, even when their true prices are actually zero. To see why, notice that the mean value of δ_t, say $\bar{\underline{\delta}} = \Sigma\underline{\delta}_t / T$, must, with probability one, not be exactly zero in any sample. Thus, the cross-sectional regression (9) actually should be written

$$\bar{r} = \hat{B}(\lambda + \bar{\delta}) + \bar{\epsilon}$$

so that $E(\hat{\lambda}) = \lambda + \bar{\delta}$ will be biased by the time series *sample* mean of the factors, $\bar{\delta}$. Of course, the bias should decrease with larger time series sample sizes, but since $\bar{\delta}$ will not be exactly zero, however large the time series, $E(\hat{\lambda}) \neq 0$ even when $\lambda = 0$.

To correct this problem, we have employed a method analagous to that of Fama and MacBeth [14] but adapted to the factor analytic framework. The Fama-MacBeth procedure calculates a cross-sectional regression like (9) *for every time period t,*

$$r_t = \hat{B}\hat{\lambda}_t + \underline{\xi}_t$$

and then uses the time series of $\hat{\lambda}_t$ to estimate the standard error of the average value of $\hat{\lambda}$. This yields an inference about whether the true λ is non-zero.

A more efficient procedure exploits the factor analysis already conducted with the time series during the estimation of $\underline{B}$. The factor loadings $\hat{B}$ are chosen such that $\hat{V} \equiv \hat{B}\,\hat{B}' + \underline{D}$ is the estimated covariance matrix of $\underline{B}\,\hat{\delta}_t + \bar{\epsilon}_t$, the disturbance term in (7). Thus, a natural generalized least squares cross-sectional regression for each day t is

$$\hat{\lambda}_t = (\hat{B}'\hat{V}^{-1}\hat{B})^{-1}\hat{B}'\hat{V}^{-1}r_t \equiv \underline{\Gamma}r_t \tag{10}$$

which yields GLS estimates of the risk premia. Furthermore, it can be proven (Lawley and Maxwell [26, pp. 88–89]) that the covariance matrix of the estimates $\hat{\lambda}_t$ from (10) is given by

$$B'\underline{V}^{-1}B. \tag{11}$$

This matrix is particularly convenient since it is constrained to be diagonal by the factor analysis. As a consequence, the estimated risk premia are mutually independent and admit simple t-tests of significance.

For instance, we will report below significance tests for

$$\bar{\lambda} \equiv \underline{\Gamma}\bar{r} \tag{12}$$

whose covariance matrix is

$$\frac{1}{T}B'\underline{V}^{-1}\underline{B}, \tag{13}$$

provided the returns are independent over time. Notice that the time series behavior of the estimated factor "scores," the $\bar{\delta}$'s, is accounted for by the matrix $\underline{V}$, thereby eliminating the problem created by non-zero $\bar{\delta}$ in the simple OLS cross-section (9).

There remain, however, some tricky econometric problems in this procedure. First, equation (11) ignores any estimation errors present in $\hat{B}$. This means essentially that the significance tests for $\hat{\lambda}$ are only asymptotically correct. There could be an understatement or an overstatement of significance for small samples. We have no way to ascertain the extent of this problem, but we doubt that it introduces a serious error because our sample sizes are "large" by usual statistical standards.

A second difficulty concerns the signs of $\hat{\lambda}$. Since the factor loadings ($\underline{B}$) are not unique with respect to sign, neither are their coefficients $\underline{\lambda}$ in (7). Any rotated set of factors would have produced just as adequate a set of loadings. This implies that no importance can be ascribed to the numerical values of $\hat{\underline{\lambda}}$; only their statistical significance is relevant.

Finally, in the cross-sectional models (10) and (12), a value for the zero-beta or risk-free coefficient, λ_0 in (7), must be assumed. It might be thought that $\hat{\lambda}_0$ could be obtained easily by adding a column of 1's to $\hat{\underline{B}}$ and computing regression (10) with an augmented matrix of loadings, $[\underline{1}:\underline{B}]$ an augmented $\underline{\Gamma}$ and the total return R_t, in place of the excess return $\underline{r}_t$, as

$$\hat{\underline{\lambda}}_t = \underline{\Gamma} \underline{R}_t,$$

where $\hat{\underline{\lambda}}_t$ now contains an estimate for λ_0 as its first element. Unfortunately, although we report the result of this regression below, it is less satisfactory because the augmented covariance matrix of the estimated risk premia is

$$[\underline{1}:\underline{B}]' \underline{V}^{-1} [\underline{1}:\underline{B}]$$

which is not diagonal except in the fortuitous case when the constant vector is orthogonal to the loadings.

The trade-off, then, is between using a rather arbitrary value of λ_0 in the cross-sectional excess return regression (10) or allowing the data to determine $\hat{\lambda}_0$ but bearing the consequence that the estimates $\hat{\underline{\lambda}}$ are no longer statistically independent. In many applications, mutual independence is merely a nicety since F-tests can be used when dependence among the coefficients is present. In our case, however, constraining the sample design to the independent case is especially important because the $\hat{\lambda}$'s at best are some unknown linear combinations of the true $\underline{\lambda}$'s and testing for the number of priced factors or non-zero λ_j's, is thereby reduced to a simple t-test.

Perhaps this will be clarified by considering the results in Table III. The top panel assumes a λ_0 of 6% per annum during the sample period, July 1962 through December 1972. The first results in Table III give the percentage of the groups in which more than a specified number of factors were associated with statistically significant risk premia, $\hat{\underline{\lambda}}$ estimated by (12) and (13). With daily data, 88.1% of the groups had at least one significant factor risk premium, 57.1% had two or more significant factors and in one-third of the groups at least three risk premia were significant. These percentages are far in excess of what would be expected by chance alone under the null hypothesis of no effect. The next row of Table III gives the relevant percentages which would be expected under this null hypothesis. If $\underline{\lambda} = 0$, the chance of observing at least a given number of $\hat{\lambda}_j$'s significant at the 95% level is the upper tail of the binomial distribution with probability of success $p = .05$. For example, the probability of observing at least two significant

Table III

Cross-sectional generalized least squares regressions of arithmetic
mean sample returns on factor loadings, (42 groups of 30
individual securities per group, 1962–72 daily returns, standard
errors of risk premia (λ) computed from time series)

1 FACTOR	2 FACTORS	3 FACTORS	4 FACTORS	5 FACTORS
I.	$\bar{R}_j - 6\% = \hat{\lambda}_1 \, \hat{b}_{j1} + \cdots + \hat{\lambda}_5 \, \hat{b}_{j5}$ (λ_0 assumed at 6%)			
Percentage of groups with at least this many factor risk premia significant at the 95% level				
88.1	57.1	33.3	16.7	4.8
Expected Percentage of groups with at least this many risk premia significant at the 95% level given no true risk premia ($\underline{\lambda} = 0$)				
22.6	2.26	.115	.003	.00003
Percentage of groups with factor's risk premium significant at the 95% level in natural order from factor analysis				
76.2	50.0	28.6	23.8	21.4
II.	$\bar{R}_j = \hat{\lambda}_0 + \hat{\lambda}_1 \, \hat{b}_{j1} + \cdots + \hat{\lambda}_5 \, \hat{b}_{j5}$ (λ_0 estimated)			
Percentage of groups with at least this many factor risk premia significant at the 95% level				
69.0	47.6	7.1	4.8	0
Percentage of groups with this factor's risk premium significant at the 95% level in natural order from factor analysis				
35.7	31.0	23.8	21.4	16.7

$\hat{\lambda}$'s, given $\underline{\lambda} = 0$, is $1 - (.95)^5 - 5(.05)(.95)^4 = .0226$. Notice that this calculation requires zero correlation among the $\hat{\lambda}_j$'s .

If, in fact, four factors are truly significant, then the 4.8 observed significance percentage for five factors (see line 1 of Table III), is almost precisely what one would expect at the 95% level. Similarly, if three are truly significant, the 16.7% of the groups in which at least four are found to be significant exceeds the 9.75% which would occur by chance alone. The disparity is much greater if less than three factors are significant. We can conclude then, that at least three factors are important for pricing, but that it is unlikely that more than four are present.

The second set of results, still with λ_0 assumed equal to 6%, report the percentage of groups in which the first, second, and remaining factors produced by the factor analysis have significant associated risk premia. As noted above, the first factor is selected as the one with the largest diagonal element in $\hat{B}'D^{-1}\hat{B}$, the second has the second largest diagonal element, and so forth, but there is no assurance that corresponding factors agree across different groups. Nevertheless, it is of some interest to examine the significance of the ordered factors and this is reported in the third line of Table III. As can be seen, all factors are significantly greater than the chance level (5%) with particularly heavy weight on the first two. The remaining three are significant, but this may be more a consequence of mixing the order of factors across the groups than of anything important.

The second part of Table III reports similar statistics but with the constant λ_0 estimated instead of assumed. Now the t statistics are no longer independent across the factors and we cannot apply the simple analysis above. But, the statistical results seem to conform well with the previous findings. Perhaps most striking is that at least two factors are significant in 47.6% of the groups while in only 7.1% are three or more significant. This suggests that the three significant factors obtained with λ_0 set equal to 6% may be an over-estimate due to the incorrect choice of the zero-beta return λ_0. When the intercept is estimated, two factors emerge as significant for pricing. However, because the $\hat{\lambda}_j$'s are not mutually independent, there is no standard of comparison for these percentages. As is to be expected, the results for the ordered factors are less significant than those for the λ_0 equal to 6% case, at least for the first and second factors produced by the factor analysis.

The next section (III) tests the APT against a specific alternative. Section IV presents a test for the equivalence of factor structure across the 42 groups.

III. Tests of the APT Against a Specific Alternative

In the previous section, we presented evidence that equity returns seem to depend on several common factors, perhaps as many as four. This many seem to be "priced", i.e., associated with non-zero risk premia which compensate for undiversifiable variation present in the generating process. Although these results are reassuring for the APT, there remains a possibility that other variables also are "priced" even though they are not related to undiversifiable risk. According to the theory, such variables should not explain expected returns; so if some were found to be empirically important, the APT would be rejected.

In this section, we report an investigation of one particular variable, the total variance of individual returns, or the "own" variance. The total variance would not affect expected returns if the APT is valid because its diversifiable component would be eliminated by portfolio formation and its non-diversifiable part would depend only upon the factor loadings and factor variances. It is a particularly good choice to use in an attempt to reject the APT because of its long-documented high positive correlation with sample mean returns.[6] If this sample correlation arises either from statistical estimation errors or else from its relation to factor loadings, the APT would enjoy an additional element of empirical support. If the correlation cannot be ascribed to these causes, however, then this would constitute evidence against the theory.

The procedure of this section is relatively straightforward: cross-sectionally (across individual assets), we regress estimates of expected returns on the five factor loading estimates described in the previous section *and* on

$$s_j = [\sum_{t=1}^{T} (R_{jt} - R_j)/T]^{1/2}, \quad j = 1, \cdots, N$$

the standard deviation of individual returns. This test is less efficient for detecting

---

[6] See, e.g., Douglas [10] and Lintner [30]. The "own" variance received very careful scrutiny in Miller and Scholes [37], and has been the object of recent theoretical inquiry in Levy [29].

"priced" factors than the factor analysis based test reported previously. Now, however, there is no alternative to using an ordinary regression approach since the extra variable s_j is not a factor loading and is not produced by the factor analysis.

Some evidence on the apparent explanatory power of the own standard deviation, s_j, is presented in Table IV. On average over the 42 groups of securities, the t-statistic (coefficient/standard error of coefficient) was 2.17 for s_j. 45.2% of the groups displayed statistically significant effects of s_j on mean sample returns at the 95% level of significance. In contrast, the F-test that at least some (one or more) factor loading had an effect on the mean return was significant at the 95% level for only 28.6% of the 42 groups.

A caution mentioned earlier in connection with all of our results should be reiterated: there was probably some positive dependence across groups, so the percentage of groups whose statistics exceed a critical value may overstate the actual significance of the relation between explanatory variables and expected returns. Nevertheless, the magnitude of the numbers would certainly appear to support a conclusion that the relation is statistically significant. The "explained"

Table IV

Cross-sectional regression[a] of estimated expected
returns on factor loadings and individual total
standard deviations of return (summary for 42
groups of 30 individual securities per group, 1962–72
daily returns)

Arithmetic Mean	Standard Error of Mean	Percentage of Groups Whose Statistic Exceeds 95% Critical Level[b]
Across 42 Groups		
t-statistic, test for most significant factor loading having no effect on expected return.		
2.19	.162	47.6
t-statistic: test for individual total standard deviation having no effect on expected return.		
2.17	.303	45.2
F-statistic: test for no effect by any factor loading on expected return (in addition to the effect of standard deviation).		
2.21	.295	28.6

[a] The regression equation for group g is

$$\bar{R}_j = \hat{\lambda}_{0g} + \hat{\lambda}_{1g}\,\hat{b}_{1j} + \cdots + \hat{\lambda}_{5g}\,\hat{b}_{5j} + \hat{\lambda}_{6g}s_j + \xi \quad j = 1, \cdots, 30$$

where $\bar{R}_j$ is the sample arithmetic mean return for security j, $\hat{b}_{kj}$ is security j's loading on factor k, the $\hat{\lambda}$'s are regression coefficients, s_j is individual asset j's total standard deviation of daily returns during the sample period and ξ_j is a residual.

[b] With 30 observations per group and six explanatory variables, the 95% critical value is 2.06 for the t-statistic and 2.64 for the F-statistic.

variation is quite high: the coefficient of multiple determination (adjusted R^2) is .743 on average over the 42 groups. Even the group with lowest explained variation has an R^2 of .561 (and recall that these are individual assets!). Without s included, the average adjusted R^2 is .563 and the minimum R^2 over the 42 groups is .166.

The apparently significant explanatory power of the "own" standard deviation (s) suggests that the arbitrage pricing theory may be false. Since arbitrageurs should be able to diversify away the non-common part of s, it should not be priced. There is reason, however, for a closer examination before rejecting the APT entirely.

A possible source of a spurious effect of the own variance on expected return is skewness in the distribution of individual returns. Positive skewness can create positive dependence between the *sample* mean and *sample* standard deviation (and vice versa for negative skewness). Miller and Scholes [37] argued convincingly that skewness could explain the sample mean's dependence on "own" variance. Our results below tend to support the Miller-Scholes argument within the APT context.

The distribution of individual daily returns are indeed highly skewed. Table V gives some sample results. As indicated there, 1213 out of 1260 individual assets, (96.3%), had positive estimated measures of skewness. There was considerable variation across assets, too. Although the sampling distribution of the skewness measure SK is not known and is difficult to tabulate even under the assumption of lognormality, there appears to be too much cross-sectional variation in SK to be ascribed to chance alone. Thus, individual assets probably differ in their population skewness. Note that intertemporal aggregation to monthly returns reduces the skewness only slightly.

Skewness is cross-sectionally correlated positively with the mean return and even more strongly with the standard deviation. Some part of this correlation may itself arise from sampling variation and some part too could be present in the population parameters. There is really no way to sort this out definitively. The strong cross-sectional regressions in the last panels of Table V suggest that attempts to expunge the spurious sampling dependence between sample mean return and standard deviation by exploiting the measured sample skewness, either as an additional variable in the cross-sectional regression or as a basis for skewness-sorted groups which might have less remaining spurious dependence, are probably doomed to weak and ambiguous results.[7] Also, such methods would be biased against finding a true effect of standard deviation, if one exists.

A procedure[8] which is charming in its simplicity and seems to resolve many of the statistical problems occasioned by skewness can be used if the observations are not too serially dependent: simply estimate each parameter from a different set of observations. In the present application, for example, we are concerned with sampling dependencies among estimates of all three parameters, expected return, factor loadings, and "own" standard deviation. If the time-series obser-

---

[7] As Martin [33] shows, using sample skewness and standard deviation both as additional explanatory variables causes severe econometric problems.

[8] We are grateful to Richard McEnally for suggesting this procedure.

Table V

Information About Skewness for Daily and Monthly Returns 1260 New York and American Listed Assets, 1962-72

Data Interval	Percent Positive	Mean	Standard Deviation	Smallest	Largest	with $\bar{R}$	with $\text{Log}_e(s_j)$
						Correlation	

Product—Moment Skewness Measure, SK

Data Interval	Percent Positive	Mean	Standard Deviation	Smallest	Largest	with $\bar{R}$	with $\text{Log}_e(s_j)$
Daily	96.3	.681	.551	−2.06	4.56	.211	.452
Monthly	90.0	.654	.688	−1.04	5.94	.212	.520

Cross-Asset Regressions

Data Interval	$\hat{b}_1$	t_{δ_1}	$\hat{b}_2$	t_{δ_2}	Adjusted R^2

$$(\bar{R}_j - \bar{R}_{.5,j})/\log_e(s_j) = \hat{b}_0 + \hat{b}_1 SK_j \quad j = 1, \cdots, 1260$$

Data Interval	$\hat{b}_1$	t_{δ_1}	$\hat{b}_2$	t_{δ_2}	Adjusted R^2
Daily	1.82	20.6	—	—	.251
Monthly	1.14	36.6	—	—	.515

$$\bar{R}_j - \bar{R}_{.5,j} = \hat{b}_0 + \hat{b}_1 SK_j + \hat{b}_2 \log_e(s_j) \quad j = 1, \cdots, 1260$$

Data Interval	$\hat{b}_1$	t_{δ_1}	$\hat{b}_2$	t_{δ_2}	Adjusted R^2
Daily	5.17	7.87	29.2	68.0	.838
Monthly	7.33	24.6	8.17	32.1	.728

Definitions:

R_{jt} = Return for asset j in interval t

T = Total number of intervals in sample

$\bar{R}_j = \sum_t R_{jt}/T$

$\bar{R}_{.5,j}$ = Sample mean after excluding the 25% smallest and 25% largest values of R_{jt}

$s_j = [\sum_t (R_{jt} - \bar{R}_j)^2/T]^{1/2}$

$SK_j = [\sum_t (R_{jt} - \bar{R}_j)^3/T]/s^3_j$

vations are temporarily uncorrelated such dependencies could be removed by using observations 1, 4, 7, 10, ... to estimate the expected return, observations 2, 5, 8, 11, ... to estimate the factor loadings, and 3, 6, 9, 12, ... to estimate the standard deviation of returns. With complete intertemporal independence, there would be no sampling covariation among the estimates and only the cross-asset population relationships would remain.

The daily returns for each asset are indeed close to independent over time. There may be some slight negative dependence but it has a low order of magnitude. Unfortunately, this is not true for the squared returns. There is positive intertemporal dependence in absolute price changes or in squared changes. This implies that the standard deviation of returns and the factor loadings estimated from non-overlapping adjacent days would still retain some sampling dependence. But since there are so many available time series observations (2619), we have the luxury of skipping days and estimating the parameters from non-overlapping observations "insulated" be at least one day. Table VI summarizes the results obtained with daily observations, using days 1, 7, 13, . . . for the estimated expected returns, observations 3, 9, 15, . . . for the factor loadings, and 5, 11, 17, . . . for the standard deviations. This has had the effect of reducing the number of time series observations used in the estimation of each parameter from 2619 to 436. Note that the factor loadings were estimated in the usual way but for covariance matrices computed only with observations 3, 9, 15, ...

These results are to be compared with those reported in Table IV where all estimates were computed from the same sample observations. Only nine of the 42 groups now display a significant t-statistic for s. Given the possibility of cross-group interdependence, this is only the weakest conceivable evidence for an effect by s on expected returns. The remaining effect drops even further when more "insulating" days are inserted between observations used to estimate the parameters. When three days are skipped rather than just one day, only seven groups out of 42 (16.7%) display significant effects for s at the 95% level. This supports

Table VI

Cross-sectional regressions of estimated expected
returns on factor loadings and individual total
standard deviations of return (summary for 42
groups of 30 individual securities per groups, 1962–72
daily observations with estimators taken from non-
overlapping subsamples)[a]

Arithmetic Mean	Standard Error of Mean	Percentage of Groups Whose Statistic Exceeds 95% Critical Level[b]
Across 42 Groups		
t-statistic: test for most significant factor loading having no effect on expected return.		
2.27	.111	57.1
t-statistic, test for individual total standard deviation of return having no effect on expected return.		
.941	.204	21.4
F-statistic, test for no effect by any factor loading on expected return (in addition to the effect of standard deviation).		
2.24	.183	31.0

[a] The estimated returns are obtained from daily observations 1, 7, 13, $\cdots$2617; the factor loadings from observations 3, 9, $\cdots$2619; the standard deviations from observations 5, 11, $\cdots$2615.

[b] The regression equation and 95% critical values are given in nn. a and b of Table IV.

the argument that serial dependence in *squared* returns may be responsible for the small remaining effect of s shown in Table VI.

In contrast to the reduced impact of standard deviation, the estimated influence of the factor loadings have increased, (though admittedly only by a small amount). For example, the most significant factor loading now has a t-statistic of at least 2.06 in 57.1% of the groups.

Again, the groups are not independent; so caution should be exercised when interpreting the results. The results are not definitive but they *are* consistent with most of the frequently-observed sampling dependence between standard deviation and mean return being attributable to effects working through factor loadings and to spurious effects due to skewness.

As a final test, we conducted an experiment similar to that developed by Fama and MacBeth [14]. Here is an outline of the procedure:

a) Using daily observations 3, 9, 15, ... the five factor loadings $\hat{b}_{1j}, \ldots \hat{b}_{5j}$ are estimated for each asset in each of the 42 groups of 30 assets.

b) Using daily observations 5, 11, 17, ... the "own" standard deviation of return s_j is computed for each asset.

c) Using observations 1, 7, 13, ... the following cross-sectional regression is computed for each group, g. $R_{jt} = \hat{\lambda}_{0gt} + \hat{\lambda}_{1gt}\hat{b}_{1j} + \ldots + \hat{\lambda}_{5gt}\hat{b}_{5j} + \hat{\lambda}_{6gt}s_j + \xi_{jt}, j = 1, \ldots 30$ within each group and for all groups $g = 1, \ldots 42$. This yields 42 time series of vectors, $\hat{\lambda}_{gt} = \hat{\lambda}_{0gt}, \ldots \hat{\lambda}_{6gt}$, of estimated factors $\hat{\lambda}_{1gt}$ through $\hat{\lambda}_{5gt}$, of the riskless interest rate and of the effect of "own" standard deviation $\hat{\lambda}_{6gt}$.

d) The time series of $\hat{\lambda}_{6gt}$ is used to compute a standard error for the mean value, i.e., for $\bar{\lambda}_{6g} = \Sigma_t \hat{\lambda}_{6gt}/T$, in order to test for the significant presence of an "own" variance effect.

The results indicate that just three of the 42 groups (7.1%) display a significant effect of s on expected return at the 95% level. Since just one less group, two out of 42, would be fewer than the number to be expected by pure chance, there seems to be little remaining reason to reject the hypothesis that individual expected returns are unaffected by the "own" variance of returns.

This procedure also could be used to estimate the significance of different factors. However, due to the factor identification problem, the time series of factor values from one group will probably not be the same as the factor values for a different group. Furthermore, the resulting tests are less powerful than the factor-analysis based tests reported in Section II. They do indicate, however, that 17 groups (40.5%) have at least one significant factor and ten groups (23.8%) have at least two significant. This is an indication of fewer significant factors than in the factor-analysis tests but such a result is to be anticipated with a less powerful method.[9]

---

[9] Following Fama-MacBeth [14], a test of market efficiency can be conducted by regarding that the $\underline{\lambda}$ as excess returns on portfolios. (They can be interpreted as portfolios that load exclusively on a given factor). The returns should be serially uncorrelated in an efficient market. We found the first ten lagged autocorrelations, each subsuming six trading days, to be insignificantly different from zero. For example, the ten lagged serial correlation coefficients of $\underline{\lambda}_{11}$, (the first factor of the first group), are .00726, .0432, −.0197, −.0123, −.0201, −.112, −.0412, −.000979, −.0624, .0739. The sample size is 430 ± 5, (depending on the lag).

IV. A Test for the Equivalence of Factor Structure Across Groups

One of the most troubling econometric problems in the two preceding sections was due to the technological necessity of splitting assets into groups. Since the calculations were made for each group separately, but over the same time interval, the results are potentially susceptible to spurious sampling dependence among the groups. Also, due to the factor identification problem, there is no good way to ascertain whether the *same* three (or four) factors generate the returns in every group. It's conceivable, (but we think unlikely) that each of the 42 groups displays three *different* factors. This would imply that the actual number of common factors is 3×42, or at least some number considerably larger than three.

Even if the APT is true, the same underlying common factors can be "rotated" differently in each group. However, there is one parameter, the intercept term (λ_0 in eq.(2)) which should be identical across groups, whatever the sample rotation of the generating factors. Recall that λ_0 should be the expected return on either the riskless rate of interest or on an asset with no sensitivity to the common factors. This suggests that a simple test of the APT and of the cross-group consistency of factor structure can involve ascertaining whether the λ_0's estimated for the 42 groups are significantly different.

Since the test must also correct for inter-group dependence, a reasonable approach would use the time series estimated intercepts from the Fama-MacBeth type cross-sectional regressions computed in the last part of Section III; (Cf. pp. 46–48). For each group g, $\hat{\lambda}_{0gt}$ is the cross-sectional intercept for day t, from a cross-sectional regression on the factor landings ($\hat{b}$'s) and the "own" standard deviation (s_j) estimated from different but interleaved observations. Since each group has a time series $\hat{\lambda}_{0g}$ whose members are possibly correlated across groups, the appropriate test is Hotelling's T^2 for differences in adjacent groups.[10] That is, let

$$Z_{g/2,t} = \hat{\lambda}_{0,g-1,t} - \hat{\lambda}_{0,g,t} \quad g = 2, 4, 6, \ldots.$$

be computed for each naturally-ordered pair of groups with a "sufficient" number of observations. We assumed that 400 was a sufficient number. There were 38 groups with at least 400 observations from the calendar observations used in the regressions (i.e., from observation 1, 7, 13, ...). Thus, there were 19 time-series for $Z_{g/2}$, ($g = 2, \ldots 38$).

The composite null hypothesis to be tested is

$$H_0: E(Z_{g/2}) = 0, g = 2, 4, \ldots 38$$

and Hotelling's T^2 conducts this test by using the quadratic form

$$T^2 = N \, \bar{\underline{Z}} \, \underline{\underline{\Sigma}}^{-1} \, \bar{\underline{Z}}$$

where $\underline{Z}$ is the vector of sample means of the $\bar{Z}_{g/2,t}$'s and $\underline{\underline{\Sigma}}$ is their sample covariance matrix. The sample size is N. Since simultaneous observations are required to compute the covariance matrix, if any stock in any of the 38 groups

---

[10] See Press [39, ch. 6] for a general explanation of Hotelling's T^2.

had a missing observation, that observation could not be used. This resulted in a further reduction to 188 simultaneous observations.

Hotelling's T^2 value for these observations was 16.9 and the corresponding F statistic with 19 and 169 degrees of freedom was located at the .298 fractile of the null distribution. Thus, there is absolutely no evidence that the intercept terms were different across groups.

However, we do admit that this test is probably quite weak. There is a very low degree of explanatory power in the daily cross-sectional regressions and thus the sampling variation of each $\hat{\lambda}_{0gt}$ is quite large. Furthermore, Hotelling's test in small samples requires multi-variate normality. It is known, however, to be asymptotically robust and in the bivariate case is robust even for quite modest sample sizes much smaller than ours; (Cf. Chase and Bulgren [7]).

V. Conclusion

The empirical data support the APT against both an unspecified alternative—a very weak test—and the specific alternative that own variance has an independent explanatory effect on excess returns. But, as we have emphasized, these tests are only the beginning and should be viewed in that light.

A number of the empirical anomalies in the recent literature could be re-examined in the context of these results. For example, the APT would predict that insofar as price-earnings ratios have explanatory power for excess returns, they must be surrogates for the factor loadings. This provides the basis for an alternative test of the APT. On the longer term agenda, the statistical underpinnings of our analysis must be shored. Work on the small sample properties of factor analysis is scarce, and for nonnormal distributions, results appear to be nonexistent.

Lastly, of course, an effort should be directed at identifying a more meaningful set of sufficient statistics for the underlying factors. While this is not a necessary component of tests of the APT, it is an interesting and worthwhile pursuit of its own.

The issue in all of this, of course, is not whether the APT is true or false. Like all the theories that are not empty, it is false that some degree of precision in the testing: if we test long enough, all interesting theories are rejected. Rather, the question is what we will learn from these tests on how well the theory performs in competition with specific alternatives. At stake is the basic intuition of the APT that systematic variability alone affects expected returns, and this is the central theme T^2 modern asset pricing theory.

Acknowledgement

The comments and suggestions of listeners to our preliminary results on this subject have been invaluable in improving many half-baked procedures. To the extent that our soufflé is finally ready to come out of the oven, we owe a particular debt to participants in seminars at Berkeley/Stanford, Laval, Karlsruhe, and Southern California, and to the participants in the conference on "new issues in the asset pricing model" held at Coeur d'Alene, Idaho, and sponsored by Washington State University. This work originated while the authors were Leslie Wong summer fellows at the University of British Columbia in 1977. Comments by Michael Brennan, Thomas Copeland and Richard McEnally have been especially helpful. Of course, no one but us can be held responsible for remaining errors.

REFERENCES

1. J. Aitcheson and J.A.G. Brown. *The Lognormal Distribution*. Cambridge: Cambridge University Press, 1957.
2. Ray Ball. "Anomalies in Relationships Between Securities' Yields and Yield—Surrogates." *Journal of Financial Economics* (June/September 1978), 103–26.
3. Fischer Black. "Capital Market Equilibrium with Restricted Borrowing." *Journal of Business* 45 (July 1972), 444–54.
4. S. Basu. "Investment Performance of Common Stock in Relation to Their Price-Earnings Ratios: A Test of the Efficient Market Hypothesis." *Journal of Finance* 23 (June 1977), p. 663–82.
5. Douglas T. Breeden. "An Inter-Temporal Asset Pricing Model with Stochastic Consumption and Investment Opportunities." Unpublished manuscript, University of Chicago, Graduate School of Business, August 1978.
6. M. J. Brennan. "Capital Asset Pricing and the Structure of Security Returns." Unpublished manuscript, University of British Columbia, May 1971.
7. G. R. Chase and William G. Bulgren. "A Monte Carlo Investigation of the Robustness of T^2." *Journal of the American Statistical Association* 66 (September 1971), 499–502.
8. John C. Cox, Jonathan E. Ingersoll, Jr. and Stephen A. Ross. "A Theory of the Term Structure." *Econometrica*. (forthcoming).
9. Peter K. Clark. "A Subordinated Stochastic Process Model with Finite Variance for Speculative Prices." *Econometrica* 41 (January 1973), 135–55.
10. George W. Douglas. "Risk in the Equity Market: An Empirical Appraisal of Market Efficiency." *Yale Economic Essays* 9 (Spring 1969), 3–45.
11. Eugene F. Fama. "Efficient Capital Markets: A Review of Theory and Empirical Work." *Journal of Finance* 25 (May 1970), 383–417.
12. Eugene F. Fama. *Foundations of Finance*. New York: Basic Books, 1976.
13. Eugene F. Fama. "The Behavior of Stock Market Prices." *Journal of Business* 38 (January 1965), 34–105.
14. Eugene F. Fama and James D. MacBeth. "Risk, Return, and Equilibrium: Empirical Tests." *Journal of Political Economy* 38 (May 1973) 607–36.
15. D. E. Farrar. *The Investment Decision Under Uncertainty*. Englewood Cliffs, N.J.: Prentice-Hall dissertation series, 1962.
16. Milton Friedman. "The Methodology of Positive Economics," in *Essays in Positive Economics*. Chicago: University of Chicago Press, 1953.
17. Adam Gehr, Jr. "Some Tests of the Arbitrage Pricing Theory." *Journal of the Midwest Finance Association* (1975), 91–105.
18. Nils H. Hakansson. "Capital Growth and the Mean-Variance Approach to Portfolio Selection." *Journal of Financial and Quantitative Analysis* 6 (January 1971), 517–557.
19. Der-Ann Hsu, Robert B. Miller, and Dean W. Wichern. "On the Stable Paretian Behavior of Stock Market Prices." *Journal of the American Statistical Association* 69 (March 1974), 108–13.
20. Karl G. Jöreskog. "Some Contributions to Maximum Likelihood Factor Analysis." *Psychometrika* 32 (December 1967), 443–82.
21. Karl G. Jöreskog and Dag Sörbom. *EFAP, Exploratory Factor Analysis Program*. National Educational Resources, Inc., 1976.
22. Benjamin F. King. "Market and Industry Factors in Stock Price Behavior." *Journal of Business* 39 (January 1966, supp.), 139–90.

23. Alan Kraus and Robert Litzenberger. "Skewness Preference and the Valuation of Risk Assets." *Journal of Finance* 31 (September 1976), 1085–1100.

24. Lawrence Kryzanowski and To Minh Chan. "General Factor Models and the Structure of Security Returns." Working paper, Concordia University, Faculty of Commerce and Administration, (September 1979).

25. Terence C. Langetieg. "An Application of a Three-Factor Performance Index to Measure Stockholder Gains from Merger." *Journal of Financial Economics* 6 (December 1978), 365–83.

26. D. N. Lawley and A. E. Maxwell. *Factor Analysis as a Statistical Method.* London: Butterworths, 1963.

27. Cheng F. Lee. "Functional Form, Skewness Effect, and the Risk-Return Relationship." Abstracted in *Journal of Financial and Quantitative Analysis.* (March 1977), 55–72.

28. Cheng F. Lee and Joseph D. Vinso. "Single vs. Simultaneous Equation Models in Capital Asset Pricing: The Role of Firm-Related Variables." *Journal of Business Research* (1980), 65–80.

29. Haim Levy. "Equilibrium in an Imperfect Market: A Constraint on the Number of Securities in the Portfolio." *American Economic Review* (September 1978).

30. John Lintner. "The Valuation of Risk Assets and the Selection of Risky Investments in Stock Portfolios and Capital Budgets." *Review of Economics and Statistics* 47 (February 1965), 13–37.

31. Robert E. Lucas, Jr. "Asset Prices in an Exchange Economy." *Econometrica* 46 (November 1978), 1429–45.

32. Benoit Mandelbrot. "The Variation of Certain Speculative Prices." *Journal of Business* 36 (October 1963), 394–419.

33. Charles G. Martin. "Ridge Regression Estimates of the *Ex Post* Risk-Return Tradeoff on Common Stock." *Review of Business and Economic Research* 13 (Spring 1978), 1–15.

34. David Mayers. "Non-Marketable Assets and Capital Market Equilibrium Under Uncertainty." 223–248 in Michael C. Jensen, ed., *Studies in the Theory of Capital Markets.* New York: Praeger, 1972.

35. Robert C. Merton. "An Inter-Temporal Capital Asset Pricing Model." *Econometrica* 41 (September 1973), 867–87.

36. Stephen L. Meyers. "A Re-examination of Market and Industry Factors in Stock Price Behaviors." *Journal of Finance* 28 (June 1973), 695–706.

37. Merton H. Miller and Myron Scholes. "Rates of Return in Relation to Risk: A Re-examination of Some Recent Findings." 47–48 in Michael C. Jensen, ed., *Studies in the Theory of Capital Markets.* New York: Praeger, 1972.

38. Jan Mossin. "Equilibrium in a Capital Asset Market." *Econometrica* 34 (October 1966), 768–83.

39. S. James Press. *Applied Multivariate Analysis.* New York: Holt, Rinehart, and Winston, Inc., 1972.

40. Marc R. Reinganum. "Misspecification of Capital Asset Pricing: Empirical Anomalies Based on Earnings Yields and Forecasts." Unpublished manuscript, Graduate School of Business, University of Chicago, 1978.

41. Richard Roll. "A Critique of the Asset Pricing Theory's Tests." *Journal of Financial Economics* 4 (May 1977), 129–76.

42. Richard Roll. "Ambiguity When Performance is Measured by the Securities Market Line." *Journal of Finance* 33 (September 1978), 1051–69.

43. Richard Roll. "Testing a Portfolio for Ex Ante Mean/Variance Efficiency." In E. Elton and M. Gruber, eds., *TIMS Studies in the Management Sciences.* Amsterdam: North-Holland, 1979.

44. Barr Rosenberg and Vinay Marathe. "Tests of Capital Asset Pricing Hypotheses." Unpublished manuscript, University of California, Berkeley, 1977.

45. Barr Rosenberg. "Extra-Market Components of Covariance in Security Returns." *Journal of Financial and Quantitative Analysis* 9 (March 1974), 263–74.

46. Barr Rosenberg and Michael Houglet. "Error Rates in CRSP and Compustat Data Bases and Their Implications." *Journal of Finance* 29 (September 1974), 1303–10.

47. Stephen A. Ross. "Return Risk, and Arbitrage." In Irwin Friend, and James L. Bicksler, eds., *Risk and Return in Finance,* I, 189–218. Cambridge, Mass.: Ballinger, 1977.

48. Stephen A. Ross. "The Arbitrage Theory of Capital Asset Pricing." *Journal of Economic Theory* 13 (December 1976), 341–60.

49. Stephen A. Ross. "The Current Status of the Capital Asset Pricing Model (CAPM)." *Journal of Finance* 33 (June 1978), 885–90.

50. William F. Sharpe. "A Simplified Model for Portfolio Analysis." *Management Science* 9 (January 1963), 277–93.

51. William F. Sharpe. "Capital Asset Prices: A Theory of Market Equilibrium Under Conditions of Risk." *Journal of Finance* 19 (September 1964), 425–42.

52. William F. Sharpe. "The Capital Asset Pricing Model: A 'Multi-Beta' Interpretation." In H. Levy and M. Sarnat, eds., *Financial Decision Making Under Uncertainty*. New York: Academic Press, 1977.

53. Ledyard R. Tucker and Charles Lewis. "A Reliability Coefficient for Maximum Likelihood Factor Analysis." *Psychometrika* 38 (March 1973), 1–10.

54. James C. Van Horne. *Financial Management and Policy*, 4th ed. Englewood Cliffs, N.J. Prentice-Hall, 1977.

PART III

CONTINGENT CLAIMS

* *

13. THE PRICING OF OPTIONS AND CORPORATE LIABILITIES

FISCHER BLACK*
and
MYRON SCHOLES†

Reprinted from *The Journal of Political Economy,* Vol. 81, No. 3 (May–June 1973), pp. 637–654, by permission of the authors and The University of Chicago Press. Copyright © 1973 by the University of Chicago.

If options are correctly priced in the market, it should not be possible to make sure profits by creating portfolios of long and short positions in options and their underlying stocks. Using this principle, a theoretical valuation formula for options is derived. Since almost all corporate liabilities can be viewed as combinations of options, the formula and the analysis that led to it are also applicable to corporate liabilities such as common stock, corporate bonds, and warrants. In particular, the formula can be used to derive the discount that should be applied to a corporate bond because of the possibility of default.

INTRODUCTION

An option is a security giving the right to buy or sell an asset, subject to certain conditions, within a specified period of time. An "American option" is one that can be exercised at any time up to the date the option expires. A "European option" is one that can be exercised only on a specified future date.

* University of Chicago, Chicago, Illinois.

† Massachusetts Institute of Technology, Cambridge, Massachusetts.

The inspiration for this work was provided by Jack L. Treynor (1961a, 1961b). We are grateful for extensive comments on earlier drafts by Eugene F. Fama, Robert C. Merton, and Merton H. Miller. This work was supported in part by the Ford Foundation.

The price that is paid for the asset when the option is exercised is called the "exercise price" or "striking price." The last day on which the option may be exercised is called the "expiration date" or "maturity date."

The simplest kind of option is one that gives the right to buy a single share of common stock. Throughout most of the paper, we will be discussing this kind of option, which is often referred to as a "call option."

In general, it seems clear that the higher the price of the stock, the greater the value of the option. When the stock price is much greater than the exercise price, the option is almost sure to be exercised. The current value of the option will thus be approximately equal to the price of the stock minus the price of a pure discount bond that matures on the same date as the option, with a face value equal to the striking price of the option.

On the other hand, if the price of the stock is much less than the exercise price, the option is almost sure to expire without being exercised, so its value will be near zero.

If the expiration date of the option is very far in the future, then the price of a bond that pays the exercise price on the maturity date will be very low, and the value of the option will be approximately equal to the price of the stock.

On the other hand, if the expiration date is very near, the value of the option will be approximately equal to the stock price minus the exercise price, or zero, if the stock price is less than the exercise price. Normally, the value of an option declines as its maturity date approaches, if the value of the stock does not change.

These general properties of the relation between the option value and the stock price are often illustrated in a diagram like Figure 1. Line *A* represents

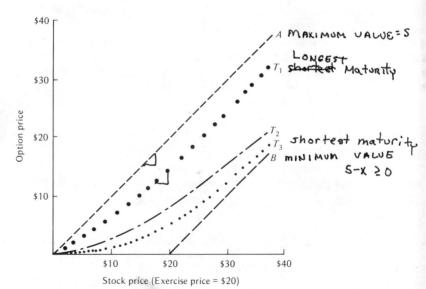

FIGURE 1.   The relation between option value and stock price.

the maximum value of the option, since it cannot be worth more than the stock. Line B represents the minimum value of the option, since its value cannot be negative and cannot be less than the stock price minus the exercise price. Lines T_1, T_2, and T_3 represent the value of the option for successively shorter maturities.

Normally, the curve representing the value of an option will be concave upward. Since it also lies below the 45° line, A, we can see that the option will be more volatile than the stock. A given percentage change in the stock price, holding maturity constant, will result in a larger percentage change in the option value. The relative volatility of the option is not constant, however. It depends on both the stock price and maturity.

Most of the previous work on the valuation of options has been expressed in terms of warrants. For example, Sprenkle (1961), Ayres (1963), Boness (1964), Samuelson (1965), Baumol, Malkiel, and Quandt (1966), and Chen (1970) all produced valuation formulas of the same general form. Their formulas, however, were not complete, since they all involved one or more arbitrary parameters.

For example, Sprenkle's formula for the value of an option can be written as follows:

$$kxN(b_1) - k^*cN(b_2)$$

$$b_1 = \frac{\ln kx/c + \frac{1}{2}v^2(t^* - t)}{v\sqrt{(t^* - t)}}$$

$$b_2 = \frac{\ln kx/c - \frac{1}{2}v^2(t^* - t)}{v\sqrt{(t^* - t)}}$$

In this expression, x is the stock price, c is the exercise price, t^* is the maturity date, t is the current date, v^2 is the variance rate of the return on the stock,[1] ln is the natural logarithm, and $N(b)$ is the cumulative normal density function. But k and k^* are unknown parameters. Sprenkle (1961) defines k as the ratio of the expected value of the stock price at the time the warrant matures to the current stock price, and k^* as a discount factor that depends on the risk of the stock. He tries to estimate the values of k and k^* empirically, but finds that he is unable to do so.

More typically, Samuelson (1965) has unknown parameters α and β, where α is the rate of expected return on the stock, and β is the rate of expected return on the warrant or the discount rate to be applied to the warrant.[2] He assumes that the distribution of possible values of the stock when the warrant matures is log-normal and takes the expected value of this distribution, cutting it off at

---

[1] The variance rate of the return on a security is the limit, as the size of the interval of measurement goes to zero, of the variance of the return over that interval divided by the length of the interval.

[2] The rate of expected return on a security is the limit, as the size of the interval of measurement goes to zero, of the expected return over that interval divided by the length of the interval.

the exercise price. He then discounts this expected value to the present at the rate β. Unfortunately, there seems to be no model of the pricing of securities under conditions of capital market equilibrium that would make this an appropriate procedure for determining the value of a warrant.

In a subsequent paper, Samuelson and Merton (1969) recognize the fact that discounting the expected value of the distribution of possible values of the warrant when it is exercised is not an appropriate procedure. They advance the theory by treating the option price as a function of the stock price. They also recognize that the discount rates are determined in part by the requirement that investors be willing to hold all of the outstanding amounts of both the stock and the option. But they do not make use of the fact that investors must hold other assets as well, so that the risk of an option or stock that affects its discount rate is only that part of the risk that cannot be diversified away. Their final formula depends on the shape of the utility function that they assume for the typical investor.

One of the concepts that we use in developing our model is expressed by Thorp and Kassouf (1967). They obtain an empirical valuation formula for warrants by fitting a curve to actual warrant prices. Then they use this formula to calculate the ratio of shares of stock to options needed to create a hedged position by going long in one security and short in the other. What they fail to pursue is the fact that in equilibrium, the expected return on such a hedged position must be equal to the return on a riskless asset. What we show below is that this equilibrium condition can be used to derive a theoretical valuation formula.

THE VALUATION FORMULA

In deriving our formula for the value of an option in terms of the price of the stock, we will assume "ideal conditions" in the market for the stock and for the option:

1. The short-term interest rate is known and is constant through time.
2. The stock price follows a random walk in continuous time with a variance rate proportional to the square of the stock price. Thus the distribution of possible stock prices at the end of any finite interval is log-normal. The variance rate of the return on the stock is constant.
3. The stock pays no dividends or other distributions.
4. The option is "European," that is, it can only be exercised at maturity.
5. There are no transaction costs in buying or selling the stock or the option.
6. It is possible to borrow any fraction of the price of a security to buy it or to hold it, at the short-term interest rate.
7. There are no penalties to short selling. A seller who does not own a security will simply accept the price of the security from a buyer, and will agree to settle with the buyer on some future date by paying him an amount equal to the price of the security on that date.

Under these assumptions, the value of the option will depend only on the price of the stock and time and on variables that are taken to be known constants. Thus, it is possible to create a hedged position, consisting of a long position in the stock and a short position in the option, whose value will not depend on the price of the stock, but will depend only on time and the values of known constants. Writing $w(x, t)$ for the value of the option as a function of the stock price x and time t, the number of options that must be sold short against one share of stock long is:

$$1/w_1(x,t). \qquad W_1 = slope \qquad (1)$$

In expression (1), the subscript refers to the partial derivative of $w(x,t)$ with respect to its first argument.

To see that the value of such a hedged position does not depend on the price of the stock, note that the ratio of the change in the option value to the change in the stock price, when the change in the stock price is small, is $w_1(x,t)$. To a first approximation, if the stock price changes by an amount Δx, the option price will change by an amount $w_1(x, t) \Delta x$, and the number of options given by expression (1) will change by an amount Δx. Thus, the change in the value of a long position in the stock will be approximately offset by the change in value of a short position in $1/w_1$ options.

As the variables x and t change, the number of options to be sold short to create a hedged position with one share of stock changes. If the hedge is maintained continuously, then the approximations mentioned above become exact, and the return on the hedged position is completely independent of the change in the value of the stock. In fact, the return on the hedged position becomes certain.[3]

To illustrate the formation of the hedged position, let us refer to the solid line (T_2) in figure 1 and assume that the price of the stock starts at $15.00, so that the value of the option starts at $5.00. Assume also that the slope of the line at that point is ½. This means that the hedged position is created by buying one share of stock and selling two options short. One share of stock costs $15.00, and the sale of two options brings in $10.00, so the equity in this position is $5.00.

If the hedged position is not changed as the price of the stock changes, then there is some uncertainty in the value of the equity at the end of a finite interval. Suppose that two options go from $10.00 to $15.75 when the stock goes from $15.00 to $20.00, and that they go from $10.00 to $5.75 when the stock goes from $15.00 to $10.00. Thus, the equity goes from $5.00 to $4.25 when the stock changes by $5.00 in either direction. This is a $.75 decline in the equity for a $5.00 change in the stock in either direction.[4]

---

[3] This was pointed out to us by Robert Merton.

[4] These figures are purely for illustrative purposes. They correspond roughly to the way Figure 1 was drawn, but not to an option on any actual security.

In addition, the curve shifts (say from T_2 to T_3 in Fig. 1) as the maturity of the options changes. The resulting decline in value of the options means an increase in the equity in the hedged position and tends to offset the possible losses due to a large change in the stock price.

Note that the decline in the equity value due to a large change in the stock price is small. The ratio of the decline in the equity value to the magnitude of the change in the stock price becomes smaller as the magnitude of the change in the stock price becomes smaller.

Note also that the direction of the change in the equity value is independent of the direction of the change in the stock price. This means that under our assumption that the stock price follows a continuous random walk and that the return has a constant variance rate, the covariance between the return on the equity and the return on the stock will be zero. If the stock price and the value of the "market portfolio" follow a joint continuous random walk with constant covariance rate, it means that the covariance between the return on the equity and the return on the market will be zero.

Thus the risk in the hedged position is zero if the short position in the option is adjusted continuously. If the position is not adjusted continuously, the risk is small, and consists entirely of risk that can be diversified away by forming a portfolio of a large number of such hedged positions.

In general, since the hedged position contains one share of stock long and $1/w_1$ options short, the value of the equity in the position is:

$$x - w/w_1. \tag{2}$$

The change in the value of the equity in a short interval Δt is:

$$\Delta x - \Delta w/w_1. \tag{3}$$

Assuming that the short position is changed continuously, we can use stochastic calculus[5] to expand Δw, which is $w(x + \Delta x, t + \Delta t) - w(x,t)$, as follows:

$$\Delta w = w_1\Delta x + \tfrac{1}{2}w_{11}v^2x^2\Delta t + w_2\Delta t. \tag{4}$$

In equation (4), the subscripts on w refer to partial derivatives, and v^2 is the variance rate of the return on the stock.[6] Substituting from equation (4) into expression (3), we find that the change in the value of the equity in the hedged position is:

$$-(\tfrac{1}{2}w_{11}v^2x^2 + w_2) \, \Delta t/w_1. \tag{5}$$

Since the return on the equity in the hedged position is certain, the return must be equal to $r \, \Delta t$. Even if the hedged position is not changed continuously, its risk is small and is entirely risk that can be diversified away, so the expected

[5] For an exposition of stochastic calculus, see McKean (1969).
[6] See Note 1.

return on the hedged position must be at the short-term interest rate.[7] If this were not true, speculators would try to profit by borrowing large amounts of money to create such hedged positions, and would in the process force the returns down to the short-term interest rate.

Thus the change in the equity (5) must equal the value of the equity (2) times $r \Delta t$.

$$-(\tfrac{1}{2}w_{11}v^2x^2 + w_2) \Delta t/w_1 = (x - w/w_1)r\Delta t. \qquad (6)$$

Dropping the Δt from both sides, and rearranging, we have a differential equation for the value of the option.

$$w_2 = rw - rxw_1 - \tfrac{1}{2}v^2x^2w_{11}. \qquad (7)$$

Writing t^* for the maturity date of the option, and c for the exercise price, we know that:

$$
\begin{aligned}
w(x,t^*) &= x - c, \quad x \geq c \\
&= 0, \qquad\quad x < c.
\end{aligned}
\qquad (8)
$$

There is only one formula $w(x,t)$ that satisfies the differential equation (7) subject to the boundary condition (8). This formula must be the option valuation formula.

To solve this differential equation, we make the following substitution:

$$
\begin{aligned}
w(x,t) = {}& e^{r(t-t^*)}y[(2/v^2)(r - \tfrac{1}{2}v^2)[\ln x/c - (r - \tfrac{1}{2}v^2)(t - t^*)], \qquad (9) \\
& -(2/v^2)(r - \tfrac{1}{2}v^2)^2(t - t^*)].
\end{aligned}
$$

With this substitution, the differential equation becomes:

$$y_2 = y_{11}, \qquad (10)$$

and the boundary condition becomes:

$$
\begin{aligned}
y(u,0) &= 0, && u < 0 \\
&= c[e^{u(1/2v^2)/(r - 1/2v^2)} - 1], && u \geq 0.
\end{aligned}
\qquad (11)
$$

The differential equation (10) is the heat-transfer equation of physics, and its solution is given by Churchill (1963, p. 155). In our notation, the solution is:

---

[7] For a thorough discussion of the relation between risk and expected return, see Fama and Miller (1972) or Sharpe (1970). To see that the risk in the hedged position can be diversified away, note that if we don't adjust the hedge continuously, expression (5) becomes:

$$-(\tfrac{1}{2}w_{11} \Delta x^2 + w_2 \Delta t)/w_1. \qquad (5')$$

Writing Δm for the change in the value of the market portfolio between t and $t + \Delta t$, the "market risk" in the hedged position is proportional to the covariance between the change in the value of the hedged portfolio, as given by expression (5'), and Δm: $-\tfrac{1}{2}w_{11} \operatorname{cov}(\Delta x^2, \Delta m)$. But if Δx and Δm follow a joint normal distribution for small intervals Δt, this covariance will be zero. Since there is no market risk in the hedged position, all of the risk due to the fact that the hedge is not continuously adjusted must be risk that can be diversified away.

$$y(u,s) = 1/\sqrt{2\pi} \int_{-u/\sqrt{2}s}^{\infty} c[e^{(u+q\sqrt{2}s)(1/2v^2)/(r-1/2v^2)} - 1]e^{-q^2/2} \, dq. \tag{12}$$

Substituting from equation (12) into equation (9), and simplifying, we find:

$$w(x,t) = xN(d_1) - ce^{r(t-t^*)}N(d_2)$$
$$d_1 = \frac{\ln x/c + (r + \tfrac{1}{2}v^2)(t^* - t)}{v\sqrt{t^* - t}} \tag{13}$$
$$d_2 = \frac{\ln x/c + (r - \tfrac{1}{2}v^2)(t^* - t)}{v\sqrt{t^* - t}}$$

In equation (13), $N(d)$ is the cumulative normal density function.

Note that the expected return on the stock does not appear in equation (13). The option value as a function of the stock price is independent of the expected return on the stock. The expected return on the option, however, will depend on the expected return on the stock. The faster the stock price rises, the faster the option price will rise through the functional relationship (13).

Note that the maturity $(t^* - t)$ appears in the formula only multiplied by the interest rate r or the variance rate v^2. Thus, an increase in maturity has the same effect on the value of the option as an equal percentage increase in both r and v^2.

Merton (1973) has shown that the option value as given by equation (13) increases continuously as any one of t^*, r, or v^2 increases. In each case, it approaches a maximum value equal to the stock price.

The partial derivative w_1 of the valuation formula is of interest, because it determines the ratio of shares of stock to options in the hedged position as in expression (1). Taking the partial derivative of equation (13), and simplifying, we find that:

$$w_1(x,t) = N(d_1). \tag{14}$$

In equation (14), d_1 is as defined in equation (13).

From equations (13) and (14), it is clear that xw_1/w is always greater than one. This shows that the option is always more volatile than the stock.

AN ALTERNATIVE DERIVATION

It is also possible to derive the differential equation (7) using the "capital asset pricing model."[8] This derivation is given because it gives more under-

---

[8] The model was developed by Treynor (1961b), Sharpe (1964), Lintner (1965), and Mossin (1966). It is summarized by Sharpe (1970), and Fama and Miller (1972). The model was originally stated as a single-period model. Extending it to a multiperiod model is, in general, difficult. Fama (1970), however, has shown that if we make an assumption that implies that the short-term interest rate is constant through time, then the model must apply to each successive period in time. His proof also goes through under somewhat more general assumptions.

standing of the way in which one can discount the value of an option to the present, using a discount rate that depends on both time and the price of the stock.

The capital asset pricing model describes the relation between risk and expected return for a capital asset under conditions of market equilibrium.[8] The expected return on an asset gives the discount that must be applied to the end-of-period value of the asset to give its present value. Thus, the capital-asset pricing model gives a general method for discounting under uncertainty.

The capital-asset pricing model says that the expected return on an asset is a linear function of its β, which is defined as the covariance of the return on the asset with the return on the market, divided by the variance of the return on the market. From equation (4) we see that the covariance of the return on the option $\Delta w/w$ with the return on the market is equal to xw_1/w times the covariance of the return on the stock $\Delta x/x$ with the return on the market. Thus, we have the following relation between the option's β and the stock's β:

$$\beta_w = (xw_1/w)\beta_x. \tag{15}$$

The expression xw_1/w may also be interpreted as the "elasticity" of the option price with respect to the stock price. It is the ratio of the percentage change in the option price to the percentage change in the stock price, for small percentage changes, holding maturity constant.

To apply the capital-asset pricing model to an option and the underlying stock, let us first define a as the rate of expected return on the market minus the interest rate.[9] Then the expected return on the option and the stock are:

$$E(\Delta x/x) = r\,\Delta t + a\beta_x\,\Delta t, \tag{16}$$
$$E(\Delta w/w) = r\,\Delta t + a\beta_w\,\Delta t. \tag{17}$$

Multiplying equation (17) by w, and substituting β_w from equation (15), we find:

$$E(\Delta w) = rw\Delta t + axw_1\beta_x\,\Delta t. \tag{18}$$

Using stochastic calculus,[10] we can expand Δw, which is $w(x + \Delta x, t + \Delta t) - w(x,t)$, as follows:

$$\Delta w = w_1\Delta x + \tfrac{1}{2}w_{11}v^2x^2\,\Delta t + w_2\,\Delta t. \tag{19}$$

Taking the expected value of equation (19), and substituting for $E(\Delta x)$ from equation (16), we have:

$$E(\Delta w) = rxw_1\Delta t + axw_1\beta_x\Delta t + \tfrac{1}{2}v^2x^2w_{11}\Delta t + w_2\Delta t. \tag{20}$$

---

[9] See Note 2.

[10] For an exposition of stochastic calculus, see McKean (1969).

Combining equations (18) and (20), we find that the terms involving a and β_x cancel, giving:

$$w_2 = rw - rxw_1 - \tfrac{1}{2}v^2x^2w_{11}. \tag{21}$$

Equation (21) is the same as equation (7).

MORE COMPLICATED OPTIONS

The valuation formula (13) was derived under the assumption that the option can only be exercised at time t^*. Merton (1973) has shown, however, that the value of the option is always greater than the value it would have if it were exercised immediately $(x - c)$. Thus, a rational investor will not exercise a call option before maturity, and the value of an American call option is the same as the value of a European call option.

There is a simple modification of the formula that will make it applicable to European put options (options to sell) as well as call options (options to buy). Writing $u(x,t)$ for the value of a put option, we see that the differential equation remains unchanged.

$$u_2 = ru - rxu_1 - \tfrac{1}{2}v^2x^2u_{11}. \tag{22}$$

The boundary condition, however, becomes:

$$\begin{aligned} u(x,t^*) &= 0, & x \geq c \\ &= c - x, & x < c. \end{aligned} \tag{23}$$

To get the solution to this equation with the new boundary condition, we can simply note that the difference between the value of a call and the value of a put on the same stock, if both can be exercised only at maturity, must obey the same differential equation, but with the following boundary condition:

$$w(x,t^*) - u(x,t^*) = x - c. \tag{24}$$

The solution to the differential equation with this boundary condition is:

$$w(x,t) - u(x,t) = x - ce^{r(t-t^*)}. \tag{25}$$

Thus the value of the European put option is:

$$u(x,t) = w(x,t) - x + ce^{r(t-t^*)}. \tag{26}$$

Putting in the value of $w(x,t)$ from (13), and noting that $1 - N(d)$ is equal to $N(-d)$, we have:

$$u(x,t) = -xN(-d_1) + ce^{-rt^*}N(-d_2). \tag{27}$$

In equation (27), d_1 and d_2 are defined as in equation (13).

Equation (25) also gives us a relation between the value of a European call and the value of a European put.[11] We see that if an investor were to buy a call and sell a put, his returns would be exactly the same as if he bought the stock on margin, borrowing $ce^{r(t-t^*)}$ toward the price of the stock.

Merton (1973) has also shown that the value of an American put option will be greater than the value of a European put option. This is true because it is sometimes advantageous to exercise a put option before maturity, if it is possible to do so. For example, suppose the stock price falls almost to zero and that the probability that the price will exceed the exercise price before the option expires is negligible. Then it will pay to exercise the option immediately, so that the exercise price will be received sooner rather than later. The investor thus gains the interest on the exercise price for the period up to the time he would otherwise have exercised it. So far, no one has been able to obtain a formula for the value of an American put option.

If we relax the assumption that the stock pays no dividend, we begin to get into some complicated problems. First of all, under certain conditions it will pay to exercise an American call option before maturity. Merton (1973) has shown that this can be true only just before the stock's ex-dividend date. Also, it is not clear what adjustment might be made in the terms of the option to protect the option holder against a loss due to a large dividend on the stock and to ensure that the value of the option will be the same as if the stock paid no dividend. Currently, the exercise price of a call option is generally reduced by the amount of any dividend paid on the stock. We can see that this is not adequate protection by imagining that the stock is that of a holding company and that it pays out all of its assets in the form of a dividend to its shareholders. This will reduce the price of the stock and the value of the option to zero, no matter what adjustment is made in the exercise price of the option. In fact, this example shows that there may not be any adjustment in the terms of the option that will give adequate protection against a large dividend. In this case, the option value is going to be zero after the distribution, no matter what its terms are. Merton (1973) was the first to point out that the current adjustment for dividends is not adequate.

WARRANT VALUATION

A warrant is an option that is a liability of a corporation. The holder of a warrant has the right to buy the corporation's stock (or other assets) on specified terms. The analysis of warrants is often much more complicated than the analysis of simple options, because:

1. The life of a warrant is typically measured in years, rather than months. Over a period of years, the variance rate of the return on the stock may be expected to change substantially.
2. The exercise price of the warrant is usually not adjusted at all for dividends.

---

[11] The relation between the value of a call option and the value of a put option was first noted by Stoll (1969). He does not realize, however, that his analysis applies only to European options.

The possibility that dividends will be paid requires a modification of the valuation formula.

3. The exercise price of a warrant sometimes changes on specified dates. It may pay to exercise a warrant just before its exercise price changes. This too requires a modification of the valuation formula.

4. If the company is involved in a merger, the adjustment that is made in the terms of the warrant may change its value.

5. Sometimes the exercise price can be paid using bonds of the corporation at face value, even though they may at the time be selling at a discount. This complicates the analysis and means that early exercise may sometimes be desirable.

6. The exercise of a large number of warrants may sometimes result in a significant increase in the number of common shares outstanding.

In some cases, these complications can be treated as insignificant, and equation (13) can be used as an approximation to give an estimate of the warrant value. In other cases, some simple modifications of equation (13) will improve the approximation. Suppose, for example, that there are warrants outstanding, which, if exercised, would double the number of shares of the company's common stock. Let us define the "equity" of the company as the sum of the value of all of its warrants and the value of all of its common stock. If the warrants are exercised at maturity, the equity of the company will increase by the aggregate amount of money paid in by the warrant holders when they exercise. The warrant holders will then own half of the new equity of the company, which is equal to the old equity plus the exercise money.

Thus, at maturity, the warrant holders will either receive nothing, or half of the new equity, minus the exercise money. Thus, they will receive nothing or half of the difference between the old equity and half the exercise money. We can look at the warrants as options to buy shares in the equity rather than shares of common stock, at half the stated exercise price rather than at the full exercise price. The value of a share in the equity is defined as the sum of the value of the warrants and the value of the common stock, divided by twice the number of outstanding shares of common stock. If we take this point of view, then we will take v^2 in equation (13) to be the variance rate of the return on the company's equity, rather than the variance rate of the return on the company's common stock.

A similar modification in the parameters of equation (13) can be made if the number of shares of stock outstanding after exercise of the warrants will be other than twice the number of shares outstanding before exercise of the warrants.

COMMON STOCK AND BOND VALUATION

It is not generally realized that corporate liabilities other than warrants may be viewed as options. Consider, for example, a company that has common stock and bonds outstanding and whose only asset is shares of common stock of a second company. Suppose that the bonds are "pure discount bonds" with no coupon, giving the holder the right to a fixed sum of money, if the corporation can pay it, with a maturity of 10 years. Suppose that the bonds contain no restrictions on the company except a restriction that the company cannot pay any dividends until after the bonds are paid off. Finally, suppose that the company plans to sell all the stock it holds at the end of 10 years, pay off the bond holders if possible, and pay any remaining money to the stockholders as a liquidating dividend.

Under these conditions, it is clear that the stockholders have the equivalent of an option on their company's assets. In effect, the bond holders own the company's assets, but they have given options to the stockholders to buy the assets back. The value of the common stock at the end of 10 years will be the value of the company's assets minus the face value of the bonds, or zero, whichever is greater.

Thus, the value of the common stock will be $w(x,t)$, as given by equation (13), where we take v^2 to be the variance rate of the return on the shares held by the company, c to be the total face value of the outstanding bonds, and x to be the total value of the shares held by the company. The value of the bonds will simply be $x - w(x,t)$.

By subtracting the value of the bonds given by this formula from the value they would have if there were no default risk, we can figure the discount that should be applied to the bonds due to the existence of default risk.

Suppose, more generally, that the corporation holds business assets rather than financial assets. Suppose that at the end of the 10 year period, it will recapitalize by selling an entirely new class of common stock, using the proceeds to pay off the bond holders, and paying any money that is left to the old stockholders to retire their stock. In the absence of taxes, it is clear that the value of the corporation can be taken to be the sum of the total value of the debt and the total value of the common stock.[12] The amount of debt outstanding will not affect the total value of the corporation, but will affect the division of that value between the bonds and the stock. The formula for $w(x,t)$ will again describe the total value of the common stock, where x is taken to be the sum of the value of the bonds and the value of the stock. The formula for $x - w(x,t)$ will again describe the total value of the bonds. It can be shown that, as the face value c of the bonds increases, the market value $x - w(x,t)$ increases by a smaller percentage. An increase in the corporation's debt, keeping the total value of the corporation constant, will increase the probability of default and will thus reduce the market value of one of the corporation's bonds. If the company changes its capital structure by issuing more bonds and using the proceeds to retire common stock, it will hurt the existing bond holders, and

---

[12] The fact that the total value of a corporation is not affected by its capital structure, in the absence of taxes and other imperfections, was first shown by Modigliani and Miller (1958).

help the existing stockholders. The bond price will fall, and the stock price will rise. In this sense, changes in the capital structure of a firm may affect the price of its common stock.[13] The price changes will occur when the change in the capital structure becomes certain, not when the actual change takes place.

Because of this possibility, the bond indenture may prohibit the sale of additional debt of the same or higher priority in the event that the firm is recapitalized. If the corporation issues new bonds that are subordinated to the existing bonds and uses the proceeds to retire common stock, the price of the existing bonds and the common stock price will be unaffected. Similarly, if the company issues new common stock and uses the proceeds to retire completely the most junior outstanding issue of bonds, neither the common stock price nor the price of any other issue of bonds will be affected.

The corporation's dividend policy will also affect the division of its total value between the bonds and the stock.[14] To take an extreme example, suppose again that the corporation's only assets are the shares of another company, and suppose that it sells all these shares and uses the proceeds to pay a dividend to its common stockholders. Then the value of the firm will go to zero, and the value of the bonds will go to zero. The common stockholders will have "stolen" the company out from under the bond holders. Even for dividends of modest size, a higher dividend always favors the stockholders at the expense of the bond holders. A liberalization of dividend policy will increase the common stock price and decrease the bond price.[15] Because of this possibility, bond indentures contain restrictions on dividend policy, and the common stockholders have an incentive to pay themselves the largest dividend allowed by the terms of the bond indenture. However, it should be noted that the size of the effect of changing dividend policy will normally be very small.

[13] For a discussion of this point, see Fama and Miller (1972, pp. 151–52).

[14] Miller and Modigliani (1961) show that the total value of a firm, in the absence of taxes and other imperfections, is not affected by its dividend policy. They also note that the price of the common stock and the value of the bonds will not be affected by a change in dividend policy if the funds for a higher dividend are raised by issuing common stock or if the money released by a lower dividend is used to repurchase common stock.

[15] This is true assuming that the liberalization of dividend policy is not accompanied by a change in the company's current and planned financial structure. Since the issue of common stock or junior debt will hurt the common shareholders (holding dividend policy constant), they will normally try to liberalize dividend policy without issuing new securities. They may be able to do this by selling some of the firm's financial assets, such as ownership claims on other firms. Or they may be able to do it by adding to the company's short-term bank debt, which is normally senior to its long-term debt. Finally, the company may be able to finance a higher dividend by selling off a division. Assuming that it receives a fair price for the division, and that there were no economies of combination, this need not involve any loss to the firm as a whole. If the firm issues new common stock or junior debt in exactly the amounts needed to finance the liberalization of dividend policy, then the common stock and bond prices will not be affected. If the liberalization of dividend policy is associated with a decision to issue more common stock or junior debt than is needed to pay the higher dividends, the common stock price will fall and the bond price will rise. But these actions are unlikely, since they are not in the stockholders' best interests.

If the company has coupon bonds rather than pure discount bonds outstanding, then we can view the common stock as a "compound option." The common stock is an option on an option on . . . an option on the firm. After making the last interest payment, the stockholders have an option to buy the company from the bond holders for the face value of the bonds. Call this "option 1." After making the next-to-the-last interest payment, but before making the last interest payment, the stockholders have an option to buy option 1 by making the last interest payment. Call this "option 2." Before making the next-to-the-last interest payment, the stockholders have an option to buy option 2 by making that interest payment. This is "option 3." The value of the stockholders' claim at any point in time is equal to the value of option $n + 1$, where n is the number of interest payments remaining in the life of the bond.

If payments to a sinking fund are required along with interest payments, then a similar analysis can be made. In this case, there is no "balloon payment" at the end of the life of the bond. The sinking fund will have a final value equal to the face value of the bond. Option 1 gives the stockholders the right to buy the company from the bond holders by making the last sinking fund and interest payment. Option 2 gives the stockholders the right to buy option 1 by making the next-to-the-last sinking fund and interest payment. And the value of the stockholders' claim at any point in time is equal to the value of option n, where n is the number of sinking fund and interest payments remaining in the life of the bond. It is clear that the value of a bond for which sinking fund payments are required is greater than the value of a bond for which they are not required.

If the company has callable bonds, then the stockholders have more than one option. They can buy the next option by making the next interest or sinking fund and interest payment, or they can exercise their option to retire the bonds before maturity at prices specified by the terms of the call feature. Under our assumption of a constant short-term interest rate, the bonds would never sell above face value, and the usual kind of call option would never be exercised. Under more general assumptions, however, the call feature would have value to the stockholders and would have to be taken into account in deciding how the value of the company is divided between the stockholders and the bond holders.

Similarly, if the bonds are convertible, we simply add another option to the package. It is an option that the bond holders have to buy part of the company from the stockholders.

Unfortunately, these more complicated options cannot be handled by using the valuation formula (13). The valuation formula assumes that the variance rate of the return on the optioned asset is constant. But the variance of the return on an option is certainly not constant; it depends on the price of the stock and the maturity of the option. Thus the formula cannot be used, even as an approximation, to give the value of an option on an option. It is possible, however, that an analysis in the same spirit as the one that led to equation (13) would allow at least a numerical solution to the valuation of certain more complicated options.

EMPIRICAL TESTS

We have done empirical tests of the valuation formula on a large body of call-option data (Black and Scholes 1972). These tests indicate that the actual prices at which options are bought and sold deviate in certain systematic ways from the values predicted by the formula. Option buyers pay prices that are consistently higher than those predicted by the formula. Option writers, however, receive prices that are at about the level predicted by the formula. There are large transaction costs in the option market, all of which are effectively paid by option buyers.

Also, the difference between the price paid by option buyers and the value given by the formula is greater for options on low-risk stocks than for options on high-risk stocks. The market appears to underestimate the effect of differences in variance rate on the value of an option. Given the magnitude of the transaction costs in this market, however, this systematic misestimation of value does not imply profit opportunities for a speculator in the option market.

REFERENCES

Ayres, Herbert F. "Risk Aversion in the Warrants Market." *Indus. Management Rev.* 4 (Fall 1963): 497–505. Reprinted in Cootner (1967), pp. 497–505.

Baumol, William J.; Malkiel, Burton G.; and Quandt, Richard E. "The Valuation of Convertible Securities." *Q.J.E.* 80 (February 1966): 48–59.

Black, Fischer, and Scholes, Myron. "The Valuation of Option Contracts and a Test of Market Efficiency." *J. Finance* 27 (May 1972): 399–417.

Boness, A. James. "Elements of a Theory of Stock-Option Values." *J.P.E.* 72 (April 1974): 163–75.

Chen, Andrew H. Y. "A Model of Warrant Pricing in a Dynamic Market." *J. Finance* 25 (December 1970): 1041–60.

Churchill, R. V. *Fourier Series and Boundary Value Problems,* 2d ed. New York: McGraw-Hill, 1963.

Cootner, Paul A. *The Random Character of Stock Market Prices.* Cambridge, Mass.: M.I.T. Press, 1967.

Fama, Eugene F. "Multiperiod Consumption-Investment Decisions." *A.E.R.* 60 (March 1970): 163–74.

Fama, Eugene F., and Miller, Merton H. *The Theory of Finance.* New York: Holt, Rinehart & Winston, 1972.

Lintner, John. "The Valuation of Risk Assets and the Selection of Risky

Investments in Stock Portfolios and Capital Budgets." *Rev. Econ. and Statis.* 47 (February 1964): 768–83.

McKean, H. P., Jr. *Stochastic Integrals.* New York: Academic Press, 1969.

Merton, Robert C. "Theory of Rational Option Pricing." *Bell J. Econ. and Management Sci.* (1973).

Miller, Merton H., and Modigliani, Franco. "Dividend Policy, Growth, and the Valuation of Shares." *J. Bus.* 34 (October 1961): 411–33.

Modigliani, Franco, and Miller, Merton H. "The Cost of Capital, Corporation Finance, and the Theory of Investment." *A.E.R.* 48 (June 1958): 261–97.

Mossin, Jan. "Equilibrium in a Capital Asset Market." *Econometrica* 34 (October 1966): 768–83.

Samuelson, Paul A. "Rational Theory of Warrant Pricing." *Indus. Management Rev.* 6 (Spring 1965): 13–31. Reprinted in Cootner (1967), pp. 506–32.

Samuelson, Paul A., and Merton, Robert C. "A Complete Model of Warrant Pricing that Maximizes Utility." *Indus. Management Rev.* 10 (Winter 1969): 17–46.

Sharpe, William F. "Capital Asset Prices: A Theory of Market Equilibrium Under Conditions of Risk." *J. Finance* 19 (September 1964): 425–42.

———. *Portfolio Theory and Capital Markets:* New York: McGraw-Hill, 1970.

Sprenkle, Case. "Warrant Prices as Indications of Expectations." *Yale Econ. Essays* 1 (1961): 179–232. Reprinted in Cootner (1967), 412–74.

Stoll, Hans R. "The Relationship Between Put and Call Option Prices." *J. Finance* 24 (December 1969): 802–24.

Thorp, Edward O., and Kassouf, Sheen T. *Beat the Market.* New York: Random House, 1967.

Treynor, Jack L. "Implications for the Theory of Finance." Unpublished memorandum, 1961. (*a*)

———. "Toward a Theory of Market Value of Risky Assets." Unpublished memorandum, 1961. (*b*)

14. AN EMPIRICAL EXAMINATION OF THE BLACK-SCHOLES CALL OPTION PRICING MODEL

JAMES D. MACBETH and LARRY J. MERVILLE*

Reprinted from *The Journal of Finance,* Vol. XXXIV, No. 5 (December 1979), pp. 1173–1186, by permission of the authors and publisher.

I. Introduction

THIS STUDY IS A descriptive analysis of how market prices of call options compare with prices predicted by the Black and Scholes [2], B-S, option pricing model. Although tests of alternative call option valuation models are not conducted, it is possible to relate some of the deviations which we observe between market and B-S model prices to predictions of other models, and thereby reconcile conflicting statements in the empirical literature regarding the relationship between market prices and B-S model prices.

The B-S model:

$$C = S \cdot N(d_1) - X e^{-r\tau} \cdot N(d_2)$$

$$d_1 = \frac{\ln\left(\dfrac{S}{X}\right) + (r + \sigma^2/2)\tau}{\sigma\sqrt{\tau}}; \qquad d_2 = d_1 - \sigma\sqrt{\tau} \tag{1}$$

has been discussed extensively in the literature. At any instant of time, C is the market value of the call option; S is the price of the underlying security; X is the exercise price; τ is the time to expiration; r is the short-term interest rate which is continuous and constant through time; σ^2 is the variance rate of return for the underlying security; $N(d_i)$ is the cumulative normal density function evaluated at d_i.

For any time interval of length d, the return on the underlying security has a normal distribution with variance $\sigma^2 d$. It is also assumed in this model that the underlying security pays no cash distributions, that there are no transaction costs in buying or selling the option or underlying security, that there are no taxes, and that there are no restrictions on short sales.

Our investigation focuses on the variance rate, σ^2. Blattberg and Gonedes [3] present evidence that σ^2 changes through time. That is, it appears that observed rates of return on common stock can be characterized as independent drawings from a normal population with presumably constant mean but changing variance. An initial step in testing the B-S model against option pricing models which do not require a constant variance rate (for example, Merton's [7] model) should be a careful documentation of how B-S model predicted prices compare with observed market prices.

The basic method of analysis is similar to that of Latané and Rendelman [6],

---

* University of Texas at Dallas. We thank Ross Lumley for computational assistance and Ruth Friedman for assistance with collection of data.

Schmalensee and Trippi [9], and Chiras and Manaster [4]. We substitute the observed market price into equation (1) and numerically solve the equation for its only unobservable quantity, the variance rate, σ^2. We find that on any given day different market prices of options written on the same underlying stock yield different values of σ^2 and that these implied variance rates, for the same option, change through time. However, our results indicate that the differences between the implied variance rates are systematically related to the difference between the stock price, S, the exercise price, X, and the time left to expiration, τ. Then, under certain assumptions, these systematic differences in variance rates are translated into systematic differences between observed market prices of call options and B-S model predicted prices.

II. The Data and Empirical Results

Our sample consists of daily closing prices of all call options traded on the Chicago Board of Trade Options Exchange for American Telephone and Telegraph (ATT), Avon Products (AVON), Eastman Kodak (ETKD), Exxon (EXXN), International Business Machines (IBM), and Xerox (XERX) from December 31, 1975 to December 31, 1976. Option prices and prices of the underlying stocks are taken from the Wall Street Journal. Dividend information comes from Standard and Poors Stock Record. The riskless return is imputed from bid and ask yields reported in the Wall Street Journal for United States Treasury Bills and is updated weekly. That is, when an option is first traded we select a Treasury Bill that expires just beyond the expiration date of the option and then follow the yield on that Bill through time. For each option expiration date we have a different riskless rate. The riskless rates are generally within ½ of 1% of one another and given the lack of sensitivity of the call price to the riskless rate, our results would be virtually identical had we used a single riskless return for a Treasury Bill with, say, one year to maturity for all expiration dates.

For each day, t, a numerical search routine is used to calculate an implied value of σ for each option price. The time to expiration and the riskless return are measured on a daily basis and the current stock price is reduced by the present value, measured by the riskless rate, of any dividends paid between t and the expiration date. At this juncture we have not explicitly addressed the issue resulting from the fact that American options may be exercised early; however, we later demonstrate that our conclusions would not be altered had we considered early exercise in the calculation of each implied value of σ.

The numerical search routine finds implied values of σ in the interval .0001 to .06.[1] For options in the money, $S > Xe^{-r\tau}$, we observe some option prices that are too low to yield a σ as large as .0001. These options are invariably deep in the money with less than ninety days to expiration.[2] We also observe some deep in the money options with less than ninety days to expiration which have implied values of σ greater than .06. Overall, we are able to find values of σ between .0001 and .06 for approximately 97% of the observed option prices. For example, we

---

[1] The range .0001 to .06 is large enough to include all reasonable values of σ.

[2] Out the money options with positive market prices will always have a positive implied variance rate.

observe 2483 separate prices for options written on IBM and traded on the CBOE in 1976. The implied value of σ exceeds .06 in only 23 cases and is less than .0001 in just 31 cases.

A. The Relationship Between the Implied Variance Rate, the Exercise Price, and the Time to Expiration

Table 1 contains a sample of the implied values of σ for IBM. Looking down a column of values of σ in Table 1 we see that the values of σ change from day to day and that on any given day the implied variance rates decline as the exercise price increases. These relationships hold for all of our option data.

To see the importance of these results, consider again the B-S model. In the valuation of a call option price there are two variables (S, τ) and three parameters (r, σ^2, X). Of the parameters, only the variance rate is tied directly to the underlying stock. Thus, consider two call options written on the same stock with the same number of days to expiration, τ. For these two options, S, r, and τ should clearly be the same values in their pricing. However; let one be in the money $(Xe^{-r\tau} < S)$ and one out of the money $(X^*e^{-r\tau} > S)$ which implies different exercise prices $(X < X^*)$. Should different exercise prices imply different variance rates? The answer must be no, as the σ^2 pertains to S not X. Therefore, in the money and out of the money options according to B-S should yield the same implied σ^2 or σ. Our empirical results show that the implied variances are different in general depending on whether or not the option is out, near, or in the money.

There also appears to be a relationship between implied variance rates and time to expiration. In Table 1 one can see a tendency for in the money options with a short time to expiration to have implied values of σ which are larger than those of options with the same exercise price but a longer time to expiration. At the same time, out of the money options with a short time to expiration tend to have implied values of σ smaller than those of options with the same exercise price but a longer time to expiration. We observe the same relationships between the implied variance rates and exercise prices in the data for the other five securities. However, the relationships between time to expiration and implied variance rates in the data for options on the other five securities is not always as systematic as it is for options written on IBM, especially as the time to expiration becomes less than one month.

B. The Relationship Between B-S Model Prices and Observed Market Prices

Black [1] states that market prices of call options "tend to differ in certain systematic ways" from the values given by the B-S model for options with less than three months to expiration and for options that are either deep in or deep out of the money. The evidence in Table 1 is consistent with Black's statement. On the basis of Black's assertion and the evidence in Table 1, we assume, for the remainder of our analysis, that the B-S model correctly prices at the money options with at least ninety days to expiration.[3] It follows from this assumption

[3] While this assumption is somewhat arbitrary, it is useful for our purpose of comparing observed market prices and B-S model prices; but it may not be appropriate for all purposes. For example, it may not be useful for a test of the B-S model against Merton's model.

Table 1

Sample Implied Values of Sigma for IBM

Date	Exercise Price	January	April	July	October	Stock Price
1006.1976	200.00	0.0	0.0	0.02103	0.0	255.12
1006.1976	220.00	0.0	0.0	0.01730	0.01655	255.12
1006.1976	240.00	0.01412	0.0	0.01362	0.01423	255.12
1006.1976	260.00	0.01263	0.0	0.01118	0.01254	255.12
1006.1976	280.00	0.01154	0.0	0.00980	0.01164	255.12
1106.1976	200.00	0.0	0.0	0.02900	0.0	257.75
1106.1976	220.00	0.0	0.0	0.02087	0.01674	257.75
1106.1976	240.00	0.01431	0.0	0.01567	0.01496	257.75
1106.1976	260.00	0.01304	0.0	0.01080	0.01272	257.75
1106.1976	280.00	0.01158	0.0	0.00979	0.01153	257.75
1406.1976	200.00	0.0	0.0	0.02841	0.0	260.25
1406.1976	220.00	0.0	0.0	0.01931	0.01869	260.25
1406.1976	240.00	0.01540	0.0	0.01472	0.01542	260.25
1406.1976	260.00	0.01289	0.0	0.01066	0.01282	260.25
1406.1976	280.00	0.01169	0.0	0.01016	0.01164	260.25
1506.1976	200.00	0.0	0.0	0.02865	0.0	259.00
1506.1976	220.00	0.0	0.0	0.02413	0.01727	259.00
1506.1976	240.00	0.01498	0.0	0.01588	0.01502	259.00
1506.1976	260.00	0.01316	0.0	0.01072	0.01317	259.00
1506.1976	280.00	0.01173	0.0	0.01063	0.01174	259.00
1606.1976	200.00	0.0	0.0	0.03368	0.0	262.37
1606.1976	220.00	0.0	0.0	0.02542	0.01947	262.37
1606.1976	240.00	0.01519	0.0	0.01630	0.01584	262.37
1606.1976	260.00	0.01287	0.0	0.01068	0.01303	262.37
1606.1976	280.00	0.01172	0.0	0.01018	0.01132	262.37
1706.1976	200.00	0.0	0.0	0.02794	0.0	267.50
1706.1976	220.00	0.0	0.0	0.01398	0.01490	267.50
1706.1976	240.00	0.01358	0.0	0.01108	0.01335	267.50
1706.1976	260.00	0.01248	0.0	0.00820	0.01220	267.50
1706.1976	280.00	0.01140	0.0	0.00983	0.01097	267.50
1806.1976	200.00	0.0	0.0	0.03929	0.0	266.25
1806.1976	220.00	0.0	0.0	0.02627	0.01835	266.25
1806.1976	240.00	0.01463	0.0	0.01790	0.01568	266.25
1806.1976	260.00	0.01323	0.0	0.01087	0.01299	266.25
1806.1976	280.00	0.01206	0.0	0.01153	0.01182	266.25
2106.1976	200.00	0.0	0.0	0.03496	0.0	270.50
2106.1976	220.00	0.0	0.0	0.02514	0.01650	270.50
2106.1976	240.00	0.01374	0.0	0.01733	0.01632	270.50
2106.1976	260.00	0.01305	0.0	0.01254	0.01324	270.50
2106.1976	280.00	0.01207	0.0	0.01186	0.01196	270.50
2206.1976	200.00	0.0	0.0	0.04245	0.0	268.75
2206.1976	220.00	0.0	0.0	0.02312	0.02017	268.75
2206.1976	240.00	0.01658	0.0	0.01412	0.01346	268.75
2206.1976	260.00	0.01336	0.0	0.01066	0.01228	268.75
2206.1976	280.00	0.01153	0.0	0.01133	0.01137	268.75
2306.1976	200.00	0.0	0.0	0.03953	0.0	271.50
2306.1976	220.00	0.0	0.0	0.02708	0.01796	271.50
2306.1976	240.00	0.01309	0.0	0.01883	0.01555	271.50
2306.1976	260.00	0.01317	0.0	0.01119	0.01374	271.50
2306.1976	280.00	0.01212	0.0	0.01199	0.01203	271.50

that the at the money implied variance rate is the proper or "true" variance rate. Then, given $\frac{\partial C}{\partial \sigma^2} > 0$, the implication of this assumption is that the B-S model must yield call option prices which exceed observed market prices for options out of the money and call option prices which are less than the observed market prices for options in the money because the implied values of σ decline as the exercise price increases.

For example, consider the IBM options traded on June 14. Panel A of Table 2 contains the market prices of the options, Panel B contains the implied values of σ, and Panel C contains the B-S model prices based on an estimated value of σ for an at the money option equal to .012848. The, in the money, $220 October option has a market price $3.60 greater than the B-S model price while the, out of the money, $280 October option has a B-S model price $1.28 greater than the market price.

Table 2 also illustrates that although in the money (out of the money) options with a short time to expiration have implied variance rates that are larger (smaller) than options with the same exercise price but at least ninety days to expiration, the dollar differences between B-S model prices and market prices of these short term options are generally less than the dollar differences between B-S model prices and market prices of options with the same exercise price but at least ninety days to expiration. For example, the implied value of σ for the $220

Table 2
IBM Option Data for June 14, 1976

	Exercise Price	Expiration Dates			
		January	April	July	October
		Market Prices			
Panel A	$200			$62.00	
	$220			$42.00	$47.50
	$240	$36.50		$23.13	$30.50
	$260	$22.00		$ 7.13	$16.13
	$280	$12.00		$ .94	$ 7.00
		Implied Values of σ			
Panel B	$200			.028412	
	$220			.019312	.018691
	$240	.015404		.014725	.015417
	$260	.012885		.010658	.012824
	$280	.011689		.010158	.011640
		Black-Scholes Model Prices			
Panel C	$200			$61.23	
	$220			$41.38	$43.90
	$240	$33.22		$22.53	$28.13
	$260	$21.95		$ 8.42	$16.15
	$280	$13.73		$ 1.90	$ 8.28
	$\tau =$	220.		33.	124.
	r (Annual) =	5.9%		5.3%	5.6%
	$S^* =$	$255.85		$260.25	258.03

S^* is the stock price less the present value of dividends of $2.25 paid September 10, and December 10.

July option is greater than the implied value for the $220 October option, but the difference between the B-S model price and the market price of these options is $.62 for the July option and $3.60 for the October option.

In order to examine the difference between the B-S model prices and observed market prices, we require the implied variance rate for an at the money option. Since we are usually unable to observe an at the money option, we deduce the variance rate for an at the money option on the basis of observed variance rates. That is, to determine an implied value of σ for an at the money option on a particular stock we estimate the following regression model each day:

$$\sigma_{ijt} = \theta_{i0t} + \theta_{i1t} m_{ijt} + \epsilon_{ijt} \qquad j = 1, 2 \cdots J \qquad (2)$$

where σ_{ijt} is the implied σ for option j on security i on day t. And

$$m_{ijt} = \frac{S_{it} - X_{ij} e^{-r\tau}}{X_{ij} e^{-r\tau}}$$

where S_{it} is the closing price of a share of security i on day t and $X_{ij} e^{-r\tau}$ is the present value at time t of the exercise price j for an option on a share of security i. The estimated values of θ_{i0t}, $\hat{\theta}_{i0t}$, is our estimate of the σ that would be implied by the B-S model on day t for an at the money option written on security i[4].

Figure 1 is an exemplary scatter diagram with the estimate regression line for the options written on IBM on June 14, 1976. Notice that $\hat{\theta}_{i0t}$ equals .012848 and that the implied values of σ for the two near the money $260 options with at least ninety days to expiration are .012885 and .012824. Typically, the number of observations, J, in these regressions is in the neighborhood of five. Given the evidence in Table 1 for IBM, it is not surprising that the R^2's from these regressions are large, generally on the order of 0.80.

$\hat{\theta}_{i0t}$ is a weighted sum of the implied values of σ for the options on security i on day t and, therefore, corresponds to the weighted average implied standard deviations of Latané and Rendelman [6], Schmalensee and Trippi [9], and Chiras and Manaster [4].

To facilitate comparisons between options on different securities we relate the difference between C_{ijt}, the market price on day t of option j on security i with exercise price X_{ij}, and the B-S model price of the same option, $C_{BS}(\hat{\theta}_{i0t})$; to the extent to which the option is in or out of the money as measured by m_{ijt}, the independent variable in equation (2). Initially, we relate m_{ijt} to v_{ijt}, the difference between the market price of an option and the B-S model price expressed as a percentage of the B-S model price.[5]

$$v_{ijt} = \frac{C_{ijt} - C_{BS}(\hat{\theta}_{i0t})}{C_{BS}(\hat{\theta}_{i0t})} \qquad (3)$$

Figure 2 is a scatter diagram of v against m for options with at least ninety days to expiration written on shares of IBM in the year 1976.[6] It appears that on

---

[4] Since the B-S model appears to fit the data best for options with at least ninety days to expiration, we include in these regressions only options with that property.

[5] When comparing B-S model prices and market prices using v_{ijt} we do not include options which have B-S model prices less than $.0625, the lowest quoted market price for options.

[6] Subscripts are omitted when there is little chance of confusion on the part of the reader.

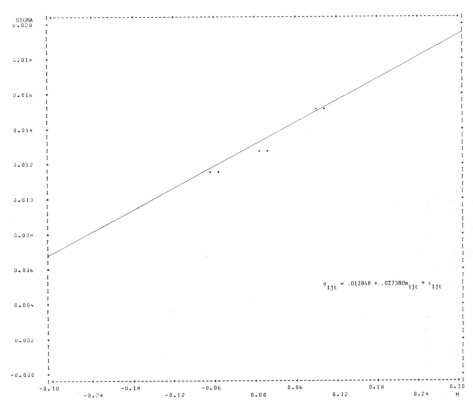

Figure 1.   Sigma values regressed on M for IBM

average v is an increasing function of m for values of m less than .05. For options on IBM that are in the money by more than five percent, the percentage difference between observed market prices and B-S model prices appears to be constant, in the neighborhood of five percent of the present value of the exercise price. Scatter diagrams for corresponding options written on the other five stocks appear almost identical to Figure 2 and are thus omitted.

Figure 3 is the same type of scatter diagram as Figure 2 but for options written on IBM with less than ninety days to expiration. The scatter in Figure 3 is basically the same as in Figure 2, but there are some out of the money options with fairly large positive values of v. Scatter diagrams for corresponding options written on the other five stocks are similar to Figure 3 except that there are more out of the money options with positive values of v. For example, out of the money options written on Xerox have nearly as many positive values of v as negative values.

Call options trade on the CBOE can be exercised at any time prior to the stated expiration date and sometimes should be exercised just prior to an ex-dividend day. Assuming that one dividend, known for certain, will be paid prior to the stated expiration date of an option, the option can be valued either by the B-S model with the stock price reduced by the present value of the future dividend (as we have done), or by the B-S model with the observed stock price and the ex-dividend date as the expiration date. The market price of the option will be

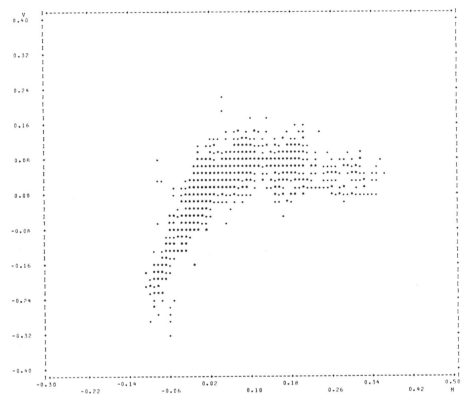

Figure 2. "V", Percent difference between the market price of call options and the Black-Scholes model price versus "M", percent in or out of the money, for options with at least ninety days to expiration, written on IBM

greater than the maximum of these two values; however, since the B-S model is the focal point of our analysis we assume that the market price equals the larger of these two values.[7] The appropriate implied variance rate will then be the smaller of the two values obtained by viewing the option in the two ways mentioned above.

Early exercise is more likely the closer the ex-dividend date is to the expiration date. Since all of our six stocks pay dividends in February, May, August and November there is at least forty-five days between an ex-dividend date and an expiration date. Therefore, apriori there is some reason to believe that our option prices will not be seriously affected by the possibility of early exercise. However, should early exercise be important, our implied value of σ for an option will be too high in the days prior to the ex-dividend date. This could affect our results in two ways. First, $\hat{\theta}_{i0t}$ will be too large and second, we will have some observations in the plots of v against m that should be deleted and replaced with observations based upon larger stock prices and shorter times to expiration.

Since we exclude options with less than ninety days to expiration from the calculation of $\hat{\theta}_{i0t}$, the early exercise effect could only affect $\hat{\theta}_{i0t}$ if it occurs at least

---

[7] Roll [8] derives an explicit valuation equation for a call option with a single known dividend to be paid before the option's expiration date.

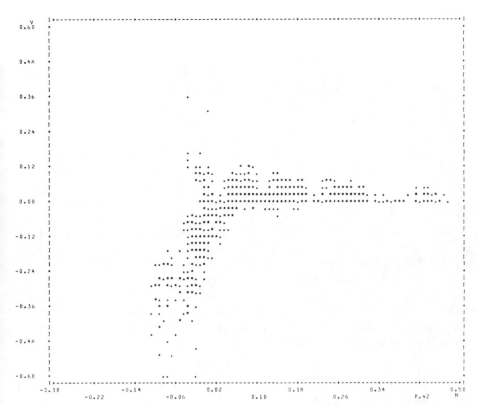

Figure 3. "V", Percent difference between market price of call options and the Black-Scholes price versus "M", Percent in or out of the money, for options with less than ninety days to expiration, written on IBM

ninety days prior to expiration. As a check, we have examined our data for the period between ninety and one hundred days prior to expiration and find no evidence of an early exercise effect. That is, if we consider that the option will be exercised just prior to the ex-dividend date and compute an implied variance rate, we invariably obtain a value larger than the implied variance we originally calculated.

Since we find no evidence of an early exercise effect in the prices of options with between ninety and one hundred days to expiration we assume that our computed values of v and m for options with at least ninety days to expiration are not contaminated by an early exercise effect. To determine whether the computed values of v and m for options with less than ninety days to expiration are affected, we have examined our data for the two weeks prior to and two weeks following ex-dividend dates. For Eastman Kodak and International Business Machines we find no evidence of an early exercise effect. However, there does appear to be some unusual price behavior for deep in the money options on the other four stocks around ex-dividend days. It is not uncommon for the price of a deep in the money option to drop suddenly to its exercise value in the week prior to the ex-dividend day even though the stock price remains essentially constant. This suggests that the option should have been exercised; however, it is difficult to explain why in the weeks prior to the ex-dividend date the price should reflect the original expiration date and then, three or four days before the ex-dividend day, suddenly reflect the day before the ex-dividend date as the expiration date. On the ex-dividend day and the days following, the option sometimes continues to trade at its exercise value and sometimes trades at a higher value.

Fortunately these days of unusual price behavior have been excluded from our sample since on days when an option trdes at its value if exercised, we are unable to compute a positive value of σ. Eastman Kodak and International Business Machines have significantly fewer instances where we are unable to impute a positive value of σ for deep in the money options. To summarize, we are unable to detect an early exercise effect in prices of options on two of our stocks. The possibility of early exercise appears to affect a small number of prices of options, with less than ninety days to expiration, on the other four stocks, but we have eliminated virtually all of these observations from our sample. Thus, had early exercise been considered for all of our options the plots in Figure 2 would look exactly the same and those in Figure 3 would look essentially the same.

To quantify the visual relationships conveyed in Figures 2 and 3 we report in Table 3 the sample means and standard deviations of v and m for in the money and out of the money options with at least ninety days to expiration (far), and less than ninety days to expiration (near) on all six stocks. To convey an idea of the dollar amounts involved we compute

$$y_{ijt} \equiv C_{ijt} - C_{BS}(\hat{\theta}_{i0t}) \tag{4}$$

and report the sample mean and standard deviation of y where N is the number of options in each category.

The statistics reported in Table 3 reinforce the visual relationships expressed in the Figures. Regardless of whether the time to expiration is at least ninety days or less than ninety days, options that are in the money have, on average, market prices which exceed B-S model prices and options that are out of the money have, on average, market prices which are less than B-S model prices.

Table 3 also contains some information regarding the effect of time to expiration on the overpricing or underpricing of options by the B-S model. Notice that in the money options with τ less than ninety days are on average deeper in the money but that they are on average underpriced by the B-S model to a smaller extent, as measured by $\bar{y}$, than options with at least ninety days to expiration. On the other hand, out of the money options with less than ninety days to expiration are on average about as far out of the money as out of the money options with at least ninety days to expiration but those with less than ninety days to expiration are on average overpriced by the B-S model to a lesser extent than those with at least ninety days to expiration. Thus, it appears that as τ approaches zero so does y even though the implied variance rates in Table 1 for options in or out of the money tend to deviate more from the implied variance rate of an at the money option. But this result is to be expected since B-S model prices and market prices converge to the minimum of zero or $S - X$ as τ approaches zero.

To investigate the relationship between changes in y and changes in m and τ, we estimate the following linear regression model

$$y_{ijt} = \alpha_0 + \alpha_1 m_{ijt} + \alpha_2 \tau_{ijt} + \epsilon_{ijt} \qquad \begin{aligned} j &= 1, 2 \cdots J \\ t &= 1, 2, \cdots T \end{aligned} \tag{5}$$

Table 3
Difference Between Market Prices and Black-Scholes Model Prices

Option Money Expiration		N	$\bar{m}$	$s(m)$	$\bar{v}$	$s(v)$	$\bar{y}$	$s(y)$
ATT								
Out	Near	120	−.04	.03	−.16	.16	$−.10	$ .12
Out	Far	420	−.04	.03	−.10	.10	−.13	.13
In	Far	875	.09	.06	.05	.08	.34	.38
In	Near	384	.11	.08	.01	.09	.19	.31
AVON								
Out	Near	283	−.08	.06	−.05	.25	−.07	.18
Out	Far	532	−.07	.06	−.07	.08	−.17	.16
In	Far	928	.13	.10	.04	.04	.28	.29
In	Near	465	.16	.13	.01	.08	.10	.29
ETKD								
Out	Near	406	−.10	.06	−.12	.25	−.10	.26
Out	Far	930	−.10	.07	−.12	.13	−.33	.30
In	Far	632	.09	.07	.03	.04	.39	.63
In	Near	376	.10	.08	.04	.06	.49	.60
EXXN								
Out	Near	230	−.06	.04	−.07	.21	−.09	.14
Out	Far	590	−.07	.05	−.10	.12	−.17	.20
In	Far	684	.08	.06	.02	.05	.16	.35
In	Near	342	.09	.07	−.01	.06	.06	.30
IBM								
Out	Near	206	−.03	.03	−.18	.16	−.83	.73
Out	Far	376	−.04	.03	−.07	.08	−.80	.83
In	Far	1096	.11	.08	.06	.04	2.09	1.55
In	Near	748	.17	.12	.03	.05	1.09	1.16
XERX								
Out	Near	294	−.11	.07	−.02	.27	−.00	.23
Out	Far	567	−.10	.07	−.07	.09	−.17	.19
In	Far	798	.16	.12	.02	.03	.23	.33
In	Near	379	.16	.12	.01	.06	.19	.34

for the various classifications of options reported in Table 3. Summary statistics from the estimated model are reported in Table 4. The estimate value of α_k is denoted $\hat{\alpha}_k$; $t(\hat{\alpha}_k)$ is the Student "t" statistic of the estimated coefficient $\hat{\alpha}_k$; $\rho(\hat{\epsilon})$ is the first order autocorrelation coefficient of the residuals; $s(\hat{\epsilon})$ is the standard error of the residuals; and R^2 is the coefficient of determination.

For in the money options $\hat{\alpha}_1$ is always positive and with one exception larger for options with at least ninety days to expiration. Note also that for in the money options the coefficient of τ, $\hat{\alpha}_2$, is, with one exception, positive. Thus, the extent to which the B-S model underprices in the money options increases with the extent to which the option is in the money and this relationship appears stronger the longer the time to expiration. On the other hand, the extent to which the B-S model underprices in the money options becomes smaller as the expiration date approaches.

Table 4

Summary Statistics from the Regression Model

$$y_{ijt} = \alpha_0 + \alpha_1 m_{ijt} + \alpha_2 \tau_{ijt} + \epsilon_{ijt} \quad \begin{array}{l} j = 12\cdots J \\ t = 12\cdots T \end{array}$$

Option Money Expiration		$\hat{\alpha}_0$	$t(\hat{\alpha}_0)$	$\hat{\alpha}_1$	$t(\hat{\alpha}_1)$	$\hat{\alpha}_2{}^*$	$t(\hat{\alpha}_2)$	$\rho(\hat{\epsilon})$	R^2	$s(\hat{\epsilon})$
ATT										
Out	Near	−.12	−3.03	− .78	−2.20	−.03	− .56	.29	.03	.12
Out	Far	−.05	−1.93	1.78	8.15	−.01	− .47	.19	.13	.12
In	Far	−.40	−9.80	4.01	24.00	.22	11.36	.36	.41	.29
In	Near	−.26	−8.86	2.46	17.99	.31	6.95	.18	.52	.21
AVON										
Out	Near	−.15	−5.97	−1.15	−7.07	−.03	− .66	.61	.15	.17
Out	Far	−.03	−1.04	.98	8.34	−.04	−3.13	−.11	.12	.15
In	Far	−.15	−4.66	1.81	21.93	.11	7.33	.09	.34	.23
In	Near	−.13	−4.25	1.10	12.38	.11	2.34	.49	.26	.25
ETKD										
Out	Near	−.17	−4.90	− .01	− .05	.14	2.36	.63	.01	.26
Out	Far	.28	7.06	1.44	10.29	−.27	−14.56	.14	.21	.27
In	Far	.23	2.44	3.00	9.21	−.07	−1.45	.25	.13	.58
In	Near	−.24	−3.75	3.65	11.24	.72	7.08	.46	.32	.49
EXXN										
Out	Near	−.11	−4.50	−1.41	−6.84	−.11	−2.82	.32	.17	.13
Out	Far	−.03	−1.04	.95	5.39	−.04	−2.74	.38	.06	.20
In	Far	−.36	−7.53	2.74	13.40	.17	7.46	.11	.23	.30
In	Near	−.23	−6.77	2.71	13.97	.06	1.16	−.01	.36	.24
IBM										
Out	Near	−.56	−4.38	4.55	2.51	−.24	−1.05	.83	.04	.72
Out	Far	.11	1.02	21.36	19.82	−.09	−1.71	.12	.51	.58
In	Far	−.25	−1.62	11.69	25.52	.63	8.40	.43	.37	1.23
In	Near	−.24	−2.51	4.47	14.50	1.25	8.41	.45	.27	.99
XERX										
Out	Near	−.13	−3.49	− .15	− .76	.21	3.33	.81	.04	.23
Out	Far	.08	2.61	.59	5.14	−.11	−7.40	.14	.10	.18
In	Far	−.16	−3.91	1.33	14.80	.10	4.91	.09	.22	.29
In	Near	−.10	−2.64	1.27	9.86	.18	2.90	.33	.23	.30

$\hat{\alpha}_2{}^* = \hat{\alpha}_2 \times 10^2$.

The estimated coefficients of m and τ for out of the money options with at least ninety days to expiration are all positive and negative, respectively. Hence, for this class of options the extent to which the B-S model price exceeds the market price increases with the extent to which the option is out of the money and decreases as the expiration date approaches.

There does not appear to be any consistent relationships between changes in y and changes in m or τ for out of the money options with less than ninety days to expiration.

The Student t statistics of the estimated coefficients in Table 4 cannot be strictly interpreted because they overstate the statistical significance of the estimated coefficients. This results from sizable positive autocorrelation in the error terms, ϵ_{ijt}, which in turn probably results from the effects of one or more explanatory variables left out of the regression model and also from the way the observations for equation (5) are loaded into our regression routine. For any regression reported in Table 3 the observations are loaded each day in order of exercise price (e.g., across the rows of Table 1 for IBM). Thus, it appears that if this unknown explanatory variable causes $y_{i,j,t}$ to be larger (smaller) than the value predicted by the estimated regression equation, then this unknown explanatory variable also tends to make $y_{i,j+1,t}$ larger (smaller) than its predicted value. Since our main intent is to describe general systematic deviations of the B-S model predicted prices from observed market prices rather than to conduct a rigorous statistical test of the B-S model, the statistics reported in Table 4 should be viewed as more descriptive than inferential.

III Summary and Conclusions

Since we have examined daily prices of options on only six underlying securities over a one year time period, inferences drawn from this research must be tentative. However, we have analyzed in excess of twelve thousand option prices and have found striking similarities in the results for options on the six different stocks; therefore, we consider this research to be one of the most extensive empirical examinations of option prices to be reported in the literature to date.

If one assumes that the B-S model correctly prices at the money options with at least ninety days to expiration, then our analysis implies that:

1. The B-S model predicted prices are on average less (greater) than market prices for in the money (out of the money) options.

2. With the lone exception of out of the money options with less than ninety days to expiration, the extent to which the B-S model underprices (overprices) an in the money (out of the money) option increases with the extent to which the option is in the money (out of the money), and decreases as the time to expiration decreases.

3. B-S model prices of out of the money options with less than ninety days to expiration are, on average, greater than market prices; but there does not appear to be any consistent relationship between the extent to which these options are overpriced by the B-S model and the degree to which these options are out of the money or the time to expiration.[8]

We emphasize that our results are exactly opposite to those reported by Black [1], wherein he states that deep in the money (out of the money) options generally have B-S model prices which are greater (less) than market prices; and, our results also conflict with Merton's [7] statement that practitioners observe B-S model prices to be less than market prices for deep in the money as well as deep

---

[8] In our analysis, we have excluded options which have B-S model prices less than $.0625. The number of excluded observations varies from three for IBM to one hundred twenty-three for Eastman Kodak. Since the lowest option price is $.0625, these options all have market prices greater than their B-S model prices. On the other hand, if market prices less than $.0625 existed these options may not be underpriced by the B-S model. Moreover, the difference between market prices and B-S model prices for these options is on average a few cents; for the one hundred twenty-three Eastman Kodak options the average price difference is $.05. Thus, the inclusion of these options in our analysis would not affect our inferences.

out of the money options. We propose that these conflicting empirical observations may, at least in part, be the result of a non-stationary variance rate in the stochastic process generating stock prices.

One call option valuation model that explicitly incorporates a non-stationary variance rate is Geske's [5] compound option model. Assuming market prices are given by this model, then B-S model prices will also equal market prices on day t provided the variance rate for day t, σ_t^2, is used in the B-S equation. Thus, the compound option model provides theoretical justification for our methodology of computing implied variance rates on a daily basis, but it still does not explain the systematic differences we observe in implied variance rates.

Nevertheless, if one accepts the hypothesis that market prices should correspond to compound option model prices, then it is possible to explain some of the apparently conflicting empirical observations on option pricing which appear in the literature. For example, if B-S model prices are calculated using a constant estimated variance rate, $\hat{\sigma}$, obtained from a time series of past returns to the underlying common stock, then on days when the true variance rate, σ_t, exceeds $\hat{\sigma}$, the B-S model price based upon $\hat{\sigma}$ will be less than the market price; but on other days, when σ_t is less than $\hat{\sigma}$, the reverse will be true. Therefore, it is easy to see how one researcher may find in the money options overpriced by the B-S model while another finds in the money options underpriced if they use different data to estimate the variance rate $\hat{\sigma}$ and/or compute B-S model prices over different time periods.

Finally, our analysis sheds some light on the apparently profitable option trading strategy of Chiras and Manaster [4]. Their strategy involves selling options that have a market price which exceeds the B-S model prices and buying options that have a market price which is less than the B-S model price. Since Chiras and Manaster do not weight the implied σ values exactly as we weight them, their B-S model price for an option is different from ours. Generally, their B-S model price exceeds our B-S model price but the differences are not large. Our analysis suggests that their trading strategy may involve selling deep in the money options and buying deep out of the money options. Whether or not this strategy yields abnormally high returns is another matter.

REFERENCES

1. Fischer Black. "Fact and Fantasy in the Use of Options." *Financial Analysts Journal*, (July-August 1975).
2. F. Black and M. Scholes. "The Pricing of Options and Corporate Liabilities." *Journal of Political Economy*, Volume 81, (1973).
3. R. C. Blattberg and N. J. Gonedes. "A Comparison of the Stable and Student Distributions as Stochastic Models for Stock Prices." *Journal of Business*, Volume 47, (1974).
4. D. Chiras and S. Manaster. "The Informational Content of Option Prices and a Test of Market Efficiency." *Journal of Financial Economics*, forthcoming.
5. R. Geske. "The Valuation of Compound Options." *Journal of Financial Economics*, forthcoming.
6. H. A. Latané and R. J. Rendleman. "Standard Deviations of Stock Price Ratios Implied in Option Prices." *Journal of Finance*, Vol. 31, No. 2, (1976).
7. R. C. Merton. "Option Pricing When Underlying Stock Returns are Discontinuous." *Journal of Financial Economics*, Vol. 3, Nos. 1 & 2, (Jan/March 1976).
8. R. Roll. "An Analytic Valuation Formula for Unprotected American Call Options on Stocks with Known Dividends." *Journal of Financial Economics*, Vol. 5, No. 2, (November 1977).
9. R. Schmalensee and R. Trippi. "Common Stock Volatility Expectations Implied by Option Premia." *The Journal of Finance*, Vol. 33, No. 1, (March 1978).

PART IV

INVESTMENT DECISIONS, FINANCING DECISIONS, AND THE COST OF CAPITAL

* *

15. THREE PROBLEMS IN RATIONING CAPITAL*

JAMES H. LORIE†
and
LEONARD J. SAVAGE‡

Reprinted from *Journal of Business,* Vol. XXVIII, No. 4
(October 1955), pp. 56–66, by permission of the authors and
publisher.

I. INTRODUCTION

Corporate executives face three tasks in achieving good financial management. The first is largely administrative and consists in finding an efficient procedure for preparing and reviewing capital budgets, for delegating authority and fixing responsibility for expenditures, and for finding some means for ultimate evaluation of completed investments. The second task is to forecast correctly the cash flows that can be expected to result from specified investment proposals, as well as the liquid resources that will be available for investment. The third task is to ration available capital or liquid resources among competing investment opportunities. This article is concerned with only this last task; it discusses three problems in the rationing of capital, in the sense of liquid resources.

1. Given a firm's cost of capital and a management policy of using this cost to identify acceptable investment proposals, which group of "independent" investment proposals should the firm accept? In other words, how should the firm's cost of capital be used to distinguish between acceptable and unacceptable investments? This is a problem that is typically faced by top management whenever it reviews and approves a capital budget.

* This work was supported in part by the Office of Naval Research and in part by Joel Dean Associates.

† Associate professor of marketing, University of Chicago, and senior consultant, Joel Dean Associates.

‡ Professor of statistics, University of Chicago.

Before presenting the second problem with which this paper deals, the use of the word "independent" in the preceding paragraph should be explained. Investment proposals are termed "independent"—although not completely accurately—when the worth of the individual investment proposal is not profoundly affected by the acceptance of others. For example, a proposal to invest in materials-handling equipment at location A may not profoundly affect the value of a proposal to build a new warehouse in location B. It is clear that the independence is never complete, but the degree of independence is markedly greater than for sets of so-called "mutually exclusive" investment proposals. Acceptance of one proposal in such a set renders all others in the same set clearly unacceptable—or even unthinkable. An example of mutually exclusive proposals would be alternative makes of automotive equipment for the same fleet or alternative warehouse designs for the same site. The choice among mutually exclusive proposals is usually faced later in the process of financial management than is the initial approval of a capital budget. That is, the decision as to which make of automotive equipment to purchase, for example, typically comes later than the decision to purchase some make of equipment.

2. Given a fixed sum of money to be used for capital investment, what group of investment proposals should be undertaken? If a firm pursues a policy of fixing the size of its capital budget in dollars, without explicit cognizance of, or reference to, its cost of capital, how can it best allocate that sum among competing investment proposals? This problem will be considered both for proposals which require net outlays in only one accounting period and for those which require outlays in more than one accounting period. In the latter case, special difficulties arise.

3. How should a firm select the best among mutually exclusive alternatives? That is, when the management of an enterprise, in attempting to make concrete and explicit proposals for expenditures of a type which is included in an approved capital budget, develops more than one plausible way of investing money in conformance with the budget, how can it select the "best" way?

After presenting our solutions to these three problems, we shall discuss the solutions implied by the rate-of-return method of capital budgeting.[1] These solutions are worthy of special attention, since they are based on a different principle from the solutions that we propose and since the rate-of-return method is the most defensible method heretofore proposed in the business literature for maximizing corporate profits and net worth.

II. THE THREE PROBLEMS

A. GIVEN THE COST OF CAPITAL, WHAT GROUP OF INVESTMENTS SHOULD BE SELECTED?

---

[1] This method was developed by Joel Dean, who has probably done more than anyone else in applying the formal apparatus of economics to the solution of capital budgeting problems in their business context.

The question of determining the cost of capital is difficult, and we, happily, shall not discuss it. Although there may be disagreement about methods of calculating a firm's cost of capital, there is substantial agreement that the cost of capital is the rate at which a firm should discount future cash flows in order to determine their present value.[2] The first problem is to determine how selection should be made among "independent" investment proposals, given this cost or rate.

Assume that the firm's objective is to maximize the value of its net worth—not necessarily as measured by the accountant but rather as measured by the present value of its expected cash flows. This assumption is commonly made by economists and even business practitioners who have spoken on the subject. It is equivalent to asserting that the corporate management's objective is to maximize the value of the owner's equity or, alternatively, the value of the owner's income from the business. Given this objective and agreement about the significance of the firm's cost of capital, the problem of selecting investment proposals becomes trivial in those situations where there is a well-defined cost of capital; namely, proposals should be selected that have positive present values when discounted at the firm's cost of capital. The things to discount are the net cash flows resulting from the investments, and these cash flows should take taxes into account.

There is nothing unusual or original about this proposed solution. It is identical with that proposed by Lutz and Lutz[3] and is an economic commonplace. Joel Dean in his writings has developed and recommended a method which typically yields the same results for this problem, although the principle of solution is somewhat different, as is discussed later in this article.

The principle of accepting all proposals having positive present value at the firm's cost of capital is obvious, since the failure to do so would clearly mean foregoing an available increment in the present value of the firm's net worth. The principle is discussed here only because it seems a useful introduction to the somewhat more complicated problems that follow. An interesting property of this principle is that adherence to it will result in the present value of the firm's net worth being at a maximum at all points in time.

B. GIVEN A FIXED SUM FOR CAPITAL INVESTMENT, WHAT GROUP OF INVESTMENT PROPOSALS SHOULD BE UNDERTAKEN?

Some business firms—perhaps most—do not use the firm's cost of capital to distinguish between acceptable and unacceptable investments but, instead, determine the magnitude of their capital budget in some other way that results in

---

[2] One of the difficulties with the concept of cost of capital is that in complicated circumstances there may be no one rate that plays this role. Still worse, the very concept of present value may be obscure.

[3] Friederich and Vera Lutz, *The Theory of Investment of the Firm* (Princeton: Princeton University Press, 1951). The solution proposed here is identical with the maximization of $V - C$, where V is the present value of future inflows and C is the present value of future outflows. This is discussed in chap. ii of the Lutz book.

fixing an absolute dollar limit on capital expenditures. Perhaps, for example, a corporate management may determine for any one year that the capital budget shall not exceed estimated income after taxes plus depreciation allowances, after specified dividend payments. It is probable that the sum fixed as the limit is not radically different from the sum that would be expended if correct and explicit use were made of the firm's cost of capital, since most business firms presumably do not long persist in policies antithetical to the objective of making money. (The profit-maximizing principle is the one that makes use of the firm's cost of capital, as described previously.) Nevertheless, there are probably some differences in the amount that would be invested by a firm if it made correct use of the firms' cost of capital and the amount that would be invested if it fixed its capital budget by other means, expressing the constraint on expenditures as being a maximum outlay. At the very least, the differences in the ways of thinking suggest the usefulness to some firms of a principle that indicates the "best" group of investments that can be made with a fixed sum of money.

The problem is trivial when there are net outlays in only one accounting period—typically, one year. In such cases, investment proposals should be ranked according to their present value—at the firm's cost of capital—per dollar of outlay required. Once investment proposals have been ranked according to this criterion, it is easy to select the best group by starting with the investment proposal having the highest present value per dollar of outlay and proceeding down the list until the fixed sum is exhausted.[4]

The problem can become more difficult when discontinuities are taken into account. For large firms, the vast majority of investment proposals constitute such a small proportion of their total capital budget that the problems created by discontinuities can be disregarded at only insignificant cost, especially when the imprecision of the estimates of incomes is taken into account. When a project constitutes a large proportion of the capital budget, the problem of discontinuities may become serious, though not necessarily difficult to deal with. This problem can become serious because of the obvious fact that accepting the large proposal because it is "richer" than smaller proposals may preclude the possibility of accepting two or more smaller and less rich proposals which, in combination, have a greater value than the larger proposal. For example, suppose that the total amount available for investment were $1,000 and that only three investment proposals had been made: one requiring a net outlay of $600 and creating an increment in present value of $1,000 and two others, each requiring a net outlay of $500 and each creating an increment in present value of $600. Under these circumstances, the adop-

---

[4] We mention, for completeness, that the outlay or the present value or both for a proposal can be negative. Proposals for which the outlay alone is negative—something for nothing—are always desirable but almost never available. Proposals for which both the outlay and present value are negative can sometimes be acceptable if something sufficiently profitable can be done with ready cash expressed by the negative outlay. The rules which we shall develop can be extended to cover such cases.

tion of the richest alternative, the first, would mean foregoing the other two alternatives, even though in combination they would create an increment in present value of $1,200 as compared with the increment of $1,000 resulting from the adoption of the richest investment alternative. Such discontinuities deserve special attention, but the general principles dealing with them will not be worked out here, primarily because we do not know them.

We shall, however, deal with the more serious difficulties created by the necessity to choose among investment proposals some of which require net cash outlays in more than one accounting period. In such cases a constraint is imposed not only by the fixed sum available for capital investment in the first period but also by the fixed sums available to carry out present commitments in subsequent time periods. Each such investment requires, so to speak, the use of two or more kinds of money—money from the first period and money from each subsequent period in which net outlays are required. We shall discuss only the case of investments requiring net outlays in two periods, for simplicity of exposition and because the principle—although not the mechanics—is the same as for investments requiring net outlays in more than two periods.

1. Let us start with a very simple case. Suppose that all the available opportunities for investment that yield a positive income can be adopted without exceeding the maximum permitted outlay in either time period one or time period two. Clearly, no better solution can be found, because all desirable opportunities have been exhausted. This simple case is mentioned not because of its practical importance, which is admittedly slight, but because it may clarify the more complicated cases that follow.

2. Next, consider a slightly more complicated case. Suppose that the opportunities available require more funds from either time period one or two than are permitted by the imposed constraints. Under these circumstances the problem becomes somewhat more complicated, but it still may not be very complicated. It is still relatively simple if (*a*) the best use of money available in period one does not exhaust the money available in period two or (*b*) the best use of money available in period two does not exhaust the money available in period one. In either case the optimum solution—that is, the solution which results in the greatest increment in the net worth of the firm, subject to the two stated constraints—is the one that makes the best possible use of the funds available for investment in one of the two time periods.

This statement is justified by the following reasoning. The imposition of additional restrictions upon the freedom of action of any agency can obviously never increase the value of the best opportunity available to that agency. In the problem at hand, this means that the imposition of an absolute dollar constraint or restriction in time period two can never make it possible to make better use of dollars available in time period one than would have been possible in the absence of that constraint. Thus, if the best possible use is made of the dollars available in time period one, the imposition of a restriction relating to time period two can never mean increased possibilities of profit from the use of funds available in time period one. Therefore, the maximization of the productivity of dollars available in time period one will constitute a maximization of productivity subject to the two constraints as well as to the one constraint. The reasoning is equally valid if we start with the constraint referring to time period two and maximize productivity of money available in that time period and then think of the effect of the additional constraint imposed for time period one.

3. Unfortunately, typical circumstances will probably make the relatively simple solutions unavailable. The solution to the relatively complex problem will—abstracting from discontinuities—require expending the full amount available for investment in each period. To illustrate how the solution is to be reached, consider the average actual net outlay of the two periods as being an outlay in a single "virtual" period and consider the average net outlay that is permitted by the constraints as being the average permitted outlay for the "virtual" period. Plan a budget for this "virtual" period according to the method of the one-period problem with which this section begins. That is, ration the capital available in the "virtual" period among the available investment opportunities so as to maximize the firm's net worth according to the principles stated in the discussion of the one-period problem. If, by accident, this budget happens to require precisely those outlays which are permitted for the first and second periods, it is easy to see that the problem has been solved. No other budget with a higher present value can be devised within the stated constraints for periods one and two.

Typically, the happy accident referred to in the preceding paragraph will not occur. The optimum use of the average amount available for investment in the two periods will typically result in expending too much in one period and not so much as is permitted in the other. Indeed, the happy accident was mentioned only as a step in explaining one method that will work. Though a simple average will almost never work, there is always some weighted average that will, and it can be found by trial and error. We shall describe in some detail a method that is mathematically equivalent to this method of weighted averages. In this method the solution is found by choosing, for suitable positive constants p_1 and p_2, those, and only those, proposals for which the following quantity is positive: $y - p_1c_1 - p_2c_2$. Here y is the present value of the proposal; c_1 and c_2 are the present values of the net outlays required in the first and second periods, respectively; and the multipliers p_1 and p_2 are auxiliary quantities for which there does not seem to be an immediate interpretation but that nonetheless help in solving the problem.[5]

Initially, the values of p_1 and p_2 will be determined by judgment. Subsequently, they will be altered by trial and error until the amounts to be expended in the first and second periods, according to the rule just enunciated, are precisely the amounts permitted by the constraints. The initial choice of

[5] The multipliers, p_1 and p_2, are closely related to what are known in mathematics and in economics as "Lagrange multipliers."

values for p_1 and p_2 is not very important, since a graphical process can usually lead rapidly to the correct values.

Certain special possibilities are worth noting. Proposals of positive present value may have negative cost, that is, release cash, for either period. Some proposals of zero or negative present value may be acceptable because they release cash for one period or both. All such possibilities are automatically covered by the rule as stated and by the rules to be given for later problems.

Finding the correct values for p_1 and p_2 is sometimes not easy—especially when combined with the problem of selecting among mutually exclusive alternatives—but the task is usually as nothing compared to the interests involved or compared to many everyday engineering problems.[6] The following example may clarify the process.

Nine investments have been proposed. The present value of the net outlays required in the first and second time periods and the present values of the investments are as shown in Table 1. The finance committee has stated that $50 and $20 will be available for capital investment in the first and second periods, respectively. We shall consider these amounts to have present values of $50 and $20, respectively. According to the principle stated above, we must now find appropriate multipliers, p_1 and p_2.

TABLE 1

INVESTMENT	OUTLAY— PERIOD 1 (c_1)	OUTLAY— PERIOD 2 (c_2)	PRESENT VALUE OF INVESTMENT
a	$12	$ 3	$14
b	54	7	17
c	6	6	17
d	6	2	15
e	30	35	40
f	6	6	12
g	48	4	14
h	36	3	10
i	18	3	12

Multipliers p_1 and p_2 were initially set at 1 and 3, respectively. With these values, only for investment d was the expression $(y - p_1c_1 - p_2c_2)$ positive and therefore acceptable. This would have resulted in net outlays of only $6 and $2 in periods one and two, respectively, Clearly, the values initially chosen for p_1 and p_2 were too great. On the other hand, values of 0.1 and 0.5 for p_1 and p_2, respectively, are too low, resulting in a positive value of $(y -$

---

[6] It is true, however, that the numbers in engineering problems are less conjectural; hence the cost of calculation is more likely to be considered worth while.

$p_1c_1 - p_2c_2$) for all investments and required outlays in periods one and two far exceeding the permitted outlays.

Values of 0.33 and 1 for p_1 and p_2 result in a near-perfect fit. The expression $(y - p_1c_1 - p_2c_2)$ is positive for investments a, c, d, f, and i. These investments require outlays of $48 and $20 in the first and second periods, as near the permitted outlays of $50 and $20 as discontinuities permit. No other group of investments that is possible within the stated constraints has a greater present value than $70, the present value of this group.[7]

C. SELECTING THE BEST AMONG MUTUALLY EXCLUSIVE ALTERNATIVES

Before monies are actually expended in fulfilment of an approved capital budget, the firm usually considers mutually exclusive alternative ways of making the generally described capital investment. When the firm is operating without an absolute limit on the dollars to be invested, the solution to the problem of selecting the best alternative is obvious. (Throughout this article, it is assumed that decisions regarding individual investment proposals do not significantly affect the firm's cost of capital.) The best alternative is the one with the greatest present value at the firm's cost of capital.

When the firm is operating subject to the constraint of an absolute dollar limit on capital expenditures, the problem is more difficult. Consider, first, the case in which there are net outlays in only one time period. The solution is found by the following process:

1. From each set of mutually exclusive alternatives, select that alternative for which the following quantity is a maximum: $y - pc$. Here y is the present value of the alternative; c is the net outlay required; and p is a constant of a magnitude chosen initially according to the judgment of the analyst. (Remember that the alternative of making no investment—that is, accepting $y = 0$ and $c = 0$—is always available, so that the maximum in question is never negative.)

2. Compute the total outlays required to adopt all the investment proposals selected according to the principle just specified.

3. If the total outlay required exceeds the total amount available, p should be increased; if the total amount required is less than the amount available for investment, p should be reduced. By trial and error, a value for p can be found that will equate the amount required for investment with that available for investment.

It should be clear that, as the value of y is increased, the importance of the product, pc, increases, with a consequent increase in the probability that in each set of mutually exclusive alternatives, an alternative will be selected that requires a smaller net outlay than is required with a smaller value for p. Thus increasing p tends to reduce the total amount required to adopt the investment proposals selected according to the principle indicated in (1)

---

[7] For the three-period problem, the relevant quantity is $(y - p_1c_1 - p_2c_2 - p_3c_3)$ rather than $(y - p_1c_1 - p_2c_2)$.

above. Conversely, reducing p tends to increase the outlay required to adopt the investment proposals selected according to this principle.

When there are net outlays in more than one period, the principle of solution is the same. Instead of maximizing the quantity $(y - pc)$, it is necessary to maximize the quantity $(y - p_1c_1 - p_2c_2)$, where again c_1 and c_2 are the net outlays in the first and second periods and p_1 and p_2 are auxiliary multipliers.

Up to this point, we have not discussed the problem of rationing capital among both independent investment proposals and sets of mutually exclusive investment proposals. Superficially, this problem seems different from the one of rationing among mutually exclusive proposals only, but in fact the problems are the same. The identity rests upon the fact that each so-called "independent" proposal is and should be considered a member of the set of proposals consisting of the independent proposal and of the always present proposal to do nothing. When independent proposals are viewed in this way, it can be seen that the case of rationing simultaneously among independent proposals and sets of mutually exclusive proposals is really just a special case of rationing among mutually exclusive proposals according to the principles outlined in the preceding paragraph.

The mechanics of solution are easily worked out. All that is required in order to make the solution the same as the solution for what we have called "mutually exclusive" sets of alternatives is that each so-called "independent" proposal be treated as a member of a mutually exclusive set consisting of itself and of the alternative of doing nothing. Once this is done, it is possible to go into the familiar routine of selecting from each set that proposal for which the express $(y - pc)$, or its appropriate modification to take account of constraints existing in more than one time period, is a maximum. Again, of course, that value of p will have to be found which results in matching as nearly as discontinuities permit the outlays required by the accepted proposals with the outlays permitted by the stated budgetary constraints.

III. SOME COMPARISONS WITH THE RATE-OF-RETURN METHOD OF CAPITAL RATIONING[8]

Since the rate-of-return method of capital rationing is fully described elsewhere, we shall describe it only briefly.[9] As in the methods described previously, attention is focused exclusively on net cash flows rather than on the data produced by conventional accounting practices. Investment proposals are ranked according to their "rate of return," defined as that rate of discounting which

---

[8] Joel Dean has pioneered in the development of methods of capital rationing that have an understandable relationship to profit maximization, in contrast to methods still quite widely used in business that rely on such criteria as pay-back, average return on book investment, etc. The method that he advocates is called the "rate-of-return" method.

[9] See Joel Dean, *Capital Budgeting* (New York: Columbia University Press, 1951); "Measuring the Productivity of Capital," *Harvard Business Review*, January–February, 1954.

reduces a stream of cash flows to zero, and selected from this ranking, starting with the highest rate of return.

The rate-of-return solution to the three problems that are the subject of this paper is discussed below.

A. GIVEN THE COST OF CAPITAL, WHAT GROUP OF INVESTMENTS SHOULD BE SELECTED?

The rate-of-return solution to the problem of selecting a group of independent proposals, given the firm's cost of capital, is to accept all investment proposals having a rate of return greater than the firm's cost of capital. This solution is necessarily identical with the solution proposed previously, except when the present value of some of the proposals is other than a steadily decreasing function of the cost of capital. An intuitive substantiation of this statement is achieved by an understanding of Figure 1. In Figure 1, I–I indicates the present value of an investment at different rates of interest; Oa is the firm's cost of capital; Ob is the rate of return on the investment; and aa' is the present value of the investment at the firm's cost of capital. It should be clear from the diagram that any proposal that has a positive ordinate (present value) at the firm's cost of capital will also have a rate of return (x-intercept) greater than the cost of capital. (However, it usually takes a little longer to find an intercept than to determine the value of an ordinate at one point.)

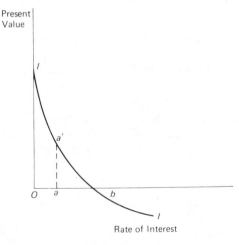

Figure 1

Under what circumstances can the present value of an investment proposal be something other than a steadily decreasing function of the cost of capital? Some investment proposals can intersect the x-axis at more than one point. In particular, investment proposals having initial cash outlays, subsequent net cash inflows, and final net cash outlays can intersect the x-axis more than once and have, therefore, more than one rate of return. Investments of this nature are rare, but they do occur, especially in the extractive industries. For example, an investment proposal might consist of an investment in an oil pump that gets a fixed quantity of oil out of the ground more rapidly than the pump currently in use. Making this investment would require an initial net outlay (for the new pump), subsequent net incremental cash inflow (larger oil production), and final net incremental cash outlay (the absence of oil production, because of its earlier exhaustion with the use of the higher-capacity new pump).[10] The present value of an investment in such a pump could look like Figure 2. In Figure 2, I–I indicates the present value of the investment; Oa is the firm's cost of capital; Ob and Oc are the two rates of return on the investment; and aa' is the present value of the investment at the firm's cost of capital.

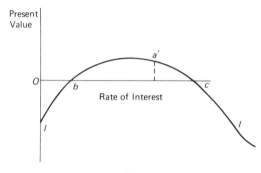

Figure 2

The reasoning behind this apparent paradox of the double rate of return is as follows:

 a) As the cost of capital of the firm approaches zero, the present value of the investment proposal approaches the algebraic sum of net cash flows and will be negative if this sum is negative.

 b) As the cost of capital increases, the present value of the final net cash outflow diminishes in importance relative to the earlier flows, and this diminution can cause the present value of the entire proposal to become positive.

 c) If the cost of capital continues to increase, the significance of all future cash flows tends to diminish, causing the present value of the proposal to approach the initial outlay as a limit.

The rate-of-return criterion for judging the acceptability of investment proposals, as it has been presented in published works, is then ambiguous or anomalous. This is in contrast to the clarity and uniform accuracy of the decisions indicated by the principle proposed earlier, which relates to the

---

[10] These incremental flows are measured with reference to the flows that would have resulted from the use of the smaller pump. Thus the final net outlay is not absolute but rather by comparison with oil (money) that would have been produced had the smaller pump been in use.

present value of an investment at the cost of capital rather than to a comparison between the cost of capital and the rate of return.[11]

B. GIVEN A FIXED SUM FOR CAPITAL INVESTMENT, WHAT GROUP OF INVESTMENT PROPOSALS SHOULD BE UNDERTAKEN?

The rate-of-return solution to the problem of allocating a fixed sum of money—without reference to cost of capital—among competing proposals is to order the proposals according to their rate of return and to proceed down the ladder thus created until the available funds are exhausted. The group of investment proposals selected by the use of this principle can be different, and probably would usually be different, from the group selected when the criterion is present value rather than rate of return. A difference between the two groups would not exist if the available capital funds were just equal to that amount which would permit investment in all those proposals having a rate of return at least equal to the firm's cost of capital and only those proposals, and if the anomalies mentioned under Section A were not present.

The preceding statements are equivalent to saying that the groups of investments that would be chosen by the use of the two principles or criteria would necessarily be the same only if the fixed sum to be invested happened to be the optimum sum and that investment of any other sum could result in selection of different groups of proposals by use of the two principles. This difference would result from the fact that the different principles can result in a different ranking of proposals within the group that would be accepted if the optimum amount were invested. Table 2 indicates the validity of the statement that the ordering of two investment proposals according to their

TABLE 2

| | NET CASH FLOWS | |
PERIOD	Investment A ($)	Investment B ($)
0– year	− 85	− 90
0–1 year	+ 17	+ 21
1–2 years	+ 35	+ 33
2–3 years	+ 68	+ 57
3–4 years	+131	+ 94
4–5 years	+216	+ 155
5–6 years	+357	+ 255
6–7 years	+546	+ 420
7–8 years	+555	+ 695
8–9 years	+345	+1,150
Present value at 20%	+606	+ 853
Rate of return (%)	66	62

[11] The rate-of-return rule could be easily modified to remove this ambiguity or anomaly by specifying that the relevant rate of return is the one at which the investment is a decreasing function of the rate of interest.

rate of return can be contrary to their ordering according to their present value per dollar of outlay.

The example of Table 2 illustrates that a proposal with a higher rate of return can have a lower present value and that, therefore, the two rules can conflict. The present-value rule maximizes the present value of the firm's net worth—by definition—and the rate-of-return rule therefore may not.

This discrepancy is undoubtedly of small practical significance. In the first place, firms that ration their capital rationally use the firm's cost of capital as the constraint rather than an absolute dollar sum, and under such rational behavior the two rules yield the same results, with the exception noted previously. (Undoubtedly, no firms long persist in setting absolute dollar constraints that differ significantly in their effects from the cost of capital constraint.) In the second place, the present values of investment proposals, expressed as functions of the cost of capital, are often thoughtful enough not to intersect above the x-axis (the rate-of-interest axis), a necessary condition for a conflict between the rate-of-return and present-value principles.

C. SELECTING THE BEST AMONG MUTUALLY EXCLUSIVE ALTERNATIVES

The rate-of-return solution to the problem of selecting the "best" among mutually exclusive investment alternatives, although occasionally tricky in practice, is simply explained as follows:

1. Compute the rate of return for that investment proposal, among the set of mutually exclusive proposals, requiring the least initial net outlay.

2. If the rate of return on the investment requiring the smallest outlay exceeds the firm's cost of capital (or other cutoff rate), tentatively accept that investment. Next compute the rate of return on the incremental outlay needed for the investment requiring the second lowest outlay. If that rate exceeds the firm's cutoff rate, accept the investment requiring the greater outlay in preference to that requiring the lesser. Proceed by such paired comparisons (based on rates of return on incremental outlay) to eliminate all but one investment.

3. If the rate of return on the proposal requiring the least outlay does not exceed the firm's cutoff rate, drop it from further consideration, and compute the rate of return for the proposal requiring the next least outlay. If that rate exceeds the firm's cutoff rate, that investment proposal becomes the bench mark for the first paired comparison. If that rate does not exceed the firm's cutoff rate, drop that proposal from further consideration. The process just described is to be repeated until either a proposal is found with a rate of return exceeding the cost of capital or until all proposals have been eliminated because their rates of return do not exceed the cutoff rate.

The rate-of-return solution to the problem of selecting the best among mutually exclusive investment alternatives is especially subject to the ambiguities and anomalies mentioned under Section A, because the costs and revenues associated with incremental investments required for proposals included in mutually exclusive sets are much more likely to have unusual time shapes and

reversals than are the costs and revenues associated with independent investments.

SUMMARY

We have given solutions to the three problems in budgeting capital so as to
maximize the net worth of the firm. The solutions that we have given differ in
principle from those implied by the rate of return method of capital rationing.
The difference in principle can lead to differences in behavior. Differences in
behavior will be rare in coping with problems of the first and third sorts and
will be relatively frequent for problems of the second sort. When differences
do exist, the rate-of-return solution does not result in maximizing the present
value of the firm's net worth.

16. ON THE THEORY OF OPTIMAL INVESTMENT DECISION[1]

J. HIRSHLEIFER*

Reprinted from *The Journal of Political Economy,* Vol.
LXVI, No. 4 (August 1958), pp. 329–52, by permission of
the author and the University of Chicago Press. Copyright,
1958, by the University of Chicago.

This article is an attempt to solve (in the theoretical sense), through the use
of isoquant analysis, the problem of optimal investment decisions (in business
parlance, the problem of capital budgeting). The initial section reviews the
principles laid down in Irving Fisher's justly famous works on interest[2] to
see what light they shed on two competing rules of behavior currently proposed
by economists to guide business investment decisions—the present-value rule

* University of Chicago
[1] I should like to express indebtedness to many of my colleagues, and especially to James
H. Lorie and Martin J. Bailey, for valuable suggestions and criticisms.
[2] Irving Fisher, *The Theory of Interest* (New York: Macmillan Co., 1930), is most widely
known. His earlier work, *The Rate of Interest* (New York: Macmillan Co., 1907), contains
most of the essential ideas.

and the internal-rate-of-return rule. The next concern of the paper is to show how Fisher's principles must be adapted when the perfect capital market assumed in his analysis does not exist—in particular, when borrowing and lending rates diverge, when capital can be secured only at an increasing marginal borrowing rate, and when capital is "rationed." In connection with this last situation, certain non-Fisherian views (in particular, those of Scitovsky and of the Lutzes) about the correct ultimate goal or criterion for investment decisions are examined. Section III, which presents the solution for multiperiod investments, corrects an error by Fisher which has been the source of much difficulty. The main burden of the analysis justifies the contentions of those who reject the internal rate of return as an investment criterion, and the paper attempts to show where the error in that concept (as ordinarily defined) lies and how the internal rate must be redefined if it is to be used as a reliable guide. On the positive side, the analysis provides some support for the use of the present-value rule but shows that even that rule is at best only a partial indicator of optimal investments and, in fact, under some conditions, gives an incorrect result.

More recent works on investment decisions, I shall argue, suffer from the neglect of Fisher's great contributions—the attainment of an optimum through balancing consumption alternatives over time and the clear distinction between production opportunities and exchange opportunities. It is an implication of this analysis, though it cannot be pursued here in detail, that solutions to the problem of investment decision recently proposed by Boulding, Samuelson, Scitovsky, and the Lutzes are at least in part erroneous. Their common error lay in searching for a rule or formula which would indicate optimal investment decisions *independently of consumption decisions*. No such search can succeed, if Fisher's analysis is sound which regards investment as not an end in itself but rather a process for distributing consumption over time.

The present paper deals throughout with a highly simplified situation in which the costs and returns of alternative individual investments are known *with certainty*, the problem being to select the scale and the mix of investments to be undertaken. To begin with, the analysis will be limited to investment decisions relating to two time periods only. We shall see in later sections that the two-period analysis can be translated immediately to the analysis of investments in perpetuities. For more general fluctuating income streams, however, additional difficulties arise whose resolution involves important new questions of principle. The restriction of the solution to perfect-information situations is, of course, unfortunate, since ignorance and uncertainty are of the essence of certain important observable characteristics of investment decision behavior. The analysis of optimal decisions under conditions of certainty can be justified, however, as a first step toward a more complete theory. No further apology will be offered for considering this oversimplified problem beyond the statement that theoretical economists are in such substantial disagreement about it that a successful attempt to bring the solution within the standard body of economic doctrine would represent a real contribution.

I. TWO-PERIOD ANALYSIS

A. BORROWING RATE EQUALS LENDING RATE (FISHER'S SOLUTION)

In order to establish the background for the difficult problems to be considered later, let us first review Fisher's solution to the problem of investment decision.[3] Consider the case in which there is a given rate at which the individual (or firm)[4] may borrow that is unaffected by the amount of his borrowings; a given rate at which he can lend that is unaffected by the amount of his loans; and in which these two rates are equal. These are the conditions used by Fisher; they represent a perfect capital market.

In Figure 1 the horizontal axis labeled K_0 represents the amount of actual or potential income (the amount consumed or available for consumption) in period 0; the vertical axis K_1 represents the amount of income in the same sense in period 1. The individual's decision problem is to choose, within the

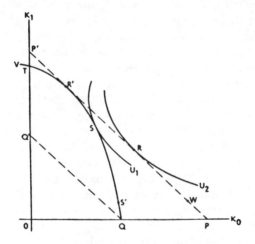

FIG. 1.—Fisher's solution

opportunities available to him, an optimum point on the graph—that is, an optimum time pattern of consumption. His starting point may conceivably be a point on either axis (initial income falling all in period 0 or all in period 1), such as points T or P, or else it may be a point in the positive quadrant (initial income falling partly in period 0 and partly in period 1), such as points W or S'. It may even lie in the second or fourth quadrants—where his initial situation involves negative income either in period 0 or in period 1.

---

[3] Fisher's contributions to the theory of capital go beyond his solution of the problem discussed in this paper—optimal investment decision. He also considers the question of the equilibrium of the capital market, which balances the supplies and demand of all the decision-making agencies.

[4] This analysis does not distinguish between individuals and firms. Firms are regarded solely as agencies or instruments of individuals.

The individual is assumed to have a preference function relating income in periods 0 and 1. This preference function would be mapped in quite the ordinary way, and the curves U_1 and U_2 are ordinary utility-indifference curves from this map.

Finally, there are the investment opportunities open to the individual. Fisher distinguishes between "investment opportunities" and "market opportunities." The former are real productive transfers between income in one time period and in another (what we usually think of as "physical" investment, like planting a seed); the latter are transfers through borrowing or lending (which naturally are on balance offsetting in the loan market). I shall depart from Fisher's language to distinguish somewhat more clearly between "production opportunities" and "market opportunities"; the word "investment" will be used in the more general and inclusive sense to refer to both types of opportunities taken together. Thus we may invest by building a house (a sacrifice of present or future income through a production opportunity) or by lending on the money market (a sacrifice of present for future income through a market or exchange opportunity). We could, equivalently, speak of purchase and sale of capital assets instead of lending or borrowing in describing the market opportunities.

In Figure 1 an investor with a starting point at Q faces a market opportunity illustrated by the dashed line QQ'. That is, starting with all his income in time 0, he can lend at some given lending rate, sacrificing present for future income, any amount until his K_0 is exhausted—receiving in exchange K_1 or income in period 1. Equivalently, we could say that he can buy capital assets—titles to future income K_1—with current income K_0. Following Fisher, I shall call QQ' a "market line."[5] The line PP', parallel to QQ', is the market line available to an individual whose starting point is P on the K_0 axis. By our assumption that the borrowing rate is also constant and equal to the lending rate, the market line PP' is also the market opportunity to an individual whose starting point is W, within the positive quadrant.

Finally, the curve $QSTV$ shows the range of productive opportunities available to an individual with starting point Q. It is the locus of points attainable to such an individual as he sacrifices more and more of K_0 by productive investments yielding K_1 in return. This attainability locus Fisher somewhat ambiguously calls the "productive opportunity curve" or "productive transformation curve." Note that in its concavity to the origin the curve reveals a kind of diminishing returns to investment. More specifically, productive investment projects may be considered to be ranked by the expression $(\Delta K_1)/(-\Delta K_0) - 1$, which might be called the "productive rate of return."[6] Here ΔK_0 and ΔK_1 represent the changes in income of periods 0 and 1 associated with the project in question.

---

[5] The slope of the market line is, of course, $-(1 + i)$, where i is the lending-borrowing rate. That is, when one gives up a dollar in period 0, he receives in exchange $1 + i$ dollars in period 1.

[6] For the present it is best to avoid the term "internal rate of return." Fisher uses the expressions "rate of return on sacrifice" or "rate of return over cost."

We may conceive of whole projects being so ranked, in which case we get the average productive rate of return for each such project. Or we may rank infinitesimal increments to projects, in which case we can deal with a marginal productive rate of return. The curve $QSTV$ will be continuous and have a continuous first derivative under certain conditions relating to absence of "lumpiness" of individual projects (or increments to projects), which we need not go into. In any case, $QSTV$ would represent a sequence of projects so arranged as to start with the one yielding the highest productive rate of return at the lower right and ending with the lowest rate of return encountered when the last dollar of period 0 is sacrificed at the upper left.[7] It is possible to attach meaning to the portion of $QSTV$ in the second quadrant, where K_0 becomes negative. Such points could not be optimal with indifference curves as portrayed in Figure 1, of course, but they may enter into the determination of an optimum. (This analysis assumes that projects are independent. Where they are not, complications ensue which will be discussed in Sections E and F below.)

As to the solution itself, the investor's objective is to climb onto as high an indifference curve as possible. Moving along the productive opportunity line $QSTV$, he sees that the highest indifference curve it touches is U_1 at the point S. But this is not the best point attainable, for he can move along $QSTV$ somewhat farther to the point R', which is on the market line PP'. He can now move in the reverse direction (borrowing) along PP', and the point R on the indifference curve U_2 is seen to be the best attainable.

The investor has, therefore, a solution in two steps. The "productive" solution—the point at which the individual should stop making additional productive investments—is at R'. He may then move along his market line to a point better satisfying his time preferences, at R. That is to say, he makes the best investment from the productive point of view and then "finances" it in the loan market. A very practical example is building a house and then borrowing on it through a mortgage so as to replenish current consumption income.

[7] An individual starting at S' would also have a "disinvestment opportunity."

[8] The present-value rule is the more or less standard guide supported by a great many theorists. The internal-rate-of-return rule, in the sense used here, has also been frequently proposed (see, e.g., Joel Dean, *Capital Budgeting* [New York: Columbia University Press, 1951], pp. 17–19). Citations on the use of alternative investment criteria may be found in Friedrich and Vera Lutz, *The Theory of Investment of the Firm* (Princeton, N. J.: Princeton University Press, 1951), p. 16. The internal-rate-of-return rule which we will consider in detail (i.e., adopt all projects and increments to projects for which the internal rate of return exceeds the market rate of interest) is *not* the same as that emphasized by the Lutzes (i.e., adopt that pattern of investments maximizing the internal rate of return). The rule considered here compares the incremental or marginal rate of return with a market rate; the other would maximize the average internal rate of return, without regard to the market rate. The latter rule will be shown to be fundamentally erroneous, even in the form the Lutzes accept as their ultimate criterion (maximize the internal rate of return on the investor's owned capital). This point will be discussed in connection with capital rationing in Sec. D, below.

We may now consider, in the light of this solution, the current debate between two competing "rules" for optimal investment behavior.[8] The first of these, the present-value rule, would have the individual or firm adopt all projects whose present value is positive at the market rate of interest. This would have the effect of maximizing the present value of the firm's position in terms of income in periods 0 and 1. Present value, under the present conditions, may be defined as $K_0 + (K_1)/(1 + i)$, income in period 1 being discounted by the factor $1 + i$, where i is the lending-borrowing rate. Since the market lines are defined by the condition that a sacrifice of one dollar in K_0 yields $1 + i$ dollars in K_1, these market lines are nothing but lines of constant present value. The equation for these lines is $K_0 + (K_1)/(1 + i) = C$, C being a parameter. The present-value rule tells us to invest until the highest such line is attained, which clearly takes place at the point R'. So far so good, but note that the rule says nothing about the "financing" (borrowing or lending) also necessary to attain the final optimum at R.

The internal-rate-of-return rule, in the form here considered, would have the firm adopt any project whose internal rate is greater than the market rate of interest. The internal rate for a project in the general case is defined as that discounting rate ρ which reduces the stream of net returns associated with the project to a present value of zero (or, equivalently, which makes the discounted value of the associated cost stream equal to the discounted value of the receipts stream). We may write

$$0 = \Delta K_0 + \frac{\Delta K_1}{1 + \rho} + \frac{\Delta K_2}{(1 + \rho)^2} + \cdots + \frac{\Delta K_n}{(1 + \rho)^n}.$$

In the two-period case ρ is identical with the productive rate of return, $(\Delta K_1)/(-\Delta K_0) - 1$. As in the discussion above, if infinitesimal changes are permitted, we may interpret this statement in the marginal sense. The marginal (two-period) internal rate of return is measured by the slope of the productive opportunity curve minus unity. In Figure 1 at each step we would compare the steepness of $QSTV$ with that of the market lines. We would move along $QSTV$ as long as, and just so long as, it is the steeper. Evidently, this rule would have us move along $QSTV$ until it becomes tangent to a market line at R'. Again, so far so good, but nothing is said about the borrowing or lending necessary to attain the optimum.

At least for the two-period case, then, the present-value rule and the internal-rate-of-return rule lead to identical answers[9] which are the same as that reached by our isoquant analysis, so far as *productive* investment decisions are concerned. The rules are both silent, however, about the market exchange between K_0 and K_1, which remains necessary if an optimum is to be achieved. This second step is obviously part of the solution. Had there been no actual

---

[9] In fact, for the two-period case the rules are identical; it is possible to show that any project (or increment to a project) of positive present value must have an internal rate of return greater than the rate of interest.

opportunity to borrow or lend, the point S would have been the best attainable, and the process of productive investment should not have been carried as far as R'. We cannot say that the rules are definitely wrong, however, since with no such market opportunities there would have been no market rate of interest i for calculating present values or for comparison with the marginal internal rate of return. It remains to be seen whether these rules can be restated or generalized to apply to cases where a simple market rate of interest is not available for unlimited borrowing and lending. But it should be observed that, in comparison with isoquant analysis, each of the rules leads to only a partial answer.

B. WHEN BORROWING AND LENDING RATES DIFFER

We may now depart from Fisher's analysis, or rather extend it, to a case he did not consider. The borrowing and lending rates are still assumed to be constant, independent of the amounts taken or supplied by the individual or firm under consideration. However, it is now assumed that these rates are not equal, the borrowing rate being higher than the lending rate.[10] In Figure 2 there is the same preference map, of which only the isoquant U_1 is shown.

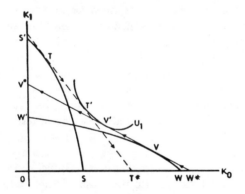

FIG. 2.—Extension of Fisher's solution for differing borrowing and lending rates.

There are now, however, two sets of market lines over the graph; the steeper (*dashed*) lines represent borrowing opportunities (note the direction of the arrows), and the flatter (*solid*) lines represent lending opportunities. The heavy solid lines show two possible sets of productive opportunities, both of which lead to solutions along U_1. Starting with amount OW of K_0, an investor

[10] If the borrowing rate were lower than the lending rate, it would be possible to accumulate infinite wealth by borrowing and relending, so I shall not consider this possibility. Of course, financial institutions typically borrow at a lower average rate than that at which they lend, but they cannot expand their scale of operations indefinitely without changing this relationship.

with a production opportunity WVW' would move along WVW' to V, at which point he would *lend* to get to his time-preference optimum—the tangency with U_1 at V'. The curve STS' represents a much more productive possibility; starting with only OS of K_0, the investor would move along STS' to T and then *borrow* backward along the dashed line to get to T', the tangency point with U_1. Note that the total opportunity set (the points attainable through any combination of the market and productive opportunities) is WVW^* for the first opportunity, and $S'TT^*$ for the second.

More detailed analysis, however, shows that we do not yet have the full solution—there is a third possibility. An investor with a productive opportunity locus starting on the K_0 axis will never stop moving along this locus in the direction of greater K_1 as long as the marginal productive rate of return is still above the borrowing rate—nor will he ever push along the locus beyond the point where the marginal productive rate of return falls below the lending rate. Assuming that some initial investments are available which have a higher productive rate of return than the borrowing rate, the investor should push along the locus until the borrowing rate is reached. If, at this point, it is possible to move up the utility hill by borrowing, productive investment should cease, and the borrowing should take place; the investor is at some point like T in Figure 2. If borrowing decreases utility, however, more productive investment is called for. Suppose investment is then carried on until diminishing returns bring the marginal productive rate of return down to the lending rate. If lending then increases utility, productive investment should halt there, and the lending take place; the investor is at some point like V in Figure 2. But suppose that now it is found that lending also decreases utility! This can only mean that a tangency of the productive opportunity locus and an indifference curve took place when the marginal productive rate of return was somewhere *between* the lending and the borrowing rates. In this case neither lending nor borrowing is called for, the optimum being reached directly in the productive investment decision by equating the marginal productive rate of return with the marginal rate of substitution (in the sense of time preference) along the utility isoquant.

These solutions are illustrated by the division of Figure 3 into three zones. In Zone I the borrowing rate is relevant. Tangency solutions with the market line at the borrowing rate like that at T are carried back by borrowing to tangency with a utility isoquant at a point like T'. All such final solutions lie along the curve OB, which connects all points on the utility isoquants whose slope equals that of the *borrowing* market line. Correspondingly, Zone III is that zone where the production solution involves tangency with a lending market line (like V), which is then carried forward by lending to a final tangency optimum with a utility isoquant along the line OL at a point like V'. This line connects all points on the utility isoquants with slope equal to that of the *lending* market line. Finally, Zone II solutions occur when a productive opportunity locus like QRQ' is steeper than the lending rate throughout Zone III but flatter than the borrowing rate throughout Zone I. Therefore, such a locus must be tangent to one of the indifference curves somewhere in Zone II.

By analogy with the discussion in the previous section, we may conclude that the *borrowing* rate will lead to correct answers (to the productive investment decision, neglecting the related financing question) under the present-value rule or the internal-rate-of-return rule—when the situation involves a Zone I solution. Correspondingly, the *lending* rate will be appropriate and lead to correct investment decisions for Zone III solutions. For Zone II solutions, however, neither will be correct. There will, in fact, be some rate between the lending and the borrowing rates which would lead to the correct results.

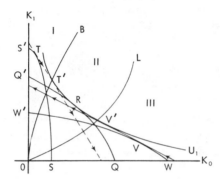

Figure 3. Three Solution Zones for Differing Borrowing and Lending Rates.

Formally speaking, we could describe this correct discount rate as the marginal productive opportunity rate,[11] which will at equilibrium equal the marginal subjective time-preference rate. In such a case neither rule is satisfactory in the sense of providing the productive solution without reference to the utility isoquants; knowledge of the comparative slopes of the utility isoquant and the productive opportunity frontier is all that is necessary, however. Of course, even when the rules in question are considered "satisfactory," they are misleading in implying that productive investment decisions can be correctly made independently of the "financing" decision.

This solution, in retrospect, may perhaps seem obvious. Where the productive opportunity, time-preference, and market (or financing) opportunities stand in such relations to one another as to require borrowing to reach the optimum, the borrowing rate is the correct rate to use in the productive investment decision. The lending rate is irrelevant because the decision on the

[11] The marginal productive opportunity rate, or marginal internal rate of return, measures the rate of return on the best alternative project. Assuming continuity, it is defined by the slope of QRQ' at R in Fig. 3. Evidently, a present-value line tangent to U_1 and QRQ' at R would, in a formal sense, make the present-value rule correct. And comparing this rate with the marginal internal rate of return as it varies along QRQ' would make the internal-rate-of-return rule also correct in the same formal sense.

margin involves a balancing of the cost of borrowing and the return from further productive investment, both being higher than the lending rate. The lending opportunity is indeed still available, but, the rate of return on lending being lower than the lowest marginal productive rate of return we would wish to consider in the light of the borrowing rate we must pay, lending is not a relevant alternative. Rather the relevant alternative to productive investment is a reduction in borrowing, which in terms of saving interest is more remunerative than lending. Similarly, when the balance of considerations dictates lending part of the firm's current capital funds, borrowing is not the relevant cost incurred in financing productive investment. The relevant alternative to increased productive investment is the amount of lending which must be foregone. While these considerations may be obvious, there is some disagreement in the literature as to whether the lending or the borrowing rate is *the* correct one.[12]

C. INCREASING MARGINAL COST OF BORROWING

While it is generally considered satisfactory to assume a constant lending rate (the investor does not drive down the loan rate as a consequence of his lendings), for practical reasons it is important to take account of the case in which increased borrowing can only take place at increasing cost. As it happens, however, this complication does not require any essential modification of principle.

Figure 4 shows, as before, a productive opportunity locus $QR'T$ and an indifference curve U_1. For simplicity, assume that marginal borrowing costs rise at the same rate whether the investor begins to borrow at the point R', S', or W' or at any other point along $QR'T$ (he cannot, of course, start borrowing at Q, having no K_1 to offer in exchange for more K_0). Under this assumption we can then draw market curves, now concave to the origin, like $R'R$, $S'S$, and $W'W$. The curve TE represents the total opportunity set as the *envelope* of these market curves, that is, TE connects all the points on the market curves representing the maximum K_0 attainable for any given K_1. By the nature of an envelope curve, TE will be tangent to a market curve at each such point. The optimum is then simply found where TE is tangent to the highest indifference curve attainable—here the curve U_1 at R. To reach R, the investor must exploit his productive opportunity to the point R' and then borrow back along his market curve to R.

The preceding discussion applies solely to what was called a Zone I (borrowing) solution in the previous section. Depending upon the nature of

---

[12] The borrowing rate (the "cost of capital") has been recommended by Dean and by Lorie and Savage (see Joel Dean, *Capital Budgeting* [New York: Columbia University Press, 1951], esp. pp. 43–44; James H. Lorie and Leonard J. Savage, "Three Problems in Rationing Capital," *Journal of Business*, XXVIII [October, 1955], 229–39, esp. p. 229). Roberts and the Lutzes favor the use of the lending rate (see Friedrich and Vera Lutz, *op. cit.*, esp. p. 22; Harry V. Roberts, "Current Problems in the Economics of Capital Budgeting," *Journal of Business*, XXX [January, 1957], 12–16).

the productive opportunity, a Zone II or Zone III solution would also be possible under the assumptions of this section. With regard to the present-value and the internal-rate-of-return rules, the conclusions are unchanged for Zone II and III solutions, however. Only for Zone I solutions is there any modification.

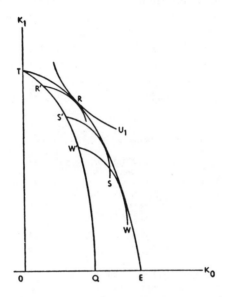

FIG. 4.—Increasing marginal cost of borrowing

The crucial question, as always, for these rules is what rate of discount to use. Intuition tells us that the rate representing *marginal* borrowing cost should be used as the discount rate for Zone I solutions, since productive investment will then be carried just to the point justified by the cost of the associated increment of borrowing.[13] That is, the slope of the envelope for any point on the envelope curve (for example, R), is the same as the slope of the productive opportunity curve at the corresponding point (R') connected by the market curve.[14] If this is the case, the discount rate determined by the slope at a tangency with U_1 at a point like R will also lead to productive investment being carried to R' by the rules under consideration. Of course, this again is a purely formal statement. Operationally speaking, the rules may not be of much value, since the discount rate to be used is not known in advance independently of the utility (time-preference) function.

[13] I should like to thank Joel Segall for insisting on this point in discussions of the problem. Note that the rate representing marginal borrowing cost is not necessarily the borrowing rate on marginal funds—an increment of borrowing may increase the rate on infra-marginal units.

[14] While this point can be verified geometrically, it follows directly from the analytic properties of an envelope curve.

To simplify notation, in this note I shall denote K_1 of Figure 4 as y and K_0 as x. The

D. RATIONING OF "CAPITAL"—A CURRENT CONTROVERSY

The previous discussion provides the key for resolving certain current disputes over what constitutes optimal investment decision under a condition of "capital rationing" or "fixed capital budget." This condition is said to exist when the firm, or individual, or perhaps department of government under consideration cannot borrow additional "capital" but is limited instead of making the best use of the "capital" already in its possession or allocated to it.[15] In theoretical literature a closely related idea is expressed by Scitovsky, who, regarding the availability of capital (in the sense of "current capital

---

equation of the productive opportunity locus may be written

$$y_0 = f(x_0). \qquad (a)$$

The family of market curves can be expressed by $y - y_0 = g(x - x_0)$, or

$$F(x,x_0) = f(x_0) + g(x - x_0). \qquad (b)$$

An envelope $y - h(x)$, is defined by the condition that any point on it must be a point of tangency with some member of the family (b). Thus we have

$$h(x) = F(x,x_0) \qquad (c)$$

$$\frac{dh}{dx} = \frac{\partial F(x,x_0)}{\partial x}. \qquad (d)$$

The second condition for an envelope is that the partial derivative of the function (b) with respect to the parameter must equal zero:

$$\frac{\partial F(x,x_0)}{\partial x_0} = 0. \qquad (e)$$

But

$$\frac{\partial F(x,x_0)}{\partial x_0} = \frac{df(x_0)}{dx_0} + (-1)\frac{dg(x - x_0)}{d(x - x_0)}.$$

Hence

$$\frac{df(x_0)}{dx_0} = \frac{dg(x - x_0)}{d(x - x_0)}.$$

Also

$$\frac{\partial F(x,x_0)}{\partial x} = \frac{dg(x - x_0)}{d(x - x_0)}.$$

So, finally,

$$\frac{df(x_0)}{dx_0} = \frac{dg(x - x_0)}{d(x - x_0)} = \frac{\partial F(x,x_0)}{\partial x} = \frac{dh}{dx}.$$

Thus the slope of the productive opportunity locus is the same as the slope of the envelope at points on the two curves connected by being on the same curve.

[15] The expression "capital rationing" was used some time ago by Hart to refer to a nonprice limitation on the acquisition of debt or equity financing (see A. G. Hart, "Anticipations, Business Planning, and the Cycle," *Quarterly Journal of Economics*, LI [1937], 273–97). His use of the term does not seem to imply a definitely fixed quantity available and can,

funds ") as the fixed factor limiting the size of the firm, proposes as the investment criterion the maximization of " profit per unit capital invested."[16] Lutz
and Lutz, in contrast, assert as their ultimate investment criterion the maximization of the rate of return on the entrepreneur's *owned* capital, which they
regard as fixed.[17]

It is of some interest to analyze these concepts in greater detail in terms of
our Fisherian model. Scitovsky defines " capital" as current capital funds
(our K_0) required to bridge the time lapse between factor input and product
output.[18] Under this definition, however, " capital" would be fixed to the
firm only under rather peculiar conditions; specifically, if there is a discontinuity in the capital funds market such that the marginal borrowing rate suddenly
becomes infinite at the firm's level of borrowings.[19] Without discontinuity,
an infinitely high marginal borrowing rate could never represent an equilibrium position for the borrower, unless indeed his preference for present
income over future income was absolute. And, of course, if the marginal borrowing rate is not infinite, current capital funds could not be said to be fixed.
Nevertheless, while this case may be considered peculiar and unlikely to arise
in any strict sense, it may be acceptable as a reasonable approximation of
certain situations which occur in practice—especially in the short run, perhaps
as a result of previous miscalculations. A division of a firm or a department
of government may at times be said to face an infinite marginal borrowing
rate once a budget constraint is reached—until the next meeting of the board
of directors or the Congress provides more funds.

On the other hand, it is difficult to decipher the Lutzes' meaning when they
speak of the firm's *owned* capital as fixed. In the Fisherian analysis, " ownership" of current or future assets is a legal form without analytical significance
—to buy an asset yielding future income, with current funds, is simply to
lend, while selling income is the same as borrowing. In a more fundamental
sense, however, we could think of the firm as " owning" the opportunity set
or at least the physical productive opportunities available to it, and this perhaps is what the Lutzes have in mind. Thus, Robinson Crusoe's house might

---

in fact, be interpreted simply as indicating a rising marginal cost of capital funds. See also
Joel Dean, *Managerial Economics* (Englewood Cliffs, N. J.: Prentice-Hall, Inc., 1951), pp.
586–600. In the sense of a definitely fixed quantity of funds, the term has been used by
various authors discussing business or government problems. See J. Margolis, "The Discount Rate and the Benefits-Cost Justification of Federal Irrigation Investment," (Department of Economics, Stanford University, Technical Report No. 23 [Stanford, Calif., 1955]);
Lorie and Savage, *op. cit.*, and R. McKean, *Efficiency in Government through Systems
Analysis* (New York: John Wiley & Sons, 1958).

[16] T. Scitovsky, *Welfare and Competition* (Chicago: Richard D. Irwin, Inc., 1951), pp.
208–9.

[17] *Op. cit.*, pp. 16–48, esp. pp. 17, 20, 42.

[18] *Op. cit.*, p. 194.

[19] Scitovsky appears to leap from the acceptable argument in the earlier part of his discussion that willingness to lend and to borrow are not *unlimited* to the unacceptable position
in his later discussion that current capital funds are *fixed* (*ibid*, pp. 193–200, 208–9).

be considered as his "owned capital"—a resource yielding consumption income in both present and future. The trouble is that the Lutzes seem to be thinking of "owned capital" as the *value* of the productive resources (in the form of capital goods) owned by the firm,[20] but owned physical capital goods cannot be converted to a capital *value* without bringing in a rate of discount for the receipts stream. But since, as we have seen, the relevant rate of discount for a firm's decisions is not (except where a perfect capital market exists) an independent entity but is itself determined by the analysis, the *capital value* cannot in general be considered to be fixed independently of the investment decision.[21]

While space does not permit a full critique of the Lutzes' important work, it is worth mentioning that—from a Fisherian point of view—it starts off on the wrong foot. They search first for an ultimate criterion or formula with which to gauge investment decision rules and settle upon "maximization of the rate of return on the investor's owned capital" on what seem to be purely intuitive grounds. The Fisherian approach, in contrast, integrates investment decision with the general theory of choice—the goal being to maximize utility subject to certain opportunities and constraints. In these terms, certain formulas can be validated as useful proximate rules for some classes of problems, as I am attempting to show here. However, the ultimate Fisherian criterion of choice—the optimal balancing of consumption alternatives over time—cannot be reduced to any of the usual formulas.

Instead of engaging in further discussion of the various senses in which "capital" may be said to be fixed to the firm, it will be more instructive to see how the Fisherian approach solves the problem of "capital rationing." I shall use as an illustration what may be called a "Scitovsky situation," in which the investor has run against a discontinuity making the marginal borrowing rate infinite. I regard this case (which I consider empirically significant only in the short run) as the model situation underlying the "capital rationing" discussion.

An infinite borrowing rate makes the dashed borrowing lines of Figures 2 and 3 essentially vertical. In consequence, the curve *OB* in Figure 3 shifts so far to the left as to make Zone I disappear for all practical purposes. There are then only Zone II and Zone III solutions. An investment-opportunity locus

---

[20] Lutz and Lutz, *op. cit.*, pp. 3–13.

[21] It is possible, however, that the Lutzes had in mind only the case in which an investor starts off with current funds but no other assets. In this case no discounting problems would arise in defining owned capital, so their ultimate criterion could not be criticized on that score. The objection raised below to the Scitovsky criterion, however—that it fails to consider the *consumption* alternative, which is really the heart of the question of investment decision—would then apply to the Lutzes' rule. In addition, a rule for an investor owning solely current funds is hardly of general enough applicability to be an ultimate criterion. The Lutzes themselves recognize the case of an investor owning no "capital" but using only borrowed funds, and for this case they themselves abandon their ultimate criterion (*ibid.*, p. 42, n. 32). The most general case, of course, is that of an investor with a productive opportunity set capable of yielding him alternative combinations of present and future income.

like WVW' in Figure 3 becomes less steep than the lending slope in Zone III, in which case the investor will carry investment up to the point V where this occurs and then lend until a tangency solution is reached at V', which would be somewhere along the curve OL of Figure 3. If an investment-opportunity locus like QRQ' in Figure 3 is still steeper than the lending rate after it crosses OL, investment should be carried until tangency with an indifference curve like U_1 is attained somewhere to the left of OL, with no lending or borrowing taking place.

In terms of the present-value or internal-rate-of-return rules, under these conditions the decisions should be based on the *lending* rate (as the discounting rate or the standard of comparison) if the solution is a Zone III one. Here lending actually takes place, since movement upward and to the left still remains desirable when the last investment with a rate of return greater than the lending rate is made. If the solution is a Zone II one, the lending rate must not be used. Investments showing positive present value at the lending rate (or, equivalently, with an internal rate of return higher than the lending rate) will be nevertheless undesirable after a tangency point equating the investment-opportunity slope and the time-preference slope is reached. The correct rate, formally speaking, is the marginal opportunity rate.

The solution changes only slightly when we consider an isolated individual like Robinson Crusoe or a self-contained community like a nation under autarchy (or like the world economy as a whole). In this situation neither borrowing nor lending is possible in our sense, only productive opportunities existing. Only Zone II solutions are then possible. This case is the extreme remove from the assumption of perfect capital markets.[22]

As in the case of the Zone II solutions arising without capital rationing, the present-value or internal-rate-of-return rules can be formally modified to apply to the Zone II solutions which are typical under capital rationing. The discount rate to be used for calculating present values or as a standard of comparison against the internal rate of project increments is the rate given by the slope of the Zone II tangency (the marginal productive rate of return); with this rate, the rules give the correct answer. But this rate cannot be discovered until the solution is attained and so is of no assistance in reaching the solution. The exception is the Zone III solution involving lending which can arise in a "Scitovsky situation." Here the lending rate should of course be used. The undetermined discount rate that gives correct results when the rules are used for Zone II solutions can, in some problems, be regarded as a kind of shadow price reflecting the productive rate of return on the best alternative opportunity not being exploited.

The reader may be curious as to why, in the Scitovsky situation, the outcome of the analysis was not Scitovsky's result—that the optimal investment

---

[22] We could, following the principles already laid down, work out without great difficulty the solution for the case in which borrowing is permitted but only up to a certain fixed limit. The effect of such a provision is to provide a kind of "attainability envelope" as in Fig. 4, but of a somewhat different shape.

decision is such as to maximize the (average) internal rate of return on the firm's present capital funds (K_0). Thus, in Figure 3, for a firm starting with OQ of K_0 and faced with the productive opportunity locus QRQ', the average rate of return (K_1 received per unit of K_0 sacrificed) is a maximum for an infinitesimal movement along QRQ', since, the farther it moves, the more the marginal and average productive rates of return fall. Such a rule implies staying at Q—which is obviously the wrong decision.

How does this square with Scitovsky's intuitively plausible argument that the firm always seeks to maximize its returns on the fixed factor, present capital funds being assumed here to be fixed?[23] The answer is that this argument is applicable only for a factor "fixed" in the sense of no alternative uses. Here present capital funds K_0 are assumed to be fixed, but not in the sense Scitovsky must have had in mind. The concept here is that no additional borrowing can take place, but the possibility of *consuming* the present funds as an alternative to investing them is recognized. For Scitovsky, however, the funds *must* be invested. If in fact current income K_0 had no uses other than conversion into future income K_1 (this amounts to absolute preference for future over current income), Scitovsky's rule would correctly tell us to pick that point on the K_1 axis which is the highest.[24] Actually, our time preferences are more balanced; there *is* an alternative use (consumption) for K_0. Therefore, even in Scitovsky situations, we will balance K_0 and K_1 on the margin—and not simply accept the maximum K_1 we can get in exchange for all our "fixed" K_0.[25] The analyses of Scitovsky, the Lutzes, and many other recent writers frequently lead to incorrect solutions because of their failure to take into account the alternative consumption opportunities which Fisher integrated into his theory of investment decision.

E. NON-INDEPENDENT INVESTMENT OPPORTUNITIES

Up to this point, following Fisher, investment opportunities have been assumed to be independent so that it is possible to rank them in any desired way. In particular, they were ordered in Figure 1 through 4 in terms of decreasing productive rate of return; the resultant concavity produced unique tangency solutions with the utility or market curves. But suppose, now, that there are two mutually exclusive sets of such investment opportunities. Thus we may consider building a factory in the East or the West, but not both—

[23] *Op. cit.*, p. 209.

[24] That is, the point Q' in Fig. 3. This result is of course trivial. Scitovsky may possibly have in mind choice among non-independent sets of investments (discussed in the next section), where each set may have a different intersection with the K_1 axis. Here a non-trivial choice could be made with the criterion of maximizing the average rate of return.

[25] Scitovsky may have in mind a situation in which a certain fraction of current funds K_0 are set apart from consumption (on some unknown basis) to become the "fixed" current capital funds. In this case the Scitovsky rule would lead to the correct result if it happened that just so much "fixed" capital funds were allocated to get the investor to the point R' on his productive transformation locus of Fig. 3.

contemplating the alternatives, the eastern opportunities may look like the locus $QV'V$, and the western opportunities like $QT'T$ in Figure 5.[26]

Which is better? Actually, the solutions continue to follow directly from Fisher's principles, though too much non-independence makes for troublesome calculations in practice, and in some classes of cases the heretofore inerrant present-value rule fails. In the simplest case, in which there is a constant borrowing-lending rate (a perfect capital market), the curve $QV'V$ is

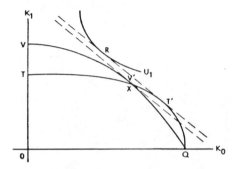

FIGURE 5. NON-INDEPENDENT INVESTMENT OPPORTUNITIES
— TWO ALTERNATIVE PRODUCTIVE INVESTMENT LOCI.

tangent to its highest attainable present-value line at V'—while the best point on $QT'T$ is T'. It is only necessary to consider these, and the one attaining the higher present-value line ($QT'T$ at T' in this case) will permit the investor to reach the highest possible indifference curve U_1 at R. In contrast, the internal-rate-of-return rule would locate the points T' and V' but could not discriminate between them. Where borrowing and lending rates differ, as in Figure 2 (now interpreting the productive opportunity loci of that figure as mutually exclusive alternatives), it may be necessary to compare, say, a lending solution at V with a borrowing solution at T. To find the *optimum optimorum*, the indifference curves must be known (in Fig. 2 the two solutions attain the same indifference curve). Note that present value is *not* a reliable guide here; in fact, the present value of the solution $V(=W^*)$ at the relevant discount rate for it (the lending rate) far exceeds that of the solution $T(=T^*)$ at its discount rate (the borrowing rate), when the two are actually indifferent. Assuming an increasing borrowing rate creates no new essential difficulty.

Another form of non-independence, illustrated in Figure 6, is also troublesome without modifying principle. Here the projects along the productive investment locus QQ' are not entirely independent, for we are constrained to adopt some low-return ones before certain high-return ones. Again, there is a possibility of several local optima like V and T, which can be compared along the same lines as used in the previous illustration.

[26] It would, of course, reduce matters to their former simplicity if one of the loci lay completely within the other, in which case it would be obviously inferior and could be dropped from consideration.

F. CONCLUSION FOR TWO-PERIOD ANALYSIS

The solutions for optimal investment decisions vary according to a two-way classification of cases. The first classification refers to the way market opportunities exist for the decision-making agency; the second classification refers to the absence or presence of the complication of non-independent productive opportunities. The simplest, extreme cases for the first classification are: (*a*) a perfect capital market (market opportunities such that lending or borrowing in any amounts can take place at the same, fixed rate) and (*b*) no market

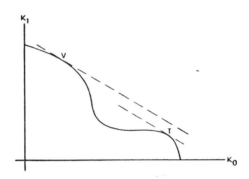

FIG. 6.—Non-independent investment opportunities—poorer projects prerequisite to better ones.

opportunities whatsoever, as was true for Robinson Crusoe. Where there is a perfect capital market, the total attainable set is a triangle (considering only the first quadrant like *OPP'* in Figure 1, just tangent to the productive opportunity locus. Where there is no capital market at all, the total attainable set is simply the productive opportunity locus itself. It is not difficult to see how the varying forms of imperfection of the capital market fit in between these extremes.

When independence of physical (productive) opportunities holds, the opportunities may be ranked in order of descending productive rate of return. Geometrically, if the convenient (but inessential) assumption of continuity is adopted, independence means that the productive opportunity locus is everywhere concave to the origin, like *QS'TV* in Figure 1. Non-independence may take several forms (see Figs. 5 and 6), but in each case that is not trivial non-independence means that the effective productive opportunity locus is not simply concave. This is obvious in Figure 6. In Figure 5 each of the two alternative loci considered separately is concave, but the effective locus is the scalloped outer edge of the overlapping sets of points attainable by either—that is, the effective productive opportunity locus runs along *QT'T* up to *X* and then crosses over *QV'V*.

With this classification a detailed tabulation of the differing solutions could be presented; the following brief summary of the general principles involved should serve almost as well, however.

1. The internal-rate-of-return rule fails wherever there are multiple tangencies—the normal outcome for non-independent productive opportunities.
2. The present-value rule works whenever the other does and, in addition, correctly discriminates among multiple tangencies whenever a perfect capital market exists (or, by extension, whenever a unique discount rate can be determined for the comparison—for example when all the alternative tangencies occur in Zone I or else all in Zone III).
3. Both rules work only in a formal sense when the solution involves direct tangency between a productive opportunity locus and a utility isoquant, since the discount rate necessary for use of both rules is the marginal opportunity rate—a product of the analysis.
4. The cases when even the present-value rule fails (may actually give wrong answers) all involve the comparison of multiple tangencies arising from non-independent investments when, in addition, a perfect capital market does not exist. One important example is the comparison of a tangency involving borrowing in Zone I with another involving lending in Zone III. Only reference to the utility map can give correct answers for such cases.
5. Even when one or both rules are correct in a not merely formal sense, the answer given is the "productive solution"—only part of the way toward attainment of the utility optimum. Furthermore, this productive decision is optimal only when it can be assumed that the associated financing decision will in fact be made.

II. A BRIEF NOTE ON PERPETUITIES

A traditional way of handling the multiperiod case in capital theory has been to consider investment decisions as choices between current funds and perpetual future income flows. For many purposes this is a valuable simplifying idea. It cannot be adopted here, however, because the essence of the practical difficulties which have arisen in multiperiod investment decisions is the *reinvestment* problem—the necessity of making productive or market exchanges between incomes in future time periods. In fact, the consideration of the perpetuity case is, in a sense, only a variant of the two-period analysis, in which there is a single present and a single future. In the case of perpetuity analysis, the future is stretched out, but we cannot consider transfer between different periods of the future.

All the two-period results in Section I can easily be modified to apply to the choice between funds and perpetuities. In the figures, instead of income K_1 in period 1 one may speak of an annual rate of income k. Productive opportunity loci and time-preference curves will retain their familiar shapes. The lines of constant present value (borrow-lend lines) are expressed by the equation $C = K_0 + (k/i)$ instead of $C = K_0 + (K_1)/(1 + i)$. The "internal rate of return" will equal $(k)/(-\Delta K_0)$. The rest of the analysis follows directly, but, rather than trace it out, I shall turn to the consideration of the multiperiod case in a more general way.

III. MULTIPERIOD ANALYSIS

Considerable doubt prevails on how to generalize the principles of the two-period analysis to the multiperiod case. The problems which have troubled the analysis of the multiperiod case are actually the result of inappropriate generalizations of methods of solution that do lead to correct results in the simplified two-period analysis.

A. INTERNAL-RATE-OF-RETURN RULE VERSUS PRESENT-VALUE RULE

In the multiperiod analysis there is no formal difficulty in generalizing the indifference curves of Figure 1 to indifference shells in any number of dimensions. Also the lines of constant present value or market lines become hyperplanes with the equation (in the most general form)

$$K_0 + \frac{K_1}{1 + i_1} + \frac{K_2}{(1 + i_1)(1 + i_2)} + \cdots + \frac{K_n}{(1 + i_1)(1 + i_2) \cdots (1 + i_n)} = C,$$

C being a parameter, i_1 the discount rate between income in period 0 and 1, i_2 the discount rate between periods 1 and 2, and so forth.[27] Where $i_1 = i_2 = \cdots i_n = i$, the expression takes on the simpler and more familiar form

$$K_0 + \frac{K_1}{1 + i} + \frac{K_2}{(1 + i)^2} + \cdots + \frac{K_n}{(1 + i)^n} = C.$$

The major difficulty with the multiperiod case turns upon the third element of the solution—the description of the productive opportunities, which may be denoted by the equation $f(K_0, K_1, \ldots, K_n) = 0$. The purely theoretical specification is not too difficult, however, if the assumption is made that all investment options are independent. The problem of non-independence is not essentially different in the multiperiod case and in the two-period case, and it would enormously complicate the presentation to consider it here. Under this condition, then, and with appropriate continuity assumptions, the productivity opportunity locus may be envisaged as a shell[28] concave to the origin in all directions. With these assumptions, between income in any two periods K_r and K_s (holding K_t for all other periods constant) there will be a two-dimensional productive opportunity locus essentially like that in Figure 1.[29]

---

[27] I shall not, in this section, consider further the possible divergences between the lending and borrowing rates studies in detail in Sec. I but shall speak simply of " the discount rate " or " the market rate." The principles involved are not essentially changed in the multiperiod case; I shall concentrate attention on certain other difficulties that appear only when more than two periods are considered. We may note that in the most general case the assumption of full information becomes rather unrealistic—e.g., that the pattern of interest rates i_1 through i_n is known today.

[28] As in the two-period case, the locus represents not all the production opportunities but only the *boundary* of the region represented by the production opportunities. The boundary consists of those opportunities not dominated by any other; any opportunity represented by an interior point is dominated by at least one boundary point.

[29] The assumption of n-dimensional continuity is harder to swallow than two-dimensional continuity as an approximation to the nature of the real world. Nevertheless, the restriction is not essential, though it is an enormous convenience in developing the argument. One possible misinterpretation of the continuity assumption should be mentioned: it does not

Now suppose that lending or borrowing can take place between any two successive periods r and s at the rate i_s. The theoretical solution involves finding the multidimensional analogue of the point R' (in Fig. 1)—that is, the point on the highest present-value hyperplane reached by the productive opportunity locus. With simple curvature and continuity assumptions, R' will be a tangency point, thus having the additional property that, between the members of any such pair of time periods, the marginal productive rate of return between K_r and K_s (holding all other K_i's constant) will be equal to the discount rate between these periods. Furthermore, if the condition is met between all pairs of successive periods, it will also be satisfied between any pairs of time periods as well.[30] Again, as in the two-period case, the final solution will involve market lending or borrowing ("financing") to move along the highest present-value hyperplane attained from the intermediate productive solution R' to the true preference optimum at R. Note that, as compared with the present value or direct solution, the principle of equating the marginal productive rate of return with the discount rate requires certain continuity assumptions.

---

necessarily mean that the only investment opportunities considered are two-period options between pairs of periods in the present or future. Genuine multiperiod options are allowable—for example, the option described by cash-flows of -1, $+4$, $+2$, and $+6$ for periods 0, 1, 2, and 3, respectively. The continuity assumption means, rather, that if we choose to move from an option like this one in the direction of having more income in period 1 and less, say, in period 3, we can find other options available like -1, $+4\,e_1$, $+2$, $+6 - e_3$, where e_1 and e_3 represent infinitesimals. In other words, from any point on the locus it is possible to trade continuously between incomes in any pair of periods.

[30] Maximizing the Lagrangian expression $C - \lambda f(K_0, \ldots, K_n)$, we derive the first-order conditions

$$
\begin{cases}
\dfrac{\partial C}{\partial K_0} = 1 & -\lambda \dfrac{\partial f}{\partial K_0} = 0 \\[2ex]
\dfrac{\partial C}{\partial K_1} = \dfrac{1}{1 + i_1} & -\lambda \dfrac{\partial f}{\partial K_1} = 0 \\[2ex]
\cdots \cdots \cdots \cdots \cdots \cdots \\[2ex]
\dfrac{\partial C}{\partial K_n} = \dfrac{1}{(1 + i_1)(1 + i_2) \ldots (1 + i_n)} & -\lambda \dfrac{\partial f}{\partial K_n} = 0.
\end{cases}
$$

Eliminating λ between any pair of successive periods:

$$
\frac{\partial f / \partial K_r}{\partial f / \partial K_s} = \frac{(1 + i_1)(1 + i_2) \cdots (1 + i_r)(1 + i_s)}{(1 + i_1)(1 + i_2) \cdots (1 + i_r)}
$$

$$
\left. \frac{\partial K_s}{\partial K_r} \right|_{\substack{K_j \\ (j \neq r,s)}} = 1 + i_s
$$

Between non-successive periods:

$$
\left. \frac{\partial K_t}{\partial K_r} \right|_{\substack{K_j \\ (j \neq r,t)}} = (1 + i_{r+1})(1 + i_{r+2}) \cdots (1 + i_{t-1})(1 + i_t).
$$

Now it is here that Fisher, who evidently understood the true nature of the solution himself, appears to have led others astray. In his *Rate of Interest* he provides a mathematical proof that the optimal investment decision involves setting what is here called the marginal productive rate of return equal to the market rate of interest *between any two periods*.[31] By obvious generalization of the result of the two-period problem, this condition is identical with that of finding the line of highest present value (the two-dimensional projection of the hyperplane of highest present value) between these time periods. Unfortunately, Fisher fails to state the qualification " between any two time-periods " consistently and at various places makes flat statements to the effect that investments will be made wherever the " rate of return on sacrifice " or " rate of return on cost " between any two options exceeds the rate of interest.[32]

Now the rate of return on sacrifice is, for two-period comparisons, equivalent to the productive rate of return. More generally, however, Fisher defines the rate of return on sacrifice in a *multiperiod* sense; that is, as that rate which reduces to a present value of zero the entire sequence of positive and negative periodic differences between the returns of any two investment options.[33] This definition is, for our purposes, equivalent to the so-called " internal rate of return."[34] This latter rate (which will be denoted ρ) will, however, be shown to lead to results which are, in general, not correct if the procedure is followed of adopting or rejecting investment options on the basis of a comparison of ρ and the market rate.[35]

B. FAILURE OF THE GENERALIZED " INTERNAL RATE OF RETURN "

Recent thinking emphasizing the internal rate of return seems to be based upon the idea of finding a purely " internal " measure of the time productivity of an investment—that is, the rate of growth of capital funds invested in a

[31] *Rate of Interest*, pp. 398–400. Actually, the proof refers only to successive periods, but this is an inessential restriction.

[32] *Ibid.*, p. 155; *Theory of Interest*, pp. 168–69.

[33] *Rate of Interest*, p. 153; *Theory of Interest*, pp. 168–69.

[34] For some purposes it is important to distinguish between the rate which sets the present value of a series of receipts from an investment equal to zero and that rate which does the same for the series of *differences* between the receipts of two alternative investment options (see A. A. Alchian, " The Rate of Interest, Fisher's Rate of Return over Cost, and Keynes' Internal Rate of Return," *American Economic Review*, XLV [December, 1955], 938–43). For present purposes there is no need to make the distinction because individual investment options are regarded as independent increments—so that the receipts of the option in question are in fact a sequence of differences over the alternative of not adopting that option.

[35] As another complication, Fisher's mathematical analysis compares the two-period marginal rates of return on sacrifice with the interest rates of return on sacrifice with the interest rates between those two periods, the latter not being assumed constant throughout. In the multiperiod case Fisher nowhere states how to combine the differing period-to-period interest rates into an over-all market rate for comparison with ρ. It is possible that just at this point Fisher was thinking only of a rate of interest which remained constant over time, in which case the question would not arise. The difficulty in the use of the " internal rate " when variations in the market rate over time exist will be discussed below.

project—for comparison with the market rate.[36] But the idea of rate of growth involves a ratio and cannot be uniquely defined unless one can uniquely value initial and terminal positions. Thus the investment option characterized by the annual cash-flow sequence $-1, 0, 0, 8$ clearly involves a growth rate of 100 per cent (compounding annually), because it really reduces to a two-period option with intermediate compounding. Similarly, a savings deposit at 10 per cent compounded annually for n years may seem to be a multiperiod option, but it is properly regarded as a series of two-period options (the "growth" will take place only if at the beginning of each period the decision is taken to reinvest the capital plus interest yielded by the investment of the previous period). A savings-account option without reinvestment would be: $-1, .10, .10, .10, \ldots, 1.10$ (the last element being a terminating payment); with reinvestment, the option becomes $-1, 0, 0, 0, \ldots, (1.10)^n$, n being the number of compounding periods after the initial deposit.

Consider, however, a more general investment option characterized by the sequence $-1, 2, 1$. (In general, all investment options considered here will be normalized in terms of an assumed \$1.00 of initial outlay or initial receipt.) How can a rate of growth for the initial capital outlay be determined? Unlike the savings-account opportunity, no information is provided as to the rate at which the intermediate receipt or "cash throw-off" of \$2.00 can be reinvested. If, of course, we use some external discounting rate (for example, the cost of capital or the rate of an outside lending opportunity), we will be departing from the idea of a purely *internal* growth rate. In fact, the use of an external rate will simply reduce us to a present-value evaluation of the investment option.

In an attempt to resolve this difficulty, one mathematical feature of the two-period marginal productive rate of return was selected for generalization by both Fisher and his successors. This feature is the fact that, when ρ (in the two-period case equal to the marginal productive rate of return $[\Delta K_1]/[-\Delta K_0] - 1$) is used for discounting the values in the receipt-outlay stream, the discounted value becomes zero. This concept lends itself to easy generalization: for any multiperiod stream there will be a similar discounting rate ρ which will make the discounted value equal to zero (or so it was thought). This rate seems to be purely internal, not infected by any market considerations. And, in certain simple cases, it does lead to correct answers in choosing investment projects according to the rule: Adopt the project if ρ is greater than the market rate r.

For the investment option $-1, 2, 1$ considered above, ρ is equal to $\sqrt{2}$, or 141.4 per cent. And, in fact, if the borrowing rate or the rate on the best alternative opportunity (whichever is the appropriate comparison) is less than $\sqrt{2}$, the investment is desirable. Figure 7 plots the present value C of the option as a function of the discounting interest rate, i, assumed to be constant

[36] Sec K. E. Boulding, *Economic Analysis* (rev. ed.; New York: Harper & Bros., 1948), p. 819.

over the two discounting periods. Note that the present value of the option diminishes as i increases throughout the entire relevant range of i, from $i = -1$ to $i = \infty$.[37] The internal rate of return ρ is that i for which the present value curve cuts the horizontal axis. Evidently, for any $i < \rho$, present value is positive; for $i > \rho$, it is negative.

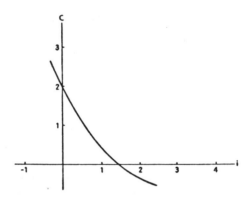

Fig. 7.—Sketch of present value of the option $-1, 2, 1$.

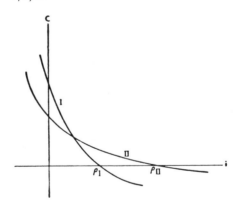

Fig. 8.—Two alternative options

However, the fact that the use of ρ leads to the correct decision in a particular case or a particular class of cases does not mean that it is correct in principle. And, in fact, cases have been adduced where its use leads to incorrect answers. Alchian has shown that, in the comparison of two investment options which are alternatives, the choice of the one with a higher ρ is not in general correct—in fact, the decision cannot be made without knowledge of the appropriate external discounting rate.[38] Figure 8 illustrates two such options,

---

[37] Economic meaning may be attached to negative interest rates; these are rates of shrinkage of capital. I rule out the possibility of shrinkage rates greater than 100 per cent however.

[38] Alchian, *op. cit.*, p. 939.

I being preferable for low rates of interest and II for high rates. The i at which the crossover takes place is Fisher's rate of return on sacrifice between these two options. But II has the higher internal rate of return (that is, its present value falls to zero at a higher discounting rate) regardless of the actual rate of interest. How can we say that I is preferable at low rates of interest? Because its present value is higher, it permits the investor to move along a higher hyperplane to find the utility optimum attained somewhere on that hyperplane. If II were adopted, the investor would also be enabled to move along such a hyperplane, but a lower one. Put another way, with the specified low rate of interest, the investor adopting I could, if he chose, put himself in the position of adopting II by appropriate borrowings and lendings together with throwing away some of his wealth.[39]

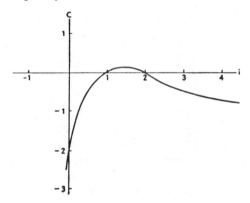

FIG. 9.—Sketch of present value of the investment option −1, 5, −6.

Even more fundamentally, Lorie and Savage have shown that ρ may not be unique.[40] Consider, for example, the investment option −1, 5, −6. Calculation reveals that this option has a present value of zero at discounting rates of both 100 per cent and 200 per cent. For this investment option present value as a function of the discounting rate is sketched in Figure 9. While

[39] Some people find this so hard to believe that I shall provide a numerical example. For investment I, we may use the annual cash-flow stream −1, 0, 4—then the internal rate of return is 1, or 100 per cent. For investment option II, we may use the option illustrated in Figure 7: −1, 2, 1. For this investment p is equal to $\sqrt{2}$, or 141.4 per cent. So the internal rate of return is greater for II. However, the present value for option I is greater at an interest rate of 0 per cent, and in fact it remains greater until the cross-over rate, which happens to be at 50 per cent for these two options. Now it is simple to show how, adopting I, we can get to the result II at any interest rate lower than 50 per cent —10 per cent, for example. Borrowing from the final time period for the benefit of the intermediate one, we can convert −1, 0, 4 to −1, 2.73, 1 (I have subtracted 3 from the final period, crediting the intermediate period with $3/1.1 = 2.73$). We can now get to option II by throwing away the 0.73, leaving us with −1, 2, 1. The fact that we can get to option II by throwing away some wealth demonstrates the superiority of I even though $\rho_{II} > \rho_I$, provided that borrowing and lending can take place at an interest rate less than the cross-over discounting rate of 50 per cent.

[40] *Op. cit.*, pp. 236–39.

Lorie and Savage speak only of "dual" internal rates of return, any number of zero values of the present-value function are possible in principle. The option $-1, 6, -11, 6$, illustrated in Figure 10, has zero present value at the discounting rates 0 per cent, and 200 per cent, for example.[41]

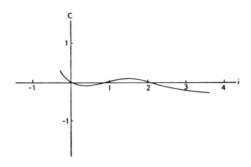

Fig. 10.—Sketch of present value of the investment option $-1, 6, -11, 6$.

In fact, perfectly respectable investment options may have *no* real internal rates (the present value equation has only imaginary roots). The option $-1, 3, -2\frac{1}{2}$ is an example; a plot would show that its present value is negative throughout the relevant range.[42] It is definitely not the case, however, that all options for which the internal rate cannot be calculated are bad ones. If we merely reverse the signs on the option above to get $1, -3, 2\frac{1}{2}$, we have an option with positive present value at all rates of discount.

These instances of failure of the multiperiod internal-rate-of-return rule (note that in each case the present-value rule continues to indicate the correct

[41] The instances discussed above suggest that the alternation of signs in the receipt stream has something to do with the possibility of multiple ρ's. In fact, Descarts' rule of signs tells us that the number of solutions in the allowable range (the number of points where present value equals zero for $i > -1$) is at most equal to the number of reversals of signs in the terms of the receipts sequence. Therefore, a two-period investment option has at most a single ρ, a three-period option at most a dual ρ, and so forth. There is an interesting footnote in Fisher which suggests that he was not entirely unaware of this difficulty. Where more than a single-sign alternation takes place, he suggests the use of the present-value method rather than attempting to compute "the rate of return on sacrifice" (*Rate of Interest*, p. 155). That any number of zeros of the present value function can occur was pointed out by Paul A. Samuelson in "Some Aspects of the Pure Theory of Capital," *Quarterly Journal of Economics*, LI (1936–37), 469–96 (at p. 475).

[42] Mathematically, the formula for the roots of a three-period option n_0, n_1, n_2 where $n_0 = -1$ is:

$$i = \frac{(n_1 - 2) \pm \sqrt{n_1^2 + 4n_2}}{2}.$$

If $-4n_2$ exceeds n_1^2, the roots will be imaginary, and an internal rate of return cannot be calculated. A necessary condition for this result is that the sum of the undiscounted cash flows be negative, but this condition should not rule out consideration of an option (note the option $-1, 5, -6$ in Fig. 9).

answer unambiguously, setting aside the question of the appropriate discounting rate which was discussed in Sec. I) are, of course, merely the symptom of an underlying erroneous conception. It is clear that the idea that ρ represents a growth rate in any simple sense cannot be true; a capital investment of $1.00 cannot grow at a rate both of 100 per cent and of 200 per cent. Even more fundamentally, the idea that ρ is a purely *internal* rate is not true either. Consider the option $-1, 2, 1$ discussed earlier, with a unique ρ equal to $\sqrt{2}$. The intermediate cash throwoff of $2.00 must clearly be reinvested externally of this option. How does the calculation of ρ handle this? This answer is that the mathematical manipulations involved in the calculation of ρ implicitly assume that all intermediate receipts, positive or negative, are treated as if they could be compounded at the rate ρ being solved for.[43] The rate ρ has been characterized rather appropriately as the "solving rate" of interest. But note that this mathematical manipulation, even where it does lead to a unique answer (and, in general, it will not), is unreasonable in its economic implications. There will not normally be other investment opportunities arising for investment of intermediate cash inflows (if required) must be obtained by borrowing at the rate ρ. The rate ρ, arising from a mathematical manipulation, will only by rare coincidence represent relevant economic alternatives.

The preceding arguments against the use of the usual concept of the "internal rate of return" do not take any account of the possibility of non-constant interest rates over time. Martin J. Bailey has emphasized to me that it is precisely when this occurs (when there exists a known pattern of future variation of i) that the internal-rate-of-return rule fails most fundamentally. For in the use of that rule all time periods are treated on a par; the only discounting is via the solving rate defined only in terms of the sequence of cash flows. But with (a known pattern of) varying future i, shifts in the relative desirability of income in different periods are brought about. In the usual formulation the internal rate of return concept can take no account of this. In fact, in such a case one might have an investment for which ρ was well defined and unique and still not be able to determine the desirability of the investment opportunity (that is, depending upon the time pattern of future interest rates, present value might be either negative or positive).

The following remarks attempt to summarize the basic principles discussed in this section.

At least in the simplest case, where we do not worry about differences between borrowing and lending rates but assume these to be equal and also constant (constant with respect to the amount borrowed or lent—not constant over time), the multidimensional solution using the present-value rule is a straightforward generalization of the two-period solution. The principle is to

---

[43] The true significance of the reinvestment assumption was brought out in Ezra Solomon, "The Arithmetic of Capital-budgeting Decisions," *Journal of Business*, XXIX (April, 1956), 124–29, esp. pp. 126–27.

push productive investment to the point where the highest attainable level of present value is reached and then to "finance" this investment by borrowing or lending between time periods to achieve a time-preference optimum.

The main burden of these remarks has been to the effect that the internal-rate-of-return rule, unlike the present-value rule, does not generalize the multi-period case if the usual definition of the internal rate ρ is adopted—that is, as that rate which sets the present value of the discounted income stream equal to zero. I have tried to show the multiperiod generalization which *would* make the internal-rate-of-return rule still correct: between *every pair* of time periods, the marginal internal rate of return in the sense of the marginal productive rate of return between those two periods, holding income in other periods constant, should be set equal to the market discount rate between those periods. That the usual interpretation of the internal-rate-of-return rule is not in general correct has been illustrated by its failure in particular cases and has been explained by exposing the implicit assumption made in the mathematical manipulation which finds ρ—that all intermediate cash flows are reinvested (or borrowed if cash flows are negative) at the rate ρ itself. In addition, ρ does not allow for varying interperiod preference rates (or interest rates) over time. This generalized multiperiod internal rate of return is, there-fore, not really internal, nor is the assumption implied about the external opportunities generally correct or even generally reasonable.

IV. CONCLUDING COMMENTS

The preceding analysis has slighted a great many questions. In addition, lack of time has precluded comparative discussion of the works of other authors, however helpful this might have been.[44]

I have not attempted to generalize the results to the multiperiod case with non-independent investments or with differing or non-constant borrowing and lending rates. On the latter points intuition suggests that whether the borrowing or lending rate in calculating present value is to be used for any time period does not depend upon any characteristics of the investment option under consideration in isolation; it depends rather upon the over-all cash position after adoption of that option as an increment. If, after such adoption, time preference dictates shifting to less income in period r and more in period t,

---

[44] I should comment, though, on the important article by Samuelson, *op. cit.* The results here are in part consistent with his, with the following main differences: (1) He limits him-self to the analysis of a single investment, whereas I consider the entire investment-consump-tion pattern over time. (2) He concludes in favor of the present-value rule, discounting at *the* market rate of interest. I have attempted to consider explicitly the problem of what to do when the borrowing and lending rates diverge, or vary as a function of the amount bor-rowed, and I do not find the present-value rule to be universally valid. Of these differences, the first is really crucial. It is the heart of Fisher's message that investments *cannot* be con-sidered in isolation but only in the context of the other investment and consumption alterna-tives available. Nevertheless, Samuelson's article suffices to refute a number of fallacies still current in this field of economic theory.

any income associated with the option in question falling in period r should be discounted back to the next earlier period at the lending rate (and that for period t at the borrowing rate). Income at any period s may then have been successively discounted at borrowing rates for a number of periods and lending rates for a number of others before being reduced to a present value.

The main positive conclusion of the paper is that the present-value rule for investment decisions is correct in a wide variety of cases (though not universally) and in a limited sense. The rule tells us to attain the highest possible level of present value, but the point at which this condition is satisfied (that is, the distribution of incomes in various time periods) is not the final solution. It is, rather, an intermediate "productive" solution which must then be modified by borrowing or lending ("financing") to find the over-all optimum. This becomes particularly clear when we consider the case where lending and borrowing rates differ and thus enter the subcontroversy between those who favor the use of present-value discounting at the cost of capital and those who would discount at the alternative lending rate. Which is correct depends upon the financing necessary to approach the time-preference optimum. Furthermore, if an tangency takes place between the productive opportunity locus and the time-preference utility isoquant at a rate between the lending and the borrowing rates, the "productive" solution requires no financing and the present-value principle is only correct in a formal sense. The present-value rule fails to give correct answers only for certain cases which combine the difficulties of non-independent investments and absence of a perfect capital market. When a perfect capital market exists, the present-value rule is universally correct in the limited sense referred to above. With independent investments but an imperfect capital market, the present-value rule will give answers which are correct but possibly only in a formal sense (the discounting rate used is not an external opportunity but an internal shadow price which comes out of the analysis).

The main negative conclusion is that the internal-rate-of-return rule for the multiperiod case is not generally correct, if the usual definition of the internal rate is adopted as that discount rate which makes the present value of the income stream associated with an investment option equal to zero. The so-called internal rate will only give correct answers in general if restricted to two-period comparisons; I have called this two-period internal rate the productive rate of return. For multiperiod investments the usual internal-rate-of-return rule (compare ρ with the market rate r) is not generally correct; however, given certain continuity assumptions, the correct answer will be arrived at by setting the marginal productive rate of return between each *pair* of time periods equal to the discount of market rate between those periods.

More important than the specific detailed conclusions is the demonstration that the Fisherian approach—the analysis of investment decisions as a means of balancing consumption incomes over time, together with the distinction between productive and market investment opportunities—is capable of solving (in the theoretical sense) all the problems posed. This solution is, furthermore, not an excrescence upon the general economic theory of choice but entirely integrated with it, constituting another dimension, so to speak. Since Fisher, economists working in the theory of investment decision have tended to adopt a mechanical approach—some plumping for the use of this formula, some for that. From a Fisherian point of view, we can see that none of the formulas so far propounded is universally valid. Furthermore, even where the present-value rule, for example, is correct, few realize that its validity is conditional upon making certain associated financing decisions as the Fisherian analysis demonstrates. In short, the Fisherian approach permits us to define the range of applicability and the shortcomings of all the proposed formulas—thus standing over against them as the general theoretical solution to the problem of investment decision under conditions of certainty.

17. THE COST OF CAPITAL, CORPORATION FINANCE, AND THE THEORY OF INVESTMENT

FRANCO MODIGLIANI

and

MERTON H. MILLER*

Reprinted from *The American Economic Review,* Vol. XLVIII, No. 3 (June 1958), pp. 261–97, by permission of the authors and the publisher.

What is the "cost of capital" to a firm in a world in which funds are used to acquire assets whose yields are uncertain; and in which capital can be obtained by many different media, ranging from pure debt instruments, representing money-fixed claims, to pure equity issues, giving holders only the right to a pro-rata share in the uncertain venture? This question has vexed at least three classes of economists: (1) the corporation finance specialist concerned with the techniques of financing firms so as to ensure their survival and growth; (2) the managerial economist concerned with capital budgeting; and (3) the economic theorist concerned with explaining investment behavior at both the micro and macro levels.[1]

In much of his formal analysis, the economic theorist at least has tended to side-step the essence of this cost-of-capital problem by proceeding as though physical assets—like bonds—could be regarded as yielding known, sure streams. Given this assumption, the theorist has concluded that the cost of capital to the owners of a firm is simply the rate of interest on bonds; and has derived the familiar proposition that the firm, acting rationally, will tend to push investment to the point where the marginal yield on physical assets is

* The authors are, respectively, professor and associate professor of economics in the Graduate School of Industrial Administration, Carnegie Institute of Technology. This article is a revised version of a paper delivered at the annual meeting of the Econometric Society, December 1956. The authors express thanks for the comments and suggestions made at that time by the discussants of the paper, Evsey Domar, Robert Eisner and John Lintner, and subsequently by James Duesenberry. They are also greatly indebted to many of their present and former colleagues and students at Carnegie Tech who served so often and with such remarkable patience as a critical forum for the ideas here presented.

[1] The literature bearing on the cost-of-capital problem is far too extensive for listing here. Numerous references to it will be found throughout the paper, though we make no claim to completeness. One phase of the problem which we do not consider explicitly, but which has a considerable literature of its own is the relation between the cost of capital and public utility rates. For a recent summary of the "cost-of-capital theory" of rate regulation and a brief discussion of some of its implications, the reader may refer to H. M. Somers [20].

equal to the market rate of interest.[2] This proposition can be shown to follow from either of two criteria of rational decision-making which are equivalent under certainty, namely (1) the maximization of profits and (2) the maximization of market value.

According to the first criterion, a physical asset is worth acquiring if it will increase the net profit of the owners of the firm. But net profit will increase only if the expected rate of return, or yield, of the asset exceeds the rate of interest. According to the second criterion, an asset is worth acquiring if it increases the value of the owners' equity, i.e., if it adds more to the market value of the firm than the costs of acquisition. But what the asset adds is given by capitalizing the stream it generates at the market rate of interest, and this capitalized value will exceed its cost if and only if the yield of the asset exceeds the rate of interest. Note that, under either formulation, the cost of capital is equal to the rate of interest on bonds, regardless of whether the funds are acquired through debt instruments or through new issues of common stock. Indeed, in a world of sure returns, the distinction between debt and equity funds reduces largely to one of terminology.

It must be acknowledged that some attempt is usually made in this type of analysis to allow for the existence of uncertainty. This attempt typically takes the form of superimposing on the results of the certainty analysis the notion of a "risk discount" to be subtracted from the expected yield (or a "risk premium" to be added to the market rate of interest). Investment decisions are then supposed to be based on a comparison of this "risk adjusted" or "certainty equivalent" yield with the market rate of interest.[3] No satisfactory explanation has yet been provided, however, as to what determines the size of the risk discount and how it varies in response to changes in other variables.

Considered as a convenient approximation, the model of the firm constructed via this certainty—or certainty-equivalent—approach has admittedly been useful in dealing with some of the grosser aspects of the processes of capital accumulation and economic fluctuations. Such a model underlies, for example, the familiar Keynesian aggregate investment function in which aggregate investment is written as a function of the rate of interest—the same riskless rate of interest which appears later in the system in the liquidity-preference equation. Yet few would maintain that this approximation is adequate. At the macroeconomic level there are ample grounds for doubting that the rate of interest has as large and as direct an influence on the rate of investment as this analysis would lead us to believe. At the microeconomic level the certainty model has little descriptive value and provides no real

[2] Or, more accurately, to the marginal cost of borrowed funds since it is customary, at least in advanced analysis, to draw the supply curve of borrowed funds to the firm as a rising one. For an advanced treatment of the certainty case, see F. and V. Lutz [13].

[3] The classic examples of the certainty-equivalent approach are found in J. R. Hicks [8] and O. Lange [11].

guidance to the finance specialist or managerial economist whose main problems cannot be treated in a framework which deals so cavalierly with uncertainty and ignores all forms of financing other than debt issues.[4]

Only recently have economists begun to face up seriously to the problem of the cost of capital *cum* risk. In the process they have found their interests and endeavors merging with those of the finance specialist and the managerial economist who have lived with the problem longer and more intimately. In this joint search to establish the principles which govern rational investment and financial policy in a world of uncertainty two main lines of attack can be discerned. These lines represent, in effect, attempts to extrapolate to the world of uncertainty each of the two criteria—profit maximization and market value maximization—which were seen to have equivalent implications in the special case of certainty. With the recognition of uncertainty this equivalence vanishes. In fact, the profit maximization criterion is no longer even well defined. Under uncertainty there corresponds to each decision of the firm not a unique profit outcome, but a plurality of mutually exclusive outcomes which can at best be described by a subjective probability distribution. The profit outcome, in short, has become a random variable and as such its maximization no longer has an operational meaning. Nor can this difficulty generally be disposed of by using the mathematical expectation of profits as the variable to be maximized. For decisions which affect the expected value will also tend to affect the dispersion and other characteristics of the distribution of outcomes. In particular, the use of debt rather than equity funds to finance a given venture may well increase the expected return to the owners, but only at the cost of increased dispersion of the outcomes.

Under these conditions the profit outcomes of alternative investment and financing decisions can be compared and ranked only in terms of a *subjective* " utility function " of the owners which weighs the expected yield against other characteristics of the distribution. Accordingly, the extrapolation of the profit maximization criterion of the certainty model has tended to evolve into utility maximization, sometimes explicitly, more frequently in a qualitative and heuristic form.[5]

The utility approach undoubtedly represents an advance over the certainty or certainty-equivalent approach. It does at least permit us to explore (within limits) some of the implications of different financing arrangements, and it does give some meaning to the "cost" of different types of funds. However, because the cost of capital has become an essentially subjective concept, the utility approach has serious drawbacks for normative as well as analytical

---

[4] Those who have taken a "case-method" course in finance in recent years will recall in this connection the famous Liquigas case of Hunt and Williams [9, pp. 193–96], a case which is often used to introduce the student to the cost-of-capital problem and to poke a bit of fun at the economist's certainty-model.

[5] For an attempt at a rigorous explicit development of this line of attack, see F. Modigliani and M. Zeman [14].

purposes. How, for example, is management to ascertain the risk preferences of its stockholders and to compromise among their tastes? And how can the economist build a meaningful investment function in the face of the fact that any given investment opportunity might or might not be worth exploiting depending on precisely who happen to be the owners of the firm at the moment?

Fortunately, these questions do not have to be answered; for the alternative approach, based on market value maximization, can provide the basis for an operational definition of the cost of capital and a workable theory of investment. Under this approach any investment project and its concomitant financing plan must pass only the following test: Will the project, as financed, raise the market value of the firm's shares? If so, it is worth undertaking; if not, its return is less than the marginal cost of capital to the firm. Note that such a test is entirely independent of the tastes of the current owners, since market prices will reflect not only their preferences but those of all potential owners as well. If any current stockholder disagrees with management and the market over the valuation of the project, he is free to sell out and reinvest elsewhere, but will still benefit from the capital appreciation resulting from management's decision.

The potential advantages of the market-value approach have long been appreciated; yet analytical results have been meager. What appears to be keeping this line of development from achieving its promise is largely the lack of an adequate theory of the effect of financial structure on market valuations, and of how these effects can be inferred from objective market data. It is with the development of such a theory and of its implications for the cost-of-capital problem that we shall be concerned in this paper.

Our procedure will be to develop in Section I the basic theory itself and to give some brief account of its empirical relevance. In Section II, we show how the theory can be used to answer the cost-of-capital question and how it permits us to develop a theory of investment of the firm under conditions of uncertainty. Throughout these sections the approach is essentially a partial-equilibrium one focusing on the firm and "industry." Accordingly, the "prices" of certain income streams will be treated as constant and given from outside the model, just as in the standard Marshallian analysis of the firm and industry the prices of all inputs and of all other products are taken as given. We have chosen to focus at this level rather than on the economy as a whole because it is at the level of the firm and the industry that the interests of the various specialists concerned with the cost-of-capital problem come most closely together. Although the emphasis has thus been placed on partial-equilibrium analysis, the results obtained also provide the essential building blocks for a general equilibrium model which shows how those prices which are here taken as given, are themselves determined. For reasons of space, however, and because the material is of interest in its own right, the presentation of the general equilibrium model which rounds out the analysis must be deferred to a subsequent paper.

I. THE VALUATION OF SECURITIES, LEVERAGE, AND THE COST OF CAPITAL

A. THE CAPITALIZATION RATE FOR UNCERTAIN STREAMS

As a starting point, consider an economy in which all physical assets are owned by corporations. For the moment, assume that these corporations can finance their assets by issuing common stock only; the introduction of bond issues, or their equivalent, as a source of corporate funds is postponed until the next part of this section.

The physical assets held by each firm will yield to the owners of the firm—its stockholders—a stream of "profits" over time; but the elements of this series need not be constant and in any event are uncertain. This stream of income, and hence the stream accruing to any share of common stock, will be regarded as extending indefinitely into the future. We assume, however, that the mean value of the stream over time, or average profit per unit of time, is finite and represents a random variable subject to a (subjective) probability distribution. We shall refer to the average value over time of the stream accruing to a given share as the return of that share; and to the mathematical expectation of this average as the expected return of the share.[6] Although individual investors may have different views as to the shape of the probability distribution of the return of any share, we shall assume for simplicity that they are at least in agreement as to the expected return.[7]

This way of characterizing uncertain streams merits brief comment. Notice first that the stream is a stream of profits, not dividends. As will become clear later, as long as management is presumed to be acting in the best interests of the stockholders, retained earnings can be regarded as equivalent to a fully subscribed, pre-emptive issue of common stock. Hence, for present purposes, the division of the stream between cash dividends and retained

---

[6] These propositions can be restated analytically as follows: The assets of the ith firm generate a stream:

$$X_i(1), \; X_i(2) \cdots X_i(T)$$

whose elements are random variables subject to the joint probability distribution:

$$\chi_i[X_i(1), \; X_i(2) \cdots X_i(t)].$$

The return to the ith firm is defined as:

$$X_i = \lim_{T \to \infty} \frac{1}{T} \sum_{t=1}^{T} X_i(t).$$

X_i is itself a random variable with a probability distribution $\phi(X_i)$ whose form is determined uniquely by χ_i. The expected return $\bar{X}_i$ is defined as $\bar{X}_i = E(X_i) = \int x_i X_i \phi_i(X_i) dX_i$. If N_i is the number of shares outstanding, the return of the ith share is $x_i = (1/N)X_i$ with probability distribution $\phi_i(x_i)dx_i = \phi_i(Nx_i)d(Nx_i)$ and expected value $x_i = (1/N)\bar{X}_i$.

[7] To deal adequately with refinements such as differences among investors in estimates of expected returns would require extensive discussion of the theory of portfolio selection. Brief references to these and related topics will be made in the succeeding article on the general equilibrium model.

earnings in any period is a mere detail. Notice also that the uncertainty attaches to the mean value over time of the stream of profits and should not be confused with variability over time of the successive elements of the stream. That variability and uncertainty are two totally different concepts should be clear from the fact that the elements of a stream can be variable even though known with certainty. It can be shown, furthermore, that whether the elements of a stream are sure or uncertain, the effect of variability per se on the valuation of the stream is at best a second-order one which can safely be neglected for our purposes (and indeed most others too).[8]

The next assumption plays a strategic role in the rest of the analysis. We shall assume that firms can be divided into "equivalent return" classes such that the return on the shares issued by any firm in any given class is proportional to (and hence perfectly correlated with) the return on the shares issued by any other firm in the same class. This assumption implies that the various shares within the same class differ, at most, by a "scale factor." Accordingly, if we adjust for the difference in scale, by taking the *ratio* of the return to the expected return, the probability distribution of that ratio is identical for all shares in the class. It follows that all relevant properties of a share are uniquely characterized by specifying (1) the class to which it belongs and (2) its expected return.

The significance of this assumption is that it permits us to classify firms into groups within which the shares of different firms are "homogeneous," that is, perfect substitutes for one another. We have, thus, an analogue to the familiar concept of the industry in which it is the commodity produced by the firms that is taken as homogeneous. To complete this analogy with Marshallian price theory, we shall assume in the analysis to follow that the shares concerned are traded in perfect markets under conditions of atomistic competition.[9]

From our definition of homogeneous classes of stock it follows that in equilibrium in a perfect capital market the price per dollar's worth of expected return must be the same for all shares of any given class. Or, equivalently, in any given class the price of every share must be proportional to its expected return. Let us denote this factor of proportionality for any class, say the kth

---

[8] The reader may convince himself of this by asking how much he would be willing to rebate to his employer for the privilege of receiving his annual salary in equal monthly installments rather than in irregular amounts over the year. See also J. M. Keynes [10, esp. pp. 53–54].

[9] Just what our classes of stocks contain and how the different classes can be identified by outside observers are empirical questions to which we shall return later. For the present, it is sufficient to observe: (1) Our concept of a class, while not identical to that of the industry is at least closely related to it. Certainly the basic characteristics of the probability distributions of the returns on assets will depend to a significant extent on the product sold and the technology used. (2) What are the appropriate class boundaries will depend on the particular problem being studied. An economist concerned with general tendencies in the market, for example, might well be prepared to work with far wider classes than would be appropriate for an investor planning his portfolio, or a firm planning its financial strategy.

class, by $1/\rho_k$. Then if p_j denotes the price and $\bar{x}_j$ is the expected return per share of the jth firm in class k, we must have:

(1)
$$p_j = \frac{1}{\rho_k} \bar{x}_j;$$

or, equivalently,

(2)
$$\frac{\bar{x}_j}{p_j} = \rho_k, \text{ a constant for all firms } j \text{ in class } k.$$

The constants ρ_k (one for each of the k classes) can be given several economic interpretations: (a) From (2) we see that each ρ_k is the expected rate of return of any share in class k. (b) From (1) $1/\rho_k$ is the price which an investor has to pay for a dollar's worth of expected return in the class k. (c) Again from (1), by analogy with the terminology for perpetual bonds, ρ_k can be regarded as the market rate of capitalization for the expected value of the uncertain streams of the kind generated by the kth class of firms.[10]

B. DEBT FINANCING AND ITS EFFECTS ON SECURITY PRICES

Having developed an apparatus for dealing with uncertain streams we can now approach the heart of the cost-of-capital problem by dropping the assumption that firms cannot issue bonds. The introduction of debt-financing changes the market for shares in a very fundamental way. Because firms may have different proportions of debt in their capital structure, shares of different companies, even in the same class, can give rise to different probability distributions of returns. In the language of finance, the shares will be subject to different degrees of financial risk or "leverage" and hence they will no longer be perfect substitutes for one another.

To exhibit the mechanism determining the relative prices of shares under these conditions, we make the following two assumptions about the nature of bonds and the bond market, though they are actually stronger than is necessary and will be relaxed later: (1) All bonds (including any debts issued by households for the purpose of carrying shares) are assumed to yield a constant income per unit of time, and this income is regarded as certain by all traders regardless of the issuer. (2) Bonds, like stocks, are traded in a perfect market, where the term perfect is to be taken in its usual sense as implying that any two commodities which are perfect substitutes for each other must sell, in equilibrium, at the same price. It follows from assumption (1) that all bonds are in fact perfect substitutes up to a scale factor. It follows from assumption (2) that they must all sell at the same price per dollar's worth of return, or what amounts to the same thing must yield the same rate of return. This rate

[10] We cannot, on the basis of the assumptions so far, make any statements about the relationship or spread between the various ρ's or capitalization rates. Before we could do so we would have to make further specific assumptions about the way investors believe the probability distributions vary from class to class, as well as assumptions about investors' preferences as between the characteristics of different distributions.

of return will be denoted by r and referred to as the rate of interest or, equivalently, as the capitalization rate for sure streams. We now can derive the following two basic propositions with respect to the valuation of securities in companies with different capital structures:

Proposition I. Consider any company j and let $\overline{X}_j$ stand as before for the expected return on the assets owned by the company (that is, its expected profit before deduction of interest). Denote by D_j the market value of the debts of the company; by S_j the market value of its common shares; and by $V_j \equiv S_j + D_j$ the market value of all its securities or, as we shall say, the market value of the firm. Then, our Proposition I asserts that we must have in equilibrium:

(3)
$$V_j = (S_j + D_j) = \overline{X}_j/\rho_k, \text{ for any firm } j \text{ in class } k.$$

That is, the *market value of any firm is independent of its capital structure and is given by capitalizing its expected return at the rate ρ_k appropriate to its class.*

This proposition can be stated in an equivalent way in terms of the firm's "average cost of capital," $\overline{X}_j/V_j$, which is the ratio of its expected return to the market value of all its securities. Our proposition then is:

(4)
$$\frac{\overline{X}_j}{(S_j + D_j)} = \frac{\overline{X}_j}{V_j} = \rho_k, \text{ for any firm } j, \text{ in class } k.$$

That is, *the average cost of capital to any firm is completely independent of its capital structure and is equal to the capitalization rate of a pure equity stream of its class.*

To establish Proposition I we will show that as long as the relations (3) or (4) do not hold between any pair of firms in a class, arbitrage will take place and restore the stated equalities. We use the term arbitrage advisedly. For if Proposition I did not hold, an investor could buy and sell stocks and bonds in such a way as to exchange one income stream for another stream, identical in all relevant respects but selling at a lower price. The exchange would therefore be advantageous to the investor quite independently of his attitudes toward risk.[11] As investors exploit these arbitrage opportunities, the value of the overpriced shares will fall and that of the underpriced shares will rise, thereby tending to eliminate the discrepancy between the market values of the firms.

By way of proof, consider two firms in the same class and assume for simplicity only, that the expected return, $\overline{X}$, is the same for both firms. Let company 1 be financed entirely with common stock while company 2 has some

---

[11] In the language of the theory of choice, the exchanges are movements from inefficient points in the interior to efficient points on the boundary of the investor's opportunity set; and not movements between efficient points along the boundary. Hence for this part of the analysis nothing is involved in the way of specific assumptions about investor attitudes or behavior other than that investors behave consistently and prefer more income to less income, *ceteris paribus*.

debt in its capital structure. Suppose first the value of the levered firm, V_2, to be larger than that of the unlevered one, V_1. Consider an investor holding s_2 dollars' worth of the shares of company 2, representing a fraction α of the total outstanding stock, S_2. The return from this portfolio, denoted by Y_2, will be a fraction α of the income available for the stockholders of company 2, which is equal to the total return X_2 less the interest charge, rD_2. Since under our assumption of homogeneity, the anticipated total return of company 2, X_2, is, under all circumstances, the same as the anticipated total return to company 1, X_1, we can hereafter replace X_2 and X_1 by a common symbol X. Hence, the return from the initial portfolio can be written as:

$$(5) \qquad Y_2 = \alpha(X - rD_2).$$

Now suppose the investor sold his αS_2 worth of company 2 shares and acquired instead an amount $s_1 = \alpha(S_2 + D_2)$ of the shares of company 1. He could do so by utilizing the amount αS_2 realized from the sale of his initial holding and borrowing an additional amount αD_2 on his own credit, pledging his new holdings in company 1 as a collateral. He would thus secure for himself a fraction $s_1/S_1 = \alpha(S_2 + D_2)/S_1$ of the shares and earnings of company 1. Making proper allowance for the interest payments on his personal debt αD_2, the return from the new portfolio, Y_1, is given by:

$$(6) \qquad Y_1 = \frac{\alpha(S_2 + D_2)}{S_1} X - r\alpha D_2 = \alpha \frac{V_2}{V_1} X - r\alpha D_2.$$

Comparing (5) with (6) we see that as long as $V_2 > V_1$ we must have $Y_1 > Y_2$, so that it pays owners of company 2's shares to sell their holdings, thereby depressing S_2 and hence V_2; and to acquire shares of company 1, thereby raising S_1 and thus V_1. We conclude therefore that levered companies cannot command a premium over unlevered companies because investors have the opportunity of putting the equivalent leverage into their portfolio directly by borrowing on personal account.

Consider now the other possibility, namely that the market value of the levered company V_2 is less than V_1. Suppose an investor holds initially an amount s_1 of shares of company 1, representing a fraction α of the total outstanding stock, S_1. His return from this holding is:

$$Y_1 = \frac{s_1}{S_1} X = \alpha X.$$

Suppose he were to exchange this initial holding for another portfolio, also worth s_1, but consisting of s_2 dollars of stock of company 2 and of d dollars of bonds, where s_2 and d are given by:

$$(7) \qquad s_2 = \frac{S_2}{V_2} s_1, \qquad d = \frac{D_2}{V_2} s_1.$$

In other words the new portfolio is to consist of stock of company 2 and of bonds in the proportions S_2/V_2 and D_2/V_2, respectively. The return from the stock in the new portfolio will be a fraction s_2/S_2 of the total return to stockholders of company 2, which is $(X - rD_2)$, and the return from the bonds will be rd. Making use of (7), the total return from the portfolio, Y_2, can be expressed as follows:

$$Y_2 = \frac{s_2}{S_2}(X - rD_2) + rd = \frac{s_1}{V_2}(X - rD_2) + r\frac{D_2}{V_2}s_1 = \frac{s_1}{V_2}X = \alpha\frac{s_1}{V_2}X$$

(since $s_1 = \alpha S_1$). Comparing Y_2 with Y_1 we see that, if $V_2 < S_1 \equiv V_1$, then Y_2 will exceed Y_1. Hence it pays the holders of company 1's shares to sell these holdings and replace them with a mixed portfolio containing an appropriate fraction of the shares of company 2.

The acquisition of a mixed portfolio of stock of a levered company j and of bonds in the proportion S_j/V_j and D_j/V_j respectively, may be regarded as an operation which "undoes" the leverage, giving access to an appropriate fraction of the unlevered return X_j. It is this possibility of undoing leverage which prevents the value of levered firms from being consistently less than those of unlevered firms, or more generally prevents the average cost of capital $\overline{X}_j/V_j$ from being systematically higher for levered than for nonlevered companies in the same class. Since we have already shown that arbitrage will also prevent V_2 from being larger than V_1, we can conclude that in equilibrium we must have $V_2 = V_1$, as stated in Proposition I.

Proposition II. From Proposition I we can derive the following proposition concerning the rate of return on common stock in companies whose capital structure includes some debt: the expected rate of return or yield, i, on the stock of any company j belonging to the kth class is a linear function of leverage as follows:

$$(8) \qquad\qquad i_j = \rho_k + (\rho_k - r)D_j/S_j.$$

That is, *the expected yield of a share of stock is equal to the appropriate capitalization rate ρ_k for a pure equity stream in the class, plus a premium related to financial risk equal to the debt-to-equity ratio times the spread between ρ_k and r.* Or equivalently, the market price of any share of stock is given by capitalizing its expected return at the continuously variable rate i_j of (8).[12]

A number of writers have stated close equivalents of our Proposition I although by appealing to intuition rather than by attempting a proof and only to insist immediately that the results were not applicable to the actual

---

[12] To illustrate, suppose $\bar{X} = 1000$, $D = 4000$, $r = 5$ per cent and $\rho_k = 10$ per cent. These values imply that $V = 10,000$ and $S = 6000$ by virtue of Proposition I. The expected yield or rate of return per share is then:

$$i = \frac{1000 - 200}{6000} = .1 + (.1 - .05)\frac{4000}{6000} = 13\frac{1}{3} \text{ per cent.}$$

capital markets.[13] Proposition II, however, so far as we have been able to discover is new.[14] To establish it we first note that by definition, the expected rate of return, i, is given by:

$$(9) \qquad i_j \equiv \frac{\overline{X}_j - rD_j}{S_j}.$$

From Proposition I, equation (3), we know that:

$$\overline{X}_j = \rho_k(S_j + D_j).$$

Substituting in (9) and simplifying, we obtain equation (8).

C. SOME QUALIFICATIONS AND EXTENSIONS OF THE BASIC PROPOSITIONS

The methods and results developed so far can be extended in a number of useful directions, of which we shall consider here only three: (1) allowing for a corporate profits tax under which interest payments are deductible; (2) recognizing the existence of a multiplicity of bonds and interest rates; and (3) acknowledging the presence of market imperfections which might interfere with the process of arbitrage. The first two will be examined briefly in this section with some further attention given to the tax problem in Section II. Market imperfections will be discussed in Part D of this section in the course of a comparison of our results with those of received doctrines in the field of finance.

Effects of the present method of taxing corporations. The deduction of interest in computing taxable corporate profits will prevent the arbitrage process from making the value of all firms in a given class proportional to the expected returns generated by their physical assets. Instead, it can be shown (by the same type of proof used for the original version of Proposition I) that the market values of firms in each class must be proportional in equilibrium to their expected return net of taxes (that is, to the sum of the interest paid and expected net stockholder income). This means we must replace each $\overline{X}_j$ in the original versions of Propositions I and II with a new variable $\overline{X}_j^\tau$ representing the total income net of taxes generated by the firm:

$$(10) \qquad \overline{X}_j^\tau \equiv (\overline{X}_j - rD_j)(1 - \tau) + rD_j \equiv \bar{\pi}_j^\tau + rD_j,$$

---

[13] See, for example, J. B. Williams [21, esp. pp. 72–73]; David Durand [3]; and W. A. Morton [15]. None of these writers describe in any detail the mechanism which is supposed to keep the average cost of capital constant under changes in capital structure. They seem, however, to be visualizing the equilibrating mechanism in terms of switches by investors between stocks and bonds as the yields of each get out of line with their "riskiness." This is an argument quite different from the pure arbitrage mechanism underlying our proof, and the difference is crucial. Regarding Proposition I as resting on investors' attitudes toward risk leads inevitably to a misunderstanding of many factors influencing relative yields such as, for example, limitations on the portfolio composition of financial institutions. See below, esp. Section I.D.

[14] Morton does make reference to a linear yield function but only ". . . for the sake of simplicity and because the particular function used makes no essential difference in my conclusions" [15, p. 443, note 2].

where $\bar{\pi}_j^\tau$ represents the expected net income accruing to the common stock-holders and τ stands for the average rate of corporate income tax.[15]

After making these substitutions, the propositions, when adjusted for taxes, continue to have the same form as their originals. That is, Proposition I becomes:

$$(11) \qquad \frac{\overline{X}_j^\tau}{V_j} = \rho_k^\tau, \text{ for any firm in class } k,$$

and Proposition II becomes

$$(12) \qquad i_j \equiv \frac{\bar{\pi}_j^\tau}{S_j} = \rho_j^\tau + (\rho_k^\tau - r)D_j/S_j$$

where ρ_k^τ is the capitalization rate for income net of taxes in class k.

Although the form of the propositions is unaffected, certain interpretations must be changed. In particular, the after-tax capitalization rate ρ_k^τ can no longer be identified with the "average cost of capital" which is $\rho_k = \overline{X}_j/V_j$. The difference between ρ_k^τ and the "true" average cost of capital, as we shall see, is a matter of some relevance in connection with investment planning within the firm (Section II). For the description of market behavior, however, which is our immediate concern here, the distinction is not essential. To simplify presentation, therefore, and to preserve continuity with the terminology in the standard literature we shall continue in this section to refer to ρ_k^τ as the average cost of capital, though strictly speaking this identification is correct only in the absence of taxes.

Effects of a plurality of bonds and interest rates. In existing capital markets we find not one, but a whole family of interest rates varying with maturity, with the technical provisions of the loan and, what is most relevant for present purposes, with the financial condition of the borrower.[16] Economic theory and market experience both suggest that the yields demanded by lenders tend to increase with the debt-equity ratio of the borrowing firm (or individual). If so, and if we can assume as a first approximation that this yield curve, $r = r(D/S)$, whatever its precise form, is the same for all borrowers, then we can readily extend our propositions to the case of a rising supply curve for borrowed funds.[17]

---

[15] For simplicity, we shall ignore throughout the tiny element of progression in our present corporate tax and treat τ as a constant independent of $(X_j - rD_j)$.

[16] We shall not consider here the extension of the analysis to encompass the time structure of interest rates. Although some of the problems posed by the time structure can be handled within our comparative statics framework, an adequate discussion would require a separate paper.

[17] We can also develop a theory of bond valuation along lines essentially parallel to those followed for the case of shares. We conjecture that the curve of bond yields as a function of leverage will turn out to be a nonlinear one in contrast to the linear function of leverage developed for common shares. However, we would also expect that the rate of increase in the yield on new issues would not be substantial in practice. This relatively slow rise would reflect the fact that interest rate increases by themselves can never be completely satisfactory

Proposition I is actually unaffected in form and interpretation by the fact that the rate of interest may rise with leverage; while the average cost of *borrowed* funds will tend to increase as debt rises, the average cost of funds from *all* sources will still be independent of leverage (apart from the tax effect). This conclusion follows directly from the ability of those who engage in arbitrage to undo the leverage in any financial structure by acquiring an appropriately mixed portfolio of bonds and stocks. Because of this ability, the ratio of earnings (*before* interest charges) to market value—*i.e.*, the average cost of capital from all sources—must be the same for all firms in a given class.[18] In other words, the increased cost of borrowed funds as leverage increases will tend to be offset by a corresponding reduction in the yield of common stock. This seemingly paradoxical result will be examined more closely below in connection with Proposition II.

A significant modification of Proposition I would be required only if the yield curve $r = r(D/S)$ were different for different borrowers, as might happen if creditors had marked preferences for the securities of a particular class of debtors. If, for example, corporations as a class were able to borrow at lower rates than individuals having equivalent personal leverage, then the average cost of capital to corporations might fall slightly, as leverage increased over some range, in reflection of this differential. In evaluating this possibility, however, remember that the relevant interest rate for our arbitrage operators is the rate on brokers' loans and, historically, that rate has not been noticeably higher than representative corporate rates.[19] The

---

to creditors as compensation for their increased risk. Such increases may simply serve to raise r so high relative to ρ that they become self-defeating by giving rise to a situation in which even normal fluctuations in earnings may force the company into bankruptcy. The difficulty of borrowing more, therefore, tends to show up in the usual case not so much in higher rates as in the form of increasingly stringent restrictions imposed on the company's management and finances by the creditors; and ultimately in a complete inability to obtain new borrowed funds, at least from the institutional investors who normally set the standards in the market for bonds.

[18] One normally minor qualification might be noted. Once we relax the assumption that all bonds have certain yields, our arbitrage operator faces the danger of something comparable to "gambler's ruin." That is, there is always the possibility that an otherwise sound concern—one whose long-run expected income is greater than its interest liability—might be forced into liquidation as a result of a run of temporary losses. Since reorganization generally involves costs, and because the operation of the firm may be hampered during the period of reorganization with lasting unfavorable effects on earnings prospects, we might perhaps expect heavily levered companies to sell at a slight discount relative to less heavily indebted companies of the same class.

[19] Under normal conditions, moreover, a substantial part of the arbitrage process could be expected to take the form, not of having the arbitrage operators go into debt on personal account to put the required leverage into their portfolios, but simply of having them reduce the amount of corporate bonds they already hold when they acquire underpriced unlevered stock. Margin requirements are also somewhat less of an obstacle to maintaining any desired degree of leverage in a portfolio than might be thought at first glance. Leverage could be largely restored in the face of higher margin requirements by switching to stocks having more leverage at the corporate level.

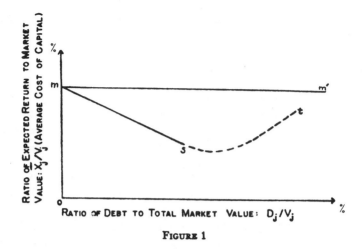

FIGURE 1

operations of holding companies and investment trusts which can borrow on terms comparable to operating companies represent still another force which could be expected to wipe out any marked or prolonged advantages from holding levered stocks.[20]

Although Proposition I remains unaffected as long as the yield curve is the same for all borrowers, the relation between common stock yields and leverage will no longer be the strictly linear one given by the original Proposition II. If r increases with leverage, the yield i will still tend to rise as D/S increases, but at a decreasing rather than a constant rate. Beyond some high level of leverage, depending on the exact form of the interest function, the yield may even start to fall.[21] The relation between i and D/S could conceivably take the form indicated by the curve MD in Figure 2, although in practice the curvature would be much less pronounced. By contrast, with a constant rate of interest, the relation would be linear throughout as shown by line MM', Figure 2.

The downward sloping part of the curve MD perhaps requires some comment since it may be hard to imagine why investors, other than those who like lotteries, would purchase stocks in this range. Remember, however, that the yield curve of Proposition II is a consequence of the more fundamental Proposition I. Should the demand by the risk-lovers prove insufficient to keep

---

[20] An extreme form of inequality between borrowing and lending rates occurs, of course, in the case of preferred stocks, which can not be directly issued by individuals on personal account. Here again, however, we would expect that the operations of investment corporations plus the ability of arbitrage operators to sell off their holdings of preferred stocks would act to prevent the emergence of any substantial premiums (for this reason) on capital structures containing preferred stocks. Nor are preferred stocks so far removed from bonds as to make it impossible for arbitrage operators to approximate closely the risk and leverage of a corporate preferred stock by incurring a somewhat smaller debt on personal account.

[21] Since new lenders are unlikely to permit this much leverage (cf. note 17), this range of the curve is likely to be occupied by companies whose earnings prospects have fallen substantially since the time when their debts were issued.

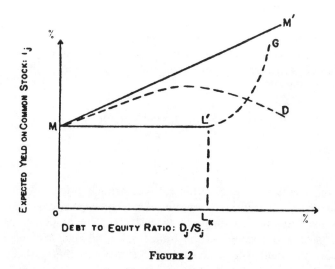

FIGURE 2

the market to the peculiar yield-curve MD, this demand would be reinforced by the action of arbitrage operators. The latter would find it profitable to own a pro-rata share of the firm as a whole by holding its stock *and* bonds, the lower yield of the shares being thus offset by the higher return on bonds.

D. THE RELATION OF PROPOSITIONS I AND Ii TO CURRENT DOCTRINES

The propositions we have developed with respect to the valuation of firms and shares appear to be substantially at variance with current doctrines in the field of finance. The main differences between our view and the current view are summarized graphically in Figures 1 and 2. Our Proposition I [equation (4)] asserts that the average cost of capital, $\overline{X}_j^{\tau}/V_j$, is a constant for all firms j in class k, independently of their financial structure. This implies that, if we were to take a sample of firms in a given class, and if for each firm we were to plot the ratio of expected return to market value against some measure of leverage or financial structure, the points would tend to fall on a horizontal straight line with intercept ρ_k^{τ}, like the solid line mm' in Figure 1.[22] From Proposition I we derived Proposition II [equation (8)] which, taking the simplest version with r constant, asserts that, for all firms in a class, the relation between the yield on common stock and financial structure, measured by D_j/S_j, will approximate a straight line with slope $(\rho_k^{\tau} - r)$ and intercept ρ_k^{τ}. This relationship is shown as the solid line MM' in Figure 2, to which reference has been made earlier.[23]

[22] In Figure 1 the measure of leverage used is D_j/V_j (the ratio of debt to market value) rather than D_j/S_j (the ratio of debt to equity), the concept used in the analytical development. The D_j/V_j measure is introduced at this point because it simplifies comparison and contrast of our view with the traditional position.

[23] The line MM' in Figure 2 has been drawn with a positive slope on the assumption that $\rho_k^{\tau} > r$, a condition which will normally obtain. Our Proposition II as given in equation (8)

By contrast, the conventional view among finance specialists appears to start from the proposition that, other things equal, the earnings-price ratio (or its reciprocal, the times-earnings multiplier) of a firm's common stock will normally be only slightly affected by "moderate" amounts of debt in the firm's capital structure.[24] Translated into our notation, it asserts that for any firm j in the class k,

(13) $$\frac{\overline{X}_j^\tau - rD_j}{S_j} \equiv \frac{\overline{\pi}_j^\tau}{S_j} = i_k^*, \text{ a constant for } \frac{D_j}{S_j} \leq L_k$$

or, equivalently,

(14) $$S_j = \overline{\pi}_j^\tau / i_k^*.$$

Here i_k^* represents the capitalization rate or earnings-price ratio on the common stock and L_k denotes some amount of leverage regarded as the maximum "reasonable" amount for firms of the class k. This assumed relationship between yield and leverage is the horizontal solid line ML' of Figure 2. Beyond L', the yield will presumably rise sharply as the market discounts "excessive" trading on the equity. This possibility of a rising range for high leverages is indicated by the broken-line segment $L'G$ in the figure.[25]

If the value of shares were really given by (14) then the over-all market value of the firm must be:

(16) $$V_j \equiv S_j + D_j = \frac{\overline{X}_j^\tau - rD_j}{i_k^*} + D_j = \frac{\overline{X}_j^\tau}{i_k^*} + \frac{(i_k^* - r)D_j}{i_k^*}$$

That is, for any given level of expected total returns after taxes $(\overline{X}_j^\tau)$ and assuming, as seems natural, that $i_k^* > r$, the value of the firm must tend to *rise* with debt;[26] whereas our Proposition I asserts that the value of the firm is completely independent of the capital structure. Another way of contrasting our position with the traditional one is in terms of the cost of capital. Solving (16) for $\overline{X}_j^\tau / V_j$ yields:

(17) $$\overline{X}_j^\tau / V_j = i_k^* - (i_k^* - r)D_j / V_j.$$

According to this equation, the average cost of capital is not independent of

---

would continue to be valid, of course, even in the unlikely event that $\rho_k^\tau < r$, but the slope of MM' would be negative.

[24] See, *e.g.*, Graham and Dodd [6, pp. 464–66]. Without doing violence to this position, we can bring out its implications more sharply by ignoring the qualification and treating the yield as a virtual constant over the relevant range. See in this connection the discussion in Durand [3, esp. pp. 225–37] of what he calls the "net income method" of valuation.

[25] To make it easier to see some of the implications of this hypothesis as well as to prepare the ground for later statistical testing, it will be helpful to assume that the notion of a critical limit on leverage beyond which yields rise rapidly, can be epitomized by a quadratic relation of the form:

(15) $$\overline{\pi}_j^\tau / S_j = i_k^* + \beta(D_j / S_j) + \alpha(D_j / S_j)^2, \qquad \alpha > 0.$$

[26] For a typical discussion of how a promoter can, supposedly, increase the market value of a firm by recourse to debt issues, see W. J. Eiteman [4, esp. pp. 11–13].

capital structure as we have argued, but should tend to *fall* with increasing leverage, at least within the relevant range of moderate debt ratios, as shown by the line *ms* in Figure 1. Or to put it in more familiar terms, debt-financing should be "cheaper" than equity-financing if not carried too far.

When we also allow for the possibility of a rising range of stock yields for large values of leverage, we obtain a U-shaped curve like *mst* in Figure 1.[27] That a yield-curve for stocks of the form *ML'G* in Figure 2 implies a U-shaped cost-of-capital curve has, of course, been recognized by many writers. A natural further step has been to suggest that the capital structure corresponding to the trough of the U is an "optimal capital structure" towards which management ought to strive in the best interests of the stockholders.[28] According to our model, by contrast, no such optimal structure exists—all structures being equivalent from the point of view of the cost of capital.

Although the falling, or at least U-shaped, cost-of-capital function is in one form or another the dominant view in the literature, the ultimate rationale of that view is by no means clear. The crucial element in the position—that the expected earnings-price ratio of the stock is largely unaffected by leverage up to some conventional limit—is rarely even regarded as something which requires explanation. It is usually simply taken for granted or it is merely asserted that this is the way the market behaves.[29] To the extent that the constant earnings-price ratio has a rationale at all we suspect that it reflects in most cases the feeling that moderate amounts of debt in "sound" corporations do not really add very much to the "riskiness" of the stock. Since the extra risk is slight, it seems natural to suppose that firms will not have to pay noticeably higher yields in order to induce investors to hold the stock.[30]

A more sophisticated line of argument has been advanced by David

---

[27] The U-shaped nature of the cost-of-capital curve can be exhibited explicitly if the yield curve for shares as a function of leverage can be approximated by equation (15) of footnote 25. From that equation, multiplying both sides by S_j we obtain: $\bar{\pi}_j^\tau = \bar{X}_j^\tau - rD_j = i_k^* S_j + \beta D_j + \alpha D_j^2/S_j$ or, adding and subtracting $i_k^* D_k$ from the right-hand side and collecting terms,

(18) $$\bar{X}_j^\tau = i_k^*(S_j + D_j) + (\beta + r - i_k^*)D_j + \alpha D_j^2/S_j.$$

Dividing (18) by V_j gives an expression for the cost of capital:

(19) $$\bar{X}_j^\tau/V_j = i_k^* - (i_k^* - r - \beta)D_j/V_j + \alpha D_j^2/S_j V_j = i_k^* - (i_k^* - r - \beta)D_j/V_j$$
$$+ \alpha(D_j/V_j)^2/(1 - D_j/V_j)$$

which is clearly U-shaped since α is supposed to be positive.

[28] For a typical statement see S. M. Robbins [16, p. 307]. See also Graham and Dodd [6, pp. 468–74].

[29] See *e.g.*, Graham and Dodd [6, p. 466].

[30] A typical statement is the following by Guthmann and Dougall [7, p. 245]: "Theoretically it might be argued that the increased hazard from using bonds and preferred stocks would counterbalance this additional income and so prevent the common stock from being more attractive than when it had a lower return but fewer prior obligations. In practice, the extra earnings from 'trading on the equity' are often regarded by investors as more than sufficient to serve as a 'premium for risk' when the proportions of the several securities are judiciously mixed."

Durand [3, pp. 231–33]. He suggests that because insurance companies and certain other important institutional investors are restricted to debt securities, nonfinancial corporations are able to borrow from them at interest rates which are lower than would be required to compensate creditors in a free market. Thus, while he would presumably agree with our conclusions that stockholders could not gain from leverage in an unconstrained market, he concludes that they can gain under present institutional arrangements. This gain would arise by virtue of the "safety superpremium" which lenders are willing to pay corporations for the privilege of lending.[31]

The defective link in both the traditional and the Durand version of the argument lies in the confusion between investors' subjective risk preferences and their objective market opportunities. Our Propositions I and II, as noted earlier, do not depend for their validity on any assumption about individual risk preferences. Nor do they involve any assertion as to what is an adequate compensation to investors for assuming a given degree of risk. They rely merely on the fact that a given commodity cannot consistently sell at more than one price in the market; or more precisely that the price of a commodity representing a "bundle" of two other commodities cannot be consistently different from the weighted average of the prices of the two components (the weights being equal to the proportion of the two commodities in the bundle).

An analogy may be helpful at this point. The relations between $1/\rho_k$, the price per dollar of an unlevered stream in class k; $1/r$, the price per dollar of a sure stream, and $1/i_j$, the price per dollar of a levered stream j, in the kth class, are essentially the same as those between, respectively, the price of whole milk, the price of butter fat, and the price of milk which has been thinned out by skimming off some of the butter fat. Our Proposition I states that a firm cannot reduce the cost of capital—i.e., increase the market value of the stream it generates—by securing part of its capital through the sale of bonds, even though debt money appears to be cheaper. This assertion is equivalent to the proposition that, under perfect markets, a dairy farmer cannot in general earn more for the milk he produces by skimming some of the butter fat and selling it separately, even though butter fat per unit weight, sells for more than whole milk. The advantage from skimming the milk rather than selling whole milk would be purely illusory; for what would be gained from selling the high-priced butter fat would be lost in selling the low-priced residue of thinned milk. Similarly our Proposition II—that the price per dollar of a levered stream falls as leverage increases—is an exact analogue of

[31] Like Durand, Morton [15] contends "that the actual market deviates from [Proposition I] by giving a changing over-all cost of money at different points of the [leverage] scale" (p. 443, note 2, inserts ours), but the basis for this contention is nowhere clearly stated. Judging by the great emphasis given to the lack of mobility of investment funds between stocks and bonds and to the psychological and institutional pressures toward debt portfolios (see pp. 444–51 and especially his discussion of the optimal capital structure on p. 453) he would seem to be taking a position very similar to that of Durand above.

the statement that the price per gallon of thinned milk falls continuously as more butter fat is skimmed off.[32]

It is clear that this last assertion is true as long as butter fat is worth more per unit weight than whole milk, and it holds even if, for many consumers, taking a little cream out of the milk (adding a little leverage to the stock) does not detract noticeably from the taste (does not add noticeably to the risk). Furthermore the argument remains valid even in the face of institutional limitations of the type envisaged by Durand. For suppose that a large fraction of the population habitually dines in restaurants which are required by law to serve only cream in lieu of milk (entrust their savings to institutional investors who can only buy bonds). To be sure the price of butter fat will then tend to be higher in relation to that of skimmed milk than in the absence of such restrictions (the rate of interest will tend to be lower), and this will benefit people who eat at home and who like skim milk (who manage their own portfolio and are able and willing to take risk). But it will still be the case that a farmer cannot gain by skimming some of the butter fat and selling it separately (firm cannot reduce the cost of capital by recourse to borrowed funds).[33]

Our propositions can be regarded as the extension of the classical theory of markets to the particular case of the capital markets. Those who hold the current view—whether they realize it or not—must assume not merely that there are lags and frictions in the equilibrating process—a feeling we certainly

[32] Let M denote the quantity of whole milk, B/M the proportion of butter fat in the whole milk, and let p_M, p_B and p_α denote, respectively, the price per unit weight of whole milk, butter fat and thinned milk from which a fraction α of the butter fat has been skimmed off. We then have the fundamental perfect market relation:

(a) $$p_\alpha(M - \alpha B) + p_B \alpha B = p_M M, \qquad 0 \le \alpha \le 1,$$

stating that total receipts will be the same amount $p_M M$, independently of the amount αB of butter fat that may have been sold separately. Since p_M corresponds to $1/\rho$, p_B to $1/r$, p_α to $1/i$, M to $\bar{X}$ and αB to rD, (a) is equivalent to Proposition I, $S + D = \bar{X}/\rho$. From (a) we derive:

(b) $$p_\alpha = p_M \frac{M}{M - \alpha B} - p_B \frac{\alpha B}{M - \alpha B}$$

which gives the price of thinned milk as an explicit function of the proportion of butter fat skimmed off; the function decreasing as long as $p_B > p_M$. From (a) also follows:

(c) $$1/p_\alpha = 1/p_M + (1/p_M - 1/p_B) \frac{p_B \alpha B}{p_\alpha(M - \alpha B)}$$

which is the exact analogue of Proposition II, as given by (8).

[33] The reader who likes parables will find that the analogy with interrelated commodity markets can be pushed a good deal farther than we have done in the text. For instance, the effect of changes in the market rate of interest on the over-all cost of capital is the same as the effect of a change in the price of butter on the price of whole milk. Similarly, just as the relation between the prices of skim milk and butter fat influences the kind of cows that will be reared, so the relation between i and r influences the kind of ventures that will be undertaken. If people like butter we shall have Guernseys; if they are willing to pay a high price for safety, this will encourage ventures which promise smaller but less uncertain streams per dollar of physical assets.

share,[34] claiming for our propositions only that they describe the central tendency around which observations will scatter—but also that there are large and *systematic* imperfections in the market which permanently bias the outcome. This is an assumption that economists, at any rate, will instinctively eye with some skepticism.

In any event, whether such prolonged, systematic departures from equilibrium really exist or whether our propositions are better descriptions of long-run market behavior can be settled only by empirical research. Before going on to the theory of investment it may be helpful, therefore, to look at the evidence.

E. SOME PRELIMINARY EVIDENCE ON THE BASIC PROPOSITIONS

Unfortunately the evidence which has been assembled so far is amazingly skimpy. Indeed, we have been able to locate only two recent studies—and these of rather limited scope—which were designed to throw light on the issue. Pending the results of more comprehensive tests which we hope will soon be available, we shall review briefly such evidence as is provided by the two studies in question: (1) an analysis of the relation between security yields and financial structure for some 43 large electric utilities by F. B. Allen [1], and (2) a parallel (unpublished) study by Robert Smith [19], for 42 oil companies designed to test whether Allen's rather striking results would be found in an industry with very different characteristics.[35] The Allen study is based on average figures for the years 1947 and 1948, while the Smith study relates to the single year 1953.

The effect of leverage on the cost of capital. According to the received view, as shown in equation (17) the average cost of capital, $\overline{X}^\tau/V$, should decline linearly with leverage as measured by the ratio D/V, at least through most of the relevant range.[36] According to Proposition I, the average cost of capital within a given class k should tend to have the same value ρ_k^τ independently of the degree of leverage. A simple test of the merits of the two alternative hypotheses can thus be carried out by correlating $\overline{X}^\tau/V$ with D/V. If the traditional view is correct, the correlation should be significantly negative; if our view represents a better approximation to reality, then the correlation should not be significantly different from zero.

---

[34] Several specific examples of the failure of the arbitrage mechanism can be found in Graham and Dodd [6, *e.g.*, pp. 646–48]. The price discrepancy described on pp. 646–47 is particularly curious since it persists even today despite the fact that a whole generation of security analysts have been brought up on this book!

[35] We wish to express our thanks to both writers for making available to us some of their original worksheets. In addition to these recent studies there is a frequently cited (but apparently seldom read) study by the Federal Communications Commission in 1938 [22] which purports to show the existence of an optimal capital structure or range of structures (in the sense defined above) for public utilities in the 1930's. By current standards for statistical investigations, however, this study cannot be regarded as having any real evidential value for the problem at hand.

[36] We shall simplify our notation in this section by dropping the subscript j used to denote a particular firm wherever this will not lead to confusion.

Both studies provide information about the average value of D—the market value of bonds and preferred stock—and of V—the market value of all securities.[37] From these data we can readily compute the ratio D/V and this ratio (expressed as a percentage) is represented by the symbol d in the regression equations below. The measurement of the variable $\overline{X}^\tau/V$, however, presents serious difficulties. Strictly speaking, the numerator should measure the expected returns net of taxes, but this is a variable on which no direct information is available. As an approximation, we have followed both authors and used (1) the average value of actual net returns in 1947 and 1948 for Allen's utilites; and (2) actual net returns in 1953 for Smith's oil companies. Net return is defined in both cases as the sum of interest, preferred dividends and stockholders' income net of corporate income taxes. Although this approximation to expected returns is undoubtedly very crude, there is no reason to believe that it will systematically bias the test in so far as the sign of the regression coefficient is concerned. The roughness of the approximation, however, will tend to make for a wide scatter. Also contributing to the scatter is the crudeness of the industrial classification, since especially within the sample of oil companies, the assumption that all the firms belong to the same class in our sense, is at best only approximately valid.

Denoting by x our approximation to $\overline{X}^\tau/V$ (expressed, like d, as a percentage), the results of the tests are as follows:

Electric Utilities $x = 5.3 + .006d$ $r = .12$
$$(\pm\ .008)$$

Oil Companies $x = 8.5 + .006d$ $r = .04.$
$$(\pm\ .024)$$

The data underlying these equations are also shown in scatter diagram form in Figures 3 and 4.

The results of these tests are clearly favorable to our hypothesis. Both correlation coefficients are very close to zero and not statistically significant. Furthermore, the implications of the traditional view fail to be supported even with respect to the sign of the correlation. The data in short provide no

[37] Note that for purposes of this test preferred stocks, since they represent an *expected* fixed obligation, are properly classified with bonds even though the tax status of preferred dividends is different from that of interest payments and even though preferred dividends are really fixed only as to their maximum in any year. Some difficulty of classification does arise in the case of convertible preferred stocks (and convertible bonds) selling at a substantial premium, but fortunately very few such issues were involved for the companies included in the two studies. Smith included bank loans and certain other short-term obligations (at book values) in his data on oil company debts and this treatment is perhaps open to some question. However, the amounts involved were relatively small and check computations showed that their elimination would lead to only minor differences in the test results.

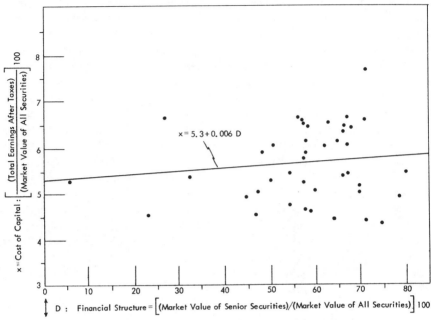

FIGURE 3.   COST OF CAPITAL IN RELATION TO FINANCIAL
STRUCTURE FOR 43 ELECTRIC UTILITIES, 1947—48

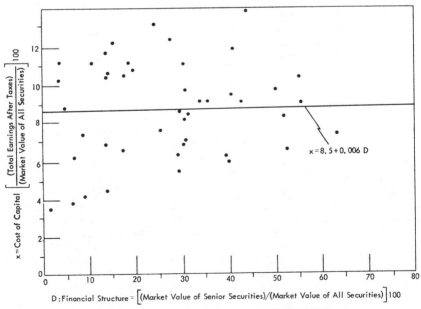

FIGURE 4.   COST OF CAPITAL IN RELATION TO FINANCIAL
STRUCTURE FOR 42 OIL COMPANIES, 1953

evidence of any tendency for the cost of capital to fall as the debt ratio increases.[38]

It should also be apparent from the scatter diagrams that there is no hint of a curvilinear, U-shaped, relation of the kind which is widely believed to hold between the cost of capital and leverage. This graphical impression was confirmed by statistical tests which showed that for both industries the curvature was not significantly different from zero, its sign actually being opposite to that hypothesized.[39]

Note also that according to our model, the constant terms of the regression equations are measures of ρ_k^τ, the capitalization rates for unlevered streams and hence the average cost of capital in the classes in question. The estimates of 8.5 per cent for the oil companies as against 5.3 per cent for electric utilities appear to accord well with a priori expectations, both in absolute value and relative spread.

The effect of leverage on common stock yields. According to our Proposition II—see equation (12) and Figure 2—the expected yield on common stock, $\bar{\pi}^\tau/S$, in any given class, should tend to increase with leverage as measured by the ratio D/S. The relation should tend to be linear and with positive slope through most of the relevant range (as in the curve MM' of Figure 2), though it might tend to flatten out if we move far enough to the right (as in the curve MD'), to the extent that high leverage tends to drive up the cost of senior capital. According to the conventional view, the yield

---

[38] It may be argued that a test of the kind used is biased against the traditional view. The fact that both sides of the regression equation are divided by the variable V which may be subject to random variation might tend to impart a positive bias to the correlation. As a check on the results presented in the text, we have, therefore, carried out a supplementary test based on equation (16). This equation shows that, if the traditional view is correct, the market value of a company should, for given $\bar{X}^\tau$, increase with debt through most of the relevant range; according to our model the market value should be uncorrelated with D, given $\bar{X}^\tau$. Because of wide variations in the size of the firms included in our samples, all variables must be divided by a suitable scale factor in order to avoid spurious results in carrying out a test of equation (16). The factor we have used is the book value of the firm denoted by A. The hypothesis tested thus takes the specific form:

$$V/A = a + b(\bar{X}^\tau/A) + c(D/A)$$

and the numerator of the ratio X^τ/A is again approximated by actual net returns. The partial correlation between V/A and D/A should now be positive according to the traditional view and zero according to our model. Although division by A should, if anything, bias the results in favor of the traditional hypothesis, the partial correlation turns out to be only .03 for the oil companies and $-.28$ for the electric utilities. Neither of these coefficients is significantly different from zero and the larger one even has the wrong sign.

[39] The tests consisted of fitting to the data the equation (19) of footnote 27. As shown there, it follows from the U-shaped hypothesis that the coefficient α of the variable $(D/V)^2/(1 - D/V)$, denoted hereafter by d^*, should be significant and positive. The following regression equations and partials were obtained:

Electric Utilities $\quad x = 5.0 + .017d - .003d^*; \ r_{xd^*.d} = -.15$

Oil Companies $\quad x = 8.0 + .05d - .03d^*; \ r_{xd^*.d} = -.14.$

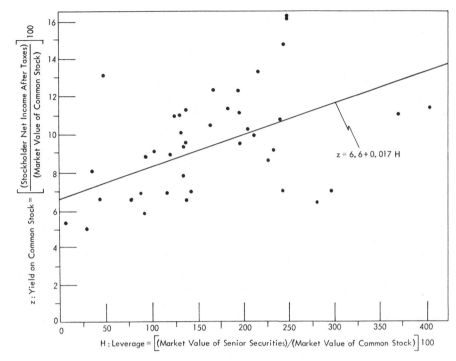

FIGURE 5. YIELD ON COMMON STOCK IN RELATION TO
LEVERAGE FOR 43 ELECTRIC UTILITIES, 1947–48

curve as a function of leverage should be a horizontal straight line (like ML') through most of the relevant range; far enough to the right, the yield may tend to rise at an increasing rate. Here again, a straight-forward correlation—in this case between $\bar{\pi}^{\tau}/S$ and D/S—can provide a test of the two positions. If our view is correct, the correlation should be significantly positive; if the traditional view is correct, the correlation should be negligible.

Subject to the same qualifications noted above in connection with $\bar{X}^{\tau}$, we can approximate $\bar{\pi}^{\tau}$ by actual stockholder net income.[40] Letting z denote in

---

[40] As indicated earlier, Smith's data were for the single year 1953. Since the use of a single year's profits as a measure of expected profits might be open to objection we collected profit data for 1952 for the same companies and based the computation of $\bar{\pi}^{\tau}/S$ on the average of the two years. The value of $\bar{\pi}^{\tau}/S$ was obtained from the formula:

$$\left(\text{net earnings in 1952} \cdot \frac{\text{assets in '53}}{\text{assets in '52}} + \text{net earnings in 1953} \right) \frac{1}{2}$$

$$\div \text{ (average market value of common stock in '53).}$$

The asset adjustment was introduced as rough allowance for the effects of possible growth in the size of the firm. It might be added that the correlation computed with $\bar{\pi}^{\tau}/S$ based on net profits in 1953 alone was found to be only slightly smaller, namely .50.

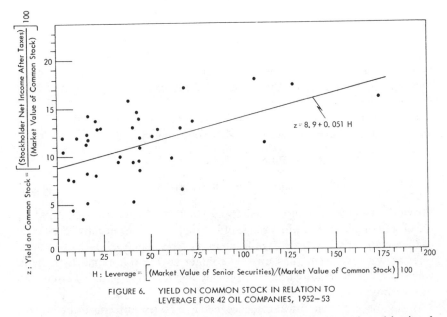

FIGURE 6. YIELD ON COMMON STOCK IN RELATION TO LEVERAGE FOR 42 OIL COMPANIES, 1952–53

each case the approximation to $\bar{\pi}^\tau/S$ (expressed as a percentage) and letting h denote the ratio D/S (also in percentage terms) the following results are obtained:

$$\text{Electric Utilities} \quad z = 6.6 + .017h \quad r = .53$$
$$(+ .004)$$

$$\text{Oil Companies} \quad z = 8.9 + .051h \quad r = .53.$$
$$(\pm .012)$$

These results are shown in scatter diagram form in Figures 5 and 6.

. Here again the implications of our analysis seem to be borne out by the data. Both correlation coefficients are positive and highly significant when account is taken of the substantial sample size. Furthermore, the estimates of the coefficients of the equations seem to accord reasonably well with our hypothesis. According to equation (12) the constant term should be the value of ρ_k^τ for the given class while the slope should be $(\rho_k^\tau - r)$. From the test of Proposition I we have seen that for the oil companies the mean value of ρ_k^τ could be estimated at around 8.7. Since the average yield of senior capital during the period covered was in the order of $3\frac{1}{2}$ per cent, we should expect a constant term of about 8.7 per cent and a slope of just over 5 per cent. These values closely approximate the regression estimates of 8.9 per cent and 5.1 per cent respectively. For the electric utilities, the yield of senior capital was also on the order of $3\frac{1}{2}$ per cent during the test years, but since the estimate of the mean value of ρ_k^τ from the test of Proposition I was 5.6 per cent, the slope should be just above 2 per cent. The actual regression estimate for the slope of 1.7 per cent is thus somewhat low, but still within one standard error of its theoretical value. Because of this underestimate of the slope and because of the large mean value of leverage ($\bar{h} = 160$ per cent) the regression estimate of the constant term, 6.6 per cent, is somewhat high, although not significantly different from the value of 5.6 per cent obtained in the test of Proposition I.

When we add a square term to the above equations to test for the presence and direction of curvature we obtain the following estimates:

Electric Utilities $\quad z = 4.6 + .004h - .007h^2$

Oil Companies $\quad z = 8.5 + .072h - .016h^2.$

For both cases the curvature is negative. In fact, for the electric utilities, where the observations cover a wider range of leverage ratios, the negative coefficient of the square term is actually significant at the 5 per cent level. Negative curvature, as we have seen, runs directly counter to the traditional hypothesis, whereas it can be readily accounted for by our model in terms of rising cost of borrowed funds.[41]

In summary, the empirical evidence we have reviewed seems to be broadly consistent with our model and largely inconsistent with traditional views. Needless to say much more extensive testing will be required before we can firmly conclude that our theory describes market behavior. Caution is indicated especially with regard to our test of Proposition II, partly because of possible statistical pitfalls[42] and partly because not all the factors that might have a systematic effect on stock yields have been considered. In particular, no attempt was made to test the possible influence of the dividend pay-out ratio whose role has tended to receive a great deal of attention in current research and thinking. There are two reasons for this omission. First, our main objective has been to assess the prima facie tenability of *our* model, and in this model, based as it is on rational behavior by investors, dividends per se play no role. Second, in a world in which the policy of dividend stabilization is widespread, there is no simple way of disentangling the true effect of dividend payments on stock prices from their apparent effect, the latter reflecting only the role of dividends as a proxy measure of long-term

[41] That the yield of senior capital tended to rise for utilities as leverage increased is clearly shown in several of the scatter diagrams presented in the published version of Allen's study. This significant negative curvature between stock yields and leverage for utilities may be partly responsible for the fact, previously noted, that the constant in the linear regression is somewhat higher and the slope somewhat lower than implied by equation (12). Note also in connection with the estimate of ρ_k^τ that the introduction of the quadratic term reduces the constant considerably, pushing it in fact below the a priori expectation of 5.6, though the difference is again not statistically significant.

[42] In our test, *e.g.*, the two variables z and h are both ratios with S appearing in the denominator, which may tend to impart a positive bias to the correlation (*cf.* note 38). Attempts were made to develop alternative tests, but although various possibilities were explored, we have so far been unable to find satisfactory alternatives.

earning anticipations.[43] The difficulties just mentioned are further compounded by possible interrelations between dividend policy and leverage.[44]

II. IMPLICATIONS OF THE ANALYSIS FOR THE THEORY OF INVESTMENT

A. CAPITAL STRUCTURE AND INVESTMENT POLICY

On the basis of our propositions with respect to cost of capital and financial structure (and for the moment neglecting taxes), we can derive the following simple rule for optimal investment policy by the firm:

Proposition III. If a firm in class k is acting in the best interest of the stockholders at the time of the decision, it will exploit an investment opportunity if and only if the rate of return on the investment, say ρ^*, is as large as or larger than ρ_k. That is, *the cut-off point for investment in the firm will in all cases be ρ_k and will be completely unaffected by the type of security used to finance the investment.* Equivalently, we may say that regardless of the financing used, the marginal cost of capital to a firm is equal to the average cost of capital, which is in turn equal to the capitalization rate for an unlevered stream in the class to which the firm belongs.[45]

To establish this result we will consider the three major financing alternatives open to the firm—bonds, retained earnings, and common stock issues—and show that in each case an investment is worth undertaking if, and only if, $\rho^* \geqq \rho_k$.[46]

Consider first the case of an investment financed by the sale of bonds. We know from Proposition I that the market value of the firm before the investment was undertaken was:[47]

$$(20) \qquad V_0 = \bar{X}_0/\rho_k$$

[43] We suggest that failure to appreciate this difficulty is responsible for many fallacious, or at least unwarranted, conclusions about the role of dividends.

[44] In the sample of electric utilities, there is a substantial negative correlation between yields and pay-out ratios, but also between pay-out ratios and leverage, suggesting that either the association of yields and leverage or of yields and pay-out ratios may be (at least partly) spurious. These difficulties however do not arise in the case of the oil industry sample. A preliminary analysis indicates that there is here no significant relation between leverage and pay-out ratios and also no significant correlation (either gross or partial) between yields and pay-out ratios.

[45] The analysis developed in this paper is essentially a comparative-statics, not a dynamic analysis. This note of caution applies with special force to Proposition III. Such problems as those posed by expected changes in r and in ρ_k over time will not be treated here. Although they are in principle amenable to analysis within the general framework we have laid out, such an undertaking is sufficiently complex to deserve separate treatment. *Cf.* note 17.

[46] The extension of the proof to other types of financing, such as the sale of preferred stock or the issuance of stock rights is straightforward.

[47] Since no confusion is likely to arise, we have again, for simplicity, eliminated the subscripts identifying the firm in the equations to follow. Except for ρ_k, the subscripts now refer to time periods.

and that the value of the common stock was:

(21) $$S_0 = V_0 - D_0.$$

If now the firm borrows I dollars to finance an investment yielding ρ^*, its market value will become:

(22) $$V_1 = \frac{\overline{X}_0 + \rho^* I}{\rho_k} = V_0 + \frac{\rho^* I}{\rho_k}$$

and the value of its common stock will be:

(23) $$S_1 = V_1 - (D_0 + I) = V_0 + \frac{\rho^* I}{\rho_k} - D_0 - I$$

or using equation (21),

(24) $$S_1 = S_0 + \frac{\rho^* I}{\rho_k} - I.$$

Hence $S_1 \gtreqless S_0$ as $\rho^* \gtreqless \rho_k$.[48]

To illustrate, suppose the capitalization rate for uncertain streams in the kth class is 10 per cent and the rate of interest is 4 per cent. Then if a given company had an expected income of 1,000 and if it were financed entirely by common stock we know from Proposition I that the market value of its stock would be 10,000. Assume now that the managers of the firm discover an investment opportunity which will require an outlay of 100 and which is expected to yield 8 per cent. At first sight this might appear to be a profitable opportunity since the expected return is double the interest cost. If, however, the management borrows the necessary 100 at 4 per cent, the total expected income of the company rises to 1,008 and the market value of the firm to 10,080. But the firm now will have 100 of bonds in its capital structure so that, paradoxically, the market value of the stock must actually be reduced from 10,000 to 9,980 as a consequence of this apparently profitable investment. Or, to put it another way, the gains from being able to tap cheap, borrowed funds are more than offset for the stockholders by the market's discounting of the stock for the added leverage assumed.

Consider next the case of retained earnings. Suppose that in the course of its operations the firm acquired I dollars of cash (without impairing the earning power of its assets). If the cash is distributed as a dividend to the

---

[48] In the case of bond-financing the rate of interest on bonds does not enter explicitly into the decision (assuming the firm borrows at the market rate of interest). This is true, moreover, given the conditions outlined in Section I.C, even though interest rates may be an increasing function of debt outstanding. To the extent that the firm borrowed at a rate other than the market rate the two I's in equation (24) would no longer be identical and an additional gain or loss, as the case might be, would accrue to the shareholders. It might also be noted in passing that permitting the two I's in (24) to take on different values provides a simple method for introducing underwriting expenses into the analysis.

stockholders their wealth W_0, after the distribution, will be:

$$(25) \qquad W_0 = S_0 + I = \frac{\overline{X}_0}{\rho_k} - D_0 + I$$

where $\overline{X}_0$ represents the expected return from the assets exclusive of the amount I in question. If however the funds are retained by the company and used to finance new assets whose expected rate of return is ρ^*, then the stockholders' wealth would become:

$$(26) \qquad W_1 = S_1 = \frac{\overline{X}_0 + \rho^* I}{\rho_k} - D_0 = S_0 + \frac{\rho^* I}{\rho_k}$$

Clearly $W_1 \gtreqless W_0$ as $\rho^* \gtreqless \rho_k$ so that an investment financed by retained earnings raises the net worth of the owners if and only if $\rho^* > \rho_k$.[49]

Consider finally, the case of common-stock financing. Let P_0 denote the current market price per share of stock and assume, for simplicity, that this price reflects currently expected earnings only, that is, it does not reflect any future increase in earnings as a result of the investment under consideration.[50] Then if N is the original number of shares, the price per share is:

$$(27) \qquad P_0 = S_0/N$$

and the number of new shares, M, needed to finance an investment of I dollars is given by:

$$(28) \qquad M = \frac{I}{P_0}.$$

As a result of the investment the market value of the stock becomes:

$$S_1 = \frac{\overline{X}_0 + \rho^* I}{\rho_k} - D_0 = S_0 + \frac{\rho^* I}{\rho_k} = NP_0 + \frac{\rho^* I}{\rho_k}$$

and the price per share:

$$(29) \qquad P_1 = \frac{S_1}{N + M} = \frac{1}{N + M}\left[NP_0 + \frac{\rho^* I}{\rho_k}\right]$$

[49] The conclusion that ρ_k is the cut-off point for investments financed from internal funds applies not only to undistributed net profits, but to depreciation allowances (and even to the funds represented by the current sale value of any asset or collection of assets). Since the owners can earn ρ_k by investing funds elsewhere in the class, partial or total liquidating distributions should be made whenever the firm cannot achieve a marginal internal rate of return equal to ρ_k.

[50] If we assumed that the market price of the stock did reflect the expected higher future earnings (as would be the case if our original set of assumptions above were strictly followed) the analysis would differ slightly in detail, but not in essentials. The cut-off point for new investment would still be ρ_k, but where $\rho^* > \rho_k$ the gain to the original owners would be larger than if the stock price were based on the pre-investment expectations only.

Since by equation (28), $I = MP_0$, we can add MP_0 and subtract I from the quantity in brackets, obtaining:

(30)

$$P_1 = \frac{1}{N + M} \left[(N + M)P_0 + \frac{\rho^* - \rho_k}{\rho_k} I \right]$$

$$= P_0 + \frac{1}{N + M} \frac{\rho^* - \rho_k}{\rho_k} I > P_0 \text{ if, and only if, } \rho^* > \rho_k.$$

Thus an investment financed by common stock is advantageous to the current stockholders if and only if its yield exceeds the capitalization rate ρ_k.

Once again a numerical example may help to illustrate the result and make it clear why the relevant cut-off rate is ρ_k and not the current yield on common stock, i. Suppose that ρ_k is 10 per cent, r is 4 per cent, that the original expected income of our company is 1,000 and that management has the opportunity of investing 100 having an expected yield of 12 per cent. If the original capital structure is 50 per cent debt and 50 per cent equity, and 1,000 shares of stock are initially outstanding, then, by Proposition I, the market value of the common stock must be 5,000 or 5 per share. Furthermore, since the interest bill is $.04 \times 5,000 = 200$, the yield on common stock is $800/5,000 = 16$ per cent. It may then appear that financing the additional investment of 100 by issuing 20 shares to outsiders at 5 per share would dilute the equity of the original owners since the 100 promises to yield 12 per cent whereas the common stock is currently yielding 16 per cent. Actually, however, the income of the company would rise to 1,012; the value of the firm to 10,120; and the value of the common stock to 5,120. Since there are now 1,020 shares, each would be worth 5.02 and the wealth of the original stockholders would thus have been increased. What has happened is that the dilution in expected earnings per share (from .80 to .796) has been more than offset, in its effect upon the market price of the shares, by the decrease in leverage.

Our conclusion is, once again, at variance with conventional views,[51] so much so as to be easily misinterpreted. Read hastily, Proposition III seems to imply that the capital structure of a firm is a matter of indifference; and that, consequently, one of the core problems of corporate finance—the problem of the optimal capital structure for a firm—is no problem at all. It may be helpful, therefore, to clear up such possible misunderstandings.

B. PROPOSITION III AND FINANCIAL PLANNING BY FIRMS

Misinterpretation of the scope of Proposition III can be avoided by remembering that this Proposition tells us only that the type of instrument used to finance an investment is irrelevant to the question of whether or not

---

[51] In the matter of investment policy under uncertainty there is no single position which represents "accepted" doctrine. For a sample of current formulations, all very different from ours, see Joel Dean [2, esp. Ch. 3], M. Gordon and E. Shapiro [5], and Harry Roberts [17].

the investment is worth while. This does not mean that the owners (or the managers) have no grounds whatever for preferring one financing plan to another; or that there are no other policy or technical issues in finance at the level of the firm.

That grounds for preferring one type of financial structure to another will still exist within the framework of our model can readily be seen for the case of common-stock financing. In general, except for something like a widely publicized oil-strike, we would expect the market to place very heavy weight on current and recent past earnings in forming expectations as to future returns. Hence, if the owners of a firm discovered a major investment opportunity which they felt would yield much more than ρ_k, they might well prefer not to finance it via common stock at the then ruling price, because this price may fail to capitalize the new venture. A better course would be a pre-emptive issue of stock (and in this connection it should be remembered that stockholders are free to borrow and buy). Another possibility would be to finance the project initially with debt. Once the project had reflected itself in increased actual earnings, the debt could be retired either with an equity issue at much better prices or through retained earnings. Still another possibility along the same lines might be to combine the two steps by means of a convertible debenture or preferred stock, perhaps with a progressively declining conversion rate. Even such a double-stage financing plan may possibly be regarded as yielding too large a share to outsiders since the new stockholders are, in effect, being given an interest in any similar opportunities the firm may discover in the future. If there is a reasonable prospect that even larger opportunities may arise in the near future and if there is some danger that borrowing now would preclude more borrowing later, the owners might find their interests best protected by splitting off the current opportunity into a separate subsidiary with independent financing. Clearly the problems involved in making the crucial estimates and in planning the optimal financial strategy are by no means trivial, even though they should have no bearing on the basic decision to invest (as long as $\rho^* \geqq \rho_k$).[52]

Another reason why the alternatives in financial plans may not be a matter of indifference arises from the fact that managers are concerned with more than simply furthering the interest of the owners. Such other objectives of the management—which need not be necessarily in conflict with those of the owners—are much more likely to be served by some types of financing arrangements than others. In many forms of borrowing agreements, for example, creditors are able to stipulate terms which the current management may regard as infringing on its prerogatives or restricting its freedom to

[52] Nor can we rule out the possibility that the existing owners, if unable to use a financing plan which protects their interest, may actually prefer to pass up an otherwise profitable venture rather than give outsiders an "excessive" share of the business. It is presumably in situations of this kind that we could justifiably speak of a shortage of "equity capital," though this kind of market imperfection is likely to be of significance only for small or new firms.

maneuver. The creditors might even be able to insist on having a direct voice in the formation of policy.[53] To the extent, therefore, that financial policies have these implications for the management of the firm, something like the utility approach described in the introductory section becomes relevant to financial (as opposed to investment) decision-making. It is, however, the utility functions of the managers per se and not of the owners that are now involved.[54]

In summary, many of the specific considerations which bulk so large in traditional discussions of corporate finance can readily be superimposed on our simple framework without forcing any drastic (and certainly no systematic) alteration of the conclusion which is our principal concern, namely that for investment decisions, the marginal cost of capital is ρ_k.

C. THE EFFECT OF THE CORPORATE INCOME TAX ON INVESTMENT DECISIONS

In Section I it was shown that when an unintegrated corporate income tax is introduced, the original version of our Proposition I,

$$\overline{X}/V = \rho_k = \text{a constant}$$

must be rewritten as:

(11) $$\frac{(\overline{X} - rD)(1 - \tau) + rD}{V} = \frac{\overline{X}^\tau}{V} = \rho_k^\tau = \text{a constant.}$$

Throughout Section I we found it convenient to refer to $\overline{X}^\tau/V$ as the cost of capital. The appropriate measure of the cost of capital relevant to investment decisions, however, is the ratio of the expected return *before* taxes to the market value, *i.e.*, $\overline{X}/V$. From (11) above we find:

(31) $$\frac{\overline{X}}{V} = \frac{\rho_k^\tau - \tau_r(D/V)}{1 - \tau} = \frac{\rho_k^\tau}{1 - \tau}\left[1 - \frac{\tau r D}{\rho_k^\tau V}\right],$$

which shows that the cost of capital now depends on the debt ratio, decreasing, as D/V rises, at the constant rate $\tau r/(1 - \tau)$.[55] Thus, with a corporate income

---

[53] Similar considerations are involved in the matter of dividend policy. Even though the stockholders may be indifferent as to payout policy as long as investment policy is optimal, the management need not be so. Retained earnings involve far fewer threats to control than any of the alternative sources of funds and, of course, involve no underwriting expense or risk. But against these advantages management must balance the fact that sharp changes in dividend rates, which heavy reliance on retained earnings might imply, may give the impression that a firm's finances are being poorly managed, with consequent threats to the control and professional standing of the management.

[54] In principle, at least, this introduction of management's risk preferences with respect to financing methods would do much to reconcile the apparent conflict between Proposition III and such empirical findings as those of Modigliani and Zeman [14] on the close relation between interest rates and the ratio of new debt to new equity issues; or of John Lintner [12] on the considerable stability in target and actual dividend-payout ratios.

[55] Equation (31) is amenable, in principle, to statistical tests similar to those described in Section I.E. However we have not made any systematic attempt to carry out such tests so far, because neither the Allen nor the Smith study provides the required information. Actually,

tax under which interest is a deductible expense, gains can accrue to stock-holders from having debt in the capital structure, even when capital markets are perfect. The gains however are small, as can be seen from (31), and as will be shown more explicitly below.

From (31) we can develop the tax-adjusted counterpart of Proposition III by interpreting the term D/V in that equation as the proportion of debt used in any additional financing of V dollars. For example, in the case where the financing is entirely by new common stock, $D = 0$ and the required rate of return ρ_k^S on a venture so financed becomes:

$$(32) \qquad \rho_k^S = \frac{\rho_k^\tau}{1 - \tau}.$$

For the other extreme of pure debt financing $D = V$ and the required rate of return, ρ_k^D, becomes:

$$(33) \qquad \rho_k^D = \frac{\rho_k^\tau}{1 - \tau}\left[1 - \tau\frac{r}{\rho_k^\tau}\right] = \rho_k^S\left[1 - \tau\frac{r}{\rho_k^\tau}\right] = \rho_k^S - \frac{r}{1 - \tau}r. \quad {}^{56}$$

For investments financed out of retained earnings, the problem of defining the required rate of return is more difficult since it involves a comparison of the tax consequences to the individual stockholder of receiving a dividend versus having a capital gain. Depending on the time of realization, a capital gain produced by retained earnings may be taxed either at ordinary income tax rates, 50 per cent of these rates, 25 per cent, or zero, if held till death. The rate on any dividends received in the event of a distribution will also be a variable depending on the amount of other income received by the stock-holder, and with the added complications introduced by the current dividend-credit provisions. If we assume that the managers proceed on the basis of reasonable estimates as to the average values of the relevant tax rates for the owners, then the required return for retained earnings ρ_k^R can be shown to be:

$$(34) \qquad \rho_k^R = \rho_k^\tau\frac{1}{1 - \tau}\frac{1 - \tau_d}{1 - \tau_g} = \frac{1 - \tau_d}{1 - \tau_g}\rho_k^S$$

Smith's data included a very crude estimate of tax liability, and, using this estimate, we did in fact obtain a negative relation between $\bar{X}/V$ and D/V. However, the correlation $(-.28)$ turned out to be significant only at about the 10 per cent level. While this result is not con-clusive, it should be remembered that, according to our theory, the slope of the regression equation should be in any event quite small. In fact, with a value of τ in the order of .5, and values of ρ_k^τ and r in the order of 8.5 and 3.5 per cent respectively (cf. Section I.E) an increase in D/V from 0 to 60 per cent (which is, approximately, the range of variation of this variable in the sample) should tend to reduce the average cost of capital only from about 17 to about 15 per cent.

[56] This conclusion does not extend to preferred stocks even though they have been classed with debt issues previously. Since preferred dividends except for a portion of those of public utilities are not in general deductible from the corporate tax, the cut-off point for new financ-ing via preferred stock is exactly the same as that for common stock.

where τ_d is the assumed rate of personal income tax on dividends and τ_g is the assumed rate of tax on capital gains.

A numerical illustration may perhaps be helpful in clarifying the relationship between these required rates of return. If we take the following round numbers as representative order-of-magnitude values under present conditions: an after-tax capitalization rate ρ_k^τ of 10 per cent, a rate of interest on bonds of 4 per cent, a corporate tax rate of 50 per cent, a marginal personal income tax rate on dividends of 40 per cent (corresponding to an income of about \$25,000 on a joint return), and a capital gains rate of 20 per cent (one-half the marginal rate on dividends), then the required rates of return would be: (1) 20 per cent for investments financed entirely by issuance of new common shares; (2) 16 per cent for investments financed entirely by new debt; and (3) 15 per cent for investments financed wholly from internal funds.

These results would seem to have considerable significance for current discussions of the effect of the corporate income tax on financial policy and on investment. Although we cannot explore the implications of the results in any detail here, we should at least like to call attention to the remarkably small difference between the "cost" of equity funds and debt funds. With the numerical values assumed, equity money turned out to be only 25 per cent more expensive than debt money, rather than something on the order of 5 times as expensive as is commonly supposed to be the case.[57] The reason for the wide difference is that the traditional view starts from the position that debt funds are several times cheaper than equity funds even in the absence of taxes, with taxes serving simply to magnify the cost ratio in proportion to the corporate rate. By contrast, in our model in which the repercussions of debt financing on the value of shares are taken into account, the *only* difference in cost is that due to the tax effect, and its magnitude is simply the tax on the "grossed up" interest payment. Not only is this magnitude likely to be small but our analysis yields the further paradoxical implication that the stockholders' gain from, and hence incentive to use, debt financing is actually smaller the lower the rate of interest. In the extreme case where the firm could borrow for practically nothing, the advantage of debt financing would also be practically nothing.

---

[57] See *e.g.*, D. T. Smith [18]. It should also be pointed out that our tax system acts in other ways to reduce the gains from debt financing. Heavy reliance on debt in the capital structure, for example, commits a company to paying out a substantial proportion of its income in the form of interest payments taxable to the owners under the personal income tax. A debt-free company, by contrast, can reinvest in the business all of its (smaller) net income and to this extent subject the owners only to the low capital gains rate (or possibly no tax at all by virtue of the loophole at death). Thus, we should expect a high degree of leverage to be of value to the owners, even in the case of closely held corporations, primarily in cases where their firm was not expected to have much need for additional funds to expand assets and earnings in the future. To the extent that opportunities for growth were available, as they presumably would be for most successful corporations, the interest of the stockholders would tend to be better served by a structure which permitted maximum use of retained earnings.

III. CONCLUSION

With the development of Proposition III the main objectives we outlined in our introductory discussion have been reached. We have in our Propositions I and II at least the foundations of a theory of the valuation of firms and shares in a world of uncertainty. We have shown, moreover, how this theory can lead to an operational definition of the cost of capital and how that concept can be used in turn as a basis for rational investment decision-making within the firm. Needless to say, however, much remains to be done before the cost of capital can be put away on the shelf among the solved problems. Our approach has been that of static, partial equilibrium analysis. It has assumed among other things a state of atomistic competition in the capital markets and an ease of access of those markets which only a relatively small (though important) group of firms even come close to possessing. These and other drastic simplifications have been necessary in order to come to grips with the problem at all. Having served their purpose they can now be relaxed in the direction of greater realism and relevance, a task in which we hope others interested in this area will wish to share.

REFERENCES

1. F. B. Allen, " Does Going into Debt Lower the ' Cost of Capital ' ?," *Analysts Jour.*, Aug. 1954, *10*, 57–61.
2. J. Dean, *Capital Budgeting*. New York 1951.
3. D. Durand, " Costs of Debt and Equity Funds for Business: Trends and Problems of Measurement " in Nat. Bur. Econ. Research, *Conference on Research in Business Finance*. New York 1952, pp. 215–47.
4. W. J. Eiteman, " Financial Aspects of Promotion," in *Essays on Business Finance* by M. W. Waterman and W. J. Eiteman. Ann Arbor, Mich. 1952, pp. 1–17.
5. M. J. Gordon and E. Shapiro, " Capital Equipment Analysis: The Required Rate of Profit," *Manag. Sci.*, Oct. 1956, *3*, 102–10.
6. B. Graham and L. Dodd, *Security Analysis*, 3rd ed. New York 1951.
7. G. Guthmann and H. E. Dougall, *Corporate Financial Policy*, 3rd ed. New York 1955.
8. J. R. Hicks, *Value and Capital*, 2nd ed. Oxford 1946.
9. P. Hunt and M. Williams, *Case Problems in Finance*, rev. ed. Homewood, Ill. 1954.
10. J. M. Keynes, *The General Theory of Employment, Interest and Money*. New York 1936.
11. O. Lange, *Price Flexibility and Employment*. Bloomington, Ind. 1944.
12. J. Lintner, " Distribution of Incomes of Corporations among Dividends, Retained Earnings and Taxes," *Am. Econ. Rev.*, May 1956, *46*, 97–113.
13. F. Lutz and V. Lutz, *The Theory of Investment of the Firm*. Princeton 1951.
14. F. Modigliani and M. Zeman, " The Effect of the Availability of Funds, and the Terms Thereof, on Business Investment " in Nat. Bur. Econ. Research, *Conference on Research in Business Finance*. New York 1952, pp. 263–309.
15. W. A. Morton, " The Structure of the Capital Market and the Price of Money," *Am. Econ. Rev.*, May 1954, *44*, 440–54.
16. S. M. Robbins, *Managing Securities*. Boston 1954.

17. H. V. Roberts, "Current Problems in the Economics of Capital Budgeting," *Jour. Bus.*, 1957, *30* (1), 12–16.
18. D. T. Smith, *Effects of Taxation on Corporate Financial Policy*. Boston 1952.
19. R. Smith, "Cost of Capital in the Oil Industry," (hectograph). Pittsburg: Carnegie Inst. Tech. 1955.
20. H. M. Somers, "'Cost of Money' as the Determinant of Public Utility Rates," *Buffalo Law Rev.*, Spring 1955, *4*, 1–28.
21. J. B. Williams, *The Theory of Investment Value*. Cambridge, Mass. 1938.
22. U.S. Federal Communications Commission, *The Problem of the "Rate of Return" in Public Utility Regulation*. Washington 1938.

18. THE COST OF CAPITAL, CORPORATION FINANCE, AND THE THEORY OF INVESTMENT: COMMENT

DAVID DURAND*

Reprinted from *The American Economic Review,* Vol. XLIX, No. 4 (September 1959), pp. 639–55, by permission of the author and the publisher.

In a recent contribution on security valuation and the cost of capital Franco Modigliani and M. H. Miller [11] (hereafter MM) have enunciated three propositions that contradict widely accepted beliefs and some earlier conclusions of mine [2]. This paper will not attempt to deny these propositions in their own properly limited theoretical context. Instead, it will analyze MM's underlying assumptions, which are subtle and restrictive; and it will indicate some of the difficulties of using these assumptions to support [11, p. 264] "an operational definition of the cost of capital and a workable theory of investment."

Of MM's propositions the first is basic. Proposition I states that, in a perfect market, the total value of all outstanding securities of a firm is independent of its capital structure. More specifically, if firm j has outstanding stock and debt instruments values at S_j and D_j and if its expected average earnings are $\overline{X}_j$ before interest, then the total value of its securities [11, p. 268, equation (3)] is

$$V_j \equiv (S_j + D_j) = \overline{X}_j/\rho_k,$$

where ρ_k is a constant capitalization factor for all firms in "equivalent return" class k. In such a class, which [11, p. 266] "plays a strategic role in the rest of the analysis," future net income per share of all firms, though

* The author is professor of industrial management, Massachusetts Institute of Technology.

subject to unknown variations, are certain to be perfectly correlated, each with every other.[1]

There are at least four devices that will aid in building a foundation under Proposition I. One is to assume that arbitrage is possible between securities in an equivalent return class. Another is to assume that a "firm" falls into none of the standard categories—proprietorship, partnership, or corporation —but is a sort of hybrid, having marketable securities like a corporation, proration of income like a partnership, and allocation of financial responsibility like neither. A third is to exclude risk. And a fourth is to assume a long-run equilibrium in which stocks sell at book value. But all of these devices are unrealistic, and MM have accepted none of them wholeheartedly. Thus, while they speak of arbitrage, MM describe a process that is not arbitrage at all, but a switch. Or again, they include all firms in one category— calling them corporations, but failing to endow them with distinctively corporate characteristics. They admit risk to the extent of minor uncertainties, but not major hazards. And finally, although they do not discuss the relation between stock prices and book value, some but not all of their treatment of dividend policy seems to assume that stocks sell at book value. This paper will expose the difficulties of justifying Proposition I for real corporations in a world where arbitrage is usually impossible, where substitutes for arbitrage are restrained and risky, and where stocks rarely sell at book value.

I. PROPOSITION I AND ARBITRAGE: AN ILLUSTRATIVE EXAMPLE

True arbitrage, when possible, is a powerful equalizer; but it is not ordinarily possible in corporate securities. To clarify the issue, this section presents an artificial example of an equivalent return class of corporations in which the possibility of arbitrage will practically guarantee Proposition I; subsequent sections will show how this example fails to account for the real problems of corporation finance.

Petrolease is a fictitious corporation whose business consists in leasing oil properties; it earns $10 per share on the average, all of which it pays out in dividends. Leverfund is a fictitious open-end investment trust, whose assets consist solely of Petrolease shares. It operates under the following conditions, some of which are unusual: (1) for every share of Petrolease that it holds, it must have outstanding one share of its own stock and one $100 bond paying interest at 5 per cent; (2) it incurs no expenses and pays out all earnings; (3) as an open-end fund, it will issue on demand one share and one bond while simultaneously acquiring, by purchase or exchange, a Petrolease

---

[1] MM offer a specific definition for an equivalent return class of debt-free firms [11, p. 266]: namely, "that the return on the shares issued by any firm in any given class is proportional to (and hence perfectly correlated with) the return on the shares of any other firm in the same class." Although MM are not equally specific for indebted firms, the obvious extension is that their returns are perfectly correlated $(Y = A + BX)$ but not proportional $(Y = BX)$.

share, or it will redeem on demand one share and one bond while divesting itself of a Petrolease share; (4) since it makes no loading charge, the buyer (or seller) of a bond and share pays (or receives) the same combined price that Leverfund pays (or receives) for a share of Petrolease; (5) in the open market, securities of both corporations trade without commissions. As a result of conditions (1) and (2), the income per share of Leverfund averages $5 and is exactly equal to the income per share of Petrolease minus $5. Thus, the incomes per share of Leverfund and Petrolease are prefectly correlated and the two corporations must belong to the same equivalent return class.

The peculiarities of Leverfund and Petrolease guarantee that an approximation to Proposition I will hold between them; together a bond and share of the one must sell for about the same price as a share of the other. Any discrepancy will provide traders with opportunities for profit, the exploitation of which will tend to reduce, and perhaps eventually eliminate, the discrepancy.

The most spectacular opportunity is through arbitrage. If a bond and share of Leverfund are selling in the open market for more than a share of Petrolease, a short-term trader can realize a quick profit by buying, say, 100 shares of Petrolease and simultaneously selling short 100 bonds and shares of Leverfund. Then, at his leisure, he exchanges his long Petrolease shares for Leverfund securities and delivers the latter against his short commitment. A single aggressive arbitrager can thus exert terrific equalizing pressure, for he can continue his operations just as long as any discrepancy remains—even to the extent of buying up and exchanging all outstanding shares of Petrolease.

But note, the effectiveness of this arbitrage depends upon equivalence in exchange between a share of Petrolease and a bond and share of Leverfund, not upon equivalence of income.[2] If, for example, personal income from bond interest were taxed at a lower rate than dividends, astute investors would prefer a bond and share of Leverfund to a share of Petrolease and would regard a price discrepancy as normal. But the arbitragers could still profit by buying Petrolease and selling Leverfund.

MM repeatedly speak of one security as a " perfect substitute " for another merely on the grounds that it represents an equal amount of income. Now, in fact, a share of Petrolease is not a perfect substitute for a bond and share of Leverfund; for one thing, a Petrolease stockholder has no vote for Leverfund directors. But owing to the possibility of exchange, a share of Petrolease is a good enough substitute for a bond and share of Leverfund, and vice versa, to

---

[2] Arbitrage between Petrolease and Leverfund belongs to the category of "kind" arbitrage. According to Weinstein [14, p. 2], a transaction of this type is defined as "the simultaneous purchase and sale of equivalent articles or securities in the same or different markets." Here the meaning of equivalence is rather special, implying that the articles or securities are essentially different but, "through the terms of their issuance or through special circumstance, may become equal to each other." Later [14, p. 66], Weinstein specifies: "By equivalent securities is meant a convertible bond or stock, a right or option warrant, or a stock of one company which may be exchanged for the stock of the same or another company."

permit the arbitrage operations that assure the validity of Proposition I between the two corporations. The importance of these details becomes apparent if Leverfund is simply transformed into a closed-end trust—bearing, say, the name Closecorp. Then, even though a share of Petrolease still stands behind a bond and share of Closecorp—maintaining income equivalence as with Leverfund—exchange is no longer possible. Neither is arbitrage, and the realization of Proposition I must depend upon other equalizing operations.

One substitute for arbitrage, to be mentioned in passing, is what might be called a hedge position,[3] to provide income without investment. If Closecorp sells at a 5 per cent premium, an operator might sell short 100 bonds and shares, investing the proceeds in 105 shares of Petrolease; then, since the income from 100 shares of Petrolease would suffice exactly to cover interest and dividend requirements on his short position, he would derive as net income the dividends from 5 shares of Petrolease. But this sort of transaction may be hard to arrange, owing to the many restrictions on short selling; and it exposes the operator to numerous risks—including the risk of being caught in a corner (cf. Macaulay [10, pp. vii–viii, 19–20]). Although corners are less frequent than formerly, the recent episode of E. L. Bruce on the American Stock Exchange indicates that some danger is still present.

Another substitute for arbitrage is the switching of investment accounts from comparatively unattractive issues into others that seem to offer a higher return for the same risk. MM commit a common error in confusing switching with arbitrage, but the distinction is important. Arbitrage can be effective if only a few professional traders are alert and aggressive. Switching, however, to be equally effective, may require the active cooperation of a large body of investors.

As an example of switching, suppose that Closecorp stock is selling in the market at 68, Closecorp bonds at 100, and Petrolease stock at 160. According to MM a leverage-loving investor who holds 300 shares of Closecorp stock outright should sell it and buy Petrolease on margin. A switch arranged according to the table below will achieve an increase of $200 in net income

Before Switching
300 Closed Corp. at $ 68   value $20,400   yielding $1,500

After Switching

340 Petrolease	at 160	54,000	yielding	3,400
Margin loan at 5% interest[4]		34,000	costing	1,700
Net investment		$20,400		$1,700

---

[3] Perhaps the use of the term "hedge" is a little loose in this context (cf. Weinstein [14, p. 76]).

[4] MM [11, p. 268] assume that the investor pays the same rate on his "bonds" (i.e., margin loan) that Leverfund pays on its bonds.

with no loss of stability; for, by arranging to pay in interest exactly $5 of his dividend receipts from each share of Petrolease, which is what Closecorp pays, the investor assures himself that his net income will exhibit exactly the same percentage fluctuations as Closecorp dividends. From such considerations MM [11, p. 270] "conclude therefore that levered companies cannot command a premium over unlevered companies because investors have the opportunity of putting the equivalent leverage into their portfolio [sic] directly by borrowing on personal account." But this is only a limited opportunity for most investors, who are deterred from aggressive margin buying by the legal and institutional restrictions placed upon it (see Section II) or by its intrinsic risks (see Section III).

Because of these deterrents, Proposition I can be no more than an inequality for Petrolease and Closecorp. In simplest terms, Closecorp securities enjoy a wider market than does Petrolease stock. Almost any investor who would buy a share of Petrolease should find a satisfactory—though not perfect—substitute in a bond and share of Closecorp, and he should willingly switch if the substitute fell to a discount.[5] Thus, as long as investors are fairly alert, Closecorp cannot sell much below Petrolease. But the reverse does not hold. Closecorp stock has a special appeal to risk-takers, and its bonds have a special appeal both to the safety-minded and to those barred from buying stock. For Closecorp to command a premium, it suffices that this specialized demand for its bonds and for its shares should exceed the available supply of these securities. After all, the essential difference between Closecorp and Leverfund is the limitation on the amount of securities that the former can issue in the short run. When Leverfund securities command a premium, the arbitragers can immediately increase the supply by buying up and exchanging Petrolease shares; they cannot do this for Closecorp.

In the long run, of course, Closecorp can expand, issuing more bonds and high-leverage shares to meet the specialized demand for these instruments; and in taking this step it will reap the benefits of low cost capital—that is until it issues enough securities to satisfy the demand. Here, then, is another substitute for arbitrage, which MM have neglected—the financial operations of corporations.

Here, also, is a paradox. If those of us who doubt the existence of equilibria advise corporate managers to remain alert and to exploit every opportunity to reduce their cost of capital by adjusting capital structure, we shall help to establish MM's equilibrium; whereas MM, by offering assurance that these opportunities do not arise, are sabotaging their own goal. Perhaps a realistic resolution to the paradox would be to recognize that any particular functional relation between total security value and capital structure is unlikely to remain stable over the long run—especially if it affords corporations an obvious opportunity to minimize capital cost by adopting one particular structure.

---

[5] There will be a few exceptions—institutions like the College Retirement Equities Fund, which are required to invest only in common stock.

Once the relation is widely recognized, everyone will attempt to exploit it; and a new relation, though not necessarily equilibrium, will result.

In practice this means that those who seek to reduce capital cost by adjusting capital structure must ascertain conditions in the current market, and act rapidly to exploit them. For instance, the stock market decline in September 1946 inaugurated a period of several years in which bonds yields were low and stock yields were high. For the first quarter of 1950, when [2] was in preparation, Standard and Poor's reported yields of 2.6 per cent for high-grade utility bonds as against dividend yields of 5.35 and earnings yields of 8.1 per cent for utility stocks. Those levels offered corporations a golden opportunity to finance with bonds. Nine years later, in the first quarter of 1959, bond yields were up to 4.3 per cent, while dividend yields and earnings yields were down to 3.9 and 5.4 per cent. The ratio of bond yields to stock yields had more than doubled. Thus, utility companies that availed themselves of the opportunity to sell bonds on comparatively favorable terms in 1950 and stock on comparatively favorable terms in 1959 must have acquired their capital at appreciably lower cost than those selling stock in 1950 and bonds in 1959.

II. MARKET IMPERFECTIONS: RESTRICTIONS ON MARGIN BUYING

MM visualize a highly competitive market, almost but not quite free of restrictions. Specifically, they write [11, pp. 280–81]:

Those who hold the current view—whether they realize it or not—must assume not merely that there are lags and frictions in the equilibrating process—a feeling we certainly share, claiming for our propositions only that they describe the central tendency around which observations will scatter—but also that there are large and *systematic* imperfections in the market which permanently bias the outcome.

Between the "current view" and their own, MM have left much middle ground. Whenever the market deviates from equilibrium, it provides someone with an opportunity for profit. But whom? MM's development of Proposition I, whether they realize it or not, accords investors exclusive rights to profit by giving them full responsibility to correct deviations from equilibrium. But why discriminate against the corporations? One likely reason, not mentioned by MM, is that market imperfections prevent corporations from issuing or redeeming securities as fast as investors can switch accounts. But even so market deviations may resist investors' corrective actions long enough for corporations to partake of the profits, unless the investors' speed is coupled with adequate volume; and a host of institutional restrictions limit the volume of switching operations that investors can arrange on short notice—especially switching from high-leverage stocks held outright into low-leverage stocks on margin, which is MM's prescribed corrective when high-leverage stocks command a premium.

Margin requirements under Regulation T can place a very substantial legal limitation on the volume of corrective margin switching that investors can generate. In the previously mentioned switch from 300 Closecorp outright at 68 into 340 Petrolease on margin at 160, the investor's equity was but 36 per cent of the total holding, which would be legally insufficient under the 90 per cent limitation in effect when this comment was prepared, or even under the 50 per cent limitation when MM published [11]. Of course, an investor with a large portfolio could legalize the transaction by hypothecating some of his other securities against his loan—but only at the expense of reducing his ability to take advantage of similar switching opportunities between other pairs of stocks.

Moreover, even the small amount of margin buying permitted some investors under Regulation T is withheld from many of our largest investors, the institutions. Mutual funds, fire and casualty companies, closed end trusts, life insurance companies, and most personal trust funds are prevented from buying stocks on margin—either by direct prohibitions in their charters or by the rather general acceptance of the prudent man rule. Together these institutional investors command a tremendous volume of investable or invested funds, most of which are simply not available for the purchase of low-leverage shares on margin, even when they fall to a discount.

MM suggest [11, pp. 278–81] that the restrictions under which institutional investors operate are, in effect, only a vehicle through which individual investors express their subjective risk preferences; cautious individuals commit their funds to conservative financial intermediaries. But this is only half the story. Nowadays, investment trusts are set up to pursue a variety of goals. An investor who wishes to plunge can entrust his savings to a high-leverage trust. The trust achieves its leverage not by buying on margin, but by selling bonds; and although the two operations are equivalent in many respects, there is an important difference. A bond issue requires time to arrange! So, if the market remains out of equilibrium long enough to provide investment trusts with extraordinary opportunities to profit by selling bonds, nonfinancial corporations can enjoy the same opportunities.

To sum up, those of us who take a middle-of-the-road view believe neither in a permanent equilibrium nor in a permanent and consistent departure from equilibrium. We suspect that switching operations by investors—hampered as they are by margin restrictions, brokers' commissions, tax considerations, and other institutional limitations—are insufficient in volume to maintain the market anywhere near equilibrium; and we regard the financing operations of nonfinancial corporations as an integral part of any equilibrating process that may be in operation. Even though corporations cannot act with the speed of a floor trader or of an aggressive investor, they can deal in large sums when they do act. Indeed, in June 1958, when MM's paper [11] appeared, margin requirements were at a 3-year low; yet the volume of loans by all commercial banks for purchasing or carrying securities ($5.6 billion reported by the Federal Reserve Board) was slightly less than the funded debt of just one corporate system ($5.7 billion for American Telephone and Telegraph).

III. THE RISKS OF MARGIN BUYING

MM would argue [11, p. 269] that the investor who switches from an outright position in Closecorp to a margined position in Petrolease incurs no additional risk, because he merely exchanges "one income stream for another stream, identical in all relevant respects but selling at a lower price." But this argument does not apply to corporate stockholders in a world of high risk, though it might apply either to stockholders in a world of low risk or to limited partners in a world of high risk. If Petrolease earnings were absolutely certain to remain above $5 per share, fluctuating only slightly about the $10 average, the income stream from Petrolease on margin would certainly equal the stream from Closecorp outright, and neither the margin lender nor the Closecorp bondholder would run any risk of default. Possibly MM had such safety in mind when they wrote [11, p. 268]: "All bonds (including any debts assumed by households for the purpose of carrying shares) are assumed to yield a constant income per unit of time, and this income is regarded as certain by all traders regardless of the issuer." But this is a strange statement for anyone who addresses himself to the question [11, p. 261]: "What is the 'cost of capital' to a firm in a world in which funds are used to acquire assets whose yields are uncertain, ... ?"

In a world where yields are really uncertain, Petrolease income may fall below $5 per share. Indeed, it may cease entirely if the oil wells run dry. If Closecorp were specially chartered as a limited partnership or joint venture with pro-rata allocation of responsibility, the outright holder of Closecorp stock would owe, in the event of financial disaster, as much to Closecorp bondholders as the margined holder of Petrolease would owe to his bank or broker. But as a corporate stockholder, the leverage-loving investor with 300 shares of Closecorp at 68 enjoys most of the benefits of a levered position in Petrolease without all of the attendant risks; for he has limited his liability to the amount of his investment, $20,400. If, however, he follows MM's advice and switches into 340 shares of Petrolease on margin at 160—regulations permitting—he incurs a liability of $34,000 for his margin loan, and his maximum loss increases to $54,400. In practice, of course, he runs little risk of losing the entire $54,400; his bank or broker, in self defense, will sell him out before Petrolease becomes worthless. But this protection against maximum loss greatly increases the risk of lesser loss. In the days when promiscuous margin buying was permitted, a temporary price decline in a generally rising market often resulted in the liquidation of over-extended accounts.

IV. THE PROBLEM OF RETENTION AND GROWTH

In the switching example, income equivalence between Closecorp and Petrolease depended on the assumption of 100 per cent dividend payout. This would be completely realistic for partnerships, since the law considers that a partner receives his pro-rata share of the firm's income, whether paid out or not; and it is almost realistic for such corporations as regulated investment trusts. But it will not do for corporations at large. MM do not actually assume 100 per cent payout; instead they say [11, p. 266]:

As will become clear later, as long as management is presumed to be acting in the best interests of the stockholders, retained earnings can be regarded as equivalent to a fully subscribed, pre-emptive issue of common stock. Hence, for present purposes, the division of the stream between cash dividends and retained earnings in any period is a mere detail.

But what do "present purposes" include? A little thought will show that they do not include the delineation of an equivalent return class, which is the cornerstone of MM's argument. Suppose, for example, that two equity-financed corporations earn regularly a definite rate ρ^* on assets of A, and that they retain no earnings. Then the assets of each will remain constant at A, and the earnings at $A\rho^*$ per year. Earnings per share will be proportional, and the two corporations must belong to the same class. But as soon as one corporation starts to retain earnings and to reinvest them profitably its assets and earnings will begin to increase; and this will suffice to transfer it into a new class, since its earnings per share will now be imperfectly correlated with those of the other corporation.

MM's proposal to regard retentions as a fully subscribed, pre-emptive stock issue will not avoid this difficulty unless stocks sell at book value. Before the corporation of the preceding paragraph started to expand, it earned $A\rho^*$—or $A\rho^*/N$ per share on N shares having book value $B_0 = A/N$. With a capitalization rate of ρ_k, the stock had a price of $P_0 = A\rho^*/\rho_k N$ and a ratio to book value of $P_0/B_0 = \rho^*/\rho_k$. Now, in the first year of its expansion, the corporation retains and reinvests $I = A\rho^*X$ to yield the same rate ρ^*; and this enables it to earn $A\rho^*(1 + \rho^*X)$. MM wish to regard I, the amount retained, as the proceeds of a stock sale, but they neglect to set the price P_f at which this hypothetical transaction is to take place—a detail, perhaps, but an important one! Except when $\rho^* = \rho_k$ and $P_0 = B_0$, no single price P_f will meet both of two requirements: first, to maintain earnings per share unchanged and thus keep the corporation in the same class; and second, to provide a genuine equation between the amount retained and the hypothetical stock issue.

A price of $P_f = B_0$, for example, will meet only the first requirement. At this price the corporation must issue new shares numbering:

$$(1) \qquad \frac{I}{B_0} = \frac{A\rho^*X}{A/N} = \rho^*NX,$$

and these together with N old shares will show the same earnings,

$$(2) \qquad \frac{A\rho^*(1 + \rho^*X)}{N(1 + \rho^*X)} = A\rho^*/N,$$

as before expansion. But the price $P_f = B_0$ will not meet the second condition because the hypothetical subscriber to this stock issue is, in effect, forced to acquire shares at B_0 when the market price is P_0; and he must either enjoy a profit $P_0 - B_0$ or suffer a loss $B_0 - P_0$.

Finding a price P_f to meet the second requirement, by equating a dollar's worth of retentions to a dollar's worth of issued stock, is difficult. Such a price will depend, when $\rho^* \neq \rho_k$ and $P_0 \neq B_0$, on the entire future growth of the corporation; and to obtain a solution, one must stipulate an arbitrary growth pattern. From the standpoint of algebra, one of the more tractable patterns is uniform growth in perpetuity, resulting from the retention and reinvestment each year of a fraction X of earnings to yield precisely ρ^*. Then the required price is given by:

$$(3) \qquad\qquad P_f = \frac{A\rho^*(1 - N)}{(\rho_k - \rho^*X)N},$$

which is a standard actuarial formula for the present value of an income stream starting at $A\rho^*(1 - X)/N$, growing at a rate ρ^*X, and discounted at ρ_k (cf. Todhunter [13, pp. 48–49]). Clearly P_f is independent of retentions only when $\rho^* = \rho_k$; then $P_f = A/N \equiv B_0$. But when $\rho^* > \rho_k$, (3) gives $P_f > B_0$, with P_f approaching infinity as ρ^*X approaches ρ_k. Thus in addition to resting on highly artificial assumptions, (3) sometimes leads to absurdities (cf. Durand [5]). Williams [15, pp. 89–94, 129–34] suggests other growth formulae, which are also artificial but avoid the absurdities.

Whether the corporation fails or succeeds in finding, for its hypothetical stock issue, the exact price P_f that meets the second requirement, any choice of $P_f \neq B_0$ will affect its earnings per share and transfer it into a new class.[6] Hence, if MM wish to include in their equivalent return classes companies expanding at various rates, or if they wish to reduce the division of corporate income between dividends and retained earnings to a mere detail, then they must assume some sort of long-run equilibrium in which $\rho^* = \rho_k$ and $P_0 = B_0$. Indeed, they have explicitly [11, pp. 288–91] assumed $\rho^* \geq \rho_k$, on the grounds that investments yielding $\rho^* < \rho_k$ are detrimental to the stockholders. They could equally well have ruled out $\rho^* > \rho_k$ on grounds of competition; if an area of investment opportunity yields $\rho^* > \rho_k$, it will attract additional capital until the discrepancy disappears. Such an argument should be no great hurdle for those who believe that the presence of "large and *systematic* imperfections in the market which permanently bias the outcome...is an assumption that economists, at any rate, will instinctively eye with some skepticism" [11, p. 281].

---

[6] Possibly this argument contains a subtlety that requires explanation. A corporation can, of course, start in a given equivalent return class, go through a period of expansion, and return to the same class at the close of its expansion—even if it earns $\rho^* > \rho_k$ on its investments. But this is not the point. It is the prospect of expansion, not the act itself, that causes the difficulty. Oddly enough, MM recognize [11, p. 290, fn. 50] that a proposed expansion may, because of its potential effect on earnings per share, influence stock prices; but they seem to have overlooked the havoc that this kind of anticipation plays with their concept of an equivalent return class.

Although an outright assumption that $\rho^* = \rho_k$ and $P_0 = B_0$ would have done much to shore up MM's theoretical argument, it would have done nothing to establish this argument as realistic or operational. In the operating world stocks do not sell at book value—not even approximately. A list recently released by the New York Stock Exchange [16] shows great variation in popular stocks—ranging from New York Central, at about one-tenth book value to International Business Machines at about seven times. This is one kind of evidence of market imperfection that is easy to obtain.

In an expanding economy where stock prices deviate from book value, the interaction between the growth rate and the ratio of price to book value is an important dynamic factor bearing on security values and the cost of capital. Writing on the utility industry, where the problem is well recognized, Tatham [12, p. 36] points out that utility stocks in recent years have generally commanded a premium over book value, thus assuring investors of a "potential increase in value and earnings during a period of expansion," which "provides one of the basic attractions of utility common stocks for investment purposes." By this "potential increase" Tatham refers specifically to growth in earnings per share resulting from successive issues of stock above book value; but he could have extended his argument to include expansion financed by borrowing or by retained earnings.[7] All this means that although retentions can often be regarded as a fully subscribed, pre-emptive stock issue, the division of earnings between dividends and retentions is anything but a mere detail when stocks do not sell at book value.

TABLE 1

REGRESSION ANALYSIS OF THE STOCKS OF 25 LARGE BANKS OUTSIDE
NEW YORK CITY, EARLY 1953

Regression Equations	Residual Sum of Squares
$\log_{10}P = .07 + .97 \log_{10}B$	.151298
$\log_{10}P = .54 + .49 \log_{10}B + .54 \log_{10}E$	.094283
$\log_{10}P = .96 + .22 \log_{10}B + .91 \log_{10}E + .70 \log_{10}D/E$	.036081

That investors do not in fact regard dividend policy as a mere detail is now attested by considerable empirical evidence (cf. Durand [3] [4], Gordon [6], Graham and Dodd [8, Ch. 34], Johnson, Shapiro, and O'Meara [9]). Table 1 summarizes a regression analysis of price P on book value B, earnings

[7] In addition to Tatham, Durand [4, Ch. 4] and Gordon and Shapiro [7] describe the mechanism by which this "potential increase" is realized and discuss its implications for the analysis of cost of capital. MM [11, pp. 288–91] describe the mechanism very clearly, but neglect the implications.

E, and dividends D, for a group of 25 bank stocks—one of six groups analyzed recently.[8] The special arrangement in the table is designed to show the successive reductions in the residual sum of squares due first to earnings, E, and then to the ratio of dividends to earnings, D/E. In particular, the reduction due to D/E (i.e., $.094283 - .036081 = .058202$) is far too great to attribute to chance (since the F-ratio $.058202 \times 21/.036081 = 33.87$ far exceeds even the $.001$ point for 1 and 21 degrees of freedom) and indicates that the payout ratio exerts a significant influence on price—even after the combined influence of book value and earnings have been taken into account. Table 2 summarizes regression analyses of four groups of public utility stocks.[9] Here the ratio of price to book value, P/B, is related to earnings over book value, E/B, and dividends over earnings, D/E. The reduction in the sum of squares is highly significant in the first two groups, but not at all significant in the last two. The combined experience of all groups taken together is significant.

TABLE 2
REGRESSION ANALYSIS OF FOUR GROUPS OF PUBLIC
UTILITY STOCKS (20 STOCKS PER GROUP), EARLY 1955

Group	Regression Equations	Residual Sum of Squares
I. Northeast	$\log_{10}P/B = 1.18 + .96 \log_{10}E/B$	.031033
	$\log_{10}P/B = 1.32 + 1.04 \log_{10}E/B = .60 \log_{10}D/E$	.017997
	$F = 17 \times .013036/.017997 = 12.314$	.013036
II. Midwest	$\log_{10}P/B = .90 + .70 \log_{10}E/B$	.019481
	$\log_{10}P/B = 1.16 + .90 \log_{10}E/B + .46 \log_{10}D/E$	.011770
	$F = 17 \times .007711/.011770 = 11.137$	.007711
III. West	$\log_{10}P/B = .97 + .77 \log_{10}E/B$	.042596
	$\log_{10}P/B = 1.11 + .87 \log_{10}E/B + .28 \log_{10}D/E$	.040625
	$F = 17 \times .001971/.040625 = .825$	.001971
IV. South	$\log_{10}P/B = 1.13 + .90 \log_{10}E/B$	.049213
	$\log_{10}P/B = 1.27 + 1.00 \log_{10}E/B + .30 \log_{10}D/E$	.041994
	$F = 17 \times .007219/.041994 = 2.922$	.007219

[8] For further analysis, see Durand [4]. The original data for this example appear in [4, p. 29, Table 5].

[9] These analyses come from a larger study on public utility stock prices and the cost of capital, financed by a grant from the Sloan Research Fund of the School of Industrial Management, Massachusetts Institute of Technology. The main results have yet to be published. The computations were performed on the I.B.M. 704 computer at the M.I.T. Computation Center.

MM are inclined to scoff at evidence like the above, arguing that [11, pp. 287–88] "in a world in which the policy of dividend stabilization is widespread, there is no simple way of disentangling the true effect of dividend payments on stock prices from their apparent effect, the latter reflecting only the role of dividends as a proxy measure of long-term earning anticipations." Are not MM trying to extinguish the fire by pouring on more fuel? In addition to the true effect, they introduce an apparent effect, which may also influence stock prices and the cost of capital—presumably by creating or correcting wrong impressions. In the earlier and less responsible days of Wall Street, an unscrupulous insider, like General Daniel E. Sickles of the Erie (cf. Dewing [1, p. 744, fn. 6]) might often attempt to mislead the public by manipulating dividends and issuing false earning statements. And even today, when blatant manipulation is far less common, psychological influences remain. If a conscientious corporation manager believes that the public is underestimating the earning power of his company and that a dividend change might improve the public's estimate, should he not make the change? There are many ways, some devious, in which dividend policy can influence stock prices and the cost of capital; and the available evidence indicates conclusively that at least some of them are effective.

Even if the available evidence does not suffice to disentangle all these influences, it offers some interesting hints. The bank stocks covered by Table 1 had an average price about 5 per cent above book value—with a range from 22 per cent below for The National Shawmut to 83 per cent above for the Bank of America. The utility stocks covered by Table 2 all sold above book value—with a range from 11 per cent for Consolidated Edison and Pennsylvania Water and Power to 222 per cent for Scranton Electric. With stocks selling above book value, a dollar retained is worth more than a dollar paid out—as implied earlier in this section—and investors seeking long-term appreciation should prefer stocks paying low dividends. If these investors dominate the market, negative regression coefficients for D/E are the natural result. The positive coefficients in Tables 1 and 2 imply dominance by another type of investor—possibly one who looks at dividend data instead of analyzing the earnings account, but more probably one with a genuine need for regular dividend income (cf. Durand [4, p. 47]). After all, there is a difference between capital gains and income—and especially between unrealized capital gains and realized income. In effect, our evidence on dividend policy is just good enough to be frustrating; it leaves us no doubt whatsoever that dividend policy exerts an influence on stock prices and the cost of capital, while failing to explain precisely how the influence is exerted.

V. PROBLEMS OF EMPIRICAL ANALYSIS

The empiricist who would investigate the cost of capital to corporations will encounter a host of obstacles, and among the first will be the gathering of reliable and pertinent data. He will find price quotations sometimes hard to acquire and often erratic or nominal—particularly quotations for corporate bonds, most of which are rather inactively traded nowadays, and some of which, the so-called private placements, are not traded at all. He will find dividend rates, although easy enough to ascertain for regular payers like American Telephone and Telegraph, very troublesome when irregular payments, stock dividends, and extras are the rule. And he will find earnings even harder than dividends to ascertain precisely, for they are subject to the vagaries of accounting practice as well as the vicissitudes of business conditions.

Another obstacle, which is crucial for MM's approach, is the difficulty of assembling a sample of corporations capable of supporting a comparative, or cross-section, type of analysis. The empirical analyst will be unable to assemble any sample meeting the rigid requirements of MM's equivalent class; but this in itself is hardly disastrous, since samples showing no variation in dividend policy and growth rate will not yield much information. The real difficulty is to find samples that are reasonably homogeneous in most respects, and yet show enough variation in growth rate, capital structure, and the like to bring out the influence of these factors. One can often find two or three, and sometimes more, corporations with characteristics sufficiently uniform to bear comparative analysis—an approach long known and used by security analysts. But if an analyst restricts his samples in order to keep them homogeneous, he must perforce keep them small; and if he attempts to expand them to the point where they are numerically satisfactory, he must pay a price in lost homogeneity. This problem arose recently in a study of 117 bank stocks (Durand [3] and [4]). A sample of 117 would be large enough to support a respectable cross-section analysis—if it were homogeneous. But a division of this sample into six subsamples, coupled with some tests for heterogeneity, revealed striking differences. Within the subsamples, moreover, there was further evidence of heterogeneity; in fact, a surprisingly large number of banks exhibited characteristics that rendered them virtually unique [4, pp. 19–20 and 60–62].

Taken all together these obstacles of sparse quotations, uncertain dividends, ambiguous earnings, and heterogeneous stock groups rather narrowly limit the ability of the empirical analyst to detect, let alone measure, the various factors affecting cost of capital. Indeed, only the strongest factors are likely to be discernible through the haze of unwanted perturbations; the subtler ones easily remain unnoticed. To date, in fact, dividend payout is one of the few factors that have proved strong enough to be repeatedly discernible; yet its specific influence is neither clear-cut nor easy to interpret. The available evidence appears inadequate to answer most of the interesting questions. Does the typical positive correlation between price and payout imply that investors are using dividend data to forecast company prospects or merely expressing an honest preference for cash income? To what extent is the price-payout relation obfuscated by growth-conscious investors, who prefer retentions to income? Can one measure reliably the price-payout relation for individual companies? And how does the conscientious manager set dividend policy to accommodate a medley of present and potential stockholders in greatly varied personal circumstances and tax brakets?

The influence, if any, of leverage on cost of capital has so far escaped detection in cross sections—both in the oils and utilities mentioned by MM, and in the bank stocks. But in view of the difficulties of empirical analysis, this is merely evidence of lack of evidence. On MM's scatter diagram [11, p. 283, Figure 3], relating cost of capital to financial structure for 43 utilities in 1947–48, the ratio of "total earnings after taxes" to "market value of all securities" (i.e., cost by MM's definition) ranges roughly from $4\frac{1}{4}$ to $7\frac{1}{2}$ per cent, with well over a third of the observations falling outside the range from 5 to $6\frac{1}{2}$ per cent. In the face of so much scatter, could anyone be assured of detecting a consistent variation of, say, $\frac{1}{4}$ per cent? And a variation in capital cost of this magnitude would not be financially insignificant to a corporation manager or a public utilities commission. On assets of $1,000,000,000 savings of $\frac{1}{4}$ per cent would amount to the tidy sum of 2,500,000 per year. I submit that MM's apparently negative cross-section evidence is essentially inconclusive—especially when history provides positive evidence of periods like 1948–50, which were unusually favorable to bond financing, and others like 1958–59, which were unusually favorable to stock financing. The real significance of the lack of evidence in these cross-sections is to warn us that many important questions in corporation finance, the cost of capital, and the theory of investment are not easily answered with available data.

VI. CONCLUSION

MM have cut out for themselves the extremely difficult, if not impossible, task of being pure and practical at the same time. Starting with a perfect market in a perfect world, they have taken a few steps in the direction of realism; but they have not made significant progress, considering their avowed purpose of achieving an "operational definition of the cost of capital." Their treatment of risk affords, perhaps, the clearest example. In allowing corporate earnings to fluctuate somewhat—presumably about a fairly definite central value—MM have postulated a world that is not 100 per cent riskless; but it is a remarkably safe world—being free from the risk of bond default, margin calls, foreclosures, or major disasters of any sort. In a world so safe, the effect of risk on the cost of capital, corporation finance, or the theory of investment is not apparent.

Or again, MM's treatment of the equilibrating mechanism in an imperfect market is unrealistic and also inconsistent. MM have endowed investors with unrestricted freedom to switch accounts whenever the market deviates from equilibrium; but for undisclosed reasons they do not extend equal freedom to corporations. If MM wish to assume a perfectly free market, they should realize that corporations unhampered by the practical costs and delays of issuing or redeeming securities can immediately exploit any departure from equilibrium, and it is then arguable that investors can never profit by switching accounts because corporate financing activities will maintain an equilibrium in which profitable switching is impossible. To be realistic, we must recognize that switching operations by investors, financing operations by corporations, and even arbitrage operations where possible, are all subject to restrictions—though not the same ones—and that each of these operations will exert some leveling effect on the market in spite of restrictions. A conscientious equilibrium theorist should advise, nay urge, all interested operators—investors or corporations—to exploit their available opportunities as vigorously as possible. MM, however, advise corporations that there is no opportunity to reduce cost of capital by judicious adjustment of capital structure; and thus they promote complacency, a form of market imperfection.

Finally, and most important, MM have underestimated the difficulty of setting up an equivalent return class, which is the cornerstone of their theory. To the practically minded, it is unthinkable to postulate the existence of two or more separate and independent corporations with income streams that can fluctuate at random and yet be perfectly correlated from now until doomsday; and the artificial example of Petrolease and Closecorp, which are not completely independent, provides no exception. But the difficulty goes much deeper. The concept of an equivalent return class, derived from notions of static equilibrium, is not adaptable to a highly dynamic economy in which stocks do not sell at book value.

Indeed, MM's approach to the cost of capital, as a ratio of current earnings to market price, is essentially static. Dynamically speaking, the cost of capital should measure the inducement—in terms of current earnings *plus long-term growth potential*—required to attract new investment fast enough to meet the needs of an expanding economy. This is the approach for a public utility commission desirous of assuring service in a growing community, for a bank supervisor worried lest the deterioration of bank capital ratios may jeopardize the ability of banks to finance expansion, and certainly for anyone concerned with the ability of this nation to maintain its position of economic leadership.

It is not easy to formulate an operational definition of the cost of capital for a dynamic economy where markets are imperfect, where price-to-book-value ratios vary from one-tenth to seven, and where investors and their advisory services discriminate between income and appreciation. Indeed, it may turn out to be impossible. But we shall make more progress in the long run by frankly recognizing the obstacles to achievement than by accepting false goals attainable by ignoring these obstacles.

REFERENCES

1. A. S. Dewing, *The Financial Policy of Corporations*, 5th ed. New York 1953, Vol. 1.
2. D. Durand, "Costs of Debt and Equity Funds for Business: Trends and Problems of Measurement" in Nat. Bur. Econ. Research, *Conference on Research in Business Finance*, New York 1952, pp. 215-47.

3. ——, " Bank Stocks and the Analysis of Covariance," *Econometrica*, Jan. 1955, *23*, 30–45.

4. ——, *Bank Stock Prices and the Bank Capital Problem*, Occasional Paper 54, Nat. Bur. Econ. Research, New York 1957.

5. ——, " Growth Stocks and the Petersburg Paradox," *Jour. Finance*, Sept. 1957, *12*, 348–63.

6. M. J. Gordon, " Dividends, Earnings, and Stock Prices," *Rev. Econ. Stat.*, May 1959, *41*, 99–105.

7. M. J. Gordon and E. Shapiro, " Capital Equipment Analysis: The Required Rate of Profit," *Manag. Sci.*, Oct. 1956, *3*, 102–10.

8. B. J. Graham and D. L. Dodd in collaboration with C. Tatham, Jr., *Security Analysis*, 3rd ed. New York 1951.

9. L. R. Johnson, E. Shapiro, and J. O'Meara, Jr., " Valuation of Closely Held Stock for Federal Tax Purposes: Approach to an Objective Method," *Univ. Penn. Law Rev.*, Nov. 1951, *100*, 166–95.

10. F. R. Maculay in collaboration with D. Durand, *Short Selling on the New York Stock Exchange* (Twentieth Century Fund, Mimeo.). New York 1951.

11. F. Modigliani and M. H. Miller, " The Cost of Capital, Corporation Finance and the Theory of Investment," *Am. Econ. Rev.*, June 1958, *48*, 261–97.

12. C. Tatham, Jr., " Book Value and Market Prices of Electric Utility Common Stocks," *Analysts Jour.*, Nov. 1953, *9*, 33–36.

13. R. Todhunter, *The Institute of Actuaries' Text-Book on Compound Interest and Annuities Certain*, 4th ed., revised by R. C. Simmonds and T. P. Thompson. Cambridge, England 1937.

14. M. H. Weinstein, *Arbitrage in Securities*. New York and London 1931.

15. J. B. Williams, *The Theory of Investment Value*. Cambridge, Mass. 1938.

16. New York Stock Exchange, " Book Value and Market Value," *The Exchange*, June 1958, *19*, 9–11.

19. THE COST OF CAPITAL, CORPORATION FINANCE, AND THE THEORY OF INVESTMENT: REPLY

FRANCO MODIGLIANI
and
MERTON H. MILLER*

Reprinted from *The American Economic Review*, Vol.
XLIX, No. 4 (September 1959), pp. 655–69, by permission
of the authors and the publisher.

In this reply to the two preceding comments, we shall concentrate on certain issues raised by David Durand. To J. R. Rose we can only apologize for having led him astray by our failure to adjust explicitly the definition of a "class" [3, p. 266, par. 2] when we introduced debt financing (Sec. I.B). We should have said more clearly, in the very beginning perhaps, that what determines membership in a class is the stream generated by the assets held by the firm, not the stream accruing to the *shares*. The two streams, of course, happen to be completely equivalent in our first special case of no borrowing, but only in that case. We hope the above emendation plus a study of Durand's numerical parable of Petrolease, Leverfund and Closecorp will clear up the misunderstanding.

We do not propose to go over Durand's comment point by point partly for reasons of space, and partly because on many issues we have little to add to (or retract from) what we originally wrote. There are, however, four issues where Durand's comments (plus correspondence we have had with many others) have led us to believe that some further elaboration of our model and our approach to the empirical problems might serve a useful purpose.

Before proceeding to this task, however, we should like to remind readers of the considerable areas of agreement between Durand and us which are easy to overlook in critical exchanges of this kind. Despite his sternly critical tone, he agrees (1) that our conclusions, which "contradict widely accepted beliefs" can be regarded as valid at least "in their own properly limited theoretical context" (see p. 640); and (2) that for all the attention that leverage has received in the literature of finance "the influence, if any, of leverage on the cost of capital has so far escaped detection" (p. 652). Not only is there agreement on these basic matters, but Durand's paper represents the kind of thoughtful and thought-provoking response we hoped we would get

* The authors are respectively, Professor and Associate Professor of Economics in the Graduate School of Industrial Administration, Carnegie Institute of Technology. They wish to thank their colleague Gert von der Linde for a number of helpful suggestions.

to the invitation in the closing paragraph of our paper. He has probed carefully to find inadequacies in our treatment of perfect markets, and he has endeavored to explore the implications of certain market imperfections for the usefulness of our approach. We feel, however, that he has not been conspicuously successful on either front, largely because he has focused on the apparent limitations of the perfect market model instead of trying to surmount these limitations by extending our basic approach.

I. THE ABILITY OF INVESTORS AND SPECULATORS TO ENFORCE PROPOSITION I

Section I of Durand's note is largely devoted to denying that the behavior of investors and speculators can be counted on to enforce Proposition I. Some of the issues raised in his discussion are largely semantic, notably whether certain transactions can or cannot properly be called arbitrage. In our paper, we chose to include under the general heading of arbitrage, the operation of simultaneously selling a commodity and replacing it with a perfect substitute because it has, in common with dictionary arbitrage, two essential features: (1) simultaneous purchase and sale of (2) perfect substitutes. We regret that our stretching of the language has annoyed Durand, who would prefer to confine this word to cases where the commodities bought and resold were identical, rather than merely perfect substitutes. Unfortunately, Durand's stretching of the word " switch " annoys us just as much because it obscures the distinction between our transaction in perfect substitutes—let us call it a " roll-over " for the sake of harmony—and ordinary switches by investors between different securities in response either to changes in tastes or to shifts of the budget line. As we tried to warn readers in our paper [3, especially n. 13] the failure to appreciate this distinction has been responsible for much of the confusion which has surrounded the analysis of capital markets.

Reservations might also be entered about his use of the word " hedge " to describe the operation, closely akin to arbitrage à la Durand-Weinstein, whereby any investor—and not the holders of the overpriced shares only—can exploit a price discrepancy by simultaneously going short on the overpriced shares and long on the undervalued ones. There is little point, however, in pursuing these terminological issues. For, whatever the nomenclature, Durand does not seem to disagree that in perfect markets[1] enough mechanisms are available to investors and speculators to prevent value discrepancies in a class from being more than ephemeral. And, on our part, we entirely agree with him that real world markets are never perfect and hence that conclusions based on the assumption of perfect markets *need not* have empirical validity.

[1] The term perfect market is to be taken in its usual sense of implying perfect information and absence of transaction costs. In addition to these standard attributes, we also require for a perfect capital market that the rate of interest (or, more generally, the rate of interest function) be the same for all borrowers and lenders. See [3, p. 268].

In particular, we have always been fully aware of the fact that, because of various "imperfections" and institutional limitations, "home-made" leverage obtained, for example, from margin buying was not identical with corporate leverage.[2] Such home-made leverage may well be inferior in some respects, though there are other respects in which it would seem to have positive advantages over corporate leverage.[3] But, in contrast to Durand, we saw little value in enumerating imperfections or trying to weight the relative merits of the two kinds of leverage. No amount of a priori speculation, we felt, could ever settle the issue of how close the substitutability is between home-made and corporate leverage, to say nothing of how close it would have to be to prevent any significant discrepancies in values from emerging. As is true elsewhere in positive economics, the most effective method of testing alternative assumptions is to test their consequences. If home-made leverage were as poor a substitute for corporate leverage as Durand and traditional doctrines (by implication) suggest, then levered companies would command a substantial premium in the market at least over some not insignificant range of capital structures. "Noise" in the data, of course, may well obscure this premium in particular samples; but if the cost advantages of (permanent) corporate borrowing were as large as traditional discussions suggest, they could and would be detected.[4] All we can say is that so far they haven't been detected; and consequently, implausible as it may seem to finance specialists, the assumption that home-made leverage of one kind or another is serving as a substitute for corporate leverage cannot yet be rejected in discussions of the cost-of-capital problem.

[2] That the concept of home-made leverage as a substitute for corporate leverage is at least not unknown to a large number of investors would seem to be indicated by the reference to it in a popular investment manual [1]. We might remind potential arbitrageurs also that margin buying is not the only way to participate in the equilibrating process. See [3, p. 262, n. 19].

[3] While an individual who pledges securities as collateral runs the risk of losing more than his original equity in the securities, the fact that his general credit stands behind the loan is one reason why interest costs on such loans are as low as they are. By the same token, the existence of limited liability forces lenders to corporations to expect somewhat higher rates and to impose more numerous and severe restrictions on corporate financial (and even operating policies) than would otherwise be the case. Not only are such restrictions unlikely to enhance the earnings prospects of levered corporations, but precisely because they cannot protect the bond-holders against temporary adversity by drafts on the wealth of the stockholders, levered corporations expose their stockholders to the risk of "gambler's ruin." See [3, p. 274, n. 18]. Similar kinds of offsetting advantages and disadvantages arise, for example, from the circumstance that the borrowing in one case may be short-term and in the other, long-term.

[4] It is important to stress that the essentially zero correlation we found between leverage and cost of capital cannot be attributed solely to noise in the data. If noise alone had been responsible, we would not have been likely to get the results we did for our tests of Proposition II (see pp. 285–286) or for the supplementary tests described in note 55. In connection with the interpretation of the empirical findings, it also strikes us to be a matter of little consequence whether the premium on levered capital structures has not been detected because it is not there or only, as Durand suggests, because it is too small to be noticed.

II. THE ROLE OF FINANCIAL OPERATIONS BY CORPORATIONS

To the above conclusion Durand raises the objection that Proposition I may hold not through the behavior of investors, but as a result of financial operations by corporations. That is, if some financial structures were to command a premium over others, this, he argues, would afford "corporate managers an opportunity to reduce their cost of capital by adjusting capital structures"; and in exploiting such opportunities, they would tend to cause the discrepancies in valuation to disappear. Hence the fact that Proposition I holds need not mean that the cost of capital is independent of financial arrangements; on the contrary, it may tend to hold because the very opposite is true.

The first point to note in connection with this line of reasoning is that it offers no support whatever for the traditional U-shaped cost-of-capital curve, the main target of our paper. For these temporary premiums, arising because the process of adjustment to equilibrium takes time in less than perfect markets, are of an entirely different sort from the permanent premiums on mixed over pure equity structures which are presumed to arise, in the traditional view, from the fact that debt money is always "cheaper" than equity money. In fact, these temporary premiums imply no lasting shape for the market cost-of-capital function, let alone the orthodox U with its unique "optimum." Depending upon where along our equilibrium horizontal line the adjustments happen to be lagging at the moment, we may have a U, an inverted U or any other shape, regular or irregular, namable or unnamable.

The next point that must be stressed is that Durand has failed to indicate explicitly what can be gained by whom and how, through adjustment of capital structures to exploit temporary bumps; or how this adjustment affects our conclusions concerning the cost of capital. As a matter of fact, he has even failed to explain what *he* means by the cost of capital—although, if taken literally, he would seem to be concerned with the cost of capital to management, whatever that might be. Nor has he provided any concrete illustrations to help us understand just what he has in mind. The only illustration given refers not to the exploitation of "bumps" prevailing at a given point of time, but to the exploitation of changes *over time* in bond and stock yields—a quite separate issue which we shall consider later. This failure to be specific is not altogether surprising. Systematic analysis would have disclosed that temporary deviations from the relation between market value and leverage implied by Proposition I, do not significantly affect our conclusions concerning the cost of capital (as defined by us), or otherwise provide management with significant opportunities to benefit stockholders through adjustment of capital structures.[5]

---

[5] While we doubt that even extremely "alert" managements, for reasons to be discussed, can reap important gains for their stockholders by exploiting the bumps, we have no doubts whatever that nonalert managements can produce losses for their stockholders. On this

By way of illustration, suppose that in a given class, total earnings were generally capitalized at 15 per cent and the market rate of interest were 5 per cent. For some reason, however, companies with leverage ratios of around 20 per cent suddenly became so popular with investors that their stocks sold at a premium. Instead of yielding the 17 per cent indicated by our equation (8), these stocks are bid up to the point where they yield only 15 per cent. This, in turn, implies that the ratio of expected return to total market value, $\overline{X}/V$, for such companies is only 13.3 per cent as compared with the 15 per cent prevailing for all other members of the class. Durand would presumably argue that companies with leverage ratios above 20 per cent could raise the total market value of their securities by selling stock and retiring bonds; and vice versa for companies with leverage below 20 per cent. Such operations would increase the supply of stock in the popular leverage range. This, in turn, would tend to satisfy the "specialized demand" and contribute to the disappearance of the premium.

But how and to what extent would this benefit the stockholders of the adjusting corporations? The effect of these manipulations would be to raise the price of their shares for as long as the premium happened to last. Such a temporary price rise, however, could offer a real advantage only to those stockholders who, like our arbitrageurs, were wise enough to dispose of the stock before the premium disappeared. The faithful stockholders would reap no gain at all (and might even be inconvenienced). It is not obvious, therefore, that a management which passed up this kind of opportunity would be derelict or complacent, especially when we take into account the cost and time lags of such capital structure adjustments and their possible conflict with the other policy considerations we mentioned [3, pp. 292–93, Sec. IIB]. And since there are no clear or strong incentives for undertaking these adjustments, little, if anything, would seem to be lost in not considering adjustments on the supply side a significant part of the equilibrating mechanism underlying Proposition I.

We may next inquire: what in our example would be the cost of capital as we have defined it, that is the minimum rate of return required for an investment to be advantageous to the stockholders? The answer to this question may appear, at first sight, to depend on the initial capital structure and on the form of financing to be adopted. The cost of capital would seem to be 13.3 per cent for companies which already have the optimum structure and propose to finance new investment with the currently popular 20 per cent debt-80 per cent equity mixture. For companies with no debt currently, a cut-off rate as low as 5 per cent might seem justified (in the sense that it would raise the market value of the shares) if the firm could, by the debt-financing

point, we actually took some pains in our Section II to warn managers that our statement that capital structure was a matter of indifference did not mean that they should become so complacent as, say, to float stock when the price of their shares was temporarily depressed, or to borrow at interest rates above the minimum obtainable in the market

of such projects, get into the popular leverage range.[6] These appearances, however, are deceptive. For, in so far as debt-free companies are concerned, unless the yield of the investment is sufficiently greater than 15 per cent, it would be possible to increase the market value per share even more by using the debt issue to buy the company's own stock. More to the point, if the bonds are used to finance new investments, then unless the yield of the projects is at least 15 per cent, the value of the stock will actually fall, once the temporary premium disappears, to less than it would have been if the investments had not been undertaken at all. Under these conditions, would Durand really be prepared to conclude that the appropriate cut-off rate for debt-free firms was anything but the same 15 per cent which would prevail everywhere in the class after the random bumps had disappeared?

For firms already in the premium zone, and thus able to finance new investment partly with "overpriced" stock the situation is more complicated. Here it can be shown that any investment yielding less than 15 per cent, but at least 13.3 per cent, might actually be slightly advantageous to the old stockholders (provided they were shrewd enough not to acquire the new issue) even after the temporary premium had disappeared. Their gain, how-ever, is made *entirely* at the expense of new stockholders to whom the management sold the temporarily overpriced shares.[7] Whether or not it is incumbent on management to engage in this sort of "exploitation" is, fortunately, an issue we need not face here since so far no one has been able to point to value discrepancies for an alert management to exploit.[8]

---

[6] If the investment yielded 5 per cent $+ \varepsilon$ (ε being any positive number), and were financed by bonds at 5 per cent interest, then the expected return to the stockholders would increase precisely by ε. Since the new structure would be in the premium range where the capitaliza-tion rate for common stock is 15 per cent, i.e., the same as the rate prevailing for the original unlevered stock, the undertaking of the investment would increase the market value of the stock by $(\varepsilon/.15)$.

[7] If the new stock issue is acquired by the old owners in proportion to their ownership, the operation will turn out to be damaging to them, the moment the bump disappears unless the investment yields at least 15 per cent. More generally, if the sale of overpriced stock is regarded as undesirable from an ethical and goodwill point of view, recourse must be had to bond or other temporary financing, just as in the reverse case of a temporary undervaluation of the stock discussed in our paper [3, p. 292]; but this course can be justified only if the investment yields no less than 15 per cent. Thus even for companies already in the premium range, there are good reasons for regarding 15 per cent as the appropriate cut-off rate or cost of capital.

[8] Durand's remarks sometimes suggest that he is concerned with another type of market imperfection, the premium attaching not to particular financial structures, but to the securi-ties of individual companies. In this case, the securities of at least some firms would have no "perfect" substitutes. Such firms would be confronted with a partly isolated and protected market entirely analogous to those underlying the theory of monopoly and of monopolistic competition; in fact, the notion of a class would then play the same role, and be subject to the same limitations as the notion of a group in the original Chamberlinian construction. Even for this type of imperfection it is not clear that the interests of the stockholders would be served by exploiting an existing premium through further issues as Durand seems to suggest (p. 643), since such a policy would reduce the market price of the shares.

There remains finally, to consider the issues raised by Durand's only concrete illustration. These issues are of an entirely different nature from the ones just discussed. They have nothing to do with the market imperfections which are supposedly Durand's main concern nor with the U-shaped cost-of-capital curve which was ours. They involve rather, the dynamic aspects of the investment and financing problem which, as repeatedly stated, we did not pretend to cover in our original paper.[9]

In the limited space available here, the most we can do is to point out that the basic conclusion of our static analysis with regard to the cost of capital will remain essentially valid even when we take into account changes over time in the capitalization rates—in so far as these changes are anticipated by the market and hence reflected in the current capitalization rates. That is to say, in general, an investment will be worth undertaking from the point of view of the current owners, if and only if its yield, ρ^*, is no smaller than the *current* capitalization rate for the class ρ_k.[10] Furthermore, this is so regardless of financial arrangements, in the sense that the criterion will lead to the highest (equilibrium) current market value for the shares no matter how the investment is financed.

Of course, future changes in interest rates and the over-all cost of capital are not always correctly anticipated by the market. Hence even though all capital structures are equally good in terms of *current* market valuations, when unanticipated changes do occur some capital structures will turn out *ex post* to have been preferable. Preferable not in the sense of enabling the *company* to secure its capital at a lower cost—for this is an essentially meaningless concept—but rather in the specific sense of being more advantageous to stockholders who bought in before the change occurred. To illustrate, a 10 per cent fall over time in the market capitalization rate ρ_k in a given class —interest rates and income expectations constant—will increase the total market value, V, by 10 per cent; and since the market value of debt is constant, it will increase the market value of the stock, S, of levered companies by even more than 10 per cent to an extent increasing with leverage.[11]

But it is one thing to say that if management can successfully guess an unexpected fall (rise) in ρ_k it can reap gains for the stockholders by adopting a levered (unlevered) capital structure, and quite another to suggest that, because of this possibility, management should be encouraged, as it were, to speculate on these changes with the stockholders' money. For such speculation can

---

[9] See e.g., [3, p. 273, n. 16]. We did, however, touch briefly on a certain class of essentially dynamic problems [3, p. 292] with a view not to solving them, but rather to showing how the analysis could be extended to handle them.

[10] The main qualification needed as a result of dynamic considerations is that when the capitalization rate is expected to fall, the static criterion is necessary but not sufficient. There are certain circumstances in which it may be preferable to postpone an investment, if such a postponement is feasible, thereby rejecting the investment now even though it currently meets the static test.

[11] It can be similarly verified that a rise in interest rates—ρ_k constant—will increase S for companies with long-term debt issued before the rise.

also reap losses when the guess is wrong. We cannot help feeling that Durand's stress on the desirability of speculative adjustments is at least partly the wisdom of hindsight. It is easy in 1959 to call attention to the gains that management might have reaped for the stockholders by having a large proportion of debt in 1950 when interest rates were only 2.6 per cent and average stock yields 8.1 per cent, knowing that stock yields fell thereafter to 5.4 per cent and bond yields rose to 4.3 per cent. Apparently, however, it was not so easy in 1950 to see that bond yields were about to rise and stock yields about to fall (or else these changes would have taken place then and there).[12] There is abundant evidence showing how hard it is for anyone to outguess the market consistently and it is obviously impossible for a majority to do so. Consequently, we, at least, are not yet convinced that corporation managers, in choosing their capital structures and planning their investment programs, should give major consideration to the possible windfall gains (or losses) they may earn for the stockholders if the current market consensus about the level of future yields should turn out to be wrong.[13]

III. DIVIDENDS, GROWTH OPPORTUNITIES AND THE THEORY OF SHARE PRICES

Durand is quite correct in pointing out that we nowhere provided an explicit description of how our model would explain relative share prices in the face of differential opportunities for growth by firms. Our omission, plus his own efforts at filling our gap, have apparently convinced him that our model cannot accomplish this task.

The fact is that the analysis can be extended in fairly straightforward fashion to accommodate growth without requiring any essential modification in the conclusions already established with the simpler model. To have developed this generalization in adequate detail, however, was impossible within the space limitations imposed on the original paper. Nor did it seem wise, in view of the controversial nature of the leverage issue, to open up a

[12] Nor does it follow, as Durand suggests, that managements choosing to issue stock rather than bonds in 1959 have advantaged their stockholders, for that will depend on the *future* course of bond yields and capitalization rates. Actually, to be certain that levered shares fared better than the others between even 1950 and 1959, we should look at the behavior of ρ_k, not of the average current yields of shares. From just the information provided by Durand, one cannot rule out the possibility that ρ_k in fact rose in this period, the lower average yield of shares reflecting merely the rise in interest rates. If so, there might have been no net advantage to the stockholders of levered companies since the rise in ρ_k might have offset the favorable effect of rising bond yields!

[13] Note that corporate managers (at least in nonfinancial corporations) who failed to engage in this type of speculation because they felt that it was not properly their function or because it was a task at which they had no comparative advantage, would not be depriving their stockholders of a potential source of gain by their failure to speculate. For, unlike the case of the "bumps," where the gains, if any, could only be reaped by financial adjustments at the corporate level, the shareholder always has the option of speculating on future market movements by arranging his own leverage position.

dividend policy dispute at the same time. Although, again for space reasons, many facets of the problem must be deferred to a forthcoming paper, we shall try to sketch out here at least enough of the theory to make it plain that no inconsistencies or peculiar assumptions about book-values are involved in the generalization.

Consider first the concept of a risk-equivalent ."class," the analogue in our analysis to the "industry" of ordinary price theory. In the more general model, two companies will be said to be in the same class at a specific point in time, t, if the elements of the streams generated by the physical assets each holds *at time t* are perfectly correlated and proportional. Membership in the class at each point in time is thus to be determined only by reference to the assets held at that point. Hence, there is no contradiction in the fact that firms in the same class are adding to their assets and income at very different rates over time.[14]

Having attached a meaning to the notion of risk-equivalence of differently growing streams we can consider the relative valuation of shares of "equal risk" but different growth potentials.[15] In order to handle, one at a time, the issues raised by Durand, we shall take for granted, until the end of this section, that investors behave rationally and that capital markets are perfect. These assumptions imply, among other things, that investors are concerned only with the total income they receive from a security and are indifferent as to whether this income takes the form of dividends or of capital gains. When such is the case, the market value of any firm will depend only on the earning power of the assets currently held and on the size and relative profitability of the investment opportunities that the firm is expected to undertake in the future.[16] More specifically, let:

[14] Note also that our definition of a class [3, p. 266] reduces to the broader definition above, in the special case in which (a) all firms in the class can acquire future income at the same terms (equivalent growth potentials) and (b) all the managements act in the best interests of the stockholders and hence pursue equivalent investment policies.

[15] In the matter of our treatment of the risk (or more properly the uncertainty) surrounding equity streams, we should like to take strong exception to Durand's observations at several points but especially in his concluding comments on page 653 that our model assumes "a remarkably safe world" and that that is why the "effect of risk on the cost of capital . . . is not apparent." We cannot see how anyone reading our discussion [pp. 265–66] could infer that we are only "Allowing corporate earnings to fluctuate somewhat—presumably about a fairly definite central value" or that we have somehow ruled out "major disaster of any sort." We did, of course, assume in our first model that *bonds* were completely riskless and perhaps this is the basis of his objections. We felt, and still feel, however, that this is an entirely satisfactory first approximation because, if for no other reason, the quantitative restrictions typically imposed by lenders to reduce their risk have in practice been remarkably successful.

Durand's impatience with our notion of a risk-equivalent class even at the level of theory (p. 653) is also puzzling. We hope that those who have tried to face up to the logical difficulties involved in applying the ordinary present-value apparatus (which is certainty analysis) to uncertain streams will recognize some merit in our risk-equivalent class as a method of dealing with some of these well-known difficulties.

[16] See, in this connection, footnote 21 below.

$\overline{X}_j(t)$ = the expected return (in the sense of our note [3, p. 265, n. 6]) of the assets held by firm j at time t;

$k_j(t)$ = the expected volume of purchases of new assets by firm j in period t, expressed for convenience as a percentage of the expected return on the assets held at t;

$\rho_j^*(t)$ = the expected rate of return on the assets acquired at t;

ρ_k = the capitalization rate in class k for the uncertain, but "non-growing" stream $\overline{X}_j(0)$ (i.e., one for which $k_j(t) = 0$ for all t). Alternatively, ρ_k may be thought of as the yield investors would earn on the securities of a company in the class with no differential earning opportunities (i.e., one for which $\rho_j^*(t) = \rho_k$ for all t regardless of $k_j(t)$.

It can then be readily shown (although the formal proof must be postponed to a forthcoming paper) that the market value of the firm will be given by:

(1) $V_j(0) \equiv S_j(0) + D_j(0)$

$$= \overline{X}_j(0)\left[\sum_{t=0}^{t=\infty}\left(1 + k_j(t)\frac{\overline{X}_j(t)}{\overline{X}_j(0)}\cdot\frac{\rho^*(t) - \rho_k}{\rho_k}\right)(1 + \rho_k)^{-t}\right].$$

It follows further from the first three definitions given above that

$$\frac{\overline{X}_j(t)}{\overline{X}_j(0)}$$

can itself be expressed entirely in terms of the quantities $k_j(\tau)$ and $\rho^*(\tau)$, $\tau = 0, 1, \ldots, t - 1$ by means of the recursive relation:

(2) $\overline{X}_j(t) = \overline{X}_j(t - 1)[1 + k_j(t - 1)\rho_j^*(t - 1)] \; t = 1, 2, \ldots, \infty.$

Hence, the value of the infinite summation in the right-hand side of (1) is, in the final analysis, a function of all the $k_j(t)$, $\rho_j^*(t)$ and ρ_k and can be conveniently denoted by $1/\psi_j(k_j(t); \rho_j^*(t); \rho_k)$. We can then rewrite (1) as:

(1') $V_j(0) = \overline{X}_j(0)/\psi_j(k_j(t); \rho_j^*(t); \rho_k)$

where the function ψ_j is defined by (1) and (2).

Equations (1) and (1') should make clear what is involved in extending our original analysis to encompass growth. Instead of the single capitalization rate for current expected earnings in the class,

$$\frac{\overline{X}_j(0)}{V_j(0)} = \rho_k \text{ for all } i$$

—this rate being also the same as the cost of capital in the class—we now get a multiplicity of composite capitalization rates

$$\frac{\overline{X}_j(0)}{V_j(0)} = \psi_j.^{17}$$

But, and this is the important point, all these composite capitalization rates for current earnings are reducible to the single cost of capital in the class ρ_k, and the parameters $\rho_j^*(t)$ and $k_j(t)$ which characterize the opportunities expected to be available and to be exploited by the firm for investing funds at a rate of return higher than the cost of capital, ρ_k.[18]

Equations (1) and (1') may also be helpful in making clearer the precise meaning of our assertion [3, p. 266] that, in perfect markets, dividend policy is a "mere detail." This statement has been misunderstood by some readers because they make the tacit, but unwarranted, assumption that the ability of the firm to exploit profitable opportunities is limited by—or at any rate intimately connected with—its dividend policy. This assumption is unwarranted because dividend retention is but one of the many sources through which expansion can be financed. Furthermore, in the absence of market imperfections such as flotation costs, and institutional factors such as tax laws, this source has no advantage or disadvantage over other sources from the point of view of the cost of funds. Hence, the possibility of exploiting opportunities is independent of dividend policy. Once a decision has been made as to which opportunities are to be exploited, the only role of dividend

[17] The function ψ_j can, of course, be specialized by making some definite assumptions about the nature of the $\rho^*_j(t)$ and the $k_j(t)$. If, for example, one assumes $\rho^*_j(t) = \rho^* = $ a constant, $k_j(t) = k = $ a constant for all t, and if one neglects leverage then (1) reduces to:

(2) $$S_j(0) = \overline{X}_j(0) \frac{1-k}{\rho_k - k\rho^*}$$ ($\rho_k > k\rho^*$ or ρ^*, whichever is smaller),

the valuation formula given by Durand. In using this simple specialization one need not be unduly concerned about Durand's "growth stock paradox" (see his reference [5]). The case in which $k\rho^* \geq \rho_k$ is not a *substantive* paradox at all, but an artifact attributable solely to the partial equilibrium nature of his analysis. In a general equilibrium framework (which we shall present in still another forthcoming paper), ρ_k, the capitalization rate, is not an independently given constant as in (1) [or the special case (2)], but a *variable*. Its actual value will be whatever is necessary to clear the market, given among other things, the growth opportunities available. If it were really true that for some corporation $k\rho^*$ was expected to remain indefinitely at say, 50 per cent per annum (k being less than one), the ρ_k for all stocks of "equal risk" would have to be at least 50 per cent. From what one knows about stock yields and growth potentials, this hardly seems an event worth worrying about; but it is in no way paradoxical.

[18] The use of the words "rate of return *higher than* ρ_k" in the above sentence is correct as long as we can expect all firms to follow an optimal investment policy, for then no firm will ever exploit opportunities yielding less than ρ_k. If so, the market price will reflect only the availability of high-yield opportunities and the capitalization rate $X_j(0)/V_j(0)$ will never be larger than ρ_k. If, however, we want to take into account the empirically relevant possibility of firms being expected to exploit "unprofitable" opportunities, then the words "higher than ρ_k" in the above sentence should be replaced by "different from ρ_k." For firms expected to adopt unprofitable investments, the market capitalization may, of course, be higher than ρ_k. On this point, see also footnote 19 below.

policy is to determine what proportion of each year's investment $k_j(t)\bar{X}_j(t)$ is to be financed from retained earnings—the equivalent of a fully subscribed preemptive issue—and what proportion from outside sources.[19] Similarly, from the point of view of the stockholder, the only significance of dividend policy is to determine how much of the earnings of the firm will accrue to him in the form of cash, and how much in the form of capital gains (or losses). We need hardly add that this explication of the "irrelevance" of dividend policy is in no way dependent, as Durand repeatedly suggests, on any special assumption about the ratio of price to book value.[20]

IV. THE EFFECT OF DIVIDENDS ON STOCK PRICES: THE EMPIRICAL FINDINGS AND THEIR INTERPRETATION

We hope that the discussion in the previous section has been sufficiently explicit, even though the formal proofs have been omitted, so that it no longer requires any great act of faith to accept our original conclusion, *viz.*, that in a world of perfect markets and rational behavior, a firm's dividend policy, other things equal, will have no effect either on the value of the firm or its cost of capital. We can then take the next step and enquire whether this conclusion is a valid or useful approximation in real-world capital markets.[21]

---

[19] Admittedly, this is not what most people have in mind when they bristle at our assertion that dividend policy is a mere detail under perfect capital markets. Their thoughts usually leap immediately to cases of the Montgomery Ward type, in which supposedly everyone but the management felt that a cessation of the hoarding policy and a more generous dividend would have raised the price of the shares. To reason this way, however, is to forget the vital *ceteris paribus*, namely *given the investment policy*. In our terminology, what was at fault was not the dividend policy as such, but the decision to invest in cash (i.e., ρ^* was too low). We doubt, in other words, that the stockholders would have been better served had management decided to finance *the same volume of hoards* not out of retained earnings, but out of new stock issues.

[20] The relation between the market value of a firm and its book value—the latter being defined not in the accounting sense, but in the economic sense of the reproduction cost of a firm's assets—will depend on many things. Some (such as drastic revaluations of a firm's prospects) do not lend themselves readily to further analysis; others (such as the relation of internal yields [the $\rho^*(t)$] to external yields [the ρ_k] can be more systematically explored by means of various specializations of equation (1). If, for example, one assumes that $\rho^*_j(t) = \rho_k$ for all j and all t then, with certain minor supplementary assumptions, one can obtain Durand's case of price equal to book-value throughout the class. This case, however (which stands in roughly the same relation to our general formulation as the "no-rent" case stands to the general theory of supply functions) is merely one of a large number of interesting possibilities.

[21] The issue under discussion—whether and to what extent market valuation is affected by current dividend policy—which is a very real issue, should not be confused with a different and entirely empty issue. This is the question whether what is capitalized is the stream of earnings and earning opportunities ratable to a share or a stream of revenues accruing to the holder of the share and consisting of cash dividends plus capital gains. This is an empty issue for it can be readily shown that both of these views, when properly stated and understood, lead to identical implications; in particular, they both imply that, given the investment policy of the firm, market valuation in perfect markets is independent of current dividend payments or long-run payout policy.

On this issue, Durand cites a number of recent empirical studies and presents some results from his own researches which, he claims, leave "no doubt whatsoever that dividend policy exerts an influence on stock prices and the cost of capital." We have to enter a strong dissent; for, as we warned in our paper [3, p. 287 and 288, n. 43] having precisely the studies he mentions in mind, the existing empirical tests are hopelessly inadequate for determining the effect, if any, of payout policy on stock prices or on the cost of capital.

What is the nature of this supposedly irrefutable evidence? It consists, by and large, of cross-section studies in which price is correlated in various ways with dividends and with *current income*. In general, dividends turn out to have high gross and net correlations with price. From this, it is concluded that our valuation formula (1), which involves earnings but not dividends, cannot be an adequate representation of reality. Note, however, that the earnings variable in our equation is not *current* earnings, X, but $\overline{X}_o$, the *expected value* of the (uncertain) earnings of the assets currently held. This difference may seem a small one at first glance, but it actually holds the main clue to the puzzle.

For if there is one thing we can assert with confidence about the firms in any sample, it is that the earnings they report for any short period like a year are affected by a great many random disturbances and temporary distortions. (See, in this connection, Durand's comment p. 651.) To the extent that these temporary disturbances are recognized as such, they will, of course, be discounted by investors and will not be reflected in market prices. Current income, in other words, is at best only an approximate and often very imperfect measure of $\overline{X}_o$, the "noise-free" earnings potential upon which rational investors would base their valuations. Furthermore, and this is what causes most of the trouble, there are many other variables which, like X, are correlated with (i.e., contain information about) the unobservable but crucial $\overline{X}_o$. In particular, whenever corporations follow a policy of stabilizing dividends—and the excellent studies of Lintner (see, e.g., [2]) leave no doubt that the majority of the publicly held corporations usually do—dividends will contain considerable information about $\overline{X}_o$, possibly even more than X. Hence, when one runs regression of price against dividends, either alone or in combination with X, significant positive coefficients would result even in a world in which we knew for certain that $\overline{X}_o$ alone was being capitalized and that dividend policy had no independent effect whatever on price.

The following example may clarify the nature of the difficulty. Suppose to take the simplest case, that we have two (unlevered) corporations with $\overline{X}_{01} = \overline{X}_{02} = \$5$ per share and with identical long-run payout policies of 40 per cent. Let us suppose that the market price of each is determined exclusively by "noise-free" earnings. If then, the capitalization rate is .1, both shares sell at \$50. Imagine now that firm 1 suffers a run of bad luck during the current year—or merely that its accountant decides to write off some assets—so that current income falls momentarily to \$3. Since management recognizes the situation as temporary, it does not take the drastic step of cutting its dividend which remains \$2. Firm 2, on the other hand, has had some temporary good fortune which pushes its income up to say \$8. Again, since the extra income is in the nature of a windfall, management does not raise the dividend above \$2, since that would not be maintainable given its 40 per cent payout target. Suppose now, given this situation and the data we have generated, we conduct one of the popular tests and see whether dividend policy affects stock prices. If we compare, say, price-earnings ratios with current dividend-payout ratios, we find:

$$\frac{P_1}{X_1} = \frac{50}{\overline{X}_{01} + 2} = \frac{50}{3} = 16.667 \qquad \frac{D_1}{X_1} = \frac{2}{3} = .667$$

$$\frac{P_2}{X_2} = \frac{50}{\overline{X}_{02} + 3} = \frac{50}{8} = 6.25 \qquad \frac{D_2}{X_2} = \frac{2}{8} = .25$$

One would certainly be tempted, from such striking results, to draw the conclusion, which we know to be false in this case, that the payout ratio (dividend policy) does have a marked effect on stock prices.[22] We get these striking results, of course, only because dividends here contain information about $\overline{X}_o$.

It is, of course, one thing to say that the informational content of dividends *could* fully account for the empirical correlations of Durand and others, and quite another to say that it *does*. At the moment, the evidence is insufficient to settle this question, as Durand himself eventually concedes (p. 651). We have some new, and we hope much sharper, tests under development, and we hope others will join us in our attempt to disentangle the two effects. But the task is by no means a simple one and definitive results may be a long time in coming.

But even if more conclusive tests were to provide adequate evidence that the apparent effect of dividends is entirely attributable to the information they convey about long-run earnings prospects, would we not, in any event, be forced to abandon our position that dividend policy has no effect on the cost of capital? That such is not the case can perhaps best be seen by considering another variable frequently used in statistical tests, to wit, the book value per share. Like dividends, this variable shows up well in correlations with P (often even when both D and X are included in the relation). But, unlike D, there seems to be little question that the effect of B is wholly informational. Or, to put it in a slightly different way, few specialists these days would argue for book value, as they do for dividends, that because of the demonstrated high correlations with price, a firm could count on raising the price of its

---

[22] For the benefit of sophisticates who know all about the dangers of spurious ratio correlation, we hasten to point out that it is not the use of ratios per se that makes dividends appear to influence price. As we shall show in more detail in our forthcoming paper, in any sample containing substantial numbers of dividend stabilizers, dividends will, in general, appear significant in relation to X regardless of the form of the test.

shares permanently, simply by writing up its book value, if nothing else changed in the situation. The word *permanently* is the important one in this context. For, in view of the customary informational content of book value, we cannot exclude the possibility that its manipulation will temporarily succeed in misleading the market.

What has been said for book value can be repeated for dividends. Because changes in dividend are usually an indication that other things have changed, they may temporarily affect the market even when other things have, in fact, not changed. Indeed, we are quite ready to believe that as many investors were gulled by Daniel Sickles' watered dividends as by Daniel Drew's watered stocks! All we argue is that changes in dividends will have such an effect only in so far as they are not perceived as manipulations and that the effect will be temporary unless the message is confirmed by deeds.

In summary, pending adequate evidence, we are not willing to accept the proposition that dividend manipulations can be exploited to lower permanently the cost of capital. For this proposition would imply either that investors are incurably irrational or that corporate managers really can fool all of the people all of the time.

V. CONCLUDING REMARKS

We are grateful to Durand for giving us this opportunity to clarify certain points in our paper and to show our approach is actually a good deal more general than he and others seem to have realized. We have been the first to stress that our paper was intended to be no more than the beginning of the attack on the cost of capital and related problems; and we have indicated areas both fundamental and applied in which the implications of our model remain to be totally or partially explored. We are as aware as Durand of the obstacles in the path. But we hope to have shown that Durand's nihilism is premature; that the framework developed in our paper has already permitted some progress; and that it represents at least a promising point of departure for a further systematic attack on the many remaining problems.

REFERENCES

1. L. Barnes, *Your Investments*. American Research Council, Larchmont, N.Y. 1959.
2. J. Lintner, "Distribution of Incomes of Corporations among Dividends, Retained Earnings and Taxes," *Am. Econ. Rev.*, May 1956, **46**, 97–113.
3. F. Modigliani and M. H. Miller, "The Cost of Capital Corporation Finance and the Theory of Investment," *Am. Econ. Rev.*, June 1958, **48**, 261–97.

20. CORPORATE INCOME TAXES AND THE COST OF CAPITAL: A CORRECTION

FRANCO MODIGLIANI
and
MERTON H. MILLER*

Reprinted from *The American Economic Review,* Vol. LIII, No. 3 (June 1963), pp. 433–43, by permission of the authors and the publisher.

The purpose of this communication is to correct an error in our paper "The Cost of Capital, Corporation Finance and the Theory of Investment" (this *Review*, June 1958). In our discussion of the effects of the present method of taxing corporations on the valuation of firms, we said (p. 272):

The deduction of interest in computing taxable corporate profits will prevent the arbitrage process from making the value of all firms in a given class proportional to the expected returns generated by their physical assets. Instead, it can be shown (by the same type of proof used for the original version of Proposition I) that the *market values of firms in each class must be proportional in equilibrium to their expected returns net of taxes (that is, to the sum of the interest paid and expected net stockholder income).* (Italics added.)

The statement in italics, unfortunately, is wrong. For even though one firm may have an *expected* return after taxes (our $\bar{X}^{\tau}$) twice that of another firm in the same risk-equivalent class, it will not be the case that the *actual* return after taxes (our X^{τ}) of the first firm will always be twice that of the second, if the two firms have different degrees of leverage.[1] And since the distribution of returns after taxes of the two firms will not be proportional, there can be no "arbitrage" process which forces their values to be proportional to their expected after-tax returns.[2] In fact, it can be shown—and this time it really will be shown—that "arbitrage" will make values within any class a function

---

* The authors are, respectively, Professor of Industrial Management, School of Industrial Management, Massachusetts Institute of Technology, and Professor of Finance, Graduate School of Business, University of Chicago.

[1] With some exceptions, which will be noted when they occur, we shall preserve here both the notation and the terminology of the original paper. A working knowledge of both on the part of the reader will be presumed.

[2] Barring, of course, the trivial case of universal linear utility functions. Note that in deference to Professor Durand (see his Comment on our paper and our reply, this *Review*, Sept. 1959, *49*, 639–69) we here and throughout use quotation marks when referring to arbitrage.

not only of expected after-tax returns, but of the tax rate and the degree of leverage. This means, among other things, that the tax advantages of debt financing are somewhat greater than we originally suggested and, to this extent, the quantitative difference between the valuations implied by our position and by the traditional view is narrowed. It still remains true, however, that under our analysis the tax advantages of debt are the *only* permanent advantages so that the gulf between the two views in matter of interpretation and policy is as wide as ever.

I. TAXES, LEVERAGE, AND THE PROBABILITY DISTRIBUTION OF AFTER-TAX RETURNS

To see how the distribution of after-tax earnings is affected by leverage, let us again denote by the random variable X the (long-run average) earnings before interest and taxes generated by the currently owned assets of a given firm in some stated risk class, k.[3] From our definition of a risk class it follows that X can be expressed in the form $\overline{X}Z$, where $\overline{X}$ is the expected value of X, and the random variable $Z = X/\overline{X}$, having the same value for all firms in class k, is a drawing from a distribution, say $f_k(Z)$. Hence the random variable X^τ, measuring the after-tax return, can be expressed as:

$$(1) \quad X^\tau = (1-\tau)(X - R) + R = (1 - \tau)X + \tau R = (1 - \tau)\,\overline{X}Z + \tau R$$

where τ is the marginal corporate income tax rate (assumed equal to the average), and R is the interest bill. Since $E(X^\tau) \equiv \overline{X}^\tau = (1 - \tau)\overline{X} + \tau R$ we can substitute $\overline{X}^\tau - \tau R$ for $(1 - \tau)\overline{X}$ in (1) to obtain:

$$(2) \qquad X^\tau = (\overline{X}^\tau - \tau R)Z + \tau R = \overline{X}^\tau\left(1 - \frac{\tau R}{\overline{X}^\tau}\right)Z + \tau R.$$

Thus, if the tax rate is other than zero, the shape of the distribution of X^τ will depend not only on the " scale " of the stream $\overline{X}^\tau$ and on the distribution of Z, but also on the tax rate and the degree of leverage (one measure of which is $R/\overline{X}^\tau$). For example, if $\mathrm{Var}\,(Z) = \sigma^2$, we have:

$$\mathrm{Var}(X^\tau) = \sigma^2(\overline{X}^\tau)^2\left(1 - \tau\,\frac{R}{\overline{X}^\tau}\right)^2$$

---

[3] Thus our X corresponds essentially to the familiar EBIT concept of the finance literature. The use of EBIT and related "income" concepts as the basis of valuation is strictly valid only when the underlying real assets are assumed to have perpetual lives. In such a case, of course, EBIT and "cash flow" are one and the same. This was, in effect, the interpretation of X we used in the original paper and we shall retain it here both to preserve continuity and for the considerable simplification it permits in the exposition. We should point out, however, that the perpetuity interpretation is much less restrictive than might appear at first glance. Before-tax cash flow and EBIT can also safely be equated even where assets have finite lives as soon as these assets attain a steady state age distribution in which annual replacements equal annual depreciation. The subject of finite lives of assets will be further discussed in connection with the problem of the cut-off rate for investment decisions.

implying that for given $\bar{X}^{\tau}$ the variance of after-tax returns is smaller, the higher τ and the degree of leverage.[4]

II. THE VALUATION OF AFTER-TAX RETURNS

Note from equation (1) that, from the investor's point of view, the long-run average stream of after-tax returns appears as a sum of two components: (1) an uncertain stream $(1 - \tau)\bar{X}Z$; and (2) a sure stream τR.[5] This suggests that the equilibrium market value of the combined stream can be found by capitalizing each component separately. More precisely, let ρ^{τ} be the rate at which the market capitalizes the expected returns net of tax of an unlevered company of size $\bar{X}$ in class k, i.e.,

$$\rho^{\tau} = \frac{(1 - \tau)\bar{X}}{V_U} \quad \text{or} \quad V_U = \frac{(1 - \tau)\bar{X}}{\rho^{\tau}}; \text{ }^{6}$$

and let r be the rate at which the market capitalizes the sure streams generated by debts. For simplicity, assume this rate of interest is a constant independent of the size of the debt so that

$$r = \frac{R}{D} \quad \text{or} \quad D = \frac{R}{r}.\text{ }^{7}$$

Then we would expect the value of a levered firm of size $\bar{X}$, with a permanent level of debt D_L in its capital structure, to be given by:

[4] It may seem paradoxical at first to say that leverage *reduces* the variability of outcomes, but remember we are here discussing the variability of total returns, interest plus net profits. The variability of stockholder net profits will, of course, be greater in the presence than in the absence of leverage, though relatively less so than in an otherwise comparable world of no taxes. The reasons for this will become clearer after the discussion in the next section.

[5] The statement that τR—the tax saving per period on the payments—is a sure stream is subject to two qualifications. First, it must be the case that firms can always obtain the tax benefit of their interest deductions either by offsetting them directly against other taxable income in the year incurred; or, in the event no such income is available in any given year, by carrying them backward or forward against past or future taxable earnings; or, in the extreme case, by merger of the firm with (or its sale to) another firm that can utilize the deduction. Second, it must be assumed that the tax rate will remain the same. To the extent that neither of these conditions holds exactly then some uncertainty attaches even to the tax savings, though, of course, it is of a different kind and order from that attaching to the stream generated by the assets. For simplicity, however, we shall here ignore these possible elements of delay or of uncertainty in the tax saving; but it should be kept in mind that this neglect means that the subsequent valuation formulas overstate, if anything, the value of the tax saving for any given permanent level of debt.

[6] Note that here, as in our original paper, we neglect dividend policy and "growth" in the sense of opportunities to invest at a rate of return greater than the market rate of return. These subjects are treated extensively in our paper, "Dividend Policy, Growth and the Valuation of Shares," *Jour. Bus.*, Univ. Chicago, Oct. 1961, 411–33.

[7] Here and throughout, the corresponding formulas when the rate of interest rises with leverage can be obtained merely by substituting $r(L)$ for r, where L is some suitable measure of leverage.

(3)
$$V_L = \frac{(1-\tau)\overline{X}}{\rho^\tau} + \frac{\tau R}{r} = V_U + \tau D_L.^8$$

In our original paper we asserted instead that, within a risk class, market value would be proportional to expected after-tax return $\overline{X}^\tau$ (cf. our original equation [11]), which would imply:

(4)
$$V_L = \frac{\overline{X}^\tau}{\rho^\tau} = \frac{(1-\tau)\overline{X}}{\rho^\tau} + \frac{\tau R}{\rho^\tau} = V_U + \frac{r}{\rho^\tau}\tau D_L.$$

We will now show that if (3) does not hold, investors can secure a more efficient portfolio by switching from relatively overvalued to relatively undervalued firms. Suppose first that unlevered firms are overvalued or that

$$V_L - \tau D_L < V_U.$$

An investor holding m dollars of stock in the unlevered company has a right to the fraction m/V_U of the eventual outcome, i.e., has the uncertain income

$$Y_U = \left(\frac{m}{V_U}\right)(1-\tau)\overline{X}Z.$$

Consider now an alternative portfolio obtained by investing m dollars as follows: (1) the portion,

$$m\left(\frac{S_L}{S_L + (1-\tau)D_L}\right),$$

is invested in the stock of the levered firm, S_L; and (2) the remaining portion,

$$m\left(\frac{(1-\tau)D_L}{S_L + (1-\tau)D_L}\right),$$

is invested in its bonds. The stock component entitles the holder to a fraction,

$$\frac{m}{S_L + (1-\tau)D_L},$$

of the net profits of the levered company or

$$\left(\frac{m}{S_L + (1-\tau)D_L}\right)[(1-\tau)(\overline{X}Z - R_L)].$$

The holding of bonds yields

$$\left(\frac{m}{S_L + (1-\tau)D_L}\right)[(1-\tau)R_L].$$

---

[8] The assumption that the debt is permanent is not necessary for the analysis. It is employed here both to maintain continuity with the original model and because it gives an upper bound on the value of the tax saving. See in this connection footnote 5 and footnote 9.

Hence the total outcome is

$$Y_L = \left(\frac{m}{(S_L + (1 - \tau)D_L)}\right)[(1 - \tau)\bar{X}Z]$$

and this will dominate the uncertain income Y_U if (and only if)

$$S_L + (1 - \tau)D_L \equiv S_L + D_L - \tau D_L \equiv V_L - \tau D_L < V_U.$$

Thus, in equilibrium, V_U cannot exceed $V_L - \tau D_L$, for if it did investors would have an incentive to sell shares in the unlevered company and purchase the shares (and bonds) of the levered company.

Suppose now that $V_L - \tau D_L > V_U$. An investment of m dollars in the stock of the levered firm entitles the holder to the outcome

$$Y_L = (m/S_L)[(1 - \tau)(\bar{X}Z - R_L)]$$
$$= (m/S_L)(1 - \tau)\bar{X}Z - (m/S_L)(1 - \tau)R_L.$$

Consider the following alternative portfolio: (1) borrow an amount (m/S_L) $(1 - \tau)D_L$ for which the interest cost will be $(m/S_L)(1 - \tau)R_L$ (assuming, of course, that individuals and corporations can borrow at the same rate, r); and (2) invest m plus the amount borrowed, i.e.,

$$m + \frac{m(1 - \tau)D_L}{S_L} = m\frac{S_L + (1 - \tau)D_L}{S_L} = (m/S_L)[V_L - \tau D_L]$$

in the stock of the unlevered firm. The outcome so secured will be

$$(m/S_L)\left(\frac{V_L - \tau D_L}{V_U}\right)(1 - \tau)\bar{X}Z.$$

Subtracting the interest charges on the borrowed funds leaves an income of

$$Y_U = (m/S_L)\left(\frac{V_L - \tau D_L}{V_U}\right)(1 - \tau)\bar{X}Z - (m/S_L)(1 - \tau)R_L$$

which will dominate Y_L if (and only if) $V_L - \tau D_L > V_U$. Thus, in equilibrium, both $V_L - \tau D_L > V_U$ and $V_L - \tau D_L < V_U$ are ruled out and (3) must hold.

III. SOME IMPLICATIONS OF FORMULA (3)

To see what is involved in replacing (4) with (3) as the rule of valuation, note first that both expressions make the value of the firm a function of leverage and the tax rate. The difference between them is a matter of the size and source of the tax advantages of debt financing. Under our original formulation, values within a class were strictly proportional to expected earnings after taxes. Hence the tax advantage of debt was due solely to the fact that the deductibility of interest payments implied a higher level of after-tax income for any given level of before-tax earnings (i.e., higher by the amount τR since $\bar{X}^\tau = (1 - \tau)\bar{X} + \tau R$). Under the corrected rule (3), however, there is an additional gain due to the fact that the extra after-tax earnings, τR, represent a sure income in contrast to the uncertain outcome $(1-\tau)\overline{X}$. Hence τR is capitalized at the more favorable certainty rate, $1/r$, rather than at the rate for uncertain streams, $1/\rho^\tau$.[9]

Since the difference between (3) and (4) is solely a matter of the rate at which the tax savings on interest payments are capitalized, the required changes in all formulas and expressions derived from (4) are reasonably straightforward. Consider, first, the before-tax earnings yield, i.e., the ratio of expected earnings before interest and taxes to the value of the firm.[10] Dividing both sides of (3) by V and by $(1 - \tau)$ and simplifying we obtain:

$$(31.c) \qquad \frac{X}{V} = \frac{\rho^\tau}{1-\tau}\left[1 - \tau\frac{D}{V}\right]$$

which replaces our original equation (31) (p. 294). The new relation differs from the old in that the coefficient of D/V in the original (31) was smaller by a factor of r/ρ^τ.

Consider next the after-tax earnings yield, i.e., the ratio of interest payments plus profits after taxes to total market value.[11] This concept was discussed extensively in our paper because it helps to bring out more clearly the differences between our position and the traditional view, and because it facilitates the construction of empirical tests of the two hypotheses about the valuation process. To see what the new equation (3) implies for this yield we need merely substitute $\overline{X}^\tau - \tau R$ for $(1 - \tau)\overline{X}$ in (3) obtaining:

$$(5) \qquad V = \frac{\overline{X}^\tau - \tau R}{\rho^\tau} + \tau D = \frac{\overline{X}^\tau}{\rho^\tau} + \tau\frac{\rho^\tau - r}{\rho^\tau}D,$$

from which it follows that the after-tax earnings yield must be:

$$(11.c) \qquad \frac{\overline{X}^\tau}{V} = \rho^\tau - \tau(\rho^\tau - r)D/V.$$

This replaces our original equation (11) (p. 272) in which we had simply

[9] Remember, however, that in one sense formula (3) gives only an upper bound on the value of the firm since $\tau R/r = \tau D$ is an exact measure of the value of the tax saving only where both the tax rate and the level of debt are assumed to be fixed forever (and where the firm is certain to be able to use its interest deduction to reduce taxable income either directly or via transfer of the loss to another firm). Alternative versions of (3) can readily be developed for cases in which the debt is not assumed to be permanent, but rather to be outstanding only for some specified finite length of time. For reasons of space, we shall not pursue this line of inquiry here beyond observing that the shorter the debt period considered, the closer does the valuation formula approach our original (4). Hence, the latter is perhaps still of some interest if only as a lower bound.

[10] Following usage common in the field of finance we referred to this yield as the "average cost of capital." We feel now, however, that the term "before-tax earnings yield" would be preferable both because it is more immediately descriptive and because it releases the term "cost of capital" for use in discussions of optimal investment policy (in accord with standard usage in the capital budgeting literature).

[11] We referred to this yield as the "after-tax cost of capital." Cf. the previous footnote.

$\bar{X}^\tau/V = \rho^\tau$. Thus, in contrast to our earlier result, the corrected version (11.c) implies that even the after-tax yield is affected by leverage. The predicted rate of decrease of $\bar{X}^\tau/V$ with D/V, however, is still considerably smaller than under the naive traditional view, which, as we showed, implied essentially $\bar{X}^\tau/V = \rho^\tau - (\rho^\tau - r)D/V$. See our equation (17) and the discussion immediately preceding it (p. 277).[12] And, of course, (11.c) implies that the effect of leverage on $\bar{X}^\tau/V$ is *solely* a matter of the deductibility of interest payments whereas, under the traditional view, going into debt would lower the cost of capital regardless of the method of taxing corporate earnings.

Finally, we have the matter of the after-tax yield on *equity* capital, i.e., the ratio of net profits after taxes to the value of the shares.[13] By subtracting D from both sides of (5) and breaking $\bar{X}^\tau$ into its two components—expected net profits after taxes, $\bar{\pi}^\tau$, and interest payments, $R = rD$—we obtain after simplifying:

$$(6) \qquad S = V - D = \frac{\bar{\pi}^\tau}{\rho^\tau} - (1 - \tau)\left(\frac{\rho^\tau - r}{\rho^\tau}\right)D.$$

From (6) it follows that the after-tax yield on equity capital must be:

$$(12.c) \qquad \frac{\bar{\pi}^\tau}{S} = \rho^\tau + (1 - \tau)[\rho^\tau - r]D/S$$

which replaces our original (12), $\bar{\pi}^\tau/S = \rho^\tau + (\rho^\tau - r)D/S$ (p. 272). The new (12.c) implies an increase in the after-tax yield on equity capital as leverage increases which is smaller than that of our original (12) by a factor of $(1 - \tau)$. But again, the linear increasing relation of the corrected (12.c) is still fundamentally different from the naive traditional view which asserts the cost of equity capital to be completely independent of leverage (at least as long as leverage remains within "conventional" industry limits).

IV. TAXES AND THE COST OF CAPITAL

From these corrected valuation formulas we can readily derive corrected measures of the cost of capital in the capital budgeting sense of the minimum prospective yield an investment project must offer to be just worth undertaking from the standpoint of the present stockholders. If we interpret earnings stream as perpetuities, as we did in the original paper, then we actually have two equally good ways of defining this minimum yield: either by the required increase in before-tax earnings, $d\bar{X}$, or by the required increase in earnings net of taxes, $d\bar{X}(1 - \tau)$.[14] To conserve space, however, as well as to

---

[12] The i_k^* of (17) is the same as ρ^τ in the present context, each measuring the ratio of net profits to the value of the shares (and hence of the whole firm) in an unlevered company of the class.

[13] We referred to this yield as the "after-tax cost of equity capital." Cf. footnote 9.

[14] Note that we use the term "earnings net of taxes" rather than "earnings after taxes." We feel that to avoid confusion the latter term should be reserved to describe what will actually appear in the firm's accounting statements, namely the net cash flow including the

maintain continuity with the original paper, we shall concentrate here on the before-tax case with only brief footnote references to the net-of-tax concept.

Analytically, the derivation of the cost of capital in the above sense amounts to finding the minimum value of $d\overline{X}/dI$ for which $dV = dI$, where I denotes the level of new investment.[15] By differentiating (3) we see that:

$$(7) \qquad \frac{dV}{dI} = \frac{1 - \tau}{\rho_\tau} \frac{d\overline{X}}{dI} + \tau \frac{dD}{dI} \geq 1 \quad \text{if} \quad \frac{d\overline{X}}{dI} \geq \frac{1 - \tau \dfrac{dD}{dI}}{1 - \tau} \rho^\tau.$$

Hence the before-tax required rate of return cannot be defined without reference to financial policy. In particular, for an investment considered as being financed entirely by new equity capital $dD/dI = 0$ and the required rate of return or marginal cost of equity financing (neglecting flotation costs) would be:

$$\rho^S = \frac{\rho^\tau}{1 - \tau}.$$

This result is the same as that in the original paper (see equation [32], (p. 294) and is applicable to any other sources of financing where the remuneration to the suppliers of capital is not deductible for tax purposes. It applies, therefore, to preferred stock (except for certain partially deductible issues of public utilities) and would apply also to retained earnings were it not for the favorable tax treatment of capital gains under the personal income tax.

For investments considered as being financed entirely by new debt capital $dI = dD$ and we find from (7) that:

$$(33.c) \qquad \rho^D = \rho^\tau$$

which replaces our original equation (33) in which we had:

$$(33) \qquad \rho^D = \rho^S - \frac{\tau}{1 - \tau} r.$$

Thus for borrowed funds (or any other tax-deductible source of capital) the marginal cost or before-tax required rate of return is simply the market rate of capitalization for net of tax unlevered streams and is thus independent of both the tax rate and the interest rate. This required rate is lower than that implied

---

tax savings on the interest (our $\overline{X}^\tau$). Since financing sources cannot in general be allocated to particular investments (see below), the after-tax or accounting concept is not useful for capital budgeting purposes, although it can be extremely useful for valuation equations as we saw in the previous section.

[15] Remember that when we speak of the minimum required yield on an investment we are referring in principle only to investments which increase the *scale* of the firm. That is, the new assets must be in the same "class" as the old. See in this connection, J. Hirshleifer, "Risk, the Discount Rate and Investment Decisions," *Am. Econ. Rev.*, May 1961, 51, 112–20 (especially pp. 119–20). See also footnote 16.

by our original (33), but still considerably higher than that implied by the traditional view (see pp. 276–77 of our paper) under which the before-tax cost of borrowed funds is simply the interest rate, r.

Having derived the above expressions for the marginal costs of debt and equity financing it may be well to warn readers at this point that these expressions represent at best only the hypothetical extremes insofar as costs are concerned and that neither is directly usable as a cut-off criterion for investment planning. In particular, care must be taken to avoid falling into the famous "Liquigas" fallacy of concluding that if a firm intends to float a bond issue in some given year then its cut-off rate should be set that year at ρ^D; while, if the next issue is to be an equity one, the cut-off is ρ^S. The point is, of course, that no investment can meaningfully be regarded as 100 per cent equity financed if the firm makes any use of debt capital—and most firms do, not only for the tax savings, but for many other reasons having nothing to do with "cost" in the present static sense (cf. our original paper pp. 292–93). And no investment can meaningfully be regarded as 100 per cent debt financed when lenders impose strict limitations on the maximum amount a firm can borrow relative to its equity (and when most firms actually plan on normally borrowing less than this external maximum so as to leave themselves with an emergency reserve of unused borrowing power). Since the firm's long-run capital structure will thus contain both debt and equity capital, investment planning must recognize that, over the long pull, *all* of the firm's assets are really financed by a mixture of debt and equity capital even though only one kind of capital may be raised in any particular year. More precisely, if L^* denotes the firm's long-run "target" debt ratio (around which its actual debt ratio will fluctuate as it "alternately" floats debt issues and retires them with internal or external equity) then the firm can assume, to a first approximation at least, that for any particular investment $dD/dI = L^*$. Hence, the relevant marginal cost of capital for investment planning, which we shall here denote by ρ^*, is:

$$\rho^* = \frac{1 - \tau_L^*}{1 - \tau} \rho^\tau = \rho^S - \frac{\tau}{1 - \tau} \rho^D L^* = \rho^S (1 - L^*) + \rho^D L^*.$$

That is, the appropriate cost of capital for (repetitive) investment decisions over time is, to a first approximation, a weighted average of the costs of debt and equity financing, the weights being the proportions of each in the "target" capital structure.[16]

---

[16] From the formulas in the text one can readily derive corresponding expressions for the required net-of-tax yield, or net-of-tax cost of capital for any given financing policy. Specifically, let $\bar{\rho}(L)$ denote the required net-of-tax yield for investment financed with a proportion of debt $L = dD/dI$. (More generally L denotes the proportion financed with tax deductible sources of capital.) Then from (7) we find:

$$(8) \qquad\qquad \bar{\rho}(L) = (1 - \tau)\frac{d\bar{X}}{dI} = (1 - L\tau)\rho^\tau$$

and the various costs can be found by substituting the appropriate value for L. In particular,

V. SOME CONCLUDING OBSERVATIONS

Such, then, are the major corrections that must be made to the various formulas and valuation expressions in our earlier paper. In general, we can say that the force of these corrections has been to increase somewhat the estimate of the tax advantages of debt financing under our model and consequently to reduce somewhat the quantitative difference between the estimates of the effects of leverage under our model and under the naive traditional view. It may be useful to remind readers once again that the existence of a tax advantage for debt financing—even the larger advantage of the corrected version—does not necessarily mean that corporations should at all times seek to use the maximum possible amount of debt in their capital structures. For one thing, other forms of financing, notably retained earnings, may in some circumstances be cheaper still when the tax status of investors under the personal income tax is taken into account. More important, there are, as we pointed out, limitations imposed by lenders (see pp. 292–93), as well as many other dimensions (and kinds of costs) in real-world problems of financial strategy which are not fully comprehended within the framework of static equilibrium models, either our own or those of the traditional variety. These additional considerations, which are typically grouped under the rubric of " the need for preserving flexibility," will normally imply the maintenance by the corporation of a substantial reserve of untapped borrowing power. The tax advantage of debt may well tend to lower the optimal size of that reserve, but it is hard to believe that advantages of the size contemplated under our model could justify any substantial reduction, let alone their complete elimination. Nor do the data indicate that there has in fact been a substantial increase in the use of debt (except relative to preferred stock) by the corporate sector during the recent high tax years.[17]

---

if we substitute in this formula the " target " leverage ratio, L^*, we obtain:

$$\bar{\rho}^* \equiv \bar{\rho}(L^*) = (1 - \tau L^*)\rho^\tau$$

and $\bar{\rho}^*$ measures the average net-of-tax cost of capital in the sense described above.

Although the before-tax and the net-of-tax approaches to the cost of capital provide equally good criteria for investment decisions when assets are assumed to generate perpetual (i.e., nondepreciating) streams, such is not the case when assets are assumed to have finite lives (even when it is also assumed that the firm's assets are in a steady state age distribution so that our X or EBIT is approximately the same as the net cash flow before taxes). See footnote 3 above. In the latter event, the correct method for determining the desirability of an investment would be, in principle, to discount the net-of-tax stream at the net-of-tax cost of capital. Only under this net-of-tax approach would it be possible to take into account the deductibility of depreciation (and also to choose the most advantageous depreciation policy for tax purposes). Note that we say that the net-of-tax approach is correct " in principle " because, strictly speaking, nothing in our analysis (or anyone else's for that matter) has yet established that it is indeed legitimate to " discount " an uncertain stream. One can hope that subsequent research will show the analogy to discounting under the certainty case is a valid one; but, at the moment, this is still only a hope.

[17] See, e.g., Merton H. Miller, "The Corporate Income Tax and Corporate Financial Policies," in *Staff Reports to the Commission on Money and Credit* (forthcoming).

As to the differences between our modified model and the traditional one, we feel that they are still large in quantitative terms and still very much worth trying to detect. It is not only a matter of the two views having different implications for corporate financial policy (or even for national tax policy). But since the two positions rest on fundamentally different views about investor behavior and the functioning of the capital markets, the results of tests between them may have an important bearing on issues ranging far beyond the immediate one of the effects of leverage on the cost of capital.

21. A RE-EXAMINATION OF THE MODIGLIANI-MILLER THEOREM

JOSEPH E. STIGLITZ*

Reprinted from *The American Economic Review,* Vol. LIX, No. 5 (December 1969), pp. 784–93, by permission of the author and the publisher.

In their classic paper of 1958, Franco Modigliani and Merton H. Miller demonstrated that the cost of capital for a firm was independent of the debt-equity ratio [13]. Although much of the subsequent discussion has focused on the realism of particular assumptions [3] [7], there have been few attempts to delineate exactly the class of assumptions under which the M-M theorem obtains.[1] In particular, five limitations of the M-M proof may be noted:

1. It depended on the existence of risk classes.
2. The use of risk classes seemed to imply objective rather than subjective probability distributions over the possible outcomes.

* Associate professor, Cowles Foundation, Yale University. This is a revised version of Cowles Foundation Discussion Paper No. 242, presented at the December 1967 meetings of the Econometric Society. The research described in this paper was carried out under grants from the National Science Foundation and from the Ford Foundation. I am deeply indebted to D. Cass, A. Klevorick, M. Miller, and W. Nordhaus for extensive discussions on these problems and detailed comments on a previous draft.

[1] Exceptions are the work of Hirschleifer [9] [10] and Robichek and Meyers [19], who used the Arrow–Debreu model (which assumes at least as many securities as states of the world) and the doctoral dissertation of G. Pye [18]. More recently Sher [21] has concerned himself with some of the difficulties raised by bankruptcy. For other general equilibrium portfolio (stock-market) models, see Sharpe [20], Lintner [11], Mossin [17], and Diamond [6].

3. It was based on partial equilibrium rather than general equilibrium analysis.
4. It was not clear whether the theorem held only for competitive markets.
5. Except under special circumstances, it was not clear how the possibility of firm bankruptcy affected the validity of the theorem.

In Section 1, we show in the context of a general equilibrium state preference model that the M-M theorem holds under much more general conditions than those assumed in their original study. The validity of the theorem does not depend on the existence of risk classes, on the competitiveness of the capital market, or on the agreement of individuals about the probability distribution of outcomes.[2]

The two assumptions which do appear to be important for our proof are (a) individuals can borrow at the same market rate of interest as firms and (b) there is no bankruptcy.[3] But it is these assumptions which appear to be the center of much of the criticism of the M-M analysis. In Section II, we show that the M-M results may still be valid even if there are limitations on individual borrowing, and in Section III, we show that the possibility of bankruptcy raises more serious problems, although the M-M theorem can still be shown to hold under somewhat more stringent conditions.

I. THE BASIC THEOREM

Consider a firm whose gross returns, X (before paying bondholders but after paying all non-capital factors of production) are uncertain. We can consider X as a function of the state of the world θ. One dollar invested in a perfectly safe bond yields a gross return of r^*, so that $r^* - 1$ is the market rate of interest. If there is any chance of bankruptcy, the nominal rate $\hat{r}$ which the firm must pay on its bonds will depend on the number issued. If principal payments plus interest exceed gross profits, X, the firm goes bankrupt, and the gross profits are divided among the bondholders.[4] Thus the gross return on a dollar invested in the bonds of the firm depends on state θ.

---

[2] Except that they must agree that there is zero probability of bankruptcy. See discussion in text.

[3] It should be clear that these assumptions are not completely independent. Presumably, one of the most important reasons individuals cannot borrow at the same rate as firms is that there is a higher probability of default.

[4] Throughout the discussion we limit ourselves to a two-period model. In a two-period model, a firm either makes its interest payments or goes bankrupt. In a multi-period model, the firm can, in addition, defer the interest or principal payments. If there is a positive probability of such deferral, the market will force the firm to pay a higher nominal rate of interest. If there are large transaction costs involved in bankruptcy or deferral, the M-M theorem would not hold. Throughout the discussion we shall assume that there are no flotation costs and no taxes.

$$\text{(1)} \qquad \bar{r}(\theta) = \begin{cases} \hat{r} & \text{if } \hat{r}\, B \le X(\theta) \\ \dfrac{X(\theta)}{B} & \text{if } \hat{r}\, B \ge X(\theta). \end{cases}$$

Earnings per dollar invested in equity in state θ are given by

$$\text{(2)} \qquad e(\theta) = \begin{cases} [X(\theta) - \hat{r}B]/E & \text{if } \hat{r}B \le X(\theta) \\ 0 & \text{if } \hat{r}B \ge X(\theta) \end{cases}$$

where E is the value of the firm's equity. The value of the firm is

$$\text{(3)} \qquad V = E + B.$$

Individuals will be assumed to evaluate alternative portfolios in terms of their income patterns across the states of nature.

We now prove the following proposition.

Assume there is no bankruptcy and individuals can borrow and lend at the market rate of interest. If there exists a general equilibrium with each firm having a particular debt-equity ratio and a particular value, then there exists another general equilibrium solution for the economy with any firm having any other debt-equity ratio but with the value of all firms and the market rate of interest unchanged.

Proof. Let w^j be the jth individual's wealth, E_i^j, the value of his shares of the ith firm, B^j the number of bonds he owns.[5] Assume the ith firm, whose value is V_i, issues B_i bonds. The jth individual's budget constraint may be written

$$\text{(4)} \qquad w_j = \sum_i E_i^j + B^j.$$

If we let $\alpha_i^j = E_i^j/E_i$, the share of the ith firm's equity owned by the jth individual, (4) becomes

$$\text{(5)} \qquad w^j = \sum_i \alpha_i^j E_i + B^j.$$

Then his income in state θ may be written

$$\text{(6)} \qquad Y^j(\theta) = \sum_{i=1}^{n} (X_i - r^*B_i)\alpha_i^j + r^*\!\left(w^j - \sum_{i=1}^{n} \alpha_i^j(V_i - B_i)\right)$$

$$= \sum_{i=1}^{n} X_i \alpha_i^j + r^*\!\left(w^j - \sum_{i=1}^{n} \alpha_i^j V_i\right).$$

If, as B_i changes, V_i remains unchanged, the individual's opportunity set does not change, and the set of α_i^j which maximizes the individual's utility is unchanged. If

[5] By convention, one bond costs one dollar.

$$\sum_j \alpha_i^j = 1$$

before, i.e., demand for shares equalled supply of shares, it still does. The total net demand for bonds is

$$\sum_i \left(w^j - \sum_i \alpha_i^j (V_i - B_i) \right) + \sum_i B_i = \sum_j w^j - \sum_i V_i.$$

If the market was in equilibrium initially,

$$\sum_j w^j - \sum_i V_i = 0,$$

i.e., excess demand equalled zero. If as the debt-equity ratio changes, all V_i remain unchanged, excess demand remains at zero.

An alternative way of seeing this is the following. We may rewrite (6) as

$$(6') \qquad Y^j(\theta) = \sum_i e_i(\theta) E_i^j + r^* \left(w^j - \sum_{i=1}^n E_i^j \right).$$

Assume now that the first firm, say, issues no bonds. If we let carets denote the values of the various variables in this situation, the opportunity set is given by

$$(6'') \qquad \hat{Y}^j(\theta) = \sum_i \hat{e}_i(\theta) \hat{E}_i^j + \hat{r}^* \left(w^j - \sum_i \hat{E}_i^j \right).$$

Assume $r^* = \hat{r}^*$, $E_i = \hat{E}_i$, $i \geq 2$. Then from (2), $e_i(\theta) = \hat{e}_i(\theta)$, $i \geq 2$. If $\hat{E}_1 = E_1 + B_1$, then the opportunity sets described by (6') and (6'') are identical. To see this, assume that for each dollar of equity he owned in the first firm in the initial situation, the individual borrows B_1/E_1 in addition to B^j

$$\text{so } \hat{B}^j = B^j + E_1^j \frac{B_1}{E_1}.$$

With the proceeds of the loan he increases his holdings of equities in the first firm, so

$$(7) \qquad \hat{E}_1^j = E_1^j + E_1^j \frac{B_1}{E_1} = E_1^j \left(\frac{V_1}{E_1} \right).$$

His income in state θ is then given by

$$(8) \qquad \begin{aligned} \hat{Y}^j(\theta) &= \frac{X_1 E_1^j}{E_1} + \sum_{i=2}^n e_i(\theta) E_i^j + r^* \left(w^j - \sum_{i=2}^n E_i^j - \frac{E_1^j V_1}{E_1} \right) \\ &= \left(\frac{X_1 - r^* B_1}{E_1} \right) E_1^j + \sum_{i=2}^n e_i(\theta) E_i^j + r^* \left(w^j - \sum_{i=1}^n E_i^j \right) \end{aligned}$$

which is identical to (6').

Since his opportunity set has not been changed as a result of the change in the debt-equity ratio of the firm, if he was maximizing his utility in the initial situation, the optimal allocation in the new situation is identical to that in the initial situation with the one modification given above.

We now need to show that the markets for the firm's equities and the market for bonds will clear. Summing (7) over all individuals, we obtain

$$\sum_j \hat{E}_1^j = \frac{V_1}{E_1} \sum_j E_1^j.$$

Thus the demand for equities has increased by a factor V_1/E_1. But since $\hat{E}_1/E_1 = V_1/E_1$, the supply has increased by exactly the same proportion, so if demand equalled supply before it also does now. Similarly, the increase in the demand for bonds by individuals equals $(B_1/E_1) \sum E_1^j = B_1$. But this exactly equals the decrease in the demand for bonds by the first firm.

It should be emphasized that in this proof, $X(\theta)$ is subjectively determined; moreover no assumptions about the size of firms, the source of the uncertainty, and the existence of risk classes have been made. The only restriction on the individual's behavior is that he evaluates alternative portfolios in terms of the income stream they generate. The two crucial assumptions were (a) all individuals agree that for all firms $X_i(\theta) > r^*B$ for all θ (see Section III); and (b) individuals can borrow and lend at the market rate of interest. This assumption is considerably weaker than the assumpton of a competitive capital market, since no assumption about the number of firms has been made: the market rate of interest need not be invariant to the supply of bonds by any single firm.

II. LIMITATIONS ON INDIVIDUAL BORROWING

One of the main objections raised to the M-M analysis is that individuals cannot borrow at the same rate of interest as firms. First, it should be noted (see [13]) that the analysis does not require that individuals actually borrow from the market, but only that they change their holdings of bonds. A problem can arise then only if an individual has *no* bonds in his portfolio.

Although the requirement that all individuals hold bonds does place restrictions on the possible debt-equity ratios of different firms, there still need not be an optimal debt-equity ratio for any single firm. Assume we have some general equilibrium situation where $B^i \geq 0$ for all j. Then so long as B_i satisfy the inequalities.

(9) $$\sum_i \alpha_i^j B_i \geq w^j - \sum_i \alpha_i^j V_i \quad \text{for all } j$$

all individuals will be lenders. If there were two firms, the constraints (9) would imply that (B_1, B_2) lie in the shaded area shown in Figure 1. For any pair of (B_1, B_2) in the region, there will exist a general equilibrium in which the values of both firms are identical to that in the original situation.

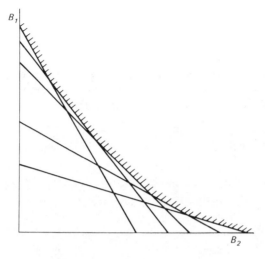

Figure 1

So far, none of our results have depended on the existence of risk classes.[6] The following two results depend on more than one firm having the same pattern of returns across the states of nature.

We shall first show that if there are two (or more) firms with the same pattern of returns and individuals can sell short, then, the two firms must have the same value, independent of the debt-equity ratio.

We follow M-M in assuming for simplicity that one of the two firms has no outstanding debt, so $V_1 = E_1$. The second firm issues B_2 bonds, so $V_2 = B_2 + E_2$.

Consider first an individual who owns α_1 of the shares of the first firm, yielding an income pattern $\alpha_1 X_1(\theta)$. If instead he purchases α_1 of the shares of the second firm, at a cost of $\alpha_1 E_2$, and buys $\alpha_1 B_2$ bonds, his income in state θ is $\alpha_1(X_2(\theta) - r^*B_2) + \alpha_1 r^*B_2 = \alpha_1 X_2(\theta)$ which is identical to his income in state θ in the previous situation. But the cost of purchasing α_1 of the shares of the first company is $\alpha_1 V_1$ which is *greater* than $\alpha_1(E_2 + B_2) = \alpha_1 V_2$ if $V_1 > V_2$. Accordingly, if V_1 were greater than V_2, all holders of shares in the first company would sell their shares and purchase shares in the second firm, driving the value of the second firm up and that of the first down. Now consider an individual who wishes to lend money. If he sells short α_2 of the shares of the second firm and buys α_2 of the shares of the first firm, he receives a perfectly safe return of[7] $-\alpha_2(X_2 - r^*B_2) + \alpha_2 X_1 = \alpha_2 r^*B_2$ at a net cost of $-\alpha_2(V_2 - B_2) + \alpha_2 V_1$ so the return per dollar is

---

[6] Two firms, i and j are in the same risk class if $X_i(\theta) = \lambda X_j(\theta)$ for all θ. In the remainder of the discussion we shall assume for convenience, that $\lambda = 1$.

[7] As usual, we assume no transactions costs and that there is no cash requirement or short sales. (See fn. 9.)

$$r^* \frac{B_2}{V_1 - (V_2 - B_2)} = r^* \frac{1}{1 + \dfrac{V_1 - V_2}{B_2}}$$

If $V_1 < V_2$, the individual can obtain a perfectly safe return in excess of r^*. It follows immediately that equilibrium in the capital market requires $V_1 = V_2$.[8] Similar arguments can be used to show the following.

If there are three or more firms in the same risk class, and the firms with the highest and lowest debt-equity ratios have the same value, then the value of all other firms must be the same.

This is true whether individuals can borrow or can sell securities short. This result rules out the possibility of a U-shaped curve relating the value of the firm to the debt-equity ratio.[9]

III. BANKRUPTCY

Bankruptcy presents a problem for the usual proofs of the M-M theorem on two accounts: first, it means that the nominal rate of interest which the firm must pay on its bonds will increase as the number of bonds increases. (M-M have treated the case where it increases at exactly the same rate for all firms and individuals.) Second, if a firm goes bankrupt, it is no longer possible for an individual to replicate the exact patterns of returns, except if he can buy on margin, using the security as collateral; and if he defaults, he only forfeits the security and none of his other assets. To see this, consider the two alternative policies considered in Section I; in the one case, the firm issues no bonds (hence no chance of default) and in the other it issues $\hat{B}$ bonds. We have shown how the individual by buying stock on margin in the latter case can exactly replicate the returns in the former situation in those states where the firm does not go bankrupt if the value of the firm is the same in the two

---

[8] This proof has the advantage that no restrictions on the sign of $X(\theta)$ need be made. Although the case of $X(\theta) < 0$ is not very interesting from an economic point of view, some authors (e.g. [21]) have drawn attention to the difficulties which arise in the original M-M proof when $X(\theta) < 0$.

[9] Taxes and bankruptcy may alter this conclusion. Recently, Baumol and Malkeil [2] have argued that if there are costs of transactions, the levered company may have a higher value than the unlevered company. They argue that if, in order to undertake the arbitrage operations required by the M-M analysis, the individual had to borrow, the total value of transactions would be greater than if the company provided the desired leverage. If there are sizeable transactions costs, in order for the net income from the two firms to be the same, the levered company must have a higher value than the unlevered firm. Transactions costs cannot be adequately analyzed in terms of the two-period model that they (and we) use, but even in the context of a two-period model, it is not clear that their point is correct. If the individual has bonds in his portfolio, or if there are two companies, one with high leverage and one with low leverage, the individual can simply change his portfolio composition.

situations. But if the firm goes bankrupt in some state, θ', in the one case his return is zero, while in the other his return per dollar invested is

$$\frac{X(\theta')}{V}\left(1 + \frac{\hat{B}}{\hat{E}}\right) - \hat{r}\frac{\hat{B}}{\hat{E}} < 0.$$

If, however, he can forfeit the security then his return will again be zero.

Of course, if the firm has a positive probability of going bankrupt, it will have to pay a higher nominal rate of interest. But if the individual is to use the security as collateral, he, too, will have to pay a higher nominal rate of interest. And indeed, it is clear that the two will be exactly the same, since the pattern of returns on the bonds in bankruptcy will be the same. Thus, we have shown that

if a firm has a positive probability of going bankrupt, and an individual can borrow using those securities as collateral (so that if his return from the securities is less than his borrowings, he can forfeit the securities) the value of the firm is invariant to the debt-equity ratio.

It should be noted that the validity of this proposition does not require 100 percent margins. The required margin is only $\hat{B}/V$.

Individuals may, of course, not be able to make the limited liability arrangements or to obtain the level of margin required by the above analysis. Then, a firm by pursuing alternative debt-equity policies may be able to offer patterns of returns which the individual cannot obtain in any other manner (i.e., by purchasing shares in one or more other firms), and the value of the firm may consequently vary as the firm changes its debt-equity ratio. In the following subsections, we consider some special situations, in which M-M results may still be valid, even though there is a finite probability of bankruptcy.

RISK CLASSES

If there are a large number of firms in the same risk class, then potentially they can all supply the same pattern of returns. If all firms maximize their value, then in market equilibrium all firms will have the same value.[10] Firms may have different debt-equity ratios and the same value for a number of reasons. For instance, assume that some individuals, for some reason or other, prefer a low debt equity-ratio, and some prefer a high debt-equity ratio. Then, some firms may have a high debt-equity ratio, some a low one. If one firm observes another firm in the same risk class with a different debt-equity ratio but a higher value, it will change its debt-equity ratio. Thus the observation that all firms in a given risk class have the same value but possibly different debt-equity ratios can be taken as evidence that firms are value

---

[10] Recall that we have assumed for expositional convenience that $X_j(\theta) = X_i(\theta)$ for all firms in the risk class.

maximizers and are in market equilibrium. It is not necessarily evidence that the arbitrage activities described by Modigliani and Miller have occurred, or that the value of the firm would be the same at some debt-equity ratio other than those actually observed.

Assume the market is in equilibrium, with $V = \rho EX$ for all members of the risk class. The securities sold by a firm are completely described by the risk class and the debt-equity ratio. A new, small firm is created, belonging to the same risk class, with mean return $\tilde{X}$. If it chooses a debt-equity ratio used by other firms in the same risk class, the price of its shares must be the same as those of the other firms (since they are identical) so its value will be $\tilde{X}\rho$. But, if it chooses some other debt-equity ratio, its value may be lower (if, for instance, there is a positive probability of bankruptcy).[11]

MEAN-VARIANCE ANALYSIS AND THE SEPARATION THEOREM

In this subsection we consider the special case where all individuals evaluate alternative income patterns in terms of their mean and variance. For simplicity, let us assume that only the first firm issues enough bonds to go bankrupt. If all individuals agree on the probability distribution of returns for each firm, it can be shown that the

...total market value of any stock in equilibrium is equal to the *capitalization* at the *risk-free interest rate r^**, of the *certainty equivalent*...of its uncertain *aggregate dollar return*;...the difference...between the expected value of these returns and their certainty equivalent is *proportional* for each company to *its aggregate risk* represented by the *sum* of the *variance* of these returns and their total covariance with those of all other stocks, and the factor of proportionality is the *same* for *all* companies in the market. [11, pp. 26–27].

This implies that

$$(10) \quad E_i + B_i = \left\{ \bar{X} - k \sum_{j=1}^{n} \mathscr{E}(X_i - \bar{X}_i)(X_j - \bar{X}_j) \right\} \Big/ r^* \qquad i = 2, \ldots, n$$

$$(11) \quad E_1 = \left\{ \bar{Z} - k \sum_{j=1}^{n} \mathscr{E}(Z - \bar{Z})(X^j - \bar{X}j) \right\} \Big/ r^*$$

$$(12) \quad B_1 = \left\{ \tilde{r}B_1 - k \sum_{j=1}^{n} \mathscr{E}(\tilde{r} - \bar{\tilde{r}}) B_1(X_j - X_j) \right\} \Big/ r^*$$

where $\mathscr{E}$ is the expectations operator,

$$Z = \max(X_1 - \tilde{r}B_1, 0), \qquad \mathscr{E}Z = \bar{Z},$$
$$\mathscr{E}X_j = \bar{X}_j, \qquad \mathscr{E}\tilde{r} = \bar{\tilde{r}},$$

and

$$k = r^* \left(\sum_i (X_i - \bar{X}_i) \Big/ \sum_i \sum_j \mathscr{E}(X_i - \bar{X}_i)(X_j - \bar{X}_j) \right).$$

[11] This also may occur with taxes if interest payments are tax deductible and if capital gains are treated preferentially. See [8].

Then adding B_1 and E_1, ((11) and (12)), we obtain

$$V_1 = E_1 + B_1 = \left\{ \overline{X}_1 - k \sum_{j=1}^{n} \mathscr{E}(X_1 - \overline{X}_1)(X_j - \overline{X}_j) \right\} \bigg/ r^*$$

independent of the debt-equity ratio.

The intuitive reason for this should be clear: it is well-known that if all individuals agree on the probability distribution of the risky assets, if there exists a safe asset, and if individuals evaluate income patterns in terms of mean and variance, the ratio in which different risky assets are purchased will be the same for all individuals, i.e. all the relevant market opportunities can be provided by the safe asset and a single mutual fund which (in market equilibrium) will contain all the risky assets, including the risky bonds. More generally, whenever the ratio in which different risky assets are purchased is the same for all individuals, then the M-M theorem will be true even with bankruptcy. For a complete discussion of the conditions under which the separation theorem obtains, see Cass and Stiglitz [4].

If, however, (a) all individuals do not agree on the probability distribution of $X_i(\theta)$ or, (b) the conditions under which the separation theorem is valid do not obtain, then the value of the firm will in general depend on the debt-equity ratio.[12]

ARROW-DEBREU SECURITIES

Arrow [1] and Debreu [5] have formulated a model of general equilibrium under uncertainty in which individuals can buy and sell promises to pay if a given state of the world occurs. See also Hirshleifer [10]. A stock market security and a bond can be viewed as a bundle of these Arrow-Debreu

---

[12] For then, issuing a risky bond (a high debt-equity ratio) changes the relevant market opportunities available to the individual. For the M-M result to be valid, the debt-equity ratio can have no real effects on the economy. But it is easy to show that the assumptions (a) marginal utility of income in each state of nature is independent of the debt-equity ratio, and (b) the value of the firm is independent of the debt-equity ratio are in general inconsistent with the first order conditions for expected utility maximization being satisfied by all individuals (if bankruptcy may occur). To see this, observe that if an individual chooses his portfolio to maximize $\mathscr{E}U(Y(\theta))$, where $U'' < 0$, then a necessary and sufficient condition for the optimal allocation (assuming short sales are allowed) may be written $\mathscr{E}U'e_i = \mathscr{E}U'r^*$, or from (2), $[\mathscr{E}U'(X_j - \hat{r}_jB_j)/\mathscr{E}U'r^* = E_j$ where $\mathscr{S}$ is defined as the set of states of nature for which $X_j(\theta) \geq \hat{r}_jB_j$. Assume $U'(Y(\theta))$ is invariant for all θ and for all individuals to the jth firm's debt-equity ratio. Then,

$$dE_j/dB_j = -\frac{\hat{r}_j}{r^*}\left(1 + \frac{d \ln \hat{r}_j}{d \ln B_j}\right)(\mathscr{E}U'/\mathscr{E}U');$$

and if the value of the firm is to be unchanged, $dE_j/dB_j = -1$. But unless all individuals have identical utility functions *and* indentical assessments of the probability of bankruptcy ($\mathscr{E}U'/\mathscr{E}U'$) will differ for different individuals, so $dE_j/dB_j = -1$ only if marginal utilities in some states of nature change for some individuals.

It should be observed that when the actions of a firm can change the opportunity set, there is no reason that firms necessarily, will maximize market value.

securities. If there is a sufficient number of different firms, equal to or greater than the number of states of nature, then the market opportunities available to the individual (by purchasing or selling short different amounts of the market securities) are identical to those of a corresponding Arrow-Debreu market. If a promise to pay one dollar in state θ has a price $p^*(\theta)$,[13] then the value of the firm's equity is

$$E = \sum_{\mathscr{S}} (X(\theta) - \hat{r}B)p^*(\theta).$$

If

$$\hat{r} = \left[1 - \sum_{\mathscr{S}'} \frac{X(\theta)}{B} p^*(\theta)\right] \Big/ \sum_{\mathscr{S}} p^*(\theta)$$

where $\mathscr{S} \equiv \{\theta \,|\, X(\theta) \geq \hat{r}B\}$, i.e. the states of nature in which the firm does not go bankrupt, and $\mathscr{S}' \equiv \{\theta \,|\, X(\theta) < \hat{r}B\}$, then

$$E = \sum_{\theta} X(\theta)p^*(\theta) - B$$

i.e.

$$V = E + B = \sum_{\theta} X(\theta)p^*(\theta)$$

independent of the debt-equity ratio.

Three observations are in order: First, individuals do not need to agree on the probability of different states of nature occurring, i.e. they may disagree on the probability distribution of the returns to any firm.[14] Second, if there are fewer firms than states of nature, whether there are as many securities as states of nature is a function of the debt-equity ratio. If there are four states of nature and two firms, and if neither firm issues enough securities to go bankrupt, then there will only be three securities, but if one of the firms goes bankrupt, there will be four. Although the latter situation will be Pareto optimal (the marginal rate of substitution between consumption in any two states identical for all individuals), the value of the firm which goes bankrupt may be larger or smaller in the former situation than in the latter.[15]

Third, if we take literally the Arrow–Debreu definition of a state of nature, there undoubtedly will be more states of nature than firms. Yet, in some sense, most of these states are not very different from one another. For example,

[13] If there are no Arrow–Debreu securities on the market, $p^*(\theta)$ is the net cost to the individual of increasing his income in state θ by one dollar, i.e. by buying and selling short different securities. If there are more securities than states of nature, market equilibrium requires that the set of market prices generated by considering any subset of market securities which span the states of nature be independent of the particular subset chosen. For a more thorough discussion of these problems, see [4].

[14] They must, however, not assign zero probabilities to different states of nature occurring.

[15] In this situation we cannot assume that firms will necessarily maximize market value. (See fn. 12.)

much of the variation in the return on stocks can be explained by the business cycle. If in any given business cycle state, the variance of the return were very small, and there were a small number of identifiable business cycle states, then the economy might look very much as if it were described by an Arrow–Debreu securities market.[16]

BANKRUPTCY AND PERFECT CAPITAL MARKETS

The usual criterion for a perfectly competitive market is that the price of a commodity or factor an individual (or firm) buys or sells be independent of the amount bought or sold and be the same for all individuals in the economy. On this basis, it has been argued that the capital market is imperfectly competitive: (a) as a firm issues more bonds the rate of interest it pays may go up; (b) individuals may have to pay a higher interest rate than firms, and some firms higher than others; (c) lending rates may differ from borrowing rates. In this section, we have, however, considered perfectly competitive capital markets (with bankruptcy) in which all three of these would be true.[17] See also [22]. Thus the possibility of bankruptcy makes somewhat questionable the interpretation of much of this evidence of an imperfect capital market. The crucial fallacy lies in the implicit assumption that one firm's bond is identical to another firm's bond, and that bonds a firm issues when it has a low debt-equity ratio and those which it issues when it has a high debt-equity ratio are the same. But they are not. They give different patterns of returns. If there is any chance of default, a bond gives a variable return (i.e., is a risky asset). Just as there is no reason to expect butter and cheese, even though they are related commodities, to have the same price, so there is no reason to expect the nominal rate of interest where there is a low debt-equity ratio to be the same as when there is a high debt-equity ratio. Even the discrepancy between borrowing and lending rates does not imply imperfect capital markets, for when a person lends to the bank and the account is insured by FDIC, he can assume there is a zero probability of bankruptcy, but when the bank lends back to the same individual, it cannot make the same assumption.

REFERENCES

1. K. J. Arrow, "The Role of Securities in the Optimal Allocation of Risk Bearing," *Rev. Econ. Stud.*, Apr. 1964, *31*, 91–96.
2. W. Baumol and B. Malkiel, "The Firm's Optimal Debt-Equity Combination and the Cost of Capital," *Quart. J. Econ.*, Nov. 1967, *18*, 547–78.
3. D. E. Brewer and J. B. Michaelson, "The Cost of Capital, Corporation Finance, and the Theory of Investment: Comment," *Amer. Econ. Rev.*, June 1965, *55*, 516–23.
4. D. Cass and J. E. Stiglitz, "The Structure of Preferences and Returns and

[16] The point is that under these conditions the individual, by diversification of his portfolio, can essentially eliminate the variations in returns within a given business cycle state.
[17] Transactions cost may also partly explain (b) and (c).

Separability in Portfolio Allocation: A Contribution to the Pure Theory of Mutual Funds," *Cowles Foundation Discussion Paper*, May 1969.

5. G. Debreu, *The Theory of Value*, New York 1959.

6. P. Diamond, "The Role of a Stock Market in a General Equilibrium Model with Technological Uncertainty," *Amer. Econ. Rev.*, Sept. 1967, *57*, 759–76.

7. D. Durand, "Cost of Capital, Corporation Finance, and the Theory of Investment: Comment," *Amer. Econ. Rev.*, Sept. 1959, *49*, 639–55.

8. D. E. Farrar and L. L. Selwyn, "Taxes, Corporate Financial Policy, and Return to Investors," *Nat. Tax J.* Dec. 1967, *20*, 444–54.

9. J. Hirshleifer, "Investment Decision under Uncertainty: Choice Theoretic Approaches," *Quart. J. Econ.*, Nov. 1965, *79*, 509–36.

10. ———, "Investment Decision under Uncertainty: Applications of the State-Preference Approach," *Quart. J. Econ.*, May 1966, *80*, 237–77.

11. J. Lintner, "The Valuation of Risk Assets and the Selection of Risky Investments in Stock Portfolios and Capital Budgets," *Rev. Econ. Statist.*, Feb. 1965, *47*, 13–37.

12. H. Markowitz, *Portfolio Selection*, New York 1959.

13. F. Modigliani and M. H. Miller, "The Cost of Capital, Corporation Finance, and the Theory of Investment," *Amer. Econ. Rev.*, June 1958, *48*, 261–97.

14. ———, "Reply to Rose and Durand," *Amer. Econ. Rev.*, Sept. 1959, *49*, 665–69.

15. ———, "Corporate Income Taxes and the Cost of Capital: A Correction," *Amer. Econ. Rev.*, June 1963, *53*, 433–43.

16. ———, "Reply to D. E. Brewer and J. B. Michaelson," *Amer. Econ. Rev.*, June 1965, *55*, 524–27.

17. J. Mossin, "Equilibrium in a Capital Asset Market," *Econometrica*, Oct. 1966, *34*, 768–83.

18. G. Pye, "Investment Rules for Corporations," doctoral dissertation, M. I. T. 1963.

19. A. A. Robichek and S. C. Myers, "Problems in the Theory of Optimal Capital Structure," *J. Finance Quant. Anal.*, June 1966, *1*, 1–35.

20. W. F. Sharpe, "Capital Asset Prices: A Theory of Market Equilibrium under Conditions of Risk," *J. Finance*, Sept. 1964, *19*, 425–42.

21. W. Sher, "The Cost of Capital and Corporation Finance Involving Risk." A paper presented at the winter meetings of the Econometric Society, Evanston, Illinois, Dec. 1968.

22. G. Stigler, "Imperfections in the Capital Market," *J. Polit. Econ.*, June 1967, *75*, 287–93.

22. PORTFOLIO ANALYSIS, MARKET EQUILIBRIUM AND CORPORATION FINANCE

ROBERT S. HAMADA*

Reprinted from *The Journal of Finance*, Vol. XXIV, No. 1 (March 1969), pp. 13–31, by permission of the author and the publisher.

I. INTRODUCTION

At least three conceptual frameworks have been developed to study the effects of uncertainty on financial and economic decision-making in recent times. Of these, the homogeneous risk-class concept constructed to eliminate the need for a general equilibrium model by Modigliani and Miller [20, 21, 22], henceforth abbreviated to MM, is most familiar to those interested in corporation finance. On the other hand, the most common basis for making personal or institutional investment decisions is the portfolio model first developed by Markowitz [16, 17]. Little has been developed rigorously to cross the finance fields using either of these two uncertainty frameworks.[1]

More recently, a third uncertainty model has been revived by Hirshleifer [8, 9, 10] and labeled the time-state preference approach.[2] This last model is undoubtedly the most general approach to uncertainty and was used by Hirshleifer [10] to prove the famous MM no-tax Proposition I. Unfortunately, thus far, this generality has its cost. Using a time-state preference formulation, it is difficult to test its propositions empirically (since markets do not exist for each state) or to derive practical decision rules for capital budgeting within the firm.

The purpose of this paper is to derive the three MM Propositions using the standard deviation-mean portfolio model in a market equilibrium context. This approach to some of the major issues of corporation finance enables us

* Graduate School of Business, University of Chicago. The generous support of the Ford Foundation and the research committee of the Graduate School of Business is gratefully acknowledged. I am indebted to Eugene Fama, Merton Miller, and Myron Scholes for their helpful comments in the preparation of this paper.

[1] The notable exception is the article by Lintner [13] which considered corporate capital budgeting questions in the context of a market equilibrium portfolio model. Lintner's treatment of this problem will be discussed in Section V.

[2] Hirshleifer restated the Arrow-Debreu [1, 4] objects of choice in the classical Irving Fisher [7] framework, where the objects of choice are consumption or income bundles at explicit times and states-of-the-world.

to derive these propositions in a somewhat more direct way than with the use of the risk-class assumption and the arbitrage proof of the MM paper. Instead, a model is substituted relating the maximization of stockholder expected utility to the selection of portfolios of assets to, finally, the financing and investment decisions within the corporation. A link will be provided between two branches of the field of finance that have so far been evolving more or less separately.

In Section II, the assumptions are enumerated and the equilibrium capital asset pricing model is presented. MM's Propositions I and II, the effects of the financing decision on equity prices, are proved in Section III for the no corporate income tax case. Section IV is devoted to the corporate tax effect on this financing decision. A derivation and discussion of the cost of capital for investment decisions within the firm (MM's Proposition III) in the no-tax case are the topics of Section V. And in Section VI, the cost of capital considering corporate taxes is derived.

II. ASSUMPTIONS AND THE EQUILIBRIUM RISK-RETURN RELATIONSHIP

A. ASSUMPTIONS

The assumptions are divided into two sets. The following are required for the portfolio-capital asset pricing model.[3]

1. There are perfect capital markets. This implies that information is available to all at no cost, there are no taxes and no transaction costs, and all assets are infinitely divisible. Also, all investors can borrow or lend at the same rate of interest and have the same portfolio opportunities.
2. Investors are risk-averters and maximize their expected utility of wealth at the end of their planning horizon or the one-period rate of return over the horizon.[4] In addition, it is assumed that portfolios can be assessed solely by their expected rate of return and standard deviation of this rate of return. Of two portfolios with the same standard deviation, the criterion of choice would lead to the selection of that portfolio with the greater mean; and of two portfolios with the same expected rate of return, the investor would select the one with the smaller risk as measured by the

---

[3] The first two sections of Fama's paper [6] is recommended as the clearest exposition of this model for the homogeneous expectations case. The extension to the case of differing judgments by investors can be found in Bierwag and Grove [2] and Lintner [14, pp. 600–601]. We shall not use the heterogeneous expectations framework here since it will not add to the primary purpose of this paper and may only serve to take the focus away from our major concern.

[4] The rate of return is defined as the change in wealth divided by the investor's initial wealth, where the change in wealth includes dividends and capital gains. Note that this is a one-period model, in common with Lintner's [13, 14] and in many respects with MM's [20, 21, 22].

standard deviation. This implies that either the investor's utility function is quadratic or that portfolio rates of return are multivariate normal.[5]

3. The planning horizon is the same for all investors and their portfolio decisions made at the same time.

4. All investors have identical estimates of expected rates of return and the standard deviations of these rates.[6]

In addition to these four assumptions, we shall require the following for the subsequent sections:

5. Expected bankruptcy or default risk associated with debt-financing, as well as the risk of interest rate and purchasing power fluctuation, are assumed to be negligible relative to variability risk on equity. Thus, the corporation is assumed to be able to borrow or lend at the same risk-free rate as the individual investor.

6. Dividend policy is assumed to have no effect on the market value of a firm's equity or cost of capital. Having made our initial assumption of perfect capital markets, it was shown by MM in [19] that this need not be an additional assumption as long as there is rational investor behavior and the financing and investment policies of the corporation can be considered independent. If assumption (5) is valid, this second requirement should be met.

7. Though future investment opportunities available to the firm at rates of return greater than the cost of capital undoubtedly are reflected in the current market price, we shall ignore them here. They can be considered a capitalized quantity independent of the issues raised by MM's three propositions as long as the firm has a long-run financing policy (if the financing mix affects the cost of capital) and if the marginal rate of return of a new investment (to be compared to the subsequently derived cost of capital) includes all, direct and indirect, contributions to cash flow provided by this investment.[7]

---

[5] See Tobin [27, pages 82–85] for a justification; the need for the restrictive normal probability distribution assumption is not strictly required, as Fama [5] has generalized much of the results of the Sharpe-Lintner model for other members of the stable class of distributions where the standard deviation does not exist. It can be further noted, as Lintner [13, pages 18–19] does, that Roy [24] has shown that investors who minimize the probability of disaster (who use the "safety-first" principle) will have roughly the same investment criterion for risky assets.

[6] See footnote 3.

[7] This latter requirement is the issue raised by Miller in [18] on Lintner's growth papers [11, 12]. Lintner assumed that the indirect effects, such as shifting the firm's investment productivity schedule to a more profitable level in all future time periods, are the same for all projects and therefore do not have to be included in the marginal rate of return of the project under consideration. Instead, we are requiring that all effects and opportunities introduced by the acceptance of this project be taken into account explicitly in the marginal rate of return. For one practical method of doing this, see Magee [15].

B. ASSET PRICES AND MARKET EQUILIBRIUM

Represent the rate of return of a portfolio or risky asset by the random variable R. From assumption (2), the expected rate of return, $E(R)$, and the standard deviation, $\sigma(R)$, of portfolios are the objects of choice; this leads to the formation, by each individual investor, of an efficient set of risky portfolios according to the principles provided by Markowitz [16, 17]. Introducing a riskless asset with a rate of return R_F leads to a new efficient set combining a single risky portfolio, M (which was on the previous efficient set), with various proportions of the risk-free asset (this includes borrowing as well as lending).

Because maximum expected utility for a risk-averter requires a tangency of his expected utility curve with this efficient set, and because all investors have the same expectations, risky portfolio M would be combined by all investors in some proportion with the riskless asset. And market equilibrium requires all outstanding, risky assets to be held in the proportion of their market value to the total market value of all assets. This is the composition of portfolio M, henceforth called the market portfolio.

From this construct, the following Sharpe-Lintner-Mossin [25, 13, 14, 23] equilibrium relationship can be derived for any individual risky asset i in the market:[8]

$$E(R_i) = R_F + \frac{[E(R_M) - R_F]}{\sigma^2(R_M)} \, \text{cov}(R_i, R_M) \tag{1}$$

Note that $\dfrac{E(R_M) - R_F}{\sigma^2(R_M)}$ is the same for all assets and can be viewed as a measure of market risk aversion, or the price of a dollar of risk. Substituting a constant λ for this expression in (1), we have:

$$E(R_i) = R_F + \lambda \, \text{cov}(R_i, R_M) \tag{1a}$$

Equation (1a) supplies us with a formal market relationship between any asset's required rate of return and its individual risk, as measured by $\text{cov}(R_i, R_M)$.

III. THE FINANCING DECISION ASSUMING NO CORPORATE TAXES

A. EFFECT OF LEVERAGE ON STOCKHOLDERS' EQUITY

This section will deal with MM's Proposition I—the effects on equity value and perceived risk as a firm alters its capital structure. The quality of equity will no longer be the same and is directly dependent on the corporation's debt-equity ratio. For this purpose, we have constructed the following: assume equilibrium exists and there is a corporation, A, with no debt in its capital

---

[8] See [6] for the derivation of equation (1).

structure. Defining S_A as the present equilibrium market value of the equity of this debt-free firm, $E(S_{AT})$ as the expected market value for this same firm one period later, $E(\text{div})$ as the expected dividends paid over this period, and $E(X_A)$ as expected earnings net of depreciation but prior to the deduction of interest and tax payments, assumptions (6) and (7) allow us to write the following relationship for the dollar return:

$$E(X_A) = E(\text{div}) + E(S_{AT}) - S_A. \qquad (2)$$

Employing the definition of the expected rate of return, we have:

$$E(R_A) \equiv \frac{E(\text{div}) + E(S_{AT}) - S_A}{S_A} = \frac{E(X_A)}{S_A} \qquad (3)$$

giving us a relation for the rate of return required by corporation A's shareholders.

Now assume that corporation A decides to alter its capital structure without changing any of its other policies. This implies its assets, both present and future, remain the same as before. All it decides to do is to simultaneously issue some debt (at the riskless rate, R_F) and purchase as much of its equity as it can with the proceeds. Let us denote the equity of this same real firm, after the issuance of debt, as B.[9] The rate of return required by the remaining stockholders is given by adjusting (2), and thus (3):

$$E(R_B) = \frac{E(X_A) - R_F D_B}{S_B} \qquad (4)$$

Two points concerning (4) should be emphasized. First, the earnings from assets is $E(X_A)$, since this is the same "real" firm as A. And secondly, the interest payments, $R_F D_B$, as noted in assumption (5), is not a random variable.

Next, from (1a), the equilibrium required rate of return-risk relationship is substituted into (3) and (4) to yield:[10]

$$R_F + \lambda \operatorname{cov}(R_A, R_M) = \frac{E(X_A)}{S_A} \qquad (3a)$$

$$R_F + \lambda \operatorname{cov}(R_B, R_M) = \frac{E(X_A) - R_F D_B}{S_B} \qquad (4a)$$

---

[9] This construction can be readily extended to the cases where a firm already has debt and is considering either increasing or decreasing the proportion of debt in its capital structure. Also, if we rigidly honor the one-period planning horizon restriction, then the situation should be more precisely worded: equilibrium at $t = 0$ with equity A included and market price for risk λ. Firm A adds debt at $t = 0 + \varepsilon$ and general equilibrium restored immediately with market risk aversion remaining the same. This comparative statics framework will be used throughout this paper.

[10] λ is not strictly equal in (3a) and (4a) since one equity, B, has been substituted for another, A. Because λ includes the effects of *all* capital assets, the substitution of B for A should have a negligible effect on the value of the market price of risk.

Intuitively, equity B should be riskier than A since its dollar return is a residual after fixed interest commitments are paid. Thus, $cov(R_B, R_M)$ should be greater than $cov(R_A, R_M)$. In addition, the expected return to the two equities are different so that it is not immediately clear what the relationship between S_A and S_B should be in equilibrium. To pursue this point, rearrange (3a) and (4a) to isolate $E(X_A)$ and equate the two relations:

$$S_A[R_F + \lambda \, cov(R_A, R_M)] = S_B\left[\lambda \, cov(R_B, R_M) + R_F\left(1 + \frac{D_B}{S_B}\right)\right] \quad (5)$$

The next step is to note the definition of the covariance:

$$cov(R_A, R_M) = E\left\{\left[\frac{X_A}{S_A} - E\left(\frac{X_A}{S_A}\right)\right][R_M - E(R_M)]\right\}$$

$$= \frac{1}{S_A} cov(X_A, R_M). \quad (6)$$

Similarly:[11]

$$cov(R_B, R_M) = \frac{1}{S_B} cov(X_A, R_M). \quad (7)$$

Substituting (6) and (7) into (5), we find:

$$S_A\left[\frac{\lambda}{S_A} cov(X_A, R_M) + R_F\right] = S_B\left[\frac{\lambda}{S_B} cov(X_A, R_M) + R_F\left(1 + \frac{D_B}{S_B}\right)\right]$$

which reduces to:

$$S_A = S_B + D_B \quad (8)$$

[11] If the "feel" for the covariance of asset earnings with R_M is difficult, we can use the definition:

$$R_M = \sum_{k=1}^{T} \frac{S_k}{S_T} R_k = \frac{1}{S_T} \sum_{k=1}^{T} X_k$$

where S_T is the market value of all capital assets and T the total number of risky assets, k, outstanding. Then:

$$cov(X_A, R_M) = \frac{1}{S_T} \sum_{k=1}^{T} cov(X_A, X_k). \quad (6a)$$

Substituting (6a) into (6) and (7), respectively, yields:

$$cov(R_A, R_M) = \frac{1}{S_A S_T} \sum_{k=1}^{T} cov(X_A, X_k) \quad (6b)$$

$$cov(R_B, R_M) = \frac{1}{S_B S_T} \sum_{k=1}^{T} cov(X_A, X_k) \quad (7a)$$

Thus we have an expression for the covariance between dollar returns. Whether we use (6) or (6b) and (7) or (7a) makes no difference since the covariance terms cancel out in the following step. The important point is the weights, $1/S_A$ and $1/S_B$, multiplying the covariances.

To complete our proof of MM's Proposition I, the relationship between V, the total market value of the firm, and earnings is required. Since by definition,

$$V = S_B + D_B$$

then from (8) and (3):

$$V = S_A = \frac{E(X_A)}{E(R_A)} \tag{9}$$

The total value of the firm depends only on the expected earnings from its assets, the uncertainty of this earning (expressed by $\text{cov}(R_A, R_M)$), and the market factors λ and R_F. The financing mix is irrelevant, given our assumptions.

Having established the entity theory of value without the use of the homogeneous risk-class assumption, we are now in a position to discuss a switching mechanism to replace the MM arbitrage operation. Substituting (4) for $E(R_i)$ and (7a) for $\text{cov}(R_i, R_M)$ in (1a), and noting that the number of shares, n_B, times the price per share, P_B, is equal to S_B, we obtain for λ:

$$\lambda = \frac{[E(X_A) - R_F D_B - n_B R_F P_B]}{\dfrac{1}{S_T} \displaystyle\sum_{k=1}^{T} \text{cov}(X_A, X_k)}. \tag{10}$$

Equation (10) is meant to emphasize the point that the ratio of the expected return (over and above the risk-free return) to the risk of any equity must be a constant and equal to λ, the market price per unit of risk, in equilibrium. Thus if P_B should, for any reason, rise above its equilibrium price, then the right-hand side of (10) would fall below λ. Investors would have an incentive to sell security B and buy any other outstanding asset from which they could obtain λ. This switching would drive down the price of B and restore the equality (10) requires in equilibrium.

Alternatively, if P_B should fall below its equilibrium price, the right-hand side of (10) would rise above λ. Since the excess rate of return for risk is now greater than what is obtainable on all other assets, investors would bid for B, driving up P_B. Thus, this switching operation is implicitly being substituted for the MM arbitrage operation in the proof presented here.[12]

B. LEVERAGE AND THE EXPECTED RATE OF RETURN

Having derived (8), to find the effect of leverage on the expected rate of return (MM's Proposition II) is merely a matter of arithmetic manipulation. Recalling that equity B is the same physical firm as A except that debt is in its capital structure, the following equilibrium conditions can be noted by substituting (6) and (7) into (1a):

---

[12] If, during the switching process prior to the restoration of equilibrium, an investor finds himself not at his maximum utility point, he would also rearrange the proportion of his riskless asset and his portfolio M.

$$E(R_A) = R_F + \frac{\lambda}{S_A} \text{cov}(X_A, R_M) \tag{11}$$

$$E(R_B) = R_F + \frac{\lambda}{S_B} \text{cov}(X_A, R_M). \tag{11a}$$

Subtracting (11) from (11a), and using our result (8), we have:

$$E(R_B) - E(R_A) = \lambda \text{cov}(X_A, R_M)\left[\frac{D_B}{S_B S_A}\right]. \tag{12}$$

From (11):

$$\lambda \text{cov}(X_A, R_M) = S_A[E(R_A) - R_F]. \tag{11b}$$

And substituting (11b) in (12), we obtain MM's Proposition II:

$$E(R_B) = E(R_A) + [E(R_A) - R_F]\left(\frac{D_B}{S_B}\right). \tag{13}$$

That is, the capitalization rate for a firm's equity, or the rate of return required by investors, increases linearly with the firm's debt-equity ratio.

IV. THE FINANCING DECISION WITH CORPORATE TAXES

Maintaining the framework of Sections II and III, the corporate tax case follows without difficulty. The rate of return, R, must be defined on an after corporate income tax basis so that individual investors will now select their portfolios with respect to after-tax expected rates of return and the standard deviation of these after-tax rates of return. Otherwise, the equilibrium risk-rate of return relationship presented in Section II will not be altered.[13]

Consideration of the firm's financing decision requires only the modification of equations (2), (3a), and (4a) to take into account the corporate tax:

$$E[X_A(1 - \tau)] = E(\text{div}) + E(S_{AT}) - S_A \tag{2a}$$

$$E(R_A) = \frac{E[X_A(1 - \tau)]}{S_A} = R_F + \lambda \text{cov}(R_A, R_M) \tag{3b}$$

$$E(R_B) = \frac{E[(X_A - R_F D_B)(1 - \tau)]}{S_B} = R_F + \lambda \text{cov}(R_B, R_M) \tag{4b}$$

where τ is the corporate tax rate and equities A and B refer to the same real firm—A with no debt and B with some debt in the capital structure.[14]

Rearranging (3b) and (4b) to isolate the tax-adjusted expected asset earnings, $(1 - \tau)E(X_A)$, and equating the two relations, we obtain:

$$S_A[R_F + \lambda \text{cov}(R_A, R_M)] = S_B\left\{\lambda \text{cov}(R_B, R_M) + R_F\left[1 + \frac{D_B}{S_B}(1 - \tau)\right]\right\}. \tag{14}$$

---

[13] Problems of Pareto optimality will not be considered here.
[14] See footnote 10.

As in the no-tax case, investigation of the two covariance terms is required next, which yields:

$$\text{cov}(R_A, R_M) = \frac{(1 - \tau)}{S_A} \text{cov}(X_A, R_M) \tag{15}$$

and[15]

$$\text{cov}(R_B, R_M) = \frac{(1 - \tau)}{S_B} \text{cov}(X_A, R_M). \tag{16}$$

Substitution of (15) and (16) into (14) gives us:

$$S_A = S_B + (1 - \tau)D_B. \tag{17}$$

Since the total market value of a firm can be expressed as:

$$V = S_B + D_B$$

we have from (17):

$$V = S_A + \tau D. \tag{18}$$

Therefore, without debt, the total value of the firm is simply S_A. As the corporation increases its leverage, the aggregate equity value for the remaining shareholders increases by τD, the government subsidy given to debt financing through tax-deductible interest payments. The entity value of the firm no longer holds.

Since the first half of (3b) gives us a relationship for S_A, we can express (18) as:

$$V = \frac{(1 - \tau)E(X_A)}{E(R_A)} + \tau D. \tag{19}$$

Again, MM's result is reproduced in a market equilibrium setting.[16]

V. INVESTMENT ANALYSIS AND THE COST OF CAPITAL ASSUMING NO CORPORATE TAXES

It was stated in assumption (2) that investors maximize their expected utility of terminal wealth. Corporation managers can increase their shareholders' utility by investing in new projects within the firm such that their stock price would rise as a result of this decision. If the stock, in addition, should change its risk characteristic, $\text{cov}(R_i, R_M)$, the stockholder can always sell his equity in the firm, realize the gain, and be better off than before. Because his wealth is now larger than originally anticipated, he is able to reach a higher utility position. Thus, to be consistent with the portfolio-asset

---

[15] See footnote 11.

[16] The effect of leverage on the expected equity rate of return (MM's Proposition II) for the corporate tax case can be derived in a manner analogous to that used in Section III B.

pricing model, the criterion for capital budgeting decisions must ensure that the change in equity value, as a result of the project selection, will at least be larger than any new equity required to finance this project.

Defining dI as the purchase cost of the incremental investment and $dE \cdot F \cdot$ as the new equity (either new stock issues or retained earnings) required to finance this investment, the capital budgeting criterion can be written as:

$$\frac{dS}{dI} \geq \frac{dE \cdot F \cdot}{dI} \tag{20}$$

for the project, dI, to be acceptable.[17]

A. DERIVATION OF THE COST OF CAPITAL

Having derived the following valuation relationship in Section III A,

$$V = \frac{E(X_A)}{E(R_A)} = \frac{E(X_A)}{R_F + \lambda \operatorname{cov}(R_A, R_M)}$$

it can be shown that:[18]

$$V = \frac{E(X_A)}{R_F} - \frac{[E(X_T) - R_F S_T] \sum\limits_{k} \operatorname{cov}(X_A, X_k)}{R_F \sigma^2(X_T)} \tag{21}$$

where X_T is the sum of dollar earnings from all risky capital assets combined. Furthermore, (21) is equivalent to:[19]

---

[17] It can be shown that this criterion is the same as the one proposed by MM, i.e. $dV/dI \geq 1$, since

$$\frac{dV}{dI} = \frac{dS}{dI} + \frac{dD}{dI} \text{ and } \frac{dE \cdot F \cdot}{dI} + \frac{dD}{dI} = 1.$$

[18] By definition,

$$\lambda = \frac{E(R_M) - R_F}{\sigma^2(R_M)}$$

and substituting

$$R_M = \sum_{k=1}^{T} \left(\frac{S_k}{S_T}\right)\left(\frac{X_k}{S_k}\right) = \frac{X_T}{S_T}, \quad \lambda = \frac{S_T[E(X_T) - R_F S_T]}{\sigma^2(X_T)}.$$

And from footnote 11,

$$\operatorname{cov}(R_A, R_M) = \frac{1}{S_A S_T} \sum_{k=1}^{T} \operatorname{cov}(X_A, X_k),$$

so that substitution and rearrangement yields (21).

In this section, the effects of the firm's investment on all of the variables will be explicitly noted—this will even include the market variables λ, S_T, and X_T. If we were to remain strictly within our initial framework, any new investment must only be a combination of what is already available in the market. Ignoring the effects on the market variables will be discussed at the end of this section.

[19] This is the same as Lintner's [13, page 26] equation (29). The subtraction of $(\lambda/S_T) \sum\limits_{k} \operatorname{cov}(X_A, X_k)$ from expected earnings adjusts for risk.

$$V = \frac{E(X_A)}{R_F} - \frac{\frac{\lambda}{S_T}\sum_k \text{cov}(X_A, X_k)}{R_F}.$$

(21a)

Since the market value of firm A's equity is part of the market value of all capital assets combined, S_T, (21a) is still not a completely reduced form. Defining:

$$S'_T = \sum_{k=A}^T S_k = \text{market value of all equity except } A,$$

then $S_T = S'_T + S_A$.

Substituting this in (21) yields:

$$S = \frac{E(X_A)\sigma^2(X_T) - [E(X_T) - R_F(S'_T - D)]\sum_k \text{cov}(X_A, X_k)}{R_F[\sigma^2(X_T) - \sum_k \text{cov}(X_A, X_k)]} - D.$$

(21b)

Applying the capital budgeting criterion (20) to (21b), solving for the dollar return on the marginal investment, and noting that $\dfrac{dD}{dI} + \dfrac{dE \cdot F \cdot}{dI} = 1$, we obtain:[20]

$$\frac{dE(X_A)}{dI} \geq R_F + \frac{\lambda}{S_T}\left[\frac{d\sum_k \text{cov}(X_A, X_k)}{dI} - Z\frac{d\sigma^2(X_T)}{dI}\right]$$

$$+ Z\left[\frac{dE(X_T)}{dI} - R_F\left(1 + \frac{dS'_T}{dI} - \frac{dD}{dI}\right)\right] \quad (22)$$

where Z is defined as

$$\frac{\sum_k \text{cov}(X_A, X_k)}{\sigma^2(X_T)} = \frac{V}{S_T}\left[\frac{E(R_A) - R_F}{E(R_M) - R_F}\right].$$

The next step is to consider the effect of this incremental investment on the expected value and variance of X_T,[21] and solve for the dollar return on the investment, $\dfrac{dE(X_A)}{dI}$, commonly called the marginal internal rate of return, on the left-hand side of the inequality. The assumption that investors maximize their expected utility leads to the criterion that the firm should make

---

[20] The term, dD/dI, in (22) does not mean that the form of financing will affect the cost of capital. It appears only because a completely general equilibrium framework is not considered here—we neglected the condition that ex ante borrowing must equal ex ante lending in the bond market so that debt floated by firm A would affect R_F and other parameters. This is truly a third-order effect which can be neglected. It will also be seen later that the dD/dI term is unimportant.

capital budgeting decisions that ensure $\dfrac{dS}{dI} \geq \dfrac{dE \cdot F \cdot}{dI}$, which in turn leads to the criterion that the expected marginal internal rate of return of a project must be larger than some quantity. This quantity, the cut-off rate for the marginal investment, or the cost of capital, is:

$$\text{cost of capital} = \frac{R_F}{1 - Z} +$$

$$\frac{\lambda}{S_T} \left\{ \frac{d \sum\limits_{k} \text{cov}(X_A, X_k)}{dI} - \left(\frac{Z}{1 - Z} \right) \left[\frac{d\sigma^2(X_T')}{dI} + \frac{d\,\text{cov}(X_T', X_A)}{dI} \right] \right\}$$

$$+ \left(\frac{Z}{1 - Z} \right) \left[\frac{dE(X_T')}{dI} - R_F \left(\frac{1 + dS_T'}{dI} - \frac{dD}{dI} \right) \right] \quad (23)$$

At this point, some approximations will be made.[22] Notice that in the denominator of the definition of Z is S_T, the aggregate market value of all capital assets combined (which includes stocks, real estate, insurance, etc.), a very large sum. Thus the last half of the second term of (23) can be assumed to be negligible since it is mutiplied by, among other things, $\dfrac{1}{S_T^2}$. In addition, the change due to an incremental investment in Firm A of the expected earnings and the market value of all assets other than A, $\dfrac{dE(X_T')}{dI}$ and $\dfrac{dS_T'}{dI}$, will be assumed to be zero when multiplied by $\dfrac{Z}{1 - Z}$, itself a very small fraction. Finally, since $\dfrac{dD}{dI}$ is bounded by one and zero, the term $\left(\dfrac{Z}{1 - Z} \right) R_F \dfrac{dD}{dI}$ will be neglected. Therefore, we are left with the approximated cost of capital expression:

---

[21] These are:

$$\frac{dE(X_T)}{dI} = \frac{dE(X_T')}{dI} + \frac{dE(X_A)}{dI}$$

and

$$\frac{d\sigma^2(X_T)}{dI} = \frac{d\sigma^2(X_T')}{dI} + \frac{d\sigma^2(X_A)}{dI} + 2 \frac{d\,\text{cov}(X_T', X_A)}{dI}$$

$$= \frac{d \sum\limits_{k} \text{cov}(X_A, X_k)}{dI} + \frac{d\sigma^2(X_T')}{dI} + \frac{d\,\text{cov}(X_T', X_A)}{dI}$$

where $X_T' = \sum\limits_{k \neq A} X_k =$ dollar earnings from all capital assets except equity A.

[22] The reason for presenting the full cost of capital equation instead of assuming away these feedback effects from the beginning is to allow the reader to judge for himself the validity of these approximations (a procedure not followed by Lintner [13] and which will be discussed shortly).

$$\text{cost of capital} = R_F + \frac{\lambda}{S_T}\left[\frac{d\sum\limits_{k}\text{cov}(X_A, X_k)}{dI}\right]. \qquad (24)$$

B. INTERPRETATION OF THE COST OF CAPITAL

Comparing (24) to the valuation equation (21a), suggests an interpretation of our derived cost of capital. If the investment is riskless, i.e., does not increase the adjustment term,

$$\frac{\lambda}{S_T}\sum_{k}\text{cov}(X_A, X_k),$$

applied by the market (in equation 21a) to account for the risk of the firm's total earnings, then the expected marginal internal rate of return of this investment must only surpass the risk-free rate of interest. By not increasing this adjustment term in (21a),

$$\frac{\lambda}{S_T}\left[\frac{d\sum\limits_{k}\text{cov}(X_A, X_k)}{dI}\right]$$

must be zero for the investment. Therefore, the second half of the cost of capital equation takes into account the effect of the specific investment on this market risk-adjustment, which is then subtracted from the new expected earnings prior to being capitalized at the riskless rate to yield the new total market value of the firm. The cost of capital is thus composed of the riskless rate plus a premium for the risk of the particular project.

We can arrive at this same intepretation by noticing that:

$$\frac{\lambda}{S_T} = \frac{V_A[E(R_A) - R_F]}{\sum\limits_{k}\text{cov}(X_A, X_k)} \qquad (25)$$

so that the risk premium in the cost of capital expression (24) is:

$$[E(R_A) - R_F]\left[\frac{\dfrac{d\sum\limits_{k}\text{cov}(X_A, X_k)}{dI}}{\dfrac{\sum\limits_{k}\text{cov}(X_A, X_k)}{V_A}}\right] \qquad (25a)$$

where $[E(R_A) - R_F]$ can be viewed as the risk premium prior to the acceptance of the project in question. Thus to obtain a project's appropriate risk premium, this existing premium is multiplied by the fractional change in the firm's risk per dollar of invested capital caused by the investment.[23]

---

[23] This discussion of the cost of capital, equation (24), gives us an interpretation of our previous approximations. All terms that were approximated to be zero were indeed second-order effects due to changes in λ caused by the investment and the inclusion of firm A's equity in S_T.

Having explained the meaning of our cost of capital, we can compare it to the one proposed by MM. They suggest using the capitalization rate for a debt-free firm; that is:

$$E(R_A) = R_F + \lambda \operatorname{cov}(R_A, R_M).$$

The use of $E(R_A)$ as the cost of capital is appropriate for any investment that preserves their valuation relationship

$$V_A = \frac{E(X_A)}{E(R_A)} = \frac{E(X_A)}{R_F + \left(\dfrac{\lambda}{S_T}\right)\left(\dfrac{1}{V_A}\right) \sum_k \operatorname{cov}(X_A, X_k)} \tag{26}$$

after the investment is accepted. Assuming that R_F, λ, and S_T are not affected by capital budgeting decisions in firm A, the type of investment that will maintain the above relation is restricted to one with the following characteristic:[24]

$$\frac{d \sum_k \operatorname{cov}(X_A, X_k)}{dI} = \frac{\sum_k \operatorname{cov}(X_A, X_k)}{V}. \tag{27}$$

The right-hand side of (27) is a measure of the existing risk per dollar invested. Therefore, we can conclude that MM's cost of capital is applicable for all new investments that have the same effect on risk per dollar invested (the left-hand side of (27)) as existing assets. Because of their use of the equivalent risk-class concept to derive the cost of capital, this conclusion is not surprising. $E(R_A)$ can be used as the cost of capital only for pure scale or non-diversifying investments that do not change the firm's risk class.

Now with a market equilibrium framework developed, we are able to obtain the cost of capital for all investments, scale-changing or otherwise. To show that our cost of capital expression will be the same as MM's result for a non-diversifying project, substitute (27) in (24) to obtain:

---

[24] The property of an investment that will preserve the linear homogeneity of (26) so that $E(R_A)$ is the correct cost of capital, can be found by differentiating the right-hand side of (26) with respect to dI

$$\frac{dI}{dV} = \frac{\left[R_F + \dfrac{\lambda}{S_T V} \sum_k \operatorname{cov}(X_A, X_k)\right] \dfrac{dE(X_A)}{dI} - E(X_A) \dfrac{\lambda}{S_T} \left\{ d\left[\dfrac{1}{V} \sum_k \operatorname{cov}(X_A, X_k)\right] / dI \right\}}{\left[R_F + \dfrac{\lambda}{S_T V} \sum_k \operatorname{cov}(X_A, X_k)\right]^2}$$

Only if

$$\frac{d\left[\dfrac{1}{V} \sum_k \operatorname{cov}(X_A, X_k)\right]}{dI} = \frac{V \dfrac{d \sum_k \operatorname{cov}(X_A, X_k)}{dI} - \left[\sum_k \operatorname{cov}(X_A, X_k)\right]\dfrac{dV}{dI}}{V^2} = 0$$

will MM's cost of capital be appropriate. Setting the numerator in the last expression equal to zero and noting that the cost of the investment, dI, must be financed by debt and/or equity so that $dI = dS + dD = dV$, condition (27) in the text is obtained.

$$\text{cost of capital} = R_F + \frac{\lambda}{S_T V} \sum_k \text{cov}(X_A, X_k)$$

$$= R_F + \lambda \, \text{cov}(R_A, R_M).$$

Lintner [13], in contrast to MM, required his investments to meet a much more stringent condition. He assumed that the change in the covariance of firm A's earnings with the earnings of all other firms caused by the marginal investment is zero; that is,[25]

$$\frac{d \sum\limits_{k \neq A} \text{cov}(X_A, X_k)}{dI} = 0$$

Then his cost of capital, in our context, becomes:

$$\text{cost of capital (Lintner)} = R_F + \frac{\lambda}{S_T} \frac{d\sigma^2(X_A)}{dI}.$$

To indicate the implication of this assumption, rearrange our (25) to obtain:

$$\sum_k \text{cov}(X_A, X_k) = S_T \frac{V_A[E(R_A) - R_F]}{\lambda} \qquad (25a)$$

which shows how large the sum of covariances must be, considering the magnitude of S_T. To suggest that the risk in all future projects is only the effect on the firm's variance is to consider only a very small part of the total riskiness of the investment. If we substitute $\sigma^2(X_A)$ for $\sum\limits_k \text{cov}(X_A, X_k)$ in (25a), the equality would hardly remain. As a result, Lintner's cost of capital is much smaller than that which would have been used for the firm had it started from scratch today. For the average investment made by the average firm, it would seem that MM's cost of capital is much more accurate than Lintner's suggested approach (even disregarding MM's proviso that it be applied only to scale-changing investments). Lintner's [13] attack on MM's work appears unjustified.[26]

[25] Lintner [13, page 23] justifies this assumption by referring to Sharpe's [26] diagonal model, whereby all assets are dependent on a common underlying market factor, D. Then:

$$R_k = \alpha_k + \beta_k R_D + \varepsilon_k \qquad k = 1, 2 \ldots, T; \qquad k \neq A$$
$$R_A = \alpha_A + \beta_A R_D + \varepsilon_A$$

and $\text{cov}(\varepsilon_A, \varepsilon_k) = \text{cov}(\varepsilon_A, R_D) = \text{cov}(\varepsilon_k, R_D) = 0$ are specified. Lintner then makes the critical assumption that the random disturbance term, ε_A, is all that can be (or is) affected by capital budgeting decisions in firm A. Then of course, $\text{cov}(R_A, R_k) = \beta_A \beta_k \sigma^2(R_D)$ and is independent of changes in $E(\varepsilon_A)$ and $\sigma(\varepsilon_A)$. But why cannot new investments affect β_A, as did previous investments? Otherwise, how did β_A get there initially? Lintner, alone, should not be criticized on this point. Many others have suggested using the Markowitz portfolio approach on the real assets of the firm and therefore ignoring all market effects on risk—for the latest example, see Cohen and Elton [3].

[26] Having assumed the major part of the risk effect of a new investment to be zero, Lintner goes on to emphasize such minor points as the covariance of an investment's earnings with concurrent projects' earnings. And just for this, he suggests using a pro-

VI. THE EFFECT OF CORPORATE TAXES ON THE COST OF CAPITAL

A. DERIVATION OF THE COST OF CAPITAL

Consideration of corporate income taxes does not require us to alter the procedure followed in Section V. The valuation formula for this case can be expressed as:[27]

$$S = \frac{(1 - \tau)E(X_A)}{R_F} + \tau D - \frac{\dfrac{\lambda}{S_T} \sum_k \text{cov}(_\tau X_A, _\tau X_k)}{R_F} - D \tag{28}$$

where after-tax asset earnings, $(1 - \tau)X$, is denoted by the left-hand subscript τ on X.

Applying the capital budgeting criterion, $\dfrac{dS}{dI} \geq \dfrac{dE \cdot F \cdot}{dI}$ to (28), rearranging, and noting that $\dfrac{dD}{dI} + \dfrac{dE \cdot F \cdot}{dI} = 1$, we obtain:

$$(1 - \tau)\frac{dE(X_A)}{dI} \geq R_F\left(1 - \tau \frac{dD}{dI}\right) + \frac{\lambda}{S_T}\left[\frac{d \sum_k \text{cov}(_\tau X_A, _\tau X_k)}{dI}\right]. \tag{29}$$

The left-hand side of (29) is the after-tax expected marginal internal rate of return of an investment and it must be at least equal to the right-hand side, otherwise stockholders' wealth will not be maximized. Therefore, the after-tax cost of capital is:

$$\text{cost of capital} = R_F\left(1 - \tau \frac{dD}{dI}\right) + \frac{\lambda}{S_T}\left[\frac{d \sum_k \text{cov}(_\tau X_A, _\tau X_k)}{dI}\right]. \tag{30}$$

---

gramming approach! Lintner also seems to have forgotten that his (and our and MM's) model is strictly valid for only one horizon period (our assumption 2) when criticizing MM and when discussing the effects of changes in R_F. Theoretically, as soon as a new investment is made by the firm, it must be financed and a new equity created. This changes the set of capital assets available to the investor and a new equilibrium (and parameters) must be determined. This is truly a major disadvantage and whether or not it invalidates the model for practical purposes awaits empirical results.

[27] Starting with equation (19), we have:

$$S = \frac{(1 - \tau)E(X_A)}{E(R_A)} + \tau D - D = \frac{(1 - \tau)E(X_A)}{R_F + \lambda \text{cov}(R_A, R_M)} + \tau D - D$$

where the subscript A represents the firm if it did not have any debt and the R's are on an after-tax basis. Since

$$\text{cov}(R_A, R_M) = \frac{1}{S_A S_T} \sum_k \text{cov}(_\tau X_A, _\tau X_k)$$

and

$$S_A = V - \tau D = S - \tau D + D,$$

equation (28) is obtained. Also, the comments made in Section V, part A, are recognized, so that we shall henceforth ignore the effects of dI on the market variables λ, S_T, and X_T.

We can interpret this result by comparing it to (28). First, consider a risk-less project; then $\dfrac{d \sum_k \text{cov}(_\tau X_A, _\tau X_k)}{dI} = 0$. Its after-tax marginal internal rate of return must be greater than only the risk-free rate less the tax subsidy given to debt financing in order for the present shareholders' equity to in-crease. The tax subsidy is the product of the dollar interest cost, $R_F \dfrac{dD}{dI}$, and the tax rate, τ. Thus, the cost of capital for a riskless project is $R_F - \tau R_F \dfrac{dD}{dI}$, the answer provided by (30).

Next, consider a project that has some risk. It will, in addition to the costs discussed for the riskless project, affect the risk adjustment term in (28). The last term in our cost of capital relation clearly considers the investment's impact on this term.

This result can be compared again to the MM cost of capital. They applied the capital budgeting criterion, $\dfrac{dV}{dI} \geq 1$, to our equation (19), to obtain:[28]

$$\text{cost of capital (MM)} = [E(R_A)]\left(1 - \tau \frac{dD}{dI}\right)$$

$$= R_F\left(1 - \tau \frac{dD}{dI}\right) + \frac{\lambda\left(1 - \tau \dfrac{dD}{dI}\right)}{S_T S_A} \sum_k \text{cov}(_\tau X_A, _\tau X_k)$$

$$(31)$$

An investment which will preserve the linear homogeneity of (19) so that (31) will be its cost of capital must satisfy the following condition:[29]

$$\frac{d \sum_k \text{cov}(_\tau X_A, _\tau X_k)}{dS_A} = \frac{\sum_k \text{cov}(_\tau X_A, _\tau X_k)}{S_A} \qquad (32)$$

As in the no-tax case, a project with this property is one that merely changes the scale of the firm. Assuming that equity was the sole source of previous capital, the right-hand side of (32) defines the risk per dollar already invested in the corporation. New investments must have this same ratio of MM's cost of capital to be applicable. In (32), proportional changes in risk are expressed on a pure equity basis; otherwise the consequence of the debt tax subsidy on effective capital required to finance the project would not be taken into con-sideration.

To show that MM's result is a special case of the cost of capital derived here, the relationship between the purchase cost of the investment, dI, and the effective capital required, dS_A, allows us to express (32) as:[30]

---

[28] See reference [20] or [22].
[29] The same procedure described in footnote 24 is used to obtain equation (32).
[30] Since dI must be financed with debt and/or equity, then $dI = dS + dD \equiv dV$. And

$$\frac{d \sum_k \text{cov}(_{\tau}X_A, _{\tau}X_k)}{dI} = \frac{\left(1 - \tau \dfrac{dD}{dI}\right) \sum_k \text{cov}(_{\tau}X_A, _{\tau}X_k)}{S_A} \tag{32a}$$

so that MM's cost of capital is obtained when (32a) is substituted in (30).

B. SUGGESTIONS FOR ESTIMATING THE COST OF CAPITAL

Nothing will be added to MM's recommendation concerning the financing of specific projects. The long-run target debt ratio, L^*, for the firm's capital structure should be recognized as the financing mix for all of the firm's investments regardless of how any individual project is financed. Then, $\dfrac{dD}{dI} = L^*$, and (30) can be expressed as:

$$\text{cost of capital} = R_F(1 - \tau L^*) + \frac{\lambda}{S_T}\left[\frac{d \sum_k \text{cov}(_{\tau}X_A, _{\tau}X_k)}{dI}\right] \tag{30a}$$

For small or nondiversifying investments, it is proposed that management assume that each effective invested dollar of the new project, dS_A, affects the covariance of the corporation's earnings with all other earnings as the average effective dollar of the corporation's existing assets, S_A, affects this covariance. Then MM's cost of capital can be used.

Major investments, in contrast to those discussed above, require a direct solution of (30a). For the risk premium, we can note the following equivalent forms:

$$\frac{\lambda}{S_T}\left[\frac{d \sum_k \text{cov}(_{\tau}X_A, _{\tau}X_k)}{dI}\right]$$

$$= \frac{\lambda}{S_T}\frac{d\,\text{cov}(_{\tau}X_A, _{\tau}X_T)}{dI}$$

$$= \frac{\lambda}{S_T}[\text{cov}(_{\tau}X_{A0} + _{\tau}X_{A1}, _{\tau}X_T + _{\tau}X_{A1}) - \text{cov}(X_{\tau A0}, _{\tau}X_T)]$$

$$= \lambda\,\text{cov}(_{\tau}X_{A1}, R_M) + \frac{\lambda}{S_T}[\text{cov}(_{\tau}X_{A0}, _{\tau}X_{A1}) + \sigma^2(_{\tau}X_{A1})] \tag{30b}$$

where $_{\tau}X_{A0}$, $_{\tau}X_{A1}$, and $_{\tau}X_T$ are defined as tax-adjusted earnings from firm A's

---

from (18), we have $dS_A = dV - \tau dD$, so that

$$dS_A = dI - \tau dD = dI\left(1 - \tau \frac{dD}{dI}\right).$$

Substituting this last expression in (32) results in (32a).

existing assets, from the new investment under consideration, and from all capital assets in the market, respectively.[31]

Use of the Sharpe [26] diagonal model is possible in estimating the project's major risk component, $\lambda \operatorname{cov}({}_\tau X_{A1}, R_M)$, if the rate of return of a value-weighted index, such as the S & P Index, can be assumed to be a "good" proxy for R_M and the systematic risk in ${}_\tau X_{A1}$ can be explained by a simple linear relationship with R_M.[32] Then:

$$_\tau X_{A1} = a + bR_M + \varepsilon \tag{33}$$

where a and b are parameters and $E(\varepsilon) = \operatorname{cov}(R_M, \varepsilon) = 0$. Applying (33) to the definition of the covariance, we have:

$$\begin{aligned}
\lambda \operatorname{cov}({}_\tau X_{A1}, R_M) &= \lambda E\{[bR_M + \varepsilon - bE(R_M)][R_M - E(R_M)]\} \\
&= \lambda b\sigma^2(R_M) \\
&= b[E(R_M) - R_F]
\end{aligned}$$

so that b and $E(R_M)$ are all that must be estimated.

VII. CONCLUSION

Two major issues of corporation finance, the financing and investment decisions of the firm, have been analyzed in this paper in the framework of the Sharpe-Lintner-Mossin market equilibrium capital asset pricing model, itself an extension of the Markowitz-Tobin portfolio model. The effects of the financing decision on aggregate equity values were the topics of Sections III and IV. The famous MM Propositions I and II were found to hold when put to the market equilibrium model, both in the no tax case (Section III) and when corporate taxes were taken into account (Section IV). Thus the assumption of homogeneous risk-classes, constructed expressly to eliminate a full-blown market equilibrium model, and the arbitrage proof are no longer necessary. In place of arbitrage, a switching operation was discussed.

Sections V and VI were devoted to developing and interpreting the cost of capital, the minimum required rate of return individual projects within the firm must surpass in order that their shareholders not suffer a decrease in

---

[31] For completeness, we should consider the covariance of the tax-adjusted earnings of project 1 with all the other projects, n, included in the year's capital budget. Then to (30b) must be added

$$\frac{\lambda}{S_T} [2 \sum_n \operatorname{cov}({}_\tau X_{A1}, {}_\tau X_n)].$$

However, this term, as well as $\operatorname{cov}({}_\tau X_{A0}, {}_\tau X_{A1})$ and $\sigma^2({}_\tau X_{A1})$, contributes very little to the cost of capital risk premium because it is multiplied by $\frac{\lambda}{S_T}$. In view of this small effect and that a programming approach is required (since this covariance is not known until the entire capital budget is determined simultaneously), we shall disregard it.

[32] We are not assuming that all of the k capital assets are related to R_M by (33). Therefore, the comments made by Fama [6] on the Sharpe-Linter conflict do not apply to the less restrictive model employed here.

expected utility. MM's recommended cost of capital was found to be a special case (for nondiversifying investments) of the one developed here, albeit a most important special case. Then comparing Lintner's cost of capital to MM's, the latter version was thought to be more accurate in the majority of cases faced by the firm. Finally, cursory suggestions to estimate the cost of capital were made.

It might be of interest to note that MM's discussions suggest an equilibrium portfolio model was implicitly being employed. For instance, they associated a rise in expected equity yields, when leverage increased, to an increased premium induced by the need to bear greater variability risk. And when discussing their arbitrage operation, we can quote [21, footnote 11]:

In the language of the theory of choice, the exchanges are movements from inefficient points in the interior to efficient points on the boundary of the investor's opportunity set; and not movements between efficient points along the boundary . . . .

That their propositions are shown to hold in the portfolio model under market equilibrium conditions a decade later (and slightly earlier for Proposition I in the time-state preference framework) should be regarded as a tribute to their partial equilibrium concept of the homogeneous risk-class.

But a word of caution is necessary in conclusion. We opened the analytical part of this paper with an enumeration of the assumptions. The results presented here are conditional on these assumptions not grossly violating reality.

REFERENCES

1. K. J. Arrow. "The Role of Securities in the Optimal Allocation of Risk-Bearing," *Review of Economic Studies*, April, 1964.
2. G. Bierwag and M. Grove. "On Capital Asset Prices: Comment," *Journal of Finance* (March, 1965), pp. 89–93.
3. K. Cohen and E. Elton. "Inter-temporal Portfolio Analysis Based on Simulation of Joint Returns," *Management Science* (Sept., 1967), pp. 5–18.
4. G. Debreu. *Theory of Value*. New York: John Wiley and Sons, 1959. Chap. 7.
5. E. Fama. "Risk, Return and General Equilibrium in a Stable Paretian Market." Unpublished manuscript, June, 1967.
6. ———. "Risk, Return and General Equilibrium: Some Clarifying Comments." *Journal of Finance* (March, 1968), pp. 29–40.
7. I. Fisher. *The Theory of Interest*. New York: Macmillan, 1930. Reprinted, Augustus M. Kelley, 1961.
8. J. Hirshleifer. "Efficient Allocation of Capital in an Uncertain World," *American Economic Review* (May, 1964), pp. 77–85.
9. ———. "Investment Decision Under Uncertainty: Choice-Theoretic Approaches," *The Quarterly Journal of Economics* (November, 1965), pp. 509–36.
10. ———. "Investment Decision Under Uncertainty: Applications of the State-Preference Approach," *The Quarterly Journal of Economics* (May, 1966), pp. 252–77.

11. J. Lintner. "The Cost of Capital and Optimal Financing of Corporate Growth," *Journal of Finance* (May, 1963), pp. 292–310.
12. ———. "Optimal Dividends and Corporate Growth Under Uncertainty," *Quarterly Journal of Economics* (February, 1964), pp. 49–95.
13. ———. "The Valuation of Risk Assets and The Selection of Risky Investments in Stock Portfolios and Capital Budgets," *Review of Economics and Statistics* (February, 1965), pp. 13–37.
14. ———. "Security Prices, Risk, and Maximal Gains from Diversification," *Journal of Finance* (December, 1965), pp. 587–615.
15. J. Magee. "Decision Trees for Decision Making," *Harvard Business Review* (July–August, 1964), pp. 126–38.
16. H. Markowitz. "Portfolio Selection," *Journal of Finance* (March 1952), pp. 77–91.
17. ———. *Portfolio Selection: Efficient Diversification of Investments.* New York: John Wiley and Sons, Inc., 1959.
18. M. Miller. "Discussion," *Journal of Finance* (May, 1963), pp. 313–16.
19. M. Miller and F. Modigliani. "Dividend Policy, Growth, and the Valuation of Shares," *Journal of Business* (October, 1961), pp. 411–33.
20. ———. "Some Estimates of the Cost of Capital to the Electric Utility Industry, 1954–57," *American Economic Review* (June, 1966), pp. 333–91.
21. Modigliani and Miller. "The Cost of Capital, Corporation Finance and the Theory of Investment," *American Economic Review* (June, 1958), pp. 261–97.
22. ———. "Corporate Income Taxes and the Cost of Capital: A Correction," *American Economic Review* (June, 1963), pp. 433–43.
23. J. Mossin. "Equilibrium in a Capital Asset Market," *Econometrica* (October, 1966), pp. 768–83.
24. A. Roy. "Safety First and the Holding of Assets," *Econometrica* (July, 1952), pp. 431–49.
25. W. Sharpe. "Capital Asset Prices: A Theory of Market Equilibrium under Conditions of Risk," *Journal of Finance* (September, 1964), pp. 425–42.
26. ———. "A Simplified Model for Portfolio Analysis," *Management Science* (January, 1963), pp. 277–93.
27. J. Tobin. "Liquidity Preference as Behavior Towards Risk," *Review of Economic Studies* (February, 1958), pp. 65–86.

23. DEBT AND TAXES*

MERTON H. MILLER†

Reprinted from *The Journal of Finance,* Vol. XXXII, No. 2
(May 1977), pp. 261–275, by permission of the author and
the publisher.

THE SOMEWHAT HETERODOX VIEWS about debt and taxes that will be presented here have evolved over the last few years in the course of countless discussions with several of my present and former colleagues in the Finance group at Chicago—Fischer Black, Robert Hamada, Roger Ibbotson, Myron Scholes and especially Eugene Fama. Charles Upton and Joseph Williams have also been particularly helpful to me recently in clarifying the main issues.[1] My long-time friend and collaborator, Franco Modigliani, is absolved from any blame for the views to follow not because I think he would reject them, but because he has been absorbed in preparing *his* Presidential Address to the American Economic Association at this same Convention.

This coincidence neatly symbolizes the contribution we tried to make in our first joint paper of nearly twenty years ago; namely to bring to bear on problems of corporate finance some of the standard tools of economics, especially the analysis of competitive market equilibrium. Prior to that time, the academic discussion in finance was focused primarily on the empirical issue of what the market *really* capitalized.[2] Did the market capitalize a firm's dividends or its earnings or some weighted combination of the two? Did it capitalize net earnings or net operating earnings or something in between? The answers to these questions and to related questions about the behavior of interest rates were supposed to provide a basis for choosing an optimal capital structure for the firm in a framework analogous to the economist's model of discriminating monopsony.

* Presidential Address, Annual Meeting of the American Finance Association, Atlantic City, N.J., September 17, 1976.

† University of Chicago.

[1] More than perfunctory thanks are also due to the many others who commented, sometimes with considerable heat, on the earlier versions of this talk: Ray Ball, Marshall Blume, George Foster, Nicholas Gonedes, David Green, E. Han Kim, Robert Krainer, Katherine Miller, Charles Nelson, Hans Stoll, Jerold Warner, William Wecker, Roman Weil, and J. Fred Weston. I am especially indebted (no pun intended) to Fischer Black.

[2] To avoid reopening old wounds, no names will be mentioned here. References can be supplied on request, however.

We came at the problem from the other direction by first trying to establish the propositions about valuation implied by the economist's basic working assumptions of rational behavior and perfect markets. And we were able to prove that when the full range of opportunities available to firms and investors under such conditions are taken into account, the following simple principle would apply: in equilibrium, the market value of any firm must be independent of its capital structure.

The arbitrage proof of this proposition can now be found in virtually every textbook in finance, followed almost invariably, however, by a warning to the student against taking it seriously. Some dismiss it with the statement that firms and investors can't or don't behave that way. I'll return to that complaint later in this talk. Others object that the invariance proposition was derived for a world with no taxes, and that world, alas, is not ours. In our world, they point out, the value of the firm can be increased by the use of debt since interest payments can be deducted from taxable corporate income. To reap more of these gains, however, the stockholders must incur increasing risks of bankruptcy and the costs, direct and indirect, of falling into that unhappy state. They conclude that the balancing of these bankruptcy costs against the tax gains of debt finance gives rise to an optimal capital structure, just as the traditional view has always maintained, though for somewhat different reasons.

It is this new and currently fashionable version of the optimal capital structure that I propose to challenge here. I will argue that even in a world in which interest payments are fully deductible in computing corporate income taxes, the value of the firm, in equilibrium will still be independent of its capital structure.

I. BANKRUPTCY COSTS IN PERSPECTIVE

Let me first explain where I think the new optimum capital structure model goes wrong. It is not that I believe there to be no deadweight costs attaching to the use of debt finance. Bankruptcy costs and agency costs do indeed exist as was dutifully noted at several points in the original 1958 article [28, see especially footnote 18 and p. 293]. It is just that these costs, by any sensible reckoning, seem disproportionately small relative to the tax savings they are supposedly balancing.

The tax savings, after all, are conventionally taken as being on the order of 50 cents for each dollar of permanent debt issued.[3] The figure one usually hears

---

[3] See, among others, Modigliani and Miller [27]. The 50 percent figure—actually 48 percent under present Federal law plus some additional state income taxes for most firms—is an upper bound that assumes the firm always has enough income to utilize the tax shield on the interest. For reestimates of the tax savings under other assumptions with respect to availability of offsets and to length of borrowing, see Kim [21] and Brennan and Schwartz [12]. The estimate of the tax saving has been further complicated since 1962 by the Investment Tax Credit and especially by the limitation of the credit to fifty percent of the firm's tax liability. Some fuzziness about the size of the tax savings also arises in the case of multinational corporations.

as an estimate of bankruptcy costs is 20 percent of the value of the estate; and if this were the true order of magnitude for such costs, they would have to be taken very seriously indeed as a possible counterweight. But when that figure is traced back to its source in the paper by Baxter [5] (and the subsequent and seemingly confirmatory studies of Stanley and Girth [36] and Van Horne [39]), it turns out to refer mainly to the bankruptcies of individuals, with a sprinkling of small businesses, mostly proprietorships and typically undergoing liquidation rather than reorganization. The only study I know that deals with the costs of bankruptcy and reorganization for large, publicly-held corporations is that of Jerold Warner [40]. Warner tabulated the direct costs of bankruptcy and reorganization for a sample of 11 railroads that filed petitions in bankruptcy under Section 77 of the Bankruptcy Act between 1930 and 1955. He found that the eventual cumulated direct costs of bankruptcy—and keep in mind that most of these railroads were in bankruptcy and running up these expenses for over 10 years!—averaged 5.3 percent of the market value of the firm's securities as of the end of the month in which the railroad filed the petition. There was a strong inverse size effect, moreover. For the largest road, the costs were 1.7 percent.

And remember that these are the *ex post*, upper-bound cost ratios, whereas, of course, the *expected* costs of bankruptcy are the relevant ones when the firm's capital structure decisions are being made. On that score, Warner finds, for example, that the direct costs of bankruptcy averaged only about 1 percent of the value of the firm 7 years before the petition was filed and when he makes a reasonable allowance for the probability of bankruptcy actually occurring, he comes up with an estimate of the expected cost of bankruptcy that is, of course, much smaller yet.

Warner's data cover only the *direct* costs of reorganization in bankruptcy. The deadweight costs of rescaling claims might perhaps loom larger if measures were available of the indirect costs, such as the diversion of the time and energies of management from tasks of greater productivity or the reluctance of customers and suppliers to enter into long-term commitments.[4] But why speculate about the size of these costs? Surely we can assume that if the direct and indirect deadweight costs of the ordinary loan contract began to eat up significant portions of the tax savings, other forms of debt contracts with lower deadweight costs would be used instead.[5]

An obvious case in point is the income bond. Interest payments on such bonds need be paid in any year only if earned; and if earned and paid are fully

---

[4] For more on this theme see Jensen and Meckling [20].

[5] A similar argument in a somewhat different, but related, context is made by Black [6, esp. pp. 330–31]. Note also that while the discussion has so far referred exclusively to "bankruptcy" costs fairly narrowly construed, much the same reasoning applies to the debt-related costs in the broader sense, as in the "agency" costs of Jensen and Meckling [20] or the "costs of lending" of Black, Miller and Posner [9].

deductible in computing corporate income tax. But if not earned and not paid in any year, the bondholders have no right to foreclose. The interest payments typically cumulate for a short period of time—usually two to three years—and then are added to the principal. Income bonds, in sum, are securities that appear to have all the supposed tax advantages of debt, without the bankruptcy cost disadvantages.[6] Yet, except for a brief flurry in the early 1960's, such bonds are rarely issued.

The conventional wisdom attributes this dearth to the unsavory connotations that surround such bonds.[7] They were developed originally in the course of the railroad bankruptcies in the 19th century and they are presumed to be still associated with that dismal process in the minds of potential buyers. As an investment banker once put it to me: "They have the smell of death about them." Perhaps so. But the obvious retort is that bit of ancient Roman wisdom: *pecunia non olet* (money has no odor). If the stakes were as high as the conventional analysis of the tax subsidy to debt seems to suggest, then ingenious security salesmen, investment bankers or tax advisers would surely long since have found ways to overcome investor repugnance to income bonds.

In sum, the great emphasis on bankruptcy costs in recent discussions of optimal capital structure policy seems to me to have been misplaced. For big businesses, at least (and particularly for such conspicuously low-levered ones as I.B.M. or Kodak), the supposed trade-off between tax gains and bankruptcy costs looks suspiciously like the recipe for the fabled horse-and-rabbit stew—one horse and one rabbit.[8]

II. TAXES AND CAPITAL STRUCTURES: THE EMPIRICAL RECORD

Problems arise also on the other side of the trade-off. If the optimal capital structure were simply a matter of balancing tax advantages against bankruptcy costs, why have observed capital structures shown so little change over time?[9]

When I looked into the matter in 1960 under the auspices of the Commission on Money and Credit (Miller [24]), I found, among other things, that the debt/asset ratio of the typical nonfinancial corporation in the 1950's was little different from that of the 1920's despite the fact that tax rates had quintu-

[6] Not quite, because failure to repay or refund the principal at maturity could trigger a bankruptcy. Also, a firm may have earnings, but no cash.

[7] See Esp. Robbins [31], [27].

[8] In this connection, it is interesting to note that the optimal debt to value ratio in the hypothetical example presented in the recent paper by E. Han Kim [21] turns out to be 42 percent and, hence, very substantially higher than the debt ratio for the typical U.S. corporation, even though Kim's calculaton assumes that bankruptcy costs would eat up no less than 40 percent of the firm's assets in the event of failure.

[9] A related question is why there appears to be no systematic cross-sectional relation between debt ratios and corporate tax rates in the countries of the European Economic Community. See Coates and Wooley [13].

pled—from 10 and 11 percent in the 1920's to 52 percent in the 1950's.[10] Such rise as did occur, moreover, seemed to be mainly a substitution of debt for preferred stock, rather than of debt for common stock. The year-to-year variations in debt ratios reflected primarily the cyclical movements of the economy. During expansions debt ratios tended to fall, partly because the lag of dividends behind earnings built up internally generated equity; and partly because the ratio of equity to debt in new financings tended to rise when the stock market was booming.

My study for the CMC carried the story only through the 1950's. A hasty perusal of the volumes of Statistics of Income available for the years thereafter suggests that some upward drift in debt ratios did appear to be taking place in the 1960's, at least in book-value terms. Some substantial portion of this seeming rise, however, is a consequence of the liberalization of depreciation deductions in the early 1960's. An accounting change of that kind reduces reported taxable earnings and, barring an induced reduction in dividend policy, will tend to push accumulated retained earnings (and total assets) below the levels that would otherwise have been recorded.[11] Thus, without considerable further adjustment, direct comparison of current and recent debt ratios to those of earlier eras is no longer possible. But suppose we were to make the extreme assumption that all the rise in debt ratios genuinely reflected policy decisions rather than changes in accounting rules. Then that would still have meant that the average nonfinancial corporation raised its ratio of long-term debt from about one-fifth to only about one-fourth of total assets during the decade.[12]

Whatever may have been the case in the 1960's, the impression was certainly widespread in the early 1970's that corporate debt ratios were rising rapidly and ominously. This was a period, after all, in which *Business Week* could devote an entire and very gloomy issue (October 12, 1974) to the theme "The Debt Economy."

Looking back now, however, with all the advantages of hindsight, the increases in debt of such concern in 1974 can be seen to be a transitory response to a peculiar configuration of events rather than a permanent shift in corporate

---

[10] The remarkable stability of corporate debt ratios in the face of huge increases in tax rates was noted by many other writers in this period. See, e.g., Sametz [22, esp. pp. 462–3] and the references there cited.

[11] Also acting in the same direction were the liberalized rules for expensing rather than capitalizing outlays for research and development. On the other hand, debt ratios would tend to be understated by the growth during the decade of off-balance-sheet debt financing, such as leasing and unfunded pension liability.

[12] For manufacturing corporations, Federal Trade Commission reports indicate that long-term debt rose during the 1960's from 12.2 percent of reported total assets to 16.6 percent. Short-term debt rose from about 7 percent to 12 percent of reported total assets over the same period. The corresponding figures for the end of 1975 were 17.9 percent for long-term debt and 10.2 percent for short-term debt. The figures here and throughout refer of course to gross debt without allowing for the substantial amounts of debt securities that are owned by manufacturing and other nonfinancial corporations.

capital structures.[13] A surge in inventory accumulation was taking place as firms sought to hedge against shortages occasioned by embargoes or price controls or crop failures. Much of this accumulation was financed by short-term borrowing—a combination that led to a sharp deterioration in such conventional measures of financial health as "quick ratios" and especially coverage ratios (since little of the return on the precautionary inventory buildup was showing up in current earnings and since inflation *per se* will automatically reduce the ratio of earnings to interest payments even with no change in the interest burden in real terms).

But this inventory buble burst soon after the famous doomsday issue of *Business Week* hit the stands—providing one more confirmation of Allen Wallis' dictum that by the time journalists become interested in an economic problem, the worst is already over. In the ensuing months, inventories have been pared, bank loans have been repaid and conventional measures of corporate liquidity have been restored to something closer to their old-time vigor. New common stock issues have been coming briskly to market as always in the past when the stock market was bouyant. Thus, when the returns for the first half of the 1970's are finally in, we are likely to be facing the same paradox we did in the 1950's—corporate debt ratios only marginally higher than those of the 1920's despite enormously higher tax rates.[14]

Actually, the cognitive dissonance is worse now than it was then. In the 1950's it was still possible to entertain the notion that the seeming failure of corporations to reap the tax advantages of debt financing might simply be a lag in adjustment. As corporate finance officers and their investment bankers sharpened their pencils, the tax savings they discovered would eventually wear down aversions to debt on the part of any others in the Boardroom still in a state of shock from the Great Depression. But hope can no longer be expected from that quarter. A disequilibrium that has lasted 30 years and shows no signs of disappearing is too hard for any economist to accept.[15] And since failure to

---

[13] For an independent reading of these events that is similar in most essential respects, see Gilbert [16].

[14] The discussion in the text has focused mainly on debt/asset ratios at book value, in the hope that book value measures might give better insight to corporate capital structure objectives than would market value measures of leverage, which are highly sensitive to changes in the level of stock prices. As of the end of 1975, tabulations prepared by Salomon Brothers in their volume *The Supply and Demand for Credit, 1976*, indicate a ratio of long-term debt to market value for all U.S. corporations (including public utilities) of 27.1 percent. (Actually, even this is a bit on the high side since the debt is measured at face value and thus does not reflect the substantial fall in the value of outstanding debt in the 1st half of the 1970's.) In 1972, at the height of the boom, the long-term debt ratio at market value was only about 17 percent. The highest recent level reached in recent years was 30 percent at the end of 1974 after a two-year fall of $500 billion in the market value of common and preferred stock.

[15] There are certainly few signs that firms were rushing to close the gap by methods as direct as exchanges of debt for their common shares. Masulis [22] was able to find only about 60 such cases involving listed corporations in the 1960's and 1970's. Most of these were concentrated during an 18-month period after the drop in the stock market in 1973; and some of these, in turn, appear more to be attempts to "go private" than to adjust the capital structure.

close the gap cannot convincingly be attributed to the bankruptcy costs or agency costs of debt financing, there would seem to be only one way left to turn: the tax advantages of debt financing must be substantially less than the conventional wisdom suggests.[16]

III. THE TAX ADVANTAGES OF DEBT FINANCING REEXAMINED

That the solution might lie in this direction was hinted at, but alas only hinted at, in the original 1958 MM paper. If I may invoke the Presidential privilege of being allowed to quote (selectively) from my earlier work, we said there in the 57th footnote:

It should also be pointed out that our tax system acts in other ways to reduce the gains from debt financing. Heavy reliance on debt in the capital structure, for example, commits a company to paying out a substantial proportion of its income in the form of interest payments taxable to the owners under the personal income tax. A debt free company, by contrast, can reinvest in the business all of its (smaller) net income and to this extent subject the owners only to the low capital gains rate (or possibly to no tax at all by virtue of the loophole at death).

We alluded to the same line of argument again briefly in the correction paper in 1963.[17] The point was developed in a more extensive and systematic way by Farrar and Selwyn [15]. Further extensions were made by Myers [30], Stapleton [37], Stiglitz [38], and in two important papers by Fischer Black [7], [8]—papers still unpublished but whose contents were communicated to me, sometimes in very forceful fashion, in the course of many arguments and discussions.

When the personal income tax is taken into account along with the corporation income tax, the gain from leverage, G_L, for the stockholders in a firm holding real assets can be shown to be given by the following expression:

$$G_L = \left[1 - \frac{(1 - \tau_C)(1 - \tau_{PS})}{1 - \tau_{PB}} \right] B_L$$

where τ_C is the corporate tax rate, τ_{PS} is the personal income tax rate applicable to income from common stock, τ_{PB} is the personal income tax rate applicable

---

[16] The resolution of the paradox offered in the CMC paper [24] was essentially one of agency costs and, in particular, that the costs of monitoring risky debt made such debt uneconomic as a market instrument.

[17] In that paper, the major weight in resolving the paradox was placed on what might be called a "precautionary" motive. Corporations were presumed to want to maintain substantial reserves of high-grade borrowing power so as not to be forced to float common stocks when they believe their stock to be undervalued. Such motives are by no means inconsistent with the explanation to be offered here.

to income from bonds and B_L is the market value of the levered firm's debt. For simplicity at this stage of the argument, all the taxes are assumed to be proportional; and to maintain continuity with the earlier MM papers, the expression is given in its "perpetuity" form.[18]

Note that when all tax rates are set equal to zero, the expression does indeed reduce to the standard MM no-tax result of $G_L = 0$. And when the personal income tax rate on income from bonds is the same as that on income from shares—a special case of which, of course, is when there is assumed to be no personal income tax at all—then the gain from leverage is the familiar $\tau_C B_L$. But when the tax rate on income from shares is less than the tax on income from bonds, then the gain from leverage will be less than $\tau_C B_L$. In fact, for a wide range of values for τ_C, τ_{PS} and τ_{PB}, the gain from leverage vanishes entirely or even turns negative!

Let me assure you that this result is no mere sleight-of-hand due to hidden trick assumptions. The gain evaporates or turns into a loss because investors hold securities for the "consumption possibilities" they generate and hence will evaluate them in terms of their yields net of all tax drains. If, therefore, the personal tax on income from common stocks is less than that on income from bonds, then the *before-tax* return on taxable bonds has to be high enough, other things equal, to offset this tax handicap. Otherwise, no taxable investor would want to hold bonds. Thus, while it is still true that the owners of a levered corporation have the advantage of deducting their interest payments to bondholders in computing their corporate income tax, these interest payments have already been "grossed up," so to speak, by any differential in the taxes that the bondholders will have to pay on their interest income. The advantage of deductibility at the one level thus merely serves to offset the disadvantages of includability at the other.[19] When the rates happen to satisfy the equation $(1 - \tau_{PB}) = (1 - \tau_C)(1 - \tau_{PS})$, the offset is one-for-one and the owners of the

---

[18] The expression can be derived in a number of ways of which the simplest is perhaps the following variant on the MM reply to Heins and Sprenkle [29]. Ownership of the fraction α of the levered corporation yields a return to the investor of $\alpha(\tilde{X} - rB_L)(1 - \tau_C)(1 - \tau_{PS})$ where $\tilde{X}$ is the uncertain return on firm's real (as opposed to financial) assets. This can be duplicated by the sum of (a) an investment of αS_U in the shares of the twin unlevered corporation, which yields $\alpha X(1 - \tau_C)(1 - \tau_{PS})$; plus (b), borrowing $\alpha B_L[(1 - \tau_C)(1 - \tau_{PS})/(1 - \tau_{PS})]$ on personal account. Since interest is deductible under the personal income tax, the net cost of the borrowing is $\alpha r B_L(1 - \tau_C)(1 - \tau_{PS})$ and thus the original levered stream has been matched.

Here and throughout, the tax authorities will be presumed to have taken the steps necessary to prevent taxable individuals or firms from eliminating their tax liabilities or converting them to negative taxes by "tax arbitrage" dodges (such as borrowing to hold tax-exempt securities) or by large-scale short-selling.

[19] An analogous argument in the context of the lease-or-buy decision is given in Miller and Upton [26]. Reasoning of essentially this kind has also long been invoked to explain the otherwise puzzling survival of preferred stock (see, among many others, Miller [24, esp. note 40, p. 431]). The fact that 85 percent of any dividends received by a taxable corporation can be excluded in computing its taxable income, pushes down the yields on preferred stocks and thereby offsets the disadvantage of nondeductibility.

corporation reap no gain whatever from their use of tax-deductible debt rather than equity capital.

But we can say more than this. Any situation in which the owners of corporations could increase their wealth by substituting debt for equity (or vice versa) would be incompatible with market equilibrium. Their attempts to exploit these opportunities would lead, in a world with progressive income taxes, to changes in the yields on stocks and bonds and in their ownership patterns. These changes, in turn, restore the equilibrium and remove the incentives to issue more debt, even without invoking bankruptcy costs or lending costs as a *deus ex machina*.

IV. TAXES AND MARKET EQUILIBRIUM

Like so many other propositions in financial economics this, too, is "obvious once you think of it." Let me belabor the obvious a bit, however, by a simple graphical example that will serve, I hope, both to illustrate the mechanism that brings the equilibrium about and to highlight some of the implications of that equilibrium.

Suppose, for simplicity, that the personal tax rate on income from stock were zero (and we'll see later that this may be a less outrageous simplification than it looks). And suppose further, again strictly for simplicity of presentation, that all bonds are riskless and that there are no transaction costs, flotation costs or surveillance costs involved in their issuance. Then in such a world, the equilibrium of the market for bonds would be that pictured in Figure 1. The quantity of bonds outstanding is measured along the horizontal axis and the rate of interest along the vertical. The demand for bonds by the investing public is given by the upward sloping curve labeled $r_d(B)$. (Yes, it *is* a demand curve

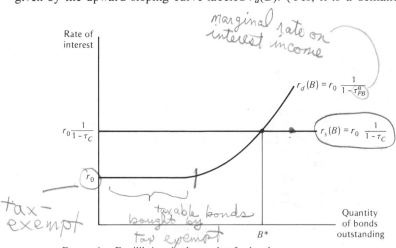

FIGURE 1. Equilibrium in the market for bonds.

even though it slopes up.) Its intercept is at r_0 which measures the equilibrium rate of interest on fully tax-exempt bonds (such as those of state and local governments). The flat stretch of the curve immediately to the right represents the demand for fully taxable corporate bonds by fully tax-exempt individuals and organizations. Clearly, these investors would be the sole holders of corporate bonds if the market interest rate on corporate debts were only r_0. Any taxable investor who wanted to hold bonds in his or her portfolio would find it preferable to buy tax-exempt bonds.

To entice these taxable investors into the market for corporate bonds, the rate of interest on such bonds has to be high enough to compensate for the taxes on interest income under the personal income tax. More precisely, for an individual whose marginal rate of personal income tax on interest income is τ_{PB}^α, the "demand rate of interest" on taxable corporate bonds would be the rate on tax exempts grossed up by the marginal tax rate, i.e., $r_0(1/(1 - \tau_{PB}^\alpha))$. Since the personal income tax is progressive, the demand interest rate has to keep rising to pull in investors in higher and higher tax brackets, thus giving the continuous, upward-sloping curve pictured.

The intersection of this demand curve with the horizontal straight line through the point $r_0/1 - \tau_C$, i.e., the tax-exempt rate grossed up by the corporate tax rate, determines the market equilibrium. If corporations were to offer a quantity of bonds greater than B^*, interest rates would be driven above $r_0/1 - \tau_C$ and some levered firms would find leverage to be a losing proposition. If the volume were below B^*, interest rates would be lower than $r_0/1 - \tau_C$ and some unlevered firms would find it advantageous to resort to borrowing.

The market equilibrium defined by the intersection of the two curves will have the following property. There will be an equilibrium level of aggregate corporate debt, B^*, and hence an equilibrium debt-equity ratio for the corporate sector as a whole. *But there would be no optimum debt ratio for any individual firm.* Companies following a no-leverage or low leverage strategy (like I.B.M. or Kodak) would find a market among investors in the high tax brackets; those opting for a high leverage strategy (like the electric utilities) would find the natural clientele for their securities at the other end of the scale. But one clientele is as good as the other. And in this important sense it would still be true that the value of any firm, in equilibrium, would be independent of its capital structure, despite the deductibility of interest payments in computing corporate income taxes.[20]

One advantage of graphical illustration is that it makes it so easy to see the answer to the following inevitable question: If the stockholders of levered corporations don't reap the benefits of the tax gains from leverage, who does? Professors of finance, of course—though only indirectly and only after cutting in their colleagues in other departments. As Figure 1 shows, universities and

[20] The details of corporate strategy and investor valuation at the micro level implied by this model are interesting in their own right, but further analysis is best deferred to another occasion.

other tax exempt organizations, as well as individuals in low tax brackets (widows and orphans?) benefit from what might be called a "bondholders' surplus." Market interest rates have to be grossed up to pay the taxes of the marginal bondholder, whose tax rate in equilibrium will be equal to the corporate rate.[21] Note that this can cut both ways, however. Low bracket individuals (and corporations) have to *pay* the corporate tax, in effect, when they want to borrow.

An equilibrium of the kind pictured in Figure 1 does not require, of course, that the effective personal tax rate on income from shares of the marginal holder be literally zero, but only that it be substantially less than his or her rate on income from bonds. As a practical matter, however, the assumption that the effective rate at the margin is close to zero may not be so wide of the mark. Keep in mind that a "clientele effect" is also at work in the market for shares. The high dividend paying stocks will be preferred by tax exempt organizations and low income investors; those stocks yielding more of their return in the form of capital gains will gravitate to the taxpayers in the upper brackets.[22] The tax rate on such gains is certainly greater than zero, in principle. But holders need pay no taxes on their gains until realized and only a small fraction of accumulated gains are, in fact, realized and taxed in any year (see, e.g., Bhatia [4, esp. note 12] and Bailey [2]). Taxes on capital gains can not only be deferred at the option of the holder—and remember that by conventional folk wisdom, 10 years of tax deferral is almost as good as exemption—but until the recent Tax Reform Act of 1976, could be avoided altogether if held until death, thanks to the rules permitting transfer of the decedent's tax basis to his or her heirs.

To the extent that the effective tax rate on income from shares is greater than zero, the horizontal line defining the equilibrium interest rate will be

---

[21] In point of fact, the spread between municipals and corporates has typically been within shouting distance of the corporate rate, though comparisons are difficult because of differences in risk (including, of course, the risk that the tax status of municipals will be changed) and though, admittedly, mechanisms of a different kind might also be producing that result. The recent study of the yield curve of U.S. Government securities by McCulloch [23] gives estimates of the marginal tax rate of holders of such bonds that are close to, but usually somewhat below the corporate rate.

[22] The data presented in the study of stock ownership by Blume, Crockett and Friend [11, esp. Table G, p. 40] are consistent with this form of clientele effect, though its magnitude is perhaps somewhat smaller than might have been expected *a priori*. They estimate, for example, that in 1971, the ratio of dividends to the market value of holdings was about 2.8 percent for individual investors with adjusted gross income of less than $15,000 as compared to 2.1 percent for those with adjusted gross incomes of $100,000 or more.

By invoking this dividend clientele effect, an argument analogous to that in Figure 1 can be developed to show that the value of a firm could be invariant to its dividend policy despite the more favorable tax treatment of capital gains than of dividends. Some gropings in that direction were made in the MM dividend paper [25, esp. pp. 431–2]. A more explicit analysis along those lines was given by Black and Scholes [10]. For a related model dealing with tax shelters on real investment see Bailey [3].

above that pictured in Figure 1. In the limiting case where the tax concessions (intended or unintended) made to income from shares were either nonexistent or so small that $(1 - \tau_C)(1 - \tau_{PS})$ implied a value for τ_{PB}^x greater than the top bracket of the personal income tax, then no interior market equilibrium would be possible. Common stock would indeed be a dominated security from the purely financial point of view, exactly as the standard micro model of the tax effect suggests. Common stock could continue to exist only by virtue of special attributes it might possess that could not be duplicated with bonds or with other forms of business organization, such as co-ops.

The analysis underlying Figure 1 can be extended to allow for risky borrowing, but there are complications. What makes things difficult is not simply a matter of risk *per se*.[23] Default risk can be accommodated in Figure 1 merely by reinterpreting all the before-tax interest rates as risk-adjusted or certainty-equivalent rates. The trouble is, rather, that bonds of companies in default will not, in general, yield the issuing stockholders their full tax shield (see MM [27, esp. note 5], Kim [21] and Brennan and Schwartz [12]). Unless the firm has past profits against which its current losses can be carried back, or unless it can escape the vigilance of the I.R.S. and unload the corporate corpse on a taxable firm, some of the interest deduction goes to waste. To entice firms to issue risky bonds, therefore, the risk-adjusted supply-rate would have to be less than $r_0(1/(1 - \tau_C))$, and presumably the more so the greater the likelihood of default.[24]

An essentially similar effect will be produced by the bankruptcy costs discussed earlier. And this will imply, among other things, that the full burden of the bankruptcy costs or lending costs is not necesssarily borne by the debtors as is frequently supposed. Part of the costs are shifted to the bond buyers in the form of lower risk-adjusted rates of interest in equilibrium.

A model of the kind in Figure 1 could, in principle, clear up most of the puzzles and anomalies discussed in Sections I and II above—the seeming disparity between the tax gains of debt and the costs of bankruptcy particularly for large low-levered corporations; the lack of widespread market interest in income bonds; and especially the failure of the average corporate debt ratio to rise substantially in response to the enormous increase in tax rates since the

[23] For the specialists in these matters, suffice it to say that in the equilibrium of Figure 1, the capital markets are, of course, assumed to be "complete." For a discussion of some of the implications of corporate taxes the deductibility of interest payments under conditions of "incomplete markets" see Hakansson [18].

[24] These effects, however, do not imply the existence of "super-premiums" for riskless bonds of the kind visualized recently by Glenn [17] and earlier by Durand [14]. Those were presumed to arise from the segmentation of the bond market and especially from the strong preferences of the institutional sector for low-risk securities. In terms of Figure 1, any such increase in the demand for safe securities would show up in the first instance as a lower value for r_0 and, hence, a lower value for the equilibrium corporate borrowing rate, $r_0/1 - \tau_C$. (See the MM 1958 article [28, especially pp. 279–80]. See also Hamada's discussion of Glenn's paper [19].)

1920's (because these increases in rates in the late 1930's as well as subsequent decreases and reincreases have generally moved both the corporate and individual rate schedules in the same direction). The model could also account as well for other of the stylized facts of corporate finance such as the oft-remarked dramatic transition of the bond market from an individual to an institution-dominated market in the late 1930's and early 1940's.[25] On the other hand, many questions clearly still remain to be answered. What about cross-sectional variations in debt ratios, for example—a subject on which surprisingly little work has yet been done?[26] Can they be explained convincingly by the market equilibrium model presented here or some variant of it? Or do the variations observed reflect some systematic part of the equilibrating process that escapes the kind of aggregate market models discussed here? What about the distribution of stocks and bonds among investors? Does ownership sort out in terms of tax status as sharply as emphasized here? Or does the need for diversification swamp the tax differences and thereby throw the main burden of the equilibration onto other factors, such as agency costs?

The call for more research traditionally signals the approaching end of a Presidential Address; and it is a tradition that I know you will want to see preserved. Let me conclude, therefore, by trying to face up, as I promised in the beginning, to the kind of complaint so often raised against market equilibrium analysis of financial policy of the type here presented: "But firms and investors don't behave that way!"

V. MARKET EQUILIBRIUM AND THE BEHAVIOR OF FIRMS AND INDIVIDUALS

If the phrase "don't behave that way" is taken to mean that firms and individuals don't literally perform the maximizing calculations that underlie the curves in Figure 1, then it is most certainly correct. No corporate treasurer's office, controller's staff, or investment banker's research team that I have ever encountered had, or could remotely be expected to have, enough reliable information about the future course of prices for a firm's securities to convince even a moderately skeptical outside academic observer that the firm's value had indeed been maximized by some specific financial decision or strategy. Given the complexities of the real-world setting, actual decision procedures are inevitably heuristic, judgmental, imitative and groping even where, as with so much of what passes for capital budgeting, they wear the superficial trappings of

---

[25] For an early account of that transition that stresses precisely the kind of tax effects that underlie Figure 1, see Shapiro [35].

[26] One of the few studies of cross-sectional differences in debt ratios is that of Schwartz and Aronson [34], but it really does little more than document the fact that utilities and railroads have substantially higher debt ratios than firms in manufacturing and mining.

hard-nosed maximization. On this score, has there ever been any doubt that the Harvard cases (and the work of Herbert Simon and his followers) give a far more accurate picture of the way things really look and get done out on the firing line than any maximizing "model of the firm" that any economist ever drew?

Why then do economists keep trying to develop models that assume rational behavior by firms? They are not, I insist, merely hoping to con their business school deans into thinking they are working on problems of business management. Rather they have found from experience—not only in finance, but across the board—that the rational behavior models generally lead to better predictions and descriptions at the level of the industry, the market and the whole economy than any alternatives available to them. Their experience, at those levels, moreover, need involve no inconsistency with the heuristic, rule-of-thumb, intuitive kinds of decision making they actually observe in firms. It suggests rather that evolutionary mechanisms are at work to give survival value to those heuristics that are compatible with rational market equilibrium, however far from rational they may appear to be when examined up close and in isolation.[27]

But we must be wary of the reverse inference that merely because a given heuristic persists, it must have some survival value and, hence, must have a rational "explanation." The MM and related invariance propositions, for example, are often dismissed on grounds that corporate finance officers would surely not show so much concern over decisions that really "don't matter." The most, however, that we can safely assert about the evolutionary process underlying market equilibrium is that harmful heuristics, like harmful mutations in nature, will die out. Neutral mutations that serve no function, but do no harm, can persist indefinitely. Neither in nature nor in the economy can the enormous variation in forms we observe be convincingly explained in simple Darwinian terms.[28]

To say that many, perhaps even most, financial heuristics are neutral is not to suggest, however, that financial decision making is just a pointless charade or that the resources devoted to financial innovations are wasted. A mutation or a heuristic that is neutral in one environment may suddenly acquire (or lose) survival value if the environment changes. The pool of existing neutral mutations and heuristics thus permits the adaptation to the new conditions to take place more quickly and more surely than if a new and original act of creation were required. Once these types and roles of heuristics in the equilibrating pro-

---

[27] Has anyone a better explanation for the puzzle of why the pay-back criterion continues to thrive despite having been denounced as Neanderthal in virtually every textbook in finance and accounting over the last 30 years?

[28] Any experienced teacher of corporate finance can surely supply numerous examples of such neutral variations. My own favorite is the captive finance company. See, e.g., the perspective discussion in Andrews [1].

cess are understood and appreciated, the differences between the institution-alist and theorist wings of our Association may be seen to be far less funda-mental and irreconcilable than the sometimes ferocious polemics of the last 20 years might seem to suggest.

REFERENCES

1. Victor L. Andrews. "Captive Finance Companies," *Harvard Business Review,* Vol. 42 (July-August 1964), 80–92.
2. Martin J. Bailey. "Capital Gains and Income Taxation," In *The Taxation of Income From Capital.* Edited by A. Harberger and M. Bailey. (Washington, D.C.: The Brookings Distribution, 1969).
3. ———. "Progressivity and Investment Yields under U.S. Income Taxation," *Journal of Political Economy,* Vol. 82, No. 6 (Nov./Dec. 1974), 1157–75.
4. Ku B. Bhatia. "Capital Gains and Inequality of Personal Income: Some Results From Survey Data," *Journal of the American Statistical Association,* Vol. 71, No. 355 (September 1976), 575–580.
5. Nevins Baxter. "Leverage, Risk of Ruin and the Cost of Capital," *Journal of Finance,* Vol. 22, No. 3 (September 1967), 395–403.
6. Fischer Black. "Bank Funds Management in an Efficient Market," *Journal of Financial Economics,* Vol. 2, No. 4 (December 1975).
7. ———. "Taxes and Capital Market Equilibrium." Working Paper No. 21A, Associates in Finance, Belmont, Masssachusetts, April 1971 (mimeo).
8. ———. "Taxes and Capital Market Equilibrium under Uncertainty," Working Paper No. 21B, Chicago, May 1973 (mimeo).
9. ———, Merton H. Miller and Richard A. Posner. "An Approach to the Regulation of Bank Holding Companies," University of Chicago, April 1976 (multilith).
10. ——— and Myron Scholes. "The Effects on Dividend Yield and Dividend Policy on Common Stock Prices and Returns," *Journal of Financial Economics,* Vol. 1, No. 1 (May 1974), 1–22.
11. Marshall E. Blume, Jean Crockett and Irwin Frend. "Stock Ownership in The United States: Characteristics and Trends," *Survey of Current Business* (November 1974), 16–40.
12. M. J. Brennan and E. S. Schwartz. "Corporate Income Taxes, Valuation and the Problem of Optimal Capital Structure," University of British Columbia, Vancouver, B.C., Canada, multilith, August 1976 (revised).
13. J. H. Coates and P. K. Wooley. "Corporate Gearing in the E.E.C.," *Journal of Business Finance and Accounting,* Vol. 2, No. 1 (Spring 1975), 1–18.
14. David Durand. "The Cost of Capital, Corporation Finance and the Invest-

ment: Comment," *American Economic Review,* Vol. 49, No. 4 (Sept. 1959), 39–55.

15. Donald Farrar and Lee L. Selwyn. "Taxes, Corporate Policy, and Returns to Investors," *National Tax Journal,* Vol. 20, No. 4 (December 1967), 444–54.

16. R. Alton Gilbert. "Bank Financing of the Recovery," *Federal Reserve Bank of St. Louis Review,* Vol. 58, No. 7, 2–9.

17. David W. Glenn. "Super Premium Security Prices and Optimal Corporate Financial Decisions," *Journal of Finance,* Vol. 31, No. 2(May 1976), 507–24.

18. Nils Hakansson. "Ordering Markets and the Capital Structures of Firms, with Illustrations," Working Paper No. 24, Institute of Business and Economic Research, University of California, Berkeley, October 1974 (multilith).

19. Robert Hamada. "Discussion," *Journal of Finance,* Vol. 31, No. 2 (May 1976), 543–46.

20. Michael C. Jensen and William H. Meckling. "Theory of the Firm: Managerial Behavior, Agency Costs and Capital Structure," University of Rochester, August 1975 (multilith).

21. Han E. Kim. "A Mean-Variance Theory of Optimum Capital Structure and Corporate Debt Capacity," Ohio State University, undated (multilith).

22. Ronald W. Masulis. "The Effects of Capital Structure Change on Security Prices," Graduate School of Business, University of Chicago, May 1976 (multilith).

23. J. Huston McCulloch, "The Tax Adjusted Yield Curve," *Journal of Finance,* Vol. 30, No. 3 (June 1975), 811–30.

24. Merton H. Miller. "The Corporation Income Tax and Corporate Financial Policies," In *Stabilization Policies,* Commission on Money and Credit, Prentice Hall, 1963.

25. ——— and Franco Modigliani. "Dividend Policy, Growth and the Valuation of Shares," *Journal of Business,* Vol. 34, No. 4 (October 1961), 411–33.

26. ——— and Charles W. Upton. "Leasing, Buying and the Cost of Capital Services." *Journal of Finance* (June 1976).

27. Franco Modigliani and Merton H. Miller. "Corporate Income Taxes and the Cost of Capital: A Correction," *American Economic Review,* Vol. 53, No. 3 (June 1963), 433–43.

28. ——— and ———. "The Cost of Capital, Corporation Finance and the Theory of Investment," *American Economic Review,* Vol. 48, No. 3 (June 1958), 261–97.

29. ——— and ———. "Reply to Heins and Sprenkle," *American Economic Review,* Vol. 59, No. 4, Part I (September 1969).

30. Stewart C. Myers, "Taxes, Corporate Financial Policy and the Return to

Investors: Comment," *National Tax Journal,* Vol. 20, No. 4 (Dec. 1967), 455–62.

31. Sidney M. Robbins. "A Bigger Role for Income Bonds," *Harvard Business Review* (November-December 1955).

32. ———. "An Objective Look at Income Bonds," *Harvard Business Review* (June 1974).

33. Arnold W. Sametz. "Trends in the Volume and Composition of Equity Finance," *Journal of Finance,* Vol. 19, No. 3 (September 1964), 450–469.

34. Eli Schwartz and J. Richard Aronson. "Some Surrogate Evidence in Support of the Concept of Optimal Financial Structure," *Journal of Finance,* Vol. 22, No. 1 (March 1963), 10–18.

35. Eli Shapiro. "The Postwar Market for Corporate Securities: 1946–55," *Journal of Finance,* Vol. 14, No. 2 (May 1959), 196–217.

36. D. T. Stanley and M. Girth. *Bankruptcy: Problems, Process, Reform.* (Washington, D.C.: The Brookings Institution, 1971).

37. R. C. Stapleton. "Taxes, the Cost of Capital and the Theory of Investment," *The Economic Journal,* Vol. 82 (December 1972), 1273–92.

38. Joseph Stiglitz. "Taxation, Corporate Financial Policy, and the Cost of Capital," *Journal of Public Economics,* Vol. 2, No. 1 (February 1973), 1–34.

39. James C. Van Horne. "Corporate Liquidity and Bankruptcy Costs," Stanford University, Graduate School of Business, Research Paper No. 205, undated (multilith).

40. Jerold Warner. "Bankruptcy Costs, Absolute Priority and the Pricing of Risky Debt Claims," University of Chicago, July 1976 (multilith).

24. THEORY OF THE FIRM: MANAGERIAL BEHAVIOR, AGENCY COSTS AND OWNERSHIP STRUCTURE

MICHAEL C. JENSEN

and

WILLIAM H. MECKLING*

Reprinted from *The Journal of Financial Economics,* Vol. 3, No. 4 (October 1976), pp. 305–360, by permission of the authors and the publisher.

This paper integrates elements from the theory of agency, the theory of property rights and the theory of finance to develop a theory of the ownership structure of the firm. We define the concept of agency costs, show its relationship to the 'separation and control' issue, investigate the nature of the agency costs generated by the existence of debt and outside equity, demonstrate who bears these costs and why, and investigate the Pareto optimality of their existence. We also provide a new definition of the firm, and show how our analysis of the factors influencing the creation and issuance of debt and equity claims is a special case of the supply side of the completeness of markets problem.

> The directors of such [joint-stock] companies, however, being the managers rather of other people's money than of their own, it cannot well be expected, that they should watch over it with the same anxious vigilance with which the partners in a private copartnery frequently watch over their own. Like the stewards of a rich man, they are apt to consider attention to small matters as not for their master's honour, and very easily give themselves a dispensation from having it. Negligence and profusion, therefore, must always prevail, more or less, in the management of the affairs of such a company.
>
> Adam Smith, *The Wealth of Nations,* 1776, Cannan Edition
> (Modern Library, New York, 1937) p. 700.

1. Introduction and summary

1.1. Motivation of the paper

In this paper we draw on recent progress in the theory of (1) property rights, (2) agency, and (3) finance to develop a theory of ownership structure[1] for the

*Associate Professor and Dean, respectively, Graduate School of Management, University of Rochester. An earlier version of this paper was presented at the Conference on Analysis and Ideology, Interlaken, Switzerland, June 1974, sponsored by the Center for Research in Government Policy and Business at the University of Rochester, Graduate School of Management. We are indebted to F. Black, E. Fama, R. Ibbotson, W. Klein, M. Rozeff, R. Weil, O. Williamson, an anonymous referee, and to our colleagues and members of the Finance Workshop at the University of Rochester for their comments and criticisms, in particular G. Benston, M. Canes, D. Henderson, K. Leffler, J. Long, C. Smith, R. Thompson, R. Watts and J. Zimmerman.

[1]We do not use the term 'capital structure' because that term usually denotes the relative quantities of bonds, equity, warrants, trade credit, etc., which represent the liabilities of a firm. Our theory implies there is another important dimension to this problem – namely the relative amounts of ownership claims held by insiders (management) and outsiders (investors with no direct role in the management of the firm).

firm. In addition to tying together elements of the theory of each of these three areas, our analysis casts new light on and has implications for a variety of issues in the professional and popular literature such as the definition of the firm, the "separation of ownership and control", the "social responsibility" of business, the definition of a "corporate objective function", the determination of an optimal capital structure, the specification of the content of credit agreements, the theory of organizations, and the supply side of the completeness of markets problem.

Our theory helps explain:

(1) why an entrepreneur or manager in a firm which has a mixed financial structure (containing both debt and outside equity claims) will choose a set of activities for the firm such that the total value of the firm is *less* than it would be if he were the sole owner and why this result is independent of whether the firm operates in monopolistic or competitive product or factor markets;

(2) why his failure to maximize the value of the firm is perfectly consistent with efficiency;

(3) why the sale of common stock is a viable source of capital even though managers do not literally maximize the value of the firm;

(4) why debt was relied upon as a source of capital before debt financing offered any tax advantage relative to equity;

(5) why preferred stock would be issued;

(6) why accounting reports would be provided voluntarily to creditors and stockholders, and why independent auditors would be engaged by management to testify to the accuracy and correctness of such reports;

(7) why lenders often place restrictions on the activities of firms to whom they lend, and why firms would themselves be led to suggest the imposition of such restrictions;

(8) why some industries are characterized by owner-operated firms whose sole outside source of capital is borrowing;

(9) why highly regulated industries such as public utilities or banks will have higher debt equity ratios for equivalent levels of risk than the average non-regulated firm;

(10) why security analysis can be socially productive even if it does not increase portfolio returns to investors.

1.2. Theory of the firm: An empty box?

While the literature of economics is replete with references to the "theory of the firm", the material generally subsumed under that heading is not a theory of the firm but actually a theory of markets in which firms are important actors. The firm is a "black box" operated so as to meet the relevant marginal conditions with respect to inputs and outputs, thereby maximizing profits, or more accurately, present value. Except for a few recent and tentative steps, however, we have no theory which explains how the conflicting objectives of the individual participants are brought into equilibrium so as to yield this result. The limitations of this black box view of the firm have been cited by Adam Smith and Alfred Marshall, among others. More recently, popular and professional debates over the "social responsibility" of corporations, the separation of ownership and control, and the rash of reviews of the literature on the "theory of the firm" have evidenced continuing concern with these issues.[2]

A number of major attempts have been made during recent years to construct a theory of the firm by substituting other models for profit or value maximization; each attempt motivated by a conviction that the latter is inadequate to explain managerial behavior in large corporations.[3] Some of these reformulation attempts have rejected the fundamental principle of maximizing behavior as well as rejecting the more specific profit maximizing model. We retain the notion of maximizing behavior on the part of all individuals in the analysis to follow.[4]

1.3. Property rights

An independent stream of research with important implications for the theory of the firm has been stimulated by the pioneering work of Coase, and extended by Alchian, Demsetz and others.[5] A comprehensive survey of this literature is given by Furubotn and Pejovich (1972). While the focus of this research has been "property rights",[6] the subject matter encompassed is far broader than that term suggests. What is important for the problems addressed here is that specification of individual rights determines how costs and rewards will be

[2]Reviews of this literature are given by Peterson (1965), Alchian (1965, 1968), Machlup (1967), Shubik (1970), Cyert and Hedrick (1972), Branch (1973), Preston (1975).

[3]See Williamson (1964, 1970, 1975), Marris (1964), Baumol (1959), Penrose (1958), and Cyert and March (1963). Thorough reviews of these and other contributions are given by Machlup (1961) and Alchian (1965).

Simon (1955) developed a model of human choice incorporating information (search) and computational costs which also has important implications for the behavior of managers. Unfortunately, Simon's work has often been misinterpreted as a denial of maximizing behavior, and misused, especially in the marketing and behavioral science literature. His later use of the term 'satisficing' [Simon (1959)] has undoubtedly contributed to this confusion because it suggests rejection of maximizing behavior rather than maximization subject to costs of information and of decision making.

[4]See Meckling (1976) for a discussion of the fundamental importance of the assumption of resourceful, evaluative, maximizing behavior on the part of individuals in the development of theory. Klein (1976) takes an approach similar to the one we embark on in this paper in his review of the theory of the firm and the law.

[5]See Coase (1937, 1959, 1960), Alchian (1965, 1968), Alchian and Kessel (1962), Demsetz (1967), Alchian and Demsetz (1972), Monsen and Downs (1965), Silver and Auster (1969), and McManus (1975).

[6]Property rights are of course human rights, i.e., rights which are possessed by human beings. The introduction of the wholly false distinction between property rights and human rights in many policy discussions is surely one of the all time great semantic flimflams.

allocated among the participants in any organization. Since the specification of rights is generally effected through contracting (implicit as well as explicit), individual behavior in organizations, including the behavior of managers, will depend upon the nature of these contracts. We focus in this paper on the behavioral implications of the property rights specified in the contracts between the owners and managers of the firm.

1.4. Agency costs

Many problems associated with the inadequcy of the current theory of the firm can also be viewed as special cases of the theory of agency relationships in which there is a growing literature.[7] This literature has developed independently of the property rights literature even though the problems with which it is concerned are similar; the approaches are in fact highly complementary to each other.

We define an agency relationship as a contract under which one or more persons (the principal(s)) engage another person (the agent) to perform some service on their behalf which involves delegating some decision making authority to the agent. If both parties to the relationship are utility maximizers there is good reason to believe that the agent will not always act in the best interests of the principal. The *principal* can limit divergences from his interest by establishing appropriate incentives for the agent and by incurring monitoring costs designed to limit the aberrant activities of the agent. In addition in some situations it will pay the *agent* to expend resources (bonding costs) to guarantee that he will not take certain actions which would harm the principal or to ensure that the principal will be compensated if he does take such actions. However, it is generally impossible for the principal or the agent at zero cost to ensure that the agent will make optimal decisions from the principal's viewpoint. In most agency relationships the principal and the agent will incur positive monitoring and bonding costs (non-pecuniary as well as pecuniary), and in addition there will be some divergence between the agent's decisions[8] and those decisions which would maximize the welfare of the principal. The dollar equivalent of the reduction in welfare experienced by the principal due to this divergence is also a cost of the agency relationship, and we refer to this latter cost as the "residual loss". We define *agency costs* as the sum of:

(1) the monitoring expenditures by the principal,[9]
(2) the bonding expenditures by the agent,
(3) the residual loss.

[7]Cf. Berhold (1971), Ross (1973, 1974a), Wilson (1968, 1969), and Heckerman (1975).

[8]Given the optimal monitoring and bonding activities by the principal and agent.

[9]As it is used in this paper the term monitoring includes more than just measuring or observing the behavior of the agent. It includes efforts on the part of the principal to 'control' the behavior of the agent through budget restrictions, compensation policies, operating rules etc.

Note also that agency costs arise in any situation involving cooperative effort (such as the co-authoring of this paper) by two or more people even though there is no clear cut principal–agent relationship. Viewed in this light it is clear that our definition of agency costs and their importance to the theory of the firm bears a close relationship to the problem of shirking and monitoring of team production which Alchian and Demsetz (1972) raise in their paper on the theory of the firm.

Since the relationship between the stockholders and manager of a corporation fit the definition of a pure agency relationship it should be no surprise to discover that the issues associated with the "separation of ownership and control" in the modern diffuse ownership corporation are intimately associated with the general problem of agency. We show below that an explanation of why and how the agency costs generated by the corporate form are born leads to a theory of the ownership (or capital) structure of the firm.

Before moving on, however, it is worthwhile to point out the generality of the agency problem. The problem of inducing an "agent" to behave as if he were maximizing the "principal's" welfare is quite general. It exists in all organizations and in all cooperative efforts – at every level of management in firms,[10] in universities, in mutual companies, in cooperatives, in governmental authorities and bureaus, in unions, and in relationships normally classified as agency relationships such as are common in the performing arts and the market for real estate. The development of theories to explain the form which agency costs take in each of these situations (where the contractual relations differ significantly), and how and why they are born will lead to a rich theory of organizations which is now lacking in economics and the social sciences generally. We confine our attention in this paper to only a small part of this general problem – the analysis of agency costs generated by the contractual arrangements between the owners and top management of the corporation.

Our approach to the agency problem here differs fundamentally from most of the existing literature. That literature focuses almost exclusively on the normative aspects of the agency relationship; that is how to structure the contractual relation (including compensation incentives) between the principal and agent to provide appropriate incentives for the agent to make choices which will maximize

---

[10]As we show below the existence of positive monitoring and bonding costs will result in the manager of a corporation possessing control over some resources which he can allocate (within certain constraints) to satisfy his own preferences. However, to the extent that he must obtain the cooperation of others in order to carry out his tasks (such as divisional vice presidents) and to the extent that he cannot control their behavior perfectly and costlessly they will be able to appropriate some of these resources for their own ends. In short, there are agency costs generated at every level of the organization. Unfortunately, the analysis of these more general organizational issues is even more difficult than that of the 'ownership and control' issue because the nature of the contractual obligations and rights of the parties are much more varied and generally not as well specified in explicit contractual arrangements. Nevertheless, they exist and we believe that extensions of our analysis in these directions show promise of producing insights into a viable theory of organization.

the principal's welfare given that uncertainty and imperfect monitoring exist. We focus almost entirely on the positive aspects of the theory. That is, we assume individuals solve these normative problems and given that only stocks and bonds can be issued as claims, we investigate the incentives faced by each of the parties and the elements entering into the determination of the equilibrium contractual form characterizing the relationship between the manager (i.e., agent) of the firm and the outside equity and debt holders (i.e., principals).

1.5. Some general comments on the definition of the firm

Ronald Coase (1937) in his seminal paper on "The Nature of the Firm" pointed out that economics had no positive theory to determine the bounds of the firm. He characterized the bounds of the firm as that range of exchanges over which the market system was suppressed and resource allocation was accomplished instead by authority and direction. He focused on the cost of using markets to effect contracts and exchanges and argued that activities would be included within the firm whenever the costs of using markets were greater than the costs of using direct authority. Alchian and Demsetz (1972) object to the notion that activities within the firm are governed by authority, and correctly emphasize the role of contracts as a vehicle for voluntary exchange. They emphasize the role of monitoring in situations in which there is joint input or team production.[11] We sympathize with the importance they attach to monitoring, but we believe the emphasis which Alchian–Demsetz place on joint input production is too narrow and therefore misleading. Contractual relations are the essence of the firm, not only with employees but with suppliers, customers, creditors, etc. The problem of agency costs and monitoring exists for all of these contracts, independent of whether there is joint production in their sense; i.e., joint production can explain only a small fraction of the behavior of individuals associated with a firm. A detailed examination of these issues is left to another paper.

It is important to recognize that most organizations are simply *legal fictions*[12] *which serve as a nexus for a set of contracting relationships among individuals.* This includes firms, non-profit institutions such as universities, hospitals and foundations, mutual organizations such as mutual savings banks and insurance companies and co-operatives, some private clubs, and even governmental bodies such as cities, states and the Federal government, government enterprises such as TVA, the Post Office, transit systems, etc.

---

[11]They define the classical capitalist firm as a contractual organization of inputs in which there is '(a) joint input production, (b) several input owners, (c) one party who is common to all the contracts of the joint inputs, (d) who has rights to renegotiate any input's contract independently of contracts with other input owners, (e) who holds the residual claim, and (f) who has the right to sell his contractual residual status.'

[12]By legal fiction we mean the artificial construct under the law which allows certain organizations to be treated as individuals.

The private corporation or firm is simply one form of *legal fiction which serves as a nexus for contracting relationships and which is also characterized by the existence of divisible residual claims on the assets and cash flows of the organization which can generally be sold without permission of the other contracting individuals.* While this definition of the firm has little substantive content, emphasizing the essential contractual nature of firms and other organizations focuses attention on a crucial set of questions – why particular sets of contractual relations arise for various types of organizations, what the consequences of these contractual relations are, and how they are affected by changes exogenous to the organization. Viewed this way, it makes little or no sense to try to distinguish those things which are "inside" the firm (or any other organization) from those things that are "outside" of it. There is in a very real sense only a multitude of complex relationships (i.e., contracts) between the legal fiction (the firm) and the owners of labor, material and capital inputs and the consumers of output.[13]

Viewing the firm as the nexus of a set of contracting relationships among individuals also serves to make it clear that the personalization of the firm implied by asking questions such as "what should be the objective function of the firm", or "does the firm have a social responsibility" is seriously misleading. *The firm is not an individual.* It is a legal fiction which serves as a focus for a complex process in which the conflicting objectives of individuals (some of whom may "represent" other oganizations) are brought into equilibrium within a framework of contractual relations. In this sense the "behavior" of the firm is like the behavior of a market; i.e., the outcome of a complex equilibrium process. We seldom fall into the trap of characterizing the wheat or stock market as an individual, but we often make this error by thinking about organizations as if they were persons with motivations and intentions.[14]

---

[13]For example, we ordinarily think of a product as leaving the firm at the time it is sold, but implicitly or explicitly such sales generally carry with them continuing contracts between the firm and the buyer. If the product does not perform as expected the buyer often can and does have a right to satisfaction. Explicit evidence that such implicit contracts do exist is the practice we occasionally observe of specific provision that 'all sales are final.'

[14]This view of the firm points up the important role which the legal system and the law play in social organizations, especially, the organization of economic activity. Statutory laws sets bounds on the kinds of contracts into which individuals and organizations may enter without risking criminal prosecution. The police powers of the state are available and used to enforce performance of contracts or to enforce the collection of damages for non-performance. The courts adjudicate conflicts between contracting parties and establish precedents which form the body of common law. All of these government activities affect both the kinds of contracts executed and the extent to which contracting is relied upon. This in turn determines the usefulness, productivity, profitability and viability of various forms of organization. Moreover, new laws as well as court decisions often can and do change the rights of contracting parties ex post, and they can and do serve as a vehicle for redistribution of wealth. An analysis of some of the implications of these facts is contained in Jensen and Meckling (1976) and we shall not pursue them here.

1.6. An overview of the paper

We develop the theory in stages. Sections 2 and 4 provide analyses of the agency costs of equity and debt respectively. These form the major foundation of the theory. Section 3 poses some unanswered questions regarding the existence of the corporate form of organization and examines the role of limited liability. Section 5 provides a synthesis of the basic concepts derived in sections 2–4 into a theory of the corporate ownership structure which takes account of the trade-offs available to the entrepreneur–manager between inside and outside equity and debt. Some qualifications and extensions of the analysis are discussed in section 6, and section 7 contains a brief summary and conclusions.

2. The agency costs of outside equity

2.1. Overview

In this section we analyze the effect of outside equity on agency costs by comparing the behavior of a manager when he owns 100 percent of the residual claims on a firm to his behavior when he sells off a portion of those claims to outsiders. If a wholly owned firm is managed by the owner, he will make operating decisions which maximize his utility. These decisions will involve not only the benefits he derives from pecuniary returns but also the utility generated by various non-pecuniary aspects of his entrepreneurial activities such as the physical appointments of the office, the attractiveness of the secretarial staff, the level of employee discipline, the kind and amount of charitable contributions, personal relations ("love", "respect", etc.) with employees, a larger than optimal computer to play with, purchase of production inputs from friends, etc. The optimum mix (in the absence of taxes) of the various pecuniary and non-pecuniary benefits is achieved when the marginal utility derived from an additional dollar of expenditure (measured net of any productive effects) is equal for each non-pecuniary item and equal to the marginal utility derived from an additional dollar of after tax purchasing power (wealth).

If the owner–manager sells equity claims on the corporation which are identical to his (i.e., share proportionately in the profits of the firm and have limited liability) agency costs will be generated by the divergence between his interest and those of the outside shareholders, since he will then bear only a fraction of the costs of any non-pecuniary benefits he takes out in maximizing his own utility. If the manager owns only 95 percent of the stock, he will expend resources to the point where the marginal utility derived from a dollar's expenditure of the firm's resources on such items equals the marginal utility of an additional 95 cents in general purchasing power (i.e., *his* share of the wealth reduction) and not one dollar. Such activities, on his part, can be limited (but probably not eliminated) by the expenditure of resources on monitoring activities by the outside stockholders. But as we show below, the owner will bear the entire wealth effects of these expected costs so long as the equity market anticipates these effects. Prospective minority shareholders will realize that the owner–manager's interests will diverge somewhat from theirs, hence the price which they will pay for shares will reflect the monitoring costs and the effect of the divergence between the manager's interest and theirs. Nevertheless, ignoring for the moment the possibility of borrowing against his wealth, the owner will find it desirable to bear these costs as long as the welfare increment he experiences from converting his claims on the firm into general purchasing power[15] is large enough to offset them.

As the owner–manager's fraction of the equity falls, his fractional claim on the outcomes falls and this will tend to encourage him to appropriate larger amounts of the corporate resources in the form of perquisites. This also makes it desirable for the minority shareholders to expend more resources in monitoring his behavior. Thus, the wealth costs to the owner of obtaining additional cash in the equity markets rise as his fractional ownership falls.

We shall continue to characterize the agency conflict between the owner–manager and outside shareholders as deriving from the manager's tendency to appropriate perquisites out of the firm's resources for his own consumption. However, we do not mean to leave the impression that this is the only or even the most important source of conflict. Indeed, it is likely that the most important conflict arises from the fact that as the manager's ownership claim falls, his incentive to devote significant effort to creative activities such as searching out new profitable ventures falls. He may in fact avoid such ventures simply because it requires too much trouble or effort on his part to manage or to learn about new technologies. Avoidance of these personal costs and the anxieties that go with them also represent a source of on the job utility to him and it can result in the value of the firm being substantially lower than it otherwise could be.

2.2. A simple formal analysis of the sources of agency costs of equity and who bears them

In order to develop some structure for the analysis to follow we make two sets of assumptions. The first set (permanent assumptions) are those which shall carry through almost all of the analysis in sections 2–5. The effects of relaxing some of these are discussed in section 6. The second set (temporary assumptions) are made only for expositional purposes and are relaxed as soon as the basic points have been clarified.

---

[15]For use in consumption, for the diversification of his wealth, or more importantly, for the financing of 'profitable' projects which he could not otherwise finance out of his personal wealth. We deal with these issues below after having developed some of the elementary analytical tools necessary to their solution.

Permanent assumptions

(P.1) All taxes are zero.

(P.2) No trade credit is available.

(P.3) All outside equity shares are non-voting.

(P.4) No complex financial claims such as convertible bonds or preferred stock or warrants can be issued.

(P.5) No outside owner gains utility from ownership in a firm in any way other than through its effect on his wealth or cash flows.

(P.6) All dynamic aspects of the multiperiod nature of the problem are ignored by assuming there is only one production–financing decision to be made by the entrepreneur.

(P.7) The entrepreneur–manager's money wages are held constant throughout the analysis.

(P.8) There exists a single manager (the peak coordinator) with ownership interest in the firm.

Temporary assumptions

(T.1) The size of the firm is fixed.

(T.2) No monitoring or bonding activities are possible.

(T.3) No debt financing through bonds, preferred stock, or personal borrowing (secured or unsecured) is possible.

(T.4) All elements of the owner–manager's decision problem involving portfolio considerations induced by the presence of uncertainty and the existence of diversifiable risk are ignored.

Define:

$X \quad = \{x_1, x_2, \ldots, x_n\}$ = vector of quantities of all factors and activities within the firm from which the manager derives non-pecuniary benefits;[16] the x_i are defined such that his marginal utility is positive for each of them;

$C(X)$ = total dollar cost of providing any given amount of these items;

$P(X)$ = total dollar value to the firm of the productive benefits of X;

$B(X) = P(X) - C(X)$ = net dollar benefit to the firm of X ignoring any effects of X on the equilibrium wage of the manager.

Ignoring the effects of X on the manager's utility and therefore on his equilibrium wage rate, the optimum levels of the factors and activities X are defined by X^* such that

$$\frac{\partial B(X^*)}{\partial X^*} = \frac{\partial P(X^*)}{\partial X^*} - \frac{\partial C(X^*)}{\partial X^*} = 0.$$

---

[16]Such as office space, air conditioning, thickness of the carpets, friendliness of employee relations, etc.

Thus for any vector $X \geq X^*$ (i.e., where at least one element of X is greater than its corresponding element of X^*), $F \equiv B(X^*) - B(X) > 0$ measures the dollar cost to the firm (net of any productive effects) of providing the increment $X - X^*$ of the factors and activities which generate utility to the manager. We assume henceforth that for any given level of cost to the firm, F, the vector of factors and activities on which F is spent are those, $\hat{X}$, which yield the manager maximum utility. Thus $F \equiv B(X^*) - B(\hat{X})$.

We have thus far ignored in our discussion the fact that these expenditures on X occur through time and therefore there are tradeoffs to be made across time as well as between alternative elements of X. Furthermore, we have ignored the fact that the future expenditures are likely to involve uncertainty (i.e., they are subject to probability distributions) and therefore some allowance must be made for their riskiness. We resolve both of these issues by defining C, P, B, and F to be the *current market values* of the sequence of probability distributions on the period by period cash flows involved.[17]

Given the definition of F as the current market value of the stream of manager's expenditures on non-pecuniary benefits we represent the constraint which a single owner–manager faces in deciding how much non-pecuniary income he will extract from the firm by the line $\bar{V}F$ in fig. 1. This is analogous to a budget constraint. The market value of the firm is measured along the vertical axis and the market value of the manager's stream of expenditures on non-pecuniary benefits, F, are measured along the horizontal axis. $0\bar{V}$ is the value of the firm when the amount of non-pecuniary income consumed is zero. By definition $\bar{V}$ is the maximum market value of the cash flows generated by the firm for a given money wage for the manager when the manager's consumption of non-pecuniary benefits are zero. At this point all the factors and activities within the firm which generate utility for the manager are at the level X^* defined above. There is a different budget constraint $\bar{V}F$ for each possible scale of the firm (i.e., level of investment, I) and for alternative levels of money wage, W, for the manager. For the moment we pick an arbitrary level of investment (which we assume has already been made) and hold the scale of the firm constant at this level. We also assume that the manager's money wage is fixed at the level W^* which represents the current market value of his wage contract[18] in the optimal compensation package which consists of both wages, W^*, and non-pecuniary benefits, F^*. Since one dollar of current value of non-pecuniary benefits withdrawn from the firm by the manager reduces the market value of the firm by \$1, by definition, the slope of $\bar{V}F$ is -1.

[17] And again we assume that for any given market value of these costs, F, to the firm the allocation across time and across alternative probability distributions is such that the manager's current expected utility is at a maximum.

[18] At this stage when we are considering a 100% owner-managed firm the notion of a 'wage contract' with himself has no content. However, the 100% owner-managed case is only an expositional device used in passing to illustrate a number of points in the analysis, and we ask the reader to bear with us briefly while we lay out the structure for the more interesting partial ownership case where such a contract does have substance.

The owner–manager's tastes for wealth and non-pecuniary benefits is represented in fig. 1 by a system of indifference curves, U_1, U_2, etc.[19] The indifference curves will be convex as drawn as long as the owner–manager's marginal rate of

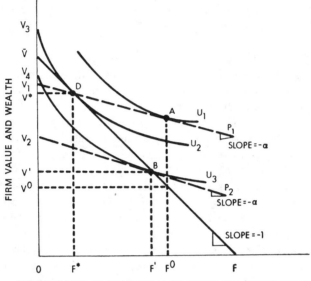

Fig. 1. The value of the firm (V) and the level of non-pecuniary benefits consumed (F) when the fraction of outside equity is $(1-\alpha)V$, and U_j ($j = 1, 2, 3$) represents owner's indifference curves between wealth and non-pecuniary benefits.

substitution between non-pecuniary benefits and wealth diminishes with increasing levels of the benefits. For the 100 percent owner–manager, this presumes that there are not perfect substitutes for these benefits available on the outside, i.e., to some extent they are job specific. For the fractional owner–manager this presumes the benefits cannot be turned into general purchasing power at a constant price.[20]

[19]The manager's utility function is actually defined over wealth and the future time sequence of vectors of quantities of non-pecuniary benefits, X_t. Although the setting of his problem is somewhat different, Fama (1970b, 1972) analyzes the conditions under which these preferences can be represented as a derived utility function defined as a function of the money value of the expenditures (in our notation F) on these goods conditional on the prices of goods. Such a utility function incorporates the optimization going on in the background which define $\hat{X}$ discussed above for a given F. In the more general case where we allow a time series of consumption, $\hat{X}_t$, the optimization is being carried out across both time and the components of X_t for fixed F.

[20]This excludes, for instance, (a) the case where the manager is allowed to expend corporate resources on anything he pleases in which case F would be a perfect substitute for wealth, or (b) the case where he can 'steal' cash (or other marketable assets) with constant returns to scale – if he could the indifference curves would be straight lines with slope determined by the fence commission.

When the owner has 100 percent of the equity, the value of the firm will be V^* where indifference curve U_2 is tangent to VF, and the level of non-pecuniary benefits consumed is F^*. If the owner sells the entire equity but remains as manager, and if the equity buyer can, at zero cost, force the old owner (as manager) to take the same level of non-pecuniary benefits as he did as owner, then V^* is the price the new owner will be willing to pay for the entire equity.[21]

In general, however, we would not expect the new owner to be able to enforce identical behavior on the old owner at zero costs. If the old owner sells a fraction of the firm to an outsider, he, as manager, will no longer bear the full cost of any non-pecuniary benefits he consumes. Suppose the owner sells a share of the firm, $1 - \alpha$, $(0 < \alpha < 1)$ and retains for himself a share, α. If the prospective buyer believes that the owner–manager will consume the same level of non-pecuniary benefits as he did as full owner, the buyer will be willing to pay $(1 - \alpha)V^*$ for a fraction $(1 - \alpha)$ of the equity. Given that an outsider now holds a claim to $(1 - \alpha)$ of the equity, however, the *cost* to the owner–manager of consuming \$1 of non-pecuniary benefits in the firm will no longer be \$1. Instead, it will be $\alpha \times \$1$. If the prospective buyer actually paid $(1 - \alpha)V^*$ for his share of the equity, and if thereafter the manager could choose whatever level of non-pecuniary benefits he liked, his budget constraint would be $V_1 P_1$ in fig. 1 and has a slope equal to $-\alpha$. Including the payment the owner receives from the buyer as part of the owner's post-sale wealth, his budget constraint, $V_1 P_1$, must pass through D, since he can if he wishes have the same wealth and level of non-pecuniary consumption he consumed as full owner.

But if the owner–manager is free to choose the level of perquisites, F, subject only to the loss in wealth he incurs as a part owner, his welfare will be maximized by increasing his consumption of non-pecuniary benefits. He will move to point A where $V_1 P_1$ is tangent to U_1 representing a higher level of utility. The value of the firm falls from V^*, to V^0, i.e., by the amount of the cost to the firm of the increased non-pecuniary expenditures, and the owner–manager's consumption of non-pecuniary benefits rises from F^* to F^0.

[21] Point D defines the fringe benefits in the optimal pay package since the value to the manager of the fringe benefits F^* is greater than the cost of providing them as is evidenced by the fact that U_2 is steeper to the left of D than the budget constraint with slope equal to -1.
That D is indeed the optimal pay package can easily be seen in this situation since if the conditions of the sale to a new owner specified that the manager would receive no fringe benefits after the sale he would require a payment equal to V_3 to compensate him for the sacrifice of his claims to V^* and fringe benefits amounting to F^* (the latter with total value to him of $V_3 - V^*$). But if $F = 0$, the value of the firm is only $\bar{V}$. Therefore, if monitoring costs were zero the sale would take place at V^* with provision for a pay package which included fringe benefits of F^* for the manager.
This discussion seems to indicate there are two values for the 'firm', V_3 and V^*. This is not the case if we realize that V^* is the value of the right to be the residual claimant on the cash flows of the firm and $V_3 - V^*$ is the value of the managerial rights, i.e., the right to make the operating decisions which include access to F^*. There is at least one other right which has value which plays no formal role in the analysis as yet – the value of the control right. By control right we mean the right to hire and fire the manager and we leave this issue to a future paper.

If the equity market is characterized by rational expectations the buyers will be aware that the owner will increase his non-pecuniary consumption when his ownership share is reduced. If the owner's response function is known or if the equity market makes unbiased estimates of the owner's response to the changed incentives, the buyer will not pay $(1-\alpha)V^*$ for $(1-\alpha)$ of the equity.

Theorem. *For a claim on the firm of $(1-\alpha)$ the outsider will pay only $(1-\alpha)$ times the value he expects the firm to have given the induced change in the behavior of the owner–manager.*

Proof. For simplicity we ignore any element of uncertainty introduced by the lack of perfect knowledge of the owner–manager's response function. Such uncertainty will not affect the final solution if the equity market is large as long as the estimates are rational (i.e., unbiased) and the errors are independent across firms. The latter condition assures that this risk is diversifiable and therefore equilibrium prices will equal the expected values.

Let W represent the owner's total wealth after he has sold a claim equal to $1-\alpha$ of the equity to an outsider. W has two components. One is the payment, S_o, made by the outsider for $1-\alpha$ of the equity; the rest, S_i, is the value of the owner's (i.e., insider's) share of the firm, so that W, the owner's wealth, is given by

$$W = S_o + S_i = S_o + \alpha V(F, \alpha),$$

where $V(F, \alpha)$ represents the value of the firm given that the manager's fractional ownership share is α and that he consumes perquisites with current market value of F. Let $V_2 P_2$, with a slope of $-\alpha$ represent the tradeoff the owner–manager faces between non-pecuniary benefits and his wealth after the sale. Given that the owner has decided to sell a claim $1-\alpha$ of the firm, his welfare will be maximized when $V_2 P_2$ is tangent to some indifference curve such as U_3 in fig. 1. A price for a claim of $(1-\alpha)$ on the firm that is satisfactory to both the buyer and the seller will require that this tangency occur along $\overline{V}F$, i.e., that the value of the firm must be V'. To show this, assume that such is not the case – that the tangency occurs to the left of the point B on the line $\overline{V}F$. Then, since the slope of $V_2 P_2$ is negative, the value of the firm will be larger than V'. The owner–manager's choice of this lower level of consumption of non-pecuniary benefits will imply a higher value both to the firm as a whole and to the fraction of the firm $(1-\alpha)$ which the outsider has acquired; that is, $(1-\alpha)V' > S_o$. From the owner's viewpoint, he has sold $1-\alpha$ of the firm for less than he could have, given the (assumed) lower level of non-pecuniary benefits he enjoys. On the other hand, if the tangency point B is to the right of the line $\overline{V}F$, the owner–manager's higher consumption of non-pecuniary benefits means the value of the firm is less than V', and hence $(1-\alpha)V(F, \alpha) < S_o = (1-\alpha)V'$. The outside owner then has paid more for his share of the equity than it is worth. S_o will be a mutually satisfactory price if and only if $(1-\alpha)V' = S_0$. But this means that the owner's post-sale wealth is equal to the (reduced) value of the firm V', since

$$W = S_0 + \alpha V' = (1-\alpha)V' + \alpha V' = V'.$$

Q.E.D.

The requirement that V' and F' fall on $\overline{VF}$ is thus equivalent to requiring that the value of the claim acquired by the outside buyer be equal to the amount he pays for it and conversely for the owner. *This means that the decline in the total value of the firm* $(V^* - V')$ *is entirely imposed on the owner–manager.* His total wealth after the sale of $(1-\alpha)$ of the equity is V' and the decline in his wealth is $V^* - V'$.

The distance $V^* - V'$ is the reduction in the market value of the firm engendered by the agency relationship and is a measure of the "residual loss" defined earlier. In this simple example the residual loss represents the total agency costs engendered by the sale of outside equity because monitoring and bonding activities have not been allowed. The welfare loss the owner incurs is less than the residual loss by the value to him of the increase in non-pecuniary benefits $(F' - F^*)$. In fig. 1 the difference between the intercepts on the Y axis of the two indifference curves U_2 and U_3 is a measure of the owner–manager's welfare loss due to the incurrence of agency costs,[22] and he would sell such a claim only if the increment in welfare he achieves by using the cash amounting to $(1-\alpha)V'$ for other things was worth more to him than this amount of wealth.

2.3. Determination of the optimal scale of the firm

The case of all equity financing. Consider the problem faced by an entrepreneur with initial pecuniary wealth, W, and monopoly access to a project requiring investment outlay, I, subject to diminishing returns to scale in I. Fig. 2 portrays the solution to the optimal scale of the firm taking into account the agency costs associated with the existence of outside equity. The axes are as defined in fig. 1 except we now plot on the vertical axis the total wealth of the owner, i.e., his initial wealth, W, plus $V(I)-I$, the net increment in wealth he obtains from exploitation of his investment opportunities. The market value of the firm, $V = V(I, F)$, is now a function of the level of investment, I, and the current market value of the manager's expenditures of the firm's resources on non-pecuniary benefits, F. Let $\overline{V}(I)$ represent the value of the firm as a function of the level of investment when the manager's expenditures on non-pecuniary benefits, F, are zero. The schedule with intercept labeled $W + [\overline{V}(I^*) - I^*)]$ and

---

[22]The distance $V^* - V'$ is a measure of what we will define as the gross agency costs. The distance $V_3 - V_4$ is a measure of what we call net agency costs, and it is this measure of agency costs which will be minimized by the manager in the general case where we allow investment to change.

slope equal to -1 in fig. 2 represents the locus of combinations of post-invest-ment wealth and dollar cost to the firm of non-pecuniary benefits which are available to the manager when investment is carried to the value maximizing

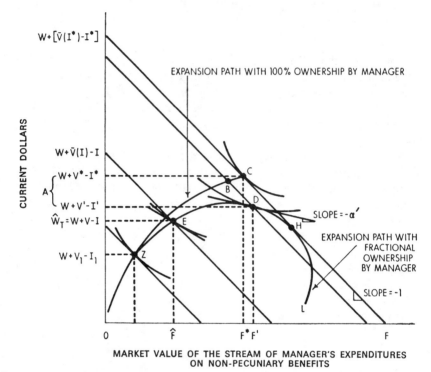

Fig. 2. Determination of the optimal scale of the firm in the case where no monitoring takes place. Point C denotes optimum investment, I^*, and non-pecuniary benefits, F^*, when invest-ment is 100% financed by entrepreneur. Point D denotes optimum investment, I', and non-pecuniary benefits, F, when outside equity financing is used to help finance the investment and the entrepreneur owns a fraction α' of the firm. The distance A measures the gross agency costs.

point, I^*. At this point $\Delta \overline{V}(I) - \Delta I = 0$. If the manager's wealth were large enough to cover the investment required to reach this scale of operation, I^*, he would consume F^* in non-pecuniary benefits and have pecuniary wealth with value $W + V^* - I^*$. However, if outside financing is required to cover the invest-ment he will not reach this point if monitoring costs are non-zero.[23]

The expansion path $OZBC$ represents the equilibrium combinations of wealth and non-pecuniary benefits, F, which the manager could obtain if he had enough

[23] I^* is the value maximizing and Pareto Optimum investment level which results from the traditional analysis of the corporate investment decision if the firm operates in perfectly competitive capital and product markets and the agency cost problems discussed here are ignored. See Debreu (1959, ch. 7), Jensen and Long (1972), Long (1972), Merton and Subrah-manyam (1974), Hirshleifer (1958, 1970), and Fama and Miller (1972).

personal wealth to finance all levels of investment up to I^*. It is the locus of points such as Z and C which represent the equilibrium position for the 100 percent owner–manager at each possible level of investment, I. As I increases we move up the expansion path to the point C where $V(I)-I$ is at a maximum. Additional investment beyond this point reduces the net value of the firm, and as it does the equilibrium path of the manager's wealth and non-pecuniary benefits retraces (in the reverse direction) the curve $OZBC$. We draw the path as a smooth concave function only as a matter of convenience.

If the manager obtained outside financing and if there were zero costs to the agency relationship (perhaps because monitoring costs were zero) the expansion path would also be represented by $OZBC$. Therefore, this path represents what we might call the "idealized" solutions, i.e., those which would occur in the absence of agency costs.

Assume the manager has sufficient personal wealth to completely finance the firm only up to investment level I_1 which puts him at point Z. At this point $W = I_1$. To increase the size of the firm beyond this point he must obtain outside financing to cover the additional investment required, and this means reducing his fractional ownership. When he does this he incurs agency costs, and the lower is his ownership fraction the larger are the agency costs he incurs. However, if the investments requiring outside financing are sufficiently profitable his welfare will continue to increase.

The expansion path $ZEDHL$ in fig. 2 portrays one possible path of the equilibrium levels of the owner's non-pecuniary benefits and wealth at each possible level of investment higher than I_1. This path is the locus of points such as E or D where (1) the manager's indifference curve is tangent to a line with slope equal to $-\alpha$ (his fractional claim on the firm at that level of investment), and (2) the tangency occurs on the "budget constraint" with slope $= -1$ for the firm value and non-pecuniary benefit tradeoff at the same level of investment.[24] As we move along $ZEDHL$ his fractional claim on the firm continues

---

[24]Each equilibrium point such as that at E is characterized by $(\hat{a}, \hat{F}, \hat{W}_T)$ where $\hat{W}_T$ is the entrepreneur's post-investment financing wealth. Such an equilibrium must satisfy each of the following four conditions:

(1) $\qquad \hat{W}_T + F = \bar{V}(I) + W - I = \bar{V}(I) - K,$

where $K \equiv I - W$ is the amount of outside financing required to make the investment I. If this condition is not satisfied there is an uncompensated wealth transfer (in one direction or the other) between the entrepreneur and outside equity buyers.

(2) $\qquad U_F(\hat{W}_T, \hat{F})/U_{W_T}(\hat{W}_T, \hat{F}) = \hat{a},$

where U is the entrepreneur's utility function on wealth and perquisites, U_F and U_{W_T} are marginal utilities and $\hat{a}$ is the manager's share of the firm.

(3) $\qquad (1-\hat{a})V(I) = (1-\hat{a})[\bar{V}(I)-\hat{F}] \geqq K,$

which says the funds received from outsiders are at least equal to K, the minimum required outside financing.

(4) Among all points $(\hat{a}, \hat{F}, \hat{W}_T)$ satisfying conditions (1)–(3), (α, F, W_T) gives the manager highest utility. This implies that $(\hat{a}, \hat{F}, \hat{W}_T)$ satisfy condition (3) as an equality.

to fall as he raises larger amounts of outside capital. This expansion path represents his complete opportunity set for combinations of wealth and non-pecuniary benefits given the existence of the costs of the agency relationship with the outside equity holders. Point D, where this opportunity set is tangent to an indifference curve, represents the solution which maximizes his welfare. At this point, the level of investment is I', his fractional ownership share in the firm is α', his wealth is $W+V'-I'$, and he consumes a stream of non-pecuniary benefits with current market value of F'. The gross agency costs (denoted by A) are equal to $(V^*-I^*)-(V'-I')$. Given that no monitoring is possible, I' is the socially optimal level of investment as well as the privately optimal level.

We can characterize the optimal level of investment as that point, I' which satisfies the following condition for small changes:

$$\Delta V - \Delta I + \alpha' \Delta F = 0. \tag{1}$$

$\Delta V - \Delta I$ is the change in the net market value of the firm, and $\alpha' \Delta F$ is the dollar value to the manager of the incremental fringe benefits he consumes (which cost the firm ΔF dollars).[25] Furthermore, recognizing that $V = \bar{V} - F$, where $\bar{V}$ is the value of the firm at any level of investment when $F = 0$, we can substitute into the optimum condition to get

$$(\Delta \bar{V} - \Delta I) - (1 - \alpha') \Delta F = 0 \tag{3}$$

as an alternative expression for determining the optimum level of investment.

The idealized or zero agency cost solution, I^*, is given by the condition $(\Delta \bar{V} - \Delta I) = 0$, and since ΔF is positive the actual welfare maximizing level of investment I' will be less than I^*, because $(\Delta \bar{V} - \Delta I)$ must be positive at I' if (3) is to be satisfied. Since $-\alpha'$ is the slope of the indifference curve at the optimum and therefore represents the manager's demand price for incremental non-pecuniary benefits, ΔF, we know that $\alpha' \Delta F$ is the dollar value to him of an increment of fringe benefits costing the firm ΔF dollars. The term $(1 - \alpha')\Delta F$ thus measures the dollar "loss" to the firm (and himself) of an additional ΔF dollars spent on non-pecuniary benefits. The term $\Delta \bar{V} - \Delta I$ is the gross increment in the value of the firm ignoring any changes in the consumption of non-pecuniary benefits. Thus, the manager stops increasing the size of the firm when the gross

---

[25]*Proof.* Note that the slope of the expansion path (or locus of equilibrium points) at any point is $(\Delta V - \Delta I)/\Delta F$ and at the optimum level of investment this must be equal to the slope of the manager's indifference curve between wealth and market value of fringe benefits, F. Furthermore, in the absence of monitoring, the slope of the indifference curve, $\Delta W/\Delta F$, at the equilibrium point, D, must be equal to $-\alpha'$. Thus,

$$(\Delta V - \Delta I)/\Delta F = -\alpha' \tag{2}$$

is the condition for the optimal scale of investment and this implies condition (1) holds for small changes at the optimum level of investment, I'.

increment in value is just offset by the incremental "loss" involved in the consumption of additional fringe benefits due to his declining fractional interest in the firm.[26]

2.4. The role of monitoring and bonding activities in reducing agency costs

In the above analysis we have ignored the potential for controlling the behavior of the owner–manager through monitoring and other control activities. In practice, it is usually possible by expending resources to alter the opportunity the owner–manager has for capturing non-pecuniary benefits. These methods include auditing, formal control systems, budget restrictions, and the establishment of incentive compensation systems which serve to more closely identify the manager's interests with those of the outside equity holders, etc. Fig. 3 portrays the effects of monitoring and other control activities in the simple situation portrayed in fig. 1. Figs. 1 and 3 are identical except for the curve BCE in fig. 3 which depicts a "budget constraint" derived when monitoring possibilities are taken into account. Without monitoring, and with outside equity of $(1-\alpha)$, the value of the firm will be V' and non-pecuniary expenditures F'. By incurring monitoring costs, M, the equity holders can restrict the manager's consumption of perquisites to amounts less than F'. Let $F(M, \alpha)$ denote the maximum perquisites the manager can consume for alternative levels of monitoring expenditures, M, given his ownership share α. We assume that increases in monitoring reduce F, and reduce it at a decreasing rate, i.e., $\partial F/\partial M < 0$ and $\partial^2 F/\partial M^2 > 0$.

Since the current value of expected future monitoring expenditures by the outside equity holders reduce the value of any given claim on the firm to them dollar for dollar, the outside equity holders will take this into account in determining the maximum price they will pay for any given fraction of the firm's

---

[26]Since the manager's indifference curves are negatively sloped we know that the optimum scale of the firm, point D, will occur in the region where the expansion path has negative slope, i.e., the market value of the firm will be declining and the *gross* agency costs, A, will be increasing and thus, the manager will not minimize them in making the investment decision (even though he will minimize them for any *given* level of investment). However, we define the *net* agency cost as the dollar equivalent of the welfare loss the manager experiences because of the agency relationship evaluated at $F = 0$ (the vertical distance between the intercepts on the Y axis of the two indifference curves on which points C and D lie). The optimum solution, I', does satisfy the condition that net agency costs are minimized. But this simply amounts to a restatement of the assumption that the manager maximizes his welfare.

Finally, it is possible for the solution point D to be a corner solution and in this case the value of the firm will not be declining. Such a corner solution can occur, for instance, if the manager's marginal rate of substitution between F and wealth falls to zero fast enough as we move up the expansion path, or if the investment projects are 'sufficiently' profitable. In these cases the expansion path will have a corner which lies on the maximum value budget constraint with intercept $\bar{V}(I^*)-I^*$, and the level of investment will be equal to the idealized optimum, I^*. However, the market value of the residual claims will be less than V^* because the manager's consumption of perquisites will be larger than F^*, the zero agency cost level.

equity. Therefore, given positive monitoring activity the value of the firm is given by $V = \bar{V} - F(M, \alpha) - M$ and the locus of these points for various levels of M and for a given level of α lie on the line BCE in fig. 3. The vertical difference between the $\bar{V}F$ and BCE curves is M, the current market value of the future monitoring expenditures.

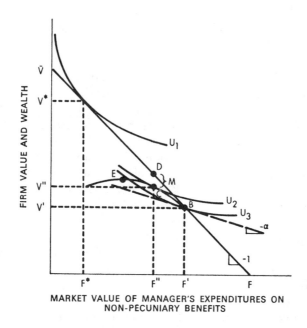

MARKET VALUE OF MANAGER'S EXPENDITURES ON
NON-PECUNIARY BENEFITS

Fig. 3. The value of the firm (V) and level of non-pecuniary benefits (F) when outside equity is $(1 - \alpha)$, U_1, U_2, U_3 represent owner's indifference curves between wealth and non-pecuniary benefits, and monitoring (or bonding) activities impose opportunity set BCE as the tradeoff constraint facing the owner.

If it is possible for the outside equity holders to make these monitoring expenditures and thereby to impose the reductions in the owner–manager's consumption of F, he will voluntarily enter into a contract with the outside equity holders which gives them the rights to restrict his consumption of non-pecuniary items to F''. He finds this desirable because it will cause the value of the firm to rise to V''. Given the contract, the optimal monitoring expenditure on the part of the outsiders, M, is the amount $D - C$. The entire increase in the value of the firm that accrues will be reflected in the owner's wealth, but his welfare will be increased by less than this because he forgoes some non-pecuniary benefits he previously enjoyed.

If the equity market is competitive and makes unbiased estimates of the effects of the monitoring expenditures on F and V, potential buyers will be indifferent between the following two contracts:

(i) Purchase of a share $(1-\alpha)$ of the firm at a total price of $(1-\alpha)V'$ and no rights to monitor or control the manager's consumption of perquisites.

(ii) Purchase of a share $(1-\alpha)$ of the firm at a total price of $(1-\alpha)V''$ and the right to expend resources up to an amount equal to $D-C$ which will limit the owner-manager's consumption of perquisites to F;.

Given contract (ii) the outside shareholders would find it desirable to monitor to the full rights of their contract because it will pay them to do so. However, if the equity market is competitive the total benefits (net of the monitoring costs) will be capitalized into the price of the claims. Thus, not surprisingly, the owner-manager reaps all the benefits of the opportunity to write and sell the monitoring contract.[27]

An analysis of bonding expenditures. We can also see from the analysis of fig. 3 that it makes no difference who actually makes the monitoring expenditures – the owner bears the full amount of these costs as a wealth reduction in all cases. Suppose that the owner-manager could expend resources to guarantee to the outside equity holders that he would limit his activities which cost the firm F. We call these expenditures "bonding costs", and they would take such forms as contractual guarantees to have the financial accounts audited by a public account, explicit bonding against malfeasance on the part of the manager, and contractual limitations on the manager's decision making power (which impose costs on the firm because they limit his ability to take full advantage of some profitable opportunities as well as limiting his ability to harm the stockholders while making himself better off).

If the incurrence of the bonding costs were entirely under the control of the manager and if they yielded the same opportunity set BCE for him in fig. 3, he would incur them in amount $D-C$. This would limit his consumption of

---

[27]The careful reader will note that point C will be the equilibrium point only if the contract between the manager and outside equity holders specifies with no ambiguity that they have the right to monitor to limit his consumption of perquisites to an amount no less than F''. If any ambiguity regarding these rights exists in this contract then another source of agency costs arises which is symmetrical to our original problem. If they could do so the outside equity holders would monitor to the point where the net value of *their* holdings, $(1-\alpha)V-M$, was maximized, and this would occur when $(\partial V/\partial M)(1-\alpha)-1 = 0$ which would be at some point between points C and E in fig. 3. Point E denotes the point where the value of the firm net of the monitoring costs is at a maximum, i.e. where $\partial V/\partial M-1 = 0$. But the manager would be worse off than in the zero monitoring solution if the point where $(1-\alpha)V-M$ was at a maximum were to the left of the intersection between BCE and the indifference curve U_3 passing through point B (which denotes the zero monitoring level of welfare). Thus if the manager could not eliminate enough of the ambiguity in the contract to push the equilibrium to the right of the intersection of the curve BCE with indifference curve U_3 he would not engage in any contract which allowed monitoring.

perquisites to F'' from F', and the solution is exactly the same as if the outside equity holders had performed the monitoring. The manager finds it in his interest to incur these costs as long as the net increments in his wealth which they generate (by reducing the agency costs and therefore increasing the value of the firm) are more valuable than the perquisites given up. This optimum occurs at point C in both cases under our assumption that the bonding expenditures yield the same opportunity set as the monitoring expenditures. In general, of course, it will pay the owner–manager to engage in bonding activities and to write contracts which allow monitoring as long as the marginal benefits of each are greater than their marginal cost.

Optimal scale of the firm in the presence of monitoring and bonding activities. If we allow the outside owners to engage in (costly) monitoring activities to limit the manager's expenditures on non-pecuniary benefits and allow the manager to engage in bonding activities to guarantee to the outside owners that he will limit his consumption of F we get an expansion path such as that illustrated in fig. 4 on which Z and G lie. We have assumed in drawing fig. 4 that the cost functions involved in monitoring and bonding are such that some positive levels of the activities are desirable, i.e., yield benefits greater than their cost. If this is not true the expansion path generated by the expenditure of resources on these activities would lie below ZD and no such activity would take place at any level of investment. Points Z, C, and D and the two expansion paths they lie on are identical to those portrayed in fig. 2. Points Z and C lie on the 100 percent ownership expansion path, and points Z and D lie on the fractional owner-ship, zero monitoring and bonding activity expansion path.

The path on which points Z and G lie is the one given by the locus of equili-brium points for alternative levels of investment characterized by the point labeled C in fig. 3 which denotes the optimal level of monitoring and bonding activity and resulting values of the firm and non-pecuniary benefits to the manager given a fixed level of investment. If any monitoring or bonding is cost effective the expansion path on which Z and G lie must be above the non-monitoring expansion path over some range. Furthermore, if it lies anywhere to the right of the indifference curve passing through point D (the zero monitor-ing–bonding solution) the final solution to the problem will involve positive amounts of monitoring and/or bonding activities. Based on the discussion above we know that as long as the contracts between the manager and outsiders are unambiguous regarding the rights of the respective parties the final solution will be at that point where the new expansion path is just tangent to the highest indifference curve. At this point the optimal level of monitoring and bonding expenditures are M'' and b''; the manager's post-investment-financing wealth is given by $W + V'' - I'' - M'' - b''$ and his non-pecuniary benefits are F''. The total gross agency costs, A, are given by $A(M'', b'', \alpha'', I'') = (V^* - I^*) - (V'' - I'' - M'' - b'')$.

2.5. Pareto optimality and agency costs in manager-operated firms

In general we expect to observe both bonding and external monitoring activities, and the incentives are such that the levels of these activities will satisfy the conditions of efficiency. They will not, however, result in the firm being run in a manner so as to maximize its value. The difference between V^*, the efficient solution under zero monitoring and bonding costs (and therefore zero agency

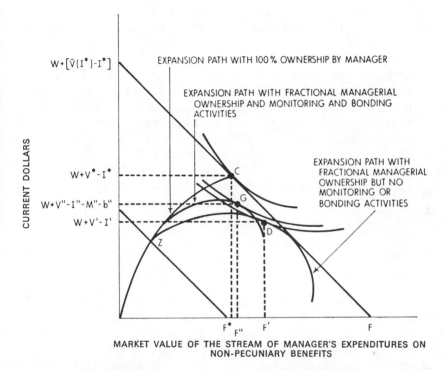

Fig. 4. Determination of optimal scale of the firm allowing for monitoring and bonding activities. Optimal monitoring costs are M'' and bonding costs are b'' and the equilibrium scale of firm, manager's wealth and consumption of non-pecuniary benefits are at point G.

costs), and V'', the value of the firm given positive monitoring costs, are the total gross agency costs defined earlier in the introduction. These are the costs of the "separation of ownership and control" which Adam Smith focused on in the passage quoted at the beginning of this paper and which Berle and Means (1932) popularized 157 years later. The solutions outlined above to our highly simplified problem imply that agency costs will be positive as long as monitoring costs are positive – which they certainly are.

The reduced value of the firm caused by the manager's consumption of perquisites outlined above is "non-optimal" or inefficient only in comparison to a world in which we could obtain compliance of the agent to the principal's wishes at zero cost or in comparison to a *hypothetical* world in which the agency costs were lower. But these costs (monitoring and bonding costs and 'residual loss') are an unavoidable result of the agency relationship. Furthermore, since they are borne entirely by the decision maker (in this case the original owner) responsible for creating the relationship he has the incentives to see that they are minimized (because he captures the benefits from their reduction). Furthermore, these agency costs will be incurred only if the benefits to the owner–manager from their creation are great enough to outweigh them. In our current example these benefits arise from the availability of profitable investments requiring capital investment in excess of the original owner's personal wealth.

In conclusion, finding that agency costs are non-zero (i.e., that there are costs associated with the separation of ownership and control in the corporation) and concluding therefrom that the agency relationship is non-optimal, wasteful or inefficient is equivalent in every sense to comparing a world in which iron ore is a scarce commodity (and therefore costly) to a world in which it is freely available at zero resource cost, and concluding that the first world is "non-optimal" – a perfect example of the fallacy criticized by Coase (1964) and what Demsetz (1969) characterizes as the "Nirvana" form of analysis.[28]

2.6. Factors affecting the size of the divergence from ideal maximization

The magnitude of the agency costs discussed above will vary from firm to firm. It will depend on the tastes of managers, the ease with which they can exercise their own preferences as opposed to value maximization in decision making, and the costs of monitoring and bonding activities.[29] The agency costs will also depend upon the cost of measuring the manager's (agent's) performance and evaluating it, the cost of devising and applying an index for compensating the manager which correlates with the owner's (principal's) welfare, and the cost of devising and enforcing specific behavioral rules or policies. Where the manager has less than a controlling interest in the firm, it will also depend upon the market for managers. Competition from other potential managers limits the costs of obtaining managerial services (including the extent to which a given manager can diverge from the idealized solution which would obtain if all monitoring and bonding costs were zero). The size of the divergence (the agency costs) will be directly related to the cost of replacing the manager. If his responsibilities require

[28]If we could establish the existence of a feasible set of alternative institutional arrangements which would yield net benefits from the reduction of these costs we could legitimately conclude the agency relationship engendered by the corporation was not Pareto optimal. However, we would then be left with the problem of explaining why these alternative institutional arrangements have not replaced the corporate form of organization.

[29]The monitoring and bonding costs will differ from firm to firm depending on such things as the inherent complexity and geographical dispersion of operations, the attractiveness of perquisites available in the firm (consider the mint), etc.

very little knowledge specialized to the firm, if it is easy to evaluate his performance, and if replacement search costs are modest, the divergence from the ideal will be relatively small and vice versa.

The divergence will also be constrained by the market for the firm itself, i.e., by capital markets. Owners always have the option of selling their firm, either as a unit or piecemeal. Owners of manager-operated firms can and do sample the capital market from time to time. If they discover that the value of the future earnings stream to others is higher than the value of the firm to them given that it is to be manager-operated, they can exercise their right to sell. It is conceivable that other owners could be more efficient at monitoring or even that a single individual with appropriate managerial talents and with sufficiently large personal wealth would elect to buy the firm. In this latter case the purchase by such a single individual would completely eliminate the agency costs. If there were a number of such potential owner–manager purchasers (all with talents and tastes identical to the current manager) the owners would receive in the sale price of the firm the full value of the residual claimant rights including the capital value of the eliminated agency costs plus the value of the managerial rights.

Monopoly, competition and managerial behavior. It is frequently argued that the existence of competition in product (and factor) markets will constrain the behavior of managers to idealized value maximization, i.e., that monopoly in product (or monopsony in factor) markets will permit larger divergences from value maximization.[30] Our analysis does not support this hypothesis. The owners of a firm with monopoly power have the same incentives to limit divergences of the manager from value maximization (i.e., the ability to increase their wealth) as do the owners of competitive firms. Furthermore, competition in the market for managers will generally make it unnecessary for the owners to share rents with the manager. The owners of a monopoly firm need only pay the supply price for a manager.

Since the owner of a monopoly has the same wealth incentives to minimize managerial costs as would the owner of a competitive firm, both will undertake that level of monitoring which equates the marginal cost of monitoring to the

[30]"Where competitors are numerous and entry is easy, persistent departures from profit maximizing behavior inexorably leads to extinction. Economic natural selection holds the stage. In these circumstances, the behavior of the individual units that constitute the supply side of the product market is essentially routine and uninteresting and economists can confidently predict industry behavior without being explicitly concerned with the behavior of these individual units.

When the conditions of competition are relaxed, however, the opportunity set of the firm is expanded. In this case, the behavior of the firm as a distinct operating unit is of separate interest. Both for purposes of interpreting particular behavior within the firm as well as for predicting responses of the industry aggregate, it may be necessary to identify the factors that influence the firm's choices within this expanded opportunity set and embed these in a formal model.' [Williamson (1964, p. 2)]

marginal wealth increment from reduced consumption of perquisites by the manager. Thus, the existence of monopoly will not increase agency costs.

Furthermore the existence of competition in product and factor markets will not eliminate the agency costs due to managerial control problems as has often been asserted [cf. Friedman (1970)]. If my competitors all incur agency costs equal to or greater than mine I will not be eliminated from the market by their competition.

The existence and size of the agency costs depends on the nature of the monitoring costs, the tastes of managers for non-pecuniary benefits and the supply of potential managers who are capable of financing the entire venture out of their personal wealth. If monitoring costs are zero, agency costs will be zero or if there are enough 100 percent owner–managers available to own and run all the firms in an industry (competitive or not) then agency costs in that industry will also be zero.[31]

3. Some unanswered questions regarding the existence of the corporate form

3.1. The question

The analysis to this point has left us with a basic puzzle: Why, given the existence of positive costs of the agency relationship, do we find the usual corporate form of organization with widely diffuse ownership so widely prevalent? If one takes seriously much of the literature regarding the "discretionary" power held by managers of large corporations, it is difficult to understand the historical fact of enormous growth in equity in such organizations, not only in the United States, but throughout the world. Paraphrasing Alchian (1968): How does it happen that millions of individuals are willing to turn over a significant fraction of their wealth to organizations run by managers who have so little interest in their welfare? What is even more remarkable, why are they willing to make these commitments purely as residual claimants, i.e., on the anticipation that managers will operate the firm so that there will be earnings which accrue to the stockholders?

There is certainly no lack of alternative ways that individuals might invest, including entirely different forms of organizations. Even if consideration is limited to corporate organizations, there are clearly alternative ways capital might be raised, i.e., through fixed claims of various sorts, bonds, notes, mortgages, etc. Moreover, the corporate income tax seems to favor the use of fixed claims since interest is treated as a tax deductible expense. Those who assert that managers do not behave in the interest or stockholders have generally not addressed a very important question: Why, if non-manager-owned shares have

---

[31]Assuming there are no special tax benefits to ownership nor utility of ownership other than that derived from the direct wealth effects of ownership such as might be true for professional sports teams, race horse stables, firms which carry the family name, etc.

such a serious deficiency, have they not long since been driven out by fixed claims?[32]

3.2. Some alternative explanations of the ownership structure of the firm

The role of limited liability. Manne (1967) and Alchian and Demsetz (1972) argue that one of the attractive features of the corporate form vis-a-vis individual proprietorships or partnerships is the limited liability feature of equity claims in corporations. Without this provision each and every investor purchasing one or more shares of a corporation would be potentially liable to the full extent of his personal wealth for the debts of the corporation. Few individuals would find this a desirable risk to accept and the major benefits to be obtained from risk reduction through diversification would be to a large extent unobtainable. This argument, however, is incomplete since limited liability does not eliminate the basic risk, it merely shifts it. The argument must rest ultimately on transactions costs. If all stockholders of GM were liable for GM's debts, the maximum liability for an individual shareholder would be greater than it would be if his shares had limited liability. However, given that many other stockholder's also existed and that each was liable for the unpaid claims in proportion to his ownership it is highly unlikely that the maximum payment each would have to make would be large in the event of GM's bankruptcy since the total wealth of those stockholders would also be large. However, the existence of unlimited liability would impose incentives for each shareholder to keep track of both the liabilities of GM and the wealth of the other GM owners. It is easily conceivable that the costs of so doing would, in the aggregate, be much higher than simply paying a premium in the form of higher interest rates to the creditors of GM in return for their acceptance of a contract which grants limited liability to the shareholders. The creditors would then bear the risk of any non-payment of debts in the event of GM's bankruptcy.

It is also not generally recognized that limited liability is merely a necessary condition for explaining the magnitude of the reliance on equities, not a sufficient condition. Ordinary debt also carries limited liability.[33] If limited liability is all that is required, why don't we observe large corporations, individually owned, with a tiny fraction of the capital supplied by the entrepreneur,

---

[32]Marris (1964, pp. 7–9) is the exception, although he argues that there exists some 'maximum leverage point' beyond which the chances of 'insolvency' are in some undefined sense too high.

[33]By limited liability we mean the same conditions that apply to common stock. Subordinated debt or preferred stock could be constructed which carried with it liability provisions; i.e., if the corporation's assets were insufficient at some point to pay off all prior claims (such as trade credit, accrued wages, senior debt, etc.) and if the personal resources of the 'equity' holders were also insufficient to cover these claims the holders of this 'debt' would be subject to assessments beyond the face value of their claim (assessments which might be limited or unlimited in amount).

and the rest simply borrowed[34] At first this question seems silly to many people (as does the question regarding why firms would ever issue debt or preferred stock under conditions where there are no tax benefits obtained from the treatment of interest or preferred dividend payments[35]). We have found that oftentimes this question is misinterpreted to be one regarding why firms obtain capital. The issue is not why they obtain capital, but why they obtain it through the particular forms we have observed for such long periods of time. The fact is that no well articulated answer to this question currently exists in the literature of either finance or economics.

The "irrelevance" of capital structure. In their pathbreaking article on the cost of capital, Modigliani and Miller (1958) demonstrated that in the absence of bankruptcy costs and tax subsidies on the payment of interest the value of the firm is independent of the financial structure. They later (1963) demonstrated that the existence of tax subsidies on interest payments would cause the value of the firm to rise with the amount of debt financing by the amount of the capitalized value of the tax subsidy. But this line of argument implies that the firm should be financed almost entirely with debt. Realizing the inconsistence with observed behavior Modigliani and Miller (1963, p. 442) comment:

> "it may be useful to remind readers once again that the existence of a tax advantage for debt financing . . . does not necessarily mean that corporations should at all times seek to use the maximum amount of debt in their capital structures. . . . there are as we pointed out, limitations imposed by lenders . . . as well as many other dimensions (and kinds of costs) in real-world problems of financial strategy which are not fully comprehended within the framework of static equilibrium models, either our own or those of the traditional variety. These additional considerations, which are typically grouped under the rubric of 'the need for preserving flexibility',

---

[34]Alchian–Demsetz (1972, p. 709) argue that one can explain the existence of both bonds and stock in the ownership structure of firms as the result of differing expectations regarding the outcomes to the firm. They argue that bonds are created and sold to 'pessimists' and stocks with a residual claim with no upper bound are sold to 'optimists'.

As long as capital markets are perfect with no taxes or transactions costs and individual investors can issue claims on distributions of outcomes on the same terms as firms, such actions on the part of firms cannot affect their values. The reason is simple. Suppose such 'pessimists' did exist and yet the firm issues only equity claims. The demand for those equity claims would reflect the fact that the individual purchaser could on his own account issue 'bonds' with a limited and prior claim on the distribution of outcomes on the equity which is exactly the same as that which the firm could issue. Similarly, investors could easily unlever any position by simply buying a proportional claim on both the bonds and stocks of a levered firm. Therefore, a levered firm could not sell at a different price than an unlevered firm solely because of the existence of such differential expectations. See Fama and Miller (1972, ch. 4) for an excellent exposition of these issues.

[35]Corporations did use both prior to the institution of the corporate income tax in the U.S. and preferred dividends have, with minor exceptions, never been tax deductible.

will normally imply the maintenance by the corporation of a substantial reserve of untapped borrowing power."

Modigliani and Miller are essentially left without a theory of the determination of the optimal capital structure, and Fama and Miller (1972, p. 173) commenting on the same issue reiterate this conclusion:

"And we must admit that at this point there is little in the way of convincing research, either theoretical or empirical, that explains the amounts of debt that firms do decide to have in their capital structure."

The Modigliani–Miller theorem is based on the assumption that the probability distribution of the cash flows to the firm is independent of the capital structure. It is now recognized that the existence of positive costs associated with bankruptcy and the presence of tax subsidies on corporate interest payments will invalidate this irrelevance theorem precisely because the probability distribution of future cash flows changes as the probability of the incurrence of the bankruptcy costs changes, i.e., as the ratio of debt to equity rises. We believe the existence of agency costs provide stronger reasons for arguing that the probability distribution of future cash flows is *not* independent of the capital or ownership structure.

While the introduction of bankruptcy costs in the presence of tax subsidies leads to a theory which defines an optimal capital structure,[36] we argue that this theory is seriously incomplete since it implies that no debt should ever be used in the absence of tax subsidies if bankruptcy costs are positive. Since we know debt was commonly used prior to the existence of the current tax subsidies on interest payments this theory does not capture what must be some important determinants of the corporate capital structure.

In addition, neither bankruptcy costs nor the existence of tax subsidies can explain the use of preferred stock or warrnts which have no tax advantages, and there is no theory which tells us anything about what determines the fraction of equity claims held by insiders as opposed to outsiders which our analysis in section 2 indicates is so important. We return to these issues later after analyzing in detail the factors affecting the agency costs associated with debt.

4. The agency costs of debt

In general if the agency costs engendered by the existence of outside owners are positive it will pay the absentee owner (i.e., shareholders) to sell out to an owner–manager who can avoid these costs.[37] This could be accomplished in principle by having the manager become the sole equity holder by repurchasing

[36]See Kraus and Litzenberger (1972) and Lloyd-Davies (1975).
[37]And if there is competitive bidding for the firm from potential owner–managers the absentee owner will capture the capitalized value of these agency costs.

all of the outside equity claims with funds obtained through the issuance of limited liability debt claims and the use of his own personal wealth. This single-owner corporation would not suffer the agency costs associated with outside equity. Therefore there must be some compelling reasons why we find the diffuse-owner corporate firm financed by equity claims so prevalent as an organizational form.

An ingenious entrepreneur eager to expand, has open to him the opportunity to design a whole hierarchy of fixed claims on assets and earnings, with premiums paid for different levels of risk.[38] Why don't we observe large corporations individually owned with a tiny fraction of the capital supplied by the entrepreneur in return for 100 percent of the equity and the rest simply borrowed? We believe there are a number of reasons: (1) the incentive effects associated with highly leveraged firms, (2) the monitoring costs these incentive effects engender, and (3) bankruptcy costs. Furthermore, all of these costs are simply particular aspects of the agency costs associated with the existence of debt claims on the firm.

4.1. The incentive effects associated with debt

We don't find many large firms financed almost entirely with debt type claims (i.e., non-residual claims) because of the effect such a financial structure would have on the owner–manager's behavior. Potential creditors will not loan $100,000,000 to a firm in which the entrepreneur has an investment of $10,000. With that financial structure the owner–manager will have a strong incentive to engage in activities (investments) which promise very high payoffs if successful even if they have a very low probability of success. If they turn out well, he captures most of the gains, if they turn out badly, the creditors bear most of the costs.[39]

To illustrate the incentive effects associated with the existence of debt and to provide a framework within which we can discuss the effects of monitoring and bonding costs, wealth transfers, and the incidence of agency costs, we again consider a simple situation. Assume we have a manager-owned firm with no debt

[38]The spectrum of claims which firms can issue is far more diverse than is suggested by our two-way classification – fixed vs. residual. There are convertible bonds, equipment trust certificates, debentures, revenue bonds, warrants, etc. Different bond issues can contain different subordination provisions with respect to assets and interest. They can be callable or non-callable. Preferred stocks can be 'preferred' in a variety of dimensions and contain a variety of subordination stipulations. In the abstract, we can imagine firms issuing claims contingent on a literally infinite variety of states of the world such as those considered in the literature on the time–state-preference models of Arrow (1964), Debreu (1959) and Hirshleifer (1970).

[39]An apt analogy is the way one would play poker on money borrowed at a fixed interest rate, with one's own liability limited to some very small stake. Fama and Miller (1972, pp. 179–180) also discuss and provide a numerical example of an investment decision which illustrates very nicley the potential inconsistency between the interests of bondholders and stockholders.

outstanding in a world in which there are no taxes. The firm has the opportunity to take one of two mutually exclusive equal cost investment opportunities, each of which yields a random payoff, $\tilde{X}_j$, T periods in the future ($j = 1, 2$). Production and monitoring activities take place continuously between time 0 and time T, and markets in which the claims on the firm can be traded are open continuously over this period. After time T the firm has no productive activities so the payoff $\tilde{X}_j$ includes the distribution of all remaining assets. For simplicity, we assume that the two distributions are log-normally distributed and have the same expected total payoff, $E(\tilde{X})$, where $\tilde{X}$ is defined as the logarithm of the final payoff. The distributions differ only by their variances with $\sigma_1^2 < \sigma_2^2$. The systematic or covariance risk of each of the distributions, β_j, in the Sharpe (1964) – Lintner (1965) capital asset pricing model, is assumed to be identical. Assuming that asset prices are determined according to the capital asset pricing model, the preceding assumptions imply that the total market value of each of these distributions is identical, and we represent this value by V.

If the owner–manager has the right to decide which investment program to take, and if after he decides this he has the opportunity to sell part or all of his claims on the outcomes in the form of either debt or equity, he will be indifferent between the two investments.[40]

However, if the owner has the opportunity to *first* issue debt, then to decide which of the investments to take, and then to sell all or part of his remaining equity claim on the market, he will not be indifferent between the two investments. The reason is that by promising to take the low variance project, selling bonds and then taking the high variance project he can transfer wealth from the (naive) bondholders to himself as equity holder.

Let X^* be the amount of the "fixed" claim in the form of a non-coupon bearing bond sold to the bondholders such that the total payoff to them, R_j ($j = 1, 2$, denotes the distribution the manager chooses), is

$$
\begin{aligned}
R_j &= X^*, \quad \text{if} \quad \tilde{X}_j \geqq X^*, \\
&= X_j, \quad \text{if} \quad \tilde{X}_j \leq X^*.
\end{aligned}
$$

Let B_1 be the current market value of bondholder claims if investment 1 is taken, and let B_2 be the current market value of bondholders claims if investment 2 is taken. Since in this example the total value of the firm, V, is independent of the investment choice and also of the financing decision we can use the Black–Scholes (1973) option pricing model to determine the values of the debt, B_j, and equity, S_j, under each of the choices.[41]

---

[40]The portfolio diversification issues facing the owner–manager are brought into the analysis in section 5 below.

[41]See Smith (1976) for a review of this option pricing literature and its applications and Galai and Masulis (1976) who apply the option pricing model to mergers, and corporate investment decisions.

Black–Scholes derive the solution for the value of a European call option (one which can be exercised only at the maturity date) and argue that the resulting option pricing equation can be used to determine the value of the equity claim on a levered firm. That is the stockholders in such a firm can be viewed as holding a European call option on the total value of the firm with exercise price equal to X^* (the face value of the debt), exercisable at the maturity date of the debt issue. More simply, the stockholders have the right to buy the firm back from the bondholders for a price of X^* at time T. Merton (1973, 1974) shows that as the variance of the outcome distribution rises the value of the stock (i.e., call option) rises, and since our two distributions differ only in their variances, $\sigma_2^2 < \sigma_1^2$, the equity value S_1 is less than S_2. This implies $B_1 > B_2$, since $B_1 = V - S_1$ and $B_2 = V - S_2$.

Now if the owner–manager could sell bonds with face value X^* under the conditions that the potential bondholders believed this to be a claim on distribution 1, he would receive a price of B_1. After selling the bonds, his equity interest in distribution 1 would have value S_1. But we know S_2 is greater than S_1 and thus the manager can make himself better off by changing the investment to take the higher variance distribution 2, thereby redistributing wealth from the bondholders to himself. All this assumes of course that the bondholders could not prevent him from changing the investment program. *If the bondholders cannot do so, and if they perceive that the manager has the opportunity to take distribution 2 they will pay the manager only B_2 for the claim X^*, realizing that his maximizing behavior will lead him to choose distribution 2.* In this event there is no redistribution of wealth between bondholders and stockholders (and in general with rational expectations there never will be) and no welfare loss. It is easy to construct a case, however, in which these incentive effects do generate real costs.

Let cash flow distribution 2 in the previous example have an expected value, $E(X_2)$, which is lower than that of distribution 1. Then we know that $V_1 > V_2$, and if ΔV, which is given by

$$\Delta V = V_1 - V_2 = (S_1 - S_2) + (B_1 - B_2),$$

is sufficiently small relative to the reduction in the value of the bonds the value of the stock will increase.[42] Rearranging the expression for ΔV we see that the

[42]While we used the option pricing model above to motivate the discussion and provide some intuitive understanding of the incentives facing the equity holders, the option pricing solutions of Black and Scholes (1973) do not apply when incentive effects cause V to be a function of the debt/equity ratio as it is in general and in this example. Long (1974) points out this difficulty with respect to the usefulness of the model in the context of tax subsidies on interest and bankruptcy cost. The results of Merton (1974) and Galai and Masulis (1976) must be interpreted with care since the solutions are strictly incorrect in the context of tax subsidies and/or agency costs.

difference between the equity values for the two investments is given by

$$S_2 - S_1 = (B_1 - B_2) - (V_1 - V_2),$$

and the first term on the RHS, $B_1 - B_2$, is the amount of wealth "transferred" from the bondholders and $V_1 - V_2$ is the reduction in overall firm value. Since we know $B_1 > B_2$, $S_2 - S_1$ can be positive even though the reduction in the value of the firm, $V_1 - V_2$, is positive.[43] Again, the bondholders will not actually lose as long as they accurately perceive the motivation of the equity owning manager and his opportunity to take project 2. They will presume he will take investment 2, and hence will pay no more than B_2 for the bonds when they are issued.

In this simple example the reduced value of the firm, $V_1 - V_2$, is the agency cost engendered by the issuance of debt[44] and it is borne by the owner–manager. If he could finance the project out of his personal wealth, he would clearly choose project 1 since its investment outlay was assumed equal to that of project 2 and its market value, V_1, was greater. This wealth loss, $V_1 - V_2$, is the "residual loss" portion of what we have defined as agency costs and it is generated by the cooperation required to raise the funds to make the investment. Another important part of the agency costs are monitoring and bonding costs and we now consider their role.

4.2. The role of monitoring and bonding costs

In principle it would be possible for the bondholders, by the inclusion of various covenants in the indenture provisions, to limit the managerial behavior

---

[43]The numerical example of Fama and Miller (1972, pp. 179–180) is a close representation of this case in a two-period state model. However, they go on to make the following statement on p. 180:

'From a practical viewpoint, however, situations of potential conflict between bondholders and shareholders in the application of the market value rule are probably unimportant. In general, investment opportunities that increase a firm's market value by more than their cost both increase the value of the firm's shares and strengthen the firm's future ability to meet its current bond commitments.'

This first issue regarding the importance of the conflict of interest between bondholders and stockholders is an empirical one, and the last statement is incomplete – in some circumstances the equity holders could benefit from projects whose net effect was to reduce the total value of the firm as they and we have illustrated. The issue cannot be brushed aside so easily.

[44]Myers (1975) points out another serious incentive effect on managerial decisions of the existence of debt which does not occur in our simple single decision world. He shows that if the firm has the option to take future investment opportunities the existence of debt which matures after the options must be taken will cause the firm (using an equity value maximizing investment rule) to refuse to take some otherwise profitable projects because they would benefit only the bondholders and not the equity holders. This will (in the absence of tax subsidies to debt) cause the value of the firm to fall. Thus (although he doesn't use the term) these incentive effects also contribute to the agency costs of debt in a manner perfectly consistent with the examples discussed in the text.

which results in reductions in the value of the bonds. Provisions which impose constraints on management's decisions regarding such things as dividends, future debt issues,[45] and maintenance of working capital are not uncommon in bond issues.[46] To completely protect the bondholders from the incentive effects, these provisions would have to be incredibly detailed and cover most operating aspects of the enterprise including limitations on the riskiness of the projects undertaken. The costs involved in writing such provisions, the costs of enforcing them and the reduced profitability of the firm (induced because the covenants occasionally limit management's ability to take optimal actions on certain issues) would likely be non-trivial. In fact, since management is a continuous decision making process it will be almost impossible to completely specify such conditions without having the bondholders actually perform the management function. All costs associated with such covenants are what we mean by monitoring costs.

The bondholders will have incentives to engage in the writing of such covenants and in monitoring the actions of the manager to the point where the "nominal" marginal cost to them of such activities is just equal to the marginal benefits they perceive from engaging in them. We use the word nominal here because debtholders will not in fact bear these costs. As long as they recognize their existence, they will take them into account in deciding the price they will pay for any given debt claim,[47] and therefore the seller of the claim (the owner) will bear the costs just as in the equity case discussed in section 2.

In addition the manager has incentives to take into account the costs imposed on the firm by covenants in the debt agreement which directly affect the future cash flows of the firm since they reduce the market value of his claims. Because both the external and internal monitoring costs are imposed on the owner-manager it is in his interest to see that the monitoring is performed in the lowest cost way. Suppose, for example, that the bondholders (or outside equity holders) would find it worthwhile to produce detailed financial statements such as those contained in the usual published accounting reports as a means of monitoring the manager. If the manager himself can produce such information at lower costs than they (perhaps because he is already collecting much of the data they desire for his own internal decision making purposes), it would pay him to agree in advance to incur the cost of providing such reports and to have their

---

[45]Black–Scholes (1973) discuss ways in which dividend and future financing policy can redistribute wealth between classes of claimants on the firm.

[46]Black, Miller and Posner (1974) discuss many of these issues with particular reference to the government regulation of bank holding companies.

[47]In other words, these costs will be taken into account in determing the yield to maturity on the issue. For an examination of the effects of such enforcement costs on the nominal interest rates in the consumer small loan market, see Benston (1977).

accuracy testified to by an independent outside auditor. This is an example of what we refer to as bonding costs.[48,49]

4.3. Bankruptcy and reorganization costs

We argue in section 5 that as the debt in the capital structure increases beyond some point the marginal agency costs of debt begin to dominate the marginal

[48]To illustrate the fact that it will sometimes pay the manager to incur 'bonding' costs to guarantee the bondholders that he will not deviate from his promised behavior let us suppose that for an expenditure of $b of the firm's resources he can guarantee that project 1 will be chosen. If he spends these resources and takes project 1 the value of the firm will be $V_1 - b$ and clearly as long as $(V_1 - b) > V_2$, or alternatively $(V_1 - V_2) > b$ he will be better off, since his wealth will be equal to the value of the firm minus the required investment, I (which we assumed for simplicity to be identical for the two projects).

On the other hand, to prove that the owner–manager prefers the lowest cost solution to the conflict let us assume he can write a covenant into the bond issue which will allow the bondholders to prevent him from taking project 2, if they incur monitoring costs of m, where $m < b$. If he does this his wealth will be higher by the amount $b - m$. To see this note that if the bond market is competitive and makes unbiased estimates, potential bondholders will be indifferent between:

(i) a claim X^* with no covenant (and no guarantees from management) at a price of B_2,
(ii) a claim X^* with no covenant (and guarantees from management, through bonding expenditures by the firm of $b, that project 1 will be taken) at a price of B_1, and
(iii) a claim X^* with a covenant and the opportunity to spend m on monitoring (to guarantee project 1 will be taken) at a price of $B_1 - m$.

The bondholders will realize that (i) represents in fact a claim on project 2 and that (ii) and (iii) represent a claim on project 1 and are thus indifferent between the three options at the specified prices. The owner–manager, however, will not be indifferent between incurring the bonding costs, b, directly, or including the covenant in the bond identure and letting the bondholders spend m to guarantee that he take project 1. His wealth in the two cases will be given by the value of his equity plus the proceeds of the bond issue less the required investment, and if $m < b < V_1 - V_2$, then his post-investment-financing wealth, W, for the three options will be such that $W_i < W_{ii} < W_{iii}$. Therefore, since it would increase his wealth, he would voluntarily include the covenant in the bond issue and let the bondholders monitor.

[49]We mention, without going into the problem in detail, that similar to the case in which the outside equity holders are allowed to monitor the manager–owner, the agency relationship between the bondholders and stockholders has a symmetry if the rights of the bondholders to limit actions of the manager are not perfectly spelled out. Suppose the bondholders, by spending sufficiently large amounts of resources, could force management to take actions which would transfer wealth from the equity holder to the bondholders (by taking sufficiently less risky projects). One can easily construct situations where such actions could make the bondholders better off, hurt the equity holders and actually lower the total value of the firm. Given the nature of the debt contract the original owner-manager might maximize his wealth in such a situation by selling off the equity and keeping the bonds as his 'owner's' interest. If the nature of the bond contract is given, this may well be an inefficient solution since the total agency costs (i.e., the sum of monitoring and value loss) could easily be higher than the alternative solution. However, if the owner–manager could strictly limit the rights of the bondholders (perhaps by inclusion of a provision which expressly reserves all rights not specifically granted to the bondholder for the equity holder), he would find it in his interest to establish the efficient contractual arrangement since by minimizing the agency costs he would be maximizing his wealth. These issues involve the fundamental nature of contracts and for now we simply assume that the 'bondholders' rights are strictly limited and unambiguous and all rights not specifically granted them are reserved for the 'stockholders'; a situation descriptive of actual institutional arrangements. This allows us to avoid the incentive effects associated with 'bondholders' potentially exploiting 'stockholders'.

agency costs of outside equity and the result of this is the generally observed phenomenon of the simultaneous use of both debt snd outside equity. Before considering these issues, however, we consider here the third major component of the agency costs of debt which helps to explain why debt doesn't completely dominate capital structures – the existence of bankruptcy and reorganization costs.

It is important to emphasize that bankruptcy and liquidation are very different events. The legal definition of bankruptcy is difficult to specify precisely. In general, it occurs when the firm cannot meet a current payment on a debt obligation,[50] or one or more of the other indenture provisions providing for bankruptcy is violated by the firm. In this event the stockholders have lost all claims on the firm,[51] and the remaining loss, the difference between the face value of the fixed claims and the market value of the firm, is borne by the debtholders. Liquidation of the firm's assets will occur only if the market value of the future cash flows generated by the firm is less than the opportunity cost of the assets, i.e., the sum of the values which could be realized if the assets were sold piecemeal.

If there were no costs associated with the event called bankruptcy the total market value of the firm would not be affected by increasing the probability of its incurrence. However, it is costly, if not impossible, to write contracts representing claims on a firm which clearly delineate the rights of holders for all possible contingencies. Thus even if there were no adverse incentive effects in expanding fixed claims relative to equity in a firm, the use of such fixed claims would be constrained by the costs inherent in defining and enforcing those claims. Firms incur obligations daily to suppliers, to employees, to different classes of investors, etc. So long as the firm is prospering, the adjudication of claims is seldom a problem. When the firm has difficulty meeting some of its obligations, however, the issue of the priority of those claims can pose serious problems. This is most obvious in the extreme case where the firm is forced into bankruptcy. If bankruptcy were costless, the reorganization would be accompanied by an adjustment of the claims of various parties and the business, could, if that proved to be in the interest of the claimants, simply go on (although perhaps under new management).[52]

[50]If the firm were allowed to sell assets to meet a current debt obligation, bankruptcy would occur when the total market value of the future cash flows expected to be generated by the firm is less than the value of a current payment on a debt obligation. Many bond indentures do not, however, allow for the sale of assets to meet debt obligations.

[51]We have been told that while this is true in principle, the actual behavior of the courts appears to frequently involve the provision of some settlement to the common stockholders even when the assets of the company are not sufficient to cover the claims of the creditors.

[52]If under bankruptcy the bondholders have the right to fire the management, the management will have some incentives to avoid taking actions which increase the probability of this event (even if it is in the best interest of the equity holders) if they (the management) are earning rents or if they have human capital specialized to this firm or if they face large adjustment costs in finding new employment. A detailed examination of this issue involves the value of the control rights (the rights to hire and fire the manager) and we leave it to a subsequent paper.

In practice, bankruptcy is not costless, but generally involves an adjudication process which itself consumes a fraction of the remaining value of the assets of the firm. Thus the cost of bankruptcy will be of concern to potential buyers of fixed claims in the firm since their existence will reduce the payoffs to them in the event of bankruptcy. These are examples of the agency costs of cooperative efforts among individuals (although in this case perhaps "non-cooperative" would be a better term). The price buyers will be willing to pay for fixed claims will thus be inversely related to the probability of the incurrence of these costs i.e., to the probability of bankruptcy. Using a variant of the argument employed above for monitoring costs, it can be shown that the total value of the firm will fall, and the owner–manager equity holder will bear the entire wealth effect of the bankruptcy costs as long as potential bondholders make unbiased estimates of their magnitude at the time they initially purchase bonds.[53]

Empirical studies of the magnitude of bankruptcy costs are almost non-existent. Warner (1975) in a study of 11 railroad bankruptcies between 1930 and 1955 estimates the average costs of bankruptcy[54] as a fraction of the value of the firm three years prior to bankruptcy to be 2.5% (with a range of 0.4% to 5.9%). The average dollar costs were $1.88 million. Both of these measures seem remarkably small and are consistent with our belief that bankruptcy costs themselves are unlikely to be the major determinant of corporate capital structures. It is also interesting to note that the annual amount of defaulted funds has fallen significantly since 1940. [See Atkinson (1967).] One possible explanation for this phenomena is that firms are using mergers to avoid the costs of bankruptcy. This hypothesis seems even more reasonable, if, as is frequently the case, reorganization costs represent only a fraction of the costs associated with bankruptcy.

In general the revenues or the operating costs of the firm are not independent of the probability of bankruptcy and thus the capital structure of the firm. As the probability of bankruptcy increases, both the operating costs and the revenues of the firm are adversely affected, and some of these costs can be avoided by merger. For example, a firm with a high probability of bankruptcy will also find that it must pay higher salaries to induce executives to accept the higher risk of unemployment. Furthermore, in certain kinds of durable goods industries the demand function for the firm's product will not be independent of the probability of bankruptcy. The computer industry is a good example. There, the buyer's welfare is dependent to a significant extent on the ability to maintain the equipment, and on continuous hardware and software development. Furthermore, the owner of a large computer often receives benefits from the software

[53]Kraus and Litzenberger (1972) and Lloyd-Davies (1975) demonstrate that the total value of the firm will be reduced by these costs.

[54]These include only payments to all parties for legal fees, professional services, trustees' fees and filing fees. They do not include the costs of management time or changes in cash flows due to shifts in the firm's demand or cost functions discussed below.

developments of other users. Thus if the manufacturer leaves the business or loses his software support and development experts because of financial difficulties, the value of the equipment to his users will decline. The buyers of such services have a continuing interest in the manufacturer's viability not unlike that of a bondholder, except that their benefits come in the form of continuing services at lower cost rather than principle and interest payments. Service facilities and spare parts for automobiles and machinery are other examples.

In summary then the agency costs associated with debt[55] consist of:

(1) the opportunity wealth loss caused by the impact of debt on the investment decisions of the firm,

(2) the monitoring and bonding expenditures by the bondholders and the owner–manager (i.e., the firm),

(3) the bankruptcy and reorganization costs.

4.4. Why are the agency costs of debt incurred?

We have argued that the owner–manager bears the entire wealth effects of the agency costs of debt and he captures the gains from reducing them. Thus, the agency costs associated with debt discussed above will tend, in the absence of other mitigating factors, to discourage the use of corporate debt. What are the factors that encourage its use?

One factor is the tax subsidy on interest payments. (This will not explain preferred stock where dividends are not tax deductible.)[56] Modigliani and Miller (1963) originally demonstrated that the use of riskless perpetual debt will increase the total value of the firm (ignoring the agency costs) by an amount equal to τB, where τ is the marginal and average corporate tax rate and B is the market value of the debt. Fama and Miller (1972, ch. 4) demonstrate that for the case of risky debt the value of the firm will increase by the market value of the (uncertain) tax subsidy on the interest payments. Again, these gains will accrue entirely to

---

[55]Which, incidentally, exist only when the debt has some probability of default.

[56]Our theory is capable of explaining why in the absence of the tax subsidy on interest payments, we would expect to find firms using both debt and preferred stocks – a problem which has long puzzled at least one of the authors. If preferred stock has all the characteristics of debt except for the fact that its holders cannot put the firm into bankruptcy in the event of nonpayment of the preferred dividends, then the agency costs associated with the issuance of preferred stock will be lower than those associated with debt by the present value of the bankruptcy costs.

However, these lower agency costs of preferred stock exist only over some range if as the amount of such stock rises the incentive effects caused by their existence impose value reductions which are larger than that caused by debt (including the bankruptcy costs of debt). There are two reasons for this. First, the equity holder's claims can be eliminated by the debtholders in the event of bankruptcy, and second, the debtholders have the right to fire the management in the event of bankruptcy. Both of these will tend to become more important as an advantage to the issuance of debt as we compare situations with large amounts of preferred stock to equivalent situations with large amounts of debt because they will tend to reduce the incentive effects of large amounts of preferred stock.

the equity and will provide an incentive to utilize debt to the point where the marginal wealth benefits of the tax subsidy are just equal to the marginal wealth effects of the agency costs discussed above.

However, even in the absence of these tax benefits, debt would be utilized if the ability to exploit potentially profitable investment opportunities is limited by the resources of the owner. If the owner of a project cannot raise capital he will suffer an opportunity loss represented by the increment in value offered to him by the additional investment opportunities. Thus even though he will bear the agency costs from selling debt, he will find it desirable to incur them to obtain additional capital as long as the marginal wealth increments from the new investments projects are greater than the marginal agency costs of debt, and these agency costs are in turn less than those caused by the sale of additional equity discussed in section 2. Furthermore, this solution is optimal from the social viewpoint. However, in the absence of tax subsidies on debt these projects must be unique to this firm[57] or they would be taken by other competitive entrepreneurs (perhaps new ones) who possessed the requisite personal wealth to fully finance the projects[58] and therefore able to avoid the existence of debt or outside equity.

5. A theory of the corporate ownership structure

In the previous sections we discussed the nature of agency costs associated with outside claims on the firm – both debt and equity. Our purpose here is to integrate these concepts into the beginnings of a theory of the corporate ownership structure. We use the term "ownership structure" rather than "capital structure" to highlight the fact that the crucial variables to be determined are not just the relative amounts of debt and equity but also the fraction of the equity held by the manager. Thus, for a given size firm we want a theory to determine three variables:[59]

[57]One other conditions also has to hold to justify the incurrence of the costs associated with the use of debt or outside equity in our firm. If there are other individuals in the economy who have sufficiently large amounts of personal capital to finance the entire firm, our capital constrained owner can realize the full capital value of his current and prospective projects and avoid the agency costs by simply selling the firm (i.e. the, right to take these projects) to one of these individuals. He will then avoid the wealth losses associated with the agency costs caused by the sale of debt or outside equity. If no such individuals exist, it will pay him (and society) to obtain the additional capital in the debt market. This implies, incidentally, that it is somewhat misleading to speak of the owner–manager as the individual who bears the agency costs. One could argue that it is the project which bears the costs since, if it is not sufficiently profitable to cover all the costs (including the agency costs), it will not be taken. We continue to speak of the owner–manager bearing these costs to emphasize the more correct and important point that he has the incentive to reduce them because, if he does, his wealth will be increased.

[58]We continue to ignore for the moment the additional complicating factor involved with the portfolio decisions of the owner, and the implied acceptance of potentially diversifiable risk by such 100% owners in this example.

[59]We continue to ignore such instruments as convertible bonds and warrants.

S_i : inside equity (held by the manager),

S_o : outside equity (held by anyone outside of the firm),

B : debt (held by anyone outside of the firm).

The total market value of the equity is $S = S_i + S_o$, and the total market value of the firm is $V = S + B$. In addition, we also wish to have a theory which determines the optimal size of the firm, i.e., its level of investment.

5.1. Determination of the optimal ratio of outside equity to debt

Consider first the determination of the optimal ratio of outside equity to debt, S_o/B. To do this let us hold the size of the firm constant. V, the actual value of the firm for a given size, will depend on the agency costs incurred, hence we use as our index of size V^*, the value of the firm at a given scale when agency costs are zero. For the moment we also hold the amount of outside financing $(B + S_o)$, constant. Given that a specified amount of financing $(B + S_o)$ is to be obtained externally our problem is to determine the optimal fraction $E^* \equiv S_o^*/(B + S_o)$ to be financed with equity.

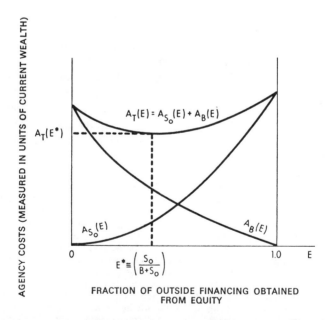

Fig. 5. Total agency costs, $A_T(E)$, as a function of the ratio of outside equity, to total outside financing, $E \equiv S_o/(B + S_o)$, for a given firm size V^* and given total amounts of outside financing $(B + S_o)$. $A_{S_o}(E) \equiv$ agency costs associated with outside equity, $A_B(E) \equiv$ agency costs associated with debt, B. $A_T(E^*) =$ minimum total agency costs at optimal fraction of outside financing E^*.

We argued above that: (1) as long as capital markets are efficient (i.e., characterized by rational expectations) the prices of assets such as debt and outside equity will reflect unbiased estimates of the monitoring costs and redistributions which the agency relationship will engender, and (2) the selling owner–manager will bear these agency costs. Thus from the owner–manager's standpoint the optimal proportion of outside funds to be obtained from equity (versus debt) *for a given level of internal equity* is that E which results in minimum total agency costs.

Fig. 5 presents a breakdown of the agency costs into two separate components: Define $A_{S_0}(E)$ as the total agency costs (a function of E) associated with the 'exploitation' of the outside equity holders by the owner–manager, and $A_B(E)$ as the total agency costs associated with the presence of debt in the ownership structure. $A_T(E) = A_{S_0}(E) + A_B(E)$ is the total agency cost.

Consider the function $A_{S_0}(E)$. When $E \equiv S_0/(B+S_0)$ is zero, i.e., when there is no outside equity, the manager's incentives to exploit the outside equity is at a minimum (zero) since the changes in the value of the *total* equity are equal to the changes in *his* equity.[60] As E increases to 100 percent his incentives to exploit the outside equity holders increase and hence the agency costs $A_{S_0}(E)$ increase.

The agency costs associated with the existence of debt, $A_B(E)$ are composed mainly of the value reductions in the firm and monitoring costs caused by the manager's incentive to reallocate wealth from the bondholders to himself by increasing the value of his equity claim. They are at a maximum where all outside funds are obtained from debt, i.e., where $S_0 = E = 0$. As the amount of debt declines to zero these costs also go to zero because as E goes to 1, his incentive to reallocate wealth from the bondholders to himself falls. These incentives fall for two reasons: (1) the total amount of debt falls, and therefore it is more difficult to reallocate any given amount away from the debtholders, and (2) his share of any reallocation which is accomplished is falling since S_0 is rising and therefore $S_i/(S_0 + S_i)$, his share of the total equity, is falling.

The curve $A_T(E)$ represents the sum of the agency costs from various combinations of outside equity and debt financing, and as long as $A_{S_0}(E)$ and $A_B(E)$ are

---

[60]Note, however, that even when outsiders own none of the equity the stockholder–manager still has some incentives to engage in activities which yield him non-pecuniary benefits but reduce the value of the firm by more than he personally values the benefits if there is any risky debt outstanding. Any such actions he takes which reduce the value of the firm, V, tend to reduce the value of the bonds as well as the value of the equity. Although the option pricing model does not in general apply exactly to the problem of valuing the debt and equity of the firm, it can be useful in obtaining some qualitative insights into matters such as this. In the option pricing model $\partial S/\partial V$ indicates the rate at which the stock value changes per dollar change in the value of the firm (and similarly for $\partial B/\partial V$). Both of these terms are less than unity [cf. Black and Scholes (1973)]. Therefore, any action of the manager which reduces the value of the firm, V, tends to reduce the value of both the stock and the bonds, and the larger is the total debt/equity ratio the smaller is the impact of any given change in V on the value of the equity, and therefore, the lower is the cost to him of consuming non-pecuniary benefits.

as we have drawn them the minimum total agency cost for given size firm and outside financing will occur at some point such as $A_T(E^*)$ with a mixture of both debt and equity.[61]

A caveat. Before proceeding further we point out that the issue regarding the exact shapes of the functions drawn in fig. 5 and several others discussed below is essentially an open question at this time. In the end the shape of these functions is a question of fact and can only be settled by empirical evidence. We outline some a priori arguments which we believe lead to some plausible hypotheses about the behavior of the system, but confess that we are far from understanding the many conceptual subtleties of the problem. We are fairly confident of our arguments regarding the signs of the first derivatives of the functions, but the second derivatives are also important to the final solution and much more work (both theoretical and empirical) is required before we can have much confidence regarding these parameters. We anticipate the work of others as well as our own to cast more light on these issues. Moreover, we suspect the results of such efforts will generate revisions to the details of what follows. We believe it is worthwhile to delineate the overall framework in order to demonstrate, if only in a simplified fashion, how the major pieces of the puzzle fit together into a cohesive structure.

5.2. Effects of the scale of outside financing

In order to investigate the effects of increasing the amount of outside financing, $B+S_o$, and therefore reducing the amount of equity held by the manager, S_i, we continue to hold the scale of the firm, V^*, constant. Fig. 6 presents a plot of the agency cost functions, $A_{S_o}(E)$, $A_B(E)$ and $A_T(E) = A_{S_o}(E) + A_B(E)$, for two different levels of outside financing. Define an index of the amount of outside financing to be

$$K = (B+S_o)/V^*,$$

and consider two different possible levels of outside financing K_0 and K_1 for a given scale of the firm such that $K_0 < K_1$.

As the amount of outside equity increases, the owner's fractional claim on the firm, α, falls. He will be induced thereby to take additional non-pecuniary benefits out of the firm because his share of the cost falls. This also increases the marginal benefits from monitoring activities and therefore will tend to increase the optimal level of monitoring. Both of these factors will cause the locus of agency costs $A_{S_0}(E; K)$ to shift upward as the fraction of outside financing, K,

---

[61]This occurs, of course, not at the intersection of $A_{S_o}(E)$ and $A_B(E)$, but at the point where the absolute value of the slopes of the functions are equal, i.e., where $A'_{S_o}(E) + A'_B(E) = 0$.

increases. This is depicted in fig. 6 by the two curves representing the agency costs of equity, one for the low level of outside financing, $A_{S_0}(E; K_o)$, the other for the high level of outside financing, $A_{S_0}(E; K_1)$. The locus of the latter lies above the former everywhere except at the origin where both are 0.

The agency cost of debt will similarly rise as the amount of outside financing increases. This means that the locus of $A_B(E; K_1)$ for high outside financing, K_1,

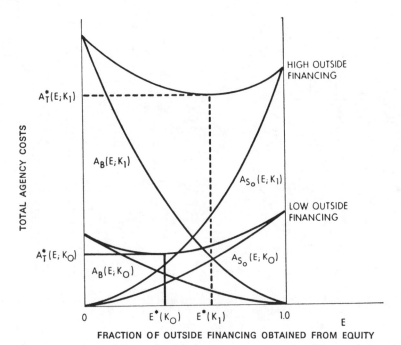

Fig. 6. Agency cost functions and optimal outside equity as a fraction of total outside financing, $E^*(K)$, for two different levels of outside financing, K, for a given size firm, $V^*: K_1 > K_0$.

will lie above the locus of $A_B(E; K_o)$ for low outside financing, K_o because the total amount of resources which can be reallocated from bondholders increases as the total amount of debt increases. However, since these costs are zero when the debt is zero for both K_o and K_1 the intercepts of the $A_B(E; K)$ curves coincide at the right axis.

The net effect of the increased use of outside financing given the cost functions assumed in fig. 6 is to: (1) increase the total agency costs from $A_T(E^*; K_o)$ to $A_T(E^*; K_1)$, and (2) to increase the optimal fraction of outside funds obtained from the sale of outside equity. We draw these functions for illustration only and are unwilling to speculate at this time on the exact form of $E^*(K)$ which gives the general effects of increasing outside financing on the relative quantities of debt and equity.

The locus of points, $A_T(E^*; K)$ where agency costs are minimized (not drawn in fig. 6), determines $E^*(K)$, the optimal proportions of equity and debt to be used in obtaining outside funds as the fraction of outside funds, K, ranges from 0 to 100 percent. The solid line in fig. 7 is a plot of the minimum total agency costs

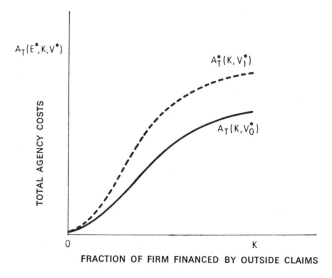

Fig. 7. Total agency costs as a function of the fraction of the firm financed by outside claims for two firm sizes, $V_1^* > V_0^*$.

as a function of the amount of outside financing for a firm with scale V_0^*. The dotted line shows the total agency costs for a larger firm with scale $V_1^* > V_0^*$. That is, we hypothesize that the larger the firm becomes the larger are the total agency costs because it is likely that the monitoring function is inherently more difficult and expensive in a larger organization.

5.3. Risk and the demand for outside financing

The model we have used to explain the existence of minority shareholders and debt in the capital structure of corporations implies that the owner–manager, if he resorts to any outside funding, will have his entire wealth invested in the firm. The reason is that he can thereby avoid the agency costs which additional outside funding impose. This suggests he would not resort to outside funding until he had invested 100 percent of his personal wealth in the firm – an implication which is not consistent with what we generally observe. Most owner–managers hold personal wealth in a variety of forms, and some have only a relatively small fraction of their wealth invested in the corporation they manage.[62] Diversification on the part of owner–managers can be explained by risk aversion and optimal portfolio selection.

If the returns from assets are not perfectly correlated an individual can reduce the riskiness of the returns on his portfolio by dividing his wealth among many different assets, i.e., by diversifying.[63] Thus a manager who invests all of his wealth in a single firm (his own) will generally bear a welfare loss (if he is risk averse) because he is bearing more risk than necessary. He will, of course, be willing to pay something to avoid this risk, and the costs he must bear to accomplish this diversification will be the agency costs outlined above. He will suffer a wealth loss as he reduces his fractional ownership because prospective shareholders and bondholders will take into account the agency costs. Nevertheless, the manager's desire to avoid risk will contribute to his becoming a minority stockholder.

5.4. Determination of the optimal amount of outside financing, K^*

Assume for the moment that the owner of a project (i.e., the owner of a prospective firm) has enough wealth to finance the entire project himself. The optimal scale of the corporation is then determined by the condition that, $\Delta V - \Delta I = 0$. In general if the returns to the firm are uncertain the owner–manager can increase his welfare by selling off part of the firm either as debt or equity and reinvesting the proceeds in other assets. If he does this with the optimal combination of debt and equity (as in fig. 6) the total wealth reduction he will incur is given by the agency cost function, $A_T(E^*, K; V^*)$ in fig. 7. The functions $A_T(E^*, K; V^*)$ will be S shaped (as drawn) if total agency costs for a given scale of firm increase at an increasing rate at low levels of outside financing, and at a decreasing rate for high levels of outside financing as monitoring imposes more and more constraints on the manager's actions.

Fig. 8 shows marginal agency costs as a function of K, the fraction of the firm financed with outside funds assuming the total agency cost function is as plotted in fig. 7, and assuming the scale of the firm is fixed. The demand by the owner–manager for outside financing is shown by the remaining curve in fig. 8. This curve represents the marginal value of the increased diversification which the manager

[62]On the average, however, top managers seem to have substantial holdings in absolute dollars. A recent survey by Wytmar (*Wall Street Journal*, August 13, 1974, p. 1) reported that the median value of 826 chief executive officers' stock holdings in their companies at year end 1973 was $557,000 and $1.3 million at year end 1972.

[63]These diversification effects can be substantial. Evans and Archer (1968) show that on the average for New York Stock Exchange securities approximately 55% of the total risk (as measured by standard deviation of portfolio returns) can be eliminated by following a naive strategy of dividing one's assets equally among 40 randomly selected securities.

can obtain by reducing his ownership claims and optimally constructing a diversified portfolio. It is measured by the amount he would pay to be allowed to reduce his ownership claims by a dollar in order to increase his diversification. If the liquidation of some of his holdings also influences the owner–manager's consumption set, the demand function plotted in fig. 8 also incorporates the marginal value of these effects. The intersection of these two schedules determines

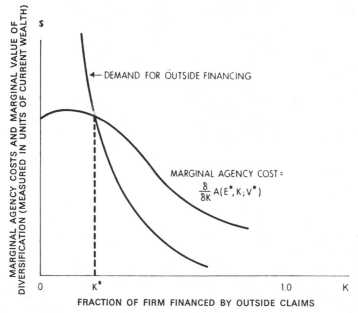

Fig. 8. Determination of the optimal amount of outside financing, K^*, for a given scale of firm

the optimal fraction of the firm to be held by outsiders and this in turn determines the total agency costs borne by the owner. This solution is Pareto optimal; there is no way to reduce the agency costs without making someone worse off.

5.5. Determination of the optimal scale of the firm

While the details of the solution of the optimal scale of the firm are complicated when we allow for the issuance of debt, equity and monitoring and bonding, the general structure of the solution is analogous to the case where monitoring and bonding are allowed for the outside equity example (see fig. 4).

If it is optimal to issue any debt, the expansion path taking full account of such opportunities must lie above the curve ZG in fig. 4. If this new expansion path lies anywhere to the right of the indifference curve passing through point G debt will be used in the optimal financing package. Furthermore, the optimal scale of the firm will be determined by the point at which this new expansion path touches the highest indifference curve. In this situation the resulting level of the owner–manager's welfare must therefore be higher.

6. Qualifications and extensions of the analysis

6.1. Multiperiod aspects of the agency problem

We have assumed throughout our analysis that we are dealing only with a single investment-financing decision by the entrepreneur and have ignored the issues associated with the incentives affecting future financing–investment decisions which might arise after the initial set of contracts are consumated between the entrepreneur–manager, outside stockholders and bondholders. These are important issues which are left for future analysis.[64] Their solution will undoubtedly introduce some changes in the conclusions of the single decision analysis. It seems clear for instance that the expectation of future sales of outside equity and debt will change the costs and benefits facing the manager in making decisions which benefit himself at the (short-run) expense of the current bondholders and stockholders. If he develops a reputation for such dealings he can expect this to unfavourably influence the terms at which he can obtain future capital from outside sources. This will tend to increase the benefits associated with "sainthood" and will tend to reduce the size of the agency costs. Given the finite life of any individual, however, such an effect cannot reduce these costs to zero, because at some point these future costs will begin to weigh more heavily on his successors and therefore the relative benefits to him of acting in his own best interests will rise.[65] Furthermore, it will generally be impossible for him to fully guarantee the outside interests that his successor will continue to follow his policies.

6.2. The control problem and outside owner's agency costs

The careful reader will notice that nowhere in the analysis thus far have we taken into account many of the details of the relationship between the part owner–manager and the outside stockholders and bondholders. In particular we have assumed that all outside equity is nonvoting. If such equity does have voting rights then the manager will be concerned about the effects on his long-run welfare of reducing his fractional ownership below the point where he loses

[64]The recent work of Myers (1975) which views future investment opportunities as options and investigates the incentive effects of the existence of debt in such a world where a sequence of investment decisions is made is another important step in the investigation of the multiperiod aspects of the agency problem and the theory of the firm.

[65]Becker and Stigler (1972) analyze a special case of this problem involving the use of nonvested pension rights to help correct for this end game play in the law enforcement area.

effective control of the corporation. That is, below the point where it becomes possible for the outside equity holders to fire him. A complete analysis of this issue will require a careful specification of the contractual rights involved on both sides, the role of the board of directors, and the coordination (agency) costs borne by the stockholders in implementing policy changes. This latter point involves consideration of the distribution of the outside ownership claims. Simply put, forces exist to determine an equilibrium distribution of outside ownership. If the costs of reducing the dispersion of ownership are lower than the benefits to be obtained from reducing the agency costs, it will pay some individual or group of individuals to buy shares in the market to reduce the dispersion of ownership. We occasionally witness these conflicts for control which involve outright market purchases, tender offers and proxy fights. Further analysis of these issues is left to the future.

6.3. A note on the existence of inside debt and some conjectures on the use of convertible financial instruments

We have been asked[66] why debt held by the manager (i.e., "inside debt") plays no role in our analysis. We have as yet been unable to incorporate this dimension formally into our analysis in a satisfactory way. The question is a good one and suggests some potentially important extensions of the analysis. For instance, it suggests an inexpensive way for the owner–manager with both equity and debt outstanding to eliminate a large part (perhaps all) of the agency costs of debt. If he binds himself contractually to hold a fraction of the total debt equal to his fractional ownership of the total equity he would have no incentive whatsoever to reallocate wealth from the debt holders to the stockholders. Consider the case where

$$B_i/S_i = B_o/S_o, \tag{4}$$

where S_i and S_o are as defined earlier, B_i is the dollar value of the inside debt held by the owner–manager, and B_o is the debt held by outsiders. In this case if the manager changes the investment policy of the firm to reallocate wealth between the debt and equity holders, the net effect on the total value of his holdings in the firm will be zero. Therefore, his incentives to perform such reallocations are zero.[67]

Why then don't we observe practices or formal contracts which accomplish

---

[66] By our colleague David Henderson.

[67] This also suggests that *some* outside debt holders can protect themselves from 'exploitation' by the manager by purchasing a fraction of the total equity equal to their fractional ownership of the debt. All debt holders, of course, cannot do this unless the manager does so also. In addition, such an investment rule restricts the portfolio choices of investors and therefore would impose costs if followed rigidly. Thus the agency costs will not be eliminated this way either.

this elimination or reduction of the agency costs of debt? Maybe we do for smaller privately held firms (we haven't attempted to obtain this data), but for large diffuse owner corporations the practice does not seem to be common. One reason for this we believe is that in some respects the claim that the manager holds on the firm in the form of his wage contract has some of the characteristics of debt.[68] If true, this implies that even with zero holdings of formal debt claims he still has positive holdings of a quasi-debt claim and this may accomplish the satisfaction of condition (4). The problem here is that any formal analysis of this issue requires a much deeper understanding of the relationship between formal debt holdings and the wage contract; i.e., how much debt is it equivalent to?

This line of thought also suggests some other interesting issues. Suppose the implicit debt characteristics of the manager's wage contract result in a situation equivalent to

$$B_i/S_i > B_o/S_o.$$

Then he would have incentives to change the operating characteristics of the firm (i.e., reduce the variance of the outcome distribution) to transfer wealth from the stockholders to the debt holders which is the reverse of the situation we examined in section 4. Furthermore, this seems to capture some of the concern often expressed regarding the fact that managers of large publicly held corporations seem to behave in a risk averse way to the detriment of the equity holders. One solution to this would be to establish incentive compensation systems for the manager or to give him stock options which in effect give him a claim on the upper tail of the outcome distribution. This also seems to be a commonly observed phenomenon.

This analysis also suggests some additional issues regarding the costs and benefits associated with the use of more complicated financial claims such as warrants, convertible bonds and convertible preferred stock which we have not formally analyzed as yet. Warrants, convertible bonds and convertible preferred stock have some of the characteristics of non-voting shares although they can be converted into voting shares under some terms. Alchian–Demsetz (1972) provide an interesting analysis regarding the use of non-voting shares. They argue that some shareholders with strong beliefs in the talents and judgements of the manager will want to be protected against the possibility that some other shareholders will take over and limit the actions of the manager (or fire him). Given that the securities exchanges prohibit the use of non-voting shares by listed firms the use of option type securities might be a substitute for these claims.

In addition warrants represents a claim on the upper tail of the distribution of

---

[68]Consider the situation in which the bondholders have the right in the event of bankruptcy to terminate his employment and therefore to terminate the future returns to any specific human capital or rents he may be receiving.

outcomes, and convertible securities can be thought of as securities with non-detachable warrants. It seems that the incentive effects of warrants would tend to offset to some extent the incentive effects of the existence of risky debt because the owner–manager would be sharing part of the proceeds associated with a shift in the distribution of returns with the warrant holders. Thus, we conjecture that potential bondholders will find it attractive to have warrants attached to the risky debt of firms in which it is relatively easy to shift the distribution of outcomes to expand the upper tail of the distribution to transfer wealth from bondholders. It would also then be attractive to the owner–manager because of the reduction in the agency costs which he would bear. This argument also implies that it would make little difference if the warrants were detachable (and therefore saleable separately from the bonds) since their mere existence would reduce the incentives of the manager (or stockholders) to increase the riskiness of the firm (and therefore increase the probability of bankruptcy). Furthermore, the addition of a conversion privilege to fixed claims such as debt or preferred stock would also tend to reduce the incentive effects of the existence of such fixed claims and therefore lower the agency costs associated with them. The theory predicts that these phenomena should be more frequently observed in cases where the incentive effects of such fixed claims are high than when they are low.

6.4. Monitoring and the social product of security analysts

One of the areas in which further analysis is likely to lead to high payoffs is that of monitoring. We currently have little which could be glorified by the title of a "Theory of Monitoring" and yet this is a crucial building block of the analysis. We would expect monitoring activities to become specialized to those institutions and individuals who possess comparative advantages in these activities. One of the groups who seem to play a large role in these activities is composed of the security analysts employed by institutional investors, brokers and investment advisory services as well as the analysis performed by individual investors in the normal course of investment decision making.

A large body of evidence exists which indicates that security prices incorporate in an unbiased manner all publicly available information and much of what might be called "private information".[69] There is also a large body of evidence which indicates that the security analysis activities of mutual funds and other institutional investors are not reflected in portfolio returns, i.e., they do not increase risk adjusted portfolio returns over a naive random selection buy and hold strategy.[70] Therefore some have been tempted to conclude that the resources expended on such research activities to find under- or over-valued securities is a social loss. Jensen (1974) argues that this conclusion cannot be

---

[69]See Fama (1970) for a survey of this 'efficient markets' literature.
[70]See Jensen (1969) for an example of this evidence and references.

unambiguously drawn because there is a large consumption element in the demand for these services.

Furthermore, the analysis of this paper would seem to indicate that to the extent that security analysis activities reduce the agency costs associated with the separation of ownership and control they are indeed socially productive. Moreover, if this is true we expect the major benefits of the security analysis activity to be reflected in the higher capitalized value of the ownership claims to corporations and *not* in the period to period portfolio returns of the analyst. Equilibrium in the security analysis industry requires that the private returns to analysis (i.e., portfolio returns) must be just equal to the private costs of such activity,[71] and this will not reflect the social product of this activity which will consist of larger output and higher *levels* of the capital value of ownership claims. Therefore, the argument implies that if there is a non-optimal amount of security analysis being performed it is too much[72] not too little (since the shareholders would be willing to pay directly to have the "optimal" monitoring performed), and we don't seem to observe such payments.

6.5. *Specialization in the use of debt and equity*

Our previous analysis of agency costs suggests at least one other testable hypothesis: i.e., that in those industries where the incentive effects of outside equity or debt are widely different, we would expect to see specialization in the use of the low agency cost financing arrangement. In industries where it is relatively easy for managers to lower the mean value of the outcomes of the enterprise by outright theft, special treatment of favored customers, ease of consumption of leisure on the job, etc. (for example, the bar and restaurant industry) we would expect to see the ownership structure of firms characterized by relatively little outside equity (i.e., 100 percent ownership of the equity by the manager) with almost all outside capital obtained through the use of debt.

The theory predicts the opposite would be true where the incentive effects of debt are large relative to the incentive effects of equity. Firms like conglomerates, in which it would be easy to shift outcome distributions adversely for bondholders (by changing the acquisition or divestiture policy) should be characterized by relatively lower utilization of debt. Conversely in industries where the freedom of management to take riskier projects is severely constrained (for example, regulated industries such as public utilities) we should find more intensive use of debt financing.

The analysis suggests that in addition to the fairly well understood role of uncertainty in the determination of the quality of collateral there is at least one other element of great importance – the ability of the owner of the collateral to

---

[71] Ignoring any pure consumption elements in the demand for security analysis.

[72] Again ignoring the value of the pure consumption elements in the demand for security analysis.

change the distribution of outcomes by shifting either the mean outcome or the variance of the outcomes. A study of bank lending policies should reveal these to be important aspects of the contractual practices observed there.

6.6. Application of the analysis to the large diffuse ownership corporation

While we believe the structure outlined in the proceeding pages is applicable to a wide range of corporations it is still in an incomplete state. One of the most serious limitation of the analysis is that as it stands we have not worked out in this paper its application to the very large modern corporation whose managers own little or no equity. We believe our approach can be applied to this case but space limitations precludes discussion of these issues here. They remain to be worked out in detail and will be included in a future paper.

6.7. The supply side of the incomplete markets question

The analysis of this paper is also relevant to the incomplete market issue considered by Arrow (1964), Diamond (1967), Hakansson (1974a, b), Rubinstein (1974), Ross (1974) and others. The problems addressed in this literature derive from the fact that whenever the available set of financial claims on outcomes in a market fails to span the underlying state space [see Arrow (1964) and Debreu (1959)] the resulting allocation is Pareto inefficient. A disturbing element in this literature surrounds the fact that the inefficiency conclusion is generally drawn without explicit attention in the analysis to the costs of creating new claims or of maintaining the expanded set of markets called for to bring about the welfare improvement.

The demonstration of a possible welfare improvement from the expansion of the set of claims by the introduction of new basic contingent claims or options can be thought of as an analysis of the demand conditions for new markets. Viewed from this perspective, what is missing in the literature on this problem is the formulation of a positive analysis of the supply of markets (or the supply of contingent claims). That is, what is it in the maximizing behavior of individuals in the economy that causes them to create and sell contingent claims of various sorts?

The analysis in this paper can be viewed as a small first step in the direction of formulating an analysis of the supply of markets issue which is founded in the self-interested maximizing behavior of individuals. We have shown why it is in the interest of a wealth maximizing entrepreneur to create and sell claims such as debt and equity. Furthermore, as we have indicated above, it appears that extensions of these arguments will lead to a theory of the supply of warrants, convertible bonds and convertible preferred stock. We are not suggesting that the specific analysis offered above is likely to be sufficient to lead to a theory of the supply of the wide range of contracts (both existing and merely potential) in the world at large. However, we do believe that framing the question of the completeness of markets in terms of the joining of both the demand and supply conditions will be very fruitful instead of implicitly assuming that new claims spring forth from some (costless) well head of creativity unaided or unsupported by human effort.

7. Conclusions

The publicly held business corporation is an awesome social invention. Millions of individuals voluntarily entrust billions of dollars, francs, pesos, etc., of personal wealth to the care of managers on the basis of a complex set of contracting relationships which delineate the rights of the parties involved. The growth in the use of the corporate form as well as the growth in market value of established corporations suggests that at least, up to the present, creditors and investors have by and large not been disappointed with the results, despite the agency costs inherent in the corporate form.

Agency costs are as real as any other costs. The level of agency costs depends among other things on statutory and common law and human ingenuity in devising contracts. Both the law and the sophistication of contracts relevant to the modern corporation are the products of a historical process in which there were strong incentives for individuals to minimize agency costs. Moreover, there were alternative organizational forms available, and opportunities to invent new ones. Whatever its shortcomings, the corporation has thus far survived the market test against potential alternatives.

References

Alchian, A.A., 1965, The basis of some recent advances in the theory of management of the firm, Journal of Industrial Economics, Nov., 30–44.

Alchian, A.A., 1968, Corporate management and property rights, in: Economic policy and the regulation of securities (American Enterprise Institute, Washington, DC).

Alchian, A.A., 1974, Some implications of recognition of property right transactions costs, unpublished paper presented at the First Interlaken Conference on Analysis and Ideology, June.

Alchian, A.A. and W.R. Allen, 1969, Exchange and production: Theory in use (Wadsworth, Belmont, CA).

Alchian, A.A. and H. Demsetz, 1972, Production, information costs, and economic organization, American Economic Review LXII, no. 5, 777–795.

Alchian, A.A. and R.A. Kessel, 1962, Competition, monopoly and the pursuit of pecuniary gain, in: Aspects of labor economics (National Bureau of Economic Research, Princeton, NJ).

Arrow, K.J., 1963/4, Control in large organizations, Management Science 10, 397–408.

Arrow, K.J., 1964, The role of securities in the optimal allocation of risk bearing, Review of Economic studies 31, no. 86, 91–96.

Atkinson, T.R., 1967, Trends in corporate bond quality, in: Studies in corporate bond finance 4 (National Bureau of Economic Research, New York).

Baumol, W.J., 1959, Business behavior, value and growth (Macmillan, New York).

Becker, G., 1957, The economics of discrimination (University of Chicago Press, Chicago, IL).

Becker, G.S. and G.J. Stigler, 1972, Law enforcement, corruption and compensation of enforcers, unpublished paper presented at the Conference on Capitalism and Freedom, Oct.

Benston, G., 1977, The impact of maturity regulation on high interest rate lenders and borrowers, Journal of Financial Economics 4, no. 1.

Berhold, M., 1971, A theory of linear profit sharing incentives, Quarterly Journal of Economics LXXXV, Aug., 460–482.

Berle, A.A., Jr. and G.C. Means, 1932, The modern corporation and private property (Macmillan, New York).

Black, F. and M. Scholes, 1973, The pricing of options and corporate liabilities, Journal of Political Economy 81, no. 3, 637–654.

Black, F., M.H. Miller and R.A. Posner, 1974, An approach to the regulation of bank holding companies, unpublished manuscript (University of Chicago, Chicago, IL).

Branch, B., 1973, Corporate objectives and market performance, Financial Management, Summer, 24–29.

Coase, R.H., 1937, The nature of the firm, Economica, New Series, IV, 386–405. Reprinted in: Readings in price theory (Irwin, Homewood, IL) 331–351.

Coase, R.H., 1959, The Federal Communications Commission, Journal of Law and Economics II, Oct., 1–40.

Coase, R.H., 1960, The problem of social cost, Journal of Law and Economics III, Oct., 1–44.

Coase, R.H., 1964, Discussion, American Economic Review LIV, no. 3, 194–197.

Cyert, R.M. and C.L. Hedrick, 1972, Theory of the firm: Past, present and future; An interpretation, Journal of Economic Literature X, June, 398–412.

Cyert, R.M. and J.G. March, 1963, A behavioral theory of the firm (Prentice Hall, Englewood Cliffs, NJ).

De Alessi, L., 1973, Private property and dispersion of ownership in large corporations, Journal of Finance, Sept., 839–851.

Debreu, G., 1959, Theory of value (Wiley, New York).

Demsetz, H., 1967, Toward a theory of property rights, American Economic Review LVII, May, 347–359.

Demsetz, H., 1969, Information and efficiency: Another viewpoint, Journal of Law and Economics XII, April, 1–22.

Diamond, P.A., 1967, The role of a stock market in a general equilibrium model with technological uncertainty, American Economic Review LVII, Sept., 759–776.

Evans, J.L. and S.H. Archer, 1968, Diversification and the reduction of dispersion: An empirical analysis, Journal of Finance, Dec.

Fama, E.F., 1970a, Efficient capital markets: A review of theory and empirical work, Journal of Finance XXV, no. 2.

Fama, E.F., 1970b, Multiperiod consumption–investment decisions, American Economic Review LX, March.

Fama, E.F., 1972, Ordinal and measurable utility, in: M.C. Jensen, ed., Studies in the theory of capital markets (Praeger, New York).

Fama, E.F. and M. Miller, 1972, The theory of finance (Holt, Rinehart and Winston, New York).

Friedman, M., 1970, The social responsibility of business is to increase its profits, New York Times Magazine, 13 Sept, 32ff.

Furubotn, E.G. and S. Pejovich, 1972, Property rights and economic theory: A survey of recent literature, Journal of Economic Literature X, Dec., 1137–1162.

Galai, D. and R.W. Masulis, 1976, The option pricing model and the risk factor of stock, Journal of Financial Economics 3, no. 1/2, 53–82.

Hakansson, N.H., 1974a, The superfund: Efficient paths toward a complete financial market, unpublished manuscript.

Hakansson, N.H., 1974b, Ordering markets and the capital structures of firms with illustrations, Institute of Business and Economic Research Working Paper no. 24 (University of California, Berkeley, CA).

Heckerman, D.G., 1975, Motivating managers to make investment decisions, Journal of Financial Economics 2, no. 3, 273–292.

Hirshleifer, J., 1958, On the theory of optimal investment decisions, Journal of Political Economy, Aug., 329–352.

Hirshleifer, J., 1970, Investment, interest, and capital (Prentice-Hall, Englewood Cliffs, NJ).

Jensen, M.C., 1969, Risk, the pricing of capital assets, and the evaluation of investment portfolios, Journal of Business 42, no. 2, 167–247.

Jensen, M.C., 1974, Tests of capital market theory and implications of the evidence. Graduate School of Management Working Paper Series no.7414 (University of Rochester, Rochester, NY).

Jensen, M.C. and J.B. Long, 1972, Corporate investment under uncertainty and Pareto optimality in the capital markets, Bell Journal of Economics, Spring, 151–174.

Jensen, M.C. and W.H. Meckling, 1976, Can the corporation survive? Center for Research in Government Policy and Business Working Paper no. PPS 76–4 (University of Rochester, Rochester, NY).

Klein, W.A., 1976, Legal and economic perspectives on the firm, unpublished manuscript (University of California, Los Angeles, CA).

Kraus, A. and R. Litzenberger, 1973, A state preference model of optimal financial leverage, Journal of Finance, Sept.

Larner, R.J., 1970, Management control and the large corporation (Dunellen, New York).

Lintner, J., 1965, Security prices, risk, and maximal gains from diversification, Journal of Finance XX, Dec., 587–616.

Lloyd-Davies, P., 1975, Risk and optimal leverage, unpublished manuscript (University of Rochester, Rochester, NY).

Long, J.B., 1972, Wealth, welfare, and the price of risk, Journal of Finance, May, 419–433.

Long, J.B., Jr., 1974, Discussion, Journal of Finance XXXIX, no. 12, 485–488.

Machlup, F., 1967, Theories of the firm: Marginalist, behavioral, managerial, American Economic Review, March, 1–33.

Manne, H.G., 1962, The 'higher criticism' of the modern corporation, Columbia Law Review 62, March, 399–432.

Manne, H.G., 1965, Mergers and the market for corporate control, Journal of Political Economy, April, 110–120.

Manne, H.G., 1967, Our two corporate systems: Law and economics, Virginia Law Review 53, March, 259–284.

Manne, H.G., 1972, The social responsibility of regulated utilities, Wisconsin Law Review V, no. 4, 995–1009.

Marris, R., 1964, The economic theory of managerial capitalism (Free Press of Glencoe, Glencoe, IL).

Mason, E.S., 1959, The corporation in modern society (Harvard University Press, Cambridge, MA).

McManus, J.C., 1975, The costs of alternative economic organizations, Canadian Journal of Economics VIII, Aug., 334–350.

Meckling, W.H., 1976, Values and the choice of the model of the individual in the social sciences, Schweizerische Zeitschrift für Volkswirtschaft und Statistik, Dec.

Merton, R.C., 1973, The theory of rational option pricing, Bell Journal of Economics and Management Science 4, no. 1, 141–183.

Merton, R.C., 1974, On the pricing of corporate debt: The risk structure of interest rates, Journal of Finance XXIX, no. 2, 449–470.

Merton, R.C. and M.G. Subrahmanyam, 1974, The optimality of a competitive stock market, Bell Journal of Economics and Management Science, Spring, 145–170.

Miller, M.H. and F. Modigliani, 1966, Some estimates of the cost of capital to the electric utility industry, 1954–57, American Economic Review, June, 333–391.

Modigliani, F. and M.H. Miller, 1958, The costs of capital, corporation finance, and the theory of investment, American Economic Review 48, June, 261–297.

Modigliani, F. and M.H. Miller, 1963, Corporate income taxes and the cost of capital: A correction, American Economic Review June, 433–443.

Monsen, R.J. and A. Downs, 1965, A theory of large managerial firms, Journal of Political Economy, June, 221–236.

Myers, S.C., 1975, A note on the determinants of corporate debt capacity, unpublished manuscript (London Graduate School of Business Studies, London).

Penrose, E., 1958, The theory of the growth of the firm (Wiley, New York).

Preston, L.E., 1975, Corporation and society: The search for a paradigm, Journal of Economic Literature XIII, June, 434–453.

Ross, S.A., 1973, The economic theory of agency: The principals problems, American Economic Review LXII, May, 134–139.

Ross, S.A., 1974a, The economic theory of agency and the principle of similarity, in: M.D. Balch et al., eds., Essays on economic behavior under uncertainty (North-Holland, Amsterdam).

Ross, S.A., 1974b, Options and efficiency, Rodney L. White Center for Financial Research Working Paper no. 3–74 (University of Pennsylvania, Philadelphia, PA).

Rubinstein, M., 1974, A discrete-time synthesis of financial theory, Parts I and II, Institute of Business and Economic Research Working Papers nos. 20 and 21 (University of California, Berkeley, CA).

Scitovsky, T., 1943, A note on profit maximisation and its implications, Review of Economic Studies XI, 57–60.

Sharpe, W.F., 1964, Capital asset prices : A theory of market equilibrium under conditions of risk, Journal of Finance XIX, Sept., 425–442.

Shubik, M., 1970, A curmudgeon's guide to microeconomics, Journal of Economic Literature VIII, June, 405–434.

Silver, M. and R. Auster, 1969, Entrepreneurship, profit and limits on firm size, Journal of Business 42, July, 277–281.

Simon, H.A., 1955, A behavioral model of rational choice, Quarterly Journal of Economics 69, 99–118.

Simon, H.A., 1959, Theories of decision making in economics and behavioral science, American Economic Review, June, 253–283.

Smith, A., 1937, The wealth of nations, Cannan edition (Modern Library, New York).

Smith, C., 1976, Option pricing: A review, Journal of Financial Economics 3, nos. 1/2, 3–52.

Warner, J.B., 1975, Bankruptcy costs, absolute priority, and the pricing of risky debt claims, unpublished manuscript (University of Chicago, Chicago, IL).

Williamson, O.E., 1964, The economics of discretionary behavior: Managerial objectives in a theory of the firm (Prentice-Hall, Englewood Cliffs, NJ).

Williamson, O.E., 1970, Corporate control and business behavior (Prentice-Hall, Englewood Cliffs, NJ).

Williamson, O.E., 1975, Markets and hierarchies: Analysis and antitrust implications (The Free Press, New York).

Wilson, R., 1968, On the theory of syndicates, Econometrica 36, Jan., 119–132.

Wilson, R., 1969, La decision: Agregation et dynamique des orders de preference, Extrait (Editions du Centre National de la Recherche Scientifique, Paris) 288–307.

25. AGENCY PROBLEMS AND THE THEORY OF THE FIRM

EUGENE F. FAMA*

Reprinted from *The Journal of Political Economy*, Vol. 88, No. 2 (April 1980), pp. 288–307, by permission of the author and the University of Chicago Press. Copyright © 1980 by the University of Chicago.

This paper attempts to explain how the separation of security ownership and control, typical of large corporations, can be an efficient form of economic organization. We first set aside the presumption that a corporation has owners in any meaningful sense. The entrepreneur is also laid to rest, at least for the purposes of the large modern corporation. The two functions usually attributed to the entrepreneur—management and risk bearing—are treated as naturally separate factors within the set of contracts called a firm. The firm is disciplined by competition from other firms, which forces the evolution of devices for efficiently monitoring the performance of the entire team and of its individual members. Individual participants in the firm, and in particular its managers, face both the discipline and opportunities provided by the markets for their services, both within and outside the firm.

Economists have long been concerned with the incentive problems that arise when decision making in a firm is the province of managers who are not the firm's security holders.[1] One outcome has been the development of "behavioral" and "managerial" theories of the firm which reject the classical model of an entrepreneur, or owner-

This research is supported by the National Science Foundation. Roger Kormendi has contributed much, and the comments of A. Alchian, S. Bhattacharya, G. Becker, F. Black, M. Blume, M. Bradley, D. Breeden, N. Gonedes, B. Horwitz, G. Jarrell, E. H. Kim, J. Long, H. Manne, W. Meckling, M. H. Miller, M. Scholes, C. Smith, G. J. Stigler, R. Watts, T. Whisler, and J. Zimmerman are gratefully acknowledged. Presentations at the finance, labor economics, and industrial organization workshops of the University of Chicago and the workshop of the Managerial Economics Research Center of the University of Rochester have been helpful. The paper is largely an outgrowth of discussions with Michael C. Jensen.

* University of Chicago

[1] Jensen and Meckling (1976) quote from Adam Smith (1776). The modern literature on the problem dates back at least to Berle and Means (1932).

manager, who single-mindedly operates the firm to maximize profits, in favor of theories that focus more on the motivations of a manager who controls but does not own and who has little resemblance to the classical "economic man." Examples of this approach are Baumol (1959), Simon (1959), Cyert and March (1963), and Williamson (1964).

More recently the literature has moved toward theories that reject the classical model of the firm but assume classical forms of economic behavior on the part of agents within the firm. The firm is viewed as a set of contracts among factors of production, with each factor motivated by its self-interest. Because of its emphasis on the importance of rights in the organization established by contracts, this literature is characterized under the rubric "property rights." Alchian and Demsetz (1972) and Jensen and Meckling (1976) are the best examples. The antecedents of their work are in Coase (1937, 1960).

The striking insight of Alchian and Demsetz (1972) and Jensen and Meckling (1976) is in viewing the firm as a set of contracts among factors of production. In effect, the firm is viewed as a team whose members act from self-interest but realize that their destinies depend to some extent on the survival of the team in its competition with other teams. This insight, however, is not carried far enough. In the classical theory, the agent who personifies the firm is the entrepreneur who is taken to be both manager and residual risk bearer. Although his title sometimes changes—for example, Alchian and Demsetz call him "the employer"—the entrepreneur continues to play a central role in the firm of the property-rights literature. As a consequence, this literature fails to explain the large modern corporation in which control of the firm is in the hands of managers who are more or less separate from the firm's security holders.

The main thesis of this paper is that separation of security ownership and control can be explained as an efficient form of economic organization within the "set of contracts" perspective. We first set aside the typical presumption that a corporation has owners in any meaningful sense. The attractive concept of the entrepreneur is also laid to rest, at least for the purposes of the large modern corporation. Instead, the two functions usually attributed to the entrepreneur, management and risk bearing, are treated as naturally separate factors within the set of contracts called a firm. The firm is disciplined by competition from other firms, which forces the evolution of devices for efficiently monitoring the performance of the entire team and of its individual members. In addition, individual participants in the firm, and in particular its managers, face both the discipline and opportunities provided by the markets for their services, both within and outside of the firm.

The Irrelevance of the Concept of Ownership of the Firm

To set a framework for the analysis, let us first describe roles for management and risk bearing in the set of contracts called a firm. Management is a type of labor but with a special role—coordinating the activities of inputs and carrying out the contracts agreed among inputs, all of which can be characterized as "decision making." To explain the role of the risk bearers, assume for the moment that the firm rents all other factors of production and that rental contracts are negotiated at the beginning of each production period with payoffs at the end of the period. The risk bearers then contract to accept the uncertain and possibly negative difference between total revenues and costs at the end of each production period.

When other factors of production are paid at the end of each period, it is not necessary for the risk bearers to invest anything in the firm at the beginning of the period. Most commonly, however, the risk bearers guarantee performance of their contracts by putting up wealth ex ante, with this front money used to purchase capital and perhaps also the technology that the firm uses in its production activities. In this way the risk bearing function is combined with ownership of capital and technology. We also commonly observe that the joint functions of risk bearing and ownership of capital are re-packaged and sold in different proportions to different groups of investors. For example, when front money is raised by issuing both bonds and common stock, the bonds involve a combination of risk bearing and ownership of capital with a low amount of risk bearing relative to the combination of risk bearing and ownership of capital inherent in the common stock. Unless the bonds are risk free, the risk bearing function is in part borne by the bondholders, and ownership of capital is shared by bondholders and stockholders.

However, ownership of capital should not be confused with owner-ship of the firm. Each factor in a firm is owned by somebody. The firm is just the set of contracts covering the way inputs are joined to create outputs and the way receipts from outputs are shared among inputs. In this "nexus of contracts" perspective, ownership of the firm is an irrelevant concept. Dispelling the tenacious notion that a firm is owned by its security holders is important because it is a first step toward understanding that control over a firm's decisions is not neces-sarily the province of security holders. The second step is setting aside the equally tenacious role in the firm usually attributed to the entre-preneur.

Management and Risk Bearing: A Closer Look

The entrepreneur (manager–risk bearer) is central in both the Jensen-Meckling and Alchian-Demsetz analyses of the firm. For example, Alchian-Demsetz state: "The essence of the classical firm is identified here as a contractual structure with: 1) joint input production; 2) several input owners; 3) one party who is common to all the contracts of the joint inputs; 4) who has the right to renegotiate any input's contract independently of contracts with other input owners; 5) who holds the residual claim; and 6) who has the right to sell his central contractual residual status. The central agent is called the firm's owner and the employer" (1972, p. 794).

To understand the modern corporation, it is better to separate the manager, the agents of points 3 and 4 of the Alchian-Demsetz definition of the firm, from the risk bearer described in points 5 and 6. The rationale for separating these functions is not just that the end result is more descriptive of the corporation, a point recognized in both the Alchian-Demsetz and Jensen-Meckling papers. The major loss in retaining the concept of the entrepreneur is that one is prevented from developing a perspective on management and risk bearing as separate factors of production, each faced with a market for its services that provides alternative opportunities and, in the case of management, motivation toward performance.

Thus, any given set of contracts, a particular firm, is in competition with other firms, which are likewise teams of cooperating factors of production. If there is a part of the team that has a special interest in its viability, it is not obviously the risk bearers. It is true that if the team does not prove viable factors like labor and management are protected by markets in which rights to their future services can be sold or rented to other teams. The risk bearers, as residual claimants, also seem to suffer the most direct consequences from the failings of the team. However, the risk bearers in the modern corporation also have markets for their services—capital markets—which allow them to shift among teams with relatively low transaction costs and to hedge against the failings of any given team by diversifying their holdings across teams.

Indeed, portfolio theory tells us that the optimal portfolio for any investor is likely to be diversified across the securities of many firms.[2] Since he holds the securities of many firms precisely to avoid having his wealth depend too much on any one firm, an individual security holder generally has no special interest in personally overseeing the detailed activities of any firm. In short, efficient allocation of risk bearing seems to imply a large degree of separation of security ownership from control of a firm.

On the other hand, the managers of a firm rent a substantial lump of wealth—their human capital—to the firm, and the rental rates for

---

[2] Detailed discussions of portfolio models can be found in Fama and Miller (1972, chaps. 6 and 7), Jensen (1972), and Fama (1976, chaps. 7 and 8).

their human capital signaled by the managerial labor market are likely to depend on the success or failure of the firm. The function of management is to oversee the contracts among factors and to ensure the viability of the firm. For the purposes of the managerial labor market, the previous associations of a manager with success and failure are information about his talents. The manager of a firm, like the coach of any team, may not suffer any immediate gain or loss in current wages from the current performance of his team, but the success or failure of the team impacts his future wages, and this gives the manager a stake in the success of the team.

The firm's security holders provide important but indirect assistance to the managerial labor market in its task of valuing the firm's management. A security holder wants to purchase securities with confidence that the prices paid reflect the risks he is taking and that the securities will be priced in the future to allow him to reap the rewards (or punishments) of his risk bearing. Thus, although an individual security holder may not have a strong interest in directly overseeing the management of a particular firm, he has a strong interest in the existence of a capital market which efficiently prices the firm's securities. The signals provided by an efficient capital market about the values of a firm's securities are likely to be important for the managerial labor market's revaluations of the firm's management.

We come now to the central question. To what extent can the signals provided by the managerial labor market and the capital market, perhaps along with other market-induced mechanisms, discipline managers? We first discuss, still in general terms, the types of discipline imposed by managerial labor markets, both within and outside of the firm. We then analyze specific conditions under which this discipline is sufficient to resolve potential incentive problems that might be associated with the separation of security ownership and control.

The Viability of Separation of Security Ownership and Control of the Firm: General Comments

The outside managerial labor market exerts many direct pressures on the firm to sort and compensate managers according to performance. One form of pressure comes from the fact that an ongoing firm is always in the market for new managers. Potential new managers are concerned with the mechanics by which their performance will be judged, and they seek information about the responsiveness of the system in rewarding performance. Moreover, given a competitive managerial labor market, when the firm's reward system is not responsive to performance the firm loses managers, and the best are the first to leave.

There is also much internal monitoring of managers by managers themselves. Part of the talent of a manager is his ability to elicit and measure the productivity of lower managers, so there is a natural process of monitoring from higher to lower levels of management. Less well appreciated, however, is the monitoring that takes place from bottom to top. Lower managers perceive that they can gain by stepping over shirking or less competent managers above them. Moreover, in the team or nexus of contracts view of the firm, each manager is concerned with the performance of managers above and below him since his marginal product is likely to be a positive function of theirs. Finally, although higher managers are affected more than lower managers, all managers realize that the managerial labor market uses the performance of the firm to determine each manager's outside opportunity wage. In short, each manager has a stake in the performance of the managers above and below him and, as a consequence, undertakes some amount of monitoring in both directions.

All managers below the very top level have an interest in seeing that the top managers choose policies for the firm which provide the most positive signals to the managerial labor market. But by what mechanism can top management be disciplined? Since the body designated for this function is the board of directors, we can ask how it might be constructed to do its job. A board dominated by security holders does not seem optimal or endowed with good survival properties. Diffuse ownership of securities is beneficial in terms of an optimal allocation of risk bearing, but its consequence is that the firm's security holders are generally too diversified across the securities of many firms to take much direct interest in a particular firm.

If there is competition among the top managers themselves (all want to be the boss of bosses), then perhaps they are the best ones to control the board of directors. They are most directly in the line of fire from lower managers when the markets for securities and managerial labor give poor signals about the performance of the firm. Because of their power over the firm's decisions, their market-determined opportunity wages are also likely to be most affected by market signals about the performance of the firm. If they are also in competition for the top places in the firm, they may be the most informed and responsive critics of the firm's performance.

Having gained control of the board, top management may decide that collusion and expropriation of security holder wealth are better than competition among themselves. The probability of such collusive arrangements might be lowered, and the viability of the board as a market-induced mechanism for low-cost internal transfer of control might be enhanced, by the inclusion of outside directors. The latter might best be regarded as professional referees whose task is to stimulate and oversee the competition among the firm's top managers. In a state of advanced evolution of the external markets that buttress the corporate firm, the outside directors are in their turn disciplined by the market for their services which prices them according to their performance as referees. Since such a system of separation of security ownership from control is consistent with the pressures applied by the managerial labor market, and since it likewise operates in the interests of the firm's security holders, it probably has good survival properties.[3]

This analysis does not imply that boards of directors are likely to be composed entirely of managers and outside directors. The board is viewed as a market-induced institution, the ultimate internal monitor of the set of contracts called a firm, whose most important role is to scrutinize the highest decision makers within the firm. In the team or nexus of contracts view of the firm, one cannot rule out the evolution of boards of directors that contain many different factors of production (or their hired representatives), whose common trait is that their marginal products are affected by those of the top decision makers. On the other hand, one also cannot conclude that all such factors will naturally show up on boards since there may be other market-induced institutions, for example, unions, that more efficiently monitor managers on behalf of specific factors. All one can say is that in a competitive environment lower-cost sets of monitoring mechanisms are likely to survive. The role of the board in this framework is to provide a relatively low-cost mechanism for replacing or reordering top managers; lower cost, for example, than the mechanism provided by an outside takeover, although, of course, the existence of an outside market for control is another force which helps to sensitize the internal managerial labor market.

The perspective suggested here owes much to, but is nevertheless different from, existing treatments of the firm in the property rights literature. Thus, Alchian (1969) and Alchian and Demsetz (1972) comment insightfully on the disciplining of management that takes place through the inside and outside markets for managers. However, they attribute the task of disciplining management primarily to the risk bearers, the firm's security holders, who are assisted to some extent by managerial labor markets and by the possibility of outside takeover. Jensen and Meckling (1976) likewise make control of man-

---

[3] Watts and Zimmerman (1978) provide a similar description of the market-induced evolution of "independent" outside auditors whose function is to certify and, as a consequence, stimulate the viability of the set of contracts called the firm. Like the outside directors, the outside auditors are policed by the market for their services which prices them in large part on the basis of how well they resist perverting the interests of one set of factors (e.g., security holders) to the benefit of other factors (e.g., management). Like the professional outside director, the welfare of the outside auditor depends largely on "reputation."

agement the province of the firm's risk bearers, but they do not allow for any assistance from the managerial labor market. Of all the authors in the property-rights literature, Manne (1965, 1967) is most concerned with the market for corporate control. He recognizes that with diffuse security ownership management and risk bearing are naturally separate functions. But for him, disciplining management is an "entrepreneurial job" which in the first instance falls on a firm's organizers and later on specialists in the process of outside takeover.

When management and risk bearing are viewed as naturally separate factors of production, looking at the market for risk bearing from the viewpoint of portfolio theory tells us that risk bearers are likely to spread their wealth across many firms and so not be interested in directly controlling the management of any individual firm. Thus, models of the firm, like those of Alchian-Demsetz and Jensen-Meckling, in which the control of management falls primarily on the risk bearers, are not likely to allay the fears of those concerned with the apparent incentive problems created by the separation of security ownership and control. Likewise, Manne's approach, in which the control of management relies primarily on the expensive mechanism of an outside takeover, offers little comfort. The viability of the large corporation with diffuse security ownership is better explained in terms of a model where the primary disciplining of managers comes through managerial labor markets, both within and outside of the firm, with assistance from the panoply of internal and external monitoring devices that evolve to stimulate the ongoing efficiency of the corporate form, and with the market for outside takeovers providing discipline of last resort.

The Viability of Separation of Security Ownership and Control: Details

The preceding is a general discussion of how pressure from managerial labor markets helps to discipline managers. We now examine somewhat more specifically conditions under which the discipline imposed by managerial labor markets can resolve potential incentive problems associated with the separation of security ownership and control of the firm.

To focus on the problem we are trying to solve, let us first examine the situation where the manager is also the firm's sole security holder, so that there is clearly no incentive problem. When he is sole security holder, a manager consumes on the job, through shirking, perquisites, or incompetence, to the point where these yield marginal expected utility equal to that provided by an additional dollar of wealth usable for consumption or investment outside of the firm. The manager is induced to make this specific decision because he pays directly for consumption on the job; that is, as manager he cannot avoid a full ex post settling up with himself as security holder.

In contrast, when the manager is no longer sole security holder, and in the absence of some form of full ex post settling up for deviations from contract, a manager has an incentive to consume more on the job than is agreed in his contract. The manager perceives that, on an ex post basis, he can beat the game by shirking or consuming more perquisites than previously agreed. This does not necessarily mean that the manager profits at the expense of other factors. Rational managerial labor markets understand any shortcomings of available mechanisms for enforcing ex post settling up. Assessments of ex post deviations from contract will be incorporated into contracts on an ex ante basis; for example, through an adjustment of the manager's wage.

Nevertheless, a game which is fair on an ex ante basis does not induce the same behavior as a game in which there is also ex post settling up. Herein lie the potential losses from separation of security ownership and control of a firm. There are situations where, with less than complete ex post settling up, the manager is induced to consume more on the job than he would like, given that on average he pays for his consumption ex ante.

Three general conditions suffice to make the wage revaluation imposed by the managerial labor market a form of full ex post settling up which resolves the managerial incentive problem described above. The first condition is that a manager's talents and his tastes for consumption on the job are not known with certainty, are likely to change through time, and must be imputed by managerial labor markets at least in part from information about the manager's current and past performance. Since it seems to capture the essence of the task of managerial labor markets in a world of uncertainty, this assumption is no real restriction.

The second assumption is that managerial labor markets appropriately use current and past information to revise future wages and understand any enforcement power inherent in the wage revision process. In short, contrary to much of the literature on separation of security ownership and control, we impute efficiency or rationality in information processing to managerial labor markets. In defense of this assumption, we note that the problem faced by managerial labor markets in revaluing the managers of a firm is much entwined with the problem faced by the capital market in revaluing the firm itself. Although we do not understand all the details of the process, available empirical evidence (e.g., Fama 1976, chaps. 5 and 6) suggests that the capital market generally makes rational assessments of the value of the firm in the face of imprecise and uncertain information. This does not necessarily mean that information processing in managerial labor markets is equally efficient or rational, but it is a warning against strong presumptions to the contrary.

The final and key condition for full control of managerial behavior through wage changes is that the weight of the wage revision process is sufficient to resolve any potential problems with managerial incentives. In this general form, the condition amounts to assuming the desired result. More substance is provided by specific examples.

Example 1: Marketable Human Capital

Suppose a manager's human capital, his stream of future wages, is a marketable asset. Suppose the manager perceives that, because of the consequent revaluations of future wages, the current value of his human capital changes by at least the amount of an unbiased assessment of the wealth changes experienced by other factors, primarily the security holders, because of his current deviations from contract. Then, as long as the manager is not a risk preferrer, these revaluations of his human capital are a form of full ex post settling up. The manager need not be charged ex ante for presumed ex post deviations from contract since the weight of the wage revision process is sufficient to neutralize his incentives to deviate.

It is important to consider why the manager might perceive that the value of his human capital changes by at least the amount of an unbiased assessment of the wealth changes experienced by other factors due to his deviations from contract. Note first that the market's assessment of such wealth changes is also its assessment of the difference between the manager's ex post marginal product and the marginal product he contracted to deliver ex ante. However, any assessment of the manager's marginal product is likely to include extraneous noise which has little to do with his talents and efforts. Without specific details on what the market takes to be the statistical process governing the evolution of the manager's talents and his tastes for consumption on the job, one cannot say exactly how far it will go in adjusting his future wages to reflect its most recent measurement of his marginal product. Assuming the market uses information rationally, the adjustment is closer to complete the larger the signal in the most recent measurement relative to the noise, but as long as there is some noise in the process, the adjustment is less than complete.[4]

Although his next wage may not adjust by the full amount of an unbiased assessment of the current cost of his deviations from con-

---

[4] Specific illustrations of this point are provided later.

tract, a manager with a multiperiod horizon may perceive that the implied current wealth change, the present value of likely changes in the stream of future wages, is at least as great as the cost of his deviations from contract. In this case, the contemporaneous change in his wealth implied by an eventual adjustment of future wages is a form of full ex post settling up which results in full enforcement of his contract. Moreover, the wage revision process resolves any potential problems about a manager's incentives even though the implied ex post settling up need not involve the firm currently employing the manager; that is, lower or higher future wages due to current deviations from contract may come from other firms.

Of course, changes in a manager's wealth as a consequence of anticipated future wage revisions are not always equivalent to full ex post settling up. When a manager does not expect to be in the labor market for many future periods, the weight of future wage revisions due to current assessments of performance may amount to substantially less than full ex post settling up. However, it is just as important to recognize that the weight of anticipations about future wages may amount to more than full ex post settling up. There may be situations where the personal wealth change perceived by the manager as a consequence of deviations from contract is greater than the wealth change experienced by other factors. Since many readers have had trouble with this point, it is well to bring it closer to home.

Economists (especially young economists) easily imagine situations where the effects of higher or lower quality of a current article or book on the market value of human capital, through enhancement or lowering of "reputation," are in excess of the effects of quality differences on the market value of the specific work to any publisher. Managers can sometimes have similar perceptions with respect to the implications of current performance for the market value of their human capital.

Example 2: Stochastic Processes for Marginal Products

The next example of ex post settling up through the wage revision process is somewhat more formal than that described above. We make specific assumptions about the stochastic evolution of a manager's measured marginal product and about how the managerial labor market uses information from the process to adjust the manager's future wages—in a manner which amounts to precise, full ex post settling up for the results of past performance.

Suppose the manager's measured marginal product for any period t is composed of two terms: (i) an expected value, given his talents, effort exerted during t, consumption of perquisites, etc.; and (ii) random noise. The random noise may in part result from measurement error, that is, the sheer difficulty of accurately measuring marginal products when there is team production, but it may also arise in part from the fact that effort exerted and talent do not yield perfectly certain consequences. Moreover, because of the uncertain evolution of the manager's talents and tastes, the expected value of his marginal product is itself a stochastic process. Specifically, we assume that the expected value, $\bar{z}_t$, follows a random walk with steps that are independent of the random noise, ϵ_t, in the manager's measured marginal product, z_t. Thus, the measured marginal product,

$$z_t = \bar{z}_t + \epsilon_t, \tag{1}$$

is a random walk plus white noise. For simplicity, we also assume that this process describes the manager's marginal product both in his current employment and in the best alternative employment.

The characteristics (parameters) of the evolution of the manager's marginal product depend to some extent on endogenous variables like effort and perquisites consumed, which are not completely observable. Our purpose is to set up the managerial labor market so that the wage revision process resolves any potential incentive problems that may arise from the endogeneity of z_t in a situation where there is separation of security ownership and control of the firm.

Suppose next that risk bearers are all risk neutral and that 1-period market interest rates are always equal to zero. Suppose also that managerial wage contracts are written so that the manager's wage in any period t is the expected value of his marginal product, $\bar{z}_t$, conditional on past measured values of his marginal product, with the risk bearers accepting the noise ϵ_t, in the ex post measurement of the marginal product. We shall see below that this is an optimal arrangement for our risk-neutral risk bearers. However, it is not necessarily optimal for the manager if he is risk averse. A risk-averse manager may want to sell part of the risk inherent in the uncertain evolution of his expected marginal product to the risk bearers, for example, through a long-term wage contract.

We avoid this issue by assuming that, perhaps because of the more extreme moral hazard problems in long-term contracts (remember that $\bar{z}_t$ is in part under the control of the manager) and the contracting costs to which these moral hazard problems give rise, simple contracts in which the manager's wage is reset at the beginning of each period are dominant, at least for some nontrivial subset of firms and managers.[5] If we could also assume away any remaining moral hazard

---

[5] Institutions like corporations, that are subject to rapid technological change with a large degree of uncertainty about future managerial needs, may find that long-term

(managerial incentive) problems, then with risk-averse managers, risk-neutral risk bearers, and the presumed fixed recontracting period, the contract which specifies ex ante that the manager will be paid the current expected value of his marginal product dominates any contract where the manager also shares the ex post deviation of his measured marginal product from its ex ante expected value (see, e.g., Spence and Zeckhauser 1971).

However, contracts which specify ex ante that the manager will be paid the current expected value of his marginal product seem to leave the typical moral hazard problem that arises when there is less than complete ex post enforcement of contracts. The noise ϵ_t in the manager's marginal product is borne by the risk bearers. Once the manager's expected marginal product $\overline{z}_t$ (= his current wage) has been assessed, he seems to have an incentive to consume more perquisites and provide less effort than are implied in $\overline{z}_t$.

A mechanism for ex post enforcement is, however, built into the model. With the expected value of the manager's marginal product wandering randomly through time, future assessments of expected marginal products (and thus of wages) will be determined in part by ϵ_t, the deviation of the current measured marginal product from its ex ante expected value. In the present scenario, where $\overline{z}_t$ is assumed to follow a random walk, Muth (1960) has shown that the expected value of the marginal product evolves according to

$$\overline{z}_t = \overline{z}_{t-1} + (1 - \phi)\epsilon_{t-1}, \tag{2}$$

where the parameter ϕ $(0 < \phi < 1)$ is closer to zero the smaller the variance of the noise term in the marginal product equation (1) relative to the variance of the steps in the random walk followed by the expected marginal product.

In fact, the process by which future expected marginal products are adjusted on the basis of past deviations of marginal products from their expected values leads to a precise form of full ex post settling up. This is best seen by writing the marginal product z_t in its inverted form, that is, in terms of past marginal products and the current noise. The inverted form for our model, a random walk embedded in random noise, is

$$z_t = (1 - \phi)z_{t-1} + \phi(1 - \phi)z_{t-2} + \phi^2(1 - \phi)z_{t-3} + \ldots + \epsilon_t, \tag{3}$$

---

managerial contracts can only be negotiated at high cost. On the other hand, institutions like governments, schools, and universities may be able to forecast more reliably their future needs for managers (and other professionals) and so may be able to offer long-term contracts at relatively low cost. These institutions can then be expected to attract the relatively risk-averse members of the professional labor force, while the riskier employment offered by corporations attracts those who are willing to accept shorter-term contracts.

so that

$$\bar{z}_t = (1 - \phi)z_{t-1} + \phi(1 - \phi)z_{t-2} + \phi^2(1 - \phi)z_{t-3} + \ldots \qquad (4)$$

(see, e.g., Nelson 1973, chap. 4, or Muth 1960).

For our purposes, the interesting fact is that, although he is paid his ex ante expected marginal product, the manager does not get to avoid his ex post marginal product. For example, we can infer from (4) that z_{t-1} has weight $1 - \phi$ in $\bar{z}_t$; then it has weight $\phi(1 - \phi)$ in $\bar{z}_{t+1}$, $\phi^2(1 - \phi)$ in $\bar{z}_{t+2}$, and so on. In the end, the sum of the contributions of z_{t-1} to future expected marginal products, and thus to future wages, is exactly z_{t-1}. With zero interest rates, this means that the risk bearers simply allow the manager to smooth his marginal product across future periods at the going opportunity cost of all such temporal wealth transfers. As a consequence, the manager has no incentive to try to bury shirking or consumption of perquisites in his ex post measured marginal product.

Since the managerial labor market is presumed to understand the weight of the wage revision process, which in this case amounts to precise full ex post settling up, any potential managerial incentive problems in the separation of risk bearing, or security ownership, from control are resolved. The manager can contract for and take an optimal amount of consumption on the job. The wage set ex ante need not include any allowance for ex post incentives to deviate from the contract since the wage revision process neutralizes any such incentives. Note, moreover, that the value of ϕ in the wage revision process described by (4) determines how the observed marginal product of any given period is subdivided and spread across future periods, but whatever the value of ϕ, the given marginal product is fully accounted for in the stream of future wages. Thus, it is now clear what was meant by the earlier claim that although the parameter ϕ in the process generating the manager's marginal product is to some extent under his control, this is not a matter of particular concern to the managerial labor market.

A somewhat evident qualification is in order. The smoothing process described by (4) contains an infinite number of terms, whereas any manager has a finite working life. For practical purposes, full ex post settling up is achieved as long as the manager's current marginal product is "very nearly" fully absorbed by the stream of wages over his future working life. This requires a value of ϕ in (4) which is sufficiently far from 1.0, given the number of periods remaining in the manager's working life. Recall that ϕ is closer to 1.0 the larger the variance of the noise in the manager's measured marginal product relative to the variance of the steps of the random walk taken by the expected value of his marginal product. Intuitively, when the variance of the noise term is large relative to that of the changes in the expected value, the current measured marginal product has a weak signal about any change in the expected value of the marginal product, and the current marginal product is only allocated slowly to expected future marginal products.

Some Extensions

Having qualified the analysis, let us now indicate some ways in which it is robust to changes in details of the model.

1. More Complicated Models for the Manager's Marginal Product

The critical ingredient in enforcing precise full ex post settling up through wage revisions on the basis of reassessments of expected marginal products is that when the marginal product and its expected value are expressed in inverted form, as in (3) and (4), the sum of the weights on past marginal products is exactly 1.0. This will be the case (see, e.g., Nelson 1973, chap. 4) whenever the manager's marginal product conforms to a nonstationary stochastic process, but the changes from period to period in the marginal product conform to some stationary ARMA (mixed autoregressive moving average) process. The example summarized in equations (1)–(4) is the interesting but special case where the expected marginal product follows a random walk so that the differences of the marginal product are a stationary, first-order moving average process. The general case allows the expected value of the marginal product to follow any more complicated nonstationary process which has the property that the differences of the marginal product are stationary, so that the marginal product and its expected value can be expressed in inverted form as

$$z_t = \pi_1 z_{t-1} + \pi_2 z_{t-2} + \ldots + \epsilon_t \tag{5}$$

$$\overline{z}_t = \pi_1 z_{t-1} + \pi_2 z_{t-2} + \ldots \tag{6}$$

with

$$\sum_{i=1}^{\infty} \pi_i = 1. \tag{7}$$

These can be viewed as the general conditions for enforcing precise full ex post settling through the wage revision process when the manager's wage is equal to the current expected value of his marginal product.[6]

2. Risk-Averse Risk Bearers

In the framework summarized in equations (5)–(7), if the manager switches firms, the risk bearers of his former firm are left with the remains of his measured marginal products not previously absorbed into the expected value of his marginal product. Nevertheless, in the way we have set up the world, the risk bearers realize that the manager's next firm continues to set his wage according to the same stochastic process as the last firm. Since this results in full ex post settling up on the part of the manager, the motive for switching firms cannot be to avoid perverse adjustments of future wages on the basis of past performance. On average, the switching of managers among firms does not result in gains or losses to risk bearers, which means that the switches are a matter of indifference to our presumed risk-neutral risk bearers.

It is, however, interesting to examine how the analysis might change when the risk bearers are risk averse and switching of managers among firms is not a matter of indifference. Suppose, for the moment, that the risk bearers offer managers contracts where, as before, the manager's wage tracks the expected value of his marginal product, but each period there is also a fixed discount in the wage to compensate the risk bearers for the risks of unfinished ex post settling up with the firm as a consequence of a possible future shift by the manager to another firm. Such an arrangement may satisfy the risk bearers, but it will not be acceptable to the manager. As long as his marginal product evolves according to equations (5)–(7), both in his current firm and in the best alternative, the manager is subject to full ex post settling up. Thus, any risk adjustment of his wage to reflect the fact that the settling up may not be with his current firm is an uncompensated loss which he will endeavor to avoid.

The manager can avoid any risk discount in his wage, and maintain complete freedom to switch among firms, by himself bearing all the risk of his marginal product; that is, he contracts to accept, at the end of each period, his ex post measured marginal product rather than its ex ante expected value so that there is, period by period, full ex post settling up with his current firm. There is such a presumption against

---

[6] When $\bar{z}_t$ follows a stationary process, the long-run average value toward which the process always tends will eventually be known with near perfect certainty. Thus, the case of a stationary expected marginal product is of little interest, at least for the purposes of ex post settling up enforced by the wage revision process.

the optimality of immediate, full ex post settling up in the literature on optimal contracting that it behooves us to examine how and why it works, and is optimal, in the circumstances under examination.

Contractual Settling Up

The literature on optimal contracting, for example, Harris and Raviv (1978, 1979), Holmström (1979), and Shavell (1979), suggests uniformly that when there is noise in the manager's marginal product, that is, when the deviation of measured marginal product from its expected value cannot be traced unambiguously and costlessly to the manager's actions (talents, effort exerted, and consumption on the job), then a risk-averse manager will always choose to share part of the uncertainty in the evaluation of his performance with the firm's risk bearers. He will agree to some amount of ex post settling up, but always less than 100 percent of the deviation of his measured marginal product from its ex ante expected value. In short, the contracting models suggest that we must learn to live with the incentive problems that arise when there is less than complete ex post enforcement of contracts.

The contracting literature is almost uniformly concerned with 1-period models. In a 1-period world, there can be no enforcement of contracts through a wage revision process imposed by the managerial labor market. The existence of this form of ex post settling up in a multiperiod world affects the manager's willingness to engage in explicit contractual ex post settling up.

For example, in the model summarized in equations (5)–(7), the manager's wage in any period is the expected value of his marginal product assessed at the beginning of the period, and the manager does not immediately share any of the deviation of his ex post marginal product from its ex ante expected value. However, because it contains information about future expected values of his marginal product, eventually the manager's current measured marginal product is allocated in full to future expected marginal products. Equivalently, in the wage revision process described by equations (5)–(7), the managerial labor market in effect acts as a financial intermediary. It withdraws portions of past accumulated measured marginal products to pay the manager a dividend on his human capital equal to the expected value of his marginal product, and implicitly provides the lending arrangements which allow the manager to spread his current measured marginal product over future periods in precisely the way the current marginal product will contribute to expected future marginal products.

Looked at from this perspective, however, the manager might simply contract to take the ex post measured value of his marginal product as his wage and then himself use the capital market to smooth his measured marginal product over future periods. Since the same asset (his human capital) is involved, the manager should be able to carry out these smoothing transactions via the capital market on the same terms as can be had in the managerial labor market. The advantage to the manager in smoothing through the capital market, however, is that he can then contract to accept full ex post settling up period by period (he is paid his measured marginal product), which means he can avoid any risk discount in his wage that might be imposed when he is paid the expected value of his marginal product with the possibility of unanticipated switches to other firms.[7]

It is important to recognize that using the capital market in the manner described above allows the manager to "average out" the random noise in his measured marginal product. Thus, when he is instead paid the expected value of his marginal product each period, and when the process generating his marginal product is described by equations (5)–(7), the manager's current measured marginal product is eventually allocated in full to future expected marginal products. This happily, but only coincidentally, resolves incentive problems by imposing full ex post settling up. The allocation of the current marginal product to future expected marginal products in fact occurs because the current marginal product has information about future expected marginal products. The weights π_i in equations (5)–(7) are precisely those that optimally extract this information and so optimally smooth or average out the purely random noise in the manager's measured marginal product. The manager can achieve the same result by contracting to be paid the measured value of his marginal product and then using the capital market to smooth his marginal product. This power of the capital market to reduce the terror in full contractual ex post settling up is lost in the 1-period models that dominate the contracting literature.

---

[7] With positive interest rates, contracting to be paid his measured marginal product and then using the capital market to smooth the marginal product over future periods dominates the contract in which the manager is paid the expected value of his marginal product. Equivalence can be restored by adjusting the expected marginal product $\bar{z}_t$ in eq. (6) for accumulated interest on the past marginal products, $z_{t-1}, z_{t-2}, \ldots$, or by prepaying the present value of interest on the deferrals of the current marginal product over future periods. Suffice it to say, however, that either accumulation or prepayment of interest complicates the problems posed by possible shifts of the manager to other firms and so may lean the system toward contracts in which the manager is paid his measured marginal product and then uses the capital market to achieve optimal smoothing.

Conclusions

The model summarized by equations (5)–(7) is one specific scenario in which the wage revision process imposed by the managerial labor market amounts to full ex post settling up by the manager for his past performance. The important general point is that in any scenario where the weight of the wage revision process is at least equivalent to full ex post settling up, managerial incentive problems—the problems usually attributed to the separation of security ownership and control of the firm—are resolved.

No claim is made that the wage revision process always results in a full ex post settling up on the part of the manager. There are certainly situations where the weight of anticipated future wage changes is insufficient to counterbalance the gains to be had from ex post shirking, or perhaps outright theft, in excess of what was agreed ex ante in a manager's contract. On the other hand, precise full ex post settling up is not an upper bound on the force of the wage revision process. There are certainly situations where, as a consequence of anticipated future wage changes, a manager perceives that the value of his human capital changes by more than the wealth changes imposed on other factors, and especially the firm's security holders, by his current deviations from the terms of his contract.

The extent to which the wage revision process imposes ex post settling up in any particular situation is, of course, an empirical issue. But it is probably safe to say that the general phenomenon is at least one of the ingredients in the survival of the modern large corporation, characterized by diffuse security ownership and the separation of security ownership and control, as a viable form of economic organization.

References

Alchian, Armen A. "Corporate Management and Property Rights." In *Economic Policy and the Regulation of Corporate Securities*, edited by Henry G. Manne. Washington: American Enterprise Inst. Public Policy Res., 1969.

Alchian, Armen A., and Demsetz, Harold. "Production, Information Costs, and Economic Organization." *A.E.R.* 62 (December 1972): 777–95.

Baumol, William J. *Business Behavior, Value and Growth.* New York: Macmillan, 1959.

Berle, Adolph A., Jr., and Means, Gardiner C. *The Modern Corporation and Private Property.* New York: Macmillan, 1932.

Coase, Ronald H. "The Nature of the Firm." *Economica*, n.s. 4 (November 1937): 386–405.

———. "The Problem of Social Cost." *J. Law and Econ.* 3 (October 1960): 1–44.

Cyert, Richard M., and March, James G. *A Behavioral Theory of the Firm.* Englewood Cliffs, N.J.: Prentice-Hall, 1963.

Fama, Eugene F. *Foundations of Finance*. New York: Basic, 1976.

Fama, Eugene F., and Miller, Merton H. *The Theory of Finance*. New York: Holt, Rinehart & Winston, 1972.

Harris, Milton, and Raviv, Artur. "Some Results on Incentive Contracts with Applications to Education and Employment, Health Insurance, and Law Enforcement." *A.E.R.* 68 (March 1978): 20–30.

———. "Optimal Incentive Contracts with Imperfect Information." Working Paper no. 70-75-76, Carnegie-Mellon Univ., Graduate School of Indus. Admin., April 1976 (rev. January 1979), forthcoming in *J. Econ. Theory*.

Holmström, Bengt. "Moral Hazard and Observability." *Bell J. Econ.* 10 (Spring 1979): 74–91.

Jensen, Michael C. "Capital Markets: Theory and Evidence." *Bell J. Econ. and Management Sci.* 3 (Autumn 1972): 357–98.

Jensen, Michael C., and Meckling, William H. "Theory of the Firm: Managerial Behavior, Agency Costs and Ownership Structure." *J. Financial Econ.* 3 (October 1976): 305–60.

Manne, Henry G. "Mergers and the Market for Corporate Control." *J.P.E.* 73, no. 2 (April 1965): 110–20.

———. "Our Two Corporate Systems: Law and Economics." *Virginia Law Rev.* 53 (March 1967): 259–85.

Muth, John F. "Optimal Properties of Exponentially Weighted Forecasts." *J. American Statis. Assoc.* 55 (June 1960): 299–306.

Nelson, Charles R. *Applied Time Series Analysis for Managerial Forecasting*. San Francisco: Holden-Day, 1973.

Shavell, Steven. "Risk Sharing and Incentives in the Principal and Agent Relationship." *Bell J. Econ.* 10 (Spring 1979): 55–73.

Simon, Herbert A. "Theories of Decision Making in Economics and Behavioral Science." *A.E.R.* 49 (June 1959): 253–83.

Smith, Adam. *The Wealth of Nations*. 1776. Cannan ed. New York: Modern Library, 1937.

Spence, Michael, and Zeckhauser, Richard. "Insurance, Information and Individual Action." *A.E.R.* 61 (May 1971): 380–87.

Watts, Ross L., and Zimmerman, Jerold. "Auditors and the Determination of Accounting Standards, an Analysis of the Lack of Independence." Working Paper GPB 7806, Univ. Rochester, Graduate School of Management, 1978.

Williamson, Oliver E. *The Economics of Discretionary Behavior: Managerial Objectives in a Theory of the Firm*. Englewood Cliffs, N.J.: Prentice-Hall, 1964.

26. THE DETERMINATION OF FINANCIAL STRUCTURE: THE INCENTIVE-SIGNALLING APPROACH

STEPHEN A. ROSS*

Reprinted from *Bell Journal of Economics,* Vol. 8, No. 1 (Spring 1977), pp. 23–40, by permission of the author and the publisher.

The Modigliani-Miller theorem on the irrelevancy of financial structure implicitly assumes that the market possesses full information about the activities of firms. If managers possess inside information, however, then the choice of a managerial incentive schedule and of a financial structure signals information to the market, and in competitive equilibrium the inferences drawn from the signals will be validated. One empirical implication of this theory is that in a cross section, the values of firms will rise with leverage, since increasing leverage increases the market's perception of value.

1. INTRODUCTION

The central results of modern corporate finance, the Modigliani-Miller irrelevancy propositions, are summarized nicely in the following quotations: "the market value of any firm is independent of its capital structure and is given by capitalizing its expected return at the rate ρ_k appropriate to its class" (Modigliani and Miller, 1958); and "the current valuation is unaffected by differences in dividend payments in any future period and thus ... dividend policy is irrelevant for the determination of market prices, given investment policy" (Miller and Modigliani, 1961).

The concept of a "risk class" has passed out of fashion with the subsequent refinement of these propositions, and they are now generally viewed as consequences of perfection and competition in financial markets. Perhaps the simplest proof of the proposition that the value of the firm is unaffected by financial structure is that if such changes, say in the debt-equity composition,

* Professor of Economics and Finance, University of Pennsylvania.

The author is grateful to the National Science Foundation for support under grant No. SOC-20292 and to the Guggenheim Foundation. The participants in the Wells Fargo Seminar, 1976, are also to be thanked along with John Cox, Mark Rubinstein, Gerald Jaynes, Sandford Grossman, the Editorial Board, and an anonymous referee for their helpful comments.

lowered value, then by purchasing the firm (or a proportion of it) and reissuing the value maximizing financial package on personal account (or as a reformed corporate structure) individuals could realize an arbitrage profit. Since such profits are inconsistent with equilibrium, the value of the firm must be constant across all financial packages, or, to put it somewhat differently, in the "inferior" situation value would be bid up to the maximum. To make the point in an alternative fashion, if individuals can issue securities in the market just as firms—they have equal access to the capital market—then they can "undo" any financial package issued by the firm to restore a given general equilibrium. In this sense nothing fundamental, e.g., firm value, can be altered by the firm's financing decisions. (See Fama for an elegant treatment of these approaches to the irrelevancy propositions, their derivation from perfect competition in financial markets, and their limitations.)

An unfortunate consequence of the Modigliani-Miller insights has been the discarding (and denial) of theories for determining the financial structure. If the theory is complete and thought to be correct, then structure is indeterminate or random in actuality, and this is a somewhat inhibiting basis on which to develop an explanation of financial structure.[1]

One possible approach to the problem is to modify the Modigliani-Miller theory to take account of the structural features of the "real world." These form the basis of the traditional view of corporate finance. Since debt payments are excluded from income in computing corporate income tax, the value of the firm should increase with the substitution of debt for equity financing.[2] Unless, however, there are offsetting costs, this has the awkward implication that the firm should be wholly debt financed. If there are true bankruptcy costs, e.g., wastage from mismanagement, or direct costs associated with reorganization and discounts in secondary markets, then such costs would act to mitigate the amount of debt financing. An optimum ratio of debt to equity trades off the tax benefits of increased debt against the costs of an increased probability of ruin.[3]

---

[1] Of course, as the Modigliani and Miller theory argues, there may simply not be a significant role for finance, but then some explanation is required of the apparently irrational effort that corporations put into the financial decisionmaking process. One of the more sobering experiences for a student of finance is to explain the irrelevancy propositions to a corporate treasurer.

[2] It is sometimes said that the irrelevancy propositions are "untrue" in a world with taxation benefits, but there is a more symmetric view that can be taken. With taxation, the government becomes a claimant to the firm's returns. Altering the private financing package now leaves the total (nonmarket) value of the firm unaltered but can increase the private market value of the firm at the expense of the public share. We are, of course, ignoring the offsetting effects of differential rates of personal taxation on capital gains and dividends in this analysis.

[3] If bankruptcy costs accrue to a third party then note 2 can be applied. Also, we should note that the Internal Revenue's view of an all debt firm is somewhat more complicated than a simple linear tax schedule would suggest. As the debt component is raised, there is an increasing chance that the debt service will lose its exemption.

But this is not an entirely satisfactory resolution of the matter either. On the one hand, it is difficult to specify exactly what the costs of bankruptcy are, particularly when it is in the interest of all parties to simply reorganize the firm.[4] Even granting that such costs might be significant, this puts a large burden on the effect of the tax benefits. Furthermore, it is rebutted by the evidence. As Jensen and Meckling (1975) observe,

Since we know debt was commonly used prior to the existence of the current tax subsidies on interest payments this theory does not capture what must be some important determinants of the corporate financial structure.[5]

Another possibility, of course, is to take a closer look at the underpinnings of the Modigliani-Miller theory itself. If changes in the financial structure of the firm affect the consumption and investment opportunity sets open to economic agents, then the pivotal role played by value maximization in arbitrage arguments may have to be rejected. Leland, Ekern and Wilson, Radner and others have examined this possibility for activity choice in models with incomplete (marginal) spanning and suggested alternative behavioral rules such as the requirement of stockholder unanimity. This is equivalent, though, to assuming that firms have monopoly power in financial markets, and it is difficult to see a definitive theory emerging from such an inherently game theoretic and strategic situation.[6] If pricing is complete and value maximization is the goal, then we will have to look elsewhere for a theory of the financial structure.

Implicit in the irrelevancy proposition is the assumption that the market knows the (random) return stream of the firm and values this stream to set the value of the firm. What is valued in the marketplace, however, is the *perceived* stream of returns for the firm. Putting the issue this way raises the possibility that changes in the financial structure can alter the market's perception. In the old terminology of Modigliani and Miller, by changing its financial structure the firm alters its perceived risk class, even though the actual risk class remains unchanged.

---

[4] Except, of course, lawyers who would be claimants in bankruptcy and, if they held debt, might oppose reorganization.

[5] These authors develop a detailed theory of financial structure that emphasizes the costs of management. We take a view that essentially ignores such costs.

[6] I have some other somewhat more narrow objections to this approach. If there are constant returns to scale in activity choice, I find it difficult to see why the firm would not simply explore the underlying state price system by "local" changes in activities. In this fashion a competitive firm could (presumably at a differential cost) map out what the relevant state prices would be. More telling, though, theories with incomplete spanning really require a careful explanation of what markets do exist. Without such an understanding, it will always be unclear whether or not, even without complete spanning, there is sufficient spanning for a value maximizing efficient equilibrium. For example, partitions associated with states idiosyncratic to individuals might be irrelevant by diversification and insurance in financial markets. (See Samuelson or Malinvaud.)

In Section 2 we shall show in a simple example how this phenomenon can be linked with the managerial incentive structure to provide a theory that determines the financial structure and is consistent with the Modigliani-Miller framework. Section 3 describes the features of a general theory and Section 4 develops a somewhat more realistic model than that of Section 2. Section 5 summarizes the paper and considers some possible extensions and generalizations.

2. A SIMPLE EXAMPLE

This section constructs a simple example that illustrates the relationships between signalling and the managerial incentive structure in the financial market. Throughout the paper we will make the usual perfect market assumptions.

Assumption 0. Financial markets are competitive and perfect with no transaction costs or tax effects.

As a consequence, no individual or firm exercises monopoly power in the financial markets and each participant acts as if demand were infinitely elastic at the quoted prices.

Suppose that the market, or the relevant corner of the market, consists of two types of firms, A and B. It is currently time 0 and at time 1, A firms will have a total return (value) of a and B firms will return b with

$$a > b.$$

For additional simplicity, we will also assume that pricing in the market is risk neutral. Hence, if riskless bonds are traded, then assets will be valued at their expected discounted value. Risk neutrality can be justified at a more primitive level by simply assuming that investors are risk neutral, but it is also possible to base it on the assumption that this sector of the market is small and independent of the overall financial market. Alternatively, we could argue that there are a sufficiently large number of firms of each type as to enable individuals to diversify away firm risk. The assumption of risk neutrality, though, is not essential; it is made largely to avoid complicating the model with the additional effects of risk-sensitive pricing.

A CERTAIN WORLD

If there is no uncertainty in the market and investors can identify the A and the B firms, then their respective values at time 0 will be given simply by

$$V_0^A = \frac{a}{1 + r},\tag{1a}$$

and

$$V_0^B = \frac{b}{1 + r} < V_0^A, \tag{1b}$$

where r is the sure rate of interest.

There is little more that needs to be said about this case. It should be clear that the valuations in (1) are unaffected by the mode of financing chosen by the firm. For example, suppose the type A firm is financed by debt, D, with a face value of F, and equity, E. The debt is the senior claimant to the firm's returns and will have a value of

$$\min \{F, a\},$$

at time 1 and the equity will claim the residual

$$\max \{a - F, 0\}.$$

The time 0 values respectively will be

$$E = \frac{\max \{a - F, 0\}}{1 + r}$$

and

$$D = \frac{\min \{a, F\}}{1 + r},$$

and, therefore

$$E + D = \frac{a}{1 + r} = V_0^A.$$

In this simple world, the Modigliani-Miller theorem is really just a restatement of Fisher's separation theorem.

UNCERTAINTY AND SIGNALLING—AN IRRELEVANCE RESULT

Suppose, now, that investors cannot distinguish A firms from B firms. If q is the proportion of A firms, suppose, too, that investors all act as though any firm has a q chance of being an A firm. The returns, a and b, are conditional on the current exogenous information. *Given* the available information at time 0, firms in the model have a q chance of being type A and a $(1 - q)$ chance of being type B. It follows that all firms will have the same value,

$$V_0 = \frac{qa + (1 - q)b}{1 + r}, \tag{2}$$

with

$$V_0^A > V_0 > V_0^B. \tag{3}$$

This result is quite robust, and it follows directly from the Modigliani-Miller propositions that valuation will be unaffected by the mode of financing.

For example, it would be ineffective for A firms to attempt to inform the market, or signal that they were of type A rather than B. The difficulty is the moral hazard that B firms would give the same false signal, once again leaving the equilibrium one where firms cannot be discriminated. Suppose that there were some activity, X^A, perhaps a financial package, that A firms could engage in and that investors would observe and use to infer a value $V_0(X^A)$ for the firm. If $V_0(X^A) > V_0$, then (by the initial symmetry) B firms would also engage in X^A and realize the initial value $V_0(X^A)$. In equilibrium, we must have $V_0(X^A) = V_0$. Equivalently, if a B firm were to follow a policy X^B for which $V_0(X^A) > V_0(X^B)$, then by purchasing the firm for $V_0(X^B)$ and using the activity X^A (e.g., refinancing it), a financier would realize a riskless capital gain of $V_0(X^A) - V_0(X^B)$.

This concept of signalling was first studied in the context of job and product markets by Akerlof and Arrow, and was developed into an equlibrium theory by Spence. It has been subsequently examined (with emphasis on the possible lack of equilibrium) in different problems by Rothschild and Stiglitz and by Riley. The joining of Modigliani-Miller arguments with moral hazard, however, does not seem to leave much room for signalling in financial markets. If the chosen mode of signalling is the financial structure, then since finance is costless, the market valuation function $V_0(\cdot)$ will be the same for A and B firms and, as we have seen, the only equlibrium will be where

$$V_0^A = V_0^B. \tag{4}$$

This result will hold in a very general setting and is not dependent on the special assumptions of the simple model. Even when the implications of financing decisions differ for the A and B firms, any such consequences, e.g., true bankruptcy costs, are realized at time 1. A financier who can buy a B firm more cheaply than an A firm would simply reissue the A financial package and avoid any of the time 1 consequences. The only time 0 equlibrium, then, is one where (4) holds and firms have identical values.

A MANAGERIAL INCENTIVE-SIGNALLING EQUILIBRIUM

One way to break out of the constraint that binds the value of A and B firms is to assume a significant role for the manager. If the manager of a firm is accountable for time 0 decisions, then there is a means of validating financial signals and avoiding the moral hazard problem. Of course, as well as being accountable the manager must also be assumed to have special or inside information about the firm's type. It would do little good to make managers bear the consequences of their decisions if they had the same information as ordinary investors. The following assumption summarizes these points.

Assumption 1. Manager-insiders are identified with firms as possessors of inside information. Furthermore, refinancing by outsiders conveys no information to the market.

In the simple model of this section we will assume that managers know their own firm's type, but have no inside information about firms other than their own. Refinancing by outsiders, including other managers, will be assumed to convey no information, i.e., it will not alter the market's perception of the firm's type. In addition to identifying a role for managers, we also have to specify exactly how they share in the consequences of their decisions.

Assumption 2. Manager-insiders are compensated by a known incentive schedule, i.e., a given rule which investors know.

Suppose that F denotes the face value of the debt issued by a firm at time 0. In our model we shall assume that managers receive the following compensation

$$M = (1 + r)\gamma_0 V_0 + \gamma_1 \left\{ \begin{array}{l} V_1 \text{ if } V_1 \geq F \\ V_1 - L \text{ if } V_1 < F \end{array} \right\}, \tag{5}$$

where V_0 and V_1 are the respective values of the firm at time 0 and at time 1, and L is a penalty assessed on the manager if the firm is bankrupt at time 1, i.e., if $V_1 < F$ and the value cannot cover the debt repayment. The constants γ_0 and γ_1 are fixed nonnegative weights.

We shall also suppose that manager-insiders actually act to maximize their incentive compensation, M, in (5). This implies, of course, that they will set a level of debt financing, F, at time 0 so as to maximize M. Since in the example there is no productive activity choice available, F is, in fact, the only decision variable at the manager's discretion. The penalty, L, associated with bankruptcy is a penalty imposed on the manager and does *not* necessarily represent any true bankruptcy cost to the firm, but if there were any such costs, then they would fit into the incentive schedule through the penalty in a very natural fashion.

Given (5) and Assumption (2), the activities of the manager are circumscribed in a number of ways. In particular, the manager cannot trade in the financial instruments issued by his own firm. If the manager were to do so, then the incentive schedule would not be given by (5). Legal rules designed to prevent managers from trading in their own firm's liabilities are generally motivated by the desire to avoid moral hazard problems, but one consequence of such avoidance is a clearer specification of the managerial incentive structure. Disclosure rules on insider trading also serve the function of clarifying the managerial incentive schedule and make it easier for investors to "read" the financial signals. (See Ross, 1976b.)

We can use (5) to establish a signalling equilibrium, in the sense introduced by Spence, in the financial market. Suppose that investors use F, the face value of the debt, as a signal of the firm's type. Let F^* be a critical level of financing, with

$$b \leq F^* < a.$$

If

$$F > F^*,$$

then we shall assume that the market perceives the firm to be of type A, and if

$$F \leq F^*,$$

the market perceives the firm to be of type B. For this to be an equilibrium we must show that investors' perceptions are accurate, i.e., all firms of type A must actually issue debt with $F^A > F^*$ and all the type B firms must set $F^B \leq F^*$.

If a firm signals itself to be of type A and if it also sets $F^A \leq a$, so that it does not risk bankruptcy unnecessarily, then

$$V_0 = V_0(F^A) = \frac{a}{1 + r}. \tag{6}$$

Similarly a firm that gives a type B signal by setting $F^B \leq b$ will have an initial value of

$$V_0(F^B) = \frac{b}{1 + r}. \tag{7}$$

The compensation of the manager of a type A firm, then, will be given by

$$M^A(F) = \begin{cases} (\gamma_0 + \gamma_1)a \text{ if } F^* < F^A \leq a, \\ \text{and} \\ \gamma_0 b + \gamma_1 a \text{ if } F^A \leq F^*. \end{cases} \tag{8}$$

The compensation of the manager of a type B firm is given by

$$M^B(F) = \begin{cases} \gamma_0 a + \gamma_1(b - L) \text{ if } F^B > F^*, \\ \text{and} \\ \gamma_0 b + \gamma_1 b \text{ if } F^B \leq b \leq F^*, \end{cases} \tag{9}$$

where we have assumed that the manager will not expose himself to bankruptcy cost unnecessarily.

Suppose, now, that the A managers choose financing levels, F^A,

$$F^* < F^A \leq a, \tag{10}$$

and the B managers choose F^B,

$$F^B \leq b. \tag{11}$$

This is a signalling equilibrium in the sense defined by Spence if neither type of manager has an incentive to change signals and if, in addition, the signals are valid, that is, the inference drawn from the signal by the market is correct. Now, an A manager will have no incentive to change since, from (10), for $F' \leq F^*$,

$$M^A(F^A) = (\gamma_0 + \gamma_1)a > M(F') = \gamma_0 b + \gamma_1 a. \tag{12}$$

With no bankruptcy costs being incurred, the manager will obviously give a signal that the firm is of type A.

Less obviously, the B type manager may not have an incentive to falsely signal that his firm is of type A. This requires that for $F' > F^*$

$$M^B(F') = \gamma_0 a + \gamma_1(b - L)$$
$$< M^B(F^B)$$
$$= (\gamma_0 + \gamma_1)b,$$

or

$$\gamma_0(a - b) < \gamma_1 L. \tag{13}$$

This is a very sensible result. The B manager signals truthfully if the marginal gain to a false signal $(a - b)$ weighted by the manager's share, γ_0, is less than the bankruptcy costs incurred, L, again weighted by the manager's share, γ_1.

This equilibrium is illustrated in Figure 1. There are, in fact, many equilibrium values (F^A, F^B). Any pair with

$$F^B \leq b,$$

and

$$b < F^A \leq a, \tag{14}$$

will do, and there is no reason to expect that one pair will be chosen uniquely (or that all firms of the same type will choose the same level of debt). This

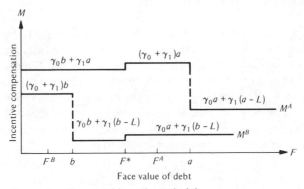

FIGURE 1.   Managerial incentives schedule.

result, however, is a feature of the simple structure of the model and will disappear in a more complex setting.

It is worth examining the criterion (13) with care. If $\gamma_1 = 0$, then managers, like investors, will maximize time 0 value. Since they share no consequences of next period's performance, they will be unable to signal and the equilibrium will degenerate into that described in (b) above. If $\gamma_0 = 0$, then (13) is satisfied for $\gamma_1 L > 0$, but oddly we may not have an equilibrium. In this case, B managers will not falsely signal, but since A managers do not care about the firm's valuation at time 0, they also have no incentive to signal correctly to differentiate their firms from firms of type B. What occurs if the inequality in (13) is reversed? Now matters become somewhat more complex and the possibility that there is no equilibrium opens up. This case can be treated, but as the next section emphasizes, the incentive schedule M is itself determined in equilibrium, and as a consequence, this particular problem does not arise in the financial incentive-signalling model.

It should also be clear now why equilibrium requires that managers be precluded from trading in their own instruments. An A manager, for example, could raise his compensation by falsely giving a B type signal and then purchasing his own stock, or a B type could give a false A signal and short his own stock. (Disclosure rules, though, enable the market to use such insider trading as a signal.) Another difference between the financial incentive-signalling model and the job signalling models is that there is no implication of inefficiency in the resulting financial equilibrium. Unlike the job signalling models where the investment in a signal is costly and, therefore, inefficient if signals serve no productive function, financial signalling is relatively costless. If L is only an incentive cost and there are no true costs to bankruptcy, this result will be quite general. In this simple example, with certain returns, even if L represents true bankruptcy costs, it is the prohibitive potential cost that validates the signal and in equlibrium neither type of firm must inefficiently risk bankruptcy to signal validly.

SETTING THE MANAGERIAL INCENTIVE SCHEDULE

Who establishes (5) as the incentive schedule for managers? In one sense this is similar to (and about as embarrassing as) asking who sets the price in a competitive market, but consider the following argument.[7] Suppose that the opportunity cost or wage of individuals who might supply their services as manager-insiders is w. If the managerial supply is perfectly elastic at w, and if managers are randomly assigned to firms with no *a priori* knowledge of firm type, then they will demand an expected wage equal to w. Once assigned to a firm, the manager learns its type and is locked to it.

---

[7] A colleague suggested, not entirely facetiously, that the financial analysts did it.

Suppose, then, that managers are all given a perfectly proportional wage schedule

$$(1 + r)\gamma_0 V_0 + \gamma_1 V_1, \qquad (15)$$

where (positive) γ_0 and γ_1 are chosen so that

$$\gamma_0 E\{V_0\} + \gamma_1 E\{V_1\} = w, \qquad (16)$$

i.e., the expected compensation equals the wage. Managers assigned to an A firm will, by (15), find it in their interest to signal the market that their firm is of type A. To do so the manager can simply alter (15) to (5) by issuing debt of face value $F > b$ and announcing that he will be liable for a penalty of L, satisfying (13) if bankruptcy occurs.

Managers of type B firms would then find their firms identified as such and, by the analysis above, with L sufficiently high they would have no incentive to follow the type A managers and signal falsely. Furthermore, since (5) is uniformly less than (15) all holders of equity in the firm would unanimously favor such a change. (In addition, the total compensation of the managerial class is unaltered in the new equilibrium.) Given (15), then, an incentive schedule like (5) (with similar implications) would arise in equilibrium. Or, to put the matter somewhat differently, (15) is not an equlibrium incentive schedule, and (5) is.

There are, of course, other alternatives to financial signalling. Without issuing any debt, for example, the A type manager could simply assert his liability of L if return falls below a. I cannot claim to have eliminated such possibilities, but finance has at least one important advantage over the simple announcement. By using debt the manager creates an instrument which is priced in the market and returns on which are realized at time 1. The manager's compensation schedule, (5), is now equivalent to a financial claim on the firm's returns, or, more precisely, a derivative security written on the equity or bonds of the firm (see Ross, 1976a). Since the manager's compensation is now directly dependent on the value of the firm's financial claims in the market and equivalent to a package of marketed claims, it is relatively simple to monitor and enforce (5) as the manager's true compensation. Implicit in the argument, of course, is the assumption that this is cheaper than monitoring and bonding an *ad hoc* assertion of liability.

In addition, while the analysis above provides a more detailed justification for the emergence of an incentive structure such as (5) in equilibrium, it remains to explain why one such as (15) was established *a priori*. What is at issue here is not the uniqueness of (5) or (15). Obviously these are not unique and are important only in terms of the incentives they give; any penalty structure on bankruptcy satisfying a condition analogous to (13) would do. A schedule like (5) would, I think, emerge from some additional features that are missing from the simple model. If the manager makes activity choices, then some incentive scheme will be required irrespective of signalling needs. Furthermore, the two-period model misses the ongoing nature of the relationship which would act to stabilize the incentive structure over time. There is no reason to believe that the resulting schedule would be linear, but, except for discount factors, it should not change form over time.

To summarize the basic argument of this section, given an *a priori* incentive structure, the type *A* manager has a further incentive to modify it in such a fashion as to permit him to differentiate his firm through the financial package. With more types than two, type *B* managers then respond in such a way as to separate their firms from type *C* firms, given the constraints imposed by the financing-incentive schedule adopted by the *A* managers, and so on down the hierarchy. We shall consider a more complex example of this below, but first it might be valuable to examine some of these issues in a more general setting.

3. A GENERAL STRUCTURE

One value of trying to put the analysis of Section 2 into a more general framework is that it forces us to think carefully about the essential features of the example. We shall stay within a two-period context, although by thinking of second period returns as discounted future values this limitation is less restrictive than might appear. (This does, however, impose a myopia condition on investors.)

The compensation of the manager, M, consists of two components, a time 0 compensation,

$$M_0(f),$$

which is a function solely of the financial claims, f, which he holds against the firm, and the time 1 returns on the claims themselves. Generally, the current compensation, M_0, is actually a composite function of the form

$$M_0(a(f), f),$$

where $a(f)$ is the market's subjective perception of firm type based upon the financial package issued by the firm. Total compensation for a type t firm is then given by

$$M^t = M_0(f) + E\{f(x_t)\}, \tag{17}$$

where x_t is the random time 1 return of the type t firm.

By valuing the incentive claim according to its expectation, we have ignored the preference structure of the manager and considerations of his reaction to uncertainty. This is an important omission since Assumption 2 effectively precludes the manager from participating in the market in the firm's claims. If the manager's risk aversion affects his evaluation of the incentive schedule, this will alter the manager's evaluation of differing financial structures, and without a complete knowledge of the preference structure, the effect of a particular incentive schedule on financial choice will be indeterminate.

There is a large literature on such incentive problems, under various headings, but it generally assumes a knowledge of the manager's von Neumann-Morgenstern utility function in setting the motivational schedule. We could consider incentive schedules designed to induce the manager to reveal his utility function, but such procedures are difficult to implement. Alternatively, it might be possible to assume a probabilistic knowledge and to develop a theory on this basis, perhaps allowing the manager to signal preferences as well as firm characteristics, but this would take us well beyond the scope of the present paper. We shall use (17), then, and justify it on the grounds that the variable compensation given by M is small relative to the manager's wealth.[8]

The final requirement is that of specifying the feasible set, A, of admissible financial packages and incentive schedules. One way to do this was suggested in the discussion at the end of Section 2. For example, A could denote the set of incentive schedules satisfying a constraint of the form of (16) on the *ex ante* expected return of the manager. The manager would now be free to choose any financial package f that satisfied such a constraint. The term feasible thus refers either to f or M, and as it is always possible to scale the equilibrium schedules in such a way that the manager's actual compensation is arbitrary, generally feasibility will be implicit in the limited financial instruments we permit.

The following definition of an equlibrium coincides with that used in the example of Section 2.

Definition. A financial incentive-signalling equilibrium is a vector $(M_0, a, f^2, \ldots, f^t)$ such that for all types t, $M^t(f^t)$ is feasible,

---

[8] Suppose that the incentive compensation considered above is a small portion of the manager's total compensation. If W denotes the manager's total wealth and U his utility function, then

$$E\{[W + M]\} \cong U(W) + U'(W)E\{M\}, \tag{i}$$

and the manager acts to maximize expected compensation. Among its other virtues, this simple procedure requires no knowledge of the manager's risk preferences.

In practice managerial bonuses are generally small compared to total wealth, but even to the extent that incentive schemes provide a large portion of the manager's compensation, what is relevant in the approximation of (i) is the variable portion that is influenced by the financial decision. A major executive in the automobile industry might receive a yearly bonus amounting to half of his total compensation, but of the total bonus, the principal portion is determined by the influence of industry effects and overall economic conditions, and the variable portion influenced by the manager's financial decisions is probably fairly small. In the jargon of capital market theory, the bonus is primarily determined by the firm's betas with the market and the industry and only secondarily by the manager's financial choices. (For those who feel that executive salaries strain the credulity of managerial productivity theory, this provides an alternate—equally plausible—explanation. Executives receive large salaries to eliminate the need for evaluating their risk preferences.)

$$\text{(i)} \quad M'(f') \geq M'(f), \text{ for all feasible } f, \qquad (18)$$

and

$$\text{(ii)} \quad a(f') = t. \qquad (19)$$

Part (i) of the definition specifies f' as the financial package chosen by firm t, given the incentive function M and the market signalling function, $a(f)$, and part (ii) is Spence's rationality criterion that the signal be valid, i.e., that a type t firm give a type t signal. Notice that in contrast with job market signalling models, the incentive function, M, as well as the signalling mechanism, a, is an object of equilibrium. Also, as argued in Section 2, it will be assumed that f' is formed from the marketed instruments of the firm to facilitate valuation and therefore monitoring and enforcement. This will link the equilibrium compensation schedule with the firm's financial structure.

To prove the existence of an incentive-signalling equilibrium is not a straightforward task and we shall not take it up here. In fact, though, as the previous example illustrates, there may be a multiplicity of equilibria. Given the incentive schedule, however, the possible *distinct* modes of financing are limited. While there are a plethora of different financial instruments, what matters is the set of incentive returns they yield. To be concrete about this, suppose that M is given as in the example of Section 2 by (5). By altering the package of financial instruments that are issued, a firm can arbitrarily affect the probability of bankruptcy, but by simply issuing debt the firm can achieve the same range of possible incentive returns, i.e., values for (5). In other words, given the incentive schedule of (5), debt and equity constitute a sufficient financial package and the incentive effects of any other package will be equivalent to those obtained by some package of debt and equity. More generally, still, in the example the signalling implications of any incentive-financial structure *pair* (a, f') will be matched by a particular pair in (5) using debt and equity. (This phenomenon of redundancy is identical to that studied by Ross, 1976a.)

In conclusion, the manager of a firm maximizes his incentive return by choosing a financial package that trades off the current value of the signal given to the market against the incentive consequences on that return. In equilibrium, firms are correctly distinguished by their financial choices. What matters, though, is not the particular package chosen, but rather the essential characteristics of the financial package, i.e., its implications for incentives. Many seemingly distinct financial packages may actually have the same incentive properties.

4. A MODEL WITH RANDOM RETURNS

THE MODEL

The two-firm model of Section 2 can be generalized by simply adding types, but one feature that makes it particularly unacceptable is the assumption that managers know the returns of their own firms with certainty. By making returns uncertain, we shall be able to create a natural incentive, analogous to bankruptcy risk, for managers to limit their debt financing to as low a value as is consistent with signalling. This will provide a clearer example of the tradeoff between signalling and incentive consequences described in Section 3.

Once again we shall assume that only expected values matter for valuation. Suppose that firms have random returns, X, uniformly distributed on $[0, t]$ where manager-insiders know their own firm's t value and there are a continuum of types $t \epsilon [c, d]$.[9] If we adopt the incentive schedule

$$M = (1 + r)\gamma_0 V_0 + \gamma_1 E \begin{Bmatrix} X \text{ if } X \geq F \\ X - L \text{ if } X < F \end{Bmatrix}, \qquad (20)$$

where F is, again, the face value of debt, then debt and equity will be sufficient instruments in the sense of Section 3.

If the type, t, of a firm is known for sure, then its current value will be given by

$$V_0 = \frac{t}{2(1 + r)}, \qquad (21)$$

hence if the signal of type is $a(F)$, from (20)

$$M = \frac{1}{2} \gamma_0 a(F) + \gamma_1 \left[\frac{1}{2} t - L \frac{F}{t} \right], \qquad (22)$$

where we have assumed that $F \leq t$. To find the optimum financial level, we assume the maximum is internal, and differentiating (22) with respect to F yields

$$\frac{1}{2} \gamma_0 a'(F) = \gamma_1 \frac{L}{t}. \qquad (23)$$

Condition (19) for signal validity requires that

$$a(F) = t. \qquad (24)$$

Conditions (23) and (24) permit us to solve for the equilibrium structure.[10] Recalling that F is a function of t in equilibrium, we can differentiate (24) and combine it with (23) to obtain the differential equation

$$F' = \frac{1}{2} \frac{\gamma_0}{\gamma_1} \frac{t}{L}, \qquad (25)$$

---

[9] The distribution, $Q(t)$, on the continuum is the probability distribution of types, t, *given* the exogenous information at time 0. For each firm in this sample, $Q(t)$ would be the probability that the firm has a type less than or equal to t. For example, if time 1 returns are based on an econometric forecast, $Q(t)$ would be that forecast for all firms in the model. Firms with different forecasts would be lumped into different samples.

[10] Conditions (23) and (24) are, in fact, formally identical to those of a model that Spence has studied. We include the solution for completeness only.

whose solution is

$$F_t = \frac{\gamma_0}{4\gamma_1} \frac{t^2}{L} + b, \tag{26}$$

where b is a constant of integration. From (24), then

$$a(F) = 2 \sqrt{\frac{\gamma_1 L}{\gamma_0}} [F - b]^{1/2}. \tag{27}$$

Since the lowest firm, with $t = c$, will clearly gain no advantage from signalling, it will set

$$F_c = 0,$$

which implies that

$$F_t = \frac{\gamma_0}{4\gamma_1 L} [t^2 - c^2]. \tag{28}$$

We must have

$$d^2 - c^2 \leq \frac{4\gamma_1 L}{\gamma_0} d, \tag{29}$$

to insure that the required financing level will not exceed t. As in the simple example, (28) implies that no manager will wish to give a false signal as long as the probability of bankruptcy is not one. By direct comparison, we also set

$$\tfrac{1}{2}\gamma_0(d - c) \leq \gamma_1 L, \tag{30}$$

which is precisely the form of (13), and implies (29).

Now, if the set of incentive schedules available to managers is given by (20) with L as a parameter, a manager of a type d firm will choose a particular incentive structure by setting L at L^* where (30) is an equality. This will just permit full discrimination and any greater L would needlessly increase bankruptcy incentive costs.[11] This completes the conditions for an equilibrium incentive-signalling pair.

----

[11] We are assuming that managers do not falsely signal when there is no positive incentive to do so and, hence, there is still discrimination when (30) is set on equality. We are also assuming that d is sufficiently great so that a c type manager must bankrupt with certainty to signal type d. Note that there is nothing inherent in the problem to assure us that (28) is a unique equilibrium.

If the density of low value firms in the sample is sufficiently small, then there might be another equilibrium with no firms issuing debt. In this case the difference between the average value and the highest value is small, and the cost to a manager of differentiating a firm would be prohibitive. Nevertheless, (28) still describes an equilibrium. While it is to the advantage of the managers of the high return firms, acting as a group, to cut their financing level, any single manager doing

As with the previous examples, the Modigliani-Miller irrelevancy theorem holds within a risk class, i.e., given t, value is determined by (21) independent of the financial structure. But, by changing F the manager-insider alters the market's perception of the firm's risk class (or type) and therefore its current value changes with F according to (27) and, by (28), there is a unique optimum level of financing for each firm type.

SOME EMPIRICAL IMPLICATIONS

Let us look at some variables whose values are often cited as tests of the Modigliani-Miller theory.

The Cost of Capital. One way to define the (average) cost of capital is by the ratio

$$\rho \equiv \frac{E\{X\}}{V_0}. \tag{31}$$

Now, irrespective of financing,

$$E\{X\} = \tfrac{1}{2}t, \tag{32}$$

and if we are in an incentive signalling equilibrium, the financial package, F, will signal type t correctly and the relevant value, V_0, for (31) will be

$$V_0 = \frac{(1/2)t}{1 + r}. \tag{33}$$

This implies, of course, that

$$\rho = 1 + r, \tag{34}$$

for all firms.

In cross section, then, the "cost of capital" will be unaffected by the financing decision, *even though the level of debt is uniquely determined.*

---

so would find that his firm value dilutes down to the lower value. (Of course, if low value firms were in elastic supply, with free entry, this problem would disappear.)

This is the same sort of structure that arises in the nonequilibrium examples of Rothschild and Stiglitz, and the financial-signalling problem would be subject to the same difficulties if a mutual fund or financial intermediary could make discriminating offers to the market as a whole, pooling intragroup risks. These matters are still unresolved and are further complicated in our setting by the endogenous nature of the incentive schedule itself, and while they are of interest to us, we shall not pursue them here. As a conjecture, though, I suspect that the problems of nonequilibrium in these models are identical to those that arise in the two-person game with nonconvex strategy spaces. By augmenting the strategy spaces available to the firms, specifically by considering randomized strategies, definitive equilibria might be found.

Bankruptcy or Incentive "L" Risk. It is also possible to determine how the risk of bankruptcy or having an incentive loss, L, varies with the level of debt. Since X is uniformly distributed, from (28)

$$P \equiv \text{Prob}\{X < F \,|\, t\} = F/t$$
$$= \frac{\gamma_0}{4\gamma_1 L} \left[t - \frac{c^2}{t} \right]. \tag{35}$$

The bankruptcy risk, P, is an increasing function of firm type, t, and equivalently of the debt level F. That the risk should increase with F is in accord with traditional theory, but that it should also increase with t may seem counterintuitive. In fact, though, it is because increasing debt brings greater risks that this can be taken as a valid signal of a more productive firm. The traditional view that higher debt lowers firm value may be correct with true dead weight bankruptcy costs for a given firm, but in equilibrium exactly the opposite is true in a cross section of firms.

The Financial Ratios. Defining the current value of debt and equity as D and E, it is easily shown that

$$D = \frac{F}{1 + r} \left[1 - \frac{F}{2t} \right],$$
$$E = \frac{1}{1 + r} \left[\frac{t}{2} - F + \frac{F^2}{2t} \right], \tag{36}$$

and

$$V_0 = D + E = \frac{1}{1 + r} \frac{t}{2}.$$

Differentiating (36) verifies that as t and, equivalently, V increase, D/E increases as well. In other words, in a cross section, value increases as the debt-equity ratio *rises*.

Despite these somewhat paradoxical results, a great deal of care must be taken in actual empirical testing. It must be stressed, first, that the firms in the model are all *ex ante* identical in that on the basis of exogenous information they each have the same probability of belonging to any given type. A corner garage cannot signal that it is General Motors simply by raising its debt-equity ratio. Furthermore, the above comparative statics hold at time 0. In a continuous time model it is certainly the case that for a given firm, with true bankruptcy costs, value will fall with increases in the debt-equity ratio; in fact D/E must approach infinity as bankruptcy is approached (in a diffusion model). Even without such costs, D/E and V will move in opposite directions. These effects will tend to counter the initial incentive-signalling effects and may make empirical testing more difficult.

5. GENERALIZATIONS, EXTENSIONS AND CONCLUSIONS

Considerable work remains, though, before the incentive-signalling model is in a form suitable for empirical testing. First, the model should be generalized to incorporate the possibility of activity choice by the manager. In the examples, the returns of the firm were specified exogenously to the manager. More generally, the manager faces a production problem as well as a financial decision and must choose an optimal activity from a given production set according to an endogenously determined investment criterion. The interplay between the incentive schedule and activity choice produces some interesting results, but in a perfect market even with incentive-signalling phenomena some Fisherian separation results should hold as well.

The introduction of activity choice also imposes a need for a more general treatment of uncertainty in the model. If we retain a competitive financial market, then the valuation rule will remain linear, but in either a state-space framework or a k-parameter theory, the tradeoff between return and risk will influence value. This, in turn, will affect both the equilibrium incentive structure and the resulting activity and financing choices. A number of these extensions are studied in Ross (1976b).

A third requirement is to specify the model intertemporally, and in continuous time. This would not only provide a natural setting for empirical work, but it would also draw on the current work on option pricing theory. For example, an incentive schedule that gave the manager a stock holding could be priced directly, as a function of the current value of the firm, V_0, from the existing literature on pricing call options. Similarly, an option to buy stock could also be priced as a function of V_0 by considering the option as an option on the firm.[12] Finally, of course, for empirical work the effects of taxation and true bankruptcy costs must be considered.[13]

---

[12] I am grateful to John Cox and Mark Rubinstein for pointing out this latter possibility to me.

[13] The model should also be extended to consider problems in personal or small firm finance as well as corporate finance. In such problems the manager is an owner, and questions of managerial risk aversion become significant. Furthermore, we cannot assume that the manager's compensation is small relative to the firm's value. Much of our intuition about finance appears to be derived from analysis at this level, where the severity of the moral hazard problem is dominant and enforcement and monitoring costs become significant. In an independent paper, Leland and Pyle have analyzed some of these issues in a model where an entrepreneur is seeking to finance a project. It is also necessary to consider the role of financial intermediaries and structural changes in the incentive signalling model. For example, in the model of Section 4, managers, while not initially risk averse, may adopt a risk averse equilibrium schedule. Such a schedule would provide incentives for managers to merge firms, and it would also open up a role for mutual funds to pool managerial risk. (See note 11 for a glimpse of some of the problems with such analyses, though.)

Gerald Jaynes has also suggested that the incentive-signalling apparatus might have implications for modelling a wide variety of economic phenomena involving general producer warranties and guarantees (that are not intrinsically financial). In the realm of purely financial signals, dividend payments, warrant offerings, earnings retention rates and all manners of financial relations between the firm and the market have signalling content.

Nevertheless, even without these extensions, the simple incentive-signalling model developed in this paper provides a theory for the determination of the financial structure of the firm. The assumptions of perfection and competition in financial markets underlie not only the Modigliani-Miller irrelevancy theory, but also the capital asset pricing models and the option pricing literature. If we must drop these assumptions to build a more realistic theory of corporate finance, then we should also be prepared to develop pricing theories in imperfect markets. The incentive-signalling model, though, provides a role for corporate finance within the framework that supports both the pricing theories and the Modigliani-Miller theory.

REFERENCES

Akerlof, G. "The Market for 'Lemons': Qualitative Uncertainty and the Market Mechanism." *Quarterly Journal of Economics* (August 1970).

―――. "A Theory of Information and Labor Markets." *Quarterly Journal of Economics,* forthcoming.

Arrow, K. J. "Some Models of Racial Discrimination in the Labor Market," in A. H. Pascal, ed., *Racial Discrimination in Economic Life,* Lexington, Mass.: Heath, 1972.

Ekern, S. and Wilson, R. "On the Theory of the Firm in an Economy with Incomplete Markets." *The Bell Journal of Economics* (Spring 1974).

Fama, "The Effects of a Firm's Investment and Financing Decisions on the Welfare of Its Securityholders." European Institute for Advanced Studies in Management Working Paper No. 75-43, December 1975.

Jensen, M. C. and Meckling, W. H. "Theory of the Firm: Managerial Behavior, Agency Costs and Ownership Structure." University of Rochester Graduate School of Management Working Paper Series #GPB-75-3, December 1975.

Leland, H. "Production Theory and the Stock Market." *The Bell Journal of Economics* (Spring 1974).

Leland, H. and Pyle, D. H. "Informational Asymmetries, Financial Structure, and Financial Intermediation." Research Program in Finance Working Paper No. 41, Graduate School of Business Adminstration, Institute of Business and Economic Research, March 1976.

Malinvaud, E. "Markets for an Exchange Economy with Individual Risks." *Econometrica* (May 1973).

Miller, M. and Modigliani, F. "Dividend Policy, Growth, and the Valuation of Shares." *Journal of Business* (October 1961).

Modigliani, F. and Miller, M. "The Costs of Capital, Corporation Finance, and the Theory of Investment." *The American Economic Review* (June 1958).

Radner, R. "A Note on Unanimity of Stockholders' Preferences Among Alternative Production Plans: A Reformulation of the Ekern-Wilson Model." *The Bell Journal of Economics* (Spring 1974).

Riley. J. G. "Competitive Signalling." *Journal of Economic Theory* (April 1975).

Ross, S. A. "Options and Efficiency." *Quarterly Journal of Economics* (February 1976a).

———. "Some Notes on Financial Incentive-Signalling Models, Activity Choice and Risk Preferences." Paper presented at the Bell Laboratories Symposium on Financial Economics, Holmdel, New Jersey, September 20–21, 1976b.

Rothschild, M. and Stiglitz, J. E. "Equilibrium in Competitive Insurance Markets; the Economics of Markets with Imperfect Information." *Quarterly Journal of Economics,* forthcoming.

Samuelson, P. "Risk and Uncertainty: A Fallacy of Large Numbers." Reprinted in *The Collected Scientific Papers,* Vol. 1, MIT Press, Cambridge, Massachusetts, 1972.

Spence, A. M. "Competitive and Optimal Responses to Signals: Analysis of Efficiency and Distribution." *Journal of Economic Theory* (March 1974).

———. *Market Signalling: Information Transfer in Hiring and Related Processes.* Cambridge: Harvard University Press, 1974.

Stiglitz, J. E. "A Re-Examination of the Modigliani-Miller Theorem." *The American Economic Review* (December 1969).

———. "Some Aspects of the Pure Theory of Corporate Finance: Bankruptcies and Takeovers." *The Bell Journal of Economics* (Autumn 1972).

———. "On the Irrelevance of Corporate Financial Policy." *The American Economic Review* (December 1974).

27. THE EFFECTS OF A FIRM'S INVESTMENT AND FINANCING DECISIONS ON THE WELFARE OF ITS SECURITY HOLDERS

EUGENE F. FAMA*

Reprinted from *The American Economic Review*, Vol. 68, No. 3 (June 1978), pp. 272–284, by permission of the author and the publisher.

In their classic article, Franco Modigliani and Merton H. Miller showed that in a perfect capital market, and given some other peripheral assumptions, the financing decisions of a firm are of no consequence. Substantial controversy followed, centered in large part on which of the peripheral assumptions are important to the validity of the theorem. For example, Joseph Stiglitz (1969, 1974) argues that in addition to a perfect market, the critical assumption is that bonds issued by individuals and firms are free of default risk. However, in chapter 4 of our book, Miller and I show that the theorem holds when debt is risky as long as stockholders and bondholders protect themselves from one another with what Fama and Miller (hereafter noted F-M) call "me-first rules."

This paper shows that me-first rules are also unnecessary. Propositions about the irrelevance of the financing decisions of firms can be built either on the assumption that investors and firms have equal access to the capital market or on the assumption that no firm issues securities for which there are not perfect substitutes from other firms. With either approach one can show that if the capital market is perfect, then (a) a firm's financing decisions have no effect on its market value, and (b) its financing decisions are of no consequence to its security holders.

The paper begins with a review of existing capital structure theorems, focusing on the work of Stiglitz and F-M. The discussion of old results has two purposes. The literature in this area has tended to become increasingly mathematical. One of the goals here is to show that the capital structure propositions in fact rest on simple economic arguments. Examining previous results also helps put the new results to be presented into perspective.

* Graduate School of Business, University of Chicago. This research is supported by the National Science Foundation. I am grateful for the comments of R. Ball, M. Blume, G. Borts, H. DeAngelo, N. Gonedes, R. Hamada, M. Jensen, S. Ross, M. Scholes, G. W. Schwert, and R. Weil. If I have any clear thoughts on the subject matter of this paper, they are due in large part to discussions with Merton H. Miller.

Finally, F-M and Stiglitz (1972) note that when firms can issue risky debt, the market value rule for the investment decisions of firms is ambiguous. With risky debt, maximizing stockholder wealth, bondholder wealth, or the combined wealth of bondholders and stockholders can imply three different investment decisions. Stiglitz argues that firms are likely to maximize stockholder wealth, even though this might be less economically efficient than maximizing combined stockholder and bondholder wealth. Miller and I leave the issue unresolved. I argue here that maximizing combined stockholder and bondholder wealth is the only market value rule consistent with a stable equilibrium, and that in its capacity as price setter the market can provide incentives for firms to choose this rule.

I. ARBITRAGE PROOFS OF THE MARKET VALUE PROPOSITION

Much of the early literature is concerned with the proposition that the market value of a firm is unaffected by its financing decisions, and most of the early proofs use arbitrage arguments. The general idea is that if the financing decisions of a firm affect its market value, there are arbitrage opportunities that can be used to produce costless instantaneous increases in wealth. Since the existence of such opportunities is inconsistent with equilibrium in a perfect capital market, one can conclude that the market value of a firm is unaffected by its financing decisions. Examples of this approach are the original "risk class" model of Modigliani and Miller and the "states of the world" model of Jack Hirshleifer (1965, 1966).

In all of the arbitrage proofs of the market value proposition, there are five common assumptions:

Assumption 1: Perfect Capital Market. There are no transactions costs to investors and firms when they issue or trade securities; bankruptcy likewise involves no costs; there are no taxes; and there are no costs in keeping a firm's management to the decision rules set by its security holders. The perfect capital market assumption is maintained throughout the paper. Thus, I shall not discuss the interesting problems that arise from the differential treatment of corporate dividend and interest payments in computing corporate taxes, or the problems that arise from the differential treatment of dividends and capital gains in computing personal taxes. Nor shall I discuss any effects of bankruptcy costs or managerial agency costs on the nature of optimal investment and financing decisions by firms.

Assumption 2: Equal Access. Individuals and firms have equal access to the capital market. This means that the types of securities that can be issued by firms can be issued by investors on personal account. For example, suppose an investor owns the same proportion of each of a firm's securities, so that he has a direct share in the firm's activities. Equal access implies that, using the firm's securities as exclusive collateral, the investor can issue the same sort of securities as the firm. If firms can issue securities that contain limited liability provisions, such provisions can also be included in securities issued by investors against their holdings in firms. Moreover, the prices of securities are determined by the characteristics of their payoff streams and not by whether they are issued by investors or firms. Equal access could logically be included as a characteristic of a perfect capital market, but it plays such an important role in capital structure propositions that it is stated separately.

Assumption 3: Complete Agreement or Homogeneous Expectations. Any information available is costlessly available to all market agents (investors and firms), and all agents correctly assess the implications of the information for the future prospects of firms and securities. For most of what we do, it would be sufficient to assume that all market agents can correctly determine when securities issued by different investors and firms are perfect substitutes, but it seems at best a short step from this to complete agreement. A perfect capital market could be taken to imply complete agreement, but it is common in the literature to state the two as separate assumptions.

Assumption 4: Only Wealth Counts. Aside from effects on security holder wealth, the financing decisions of a firm do not affect the characteristics of the portfolio opportunities available to investors. Thus the effects of a firm's financing decisions on the welfare of its security holders can be equated with effects on security holder wealth. This assumption is only precise in the context of models that say which characteristics of portfolio opportunities are of concern to investors. We need not be so specific. For our purposes it is sufficient to assume that the capital market satisfies whatever conditions are necessary to ensure the desired correspondence between wealth and welfare. Moreover, we shall see that one of the contributions of more recent treatments of capital structure propositions is to show that this assumption is unnecessary.

Assumption 5: Given Investment Strategies. To focus on the effects of a firm's financing decisions on the welfare of its security holders, all proofs of capital structure porpositions take the investment strategies of firms as given. Although decisions to be made in the future are unknown, the rules that firms use to make current and future investment decisions are given. In addition, investment decisions are made independently of how the decisions are financed. In the last section of the paper, we consider the nature of optimal investment strategies for firms.

Stiglitz (1974, Theorem 2) gives the most general arbitrage proof that Assumptions 1–5 imply that the market value of a firm is unaffected by its financing decisions. Suppose there is an optimal capital structure for the firm, but the firm does not choose this capital structure. Any investor can provide the optimal capital structure to the market by buying equal proportions of the firm's securities and then issuing the optimal proportions on personal account. If the market value of the firm were less than the value implied by an optimal capital structure, by providing the optimal capital structure to the market, the investor could earn an arbitrage profit. Since every investor has an incentive to exploit such opportunities and since exploitation is costless, their existence is inconsistent with a market equilibrium. In equalibrium, the market value of a firm is always the value implied by an optimal capital structure, irrespective of the capital structure chosen by the firm. Thus, at least with respect to its effects on the firm's market value, any choice of capital structure by the firm is as good as any other.

II. MARKET VALUE AND SECURITY HOLDER INDIFFERENCE

In the fourth chapter of our book, Miller and I show that the absence of a relationship between a firm's market value and its financing decisions does not in itself imply that the financing decisions are of no consequence to the firm's security holders. When the firm can issue risky debt, it may be able to use its financing decisions to shift wealth from its bondholders to its stockholders or vice versa.

To illustrate, assume a discrete time world in which the firm can issue two general types of securities, bonds and common stock. Given a perfect capital market and a market where the financing decisions of a firm do not affect the important characteristics of the portfolio opportunities available to investors, there is nothing the firm can do with its financing decisions at time t that will help or hurt investors who buy the firm's securities at time t. Thus it suffices to examine the effects of the firm's financing decisions at t on the wealths of investors who have held its securities from $t - 1$.

Let $S_{t-1}(t)$ and $B_{t-1}(t)$ be the market values at time t of the firm's common stock and bonds outstanding from $t - 1$. The combined value of these old stocks and bonds at t is the market value of the firm $V(t)$, less the value of new bonds issued at t, $b(t)$, less the market value of new common stock $s(t)$:

$$S_{t-1}(t) + B_{t-1}(t) = V(t) - b(t) - s(t) \tag{1}$$

The firm also makes dividend and interest payments at t, and we assume these are made only on securities outstanding from $t - 1$. Total dividend payments $D(t)$ and interest payments R(t) are defined by

$$D(t) + R(t) = X(t) - I(t) + b(t) + s(t) \tag{2}$$

where $X(t)$ is net cash income at t (cash revenues minus cash costs), and $I(t)$ is the cash outlay for investment. Adding (1) and (2), the total wealth at time t associated with common stock and bonds outstanding from $t - 1$ is

$$[D(t) + S_{t-1}(t)] + [R(t) + B_{t-1}(t)] = X(t) - I(t) + V(t) \tag{3}$$

Since all capital structure propositions take the firm's investment strategy as given, $I(t)$ does not depend on financing decisions at t. The net cash earnings $X(t)$ are the result of past investment decisions and so are independent of financing decisions at t. Assumptions 1–5 ensure that the value of the firm $V(t)$ is unaffected by its financing decisions. Since $X(t)$, $I(t)$, and $V(t)$ are all independent of financing decisions at t, we can conclude from (3) that the combined wealth of old bondholders and stockholders at time t is independent of the firm's financing decisions at t.

However, there might be financing decisions that the firm can make at time t that change the nature of the claims represented by the bonds outstanding from t − 1 and so shift wealth from bondholders to stockholders or vice versa. For example, suppose the firm's old bonds are free of default risk if no new debt is issued, but the firm can issue new debt that has the effect of imposing default risk on the old bonds. The new debt thus brings about a change in the characteristics of the old debt which we would expect to lead to a lower value of $B_{t-1}(t)$. Since the combined wealth of the old bonds and stocks in independent of the financing decision, issuing the new debt has the effect of shifting wealth from the old bondholders to the old stockholders. Alternatively, suppose the old debt is already subject to default risk, and at time t the firm retires some of it but not the entire amount. In the event of bankruptcy at a future date, each of the remaining bonds recovers more than if some of the old bonds are not retired at t. When a firm announces such a financing decision at t, we would expect the value $B_{t-1}(t)$ of all the old bonds to be higher than when no retirement takes place. Thus given constant total wealth, the financing decision implies a shift of wealth from the old stockholders to the old bondholders. In short, the fact that the market value of a firm is independent of its financing decisions does not necessarily imply that the financing decisions are a matter of indifference to the firm's security holders.

Given the world of Assumptions 1–5, the indifference proposition will hold if we restrict the types of securities that can be issued by firms so as to guarantee that the characteristics of the payoffs on the firm's old bonds are unaffected by its financing decisions at t. One way to accomplish this is to assume that all debt is free of default risk, which is the approach taken by Stiglitz (1969, 1974). In chapter 4 of our book, however, Miller and I show that the desired result is obtained when investors protect themselves with me-first rules. For example, bondholders insist that any new debt issued is junior to existing debt—in the event of bankruptcy, older bonds are paid off before newer bonds. The stockholders in their turn insist that the firm does not use its financing decisions to improve the positions of any bondholders. For example, if the firm wants to retire debt before its maturity, junior issues must be retired before senior issues, and any issues retired must be retired in full. We formalize these statements with a new assumption.

Assumption 6. A firm's stockholders and bondholders protect themselves from one another with costlessly enforced me-first rules which ensure that the characteristics of the payoffs on the firm's outstanding bonds are unaffected by changes in its capital structure.

In sum, Assumptions 1–5 are sufficient to conclude that the market value of a firm is unaffected by its financing decisions. Risk-free debt or the me-first rules of Assumption 6 then lead to the somewhat stronger conclusion that the financing decisions of the firm are a matter of indifference to all of its security holders.

III. THE IRRELEVANCE OF A FIRM'S DIVIDEND DECISIONS

A firm's dividend decision at any time t is part of its financing decision. The preceding analysis implies that when a firm's securities are protected by me-first rules, the firm's dividend decision at t determines how the wealth of its shareholders is split between $D(t)$ and $S_{t-1}(t)$, but the sum of the two components of shareholder wealth is unaffected by the dividend decision. In short, dividend decisions are a matter of indifference to the firm's security holders whenever financing decisions are a matter of indifference.

However, dividend decisions can be a matter of indifference even when other aspects of the firm's financing decisions are of some consequence. Consider a world where the market value of a firm $V(t)$ is unaffected by its financing decisions, but the firm has risky debt outstanding which is not protected by me-first rules. By issuing more or less new bonds $b(t)$ at time t, the firm can affect the value of its old bonds $B_{t-1}(t)$, which in turn affects the split of wealth between its old bonds and its old stock. Any such effects on the wealths of old bonds and stocks are, however, due entirely to the choice of $b(t)$. Since the firm can issue more or less new stock $s(t)$ at time t, we can see from equation (2) that the choice of $b(t)$ need not affect the decision about the dividend $D(t)$. We can see from equations (1) to (3) that given any decision about $b(t)$ and its implication for $B_{t-1}(t)$, the dividend decision again just affects the split of shareholder wealth between dividends and capital value.

Keep in mind that we are taking the investment strategy of the firm as given. For example, if a firm that has risky bonds outstanding unexpectedly increases its dividend by selling off assets, there is a shift in wealth from bondholders to stockholders. However, the shift should be attributed to the investment decision, the sale of assets, rather than to the dividend decision since the same shift of wealth takes place, but in the form of a capital gain instead of a dividend, if the firm announces that the proceeds from the sale of assets will be used to repurchase shares.

IV. DROPPING THE "ONLY WEALTH COUNTS" ASSUMPTION

Beginning with Modigliani and Miller, proofs of capital structure propositions generally include the Assumption 4 that aside from effects on security holder wealth, the financing decisions of firms do not affect the characteristics of the portfolio opportunities available to investors. Thus, the effects of financing decisions on security holder welfare can be evaluated in terms of their effects on security holder wealth. An exception to this approach is Stiglitz (1969, 1974) who shows that assumptions that lead to capital structure propositions also imply a world where the protfolio opportunities facing investors are unaffected by the financing decisions of firms. Formally:

Theorem 1. *Suppose the capital market is perfect in the sense of Assumption 1, the equal access and complete agreement provisions, Assumptions 2 and 3, hold, the investment strategies of firms are given in the sense of Assumption 5, and debt is either free of default risk or investors insist on the me-first rules of Assumption 6. Then the characteristics of a general equilibrium, that is, the market values of firms, the positions that investors take in firms and the costs of these positions, are unaffected by the financing decisions of firms. Thus, the financing decisions of firms are of no consequence to investors.*

The intuition of the argument of Stiglitz' theorem is that when investors and firms have equal access to the capital market, the positions in firms that can be created and traded among investors are determined by the investment strategies of firms, and the possibilities are the same for any set of financing decisions by firms. Thus, the financing decisions of firms have no effect on the set of general equilibria that can be acheived in the capital market.

Moreover, once a general equilibrium has been achieved, implying an optimal set of holdings in firms by investors, there is no reason why changes in the financing decisions of firms should move the market to a different general equilibrium. When firms perturb a general equilibrium by changing their financing decisions, their actions neither expand nor contract the types of positions in firms that can be created by investors. It follows that an optimal response to the changes in the financing decisions of firms occurs when the general equilibrium remains unchanged. Specifically, the market responds by leaving the values of firms and their previously existing bonds unchanged. Investors respond by exactly reversing the changes in the financing decisions of firms on personal account so that the positions of investors in firms are unaffected by the changes in the financing decisions of firms.

The formal proof of Theorem 1 requires that changes in the financing decisions of firms can be reversed by investors on personal account. For this, the equal access Assumption 2 is required, but it is also assumed either that bonds are free of default risk (the assumption that Stiglitz (1974) uses in his proof of Theorem 1) or that investors insist on and costlessly enforce appropriate me-first rules (the extension of Stiglitz's analysis suggested by F-M). In the presence of risky bonds and in the absence of me-first rules, the firm can use changes in its financing decisions to, in effect, expropriate the positions of bondholders to the benefit of stockholders, or vice versa. And the expropriations cannot always be neutralized by investors on personal account.

For example, suppose the firm increases the dividend paid to stockholders at time t by issuing new bonds that have the same priority as the firm's old bonds in the event of bankruptcy. Even if the shareholders use the increase in dividends to repurchase the new bonds issued by the firm, things are not as they were. The new bonds are still outstanding, so that in the event of bankruptcy each of the old bonds gets less than if no new bonds are issued. By issuing new bonds that have equal priority with the old bonds, the firm has expropriated part of the holdings of the old bondholders to the benefit of its stockholders. Other examples, some involving expropriations of stockholder positions to the benefit of bondholders, are easily constructed.

V. CAPITAL STRUCTURE PROPOSITIONS WITHOUT ME-FIRST RULES

The assumptions that debt is free of default risk or security holders protect themselves with me-first rules are, however, arbitrary restrictions on the types of securities that can be issued. Some firms or investors may want to issue unprotected bonds, and, appropriately priced, other investors may be willing to hold them. It is now argued that such restrictions on investment opportunities are unnecessary, and this is the first new result of the paper.

Theorem 2. Suppose the capital market is perfect in the sense of Assumption 1, the equal access and complete agreement provisions, Assumptions 2 and 3, hold, and the investment strategies of firms are given in the sense of Assumption 5. Then the characteristics of a general equilibrium, that is, the market values of firms, the positions that investors take in firms and the costs of these positions, are unaffected by the financing decisions of firms. Thus, the financing decisions of firms are of no consequence to investors.

To establish the theorem we return to time 0, the time when the first firms are organized and before they have issued any securities. The firms choose their investment strategies and then they go into the capital market for the resources to finance these investment strategies. At this point it is clear that given a perfect capital market and geven equal access to the market by individuals and firms, the financing decisions of firms have no effect on the nature of a general equilibrium. The positions in firms that investors create and hold, the prices of these positions, and thus the market values of firms are independent of the financing decisions of firms.

If unprotected securities are issued at time 0, then when time 1 comes along firms may be able to use their financing decisions to affect the positions of their security holders. When they hold the securities of a firm that are not protected by me-first rules, investors would of course prefer that the firm not engage in financing decisons at time 1 that have the effect of expropriating their positions; or, they would rather that the firm expropriate to their benefit the positions of other investors. But all of this is irrelevant, once we reconsider how it happened that at time 0 some investors put themselves into positions that could be expropriated at time 1. In an equal access market, the financing decisions of firms affect neither the variety of securities that could be traded at time 0 nor the instruments that are chosen by investors. If the positions that investors want to hold in firms are not offered by the firms, investors can buy up the securities of firms and create their desired positions in trades among themselves. Thus, the positions, protected and unprotected, that investors take in firms at time 0 are the same irrespective of the financing decisions of firms at time 0. If at time 1 some investors profit from or are hurt by unprotected positions taken at time 0, all of this happens to exactly the same extent for any set of financing decisions by firms at time 0.

Likewise, at time 1 firms cannot use their financing decisions to affect the positions in firms that investors choose to carry forward to time 2. Given an equal access market, investors can refinance any firm, buying equal proportions of all its securities, and then issuing preferred proportions on personal account. Thus the types and quantities of claims against firms that investors carry forward from time 1 to time 2 are independent of the financing decisions of firms at time 1. If expropriations take place at time 2 as a result of positions taken at time 1, the same investors are helped or hurt by these expropriations and to exactly the same extent when the unprotected securities are issued at time 1 by firms as when they are issued by investors in trades among themselves.

The arguments are general. When investors and firms have equal access to the capital market, at any point in time the positions that investors take in firms, the prices of these positions and thus the market values of firms are unaffected by the financing decisions of firms. Since the financial history of any investor—what happens to him in the market through time—is unaffected by the financing decisions of firms, the financing decisions of firms are of no consequence to investors.

In all versions of the capital structure propositions discussed so far, equal access to the capital market by investors and firms is assumed. However, the assumption is stronger when debt is neither free of default risk nor protected by me-first rules. One is likewise leaning harder on the complete agreement assumption. Investors must be able to specify the details of potentially expropriative contracts in the same way as firms. If investors issue unprotected bonds against their holdings in firms, they subsequently expropriate (for example, issue more unprotected bonds) in the same circumstances as would the firms. This requires either that the conditions or states of the world in which expropriations will take place at any time t are stated explicitly in loan contracts or that investors make accurate assessments of the probabilities and extent of expropriations in different future states of the world. Probabilistically speaking, neither issuers nor purchasers of loan contracts are ever "fooled" by anything that happens during the life of a contract, and the price of a contract always properly reflects the possibilities for future expropriations.

I now show that the capital structure propositions can be established without the equal access assumption. The cost, however, is a new assumption which precludes a firm from issuing any securities monopolistically. In effect, we set up conditions that lead to a capital market which is perfectly competitive with respect to the financing decisons of a firm.

VI. CAPITAL STRUCTURE PROPOSITIONS WITHOUT EQUAL ACCESS

In Theorem 2, as in Theorem 1, the portfolio opportunities facing investors turn out to be independent of the financing decisions of firms. However, firms can still be monopolists in their investment decisions. A firm may have access to investment opportunities that allow it to create securities with payoff streams whose characteristics cannot be replicated by other firms. Nevertheless, when there is equal access to financial markets, investors can issue the same claims against their holdings in firms that the firms themselves can issue. As a consequence, once firms have chosen their investment strategies, there is nothing further they can do through their financing decisions to affect the opportunity set facing investors.

If this result is to hold when the equal access assumption is dropped, we must restructure the world in such a way that the actions that investors (with equal access) take to free the investment opportunity set from any effects of financing decisions by firms, can be taken instead by firms. To accomplish this, firms are no longer allowed to issue securities for which there are not perfect substitutes issued by other firms. This implies that firms can no longer have monopolistic access to investment opportunities. Firms must also be given the motivation to act in the manner that leads to the validity of the capital structure propositions. In contrast, in an equal access world, once firms choose their investment strategies, what then happens when they get themselves to the capital market is beyond their control.

The specific new assumptions are:

Assumption 7. No firm produces any security monopolistically. There are always perfect substitutes issued by other firms. Moreover, if a firm shifts its capital structure, substituting some types of securities for others, its actions can be exactly offset by other firms who carry out the reverse shift, with the result that aggregate quantities of each type of security are unchanged.

Assumption 8. The goal of a firm in its financing decisions is to maximize its total market value at whatever prices for securities it sees in the market. Since firms are shown to be perfectly competitive in the capital market, the assumption is unobjectionable.

The arguments in the proof of the theorem that follows are similar to those used by the author and Arthur Laffer in discussing sufficient conditions for perfect competition in product markets in a world of perfect certainty. Also relevant are papers by the author (1972) and Fischer Black and Myron Scholes.

Theorem 3. Suppose the capital market is perfect in the sense of Assumption 1, the complete agreement assumption, Assumption 3, holds, the investment strategies of firms are given in the sense of Assumption 5, and Assumptions 7 and 8 also hold. Then given a general equilibrium in the capital market at any time t: (a) *The market value of a firm is unaffected by changes in its financing decisions;* (b) *the financing decisions of a firm are of no consequence to investors; that is, the firm's financing decisions do not affect what happens to any investor through time; and* (c) *the capital market is perfectly competitive in the sense that aggregate supplies and prices of different types of securities are unaffected by changes in the financing decisions of a firm.*

Consider first the case where debt is free of default risk or investors protect themselves from one another with the me-first rules of Assumption 6. Suppose the capital market achieves a general equilibrium at time t and then, for whatever reason, some firm perturbs the equilibrium by changing its capital structure.

In the original equilibrium, firms, including the firm that subsequently shifts, chose securities so as to maximize their market values at the original equilibrium values of security prices. This means that at the original prices, the new securities that the shifting firm issues had exactly the same market value as the securities it no longer issues. It also means that the market can achieve a "new" general equilibrium if other firms instantly respond to the disturbance of the initial equilibrium by exactly offsetting the change in the shifting firm's capital structure, and if the prices of securities remain at their old equilibrium values. When this happens, the market value of any firm is the same as it was in the old general equilibrium, and firms have no further incentives to change their capital structures. In addition, since debt is assumed to be either free of default risk or securities are protected by me-first rules, the wealths of individual investors are the same in the new general equilibrium as in the old. Since the aggregate supplies and prices of different securities are unchanged, each investor can choose a portfolio identical to the one chosen in the initial general equilibrium; just the names of the firms issuing particular types of securities may be different. In short, with me-first rules and the perfectly competitive capital market produced by the offsetting financing decisions of other firms, investors are completely immunized from any effects of shifts in the financing decisions of any firm.

The same analysis applies in the absence of me-first rules, once we understand the restrictions implied by the perfect substitutes Assumption 7. In particular, the fact that different firms issue securities at time t − 1 that are perfect substitutes does not imply that these firms make the same financing decisions at time t. However, if unprotected securities issued by different firms at t − 1 are perfect substitutes, any expropriations that take place at time t must be the same for all of these firms. It follows that if a firm issues unprotected securities at any time t − 1, the expropriations that take place in any given state of the world at time t must be the same for all financing decisions that the firm might make in that state at t.

Suppose now that time t comes along, the state of the world is known, firms make their financing decisions, and a general equilibrium set of securities prices and values of firms is determined. Some firm then perturbs the general equilibrium by shifting its capital structure. Given what was said above, even though the firm may have unprotected securities in its capital structure, the shift cannot cause expropriations of security holder positions beyond those associated with the firm's original financing decisions at t. Thus, just as in the case where debt is risk free or securities are protected by me-first rules, the market can reattain a general equilibrium if other firms exactly offset the change in the shifting firm's capital structure, leaving aggregate supplies and prices of different securities unchanged. Since no new expropriations take place, the wealths of investors are also unchanged, and each investor can choose a portfolio identical to the one chosen in the initial general equilibrium.

In the initial general equilibrium that follows the occurrence of a state of the world at time t, the positions of a firm's security holders are, of course, affected by any expropriative financing decisions. But in the world of the complete agreement Assumption 3, investors properly assessed the possibilities for future expropriations when they decided to hold the firm's securities at times t − 1, and these possibilities were properly reflected in the prices of the securities at t − 1. If the firm hadn't issued these potentially expropriative securities, its security holders would have purchased perfect substitutes from other firms. Thus the financing decisions of any firm are of no consequence to any investor in the sense that what happens to any investor through time happens irrespective of the financing decisions of any particular firm.

VII. SOME PERSPECTIVE ON CAPITAL STRUCTURE PROPOSITIONS

Given a perfect capital market, and given the investment strategies of firms, there are two approaches that lead to the conclusions that the market value of a firm is unaffected by its financing decisions, and a firm's financing decisions are of no consequence to its security holders. One approach is based on the assumption that investors and firms have equal access to the capital market. The other assumes that no firm offers securities to the market for which there are not perfect substitutes from other firms. The fundamental argument in both approaches is that, given the investment strategies of firms, there are mechanisms that insulate the opportunity set facing investors from any effects of the financing decisions of firms. With the equal access assumption, the off-setting actions that produce this result can come from investors or firms, while in the perfect substitutes approach, changes in the financing decisions of a firm are offset by other firms.

The types of capital structure propositions obtained with the two approaches are somewhat different. With equal access one gets statements about the effects of the financing decisions of all firms. When investors and firms have equal access to the capital market, then given the investment strategies of firms, the positions in firms that can be traded among investors are independent of the financing decisions of firms. As a consequence, the characteristics of a general equilibrium in the capital market are unaffected by the financing decisions of firms. In contrast, with the perfect substitutes approach, only firms issue securities so one can't conclude that the characteristics of a general equilibrium are independent of the financing decisions of all firms. One is limited to partial equilibrium statements about the irrelevance of the financing decisions of any individual firm.

The analysis here goes beyond earlier treatments in several respects. First, although earlier approaches generally use both assumptions in one form or another, it is evident from the work of Stiglitz (1969, 1974) that in an equal access market, the validity of the capital structure propositions does not also require the perfect substitutes assumption. However, Stiglitz argues that it is necessary to assume debt is risk free if the financing decisions of firms are to be a matter of indifference to security holders. The analysis here shows that in an equal access market, even the me-first rules of F-M are unnecessary restrictions on the types of securities that can be issued. In essence, in an equal access market investors can and will choose the same positions, protected and unprotected, irrespective of the financing decisions of firms. Thus, the fact that firms might issue unprotected securities does not invalidate the proposition that the financing decisions of firms are a matter of indifference to investors.

In a recent paper, Frank Milne argues that with the perfect substitutes assumption, the proposition that the market value of a firm is independent of its financing decisions does not also require the equal access assumption. However, Milne's framework is less general than that examined here. First, he allows unrestricted short selling of all securities, an assumption close to equal access. To emphasize the power of the perfect substitutes assumpton, in the analysis presented here securities are only issued by firms. Second, Milne assumes that the capital market is perfectly competitive, whereas we show how the actions of firms lead to a world where the total supplies and prices of securities of different types are unaffected by the financing decisions of any individual firm. Showing how the existence of perfect substitutes leads to such a strong form of perfect competition seems a substantial enrichment of the analysis. Finally, Milne works in a one-period context and investors do not come into the period already holding the securities of firms. In this world, the analytical difficulties that arise from potential expropriations of security holder positions never have to be faced. In contrast, I analyze the capital structure propositions in a multiperiod framework where firms are allowed to issue unprotected securities. It is shown that with the strong form of perfect competition in the capital market that arises from the perfect substitutes assumption, the financial history of any investor, that is, the protected and unprotected portfolio positions that he takes through time, are unaffected by the financing decisions of any individual firm.

Many have quarreled with the realism of the equal access assumption. (See, for example, the comments of David Durand on the Modigliani and Miller paper.) One can certainly also quarrel with the perfect substitutes assumption. It would seem that if for any securities issued by a firm there are perfect substitutes issued by other firms, then either there exist risk classes of firms in the sense of Modigliani and Miller (that is, there are classes of firms wherein the net cash flows of different firms are perfectly correlated) or the markets for contingent claims discussed by Hirshleifer cover all possible future states of the world. The existence of such risk classes or of complete markets for contingent claims is questionable.

In economics, however, formal propositions never provide pictures of the world that are realistic in all their details. The role of such propositions is to pinpoint the factors that can lead to certain kinds of results. In this view, the analysis of capital structure propositions suggests two factors that push the capital market toward equilibria where the market values of firms are independent of their financing decisions, and where the financing decisions of firms are of no consequence to their security holders. The first factor covers any possibilities investors have to issue claims against the securities of firms that they hold. The second is the natural incentive of firms to provide the types of securities desired by investors, and the ability of firms to provide securities that are close substitutes for those of other firms. In pure form, and in combination with a perfect capital market where contracts are costlessly written and enforced, either of these factors leads to irrelevance of capital structure propositions. In less pure form, but perhaps acting together, they are factors that help to push the market in the direction of the capital structure propositions.

VIII. THE MARKET VALUE RULE FOR INVESTMENT DECISIONS

The previous sections discuss the financing decisions of firms, given their investment strategies. I turn now to problems that arise in determining an optimal investment strategy when the capital market is perfect and when a firm can affect the portfolio opportunities facing its security holders only through the effects its investment decisions have on the wealths of its security holders. All other characteristics of portfolio opportunities are assumed to be unaffected by the investment and financing decisions of the firm.

Given that the investment decisions of a firm only affect the wealths of its security holders, the objectives of the security holders are clear. More wealth is better than less. In chapter 4 of our book, however, Miller and I point out that the "maximize securityholder wealth" rule can be ambiguous when the firm has risky debt. The firm might be able to use its investment decisions to make its previously issued bonds more or less risky and so to shift wealth from bondholders to stockholders or vice versa. One can easily construct examples where the rules "maximize stockholder wealth," "maximize bondholder wealth," and "maximize combined stockholder-bondholder wealth" all lead to different investment decisions.

A. THE PRESSURE OF POSSIBLE TAKEOVERS

We can apply the argument of Ronald Coase to show that of the three market value rules, only the rule maximize combined stockholder-bondholder wealth is consistent with a stable capital market equilibrium. Note first that when the capital market is perfect and when the characteristics of portfolio opportunities are independent of the actions of any individual firm, there is nothing the firm can do with its investment decision at t to help or hurt investors who buy its securities at t. Thus it suffices to examine the effects of the firm's investment decision at t on investors who have held its securities from $t - 1$.

From equation (3), the combined wealth at time t of the firm's bonds and stocks outstanding from $t - 1$ is $X(t) + V(t) - I(t)$. Since net cash earnings $X(t)$ are assumed to result from past decisions, they are unaffected by the investment decision at t. Thus maximum combined stockholder-bondholder wealth implies maximizing $V(t) - I(t)$, the excess of the market value of the firm at t over the investment outlays needed to generate that market value.

Suppose the firm is controlled by its stockholders, and they choose the rule maximize stockholder wealth. It will pay for the firm's bondholders to buy out the stockholders, paying them the value their shares would have under the rule maximize stockholder wealth. If the bondholders then maximize $V(t) - I(t)$, we can see from (3) that their wealth is larger than if they had allowed the shareholders to proceed with the investment rule maximize stockholder wealth. The same arguments apply, but with the roles of the stockholders and bondholders reversed, when the firm is initially controlled by its bondholders who wish to follow the rule maximize bondholder wealth. Alternatively, if the firm announces an investment rule other than "maximize $V(t) - I(t)$," it pays for outsiders to buy up the firm's securities and then to switch to the rule maximize $V(t) - I(t)$. The outsiders can even afford to pay a premium for the firm as long as it is no greater than the difference between the maximum value of $V(t) - I(t)$ and the value of $V(t) - I(t)$ under the investment policy chosen by the firm.

B. THE PRESSURES APPLIED BY THE MARKET IN ITS CAPACITY AS PRICE SETTER

Potential takeovers are not the only pressure pushing the firm toward the investment rule maximize $V(t) - I(t)$. In its role as price setter, the market has an additional way to motivate the firm to maximize the total wealth of its security holders.

Consider the firm's bondholders. When the firm issues bonds, the price of a given promised stream of payments depends on the investment strategy that the market perceives the firm to follow. If the firm in fact follows this strategy, the investment strategy is of no consequence to the bondholders. If they had the choice again, with the same uncertainties about the future, they would choose to hold the firm's bonds or perfect substitutes for them. In a capital market where the investment and financing decisions of a firm do not affect the portfolio opportunities facing investors, such perfect substitutes exist or they can be created from the securities of other firms. Since the market for shares is likewise a market of perfect substitutes, given that a firm sticks to the investment strategy that investors perceive it to follow, the choice of strategy is of no consequence to those who purchase its shares when it is an ongoing firm. In this stiuation, the choice of an investment strategy by the firm affects only the firm's original shareholders or organizers, those who own the rights to its investment opportunities before any securities are issued.

Let us return, then, to the point, call it time 0, when the firm is organized. The firm wishes to choose the investment strategy that maximizes the wealth of its organizers. The wealth of the organizers is $V(0) - I(0)$, the difference between the value of the firm and the investment outlays necessary at time 0 to generate that value. Thus the optimal investment decision at time 0 is to maximize $V(0) - I(0)$.

The value of the firm $V(0)$ depends also on the investment strategy the market thinks the firm will follow at time 1. Since the wealth at time 1 of securities outstanding from time 0 is $X(1) + V(1) - I(1)$, the value of the firm at time 0 is just the market value at time 0 of the distribution of $X(1) + V(1) - I(1)$. The earnings $X(1)$ observed at time 1 are a consequence of the investment decision taken at time 0. In every possible state of the world at time 1, the policy "maximize $V(1) - I(1)$" obviously produces as large a value of $V(1) - I(1)$ as any other investment strategy. It follows that if the firm's statements about investment policy are accepted by the market, the announcement at time 0 that the firm will maximize $V(1) - I(1)$ at time 1 maximizes the contribution of the investment decision at time 1 to $V(0)$ and thus to $V(0) - I(0)$.

Since the market value of the firm at time 1 is just the market value of the distribution of $X(2) + V(2) - I(2)$, $V(1)$ and thus $V(1) - I(1)$ depend in turn on the investment strategy that will be followed at time 2. Arguments analogous to those above imply that the announcement, at time 0, that the firm will maximize $V(1) - I(1)$ at time 1 implies the announcement, at time 0, that it will maximize $V(2) - I(2)$ at time 2. In short, to maximize $V(0) - I(0)$, the wealth of its organizers at time 0, the firm must convince the market that its investment strategy in each future period will likewise be maximize $V(t) - I(t)$. If the firm sticks to this strategy, this means that at any time t it chooses the investment decisions that maximize the combined wealth of bonds and stocks outstanding from $t - 1$.

Using the analysis of "agency costs" provided by Michael Jensen and William Meckling one can argue that the essence of the potential problems surrounding conflicting stockholder-bondholder interests is that once time 0 passes it will be difficult for the stockholders to resist the temptation to try to carry out an unexpected shift from the rule maximize $V(t) - I(t)$ to the rule maximize stockholder wealth. But the market has the means to motivate firms to stay in line. To maximize $V(0) - I(0)$, the wealth of its organizers, the firm must convince the market that it will always follow the investment strategy maximize $V(t) - I(t)$. The market realizes that the firm might later try to shift to another stragegy and it will take this into account in setting $V(0)$. To get the market to set $V(0)$ at the value appropriate to the strategy maximize $V(t) - I(t)$, the firm will have to find some way to guarantee that it will stay with this strategy.

The important point is that the onus of providing this guarantee falls on the firm. In pricing a firm's securities, a well-functioning market will, on average, appropriately charge the firm in advance for future departures from currently declared decision rules. The firm can only avoid these discounts in the prices of its securities to the extent that it can provide concrete assurances of its forthrightness. Thus, firms have clear-cut incentives to evolve mechanisms to assure the market that statements of policy can be taken at face value, and they have incentives to provide these assurances at lowest possible cost. In a multiperiod world, this might not be so difficult since firms continually have opportunities to behave in ways that reinforce their credibility.

Remember also that if the firm does not follow the strategy maximize $V(t) - I(t)$, it pays for outsiders to acquire the firm and then switch to this strategy. The outsiders are then in the position of the firm's organizers. That is, the firm will not be priced at the value implied by the strategy maximize $V(t) - I(t)$ unless the market is convinced that the firm will adhere to this strategy in future periods. If other forms of assurance prove difficult or costly, one possibility is to finance the firm entirely with equity, or more generally, never to issue risky debt. Then the rules maximize stockholder wealth and maximize $V(t) - I(t)$ coincide.

REFERENCES

F. Black and M. Scholes, "The Effect of Dividend Yield and Divident Policy on Common Stock Prices and Returns," *J. Finan. Econ.,* May 1974, *1,* 1–22.

R. H. Coase, "The Problem of Social Cost," *J. Law Econ.,* Oct. 1960, *3,* 1–44.

D. Durand, "The Cost of Capital in an Imperfect Market: A Reply to Modigliani and Miller," *Amer. Econ. Rev.,* June 1959, *49,* 639–55.

Eugene F. Fama, "Perfect Competition and Optimal Production Decisions under Uncertainty," *Bell J. Econ.,* Autumn 1972, *3,* 509–30.

———— and A. B. Laffer, "The Number of Firms and Competition," *Amer. Econ. Rev.,* Sept. 1972, *62,* 670–74.

———— and Merton H. Miller, *The Theory of Finance,* New York 1972.

J. Hirshleifer, "Investment Decisions under Uncertainty: Choice Theoretic Approaches," *Quart. J. Econ.,* Nov. 1965, *79,* 509–36.

————, "Investment Decisions under Uncertainty: Applications of the State-Preference Approach," *Quart. J. Econ.,* May 1966, *80,* 237–77.

M. C. Jensen and W. H. Meckling, "Theory of the Firm: Managerial Behavior, Agency Costs and Ownership Structure," *J. Finan. Econ.,* Oct. 1976, *3,* 305–60.

F. Milne, "Choice over Asset Economics: Default Risk and Corporate Leverage," *J. Finan. Econ.,* June 1975, 2, 165–85.

F. Modigliani and M. H. Miller, "The Cost of Capital, Corporation Finance, and the Theory of Investment," *Amer. Econ Rev.,* June 1958, *48,* 261–97.

J. C. Stiglitz, "A Re-Examination of the Modigliani-Miller Theorem," *Amer. Econ. Rev.,* Dec. 1969, *59,* 784–93.

————, "Some Aspects of the Pure Theory of Corporate Finance: Bankruptcies and Take-overs," *Bell J. Econ.,* Autumn 1972, *3,* 458–82.

————, "On the Irrelevance of Corporate Financial Policy," *Amer. Econ. Rev.,* Dec. 1974, *64,* 851–66.

28. MARKET IMPERFECTIONS, AGENCY PROBLEMS, AND CAPITAL STRUCTURE: A REVIEW

AMIR BARNEA*, ROBERT A. HAUGEN, and LEMMA W. SENBET

Reprinted from *Financial Management*, Vol. 10, No. 3 (Summer 1981), pp. 7–22, by permission of the authors and the publisher.

INTRODUCTION

Prediction of the effect of capital structure on the market value of the firm remains elusive despite much research over the past three decades. On the one hand, Modigliani and Miller [35] demonstrate that under perfect capital markets—free entry, equal access to information, and absence of transaction costs and taxes—the choice among various financial instruments is inconsequential to the value of the firm. This powerful result is reinforced by Stiglitz [45], who shows that financial policies are irrelevant even with risky debt, provided the investment opportunity set remains unchanged by financial policy. His proof further implies that corporate decisions relating to the maturity structure of debt as well as other complexities which characterize financial instruments do not affect frim value.[1] On the other hand, real world corporations engage in

* Amir Barnea is on the Faculty of Management at Tel-Aviv University. During the writing of this paper, he was visiting at the Graduate School of Business at the University of Wisconsin at Madison, where his co-authors teach. The authors wish to acknowledge many helpful comments and suggestions from a reader for this journal and from the participants in the Finance Workshop at the University of Wisconsin-Madison. This tutorial article was solicited by the editors, who are grateful for the authors' response.

[1] Many apparent explanations of the observable complex structure of financial instruments are not consistent with the Stiglitz framework. For example, *call provisions* on corporate debt are commonly attributed to interest rate uncertainty, suggesting that since stockholders are able to reap the added value of the bond caused by a decrease in interest rates, they gain, and bondholders lose commensurately, in an *ex ante* sense. However, in the Stiglitz framework, when arbitrage profits are fully exploited, the value of a non-callable bond will always equal the value of a callable bond plus the value of the call privilege. That is, stockholders pay at issuance an amount which reflects the full value of the call privilege. Also the common explanation of the *maturity structure* of a debt is a "habitat" argument, which implies that "optimal" debt maturity is achieved at the point where debt and asset maturities are matched so as to minimize the uncertainty associated with interest rate fluctuations [36]. Again, however, in the framework of perfect markets, there is no basis for an "optimal" maturity structure.

active financial management which manifests itself in the form of cross-sectional variations in debt ratios, differing debt maturity structures across industries, and complex financial contractual arrangements (*e.g.,* call provisions, convertibility features, sinking fund arrangements, warrants, or preferred stock).

There are two alternative explanations for the discrepancy between theory and reality. The first asserts that corporate reliance on complex financial instruments is merely an artifact of market equilibrium and by itself does not provide evidence for the relevance of the corporate financial policies. According to this argument, the multiplicity of financial instruments emerges from situations of disequilibrium in which (certainty equivalent) yield differentials temporarily exist. Corporations engage in activities that are aimed to capture arbitrage profits by providing more of the desired instrument. These supply adjustments continue until equilibrium is reached where the choice among financial arrangements no longer affects the market value of the firm. Still, at this point, corporations are financed by a variety of financial instruments so that complex financial structures may be observed. The second explanation of complex financial structures centers on imperfections in the functioning of the capital market. The link between specific types of market imperfections and corporate financial policies is the subject of this paper.

The introduction of imperfections to rationalize corporate decisions is not new. Finance texts provide criteria for optimal capital budgeting decisions. But such criteria can be justified only if the product and factor markets are imperfect in the sense that they are subject to barriers to entry, scale economies, information monopoly, and so on. Only then can positive net present values occur. By the same token, an explanation for the resources expended to identify optimal financial decisions must rely on market imperfections or frictions. One example of an imperfection is the tax code which, in recognizing interest as an allowable expense, favors debt over equity financing.[2] The focus of our paper is on *another* class of market imperfections, namely, agency problems stemming from the ownership structure of the firm.

Agency problems may exist when a principal, or group of principals, employs an agent to perform a service which necessitates delegating decision-making authority to the agent. These problems arise from conflicts of interests between the agent and the principal, or they can occur among the principals themselves. The analysis of the impact of these conflicts of interest on corporate decisions is based on two fundamental assumptions. First, owners and agents behave according to their own self-interest; and second, each of the participants in the activities of the firm is rational and capable of forming unbiased expectations regarding the future wealth. The agency literature identifies situations where

---

[2] Differential tax treatment of equity and debt *by itself* is not sufficient to explain observed corporate financial policies since it implies either the dominance of debt over equity financing or, as Miller [31] has recently shown, supply adjustments by value-maximizing corporations can eliminate any gain from leverage at a particular firm level.

conflicts of interest coupled with self interested behavior and rational expectations result in suboptimal business decisions. When this occurs, agency problems create "agency costs."

The agency problems considered in this paper arise from three sources. *First,* market imperfections may lead to an inability of management (the agent) to reveal the exact nature of the firm to debt and equity financiers (the principals) costlessly. This is a problem of informational asymmetry [20, 29, 39, 40, 44].

Second, the existence of debt financing under limited liability generates 1) stockholder incentives to accept suboptimal and high-risk projects which transfer wealth from bondholders to stockholders [15, 23], 2) stockholder incentives to forgo new profitable investments when previously issued debt is supported by the existing assets and the option to undertake these investments [8, 37], and 3) bankruptcy costs associated with resolving stockholder–bondholder disputes if insolvency occurs [5, 19, 23, 24, 27, 28, 42, 48].

Third, partial ownership of the firm by an owner-manager may provide him or her an incentive to consume non-pecuniary benefits or perquisites beyond that which a manager who is the sole owner of the firm would consume [21, 23].

Agency problems result in a reduction in market value *if* the markets for financial and human capital are unable to resolve the problems costlessly. One market mechanism that can mitigate agency problems is the takeover process. An impediment to this mechanism exists in the form of the "free rider" problem (see [16]). While we discuss the "free rider" problem in detail later, our analysis focuses on the agency problems that remain unresolved after natural market forces have operated to the full extent possible. Attempts to control these residual problems yield 1) complex contracts which may partially resolve them, 2) differential yields among various types of financial instruments, and 3) complex (and possibly optimal) capital structure.

THE NATURE OF AGENCY PROBLEMS

Debtholders are assumed to be rational in anticipating agency problems and in pricing agency costs into the value of their financial claims. In this framework, it should come as no surprise that stockholders might bear the full consequences of all unresolved agency problems.

THE AGENCY PROBLEM OF INFORMATIONAL ASYMMETRY

Consider a management that seeks to finance a project by selling securities, while the true nature of the return distribution of the project is unknown to the outside market. Management possesses valuable information about the project which is unavailable to the market. If this information were revealed to the market without ambiguity, the market would value the project at V_A. Otherwise, the market is unable to distinguish this project from another *less* profitable project with a value of V_B. This is a problem of informational asymmetry. It does not imply that management has better or more information than the market, but that it possesses some information that is valuable but unavailable to the market, without which the market cannot identify the true nature of the project before it is undertaken.

This asymmetry may be resolved, at a cost, through various "signaling mechanisms." In the absence of an unambiguous signal, however, management will obtain less for securities sold than their "fair value" reflected in the true nature of project A. The difference between the "fair" price and the actual price is the agency cost associated with informational asymmetry, and it exists for the issuance of debt as well as new equity securities, provided that there is a differential probability of bankruptcy for the two projects.

It should perhaps be noted here that this particular agency problem is unique, because unlike the others, it cannot be resolved costlessly through arbitrage in the financial markets. Consequently, this problem may be more significant than the others in terms of inducing yield differentials between securities and optimal capital structure. We wish to emphasize that a going concern faces a continuing problem of informational asymmetry. The problem is not merely one of identifying the nature of new projects, but also one of identifying the nature of the current distribution of returns to the entire firm whenever additional financing is needed.

AGENCY PROBLEMS ASSOCIATED WITH DEBT FINANCING UNDER LIMITED LIABILITY

The Incentive of Stockholders to Bear Unwarranted Risk. The fact that stockholders may benefit by investing in high-risk projects is best demonstrated by considering equity as a European-type call option to buy back the entire firm from the debtholders at maturity, at an exercise price equal to the face value of the debt. The debtholders can be viewed as buying the assets of the firm and issuing the call option (equity) on these assets. It is easy to understand this if the debt is in the form of pure discount bonds so that the time to expiration of the option (equity) is the maturity date of the bonds. As (in the framework of the option pricing model of Black and Scholes [7]) the value of this call option increases with the variance of the cash flows of the underlying assets, stockholders will increase the market value of equity, at the expense of debtholders, by selecting high-risk projects. For expositional purposes, suppose that two projects with differing risks are available to the firm. If both low- and high-risk projects available to the firm have the same market value, the choice does not affect the total value of the firm. It affects only the distribution of the value between bondholders and stockholders. Rational bondholders recognize the investment alternatives and stockholder risk incentives, and thus offer a price for the debt that reflects the distribution of wealth given adoption of the high-variance project. In any case, because both projects command the same value, no cost is incurred by either party.

The situation is more serious, however, if the high-variance project commands a lower market value, say $9 as opposed to $10 for the low-variance project. Suppose that for a given face value and coupon, the price of debt is $5 if priced in accordance with the adoption of the superior (but low-risk) project but $3 if priced with the presumption that the inferior (but high-risk) project is adopted. If bondholders have no means of neutralizing the stockholder incentive for risk shifting, they would presume that the inferior (but higher-risk) project will be adopted, and hence offer a price of $3. Unlike the previous case, the price reflects not only the higher-risk from which equityholders benefit but also the inferiority of the project in terms of current value. If stockholders wish to finance the superior project, they will lose, because the bond price will go up to $5 from $3, and commensurately the stock price will decline from $6 to $5. Thus, they are forced to adopt the inferior project with a value differential of $1. This differential is an agency cost which, on the surface, appears to be borne by stockholders.

The Incentive of Stockholders to Forgo Profitable Investments. This case considers a firm that holds an option on future investment opportunities [37]. Based on those opportunities, the firm issues debt (at time t = 0) with a face value of D which matures (at t = 2) *after* the true market value of the investments is revealed (at t = 1). This debt is *entirely* supported by future investment opportunities. At t = 1 the firm faces a decision whether to exercise the option (*i.e.,* undertake the investment). In the absence of debt financing, the firm accepts any investment for which the market value net of the required dollar investment is positive. But given the outstanding debt, stockholders maximize thier wealth by accepting an investment only if its *net* market value exceeds D. Otherwise, it is in their best interests to default. Thus, the presence of debt in the capital structure causes the firm to forgo any investments for which the (positive) net market value is lower than D. Obviously rational bondholders recognize the increased probability of default on their claims and discount it in the price they are willing to offer the firm for its bonds. Consequently, the stockholders, once again, are apparently forced to suffer the full burden of this agency cost.

Suboptimal future investments can also occur when the currently outstanding debt is issued against the currently held assets [8]. This is unlike the previous case in which debt is entirely supported by future investments. Stockholders, however, cannot capture the full benefits of future investment opportunities, because they partially accrue to bondholders in the form of a reduction in the probability of default. Consequently, investment incentives may be curtailed despite the possibility that these opportunities generate a positive net present value for the firm as a whole. As before, equityholders suffer the full burden of the associated agency cost, because bondholders are unwilling to pay for future benefits due to the moral hazard problem.

Bankruptcy Costs. It is well known that if the transfer of ownership from stockholders to bondholders under default is costless, the mere possibility of bankruptcy should have no impact on the capital structure decision [3, 4, 13, 18, 33, 45]. Since it is impossible, though, to write contracts which specify, clearly and unambiguously, the rights of claimholders under all contingencies, one or more of the parties may precipitate a dispute that may be resolved in the process of formal bankruptcy proceedings. These proceedings are not cost-less; they involve a legal process which itself consumes a portion of the remaining value of the firm's assets. Moreover, the formal process of transferring ownership may disrupt the normal activities of the firm, precipitating a deterioration in long-standing customer and supplier relationships.

As significant as the costs associated with formal bankruptcy proceedings may be, they should not be confused with the costs associated with *liquidating* the firm's assets [19]. Bankruptcy and liquidation are best considered as distinct and independent events. Neither event is necessarily sufficient to trigger the other. The firm liquidates if and only if the market value of the firm as a going concern falls below its dismantled value under liquidation. Many authors have attributed the costs associated with distress sale of the assets of the firm to the event of bankruptcy [24, 27, 28, 42]. This is inappropriate, because while the proportion of debt in the capital structure affects the probability of bankruptcy, in no way does it affect the probability of liquidation. Liquidation is, in a complete sense, a mere capital budgeting decision. There is no *necessary* link between the decision to liquidate and the ability to pay off debt claims. A firm on the brink of bankruptcy should be liquidated only if the value of its assets as a going concern net of the reorganization costs is below the dismantled value under liquidation. By the same token, a non-bankrupt which fits this same test must be liquidated. At any rate, the expected value of bankruptcy costs, if any, can be said to be borne by equityholders if debt is sold to rational investors. Bankruptcy costs are identical to other agency costs in this respect.

THE AGENCY PROBLEM ASSOCIATED WITH PARTIAL OWNERSHIP WITH
CONTROLLING INTERESTS

Consider an owner-manager who uses external equity financing but retains complete control of the firm [23]. The manager behaves so as to maximize his utility from 1) money wages (which are assumed to be fixed), 2) the market value of his firm, and 3) on-the-job perquisites (which are assumed to be *inseparable* from the firm).[3] *As sole owner,* the manager fully bears the cost associated with additional perquisite consumption, and he seeks a utility maximizing combination of the rewards described above. This balance is upset,

---

[3] A good example of a "perk" of this type is expanding the owner-manager's span of control beyond the level that would maximize firm value. The manager may value the social prestige and power accompanying his position as chief executive officer and may be hesitant to delegate authority, even when it would increase the market value of the firm to do so.

however, once the manager sells a fraction of his common shares to outsiders. This is the case, because, while he continues to enjoy the full benefit of additional perquisite consumption, he bears only *his* proportional ownership fraction of the associated reduction in the value of the firm's stock.

With rational expectations, outsiders are aware of the owner-manager's incentive to increase "perk" consumption. They make unbiased estimates of the costs associated with the increased perk consumption, and they pass these costs back to the owner-manager in full, in the form of a commensurate reduction in the price they are willing to pay for the securities he initially desires to sell. The manager is left with a combination of benefits in the form of dollar wealth and perquisites that is undesirable relative to his optimal combination as sole owner. Thus, in attempting to finance the firm through sale of common stock, he suffers a welfare loss that may be described as an agency cost. A similar problem occurs if the owner-manager seeks financing through debt securities. Given limited liability, if the probability of default on the debt increases with increased perk consumption, the manager bears only a (decreasing) fraction of the associated cost. Again, however, with symmetric rationality, that portion of the costs not borne directly will be incurred when the securities are issued in the form of lowered proceeds of sale.

Agency problems have been classified in this section by their origin. A related classification emphasizes the financial asset (equity or debt) which is subject to a particular agency problem. The agency problems of equity appear under informational asymmetry and under excessive perk consumption. The agency problems of debt are associated with these as well as with risk incentives and bankruptcy problems. The fixed nature of the debt claim in conjunction with limited liability is the prime source for the risk incentive and bankruptcy problems.

MARKET SOLUTIONS TO AGENCY PROBLEMS

Here we will assess the role that well-functioning markets for capital and labor may play in reducing or eliminating the costs involved in specific agency problems. In essence, we argue that, if markets are well-functioning, sufficient pressures are present to force management to carry out decisions on the basis on the interests of all securityholders. Thus, costs arising from conflicts of interest are resolved.

THE MARKET FOR FINANCIAL CAPITAL

Agency problems associated with debt financing under limited liability may be resolved by natural forces in the capital market. Assume management seeks to maximize stockholder welfare by switching to projects characterized by relatively high variance and relatively low value. In anticipation of these decisions, the total value of the firm declines as a net result of an increase in the value of the common stock and a more than proportionate decrease in the value of the outstanding debt. It is now in the interests of bondholders to acquire controlling interest in the common stock and to make decisions that maximize *firm* value [2, 13]. In doing so, they capture a pure benefit (an arbitrage profit) from increased value.

Existing common stockholders, of course, may also force management into a decision to maximize firm value. In fact, in view of possible impediments to "market pressure" that we shall discuss, stockholders seem to have a *comparative advantage* in carrying out the process. If each individual stockholder imputes rationality to other stockholders, it is in his interests to acquire debt in the firm (at a reduced price which reflects the impending *suboptimal* investment decision) in proportion to the fractional amount of debt contained in the firm's capital structure. Once a controlling majority of stockholders have done this, management must shift to an optimal investment decision, and these rational stockholders reap arbitrage profits.

When equityholders buy up the bonds of the firm on a *pro rata* basis, debt possibly loses its economic distinction and bondholders essentially become equityholders. However, for a firm with dispersed ownership, the Internal Revenue Code recognizes the debt as legitimate, and hence tax deduction of interest payments is still intact. Moreover, as far as an owner-manager is concerned, purchasing debt in proportion to his equity share has no impact on his propensity to consume perks if the debt is riskless, and it actually reduces the propensity if the probability of default on the debt is positive.[4]

A similar arbitrage argument can be evoked in the context of the agency cost associated with bankruptcy [19]. The argument states that if the costs of *formal* reorganization are indeed significant, it is in the interest of managers to adjust to an optimal capital structure by reorganizing the firm *informally* through purchase and sale of the bonds and the stock of the firm at prevailing capital market prices. If the manager fails to do so and the market values of the securities of the firm are reduced to reflect the costs of formal bankruptcy, it is in the interests of outsiders to take over the firm and initiate an informal reorganization. This can be accomplished by buying the bonds and the stock at their discounted market values. By acquiring all the claims to the firm, the dispute can be avoided and the expected bankruptcy cost can be captured as an arbitrage profit.

THE MARKET FOR HUMAN CAPITAL

Agency problems associated with informational asymmetry and managerial perk consumption may be resolved via the operation of well-functioning markets for human capital. Consider the problem of excessive perk consumption.

---

[4] On the other hand, if investors are forced to hold fixed proportions of debt and equity, they may suffer diversification costs as their portfolios deviate from the desired, utility-maximizing, weights.

This problem must be of no consequence if the managerial labor market is efficient in the sense that the managerial wage reflects an unbiased estimate of his expected marginal product. In this case, the present value of the manager's future wages adjusts fully to reflect "shirking" or excessive perk consumption. In such an efficient labor market, the adjustment in the manager's wage provides for a full *ex post* settling up, so that the manager is disciplined to behave in the optimal interests of the firm [12].

It doesn't seem to be widely recognized that discipline in this form by the labor market provides a solution to the problem of informational asymmetry as well. In this case, the manager has a problem of communicating the true nature of the firm without moral hazard. If the manager fully suffers the consequences of attempts to deceive the market through changes in the value of his human capital, the moral hazard problem disappears. This may explain why managers want the Board of Directors to verify their honesty. The Board may be viewed as improving the functioning of labor markets in resolving the problem of informational asymmetry. Therefore, in the presence of a well-functioning labor market, managers are motivated to tell the truth with or without a specific managerial incentive compensation scheme that is tied to bankruptcy such as discussed in [39]. Thus, the link between financial structure and informational asymmetry disappears.

IMPEDIMENTS TO SPONTANEOUS MARKET SOLUTIONS OF AGENCY PROBLEMS

Impediments may exist which serve to block a natural and costless resolution to agency problems in the *capital* market. Consider first the agency problem associated with excessive perk consumption by an owner-manager. It would seem at first that outsiders are in a position to capture an arbitrage profit by purchasing all the securities of the firm and replacing the owner with a manager who will run the firm to maximize shareholder wealth. It must be remembered, however, that in order to surrender his controlling interest in the firm, the owner-manager demands compensation, over and above the fair market value of his securities, for his "managerial rights." Recall, that the manager derives utility from perk consumption as well as from the dollar wealth represented by his security holdings. Moreover, the combined utility from both exceeds the utility he can derive from reducing perk consumption to zero and maximizing the value of the firm. Consequently, he will not surrender the firm at a price that reflects this maximized value, and hence the natural capital market mechanism is impeded.

The nature of the personal income tax may also impede the market mechanism. Capital gains are taxed when realized and, if the market value of the stock has appreciated, a controlling majority of stockholders may be locked into their existing investment in the firm. By holding their shares they are in effect benefiting from an interest-free loan from the government (the capital gains tax they do not have to pay) and they will demand a price for their stock that is higher than the prevailing equilibrium market price in order to surrender this benefit. One may counter this argument with an assumption of unlimited short selling, but it is difficult to imagine how one can force a takeover of *controlling interest* in the shares of the firm even when the potential acquirer is aided by additional supply brought on by short selling.

This impediment is not as effective in blocking market mechanisms as solutions to the agency problems of debt associated with bankruptcy. The securityholders of a bankrupt firm are likely to have already suffered accrued capital losses, and hence they are not "locked in" in terms of taxes.

Still another impediment to the threat of takeover, which underlies many of the market solutions to agency problems, is implied by the "free rider" problem [16, 17]. In a standard definition, a free rider is one who benefits from actions or costs borne by others. In other words, a free rider gets a "free lunch," so to speak. In the context of this paper, a free rider is an individual who attempts to benefit at the expense of his fellow securityholders by blocking a process which is in the general interests of all parties. It is not surprising that free riders themselves are discouraged through the legislative and judicial process. Consider the case where the takeover process is initiated by an outsider, say another firm. Suppose the target firm's bankruptcy is imminent and that the total value of all securities of the firm reflects the expected costs of formal bankruptcy. Corporate charters commonly provide for acceptance of merger bids by majority vote of existing stockholders. Free riders can be prevented from blocking the takeover process by tendering an offer to existing stockholders at a slight premium over the prevailing market price. A controlling majority of stockholders need only respond favorably to the offer in order to formally merge the two firms. In legal terms, minority stockholders may now be "cashed out" of the arrangement on the basis of the market value of the firm prior to merger. In fact, if one assumes that the capital market functions perfectly, it is in the interest of securityholders to write corporate charters that severely restrict the ability of shareholders to "free ride." By allowing successful raiders to "cash out" free riders at unfavorable terms, securityholders increase the probability of attempted takeovers, and motivate existing management to maximize the value of the firm and thus reduce agency costs.

On the other hand, if the market for takeovers is not perfectly competitive, such charters may not be optimal, as they may reduce the expected value of the takeover bid. The importance of the "free rider" problem thus hinges on the functioning of the capital market. It is worth noting that an unimpeded operation of the takeover mechanism is the cornerstone of all financial theories which produce valuation models based on the elimination of arbitrage profits. In this regard, the importance of the "free rider" problem as an impediment in the capital market extends beyond the issue of agency problems.

Impediments may also block managerial discipline arising from the market for *human capital*. For example, senior corporate officers are usually not individuals in the early stages of their career. If retirement is a relatively short period away, a *simple* contract which specifies the manager's wage as his expected marginal product may be inappropriate to ensure a complete *ex post* marginal products may be required. In addition, a complete *ex post* settling up. A more complex contract which makes the manager's retirement benefits a function of his *ex post* settling up for a wage readjustment depends on perfect and costless information in the labor market on past performance of each and every executive. If such information is not available, or if it is costly, firms may err in assessing managers, and a complete *ex post* settling up is no longer achieved for managers who change employers. Finally, we note the difficulty in assessing top level management given the sweeping impact of their decisions on corporate performance. It is possible that the magnitude and variability of corporate performance measures may not allow for meaningful estimation of managers' excessive perk consumption. In this case, managers are able to consume perks without the threat of an accompanying loss in the value of their human capital.

In the face of these impediments, one must admit some possibility of a blockage to natural resolution of agency problems by markets.

AGENCY PROBLEMS AND OPTIMAL CAPITAL STRUCTURE

Marginal agency costs of debt are commonly considered to be an increasing function of the amount of debt employed in the capital structure. This is true in the case of bandruptcy, as the expected marginal costs associated with bankruptcy depend on the probability of bankruptcy, which is an increasing function of the amount of debt relative to equity. In terms of the risk incentive and the forgone growth opportunities problems, *marginal* agency costs of debt depend on the investment opportunity set facing the firm. For the risk incentive problem [15] this is immediately observed by ordering projects according to their net market value and level of risk. The change in net market value which is associated with a shift to a higher risk project will determine the magnitude of marginal agency costs.

On the other hand, if debt is used to signal the true nature of the firm [39] an increase in the amount of debt may *reduce* the agency costs associated with informational asymmetry. The rate of reduction, *i.e.*, the marginal agency costs associated with informational asymmetry, depends on the distribution of capital structures among firms which remain undistinugished by the market. This distribution determines the signaling value of marginal units of debt which are used to identify the true value of the firm.

These relationships between the agency costs of debt and the amount of debt give rise to an optimal capital structure in three distinct ways. *First*, agency costs (in particular bankruptcy costs) may serve as an offset against the tax advantage of debt financing, and hence the corner solution (99.99 . . .% debt in capital structure) implied by the traditional Modigliani–Miller [34] tax-adjusted valuation model breaks down. The interior optimum arises from the tradeoff between the tax subsidy which is an increasing function (at a decreasing rate) of the amount of debt employes and the agency costs which are also an increasing fuction (at an increasing rate) of the amount of debt. *Second,* an optimal capital structure can result from the tradeoff between agency costs of debt on the one hand and agency costs of equity on the other hand, even in a taxless world. *Third,* a positive theory of capital structure can emerge in the process of signaling to the market the true nature of the firm when there is informational asymmetry.

THE TRADEOFF BETWEEN TAX SAVINGS AND BANKRUPTCY COSTS

For some 15 years, agency costs in the form of bankruptcy costs have been offered as a link between observed firm debt policies and the Modigliani–Miller theorem under corporate taxes. The MM theorem depicted in Figure 1 predicts that the value of the levered firm, V_L, increases linearly with debt, D, so as to

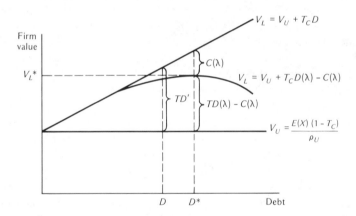

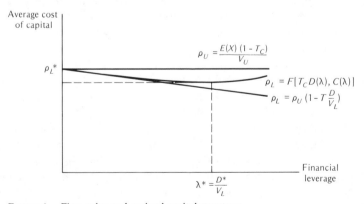

FIGURE 1.   Firm value and optimal capital structure.

exceed the value of the unlevered (but otherwise equivalent) firm by a tax subsidy, $T_C D$, where T_C is the marginal corporate tax rate uniform across all corporations. Thus this theorem leads to a corner solution in which a nearly 100% debt/value ratio is desirable. Given possibility of costly bankruptcy, however, an optimal capital structure obtains when the present value of expected tax savings is offset at the margin by the present value of expected incremental bankruptcy costs [5, 25, 27, 42]. Assuming that bankruptcy costs exist, the value of the firm, V_L, is shown in Figure 1 as a concave function of the amount of debt employed. The present value of expected bankruptcy costs, C, is an increasing function (at an *increasing* rate) of the financial leverage, λ, while the tax subsidy $T_C D(\lambda)$ is also increasing with D. These phenomena manifest themselves in both the value and the cost of capital of the firm. At the optimum, the level of debt, D*, maximizes the value of the firm (V*) or equivalently minimizes the cost of capital ($\rho_L{}^*$).

It should be noted here that this tradeoff results in an (interior) optimal capital structure regardless of the magnitude of bankruptcy costs. This is true because, even if these costs are small, at some finite degree of leverage the present values of expected bankruptcy cost and the expected value of the tax subsidy may offset each other at the margin. However, the preceding arguments have been employed in order to reconcile existing financial theory with contemporary financial structures for observed firms. In the context of the actual probabilities of default, and the models employed by those advocating a bankruptcy cost–tax subsidy tradeoff, one must allege that the costs associated with bankruptcy are large. Limited efforts have been made to document their magnitude [48], but in any case the *traditional* arguments concerning bankruptcy costs and the tax subsidy rest on a significant breakdown of the arbitrage process described earlier. However, as we shall see below, if one evokes arguments pursuant to an equilibrium [31] in which bond yields are grossed up to reflect the tax advantage of debt at the corporate level, one *begins* from a position of indifference to debt *vis-à-vis* equity financing. This being the case, even an expected agency cost which is relatively small can result in an optimal capital structure, assuming that transaction costs associated with search for an optimal capital structure are negligible. However, it is still the case that agency costs of small magnitude have low impact on the *value of the firm*.

THE TRADEOFF BETWEEN AGENCY COSTS OF DEBT AND AGENCY COSTS OF EQUITY

It would seem that, in a taxless world with agency problems of debt financing, we should have a corner solution to the capital structure decision in which equity financing dominates debt. This view is limited, because it ignores the possibility that equity financing may be characterized by significant agency costs. Agency problems of informational asymmetry and managerial perquisite consumption are endemic to equity financing as well. Capital structure policies that merely substitute equity for debt are trading off agency costs of debt against agency costs of equity [23].

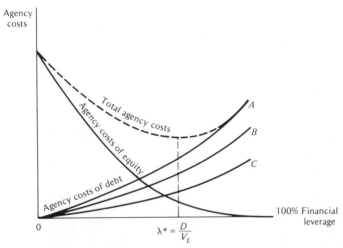

FIGURE 2.   Optimal capital structure with agency costs of equity and debt. A = bankruptcy costs; B = investment incentive costs; C = risk incentive costs.

The tradeoff is depicted in Figure 2 in which marginal agency costs of equity and debt are shown as rising functions of equity and debt, respectively. It is no longer necessary that debt financing have a tax advantage for an optimal capital structure. The advantage here is the reduction in the agency cost of equity. This advantage is offset at the margin by the incremental disadvantage of debt financing in the form of its own agency costs. In Figure 2 the optimum, λ^*, is reached when the present value of the sum of the expected agency costs of equity and debt is minimized. Thus, agency costs alone without tax considerations may give rise to an optimal capital structure.

FINANCIAL SIGNALING AND OPTIMAL CAPITAL STRUCTURE

Various signaling mechanisms may be used to resolve the problem of informational asymmetry. The capital structure itself may be used as a signaling device to convey, without moral hazard, the true nature of the projects (firms). For instance, a proper role of financial structure as a signal can be ensured through a managerial incentive schedule with an associated penalty tied to the occurrency of bankruptcy [39]. The "bankruptcy" penalty, which is built into the schedule, ensures a truthful signal by a manager who behaves rationally. The incentive problem associated with managerial announcements relating to firm profitability is resolved. In this framework, debt financing allows firms to signal the quality of their projects. For a firm with superior projects, additional debt financing is beneficial as it reduces the costs associated with informational asymmetry.

Another approach asserts that the entrepreneur's fractional equity ownership signals his personal evaluation of the project [29]. It is argued that there exists an optimal fractional ownership that correctly signals the true return stream of the project. This mechanism requires a prespecified schedule depicting the expected return on the project as a function of the entrepreneur's fractional ownership and an assumption that his utility function is known to the market.

While in the first two explanations of optimal capital structure the relationship between the capital structure and the value of the firm is *causal,* the signaling explanation suggests merely a *statistical* relationship. In the latter case, if financial structure serves as a signal, the value of the firm would respond to changes in financial structure caused by a change in the market's *perceptions* and not because of a *real* change in the return stream.

COMPLEX FINANCIAL CONTRACTS AS SOLUTIONS TO AGENCY PROBLEMS

The failure of markets to provide complete and costless solutions to agency problems suggests that a class of securityholders may require additional assurances against possible expropriation of their wealth by another class. Such assurances, and a commensurate reduction in agency costs, can be obtained through complex financial (and management compensation) contracts. Our discussion of the role of complex financial contracts in reducing agency costs covers call provisions, conversion privileges, income bonds, and the maturity structure of debt. By no means is this list exhaustive. For instance, we do not discuss avenues such as debt renegotiations or leasing arrangements which may be useful in resolving agency problems of debt financing.

The notion that complex contracts evolve in order to reduce agency problems has the potential to explain many real world contractual arrangements. The literature includes analyses of bond covenants (e.g., contractual limitations on managers' incentive to take unwarranted risk) as a means of reducing the agency problems associated with risk incentives. Management compensation contracts are known as examples of arrangements that are beneficial in reducing agency problems when labor markets fail to provide appropriate solutions. Corporate bylaws include provisions that limit minority stockholders' options to block prospective takeovers or to act as "free riders" as discussed earlier.

CALL PROVISIONS IN CORPORATE DEBT

The call provision can be explained as a means of resolving the agency problems associated with informational asymmetry and risk incentives.[5] Consider

---

[5] It should be pointed out that, with respect to all the agency problems discussed above, shortening the maturity of the debt accomplishes the same task as the call strategy does. The issues of debt maturity structure and call provisions belong to the same family in that both are alternative solutions to specific agency problems [2].

first the case of informational asymmetry. Managers know that the firm is worth $V(A)$; the market, however, is uncertain about the firm's worth and hence is unable to distinguish it from the worth of an alternative firm, $V(B)$, where $V(B) < V(A)$. Management seeks to finance the firm with debt maturing in T periods. The true nature of the firm will be revealed to the market at some point prior to T. If the debt is risky, it must be sold in the market at less than its true value. The agency cost associated with the asymmetry is $V_D(A) - V_D(B)$, where $V_D(\cdot)$ is the market value of the debt, given the information set.

Management can mitigate the agency cost by attaching a call provision which provides the right to repurchase the bond at a specified price at a point in time immediately following the point at which the true nature of the firm is revealed. Thus, the stockholders of the firm take a long position in the call option and a short position in the debt. Note that the market undervalues both the call option and the debt, because they are both valued with the presumption that the value of firm is $V(B)$. The stockholders suffer a cost in amount $V_D(A) - V_D(B)$, but they recapture it, in part, through the undervaluation of the call option, $V_C(A) - V_C(B)$, where $V_C(A)$ and $V_C(B)$ are the values of call provisions associated with $V(A)$ and (B), respectively. The partial recapture is possible because of a lag in the revelation of the true nature of the firm. The call is effective in mitigating the transfer of wealth, however, only to the extent that the true nature of the firm is revealed prior to the maturity date of the debt. If the maturity and revelation dates coincide, there will be no recapture of the agency cost.

The call provision can also be used to eliminate the incentive to shift to high-risk (but low-value) investments in order to transfer wealth from bondholders to stockholders. In the absence of a call provision, the shift to a high-risk investment may reduce the total value of the firm but may alter the relative values of debt and equity such that the value of equity is actually greater after the shift. The prescence of a call option may eliminate the incentive entirely, because the value of this option declines with the value of the debt. Given that stockholders have a long position in this option, the option may be designed so that the decline in its value more than offsets the increase in the value of the stock that would take place. In this way, the risk incentive problem is neutralized, and the agency cost disappears.

The call provision may also be used to eliminate the incentive to forgo otherwise profitable investment opportunities. If the debt matures after the future investment decision is to be made, the benefits of the decision partly accrue to debtholders by a reduction in the probability of default and a corresponding increase in the value of the debt. This benefit may once again be recaptured by attaching a call provision to be debt, which gives management the right to recall the debt at a stated price at the time when the investment decision is made.

While callable debt may not restore the value of the firm to the value which exists under all equity financing, the issuance of callable debt can be shown to dominate the issuance of non-callable debt [8]. It should be noted that call provisions may also resolve the agency problems associated with forgone growth opportunities if the debt issued is supported entirely by these opportunities [2, 37].

CONVERTIBLE SECURITIES

Convertible securities may reduce agency problems associated with excessive perk consumption by an owner–manager. Suppose the manager sells a fraction $(1 - \alpha)$ of the stock to outsiders, and he retains a fraction α of the stock for himself. The change in the manager's wealth, VW, in response to a change in the value of the firm, V, is now given by $\dfrac{\partial Vw}{\partial V} + \alpha$, and the smaller α, the less the effect of his perk consumption on his own *monetary* wealth. The manager, though, can align his own interests with those of external securityholders if he raises capital by offering to outside capital contributors the following financial instruments.

The manager holds a positive position in a call option along with his positive position in α% of the outstanding common stock. He holds a negative position in a put option which is to be held long by outsiders. If the manager increases consumption of perks, he will a) decrease the value of his common stock, b) decrease the value of his call option, and c) increase the value of the put option which can be viewed as the manager's liability. The options can be designed so that the following condition holds: $\partial VW/\partial V = \alpha + \partial V_c/\partial V - \partial V_p/\partial V = 1$, where V_c and V_p are the values of the call and the put options, respectively. In this sense the manager's incentive to consume perks is restored to that of his original position as sole owner. Outsiders will recognize that the manager will consume perks at a level consistent with that of sole ownership, and hence price the securities accordingly. Once again the agency cost is reduced.

It should be apparent that if the contract is *continuously* readjusted, outside capital contributors end up holding a riskless position in the firm. However, the solution does not call for continuous readjustments. The contract may be viewed as a solution to the single-period world of Jensen and Meckling in which decisions relating to investment, financing, and the nature of the productive process are made simultaneously at the beginning of the period and are not altered throughout the productive period. Moreover, the contract is readily generalizable to a multiperiod framework where *discrete* time readjustments of contractual positions are feasible, given that the productive decisions and the corresponding incentive problems occur through discrete time.

While the issuance of stock options may be used to resolve the agency problem associated with the consumption of perquisites, stock options may create an incentive for the manager to engage in either high- or low-risk investment programs. This incentive problem is analogous to the wealth transfer problem associated with the existence of risky debt in the capital structure. It can be shown, however, that the stock options can be designed so as to simultaneously solve the problems associated with perk consumption and risk-taking [21].

The put–call financial package may seem unusual, but it actually represents a financial strategy that is often observed. The use of the call option is analogous to the actual use of executive stock options in managerial compensation. The put option, in combination with the fraction of the stock held by the outsiders, can be thought of as a surrogate for the convertible bond. If the terminal value of the firm exceeds the exercise price of the put, the put is worthless, and the outsiders remain as common stockholders holding a fractional interest in the common stock of the firm. This outcome represents conversion of the bond into a fractional interest in the firm's common stock. If, on the other hand, the firm value falls below the exercise price, the outsiders exercise their claim and sell the firm to the manager at the exercise price. This represents the case where conversion is unprofitable and bondholders exercise their fixed claim.

INCOME BONDS

The agency cost associated with bankruptcy may also call for the issuance of a complex debt instrument [31]. The obvious analogue of this complexity in the context of bankruptcy problems is the issuance of income bonds. Interest payments on these bonds are required only if earned. Income bonds can, however, trigger bankruptcy at maturity from the firm's failure to meet principal payments. Perpetual income bonds would seem to satisfy this deficiency, but, even prior to maturity, income bonds can trigger technical default if available cash is incommensurate with current earning and hence is insufficient to meet current interest payments. Income bonds are rarely issued by firms, possibly because 1) they are unable to fully resolve bankruptcy problems, and 2) natural market mechanisms are relatively efficient in resolving these problems.

Unlike income bonds, interest on conventional coupon bonds is payable irrespective of the level of current earnings, or default would occur. Because each coupon payment can be regarded as a bond, there is a higher probability of bankruptcy with conventional bonds than with income bonds. Income bonds are similar to preferred stock, but, unlike the latter, they carry the tax benefit of interest payment deduction.

THE EFFECT OF AGENCY PROBLEMS ON EQUILIBRIUM PRICING IN FINANCIAL MARKETS

Miller [32] has extended the notion of tax-induced differential returns into a general equilibrium framework in which firms adjust the amount of bonds offered in response to differential yields on equity and debt. He shows that, in the presence of the corporate income tax subsidy on debt financing, yields on corporate debt are "grossed up" to reflect the tax subsidy in such a way as to cause individual firms to be indifferent between debt and equity financing. There is, nonetheless, an economy-wide optimal debt outstanding. As a direct result of the equilibrating process, the tax subsidy that is shifted away from the stockholders is captured by bondholders in the form of increased yields on corporate debt.

This equilibrium can be explained in terms of Figure 3, which plots *certainty equivalent* interest rates on the vertical axis and quantities of total corporate debt demanded and supplied on the horizontal axis. Assume two types of securities are available: common stock whose returns are tax-exempt and bonds whose returns are taxable at varying rates. The certainty equivalent return on common stock is given by r^*. Tax-exempt institutions may exist that are willing to demand corporate debt as an investment in aggregate amount D'' at a certainty equivalent rate equal to that available on common stock. Additional demand, stemming from investment by individual investors in progressively higher tax brackets, can be generated by offering progressively higher yields on corporate bonds. The upward sloping demand curve reflects the progressive nature of the personal income tax.

The supply curve for corporate debt is horizontal at a rate of interest equal to $r^* (1 - \tau_c)$ where τ_c is the corporate income tax rate, which is presumed to be uniform. The supply curve is horizontal, because corporations are assumed to be wealth maximizers, and because the corporate tax rate is uniform across all corporations. Consequently, if the yield on corporate debt falls slightly below $r^*/(1 - \tau_c)$, it is in the interest of all wealth maximizing firms to finance their investments entirely with debt. On the other hand, if the yield rises slightly above $r^*/(1 - \tau_c)$, corporate debt completely disappears from the mar-

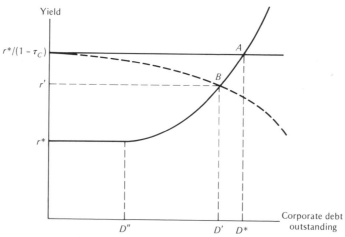

FIGURE 3. Equilibrium in corporate bond market.

ket. The horizontal supply curve intersects the upward-sloping demand curve at A, and the equilibrium yield is given by $r^*/(1 - \tau_c)$. At this rate individual firms are indifferent between issuing debt or equity to finance their investments.

The Miller equilibrium follows only in the absence of agency problems associated with debt financing. If agency costs are not completely resolved by natural market forces, it can be shown [1, 10] that they will manifest themselves in yield differentials between securities which differ in terms of their inherent ability to resolve the problems. To illustrate this point, suppose that equity financing involves no agency cost, but that debt financing involves firm-specific agency costs which increase with the relative amount of debt in the capital structure. If firms face agency costs of this type, they are no longer indifferent between equity and debt financing when debt yields $r^*/(1 - \tau_c)$, and the supply curve is no longer horizontal. For each rate of interest on corporate debt, $r_c < r^*/(1 - \tau_c)$, firms increase the amount of debt in their capital structures until the agency cost as a percent of marginal debt financed, $\theta(D)$, is equal to $r^*/(1 - \tau_c) - r_c$. As long as rates are lower, it pays each firm to issue more debt so that aggregate supply is increased. Every point on the broken, downward-sloping supply curve of Figure 3 represents the quantity of debt supplied as firms optimize their capital structures. As the interest rate on corporate debt falls, there is a general increase across all firms in the optimal amount of debt in capital structures. Equilibrium occurs at B, the intersection of the upward-sloping demand curve with the downward-sloping supply curve.

Unlike the Miller equilibrium, optimal capital structures exist for individual firms as well as for the corporate sector as a whole as denoted by D'. While the analysis here is carried out in terms of pure debt and equity instruments, the analysis may be generalized to equilibrium yield differentials and optimal capital structure proportions involving a wide variety of financial contracts.

The expected value of the agency costs need not be large to induce complexity in financial contracts and optimal capital structure. In the absence of agency problems, management faces alternative contracts and capital structures with indifference. The presence of even minor residual costs associated with agency problems may serve to explain the complexity of capital structure, as managers attempt to balance these costs with yield differentials on alternative contracts. Thus, it is possible to observe corporations engaging in capital structure decisions even if markets are reasonably (but not strictly) proficient in disciplining managers to act in the interest of all securityholders. The effect of financial decisions on the value of the firm may be *insignificant* but still *sufficient* to explain a) why corporations engage in capital structure decision-making, b) complexities in financial contracts, and c) clustering of capital structure characteristics by industry so long as there are no costs involved in financial contracting.

Another property of our equilibrium relates to a sharing of the agency costs among the securityholders. It is apparent from Figure 3 that the agency costs associated with debt financing may be shifted to the bondholders in the form of reduced equilibrium yields on corporate debt. This conclusion stands in direct contradiction to the long held point of view that stockholders bear the agency costs of debt financing. The reader should recall that the belief that stockholders reap the tax subsidy associated with debt financing was also long held, until Miller's equilibrium analysis showed that the tax subsidy, like the agency cost, is shifted to bondholders.

We emphasize that this equilibrium analysis is still partial in the sense that the equity rate of return is taken as given. This is similar to the Jensen–Meckling [23] agency cost incidence analysis where the interest rate (state prices) for bond payoffs is taken as given. Obviously, any definite statement regarding the final incidence of agency costs and debt tax subsidy must rely on a general equilibrium analysis where the rate of return on equity is endogenously determined.

POLICY IMPLICATIONS OF THE SHIFTING OF AGENCY COSTS

Agency costs are real factor costs that affect production decisions. Optimal resource allocation in the economy requires that firms act to reduce agency costs up to the level where the marginal costs associated with the reduction are equal to the marginal benefits. If the agency costs associated with debt financing are shifted to bondholders, what are the benefits associated with reducing agency costs to those who control production and financing decisions?

Consider Figure 4 which depicts the realtionship between marginal and average agency costs as a function of the amount of debt in the capital structure of an individual firm. Given a particular (certainty-equivalent) rate of interest on corporate debt, one can compute the differential, θ^*, between this

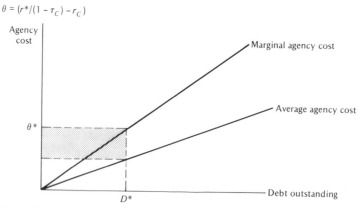

FIGURE 4. Determination of the Financiers' Surplus.

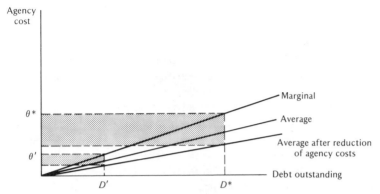

FIGURE 5. Determination of the Financiers' Surplus.

rate and the rate required to induce debt financing in the absence of agency costs $r^*/(1 - \tau_c)$. The differential, θ^*, may be interpreted as the benefit of debt financing associated with the tax subsidy. The individual firm issues debt until the marginal agency cost associated with the last unit of debt issued is equal to this (constant) marginal benefit. The amount of debt issued is thus D^*, and the stockholders of the firm gain a surplus associated with debt financing which is represented by the shared area of Figure 4.

Suppose that the firm now acts to reduce its agency costs by introducing some mechanism by which its management can be costlessly monitored by securityholders. Presume also that this mechanism cannot be imitated by other firms. In this case, the agency costs of debt financing are reduced, as represented in Figure 5, and the magnitude of the financiers' surplus is increased as long as the differential θ^* remains intact. In this case, stockholders have an incentive to institute the monitoring activity.

Suppose, instead, that the monitoring mechanism is easily imitated by other firms. Note that this represents a departure from our initial assumption that individual firms are price takers in the capital market. The adoption of the new mechanism by all firms will shift the supply curve of Figure 3 upward in the direction of the horizontal supply curve at $r^*/(1 - \tau_c)$. The equilibrium rate of interest on corporate debt rises to reflect the diminished importance of the agency problems. Consequently, the differential, θ^*, falls to some level θ'. The change in the magnitude of the financiers' surplus is determined by two offsetting effects: The reduction in agency costs, which increases the surplus, and the reduction in the yield differential, which decreases the surplus. As was shown in [1], the dollar change in the surplus depends on the elasticities of the demand and supply curves for corporate debt. It is possible that the surplus will fall below its initial level of Figure 5. In this special case, stockholders are actually penalized by introducing the costless monitoring mechanism.

It would seem that stockholder incentives to reduce agency problems are related to the speed at which other firms can imitate the financial innovation. Most financial innovations are easily imitated by other firms, which would seem to be true especially for modifications in generally accepted accounting principles. Accounting is one of many monitoring systems that may serve to reduce agency problems. It would appear that, as acceptance of modifications in this system is by definition widespread, improvements in accounting designed solely to increase its effectiveness in monitoring management may not be in the interest of managers attempting to maximize stockholder wealth, even if these modifications are *costless*. This same point would seem to hold for some government regulations of the securities markets such as prospectus requirements, full disclosure provisions, and mandatory provisions in indentures associated with debt financing. One may expect to see managerial opposition to these requirements even if such requirements are considered desirable on the basis of social costs and benefits.

CONCLUSION

Agency problems derive from conflicts of interest between individuals associated with the firm. Many of these conflicts can be resolved in a spontaneous and costless fashion by the markets for financial and human capital. If frictions exist in these markets, however, the agency problems may give rise to potential costs.

These costs can be minimized through complex contractual arrangements between the parties in conflict. Thus, agency problems may explain the evolution of complexities in capital structure such as conversion and call privileges in corporate debt. Financial contracts which differ in terms of their inherent ability to resolve agency problems may sell at differential equilibrium prices or yields in the market place. The financial manager reaches an optimal capital structure when, at the margin for each class of contract, the costs associated with agency problems are balanced by the benefits associated with existing yeild differentials and tax exposure.

REFERENCES

1. A. Barnea, R. Haugen, and L. Senbet, "An Equilibrium Analysis of Debt Financing Under Costly Tax Arbitrage and Agency Problems," forthcoming in the *Journal of Finance* (June 1981).
2. A. Barnea, R. Haugen, and L. Senbet, "A Rationale for Debt Maturity Structure and Call Provisions in the Agency Theoretic Framework," *Journal of Finance* (December 1980), pp. 1223–1234.
3. D. Baron, "Default Risk, Home-made Leverage, and the Modigliani–Miller Theorem," *American Economic Review* (March 1974), pp. 176–182.

4. D. Baron, "Default Risk and the Modigliani–Miller Theorem: A Synthesis," *American Economic Review* (March 1976), pp. 204–212.
5. N. Baxter, "Leverage, Risk of Ruin and the Cost of Capital," *Journal of Finance* (September 1967), pp. 395–404.
6. S. Bhattacharya, "Imperfect Information, Dividend Policy, and the 'Bird in the Hand' Fallacy," *Bell Journal of Economics* (Spring 1979), pp. 259–270.
7. F. Black and M. Scholes, "The Pricing of Options and Corporate Liabilities," *Journal of Political Economy* (May-June 1973), pp. 637–654.
8. Z. Bodie and R. Taggart, "Future Investment Opportunities and the Value of the Call Provision on a Bond," *Journal of Finance* (September 1978), pp. 1187–1200.
9. W. Boyce and A. Kalotay, "Tax Differentials and Callable Bonds," *Journal of Finance* (September 1979), pp. 825–838.
10. H. DeAngelo and R. Masulis, "Optimal Capital Structure Under Corporate and Personal Taxation," *Journal of Financial Economics* (March 1980), pp. 3–30.
11. E. Elton and M. Gruber, "The Economic Value of the Call Option," *Journal of Finance* (September 1972), pp. 891–901.
12. E. Fama, "Agency Problems and the Theory of the Firm," *Journal of Political Economy* (April 1980), pp. 288–307.
13. E. Fama, "The Effects of a Firm's Investment and Financing Decisions on the Welfare of its Security Holders," *American Economic Review* (June 1978), pp. 272–284.
14. E. Fama and M. Miller, *The Theory of Finance,* New York, Holt, Rinehart and Winston, 1972.
15. D. Galai and R. Masulis, "The Option Pricing Model and the Risk Factor of Stock," *Journal of Financial Economics* (January-March 1976), pp. 53–81.
16. S. Grossman and O. Hart, "Take-Over Bids, The Free-Rider Problem and the Theory of the Corporation," *Bell Journal of Economics* (Spring 1980), pp. 42–64.
17. S. Grossman and J. Stiglitz, "On Value Maximization and Alternative Objectives of the Firm," *Journal of Finance* (May 1977), pp. 389–402.
18. K. Hagen, "Default Risk, Home-made Leverage, and the Modigliani–Miller Theorem: A Note," *American Economic Review* (March 1976), pp. 199–203.
19. R. Haugen and L. Senbet, "The Insignificance of Bankruptcy Costs to the Theory of Optimal Capital Structure," *Journal of Finance* (May 1978), pp. 383–393.
20. R. Haugen and L. Senbet, "New Perspectives on Informational Asymmetry and Agency Relationships," *Journal of Financial and Quantitative Analysis* (November 1979), pp. 671–694.
21. R. Haugen and L. Senbet, "Resolving the Agency Problems of External Capital through Stock Options," forthcoming in the *Journal of Finance.*

22. R. Higgins and L. Schall, "Corporate Bankruptcy and Conglomerate Merger," *Journal of Finance* (March 1975), pp. 93–113.
23. M. Jensen and W. Meckling, "Theory of the Firm: Managerial Behavior, Agency Costs and Ownership Structure," *Journal of Financial Economics* (October 1976), pp. 305–360.
24. E. Kim, "A Mean–Variance Theory of Optimal Capital Structure and Corporate Debt Capacity," *Journal of Fiannce* (March 1978), pp. 45–64.
25. E. Kim, W. Lewellen, and J. McConnell, "Financial Leverage Clienteles: Theory and Evidence," *Journal of Financial Economics* (March 1979), pp. 83–109.
26. A. Kraus, "The Bond Refunding Decision in an Efficient Market," *Journal of Financial and Quantitative Analysis* (December 1973), pp. 793–806.
27. A. Kraus and R. Litzenberger, "A State-Preference Leverage," *Journal of Finance* (September 1973), pp. 911–922.
28. W. Lee and H. Barker, "Bankruptcy Costs and the Firm's Optimal Debt Capacity: A Positive Theory of Capital Structure," *Southern Economic Journal* (April 1977), pp. 1453–1465.
29. H. Leland and D. Pyle, "Informational Asymmetries, Financial Structure, and Financial Intermediation," *Journal of Finance* (May 1977), pp. 371–387.
30. J. McCulloch, "The Tax-Adjusted Yield Curve," *Journal of Finance* (June 1975), pp. 811–830.
31. M. Miller, "Debt and Taxes," *Journal of Finance* (May 1977), pp. 261–275.
32. M. Miller and M. Scholes, "Dividends and Taxes," *Journal of Financial Economics* (March 1978), pp. 333–364.
33. F. Milne, "Choice Over Assets Economies: Default Risk and Corporate Leverage," *Journal of Financial Economics* (June 1975), pp. 165–185.
34. F. Modigliani and M. Miller, "Corporation Income Taxes and the Cost of Captial: A Correction," *American Economic Review* (June 1963), pp. 433–443.
35. F. Modigliani and M. Miller, "The Cost of Capital, Corporation Finance, and the Theory of Investment," *American Economic Review* (June 1958), pp. 261–297.
36. F. Modigliani and R. Sutch, "Innovations in Interest Rates Policy," *American Economic Review* (May 1966), pp. 178–197.
37. S. Myers, "Determinants of Corporate Borrowing," *Journal of Financial Economics* (November 1977), pp. 147–176.
38. G. Pye, "The Value of Call Deferment on a Bond: Some Empirical Results," *Journal of Finance* (December 1967), pp. 623–636.
39. S. Ross, "The Determination of Financial Structure: The Incentive–Signalling Approach," *The Bell Journal of Economics* (Spring 1977), pp. 23–40.

40. S. Ross, "The Economic Theory of Agency: The Principal's Problem," *American Economic Review* (May 1973), pp. 134–139.
41. S. Ross, "Some Notes on Financial Incentive–Signalling Models," *Journal of Finance* (June 1978), pp. 777–792.
42. J. Scott, "A Theory of Optimal Capital Structure," *Bell Journal of Economics* (Spring 1976), pp. 33–54.
43. C. Smith and J. Warner, "On Financial Contracting: An Analysis of Bond Covenants," *Journal of Financial Economics* (June 1979), pp. 117–161.
44. M. Spence, *Market Signalling: Information Transfer in Hiring and Related Processes,* Cambridge, Harvard University Press, 1974.
45. J. Stiglitz, "On the Irrelevance of Corporate Financial Policy," *American Economic Review* (December 1974), pp. 851–866.
46. J. Stiglitz, "A Re-examination of the Modigliani–Miller Theorem," *American Economic Review* (December 1979), pp. 784–793.
47. R. Taggart, "Taxes and Corporate Capital Structure in an Incomplete Market," *Journal of Finance* (June 1980), pp. 645–659.
48. J. Warner, "Bankruptcy Costs: Some Evidence," *Journal of Finance* (May 1977), pp. 239–276.
49. H. Weingartner, "Optimal Timing of Bond Refunding," *Management Science* (March 1967), pp. 511–524.

V

DIVIDENDS

* *

29. OPTIMAL INVESTMENT AND FINANCING POLICY

M. J. GORDON*

Reprinted from *The Journal of Finance,* Vol. XVIII, No. 2 (May 1963), pp. 264–72, by permission of the author and the publisher.

In two papers[1] and in a recent book[2] I have presented theory and evidence which lead to the conclusion that a corporation's share price (or its cost of capital) is not independent of the dividend rate. As you may know, MM (Modigliani and Miller) have the opposite view, and they argued their position at some length in a recent paper.[3] Moreover, the tone of their paper made it clear that they saw no reasonable basis on which their conclusion could be questioned. Since they were so sure of their conclusion, it would seem advisable for me to review carefully my thinking on the subject, and this meeting appears to be a good time and place to do so.

I.

Let us begin by examining MM's fundamental proof that the price of a share is independent of its dividend. They defined the value of a share at $t = 0$ as the present value of (1) the dividend it will pay at the end of the first period, D_1, plus (2) the ex-dividend price of the share at the end of the period, P_1:

$$P_0 = \frac{1}{1 + k} [D_1 + P_1].\tag{1}$$

* Professor of business economics, University of Rochester.

[1] "Dividends, Earnings and Stock Prices," *Review of Economics and Statistics,* May, 1959, pp. 99–105; "The Savings, Investment and Valuation of the Corporation," *ibid.,* February, 1962, pp. 37–51.

[2] *The Investment Financing and Valuation of the Corporation* (Homewood, Ill.: R. D. Irwin, 1962).

[3] "Dividend Policy, Growth, and the Valuation of Shares," *Journal of Business,* October, 1961, pp. 411–33.

They then asked what would happen if the corporation, say raised its dividend but kept its investment for the period constant by selling the additional number of shares needed to offset the funds lost by the dividend increase. They demonstrated that the ex-dividend price of the stock at the end of the period would go down by exactly the same amount as the increase in the dividend. Since the sum $D_1 + P_1$ remains the same, P_0 is unchanged by the change in the dividend.

I will not review their proof of the theorem in detail because I find nothing wrong with it under the assumption they made that the future is certain. However, after proving the theorem a number of times under different conditions, they withdrew the assumption of certainty and made the dramatic announcement, "our first step, alas, must be to jettison the fundamental valuation equation."[4] Under uncertainty, they continued, it is not "at all clear what meaning can be attached to the discount factor...."[5] The implication which they made explicit in discussing my work is that under uncertainty we cannot represent investors as using discount rates to arrive at the present value of an expectation of future receipts.

It would seem that all is lost. But no! On the very next page we are told that their "fundamental conclusion need not be modified merely because of the presence of uncertainty about the future course of profits, investment, or dividends...."[6] By virtue of the postulates of "imputed rationality" and "symmetric market rationality," it remains true that "dividend policy is irrelevant for the determination of market prices."[7]

Their paper continued with a discussion of market imperfections, in which they note that the most important one, the capital gains tax, should create a preference for low payout rates. They concede that it may nevertheless be true that high payout rates sell at a premium, but they found "... only one way to account for it, namely as a result of systematic irrationality on the part of the investing public." They concluded with the hope that "... investors, however naive they may be when they enter the market, do sometimes learn from experience; and perhaps, occasionally even from reading articles such as this."[8]

It would seem that under uncertainty they might have been less sure of their conclusion for two reasons. First, under uncertainty an investor need not be indifferent as to the distribution of the one-period gain on a share between the dividend and price appreciation. Since price appreciation is highly uncertain, an investor may prefer the expectation of a \$5 dividend and a \$50 price to a zero dividend and a \$55 price without being irrational. Second, the expectation of a stock issue at $t = 1$ may have a depressing influence on the price at $t = 0$. What MM did was both change the dividend and change the number of new shares issued. Can we be so sure that the price of a share will not change when these two events take place?

---

[4] Miller and Modigliani, *op. cit.*, p. 426.
[5] *Ibid.*, p. 427.   [6] *Ibid.*, p. 428.   [7] *Ibid.*, p. 429.   [8] *Ibid.*, p. 432.

II.

Let us turn now to the proof of the MM position on the dividend rate that I presented in my *RES* paper and book. The reasons for presenting this proof will be evident shortly. Consider a corporation that earned Y_0 in the period ending at $t = 0$ and paid it all out in dividends. Further, assume that the corporation is expected to continue paying all earnings in dividends and to engage in no outside financing. Under these assumptions the company is expected to earn and pay Y_0 in every future period. If the rate of return on investment that investors require on the share is k, we may represent the valuation of the share as follows:

$$P_0 = \frac{Y_0}{(1+k)^1} + \frac{Y_0}{(1+k)^2} + \frac{Y_0}{(1+k)^3} + \cdots + \frac{Y_0}{(1+k)^t} + \cdots. \qquad (2)$$

We may also say that k is the discount rate that equates the dividend expectation of Y_0 in perpetuity with the price P_0.

Next, let the corporation announce at $t = 0$ that it will retain and invest $Y_1 = Y_0$ during $t = 1$ and that it expects to earn a rate of return of $k = Y_0/P_0$ on the investment. In each subsequent period it will pay all earnings out in dividends. Share price is now given by the expression

$$P_0 = \frac{0}{(1+k)^1} + \frac{Y_0 + kY_0}{(1+k)^2} + \frac{Y_0 + kY_0}{(1+k)^3} + \cdots + \frac{Y_0 + kY_0}{(1+k)^t}. \qquad (3)$$

Notice that the numerator of the first term on the right side is zero. It is the dividend and not the earnings in the period, since the investor is correctly represented as using the dividend expectation in arriving at P_0. If he were represented as looking at the earnings expectation, then as Bodenhorn[9] noted, he would be double-counting the first period's earnings.

It is evident that, as a result of the corporation's decision, the investor gives up Y_0 at the end of $t = 1$ and receives, in its place, kY_0 in perpetuity. The distribution of dividends over time has been changed. It is also evident that kY_0 in perpetuity discounted at k is exactly equal to Y_0. Hence P_0 is unchanged, and the change in the distribution over time of the dividends had no influence of share price. In general, the corporation can be expected to retain and invest any fraction of the income in any period without share price being changed as a consequence, so long as r, the return on investment, is equal to k. If $r > k$ for any investment, P_0 will be increased, but the reason is the profitability of investment and not the change in the time distribution of dividends.

Assume now that when the corporation makes the announcement which changes the dividend expectation from the one given by equation (2) to the one given by equation (3), investors raise the discount rate from k to k'. For the

---

[9] Diran Bodenhorn, " On the Problem of Capital Budgeting," *Journal of Finance*, December, 1959, pp. 473–92.

moment let us not wonder why the discount rate is raised from k to k', i.e., why the rate of return investors require on the share is raised as a consequence of the above change in the dividend expectation. If this takes place, equation (3) becomes

$$P'_0 = \frac{0}{(1 + k')^1} + \frac{Y_0 + kY_0}{(1 + k')^2} + \frac{Y_0 + kY_0}{(1 + k')^3} + \cdots + \frac{Y_0 + kY_0}{(1 + k')^t} + \cdots . \quad (3a)$$

It is clear that with $k' > k$, $P'_0 < P_0$.

Let us review what happened. The dividend policy changed: the near dividend was reduced, and the distant dividends were raised. This caused a rise in the discount rate, and the result was a fall in the price of the share. I, therefore, say that the change in dividend policy changed the share's price.

In response to this argument, MM stated that I fell into "the typical confounding of dividend policy with investment policy."[10] I don't understand their reasoning. It is well known that when the rate of return on investment is set equal to the discount rate, changing the level of investment has no influence on share price. By this means, I neutralized the profitability of investment. It seems to me perfectly clear that I did not confound investment and dividend policy; I changed the discount rate. Share price changed with the dividend rate in the above example because the discount rate was changed. The issue, therefore, is whether the behavior of investors under uncertainty is correctly represented by a model in which the discount rate that equates a dividend expectation with its price is a function of the dividend rate.

I cannot categorically state that k is a function of the rate of growth in the dividend, i.e., the dividend rate, but I can present some theoretical considerations and empirical evidence in support of the theorem. It seems plausible that (1) investors have an aversion to risk or uncertainty, and (2), given the riskiness of a corporation, the uncertainty of a dividend it is expected to pay increases with the time in the future of the dividend. It follows from these two propositions that an investor may be represented as discounting the dividend expected in period t at a rate of k_t, with k_t not independent of t. Furthermore, if aversion to risk is large enough and/or risk increases rapidly enough with time, k_t increases with t.

It is therefore possible, though not certain, that investor behavior is correctly approximated by the statement that, in arriving at the value of a dividend expectation, they discount it at the rates k_t, $t = 1, 2 \ldots$, with $k_t > k_{t-1}$. In this event the single discount rate we use in stock value models is an increasing function of the rate of growth in the dividend. In short, dividend policy influences share price. To illustrate the conclusion, let us rewrite equation (2):

$$P_0 = \frac{Y_0}{(1 + k_1)^1} + \frac{Y_0}{(1 + k_2)^2} + \frac{Y_0}{(1 + k_3)^3} + \cdots \frac{Y_0}{(1 + k_t)^t} + \cdots . \quad (4)$$

We now look on the k of equation (2) as an average of the k_t of equation (4)

[10] Miller and Modigliani, *op. cit.*, p. 425.

such that if the entire dividend expectation is discounted at this single rate, it results in the same share price. The discount rate k is an average of the k_t with Y_0, the weight assigned to each item.

Once again let the corporation retain $Y_1 = Y_0$ and invest it to earn $k Y_0$ per period in perpetuity. Using the sequence of discount rates k_t, the same as that appearing in equation (4), the valuation of the new dividend expectation becomes

$$P_0' = \frac{0}{(1 + k_1)^1} + \frac{Y_0 + k Y_0}{(1 + k_2)^2} + \frac{Y_0 + k Y_0}{(1 + k_3)^3} + \cdots + \frac{Y_0 + k Y_0}{(1 + k_t)^t} + \cdots . \quad (5)$$

The shareholder gives up Y_0 and gets $k Y_0$ in perpetuity, but the latter is now discounted at the rates k_t, $t = 2 \to \infty$, and it can be shown that $k Y_0$ so discounted is less than Y_0. Hence $P_0' < P_0$, and dividend policy influences share price. It also can be shown that k', the new average of the same k_t, is greater than k. In general, reducing the near dividends and raising the distant dividends (lowering the dividend rate) changes the weights of the k_t and raises their average.

III.

To summarize the theoretical part of my argument, I started with two assumptions: (1) aversion to risk and (2) increase in the uncertainty of a receipt with its time in the future. From these assumptions I proceeded by deductive argument to the proposition that the single discount rate an investor is represented as using to value a share's dividend expectation is an increasing function of the rate of growth in the dividend. The consequence of the theorem is that dividend policy per se influences the value of a share. The assumptions have enough intuitive merit, I believe, that the theorem may in fact be true.

Before proceeding to the empirical evidence, I would like to comment briefly on two other criticisms MM directed at my argument. First, they differentiated between my "purely subjective discount rate and the objective market-given yields" and stated: "To attempt to derive valuation formulas from these purely subjective discount factors involves, of course, an error...."[11] My assumptions and empirical results may be questioned, but where is the error? Does the theorem fail to follow from the assumptions? Why, as they suggest, is it logically impossible for an investor to arrive at the value of a share by estimating its future dividends and discounting the series at a rate appropriate to its uncertainty?

The following MM criticism of my argument I find even more confusing. They stated: "Indeed if they [investors] valued shares according to the Gordon approach and thus paid a premium for higher payout ratios, then holders of the low payout shares would actually realize consistently higher returns on their investment over any stated interval of time."[12] Under this reasoning two shares cannot sell at different yields regardless of how much they differ in risk because the holders of the higher-yield share would "actually realize

[11] *Ibid.*, p. 424.
[12] *Ibid.*, p. 425.

consistently higher returns over any stated interval of time." Do MM deny that investors have an aversion to risk?

To test the theorem empirically, I proceeded as follows. The valuation of a share may be represented by the expression

$$P_0 = \int_0^\infty D_t e^{-kt} \, dt, \tag{6}$$

[handwritten annotation: indicates an integral; that it is calculus notation]

where D_t is the dividend expected in period t and k is an operator on the D_t that reduces them to their present value to the investor. Equation (6) is a perfectly general statement that is not open to question. However, to use the equation in empirical work, we must specify how investors arrive at D_t from observable variables. For this, I assumed that investors expect a corporation will: (1) retain the fraction b of its income in each future period; (2) earn a rate of return, r, on the common equity investment in each future period; (3) maintain the existing debt-equity ratio; and (4) undertake no new outside equity financing. Under the above assumptions the current dividend is $D_0 = (1 - b) Y_0$, and its rate of growth is br. Further, the entire dividend expectation is represented by these two variables, and equation (6) is equal to:

$$P_0 = \frac{(1 - b) Y_0}{k - br}. \tag{7}$$

The above four assumptions may be criticized as being too great a simplification of reality. I have admitted their limitations, and I welcome improvement, but I know of no other empirical model that contains as rich and accurate a statement of the dividend expectation provided by a share. Most empirical work, including the published work of MM, represents the investor as expecting that the corporation will pay all earnings in dividends and engage in no outside financing. They, therefore, also ignore the influence of the profitability of investment on share price. This model incorporates a prediction of the corporation's investment and rate of return on the investment in each future period. The expected investment in period t is the fraction b of the period's income plus the leverage on the retention that maintains the corporation's existing debt-equity ratio. Further, the influence of this retention and borrowing on the dividend expectation is incorporated in the model.

The interesting thing about the model as it stands is that it is consistent with the MM position and should provoke no objection. To see this, let us make their assumption that k is independent of b and, to neutralize the profitability of investment, let $r = k$. In this model, dividend policy is represented by b the retention rate, so that, if we take the derivative of P_0 with respect to b, we establish the relation between share price and the dividend rate. We find that $\partial P/\partial b = 0$. The value of a share is independent of the dividend rate—exactly what MM argue.

One can use this model in empirical work under the assumption that k is independent of br. I did and obtained poor results. Since I found good theoretical grounds for believing that k is an increasing function of br, it would seem reasonable to explore the hypothesis, and that is what I did. If k is an increasing function of br, we can write equation (7) as

$$P_0 = A_0[(1 - b)Y_0][1 + br]^{\alpha_2}. \tag{8}$$

In this expression, A_0 represents the influence of all variables other than the current dividend, $(1 - b)Y_0$, and its rate of growth, br. When $b = 0$, P_0 is the multiple A_0 of Y_0. As br increases, the dividend, $(1 - b)Y_0$, falls and br rises, the former lowering price and the latter raising price. Whether P_0 rises or falls with b depends on r, the profitability of investment, and on α_2. The expression α_2 may be looked on as how much investors are willing to pay for growth. Its value depends on how fast the k_t rise with t, that is, on how fast uncertainty increases with time and on the degree of investor aversion to risk.

It should be noted that equation (8) is not merely a stock value model. Given the investor's valuation of a share, A_0 and α_2, and, given the profitability of investment, r, the model may be used t῀ find the retention rate (equal to the investment rate under our assumptions) that maximizes the value of a share. Extensions of the model developed elsewhere[13] allow its use to find the investment and the financing, retention, debt, and new equity that maximize share price.

The empirical results I obtained with the above model have been published in detail,[14] and all I will say here is that they are very good. Although the results compare favorably with earlier work, they are not good enough to settle the question. MM[15] and Benishay[16] have pointed out that my independent variables are not free of error, and the consequence is that the parameter estimates have a downward basis. Kolin[17] has reported that his empirical work revealed no relation between dividend policy and share price. As things stand, I would say that the influence of dividend policy on share price is a question that requires further study. The axiomatic basis of the MM position is certainly not so powerful as to force the acceptance of their conclusions.

IV.

I should like to close with a brief comment on the two major camps that are emerging with respect to the theory of corporation finance. In both camps optimal policy is taken as the policy that maximizes the value of the corporation. Although corporations may not make investment and financing decisions with only this objective in mind, managements are certainly not indifferent to the prices at which their corporations' securities sell. Hence the policy question posed has practical significance.

[13] M. J. Gordon, *The Investment, Financing and Valuation of the Corporation* (Homewood, Ill.: R. D. Irwin, 1962).

[14] *Ibid.*

[15] Franco Modigliani and Merton Miller, "The Cost of Capital Corporation Finance, and Theory of Investment: Reply," *American Economic Review*, September, 1959, pp. 655–69.

[16] Haskel Benishay, "Variability in Earnings-Price Ratios: Reply," *American Economic Review*, March, 1962, pp. 209–16.

[17] Marshal Kolin, *The Relative Price of Corporate Equity* (Boston: Harvard Business School).

In one camp, where we find MM, it is argued that a corporation's cost of capital is a constant—i.e., independent of the method and level of financing. Optimal policy is the investment that equates the marginal return on investment with this cost of capital. The inescapable conclusion is that financing policy is not a problem. The opposite position is that a corporation's cost of capital varies with the method and level of financing. My judgment is that the theoretical and empirical evidence we have favors this position.

However, regardless of which view prevails, the battle should be lively and productive. For a long time the position that cost of capital is a constant was held almost exclusively by economists, who were sophisticated in methods of theoretical and econometric analysis but knew little of finance. By contrast, the position that the cost of capital is a variable was held by finance men, who were familiar with their subject but not with advanced methods of theoretical and empirical research. People in each group talked only to those who agreed with them, and in consequence not much was said. The situation has changed, it will change further, and the promise is that the lively debate and active research in progress will advance our knowledge on the subject.

30. DIVIDEND POLICY, GROWTH, AND THE VALUATION OF SHARES*

MERTON H. MILLER†
and
FRANCO MODIGLIANI‡

Reprinted from *The Journal of Business of the University of Chicago,* Vol. XXXIV, No. 4 (October 1961), pp. 411–33, by permission of the authors and the University of Chicago Press. Copyright 1961 by the University of Chicago.

The effect of a firm's dividend policy on the current price of its shares is a matter of considerable importance, not only to the corporate officials who must set the policy, but to investors planning portfolios and to economists seeking to understand and appraise the functioning of the capital markets. Do companies with generous distribution policies consistently sell at a premium over those with niggardly payouts? Is the reverse ever true? If so, under what conditions? Is there an optimum payout ratio or range of ratios that maximizes the current worth of the shares?

Although these questions of fact have been the subject of many empirical studies in recent years no consensus has yet been achieved. One reason appears to be the absence in the literature of a complete and reasonably rigorous statement of those parts of the economic theory of valuation bearing directly on the matter of dividend policy. Lacking such a statement, investigators have not yet been able to frame their tests with sufficient precision to distinguish adequately between the various contending hypotheses. Nor have they been able to give a convincing explanation of what their test results do imply about the underlying process of valuation.

In the hope that it may help to overcome these obstacles to effective empirical testing, this paper will attempt to fill the existing gap in the theoretical literature on valuation. We shall begin, in Section I, by examining the effects of differences in dividend policy on the current price of shares in an ideal economy characterized by perfect capital markets, rational behavior, and perfect certainty. Still within this convenient analytical framework we shall go on in Sections II and III to consider certain closely related issues that

* The authors wish to express their thanks to all who read and commented on earlier versions of this paper and especially to Charles C. Holt, now of the University of Wisconsin, whose suggestions led to considerable simplification of a number of the proofs.

† Professor of finance and economics, University of Chicago.

‡ Professor of economics, Northwestern University.

appear to have been responsible for considerable misunderstanding of the role of dividend policy. In particular, Section II will focus on the longstanding debate about what investors "really" capitalize when they buy shares; and Section III on the much mooted relations between price, the rate of growth of profits, and the rate of growth of dividends per share. Once these fundamentals have been established, we shall proceed in Section IV to drop the assumption of certainty and to see the extent to which the earlier conclusions about dividend policy must be modified. Finally, in Section V, we shall briefly examine the implications for the dividend policy problem of certain kinds of market imperfections.

I. EFFECT OF DIVIDEND POLICY WITH PERFECT MARKETS, RATIONAL BEHAVIOR, AND PERFECT CERTAINTY

The meaning of the basic assumptions. Although the terms "perfect markets," "rational behavior," and "perfect certainty" are widely used throughout economic theory, it may be helpful to start by spelling out the precise meaning of these assumptions in the present context.

1. In "perfect capital markets," no buyer or seller (or issuer) of securities is large enough for his transactions to have an appreciable impact on the then ruling price. All traders have equal and costless access to information about the ruling price and about all other relevant characteristics of shares (to be detailed specifically later). No brokerage fees, transfer taxes, or other transaction costs are incurred when securities are bought, sold, or issued, and there are no tax differentials either between distributed and undistributed profits or between dividends and capital gains.
2. "Rational behavior" means that investors always prefer more wealth to less and are indifferent as to whether a given increment to their wealth takes the form of cash payments or an increase in the market value of their holdings of shares.
3. "Perfect certainty" implies complete assurance on the part of every investor as to the future investment program and the future profits of every corporation. Because of this assurance, there is, among other things, no need to distinguish between stocks and bonds as sources of funds at this stage of the analysis. We can, therefore, proceed as if there were only a single type of financial instrument which, for convenience, we shall refer to as shares of stock.

The fundamental principle of valuation. Under these assumptions the valuation of all shares would be governed by the following fundamental principle: the price of each share must be such that the rate of return (dividends plus capital gains per dollar invested) on every share will be the same throughout the market over any given interval of time. That is, if we let

$d_j(t)$ = dividends per share paid by firm j during period t

$p_j(t)$ = the price (ex any dividend in $t-1$) of a share in firm j at the start of period t, we must have

$$\frac{d_j(t) + p_j(t + 1) - p_j(t)}{p_j(t)} = \rho(t) \text{ independent of } j; \tag{1}$$

or equivalently,

$$p_j(t) = \frac{1}{1 + \rho(t)} [d_j(t) + p_j(t + 1)] \tag{2}$$

for each j and for all t. Otherwise, holders of low-return (high-priced) shares could increase their terminal wealth by selling these shares and investing the proceeds in shares offering a higher rate of return. This process would tend to drive down the prices of the low-return shares and drive up the prices of high-return shares until the differential in rates of return had been eliminated.

The effect of dividend policy. The implications of this principle for our problem of dividend policy can be seen somewhat more easily if equation (2) is restated in terms of the value of the enterprise as a whole rather than in terms of the value of an individual share. Dropping the firm subscript j since this will lead to no ambiguity in the present context and letting

$n(t)$ = the number of shares of record at the start of t

$m(t + 1)$ = the number of new shares (if any) sold during t at the ex dividend closing price $p(t + 1)$, so that

$n(t + 1) = n(t) + m(t + 1)$

$V(t) = n(t) p(t)$ = the total value of the enterprise and

$D(t) = n(t) d(t)$ = the total dividends paid during t to holders of record at the start of t,

we can rewrite (2)

$$V(t) = \frac{1}{1 + \rho(t)} [D(t) + n(t)p(t + 1)]$$

$$= \frac{1}{1 + \rho(t)} [D(t) + V(t + 1) - m(t + 1)p(t + 1)]. \tag{3}$$

The advantage of relating the fundamental rule in this form is that it brings into sharper focus the three possible routes by which current dividends might affect the current market value of the firm $V(t)$, or equivalently the price of its individual shares, $p(t)$. Current dividends will clearly affect $V(t)$ via the first term in the brackets, $D(t)$. In principle, current dividends might also affect $V(t)$ indirectly via the second term, $V(t + 1)$, the new ex dividend market value. Since $V(t + 1)$ must depend only on future and not on past events, such could be the case, however, only if both (a) $V(t + 1)$ were a function of future dividend policy and (b) the current distribution $D(t)$ served to convey some otherwise unavailable information as to what that future dividend policy would be. The first possibility being the relevant one from the standpoint of assessing the effects of dividend policy, it will clarify matters to assume, provisionally, that the future dividend policy of the firm is known and given for $t + 1$ and all subsequent periods and is independent of the actual dividend decision in t. Then $V(t + 1)$ will also be independent of the current dividend decision, though it may very well be affected by $D(t + 1)$ and all subsequent distributions. Finally, current dividends can influence $V(t)$ through the third term, $-m(t + 1) p(t + 1)$, the value of new shares sold to outsiders during the period. For the higher the dividend payout in any period the more the new capital that must be raised from external sources to maintain any desired level of investment.

The fact that the dividend decision effects price not in one but in these two conflicting ways—directly via $D(t)$ and inversely via $-m(t) p(t + 1)$—is, of course, precisely why one speaks of there being a dividend policy *problem*. If the firm raises its dividend in t, given its investment decision, will the increase in the cash payments to the current holders be more or less than enough to offset their lower share of the terminal value? Which is the better strategy for the firm in financing the investment: to reduce dividends and rely on retained earnings or to raise dividends but float more new shares?

In our ideal world at least these and related questions can be simply and immediately answered: the two dividend effects must always exactly cancel out so that the payout policy to be followed in t will have *no* effect on the price at t.

We need only express $m(t + 1) \cdot p(t + 1)$ in terms of $D(t)$ to show that such must indeed be the case. Specifically, if $I(t)$ is the given level of the firm's investment or increase in its holding of physical assets in t and if $X(t)$ is the firm's total net profit for the period, we know that the amount of outside capital required will be

$$m(t + 1)p(t + 1) = I(t) - [X(t) - D(t)]. \tag{4}$$

Substituting expression (4) into (3), the $D(t)$ cancel and we obtain for the value of the firm as of the start of t

$$V(t) \equiv n(t)p(t) = \frac{1}{1 + \rho(t)} [X(t) - I(t) + V(t + 1)]. \tag{5}$$

Since $D(t)$ does not appear directly among the arguments and since $X(t)$, $I(t)$, $V(t + 1)$ and $\rho(t)$ are all independent of $D(t)$ (either by their nature or by assumption) it follows that the current value of the firm must be independent of the current dividend decision.

Having established that $V(t)$ is unaffected by the current dividend decision it is easy to go on to show that $V(t)$ must also be unaffected by any future dividend decision as well. Such future decisions can influence $V(t)$ only via their effect on $V(t + 1)$. But we can repeat the reasoning above and show that $V(t + 1)$—and hence $V(t)$—is unaffected by dividend policy in $t + 1$; that $V(t + 2)$—and hence $V(t + 1)$ and $V(t)$—is unaffected by dividend policy in $t + 2$; and so on for as far into the future as we care to look. Thus, we may conclude that given a firm's investment policy, the dividend payout policy it chooses to follow will affect neither the current price of its shares nor the total return to its shareholders.

Like many other propositions in economics, the irrelevance of dividend policy, given investment policy, is "obvious, one you think of it." It is, after all, merely one more instance of the general principle that there are no "financial illusions" in a rational and perfect economic environment. Values there are determined solely by "real" considerations—in this case the earning power of the firm's assets and its investment policy—and not by how the fruits of the earning power are "packaged" for distribution.

Obvious as the proposition may be, however, one finds few references to it in the extensive literature on the problem.[1] It is true that the literature abounds with statements that in some "theoretical" sense, dividend policy ought not to count; but either that sense is not clearly specified or, more frequently and especially among economists, it is (wrongly) identified with a situation in which the firm's internal rate of return is the same as the external or market rate of return.[2]

A major source of these and related misunderstandings of the role of the dividend policy has been the fruitless concern and controversy over what investors "really" capitalize when they buy shares. We say fruitless because as we shall now proceed to show, it is actually possible to derive from the basic principle of valuation (1) not merely one, but several valuation formulas each starting from one of the "classical" views of what is being capitalized by investors. Though differing somewhat in outward appearance, the various formula can be shown to be equivalent in all essential respects including, of course, their implication that dividend policy is irrelevant. While the controversy itself thus turns out to be an empty one, the different expressions do have some intrinsic interest since, by highlighting different combinations of variables they provide additional insights into the process of valuation and they open alternative lines of attack on some of the problems of empirical testing.

II. WHAT DOES THE MARKET "REALLY" CAPITALIZE?

In the literature on valuation one can find at least the following four more or less distinct approaches to the valuation of shares: (1) the discounted cash flow approach; (2) the current earnings plus future investment opportunities approach; (3) the stream of dividends approach; and (4) the stream of earnings approach. To demonstrate that these approaches are, in fact, equivalent it will be helpful to begin by first going back to equation (5) and developing from it a valuation formula to serve as a point of reference and comparison. Specifically, if we assume, for simplicity, that the market rate of yield $\rho(t) = \rho$

---

[1] Apart from the references to it in our earlier papers, especially [16], the closest approximation seems to be that in Bodenhorn [1, p. 492], but even his treatment of the role of dividend policy is not completely explicit. (The numbers in brackets refer to references listed below, pp. 365–366).

[2] See below p. 354.

for all t,[3] then, setting $t = 0$, we can rewrite (5) as

$$V(0) = \frac{1}{1 + \rho}[X(0) - I(0)] + \frac{1}{1 + \rho} V(1). \tag{6}$$

Since (5) holds for all t, setting $t = 1$ permits us to express $V(1)$ in terms of $V(2)$ which in turn can be expressed in terms of $V(3)$ and so on up to any arbitrary terminal period T. Carrying out these substitutions, we obtain

$$V(0) \sum_{t=0}^{T-1} \frac{1}{(1 + \rho)^{t+1}} [X(t) - I(t)] + \frac{1}{(1 + \rho)^T} V(T). \tag{7}$$

In general, the remainder term $(1 + \rho)^{-T} V(T)$ can be expected to approach zero as T approaches infinity[4] so that (7) can be expressed as

$$V(0) = \lim_{T \to \infty} \sum_{t=0}^{T-1} \frac{1}{(1 + \rho)^{t+1}} [X(t) - I(t)], \tag{8}$$

which we shall further abbreviate to

$$V(0) = \sum_{t=0}^{\infty} \frac{1}{(1 + \rho)^{t+1}} [X(t) - I(t)]. \tag{9}$$

The discounted cash flow approach. Consider now the so called discounted cash flow approach familiar in discussions of capital budgeting. There, in valuing any specific machine we discount at the market rate of interest the stream of cash receipts generated by the machine; plus any scrap or terminal value of the machine; and minus the stream of cash outlays for direct labor, materials, repairs, and capital additions. The same approach, of course, can also be applied to the firm as a whole which may be thought of in this context as simply a large, composite machine.[5] This approach amounts to defining the value of the firm as

$$V(0) = \sum_{t=0}^{T-1} \frac{1}{(1 + \rho)^{t+1}} [\mathcal{R}(t) - \mathcal{O}(t)] + \frac{1}{(1 + \rho)^T} V(T), \tag{10}$$

[3] More general formulas in which $\rho(t)$ is allowed to vary with time can always be derived from those presented here merely by substituting the cumbersome product.

$$\prod_{\tau=0}^{t} [1 + \rho(\tau)] \text{ for } (1 + \rho)^{t+1}.$$

[4] The assumption that the remainder vanishes is introduced for the sake of simplicity of exposition only and is in no way essential to the argument. What is essential, of course, is that $V(0)$, i.e., the sum of the two terms in (7), be finite, but this can always be safely assumed in economic analysis. See below, n. 14.

[5] This is, in fact, the approach to valuation normally taken in economic theory when discussing the value of the *assets* of an enterprise, but much more rarely applied, unfortunately, to the value of the liability side. One of the few to apply the approach to the shares as well as the assets is Bodenhorn in [1], who uses it to derive a formula closely similar to (9) above.

where $\mathscr{R}(t)$ represents the stream of cash receipts and $\mathcal{O}(t)$ of cash outlays, or, abbreviating, as above to

$$V(0) = \sum_{t=0}^{\infty} \frac{1}{(1+\rho)^{t+1}} [\mathscr{R}(t) - \mathcal{O}(t)]. \tag{11}$$

But we also know, by definition, that $[X(t) - I(t)] = [\mathscr{R}(t) - \mathcal{O}(t)]$ since, $X(t)$ differs from $\mathscr{R}(t)$ and $I(t)$ differs from $\mathcal{O}(t)$ merely by the "cost of goods sold" (and also by the depreciation expense if we wish to interpret $X(t)$ and $I(t)$ as net rather than gross profits and investment). Hence (11) is formally equivalent to (9), and the discounted cash flow approach is thus seen to be an implication of the valuation principle for perfect markets given by equation (1).

The investment opportunities approach. Consider next the approach to valuation which would seem most natural from the standpoint of an investor proposing to buy out and operate some already-going concern. In estimating how much it would be worthwhile to pay for the privilege of operating the firm, the amount of dividends to be paid is clearly not relevant, since the new owner can, within wide limits, make the future dividend stream whatever he pleases. For him the worth of the enterprise, as such, will depend only on: (a) the "normal" rate of return he can earn by investing his capital in securities (i.e., the market rate of return); (b) the earning power of the physical assets currently held by the firm; and (c) the opportunities, if any, that the firm offers for making additional investments in real assets that will yield more than the "normal" (market) rate of return. The latter opportunities, frequently termed the "good will" of the business, may arise, in practice, from any of a number of circumstances (ranging all the way from special locational advantages to patents or other monopolistic advantages).

To see how these opportunities affect the value of the business assume that in some future period t the firm invests $I(t)$ dollars. Suppose, further, for simplicity that starting in the period immediately following the investment of the funds, the projects produce net profits at a constant rate of $\rho^*(t)$ per cent of $I(t)$ in each period thereafter.[6] Then the present worth as of t of the (perpetual) stream of profits generated will be $I(t)\,\rho^*(t)/\rho$, and the "good will" of the projects (i.e., the difference between worth and cost) will be

$$I(t)\frac{\rho^*(t)}{\rho} - I(t) = I(t)\left[\frac{\rho^*(t) - \rho}{\rho}\right].$$

The present worth as of now of this future "good will" is

$$I(t)\left[\frac{\rho^*(t) - \rho}{\rho}\right](1 + \rho)^{-(t+1)},$$

---

[6] The assumption that $I(t)$ yields a uniform perpetuity is not restrictive in the present certainty context since it is always possible by means of simple, present-value calculations to find an equivalent uniform perpetuity for any project, whatever the time shape of its actual returns. Note also that $\rho^*(t)$ is the *average* rate of return. If the managers of the firm are behaving rationally, they will, of course, use ρ as their cut-off criterion (cf. below p. 347). In this event we would have $\rho^*(t) \geq \rho$. The formulas remain valid, however, even where $\rho^*(t) < \rho$.

and the present value of all such future opportunities is simply the sum

$$\sum_{t=0}^{\infty} I(t) \frac{\rho^*(t) - \rho}{\rho} (1 + \rho)^{-(t+1)}.$$

Adding in the present value of the (uniform perpetual) earnings, $X(O)$, on the assets currently held, we get as an expression for the value of the firm

$$V(0) = \frac{X(0)}{\rho} + \sum_{t=0}^{\infty} I(t) \frac{\rho^*(t) - \rho}{\rho} (1 + \rho)^{-(t+1)}. \tag{12}$$

To show that the same formula can be derived from (9) note first that our definition of $\rho^*(t)$ implies the following relation between the $X(t)$:

$$X(1) = X(0) + \rho^*(0)I(0),$$
$$\dotfill$$
$$X(t) = X(t-1) + \rho^*(t-1)I(t-1)$$

and by successive substitution

$$X(t) = X(0) + \sum_{\tau=0}^{t-1} \rho^*(\tau)I(\tau),$$

$$t = 1, 2 \cdots \infty.$$

Substituting the last expression for $X(t)$ in (9) yields

$$V(0) = [X(0) - I(0)](1 + \rho)^{-1}$$

$$+ \sum_{t=1}^{\infty} \left[X(0) + \sum_{\tau=0}^{t-1} \rho^*(\tau)I(\tau) - I(t) \right] (1 + \rho)^{-(t+1)}$$

$$= X(0) \sum_{t=1}^{\infty} (1 + \rho)^{-t} - I(0)(1 + \rho)^{-1}$$

$$+ \sum_{t=1}^{\infty} \left[\sum_{\tau=0}^{t-1} \rho^*(\tau)I(\tau) - I(t) \right] (1 + \rho)^{-(t+1)}$$

$$= X(0) \sum_{t=1}^{\infty} (1 + \rho)^{-t} + \sum_{t=1}^{\infty} \left[\sum_{\tau=0}^{t-1} \rho^*(\tau)I(\tau) - I(t-1) \right.$$

$$\times (1 + \rho) \Big] (1 + \rho)^{-(t+1)}.$$

The first expression is, of course, simply a geometric progression summing to $X(0)/\rho$, which is the first term of (12). To simplify the second expression note that it can be rewritten as

$$\sum_{t=0}^{\infty} I(t) \left[\rho^*(t) \sum_{\tau=t+2}^{\infty} (1 + \rho)^{-\tau} - (1 + \rho)^{-(t+1)} \right].$$

Evaluating the summation within the brackets gives

$$\sum_{t=0}^{\infty} I(t)\left[\rho^*(t)\frac{(1+\rho)^{-(t+1)}}{\rho} - (1+\rho)^{-(t+1)}\right]$$

$$= \sum_{t=0}^{\infty} I(t)\left[\frac{\rho^*(t)-\rho}{\rho}\right](1+\rho)^{-(t+1)},$$

which is precisely the second term of (12).

Formula (12) has a number of revealing features and deserves to be more widely used in discussions of valuation.[7] For one thing, it throws considerable light on the meaning of those much abused terms "growth" and "growth stocks." As can readily be seen from (12), a corporation does not become a "growth stock" with a high price-earning ratio merely because its assets and earnings are growing over time. To enter the glamor category, it is also necessary that $\rho^*(t) > \rho$. For if $\rho^*(t) = \rho$, then however large the growth in assets may be, the second term in (12) will be zero and the firm's price-earnings ratio would not rise above a humdrum $1/\rho$. The essence of "growth" in short, is not expansion, but the existence of opportunities to invest significant quantities of funds at higher than "normal" rates of return.

Notice also that if $\rho^*(t) < \rho$, investment in real assets by the firm will actually reduce the current price of the shares. This should help to make clear among other things, why the "cost of capital" to the firm is the same regardless of how the investments are financed or how fast the firm is growing. The function of the cost of capital in capital budgeting is to provide the "cut-off rate" in the sense of the minimum yield that investment projects must promise to be worth undertaking from the point of view of the current owners. Clearly, no proposed project would be in the interest of the current owners if its yield were expected to be less than ρ since investing in such projects would reduce the value of their shares. In the other direction, every project yielding more than ρ is just as clearly worth undertaking since it will necessarily enhance the value of the enterprise. Hence, the cost of capital or cut-off criterion for investment decisions is simply ρ.[8]

Finally, formula (12) serves to emphasize an important deficiency in many recent statistical studies of the effects of dividend policy (such as Walter [19] or Durand [4, 5]). These studies typically involve fitting regression equations in which price is expressed as some function of current earnings and dividends.

---

[7] A valuation formula analogous to (12) though derived and interpreted in a slightly different way is found in Bodenhorn [1]. Variants of (12) for certain special cases are discussed in Walter [20].

[8] The same conclusion could also have been reached, of course, by "costing" each particular source of capital funds. That is, since ρ is the going market rate of return on equity any new shares floated to finance investment must be priced to yield ρ; and withholding funds from the stockholders to finance investment would deprive the holders of the chance to earn ρ on these funds by investing their dividends in other shares. The advantage of thinking in terms of the cost of capital as the cut-off criterion is that it minimizes the danger of confusing "costs" with mere "outlays."

A finding that the dividend coefficient is significant—as is usually the case—is then interpreted as a rejection of the hypothesis that dividend policy does not affect valuation.

Even without raising questions of bias in the coefficients,[9] it should be apparent that such a conclusion is unwarranted since formula (12) and the analysis underlying it imply only that dividends will not count given current earnings *and growth potential.* No general prediction is made (or can be made) by the theory about what will happen to the dividend coefficient if the crucial growth term is omitted.[10]

The stream of dividends approach. From the earnings and earnings opportunities approach we turn next to the dividend approach, which has, for some reason, been by far the most popular one in the literature of valuation. This approach too, properly formulated, is an entirely valid one though, of course, not the only valid approach as its more enthusiastic proponents frequently suggest.[11] It does, however, have the disadvantage in contrast with previous approaches of obscuring the role of dividend policy. In particular, uncritical use of the dividend approach has often led to the unwarranted inference that, since the investor is buying dividends and since dividend policy affects the amount of dividends, then dividend policy must also affect the current price.

Properly formulated, the dividend approach defines the current worth of a share as the discounted value of the stream of dividends to be paid on the share in perpetuity. That is

$$p(t) = \sum_{\tau=0}^{\infty} \frac{d(t+\tau)}{(1+\rho)^{\tau+1}}. \tag{13}$$

To see the equivalence between this approach and previous ones, let us first restate (13) in terms of total market value as

$$V(t) = \sum_{\tau=0}^{\infty} \frac{D_t(t+\tau)}{(1+\rho)^{\tau+1}}, \tag{14}$$

[9] The serious bias problem in tests using current reported earnings as a measure of $X(0)$ was discussed briefly by us in [16].

[10] In suggesting that recent statistical studies have not controlled adequately for growth we do not mean to exempt Gordon in [8] or [9]. It is true that his tests contain an explicit "growth" variable, but it is essentially nothing more than the ratio of retained earnings to book value. This ratio would not in general provide an acceptable approximation to the "growth" variable of (12) in any sample in which firms resorted to external financing. Furthermore, even if by some chance a sample was found in which all firms relied entirely on retained earnings, his tests then could not settle the question of dividend policy. For if all firms financed investment internally (or used external financing only in strict proportion to internal financing as Gordon assumes in [8]) then there would be no way to distinguish between the effects of dividend policy and investment policy (see below p. 354).

[11] See, e.g., the classic statement of the position in J. B. Williams [21]. The equivalence of the dividend approach to many of the other standard approaches is noted to our knowledge only in our [16] and, by implication, in Bodenhorn [1].

where $D_t(t + \tau)$ denotes that portion of the total dividends $D(t + \tau)$ paid during period $t + \tau$, that accrues to the shares of record as of the start of period t (indicated by the subscript). That equation (14) is equivalent to (9) and hence also to (12) is immediately apparent for the special case in which no outside financing is undertaken after period t, for in that case

$$D_t(t + \tau) = D(t + \tau) = X(t + \tau) - I(t + \tau).$$

To allow for outside financing, note that we can rewrite (14) as

$$V(t) = \frac{1}{1 + \rho} \left[D_t(t) + \sum_{\tau=1}^{\infty} \frac{D_t(t + \tau)}{(1 + \rho)^\tau} \right]$$

$$= \frac{1}{1 + \rho} \left[D(t) + \sum_{\tau=0}^{\infty} \frac{D_t(t + \tau + 1)}{(1 + \rho)^{\tau+1}} \right]. \tag{15}$$

The summation term in the last expression can be written as the difference between the stream of dividends accruing to all the shares of record as of $t + 1$ and that portion of the stream that will accrue to the shares newly issued in t, that is,

$$\sum_{\tau=0}^{\infty} \frac{D_t(t + \tau + 1)}{(1 + \rho)^{\tau+1}} = \left(1 - \frac{m(t + 1)}{n(t + 1)} \right) \sum_{\tau=0}^{\infty} \frac{D_{t+1}(t + \tau + 1)}{(1 + \rho)^{\tau+1}} \tag{16}$$

But from (14) we know that the second summation in (16) is precisely $V(t + 1)$ so that (15) can be reduced to

$$V(t) = \frac{1}{1 + \rho} \left[D(t) + \left(1 - \frac{m(t + 1)p(t + 1)}{n(t + 1)p(t + 1)} \right) V(t + 1) \right]$$

$$= \frac{1}{1 + \rho} [D(t) + V(t + 1) - m(t + 1)p(t + 1)], \tag{17}$$

which is (3) and which has already been shown to imply both (9) and (12).[12]

There are, of course, other ways in which the equivalence of the dividend approach to the other approaches might have been established, but the method presented has the advantage perhaps of providing some further insight into the reason for the irrelevance of dividend policy. An increase in current dividends, given the firm's investment policy, must necessarily reduce the

[12] The statement that equations (9), (12), and (14) are equivalent must be qualified to allow for certain pathological extreme cases, fortunately of no real economic significance. An obvious example of such a case is the legendary company that is expected *never* to pay a dividend. If this were literally true then the value of the firm by (14) would be zero; by (9) it would be zero (or possibly negative since zero dividends rule out $X(t) > I(t)$ but not $X(t) < I(t)$); while by (12) the value might still be positive. What is involved here, of course, is nothing more than a discontinuity at zero since the value under (14) and (9) would be positive and the equivalence of both with (12) would hold if that value were also positive as long as there was some period T, however far in the future, beyond which the firm would pay out $\varepsilon > 0$ per cent of its earnings, however small the value of ε.

terminal value of existing shares because part of the future dividend stream that would otherwise have accrued to the existing shares must be diverted to attract the outside capital from which, in effect, the higher current dividends are paid. Under our basic assumptions, however, ρ must be the same for all investors, new as well as old. Consequently the market value of the dividends diverted to the outsiders, which is both the value of their contribution and the reduction in terminal value of the existing shares, must always be precisely the same as the increase in current dividends.

The stream of earnings approach. Contrary to widely held views, it is also possible to develop a meaningful and consistent approach to valuation running in terms of the stream of earnings generated by the corporation rather than of the dividend distributions actually made to the shareholders. Unfortunately, it is also extremely easy to mistate or misinterpret the earnings approach as would be the case if the value of the firm were to be defined as simply the discounted sum of future total earnings.[13] The trouble with such a definition is not, as is often suggested, that it overlooks the fact that the corporation is a separate entity and that these profits cannot freely be withdrawn by the shareholders; but rather that it neglects the fact that additional capital must be acquired at some cost to maintain the future earnings stream at its specified level. The capital to be raised in any future period is, of course, $I(t)$ and its opportunity cost, no matter how financed, is ρ per cent per period thereafter. Hence, the current value of the firm under the earnings approach must be stated as

$$V(0) = \sum_{t=0}^{\infty} \frac{1}{(1 + \rho)^{t+1}} \left[X(t) - \sum_{\tau=0}^{t} \rho I(\tau) \right].$$ (18)

That this version of the earnings approach is indeed consistent with our bsaic assumptions and equivalent to the previous approaches can be seen by regrouping terms and rewriting equation (18) as

$$V(0) = \sum_{t=0}^{\infty} \frac{1}{(1 + \rho)^{t+1}} X(t) - \sum_{t=0}^{\infty} \left(\sum_{\tau=t}^{\infty} \frac{\rho I(t)}{(1 + \rho)^{\tau+1}} \right)$$

$$= \sum_{t=0}^{\infty} \frac{1}{(1 + \rho)^{t+1}} X(t) - \sum_{t=0}^{\infty} \frac{1}{(1 + \rho)^{t+1}}$$

$$\times \left(\sum_{\tau=0}^{\infty} \frac{\rho I(t)}{(1 + \rho)^{\tau+1}} \right).$$ (19)

[13] In fairness, we should point out that there is no one, to our knowledge, who has seriously advanced this view. It is a view whose main function seems to be to serve as a "straw man" to be demolished by those supporting the dividend view. See, e.g., Gordon [9, esp. pp. 102–3]. Other writers take as the supposed earnings counter-view to the dividend approach not a relation running in terms of the *stream* of earnings but simply the proposition that price is proportional to current earnings, i.e., $V(0) = X(0)/\rho$. The probable origins of this widespread misconception about the earnings approach are discussed further below (p. 354).

Since the last inclosed summation reduces simply to $I(t)$, the expression in turn turn reduces to simply

$$V(0) = \sum_{t=0}^{\infty} \frac{1}{(1 + \rho)^{t+1}} [X(t) - I(t)], \tag{20}$$

which is precisely our earlier equation (9).

Note that the version of the earnings approach presented here does not depend for its validity upon any special assumptions about the time shape of the stream of total profits or the stream of dividends per share. Clearly, however, the time paths of the two streams are closely related to each other (via financial policy) and to the stream of returns derived by holders of the shares. Since these relations are of some interest in their own right and since misunderstandings about them have contributed to the confusion over the role of dividend policy, it may be worthwhile to examine them briefly before moving on to relax the basic assumptions.

III. EARNINGS, DIVIDENDS, AND GROWTH RATES

The convenient case of constant growth rates. The relation between the stream of earnings of the firm and the stream of dividends and of returns to the stockholders can be brought out most clearly by specializing (12) to the case in which investment opportunities are such as to generate a constant rate of growth of profits in perpetuity. Admittedly, this case has little empirical significance, but it is convenient for illustrative purposes and has received much attention in the literature.

Specifically, suppose that in each period t the firm has the opportunity to invest in real assets a sum $I(t)$ that is k per cent as large as its total earnings for the period; and that this investment produces a perpetual yield of ρ^* beginning with the next period. Then, by definition

$$X(t) = X(t - 1) + \rho^* I(t - 1) = X(t - 1)[1 + k\rho^*]$$
$$= X(0)[1 + k\rho^*]^t \tag{21}$$

and $k\rho^*$ is the (constant) rate of growth of total earnings. Substituting from (21) into (12) for $I(t)$ we obtain

$$V(0) = \frac{X(0)}{\rho} + \sum_{t=0}^{\infty} \left(\frac{\rho^* - \rho}{\rho}\right) kX(0)[1 + k\rho^*]^t (1 + \rho)^{-(t+1)}$$
$$= \frac{X(0)}{\rho} \left[1 + \frac{k(\rho^* - \rho)}{1 - \rho} \sum_{t=0}^{\infty} \left(\frac{1 + k\rho^*}{1 + \rho}\right)^t\right]. \tag{22}$$

Evaluating the infinite sum and simplifying, we finally obtain[14]

$$V(0) = \frac{X(0)}{\rho} \left[1 + \frac{k(\rho^* - \rho)}{\rho - k\rho^*}\right] = \frac{X(0)(1 - k)}{\rho - k\rho^*}, \tag{23}$$

---

[14] One advantage of the specialization (23) is that it makes it easy to see what is really involved in the assumption here and throughout the paper that the $V(0)$ given by any of our summation formulas is necessarily finite (cf. above, n.4). In terms of (23) the condition is

which expresses the value of the firm as a function of its current earnings, the rate of growth of earnings, the internal rate of return, and the market rate of return.[15] Note that (23) holds not just for period 0, but for every t. Hence if $X(t)$ is growing at the rate $k\rho^*$, it follows that the value of the enterprise, $V(t)$, also grows at that rate.

The growth of dividends and the growth of total profits. Given that total earnings (and the total value of the firm) are growing at the rate $k\rho^*$ what is the rate of growth of dividends per share and of the price per share? Clearly, the answer will vary depending on whether or not the firm is paying out a high percentage of its earnings and thus relying heavily on outside financing. We can show the nature of this dependence explicitly by making use of the

---

clearly $k\rho^* < \rho$, i.e., that the rate of growth of the firm be less than market rate of discount. Although the case of (perpetual) growth rates greater than the discount factor is the much-discussed "growth stock paradox" (e.g. [67]), it has no real economic significance as we pointed out in [16, esp. n.17, p. 664]. This will be apparent when one recalls that the discount rate ρ, though treated as a constant in partial equilibrium (relative price) analysis of the kind presented here, is actually a variable from the standpoint of the system as a whole. That is, if the assumption of finite value for all shares did not hold, because for some shares $k\rho^*$ was (perpetually) greater than ρ, then ρ would necessarily rise until an over-all equilibrium in the capital markets had been restored.

[15] An interesting and more realistic variant of (22), which also has a number of convenient features from the standpoint of developing empirical tests, can be obtained by assuming that the special investment opportunities are available not in perpetuity but only over some finite interval of T periods. To exhibit the value of the firm for this case, we need only replace the infinite summation in (22) with a summation running from $t = 0$ to $t = T - 1$. Evaluating the resulting expression, we obtain

$$V(0) = \frac{X(0)}{\rho}\left\{1 + \frac{k(\rho^* - \rho)}{\rho - k\rho^*}\left[1 - \left(\frac{1 + k\rho^*}{1 + \rho}\right)^T\right]\right\} \tag{22a}$$

Note that (22a) holds even if $k\rho^* > \rho$, so that the so-called growth paradox disappears altogether. If, as we should generally expect, $(1 + k\rho^*)/(1 + \rho)$ is close to one, and if T is not too large, the right hand side of (22a) admits of a very convenient approximation. In this case in fact we can write

$$\left[\frac{1 + k\rho^*}{1 + \rho}\right]^T \cong 1 + T(k\rho^* - \rho)$$

the approximation holding, if, as we should expect, $(1 + k\rho^*)$ and $(1 + \rho)$ are both close to unity. Substituting this approximation into (22a) and simplifying, finally yields

$$V(0) \cong \frac{X(0)}{\rho}\left[1 + \frac{k(\rho^* - \rho)}{\rho - k\rho^*}T(\rho - k\rho^*)\right]$$

$$= \left[\frac{X(0)}{\rho} + kX(0)\left(\frac{\rho^* - \rho}{\rho}\right)T\right]. \tag{22b}$$

The common sense of (22b) is easy to see. The current value of a firm is given by the value of the earning power of the currently held assets plus the market value of the special earning opportunity multiplied by the number of years for which it is expected to last.

fact that whatever the rate of growth of dividends per share the present value of the firm by the dividend approach must be the same as by the earnings approach. Thus let

> g = the rate of growth of dividends per share, or, what amounts to the same thing, the rate of growth of dividends accruing to the shares of the current holders (i.e., $D_o(t) = D_o(0)[1 + g]^t$);
> k_r = the fraction of total profits retained in each period (so that $D(t) = X(0)[1 - k_r]$);
> $k_e = k - k_r$ = the amount of external capital raised per period, expressed as a fraction of profits in the period.

Then the present value of the stream of dividends to the original owners will be

$$D_0(0) \sum_{t=0}^{\infty} \frac{(1 + g)^t}{(1 + \rho)^{t+1}} = \frac{D(0)}{\rho - g} = \frac{X(0)[1 - k_r]}{\rho - g}. \tag{24}$$

By virtue of the dividend approach we know that (24) must be equal to $V(0)$. If therefore, we equate it to the right hand side of (23), we obtain

$$\frac{X(0)[1 - k_r]}{\rho - g} = \frac{X(0)[1 - (k_r + k_e)]}{\rho - k\rho^*}$$

from which it follows that the rate of growth of dividends per share and the rate of growth of the price of a share must be[16]

$$g = k\rho^* \frac{1 - k_r}{1 - k} - k_e\rho \frac{1}{1 - k}. \tag{25}$$

Notice that in the extreme case in which all financing is internal ($k_e = 0$ and $k = k_r$), the second term drops out and the first becomes simply $k\rho^*$. Hence the growth rate of dividends in that special case is exactly the same as that of total profits and total value and is proportional to the rate of retention k_r. In all other cases, g is necessarily less than $k\rho^*$ and may even be negative, despite a positive $k\rho^*$, if $\rho^* < \rho$ and if the firm pays out a large fraction of its income in dividends. In the other direction, we see from (25) that even if a firm is a "growth" corporation ($\rho^* > \rho$) then the stream of dividends and price per share must grow over time even though $k_r = 0$, that is, even though it pays out *all* its earnings in dividends.

---

[16] That g is the rate of price increase per share as well as the rate of growth of dividends per share follows from the fact that by (13) and the definition of g

$$p(t) = \sum_{\tau=0}^{\infty} \frac{d(t + \tau)}{(1 + \rho)^{\tau+1}} = \sum_{\tau=0}^{\infty} \frac{d(0)[1 + g]^{t+\tau}}{(1 + \rho)^{\tau+1}}$$

$$= (1 + g)^t \sum_{\tau=0}^{\infty} \frac{d(\tau)}{(1 + \rho)^{\tau+1}} = p(0)[1 + g]^t.$$

The relation between the growth rate of the firm and the growth rate of dividends under various dividend policies is illustrated graphically in Figure 1 in which for maximum clarity the natural logarithm of profits and dividends have been plotted against time.[17]

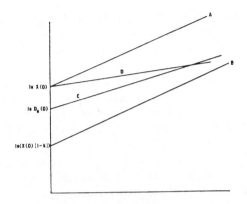

FIG. 1.- Growth of dividends per share in relation to growth in total earnings:

A. Total earnings: $\ln X(t) = \ln X(0) + k\rho^*t;$

B. Total earnings minus capital invested: $\ln [X(t) - I(t)] = \ln X(0) [1 - k] + k\rho^*t;$
   Dividends per share (all financing internal): $\ln D_0(t) = \ln D(0) + gt = \ln X(0) [1 - k] + k\rho^*t;$

C. Dividends per share (some financing external): $\ln D_0(t) = \ln D(0) + gt;$

D. Dividends per share (all financing external): $\ln D_0(t) = \ln X(0) + [(k/1 - k) (\rho^* - \rho)]t.$

Line A shows the total earnings of the firm growing through time at the constant rate $k\rho^*$, the slope of A. Line B shows the growth of (1) the stream of total earnings minus capital outlays and (2) the stream of dividends to the original owners (or dividends per share) in the special case in which all financing is internal. The slope of B is, of course, the same as that of A and the (constant) difference between the curves is simply $\ln(1 - k)$, the ratio of dividends to profits. Line C shows the growth of dividends per share when the firm uses both internal and external financing. As compared with the pure retention case, the line starts higher but grows more slowly at the rate g given by (25). The higher the payout policy, the higher the starting position and the slower the growth up to the other limiting case of complete external financing, Line D, which starts at $\ln X(0)$ and grows at a rate of $(k/1 - k) \cdot (\rho^* - \rho)$.

The special case of exclusively internal financing. As noted above the growth rate of dividends per share is not the same as the growth rate of the firm except in the special case in which all financing is internal. This is merely one of a number of peculiarites of this special case on which, unfortunately, many writers have based their entire analysis. The reason for the preoccupation with this special case if far from clear to us. Certainly no one would

[17] That is, we replace each discrete compounding expression such as $X(t) = X(0) \times [1 + k\rho^*]^t$ with its counterpart under continuous discounting $X(t) = X(0)e^{k\rho^*t}$ which, of course, yields the convenient linear relation in $X(t) = \ln X(0) + k\rho^*t.$

suggest that it is the only empirically relevant case. Even if the case were in fact the most common, the theorist would still be under an obligation to consider alternative assumptions. We suspect that in the last analysis, the popularity of the internal financing model will be found to reflect little more than its ease of manipulation combined with the failure to push the analysis far enough to disclose how special and how treacherous a case it really is.

In particular, concentration on this special case appears to be largely responsible for the widely held view that, even under perfect capital markets, there is an optimum dividend policy for the firm that depends on the internal rate of return. Such a conclusion is almost inevitable if one works exclusively with the assumption, explicit or implicit, that funds for investment come *only* from retained earnings. For in that case *dividend policy* is indistinguishable from *investment policy*; and there is an optimal investment policy which does in general depend on the rate of return.

Notice also from (23) that if $\rho^* = \rho$ and $k = k_r$, the term $[1 - k_r]$ can be canceled from both the numerator and the denominator. The value of the firm becomes simply $X(0)/\rho$, the capitalized value of current earnings. Lacking a standard model for valuation more general than the retained earnings case it has been all too easy for many to conclude that this dropping out of the payout ratio $[1 - k_r]$ when $\rho^* = \rho$ must be what is meant by the irrelevance of dividend policy and that $V(0) = X(0)/\rho$ must constitute the "earnings" approach.

Still another example of the pitfalls in basing arguments on this special case is provided by the recent and extensive work on valuation by M. Gordon.[18] Gordon argues, in essence, that because of increasing uncertainty the discount rate $\hat{\rho}(t)$ applied by an investor to a future dividend payment will rise with t, where t denotes not a specific date but rather the distance from the period in which the investor performs the discounting.[19] Hence, when we use a single uniform discount rate ρ as in (22) or (23), this rate should be thought of as really an average of the "true" rates $\hat{\rho}(t)$ each weighted by the size of the expected dividend payment at time t. If the dividend stream is growing exponentially then such a weighted average ρ would, of course, be higher the greater the rate of growth of dividends g since the greater will then be the portion of the dividend stream arising in the distant as opposed to the near future. But if all financing is assumed to be internal, then $g = k_r \rho^*$ so that given ρ^*, the weighted average discount factor ρ will be an increasing function

[18] See esp. [8]. Gordon's views represent the most explicit and sophisticated formulation of what might be called the "bird-in-the-hand" fallacy. For other, less elaborate, statements of essentially the same position see, among others, Graham and Dodd [11, p. 433] and Clendenin and Van Cleave [3].

[19] We use the notation $\hat{\rho}(t)$ to avoid any confusion between Gordon's purely subjective discount rate and the objective, market-given yields $\rho(t)$ in Sec. I above. To attempt to derive valuation formulas under uncertainty from these purely subjective discount factors involves, of course, an error essentially analogous to that of attempting to develop the certainty formulas from "marginal rates of time preference" rather than objective market opportunities.

of the rate of retention k_r which would run counter to our conclusion that dividend policy has no effect on the current value of the firm or its cost of capital.

For all its ingenuity, however, and its seeming foundation in uncertainty, the argument clearly suffers fundamentally from the typical confounding of dividend policy with investment policy that so frequently accompanies use of the internal financing model. Had Gordon not confined his attention to this special case (or its equivalent variants), he would have seen that while a change in dividend policy will necessarily affect the size of the expected dividend payment on the share in any future period, it need not, in the general case, affect either the size of the *total* return that the investor expects during that period or the degree of uncertainty attaching to that total return. As should be abundantly clear by now, a change in dividend policy, given investment policy, implies a change only in the distribution of the total return in any period as between dividends and capital gains. If investors behave rationally, such a change cannot affect market valuations. Indeed, if they valued shares according to the Gordon approach and thus paid a premium for higher payout ratios, then holders of the low payout shares would actually realize consistently higher returns on their investment over any stated interval of time.[20]

Corporate earnings and investor returns. Knowing the relation of g to $k\rho^*$ we can answer a question of considerable interest to economic theorists, namely: What is the precise relation between the earnings of the corporation in any period $X(t)$ and the total return to the owners of the stock during that period?[21] If we let $G_t(t)$ be the capital gains to the owners during t, we know

---

[20] This is not to deny that growth stocks (in our sense) may well be "riskier" than non-growth stocks. But to the extent that this is true, it will be due to the possibly greater uncertainty attaching to the size and duration of future growth opportunities and hence to the size of the future stream of total returns quite apart from any questions of dividend policy.

[21] Note also that the above analysis enables us to deal very easily with the familiar issue of whether a firm's cost of equity capital is measured by its earnings/price ratio or by its dividend/price ratio. Clearly, the answer is that it is measured by neither, except under very special circumstances. For from (23) we have for the earnings/price ratio

$$\frac{X(0)}{V(0)} = \frac{\rho - k\rho^*}{1 - k},$$

which is equal to the cost of capital, ρ, only if the firm has no growth potential (i.e., $\rho^* = \rho$). And from (24) we have for the dividend/price ratio

$$\frac{D(0)}{V(0)} = \rho - g,$$

which is equal to ρ only when $g = 0$; i.e., from (25), either when $k = 0$; or, if $k > 0$, when $\rho^* < \rho$ and the amount of external financing is precisely

$$k_e \frac{\rho^*}{\rho} k[1 - k_r],$$

so that the gain from the retention of earnings exactly offsets the loss that would otherwise be occasioned by the unprofitable investment.

that

$$D_t(t) + G_t(t) = X(t)(1 - k_r) + gV(t) \qquad (26)$$

since the rate of growth of price is the same as that of dividends per share. Using (25) and (26) to substitute for g and $V(t)$ and simplifying, we find that

$$D_t(t) + G_t(t) = X(t)\left[\frac{\rho(1 - k)}{\rho - k\rho^*}\right]. \qquad (27)$$

The relation between the investors' return and the corporation's profits is thus seen to depend entirely on the relation between ρ^* and ρ. If $\rho^* = \rho$ (i.e., the firm has no special "growth" opportunities), then the expression in brackets becomes 1 and the investors returns are precisely the same as the corporate profits. If $\rho^* < \rho$, however, the investors' return will be less than the corporate earnings; and, in the case of growth corporations the investors' return will actually be greater than the flow of corporate profits over the interval.[22]

Some implications for constructing empirical tests. Finally the fact that we have two different (though not independent) measures of growth in $k\rho^*$ and g and two corresponding families of valuation formulas means, among other things, that we can proceed by either of two routes in empirical studies of valuation. We can follow the standard practice of the security analyst and think in terms of price per share, dividends per share, and the rate of growth of dividends per share; or we can think in terms of the total value of the enterprise, total earnings, and the rate of growth of total earnings. Our own

---

[22] The above relation between earnings per share and dividends plus capital gains also means that there will be a systematic relation between retained earnings and capital gains. The "marginal" relation is easy to see and is always precisely one for one regardless of growth or financial policy. That is, taking a dollar away from dividends and adding it to retained earnings (all other things equal) means an increase in capital gains of one dollar (or a reduction in capital loss of one dollar). The "average" relation is somewhat more complex. From (26) and (27) we can see that

$$G_t(t) = k_r X(t) + k X(t)\frac{\rho^* - \rho}{\rho - k\rho^*}.$$

Hence, if $\rho^* = \rho$ the total capital gain received will be exactly the same as the total retained earnings per share. For growth corporations, however, the capital gain will always be greater than the retained earnings (and there will be a capital gain of

$$k X(t)\left[\frac{\rho^* - \rho}{\rho - k\rho^*}\right]$$

even when all earnings are paid out). For non-growth corporations the relation between gain and retentions is reversed. Note also that the absolute difference between the total capital gain and the total retained earnings is a constant (given, ρ, k and ρ^*) unaffected by dividend policy. Hence the *ratio* of capital gain to retained earnings will vary directly with the payout ratio for growth corporations (and vice versa for non-growth corporations). This means, among other things, that it is dangerous to attempt to draw inferences about the relative growth potential or relative managerial efficiency of corporations solely on the basis of the ratio of capital gains to retained earnings (cf. Harkavy [12, esp. pp. 289–94]).

preference happens to be for the second approach primarily because certain additional variables of interest—such as dividend policy, leverage, and size of firm—can be incorporated more easily and meaningfully into test equations in which the growth term is the growth of total earnings. But this can wait. For present purposes, the thing to be stressed is simply that two approaches, properly carried through, are in no sense *opposing* views of the valuation process; but rather equivalent views, with the choice between them largely a matter of taste and convenience.

IV. THE EFFECTS OF DIVIDEND POLICY UNDER UNCERTAINTY

Uncertainty and the general theory of valuations. In turning now from the ideal world of certainty to one of uncertainty our first step, alas, must be to jettison the fundamental valuation principle as given, say, in our equation (3)

$$V(t) \frac{1}{1 + \rho(t)} [D(t) + n(t)p(t + 1)]$$

and from which the irrelevance proposition as well as all the subsequent valuation formulas in Sections II and III were derived. For the terms in the bracket can no longer be regarded as given numbers, but must be recognized as "random variables" from the point of view of the investor as of the start of period t. Nor is it at all clear what meaning can be attached to the discount factor $1/[1 + \rho(t)]$ since what is being discounted is not a given return, but at best only a probability distribution of possible returns. We can, of course, delude ourselves into thinking that we are preserving equation (3) by the simple and popular expedient of drawing a bar over each term and referring to it thereafter as the mathematical expectation of the random variable. But except for the trivial case of universal linear utility functions we know that $V(t)$ would also be affected, and materially so, by the higher order moments of the distribution of returns. Hence there is no reason to believe that the discount factor for expected values, $1/[1 + \rho(t)]$, would in fact be the same for any two firms chosen arbitrarily, not to mention that the expected values themselves may well be different for different investors.

All this is not to say, of course, that there are insuperable difficulties in the way of developing a testable theory of rational market valuation under uncertainty.[23] On the contrary, our investigations of the problem to date have convinced us that it is indeed possible to construct such a theory—though the construction, as can well be imagined, is a fairly complex and space-consuming task. Fortunately, however, this task need not be undertaken in this paper

---

[23] Nor does it mean that all the previous certainty analysis has no relevance whatever in the presence of uncertainty. There are many issues, such as those discussed in Sec. I and II, that really relate only to what has been called the pure "futurity" component in valuation. Here, the valuation formulas can still be extremely useful in maintaining the internal consistency of the reasoning and in suggesting (or criticizing) empirical tests of certain classes of hypotheses about valuation, even though the formulas themselves cannot be used to grind out precise numerical values for specific real-world shares.

which is concerned primarily with the effects of dividend policy on market valuation. For even without a full-fledged theory of what *does* determine market value under uncertainty we can show that dividend policy at least is *not* one of the determinants. To establish this particular generalization of the previous certainty results we need only invoke a corresponding generalization of the original postulate of rational behavior to allow for the fact that, under uncertainty, choices depend on expectations as well as tastes.

"*Imputed rationality*" and "*symmetric market rationality.*" This generalization can be formulated in two steps as follows. First, we shall say that an individual trader "imputes rationality to the market" or satisfies the postulate of "imputed rationality" if, in forming expectations, he assumes that every other trader in the market is (a) rational in the previous sense of preferring more wealth to less regardless of the form an increment in wealth may take, and (b) imputes rationality to all other traders. Second, we shall say that a market as a whole satisfies the postulate of "symmetric market rationality" if every trader both behaves rationally and imputes rationality to the market.[24]

Notice that this postulate of symmetric market rationality differs from the usual postulate of rational behavior in several important respects. In the first place, the new postulate covers not only the choice behavior of individuals but also their expectations of the choice behavior of others. Second, the postulate is a statement about the market as a whole and not just about individual behavior. Finally, though by no means least, symmetric market rationality cannot be deduced from individual rational behavior in the usual sense since that sense does not imply imputing rationality to others. It may, in fact, imply a choice behavior inconsistent with imputed rationality unless the individual actually believes the market to be symmetrically rational. For if an ordinarily rational investor had good reason to believe that other investors would not behave rationally, then it might well be rational for him to adopt a strategy he would otherwise have rejected as irrational. Our postulate thus rules out, among other things, the possibility of speculative "bubbles" wherein an individually rational investor buys a security he knows to be overpriced (i.e., too expensive in relation to its expected *long-run* return to be attractive as a permanent addition to his portfolio) in the expectation that he can resell it at a still more inflated price before the bubble bursts.[25]

---

[24] We offer the term "symmetric market rationality" with considerable diffidence and only after having been assured by game theorists that there is no accepted term for this concept in the literature of that subject even though the postulate itself (or close parallels to it) does appear frequently. In the literature of economics a closely related, but not exact, counterpart is Muth's "hypothesis of rational expectations" [18]. Among the more euphonic, though we feel somewhat less revealing, alternatives that have been suggested to us are "putative rationality" (by T. J. Koopmans), "bi-rationality" (by G. L. Thompson), "empathetic rationality" (by Andrea Modigliani), and "pan-rationality" (by A. Ando).

[25] We recognize, of course, that such speculative bubbles have actually arisen in the past (and will probably continue to do so in the future), so that our postulate can certainly not be taken to be of universal applicability. We feel, however, that it is also not of universal inapplicability since from our observation, speculative bubbles, though well publicized when they occur, do not seem to us to be a dominant, or even a fundamental, feature of actual

The irrelevance of dividend policy despite uncertainty. In Section I we were able to show that, given a firm's investment policy, its dividend policy was irrelevant to its current market valuation. We shall now show that this fundamental conclusion need not be modified merely because of the presence of uncertainty about the future course of profits, investment, or dividends (assuming again, as we have throughout, that investment policy can be regarded as separable from dividend policy). To see that uncertainty about these elements changes nothing essential, consider a case in which current investors believe that the future streams of total earnings and total investment whatever actual values they may assume at different points in time will be identical for two firms, 1 and 2.[26] Suppose further, provisionally, that the same is believed to be true of future total dividend payments from period one on so that the only way in which the two firms differ is possibly with respect to the prospective dividend in the current period, period 0. In terms of previous notation we are thus assuming that

$$\tilde{X}_1(t) = \tilde{X}_2(t) \qquad t = 0 \cdots \infty$$

$$\tilde{I}_1(t) = \tilde{I}_2(t) \qquad t = 0 \cdots \infty$$

$$\tilde{D}_1(t) = \tilde{D}_2(t) \qquad t = 1 \cdots \infty$$

the subscripts indicating the firms and the tildes being added to the variables to indicate that these are to be regarded from the standpoint of current period, not as known numbers but as numbers that will be drawn in the future from the appropriate probability distributions. We may now ask: "What will be the return, $\tilde{R}_1(0)$ to the current shareholders in firm 1 during the current period?" Clearly, it will be

$$\tilde{R}_1(0) = \tilde{D}_1(0) + \tilde{V}_1(1) - \tilde{m}_1(1)\tilde{p}_1(1). \qquad (28)$$

But the relation between $\tilde{D}_1(0)$ and $\tilde{m}_1(1)\,\tilde{p}_1(1)$ is necessarily still given by equation (4) which is merely an accounting identity so that we can write

$$\tilde{m}_1(1)\tilde{p}_1(1) = \tilde{I}_1(0) - [\tilde{X}_1(0) - \tilde{D}_1(0)], \qquad (29)$$

and, on substituting in (28), we obtain

$$\tilde{R}_1(0) = \tilde{X}_1(0) - \tilde{I}_1(0) + \tilde{V}_1(1) \qquad (30)$$

---

market behavior under uncertainty. That is, we would be prepared to argue that, as a rule and on the average, markets do not behave in ways which do not obviously contradict the postulate so that the postulate may still be useful at least as a first approximation, for the analysis of long-run tendencies in organized capital markets. Needless to say, whether our confidence in the postulate is justified is something that will have to be determined by empirical tests of its implications (such as, of course, the irrelevance of dividend policy).

[26] The assumption of two identical firms is introduced for convenience of exposition only, since it usually is easier to see the implications of rationality when there is an explicit arbitrage mechanism, in this case, switches between the shares of the two firms. The assumption, however, is not necessary and we can, if we like, think of the two firms as really corresponding to two states of the same firm for an investor performing a series of "mental experiments" on the subject of dividend policy.

for firm 1. By an exactly parallel process we can obtain an equivalent expression for $\tilde{R}_2(0)$.

Let us now compare $\tilde{R}_1(0)$ with $\tilde{R}_2(0)$. Note first that, by assumption, $\tilde{X}_1(0) = \tilde{X}_2(0)$ and $\tilde{I}_1(0) = \tilde{I}_2(0)$. Furthermore, with symmetric market rationality, the terminal values $\tilde{V}_i(1)$ can depend only on prospective future earnings, investment and dividends from period 1 on and these too, by assumption, are identical for the two companies. Thus symmetric rationality implies that every investor must expect $\tilde{V}_1(1) = \tilde{V}_2(1)$ and hence finally $\tilde{R}_1(0) = \tilde{R}_2(0)$. But if the return to the investors is the same in the two cases, rationality requires that the two firms command the same current value so that $V_1(0)$ must equal $V_2(0)$ regardless of any difference in dividend payments during period 0. Suppose now that we allow dividends to differ not just in period 0 but in period 1 as well, but still retain the assumption of equal $\tilde{X}_i(t)$ and $\tilde{I}_i(t)$ in all periods and of equal $\tilde{D}_i(t)$ in period 2 and beyond. Clearly, the only way differences in dividends in period 1 can effect $\tilde{R}_i(0)$ and hence $V_i(0)$ is via $\tilde{V}_i(1)$. But, by the assumption of symmetric market rationality, current investors know that as of the start of period 1 the then investors will value the two firms rationally and we have already shown that differences in the current dividend do not affect current value. Thus we must have $\tilde{V}_1(1) = \tilde{V}_2(1)$—and hence $V_1(0) = V_2(0)$—regardless of any possible difference in dividend payments during period 1. By an obvious extension of the reasoning to $\tilde{V}_i(2)$, $\tilde{V}_i(3)$, and so on, it must follow that the current valuation is unaffected by differences in dividend payments in any future period and thus that dividend policy is irrelevant for the determination of market prices, given investment policy.[27]

Dividend policy and leverage.   A study of the above line of proof will show it to be essentially analogous to the proof for the certainty world, in which as we know, firms can have, in effect, only two alternative sources of investment funds: retained earnings or stock issues. In an uncertain world, however, there is the additional financing possibility of debt issues. The question naturally arises, therefore, as to whether the conclusion about irrelevance remains valid even in the presence of debt financing, particularly since there may very well be interactions between debt policy and dividend policy. The answer is that it does, and while a complete demonstration would perhaps be too tedious and repetitious at this point, we can at least readily sketch out the main outlines of how the proof proceeds. We begin, as above, by establishing the conditions from period 1 on that lead to a situation in which $\tilde{V}_1(1)$ must be brought into equality with $\tilde{V}_2(1)$ where the V, following the approach in our

[27] We might note that the assumption of symmetric market rationality is sufficient to derive this conclusion but not strictly necessary if we are willing to weaken the irrelevance proposition to one running in terms of long-run, average tendencies in the market. Individual rationality alone could conceivably bring about the latter, for over the long pull rational investors could enforce this result by buying and holding " undervalued " securities because this would insure them higher long-run returns when eventually the prices became the same. They might, however, have a long, long wait.

earlier paper [17], is now to be interpreted as the total market value of the firm, debt plus equity, not merely equity alone. The return to the original investors taken as a whole—and remember that any individual always has the option of buying a proportional share of both the equity and the debt—must correspondingly be broadened to allow for the interest on the debt. There will also be a corresponding broadening of the accounting identity (4) to allow, on the one hand, for the interest return and, on the other, for any debt funds used to finance the investment in whole or in part. The net result is that both the dividend component and the interest component of total earnings will cancel out making the relevant (total) return, as before, $[\tilde{X}_i(0) - \tilde{I}_i(0) + \tilde{V}_i(1)]$ which is clearly independent of the current dividend. It follows, then, that the value of the firm must also therefore be independent of dividend policy given investment policy.[28]

The informational content of dividends. To conclude our discussion of dividend policy under uncertainty, we might take note briefly of a common confusion about the meaning of the irrelevance propossition occasioned by the fact that in the real world a change in the dividend rate is often followed by a change in the market price (sometimes spectacularly so). Such a phenomenon would not be incompatible with irrelevance to the extent that it was merely a reflection of what might be called the "informational content" of dividends, an attribute of particular dividend payments hitherto exluded by assumption from the discussion and proofs. That is, where a firm has adopted a policy of dividend stabilization with a long-established and generally appreciated "target payout ratio," investors are likely to (and have good reason to) interpret a change in the dividend rate as a change in management's views of future profit prospects for the firm.[29] The dividend change, in other words, provides the occasion for the price change though not its cause, the price still being solely a reflection of future earnings and growth opportunities. In any particular instance, of course, the investors might well be mistaken in placing this interpretation on the dividend change, since the management might really only be changing its payout target or possibly even attempting to "manipulate" the price. But this would involve no particular conflict with the irrelevance proposition, unless, of course, the price changes in such cases were not reversed when the unfolding of events had made clear the true nature of the situation.[30]

---

[28] This same conclusion must also hold for the current market value of all the shares (and hence for the current price per share), which is equal to the total market value minus the given initially outstanding debt. Needless to say, however, the price per share and the value of the equity at *future* points in time will not be independent of dividend and debt policies in the interim.

[29] For evidence on the prevalance of dividend stabilization and target ratios see Lintner [15].

[30] For a further discussion of the subject of the informational content of dividends, including its implications for empirical tests of the irrelevance proposition, see Modigliani and Miller [16, pp. 666–68].

V. DIVIDEND POLICY AND MARKET IMPERFECTIONS

To complete the analysis of dividend policy, the logical next step would presumably be to abandon the assumption of perfect capital markets. This is, however, a good deal easier to say than to do principally because there is no unique set of circumstances that constitutes "imperfection." We can describe not one but a multitude of possible departures from strict perfection, singly and in combinations. Clearly, to attempt to pursue the implications of each of these would only serve to add inordinately to an already overlong discussion. We shall instead, therefore, limit ourselves in this concluding section to a few brief and general observations about imperfect markets that we hope may prove helpful to those taking up the task of extending the theory of valuation in this direction.

First, it is important to keep in mind that from the standpoint of dividend policy, what counts is not imperfection per se but only imperfection that might lead an investor to have a systematic preference as between a dollar of current dividends and a dollar of current capital gains. Where no such systematic preference is produced, we can subsume the imperfection in the (random) error term always carried along when applying propositions derived from ideal models to real-world events.

Second even where we do find imperfections that bias individual preferences—such as the existence of brokerage fees which tend to make young "accumulators" prefer low-payout shares and retired persons lean toward "income stocks"—such imperfections are at best only necessary but not sufficient conditions for certain payout policies to command a permanent premium in the market. If, for example, the frequency distribution of corporate payout ratios happened to correspond exactly with the distribution of investor preferences for payout ratios, then the existence of these preferences would clearly lead ultimately to a situation whose implications were different in no fundamental respect from the perfect market case. Each corporation would tend to attract to itself a "clientele" consisting of those preferring its particular payout ratio, but one clientele would be entirely as good as another in terms of the valuation it would imply for the firm. Nor, or course, is it necessary for the distributions to match exactly for this result to occur. Even if there were a "shortage" of some particular payout ratio, investors would still normally have the option of achieving their particular saving objectives without paying a premium for the stocks in short supply simply by buying appropriately weighted combinations of the more plentiful payout ratios. In fact, given the great range of corporate payout ratios known to be available, this process would fail to eliminate permanent premiums and discounts only if the distribution of investor preferences were heavily concentrated at either of the extreme ends of the payout scale.[31]

---

[31] The above discussion should explain why, among other reasons, it would not be possible to draw any valid inference about the relative preponderance of "accumulators" as opposed to "income" buyers or the strength of their preferences merely from the weight attaching to dividends in a simple cross-sectional regression between value and payouts (as is attempted in Clendenin [2, p. 50] or Durand [5, p. 651]).

Of all the many market imperfections that might be detailed, the only one that would seem to be even remotely capable of producing such a concentration is the substantial advantage accorded to capital gains as compared with dividends under the personal income tax. Strong as this tax push toward capital gains may be for high-income individuals, however, it should be remembered that a substantial (and growing) fraction of total shares outstanding is currently held by investors for whom there is either no tax differential (charitable and educational institutions, foundations, pension trusts, and low-income retired individuals) or where the tax advantage is, if anything, in favor of dividends (casualty insurance companies and taxable corporations generally). Hence, again, the "clientele effect" will be at work. Furthermore, except for taxable individuals in the very top brackets, the required difference in before-tax yields to produce equal after-tax yields is not particularly striking, at least for moderate variations in the composition of returns.[32] All this is not to say, of course, that differences in yields (market values) caused by differences in payout policies should be ignored by managements or investors merely because they may be relatively small. But it may help to keep investigators from being too surprised if it turns out to be hard to measure or even to detect any premium for low-payout shares on the basis of standard statistical techniques.

Finally, we may note that since the tax differential in favor of capital gains is undoubtedly the major *systematic* imperfection in the market, one clearly cannot invoke "imperfections" to account for the difference between our irrelevance proposition and the standard view as to the role of dividend policy found in the literature of finance. For the standard view is not that low-payout companies command a premium; but that, in general, they will sell at a discount![33] If such indeed were the case—and we, at least, are not prepared to concede that this has been established—then the analysis presented in this paper suggests there would be only one way to account for it; namely, as the result of systematic irrationality on the part of the investing public.[34]

To say that an observed positive premium on high payouts was due to

---

[32] For example, if a taxpayer is subject to a marginal rate of 40 per cent on dividends and half that or 20 per cent on long-term capital gains, then a before-tax yield of 6 per cent consisting of 40 per cent dividends and 60 per cent capital gains produces an after-tax yield of 4.32 per cent. To net the same after-tax yield on a stock with 60 per cent of the return in dividends and only 40 per cent in capital gains would require a before-tax yield of 6.37 per cent. The difference would be somewhat smaller if we allowed for the present dividend credit, though it should also be kept in mind that the tax on capital gains may be avoided entirely under present arrangements if the gains are not realized during the holder's lifetime.

[33] See, among many, many others, Gordon [8, 9], Graham and Dodd [11, esp. chaps. xxxiv and xxxvi], Durand [4, 5], Hunt, Williams, and Donaldson [13, pp. 647–49], Fisher [7], Gordon and Shapiro [10], Harkavy [12], Clendenin [2], Johnson, Shapiro, and O'Meara [14], and Walter [19].

[34] Or, less plausibly, that there is a systematic tendency for external funds to be used more productively than internal funds.

irrationality would not, of course, make the phenomenon any less real. But it would at least suggest the need for a certain measure of caution by long-range policy-makers. For investors, however naive they may be when they enter the market, do sometimes learn from experience; and perhaps, occasionally, even from reading articles such as this.

REFERENCES

1. Bodenhorn, Diran. "On the Problem of Capital Budgeting," *Journal of Finance*, XIV (December, 1959), 473–92.
2. Clendenin, John. "What Do Stockholders Like?" *California Management Review*, I (Fall, 1958), 47–55.
3. Clendenin, John, and Van Cleave, M. "Growth and Common Stock Values," *Journal of Finance*, IX (September, 1954), 365–76.
4. Durand, David. *Bank Stock Prices and the Bank Capital Problem.* ("Occasional Paper," No. 54) New York: National Bureau of Economic Research, 1957.
5. ——. "The Cost of Capital and the Theory of Investment: Comment," *American Economic Review*, XLIX (September, 1959), 639–54.
6. ——. "Growth Stocks and the Petersburg Paradox," *Journal of Finance*, XII (September, 1957), 348–63.
7. Fisher, G. R. "Some Factors Influencing Share Prices," *Economic Journal*, LXXI, No. 281 (March, 1961), 121–41.
8. Gordon, Myron. "Corporate Saving, Investment and Share Prices," *Review of Economics and Statistics* (forthcoming).
9. ——. "Dividends, Earnings and Stock Prices," *ibid.*, XLI, No. 2, Part I (May, 1959), 99–105.
10. Gordon, Myron, and Shapiro, Eli. "Capital Equipment Analysis: The Required Rate of Profit," *Management Science*, III, 1956, 102–10.
11. Graham, Benjamin, and Dodd, David. *Security Analysis.* 3rd ed. New York: McGraw-Hill Book Company, 1951.
12. Harkavy, Oscar, "The Relation between Retained Earnings and Common Stock Prices for Large Listed Corporations," *Journal of Finance*, VIII (September, 1953), 283–97).
13. Hunt, Pearson, Williams, Charles, and Donaldson, Gordon. *Basic Business Finance.* Homewood, Ill.: Richard D. Irwin, 1958.
14. Johnson, L. R., Shapiro, Eli, and O'Meara, J. "Valuation of Closely Held Stock for Federal Tax Purposes: Approach to an Objective Method," *University of Pennsylvania Law Review*, C, 166–95.
15. Lintner, John. "Distribution of Incomes of Corporations among Dividends, Retained Earnings and Taxes," *American Economic Review*, XLVI (May, 1956), 97–113.
16. Modigliani, Franco, and Miller, Merton. "The Cost of Capital, Corporation Finance and the Theory of Investment: Reply," *American Economic Review*, XLIX (September, 1959), 655–69.
17. ——. "The Cost of Capital, Corporation Finance and the Theory of Investment," *ibid.*, XLVIII (1958), 261–97.
18. Muth, John F. "Rational Expectations and the Theory of Price Movements," *Econometrica* (forthcoming).

19. Walter, James E. "A Discriminant Function for Earnings-Price Ratios of Large Industrial Corporations," *Review of Economics and Statistics*, XLI (February, 1959), 44–52.

20. ——. "Dividend Policies and Common Stock Prices," *Journal of Finance*, XI (March, 1956), 29–41.

21. Williams, John B. *The Theory of Investment Value*. Cambridge, Mass.: Harvard University Press, 1938.

31. DIVIDENDS AND TAXES

MERTON H. MILLER
and
MYRON S. SCHOLES*

Reprinted from the *Journal of Financial Economics,* Vol. 6,
No. 4 (December 1978), pp. 333–364, by permission of the
authors and the publisher.

We present sufficient conditions for taxable investors to be indifferent to dividends despite tax differentials in favor of capital gains (Strong Invariance Proposition). The conditions include two 'seemingly unrelated' provisions of the Internal Revenue Code: (1) the limitation of interest deductions to investment income received and (2) the tax-free accumulation of wealth at the before-tax interest rate on investments in life insurance. Although we use insurance for simplicity in the proof, many tax-equivalent investment vehicles now exist, notably pension funds. Our analysis suggests that the personal income tax is approaching a consumption tax with further drift likely.

1. Introduction

The dividend policies of U.S. corporations have long been a puzzle to finance specialists. In 1976, for example, those corporations paid the Treasury 43 percent of their earnings of $111 billion in corporation income taxes. From the after-tax remainder, they then paid out $31 billion in dividends, thereby subjecting a substantial fraction of their stockholders to still another tax bite under the personal income tax.[1] This seemingly masochistic dividend payout policy cannot convincingly be attributed to a dearth of opportunities to reinvest those dividends profitably within the corporate sector – a reinvestment that would have transformed the taxable dividends into untaxed, or at least long deferred capital appreciation, subject

* University of Chicago, Chicago, Illinois.

In the months since the first draft of this paper was circulated we have received valuable comments and criticism from our colleagues at the University of Chicago, from colleagues at a number of other schools where we presented the paper and from the many others who sent their reactions along in correspondence (an indication of the intense concern with the subject of personal tax planning among academics these days). The list of those to whom we are indebted (some 67 individuals) is far too long to be spelled out in detail here, but they know who they are; and they know we know who they are. We acknowledge with thanks their help and interest. Our thanks also to the editor of this Journal and to the two referees who reviewed the manuscript in detail.

[1] The source for the estimates in this paragraph is the study *Prospects for the Credit Markets in 1977,* by Kaufman, McKeon and Cohen (1977).

to rates substantially below those on dividends. For at the same time that corporations were shovelling $31 billion of dividends out the front door, they were raking some $47 billion in through the back door in the form of new equity issues, new bond issues and new bank credit.[2] Nor can the failure to transform dividends into capital gains convincingly be attributed to a mismatching of the funds and opportunities within the corporate sector. The firms with limited internal opportunities could have benefited their taxable stockholders by using the dividend money to buy the securities of the firms with profitable growth potential. Lest it be objected that the Internal Revenue Service would then have countered with Internal Revenue Code Sections 531 and 532 – the penalty tax for improper accumulation of surplus – it should be noted that these sections are invoked only where the firm's dividend policy is set by a single dominant shareholder (or small group of large holders). Thus they pose no threat to the large, widely-held corporations that actually pay most of the dividends. More serious than the paper-tiger Sections 531 and 532 perhaps is the prospect of harassment by the Anti-Trust Division if companies such as IBM were to start buying shares in their customers or competitors. But such cash-rich firms have a simple way to avoid hassles with the Justice Department over their purchases of shares in other companies, to wit, buying their own shares instead. True, premiums may have to be offered if the tender route were used, and tax pitfalls must be avoided (such as the proportionate buy-backs which may be treated as dividends under IRC Section 302), but the difficulties are certainly not prohibitive as the recent huge share purchase by IBM amply demonstrates.

Nor can the continued outpouring of dividends by the corporate sector convincingly be explained by invoking 'clientele effects' of the kind suggested in the original MM (Miller and Modigliani) dividend paper (1961) or in Long (1977) under which the high payout shares gravitate to investors in low tax brackets and *vice versa*. Evidence of such clientele effects does exist – weak in the study of Blume, Corckett and Friend (1974) and somewhat stronger in the recent paper by Pettit (1977) – but the separation of shareholdings by dividend yield is nowhere as sharp as the raw tax differentials might seem to suggest.[3]

Perhaps most baffling of all has been the reaction of investors to the succession of proposals for tax reform that the Treasury leaked out during the summer and autumn of 1977. Relief from double taxation of dividends via dividend credits was to have been a major conciliatory gesture

[2] In fairness to the electric utility industry whose members have long been the most conspicuous followers of these policies, it is perhaps worth noting that a non-trivial fraction of their dividends have been treated for tax purposes as non-taxable returns of capital in recent years, thanks to large deductions for depreciation.

[3] A closely related puzzle is the failure of the presumed large tax disadvantage of dividends to leave a more easily detectable track in the prices or returns of shares. See, e.g., Black and Scholes (1974). Attempts to detect and measure the tax-induced differentials in before-tax returns are the subject of very active research at the moment.

to 'business' by the Administration in these plans, coupled with some surtax reduction, but also some compensatory increases in the capital gains tax. The intended beneficiaries of this relief, however, showed so little enthusiasm for the dividend credits and so much hostility to the compensating capital gains tax adjustments that the Administration abandoned the whole subject in dismay. The Revenue Act that eventually emerged in the autumn of 1978 gave substantial further relief to capital gains, but none whatever to dividends.

We doubt that any single or simple explanation can account for these and other puzzling aspects of corporate and investor policies with respect to dividends. But we do intend in this paper to call attention to one piece of the puzzle that seems to have been overlooked, namely, that by exploiting some 'seemingly unrelated' features of the personal income tax investors have opportunities to reduce the tax penalty on dividends relative to capital gains and, in the limit, to remove that penalty entirely.

Although pondering the dividend puzzles led us originally to these provisions, the provisions themselves have a significance far beyond that context. They are, it turns out, signs of a fundamental and almost certainly irreversible evolution of the structure of the personal income tax in the last twenty years. In fact, we shall argue that even the term income tax is no longer appropriate as a description of present law. We have already moved further from the accretion concept of income associated with Henry Simons (1936) and closer to the consumption concept of Irving Fisher (1937) than recent academic and legislative discussions of tax reform have recognized.

The logical organization for a paper with our objectives would presumably be to lead off with a description and explanation of those features of the tax law that are critical to the argument. Thanks to recent reforms and simplifications, however, any survey of the relevant provisions and their interactions is likely to bog down quickly in a mass of detail and qualifications. Rather than risk losing readers in these swamps, we shall begin by sketching out a simple economy, whose tax and institutional features are similar in broad-brush strokes to those of our own economy and, yet, in which the personal tax on dividends can be shown to disappear entirely. Having demonstrated the essential features of the conversion mechanism, we can then turn to the more tedious task of reviewing the current Internal Revenue Code and especially the extent to which it departs from the idealizations underlying our simple model. We conclude with some reflections on tax evolution and tax reform.

2. Dividend policy and stockholder wealth

As promised, we begin by sketching out a simple model in which the seeming tax discrimination against dividends is completely neutralized.

2.1. The initial assumptions

Consider a world in which all corporate capital is owned by a single, unlevered firm (or equivalently by a mutual 'index fund' that holds the shares of the underlying operating corporations). At the start of any period the firm has in hand resources from previous earnings in the amount of X_t that it can use to pay current dividends, D_t, or to invest in productive assets, I_t. Amounts so invested will generate an uncertain flow of resources next period of $\tilde{X}_{t+1}$ which, in turn, may then be either paid out as dividends or reinvested and so on. In addition to these sources and uses of resources, the firm may raise funds by selling additional shares, ΔS_{t+1} (the subscript $t+1$ serving as a reminder that any new shares sold are to be considered ex the dividend D_t); or it may disburse funds without a dividend declaration by buying back shares, in which case $\Delta S_{t+1} < 0$. No transaction costs are incurred by the firm or by investors in these or other dealings in shares. An no 'information effects' are introduced by the firm's dividend decision.[4]

The shares in the firm are held by a class of investors with high risk-tolerance that we shall call 'accumulators'. By contrast, that class of investors that we shall call 'retired persons' and 'widows and orphans' have low risk-tolerance and hold only low-risk, debt securities. Since we have assumed the firm to be unlevered, the sole source of these debt securities will be the accumulators who lever up their own holdings of shares in the firm. The riskless rate of interest, for which we shall use the symbol r, will equilibrate the demand and supply of debt securities between the two groups. If the accumulators are eager to accept higher risks in return for greater prospective returns, then their rush to borrow will tend to push r up. Should the accumulators turn timid, however, the retirees will have to accept very low interest rates to entice the accumulators to generate debt securities by levering their portfolios.[5]

In addition to investing in stocks and bonds, accumulators may also hold 'insurance policies', either of the straight-life or of the endowment kind. Such policies are intended to be riskless investments, and the insurance companies that issue the policies will be assumed to hold only riskless debt securities (issued by accumulators) in their own portfolios.

As for the tax regime, assume initially a personal income tax on wages, salaries and investment income, defined as dividends and interest received, with interest payments deductible up to the amount of investment income received. No tax is levied on the investment income of insurance companies

---

[4] The basic framework is thus essentially that of the MM dividend article (1961), except that we are working here with a mutual fund rather than individual companies. As will become clear shortly, this distinction is not important; and it actually can serve to dramatize that our results here do not depend on 'clientele effects'.

[5] The equilibrating interest rate we are discussing here is, of course, the real interest rate. The nominal interest also plays an important role in the equilibrating process, but it is of a very different kind. [See Fama and Farber (1978).]

while the insurance is kept in force. Further, assume that decumulation of an insurance policy whether by exercise of rights to the cash surrender value[6] or by conversion of a policy to a retirement annuity is not deemed a taxable realization, nor is any tax levied on the insurance proceeds received by the widow and orphan beneficiaries of a deceased accumulator. Realized capital gains from stocks or any other source are taxed at a rate normally substantially less than that on ordinary income; and to dramatize that spread, we shall assume that the rate on capital gains is actually zero.

2.2. Strong Invariance Proposition

The assumptions above are sufficient to establish the following strong dividend invariance proposition; given the firm's investment decision, the firm's dividend decision will have no effect on the wealth or economic welfare of its shareholders. The validity of this proposition can be demonstrated in any of a number of ways of which the simplest and most revealing is to show that a change in the firm's dividend decision will leave every (rational) investor's wealth unchanged regardless of his or her initial portfolio composition.[7]

Suppose then that the firm has announced its investment decision, I_t, and its dividend decision, D_t. Had it chosen a higher level of dividends, D'_t, the firm would have had to finance these additional payments by floating more new shares or by buying back fewer old shares than under the original program. Under either financing strategy, long-familiar MM analysis implies that the choice of the higher level of dividends and its concomitant financing would increase the dividend yield of the stock relative to the capital gain yield. In a no-tax world, this transformation of capital gains into dividends would have no effect on any investor's wealth or consumption pattern. The investor's short-run *cash flow* would be altered, of course, but the original cash position could always be restored without disturbing the consumption plan by an offsetting transaction in the capital markets (in this case, by using the additional dividend to buy an aliquot portion of the additional shares issued or by selling fewer shares back to the firm).

Consider now the same events from the standpoint of a fully taxable accumulator. By assumption, all such investors hold levered portfolios. And suppose, initially, that the investor is so extremely risk tolerant and hence so

---

[6]The cash surrender value or, as we shall usually call it, the accumulated saving component of a straight-life or endowment policy arises because the level premium paid by the policy holder in the early years of the contract exceeds the cost of the component representing pure insurance (and associated options).

[7]For simplicity, we shall restrict attention to the single-period case. The proof can be generalized to the multi-period case by forward induction as in the original MM dividend article, subject to the additional assumptions and limitations there described.

highly levered that interest payments actually exceed dividend receipts. By assumption, interest deductions are limited to the amount of investment income received. The additional dividends, therefore, serve to generate additional allowable deductions dollar for dollar leaving the investor's aggregate tax liability completely unaffected. The investor's before-tax cash flow will be affected but, as before, these changes can be offset by capital market transactions that will have no tax consequences under our assumptions.

Consider next an accumulator whose interest deductions exactly equalled dividend receipts before the dividend increase. If the investor did nothing to offset that dividend increase, an increase in taxes payable would indeed occur. But the tax increase can be avoided by bringing the level of interest payments back up to the point where the allowable deductions completely wash out the taxable dividends. Such a step might at first light seem to mean an increase in the risk assumed as well. But the investor's original risk position can always be restored by the simple expedient of using the proceeds of the additional borrowing to purchase an insurance policy whose saving component has equal value. Putting this riskless, tax-deferred saving component of the insurance policy on the asset side of the investor's balance sheet will thus obviate any change in the *net* leverage position either for the individual or for the economy as a whole.[8] Furthermore, the same reasoning shows that we can rule out as irrational any accumulator portfolios with interest payments less than dividends received, since their owners would be wasting resources in unnecessary taxes. Since the cases we have considered are mutually exclusive and exhaustive, we have shown that an increase in the firm's dividend from D_t to D'_t will have no effect on the wealth of any shareholder.

The proof for a dividend change in the other direction is even simpler since there is no need to adjust the leverage. Cuts in the dividend merely cause redundant interest deductions to emerge or to increase in amount, but have no effect on taxes actually paid. Cash flow can be restored by any investor with no tax consequences by reducing planned purchases of new shares (or by increasing planned sales if the firm's cash flow constraint had dictated a buy-back of its shares). Thus, neither dividend cuts nor dividend increases have any effect on the wealth or welfare of the shareholders, despite the difference in the tax treatment of dividends and capital gains.

[8]In treating the saving component as if it were a separate, free-standing security, we are in effect assuming that accumulators also have pure term insurance policies (in amounts chosen for reasons other than simple wealth accumulation); and that when more straight-life or endowment insurance is purchased for restoring portfolio balance, the term insurance component of the policy is offset by a reduction in term insurance proper. Alternatively, the individual investor may be viewed as owning a set of straight life or endowment policies and making the portfolio adjustments by raising or lowering the amount of borrowings against the cash surrender values. We shall have more to say on these points in later sections.

2.3. *Homemade   leverage   and   the   transformation   of   dividends   into   capital gains*

Like most propositions in finance, this one, too, is obvious once you think of it. What has perhaps kept us all these years from seeing how obvious it really is, has been the tendency to treat dividend policy and debt policy as two separate problems, both at the level of the firm and at the level of the individual. This compartmentalization was probably necessary for efficiency in coming to grips initially with problems of such complexity. And it undoubtedly made easier to see such important points as how a firm's dividend policy, given its investment policy, serves to partition the stockholder's return between dividends and capital gains; or how 'homemade' leverage by individual investors can substitute for leverage at the corporate level (or offset it). But the price paid for these gains from specialization was an obscuring of the interaction between dividend policy and homemade leverage – to wit, the ability of homemade leverage to transform dividends into capital gains.

This transformation is one of the two key blades in the proof of our invariance proposition and may perhaps be worth illustrating separately at this point. Consider, then, an investor with a net worth of $25,000, invested initially in 2,500 shares each selling currently for $10 and expected to yield $0.40 per share in dividends and $0.60 per share in price appreciation, for a combined expected rate of return of 10 percent. Suppose the investor were to borrow $50,000 at an assumed market rate of interest of 6 percent and invest the proceeds in 5,000 additional shares of the same stock.[9] The investor's opening balance sheet and pro forma closing balance sheet would be:

Opening Balance Sheet

Assets		Liabilities
7,500 shares @ 10:	$75,000	$50,000 Loan
		$25,000 Net worth
Total	$75,000	$75,000

---

[9]For simplicity of presentation we have constructed the example with the interest rate greater than the dividend yield. That assumption is not essential, however, for reasons that will become clear shortly. Whether the amount of homemade leverage required for the present and following examples could in fact be generated under present institutional arrangements will be considered later.

Pro Forma Closing Balance Sheet

Assets		Liabilities
7,500 shares @ 10.60:	$79,500	$50,000 Loan
Accrued dividends		
@ 0.40 per share	$ 3,000	$ 3,000 Accrued interest
		$29,500 Net worth
Total	$82,500	$82,500

If the position were closed out at the end of the year, the relevant portions of the investor's pro forma tax return would be:

Ordinary income		Capital gains (schedule D)	
Dividends received	$3,000	Sale of 7,500 shares @ $10.60	$79,500
Less: Interest expense	$3,000	*Less:* Original basis @ $10.00	$75,000
Net ordinary income	$ 0	Net capital gain	$ 4,500

And if the investor continued the position (as presumably would be the case for one of our accumulators), the entire return on the shares would take the form of unrealized capital gains.

The cost of converting dividends to capital gains by this route is, of course, an increase in the risk. The after-tax income received by a levered investor can be expressed as

$$Y = gS + d(1-t)S - r(1-t)B, \tag{1}$$

where g is the capital gain yield on the shares, S is the initial value of the shares, d is the before-tax dividend yield, t is the tax rate, r is the interest rate, and B is the initial value of the borrowing incurred to carry the shares. Letting $W \equiv S - B$ stand for the investor's net worth and letting $R \equiv d + g$ represent the before-tax rate of return on the share, the relation between the after-tax rate of return on net worth and investor's stock/net worth ratio, $S/W \equiv s$, becomes

$$Y/W \equiv y = r(1-t) + (R - r + t(r-d))s. \tag{2}$$

A value of $s = 0$ would signify a portfolio wholly in bonds with rate of return $r(1-t)$; $s = 1$ implies a portfolio consisting entirely of stocks (with neither leverage nor positive holdings of bonds) and yields a rate of return of $R - td$; $s > 1$ corresponds to a levered portfolio. In the simple special case in which the dividend portion of the uncertain return on the shares is taken as known, the standard deviation of the rate of return on net worth will be proportional to s (i.e., $\sigma_y = \sigma_R s$). Hence s can serve as a surrogate for σ_y and the investor's trade-off between expected return and risk in that sense becomes the convenient linear expression

$$E(y) = r(1 - t) + (E(R) - r + t(r - d))s. \tag{3}$$

Fig. 1 shows the opportunity set (3) for a taxable and a non-taxable investor in the absence of the insurance mechanism described earlier. In the normal case in which $r > d$, the two curves will cross at the positive leverage ratio $s = r/(r - d)$ where interest deductions will exactly equal dividends received.[10] If interest deductions are limited by dividends received, as

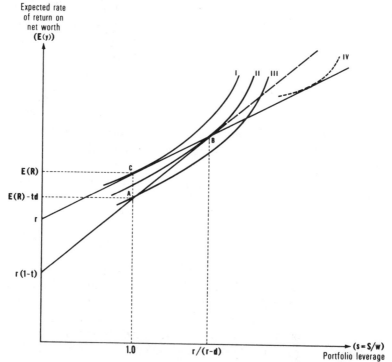

Fig. 1. Opportunity set for taxable and non-taxable investors: Expected return versus portfolio leverage (risk).

[10]For $r = d$ the two curves will be parallel; and for $r < d$ the slope of the taxable curve will be flatter than that of the non-taxable curve, implying that no cross-over occurs at any positive value for s. To offset the dividend receipts against the interest payments when $d \geqq r$ would require leverage ratios so high that the net equity in the share was actually negative.

assumed in our model, the portion of the taxable curve beyond the cross-over point indicated by the broken line will be inadmissible.

The steeper slope of the taxable curve signifies that the cost of leverage *relative to* return is less for taxable than for non-taxable investors. Standard reasoning about substitution would thus suggest that taxable individuals, *ceteris paribus*, would make that substitution and, to that extent, blunt the tax penalty on dividend income. In terms of fig. 1, the welfare loss to a taxable 'representative' investor with $s = 1$ (i.e., to an investor 'holding the market') would be measured by the difference between indifference curves I and II; and not by I and III. The representative investor pictured would still prefer, of course, to have the firm eliminate the dividend; but the welfare gain would be less than the simple comparison of before-tax and after-tax returns on the dividend-paying share might suggest.[11]

But even this much pressure on management to cut back dividends might vanish entirely if our accumulators are sufficiently risk-tolerant. Such investors might have indifference curves of the kind labeled IV in fig. 1 calling for leverage ratios so high that interest payments actually exceed dividends received. Investors in this zone are effectively tax-exempt (by virtue of our having set the capital gains rate at zero) and hence they are as unconcerned about the firm's choice of split between dividends and capital gains as any other tax-exempt investors would be. In the more general case, in which the capital gains rate was greater than zero, the taxable investor's opportunity set would be below the non-taxable set throughout its entire length. But as long as the nominal rate on capital gains did not exceed that on dividends, the firm's dividend policy would still be a matter of no concern, within wide limits, to those taxpayers willing to assume the risks of a highly levered portfolio position.

2.4. The role of insurance: Risk-free and tax-free accumulation

Having seen what homemade leverage can and cannot accomplish by itself, the role of insurance in our proof can now be more readily understood. Its role is actually a double one. On the one hand, investment in insurance serves to control the risk level of the portfolio and, in particular, to neutralize any added risk the investor would have to assume by using homemade leverage to convert dividends to capital gains. To return to our previous numerical example, suppose that our investor wanted to eliminate taxable dividends and still bear no more risk than in the original unlevered portfolio. This goal could be achieved by borrowing $16,667 and investing that amount in riskless insurance at the riskless rate of interest. The opening balance sheet and pro forma tax return for an investor who plans to

---

[11] By the same token, any observed difference in equilibrium between the before-tax returns on dividend-paying and non-dividend-paying stocks would be smaller than the nominal tax differential between dividends and capital gains for the marginal investor.

continue to hold the stock will then be:

Opening Balance Sheet

Assets		Liabilities	
2,500 shares @ $10:	$25,000	$16,667 Loan	
Insurance	$16,667	$25,000 Net worth	
Total	$41,667	$41,667	

Pro Forma Tax Return

Dividends received @ $0.40 per share	$1,000
Less: Interest payments on loan at 6%	$1,000
Net taxable income	$ 0

Thus the investor will have no net leverage and no net taxable income. But the investor's after-tax net income in the Simons (1936) sense will be $2,500 — the sum of the $1,500 of unrealized appreciation on the shares *plus* the $1,000 of interest not subject to tax that is earned on the insurance investment.[12] Insurance, in sum, serves not only to offset leverage,[13] but to

---

[12]Obviously, costs must be incurred to make these adjustments, but they are essentially the costs of portfolio rebalancing generally rather than special consequence of our use of insurance as the balancing investment. It is true that conventional wisdom regards insurance as being a particularly costly investment vehicle as typified in the well-known sneer that insurance is the only commodity that is sold rather than bought. But the required portfolio adjustments can be made in many cases, not by instituting or cancelling policies, but merely by raising or lowering the amount of borrowing outstanding against the cash-surrender value of existing policies. The costs of the standardized policies mainly take the form of front-end load on the first premium. Even if the financial advice and other services provided by the insurance agent are assumed to be worthless, the initial lump-sum cost works out to only a few basis points of annual yield when the policy is held for a long period of years. And, of course, the upper bracket investors who are our main concern do not buy the standardized policies. Not only are the costs per dollar of insurance substantially lower on large, tailor-made policies, but if the investor happens to be a corporate official, the costs of working out the deal are often provided as a non-cash non-taxable fringe benefit. Remember also in comparing promised yields on insurance policies with those of ordinary securities that the typical insurance contract is providing the buyer with valuable option, guarantee and conversion features. In tailor-made policies the essence of the negotiation usually lies precisely in the trade-off between these options and straight yield.

[13]The role of insurance in offsetting leverage involves more, of course, than merely the marginal adjustments to changes in dividends in our examples. Insurance, by eliminating one of the risks attaching to the human capital, permits accumulators to take a more aggresive, levered position in their investment portfolios.

provide investors the opportunity of tax-free accumulation at the *before-tax* rate of interest.

The second role of insurance in our invariance proposition may well have been obscured by our assumption that the tax rate on capital gains was zero. At that rate, but only that rate, levering via borrowing and unlevering via insurance will have the same tax consequences – viz., the elimination of the tax on dividend income. Were the capital gains rate not zero, the mechanism in our proof could still be used to reduce taxes, but investors would no longer be indifferent to the firm's choice of dividend policy. In fact, even though the seeming differential against dividends and in favor of capital gains were quite substantial, investors would prefer the firm to pay out as much of its earnings in dividends as they could offset against personal interest payments.[14]

The role of insurance as a vehicle for accumulation at the before-tax rate should also make clear why limits on deductions for interest were necessary for the proof of the strong invariance proposition and are less arbitrary than may appear at first sight. Were it not for the assumed interest limitation, the income tax could in principle be gutted completely. Taxpayers would borrow until the tax shield on the interest payments had reduced their tax liabilities to zero. Since the proceeds of the borrowing are held in insurance, no risks are incurred by either the taxpayer-borrowers or their creditors. The operation would be pure arbitrage. True, even with the limitation on interest deductions of the kind we have assumed, the taxpayers in our model are still engaging in a form of arbitrage. But it is a weaker form of arbitrage, closer in spirit to what Miller and Upton (1976) have dubbed 'tax subsidies', that is, provisions allowing the taxes on a particular activity (e.g., hobby-loss farms) to go to zero, but not to generate deductions that spill over into other, unrelated activities.

2.5. Alternative vehicles for tax-free and risk-free accumulation

We chose the ordinary life insurance contract as the vehicle for risk-free and tax-free accumulation (at the before-tax rate) in our model because that

[14]In principle, the firm could pay out all of its earnings in dividends, but that would imply $d \geq r$; and, as noted earlier, offsetting the dividends with interest payments under these conditions would require incurring debts in excess of the value of the collateral. Also militating against the complete payout policy is the fact that high leverage ratios mean more frequent sales in response to fluctuations in market values and dividend flows. Investors would thereby lose some of the deferral of tax on unrealized capital gains that is the main tax advantage of return in that form. There may well be other costs to the highly levered investor being forced to sell because of a cut in dividends as suggested by the recent misfortunes of Bert Lance and Richard Kattel (see *Fortune*, June 5, 1978, especially p. 108). And, of course, there are costs for the firm due to more frequent flotations.

For completeness, one other circumstance may be noted in which investors might be indifferent to the firm's choice of dividend policy despite a non-zero capital gains tax. Such might be the case if the costs of maintaining leverage and/or the costs of portfolio rebalancing via insurance described in footnote 12 were equivalent to the capital gains tax in terms of annual yield foregone.

contract is ubiquitous and familiar. But life insurance is by no means the only existing financial instrument that might have served to tell the story. One alternative might have been the single-premium deferred annuity contract which permits insurance companies, in effect, to offer essentially the same tax-free accumulation and decumulation features as ordinary life insurance, but without the tie-in sale of term insurance and assorted renewal options. Another, less recondite alternative might have been the retirement benefit plans with deductible contributions that are now almost universal throughout the private sector. At first sight, such pension plans might appear to be substantially inferior to the insurance contracts in our model because the pension benefits paid out are normally intended to be taxable. But a closer look will show that pension plans are indeed equivalent to insurance in the context of our dividend model as an opportunity for offsetting leverage by risk-free accumulation at the before-tax rate.

Consider, for example, a simple two-period 'life-cycle' model in which the first period is the earning and accumulation phase and the second is the retirement phase. If an individual wage-earner spent c_1 for consumption during the first phase and placed the remainder of his or her after-tax wage income in common stock and insurance, consumption during the retirement period would be

$$c_2 = [w_1(1-t) - c_1](1+r),$$

where w_1 is the individual's wage income, t is the average income tax rate, and r is the *before-tax* rate of return. Suppose that instead of buying insurance the individual participated in a pension plan to which contributions are deductible currently, with taxes on the contributions and accumulated earnings of the fund deferred until received during retirement. Period 1 consumption would be

$$c_1 = (w_1 - z_1)(1-t),$$

where $z_1 = w_1 - c_1/(1-t)$ is the value of the tax deductible contributions to the pension fund. Consumption in period 2 would be

$$c_2 = z_1(1+r)(1-t)$$
$$= [w_1(1-t) - c_1](1+r),$$

exactly as in the insurance case. In sum, investing after-tax dollars in insurance at the before tax rate is equivalent to investing before-tax dollars in pension funds with tax deferred until withdrawal.

This equivalence holds exactly, of course, only if the tax rate is uniform over the entire life cycle. With a progressive income tax schedule, the pension route would presumably be somewhat superior, if only because the years with the highest deductions for saving are likely to be the years of the highest earned income and, hence, of the highest marginal rates. But the presumption is not absolute and might well be offset or more than offset by the general inflationary creep of effective tax rates over time. In any event, these problematic advantages and disadvantages from the differences in patterns of taxable income over time under the two approaches are of only second-order significance for our purposes and we shall continue to treat the two modes of accumulation as essentially interchangeable.[15]

Note finally that our use of the term 'pension plan' is merely suggestive, not restrictive. The pension plan of our equivalence relation is simply the prototypical 'tax shelter', combining front-end deductions with tax deferral in an investment vehicle that does not require the investor to assume great risks to obtain the tax benefits.

2.6. Allowing for a corporate income tax and corporate borrowing

Would the strong dividend-invariance proposition continue to hold when a corporate income tax and corporate borrowing are introduced to our model? And, if so, would a debt-invariance proposition like that in Miller (1977) also hold in that kind of a world? The answer to both questions is yes, but not a robust yes. Even seemingly slight changes in the critical assumptions can swing the system to corner solutions, and not always the same corner.

The critical conditions for the simultaneous holding of both invariance propositions are: (1) that the rate of tax on capital gains be zero; (2) that accumulators have the ability to launder out the personal tax on dividends via insurance or pension plans; and (3) that some fully taxable individuals be willing to hold taxable bonds. The first two conditions imply that the effective marginal rate of personal tax on the income from shares will be zero regardless of how the firm partitions the return between dividends and capital gains. The third condition makes possible a marginal investor whose effective marginal tax rate on bonds is equal to the corporate tax rate. Given such an investor, precisely that combination of tax rates (viz., $t_{corp} = t_{bonds}$ and $t_{stock} = 0$) would emerge that Miller (1977) has shown imply an optimal interior debt/equity ratio for the corporate sector as a whole, but not for any particular firm within it.[16]

---

[15]In the context of the dividend problem, but not in some of the broader applications of the equivalence proposition, we also require for strict equivalence that pension fund investments be restricted to riskless assets whenever the capital gains tax is not zero. In the absence of such restrictions or of tight limits on contributions to such pension plans, the plans would become the most efficient form for holding all assets including common stock; and the dividend problem would cease to exist.

[16]In this equilibrium any leverage in excess of that required for washing out the tax on dividend payments will be supplied by the corporate sector. Accumulators with high risk tolerance, like those with indifference curve IV in fig. 1, would prefer to hold levered shares rather than let their interest deductions go to waste, regardless of their tax bracket (although, of course, there may be other costs to such a strategy).

Conditions (1) and (2), which have already been discussed at length, are relatively straightforward. Either the tax law permits them, or it does not. But it is harder than may appear at first sight to construct a plausible scenario in which there are willing holders of taxable bonds so that condition (3) would hold along with (1) and (2). After all, the same strategy used to launder out the tax on dividends could be used by either accumulators or retirees to launder out interest income. That leaves only the widows and orphans as possible holders of taxable bonds. And there would be little hope from that direction either if it were simply a matter of their consuming the decedent's accumulated capital over their own lifetimes. For a variety of reasons, however, including estate-tax avoidance, the accumulator may wish to leave only the income from the property to the current heirs with the capital left intact for the benefit of future descendants. Trust funds established to meet such objectives are not 'persons' and will be unable, of course, to utilize the insurance or retirement pension routes to tax-free accumulation and de-cumulation. But the fact that the trust will be taxed on its investment income may well be considered by the grantor to be a cost worth bearing in the light of the non-tax (or at least non-income tax) benefits of the trust arrangement.

If condition (3) did not hold, the tax system would become one in which interest income were exempt. For such a case, the optimal debt policy for any corporation would be the corner solution of 100 percent financing by interest-bearing securities. With common stock thus squeezed out, the problem of optimal dividend policy would be solved in a sense by ceasing to exist.

If conditions (2) and (3) hold, but not condition (1) – i.e., if the capital gains rate is greater than zero – the debt equilibrium of Miller (1977) could still obtain, provided the capital gains rate were not too high, but the dividend equilibrium becomes similar to the debt equilibrium. That is, there would be an optimum amount of dividends for the corporate sector as a whole – to wit (see section 2.4), the maximum amount that investors can use to offset the personal interest payments on their portfolio of common stocks – but not for any particular firm. If conditions (1) and (3) hold, but not the condition (2) that permits the dividends to be laundered, then the debt equilibrium remains, but dividend equilibrium swings back to the corner in which dividends are zero.[17]

Clearly, many more combinations of assumptions and their effects on the general equilibrium might merit discussion. But this sampling is surely

---

[17]Once again (see the previous footnote) the limitation on interest deductions would make personal leverage less efficient than corporate leverage for risk-tolerant accumulators regardless of tax bracket; but, of course, with condition (2) absent and laundering ruled out, there would be no need for an interest limitation. The model in Miller (1977) is essentially of the latter kind; that is, one that meets conditions (1) and (3) but has no limitations on personal interest deductions (other than the general 'no arbitrage' rule preventing borrowing to hold tax-exempt bonds).

enough to make our main point: that the effects of taxes on the optimal financial policies of firms are far less obvious than the simple comparison of tax differentials might seem to suggest. We can now turn first to see where we now stand with respect to the key tax provisions, and then to speculate on where we seem to be drifting.

3. A closer look at the critical tax provisions

3.1. The deductibility of interest payments

The assumptions with respect to the deductibility of interest payments in our model were patterned on those in the current IRC section 163(d). In some ways, that section is more restrictive than our assumption and in some ways it is less so.

It may be more restrictive for some taxpayers to the extent that the taking of interest deductions to wipe out the tax on investment income may lead to a loss of the benefits of the maximum marginal tax rate (currently 50 percent) on personal service income under IRC Section 1348. What causes the benefit to be lost is the requirement that in computing the maximum tax on personal service income (hereafter *PSI*), all itemized deductions must be prorated between *PSI* and other income.

An example may be helpful. Suppose a taxpayer has $250,000 of *PSI* (defined as the sum of wages, salaries, professional fees, income from pensions and tax qualified annuities as well as some forms of deferred compensation) plus $50,000 of dividend income against which $50,000 of interest deductions were currently offset. Under present rates, the marginal tax rate on a joint return exceeds 50% at $55,200. Assume that other itemized deductions were equal to the zero bracket amount. If all the interest deductions could be netted against the dividend receipts, the tax would be $18,060 on the first $55,200 of taxable income plus 50% on the remaining $194,800 of taxable *PSI* for a total of $115,460. But the amount of *PSI* subject to the maximum tax is actually defined as total taxable income times the ratio of *PSI* to adjusted gross income. In our example we have:

PSI	$250,000
Dividends	$ 50,000
Adjusted gross income (*AGI*)	$300,000
Interest deductions	$ 50,000
Taxable income (*TI*)	$250,000

so that personal service income subject to the maximum tax is $TI \cdot PSI/AGI = \$250,000 \cdot \$250,000/\$300,000 = \$208,333$. The tax on $208,333 is $94,627, [$18,060 plus $0.5 \cdot (\$208,333 - \$55,200)$]. The tax on the remaining $41,667 is computed as the difference between the tax table tax (schedule Y) on $250,00 minus the tax table tax on $208,333 which is $29,167 (70% of $41,667), for a total tax of $123,794. This is an additional $8,334 over the netting alternative.

But while Congress taketh away, it also giveth. Under IRC Section 163(d) taxpayers are allowed up to an additional $10,000 of interest deductions over and above investment income received. If in our example, the taxpayer were to incur interest deductions of $60,000, redoing the maximum tax computations would result in a tax of $118,428. The effective tax on dividend income for this taxpayer is approximately 6% [($118,428 - $115,460)/$50,000]. The larger is *PSI* relative to dividends the lower the effective tax and the more complete is the conversion of dividends into capital gains. For taxpayers whose income is close to $55,000, use of part or all of this extra $10,000 of interest deductions would bring the total tax bill to the same amount as if interest were netted against investment income.[18]

Although the proration requirement (even softened by the $10,000 of additional interest deductions) makes the actual law somewhat more restrictive than our model, other respects exist in which the present law is somewhat less restrictive. Investment income includes dividends, interest, rents from net lease property, royalties, net short-term capital gains from investment property and amounts recaptured as ordinary income from the sale or exchange of investment property. Not only does each taxpayer have the $10,000 of excess interest deduction ($5,000 a year for married persons filing separate returns) to work with, but interest on mortgages or other 'personal indebtedness' is not considered in computing the limit on interest deductions. Hence, for a large number of taxpayers, particularly in the early stages of the life cycle, interest deductions will substantially exceed investment income.[19]

3.2. The tax treatment of life insurance

The tax treatment of insurance in our model was patterned closely, like

[18]Taxpayers with large stockholdings and with life-time planning goals that include more than merely retirement objectives can use multiple non-grantor *inter vivos* trusts and personal holding companies to retain stock within a family and still reduce the effective tax on dividends. For example, the creation of a charitable front-end annuity trust allows the grantor a current deduction for the present value of income (dividends) given to charity. The assets (and, of course, the capital gains thereon) revert to the grantor at the end of the specified period.

[19]In principle, taxpayers could indeed use the interest deduction on personal indebtedness to wipe out their entire income tax (along lines noted in section 2.4 above). As a practical matter, however, the agency costs of unsecured borrowing as described, for example, in Jensen and Meckling (1976) and Black, Miller, and Posner (1978), serve as an effective limit to arbitrage of that kind.

that of the interest deduction, on the actual current provisions of the Internal Revenue Code. At first sight, such might not seem to be the case since insurance companies are not in fact exempt from corporate income tax as we have assumed. But the taxes insurance companies must pay under IRC Section 801–820 are levied on their underwriting gains and losses and on any earnings that can be attributed to the equity capital invested in the insurance company itself, considered as a business enterprise. The investment earnings on the insurance reserves of the *policyholders*, however, which correspond to the accumulated savings component of insurance in our model are indeed effectively tax exempt, as we assumed.

As for the policyholder's tax status, we assumed that the earnings that were accumulated tax-free while the insurance was in force would not be subject to further tax when the insurance is terminated or the savings portion withdrawn. Actual current law is in some respects more generous and in some respects less generous to policyholders. The amounts received by reason of the death of the insured under a life insurance contract are not included in either the decedent's or the beneficiary's gross income (IRC Section 101), though the proceeds will be considered part of the decedent's estate for estate tax purposes if the decedent retained any 'incidents of ownership' of the policy. If the proceeds are paid in installments that include interest earned after the insured's death, that portion of the interest is taxable to the beneficiary when received. However, if the proceeds of the policy are to be paid over a period of time (with interest), the first $1,000 of interest received per year is excludable from tax by a surviving spouse.[20]

In principle, moreover, the accumulated proceeds can be withdrawn steadily for consumption without incurring income tax by borrowing against the cash-surrender value of the policy. It is true that the Code rules out interest deductions for debts incurred (from the insurer or otherwise) to purchase or carry life insurance bought under a plan that contemplates 'systematic' borrowing of all or part of the cash-surrender value of the policy.[21] But the interest deduction is not necessary for the tax-free decumulation. Since the cash-surrender value (including policy dividends) will grow at the before-tax interest rate, the retiree can gut the policy's cash-surrender value by borrowing against it, washing the interest accruals on the

---

[20]In addition, the rules for computing the portion of the annuity that is return of capital give higher exclusions in the early years than would be the case under strict application of the capital recovery factor.

[21]For whole life policies there are several tests for tax qualifying borrowing as 'nonsystematic', IRC Section 264. The most important is that no more than three of the first seven premiums be financed by borrowing (thus, incidentally ruling out deductions for borrowing on single premium annuities). Young accumulators after meeting these restrictions can convert a whole-life policy into a low cost term insurance policy, by borrowing the cash value of the policy and deducting the interest. But, of course, one cannot have the cake and eat it too. Any policy so converted and maintained could not also be used for savings or for controlling portfolio leverage as in our dividend model.

policy loan against the untaxed growth in the cash value of the policy. It is easy to show that the retiree can create his own personal, level tax-free annuity by setting the amount borrowed per year equal to the initial cash-surrender value multiplied by the appropriate capital recovery factor.

On the other hand, the law is less generous than our model for those using insurance savings to provide for their own consumption rather than those of their heirs if a straight-life insurance policy is terminated for its cash-surrender value or if an endowment policy is allowed to mature. In such cases, any excess of the amount received (the cash-surrender value plus all previous policy dividends) over the total of premiums paid is taxed at regular rates[22] (IRC Section 72). However, the ability to create a personal level or variable annuity by gutting the cash-surrender value as above usually dominates this route to realizing the cash-surrender value of the policy.[23]

For single premium annuity contracts (which have no term insurance component), all earnings on amounts in the policy accumulate tax-free. The contract holder pays no tax until the annuity starts and the cost basis has been fully returned. But the holder need not take the contract annuity to be able to realize the value of the policy. The holder can instead create a home-made annuity by borrowing from the insurance company against the cash-surrender value exactly as in the case of straight life insurance. Only, if he were so unfortunate as to live beyond the latest date specified for the start of the contract annuity (generally age 85) would he receive a taxable payment. Even then, however, it is not yet clear what the IRS and the courts would require to be included in income on receipt of the contract annuity. If the equity value of the policy (that is, the contract amount *less* loan value) were held to be the base for the annuity payments – a treatment for which there is already some precedent in the law in IRC Section 72 – the tax consequences would of course be trivial. As for treatment in the year of death, we know that life insurance proceeds are not income under IRC Section 101, but it is not yet clear for single premium annuities whether the contract amount, the net equity value or neither would be income to the decedent. What is clear, however, is that any remaining equity or the present value of an annuity to be received by a beneficiary is an estate asset.

---

[22]The ability to utilize endowment policies for the kinds of tax-free leverage adjustments considered in our model will be less than for straight life policies because of the large flow of 'dividends' on the policy as the pure insurance component gets smaller. Such policy dividends are considered as a return of capital (i.e., of premiums paid) rather than a receipt of income only as long as total dividends paid fall short of total premiums. Once the dividends exceed the premiums, the dividends are taxed as ordinary income and the policy becomes essentially a bond for present purposes. However, this will generally occur during retirement. The use of the home-made annuity, returning the dividend to pay the interest due, eliminates the problem (at least up to second-order timing effects).

[23]At retirement the policy may have more remaining term insurance than desired, but under IRC Section 1035 one life insurance contract can be exchanged tax-free for another life insurance or endowment policy with lower term component.

3.3. The tax treatment of employee retirement benefit plans and pension plans

Any self-employed individual – and remember that this includes college professors to the extent of their outside income from consulting or taxidriving – may set up a so-called Keogh plan for retirement saving. Taxpayers who can avail themselves of such plans have an opportunity for accumulation that is equivalent in tax benefits to insurance. Taxes on the investment income earned on the savings in the plan are deferred until retirement and contributions to the fund can be deducted from current taxable income, IRC Section 404. Under present law contributions to such plans are limited to a maximum of $7,500 per year or 15 percent of income from self-employment (up from $2,500 and 10 percent under the original legislation in 1962).

Although Keogh plans can provide only self-employed taxpayers with a route for tax-free accumulation that is equivalent to insurance,[24] the plans were intended originally to give the self-employed some of the same opportunities for tax-favored accumulation that had earlier been made available to employees via pension and related plans. Under IRC Section 401–415, which now govern such pension plans, any employer may set up a 'qualified retirement plan for employees' (following rules and procedures established by the Employee Retirement Income Security Act (ERISA) of 1974). If a plan qualifies, employees are not taxed currently either on the employer contributions or on the investment earnings of the accumulated funds. Taxes are paid by the employee only on the amounts actually received, presumably after retirement. The employer, on the other hand, may deduct contributions to the plan from current income, subject to certain limits. For so-called *defined benefits plans* (essentially pension plans), contributions are deductible only if the maximum yearly retirement benefit payable to any employee is no greater than the smaller of $90,150 (inflation adjusted for years subsequent to 1978), and the maximum of 100 percent of the average of the highest 3 years of salary and $10,000. For so-called *defined contributions plans* (including most profit-sharing plans) the allowed contribution is the lesser of 25 percent of earned income and $30,050 (inflation adjusted for years subsequent to 1978).[25] For combination plans, the rules are complicated, but the tax authorities with whom we have discussed the

---

[24]Keogh plans are easy to institute, but they are less flexible than insurance. Withdrawals cannot be made from a Keogh plan until age $59\frac{1}{2}$ without incurring a penalty excise tax of 10 percent (except under unusual circumstances).

[25]The self-employed were limited originally to defined contribution plans, but are now permitted to establish defined benefit plans (IRC Section 401). The benefit limitations are the same as for a corporate plan, but the defined benefits must adhere to guidelines that permit a plan to build up benefits based on a percentage of each year's actual earned income up to a maximum of $50,000. Contributions to the defined benefit plan in the early years can exceed the $7,500 Keogh limits by amounts that depend on actuarial assumptions; but future contributions would have to be reduced if earnings exceeded these actuarial assumptions so that no clear dominance exists of one alternative over the other.

matter tell us that the 25 percent rule would normally be a close approximation to the actual formula. However, for an employee starting a plan later in his or her working years, the initial contribution may be considerably larger because of provisions that allow catching up.

These possibilities for tax-deferred accumulation take on particular significance for our point in this paper in the light of the rapid spread in recent years of the personal service corporation among doctors, dentists and other high-income professional occupations.[26] As long as the owner-operators take pains to avoid benefit formulas that are too blatantly discriminatory in their own favor *vis-à-vis* any employees, they can get all the essential tax advantages of a Keogh plan with far more generous limits (currently the smaller of 25 percent of income and $30,050 with this year's cost-of-living adjustment). In fact, the limits are so generous that many such high-income professionals may well have no need to use the tax-deferred funds to engage in the kind of leverage adjustment we described to eliminate the current tax on their dividend income. They can accomplish that goal directly by investing all or part of their plan's funds in common stocks.

Executives and officers in ordinary corporations will normally have far less direct control over year-to-year contributions to their tax-deferred accumulation funds than those in independent professional practice. But the distinction must not be exaggerated. At the higher echelons, at least, executive compensation schemes are subject to negotiation; and it is hard to believe that tax-conscious executives do not make the trade-offs without some regard for the rest of their current portfolio position, including its leverage.[27]

Nor is it necessary that individuals participate in a formal 'plan' to obtain the benefits of tax-free accumulation at the risk-free rate. Under present law, individuals covered by no plan may set up Individual Retirement Accounts (I.R.A.'s) with allocations to such accounts currently limited to 15 percent of income up to $1,500 per year or $875 each for working and non-working spouse, IRC Section 219. But the law permits transfers of lump-sum distributions from qualified employer's plans and IRC Section 403(b) plans

---

[26]Employees of tax-exempt institutions, IRC Section 501(c), (3), such as university professors, can establish tax-deferred annuity contract accounts with organizations such as T.I.A.A. or C.R.E.F., IRC Section 403(b). These are defined contribution plans with limits for exclusion from income which are approximately 25 percent of taxable salary income. Supplemental retirement annuities, available under 403(b), can be surrendered at any time and included in income when received.

[27]For example, under IRC Section 83, an executive could agree to receive a grant of restricted company stock in lieu of a salary increase. The executive includes the market value of the common stock in personal service income only when the restrictions lapse. Any dividends paid on restricted stock during the restriction period (and those dividends, too, would be subject to negotiation) are included in personal service income. The basis of the stock for future capital gains treatment is market value when the restrictions lapse. This, in effect, is virtually a Keogh plan. The corporation can be shown to be indifferent for tax purposes between a salary payment and a restricted stock grant of equal before-tax present value.

to an I.R.A. without tax on the roll-over, so the potential for I.R.A.'s is a good deal larger than might appear at first sight. Not only are earnings on I.R.A.'s exempt from income tax currently, but the value of an annuity receivable by a beneficiary (other than an executor) under an I.R.A. is excluded from the decedent's gross estate if the annuity payments to the survivor extend beyond three years. The election to receive a survivor annuity can be made by the executor of the estate before an estate tax return is filed. This election does not result in a taxable gift either before or after death, and the survivor includes the annuity amounts in income.[28]

3.4. Other means to defer tax: Alternatives to insurance and pension plans

Many other investment forms exist that would be almost, but not quite as good as insurance or pension plans for the purposes of our model. Investments in this category range from the humble and familiar Series E. U.S. Savings Bond to supersophisticated tax shelters, broadly construed.

Series E bonds, which are issued at a discount, currently yield 6.0 percent to maturity of 5 years compounded semiannually and give the holder two options with respect to reporting the interest for tax purposes: (1) the increase in redemption value may be reported as interest income each year; or (2) the entire difference between redemption value and purchase price may be reported as income in the year redeemed or matured. Not only does the second option provide 5 years of tax-free accumulation, but automatic extensions (with interest yields adjusted to their current levels) are available in 10-year increments up to an additional 30 years without tax or other penalty on the roll-over. In the event of the holder's death, the accumulated interest can be entered into taxable income in a lump sum in the decedent's final income tax return; or it can be passed on without tax at that point to the beneficiary who in turn can utilize any remaining portion of the 35 years of tax-deferred accumulation. Should the holder choose to cease accumulation at any point and begin to consume the proceeds, he or she may choose to convert from Series E bonds to Series H Current Income Bonds of 10-year maturity, that pay interest in cash semiannually. Taxes are due on that interest as it is paid, but the tax on the previously accumulated interest may be deferred until the Series H bonds mature or are redeemed. Thus, Series E bonds are similar to insurance in providing tax-free accumulation on after-tax dollars at the riskless rate, but are subject to higher taxes potentially, when the accumulation period ends.

Tax shelters, whether in farming, oil and gas, timber, real estate or other business ventures have the common property of allowing fast write-offs for non-cash flow items such as depreciation or depletion. These non-cash flow

---

[28]The Revenue Act of 1978 allows an employer to establish a simplified pension plan using I.R.A. accounts. If the employer contributes less than regular I.R.A. limits, the employee can contribute an additional amount up to the minimum of $7,500 and 15 percent of compensation.

deductions reduce current taxable income in a manner entirely analogous to the before-tax contributions to a Keogh plan. If all the initial cost of the investment were deductible from taxable income and future income from the investment were includable in personal service income, the analogy between tax shelters and Keogh plans would be exact. With the exception of intangible drilling costs associated with oil and gas programs, however, investment costs must be depreciated rather than expensed. But with investment tax credits and accelerated depreciation, the present value of these non-cash deductions is likely to be of the same order of magnitude as the cost of the investment. For any particular high tax bracket· investor, of course, a tax shelter investment may be more or less advantageous than a Keogh plan investment of the same risk and expected before tax return. Accelerated depreciation on real property and on all leased personal property, percentage depletion, intangible drilling costs and excess amortization, in excess of more conservative alternatives such as straight line depreciation are tax preference items subject to the minimum tax, IRC Section 57 and reduce income that is taxable at the maximum rate of 50 percent, IRC Section 1348. The investment income from a shelter is taxed like a dividend. But, on sale of the shelter asset, capital gains rates may apply and this is more advantageous than Keogh plan tax treatment. The net advantage of a tax shelter over a Keogh plan depends on the capital gains tax, investment tax credits, depreciation and possibly other taxes resulting from recapture and tax preferences.[29]

Investments in human capital also have some of the properties of tax shelters. Property and state taxes are deductible and these taxes pay for the largest fraction of public education. Expenses for on-the-job training and apprenticeships are deductible by employers as are the tuition grants by corporations for continuing education that are now becoming standard. An individual may deduct educational expenses that are job related and required to maintain employment, but not to meet the minimum educational requirements for employment qualification, IRC Reg. 1.162. An employee will be considered to have received taxable income if the employee is reimbursed or an employer pays for non-qualifying educational expenses. But if the education is deemed qualifying, an employer may deduct such expenses as business expense not subject to withholding and an employee need not include them in income, IRC Reg. 31.3121. Since these distinctions led to much quibbling, the Revenue Act of 1978 eliminated the distinctions between job related and personal educational expenses for employer plans that are

---

[29]The Tax Reform Act of 1976 and the Revenue Act of 1978 did not eliminate tax shelters which, as we have seen, are in principle just variations of the Keogh plan. The changes were enacted to restrict abuses of the shelter investment which could make the shelter superior to a Keogh investment. For example, an artificially high depreciation basis generated by using non-recourse loans could result in deductions whose present value were large enough to shelter other source income and earn more than the competitive before-tax return on investment.

provided generally and only to employees. However, individuals, once past the full time student stage, will still have to distinguish between job related and personal educational expenses.

University or post-graduate education can be financed either with before-tax dollars or out of after-tax dollars with some tax benefits. The use of educational benefit trusts established either by corporations for employees or by parents for children can reduce the tax rate substantially on accumulation within the trust. For an employee educational benefit trust, employer contributions to fund trust investments usually in annuities, are corporate expenses in the year made if these benefits are generally available to a class of employees and are taxable income when paid to the employee for the education of children, IRC Reg. 1.162–10. Thus these payments for education are in before-tax dollars as in a Keogh plan. A parent may establish a non-grantor trust, sometimes called a Clifford trust, for the benefit of children. This trust is set up with after-tax dollars, but enables the parent to use the low tax bracket of a child or trust to accumulate a fund for education (or for other purposes). If the trust is a simple trust, the child files a tax return including all trust income as his or her own. In addition to a low bracket, the first $1,000 of investment income plus a $100 dividend exclusion is exempt from tax.

3.5. The tax treatment of realized capital gains and losses

Perhaps the biggest single discrepancy between the current tax law and the tax provisions of our strong invariance model is our assumption that the tax rate on realized capital gains is the same as that on unrealized capital gains (both being taken as zero for simplicity). In a strictly literal sense, that assumption *does* apply, of course, to the extent that the accumulation is aimed at estate building rather than providing retirement income. No income tax is paid on insurance proceeds and, until the Tax Reform Act of 1976, no capital gains tax was due on any unrealized gains accumulated in the securities portfolio of the decedent. The Tax Reform Act of 1976 made the value of listed securities as of December 31, 1976, the carry-over basis for income tax purposes, in the case of a gain, in the hands of legatees, IRC Section 1023. Because the required regulations would have been extremely complex (and bitterly contested), the Revenue Act of 1978 postponed the application of IRC Section 1023 to December 31, 1979, by which time Congress will have reviewed the whole concept of carry-over basis. Thus, until tax year 1980 at least (and quite possibly not even then[30]), some part of

[30]The drafters of the 1976 legislation seem to have overlooked, among other things, the fact that carrying over the basis of property against which liabilities have been incurred could convert bequests of those assets to 'white elephants'. That is, the value of the gift to the donee could be negative if the mortgage plus the capital gain liability exceeded the value of the property. Of course, under those conditions a gift to a tax-exempt charity becomes an obvious choice, though a spiteful donor might well be tempted to bequeath the property to a member of the Ways and Means Committee.

the gains that have escaped capital gains tax in the hands of the accumulator will not face capital gains tax in the hands of the heirs because of the step-up in basis to fair market value at time of death.

For those whose accumulation objective is that of providing for consumption during the retirement period, the tax on any accumulated gains realized to provide the wherewithal for that consumption will not in general be zero. It is difficult, however, to state briefly what the rate *will* be. For long-term gains (currently defined as gains on assets held more than 12 months) the normal presumption has been that the rate was half that of the individual's regular rates (because only one-half of any net long-term capital gain was included in taxable income, IRC Section 1202). With the Revenue Act of 1978, only 40 percent of any net long-term capital gain is includable in taxable income, so the rate for most taxpayers will be 40 percent of the individual's regular rates. For high tax bracket investors, prior to the Revenue Act of 1978, the effective rate might have been considerably greater if the taxpayer ran afoul of the minimum tax on so-called preference items. Under IRC Section 56, preference items (which included the untaxed portion of long-term capital gains) exceeding the larger of one-half the federal income tax as computed and $10,000 were taxed at a flat 15 percent. The new law excludes the untaxed portion of long-term capital gains (and adjusted excess itemized deductions) from the add-on minimum tax. Prior to the Revenue Act of 1978, preference items, such as the untaxed portion of capital gains, reduced income eligible for the maximum tax, dollar-for-dollar, effectively increasing the capital gains rate, IRC Section 1348. The Revenue Act of 1978 excludes the untaxed portion of capital gains as a preference item in computing the maximum tax and the minimum add-on-tax. Untaxed capital gains become part of a new alternative minimum tax which becomes effective in 1979, IRC Section 55. The alternative minimum tax is computed by adding to taxable income the sum of tax preferences for untaxed capital gains and excess itemized deductions and applying a flat percentage to this sum, for example, 25 percent if such income exceeds $100,000. While it was claimed that the old capital gains rate might exceed 49 percent, the new maximum effective capital gains rate is 28 percent. The individual pays the larger of the regular tax (income plus add-on-minimum tax) and the alternative minimum tax.

On the other hand, the effective tax on long-term capital gains may well be less than 40 percent of the taxpayer's regular rate if the rate is interpreted in the long-run sense. Consider, for example, an investor who holds a security growing in value at a rate of 10 percent per year before taxes. A 20 percent tax on capital gains paid on a one-time realization 30 years later would be equivalent to an annual rate of tax on the unrealized accruals of only 8 percent. The higher the rate of return and the longer the horizon, the lower the effective annual rate of tax. In addition, the holder of securities retains the initiative with respect to the timing of realizations. Realization of gains can be timed to coincide with years in which other income is low or itemized deduction are high. Current tax law also allows the taxpayer to deduct net capital losses up to $3,000 a year, IRC Section 1211 (technically, the sum of the excess of net short-term capital loss over net long-term capital gain and 40 percent of the excess of net long-term capital loss over net short-term capital gain). Taking losses short-term and letting the 'winners' ride reduces the present value of the capital gains tax (and for well-diversified portfolios of moderate size may even make the tax effectively negative). In addition, charitable donations of appreciated securities at full value (without realization of a capital gain) provide satisfactions equivalent to personal consumption for many security owners.[31]

3.6. The trade-off between income taxes and estate taxes

In a world with a corporate income tax, we have seen that the nature of the equilibrium can be drastically affected by the presence or absence of a group of high-bracket investors willing to hold taxable corporate bonds. Such a group can arise quite naturally once we allow for estate and gift taxes along with taxes on income. The attempt to minimize the *combined* impact of the two sets of taxes may well make it worthwhile to trade income tax penalties for estate tax benefits.[32]

Testamentary trusts created by will or *inter vivos* trusts (living trusts) are the major vehicles for effecting this trade-off. Testamentary trusts cannot use insurance or Keogh plans to obtain tax-free investment income or to balance risk like our accumulators. Since the trustees and executors are also bound

[31]A related device commonly used by high bracket taxpayers to avoid capital gains tax is to establish charitable remainder annuity trusts and unitrusts, IRC Section 664. In high-income years, taxpayers wishing to donate to charity in the future establish these trusts obtaining a current deduction for the fair market value of the property to be given in the future, less the present value of the annuity or percentage that the trust must pay out to non-charitable income beneficiaries.

[32]This interaction between the estate tax and the income tax also becomes important in considering the new carry-over basis rules on capital assets, IRC Section 1023. Under the old rules (pre-1976) a capital gains tax was paid on assets sold prior to death, but the size of the estate and the estate tax was thereby lower. Alternatively, no capital gains tax was paid prior to death, but the estate tax was larger. To avoid creating incentives to sell appreciated assets prior to death, the new carry-over basis rules enacted in the Tax Reform Act of 1976 (but whose implementation has been postponed, possibly indefinitely) increase the basis on each appreciated asset by the amount of estate tax attributable to the gain. This increases the carry-over basis and thus reduces the resultant capital gain on a future sale of the asset. The minimization of the combined income and estate tax is also an important consideration in whether or not to use the special ten-year averaging rule under IRC Section 402 on liquidation of a pension plan account. The surrender of the account may result in lower income tax for certain individuals, but may result in higher estate tax since survivors could no longer elect to exclude the pension assets from an estate. For a further discussion of the fascinating details of the interaction between the income tax and the estate and gift taxes, see Cooper (1977).

by law to keep the trust assets in low-risk securities, the typical trust portfolio will be found to be heavily invested in bonds (primarily taxable bonds for low tax-bracket trusts and primarily municipals for those in high tax brackets).[33]

As against their potential income tax disadvantages, trusts offer two major types of estate tax savings. A marital deduction trust escapes the first round of the estate tax (though any remaining assets of the trust would be subject to estate tax on the death of the surviving spouse). The maximum marital deduction is currently limited to the larger of $250,000 or one-half the estate. At current rates, a taxable estate of $500,000 with a marital deduction of $250,000 will realize immediate estate tax savings of $85,000 if a marital deduction trust were used. In addition, any of the remaining portion not in the marital trust can be placed in a continuing trust with the provision, for example, that the income be paid to the surviving spouse, and that any assets remaining in the trust on the death of that spouse be paid to other beneficiaries as designated by the will. As long as the assets remain in the trust, they escape further estate taxation on the death of any beneficiary named in the will (and in some cases this provision can apply as well to generations yet unborn). It is easy to construct examples showing that it is advantageous for a survivor to pay a 46 percent income tax on the bond income of the estate trust to obtain these substantial estate tax advantages.[34]

3.7. Summary and conclusion

Our survey of the relevant provisions of the Internal Revenue Code shows that the key tax features of the theoretical models in section 2 do indeed have close or exact counterparts in the current tax law. Nor should this occasion much surprise. As we have hinted at various points, we chose the key tax features that drive the theoretical models with the current Code provisions very much in mind. These provisions have been seen to be less generous in some details than those of the model and to be more generous in others; but the similarity in the essentials should be apparent.

---

[33]In 1976, personal trusts and estate assets in well over one million separate accounts at commercial banks exceeded $192 billion. In addition, *inter vivos* trust assets exceeded $80 billion. Approximately 55 percent of assets in trust accounts were in stocks and the remainder in real estate, savings accounts and bonds (including some $25 billion of corporate obligations). [See U.S. Federal Deposit Insurance Corporation (1976).]

[34]A transfer tax was imposed by the Tax Reform Act of 1976 on generation-skipping trusts created after June 11, 1976, IRC Sections 2601–2622. If generation C benefits from a trust on the death of generation B who received benefits from generation A, a tax may be imposed on the remaining assets in the trust passing to C. If generation C were a grandchild to generation A, a $250,000 exclusion from tax is allowed for each generation B child of A. This transfer tax, however, does not apply to what have been called generation-jumping trusts in which part of the estate of generation A hops over generation B directly to C and/or D. By hopping, skipping and jumping grantors can still exploit the trust device to leave assets to many succeeding generations without double estate taxation.

How many dividend receivers are deliberately utilizing the double-bladed tactics of the model at the moment and how much their actions are reducing the pressures on corporate managements to ·find alternatives to the payment of taxable dividends is hard to say. We can be reasonably sure, of course, that the conditions of our strong invariance proposition did not hold exactly prior to 1969 since it was only in that year that Congress moved to restrict the tax advantages of unlimited interest deductions by imposing the interest limitation. The additional allowable deductions for interest paid over and above investment income received – $25,000 on a joint return under the 1969 Act, later reduced to $10,000 by the Tax Reform Act of 1976 – mean that at current margin limits, interest rates and dividend yields, the interest limit is likely to be binding only for holders of very large blocks of shares. But an astonishing fraction of the stock held by non-institutional investors is in fact held in blocks of great size.[35] And a non-trivial fraction of these blocks, in turn, are likely to represent the holdings of the senior corporate officials who actually make the dividend decisions.

Although the complete wealth holdings and transaction records of such large-block holders are not available for direct study, we can at least look to the aggregate data for evidence on the current usage of each of the two blades taken separately. Brokers' loans, for example, are currently close to $11 billion, implying a flow of dividend-offsetting interest payments from this source alone of a billion dollars or so. A recent Treasury study, *'High Income Tax Returns: 1974 and 1975'* (1977), of returns of wealthy individuals paying low taxes found interest deductions to be one of the major factors responsible.[36]

As for the second blade, tax-free accumulation, usage is now almost universal. So many and so varied, in fact, are the devices for tax-free accumulation, so large are the amounts invested in such devices and so

---

[35]Blume and Friend (1978, p. 10) report that: 'In 1971, those families with stock portfolios valued above $1 million owned fully 40 percent of all individually held stock. These families represented at most 1.1 percent of all families owning stock but, of course, a very much smaller percentage of the population as a whole. Those families with stock portfolios valued at more than $100,000 owned roughly 80 percent of all individually held stock and represented at most 14.2 percent of all households owning stock. In contrast, over half the families owning stock had portfolios of less than $10,000, but they held only 2.4 percent of the market value of all individually held stock.'

[36]The tabulations presented there and in *Statistics of Income*, 1973, also show, however, that taxpayers exist even in the very highest income groups for whom receipts of taxable dividends are substantially larger than interest deductions. The taxes paid on these returns are too large to be attributed plausibly either to ignorance or to the costs of our dividend laundering strategy. The holdings in question may perhaps represent family trusts of the kind described above (section 2.6). If not, we may perhaps be seeing there a confirmation of Henry Simons' belief that some rich people derive more satisfaction from bragging about the high taxes they pay than they would from spending them. It is perhaps also worth noting that in the aggregate, deductions for interest paid in 1973 on returns with itemized deductions actually came to more than twice the amount of dividends reported.

rapidly are they growing that we have been driven to a conclusion that transcends in important respects the dividend issues that were our initial motivating concern. To put it bluntly, the 'income' tax is dead. We turn now to the post-mortem and to the identification of the tax that has succeeded it.

4. Tax-free accumulation and the problem of tax reform

To give a precise, descriptive name to the tax system that has displaced the income tax is not easy because the new system is still evolving rapidly and has yet to shed all the vestiges of its earlier incarnation. The core component of the new system can be characterized in either of two equivalent ways, depending on the choice of paradigm for tax-free accumulation (see section 2.5 above). Under the 'insurance' scenario, the tax becomes essentially a *wage tax* since no tax is paid on the investment income earned on the after-tax dollars put into insurance reserves.[37] Under the 'pension plan' scenario, the tax becomes essentially a *consumption tax* since savings allocated to pension plans are deductible from taxable income. The two taxes are, of course, two sides of the same coin in a strict life-cycle world – because lifetime consumption in such a world is merely 'smoothed-out' wage income (subject once again to the qualifications noted earlier about progressivity and changes in effective rates over time).

In the standard life-cycle model the instruments for smoothing are called by the general term 'securities' (and we have for the most part followed that practice here), but the drift away from the strict principles of income taxation has by no means been confined to the returns on securities in the narrow sense. The service returns on that huge chunk of social capital invested in owner-occupied housing and consumer durables are completely exempt. The price appreciation component of housing is tax-deferred and under the Revenue Act of 1978 every taxpayer has a once-per-lifetime exemption of $100,000 of housing capital gains. Even some of the investment in human capital is sheltered. The deductibility of local property taxes, which seems so anomalous in an income tax, can be considered a way for many families to put before-tax dollars into investments in education; and, as noted earlier, during our survey of tax benefits, tuition reimbursement for college and graduate school training of employees has become a common fringe benefit.

At a time when the heavy tax bite on income from capital is being blamed by many for the low levels of stock prices and business real investment in recent years, it may seem ironic for us to be stressing the evolution of the income tax towards a wage or consumption tax under which the 'double

---

[37]Note, incidentally, that Social Security does indeed have some of the properties of 'insurance' in this sense. Workers pay a tax on their wage income and the Social Security benefits received are tax-exempt.

taxation of saving' is eliminated. But remember that the tax system still includes a corporate income tax. And it includes a capital gains tax whose realization criterion gives it many of the properties of a penalty tax on the efficient redeployment of capital from industry to industry and from the old to the young.[38]

Keep in mind also that while the process of converting the income tax to a wage/consumption tax is well-begun and continuing apace, the transition is still incomplete. To see where we stand at the moment, note that the policy reserves of insurance companies and reserves of pension plans currently exceed $679 billion, up by nearly $200 billion since the end of 1973. The policy reserves of life insurance companies amount to some $167 billion;[39] the total assets of non-insured pension funds are $182 billion; the total assets of insured pension reserves are $98 billion; and the pension reserves of federal, state and municipal public funds are $232 billion.[40] If we assume an average earnings rate of 7 percent, the exempt investment income on these funds would be about $47 billion currently, as compared with a total investment income of $73 billion reported on personal income tax returns for 1976 (not all of which, of course, was actually subject to tax). This estimate of exempt investment income, moreover, is a lower bound, since it does not include the earnings on Individual Retirement Accounts, Keogh plan accounts, or the unfunded liabilities of corporate and government pension plans.[41]

The erosion of the income tax that we have been describing has not escaped the attention of the Treasury nor of the academic public finance specialists, but their reactions have been mixed. Some have deplored this drift away from a tax based on the Simons accretion concept of personal income. But efforts to reverse (or even slow) the drift by a tax reform package under the banner of a broad-based income tax with 'equal treatment of equal incomes' have failed. Promises of lower rates, in return for the removal of benefits and exemptions, are simply not credible in today's political climate (if, indeed, they ever were). One shudders to think of the Congressional reaction had recent tax reform proposals contained any serious attack on the huge amounts of exempt investment income in insurance reserves and pension funds.

[38]In the latter connection, remember that while the capital gains tax will be low in a present-value sense to a young taxpayer with a long accumulation horizon, the effective weight of the tax on portfolio decisions increases steadily as time for decumulation approaches. By the logic of the life-cycle model, investors approaching retirement will hold a sizeable chunk of total appreciated assets. And their interest (and political clout) in getting capital gains reduced will be substantial.

[39]*Life Insurance Fact Book* (1977).

[40]*Statistical Bulletin*, Securities and Exchange Commission (1978).

[41]A substantial amount of income from capital also escapes taxation during the decumulation phase thanks to special additional exemptions for the elderly. Under present law, two taxpayers over 65 filing a joint return would be able to exempt $7,200 per year of investment income (equivalent to the earnings on a savings account of about $100,000).

Another wing of opinion has recognized the futility of attempts to turn the clock back to the Simons accretion concept and has called instead for completion of the movement from income tax to a consumption tax or expenditure tax.[42] For them, the shift from an income tax to Fisher's (1937) consumption tax is more than merely making the best of an irreversible erosion of the tax take on investment income. They see the change as having positive economic advantages in reducing the disincentives to saving and capital accumulation; and as having the additional ethical advantages epitomized in the dictum calling for taxes on what people take out of the common pool rather than what they put in.

But while the proponents of the consumption tax have a strong case on economic and ethical grounds they, too, appear to have underestimated the extent of the drift that has already occurred. Their policy proposals, as a consequence, have typically called for thoroughgoing structural 'reform' of the present law, scrapping much of the Code and building a new tax system based on the cash flow statement and the balance sheet (especially the net worth reconciliation). They see internal consistency as requiring drastic modification of some long-standing features of the current Code (notably the treatment of housing and of capital gains) and as forcing the creation of new sections to deal with such nonstandard cases as consumption financed with borrowings. Grandiose reform schemes of this kind, however, are as doomed to futility as the broad-based income tax. The present Internal Revenue Code may be of monstrous complexity and its internal inconsistencies may offend the academic purists, but it is an old tax. We have learned to live with it and have become attached to those provisions that soften, or at least seem to soften the blows in our own direction.

Fortunately, however, a simple way to complete most of the transition to a consumption tax and yet still keep the present Code and its vested interests intact is suggested by the thrust of this paper: allow substantial additional voluntary contributions to pension-type plans or I.R.A.'s (and eliminate the current penalties on early withdrawal at least on the voluntary contributions). Not only does this proposal have the virtue of simplicity for all concerned, but to recommend it at this time is really only a matter of accelerating the inevitable. The revenue acts of recent years have steadily extended and broadened the provisions sheltering retirement savings[43] and the

---

[42]See, e.g., Andrews (1974) and the comment on Andrews' article by Warren (1974). Many of the same forces that have moved the U.S. income tax towards a consumption or expenditure tax have also been at work in Great Britain. See in this connection Kay and King (1978) who, like Andrews, recommend going the rest of the way. A proposal for an expenditure tax was one of the two main options in the Treasury volume *Blueprints for Basic Tax Reform* (1976) prepared in the closing days of the Ford administration.

[43]It is no accident, of course, that these extensions have coincided with a period of rapid inflation. Without this form of tax relief the real after-tax rate of return on saving would have been substantially negative.

standard legislative dynamics of equalizing the benefits to 'similar' groups promises more to come. The tax system that eventually emerges from this process will, it is true, be a strange amalgam and far less logical in its details than the elegant schemes for consumption or expenditure taxes that are described in the public finance literature. But under present political and economic realities, insisting on a major overhaul of the tax system so that the remaining anomalies can be removed would indeed be making the best the enemy of the better.

References

Andrews, W.D., 1974, A consumption-type or cash flow personal income tax, Harvard Law Review 87, no. 6, 1113–1188.

Black, F. and M. Scholes, 1974, The effects of dividend yield and dividend policy on common stock prices and returns, Journal of Financial Economics 1, no. 1, 1–22.

Black, F., M.H. Miller and R.A. Posner, 1978, An approach to the regulation of bank holding companies, Journal of Business 51, no. 3, 379–412.

Blume, M.E., J. Crockett and I. Friend, 1974, Stock ownership in the United States: Characteristics and trends, Survey of Current Business, Nov., 16–40.

Blume, M.E. and I. Friend, 1978, The changing role of the individual investor, A Twentieth Century Fund report (Wiley, New York).

Cooper, G., 1977, A voluntary tax: New perspectives on sophisticated estate tax avoidance, Columbia Law Review 77, no. 2, 161–247.

Fama, E.F. and A. Farber, 1978, Money, bonds and foreign exchange, Center for Research in Security Prices Working Paper no. WP5 (Graduate School of Business, University of Chicago, Chicago, IL).

Fisher, I., 1937, Income in theory and income taxation in practice, Econometrica V, Jan., 47–48.

Jensen, M.C. and W.H. Meckling, 1976, Theory of the firm: Managerial behavior, agency costs and ownership structure, Journal of Financial Economics 3, no. 4, 305–360.

Kay, J.A. and M.A. King, 1978, The British tax system (Oxford University Press, Oxford).

Life Insurance Fact Book, 1977 (American Council of Life Insurance, Washington, DC).

Long, J.B., Jr., 1977, Efficient portfolio choice with differential taxation of dividends and capital gains, Journal of Financial Economics 5, no. 1, 25–53.

Miller, M.H. and F. Modigliani, 1961, Dividend policy, growth and the valuation of shares, Journal of Business 34, no. 4, 411–433.

Miller, M.H., 1977, Debt and taxes, Journal of Finance 32, no. 2, 261–275.

Miller, M.H. and C.W. Upton, 1976, Leasing, buying and the cost of capital services, Journal of Finance 31, no. 3, 761–786.

Pettit, R.R., 1977, Taxes, transaction costs and the clientele effect of dividends, Journal of Financial Economics 5, no. 3, 419–436.

Salomon Brothers, 1977, Prospects for the credit markets in 1977, compiled by: H. Kaufman, J. McKeon and J. Cohn (Salomon Brothers, New York).

Simons, H.C., 1938, Personal income taxation (University of Chicago Press, Chicago, IL).

U.S. Department of the Treasury, 1977, Blueprints for basic tax reform (Government Printing Office, Washington, DC).

U.S. Department of the Treasury, 1976, Statistics of income, 1973 (Government Printing Office, Washington, DC).

U.S. Department of the Treasury, 1977, High income tax returns: 1974 and 1975 (Government Printing Office, Washington, DC).

U.S. Federal Deposit Insurance Company, 1976, Trust assets of insured commercial banks (Government Printing Office, Washington, DC).

U.S. Securities and Exchange Commission, 1978, Statistical Bulletin 37, no. 5.

Warren, A.C., Jr., 1975, Fairness and a consumption-type or cash flow personal income tax, Harvard Law Review 88, no. 5, 931–947.

32. THE EFFECT OF PERSONAL TAXES AND DIVIDENDS ON CAPITAL ASSET PRICES: THEORY AND EMPIRICAL EVIDENCE

ROBERT H. LITZENBERGER*
KRISHNA RAMASWAMY†

Reprinted from the *Journal of Financial Economics*, Vol. 7, No. 2 (June 1979), pp. 163–195, by permission of the authors and the publisher.

This paper derives an after tax version of the Capital Asset Pricing Model. The model accounts for a progressive tax scheme and for wealth and income related constraints on borrowing. The equilibrium relationship indicates that before-tax expected rates of return are linearly related to systematic risk and to dividend yield. The sample estimates of the variances of observed betas are used to arrive at maximum likelihood estimators of the coefficients. The results indicate that, unlike prior studies, there is a strong positive relationship between dividend yield and expected return for NYSE stocks. Evidence is also presented for a clientele effect.

1. Introduction

The effect of dividend policy on the prices of equity securities has been an issue of interest in financial theory. The traditional view was that investors prefer a current, certain return in the form of dividends to the uncertain prospect of future dividends. Consequently, they bid up the price of high yield securities relative to low yield securities [see Cottle, Dodd and Graham (1962) and Gordon (1963)]. In their now classic paper Miller and Modigliani (1961) argued that in a world without taxes and transactions costs the dividend policy of a corporation, given its investment policy, has no effect on the price of its shares. In a world where capital gains receive preferential treatment relative to dividends, the Miller–Modigliani 'irrelevance proposition' would seem to break down. They argue, however, that since tax rates vary across investors each corporation would attract to itself a clientele of investors that most desired its dividend policy. Black and Scholes (1974) assert that corporations would adjust their payout policies until in equilib-

* Stanford University, Stanford, California.
† Bell Telephone Laboratories, Murray Hill, New Jersey,
We thank Roger Clarke, Tom Foregger, Bill Schwert, William Sharpe, and the referee, Michael Brennan, for helpful comments, and Jim Starr for computational assistance. Any remaining errors are the author's responsibility.

rium the spectrum of policies offered would be such that any one firm is unable to affect the price of its shares by (marginal) changes in its payout policy. '

In the absence of taxes, capital asset pricing theory suggests that individuals choose mean-variance efficient portfolios. Under personal income taxes, individuals would be expected to choose portfolios that are mean-variance efficient in after-tax rates of return. However, the tax laws in the United States are such that some economic units (for example, corporations) would seem to prefer dividends relative to capital gains. Other units (for example, non-profit organizations) pay no taxes and would be indifferent to the level of yield for a given level of expected return. The resulting effect of dividend yield on common stock prices seems to be an empirical issue.

Brennan (1973) first proposed an extended form of the single period Capital Asset Pricing Model that accounted for the taxation of dividends. Under the assumption of proportional individual tax rates (not a function of income), certain dividends, and unlimited borrowing at the riskless rate of interest (among others) he derived the following equilibrium relationship:

$$E(\tilde{R}_i) - r_f = b\beta_i + \tau(d_i - r_f), \tag{1}$$

where $\tilde{R}_i$ is the before tax total return to security i, β_i is its systematic risk, $b = [E(R_m) - r_f - \tau(d_m - r_f)]$ is the after-tax excess rate of return on the market portfolio, r_f is the return on a riskless asset, d_i is the dividend yield on security i, and the subscript m denotes the market portfolio. τ is a positive coefficient that accounts for the taxation of dividends and interest as ordinary income and taxation of capital gains at a preferential rate.

In empirical tests [of the form (1)] to date, the evidence has been inconsistent. Black and Scholes (1974, p. 1) conclude that

> '...it is not possible to demonstrate that the expected returns on high yield common stocks differ from the expected returns on low yield common stocks either before or after taxes.'

Alternatively, stated in terms of the Brennan model, their tests were not sufficiently powerful either to reject the hypothesis that $\tau = 0$ or to reject the hypothesis that $\tau = 0.5$. Rosenberg and Marathe (1978) attribute the lack of power in the Black–Scholes tests to (a) the loss in efficiency from grouping stocks into portfolios and (b) the inefficiency of their estimating procedures, which are equivalent to Ordinary Least Squares. Using an instrumental variables approach to the problem of errors in variables and a more complete specification of the variance–covariance matrix (of disturbances in the regression), Rosenberg and Marathe find that the dividend term is statistically significant. Both the Rosenberg and Marathe and the Black and Scholes studies use an average dividend yield from the prior twelve month period as a surrogate for the expected dividend yield. Since most dividends are paid quarterly, their proxy understates the expected dividend yield in ex-dividend months and overstates it in those months that a stock does not go ex-dividend, thereby reducing the efficiency of the estimated coefficient on the dividend yield term. Both studies (Rosenberg and Marathe in using instrumental variables, and Black–Scholes in grouping) sacrifice efficiency to achieve consistency.

The present paper derives an after-tax version of the Capital Asset Pricing Model that accounts for a progressive tax scheme and both wealth and income related constraints on borrowing. Alternative econometric procedures are used to test the implications of this model. Unlike prior tests of the CAPM, the tests here use the variance of the observed betas to arrive at maximum likelihood estimators of the coefficients. Consistent estimators are obtained without loss of efficiency. Also, for ex-dividend months the expected dividend yield based on prior information is used, and for other months the expected dividend yield is set equal to zero. While the estimate of the coefficient of dividend yield is of the same order of magnitude as that found in Black and Scholes, and lower than that found by Rosenberg and Marathe, the t-value is substantially larger, indicating a substantial increase in efficiency. Furthermore, the tests are consistent with the existence of a clientele effect, indicating that the aversion for dividends relative to capital gains is lower for high yield stocks and higher for low yield stocks. This is consistent with the Elton and Gruber (1970) empirical results on the ex-dividend behavior of common stocks.

2. Theory

This section derives a version of the Capital Asset Pricing Model that accounts for the tax treatment of dividend and interest income under a progressive taxation scheme. Two types of constraints on individual borrowing are imposed. The first constrains the maximum interest on riskless borrowing to be equal to the individual's dividend income, and the second is a margin requirement that restricts the fraction of security holdings that may be financed through borrowing. In previous published work, Brennan (1973) derives an after-tax version of the Capital Asset Pricing Model with unlimited borrowing and with constant tax rates which may vary across individuals.[1] Under his model when interest on borrowing exceeds dividend income the investor would pay a negative tax. The theoretical model

---

[1]Brennan (1970) also derives a model with a progressive tax scheme. However, he neither considers constraints on borrowing nor the limiting of interest deduction on margin borrowing to dividend income. Consideration of the limit on the interest tax deduction to dividend income combined with a positive capital gains tax would result in a preference for dividends by those individuals whose interest payments exceed their dividend income.

developed here may be viewed as an extension of the Brennan analysis to account for constraints on borrowing along with a progressive tax scheme. Special cases of the model are examined, where the income related constraint and/or the margin constraint on individual borrowing are removed.

The following assumptions are made:

(A.1) Individuals' Von Neumann–Morgenstern utility functions are monotone increasing strictly concave functions of after-tax end of period wealth.

(A.2) Security rates of return have a multivariate normal distribution.

(A.3) There are no transactions costs, and no restrictions on the short sale of securities, and individuals are price takers.

(A.4) Individuals have homogeneous expectations.

(A.5) All assets are marketable.

(A.6) A riskless asset, paying a constant rate r_f, exists.

(A.7) Dividends on securities are paid at the end of the period and are known with certainty at the beginning of the period.

(A.8) Income taxes are progressive and the marginal tax rate is a continuous function of taxable income.

(A.9) There are no taxes on capital gains.

(A.10) Constraints on individuals' borrowing are of the form:
    (i) A constraint that the interest on borrowing cannot exceed dividend income, called the income constraint on borrowing, and/or
    (ii) a margin constraint that the individual's net worth be at least a given fraction of the market value of his holdings of risky securities.

Assumptions (A.1) through (A.6) are standard assumptions of the Capital Asset Pricing Model. Assumptions (A.1) and (A.2) taken together imply that preferences can be described over the mean and the variance of after-tax end of period wealth. Under these conditions individuals prefer more mean return and are averse to the variance of return. The individual's marginal rate of substitution between the mean and variance of after-tax end of period wealth, at the optimum, can be written as the ratio of his global risk tolerance to his initial period wealth. That is, if $u_k(W_1^k)$ is the kth individual's utility function in terms of after-tax end of period wealth, $f^k(\mu_k, \sigma_k^2)$ is his objective function in terms of the mean and variance of the after-tax portfolio return, and W^k is his initial wealth,

$$f_1^k / - 2f_2^k = \theta^k / W^k, \tag{2}$$

where $\theta^k = -E(u')/E(u'')$ is the individual's global risk tolerance at the optimum [see Gonzalez-Gaverra (1973) and Rubinstein (1973)]. (A.7) implies that dividends are announced at the beginning of the period and paid at its end. Since firms display relatively stable dividend policies this may be a reasonable approximation for a monthly holding period.

Assumption (A.8) closely resembles the tax treatment of ordinary dividends in the U.S. The $100 dividend exclusion is ignored, since the small magnitude of the exclusion implies that for the majority of stockholders the marginal tax rate applicable to ordinary income is the same as that applied to dividends. Assumption (A.9) abstracts from the effects of capital gains taxes. Since capital gains are taxed only upon realization, their treatment in a single period model is not possible. It is, however, straightforward to model a capital gains tax on an accrual basis [see Brennan (1973)]. Since most capital gains go unrealized for long periods, this would tend to overstate the effect of the actual tax. Noting that the ratio of realizations to accruals is small, and that capital gains are exempt from tax when transferred by inheritance, Bailey (1969) has argued that the effective tax is rather small.

Under assumption (A.8), the kth individual's average tax rate, t^k, is a non-decreasing function of his taxable end of period income Y_1^k,

$$t^k = g(Y_1^k),$$

$$g(0) = 0, \qquad g'(Y_1^k) = 0 \quad \text{for} \quad Y_1^k \leq 0,$$

$$> 0 \quad \text{for} \quad Y_1^k > 0. \tag{3}$$

The kth individual's marginal tax rate, written T^k, is the first derivative of taxes paid with respect to taxable income. This is equal to the average tax rate plus the product of taxable income and the derivative of the average tax rate,

$$T^k \equiv d(t^k Y_1^k)/dY_1^k = t^k + Y_1^k g'(Y_1^k). \tag{4}$$

The margin constraint in assumption (A.10–ii) resembles institutional margin restrictions. By (A.10–i), borrowing is constrained up to a point where interest paid equal dividends received. This constraint incorporates the casual empirical observation that loan applications require information on income (which this constraint accounts for) in addition to information on wealth (which the margin constraint accounts for). One or both of the constraints may be binding, for a given individual. This formulation allows the analysis of an equilibrium with both constraints, with only one of them imposed or with no borrowing constraints.

The following notation is employed:

$\tilde{R}_i$ = the total before tax rate of return on security i, equal to the ratio of the value of the security at the end of the period plus dividends over its current value, less one,

d_i = the dividend yield on security i, equal to the dollar dividend divided by the current price,

X_i^k = the fraction of the kth individual's wealth invested in the ith risky asset, $i = 1, 2, ..., N$ (a negative value is a short sale),

X_f^k = the fraction of the kth individual's wealth invested in the safe asset (a negative value indicates borrowing),

$\tilde{R}_p^k$ = the before-tax rate of return on the kth individual's portfolio,

W^k = the kth individual's initial wealth, and

$f^k(\mu_k, \sigma_k^2)$ = the kth individual's expected utility function defined over the mean and variance of after-tax portfolio return, μ_k and σ_k^2, respectively.

The kth individual's ordinary income is then

$$Y_1^k = W^k \left(\sum_i X_i^k d_i + X_f^k r_f \right). \tag{5}$$

The mean after-tax return on the individual's portfolio is

$$\mu_k = \sum X_i^k E(\tilde{R}_i) + X_f^k r_f - t^k \left(\sum_i X_i^k d_i + X_f^k r_f \right), \tag{6}$$

and under assumption (A.7) the variance of after-tax return is

$$\sigma_k^2 = \sum_j \sum_i X_i^k X_j^k \operatorname{cov}(\tilde{R}_i - d_i t^k, \tilde{R}_j - d_j t^k)$$

$$= \sum_j \sum_i X_i^k X_j^k \operatorname{cov}(\tilde{R}_i, \tilde{R}_j). \tag{7}$$

By assumption (A.10–i) the income constraint on borrowing is

$$W^k \left\{ \sum_i X_i^k d_i + X_f^k r_f \right\} \geq 0, \tag{8}$$

and the margin constraint on borrowing is

$$W^k \left\{ (1 - \alpha) \sum_i X_i^k + X_f^k \right\} \geq 0, \tag{9}$$

where α, $0 < \alpha < 1$, is the margin requirement on the individual. As pointed out earlier, one or both of these constraints may be binding.

The kth individual's optimization problem is stated in terms of the following Lagrangian:

$$\mathscr{L}^k \equiv f^k(\mu_k, \sigma_k^2) + \lambda_1^k \left[1 - \sum_i X_i^k - X_f^k \right] \tag{10}$$

$$+ \lambda_2^k \left[\sum_i X_i^k d_i + X_f^k r_f - S_2^k \right] + \lambda_3^k \left[(1-\alpha) \sum_i X_i^k + X_f^k - S_3^k \right],$$

where

λ_1^k = the Lagrange multiplier on the kth individual's budget,

λ_2^k, S_2^k = the Lagrange multiplier and non-negative slack variable for the income related constraint on the kth individual's borrowing, respectively (when the constraint is binding $\lambda_2^k > 0$ and $S_2^k = 0$, and when it is not binding $\lambda_2^k = 0$ and $S_2^k \geq 0$), and

λ_3^k, S_3^k = the Lagrange multipler and non-negative slack variables for the margin constraint on the kth individual's borrowing, respectively; again if the constraint is binding (not binding), $\lambda_3^k > (=) 0$ and $S_3^k = (\geq) 0$.

The stationary points satisfy the following first order conditions:

$$\frac{\partial \mathscr{L}^k}{\partial X_1^k} = f_1^k \{ E(\tilde{R}_i) - [t^k + Y_1^k g'(Y_1^k)] d_i \} - \lambda_1^k + \lambda_2^k d_i$$

$$+ \lambda_3^k (1-\alpha) + 2 f_2^k \sum_j X_j^k \text{cov}(\tilde{R}_i, \tilde{R}_j) = 0, \qquad i = 1, 2, \ldots, N, \tag{11}$$

$$\frac{\partial \mathscr{L}^k}{\partial X_f^k} = f_1^k \{ r_f - [t^k + Y_1^k g'(Y_1^k)] r_f \} - \lambda_1^k + \lambda_2^k r_f + \lambda_3^k = 0, \tag{12}$$

where $f_1^k \equiv \partial f^k(\mu_k, \sigma_k^2)/\partial \mu_k$, $f_2^k \equiv \partial f^k(\mu_k, \sigma_k^2)/\partial \sigma_k^2$. The other first order conditions are the constraints and specify the signs of the Lagrangian multipliers and are omitted here. The progressive nature of the tax scheme [assumption (A.8)] ensures that the mean variance efficient frontier in after-tax terms is concave, and this together with risk aversion from assumption (A.8) is sufficient to guarantee the second order conditions for a maximum.

Recall the following relationships: (i) the marginal tax rate, $T^k = [t^k + Y_1^k g'(\cdot)]$, (ii) the covariance $\sum_j X_j^k \text{cov}(\tilde{R}_i, \tilde{R}_j) = \text{cov}(\tilde{R}_i, \tilde{R}_p^k)$, and (iii) the global risk tolerance $\theta^k = W^k(f_1^k/-2f_2^k)$. Subtracting relation (12) from relation (11) and re-arranging terms yields

$$\{ E(\tilde{R}_i) - r_f \} = \alpha(\lambda_3^k/f_1^k) + (W^k/\theta^k)\text{cov}(\tilde{R}_i, \tilde{R}_p^k)$$

$$+ [T^k - (\lambda_2^k/f_1^k)](d_i - r_f). \tag{13}$$

Relation (13) must be satisfied for the individual's portfolio optimum.

Market equilibrium requires that relation (13) holds for all individuals, and that markets clear. For markets to clear all assets have to be held which implies the conservation relation (14) that requires the value weighted average of all individuals' portfolios be equal to the market portfolio,

$$\sum_k (W^k/W^m)\tilde{R}_p^k = \tilde{R}_m, \tag{14}$$

or

$$\sum_k W^k \tilde{R}_p^k = W^m \tilde{R}_m,$$

where

$$\sum_k W^k \equiv W^m.$$

Multiplying both sides of relation (13) by θ^k, summing over all individuals, using the conservation relation (14) and re-arranging terms yields

$$E(\tilde{R}_i) - r_f = a + b\beta_i + c(d_i - r_f), \tag{15}$$

where

$$\beta_i \equiv \text{cov}(\tilde{R}_i, \tilde{R}_m)/\text{var}(\tilde{R}_m),$$

$$a \equiv \alpha \sum_k (\theta^k/\theta^m)(\lambda_3^k/f_1^k),$$

$$b \equiv \text{var}(\tilde{R}_m)(W^m/\theta^m).$$

$$c \equiv \sum_k (\theta^k/\theta^m)[T^k - (\lambda_2^k/f_1^k)],$$

$$\theta^m \equiv \sum_k \theta^k.$$

The term 'a', the intercept of the implied security market plane, is the fractional margin requirement α times the weighted average of the ratios of individual shadow prices on the margin constraint and the expected marginal utility of mean return. The weights, (θ^k/θ^m), are proportional to individuals' global risk tolerances. When $\alpha > 0$ and the constraint is binding for some individuals, $\lambda_3^k > 0$ for some k, a is positive. In the absence of margin requirements $(\alpha = 0)$ or when the margin constraint is not binding for all individuals, $(\lambda_3^k = 0)$ for all k), $a = 0$.

Interpreting eq. (15), 'a' is the excess return on a zero beta portfolio (relative to the market) whose dividend yield is equal to the riskless rate, i.e.,

$a = E(\tilde{R}_z) - r_f$. The term 'b', the coefficient on beta is equal to the product of the variance of the rate of return on the market portfolio and global market relative risk aversion, i.e., $b = \mathrm{var}(\tilde{R}_m)(W^m/\theta^m)$. Since relation (15) also holds for the market portfolio, b may be alternatively expressed as $b = [E(R_m) - r_f - c(d_m - r_f) - a]$. If '$c$' is interpreted as a tax rate, b may be viewed as the expected after-tax rate of return on a hedge portfolio which is long the market portfolio and short a portfolio having a zero beta and a dividend yield equal to the riskless rate of interest; i.e., $b = [E(\tilde{R}_m) - E(\tilde{R}_z) - c(d_m - d_z)]$. The term '$c$' is a weighted average of individual's marginal tax rates ($\sum_k (\theta^k/\theta^m) T^k$), less the weighted average of the individual's ratios of the shadow price on the income related borrowing constraint and the expected marginal utility of mean portfolio return $\sum_k (\theta^k/\theta^m)(\lambda_2^k/f_1^k)$. For the cases where the income related margin constraint is either non-existent or non-binding for all individuals, c is simply the weighted average of marginal tax rates, and is positive. Otherwise, the sign of 'c' depends on the magnitudes of these two terms. Define B as the set of indices of those individuals k for whom the income related constraint is binding: and define N (*not B*) as the set of indices for which the constraint is non-binding. Now for $k \in B$, $\lambda_2^k > 0$, $Y_1^k = 0$ and $T^k = t^k = 0$. And for $k \in N$, $\lambda_2^k = 0$, $Y_1^k \geqq 0$ and $T^k \geqq t^k \geqq 0$. Hence

$$c = \sum_{k \in N} \frac{\theta^k}{\theta^m} T^k - \sum_{k \in B} \frac{\theta^k}{\theta^m} \frac{\lambda_2^k}{f_1^k}. \tag{16}$$

The individuals in N may be viewed as a clientele that prefers capital gains to dividends. The individuals in B may be viewed as a clientele that shows a preference for dividends: in the context of this model, these individuals wish to borrow more than the income related constraint allows them, and increased dividends serve to increase their debt capacity without additional tax obligations. To this point corporate dividend policies have been treated as exogenous in this model.

Now consider supply adjustments by value maximizing firms. If $c > 0$ ($c < 0$) firms could increase their market values by decreasing (increasing) cash dividends and increasing (decreasing) share repurchases or decreasing (increasing) external equity flotations. Value maximizing firms (in absence of any restrictions the IRS may impose) would adjust the supply of dividends until an equilibrium was obtained where

$$\sum_{k \in N} (\theta^k/\theta^m) T^k = \sum_{k \in B} (\theta^k/\theta^m)(\lambda_2^k/f_1^k). \tag{17}$$

When condition (17) is satisfied an individual firm's dividend decision does not affect its market value, $c=0$ and dividend yield has no effect on the before tax rate of return on any security.[2]

Under unrestricted supply effects, $c=0$ and the equilibrium relationship (15) reduces to the before tax zero beta version of the Capital Asset Pricing Model:

$$E(\tilde{R}_i) = (a + r_f)(1 - \beta_i) + E(\tilde{R}_m)\beta_i. \tag{18}$$

Note that this obtains in the presence of taxes. Long (1975) has studied conditions under which the before tax and after-tax mean variance efficient frontiers are identical for any individual. He does not, however, study the equilibrium as is done here: for even though the before tax and after-tax individual mean variance frontiers are not identical, (18) demonstrates that prices are found as if there is no tax effect.

In the case where there are no margin constraints, $a=0$, and relation (18) reduces to the before tax traditional Sharpe–Lintner version of the Capital Asset Pricing Model,

$$E(\tilde{R}_i) = r_f + [E(\tilde{R}_m) - r_f]\beta_i. \tag{19}$$

Return now to the case where the income related borrowing constraint is absent. Then, in (16), $c = \sum_k T^k(\theta^k/\theta^m) \equiv T^m$, the 'market' marginal tax bracket: and the relation reduces to an after-tax version of the Black (1972), Lintner (1965), Vasicek (1971) zero beta model,

$$E(\tilde{R}_i) - T^m d_i = [r_f(1 - T^m) + a](1 - \beta_i) + (E(\tilde{R}_m) - T^m d_m)\beta_i. \tag{20}$$

When there is no margin constraint or when it is non-binding for all individuals, $a=0$, and relation (20) reduced to an after-tax version of the Sharpe (1964), Lintner (1965) model,

$$E(\tilde{R}_i) - T^m d_i = [r_f(1 - T^m)] + [E(\tilde{R}_m) - T^m d^m - r_f(1 - T^m)]\beta_i. \tag{21}$$

However, in none of these cases is T^m a weighted average of individual

[2]Note, however, that this equilibrium, where dividends do not affect before tax returns, may not exist. For example, the income constraint may be binding for no one even when dividends are zero. If all individuals had the same endowments and had the same utility functions this constraint would be non-binding for all individuals.

This argument is in the spirit of the 'supply effect' alluded to in Black and Scholes (1974). Unlike the recent argument in Miller and Scholes (1977) for a zero dividend effect, the present argument does not depend on an artificial segmentation of accumulators and non-accumulators, and the existence of tax-sheltered lending opportunities with zero administrative costs. The major problem with the argument here is that with the existence of two distinct clienteles, one preferring higher dividends and the other preferring lower dividends, shareholders would not agree on the direction in which firms should change their dividend. Thus the assertion of value maximizing behavior by firms does not have a strong theoretical basis.

average tax rates. It is only when taxes are simply proportional to income that $T^k = t^k$, and relation (21) is identical to the equilibrium implied by Brennan (1973), who assumes a constant tax rate that may differ across investors.

3. Empirical tests

From the theory, the equilibrium specification to be tested is

$$E(\tilde{R}_i) - r_f = a + b\beta_i + c(d_i - r_f). \tag{22}$$

The hypotheses are $a > 0$, $b > 0$, and in the absence of the income related constraint on borrowing $c > 0$.

In obtaining econometric estimates of a, b and c, two problems arise. The first is that expectations are not directly observed. The usual procedure is to assume that expectations are rational and that the parameters a, b and c are constant over time; the realized returns are used on the left-hand side

$$\tilde{R}_{it} - r_{ft} = \gamma_0 + \gamma_1 \beta_{it} + \gamma_2 (d_{it} - r_{ft}) + \tilde{\varepsilon}_{it}, \qquad i = 1, 2, \ldots, N_t,$$
$$t = 1, 2, \ldots, T, \tag{23}$$

where $\tilde{R}_{it}$ is the return of security i in period t, β_{it} and d_{it} are the systematic risk and the dividend yield of security i in period t respectively. The disturbance term $\tilde{\varepsilon}_{it}$ is $\tilde{R}_{it} - E(\tilde{R}_{it})$, the deviation of the realized return from its expected value. The coefficients γ_0, γ_1 and γ_2 correspond to a, b and c. The variance of the column vector of disturbance terms, $\tilde{\varepsilon} \equiv \{\tilde{\varepsilon}_{it} : i = 1, 2, \ldots, N_t, t = 1, \ldots, T\}$, is not proportional to the identity matrix, since contemporaneous covariances between security returns are non-zero and return variances differ across securities. (Note that in order to conserve space '$\{ \cdot \}$' is used to denote a column vector.) This means that ordinary least squares (OLS) estimators are inefficient, for either a cross-sectional regression in month t, or a pooled time series and cross-sectional regression. The computed variance of the OLS estimator (based on the assumption that the variance of $\tilde{\varepsilon}$ is proportional to the identity matrix) is not equal to the true variance of the estimator.

The second problem is that the true population β_{it}'s are unobservable. The usual procedure uses an estimate from past data, and this estimate has an associated measurement error. This means that the OLS estimates will be biased and inconsistent. The method used in tackling these problems is discussed in this section.

To fix matters, assume that data exist for rates of return, true betas and for dividend yields in periods i, $i = 1, 2, \ldots, N_t$, securities in each period t, $t = 1, \ldots, T$. Define the vector of realized excess returns as

$$\tilde{R} \equiv \{\tilde{R}_1 \tilde{R}_2, \ldots, \tilde{R}_t, \ldots, \tilde{R}_T\},$$

where

$$\tilde{R}_t \equiv \{(\tilde{R}_{1t} - r_{ft})(\tilde{R}_{2t} - r_{ft})(\tilde{R}_{it} - r_{ft}), \ldots, (\tilde{R}_{N_t t} - r_{ft})\},$$

and the matrices X of explanatory variables as

$$X \equiv \{X_1 X_2, \ldots, X_t, \ldots, X_T\},$$

where

$$X_t \equiv \begin{bmatrix} 1 & \beta_{1t} & (d_{1t} - r_{ft}) \\ 1 & \beta_{2t} & (d_{2t} - r_{ft}) \\ \vdots & \vdots & \vdots \\ 1 & \beta_{N_t t} & (d_{N_t t} - r_{ft}) \end{bmatrix}.$$

By defining the vector of regression coefficients as $\Gamma = \{\gamma_0 \, \gamma_1 \, \gamma_2\}$ one can write the pooled time series and cross-sectional regression as

$$\tilde{R} = X\Gamma + \tilde{\varepsilon}, \tag{24}$$

where

$$\tilde{\varepsilon} \equiv \{\tilde{\varepsilon}_1 \tilde{\varepsilon}_2, \ldots, \tilde{\varepsilon}_t, \ldots, \tilde{\varepsilon}_T\},$$

and

$$\tilde{\varepsilon}_t \equiv \{\tilde{\varepsilon}_{1t} \tilde{\varepsilon}_{2t}, \ldots, \tilde{\varepsilon}_{it}, \ldots, \tilde{\varepsilon}_{N_t t}\}.$$

It is assumed that

$$E(\tilde{\varepsilon}) = 0,$$

and that

$$E(\tilde{\varepsilon}_t \tilde{\varepsilon}_t') = V_t,$$

some symmetric positive definite matrix of order $(N_t \times N_t)$. It is also assumed that security returns are serially uncorrelated, so that

$$E(\tilde{\varepsilon}_{it} \tilde{\varepsilon}_{js}) = 0 \quad \text{for} \quad t \neq s.$$

This means that the variance–covariance matrix $V \equiv E(\tilde{\varepsilon} \tilde{\varepsilon}')$ is block diagonal, with the off-diagonal blocks being zero. The matrices V_t appears along the diagonal of V.

It is well known that the estimator for Γ which is linear in $\tilde{R}$, unbiased and has minimum variance is unique, and is given by the Aitken or Generalized Least Squares estimator (GLS),

$$\hat{\Gamma} = (X'V^{-1}X)^{-1}X'V^{-1}\tilde{R}.$$

(25)

From the block diagonal nature of V, it follows that V^{-1} is also block diagonal. The matrices V_t^{-1}, $t=1,2,\ldots,T$, appear along the diagonal of V^{-1}, with the off-diagonal blocks being zero. Assuming that Γ is an intertemporal constant, $\hat{\Gamma}$ can be estimated by efficiently pooling T independent GLS estimates of Γ, namely $\hat{\Gamma}_1, \hat{\Gamma}_2,\ldots,\hat{\Gamma}_t,\ldots,\hat{\Gamma}_T$, obtained by using cross-sectional data in periods $1,2,\ldots,t,\ldots,T$,

$$\hat{\Gamma}_t = (X_t'V_t^{-1}X_t)^{-1}X_t'V_t^{-1}\tilde{R}_t, \qquad t=1,2,\ldots,T.$$

(26)

That is, the monthly estimators $\hat{\gamma}_{kt}$ for γ_k, $k=0$, 1 or 2, are serially uncorrelated, and the pooled GLS estimator $\hat{\gamma}_k$ is found as the weighted mean of the monthly estimates, where the weights are inversely proportional to the variances of these estimates,

$$\hat{\gamma}_k = \sum_{t=1}^{T} Z_{kt}\hat{\gamma}_{kt},$$

(27)

$$\text{var}(\hat{\gamma}_k) = \sum_{t=1}^{T} Z_{kt}^2 \,\text{var}(\hat{\gamma}_{kt}),$$

(28)

$$Z_{kt} = [\text{var}(\hat{\gamma}_{kt})]^{-1} \Big/ \sum_{t} [\text{var}(\hat{\gamma}_{kt})]^{-1}.$$

(29)

For some of the results presented in section 4 each $\hat{\gamma}_{kt}$ is assumed to be drawn from a stationary distribution, and the estimates of $\hat{\gamma}_k$ and its variance are

$$\hat{\gamma}_k = \sum_{t=1}^{T} (\hat{\gamma}_{kt}/T),$$

(30)

$$\hat{\sigma}^2(\hat{\gamma}_k) = \left[\sum_{t=1}^{T} (\hat{\gamma}_{kt}-\hat{\gamma}_k)^2/T(T-1)\right], \qquad k=0,1,2.$$

(31)

A useful portfolio interpretation can be given to each of the GLS estimators $\hat{\Gamma}_t$ in (26). Choose any matrix numbers of order $N_t \times N_t$, say W_t^{-1}, such that $(X_t' W_t^{-1} X_t)^{-1}$ exists. Construct an estimator, using cross-sectional data in period t, as

$$(X_t' W_t^{-1} X_t)^{-1} X_t' W_t^{-1} \tilde{R}_t. \tag{32}$$

This estimator is linear in $\tilde{R}_t$ and unbiased for Γ. This estimator is a linear combination of realized security excess returns in period t. From the fact that

$$(X_t' W_t^{-1} X_t)^{-1} X_t' W_t^{-1} X_t = I, \tag{33}$$

where I is the identity matrix, it follows that the estimator for γ_0 in (32) is the realized excess return on a zero beta portfolio having a dividend yield equal to the riskless rate. Similarly, the estimator for γ_1 is the realized excess return on a hedge portfolio that has a beta of one and dividend yield equal to zero; and that for γ_2 is the realized excess return on a hedge portfolio having a zero beta and a dividend yield equal to unity. This interpretation[3] can be given to any estimator of the form (32). When W_t^{-1} (or, equivalently, the portfolio weights discussed above) is chosen so as to minimize the variance of the portfolio return, the resulting estimator is the GLS estimator. This is because portfolio estimates as in (32) are linear and unbiased by construction, and by the Gauss–Markov theorem the GLS estimator is the unique minimum variance estimator among linear unbiased estimators [see Amemiya (1972)].

It is not possible to specify the elements of the variance–covariance matrix V_t a priori. The task of estimating these elements is greatly simplified by assuming that the Sharpe single index model is a correct description of the return generating process. The process that generates returns at the beginning of period t is assumed to be as follows:

$$\tilde{R}_{it} = \alpha_{it} + \beta_{it} \tilde{R}_{mt} + \tilde{e}_{it}, \qquad i = 1, 2, \ldots, N_t, \tag{34}$$

$$\text{cov}(\tilde{e}_{it}, \tilde{e}_{jt}) = 0, \qquad i \neq j,$$
$$= s_{ii}, \qquad i = j, \tag{35}$$

$$\alpha_{it} = E(\tilde{R}_{it} | R_{mt} = 0).$$

With this specification the element in the ith row and the jth column of V_t, written as $V_t(i, j)$, is given by

$$V_t(i, j) = \beta_{it} \beta_{jt} \sigma_{mm}, \qquad i \neq j, \qquad i, j = 1, 2, \ldots, N_t, \tag{36}$$
$$= \beta_{it}^2 \sigma_{mm} + s_{ii}, \qquad i = j,$$

[3]For a similar interpretation, see Rosenberg and Marathe (1978).

where

$$\sigma_{mm} \equiv \text{var}(\tilde{R}_{mt}).$$

Under these conditions the GLS estimator of Γ obtained by using data in period t reduces to

$$\hat{\Gamma}_t = (X_t' \Omega_t^{-1} X_t)^{-1} X_t' \Omega_t^{-1} R_t, \qquad (37)$$

where Ω_t is a diagonal matrix of order $(N_t \times N_t)$, whose element in the ith row and jth column is given by

$$\begin{aligned}\Omega_t(i,j) &= 0, & i \neq j, \\ &= s_{ii}, & i = j,\end{aligned} \quad i, j = 1, 2, \ldots, N_t. \qquad (38)$$

In appendix A it is shown that this estimator is the GLS estimator for Γ. That is, under the assumptions of the single index model, the estimator minimizes the 'residual risk' of three portfolio returns, subject to the constraint that the expected returns on these portfolios are γ_0, γ_1 and γ_2 respectively. This estimator can be constructed as a heteroscedastic transformation on $\tilde{R}_t$ and X_t. Define the matrix P_t of order $(N_t \times N_t)$ whose elements are given by

$$\begin{aligned}P_t(i,j) &= \phi/s_i \equiv \phi/\sqrt{s_{ii}}, & i = j \\ &= 0, & i \neq j,\end{aligned} \qquad (39)$$

where ϕ is a positive scalar. Then $\hat{\Gamma}_t$ can also be arrived at from the OLS regression on the transformed variables,

$$\tilde{R}_t^* = X_t^* \Gamma + \tilde{\varepsilon}_t^*, \qquad (40)$$

where

$$\tilde{R}_t^* = P\tilde{R}_t \quad \text{and} \quad X_t^* = PX_t.$$

This is equivalent to deflating the variables in the ith rows of $\tilde{R}_t$ and X_t by a factor proportional to the residual standard error s_i. Note that Black and Scholes (1974), who used the portfolio approach, assumed in addition to the single index model that the 'residual' risks of all securities were equal: that is, they assumed that $s_{ii} = s^2$ for all i. Therefore, the Black–Scholes estimator reduces to OLS on the untransformed variables.

Errors in variables. Since true population β_{it} variables are unobserved, estimates of this variable, $\tilde{\beta}_{it}$ are obtained from historical data. The estimated beta is assumed equal to the true beta plus a measurement error $\tilde{v}_{it}$,

$$\tilde{\beta}_{it} = \beta_{it} + \tilde{v}_{it}. \tag{41}$$

The presence of measurement error causes a misspecification in OLS and GLS estimators, and the resulting estimates of Γ are biased and inconsistent [see, for example, Johnston (1972), for a discussion of the bias in the coefficients of a variable without error, here dividend yield, see Fisher (1977)]. The estimates $\tilde{\beta}_{it}$ are obtained from a regression of $\tilde{R}_{i\tau}$ on the return of the market portfolio $\tilde{R}_{m\tau}$ from data prior to period t,

$$\tilde{R}_{i\tau} = \alpha_{it} + \beta_{it}\tilde{R}_{m\tau} + \tilde{e}_{i\tau}, \qquad \tau = t-60, \ t-59, \dots, t-1. \tag{42}$$

Since the single index model is assumed, $\text{cov}(\tilde{e}_{i\tau}, \tilde{e}_{j\tau}) = 0$ and hence $\text{cov}(\tilde{v}_{it}, \tilde{v}_{jt}) = 0$. If the joint probability distribution between security rates of return and market return is stationary, the variance of the measurement error $\text{var}(\tilde{v}_{it})$ is proportional to the variance of the residual risk term $\text{var}(\tilde{e}_{i\tau})$, for each i. Since month t is not used in this time series regression, $\text{cov}(\tilde{\varepsilon}_{it}, \tilde{v}_{it}) = 0$. Note that this time series regression yields a measured beta, $\tilde{\beta}_{it}$, its variance $\text{var}(\tilde{v}_{it})$ and the variance of the residual risk term $\text{var}(\tilde{e}_{i\tau}) = s_{ii}$.

Consistent with prior empirical studies, the assumption $E(\tilde{e}_{i\tau}) = 0$ has been made. However, it is recognized that if the 'market return' used in (42) is not the true market return, then the estimate of β_{it} may be biased, as has been observed by Sharpe (1977), Mayers (1972) and Roll (1977).

Because of errors in variables, most previous empirical tests have grouped stocks into portfolios. Since errors in measurement in betas for different securities are less than perfectly correlated, grouping risky assets into portfolios would reduce the asymptotic bias in OLS estimators. However, grouping results in a reduction of efficiency caused by the loss of information. The efficiency of the OLS estimator of the coefficient of a single independent variable is proportional to the cross sectional variation in that independent variable (beta). For the two independent variables case (dividend yield and beta), Stehle (1976) has shown that the efficiency of the OLS estimator of the coefficient of a given independent variable, using grouped data, is proportional to the cross-sectional variation in that variable unexplained by the variation in the other independent variable. Since the within group variation in dividend yield unexplained by beta is eliminated, the efficiency of the estimate of the dividend yield coefficient using grouped data is lower than that using all the data.[4] For this reason the present study

---

[4]The variance of the OLS estimator of the second independent variable (dividend yield) is equal to the variance of the error term divided by the portion of its variation that is unexplained by the first independent variable (beta). Therefore, unless the independent variables are

does not use the grouping approach to errors in variables. Instead, use is made of the measurement error in beta to arrive at a consistent estimator for Γ.

In constructing the GLS estimator $\hat{\Gamma}_t$ in (37), each variable has been deflated by a factor proportional to the residual standard deviation. The factor of proportionality was an arbitrary positive scalar. The structure of our problem is such that the standard error of measurement in $\tilde{\beta}_{it}$, $\partial_i = (\text{var}(\tilde{v}_{it}))^{\frac{1}{2}}$, is proportional to the standard deviation of residual risk, $s_i = (\text{var}(\tilde{e}_{it}))^{\frac{1}{2}}$. That is, if the time series regression model satisfies the OLS assumptions,

$$
\partial_i = s_i \left/ \left(\sum_{\tau=t-60}^{t-1} (R_{m\tau} - \bar{R}_m)^2 \right)^{\frac{1}{2}} \right. ,
\tag{43}
$$

where $\bar{R}_m$ is the sample mean of the market return in the prior 60 month period.[5] Assume that ∂_i is known and let

$$
\phi = s_i / \partial_i,
\tag{44}
$$

in the definition of P in (39). Thus each variable in the rows of $\tilde{R}_t$ and X_t is now deflated by the standard deviation of the measurement error in β_{it}. If $\tilde{\beta}_{it}$ is used in place of β_{it} (unobserved), the measurement error in the deflated independent variable, $\tilde{\beta}^* = \tilde{\beta}_{it}/\partial_i$ will now have unit variance.

Call the matrix of regressors used $\tilde{X}_t^*$, which is simply X_t^* with $\tilde{\beta}_{it}$ replacing β_{it}. Then

$$
\tilde{X}_t^* = X_t^* +
\begin{bmatrix}
0 & \tilde{v}_{1t}/\partial_1 & 0 \\
0 & \tilde{v}_{2t}/\partial_2 & 0 \\
\vdots & \vdots & \vdots \\
0 & \tilde{v}_{N_t t}/\partial_{N_t} & 0
\end{bmatrix},
\tag{45}
$$

where $\text{var}(\tilde{v}_{it}/\partial_i) = 1$. Then the computed overall estimator

---

uncorrelated sequential grouping procedures as used by Black and Scholes (1974) are inefficient relative to grouping procedures that maximize the between group variation in dividend yield that is unexplained by the between group variation in beta.

[5]In the actual estimation, risk premiums were used. That is, $\tilde{R}_{it} - r_{ft}$ was regressed on $\bar{R}_{m\tau} - r_{f\tau}$ to estimate β_{it}, as explained in section 4 below. Thus in the computation in (43), $(R_{m\tau} - r_{f\tau} - \bar{R}_m - r_f)^2$ is used in place of $(R_{m\tau} - \bar{R}_m)^2$.

$$\hat{\Gamma} = \sum_{t=1}^{T} (\hat{\Gamma}_t / T),$$ (46)

where

$$\hat{\Gamma}_t = (\tilde{X}_t^{*\prime} \tilde{X}_t^*)^{-1} \tilde{X}_t^{*\prime} \tilde{R}_t^*$$ (47)

is inconsistent. This is because

$$\operatorname*{plim}_{N_t} \tilde{\Gamma}_t = \left(\Sigma_{X_t^* X_t^*} + \begin{pmatrix} 0 & 0 & 0 \\ 0 & 1 & 0 \\ 0 & 0 & 0 \end{pmatrix} \right)^{-1} \frac{X_t^{*\prime} \tilde{R}_t}{N_t},$$ (48)

where

$$\Sigma_{X_t^* X_t^*} = \operatorname*{plim}_{N_t} \frac{X_t^{*\prime} X_t^*}{N_t}.$$

This says that each cross sectional estimator is biased even in large samples. Hence the overall estimator, being an arithmetic mean of the cross-sectional estimators, is inconsistent.

Consider the following estimator in each cross sectional month:

$$\hat{\Gamma}_t = \left(\frac{\tilde{X}_t^{*\prime} \tilde{X}_t^*}{N_t} - \begin{pmatrix} 0 & 0 & 0 \\ 0 & 1 & 0 \\ 0 & 0 & 0 \end{pmatrix} \right)^{-1} \frac{\tilde{X}_t^{*\prime} R_t^*}{N_t}.$$ (49)

Then

$$\operatorname*{plim}_{N_t} \hat{\Gamma} = \frac{X_t^{*\prime} \tilde{R}_t}{X_t^{*\prime} X_t^*},$$ (50)

and

$$E\left(\operatorname*{plim}_{N_t} \hat{\Gamma}_t \right) = \frac{X_t^{*\prime} E(\tilde{R}_t^*)}{X_t^{*\prime} X_t^*} = \Gamma.$$ (51)

Thus each cross-sectional estimator is unbiased, in large samples, for Γ. Note that a portfolio interpretation can also be given to (47). Since

$$\operatorname*{plim}_{N_t} \left(\frac{\tilde{X}_t^{*\prime} \tilde{X}_t^*}{N_t} - \begin{bmatrix} 0 & 0 & 0 \\ 0 & 1 & 0 \\ 0 & 0 & 0 \end{bmatrix} \right)^{-1} \frac{\tilde{X}_t^{*\prime} X_t^*}{N_t} = I,$$ (52)

it follows that the estimator for γ_0 in (47) is the realized excess return on a normal portfolio that has, in probability limit, a zero beta and a dividend yield equal to the riskless rate. Similarly the estimator for γ_1 (or γ_2) is the realized excess return on a hedge portfolio that has, in probability limit, a beta of one (or zero) and a dividend yield equal to zero (or unity).

The overall estimator,

$$\hat{\Gamma} = \sum_{t=1}^{T} (\hat{\Gamma}_t/T),\qquad(53)$$

combines T independent estimates, and is consistent,

$$\underset{T}{\text{plim}}\left[\underset{N_t}{\text{plim}} \sum_{t=1}^{T} (\hat{\Gamma}_t/T)\right] = \Gamma.\qquad(54)$$

It is shown in appendix B that, if $\hat{v}_{it}$ and $\tilde{\varepsilon}_{it}$ are jointly normal and independent, then $\hat{\Gamma}_t$ is the maximum likelihood estimator (MLE) for Γ, using data in period t.

4. Data and results

Data on security rates of return (R_{it}) were obtained from the monthly return tapes supplied by the Center for Research in Security Prices (CRSP) at the University of Chicago. The same service provides the monthly return on a value weighted index of all the securities on the tape, and this index was used as the market return (R_{mt}) for the time series regressions. From January 1931 until December 1951, the monthly return on high grade commercial paper was used as the return on the riskless asset (r_{ft}): from January 1952 until December 1977 the return on a Treasury Bill (with one month to maturity) was used for r_{ft}. Estimates of each security's beta, $\hat{\beta}_{it}$, and its associated standard error were obtained from regressions of the security excess return on the market excess return for 60 months prior to t,

$$\tilde{R}_{i\tau} - r_{f\tau} = \alpha_{it} + \beta_{it}(\tilde{R}_{m\tau} - r_{f\tau}) + \tilde{e}_{i\tau}, \qquad \tau = t - 60, t - 59, \ldots, t - 1. \qquad (55)$$

This was repeated for all securities on the CRSP tapes from $t = 1$ (January 1936) to $t = T = 504$ (December 1977). January 1936 was chosen as the initial month for (subsequent) cross-sectional regressions because that was when dividends first became taxable.

To conduct the cross-sectional regression, the dividend yield variable (d_{it}) was computed from the CRSP monthly master file. This is

$$d_{it} = 0,$$

if in month t, security i did not go ex-dividend; or if it did, it was a non-recurring dividend not announced prior to month t;

$$d_{it} = D_{it}/P_{it-1},$$

if in month t, security i went ex-dividend, and the dollar taxable dividend D_{it} per share was announced prior to month t; and

$$d_{it} = \hat{D}_{it}/P_{it-1},$$

if in month t security i went ex-dividend and this was a recurring dividend not previously announced. Here $\hat{D}_{it}$ was the previous (going back at most 12 months), recurring, taxable dividend per share, adjusted for any changes in the number of shares outstanding in the interim; where P_{it-1} is the closing price in month $t-1$.

This construction assumes that the investor knows at the end of each month whether or not the subsequent month is an ex-dividend month for a recurring dividend. However, the surrogate for the dividend is based only on information that would have been available ex ante to the investor.

The cross-sectional regressions in each month provide a sequence of estimates $\{(\hat{\gamma}_{0t}, \hat{\gamma}_{1t}, \hat{\gamma}_{2t}), \ t = 1, 2, \ldots, 504\}$. Three such sequences are available: the first uses OLS, the second uses GLS and the third uses maximum likelihood estimation. The econometric procedures developed in section 3 apply equally well to the single variable regression, excess returns on beta alone. This corresponds to a test of the two factor Capital Asset Pricing Model, as in Black, Jensen and Scholes (1972) and Fama and MacBeth (1973),

$$\tilde{R}_{it} - r_{ft} = \gamma_0' + \gamma_1' \beta_{it} + \tilde{u}_{it}, \qquad i = 1, 2, \ldots, N_t, \quad t = 1, 2, \ldots, 504, \qquad (56)$$

where $\tilde{u}_{it}$ is the deviation of $\tilde{R}_{it}$ from its expected value. These cross sectional regressions provide three sequences $\{(\hat{\gamma}_{0t}, \hat{\gamma}_{1t}), \ t = 1, 2, \ldots, 504\}$, the first using OLS, the second using GLS and the third using maximum likelihood estimation.

The estimated coefficients were shown to be realized excess rates of return on portfolios (with certain characteristics)[6] in month t. It is assumed that the excess rates of return on these portfolios are stationary and serially uncorrelated. Under these conditions the most efficient estimators of the

---

[6]See section 3, and also appendix A.

expected excess return on these portfolios would be the unweighted means of the monthly realized excess returns. The sample variance of the mean is computed as the time series sample variance of the respective portfolio returns divided by the number of months,

$$\hat{\gamma}_k = \sum_{t=1}^{504} \hat{\gamma}_{kt} \bigg/ 504, \qquad k = 0, 1, 2, \tag{57}$$

$$\mathrm{var}(\hat{\gamma}_k) = \sum_{t=1}^{504} (\hat{\gamma}_{kt} - \hat{\gamma}_k)^2 / (504 \cdot 503). \tag{58}$$

A similar computation is made for $\hat{\gamma}_0'$ and $\hat{\gamma}_1'$.

The three sets of estimators of γ_0, γ_1 and γ_2 (and of γ_0' and γ_1') and their respective t-statistics for the overall period January 1936 to December 1977 are provided in Panel A (Panel B) of table 1.

Table 1

Pooled time series and cross section estimates of the after-tax and the before-tax CAPM: 1936–1977.[a]

Procedure	Panel A: After-tax model			Panel B: Before-tax model	
	$\hat{\gamma}_0$	$\hat{\gamma}_1$	$\hat{\gamma}_2$	$\hat{\gamma}_0'$	$\hat{\gamma}_1'$
OLS	0.00616	0.00268	0.227	0.00681	0.00228
	(4.37)	(1.51)	(6.33)	(4.84)	(1.26)
GLS	0.00446	0.00344	0.234	0.00516	0.00302
	(3.53)	(1.87)	(8.24)	(4.09)	(1.63)
MLE	0.00363	0.00421	0.236	0.00443	0.00369
	(2.63)	(1.86)	(8.62)	(3.22)	(1.62)

[a]*Notes*: The after-tax version corresponds to the regression

$$\tilde{R}_{it} - r_{ft} = \gamma_0 + \gamma_1 \beta_{it} + \gamma_2 (d_{it} - r_{ft}) + \tilde{\varepsilon}_{it}, \qquad i = 1, 2, \ldots, N_t, \ t = 1, 2, \ldots, T.$$

The before-tax version corresponds to the regression

$$R_{it} - r_{ft} = \gamma_0' + \gamma_1' \beta_{it} + \tilde{\mu}_{it}, \qquad i = 1, 2, \ldots, N_t, \ t = 1, 2, \ldots, T.$$

Each regression above is performed across securities in a given month. This gives estimates $\{\hat{\gamma}_{0t}, \hat{\gamma}_{1t}, \hat{\gamma}_{2t}; \ t = 1, 2, \ldots, T\}$ and $\{\hat{\gamma}_{0t}', \hat{\gamma}_{1t}'; \ t = 1, 2, \ldots, T\}$. The reported coefficients are arithmetic averages of this time series: for example,

$$\hat{\gamma}_1 = \sum_{t=1}^{T} \frac{\hat{\gamma}_{1t}}{T},$$

where $T = 504$, t-statistics are in parentheses under each coefficient, and they refer to $t(\hat{\gamma}_j)$, where $j = 1, 2, 3$.

The OLS and GLS estimators are biased and inconsistent due to measurement error in beta. The maximum likelihood estimators are consistent: consistency is a large sample property and for this study the monthly cross sectional regressions have between 600 and 1200 firms, and there were 504 months.[7] In Panel A, table 1, the MLE estimator of γ_1 is about 60 percent greater than the corresponding GLS estimator. Consistent with prior studies, the MLE estimator of γ_1 is significantly positive, indicating that investors are risk averse. Also consistent with prior studies, the MLE estimator of γ_0 is significantly positive. In Panel B, tests of the two factor model are presented. Note that in both panels, the GLS procedure results in an increase in the efficiency of the estimator of γ_1, which is $\hat{\gamma}_1$ ($\hat{\gamma}_1'$) in Panel A (Panel B). Consistent with prior tests of the traditional version of the Capital Asset Pricing Model, the null hypothesis that $\gamma_0' = 0$ is rejected. Consistent with investor risk aversion $\hat{\gamma}_1'$ is significantly positive at the 0.1 level. Explanations for a positive intercept ($\gamma_0 > 0$) include, in addition to margin constraints on borrowing, misspecification of the market porfolio [see Mayers (1972), Sharpe (1977) and Roll (1977)], or beta serving as a surrogate for systematic skewness [see Kraus and Litzenberger (1976)].

The coefficient of the excess dividend yield variable, $\hat{\gamma}_2$, (Panel A) is highly significant under all the estimating procedures. The standard errors of the GLS and maximum likelihood estimators of γ_2 are about 25 percent smaller than that of the OLS estimator. The magnitude of the coefficient indicates that for every dollar of taxable return investors require between 23 and 24 cents of additional before tax return.

While the finding of a significant dividend coefficient contrasts with the Black–Scholes (1974) finding of an insignificant dividend effect, the magnitude of the coefficient in table 1 is consistent with their study. The dividend yield (independent) variable they used was $(d_i - d_m)/d_m$, where d_m was the average dividend yield on stocks. Since the coefficient they found was 0.0009, and the average annual yield in their period of study (1936–1966) was 0.048, their estimate of γ_2 can be approximated by 0.0009/(0.048/12), or 0.225.

It has been assumed that the variance of the estimator of Γ is constant over time. If, due to the quarterly patterns in the incidence of dividend payments, the variances of the estimators are not constant, the equally weighted estimators in (50) are inefficient relative to an estimator that accounts for any seasonal pattern in the variance. Since dividends are usually paid once every quarter, it is possible to compute three independent estimates of Γ by averaging the coefficients obtained in only the first, only the second and only the third month of each quarter. These three estimates of Γ may be weighted by the inverse of their variances to obtain a more efficient estimator. This is provided in table 2. As can be seen from this table,

[7]Consistency here is with respect to the overall estimator so one takes probability limits with respect to t and with respect to N_t. See section 3.

the overall estimator for γ_2 is very close to the MLE estimate in table 1. The estimate of the standard error of $\hat{\gamma}_2$ is approximately the same for the first two months, but about 30 percent less for the third month.

Table 2

Pooled time series and cross section estimates of the after-tax CAPM: 1936–1977 (based on quarterly dividend patterns).[a]

Month of quarter	$\hat{\gamma}_0$	$\hat{\gamma}_1$	$\hat{\gamma}_2$
First	0.00748	0.00770	0.28932
	(0.00234)	(0.00379)	(0.05418)
Second	0.00212	0.00071	0.23531
	(0.00232)	(0.00335)	(0.05034)
Third	0.00134	0.00399	0.18940
	(0.00248)	(0.00453)	(0.03534)
Overall	0.00373	0.00383	0.22335
estimate	(0.00137)	(0.00219)	(0.02552)

[a]Notes: The after-tax version corresponds to the regression

$$\tilde{R}_{it} - r_{ft} = \gamma_0 + \gamma_1 \beta_{it} + \gamma_2 (d_{it} - r_{ft}), \quad i = 1, 2, \ldots, N_t.$$

This regression is performed across securities in a given month t. Maximum likelihood estimation is used. The reported coefficients are arithmetic averages of the coefficients obtained over time (see note to table 1). The first three rows use the estimates from only the first, only the second and only the third months of each quarter. There are 168 months' estimates in each row. Standard errors are in parentheses under each coefficient. The 'overall estimates' use the estimates in each row above, weighted inversely by their variances.

It may be inappropriate to treat γ_2 as an intertemporal constant: in the absence of income related constraints on borrowing, γ_2 is a weighted average of individuals' marginal tax rates, which may have changed over time. Assume that investors have utility functions that display decreasing absolute risk aversion and non-decreasing relative risk aversion. Assume in addition that the distribution of wealth is independent of individual utility functions. Under these conditions the weight of the marginal tax rates of individuals in the higher tax brackets would be greater than that of individuals in lower tax brackets. Holland (1962) has shown that from 1936 to 1960 there was no pronounced upward trend in the marginal tax rates of individuals with taxable income in excess of $25,000. To examine empirically whether there is evidence of an upward trend in γ_2 over time, the maximum likelihood results are presented for six subperiods in table 3. The estimators of γ_2 for the subperiods were consistently positive and, except for the 1/1955 to 12/1961 period, significantly different from zero. There does not appear to be a trend to the estimate.

Table 3

Pooled time series and cross section estimates of the after-tax CAPM (for 6 subperiods).[a]

Period	$\hat{\gamma}_0$	$\hat{\gamma}_1$	$\hat{\gamma}_2$
1/36–12/40	−0.00287 (−0.52)	0.00728 (0.65)	0.335 (2.64)
1/41–12/47	0.00454 (1.44)	0.00703 (1.59)	0.408 (7.35)
1/48–12/54	0.00528 (2.77)	0.00617 (1.45)	0.158 (4.37)
1/55–12/61	0.01355 (5.62)	−0.00316 (−0.78)	0.018 (0.32)
1/62–12/68	−0.00164 (−0.47)	0.01063 (1.95)	0.171 (2.33)
1/69–12/77	0.00166 (0.47)	−0.00045 (−0.09)	0.329 (6.00)

[a]Notes: The after-tax version corresponds to the regression

$$\tilde{R}_{it} - r_{ft} = \gamma_0 + \gamma_1 \beta_{it} + \gamma_2 (d_{it} - r_{ft}) + \tilde{\varepsilon}_{it}, \quad i = 1, 2, \ldots, N_t, \ t = 1, 2, \ldots, T.$$

Maximum likelihood estimation is used for the cross sectional regression. The reported coefficients are arithmetic averages of the coefficients estimated in the months in the period (see note to table 1). t-statistics are in parentheses under each coefficient.

It is possible that the positive coefficient on dividend yield is not a tax effect and that in non-ex-dividend months the effect completely reverses itself. If dividends are paid quarterly there would. be twice as many non-ex-dividend months as ex-dividend months. Thus, a complete reversal would require a negative effect on returns in each non-ex-dividend month that is half the absolute size of the effect in an ex-dividend month. It is also possible that a stock's dividend yield is a proxy for the covariance of its return with classes of assets not included in the value weighted index of NYSE stocks used to calculate betas in the present study. If the coefficient on dividend yield is entirely due to the effects of omitted assets, the effect in non-ex-dividend months should be positive and the same size as the effect in ex-dividend months.

In order to test whether there is a reversal effect or a re-inforcing effect in non-ex-dividend months the following cross-sectional regression was estimated:

$$\tilde{R}_{it} - r_{ft} = \gamma_0 + \gamma_1 \tilde{\beta}_{it} + \gamma_2 \{\delta_{it} d_{it}^0 - r_{ft}\} + \gamma_3 \{(1 - \delta_{it}) d_{it}^0\} + \tilde{\varepsilon}_{it},$$

$$i = 1, 2, \ldots, N_t, \qquad (59)$$

where

$$d_{it}^0 = D_{it}/P_{it-1},$$

if a dividend was announced prior to month t, to go ex-dividend in month t;

$$d_{it}^0 = \hat{D}_{it}/P_{it-1}$$

otherwise; and

$$\delta_{it} = 1,$$

if month t was an ex-dividend month for a recurring dividend;

$$\delta_{it} = 0,$$

otherwise.

The variable $(1-\delta_{it})d_{it}^0$ is intended to pick up the effect of a dividend payment in subsequent, non-ex-dividend months. The variable $\delta_{it}d_{it}^0$ is identical to d_{it}, the variable used earlier. If dividends are paid quarterly, and γ_3 is negative and has an absolute value half the size of γ_2, then one can conclude that there is a complete reversal over the course of the quarter so that there is no net tax effect. On the other hand, if there is no reversal, γ_3 should not be significantly negative.

The MLE estimates of the coefficients in (52) are presented in table 4. The estimated value of $\hat{\gamma}_3$ is positive and significantly different from zero: this rejects the hypothesis that there is complete reversal.

The significant positive γ_3 is evidence of a re-inforcing effect in non-ex-dividend months. If the coefficient on dividend yield is entirely attributable

Table 4

Pooled time series and cross section test of the reversal effect of dividend yield: 1936–1977.[a]

$\hat{\gamma}_0$	$\hat{\gamma}_1$	$\hat{\gamma}_2$	$\hat{\gamma}_3$
0.00184	0.00493	0.32784	0.10321
(1.29)	(2.17)	(7.31)	(2.87)

[a]Notes: The regression performed in each month is

$$\tilde{R}_{it} - r_{ft} = \gamma_0 \gamma_1 \beta_{it} + \gamma_2 \{\delta_{it}d_{it}^0 - r_{ft}\} + \gamma_3 (1-\delta_{it})d_{it}^0 + \tilde{\varepsilon}_{it}, \qquad i = 1, 2, \ldots, N_t,$$
$$t = 1, 2, \ldots, T.$$

Maximum likelihood estimation is used for the cross-sectional regression. The reported coefficients are arithemetic averages of the coefficients in each month (see note to table 1). t-statistics are in parentheses under each coefficient.

to the effect of omitted assets γ_3 should be the same order of magnitude as γ_2. If the effect in ex-dividend months exceeds the combined effect in the subsequent two non-ex-dividend months γ_2 should be more than twice as large as γ_3. $\hat{\gamma}_2 - 2\hat{\gamma}_3$ is 0.1214 and has a t-value of 2.79. Thus, the effect in an ex-dividend month is more than twice the size of the effect in a non-ex-dividend month. This evidence suggests that the coefficient on dividend yield in ex-dividend months is not solely attributable to the effects of missing assets and that the effect in an ex-dividend month exceeds the combined effect in the subsequent two non-ex-dividend months. If the effect in non-ex-dividend months is asserted to be entirely due to the effect of missing assets, the difference $\hat{\gamma}_2 - \hat{\gamma}_3 = 0.225$ is an estimate of the tax effect. However, further theoretical work on the combined effects of transaction costs and personal taxes in a multi-period valuation framework is required to be able to understand the cause of a significant yield effect in non-ex-dividend months. For the present it seems reasonable to conclude that 0.225 is a lower bound estimate of the tax effect.[8]

The empirical evidence presented by Elton and Gruber (1970) on the ex-dividend behavior of common stocks suggests that the coefficient on the excess dividend yield term may be a decreasing function of yield. The theoretical rationale for this effect is that investors in low (high) tax brackets invest in high (low) dividend yield stocks: a possible explanation is that institutional restrictions on short sales results in a segmentation of security holdings according to investors' tax brackets. To provide a simple test of this 'clientele' effect, the coefficient c in (22) is hypothesized to be a linear decreasing function of the ith security's dividend yield. That is c, which is now dependent on i, is written c_i and given by

$$c_i = k - hd_i, \tag{60}$$

where k, $h > 0$, and the hypothesized relationship is

$$E(\tilde{R}_i) - r_f = a + b\beta_i + (k - hd_i)(d_i - r_f). \tag{61}$$

The econometric model is

<hr>

[8]It might be argued that the persistent dividend effect is due to the fact that the dividend variable used incorporates knowledge of the ex-dividend month, which the investor may not have. To test whether this introduces spurious correlations between yields and returns the variable $(d_{it}^0/3)$ was used in the cross-sectional regression (23). The variable does not incorporate knowledge of the ex-dividend month except when it was announced. It is divided by 3 so as to distribute the yield over the three months of every quarter. The overall estimate (1936–1977) of γ_2 is 0.39, with a t-value of 3.57: one cannot attribute the earlier results due to knowledge of ex-dividend months. This is consistent with the Rosenberg and Marathe (1978) study. Note that this estimate is lower than the total effect in table 4, which is $\hat{\gamma}_2 + 2\hat{\gamma}_3 = 0.52$. The lower estimate is attributable to constraining the coefficient on yield to be the same in non-ex-dividend months and ex-dividend months.

$$\tilde{R}_{it} - r_{ft} = \gamma_0 + \gamma_1 \beta_{it} + \gamma_2 (d_{it} - r_{ft})$$
$$+ \gamma_4 d_{it}(d_{it} - r_{ft}) + \tilde{\varepsilon}_{it}, \qquad i = 1, 2, \ldots, N_t, \qquad (62)$$

where the estimate of k is γ_2 and that for $-h$ is γ_4. The maximum likelihood approach is used in each cross sectional regression, and the pooled estimates presented in table 5.

Table 5

Pooled time series and cross section test of the clientele effect: 1936–1977.[a]

$\hat{\gamma}_0$	$\hat{\gamma}_1$	$\hat{\gamma}_2$	$\hat{\gamma}_4$
0.00365	0.00425	0.336	−6.92
(2.65)	(1.88)	(6.60)	(−1.70)

[a]*Notes*: This corresponds to the following cross-sectional regression in each month:

$$\tilde{R}_{it} - r_{ft} = \gamma_0 + \gamma_1 \beta_{it} + \gamma_2 (d_{it} - r_{ft}) + \gamma_4 d_{it}(d_{it} - r_{ft}) + \tilde{\varepsilon}_{it}, \qquad i = 1, 2, \ldots, N_t,$$
$$t = 1, 2, \ldots, T.$$

Maximum likelihood estimation is used for the cross-sectional regression. The reported coefficients are arithmetic averages of the coefficients in each month (see note in table 1). t-statistics are in parentheses under each coefficient.

Consistent with the existence of a clientele effect, the maximum likelihood estimate of γ_2 is significantly positive and that of γ_4 is significantly negative, both at the 0.05 level. The magnitude of $\hat{\gamma}_4$ suggests that for every percentage point in yield the implied tax rate for ex-dividend months declines by 0.069. For example, if the annual yield was 4 percent, the implied tax rate would be approximately $0.336 - 6.92 \ (0.04/4) = 0.268$, assuming quarterly payments. The empirical evidence supporting a clientele effect suggests the need for further research that rigorously derives an equilibrium model that incorporates institutional restrictions on short sales, along with personal taxes.

5. Conclusion

In this paper, an after-tax version of the Capital Asset Pricing Model is derived. The model extends the Brennan after-tax version of the CAPM to incorporate wealth and income related constraints on borrowing along with a progressive tax scheme. The wealth related constraint on borrowing causes the expected return on a zero-beta portfolio (having a dividend yield equal to the riskless rate) to exceed the riskless rate of interest. The income related constraint tends to offset the effect that personal taxes have on the equilibrium structure of share prices. The equilibrium relationship indicates that the before tax expected return on a security is linearly related to its systematic risk and to its dividend yield. Unrestricted supply adjustments in corporate dividends would result in the before tax version of the CAPM, in a world where dividends and interest are taxed as ordinary income. If income related constraints are non-binding and/or corporate supply adjustments are restricted, the before tax return on a security would be an increasing linear function of its dividend yield.

Unlike prior tests of the CAPM that used grouping or instrumental variables to correct for measurement error in beta, this paper uses the sample estimate of the variance of observed betas to arrive at maximum likelihood estimates of the coefficients in the relations tested. Unlike prior studies of the effect of dividend yields on asset prices, which used average monthly yields as a surrogate for the expected yield in both ex-dividend and non-ex-dividend months, the expected dividend yield based on prior information is used for ex-dividend months and is set to zero for other months.

The results indicate that there is a strong positive relationship between before tax expected returns and dividend yields of common stocks. The coefficient of the dividend yield variable was positive, less than unity, and significantly different from zero. The data indicates that for every dollar increase in return in the form of dividends, investors require an additional 23 cents in before tax return. There was no noticeable trend in the coefficient over time. A test was constructed to determine whether the effect of dividend yield reverses itself in non-ex-dividend months, and this hypothesis was rejected. Indeed, the data indicates that the effect of a dividend payment on before tax expected returns is positive in both the ex-dividend month and in the subsequent non-ex-dividend months. However, the combined effect in the subsequent non-ex-dividend months is significantly less than the effect in the ex-dividend month.

Evidence is also presented for a clientele effect: that is, that stockholders in higher tax brackets choose stocks with low yields, and vice versa. Further work is needed to derive a model that implies the existence of such clienteles and to test its implications.

Appendix A

In this appendix it is shown that the estimator for Γ, given by

$$\hat{\Gamma}_t = (X_t' \Omega_t^{-1} X_t)^{-1} X_t' \Omega_t^{-1} \tilde{R}_t,$$

using data in period t, is the Generalized Least Squares (GLS) estimator for Γ under the assumption of the single index model. It was shown in section 3 of the paper that each estimated coefficient corresponds to the realized excess return of a specific portfolio. Suppose portfolio weights $\{h_{it}, i = 1, 2, \ldots, N_t\}$ are chosen in each period, for investment in assets $i = 1, 2, \ldots, N_t$. Using eq. (23) from the text the excess return on such a portfolio is given by

$$\sum_i h_{it}(\tilde{R}_{it} - r_{ft}) = \gamma_0\left(\sum_i h_{it}\right) + \gamma_1\left(\sum_i h_{it}\beta_{it}\right)$$

$$+ \gamma_2\left[\sum_i h_{it}(d_{it} - r_{ft})\right] + \sum_i h_{it}\tilde{\varepsilon}_{it}.$$

The expected excess return on this portfolio is

$$\gamma_0 \quad \text{if} \quad \sum_i h_{it} = 1, \quad \sum_i h_{it}\beta_{it} = 0, \quad \sum_i h_{it}(d_{it} - r_{ft}) = 0,$$

$$\gamma_1 \quad \text{if} \quad \sum_i h_{it} = 0, \quad \sum_i h_{it}\beta_{it} = 1, \quad \sum_i h_{it}(d_{it} - r_{ft}) = 0,$$

$$\gamma_2 \quad \text{if} \quad \sum_i h_{it} = 0, \quad \sum_i h_{it}\beta_{it} = 0, \quad \sum_i h_{it}(d_{it} - r_{ft}) = 1.$$

Under the assumption of the single index model, the variance of the return on such a portfolio is, from eq. (36) in the text,

$$\text{var}\left(\sum_i h_{it}(\tilde{R}_{it} - r_{ft})\right) = \left(\sum_i h_{it}\beta_{it}\right)^2 \sigma_{mm} + \sum_i h_{it}^2 s_{ii}.$$

Suppose one wishes to minimize the variance of the excess return on such a portfolio subject to the condition that the expected excess return on the portfolio is, in turn, γ_0, γ_1 or γ_2. This condition enforces $\sum_i h_{it}\beta_{it}$ to be either zero or unity. Hence minimizing

$$\left(\sum_i h_{it}\beta_{it}\right)^2 \sigma_{mm} + \sum_i h_{it}^2 s_{ii},$$

subject to the unbiasedness condition, is equivalent to minimizing

$$\sum_i h_{it}^2 s_{ii},$$

the 'residual risk' of the portfolio subject to the unbiasedness condition. Thus, one is using the residual risk of the portfolio as the minimand and enforcing the unbiasedness condition. By construction, Ω_t is the diagonal matrix of the residual variances s_{ii}, and by construction, $\hat{\Gamma}_t$ is linear and unbiased for Γ. The variance of the estimator has been minimized under the single index model. But by the Gauss–Markov theorem, the GLS estimator [using the full matrix V_t in (36) as the variance–covariance matrix] is the unique minimum variance estimator among linear and unbiased estimators. Hence $\hat{\Gamma}_t$ is the GLS estimator for Γ, under the assumption of the single index model.

Appendix B

In this section, it is shown that under certain conditions, $\hat{\Gamma}_t$ in (49) is the maximum likelihood estimator for Γ in period t.

First, note that there are no errors in the measurement of β, then if security returns are multivariate normal, then the GLS estimator in (37) is also the maximum likelihood estimator [see Johnston (1972)].

Suppose now there are errors in the measurement of β. Then one can use the transformation P defined in (39), with $\phi = s_i/\sigma_i$, to write the model as

$$\tilde{R}^*_{it} = \gamma_0 p^*_{it} + \gamma_1 \beta^*_{it} + \gamma_2 d^*_{it} + \tilde{\varepsilon}^*_{it}, \tag{B.1}$$

and the observed beta as

$$\bar{\beta}^*_{it} = \beta^*_{it} + \tilde{v}^*_{it}, \tag{B.2}$$

where

$$\tilde{R}^*_{it} = (\tilde{R}_{it} - r_{ft})/\sigma_i, \quad p^*_{it} = 1/\sigma_i, \quad \beta^*_{it} = \beta_{it}/\sigma_i,$$

$$\bar{\beta}^*_{it} = \bar{\beta}_{it}/\sigma_i, \quad d^*_{it} = (d_{it} - r_{ft})/\sigma_i, \quad \tilde{\varepsilon}^*_{it} = \tilde{\varepsilon}_{it}/\sigma_i,$$

and

$$\tilde{v}^*_{it} = \tilde{v}_{it}/\sigma_i.$$

Define the variable

$$m_{xy} = \sum_{i=1}^{N_t} x_{it} y_{it} \Big/ N_t, \tag{B.3}$$

as the raw co-moment for a given sequence $\{(x_{it}, y_{it}), \ i = 1, 2, \dots, N_t\}$. Then from (B.1) and (B.2),

$$m_{\tilde{R}^* p^*} = \gamma_0 m_{p^* p^*} + \gamma_1 m_{p^* \beta^*} + \gamma_2 m_{d^* p^*} + m_{\tilde{\varepsilon}^* p^*}, \tag{B.4}$$

$$m_{\tilde{R}^* \bar{\beta}^*} = \gamma_0 [m_{\beta^* p^*} + m_{v^* p^*}] + \gamma_1 [m_{\beta^* \beta^*} + m_{\tilde{v}^* \beta^*}]$$
$$+ \gamma_2 [m_{d^* \beta^*} + m_{d^* \tilde{v}^*}] + m_{\beta^* \tilde{\varepsilon}^*} + m_{\tilde{v}^* \tilde{\varepsilon}^*}, \tag{B.5}$$

$$m_{\tilde{R}* d*} = \gamma_0 m_{p* d*} + \gamma_1 m_{\beta* d*} + \gamma_2 m_{d* d*} + m_{\tilde{\varepsilon}* d*}, \tag{B.6}$$

$$m_{\tilde{\beta}* p*} = m_{\beta* p*} + m_{\tilde{v}* p*}, \tag{B.7}$$

$$m_{\tilde{\beta}* \tilde{\beta}*} = m_{\beta* \beta*} + 2m_{\beta* v*} + m_{\tilde{v}* \tilde{v}*}, \tag{B.8}$$

$$m_{d* \tilde{\beta}*} = m_{d* \beta*} + m_{d* v*}. \tag{B.9}$$

In these six equations, take expectations and use the fact that

$$E(\tilde{v}_{it}^*) = E(\tilde{\varepsilon}_{it}^*) = 0,$$
$$E(\tilde{v}_{it}^* \tilde{\varepsilon}_{it}^*) = 0, \tag{B.10}$$
$$E(\tilde{v}_{it}^* \tilde{v}_{it}^*) = E[\tilde{v}_{it}^2/\sigma_i^2] = 1.$$

The left-hand side of each of (B.4) through (B.9), after taking expectations, corresponds to the population co-moments of the subscripted variables.

If v_{it} and ε_{it} are independently normally distributed, then the corresponding sample moment is a maximum likelihood estimator of the population parameter. Replace these expected values by their maximum likelihood estimates. There are now six equations for the six unknown parameters γ_0, γ_1, γ_2, $m_{\beta* \beta*}$, $m_{\beta* d*}$, and $m_{\beta* p*}$. They can be solved for the coefficients of interest from the following 'normal' equations, which are in terms of observed sample estimates

$$m_{\tilde{R}* p*} = \gamma_0 m_{p* p*} + \gamma_1 m_{\tilde{\beta}* p*} + \gamma_2 m_{d* p*}, \tag{B.11}$$

$$m_{\tilde{R}* \tilde{\beta}*} = \gamma_0 m_{p* \tilde{\beta}*} + \gamma_1 (m_{\tilde{\beta}* \tilde{\beta}*} - 1) + \gamma_2 m_{d* \tilde{\beta}*}, \tag{B.12}$$

$$m_{\tilde{R}* d*} = \gamma_0 m_{p* d*} + \gamma_1 m_{\tilde{\beta}* d*} + \gamma_2 m_{d* d*}. \tag{B.13}$$

and are themselves maximum likelihood [see Mood et al. (1974, p. 285)].

The solution to this set gives estimates $\hat{\gamma}_{kt}$, $k = 0, 1, 2$, which are embodied in (49). They are functions of maximum likelihood estimates. Note that in addition to (B.4) through (B.9), one could write an equation for $m_{\tilde{R}* \tilde{R}*}$,

$$m_{\tilde{R}* \tilde{R}*} = \gamma_0^2 m_{p* p*} + \gamma_1^2 m_{\beta* \beta*} + \gamma_2^2 m_{d* d*} + 2\gamma_0 \gamma_1 m_{p* \beta*}.$$
$$+ 2\gamma_0 \gamma_2 m_{p* d*} + 2\gamma_1 \gamma_2 m_{\beta* d*} + 2\gamma_0 m_{p* \tilde{\varepsilon}*} + 2\gamma_1 m_{\beta* \tilde{\varepsilon}*} \tag{B.14}$$
$$+ 2\gamma_2 m_{d* \tilde{\varepsilon}*} + m_{\tilde{\varepsilon}* \tilde{\varepsilon}*}.$$

If we take expectations, using (B.10) and the fact that

$$E\left(m_{\tilde{\varepsilon}^* \tilde{\varepsilon}^*}\right) = E\left(\sum_{i=1}^{N_t} \frac{\tilde{\varepsilon}_{it}^2}{\partial_i^2 N_t}\right)$$

$$= \frac{1}{N_t} \sum_{i=1}^{N_t} \frac{E(\tilde{\varepsilon}_{it}^2)}{\partial_i^2} = \frac{1}{N_t} \cdot N_t \phi^2 = \phi^2,$$

we have

$$E(m_{\tilde{R}^* \tilde{R}^*}) = \gamma_0^2 m_{p^* p^*} + \gamma_1^2 m_{\beta^* \beta^*} + \gamma_2^2 m_{d^* d^*} + 2\gamma_0 \gamma_1 m_{p^* \beta^*}$$

$$+ 2\gamma_0 \gamma_2 m_{p^* d^*} + 2\gamma_1 \gamma_2 m_{\beta^* d^*} + \phi^2, \tag{B.15}$$

where ϕ^2 is assumed known.

By writing down the likelihood function and maximizing it for an analogous case, Johnston (1963) demonstrates a maximum likelihood estimator over the parameter space $(\gamma_0, \gamma_1, \gamma_2, \beta_{it}$ for $i = 1, 2, \ldots, N_t, \phi)$. This has the undesirable characteristic that the parameter space grows with the sample size.[9] It turns out in our problem that ϕ is assumed known. If this ϕ satisfies (B.15), when in (B.15) we use the sample co-moment estimates for the population parameters, then Johnston's M.L. procedure coincides with the solution to (B.11) through (B.13). Whereas our estimators are linear in the returns and can be interpreted as portfolios, the expanded parameter space estimator in Johnston is non-linear and has no such analog to theory. Thus conditional on ϕ^2 coinciding with the residual variation in the sample, using our estimates, the estimator in (49) is a maximum likelihood estimator over the parameter space $(\gamma_0, \gamma_1, \gamma_2)$.

[9]See Kendall and Stuart (1973, especially pp. 62 and 402).

References

Amemiya, T., 1972, Theory of econometrics: Lecture notes, Unpublished manuscript (Department of Economics, Stanford University, Stanford, CA).

Bailey, M.J., 1969, Capital gains and income taxation, in: A.C. Harberger and M.J. Bailey, The taxation of income from capital (Brookings Institution, Washington, DC) 11–49.

Black, F., 1972, Capital market equilibrium with restricted borrowing, Journal of Business 45, 444–454.

Black, F., M. Jensen and M. Scholes, 1972, The capital asset pricing model: Some empirical tests, in: M. Jensen, ed., Studies in the theory of capital markets (Praeger, New York) 79–121.

Black, F. and M. Scholes, 1974, The effects of dividend yield and dividend policy on common stock prices and returns, Journal of Financial Economics 1, 1–22.

Blume, M. and I. Friend, 1973, A new look at the capital asset pricing model, Journal of Finance 28, 19–33.

Brennan, M.J., 1973, Taxes, market valuation and corporate financial policy, National Tax Journal 23, 417–427.

Brennan, M.J., 1970, Investor taxes, market equilibrium and corporation finance, Unpublished Ph.D. Dissertation (Massachusetts Institute of Technology, Cambridge, MA).

Cottle, S., D.L. Dodd and B. Graham, 1962, Security analysis: Principles and techniques (McGraw-Hill, New York).

Elton, E. and Gruber, 1970, Marginal stockholder tax rates and the clientele effect, Review of Economics and Statistics 52, 68–74.

Fama, E.F. and J.D. MacBeth, 1973, Risk, return and equilibrium: Empirical tests, Journal of Political Economy 71, 607–636.

Fama, E.F. and M.H. Miller, 1972, The theory of finance (Holt, Rinehart and Winston, New York).

Fisher, F.M., 1977, The effect of simple specification error on the coefficients of 'unaffected' variables, Working Paper no. 194 (Department of Economics, Massachusetts Institute of Technology, Cambridge, MA).

Friend, I. and M. Blume, 1970, Measurement of portfolio performance under uncertainty, American Economic Review, 561–575.

Gonzalez-Gaverra, N.G., 1973, Inflation and capital asset market prices: Theory and tests, Unpublished Ph.D. Dissertation (Graduate School of Business, Stanford University, Stanford, CA).

Gordon, M.J., 1963, Optimal investment and financing policy, Journal of Finance 18, 264–272.

Holland, D.M., 1962, Dividends under the income tax (NBER, Princeton, NJ).

Johnston, J., 1963, Econometric methods (McGraw-Hill, New York).

Johnston, J., 1972, Econometric methods (McGraw-Hill, New York).

Kendall, M.G. and A. Stuart, 1973, The advanced theory of statistics (Hafner, New York).

Kraus, A. and R.H. Litzenberger, 1976, Skewness preference and the valuation of risk assets, Journal of Finance 31, 1085–1100.

Lintner, J., 1965, The valuation of risk assets and the selection of risky investments in stock portfolios and capital budgets, Review of Economics and Statistics 47, 13–37.

Litzenberger, R.H. and J.C. Van Horne, 1978, Elimination of the double taxation of dividends and corporate financial policy, Journal of Finance 34, 737–749.

Long, J., 1975, Efficient portfolio choice with differential taxation of dividends and capital gains, Journal of Financial Economics 5, 25–53.

Mayers, D., 1972, Non-market assets and capital market equilibrium under uncertainty, in: M.C. Jensen, ed., Studies in the theory of capital markets (Praeger, New York).

Miller, M. and M. Modigliani, 1961, Dividend policy growth, and the valuation of shares, Journal of Business 4, 411–433.

Miller, M. and M. Scholes, 1972, Rates of return in relation to risk: A re-examination of some recent findings, in: M. Jensen, ed., Studies in the theory of capital markets (Praeger, New York).

Miller, M. and M. Scholes, 1977, Dividends and taxes, Working Paper no. 8 (University of Chicago, Chicago, IL).

Mood, A., F.S. Graybill and D.C. Boes, 1974, Introduction to the theory of statistics (McGraw-Hill, New York).

Roll, R., 1977, A critique of the asset pricing theory's tests, Journal of Financial Economics 4, 129–176.

Rosenberg, B. and V. Marathe, 1978, Test of capital asset pricing hypotheses, Journal of Financial Research, forthcoming.

Rubinstein, M., 1973, A comparative statics analysis of risk premiums, Journal of Business 46.

Sharpe, W.F., 1964, Capital asset prices: A theory of market equilibrium under conditions of risk, Journal of Finance 19, 425–442.

Sharpe, W.F., 1977, The capital asset pricing model: A multi-beta interpretation, in: H. Levy and M. Sarnat, eds., Financial decision making under uncertainty (Academic Press, New York).

Stehle, R.D., 1976, The valuation of risk assets in an international capital market: Theory and tests, Unpublished Ph.D. Dissertation (Graduate School of Business, Stanford, CA).

Vasicek, O., 1971, Capital market equilibrium with no riskless borrowing, Wells Fargo Bank Memorandum (San Francisco, CA).